Handbook for Raising Capital

Financing Alternatives for Emerging and Growing Businesses

Handbook for Raising Capital

Financing Alternatives for Emerging and Growing Businesses

Edited by
Lawrence Chimerine
Robert F. Cushman
Howard D. Ross

DOW JONES-IRWIN
Homewood, Illinois 60430

ISBN 0–87094–705–2

Library of Congress Catalog Card No. 86–71216

Printed in the United States of America

1 2 3 4 5 6 7 8 9 0 K 4 3 2 1 0 9 8 7

PREFACE

The major problem that many businesses have today is their inability to obtain adequate financing for expansion and, in some cases, for ongoing operations. Time and time again, it has been proved that financing is the most important factor in building a business—or watching it fail.

Today, more companies than ever are competing for available credit while large budget deficits have, in fact, reduced the amount of credit available to the private sector. Add to this the creative and innovative credit instruments presently being utilized, and it becomes apparent that charting a path to the best and cheapest way to finance is not easy.

This book discusses virtually all of the options available to small and midsized businesses, the advantages and disadvantages of each alternative, and the strategies to be employed by companies seeking financing.

Few, if any, individuals have the training, background, and knowledge to do justice to issues of so broad a scope. The conscientious businessowner and, for that matter, the advising professional desiring to proceed with understanding and confidence have hungered for readily available, readable information pertaining to financing alternatives in a single source. This need could only be met through a collaboration of well-qualified specialists.

The accountants, bankers, businesspeople, and lawyers who wrote these chapters were chosen with two criteria in mind: first, they had to be outstanding authorities within their fields, with proper qualifications and the requisite expertise to write their particular chapters; and second, they had to be able to write in understandable, nontechnical language.

THE BOOK CONTAINS THE FOLLOWING CHAPTERS:

Chapter 1: Borrowing from Banks

Bank loans still represent the most significant source of capital for most small and middle-sized businesses. However, in view of the increased risks throughout the economy, many financial institutions are exercising greater caution in their lending activities. Mr. Howard discusses what businesses should do in order to maximize their access to bank capital, including what factors influence bankers' lending decisions and what materials should be used in presentations to banks. Many companies are originally turned down for bank financing: Mr. Howard also discusses what can be done to have such decisions reversed.

Chapter 2: Private Placements

Private placements are frequently an important source of equity financing for the emerging business. In the early stages of a company's growth, private equity placements are frequently made to individuals and represent the first sophisticated form of financing for the young business. Planning for successful private placements is extremely important, and such issues as selling the deal, valuation, and complying with securities laws and regulations must be considered. This chapter provides a thorough discussion of how private placements can be successfully accomplished.

Chapter 3: S Corporations

The use of an S corporation can play a significant role in raising capital for the emerging business. The S corporation provides many of the legal advantages of the regular corporation, but also provides a way for a company's initial losses to be funneled out to the S corporation shareholders. This chapter discusses the technical aspects of S corporations, when they make sense for the emerging business, and what their advantages and disadvantages are. Taxation of S corporations can be fairly complex and they must be clearly understood before S corporation status is elected.

Chapter 4: Lease Financing

In 1984, more than $70 billion of capital equipment was leased in the United States. Leasing is one of the most important methods of financing capital formation in our economy, and the executive of an emerging company must have a basic understanding of how to employ leasing to maximize the company's performance.

Chapter 5: Government-Assisted Financing

The federal government has a number of programs available to assist in the funding of new small businesses as well as business development and research activities. Mr. Swain, chief counsel for advocacy at the U.S. Small Business Administration, describes these programs in his chapter on the role of the federal government in small business financing. His focus is on the conditions that underlie the availability of government funding of these programs, as well as how an existing or prospective entrepreneur may have access to these funds. Costs and repayment terms are also discussed. Because of the increasingly competitive environment, in recent years many state governments have begun to make capital available to new and emerging businesses.

Mr. Plosila, using Pennsylvania programs as a prime example, discusses the different types of financing available from state and local governments, as well as how these funds can be put to use. Both tax-exempt and nontax-exempt funding are discussed in detail. In addition, Mr. Plosila discusses the requirements for such funding, the advantages of using it, and the costs associated with it.

Chapter 6: Industrial Development Bond Financing

Mr. Ellinwood and Mr. Price discuss the technique whereby state and local governments allow a private user to benefit from the government's status as a tax-exempt entity as well as its ability to issue debt obligations at tax-exempt rates.

Chapter 7: Venture Capital Financing

This chapter focuses extensively on the relationship between the entrepreneur and the venture capital provider, with particular reference to what each requires from the other. Mr. Adler's company manages venture capital funds with approximately $200 million of contributed capital and has nearly 60 investments in technology companies, with board membership in 33. The insights he provides as to what venture capitalists look for and how to work with venture capitalists are invaluable.

Mr. Pratt lays out the elements of the basic business plan and other information that venture capitalists need when considering investment decisions. He also discusses the current structure of the venture capital industry—where the money is, who has it, and where it goes.

Mr. Miller discusses how he used venture capital to build the highly successful and profitable Universal Health Services, of which he is chairman. In particular, he focuses on the decisions that he had to make and the process he went through in searching out venture capitalists, finding the appropriate one, putting together the business plan the venture capitalists required, as well as how he invested the funds wisely. He also discusses the ongoing relationship between his firm and the venture capitalists, and how that relationship can be used most effectively to assure the success of his firm.

Chapter 8: Corporate Joint Ventures

Frequently the path a small business with high growth potential takes to become a successful public company is a joint venture with a publicly held corporation. Mr. Kraftson and Mr. Giacco discuss how Safeguard Scientifics Inc., a New York Stock Exchange company, enables entrepreneurs to raise capital from the initial meeting and ensures the successful conclusion of the joint venture.

Chapter 9: Going Public

Mr. Berkeley, the managing director of Alex, Brown & Sons, Inc., addresses perhaps the most key issue affecting many small and growing companies, namely, when and how to go public. He focuses on the planning issues, particularly how to determine when market conditions as well as company conditions are most beneficial for public offering. In addition, he describes in detail virtually all of the information that is necessary to prepare for a public offering, as well as how to determine how much of the company should be sold to the public and how the proceeds should be used.

Chapter 10: Mergers and Acquisitions

Megamergers and acquisitions have now become a major part of the American business scene, unlikely to disappear for many years. They not only reflect the economic restructuring going on in the United States, particularly due to the need to improve efficiency and productivity, but they also increasingly have been used as a source of capital. Mr. Sears explores mergers and acquisitions primarily from the latter point of view—how current merger and acquisition techniques can be used to raise capital for other purposes. His chapter is perhaps the most comprehensive explanation currently available, describing the entire process from the conception of a possible merger or acquisition until its completion, with particular emphasis on finding the right partners and how to negotiate the best deal. Mr. Berger deals with the accounting and tax issues relevant to business combinations.

Chapter 11: Divestitures

Mr. Hoffman deals with the key considerations and factors leading to the divestment of a subsidiary or division. The key factors fall into the following categories: economic, psychological, operational, strategic, and governmental. Mr. Hoffman also discusses how to implement a divestment program.

Because of numerous structural changes and competitive pressures, more and more companies are in the process of restructuring their businesses. In many cases, this includes divesting existing divisions, operations, or other parts of the business. Mr. Van Wyck deals with the major considerations relating to divestiture, including when it is appropriate and how to locate buyers who offer the most potential. He includes a discussion of such issues as preparing the offering memorandum, presenting appropriate financial information, and the different selling techniques that can be used.

Two of the major factors to consider in corporate restructuring through divestiture are the legal aspects and tax and accounting considerations. Mr. Mulvihill discusses these issues in depth. In particular, he focuses on antitrust considerations and other legal issues, as well as on federal and state tax issues. Issues relating to contracts, such as the assignment of existing contracts and their implications, are also discussed at length.

Chapter 12: Leveraged Buyouts

Few, if any, financing alternatives involve the interplay of so many business and legal complexities as leveraged buyouts. Mr. Quigley and Mr. Klaus focus on a practical overview of these issues and the transactional context in which they arise.

Chapter 13: Asset-Based Financing

Asset-based lending is a form of financing that has experienced tremendous growth and popularity in recent years. It can be a primary source of cash for the emerging business. This chapter discusses the winning characteristic in obtaining this form of financing.

Chapter 14: Long-Term Borrowing

Declines in interest rates in recent years, as well as the proliferation of new types of long-term bond instruments, have again made the long-term market a viable source of funding for many corporations. Mr. Meads, of Drexel Burnham, discusses all aspects of long-term funding, including the available instruments and sources and the associated risks and costs. In addition, he compares various types of long-term financing with other financing techniques.

Chapter 15: Finance Company Borrowing

Finance companies can be a new major source of funds for small and growing businesses. Mr. Roncoroni, vice president of Beneficial Business Credit Corporation, discusses how this source of funds can be tapped more effectively. He notes the differences between traditional banking and finance companies, details the different types of loans that are available from finance companies, and, finally, discusses what finance companies need from the ultimate borrower.

Chapter 16: Real Estate Financing

Raising capital in the current real estate climate involves skillfully combining traditional techniques with new creative financing procedures. Messrs. Blumberg and Salmon discuss the variety of entities and objectives that creates the opportunity for diverse methods of raising capital in today's dynamic real estate environment.

Chapter 17: Financing Corporate Construction Projects

Money market conditions, tax laws, and accounting regulations are always subject to change. The corporate construction project provides unique flexibility and a particular opportunity to employ the most effective financing techniques achievable under whatever overall conditions apply at a given point in time.

Chapter 18: Convertibles and Warrants

In this chapter Mr. Schechter describes in detail the use of convertibles and warrants which are valuable financial tools for any company. They provide a flexible security that by its nature can be tailored to meet the issuer's needs and requirements. They can be used in all types and sizes, and unlike common stock or straight debt, they can be the security that is almost all things to all people.

Chapter 19: ESOP Financing

The Employee Stock Ownership Plan (ESOP) has become a much discussed and utilized financing vehicle for a host of corporate finance transactions. Messrs. Newberg and Mufson present the fundamentals of an ESOP and raise the readers' cognizance of how cost-effective financing can be obtained through the use of an ESOP.

Chapter 20: Letter of Credit Financing

This chapter provides discussions of the use of letter of credit financing to expand the trade credit of growing businesses. Mr. Beaumont analyzes domestic and international letters of credit and discusses how each are used and their applicable terms and conditions.

Chapter 21: Commercial Paper

Commercial paper is a short-term unsecured promissory note with a fixed maturity. Issued primarily by large corporations of the highest creditworthiness, commercial paper is sold as an alternative to short-term bank credit. In this chapter Mr. Murphy examines the commercial paper market with the primary emphasis on factors of interest to a prospective commercial paper issuer.

Chapter 22: Selling the Business

It is virtually certain that every successful business owner has at one time or another considered selling his or her business—many entrepreneurs face this decision on a regular basis. Mr. Kendall's chapter focuses extensively on the factors that should be considered in making this decision, as well as on the appropriate timing once a decision to sell is made. In addition, it provides useful tips on how to find the appropriate buyer and, most importantly, how to structure the relationship in order to maximize financial benefits and to ensure the continued success of the business after the sale.

Chapter 23: Raising Foreign Capital

Foreign investors have become more willing to invest in new and growing businesses in the United States in recent years. Mr. Delacave, chairman, The Alva Investment Trust, discusses how foreign sources can be approached. He discusses how the requirements and the information that must be supplied vary from what is typical in the United States.

Chapter 24: Futures, Options, and Swaps

New tools and financing procedures have proliferated in recent years. Among them are futures, options, and swaps. This chapter focuses on how these new methods can be used to assist in the financing process, as well as how companies can more effectively manage interest rate risk. These tools are particularly useful to small and growing companies, who must fund their growth with extensive borrowing in today's uncertain and volatile economic and financial market environment.

The editors believe that we have chosen wisely and well, and that, through the generous efforts and skill of the distinguished coauthors, we have, in this volume, developed a reference work that without cooperative effort could never have been completed.

We are indebted to each of our coauthors, whose reward is filling the void.

Lawrence Chimerine
Robert F. Cushman
Howard Ross

Philadelphia, Pa., 1986

ABOUT THE EDITORS

Lawrence Chimerine

Dr. Chimerine is currently chairman and chief economist of Chase Econometrics. He is also president of the Monetary Policy Forum, chairman of the Economic Planning Council of the International Management and Development Institute, a member of the Conference Board Economic Forum, and a member of the Advisory Board of Proposition One. He is also an adviser to many government agencies, including membership on the Economic Policy Board of the Department of Commerce and the Census Advisory Committee for the Bureau of the Census. He advises numerous senators and congressmen and presents testimony on a regular basis to the Senate and House Budget Committees, the Joint Economic Committee, and many other congressional committees. Dr. Chimerine appears regularly on such television programs as "Wall $treet Week," "Moneyworld," "Good Morning, America," "Moneyline," and "Business Times," and has delivered numerous speeches to organizations such as the Detroit Economic Club, the Chief Executives Organization, and the Vail Symposium.

Robert F. Cushman

Robert F. Cushman is a partner in the national law firm of Pepper, Hamilton & Scheetz and is a recognized specialist and lecturer on all phases of real estate and construction law. He serves as legal counsel to numerous trade associations, including the American Construction Owners Association, as well as many major construction, development, and bonding companies. Mr. Cushman is the co-editor of *A Guide to the Foreign Investor* and of *High Tech Real Estate,* both published by Dow Jones-Irwin, as well as many other handbooks and guides in the insurance, real estate, and construction fields.

Mr. Cushman, who is a member of the Bar of the Commonwealth of Pennsylvania and who is admitted to practice before the Supreme Court of the United States and the United States Court of Claims, has served as executive vice president and general counsel to the Construction Industry Foundation, as well as regional chairman of the Public Contract Law Section of the American Bar Association.

Howard D. Ross

Howard Ross is a partner in the Philadelphia office of Arthur Andersen & Co. Mr. Ross specializes in servicing the owner-managed business in accounting, text planning, and finance. He has extensive experience in counseling emerging companies in financing strategy and investment structure. Mr. Ross has participated in numerous seminars on financing the growth company, with special emphasis on venture capital and going public. He is a member of Arthur Andersen's high technology industry team and mergers and acquisitions practice. Mr. Ross is a graduate of the Wharton School of the University of Pennsylvania and is a CPA.

CONTENTS

Handbook for Raising Capital

Financing Alternatives for Emerging and Growing Businesses

CHAPTER **1**

Borrowing from Banks: The Prime Source

Graeme K. Howard, Jr.
Partner
Howard, Lawson & Co.
Philadelphia, Pa.

Graeme K. Howard, Jr., is a partner in Philadelphia-based Howard, Lawson & Co., a nationally recognized corporate finance firm that has assisted over 500 privately held firms in raising growth capital. Howard, Lawson & Co. were the founding publishers of *Going Public: The IPO Reporter,* the leading authority on the initial public offering market, and *Private Placements,* a biweekly newsletter that reports on recent venture capital financings. Venture Associates, of which Howard & Company is general partner, guides the activities of over 20 early-stage companies, providing equity and debt financing from individuals and institutions through Venture Placements, Inc., a wholly owned NASD broker-dealer. Graeme Howard is a graduate of Amherst College and Yale Law School. He practiced law in the Netherlands, New Haven, and Philadelphia, and then became a partner in the corporate finance department of a regional investment banking firm before founding Howard, Lawson & Co. in 1972.

The typical growing enterprise's largest single source of external capital is a commercial bank. Yet growing businesses have a more difficult time establishing satisfactory banking relationships than do their larger counterparts. The difficulty is as often due to the image that a growing business conveys to a prospective lender as it is to that enterprise's creditworthiness. A business needing capital is not a beggar. Money is a commodity used in business, and banks are renters of that commodity, in competition with other banks and other sources of money. Therefore, a growing business should approach the acquisition of money in the same way it approaches the acquisition of raw materials or equipment.

Business and banking are more than alliterative. Most of the capital (other than retained earnings) that supports businesses comes from banks. Although getting risk capital from venture firms or taking your company public may have a lot of glamour, it is the commercial bankers who supply most of the money for business growth.

ARE BANKERS HUMAN?

"The bank is on the phone," says your secretary. For many executives, the announcement that the bank is calling is bad news. Nearly every business person is dependent on a banker for all or the bulk of his or her company's external capital. When the bank is calling, it usually means a dirge will be heard: the loan is in default; the loan officer didn't like the last financial statements (if they were even sent); or the request for an increase in the credit line has been turned down.

Most small and medium-sized businesses depend on a bank for capital to grow (or even survive). This has created a set of perspectives about banks and banking that is out of line with reality. *The reality is that banks are businesses and bankers are businesspeople.* But their product happens to be money—and money has always had a strange effect on people. This is because money is a medium of exchange and can be used to translate one valuable thing into another valuable thing, a kind of sorcery that still bedevils the ordinary mortal.

The language of banking is also strange to many businesspeople. The jargon of sinkers, silver bullets, and affirmative covenants can be confusing, but the real problem lies in the fact that the basic talk of bankers is in numbers and the numbers are those found in balance sheets, P&Ls, financial ratios, and cash flow forecasts. This part of the numbers game is seldom the strong suit of the entrepreneur. The person who starts his own business is usually a convincing salesman, a practical inventor, or a creative engineer. He can either make or sell well. *If only he didn't have to keep books, he would be happy.* A successful entrepreneur is often a good talker. He can convince his prospective customers that his product or service is the one they can't do without. And he can motivate his employees and staff to work hard to produce the goods or services he has sold. He knows the top end of his balance sheet—how much cash he has, how much his customers owe him, how much he owes his suppliers–and what his monthly "nut" or break-even point is. As long as he doesn't have to borrow any money or bring in outside investors he is a happy man, wrestling with adversaries he knows and understands: his customers and suppliers.

But when he needs some money because he can't collect his receivables any faster or slow-pay his suppliers any longer, it means a trip to the bank. And there, across the desk, is a banker: the person who can now make or break the entrepreneur's business. Because bankers have created a kind of smoke screen made up of symbols, social class, and the money myth, the entrepreneur often sees the banker as either a superman (if he delivers the needed cash) or a subhuman (if he does not).

Although there have been many reports to the contrary, *bankers are human beings and their banking business is fraught with perils* just as dangerous as those confronted by a manufacturer, wholesaler, retailer, or service company. The fact that banking is a business run by people has been proved over the last few years as go-go banking went aground on the same shoals as go-go companies and go-go brokerage firms. When the wheel suddenly stopped turning, some of the players fell off. Continental Illinois Bank was the most notorious disaster, but many large banks whose names have always stood for propriety, rectitude, and strength were wounded and are still bleeding internally.

The important lesson for businessmen is not that bankers have large incisors to draw off profits from business, but rather once the smoke has been blown away, bankers are revealed as human beings and banks as businesses. It does no good to treat bankers like Count Dracula on the one hand or like Captain Marvel on the other.

Beneficial Borrowing Combines Buying and Selling

The key to successful borrowing is a combination of normal purchasing procedures and marketing techniques. The marketing and sales approach is needed to convince the banker that he will derive benefits from lending to you (low risk, attractive rate, few administrative costs, no worries) while the purchasing procedures must be used by you to ensure that you get the best benefits from the banker (the most money possible at the lowest possible rate with as little administrative cost to you as possible, and no worries that the loan will be yanked).

What is sometimes confusing is that these two sets of tasks appear to be contradictory. But *borrowing is no more contradictory than many situations in business where buying and selling get mixed up.* At the simplest level (for example, a retail cash sale) money and a product change hands. The customer peeks to see that in fact he got a Big Mac and not a Quarter Pounder. The cashier, who in ancient times would have bitten the coin to test it for worthiness, now slips that $20 bill under an ultraviolet light to see if it is counterfeit. The transaction creates no credit problems.

Put Yourself in His Place. A more complicated case illustrates the quandary of the banker. For purposes of illustration, assume your company processes a petroleum additive that helps make machinery run more efficiently—a kind of industrial STP. A buyer from abroad, speaking a strange language, wishes to buy your additive, but he wants you to extend credit for 180 days. You know that by the end of the six months he will have used up the additive. In theory, he should have made more than enough in added profits to pay you. But he is unknown to you, so you check him out carefully. Your investigation shows that he pays his bills regularly. You make delivery of your additive and now you wait. You know that each day he is using up your product, but there is nothing you can do but wait. You can't really gripe yet—the payment date has not even arrived—but that doesn't stop you from worrying, and any negative rumors you hear about your customer are amplified as you wake up in the middle of the night wondering what you'll do if he doesn't pay.

Your banker is in a similar situation. He also deals in an additive that should increase profits, called money. He delivers his product to people who speak strange tongues (the technical jargon of the particular borrower's industry). He is told by his customers that at the end of 6, 12, or 36 months, the product (money) will be returned to the banker and that in the meantime he will be paid a fee for letting the borrower use it. The banker checks out this prospective borrower and finds that he has paid his bills regularly in the past. The borrower tells him how good his company is and how the additive will make his business much more profitable. The banker looks around and this prospective borrower seems as good or better than anyone else knocking on his door, so he lends him the money.

A Banker Scorned. Over the next few months, the banker's vivid memory of the enthusiastic advances of the borrower wanes. The borrower doesn't call in regularly to tell the banker how he is doing and the banker begins to worry. There is nothing the banker can do, however, because the loan has not matured. If, however, the interest is a couple of days late, the banker becomes agitated ("Why can't he pay his monthly interest on time when I just loaned him 120 times that amount?"). Any adverse rumors about the borrower are magnified in the banker's mind and he wakes up in a sweat.

After the Loan Has Closed. But the banker has a real problem. Because banks have promoted an image of sanctity and strength, they are not allowed to show that they are really in a worrying business. Bankers are like parents who can only hope for the best after advancing their college-bound teenager an entire year's allowance on the matriculating student's promise that he or she will use the money only for clothes, books, tuition, room and board, and incidentals necessary to an ascetic, parent-approved lifestyle. As soon as the banker gives the borrower his "allowance," based on a litany of promises that the businessman thinks is original ("My forecasts are very conservative"; "There's no way you won't be repaid"), the banker fantasizes that the businessman rushes back to his office, announces that he has gotten the money, orders the checks that have been "in the mail" for weeks to finally be posted, accepts the hurrahs of his employees for once again turning the alchemist's trick of transforming a promise into gold, and then turns to his senior executives and says, "Now that we got the money, how will we use it?" In his nightmare, the banker dreams that after paying enough bills to get off COD with the suppliers, repaying a small but very high-interest loan that was necessary to meet a couple of payrolls when business was slack, and paying a few miscellaneous bills that had been hidden in drawers at the time of the last audit, there is about 30 percent of the loan left. Half of that is allocated to develop a new product that can't miss, and the rest is put into making initial lease payments on the machinery that the loan was supposed to have funded in full.

Contrary to this banker's fantasy, most businessmen, like their children, generally hew to the middle of the road. But that doesn't prevent your banker from having recurring nightmares that end in catastrophe for his borrower, nonrepayment of the loan that he approved, another write-off his bank can't afford (or more money down the drain to keep the company afloat until the bank's bad loan reserves catch up with their unrecognized write-offs), and a pink slip for him or lifelong banishment to the branch located in financial Siberia.

Perspective Is the Key

The most successful bankers and borrowers have taken the trouble to learn the perspectives of the other party in a loan transaction. The first step in being able to borrow profitably from a bank is to know how banks lend profitably to their customers. You can read further in this field by referring to the Suggested Reading section that follows this chapter, which lists books and periodicals about how banks and bank lending work, from the banker's point of view. For a one-hour investment of time, you can learn the basics of lending by reading a 67-page brochure, "A Bankers Guide to Commercial Loan Analysis," a primer for new commercial lenders published by the American Bankers Association (202-467-4000).

You Know How You Feel as a Creditor. There is a particularly difficult hurdle for businessmen to overcome in getting a realistic handle on how bankers and banks really operate. A successful businessman has a well-developed ego that is pridefully based on his demonstrated capacity to invent, develop, produce, and sell a product, and then motivate and administer people to make and deliver it. All through his career, the entrepreneur hones these skills. But when it finally comes time to do fruitful battle with his banker, he knows that he is playing a weaker hand than he should. Even the successful businessman may feel ignorant and bedeviled in the area of finance and it is hard for him to admit that he doesn't know as much as he should about his balance sheet; his flow of funds and P&L statements; his financial ratios; his past, present, or future cash flow; or any of the other "irrelevancies" that bankers want to explore before they turn over the wampum.

Most successful businessmen are quick studies. Unfortunately, even a bright, fluent businessman has to spend longer than he wishes learning the money business and he very often has to start in financial kindergarten even though he is a Ph.D., *summa cum laude,* in the operational and administrative aspects of his successful company. He has to learn the language of finance from the ground up. If he doesn't, he will be confused or simply memorize slick phrases ("The RMA

Annual Statement Studies shows my subordinated debt/capital funds ratio to be above the first quartile in my SIC group"). Learning a new language takes time, but once one begins traveling in the country of finance, one seldom returns, so it is better to take a Berlitz crash course to match your fluency in sales and production than to rely on interpreters (brokers) for the remainder of your business career.

In counseling hundreds of businesspeople who have embarked on this challenging and exciting trip into the realities of finance, I find that certain questions recur. A systematic, comprehensive text on bank borrowing would run to many volumes and have to be loose leaf to keep up with changes in rates, terms, conditions, structure, and availability. But the answers to some of the standard questions that puzzle businesspeople may serve as a foundation on which they can build their own principles to get more principal. This chapter deals with the key elements in raising more money, at the least cost, and with the easiest terms and conditions, and it shows you how to make raising money as orderly and effective a procedure as making and selling your products. First, an overview of 17 steps to successful bank borrowing is presented. Second, we review key factors that bankers consider in making a loan (p. 18). Third, we present an analysis of The Debtors Dozen: procedures to be followed in selecting your banks (p. 20). Fourth, we explain how to make a winning bank loan presentation (p. 35). Fifth, we mix a batch of financing dynamite: the one-page loan proposal (p. 42). Sixth, we offer some tips on postloan activities (p. 46). Seventh, we tell you what you should do if you are turned down for a loan (p. 48). Eighth, we explain how to cope with a "problem" loan (p. 50). Ninth, we analyze 13 main gripes that businesspeople have about banks and what to do about them (p. 51). Finally, we offer a list of the most important books and periodicals published on commercial bank loans (p. 55).

SEVENTEEN STEPS TO SUCCESSFUL BORROWING

Here, in summary, are the 17 steps in a successful program of raising capital from a bank:

1. Decide whether you really want your company to grow so fast that it *requires* additional bank financing.
2. Determine *how much* money your company needs and *when.*
3. Set up a *schedule and cash budget* for raising capital.
4. Conduct a modest and quick financial *market research* program.
5. Prepare a *corporate profile.*
6. Decide on the *type of debt* securities you will issue for the capital you will receive.

7. Establish the *rates, terms, and conditions* you will propose to the bank.
8. Prepare a *written loan proposal.*
9. Select the *type of bank* to which you will make your loan proposal.
10. Select *specific banks* for solicitation of interest.
11. Prepare management's *presentation.*
12. Prepare a preliminary *schedule* for the proposed meetings with banks.
13. *Invite banks* to meet with you at your offices.
14. Make *initial presentations* to each bank.
15. *Negotiate.*
16. *Close.*
17. Establish a *healthy continuing relationship* with your banker.

And now, let's look at each of these steps.

1) Decide whether You Really Want Your Company to Grow So Fast that It Requires Additional Bank Financing. If your company is healthy and growing 10 to 15 percent per annum on its present capital base, you may be wise to consider *not* borrowing to grow faster. Remember, there is no law that says you must grow your company at a whirlwind pace, even though that objective is an important part of our national mythology that says bigger is always better. This is the time to decide if you really need to grow so fast that you must increase your need for external financing.

To do so, first set a target for the value of your company's stock in five years. Then compute the net income you will be earning five years out, growing at your current rate. Multiply that net income by 10 (a midrange price-earnings ratio) to establish your forecast company value. If your target value is pretty close to your forecast value, give heavy consideration to financing growth out of profits, and thus avoid risks involved in possibly overleveraging your company. It is always easier to borrow money than to repay it. *You may not want to risk your company (your major asset) if you are already growing at a healthy rate.* Your accountant, investment banker, or financial consultant can help you on this key first step in deciding whether to raise additional external capital. (See p. 10 for example.)

2) Determine How Much Money You Need and When. If you have decided that your present capitalization is insufficient to reach the stock value and profit objective you seek, prepare a cash flow forecast that is realistic. If you or your chief financial officer can't do a cash flow forecast, ask your auditor or financial adviser to help

Example

Target for your company's value in five years:	$4,000,000
Net income after tax, most recent year:	$200,000
Historical and predicted growth rate without additional external capital:	12% per year compounded annually
Projected net income in five years:	$353,000 ($200,000 + 12% compounded annually)
Assumed multiple of earnings:	10 times net income after tax
Projected value for company in five years:	$3,530,000 (10 times $353,000)
Shortfall between target value ($4,000,000) and projected value ($3,530,000):	$470,000

In this example it would *not* make sense to borrow heavily to grow faster because the risks in higher leveraging are unnecessary to reach within 11.7 percent of your value objectives.

you. The basis for a cash flow is your written business plan and financial (P&L and balance sheet) forecasts. In preparing the cash flow forecasts, use the written assumptions prepared by the senior management of your company and then let the numbers run out where they may, regardless of how little or how much money the resulting cash flow forecast shows you need. Do not prepare a cash flow forecast on the basis of your estimate of how much you can borrow. *Never try to guess how much money a bank will lend you.* Different bankers will loan the same company widely varying amounts. Your job is to figure out how much money your company will need if realistic projections are made, not to let the banker decide how much he will lend you.

Many businessmen feel that cash flow forecasts are bunk. Although detailed forecasts seldom come true, they are the best and only tool you have to plot your cash needs in the future. If your cash flow forecasting is made as much a part of your business as calling on major customers, your forecasts will soon become good friends that guide you through financial mazes. *So few companies prepare well-grounded cash flow statements for presentation to a bank that a realistic set of them will go far in getting you the loan you need.* For a free set of instructions on how to prepare a business plan and cash flow forecasts, ask for "How to Develop a Business Plan," published by Arthur Andersen & Co., 215-241-7453.

3) Set Up a Schedule and Cash Budget for Raising Capital. A successful campaign to borrow more money from a commercial bank, mutual savings bank, or S&L requires time and money. You can prepare a schedule by assigning target dates to each of the 17 steps listed here. Count on 45 to 90 days from the time you start doing your realistic cash flow forecasting until receiving a commitment on the loan.

A cash budget should also be prepared because there will normally be out-of-pocket costs for legal, accounting, and consulting advice, not to mention opportunity costs—the profits lost to the company because its senior executives are working on the financing program instead of on revenue-producing activities. Raising money is costly, whether it shows directly or indirectly. Recognizing that these costs exist at the outset will help you to control them during the process.

4) Conduct a Modest and Quick Financial Market Research Program. This consists of telephone calls to a number of banks. Each conversation by you or your adviser should investigate the bank's interest in making a loan of the size you need to a company in your industry.

If there is a general interest, tell the banker you are now putting together your business plan and cash flow forecast and will invite him to come out when they are completed. This process gives you a basic idea as to whether there will be interest in your banking business, without making significant disclosures. For further details on this step, see page 31 in the section dealing with bank selection.

5) Prepare a Corporate Profile. A corporate profile is the basic document a company uses to convince lenders (or investors) that they should provide capital to the company. It is similar to the prospectus a public company uses to sell its securities to the public, but is more detailed and includes a business plan and financial forecasts.

The corporate profile is the most important weapon in your arsenal for raising capital. Its objective is to provide the banker with all the information he needs, in writing, to make a preliminary credit decision and to support him when he makes an affirmative presentation to the loan commitment committee of the bank.

A corporate profile has a number of benefits in addition to selling the bank on your proposal:

a. The facts in a corporate profile provide a realistic basis for corporate planning (both financial and operational).
b. The corporate profile gives each of your operating managers a clearer and more accurate overview of the company's operations.
c. Management learns to think about the company with an outsider's perspective.

As the quality of a corporate borrower's management is the single most important factor in a banker's decision to lend (see page 18), the corporate profile is an immense help in persuading lenders that management knows what it is doing (even if the company has not achieved high profits).

The corporate profile doesn't have to be fancy. Some of the best are contained in a simple loose-leaf notebook. What's important is the contents. Your corporate profile should contain the following information: table of contents, summary of profile, history of the company, financial results (last five years), summary of operations, products, line(s) of business, market and industry data, competition, marketing and sales, customers, plant and equipment, manufacturing process (or service methods or distribution process for wholesalers /retailers), suppliers, research and development, ownership, board of directors, management, employees and labor relations, litigation, professional advisers and references, management information systems and financial administration, financing history, most recent audit reports (a bank will want reports of the last five years), most recent unaudited financial statements, management's analysis of financial statements, comparison of company with Robert Morris Annual Statement Studies (see p. 41), business plan, financial and cash flow forecasts, and capital requirements. Ask for "Corporate Profile" (215-988-0010).

Putting this information together is costly in terms of management time, but its benefits far outweigh its costs. The corporate profile puts you in the driver's seat in your presentations to and negotiations with your prospective bankers.

6) Decide on the Type of Debt Securities You Will Issue for the Capital You Will Receive. This is usually known as "structuring the deal." If you don't know whether you should get a short-term credit line, a medium-term revolving credit, or a longer-term loan with or without a sinking fund, better get advice from your lawyer, auditor, or financial consultant. This step is fairly technical and following general rules is dangerous.

Draw on the experience of all your professional advisers, but make up your own mind only after *you* understand the consequences of each type of debt and recognize the benefits and the danger points in each. Do not rely on a sole adviser: Be your own decision maker, because *you* have to live with the repayment schedules, terms, and conditions, not your advisers.

7) Establish the Rates, Terms, and Conditions You Will Propose to the Bank. Start with some research. A great place to begin is by obtaining the Federal Reserve Bulletin, published monthly by the

Federal Reserve Board. (Single copies are available for $2.50 from Publications Services, Federal Reserve System, Washington, D.C. 20551, and are available in most libraries.) Among its wealth of financial reports, the Bulletin reports on what's really going on in the commercial lending marketplace. The Bulletin publishes special tables every few months, entitled "Terms of Lending at Commercial Banks," that give you the data on commercial loan activity on *all* banks (amount and average size) for a representative week three months earlier, along with maturities and *loan rates,* broken down by term and size of loan. The report also indicates the number, amount, and rate of loans made *at below prime rate* (see top of p. 15).

Exhibit 1 shows such a report published in August 1985. As an example, line 24 indicates that floating rate, short-term (less than one year) loans between $500,000 and $1 million made during the week of May 6–10, 1985, carried a weighted average effective interest rate of 11.54 percent (long-term 11.51 percent), which was one percentage point above the prime rate of 10.5 percent. Those of you who were paying more than P + 1 for your money at that time were paying above the average.

You will also find a table in the Bulletin detailing the movements of the prime rate. By correlating the two tables, you will get a good feel for how many points above (and below) prime rate banks are charging for a variety of types and sizes of loans. This should help you determine what you believe will be an acceptable rate to propose to your banker. For additional information on interest rate trends, read "Blue Chip Financial Forecasts" (see the Suggested Reading section at the end of this chapter).

Terms and conditions will differ with the type of loan you are requesting. Your professional advisers can help you outline what they should be. Remember, many conditions that banks "set" are often negotiable. Make sure that before any meeting with a banker, you understand the consequences of this "boilerplate" material, which is all too often glossed over by borrowers until the day their failure to review these critical provisions puts them in technical default on their loans. Any important terms and conditions should be highlighted in your written loan proposal. Even a technical default puts your banker in the driver's seat—and you may not like him as chauffeur. Homework in this area can't be stressed enough.

8) Prepare a Written Loan Proposal. Many executives simply tell their banker they need a certain amount of money and let the lender work out the terms. Or worse, they ask the banker to tell them how much they can borrow. That's like setting prices by asking your customers how much they want to pay for your product. By submitting

EXHIBIT 1 Federal Reserve Bulletin Report*

A70 Special Tables □ August 1985

4.23 TERMS OF LENDING AT COMMERCIAL BANKS Survey of Loans Made, May 6–10, 1985[1]

A. Commercial and Industrial Loans

Characteristics	Amount of loans (thousands of dollars)	Average size (thousands of dollars)	Weighted average maturity[2]	Loan rate (percent)		
			Days	Weighted average effective[3]	Standard error[4]	Inter-quartile range[5]
ALL BANKS						
1 Overnight[6]	17,044,661	3,695	*	8.95	.53	8.60–9.14
2 One month and under	7,421,894	412	16	9.68	.36	8.88–9.89
3 Fixed rate	5,705,205	437	16	9.57	.48	8.88–9.79
4 Floating rate	1,716,689	346	15	10.07	.25	8.98–11.06
5 Over one month and under a year	9,302,512	66	146	11.26	.44	9.52–12.62
6 Fixed rate	4,532,255	45	102	11.04	.49	9.35–12.49
7 Floating rate	4,770,257	117	188	11.48	.43	10.92–12.62
8 Demand[7]	4,368,947	152	*	11.09	.25	9.76–12.13
9 Fixed rate	837,252	211	*	9.60	.69	8.84–11.07
10 Floating rate	3,531,695	142	*	11.44	.10	11.02–12.19
11 **Total short term**	**38,138,014**	**198**	**44**	**9.90**	**.34**	**8.74–11.02**
12 Fixed rate (thousands of dollars)	27,924,391	230	21	9.43	.38	8.60–9.52
13 1–24	660,021	7	106	14.12	.28	13.31–15.03
14 25–49	312,283	33	119	13.38	.22	12.68–14.48
15 50–99	319,243	72	120	13.27	.33	12.37–14.03
16 100–499	678,332	166	65	12.83	.62	11.49–14.54
17 500–999	314,672	674	48	10.39	.25	9.26–11.07
18 1000 and over	25,639,840	7,695	15	9.11	.18	8.60–9.34
19 Floating rate (thousands of dollars)	10,213,623	144	138	11.19	.30	9.62–12.14
20 1–24	347,875	9	154	13.12	.34	12.13–14.37
21 25–49	378,884	33	142	12.73	.07	12.13–13.25
22 50–99	637,308	66	174	12.70	.26	12.00–13.80
23 100–499	1,838,317	182	186	12.22	.22	11.30–12.89
24 500–999	729,940	670	148	11.54	.11	11.02–12.13
25 1000 and over	6,281,299	3,898	119	10.49	.31	9.20–11.57
			Months			
26 **Total long term**	**4,775,340**	**134**	**55**	**11.03**	**.56**	**9.37–12.01**
27 Fixed rate (thousands of dollars)	1,718,901	79	53	11.26	1.17	9.22–11.73
28 1–99	323,533	15	41	16.01	1.27	14.37–15.17
29 100–499	51,108	228	48	12.83	.95	11.30–13.88
30 500–999	39,249	637	57	11.77	.70	10.92–13.24
31 1000 and over	1,305,011	7,536	56	10.00	.69	9.18–11.20
32 Floating rate (thousands of dollars)	3,056,438	220	56	10.90	.47	9.54–12.13
33 1–99	248,881	22	45	13.13	.32	12.13–14.93
34 100–499	372,075	180	51	12.19	.14	11.57–12.75
35 500–999	140,768	638	43	11.51	.34	10.92–12.28
36 1000 and over	2,294,715	5,887	58	10.42	.48	9.42–11.30

* This table includes data from *all* banks that are members of the Federal Reserve System. The table provides fixed and floating interest rates for short-term, demand, and long-term loans (by size of loans). Note that loans *below* prime rate are singled out for review.

SOURCE: Federal Reserve Bulletin.

EXHIBIT 1 *(concluded)*

			Days	Loan rate (percent)		Prime rate[9]
				Effective[3]	Nominal[8]	
LOANS MADE BELOW PRIME[10]						
37 Overnight[6]	16,675,173	10,463	*	8.89	8.52	10.50
38 One month and under	6,426,340	3,935	15	9.26	8.87	10.50
39 Over one month and under a year	3,897,293	448	113	9.52	9.17	10.62
40 Demand[7]	1,265,545	465	*	9.13	8.78	10.69
41 Total short term	**28,264,351**	**1,929**	**21**	**9.07**	**8.70**	**10.53**
42 Fixed rate	25,093,778	2,209	15	9.05	8.67	10.52
43 Floating rate	3,170,573	964	76	9.29	8.91	10.61
			Months			
44 Total long term	**2,264,102**	**917**	**53**	**9.49**	**9.19**	**10.56**
45 Fixed rate	937,474	434	41	9.46	9.30	10.62
46 Floating rate	1,326,628	1,309	61	9.50	9.11	10.51

a clear, detailed loan proposal, you will both impress your banker and gain the upper hand in negotiations. The proposal should have all the elements of the deal and be prepared well in advance of your meeting with the banker. A detailed loan proposal includes:

- Identity of borrower.
- Amount.
- Use of proceeds.
- Types of loan.
- Closing date.
- Term.
- Rate.
- Takedown.
- Collateral.
- Guarantees.
- Repayment schedule.
- Source of repayment.

The one-page proposal is such an important part of a successful borrowing program that a special section starting on page 42 provides details.

9) Select the Type of Bank to Which You Intend to Make Your Loan Proposals. Banks are not a homogeneous group. They can be divided into several groups: local, regional, national, and foreign commercial banks, and mutual savings banks and S&Ls. (Don't forget, mutual savings banks and S&Ls now have broad commercial lending powers, and in some locales they are becoming aggressive business lenders. See page 24 for details on the selection of your bank.

10) Select Specific Banks for Solicitation of Interest. Depending on your corporate needs, you may want to concentrate on a specific group of banks that have targeted companies like yours for reducing their excess inventory of money. (Never forget that bankers have inventory problems like every other company in the world.)

In general, your present bank should always be at the top of your list. Unless relations with your loan officer have deteriorated so badly that you believe continued business is fruitless, always include your present bank in any capital search. (That, however, doesn't preclude considering other banks. No matter what the size of your company, you should always have more than one bank.)

Working from your selection of bank types accomplished in Step 9, select the actual institutions you'd like to contact. As you make this list, keep an open mind. Banks are more competitive than ever, and the so-called middle market or emerging growth company is their latest love. If you are a pessimistic type, don't let your own "worst case" imagination keep your company from getting the best deal from the most aggressive banker. There is no loss in being turned down by a few banks before zeroing in on the bank that needs the interest from your loans to meet its revenue forecasts.

11) Prepare for Management's Presentation. A good presentation should take from two to six hours. It will include five sections: a description of operations, a review of results of operations and financial condition, business plan and cash flow forecasts, analysis of the bank's capabilities (while the banker is studying you, you should be examining and questioning him!), and the loan proposal itself.

In this day of the PC and Lotus, most companies already have some form of business plan, the major document involved in the presentation, and preparation will primarily entail top management discussing their roles in the presentation and putting together a loan proposal. See page 35 for details on how to make a winning presentation to your banker.

12) Prepare a Preliminary Schedule for the Proposed Meetings with Banks. The major step here is to make sure your management team will be available to participate in presentations on specific days. Set up a schedule before calling the banks. Having your financial vice president in Bermuda the day a calling officer visits at your request will not be impressive.

Also consider the time you and your team will devote to the presentation. Don't put together a schedule so tightly packed that it detracts from operations. Give yourselves time for the company's well-being as well as your capital search.

13) Invite Banks to Meet with You at Your Offices. The solicitation of interest can be a telephone call to a lending vice president.

Describe your company, its line of business, and location; generally describe revenues, net income, assets, and shareholder equity; and ask if the bank would have interest in discussing a financing proposal.

The telephone is not the time to give the banker the details of any proposal. You should merely determine if his institution has sufficient interest in visiting a company like yours for a full-scale presentation.

If there is interest, set up a meeting, but *always make your loan presentation to a banker on your own turf.* When you make your first presentations to any banker, insist that he come to your headquarters. Later discussions may take place at the bank, but you and your management team will be more comfortable in home territory and you will be able to impress the banker with your operations.

14) Make Initial Presentations. The first presentation may have some rough spots, but you will improve with practice. Keeping that in mind, though, you may want to schedule your first two presentations to banks you believe are not so likely to want to deal with you.

15) Negotiate. In bank loans, negotiations are key. A bank that makes a proposal to your firm will very likely supply what is more or less a form agreement. There may be minor alternatives to fit the specific borrowing situations. *Your* written loan proposal—which the bank sees first—should spell out what your company is looking for in terms of rate, terms, and conditions.

Rate and particularly availability will be determined by several factors, not the least of which is your skill as a negotiator and the extent to which the bank believes it is competing for your business. Don't be timid. If a bank rejects your proposal on a rate basis, you can always call them back and reopen negotiations later.

Crucial in all your negotiations is to remember your role—that of *customer.* Banks are one of your suppliers—in this case, they supply capital. But just as you force suppliers to bid on the materials you need to ensure you get the best deal and best working relationship, so it should be with your banker. Don't let him have the upper hand. Remember: He is the seller and you are the buyer.

16) Close. Depending on the type of loan and bank, closing may be quite formal, with sheaves of documents, or it may be a short letter reviewing the agreement. In either case, all closing documents should be reviewed by your professional advisers before you sign them and return them to the bank.

17) Establish a Healthy Continuing Relationship with Your Bankers. Don't let the romance go out of the relationship with your banker as soon as you have the bank's money in your account. Smart executives continue to meet regularly with their loan officer and make full disclosure on a regular basis. To a loan officer handling multiple accounts, this is an endearing gesture. You have his money and, for all he knows, the next time he hears from you, it will be to report you're in default. By keeping the channels of communication open, your banker is likely to be much more responsive to your next capital request. Once you get that check, don't burn your bridges. See page 48 for steps to follow if your loan proposal is not accepted.

KEY FACTORS BANKERS CONSIDER IN MAKING A POSITIVE LOAN DECISION

In a survey in which commercial lending officers listed the most important elements in saying "yes" to a loan proposal, the top four were:

1. Quality of management.
2. Existence of proper accounting systems.
3. Trend of market demand for borrower's products and services.
4. Management structure.

Quality of the Management. Every banker that answered the survey said that this was the key factor in determining whether to make a loan. If your banker turns you down, ask yourself if you are the kind of manager (both in reality and in the kind of impression you make) to whom you would entrust bank funds if you were a banker. Have you gone to the trouble to prepare resumes for your key managers? Has your banker met and talked to your executives so he knows that you are not a one-man band? If you have managers, have you trained them to respond intelligently to the questions that bankers will ask? Do you let your banker talk to your executives out of your presence so that the banker knows you trust them? When you and your managers talk to your bankers, do you make full disclosure of your problems (as well as your opportunities) and discuss how you intend to meet those challenges? If you and your managers can't sell yourselves, you will have an uphill battle selling your company's financial statements.

Existence of Proper Accounting Systems. The second most important factor is your company's accounting system. The focus here is on whether management receives accurate, relevant, and timely financial information on which to base company decision making. These are the daily, weekly, and monthly reports that affect "real world" decisions, not the audit report (which placed 13th in the list of factors). Many businessmen won't share with their bankers the informal reports they receive from their subordinates (or which they prepare themselves) because they aren't typed and done up with covers and ribbons, but these reports are the lifeblood of management. That's what the banker needs to see and discuss so he can be sure that you understand your business and can move quickly to put out fires or seize opportunities. Also included in this area, of course, are your periodical accounting reports, which should show your after-tax net income and balance sheet position on a monthly basis. Always review your chart of accounts with your banker so he knows that you understand the makeup of your financial statements. If you can't explain it to your banker, you may want to ask yourself if you are using your financial statements as key elements in deciding your company's future or merely as historical window dressing to rationalize "gut" decisions.

Trend of Market Demand. The next factor that will be given special consideration by your banker is the trend of demand for your product in the marketplace. If you are supplying a product or service that is enjoying an upward demand curve, make sure you can document this important information with government, trade association, or private market research figures. Have you made a survey of your customers' purchasing forecasts? What will happen if your loan officer asks the bank's research department for a reading on the trend of your marketplace? Will it be bullish or pessimistic? If the overall market trend is level or declining (and you are forecasting increased sales), what program have you devised to work against the adverse trend? Here is a chance to show off your marketing and selling skills to convince your banker that you can beat out the competition.

Management Structure. The way you organize your company and delegate authority and responsibility is the fourth most important factor. If your company is successful, there is no need to prepare a "make believe" organizational chart. But you should list the major functions of each executive and give these words some life by letting each executive describe the actual projects (one-shot, periodic, and continuous) for which he has responsibility. In smaller companies, everyone has a number of functions, and the banker knows and expects that to be the case, but indicate the degree of delegation that is used to keep the senior manager's time available for major decisions.

The bankers surveyed felt that the above four factors had priority over all others. After these four, they ranked the following nine factors in the order listed.

5. Adequate insurance (to preserve assets in case of catastrophic losses).
6. Staffing of the management structure (will there be skilled personnel to support future growth?).
7. Minimum working capital or current ratio level (will there be enough money, assuming the loan is made, to assure that the company will not only survive but be able to grow?).
8. Priority over other creditors.
9. Present level of demand for the borrower's products or services.
10. Current profitability.
11. Current and future cash flow.
12. Receipt of financial statements at periodic intervals.
13. A certified audit.

If your loan is turned down, examine your company's operations and the presentation you made to your bank and see how you measure up to these factors. Put yourself behind your banker's desk. Remember that he wants to lend money. Don't always blame the banker. If he turns you down, make sure you find out the real reasons based on what he says and your analysis of your company's batting average based on the factors listed above.

HOW TO SELECT YOUR COMMERCIAL BANK

The selection of a lead commercial bank is the most important financing step in a company's development. There are several situations in which a company may initiate the process of selecting a commercial bank: The company may have been profitable from the start of operations and has now reached a point where debt capital is needed for the first time (don't you wish!); or the company may have been a borrower for many years but has now decided to establish a new banking relationship for any of the following reasons:

- The banks' unwillingness to lend what's needed.
- Personality clashes with its loan officer.
- Unreasonable rates, terms, and conditions.
- Policy differences over rate of corporate growth.
- Legal loan limits.
- Loan or credit limits imposed due to the bank's bad loan position.

Regardless of the reason, senior managers of most businesses periodically face the challenge of selecting a commercial bank.

What to Do about Your Present Bank

Although competition among banks is intense, a company should not replace its existing bank lightly. In determining whether a new banking relationship should be established, a company should first evaluate its existing bank.

There are some reasons that are "automatics" for triggering selection of a new bank, but in many cases, dissatisfaction is nothing more than company management not understanding the motivations of bankers and the policies and procedures of their bank. *It does little good to select a new bank after a whirlwind courtship only to find the disease that infected the relationship with your former bank is still virulent.*

If your appraisal of your bank (described later in this article) suggests that your present bank has not been responsive to your changing patterns of demand or does not seem able or willing to support your growth plans, then it is time to select a new bank.

Changing banks can be traumatic. Management will find itself worrying that if the present bank discovers it is searching for a new one, the present line of credit will be called—or worse, if a new bank can't be found, then the company's current bank will tighten the screws and make a difficult situation intolerable.

The likelihood of discovery *can* be minimized. Although bankers trade information, they are also competitors. In this day of head-to-head battles between banks for loans of even marginal borrowers, every banker assumes that his borrowers will be avidly pursued by other lenders. Bankers seeking new corporate customers recognize, however, that a shift from one lending source to another is a delicate matter. Although there can be no absolute guarantee, bankers generally will respect a request that no contacts be made with your present bank. Further, if your company's relationship with its current bankers is that bad, then your sorrowful lender may *welcome* a replacement.

The process of selecting a new bank can be made less hazardous if the borrower is completely prepared before contacts are made with new bankers. *To be fully prepared, before any contacts are made you should have prepared or updated your corporate profile, business plan, financial forecast, and loan proposal.*

Since these preparations are time-consuming for management and may be costly if outside assistance is required, it is important to know beforehand whether banks will want to at least explore becoming your lead lender. That can be determined in short order by having you (or, if you want to remain invisible, an outside adviser, lawyer, auditor, or consultant) call the banks you have selected as likely candidates and ask their senior loan officer if the bank would be interested in reviewing a loan proposal from an unnamed client with your characteristics and loan requirements. The banker can be provided with some general information, including your industry, location, revenue range, net worth, and approximate loan requirements. From the responses, the company can decide on the number of banks to invite and the order of march. With banks awash with deposits, you may be pleasantly surprised at the reception you get from new bankers.

The Debtor's Dozen

A program to select a commercial bank can be divided into 12 steps, The Debtor's Dozen. These steps apply equally well to small and large companies. The amount of time and money spent on each step is a function of the resources of the company, the size of the loan, and the experience/skill level of the management. The dozen steps are laid out in summary form here and then covered in detail.

1. Prepare a *financial sources notebook* and establish your *financial sources information files.*
2. Determine which local, regional, and national banks are active in your area and, more specifically, are soliciting loans of the type your company needs.
3. List the specific characteristics you seek in your lead bank.
4. Make a preliminary evaluation of the banks you have listed.
5. Use your lawyer, auditor, investment banker, financial consultant, or fellow businessmen to help you in evaluation (and later in making initial contacts if needed).
6. After preliminary evaluation, list the banks in order of preference.
7. Contact banks by telephone to obtain indications of interest.
8. Select three to seven banks (usually including your present bank) to which to make presentations.
9. Make presentations.
10. After each presentation, evaluate the bank in writing.
11. Compare the characteristics, advantages, and disadvantages of each bank.
12. Make your final selection. Then negotiate and close the loan.

There are three additional follow-up steps to selecting your banker.

13. Select your second or backup bank and continue a program of contacts.
14. Continue to evaluate your bank—and review your own company's operations and progress from your banker's perspective.
15. Continue a regular program of meetings with your bank to ensure a healthy relationship.

Prepare a Financial Sources Notebook and Open Financial Sources Information Files. It's true that many banking relationships have been born out of happenstance. In an industry where there are more than 14,000 commercial banks (plus S&Ls and savings banks), each renting an identical product (money), it is foolhardy to let irrelevant quirks dictate the limits of your search for the best possible source of the least expensive supply of external capital.

To take advantage of this strong competitive position that borrowers hold, begin by setting up a *financial sources notebook.* (Your controller should take responsibility for this step.) The best method is to use a colored tab separator for each of the following sources:

- Commercial banks.
- Savings banks.
- S&Ls.
- Commercial finance companies.
- Insurance companies.
- Investment banks.
- Venture capital investors.
- Government programs.

Then prepare white tab separators for each specific financial institution you now deal with or know of and place each white tab separator behind the appropriate colored category separator.

Behind each white separator, place a control sheet with the name, address, and telephone number of the institution, and list the name, title, location, and direct-dial telephone number of each officer with whom you have made contact (or with whom you intend to make contact). Behind the control sheet, put notes of telephone calls and meetings as they occur.

As new sources are located or as additional officers are contacted, update your notebook. *For most companies, financing is episodic and the CFO's memory needs support to keep track of prior contacts.* Your financial sources notebook should be kept at hand and updated as you go along, not prepared and then filed away to gather dust. The notebook is the springboard for any financing program.

The *financial sources information files* should be set up using a hanging file system with a separate file for each institution. The files should hold annual and quarterly reports, newsletters, and other information on each institution, as well as a correspondence clip for formal communications, memos, and so on. These files are backup for the financial sources notebook and give you easy access to up-to-date information on sources for both regular and emergency use.

This well-organized system is a key to a successful financing campaign.

Determine Which Banks Are Actively Soliciting Loans of the Type Your Company Needs. This step determines how many and which banks may be interested in financing your operations. The key to any rational program of commercial bank selection is that there will be competition for your business. If there is no competition for your business, then you are a beggar and not a chooser. Competition among banks is intense. It is poor management not to select your bank in a competitive atmosphere. In order to do this, it is necessary to list the banks that may have at least an initial interest in your company.

From a borrower's point of view, it is helpful to consider banks as being local, regional, or national in character. (This refers to the geographical scope of a bank's activities, not whether they are chartered as state or national banks.)

- *Local banks* are those institutions with headquarters or branches located in the immediate locale of the borrower's main offices or factories.
- *Regional banks* are those banks located within 50 to 100 miles of the borrower's main office, whose lending activities (through calling officers) cover the borrower's city.
- *National banks* are larger banks, normally located in major cities outside the borrower's state or region, that solicit larger loans of various types across the country. These larger, money-center banks solicit either through traveling loan officers or through loan production offices (LPOs), which are representative offices with permanent staffs.

To get a list of *all* possible banks that may become your lead lender, you should purchase (or review at your local library) a bank directory, such as the *Rand McNally International Bankers Directory* or *Polk's World Bank Directory.* These lists are arranged by state and city and provide up-to-date information on the resources, branches, and senior officers of banks.

For local banks, the quickest way is to go to the Yellow Pages. (The Yellow Pages will often list not only banks that are headquartered or have branches in your city but also regional banks that are soliciting business in your area.) Make a list of such local banks, regardless of size, and place the list in the "Commercial Bank" section in your financial sources notebook.

The identification of regional banks requires slightly more homework. Using a map, list the five largest cities within 50 to 100 miles. Then make a list of the larger banks in these cities using a bank directory as the source. This may require a trip to the library or purchase of a bank directory, but the investment of time or money is well worth it in order to have an inclusive list of banks outside your city but within your region. (A shortcut is to call the local Chamber of Commerce in each city.) This list of regional banks should be inserted in your financial sources notebook. These regional banks are often the most competitive when it comes to rate and availability.

The last group of banks consists of those outside your locale or region that actively solicit business in your area. You should be able to find them at the same time you are researching regional banks at the library or with a bank directory. These banks are national in their marketing scope. Normally located in money centers such as New York, Los Angeles, Chicago, Philadelphia, Pittsburgh, Detroit, Boston, Dallas, Cleveland, San Francisco, and Houston, commercial loan departments of these banks are organized either on a geographic, functional, or industry basis, or sometimes in some combination of the three. In a typical loan department of these major banks, there will be (1) a metropolitan or regional division that handles clients within the city and suburbs or Federal Reserve district, and (2) loans to major borrowers, especially outside the headquarters city of the bank. They use loan production officers in various cities to solicit business in the region, review proposals, and coordinate communications between the borrower and an industry specialist located at bank headquarters. The list of these national banks that operate in your region should be placed behind the list of regional banks in the financial sources notebook. These national banks usually are looking for loans of $1 million or more. Don't forget U.S. branches of foreign banks if you borrow over $1 million and are creditworthy. They are among the most aggressive when it comes to rates.

As a result of this investment of time you will have a list of prospective lead lenders consisting of 3 to 15 local banks (depending on banking activity in your city), 5 to 10 regional banks, and a list of national banks that operate in your area. From these banks, three to five should be selected for your presentations.

List the Specific Characteristics You Seek in Your Lead Bank. In choosing a commercial bank, many business borrowers consider only a few of the broad array of characteristics that differentiate one bank from another. The decision as to which bank is best for your company should be made by management only after the characteristics you seek in your commercial bank have been listed in writing. By considering these characteristics in advance and measuring each prospective lender against them, you can avoid falling into a trap where one factor (rate or amount, for example, or the personal charm of a loan officer) is given more weight than it should be. The best banking relationship is a lasting one, and a wise initial choice will help to avoid the trauma that is associated with a shift in banks.

When the management of a company is deciding on a key piece of equipment to purchase or a new building to lease, all sorts of checklists are used and conferences held to make certain that the machine or factory will meet a long list of requirements. *Use of a similar system will help business borrowers avoid gross errors in their choice of a lead bank.*

Listed below are sets of questions that will provide a framework for deciding what bank characteristics are most important to your company. *Remember that banks are very different from one another.* It is these distinctions that make choosing a bank so important.

The characteristics that should be considered fall into six categories: (1) financial condition and results of operations; (2) loan policies and lending activities; (3) organization; (4) the relationship of your company to the bank; (5) disclosure policies of the bank; and (6) other services of the bank.

These characteristics can be elicited by a list of questions that can be answered from materials published by the bank (e.g., annual and quarterly reports to shareholders and Form 10-K, all of which are available without cost, from the bank's investor relations department), or in interviews with the bank's representatives, other business borrowers dealing with the bank, or your legal, accounting, or financial advisers.

Financial Condition and Operating Results of the Bank

- At what rate has the bank been growing?
- Is the bank record of profitability better or worse than other banks of its size *(a)* nationally? *(b)* regionally? *(c)* locally?
- Was the bank a go-go bank that is now slowing?
- Is the bank owned by a holding company? Since when? Has the holding company been a success? What do the other subsidiaries of the holding company do: *(a)* commercial finance? *(b)* leasing? *(c)* other?
- If publicly traded, *(a)* has stock price been rising or declining? *(b)* Is the bank's price-earnings ratio at or below that of similar banks? Has the bank or holding company had any unfavorable or "surprise" news announcements in the past two years?
- Has the bank grown by internal expansion or acquisition of other banks?
- How do the bank's key operating ratios compare with those of other banks?
- What is the relationship of loans to deposits?
- What is the relationship of the loan reserve to the loan portfolio?
- How do the bank's total resources rank with other banks in the marketing area?
- Which agencies regulate the bank? *(a)* Federal Reserve; *(b)* Comptroller of the Currency; *(c)* Federal Deposit Insurance Corporation; *(d)* State Banking Department; *(e)* Securities and Exchange Commission.

- Is the bank organized as a state or national bank?
- What amount of the loan portfolio is in *(a)* loans to lesser developed countries; *(b)* oil and gas related loans; and *(c)* loans to troubled companies, including those in Chapter 11?
- Has the bad debt reserve (provision for loan losses) recently been increased?
- Have write-offs (net loan losses) increased?
- Is the bank on the "problem" list of a regulatory body?
- From what sources (and in what proportions) does the bank generate the cash it lends to borrowers? *(a)* checking accounts; *(b)* savings accounts; *(c)* certificates of deposit; *(d)* federal funds (overnight borrowings from other banks); *(e)* notes or other long-term debt; *(f)* equity; *(g)* other sources.

What effect will the preceding factors have on:

Size of loans.

Interest rates.

Terms and conditions.

Mental state of loan officers.

Loan commitment committee procedures and decisions.

Loan Policies and Lending Activities

- Is the bank known as a retail bank (dealing primarily with individuals) or a wholesale bank (dealing with corporate customers)?
- What is the bank's legal limit for loans?
- What is the house limit for loans?
- What are the procedures used for making loans?
- How did the bank treat its customers when prime rose to 20 percent?
- In addition to normal commercial loans, does the bank make the following types of loans to regular customers?

Industrial real estate mortgages.
  Construction mortgages.
  Long-term mortgages.
    Conventional.
    Tax exempt via local, regional, or state authorities.
Term loans.
  Secured.
  Unsecured.

New product development loans.

Loans to finance acquisitions.

Home mortgages to company employees at below-market rates or with longer-than-normal maturities.

- What is the *(a)* smallest loan, *(b)* median or mainstream loan, and *(c)* largest loan that each of the divisions or departments listed below will make?

  Commercial loan department.
  Branch.
  Regional department.
  Metropolitan department.
  National or U.S. department.
  Secured lending department.

- For each department listed above, what would a "mainstream" company (the business borrower) be likely to show in its financial statements for revenues, net income, and net worth?

Organization and Reputation of the Bank

- Have there been recent changes in top management in the bank? If so, will this trigger policy changes?
- Is there rapid turnover of personnel in the commercial loan department?
- Is the commercial loan department organized by *(a)* region? *(b)* industry? *(c)* revenues? *(d)* size of loan?
- Does the bank have a national department? Who is the senior officer? How many loan officers? What is the geographical reach? What is the minimum-sized loan?
- Does the bank have any loan production offices (LPOs) located outside its headquarters state? Where is the nearest office? What does the LPO do: *(a)* solicit loan business? *(b)* structure deals? *(c)* participate in follow-up activities?
- Who makes the decisions in the various branches or departments?*(a)* One officer? *(b)* two officers? *(c)* three officers? *(d)* commitment committee? *(e)* board of directors?
- Will the bank's branch system be helpful? How many branches are there? Where are they located? Hours of operations?
- What is the bank's reputation among *(a)* regulators? *(b)* customers? *(c)* other banks?
- What is the bank's reputation for:

  Rendering promised services?
  Supporting companies that grow?
  Supporting companies that get into trouble?
  Setting interest rates above or below market?
  Demanding tougher-than-usual conditions?
  Speed of decision?
  Candor and openness?

Requiring paydowns?
Requiring compensating balances?
Imaginative financing?
Supporting customers when credit is tight?
Quality of management?
Quality of loan officers?

The Relationship of Your Company and the Bank. How important will your company's business be to the bank in terms of:

a. Amount of deposits.
b. Peripheral business (trusts, estates, personal deposits, etc.)
c. Size of loan.
d. Profitability of loan.
e. Risk of loan.
f. Prestige of borrower.

How well do your company's officers or directors know the following?

a. Chairman and president of the bank.
b. Other senior officers.
c. Line loan officers.
d. Members of the regional or functional advisory boards.
e. Bank directors: Are directors "operating" types or "pin-stripers"? Is the board dominated by the officers or by outside directors?

Disclosure Policies of the Bank. An important element in any bank relationship is the policy of disclosure that will be followed by the bank and its borrower. This policy raises the following issues:

- Does the bank disclose changes in lending policies to its borrowers?
- Does the bank have a deposit/loan relationship with your competitors, suppliers, or customers?
- How much information will the bank require for its files?
- Will any sensitive information be made available to others without the knowledge of the borrower?
- What methods are used to ensure that sensitive materials will be kept confidential?
- How will the bank respond to inquiries from suppliers or customers for credit information (either directly or via the other party's bank)?
- Will the company be notified of requests for credit information and given the substance of the bank's reply?

Other Services of the Bank. What services can the bank render in addition to normal commercial loans?

- *SBIC.* Does the bank own or participate in a Small Business Investment Company that can provide subordinated debt or equity?
- *Corporate finance.* Is there a corporate finance department that will assist in corporate planning, valuations, raising long-term debt, acquisitions, and disposition?
- *Trust and estates.* Is there a strong trust department for managing pension and profit-sharing plans and planning estate programs for the owner/managers?
- *Cash management.* How sophisticated are the cash management services rendered by the bank?
- *Registrar and transfer.* Does the bank have an efficient stock registrar and transfer agent department for public companies?
- *Commercial finance.* Does the bank own a commercial finance subsidiary (or is secured lending a part of normal loan activities)?
- *Lease financing.* Is there a leasing department? If so, is it fully staffed and funded or does the bank work through a leasing service? Does the department arrange *(a)* vendor ("sales-aid" or "lease marketing") programs? *(b)* vendor rental programs? *(c)* leveraged leasing programs? *(d)* investor's leasing programs (third-party financial sources)? *(e)* leasing programs abroad? *(f)* fleet leasing? *(g)* equipment leasing? or *(h)* sale/leaseback of equipment or land and buildings?
- *International.* Can the bank support your company's current or proposed international operations through *(a)* import financing? *(b)* export financing? *(c)* documentation? *(d)* planning? *(e)* Eurodollar financing? or *(f)* EXIM (Export/Import) Bank financing?

Although some of these characteristics may not be relevant to your bank selection, giving consideration to them will help avoid major problems later as your company grows or its needs change.

Make Preliminary Evaluation of Prospective Banks. You have prepared a list of local, regional, and national banks active in your area. The next step is to make a preliminary evaluation of these banks. Draw up a bank analysis checklist using the criteria you have decided are important, based on the questions listed above.

Use Your Lawyer, Auditor, Investment Banker, Financial Consultant, or Fellow Businessmen to Help You in Evaluation. Your advisers and peers can help in the early stages by providing information on the bankers they know. Remember that each person's views will be colored by his experience with the bank, but all views can help. Further down the line, they may also be able to provide a helpful introduction, but for now, you want hard facts.

Use the bank checklist to prompt questions and when you get an opinion ("First National won't support growth companies whose net worth lags behind sales increases"), inquire whether it is based on hearsay, a single episode, or several experiences.

An important aid that your advisers can provide is the name or names of other clients who share your operating characteristics and who have dealt successfully with various banks. They can tell you not just which is a good bank, but who is a good *banker*. The key to a successful banking relationship is finding a banker who is your ally and understands your business, while avoiding any bankers who are fearful of your company or its unique borrowing characteristics.

If you feel you need more information consider joining the *Financial Executives Institute*. It can provide some new channels for your network. The FEI can be reached at 212-953-0500, or by writing 633 Third Avenue, New York, N.Y. 10017.

After Preliminary Evaluation by You and Your Advisers, List the Banks in Order of Preference. The most important factor to consider will depend on your particular borrowing situation, but the interest of the banker you speak to on the phone should be of major importance in this first ranking. Many of the characteristics in your bank checklists will be missing at this early stage, so the rankings must be done in a rough fashion. As the process continues, however, the checklists should be used as the basic analytical tool.

Contact Banks by Telephone to Obtain Indications of Interest. Call the head of the commercial lending department (the name should be in the annual report). Identify yourself and your company. If you have a reference, such as one of your advisers, say that he suggested you call. State that the purpose of your call is to inquire if the bank would have any interest in considering a loan proposal from your company.

The bank executive will ask for background on your company. Give him your line of business, a revenue range, size of loan, and use of proceeds. Give him your location and ask to be put in touch with a loan officer familiar with your industry. Tell him you would prefer to work with a loan officer at the main office rather than a branch (because you prefer to avoid revolving loan officers). He may ask if you have an existing banking relationship. Answer that you do and would be glad to discuss your reasons for wanting to change when you meet.

If you don't want to identify your company for fear the bank will contact your present bank, which may then call your loan, have an adviser make a "blind" call to the prospect bank for you, outlining your company and its needs.

Keep in mind that you have only a limited purpose in this first call. You want to find out if there is general interest on the bank's part in lending to a company like yours. *Don't try and close the loan on the phone.* If the banker asks you to send information, tell him you have prepared full documentation on your company and a written loan proposal and that you would like to provide it all at one time. Ask if you can talk to a loan officer and arrange an appointment for him to visit your offices.

Note: At some point a new bank will want to know why you want to terminate your relationship with your current bank. Typical reasons that bankers find acceptable are: personality conflict with your loan officer, who is new to the account; many changes in account officers; unwillingness on the bank's part to support your company's growth rate; a loan officer who doesn't have the time or experience with your industry to handle the company's special needs; or a change in the bank's lending policies or senior management.

Select Three to Seven Banks (Usually Including Your Present Bank) for Presentations. It's best to try and pick at least one local, one regional, and one national bank for presentations. Schedule presentations over a two-week period. Full presentations are time-consuming, up to a full day, and should not come so close together as to pull you away from the operations of your business.

Unless you have made an irrevocable decision not to continue with your current bank, it should be given a full presentation. Don't underestimate the impact your new or revised corporate profile, business plan, forecasts and loan proposal can have on your banker. He's juggling anywhere from 50 to 200 accounts, and unless you're either very good or very bad, he may not know you as well as he might. And don't forget that when he meets his competitor in your lobby, his desire to keep your account will make him sharpen his pencil.

Make Presentations. For a complete review of how to make a winning bank loan presentation, see page 35.

After Each Presentation, Evaluate the Bank in Writing. Now it's time to go back to your bank evaluation form and fill in the missing blanks. Be sure to add intangibles: The "feel" you get for the bank is important and should be noted. Consider the personal chemistry involved and whether the bank has enthusiasm for your industry.

Compare the Characteristics of the Banks and Then Determine the Advantages and Disadvantages of Each. Your checklist will help. Make sure you make the evaluation in the "cool." It is important not to make your decisions while under the lotuslike charm of an aggressive loan officer.

Although your first inclination will be to put interest rate at the top of the list, its impact actually is negligible. Remember: 1 percent on a $1 million loan is only $10,000 per year. Compare that with the lender's apparent willingness to pony up more money when your company finds itself short of cash—a situation that can occur if your revenues either decrease or increase very rapidly.

You should expect to receive proposals from more than one bank. At this stage, there is room for you to respond and tell them what deficiencies you find in their proposals. *Be firm:* You may scare off a banker, but it is an important step to let a banker know at the beginning of your relationship that you are buying his services and you expect him to be responsive.

Make Your Final Selection, Negotiate, and Then Close the Loan. In negotiating with banks, the point should be made that you are having discussions with other banks. This should be stated at the time of the initial presentation. Although no one likes competition, bankers will get irritated *only* if it comes to them as a surprise at a later stage.

In addition, the knowledge that there is competition will normally add a crispness and clarity to their response that is often lacking if they think they are the only bank in the running.

Remember that you are *negotiating* a loan. When a bank makes a proposal to you, it is just that—a proposal. If there are restrictive covenants you find disagreeable, let them know.

Every banker would love to have 100 percent security on every loan, but that doesn't mean you have to be a secured borrower. Come back with a counter proposal, reminding the banker of the strengths of your company and telling him what you want.

Select Your Second or Backup Bank. A second bank? Think of it this way: If your vice president of purchasing dealt with only a single supplier who provided something that was an absolute necessity for your day-to-day operations, you would fire him. You are the purchasing agent for your company's capital requirements, and if you deal with only one bank, you are taking risks that you can and should avoid.

The technique for establishing a potential or active secondary banking source is based on the same procedure as for establishing your primary bank. First, determine the level of activity you will require from your second bank. Will it be limited to meetings with bank representatives or will it involve (in increasing order of importance): a corporate officer's account; a money market account; a collection account; an active checking account; a small installment loan to finance company cars or equipment; a small, unsecured line of credit for a subsidiary or new operation guaranteed by the parent; participation in a mortgage; or participation in the firm's main line of credit or term loan?

Part of the objective here is to give the second bank signals that if you are ever dissatisfied with your main bank, you would turn to them. *Do this by increasing the intensity of your relationship with them,* slowly, but regularly. But you don't have to oversell them. They probably will be happy with the knowledge they have a leg up in the event of a change with your lead bank.

Continue to Evaluate Your Bank. Don't put the financial sources notebook away and lock up the files. Your company is a living, growing thing. The need to review your financial relationships is ongoing.

Establish a quarterly (at least) review of your company's operations and progress from your banker's perspective. This entails looking at your operating performance—ratio analysis is a bank's favorite tool—to see whether your company looks better or worse to a banker. Remember to compare yourself to other borrowers by preparing a spreadsheet using the Robert Morris Associates Annual Statement Studies (see the Suggested Reading section at the end of this chapter). If your financial picture has been improving or you look a lot better than the RMA averages, you may want to consider renegotiating your line.

Continue a Regular Program of Meetings with Your Bank to Ensure a Continuing Healthy Relationship. Meet with your banker on at least a quarterly basis, and possibly more often. Most alert firms that are on steep growth curves and need regular inputs of capital see their bankers monthly. If there is bad news, let your banker know early instead of late. Bankers hate nasty surprises. If you foresee a problem and let your banker know early, he will appreciate both your farsightedness in picking out the problem and your forthrightness in telling him. If there is good news, these meetings become the perfect avenue to review it and begin discussions about changing your lending terms.

These meetings also can provide an early warning system if your relationship with your banker is deteriorating because of problems he has. It's better to know soon and try to salvage the relationship or (at the worst) be prepared to find a new bank or banker.

HOW TO MAKE A WINNING BANK LOAN PRESENTATION

Many borrowers become confused when they read in the press that bankers say there's plenty of money to lend and then get turned down when they go to their bank asking for an increase in their line of credit.

Why the turndown? The answer may be as simple as the fact that the borrower just didn't give his account officer the "ammunition" he needed to get an OK from the bank's loan commitment committee. Bankers do want to lend money, but many business borrowers don't do the preparation needed to convince their banker. *An effective presentation to your loan officer is a key step in increasing your line or getting a loan from a new bank.* A note of caution: A good presentation is always based on full disclosure, so it won't help a company to paint a rosy picture and then have to divulge that also in its garden are plenty of nettles, weeds, and stones (with creepy crawlies underneath). But if your company is capable of profitability, even if it is currently just breaking even or losing money, then a good presentation may be the difference between getting your loan instead of a turndown.

There are 10 important elements to your face-to-face presentation to a banker:

1. Place.
2. Time.
3. Participants.
4. Agenda.
5. Meeting procedure.
6. Selling of your operational capacity.
7. Evaluation of the bank.
8. Financial presentation.
9. Business plan, forecasts, and capital requirements.
10. Loan proposal.

The Place. Management should always present at its offices, *not* at the bank and certainly *never* over the telephone or by simply sending written materials to the bank. Presentations should always be face to face and *on your turf.* With bankers doing more marketing of their services, it should be easy to get them to come to your place of business. You will be more comfortable at your own headquarters; you can show off your products, facilities, and key staff; and you have the "home field" advantage where you are most confident.

The Time. A good presentation will take from two to six hours. Start at 9 or 9:30 A.M. so the banker sees you before going to the office, where he may receive bad news about some other loan going sour. Make sure he commits to hear the entire process. Bankers are hard pressed for time, but most will commit the time if told in advance you have a full presentation, including a corporate profile, business plan, financial forecasts, and a specific loan proposal, and you will have your management team ready to meet and present the facts he needs to make a credit decision.

Participants. All key members of management should participate. Don't be leery of operating managers because you're afraid they might put their feet in their mouths during a presentation. A policy of full disclosure with your banker means displaying the quality of your management team—that will be an important factor in your banker's decision. Don't worry, your sales and production managers, even if they aren't too smooth, are the best communicators of your company's strengths in their respective departments. Besides, bankers are wary of a one-man show.

The Agenda. Any efficient meeting should have a written agenda. It will outline for the banker what he will be seeing or doing during the visit. An effective format is shown in Exhibit 2.

Do not send any material to the banker before the meeting. He will ask you to do so, but resist the temptation. Tell him that all information will be made available at the meeting. If it is a new bank for your firm, send product information and indicate the range of your revenues and the amount you wish to borrow in a letter. The banker will pull a D&B, of course, but you want him to arrive with the minimum of preconceived (and very often incorrect) notions in his head.

Meeting Procedure. Hand the prepared agenda to the banker and review it with him so that he understands the ground rules. The banker will generally want to see your financials and loan proposal immediately. Tell him you will get to that later, after he has had a chance to dig into your operations so as to make the financials and proposal more meaningful. The key here is to make sure that *you* run the meeting and follow *your* agenda.

EXHIBIT 2 Sample Agenda

GKH MANUFACTURING COMPANY
Two Penn Center Plaza
Philadelphia, Pa. 19102

Banker
President
Chief Financial Officer

1. Introductions.
2. Events leading to meeting.
3. Purpose and ground rules of the meeting.
4. Key events in the history of the company.
5. Summary profile of management.
6. Analysis of company operations:
   a. Products or services.
   b. Lines of business.
   c. Market and industry.
   d. Competitors.
   e. Marketing.
   f. Manufacturing processes.
   g. Suppliers.
   h. Management (in more detail).
   i. Employees and labor relations.
   j. Litigation.
   k. Professional advisers and references.
7. Lunch (or break).
8. Management information systems and financial administration.
9. Financing history.
10. Analysis of most recent audited financial statements and interim statements.
11. Comparison of company with similar companies.
12. Business plan, forecasts, and capital requirements.
13. Loan proposal.

The Selling of the Company's Operational Capacities. Reproduce the most important pages of your corporate profile dealing with operations and management, and hand them to the banker *one at a time,* in the order listed in the agenda. Let him read the material on each page. Then read the material out loud and ask him if he has any questions. Each manager should present the information in the area of the business for which he has responsibility. The president and chief financial officer should not hog the show.

This is the chance to make your banker truly understand your business. Convince him that you and your managers really know your industry and how to operate your company profitably in your market.

Don't oversell. Let the facts do that for you. Many bankers get smoke from their customers. *You will stand out as a good manager and thus a good loan prospect* if you give the banker facts. Be sure you make full disclosure. Tell the banker your problems as well as your successes and opportunities. The good points should outweigh the bad points, and you will get a high rating from the loan officer for telling the truth.

If you make full disclosure of problem areas *before* the loan, you will not have to surprise your banker later with a bombshell of bad news. *Bankers know how to live with bad news, but they can't stand surprises.* Take this opportunity to explain problems you have and how you intend to overcome them. Bankers know better than anyone that although popular pictures of businessmen may show them seizing grand opportunities, the realities are that managers spend most of their time (as do bankers) trying to handle problems.

The entire process of making certain your banker understands the operations of your business will take from one to three hours. Do not hurry the explanations. A banker who does not understand the key elements of your business will be a nervous banker.

The Evaluation of the Bank. By lunchtime the banker should have a good understanding of your business operations. At lunch he will try to pin you down on what your loan proposal is. Postpone discussion of that until after you have reviewed the financials in the afternoon. Instead, direct a series of questions to him about the bank's operations, policies, and decision-making processes. (Before the meeting, carefully read the annual report of the bank.)

There are two reasons for using the technique of "grilling" your banker. First, you want to get this information to better know the likelihood of your getting a loan and how it will be administered. Second, it is a show of confidence that you are willing to ask your prospective money supplier the same kind of hard questions that you would ask a supplier of any other kind of product or service. Here are some of the questions that you should ask your banker.

Does your bank have a deposit or loan relationship with any of our competitors, suppliers, or customers?

If so, how is information kept confidential?

Do you act as loan officer to any of these competitors?

Have you ever worked with companies similar to ours either in terms of operations, size, or growth?

Could you give us some of the company names so we could ask them about their relationship with your bank?

What is your bank's legal loan limit?

What is the "mainstream" loan for your bank?

What is the normal loan size you handle personally?

Will we be working through a branch or the main office?

Who will be our account officer if it is not you?

If it is you, who will be your backup in your absence?

To whom do you report?

What is your personal lending authority?

If you are interested in our loan, what are the normal steps leading to a decision and how long will it take?

Is your bank actively seeking loans at this time?

What jobs have you held at the bank?

If you were our loan officer and then were promoted, would you continue to service our account?

There have been some press reports that some banks have loan difficulties that may prevent them from making normal loans. What is the situation with bad loans at your bank?

What are the services that your bank can render to us in addition to carrying our deposits and making commercial loans?

One of the effects of this kind of questioning is that it forces the banker to "sell" his bank to you. This is important from a negotiating point of view. Banks operate in different ways and the loan officer will have to defend his bank's policies.

At the end of the questioning, ask him how he feels generally about your company now that he has had a chance to review the operations. Have one of your associates at lunch take notes. There will be many signals in his statements to help you understand better how bankers react to your presentation and to your company's operations.

The Financial Presentation. After lunch (or the break) it is time to review the financial situation of the company. Begin by reviewing your management information system and financial administration by showing the banker each of the reports prepared internally by the company. The accounting system and its input are the second most important factor (management is first) considered by bankers in making decisions about loans, so it is critical that the banker understands how you keep track of your business operations from a financial and informational point of view.

Then present the financing history of the company, indicating how and why the company has been financed (internally and externally) up until now. Review the current status of any loans outstanding to banks and your history of meeting interest and principal payments.

The most recent audited statement should then be distributed. Leave the conference room so as to give the banker plenty of time to read it. After he has reviewed it but before he asks questions about it, go through *each* of the items on the balance sheet and P&L explaining what they represent. Each company uses a slightly different chart of accounts and follows different accounting principles. It is important that he understands your numbers and their makeup as well as your operations. It is also an important plus if you can explain your financials. Many owner/managers know their internal operating numbers but never spend time on their formal financials.

The most recent unaudited report should then be handed to the banker. This is the time to explain what has been happening to your company in the period since the last audit. Make sure that you relate the balance sheet and income statement to the morning discussion of operations. Hammer home that you understand your financial statements and that you use them as planning and control tools.

After he has a good understanding of your financial statements, hand the banker a sheet comparing your results of operations and financial condition with those published in the Robert Morris Associates Annual Statement Studies, which analyze the financial statements of 80,000 business borrowers active in nearly 300 lines of business, including yours (see Exhibit 3). For about $30 you can place yourself on a par in appraising the risks a banker feels he may take in lending to your company (215-665-2850).

The banker's credit department will run these comparisons in any event, and to the extent that your numbers are not typical of your industry, you must rationalize these differences, good or bad, at the outset of your relationship with a bank. It is better to do this at the time of the presentation than to let your banker later draw his own, perhaps erroneous, conclusions as to why there are significant differences between your company and other companies in your industry.

Business Plan, Forecasts, and Capital Requirements. Your business plan should be short, consisting primarily of the policies you intend to follow over the next few years in order to meet your stated objectives. One or two pages may be sufficient, especially if your presentation up to this point has persuaded your banker that you know how to manage your company and take advantage of the opportunities.

Financial forecasts, on the other hand, must have detailed written assumptions that drive the schedules of revenues, profit/losses, cash flow, and balance sheets. *The capital requirements should be the*

EXHIBIT 3 Robert Morris Associates Annual Statement Study

MANUFACTURERS - ELECTRONIC COMPONENTS & ACCESSORIES SIC# 3671 (72,74,76,77)

Current Data

209(6/30-9/30/83) 251(10/1/83-3/31/84)

	0-1MM		1-10MM		10-50MM		50-100MM		ALL	ASSET SIZE
	122		239		74		25		460	NUMBER OF STATEMENTS
	%		%		%		%		%	**ASSETS**
	9.8		7.7		13.5		12.1		9.4	Cash & Equivalents
	30.8		29.5		25.1		21.9		28.7	Accts. & Notes Rec. - Trade(net)
	26.6		26.9		26.0		27.3		26.7	Inventory
	2.5		2.1		4.1		3.5		2.6	All Other Current
	69.7		66.2		68.6		64.8		67.4	Total Current
	24.4		27.2		24.5		30.0		26.2	Fixed Assets (net)
	.6		.6		.5		.9		.6	Intangibles (net)
	5.4		6.0		6.4		4.3		5.8	All Other Non-Current
	100.0		100.0		100.0		100.0		100.0	Total
										LIABILITIES
	12.5		10.2		7.1		4.4		10.0	Notes Payable-Short Term
	3.9		3.7		2.2		1.5		3.4	Cur. Mat.-L/T/D
	16.6		15.8		9.9		8.9		14.7	Accts. & Notes Payable - Trade
	8.2		8.9		7.3		6.8		8.3	Accrued Expenses
	4.4		4.2		2.7		2.7		3.9	All Other Current
	45.5		42.8		29.3		24.2		40.3	Total Current
	11.3		15.2		11.8		11.7		13.4	Long Term Debt
	1.3		2.8		3.1		7.2		2.7	All Other Non-Current
	41.9		39.2		55.8		56.9		43.5	Net Worth
	100.0		100.0		100.0		100.0		100.0	Total Liabilities & Net Worth
										INCOME DATA
	100.0		100.0		100.0		100.0		100.0	Net Sales
	63.7		65.8		65.1		63.6		65.0	Cost Of Sales
	36.3		34.2		34.9		36.4		35.0	Gross Profit
	31.1		26.3		27.4		27.8		27.8	Operating Expenses
	5.3		7.8		7.5		8.6		7.1	Operating Profit
	.5		1.5		.8		-.5		1.0	All Other Expenses (net)
	4.8		6.3		6.7		9.1		6.1	Profit Before Taxes
										RATIOS
	2.5		2.3		4.8		4.1		2.7	
	1.5		1.5		2.7		2.8		1.7	Current
	1.1		1.2		1.7		2.1		1.2	
	1.5		1.4		2.4		2.1		1.5	
	.9		.9		1.4		1.3		1.0	Quick
	.6		.6		.9		1.0		.6	
35	10.4	**46**	7.9	**55**	6.6	**56**	6.5	**46**	8.0	
53	6.9	**58**	6.3	**69**	5.3	**73**	5.0	**59**	6.2	Sales/Receivables
69	5.3	**73**	5.0	**87**	4.2	**81**	4.5	**74**	4.9	
38	9.6	**49**	7.5	**69**	5.3	**78**	4.7	**50**	7.3	
60	6.1	**83**	4.4	**114**	3.2	**140**	2.6	**83**	4.4	Cost of Sales/Inventory
104	[illegible]	**128**	2.8	**171**	2.1	**[illegible]**	1.0	**105**	[illegible]	
21	17.1	**25**	14.8	**26**	14.2	**21**	17.5	**24**	15.5	
38	9.6	**40**	9.1	**39**	9.4	**36**	10.1	**39**	9.3	Cost of Sales/Payables
64	5.7	**61**	6.0	**49**	7.5	**60**	6.1	**61**	6.0	
	4.7		4.2		1.8		1.8		3.6	
	10.1		8.3		3.4		3.1		6.9	Sales/Working Capital
	33.7		20.5		6.9		4.4		18.8	
	8.0		7.9		13.2		12.4		8.6	
(99)	3.5	(210)	3.7	(65)	3.8	(24)	5.3	(398)	3.7	EBIT/Interest
	1.7		1.5		1.3		2.8		1.6	
	5.6		6.9		20.9		26.2		9.5	
(62)	2.7	(170)	3.0	(52)	5.0	(20)	11.9	(304)	3.2	Cash Flow/Cur. Mat. L/T/D
	1.2		1.6		1.8		3.0		1.6	
	.3		.3		.3		.4		.3	
	.6		.7		.4		.6		.6	Fixed/Worth
	1.1		1.3		.8		.7		1.1	
	.6		.8		.4		.4		.6	
	1.5		1.9		.7		.7		1.4	Debt/Worth
	3.2		3.1		1.8		1.0		2.7	
	45.7		52.1		31.2		34.4		46.7	
(119)	23.6	(234)	28.2		18.1		16.7	(452)	24.4	% Profit Before Taxes/Tangible Net Worth
	9.3		6.2		3.2		11.8		6.2	
	15.4		16.2		15.9		18.5		15.9	
	8.7		9.1		8.1		9.0		9.0	% Profit Before Taxes/Total Assets
	3.7		2.6		1.2		6.8		2.6	
	21.7		13.9		10.5		6.2		14.1	
	9.2		7.2		5.0		3.5		7.0	Sales/Net Fixed Assets
	5.4		3.9		3.6		2.7		3.9	
	2.7		2.3		1.8		1.4		2.3	
	2.2		1.8		1.2		1.1		1.8	Sales/Total Assets
	1.7		1.4		.9		.9		1.3	
	1.4		1.4		1.8		2.4		1.6	
(108)	2.4	(219)	2.7	(64)	3.3	(24)	3.9	(415)	2.7	% Depr., Dep., Amort./Sales
	4.2		4.1		4.4		5.7		4.2	
	1.2		.7		.5		1.0		.8	
(67)	2.5	(94)	1.3	(22)	1.3	(11)	1.2	(194)	1.7	% Lease & Rental Exp/Sales
	3.9		2.4		2.6		2.2		3.2	
	4.9		2.5						3.0	
(49)	8.0	(66)	5.0					(116)	5.7	% Officers' Comp/Sales
	9.9		7.5						9.1	
	147346M		1342807M		2185771M		2009741M		5685665M	Net Sales ($)
	65446M		747576M		1729138M		1739220M		4281380M	Total Assets ($)

M = $thousand MM = $million

All balance sheet and income items are defined so you can adjust your company's accounts to match up with those of 460 of your fellow bank borrowers.

All these ratios are explained in detail so you can compute your own balance sheet, income, and combination ratios, and compare them to those of 460 companies active in your line of business.

The significance of these ratios to your banker is also explained so that you can understand your banker's concern when your performance or financial condition (or their relationship to one another) is out of whack with other borrowers.

The previous five years' data, under the heading Comparative Historical Data, is not shown here.
SOURCE: RMA Annual Statement Studies, published by Robert Morris Associates (215-665-2850).

amount your forecasts show you need, not the amount you estimate the bank will lend you.

Loan Proposal. The next step is to present the loan proposal and ask the banker for his preliminary conclusions. In the following section of this chapter, a complete guide to putting together a winning loan proposal is presented.

THE ONE–PAGE LOAN PROPOSAL: FINANCING DYNAMITE

The most important handout in your presentation to a banker is your one-page loan proposal. When you hand him your proposal across your conference room table, three things happen: (1) you are showing him that you understand the financing elements of your business; (2) you have made his life easier because he doesn't have to guess your capital requirements and your payback expectations; and (3) you are seizing the initiative in a negotiating setting by presenting a clear, concise, complete proposal *in writing,* which gives it power.

The most egregious error committed by an entrepreneur or CFO seeking capital is to ask the banker how much you should raise, or ask for an indeterminant amount ("I need two to four hundred thousand dollars"). You would never ask your suppliers of raw materials or components to tell you what you need. As a purchaser, you tell your supplier what you need and what you want to pay, especially if there is heavy competition among your suppliers. The same practice applies to the major supplier of capital, your friendly bank. You need to tell *him* how much you need, when, for what, the price you wish to pay, and your plan for repayment (see Exhibit 4).

The one-page loan proposal is financing dynamite because it blows away all the superfluous chaff and gets at the deal itself. Your banker will appreciate it and it gives you the upper hand in negotiations.

Remember, there is no point in being timid or defensive when you present your loan proposal. Your banker will be impressed if you confidently and persuasively make him a proposal instead of having him figure out how much you need. Don't try to guess how much your banker will lend you and then tailor your proposal to meet that imagined limit. Always ask for what your cash flow requirements tell you your company needs. If your loan proposal is backed up by your cash flow forecasts, you have cleared an important hurdle. When you present your loan proposal, give the highlights orally and then hand the written proposal to him. Then let him read and comment. Don't defend it, let him share his reactions. You have made your best pitch, now listen. Write down his comments or criticisms. Keep your mouth buttoned. The longer he talks, the more you will learn. If you don't know his objections, you can't plan to overcome them.

After he has finished his comments, ask him what the next steps are and ask him specifically, "Will you recommend this loan to your commitment committee?" and then, "Do you believe the commitment committee will accept this proposal?"

Then tell him you will call him on a specific date *and time* (about one week hence) to follow up. Having made this telephone appointment, it is not a sign of weakness for you to call him. At the start of that call you should deliver some good news that has occurred during the week, so there is an optimistic note to that conversation. Then put on your selling hat if he isn't already sold on you, your management, and your company.

The loan proposal should be short: Everything the banker needs to know can fit on one page. Avoid legal language, but cover all the key elements of the loan agreement to prevent misunderstandings when the formal document or commitment letter is prepared.

The loan proposal shown in Exhibit 4 is for a rapidly growing manufacturing company with revenues of $2.7 million that is marginally profitable, and whose cash flow forecast shows it will need to borrow a maximum of $535,000 over the next period, up from $200,000 in the current year.

Note that this is *your proposal* to the bank, not a humble request. You and the bank are equals in this arena, and in most cases, because of intense competition among bankers for loans, the borrower is in the driver's seat.

Date of Proposal. The company is starting the process of satisfying its capital requirements when the company still has a cushion, several months before it will start to need the extra capital.

Borrower. If there are sister corporations or a parent-subsidiary corporate structure, choose the company that will generate the most cash for repayment and that has the best credit features.

Amount and Use of Proceeds. Be specific on the amount and the uses of proceeds. Be sure there is some contingency funding. Don't ask for too little. Always ask for enough to fund your business plan. Don't guess your borrowing capacity. *You must ask for what you need.*

Type of Loan. Ask your lawyer, accountant, or financial adviser to help you select the optimum structure: line of credit, revolver, term loan, or combination. If in doubt, ask for a three-year revolving line of credit. For structuring assistance call 215-988-0010.

EXHIBIT 4 Loan Proposal

Date of proposal:	June 15, 1986	
Borrower:	GKH Manufacturing Company	
Amount:	$535,000	
Use of proceeds:	For increased receivables: up to	$200,000
	For increased inventory: up to	125,000
	For new marketing programs: up to	85,000
	For equipment (include a schedule)	75,000
	Contingency:	50,000
		$535,000
Type of loan:	Revolving line of credit	
Closing date:	June 30, 1986	
Term:	Three years	
Rate:	Prime; no compensating balances; no fees	
Takedown:	$150,000 at closing $200,000 on September 1 $135,000 on November 1	
Collateral:	None—company will agree not to pledge its receivables or inventory	
Guarantees:	None	
Repayment schedule:	$535,000 or balance of line on third anniversary	
Source of funds for repayment:	a. Cash in excess of that needed for operations generated during the loan period (see cash flow forecasts); or b. Renewal and increase of line of credit if company's growth is profitable, with a portion converted to a five-year term loan with a straight line amortization.	
Contingency source of repayment:	a. Loan from commercial finance company secured by accounts receivable and inventory; or Sale and leaseback of plant and equipment.	

Closing Date. Specify the date you need the cash or commitment. How will the loan affect your balance sheet? Do you want it on your year-end statement? Banks can make a final decision in two to four weeks after you give them your corporate profile. Always set a short time fuse so that you are pressing them for a decision. That sets the correct negotiating posture for you. Always have a three- to four-month cushion before you actually need to use the money.

Term. The term of the loan should reflect when your operating cash flow forecast indicates that you can repay the loan. Add some extra time for problems or ask for the option to convert the line of credit into a term loan.

Rate. The rate should be at the low end of the "reasonable" range. Creditworthy companies should be at prime or, in most cases, below prime with the rate being measured off Fed funds. Marginal credits should ask for P + .5 percent. The banker won't be bashful about asking for more but you want to make the opening move. Always indicate there will be neither compensating balances nor commitment fees.

Takedown. Be sure to state how much you will take down at or near closing so your banker doesn't get nervous if he anticipates only minimal takedowns in the early stages of the loan. Note: The $50,000 contingency is not scheduled for takedown.

Collateral. In this case, the company did not want a financing statement filed because it would be a negative signal for current and prospective suppliers, so it proposed a promise not to pledge current assets. Never over collateralize your loans, because if you need more capital and you have pledged all of your assets already, there is no incentive to lend you more money.

Guarantees. These are touchy for both banker and bankee. Open negotiations by stating that guarantees are unnecessary because *(a)* the owners are trustworthy and *(b)* the company's financial statements are sufficient to support the loan without a guarantee. If the banker is adamant, list the events (e.g. 1:2 current ratio and 3:1 debt-to-equity ratio) that will trigger release or reduction of the guarantee. Ask for a simple guarantee. Do not sign a surety.

Repayment Schedule. Always ask for a "balloon" repayment (no principal repayments until the end of the term) except for equipment loans, where new technology should reduce your expenses and provide regular cash to repay the debt. As equipment is only 14 percent of this loan, the proposal is for a balloon.

Source of Repayment. Your banker always wants to know from what sources he will be repaid. Always show your preferred method(s) and your contingency method(s).

Borrowers sometimes feel uncomfortable in preparing such a specific loan proposal because they are fearful of rejection. Instead of rejection, however, this approach will make your banker respect your financing skills and put you in the lead in your negotiations with your banker. For assistance call 215-988-0010.

CLOSING AND THEREAFTER: 31 WAYS TO MAKE YOUR BANKER NERVOUS AND FINALLY CALL YOUR LOAN

Your loan proposal has been accepted and you have your loan commitment from your banker. By following the procedures in this chapter you have raised enough capital to thrust your company even higher on its growth curve. But remember that a loan is more than a closing ceremony. In fact, that is a misnomer. When your first takedown on your new loan occurs, you should not consider it a closing but as an "opening," the opening of a strong relationship with your bank and banker based on his full understanding of your business and your full disclosure, *which must continue.*

When you take courage and share your difficulties as well as your triumphs with your banker, your relationship will be greatly strengthened. But if you don't work hard on your continued close (but open) relationship, you may find you have a nervous banker on your hands, and *there is no animal more dangerous than a nervous banker.* If you want the excitement, challenge, and risk of dealing with a nervous banker, perform one or more of the following acts. *Here are 31 ways to make your banker nervous and finally call your loan.* Don't say you weren't warned!

1. Send your audit report dated June 30 to your banker in time for Christmas.
2. Never send him your interim financial statements.
3. Let him read about your company's fire, embezzlement, or product liability litigation in the paper; then call him and don't mention it.
4. Tell your friends you hate bankers in general but your ultimate hate is your current jackass of a loan officer. They'll pass the compliment on to him.
5. Always pay your interest late, preferably after you get a call from the collection department.
6. Skip one interest payment annually to check the alertness of the bank's accounting department.
7. Call to gripe whenever the prime rate goes up, but never say thank you when the rate is declining.
8. Spend the proceeds of your loan on items other than those agreed upon.
9. Change auditors frequently, each time to one of lesser reputation and capability.
10. Each time you change accountants, drastically modify your chart of accounts so that year-to-year figures are impossible to compare.

11. Violate one of the covenants of your loan agreement, especially the one in which you promised not to pledge any assets and not to borrow from anyone else.
12. Never call your banker.
13. Never return your banker's telephone calls.
14. At the closing of the loan, when the banker hands you a check, shout "Whoopee!" and call your company and tell them that everything is OK now because you got the loot.
15. Operate your business so that your current ratio deteriorates, your working capital declines, and all other ratios look worse on a quarterly basis—then tell your banker that business is great.
16. Lie to your banker.
17. Tell your banker that your profits would have been higher but you artificially inflated your expenses to cheat Uncle Sam out of taxes.
18. When you finally give him outdated financial statements, make sure the only footnote states that you are delinquent in filing and paying withholding taxes to the IRS.
19. Call your banker once a month with a bad surprise that you knew about long before.
20. Never meet your forecasts. To insure this, always inflate your forecasts.
21. Always have the IRS intelligence division examining your books when your loan officer visits.
22. Have a fire.
23. If you send interim statements, make sure the account titles are different from those in the audit report, so comparisons can't be made.
24. Bounce a large check one month after you have taken down a term loan.
25. Transfer the bulk of your cash to another bank.
26. Stretch your payables to the breaking point so your suppliers call your banker to see if your bank is still supporting your company.
27. Buy three years' inventory.
28. Start developing a new product not allied to your field.
29. Acquire your brother's company for cash.
30. Sell assets and invest the proceeds in marketing a new, untried product.
31. Call in with some more bad surprises.

This litany of lament leads to a last list of loan legends, to which more than lip service must be paid: send in your monthly financials

(82 percent of bankers in a survey said their major complaint was not getting them); call your banker on the first of the month and report good *and* bad news; warn your banker far in advance of when you will need an increase in your loan limits; don't be afraid to remind him that other banks are calling on you; identify and start presenting to your "next" loan officer (so that when your present officer is transferred or promoted, *you* won't have a surprise because a new banker arrives on your doorstep just when you are going for an increased line of credit).

WHAT YOU SHOULD DO IF YOUR BANKER TURNS DOWN YOUR LOAN

If your loan proposal is turned down, list in writing the reasons you think your proposal was rejected and then ask yourself these questions:

1. *Does my company really need to borrow?* Instead, can collection of receivables be expedited? Can inventory levels be reduced? Is new plant and equipment necessary? Are new marketing programs efficient? Can overhead be trimmed? Are R&D expenses too high? Can accounts payable be stretched? Many companies borrow because profits are lower than they would be if the owner/manager went to work with a sharp pencil and made tough decisions as to whether people and programs were contributing to today's profits. Keep in mind that no interest has to be paid on profits reinvested in the business.

2. *Did I describe my company clearly and comprehensively?* Many borrowers complain that their bankers don't understand their companies' operations. Remember that a typical loan officer will be responsible for administering from 50 to 200 commercial loans. To be a successful borrower, you can't expect your banker to come on the scene already possessed of a deep knowledge of your industry or your operations. It may not seem fair, but it is up to you to educate him quickly and effectively. This educational process should combine oral and written explanations. Your corporate profile and your management presentation are two tools you must have and use, and if these are below standard, improve them before making a new proposal or going to another bank.

3. *Do I understand my bank?* When you go to sell your product or service, you find out everything there is to know about your customer. Have you done the same kind of homework regarding your bank? Do you know your bank's legal loan limit; size of its "mainstream" loans; its industry likes and dislikes; its decision-making process; the reputation in the bank of you and your company; your bank's internal growth policies and its current desire (or need) to make loans; whether it is on the Federal Reserve's "watch" list?

4. *Do I know my loan officer?* Has he recently been burned with a bad loan, especially in your industry? What are the factors he considers to be critical in making a loan? Does he think you make full disclosures to him? Have you ever surprised him with bad news? What are his responsibilities, his personal objectives, his salary? Do you treat your loan officer like a demigod or a leper? (He is neither. He is simply a human beset with all the hang-ups and problems that you have, except that he is surrounded by a smoke screen that you must penetrate to find out what really motivates him.) In a company that has excellent prospects, the missing link is capital. You must spend the time to learn about your loan officer, because he is the key to rapid corporate growth.

5. *Did I make a realistic loan proposal, or did I just tell my banker I needed more money?* Was your loan proposal written? Did it include the elements that are absolute requirements in such a request? Did each of the key elements have written and oral backup? Was the loan proposal one that on its face appeared bankable? Was it a "mainstream" loan you asked for, or was it one that your bank doesn't ordinarily make? If you were your banker, how would you have responded to your loan proposal? Make sure that your loan proposal states how much you need; when you need it; what you are going to use the money for; the interest rate (and fees) you are willing to pay; the collateral (and guarantees) that will secure a loan; the schedule of repayment; and the sources from which repayments will be made (and how you will pay back the loan if that source dries up).

6. *Do I need a new loan officer or a new bank?* This is usually the first reaction a business borrower has when his bank rejects his loan application. If, after you hold up a straight mirror to your company, to your management, and to your efforts to work with your banker, you conclude that your loan proposal is realistic, then consider asking for a new loan officer and seek out a new banking (or commercial financing) source at the same time. The best procedure for getting a new loan officer is to call the head of the commercial loan department of your bank (or the regional department head in a larger bank) and tell him you wish to meet with him and your current loan officer to discuss your banking relationship. Tell him that you wish to be assigned a new loan officer and why. Give him enough facts on the phone to show that you have a reasonable set of complaints. Then tell him you want to phone your current loan officer and inform him of this call. In some cases the supervisor will prefer to meet with your present loan officer. Try and meet the supervisor as soon after the call as possible. When you see the supervisor (he should be at least a vice president in rank), give him a written history of your relations with the bank, review your corporate profile with him, show

him your written loan proposal that was rejected, and then list the reasons why a new loan officer will help you and the bank.

Prior to asking for a new loan officer, test the banking market to see if there are other banks that will be interested in your business. This will give you insight into who is at fault. Should all the blame be placed on your banking officer's shoulders or were you a contributor to the deteriorating loan relationship? Don't forget to check with commercial finance companies as a backup, in case the disagreement with your present bank escalates and you need to replace your existing source pronto.

WHAT DO YOU DO IF YOU CAN'T REPAY YOUR LOAN?

What do you do if your loan is coming due and you can only repay a small portion of the principal at the maturity date? In this case, call (don't write, it will take too long) the Bankers Publishing Company, Boston, Mass., 617-426-4495, and ask to have *Commercial Problem Loans,* by Robert H. Behrens, sent to you (in a plain brown wrapper). This book was first published in 1974 but is still timely (except that bankers are even more nervous about bad loans than they were when the book was written). This will give you a banker's view of how banks identify a bad loan, how they administer it, and how they collect. Try not to get ill while reading the section on bankruptcy, which (thankfully) is short.

What do you do if your company is in trouble? Prepare a plan. If you are depressed, confused, or frightened, get help from your auditor, lawyer, financial consultant, or other businessmen. If you are clinically depressed (can't make decisions, low energy level, wake up early and think bad thoughts, feel unworthy, etc.), then see your doctor and get referred to the best therapist in town. Your potential business failure may have triggered some hidden guilt feelings that will exacerbate your depression and make you unable to manage effectively at a time when you must be at your peak.

The plan you and your advisers prepare must be based on a realistic appraisal of your situation. If the plan requires a stretch-out of the loan, don't be afraid to ask for it. Make sure you ask for and get enough relief so that you can make your company checkbook profitable again. Don't fall for the temptation of borrowing at absurdly high interest rates to save a bad business. Those lenders are even more effective collectors of principal than your bank.

Ask yourself why you got into your pickle. If it was because you are not a good manager (but are a good salesman, inventor, or engineer), hire a good manager who has a history of turning around companies, or bring in a management consultant to teach you how to be more effective. Bankers like a new face.

Make sure that in your presentation there is something that will help the banker keep faith and assure him that he will ultimately get his money back, such as an honest increase in your market projections, a new product, or a cost-cutting program. The most important element in this type of loan situation is for the chief executive officer to recognize that he has a problem, and to get professional help in solving it.

WHAT ARE THE 13 MAIN GRIPES THAT BUSINESSMEN HAVE ABOUT BANKS AND WHAT SHOULD YOU DO ABOUT THEM?

Over the last 20 years I have kept track of the most often voiced gripes that businessmen have about their most active suppliers of capital. Here they are, with suggestions about taking care of them.

Gripe No. 1: My bank always lends me 80 percent of the money I need.

If your bank is always willing to make a loan to you but for less than you request, first of all ask your loan officer why, and if the explanation doesn't make sense then ask to be told by his supervisor. If your loan officer is pulling punches, his supervisor may be willing to expose the truth. To avoid this problem of submarginal loan commitments, make sure that you are preparing professional, accurate cash flow forecasts. If they are correct, take them to another banker and see if he will lend you what you need. A loan commitment by your present bank for less than you need may signify a nervous banker. Ask yourself if you have committed any of the 31 sins listed on page 46.

Gripe No. 2: My loan officer doesn't understand my business and asks me a lot of foolish questions.

Although it is unfair, you must take the time to teach your banker (and each new loan officer assigned to you) how your business works. This has to be more than a bull session. If you are not already using a corporate profile to tell your company's story, start now.

Gripe No. 3: Why should I prepare cash flow forecasts for my bank when I don't believe in them myself?

There are two key parts to a cash flow forecast: the assumptions and the computations. Management must make the assumptions. If you are in a business where it is difficult to make assumptions, then your cash flow forecasts will only be good for a short term. In that case you have to indicate to your bank that you are setting targets (where you hope to be), not making predictions (where you are reasonably certain you will be). If the problem is in format or computation, then get a professional to help you.

Gripe No. 4: I got my line of credit but now I have revolving loan officers. Why can't the bank let me stick with one for longer than a year?

There is very little that can be done about revolving loan officers. Make sure when you get a new loan officer that he is unlikely to be transferred, promoted, or fired in the predictable future. It is more important to be prepared for substitute loan officers than to have the unrealistic hope that you will have a single loan officer over a period longer than a year or two. If the latter occurs, it should be considered a luxury. In general, plan for new loan officers and make sure that the next most likely loan officer is briefed by your current loan officer on a regular basis and meets with you at least once a year.

Gripe No. 5: Why does my banker give me the fisheye when I tell him that we would have shown a profit if we hadn't understated our inventory, expensed capital items, and put personal expenses on the company's financials?

Bankers properly feel that a company that cheats Uncle Sam may cheat its bank.

Gripe No. 6: I think my banker is getting nervous but I don't see why.

If you are able to sense that your banker is getting nervous, you should be able to discern the reason by giving him a full presentation, as though he were a new lender. His questions will tell you his areas of concern.

Gripe No. 7: My loan officer told me last week that the loan would definitely get through the commitment committee, but he just called to say it had been rejected.

After you have climbed down from the ceiling (where you had every right to be upon hearing that kind of message) consider the following.

First, unless the loan officer has absolute authority, never get your hopes up about a loan until the check is in hand or the loan agreement signed. Second, remember that it is your job to make your loan officer a good salesman. If he thought he was going to do a good job and he failed, the problem may be that he is not privy to the real policies of his bank, which may be much more conservative than implied by the policy statements issued by the bank to its loan officers (whom the bank does not wish to make so nervous that they look for jobs elsewhere). The most likely reason, however, is that you are not using a corporate profile and did not prepare a written proposal. This meant that the loan officer went into the commitment committee meeting without sufficient support provided by you.

Gripe No. 8: I hear that other companies whose owners know the bank's senior officers well and entertain them a great deal get loans while we get turned down.

Whether you should entertain your banker is a decision that is up to you, based on his personality and yours. Regardless of how you do it, however, you must know your banker both as a person and as a loan technician.

Why waste your time talking to bankers except during the week before you need money? There are several reasons. Your banker is responsible for 50–100 (or more) loan accounts. When he takes your next loan proposal to his loan committee or to another officer for joint approval, he is your salesman. If you are "just another account," he isn't going to go to bat for you to the same degree as if you had gone out of your way to make certain he knows all there is to know about your company and its future. Your loan officer knows that the key to getting the loan repaid is the commitment of able management. When the chairman of the loan committee asks your loan officer if the proposed loan isn't a bit on the heavy side, your loan officer can carry the day if he can truthfully say that the management of the company is dedicated to success and has a real understanding of the need to repay the loan on schedule. (You should also meet, socially or otherwise, a couple of your loan officer's peers in the bank as well as his immediate supervisor. When you get caught in the revolving-loan-officer game, you must know the supervisor to get proper attention.)

Many bankers love golf or tennis and may view your invitation to activities such as these as a welcome excuse to get a rest from the bad loans on their books. But regardless of the context, your interest in your banker as a human being will pay off many times over in the future. Other companies have started this program of treating bankers like human beings many years ago. You can't catch up overnight, but you can start your program now.

Gripe No. 9: Why does my bank still want me to guarantee my company's line of credit when my firm is profitable and has substantial net worth?

Banks hate to give up an owner's guarantee. You would feel the same way if you were in their position. The most effective way to rid yourself of the guarantee is to have an offer from another bank to take on the loan without a guarantee or set an event that will trigger cancellation of the guarantee.

Gripe No. 10: My friendly loan officer says he'll give me the loan but the rate he is asking is three points over prime, plus a 1 percent commitment fee, plus 1 percent on the unloaned balance—and he says that the rate and fees are fair.

Call other companies of approximately your size and tell them your situation. They probably will not tell you what rate they are getting but they certainly will react strongly to the rate that you are being offered. This should provide you with enough information to get an idea as to your position. Review Exhibit 1, the Federal Reserve Bulletin, for some guidance. The best way to find out whether or not a loan offer is fair is to get better offers from other banks.

Gripe No. 11: Why does the bank always tie its loans to prime rate instead of giving me a fixed rate?

Banks used to be more willing to give fixed rate loans, but so many of them got burned when interest rates skyrocketed a couple of years ago that most banks gave them up. Now, however, fixed rate loans have returned. Some banks are willing to put a ceiling on loans or to postpone payment of interest above a certain rate until the time the loan matures.

Gripe No. 12: I have been a depositor at my bank for years, but when I went to them for a loan, they turned me down cold.

You have every right to be irritated and angry at your bank. You should call the president and complain. But before you do that, make sure that you have prepared your corporate profile and loan proposal. Your expectations were higher than they should have been. If you are not a current borrower, don't expect to be given instant credit (even if you are a heavy depositor) without a full-scale selling job to the bank.

Gripe No. 13: My banker tells me my account is unprofitable, yet I am paying him two points over prime.

Ask the banker to bring out the profit sheet on your loan. Most loans are evaluated for profitability by banks and the effective yield after expenses is computed. The banker may just be trading with you. If he isn't, the bank may be rendering services to you that it didn't expect to give, or it may be inefficient. Consider going to another bank. This may be a signal that you should be increasing the intensity of your relationship with your second bank.

SUGGESTED READING*

Periodicals

Entries include title, frequency of publication, one-year rate, and telephone number.

ABA Banking Journal (monthly), $20 (212 620 7200).

**ABA Report to Commercial Lenders* (monthly), $49.50 (202-467-4000).

Bank Letter (weekly), $1,020 (212-303-3233).

**Bank Loan Officers Reports* (monthly), $84 (1-800-225-2363)

The Bankers Magazine (bimonthly), $60 (1-800-225-2363)

Blue Chip Financial Forecasts (monthly), $244 (703-523-5400)

The Business Owner (monthly), $66 (516-681-2111)

Cashflow (monthly), $50 (312-998-6688)

CFO: The Magazine for Chief Financial Officers (monthly), $30 (617-542-0660)

Corporate Finance Week (weekly), $1,020 (212-303-3300)

FE: The Magazine for Financial Executives (monthly), $33 (201-898-4625)

Federal Reserve Bulletin (monthly), $20 (202-452-3000)

Inc. (monthly), $24 (1-800-525-0643)

**The Journal of Commercial Bank Lending* (monthly), $28 (215-665-2850)

Venture (monthly), $18 (1-800-247-5470)

Books

Almanac of Business and Industrial Financial Ratios, by LEO TROY. Prentice-Hall, Old Tappan, NJ 07675 (201-592-2000), $35.00.

American Banking, by CLAIN STEFANELLI. Acropolis Books, Ltd., Colortone Building, 2400 17th Street, N.W., Washington, DC 20009 (202-387-6800), $14.95.

Analyzing Financial Statements, by CLIFTON H. KREPS, JR., and RICHARD F. WACHT. American Institute of Banking, American Bankers Association, 1120 Connecticut Avenue, Washington, DC 20036 (202-467-4000), $33.00.

---

* Asterisk indicates recommended basic reading.

**Asset Based Lending.* American Bankers Association, 1120 Connecticut Avenue, N.W., Washington, DC 20036 (202-467-4000); Student Handbook, $19.50; Lender's Guide, $18.00.

Bank Officers Handbook of Commercial Banking Law, by FREDERICK K. BEUTEL. Warren, Gorham & Lamont, 210 South Street, Boston, MA 02111 (800-225-2363), $58.00.

**Bankers Guide to Commercial Loan Analysis.* American Bankers Association, 1120 Connecticut Avenue, N.W., Washington, DC 20036 (202-467-4000), $12.00.

Bankers Guide to Financial Statements, by THOMAS J. O'MALLEY. Bankers Publishing Company, 210 South Street, Boston, MA 02111 (617-426-4495), $42.00.

The Bankers Handbook, by WILLIAM H. VAUGHN and CHARLES WALKER. Dow Jones-Irwin, 1818 Ridge Road, Homewood, IL 60430 (312-798-6000), $50.00.

Bankers Handbook of Federal Aids to Financing, by HARMON S. SPOLAN. Warren, Gorham & Lamont, 210 South Street, Boston, MA 02111 (800-225-2363), out of print.

Banking For The Non-Banker, by DON H. ALEXANDER. DHA & Associates, P.O. Box 1861, Seattle, WA 98111 (206-682-0620), $6.50.

Business Loan Workouts. Practicing Law Institute, 810 7th Avenue, New York, NY 10019 (212-765-5700), $35.00.

Business Loans, by RICK STEPHAN HAYES. Van Nostrand Reinhold, 7625 Empire Drive, Florence, KY 41042 (606-525-6600), $24.95.

Classics in Commercial Bank Lending, Robert Morris Associates. The National Association of Bank Loan and Credit Officers, 1616 PNB Building, Philadelphia, PA 19107 (215-665-2850), two volumes, $73.00.

Commercial Banking, by EDWARD W. REID. Prentice-Hall, Old Tappan, NJ 07675 (201-592-2000) $30.95.

Commercial Loan Documentation, by WILLIAM C. HELMAN, Practicing Law Institute, 810 South Avenue, New York, NY 10019 (212-765-5700), $40.00.

Commercial Loan Review Procedures. Robert Morris Associates, P.O. Box 8500, S1140, Philadelphia, PA 19178 (215-665-2850), $12.00.

Commercial Problem Loans, by ROBERT H. BEHRENS. Bankers Publishing Company, 210 South Street, Boston, MA 02111 (617-426-4495), $41.00.

Corporate Banking: A Practical Approach to Lending, by J. M. MCDONALD and JOHN E. MCKINLEY. American Institute of Banking, American Bankers Assn., 1120 Connecticut Avenue, N.W., Washington, DC 20036 (202-467-4000), $33.00.

Encyclopedia of Banking and Finance, by GLEN G. MUNN and F. L. GARCIA. Bankers Publishing Company, 210 South Street, Boston, MA 02111 (617-426-4495), $89.00.

The Federal Reserve System, Purposes and Functions. Publications Services Division of Administrative Services, Board of Governors of the Federal Reserve System, Mail Stop 138, Washington, DC 20551 (202-452-3000), no charge.

Fundamental Principles of Commercial Credit. American Bankers Association, 1120 Connecticut Avenue, N.W., Washington, DC 20036 (202-467-4000), $7.50.

**Fundamentals of Analyzing Financial Statements.* American Bankers Association, 1120 Connecticut Avenue, N.W., Washington, DC 20036 (202-467-4000), Students Handbook, $19.50; Leader Guide, $18.00.

How to Analyze a Bank Statement, by F. L. GARCIA. Bankers Publishing Company, 210 South Street, Boston, MA 02111 (617-426-4495), $41.50.

**Introduction to Commercial Lending,* by LEWIS MANDELL and BARRY E. WOOD. American Institute of Banking, American Bankers Association, 1120 Connecticut Avenue, N.W., Washington, DC 20036 (202-467-4000), Text, $27.00; Instructors Manual, $12.00.

**Introduction to Commercial Loan Documentation.* American Bankers Association, 1120 Connecticut Avenue, N.W., Washington, DC 20036 (202-467-4000), Text, $15.00; Leaders Guide, $11.25.

Key Business Ratios. Dun & Bradstreet, Dun's Financial Profiles, Number One Diamond Hill Road, Murray Hill, NJ 07974-0027 (201-665-5000), $250.00.

Lending to Different Industries. Robert Morris Associates, P.O. Box 8500, S1140, Philadelphia, PA 19178 (215-665-2850), $48.00.

Loan Interviewing Training Program Handbook. American Bankers Association, 1120 Connecticut Avenue, N.W., Washington, DC 20036 (202-467-4000), $15.00.

Loan Officer Development Seminar. American Bankers Association, 1120 Connecticut Avenue, N.W., Washington, DC 20036 (202-467-4000), Text, $105.00; Leaders Guide with cassette, $135.00.

Modern Banking Forms, by JACK KUSNET and JUSTINE J. ANTOPOL. Warren, Gorham & Lamont, 210 South Street, Boston, MA 02111 (800-225-2363), three volumes, $145.00.

The Prime: Myth and Reality, by GERALD C. FISHER. Temple University School of Business Administration, Philadelphia, PA 19122.

Rand McNally International Bankers Directory. P.O. Box 7600, Chicago, IL 60680 (312-267-6868), $190.00.

RMA Annual Statement Studies. Robert Morris Associates, P.O. Box 8500, S1140, Philadelphia, PA 19178 (215-665-2850), $29.50.

Short-Term Business Borrowing: Sources, Terms & Techniques, by WILLIAM A. MACPHEE. Dow Jones-Irwin, 1818 Ridge Road, Homewood, IL 60430 (312-798-6000), $30.00.

**Small Business Financing.* American Bankers Association, 1120 Connecticut Avenue, N.W., Washington, DC 20036 (202-467-4000), $97.50.

Structuring Commercial Loan Agreements, by ROBERT TITGHE. Warren, Gorham & Lamont, 210 South Street, Boston, MA 02111 (800-225-2363), $72.00.

CHAPTER 2

Private Placements

Gerald Chalphin
Pepper, Hamilton & Scheetz
Philadelphia, Pa.

Gerald Chalphin practices law with Pepper, Hamilton & Scheetz in Philadelphia, Pa., where he specializes in securities, corporate and general business law. He is a graduate of the Columbia University School of Law and Kenyon College. Mr. Chalphin serves as Pennsylvania State Liaison for the American Bar Association's State Regulation of Securities Committee and also is a member of the American Bar Association's Small Business Committee and the Philadelphia Bar Association's Securities Regulation Committee. Mr. Chalphin is a member of Phi Beta Kappa.

Graeme K. Howard, Jr.
Partner
Howard, Lawson & Co.
Philadelphia, Pa.

Graeme K. Howard, Jr., is a partner in Philadelphia-based Howard, Lawson & Co., a nationally recognized corporate finance firm that has assisted over 500 privately held firms in raising growth capital. Howard, Lawson & Co. were the founding publishers of *Going Public: The IPO Reporter,* the leading authority on the initial public offering market, and *Private Placements,* a biweekly newsletter that reports on recent venture capital financings. Venture Associates, of which Howard & Company is general partner, guides the activities of over 20 early-stage companies, providing equity and debt financing from individuals and institutions through Venture Placements, Inc., a wholly owned NASD broker-dealer. Graeme Howard is a graduate of Amherst College and Yale Law School. He practiced law in the Netherlands, New Haven, and Philadelphia, and then became a partner in the corporate finance department of a regional investment banking firm before founding Howard, Lawson & Co. in 1972.

When a businessman can't borrow any more from his bank or other short-term lending sources, there are two forks in the financing road. One is to slow his growth to stay within his short-term borrowing ceiling, and the other is to seek long-term debt or permanent capital (equity) for his company. If the latter path is taken, the entrepreneur must learn to live with capital providers who may take a demanding and intrusive role in his company's goals and operations, all within a complex set of legal rules designed to make him see red before he gets his hands on the green.

Long-term debt and equity may come from many sources and be bundled in different forms. The private placement (sale) by a company of its securities (stock or debt) to individuals is the method for raising capital described in this chapter. In subsequent chapters you will find information and procedures for obtaining financing from public offerings made through investment bankers, from professionally managed venture capital funds like Venrock, Adler & Co. and Kleiner Perkins, and from other sources.

The term *private placement* has its roots both in the legal and marketing aspects of offerings to individuals on a private basis. A private placement is made to a relatively few purchasers so that its marketing is on a more limited, less formal, and more targeted basis than a public offering. Legally, a different set of rules will apply to private placements compared to public offerings as to the registration of the offering with regulators (federal and state securities commissions), the form and degree of disclosure to prospective purchasers, and the size of the offering and the number of purchasers.

A mainstream private placement will have the characteristics shown in Exhibit 1.

WHAT ARE THE KEY ELEMENTS IN A SUCCESSFUL PRIVATE PLACEMENT OF SECURITIES TO INDIVIDUAL INVESTORS?

There are four main elements in the successful completion of a private placement. The key steps are (1) planning, (2) preparation, and (3) marketing, while (4) complying with federal and state securities laws and regulations.

Planning

Planning includes the following:

1. Learning.
2. Assigning management responsibilities.
3. Setting objectives.
4. Scheduling.
5. Budgeting.

You can *learn* about the process by *(a)* reading (see the Suggested Reading section at the end of this chapter), *(b)* holding discussions with entrepreneurs who have recently completed private placements, *(c)* attending seminars on the financial and legal aspects of private placements, and *(d)* holding preliminary meetings with prospective intermediaries and investors. Companies recently completing private placements are listed in *Venture* and *Private Placements,* and case studies appear in *Inc.* magazine and other entrepreneurial publications. In states requiring registration, the state securities commission will often publish the names of such companies. Regulation D filings, available at the Securities and Exchange Commission or through Dis-

EXHIBIT 1 Private Placement Characteristics

Offerer (the "company")	A corporation (sole proprietorships can't offer securities). Limited partnerships (LPs) may be used by sponsoring companies that act as general partners. The LP will normally fund R&D or marketing expenses "off the balance sheet" of the sponsoring company.
Company's line of business	A product or service that nontechnical individuals can understand (or be made to understand).
Company's stage of development	Usually start-up, early stage, or nearly ready to go public.
Company's prospects	Excellent growth potential.
Amount raised	$50,000 to $1 million. Amounts over $500,000 tend to be placed with venture capital funds, providing the management, line of business, and prospects meet their relatively narrow requirements.
Company's ownership	Privately held (large public companies make placements to institutions).
Security offered	Common stock, convertible preferred stock, or subordinated debentures with a conversion feature or warrants.
Investors	If $50,000–$150,000: to be raised from management, family, friends. If $150,000–$250,000: to be raised from friends of friends, clients of professional advisers, successful entrepreneurs, and recent recipients of funds (e.g., from sale of company, initial public offering, or estate). If $250,000–$1 million: to be raised from wealthy individuals through intermediaries (investment bankers, broker-dealers, financial consultants), usually with a commission or fee.
Disclosure	All facts necessary to make a rational investment decision (no material misstatement of fact, no material omission of facts needed to make investment decision).
Documents	A private placement memorandum (PPM) is often used to make disclosure of risks and negatives. The PPM is usually *not* a selling document.
Timing	Three to six months from initial decision until closing.

closure (202-783-6297), also provide names of companies active in the private placement process.

Assignment of managerial responsibility is very important in achieving a successful private placement. As in any business project, the buck has to stop somewhere, and it is usually the chief financial officer (CFO) who takes the heat, but because of the tremendous impact a private placement will have on the future of his company, the chief executive officer (CEO) will also be active, especially in seed or start-up companies.

Whoever is responsible must establish the objectives, time schedule, and cash budget for the private placement.

The *objectives* may be rather vague at the outset, but it is the

CEO/CFO team that continually reassesses the objectives and makes them more specific. The objectives will include the amount to be raised, the sources of capital to be approached, the security to be issued to attract the capital that is needed, and the valuation to be assigned to the company.

Scheduling is critical, because most entrepreneurs start too late and then expect the process to be completed next Monday (so that checks being issued this Friday won't bounce). A private placement normally takes three to six months and can drag on for what seems to be an infinite period of time. It is important that the CFO not be optimistic in his scheduling; otherwise he may launch his company on a steep flight path before the fuel has been put in the rockets. The CEO needs to make a detailed schedule of activities described in the rest of this chapter to avoid post-takeoff crashes. A realistic schedule will prevent *angst* during the process. A general rule: It will take two to four times longer than you think to raise one half the money you seek.

Budgeting is a private placement requirement because it takes money and resources to raise money. There are two types of costs: out-of-pocket expenses, and opportunity or management costs. Cash expenses can include legal, accounting, consulting, and investment banking expenses, some of which may be up front or in the form of retainers (which can usually be avoided through competition), monthly or hourly charges, or contingency fees. Although a company may hope to pay for such services on the never-never plan if the deal fails, it is always best to have a specific and written agreement with your professional advisers, which should always have a well-defined "kill fee" to cover sad endings (e.g., 50 percent of the normal fees, not to exceed $2,500, will be paid in eight monthly payments starting six months after termination of the offer by the company).

Note that the planning process itself is not expensive, but the CEO and managers very often skip it, then plunge forward, down, and out because they were unnecessarily foolhardy and unorganized. A little dab of planning will pay off handsomely in an effective private placement program.

Preparation

If, after planning is complete, you decide to go for it, your management team, headed by its CEO/CFO leaders, must begin the normally extensive *preparations* that will lead to *marketing* the offering. There are eight steps in preparing a private placement to wealthy individuals (at least, they were wealthy before investing in your company). The first two are almost always skipped, with disastrous results to the company and its managers.

1. List 10–20 prospective individual investors.
2. Contact these prospects by telephone to qualify them as investors and obtain indications of interest in your offering.
3. Prepare or update the corporate profile.
4. Prepare or update the business plan.
5. Prepare the P&L and balance sheet forecasts (with written assumptions and schedules).
6. Prepare the cash flow forecasts (with written assumptions and schedules).
7. Establish the capital requirements for your company.
8. Prepare the investment proposal.

The fatal flaw in financings that flounder, flail, founder, and finally fail is in management's total disregard of the market (the prospective purchasers of stock), as demonstrated by management's complete denial of the need to determine, prior to making a business plan and private placement memorandum, if anyone has the capacity or interest to invest in the company.

When a management team decides to introduce a product, they will conduct competitive studies, pricing and feature analyses, and sophisticated psychological surveys; hold focus groups; run test markets and what-if programs, all to be sure that their prospective customers want to buy their product before they begin the process of building a plant, buying new equipment, and hiring expensive consultants.

These well-known marketing principles should be applied to a private placement, but seldom are, even though these qualifying steps are neither expensive nor time-consuming. Entrepreneurs and CEO/CFO teams who fail to use kindergarten market research in raising private capital do so because they are either hopelessly naive or totally fearful. If they are innocent enough to believe that everyone will want to get into their Compu-Image Corp. or Kabbage Patch Rip-Off, Inc., then these infinite number of prospective investors need only be told the idea (after signing a three-page nondisclosure agreement, of course), and the company will promptly sell out their 20-year, three percent subordinated debentures with warrants to buy .01 percent of the company—so who needs to ask if anyone is interested when the whole world will be? Fearful business owners, on the other hand, are afraid that everyone will say *nyet,* pound their shoes on the table, and laugh at the idea of investing in the company, leaving management humiliated and bankrupt—so who wants to be the finder of such awful news? In either case scarce resources are prematurely shifted from developing, selling, and manufacturing a product (or rendering a service) to a hara-kiri form of financing in which company cash and an eternity of management's time are used to prepare corporate profiles, business plans, and private placement memoranda for an audience that isn't there.

Always check to see if there is a group of qualified and interested investors before beginning all the rest of the preparation steps.

Note that the first two steps in the proper preparation of a private placement, described below, will promptly solve these problems.

First, *prepare a list of 10–20 prospective individual investors.* The list will include 10 "insiders," such as yourself, your management team, your families, and your wealthy friends; plus 10 "outsiders," comprised of successful local entrepreneurs still running their businesses, local business owners who have sold their businesses or sold shares in an initial public offering, two fifth-generation passive owners of local businesses, and a few prospects suggested by your lawyer or your accountant.

Having prepared the list, your second step is to *call each prospect to determine his capacity and interest in your deal.* The questions to ask, directly and with confidence, are:

Are you an investor?

Have you ever invested in private companies? If so, with what characteristics, line of business, revenues, net income, or net worth?

If not, would you consider an investment in a private company?

What would be your comfort zone for such an investment (e.g., $10,000, $25,000, or $100,000)?

Even if the prospect says he is not interested, tell him about your deal and ask him for the names of two people he thinks might be interested. Never hang up without describing the deal and getting at least two names, so that you extend your prospect list with each call. That makes a rejection palatable because you now have more people to call.

Your description of your deal should be short. For example:

> My company, Sundial Technology, is planning to design, develop, manufacture, and sell laser-driven, microprocessor-controlled timing and telemetry (T&T) devices for use in commercial and military ground-to-air control environments, and we have our first order from the United States Air Force. In a month or so the company, which is owned by its founders (we are all from ABC Corp., the leader in the T&T field), will offer 200,000 shares at $1 per share to raise $200,000. The founders own 400,000 shares, so the investors will receive one third of the company. (Computation: 200,000 (shares offered) divided by 600,000 (total shares) = 33⅓ percent.) The $200,000 will be used to fill the first USAF order for six units at $50,000 each, which will generate $300,000 in revenues in the first three months, and to add sales personnel to enter the commercial market. Our

> target is to build a company that, in its fifth year, will have revenues of $16 million with net income of 8 percent after tax or $1,280,000, which, if achieved, would give the company a value of approximately $12 million (at 10 times net after-tax profits). We are now preparing our formal business plan. Would you be willing to consider purchasing a portion of this private placement, approximately $________ (the investor's comfort zone)?

The individual's response will tell you whether you have a suspect, a prospect, or a "live one." In addition, the CEO should call some local investment bankers for interest in serving as an intermediary in the sale of the shares to its wealthy customers. This is also a test of interest. Does the investment banker ask to come and see you right away, or does his voice go cold, his manner become abrupt, his cordiality seem forced? Regardless of his degree of interest, set up an appointment to present the materials you are preparing.

Remember the golden rule of raising money: Before starting on the production of corporate profiles, business plans, forecasts, and private placement memoranda, you should have preliminary indications of interest for three to four times the amount of money you seek. Don't dive into other preparations until you have an identified a "market." Don't be fooled by your own hopes. Satisfy yourself that people will listen to your presentation. Don't prepare your Broadway show until some people have said they might buy tickets.

The rest of your preparation steps (before actively marketing your private placement) are documentary in form. Update or prepare for the first time a *corporate profile.* This is *not* a private placement memorandum but is prepared by businessmen for businessmen/investors. It is not a "legal" document. (Refer to Chapter 1, page 11 for a short description of the contents of a corporate profile). If you need help preparing a corporate profile, ask your corporate finance consultant or your accountant to help you.

Next, prepare a *business plan.* There are many texts that describe how to prepare a business plan. Remember that it should be *your* operating plan, not what you think investors want your business plan to represent. For a free monograph on business planning, call Arthur Andersen (215-241-7300) or read Kravitt's *How to Raise Capital: Preparing and Presenting the Business Plan.*[1]

The quantitative portion of your business plan will be reflected in your *P&L and balance sheet forecasts,* which will include written assumptions and schedules. Beware of spending more time working on the PC software program than on the business program itself. It's

---

[1] Gregory I. Kravitt, Jeffrey E. Grossman, Karl P. Keller, Korak Mitra, Edward A. Raha, and Adam E. Robins, *How to Raise Capital: Preparing and Presenting the Business Plan* (Homewood, Ill.: Dow Jones-Irwin), 1984.

the thought behind the numbers that counts, not 70 sheets of number-crammed spreadsheets. Investors invest in management; they are not Lotus eaters, no matter how impressive the numbers appear to be.

Your *cash flow forecasts* will be given special scrutiny by investors. The cumulative bottom line should show your deepest cash hole, from whence you can determine your *capital requirements* and thus the use of proceeds for your *investment proposal.* An investment proposal should contain the date of the proposal, offerer, amount, security offered, shares outstanding prior to offering, offering, price per share, use of proceeds, closing date, and (subject to legal considerations) projected operating results that summarize the extensive backup in the business plan and financial forecasts. See Exhibits 2 and 3 for examples.

Marketing

With the documentary preparations completed, marketing of the securities to be offered in the private placement must proceed promptly while the business plan and forecasts are still timely.

The marketing process can be divided into eight steps, which occur more or less in chronological order:

1. Select sources.
2. Schedule meetings during follow-up telephone call.
3. Write contact letters.
4. Conduct informational meetings.
5. Negotiate, restructure, and reprice, if necessary.
6. Conduct more negotiations.
7. Close.
8. Establish methods of communications with new security holders.

The *selection of sources* began early in the process with the identification of 10 to 20 "insiders" and "outsiders." Now it is time to add to that list. Unfortunately, you cannot advertise legally because that could be construed as an offering to the public (although you will see ads soliciting capital in *The Wall Street Journal* Mart and other publications). Other sources of names of investors are: local venture capital clubs (call 212-319-9220 for club locations); lists of past investors in limited partnerships, available from commercial list compilers (your ad agency can get you list catalogues, but most of those investors are tax shelter–oriented and averse to risk); informal networks of venture investors; investors in other growth companies in your locale; and other directories of (hopefully) wealthy individuals (country club members, luxury auto owners, yacht owners, aircraft owners, or social registrants).

EXHIBIT 2 Offering Proposal to Equity Investors for Start-Up Financing (see p. 64)

Date of proposal:	August 1, 1986
Offeror:	Sundial Technology, Inc.
Amount:	$200,000
Security:	Common stock
Shares outstanding (prior to offering):	400,000
Offering:	200,000 shares ($33\frac{1}{3}$ percent of 600,000 shares outstanding after the offering)
Price per share:	$1.00
Use of proceeds:	Manufacturing of timing and telemetry devices to satisfy United States Air Force contract; marketing expenses to penetrate the commercial market
Closing date:	September 30, 1986

	Fiscal Year Ended September 30 (000s, Except Earnings per Share)				
	1986	*1987*	*1988*	*1989*	*1990*
Projected operating results:					
Revenues	$ -0-	$ 560	$2,750	$7,540	$16,315
Net Income	(180)	(110)	270	377	1,280
Earnings per share (EPS)*	(.45)	(.18)	.45	.63	2.13
Price-earnings ratios: (based on $1.00 price and EPS for year ended, e.g., $1.00 divided by $0.45 = 2.2x)	N/A	N/A	2.2x	1.6x	.5x
Value of $200,000 investment at P/E ratio of 10:	N/A	N/A	$ 900	$1,256	$ 4,266

(e.g., for 1988,
10 × $270,000 (net income) = $2,700,000 (total company value)
× $33\frac{1}{3}$% (% of company owned by investors) = $900,000)*

* Excludes dilution from further financings, if any.

Profile of Typical Private Placement Investors. According to a survey reported in *Informal Risk Capital in New England,* Professor William E. Wetzel of the University of New Hampshire suggests the "following *profile of the mythical 'typical' informal investor.*"

1. Age 47.
2. Education: Postgraduate degree, often technical.
3. Previous management experience with start-up ventures.
4. Invests approximately $25,000 in any one venture.

EXHIBIT 3 Offering Proposal to Equity Investors for Bridge Financing

Date of proposal:	August 1, 1986
Offerer:	CAD/CAM Services, Inc.
Amount:	$500,000
Security:	10 percent noncumulative convertible preferred shares, convertible into 100,000 shares of common stock, with an investor's put at $10 per share in the fifth year and a forced conversion at an IPO.
Common shares outstanding (prior to offering):	1,000,000
Offering:	100,000 preferred shares (9.1 percent of the 1,100,000 fully diluted shares outstanding after the offering)
Price per preferred share:	$5.00
Use of proceeds:	Purchase of fixed assets; start-up costs and working capital for new service centers; expenses for initial public offering
Closing date:	September 30, 1986

	Fiscal Year Ended September 30 (000s, Except Earnings per Share)				
	1986	*1987*	*1988*	*1989*	*1990*
Projected operating results:					
Revenues	$2,399	$5,248	$11,941	$20,072	$24,462
Net income	205	540	1,541	2,956	4,130
Earnings per share (EPS) (fully diluted)*	.20	.49	1.32	2.69	3.75
Price-earnings ratios: (based on $5.00 price and EPS for the year just ended, e.g., $5.00 ÷ $0.20 = 25x)	25x	10x	4x	2x	1x
Value of $500,000 investment at end of each year assuming P/E ratio of 15x: (e.g., for 1988, 15 × $1,541,000 = $23,115,000 × 9.1% = $2,103,465)*	N/A	$ 737	$ 1,929	$ 4,034	$ 5,637

* Excluding additional dilution from IPO or later financing.

5. Invests approximately once a year.
6. Typically participates with other financially sophisticated individuals.
7. Prefers to invest in start-up and early-stage situations.

8. Willing to finance technology-based inventors if technology and markets are familiar.
9. Limited interest in financing established, moderate growth, small firms.
10. Strong preference for manufacturing ventures, high technology in particular.
11. Invests close to home—within 300 miles and usually within 50 miles.
12. Maintains an active professional relationship with portfolio ventures, typically in a consulting role or by serving on a board of directors.
13. Diversification and tax-sheltered income are not important objectives.
14. Expects to liquidate investment in five to seven years.
15. Looks for compound annual rates of return on individual investments ranging from 50+ percent from inventors, to 20 to 25 percent from established firms.
16. Looks for minimum portfolio returns of about 20 percent.
17. Often will accept limitations on financial returns in exchange for nonfinancial rewards.
18. Learns of investment opportunities primarily from friends and business associates.[2]

Professor Wetzel also states:

> Situations suggesting a (successful) search for risk capital from an appropriate individual, or group of individuals, include the following:
>
> 1. Financing technology-based inventors prior to commercialization of an invention or innovation.
> 2. Financing business start-ups, especially for firms with 5- to 10-year sales potential between $2 million and $20 million and requiring between $50,000 and $500,000 of risk capital.
> 3. Financing business start-ups with the prospect of receiving psychic income in addition to adequate financial rewards. Examples of nonfinancial incentives for informal investors include the creation of jobs in a community experiencing chronic unemployment, participating in the commercialization of a socially useful new technology or innovation, and the satisfaction of playing an active role in the entrepreneurial process.
> 4. Financing privately held, established businesses growing too fast to finance from retained earnings but not fast enough to attract institutional venture investors. Attractive, but troublesome growth rates, tend to fall between 10 percent and 30 percent per year.[3]

---

[2] William E. Wetzel, *Informal Risk Capital in New England,* NTIS Accession No.: PB81–196149 (Springfield, Va.: NTIS).

[3] Ibid.

A *telephone call* to each of these prospects (within legal offeree limits, but these calls and follow-up letters may not be considered as offers by your counsel) should qualify the investor and outline the deal. This call should establish a date for the prospect to visit you at your offices (no matter how humble, it is your turf).

The *contact letter* should summarize your telephone call to make sure you heard each other correctly and to remind the prospect of his indication of interest or willingness to refer you to others. The contact letter should confirm the meeting time and place and contain a map with directions.

Informational meetings should follow a format similar to that used with banks (see Chapter 1, p. 35), except that the time may be shorter because nonprofessional individual investors may be more interested in the chemistry with the entrepreneurs and ask fewer questions about the technology and business operations. Make certain that these meetings are dialogues with your prospects, not lectures. Let them share their ideas with you. Sell by listening. An important element in investments by individuals is the fun of being part of an exciting crapshoot. These investors will usually recognize that when they sign their check to invest in a seed or early-stage company, they have parted forever with that money. Thus, their investment is often a ticket to an entrepreneurial show, a sort of voyeuristic venture.

If the investors like you, your company, and its prospects, negotiations will ensue, with possible restructuring and repricing (if you are in a weak bargaining position, have priced your security unreasonably, or have too few prospects to be a chooser). Your financial adviser, lawyer, and accountant can help you determine if any shift in pricing is needed.

After *more negotiations* you will finally have indications of interest, oral commitments, or even subscription agreements signed by your investors. At this stage, you may meet the prospective investor's accountant, lawyer, financial adviser, or friend, each of whom has no earthly reason to recommend such a wacky investment. Suddenly your enthusiastic investor will start to play a game of hare and hounds because he is unwilling to tell you he has succumbed to the nay-saying qualities of his advisers. The antidote: Ask your waning investor to let you talk directly to the adviser, with your investor present, and take on the no-man head to head and turn him into *your* advocate.

Then you can go promptly to *closing,* where you exchange your company's securities for the checks of your happy investors, right? Wrong! Now begins the chase. Individual investors will change their minds, leave the country for Alaskan hunting trips, embark on the *Queen Elizabeth II* for 80 days, suffer an emotional or economic loss, and generally make closing a comedy/tragedy that will seem funny, but only months later, providing all the commitments are actually fulfilled. Do not count on any money until the investor's check clears the bank. Don't be surprised when a millionaire's check bounces as he moves his wealth from one account to another.

When Should a Company Use an Intermediary to Help in a Private Placement? If the CEO/CFO management team needs help in structuring or pricing the private issue of securities, use of a consultant/intermediary is called for. These include independent corporate financial consultants, corporate finance subsidiaries of commercial banks, and corporate finance departments of investment bankers (as well as your lawyer and accountant). No matter which type you use, before making a choice:

1. Beware of "money brokers" who use slick jargon, drop names, represent "mystery" financiers from the Middle East. They will always want a down payment for expenses, very often just before closing, which (after *your* check clears) is then postponed indefinitely.
2. Always talk to at least three references who have made private placements using the intermediary. Ask them tough questions about the intermediary's performance.
3. Always ask your lawyer and accountant to check out prospective intermediaries as well.
4. Never retain an intermediary until you have interviewed two or three of them at *their* offices.
5. Always have a written contract. Make sure that it includes who will do what; who the point man will be for your company and for the intermediary; the out-of-pocket expenses, hourly fees, and/or contingent fees you will pay; the event(s) that will trigger the fee; the details of confidentiality and exclusivity; term of the agreement; and termination events.

WHAT ARE THE LEGAL REQUIREMENTS IN A PRIVATE PLACEMENT TO INDIVIDUALS?

The legal requirements for a private placement vary depending on a number of factors, including where the offerees/purchasers live, the size of the offering, the kind of issuer, the relationship, if any, of the offerees/purchasers to the issuer, the investment sophistication and economic substance of the purchasers, whether a broker-dealer is used as an intermediary, and other matters. However, the single most important thing to remember about legal requirements is that there is concurrent (i.e., dual and simultaneous) regulation at both the federal and state levels. It is this concurrent regulation that probably causes more legal problems in private financings than anything else.

The federal regulation derives primarily from the Securities Act of 1933 (the 1933 Act) and, to a slightly lesser extent, the Securities Exchange Act of 1934 (the 1934 Act), each of which is administered by the Securities and Exchange Commission (SEC). State regulation derives from the state securities (or blue sky) laws, which have been enacted in one form or another by all of the states as well as the Commonwealth of Puerto Rico and the District of Columbia, and which are administered by designated state agencies, departments, or bureaus. Lastly, rules of organizations such as the National Association of Securities Dealers, Inc. also play a part to some extent in the private formation of capital.

The single most important aspect of the 1933 Act that affects private offerings is the SEC's Regulation D, adopted in 1982. This series of rules had the effect of collecting, codifying, and integrating into one generally consistent and coherent whole, the diverse judicial and administrative interpretations of the "private placement" exemption from SEC registration set forth in Section 4(2) of the 1933 Act while, at the same time, implementing the congressional mandate set forth in Section 3(b) of the 1933 Act. Since the overly simplistic language of Section 4(2) ("transactions by an issuer not involving any public offering") and the subjective standards of its prior rulemaking effort in this area had caused much confusion and uncertainty regarding the necessity for SEC registration of covered securities financings, Regulation D has caused a much needed regeneration of the private placement method of capital formation. In addition, the 1933 Act also contains an exemption from registration in Section 3(a)(11) for offerings conducted entirely within one state; however, judicial interpretations of the statutory provision coupled with the very strict requirements of SEC Rule 147, have rendered this exemption functionally useless in all but a very small number of transactions.

Regulation D technically consists of six rules covering, respectively, common definitions (Rule 501), disclosure and other common general requirements (Rule 502), filing of a notice of the offering with the SEC (Rule 503), offerings of up to $500,000 in amount (Rule 504), offerings of up to $5 million in amount (Rule 505), and offerings with no limit on the amount sold (Rule 506). Since the adoption of Regulation D, private placements have come to be known by the particular part of Regulation D under which the exemption from registration is claimed (e.g., "a Rule 505 transaction"). Also, since Regulation D was adopted under Section 3(b) of the 1933 Act as well as Section 4(2), the term *private placement* is inaccurate; the correct term is *limited offering,* unless the offering only meets the requirements of Rule 506.

Probably the most important contribution by Regulation D to the promotion of private placements to individuals is the creation of the concept of the *accredited investor.* By creating an objective standard for determination of those investors who, by virtue of either economic clout or relationship to the issuer of the securities, do not need the investor protections resulting from the registration process, the SEC made life immeasurably easier for those who structure and plan private placements. The definition of accredited investor includes not only banks, insurance companies, investment companies, and other institutional investors, but also individuals who meet specified income, net worth, investment size, or relationship-to-the-issuer tests. The financial tests are any of the following: an individual who alone or jointly with spouse has a net worth of $1 million; an individual with income in the past two years and the current year of more than $200,000 per year; and an individual who invests at least $150,000 payable within five years of the date the investment is made so long as the investment does not exceed 20 percent of the investor's net worth. Individuals who are directors or executive officers of the issuer of the securities also are accredited investors (as are general partners of a limited partnership that is the issuer).

The importance of having accredited investors among those who purchase the offered securities arises in two ways. First, if the only purchasers in the offering are accredited investors, there are no specific disclosures about the issuer's business that must be made to investors. Second, no matter how the offering is conducted under Regulation D, for federal purposes an unlimited number of accredited investors may purchase the securities. Consequently, offering costs are lowered and a larger amount of money typically can be raised if the offering is made only to accredited investors.

Unfortunately for most growing businesses, an offering made solely to accredited investors is an impossibility. Therefore, the issuer must comply with the disclosure requirements of Rule 502, unless the offering is conducted under Rule 504 (i.e., less than $500,000 in securities are offered). For most issuers using Regulation D for offerings to individuals, those requirements mean the preparation of a disclosure document (called a private placement or limited offering memorandum) that, subject to so-called materiality considerations, contains the same textual information as the prospectus portion of a typical registration statement filed with the SEC. Fortunately, however, Rule 502 does not require an issuer to provide the full audited financial statements for the same periods as are needed for a full registration statement (in some instances not even an audited balance sheet may be required!), even though audited financial statements for one or two fiscal years usually must be provided. The materiality considerations refer to, in lay terms, the importance to investors of particular information that might be provided about a business in the offering memorandum. For most businesses in the "start-up" or development stages, the information that is most material to investors usually relates to management backgrounds, use of offering proceeds, present and projected business operations (products, services, research or development efforts) and prospects, competition, management compensation, share ownership, the security being offered, underwriting arrangements, and the risk factors relating to the business summarized earlier in this chapter. Within certain limits, the required disclosures may be presented in any order.

Rule 503 requires the filing of a notice (the Form D) with the SEC within 15 days after the first sale of securities in a Regulation D offering and every six months thereafter until the offering ends. Since the SEC takes an expansive view of when a sale occurs for Regulation D purposes, the practice has developed of filing the Form D at the commencement of the offering. The SEC has said that the Form D filing requirement is used for statistical, and not enforcement, purposes.

One other requirement imposed by Regulation D that usually applies is a prohibition against general solicitation or general advertising in connection with Regulation D offerings. This means that most customary business methods and techniques for locating consumers and customers such as direct mail campaigns, "cold" calls, and the like cannot be used to locate investors. Consequently, it is harder to find investors, and intermediaries frequently must be used to place the securities.

As mentioned previously, Rule 504 relates to offerings of up to $500,000 of securities. Unlike Rule 505 and Rule 506 offerings made to nonaccredited investors, Rule 504 does not require that any specific disclosures be made. Also, if an offering under Rule 504 is registered for public sale in accordance with applicable blue sky laws, the usual general solicitation and general advertising prohibitions mentioned previously will not apply. There is no limit on the number of purchasers in a Rule 504 offering.

Rule 505, on the other hand, imposes the specific disclosure requirements previously mentioned if any securities are sold to nonaccredited investors. There is a $5 million limit on the amount of securities offered, as well as disqualifications against availability of the exemption if principals of the issuer have committed designated sins. An unlimited number of accredited investors may purchase securities in a Rule 505 offering, but no more than 35 nonaccredited investors may purchase.

Rule 506 has no dollar limitation on the amount of securities sold, but it does have the same number of purchaser limitations and disclosure requirements as Rule 505 offerings. Furthermore, Rule 506 requires the issuer to make an investment sophistication determination with respect to all nonaccredited investors.

An offering may comply simultaneously with Rules 504, 505, and 506, or it may comply with only one of those rules. However, the failure to comply with Regulation D does not mean that no exemption from registration under the 1933 Act is available. The offering may be exempt under the statute itself. Nonetheless, due to its relative clarity, as well as its availability, the vast majority of present day private offerings to individuals are structured and conducted to comply with Regulation D.

As mentioned previously, the concurrent regulation reflected in state securities or blue sky laws likely causes more legal problems in noninstitutional private financings than any other cause. This has occurred primarily because of a lack of uniformity in the requirements imposed by the states. Frequently, offerings that can be made without any filing or review in one state are completely prohibited or are deemed fraudulent if made in an adjacent state. Some blue sky laws or regulations impose requirements that no other state has, and sometimes provisions that otherwise apply widely have no force or effect in a given jurisdiction.

As a result of the foregoing, it is difficult to generalize about the application of blue sky laws. However, some points can be made. First, about two thirds of the blue sky jurisdictions have adopted, by law or regulation, some form of regulation designed to coordinate with Regulation D. Generally, those regulations permit offerings that meet the requirements of Rule 505 to be conducted without substantial changes other than relatively minor additional investor suitability determinations or "bad boy" disqualifications.

Unfortunately, however, a significant number of blue sky laws grant broad discretionary authority to the administering agency to prevent offerings that are not "fair, just, or equitable." As a consequence, these agencies engage in a process of so-called merit review, whereby determinations are made regarding the investment merit of each particular offering. Those offerings that do not comply with the applicable guidelines may be prevented from being made in that state. The applicable guidelines usually relate to matters such as promoter's compensation, dilution, restrictions on transfer of promoter's shares, and financial reporting.

In recent years, much progress has been made toward greater uniformity in the blue sky laws. However, changes in the political landscape or tides frequently result in radical changes in blue sky laws or administrative policies. Consequently, whenever an offering is being structured, attention must be given to the then current laws and regulations of the jurisdiction(s) in which the securities will be offered and sold.

WHAT SECURITIES CAN BE SOLD IN A PRIVATE PLACEMENT?

It is axiomatic that the kinds of securities that are sold in a private placement (or through any other mechanism, for that matter) are, primarily, a function of what is saleable and, secondarily, a function of what the issuer's principals are willing to give up in the way of control and/or future profits. In either case, the actual securities that are sold result (except in certain extreme instances) from business considerations (and negotiation) rather than legal requirements. The following merely summarizes the more salient features of various kinds of securities. Many variations within kinds and hybrids between kinds are possible; the limitations on creativity result more from lack of imagination than law.

Notes. Generally, these are unsecured (i.e., not collateralized) debt obligations with maturity terms that are short (one year or less) to intermediate (five years or so). Frequently, depending on the issuer, these may be accompanied by the guarantee of debt service by a third party, usually a controlling person.

Bonds. Generally, these are long-term debt obligations secured by one or more mortgages or security interests in specified hard assets (usually property, plant, or equipment). However, sometimes the term refers merely to a long-term unsecured debt obligation.

Debentures. Generally, these are intermediate to long-term unsecured debt obligations which carry a higher rate of interest than more "senior" debt obligations (unless they are convertible). Investors purchase these based on their belief that the issuer intends and will be able to live up to its payment obligation.

Preferred Stock. In contrast to notes, bonds, or debentures, which by definition carry with them the issuer's *obligation* to pay money, preferred stock, like all equity, carries with it *no obligation* to pay money. Only if the issuer decides to pay money and is legally able to do so may the issuer declare dividends (i.e., make payments on shares of preferred stock); furthermore, the dividends payable may be fixed or variable. However, unlike interest payments on notes, bonds, debentures, or other forms of debt, dividend payments on preferred stock are not deductible for tax purposes by the corporation.

Consequently, the payment of dividends subjects the issuing corporation and the holder of preferred stock to the double taxation of dividends. The one advantage of preferred stock that makes it desirable to investors is that it has a priority over common stock in respect to dividend payments and distributions of assets in liquidation. Also, because the issuance of preferred stock improves an issuer's debt-equity ratio, preferred stock is often issued where debt is already or will be used in the business plan.

Common Stock. This is the fundamental equity of the issuer representing not only ultimate control over the issuer's business and operations, but also the basic risk capital invested in the business. Generally, but not always, voting rights accompany shares of common stock. However, on liquidation, distributions are made last (if at all) to those who have invested in common stock.

Warrants. Generally, these are contract rights that permit the holder to purchase shares of common stock in the future on terms and conditions determined at the time the warrants are issued. Thus, warrants function in the same way as stock options, although warrants typically have terms lasting 5 to 10 years. Frequently, warrants are issued to provide an "equity kicker" (i.e., a share in possible capital appreciation) for investors who otherwise are investing in straight debt obligations.

Other Features or Rights

Except in very rare instances resulting more from poor planning than anything else, issuers may add innumerable features or rights to their securities. The most common examples relate to conversion, redemption, voting, and dissolution preferences.

Conversion. Convertibility of a security into another security usually is offered for three reasons. First, it permits the holder of a fixed income instrument such as a debenture or (typical) preferred stock to participate in possible capital appreciation. Second, it usually lowers the interest or dividend rate for the fixed income instrument, thereby reducing the economic cost borne by the issuer. Third, after conversion, the issuer's debt-equity ratio is improved, thereby permitting new leverage, if desired. Usually, convertibility is offered with debentures or preferred stock that can be converted into common stock.

Redemption. Redemption is the economic buy-in by the issuer of the security (usually debt or preferred stock) upon specific terms or conditions prior to the maturity of the security. Redemption usually is obligatory on the issuer if certain events (within or without the issuer's control) occur, but can be optional if desired by the issuer. Frequently, if convertible securities are to be sold, issuers will want the right to redeem the securities in order to get rid of the debt obligation (and thereby improve their debt-equity ratio) through payment or conversion.

Voting. Voting rights usually attach to common stock, but not always. Particularly in small companies, classes of nonvoting common stock often are created to represent the equity, risk capital investment without possession of control over the corporation. Sometimes preferred stock shares have voting rights, especially if dividends are not declared and paid for specified periods.

Dissolution Preferences. Of course, debt obligations are repaid in liquidation prior to payments on equity securities. However, preferred stocks commonly carry preferences in liquidation that require specified payments before holders of common stock get anything.

SUGGESTED READING

Books

A Businessman's Guide to Capital Raising under the Securities Laws, by MICHAEL M. COLEMAN and IRVING P. SELDIN, 54 pp., Packard Press (215-236-2000). An excellent introduction prepared by lawyers for businessmen, with a 21-page overview of the process and analyses of the available registration exemptions.

The Corporate Finance Sourcebook, edited by The Zehring Company, annual, approx. 900 pp., $185.00 (312-256-6067). Out of 15 sections, 4 are useful to companies raising private capital, including "Venture Capital—600 firms actively seeking high risk investments," "Major Private Lenders—investment and private loan criteria of 111 top insurance lenders," "Investment Banks—220 firms which managed public offerings and private placements to individuals," and "Pension Managers—300 managers of Fortune 500 pension assets."

How to Raise Capital: Preparing and Presenting the Business Plan, by GREGORY I. KRAVITT, et al., 187 pp., $24.95, Dow Jones-Irwin (312-798-6000). An excellent approach to business planning based on a question and answer approach to preparation of the basic financial tool.

Informal Risk Capital in New England, by WILLIAM E. WETZEL, 80 pp., $20.00, National Technical Information Service (NTIS), U.S. Dept. of Commerce, 5285 Post Royal Road, Springfield, VA 22161 (NTIS Accession No.: PB81–196149). The first empirical study of how individual investors and small growth companies come together.

Limited Offering Exemptions: Regulation D, by William Hicks, 658 pp., $55.00, Clark Boardman & Co., Ltd. (212-929-7500). Analyzes Regulation D, adopted by the SEC in 1982. Designed to ease the burdens of making exempt offerings (private placements) by small businesses under three new rules (504, 505, and 506) that provide a safe harbor for unregistered offerings.

Pratt's Guide to Venture Capital Sources, edited by Stanley E. Pratt and Jane K. Morris, annual, approx. 600 pp., $99.00, Venture Economics, Inc. (617-431-8100). Pratt's guide is aimed toward raising professionally managed venture capital funds. Several chapters are helpful for companies seeking capital by offering private placements to individuals, including "Preparing a Business Plan," "Structuring the Financing," and "The Pricing of a Venture Capital Investment." The latter provides a detailed method for pricing a deal.

R&D Partnerships: Structuring the Transaction, by Lee R. Petillon and Robert Joe Hull, approx. 600 pp., $85.00. Clark Boardman Co., Ltd. (212-929-7500). Provides comprehensive materials on R&D limited partnerships including advantages and disadvantages, tax aspects, alternatives, accounting and securities aspects, documents.

Venture Capital and Small Business Financings, by Robert J. Haft, approx. 400 pp., $85.00, Clark Boardman Co., Ltd. (212-929-7500). The narrative includes: choosing the business financing format, long-term investment under The Small Business Investment Company Act of 1958, term loan agreements, federal securities law, disclosure and due diligence, and state blue sky regulation. Forms include various types of preferred stocks, antidilution provisions, conversion rights, warrants, and so on. Appendixes include statutes and regulations.

Venture's Guide to Investing in Private Companies: A Financing Manual for the Entrepreneurial Investor, by Arthur Lipper III, with George Ryan, 279 pp., $25.00, Dow Jones-Irwin (312-798-6000). Reading this will give the entrepreneur an understanding of the perils and pitfalls investors in his company may face. Subjects include: finding private company investment opportunity, evaluating the investment opportunities, evaluating the entrepreneur and management team, structuring the deal, refinancing, negotiations, and monitoring. Appendixes review: "What's my business worth," "Prestartup Seed Capital," "Informal Investors—When and Where to Look," and "Angels and Informal Risk Capital."

Periodicals

Corporate Financing Week, weekly, published by Institutional Investor, Inc. (212-303-3300), $1,050.00 per annum, 10–24 pp. per issue. Includes short articles on recent transactions involving corporate finance activities of primarily larger public companies.

Institutional Investor, monthly, published by Institutional Investor, Inc. (212-303-3300), $135.00 per annum, approx. 350 pp. per issue. Includes longer articles on activities of institutional investors, corporate finance, and M&A transactions.

Investment Dealer's Digest, weekly, published by Dealers' Digest, Inc. (212-229-1200), $195.00 per annum, approx. 50 pp. per issue. Includes a list of private placements by primarily public companies purchased by institutional investors.

Private Placements, biweekly, published by Dealers' Digest, Inc. (212-229-1200) $450 per annum, 16 pp. per issue. Includes: profile of nine recent equity-based private placements to venture capital funds and individuals, showing 42 characteristics of each transaction.

Venture, the Magazine for Entrepreneurs, monthly, published by Venture Magazine, Inc. (212-682-7373), $18.00 per annum, approx. 140 pp. Includes profiles of private placements by smaller, privately held growth companies.

CHAPTER 3

S Corporations

INTRODUCTION
- History of S Corporations
- The Subchapter S Revision Act of 1982

QUALIFICATION FOR S CORPORATION STATUS

ELECTION OF S CORPORATION STATUS
- Timing of the Election
- Shareholder Consents

EFFECT AND CONSEQUENCES OF THE ELECTION ON THE CORPORATION
- Taxable Year of Electing Corporation
- Taxability of the Corporation
- Taxable Income of an S Corporation

EFFECT AND CONSEQUENCES OF ELECTION ON SHAREHOLDERS
- Pass-Through of Losses
- Shareholder Basis
- Distributions

REVOCATION AND TERMINATION OF S CORPORATION STATUS
- Voluntary Revocation
- Involuntary Termination
- Treatment of an S Termination Year
- Reelection after Revocation or Termination
- Passive Income Test

ADVANTAGES
- State Taxes
- Accumulated Earnings Tax
- Unreasonable Compensation
- Income Shifting
- Capital Gains
- Start-Up Losses

DISADVANTAGES

OTHER CONSIDERATIONS

CONCLUSION

Bruce J. McKenney
Partner
Arthur Andersen & Co.
Philadelphia, Pa.

Bruce J. McKenney is a tax partner. He joined the Cincinnati office of Arthur Andersen & Co. upon graduation from Michigan State University in 1974, and was promoted to manager in 1979. He transferred to the Philadelphia office in 1982 and was admitted to the firm in 1985.

Mr. McKenney specializes in the taxation of closely held businesses and their shareholders. He is a member of Arthur Andersen's S Corporation Specialty Team.

Mr. McKenney is a CPA and a member of the AICPA.

INTRODUCTION

History of S Corporations

Subchapter S was originally enacted in 1958 to permit the owners of certain "small" businesses to select the most suitable form for conducting their business operations without undue concern for federal income tax consequences. Congress recognized that the corporate form often represented the only practical option available to an entrepreneur because of the protection that it afforded from personal liability. This protection, however, was purchased at a very real cost. That cost was the severance of the business from its owner and its conversion into an entirely separate taxable entity, resulting in the double taxation of business earnings—a first tax at the corporate level and a second tax at the shareholder level when the income was withdrawn as a dividend or realized as a capital gain on sale or liquidation. The potential impact of this double tax was increased by the limit placed upon the amount of earnings that can be withdrawn from the business as tax deductible salary.

Further, the separate taxpayer status of a traditional corporation required that business losses be captured within the entity and, thereafter, be available only as a deduction against future corporate income. If the corporation never became profitable, the shareholders were restricted to capital loss treatment on their investment, except for the limited ordinary loss treatment that is available in the case of complete worthlessness.[1]

On the other hand, the partnership form was a possible, but often tenuous, alternative. The partnership form does not have the tax disadvantages of a corporation. However, it also does not provide protection from personal liability. While a limited partnership provides liability protection for passive owners (the limited partners), this form of business is often impractical since someone, or some entity, must be a general partner with unlimited personal liability. Furthermore, a partner active in the business cannot qualify as a limited partner.

Subchapter S was Congress' attempt to create a form of business entity that combined some of the most desirable attributes of the corporate and partnership forms. As such, it accorded shareholders the same protection from personal liability as a regular corporation and it imposed a conduit approach with respect to income and losses resulting in a single level of taxation roughly analogous to the partnership form.

However, though S corporations were frequently referred to as corporations taxed like partnerships (or pseudo corporations), these terms were misleading and confusing. In fact, S corporations were not really anything like partnerships, but were unique, hybrid entities for federal income tax purposes. The complexity of the rules governing S corporations and their shareholders, coupled with the significantly higher effective tax rates previously imposed upon individuals (as opposed to regular corporations), tended to limit the use of Subchapter S to small businesses having marginal profitability or to start-up situations where business losses were anticipated in the early years of the enterprise and the shareholders wished to be able to deduct those losses on their individual returns.

With the passage of the Economic Recovery Tax Act of 1981 reducing the highest marginal individual income tax rate to 50 percent, renewed attention was focused on Subchapter S. In light of this, Congress chose to reform the technical provisions governing such corporations to allow for their expanded use by the business community.

The Subchapter S Revision Act of 1982

The Subchapter S Revision Act of 1982 (the 1982 act) made radical changes in Subchapter S and brought it much closer to its originally

[1] IRC Sec. 1244.

EXHIBIT 1 After-Tax Cash to Shareholders

	Regular Corporation		
	Ordinary Dividend	*Long-Term Capital Gain on Sale or Liquidation*	*S Corporation*
Corporate tax	$209,750	$209,750	–0–
Individual tax	145,125	58,050	$250,000
Shareholders keep	$145,125	$232,200	$250,000

stated goal. An S corporation (the new official title) is now a true conduit entity, much the same as a partnership. The character of each separate item of income, gain, deduction, loss, credit, and so on, passes through to the shareholders, and the nature and timing of actual distributions to shareholders, previously an area of extreme complexity creating several traps for the unwary, is of much less concern than before.

In light of the above, every closely held business (whether presently incorporated or not) that meets or can meet the S corporation qualifications should consider or reconsider Subchapter S.

Subchapter S is much simpler than before, and most of the traps contained in the prior law have been eliminated. Furthermore, even though the corporate income tax, considered alone, will usually be less than that of the shareholders (a regular corporation will usually benefit from the graduated corporate tax rates on the first $100,000 of taxable income, whereas the shareholders will often be taxed upon their ratable share of business income at the top marginal rate of 50 percent), the second tax will be imposed sooner or later when the corporate income finds its way to the shareholders.[2] Exhibit 1 is a simplified comparison for a corporation with taxable income of $500,000.

A regular corporation that has $500,000 of taxable income will pay a corporate tax of $209,750, thereby leaving $290,250 for distribution to its shareholders. If this is distributed to shareholders in the form of a dividend, the shareholder in a 50 percent tax bracket would pay $145,125 in tax, leaving only $145,125 in his or her pocket (a combined corporate and individual tax of $353,875, over 70 percent). If the stock is sold for $290,250, and assuming the shareholder has zero basis in the stock, the shareholder would pay a maximum 20

[2] The only way to avoid the second tax would be to die, leaving the estate of the deceased shareholder with a step-up in basis of the S corporation stock. If the stock were sold at this time, there would be no capital gain. Given the alternative, the second tax may not be that bad after all.

percent capital gain tax of $58,050, leaving $232,200 in his or her pocket (a combined corporate and individual tax of $267,800, over 53 percent).[3] A sale of stock, while certainly more attractive than a dividend in cashing in on corporate profits, is often not a permitted or even desired alternative. As an S corporation, the corporate income is taxed only once, at the shareholder level, resulting in a maximum tax of 50 percent and $250,000 in the pocket of the shareholders.

S corporations offer an alternative form of conducting business and have definite advantages and disadvantages over regular corporations, partnerships, and other forms of business. The remainder of this chapter will address the technical requirements of S corporations, the taxation of S corporations and their shareholders, and the advantages and disadvantages of S corporations.

QUALIFICATION FOR S CORPORATION STATUS

The S corporation is a creature of the federal income tax law. As such, its qualifications are expressly contained in the Internal Revenue Code. Sec. 1361(b)(1) defines an S corporation in terms of the following criteria:

- It must be a domestic corporation.
- It must not be an "ineligible corporation."
- It must not have more than 35 shareholders.
- All shareholders must be individuals, estates, or certain trusts.
- A nonresident alien may not be a shareholder.
- Only one class of stock may be outstanding.

Domestic Corporation. A domestic corporation is one created or organized in the United States under the laws of any state. A corporation existing under the laws of any foreign jurisdiction will not qualify, even if it has assets or does business in the United States.

Ineligible Corporation. Sec. 1361(b)(2) details various types of corporations that *may not* elect S corporation status. These include:

- A member of an affiliated group as defined under Sec. 1504; that is, a parent/subsidiary relationship where the parent owns 80 percent or more of the voting power and 80 percent or more of the total value of the stock outstanding. An S corporation may own stock of another corporation so long as it owns less

[3] While the actual value of the stock may bear no direct relation to undistributed or retained earnings, and in most cases will exceed such, that portion of the selling price represented by the undistributed earnings will in effect be taxed at capital gain rates.

than 80 percent of the voting power *or* less than 80 percent of the total value of the stock outstanding.

- A financial institution to which Sec. 585 or 593 applies; that is, banks and savings and loan organizations.
- An insurance company.
- A possessions corporation.
- A corporation owning stock in inactive corporations.[4] However, an S corporation may own stock of an inactive corporation that has not begun business and does not have gross income (e.g., a "name-saving" corporation formed in another state).

Limitation on Number of Shareholders. An S corporation may have no more than 35 shareholders. For purposes of this test, stock owned by a husband and wife, or their estates, is considered to be owned by one shareholder for purposes of the S corporation shareholder limit.[5] It makes no difference whether the stock is owned jointly or separately. The grantor of a grantor trust is treated as the shareholder and each beneficiary of a voting trust is counted as a shareholder.[6]

Limitation On Types of Shareholders. From its inception, Congress determined that the unique "flow-through" benefits accorded shareholders of S corporations should be limited exclusively to individuals. As such, the privileges of S corporation status have been denied to any corporation having as a shareholder another corporation, partnership, trust, or estate (except for a brief period of administration). Certain grantor trusts (where the grantor-shareholder is deemed to be the owner of the trust property for federal income tax purposes), have been added to the list of permissible shareholders. This limited liberalization of the ownership requirements was both logical and consistent with legislative intent, since the grantors of such trusts are taxed individually on trust income and, for tax purposes, the trust does not exist as a taxable entity independent of the grantor. Some of the most meaningful changes wrought by recent legislation have been those increasing the types of permissible holders of S corporation stock. However, with the single exception of an estate, the law continues to require that the recipient of flow-through benefits derived from an S corporation be an individual, rather than an entity.

Only the following may be shareholders of an S corporation.[7] A corporation having a shareholder not listed cannot elect S corporation

---

[4] Sec. 1361(c)(6).

[5] Sec. 1361(c)(1).

[6] Sec. 1361(c)(2)(B)(iv).

[7] Sec. 1361(b).

status, and an S corporation election will terminate if stock is acquired by an entity not listed below:

- An individual.
- The estate of a deceased individual shareholder.
- A trust, all of which is treated as owned by an individual who is a citizen or resident of the United States under Sections 671–679. Such trusts include a true grantor trust, whether revocable or irrevocable, or a trust for which someone other than the grantor is the deemed owner.[8] Further, since a grantor trust will continue to qualify for only 60 days following the grantor's death (for two years if the entire corpus is included in the grantor's gross estate), it is imperative that the trust instrument include a provision to permit the trustee to distribute the stock to a qualifying person if the S corporation election is to be preserved.
- A voting trust.[9]
- A trust receiving stock under the terms of a will, but only for the 60-day period following the transfer.[10]
- The estate of an individual in bankruptcy.[11]
- A Qualified Subchapter S Trust (QSST).[12]

Qualified Subchapter S Trust. Prior to 1981, one of the principal deterrants to the use of Subchapter S was the limited ability to use a trust as a holding vehicle. An owner of an S corporation wanting to transfer stock ownership to children or grandchildren was forced to make either an outright gift or a gift to a trust over which the beneficiary had sufficient control so as to be deemed the owner of the property under Sec. 678. Often such a course of action was perceived as unacceptable from a family standpoint. The use of long-term, irrevocable trusts, a device commonly available with respect to all other assets, was simply not available with regard to S corporation stock. The QSST was specifically designed to address this problem. A QSST is a trust that owns stock in one or more S corporations and all the income of which is distributed (or is required to be distributed) currently to one individual who is a citizen or a resident of the United States. The introduction of the QSST allows owners of S corporations the flexibility, long available to shareholders of regular

---

[8] Sec. 678.

[9] Sec. 1361(c)(2)(A)(iv).

[10] Sec. 1361(c)(2)(A)(iii).

[11] Sec. 1361(c)(3).

[12] Sec. 1361(d).

corporations, to transfer shares of corporate stock to long-term irrevocable trusts, thereby removing control over the stock from their intended individual donees for a period of time. The QSST is an ideal receptacle for gifts where the intended donee is a minor child or grandchild or an individual whose financial abilities are in question. The documentation requirements of a QSST are quite strict, and failure to comply with them will result in termination of S corporate status. The terms of the trust must require the following:

- During the life of the current income beneficiary there shall be only one income beneficiary of the trust.
- Any trust corpus distributed during the life of the income beneficiary must be distributed only to such beneficiary.
- The income interest of the current income beneficiary shall terminate on the earlier of his or her death or termination of the trust.
- Upon the termination of the trust during the life of the current income beneficiary, the trust shall distribute all of its assets to that beneficiary.[13]

It should be noted that a QSST need not be required to distribute all of the income currently by its terms. A trust can still qualify if the income distribution is discretionary and the trustee actually distributes all of the income annually. Conversely, a simple trust may qualify regardless of whether the income is actually distributed, because the trust income is taxed to the beneficiary whether distributed or not under Sec. 652(a).

May Not Be a Nonresident Alien. A corporation that has a nonresident alien as a shareholder cannot qualify for the S corporation election. A nonresident alien is anyone who is not a U.S. citizen and who does not live in the 50 states or the District of Columbia.

One Class of Stock. Another inhibiting factor to the use of Subchapter S was the requirement that only a single class of stock be outstanding. This prevented the utilization of such estate-freezing techniques as preferred stock recapitalizations and family holding corporations. In addition, since the vote existed on a per share basis, control was purely a function of equitable stock ownership. The 1982 act did not change the single class of stock rule, but did provide some flexibility with respect to voting rights. Now, a corporation shall not be treated as having more than one class of stock solely because there are differ-

[13] Sec. 1361(d)(3).

ences in voting rights among the shares of common stock.[14] Nonvoting common stock issued to nonmanagement shareholders will enable the management shareholders to keep control of the corporation.

ELECTION OF S CORPORATION STATUS

In addition to meeting all the requirements above, a corporation must file a timely election to gain S corporation status[15] and all shareholders must consent to the election.[16]

Timing of the Election

The election may be filed anytime on or before the 15th day of the third month of the first taxable year for which the election is to be effective or any time during the preceding taxable year.[17] All the requirements of an S corporation must be met on the first day of the taxable year and every day thereafter. An election that is filed after the two-and-a-half-month limit, or a defective election filed within the first two and a half months, will be considered a timely election for the following taxable year provided that all the S corporation requirements are met at the time the election is made and thereafter.[18]

There is absolutely no statutory authority for an extension of time to file the election. A newly formed corporation can file an S corporation election only during the first two and a half months of its first taxable year if it is to be effective for that year. An election is invalid if it is filed before the corporation is considered to be in existence for federal income tax purposes. A corporation's initial taxable year for federal income tax purposes begins on the earliest of the following dates on which it has shareholders, acquires assets, or begins doing business.[19]

Shareholder Consents

All shareholders as of the date of the election must consent to the election.[20] Any shareholder who owns stock at the beginning of the

---

[14] Sec. 1361(c)(4).
[15] Sec. 1362(a)(1).
[16] Sec. 1362(a)(2).
[17] Sec. 1362(b)(1).
[18] Sec. 1362(b)(2) and (3).
[19] Reg. 1.1372-2(b)(1).
[20] Sec. 1362(a)(2).

taxable year for which the election is effective, but not as of the date of election, must also consent.[21]

Unlike the election itself, the IRS will grant extensions to file consents.[22] Since an extension of time to file consents may be obtained, the S corporation election should always be filed on time along with the shareholder consents that are available by that date. The remaining consents should be filed as soon thereafter as possible, consistent with the extension requirements of the regulations.

EFFECT AND CONSEQUENCES OF THE ELECTION ON THE CORPORATION

Taxable Year of Electing Corporation

An S corporation election requires adoption of a "permitted" taxable year in order for the election to be effective.[23] The general rule is that S corporations must report on a calendar year.[24] Further, a fiscal year is allowable only upon establishment of a business purpose to the satisfaction of the secretary.[25] However, Rev. Proc. 83-25 permits the adoption of certain fiscal years without specific advance approval by the IRS.[26]

The use of a fiscal year-end other than a calendar year can result in a significant tax deferral since income of an S corporation is reported by its shareholders in the year within which ends the corporation's year.[27] For example, an S corporation with a January 31 fiscal year-end will achieve an 11-month deferral of income (i.e. income earned during February through December will be reported by the shareholders in the following calendar year).

Taxability of the Corporation

S corporations are generally exempt from federal income taxes, with the following exceptions:[28]

- The investment tax credit recapture on assets acquired in non-electing years.

---

[21] Sec. 1362(b)(2)(B)(ii).

[22] Reg. 18.1362-2(c).

[23] Sec. 1378(a)(2).

[24] Sec. 1378(b)(1).

[25] Sec. 1378(b)(2).

[26] 1983-1 C.B.

[27] Sec. 1366(a)(1).

[28] Sec. 1363(a).

- The tax imposed on capital gains by Sec. 1374 and any related minimum tax.
- The tax on excess net passive income under Sec. 1375 (see later discussion on passive income test).

The capital gain tax under Sec. 1374 has limited application. First, the long-term capital gain at the S corporation level must exceed both $25,000 and 50 percent of the corporation taxable income for the year. Second, the taxable income for the year must exceed $25,000. Furthermore, an S corporation is not subject to the tax if it has been an S corporation for three taxable years preceding the year of the gain or from inception. If the S corporation is subject to the tax, the tax is computed as the lesser of the alternative tax (28 percent) applied to that portion of the gain in excess of $25,000, or the regular corporate tax on all taxable income.

The tax paid by the S corporation reduces the amount of capital gain reported to the shareholders for inclusion in their individual returns. Therefore, the capital gains tax imposed by Sec. 1374 does not cause a true double tax. In fact, as discussed later, the combined S corporation and individual tax will be less than if the gain is distributed as a dividend by a regular corporation.

Taxable Income of an S Corporation

The taxable income of an S corporation is computed in the same manner as that of an individual, except that[29] the following deductions are not allowed to S corporations:[30]

- Personal exemptions.
- Charitable contributions.
- Net operating losses.[31]
- Depletion with respect to oil and gas wells.[32]
- Foreign taxes.[33]

EFFECT AND CONSEQUENCES OF ELECTION ON SHAREHOLDERS

The express intent underlying an election of S corporation status is to place the corporate shareholders in a position of rough equivalency,

[29] Sec. 1363(b).
[30] Sec. 1363(b)(2).
[31] Sec. 172.
[32] Sec. 611.
[33] Sec. 901.

for federal income tax purposes, to the partners of a partnership. While the 1982 act went a long way toward realizing this goal, significant differences continue to exist.

Under the new conduit approach, any item of income, gain, loss, deduction, or credit that can effect that tax liability of any shareholder must be separately stated. Items considered separately include, but are not limited to, the following:

- Gross income (wherever necessary to determine the gross income of the shareholder).
- Investment interest.
- Sec. 1231 gains and losses.
- Charitable contributions.
- Tax-exempt interest.
- Depletion.
- Foreign income and loss.
- Expensing of depreciable assets.
- Foreign taxes.
- Foreign tax credits.
- Investment tax credit.
- Jobs tax credit.
- Preference items.

Pass-Through of Losses

The pass-through of losses results in a deduction at the shareholder level only to the extent the loss does not exceed the sum of the shareholder's basis in stock of the S corporation and of any loans he may have made to the corporation.[34] Any loss that exceeds this limitation carries over indefinitely.[35] This carryover occurs at the corporate level but is identified with the individual shareholder, recognizing that such carryovers may arise disproportionately to individual shareholders.

Shareholder Basis

A shareholder's tax basis of his interest in an S corporation is important not only for determining gain or loss upon sale or disposition, but also for calculating the actual amount of his pro rata share of corporate losses that may be deducted on his individual federal income tax return. Initially, this basis is equal to the acquisition cost of the corporate stock, plus his basis in any S corporation debt obligations of which he is the creditor. (Unlike a partnership, a shareholder of

---

[34] Sec. 1366(d)(1).

[35] Sec. 1366(d)(2).

an S corporation never receives basis for corporate debt to third parties.) Basis, however, is not a static concept determinable solely with reference to historical events. Much more closely akin to a partnership, the flow-through of corporate income and loss to any S corporation shareholder makes basis a dynamic and continually changing amount. As a general rule, income and gain items increase the shareholder's basis in stock, and loss or deduction items decrease the basis in stock.[36] Decreases in basis cannot reduce the basis of stock below zero. The flow-through of additional deductions, losses, and so on, is applied to reduce the basis of loans by the shareholder to the S corporation.[37] Losses that exceed the combined basis of stock and debt are not currently deductible by the shareholder, but are carried forward.

If there has been a reduction in the basis of debt under the rule described above, subsequent increases in basis as a result of income, gain, and so forth, are applied first to restore the reduction in basis of debt before being applied to increase the basis of stock.[38]

Distributions

Prior to the 1982 act, the basic mechanism for recognizing income at the shareholder level was through distributions—either actual distributions made during the year, or constructive distributions as of the last day of the year. After the 1982 act, the requirement to make distributions in accordance with specific rules as to timing no longer applies and distributions will generally be treated more like those from partnerships.

Different rules apply to S corporations with earnings and profits and those without. Generally, an S corporation after the 1982 act will not generate earnings and profits. However, an S corporation that was once a regular corporation or was an S corporation prior to the 1982 act can have earnings and profits.

For an S corporation without earnings and profits, distributions are tax free to the extent they do not exceed the shareholder's basis in stock.[39] Distributions in excess of stock basis are treated as gain from the sale or exchange of property, either long-term or short-term capital gain depending on the holding period of the stock.[40]

For an S corporation with earnings and profits, distributions are

---

[36] Sec. 1367(a).
[37] Sec. 1367(b)(2)(A).
[38] Sec. 1367(b)(2)(B).
[39] Sec. 1368(b).
[40] Sec. 1368(b)(2).

treated first as tax-free return of basis and then as capital gain until the total of such distributions equals the amount of the Accumulated Adjustment Account (AAA).[41] Distributions in excess of AAA are treated as dividend distributions to the extent they do not exceed accumulated earnings and profits.[42] Once all of the accumulated earnings and profits have been distributed, additional distributions are treated in the same manner as an S corporation having no earnings and profits.[43]

An S corporation may elect to distribute accumulated earnings and profits before any distributions of AAA.[44]

The AAA generally represents the undistributed income of an S corporation since the 1982 act. The AAA is maintained at the corporate level and is credited for items of income and reduced for items of expense in a manner similar, but not identical, to adjustments to basis under Sec. 1367.[45]

REVOCATION AND TERMINATION OF S CORPORATION STATUS

Termination of an S corporation election can be accomplished by formal revocation,[46] by a corporation ceasing to be a small business corporation,[47] or by violation of the new passive investment income rules.[48]

Voluntary Revocation

A planned termination may be accomplished by voluntary revocation. An S corporation election may be terminated with the consent of shareholders owning more than one half of the corporation's stock. The corporation must file a statement of revocation (there is no official form) with the District Director who received the original election form. The statement of revocation must be accompanied by a statement of consent signed by shareholders owning more than 50 percent of the corporation's stock.[49]

A revocation will be effective for the entire taxable year if it is

---

[41] Sec. 1368(c)(1).

[42] Sec. 1368(c)(2).

[43] Sec. 1368(c)(3).

[44] Sec. 1368(e)(3).

[45] Sec. 1368(e)(1)(A).

[46] Sec. 1362(d)(1).

[47] Sec. 1362(d)(2).

[48] Sec. 1362(d)(3).

[49] Sec. 1362(d)(1)(B).

filed on or before the 15th day of the third month of the taxable year. A revocation filed after that date will be effective for the following taxable year and all subsequent years.[50] The statement of revocation may provide for a prospective effective date in the taxable year in which the revocation is filed other than the first day of a taxable year. This will cause a splitting of the tax year into a short S corporation year and a short regular corporation year.[51]

Involuntary Termination

If an S corporation ceases to possess any one of the attributes required of a "small business corporation," its election will automatically be terminated. If an election is terminated under the rules of Sec. 1362(d)(3) (passive income limitation—see below) or Sec. 1362(d)(2) (ceasing to be a small business corporation), and the Secretary determines that the termination is inadvertent, the election can be salvaged retroactively. In such cases, the committee reports to the 1982 act require the IRS to be reasonable in granting waivers where no tax avoidance results from allowing continued S corporation treatment. Under such circumstances, the corporation must take steps to requalify as a small business corporation within a reasonable period of time after discovery of the event that resulted in the termination,[52] and the corporation and all shareholders during the retroactive period must agree to any adjustments required by the Secretary.[53]

Treatment of an S Termination Year

An S termination year is defined as any taxable year of a corporation in which a termination of an election to be treated as an S corporation takes effect, other than on the first day of a taxable year.[54] A termination effective any time other than the first day of a year will result in a short S corporation year and a short regular corporation year, the regular corporation year beginning on the date of the terminating event.

The allocation of income between the S short year and regular short year is on a pro rata, per share, per day basis. An election to use an actual allocation based on the corporation's books and records can be made and the election will be valid only if all shareholders

---

[50] Sec. 1362(d)(1)(C).

[51] Sec. 1362(d)(1)(D).

[52] Sec. 1362(f)(3).

[53] Sec. 1362(f)(4).

[54] Sec. 1362(e)(4).

at any time during the S short year and all shareholders on the first day of the regular short year consent to the election.[55] If actual accounting is contemplated, an agreement should be worked out in advance of an acquisition by outside shareholders or another corporation due to the requirement that the election must be unanimous.

Reelection after Revocation or Termination

Once an election is revoked or terminated, a new S corporation election cannot be made until the fifth year following the year for which termination was effective unless the IRS consents.[56] However, the inadvertent termination rules of Sec. 1362(f) may provide relief in some cases.

The IRS will generally not grant permission for a new election within the five-year period unless more than 50 percent of the stock is owned by shareholders who did not own any stock upon termination or the terminating event was outside the control of the shareholders.[57]

Passive Income Test

Prior to the 1982 act, the receipt by an S corporation of passive investment income in excess of 25 percent of its gross receipts constituted another cause of automatic termination. Now, the presence of significant amounts of passive investment income will have differing consequences depending on whether the electing corporation has "Subchapter C earnings and profits," that is, whether it once was a regular corporation or has acquired a regular corporation in a nontaxable reorganization.

An S corporation election will now terminate only if an S corporation has both passive investment income in excess of 25 percent of its total gross receipts for each of three consecutive taxable years, and Subchapter C earnings and profits at the close of each of the three years.[58] The election will then terminate as of the beginning of the fourth taxable year. Further, excess "passive net income" (that attributable to passive investment income in excess of 25 percent of gross receipts) will be taxed at the corporate level for any taxable years for which the election is not terminated.[59] The highest corporate rate (currently 46 percent) will apply and the tax will reduce the

---

[55] Sec. 1362(e)(3).

[56] Sec. 1362(g).

[57] Reg. 1.1372-5(a).

[58] Sec. 1362(d)(3).

[59] Sec. 1375.

amounts flowing through to the shareholders. The tax applies for any year the corporation "fails" the test, regardless of whether it is for one, two, or three years.[60]

In applying this test, it must be recognized that "gross receipts" is not the same as gross income. Gross receipts generally include "the total amount received or accrued under the method of accounting used by the corporation in computing its taxable income." Thus, the total amount of receipts is not reduced by returns and allowances, costs or deductions. Gross receipts include amounts received or accrued, whether or not they are included in gross income. Gross receipts do not include amounts received as a loan, loan repayment, contribution to capital, or for issuance of the corporation's stock.

The definition of passive investment income specifically includes:

- Royalties.
- Rents.
- Dividends.
- Interest.
- Annuities.
- Gains from sales or exchanges of stock or securities. If both gains and losses exist on stock or security transactions, only the gain transactions are considered.[61]

ADVANTAGES

As indicated in the introduction, the principal advantage of an S corporation is that it eliminates the double taxation of corporate income. In addition, there are several other advantages to bring an S corporation that, depending on the particular characteristics of the corporation and its shareholders, can be of significant benefit over the regular corporate structure.

State Taxes

While Subchapter S is a federal tax concept, many states automatically adopt the federal statute or have adopted provisions similar to the federal law. Other states do not recognize Subchapter S and tax the corporations as regular corporations. Corporations with multistate operations may have the shareholders pay tax in some states and the corporation paying tax in other states. While a complete analysis of the complexities in this area is beyond the scope of this chapter, it

---

[60] Sec. 1375(a).

[61] Reg. 1.1372-4(b)(5)(i).

is an area that requires consideration by the shareholders and their tax planners before adoption of S corporation status.

Adopting S corporation status could save state income taxes in situations where the state has adopted the S corporation provisions and the state corporate tax rate exceeds the individual tax rate (or where the state has no individual income taxes at all.) In many cases, the state tax savings could exceed the increased federal taxes.

Accumulated Earnings Tax

One might suggest that if a regular corporation never distributes its earnings in the form of a dividend, there will never be double taxation. In fact, the lower corporate tax rates, particularly on the first $100,000 of taxable income, encourages the accumulation of income at the corporate level. However, there is a penalty tax called the accumulated earnings tax levied on corporations, in addition to the regular corporate tax, on income that a corporation accumulates beyond the reasonable needs of its business. This tax is equal to 27.5 percent on the first $100,000 of accumulated taxable income and 38.5 percent on the accumulated taxable income in excess of $100,000. S corporations are exempt from accumulated earnings tax.[62] Thus, a regular corporation with an accumulated earnings problem can avoid this problem for the future by electing S corporation status.

Unreasonable Compensation

Similar to the issue of accumulated earnings, another technique sometimes used to avoid double tax is to pay out all the corporate income in the form of salaries and wages. Since salaries and wages are deductible at the corporate level, there is no corporate tax on this income. If the salary paid to an employee/shareholder is unreasonably high, the IRS could recast all or a portion of the salary as a dividend.[63] By electing to be an S corporation, there is no corporate tax and all the income is reported by the shareholders whether distributed or not. There is no benefit to the IRS to restructure some of the compensation as distributions.

Income Shifting

By structuring the ownership of an S corporation, income can be directed to children, grandchildren, or other low income bracket taxpay-

---

[62] Sec. 1363(a).

[63] Reg. Sec. 1.162-7(b)(1).

ers. This can even be achieved without affecting the control of the corporation. This is done through the use of nonvoting common stock. The only potential constraint in this area is where one of the shareholders is providing services or capital to the corporation and is not being adequately compensated. The IRS can make adjustments to such individual shareholders to reflect the value of the services performed.[64]

Capital Gains

The maximum capital gains rate for corporations is presently 28 percent, whereas the maximum capital gains rates for individuals is 20 percent. As discussed above, an S corporation can be liable for capital gains tax under certain circumstances. Even where there is a capital gains tax at the S corporation level, if the capital gain proceeds are to be distributed to the shareholders, the combined S corporation/shareholder tax will be less than the combined regular corporation/shareholder tax. A "one-shot" S corporation election in the year of the gain may be advisable. For example, assume a corporation with a net long-term capital gain of $100,000 that it wishes to distribute to its shareholders. Further assume that the S corporation will be subject to the Sec. 1374 tax and the shareholders are in a 50 percent tax bracket. The after-tax proceeds in the hands of the shareholder as an S corporation and a regular corporation are shown in Exhibit 2.

EXHIBIT 2 After-Tax Proceeds to Shareholders

	S Corporation	*Regular Corporation*
Gain	$100,000	$100,000
Corporate tax	21,000	28,000
Net gain distributed to shareholder	$ 79,000	$ 72,000
Shareholder tax	15,800 (20%)	36,000 (50%)
Net after-tax proceeds	$ 63,200	$ 36,000

Start-Up Losses

Many new businesses generate losses during the early years of operations. A regular corporation can carry such losses forward to offset taxable income in the future. Through the use of an S corporation, the shareholders can receive direct current benefit from these losses and, in fact, could generate more tax benefit because of the higher

[64] Sec. 1366(e).

tax rates at the shareholder level. The losses are deductible at the shareholder level to the extent of their basis in stock and direct indebtedness to the S corporation. In structuring the financing of a new venture considering S corporation status, the amount of losses should be estimated and the corporation financed accordingly. That is, if debt is going to be required, the shareholders should consider having themselves borrow the money directly from an outside lender and then loan the funds to the S corporation to provide the required basis to deduct the losses. Furthermore, the shareholders must have enough income from other sources to absorb the S corporation losses or the benefit will be deferred.

DISADVANTAGES

While there are many advantages of operating as an S corporation, there are also many disadvantages. As mentioned above, there are many qualification criteria needed to become an S corporation. Most notably, there are the restrictions on the corporation structure; that is, there can only be certain kinds of shareholders, you can only have 35 shareholders, can only have one class of stock, and so on. These restrictions in and of themselves create significant difficulties in raising capital from conventional sources, that is, venture capital corporations, partnerships, and other equity investors.

Another disadvantage of operating as an S corporation is the possibility of having the election revoked inadvertently and thereby causing significant tax problems to the shareholders who may have structured their personal financial planning to maximize the benefit of the income or losses being reported out of the S corporation.

OTHER CONSIDERATIONS

See Exhibit 3 for the listing of the nontax considerations for comparison of a regular corporation, an S corporation, and a partnership. See Exhibit 4 for a listing of the tax considerations for a comparison of a regular corporation, an S corporation, and a partnership.

CONCLUSION

An S corporation offers unique tax and nontax considerations for operations of a business. The typical types of financing needed in a startup venture offer some limitations to the use of S corporations. However, if these can be overcome, the significant tax advantages of operating in S corporation form could far outweigh the inconveniences and potential costs of conventional financing.

EXHIBIT 3 Nontax Considerations for Comparison of a Regular Corporation, an S Corporation, and a Partnership

Factor	*Regular Corporation*	*S Corporation*	*Partnership*
Life	Unlimited or perpetual unless limited by state law or terms of its charter.	Same as a regular corporation. Election may be revoked or terminated without affecting continuity of life.	Generally set up for a specific, agreed term. Usually will be terminated by death, withdrawal, insolvency, or legal disability of a general partner.
Entity	Completely separate from owners and recognized as such.	Same as regular corporation.	Generally recognized as separate by the business community, but not for all purposes.
Liability of owners	Limited. Shareholders are generally sheltered from liabilities of the corporation.	Same as regular corporation.	Each general partner is fully liable as an individual for all partnership debts. A limited partner's liability is usually limited to the amount of his capital contribution.
Ease and effect of transfer of ownership interest	Generally, stock is easily and readily transferable and transfer has no effect on the corporate entity.	Same as regular corporation. Considerations must be given to the effect of any transfer on the election, to ensure that it does not result in an unintended termination.	Transfer may require approval of all other partners and may result in termination of old partnership and creation of a new one.
Availability of outside capital or financing	May sell stock or bonds to the public and there is no limit on the number of shareholders allowed.	Limited in that there can be only one class of stock outstanding and no more than 35 shareholders. The corporation can issue debt so long as it is not considered a second class of stock.	Limited to borrowing from partners or outsiders, or to admitting new partners who contribute additional capital.
Management of business operations	Much flexibility. Control can be exercised by a small number of officers without having to consult other owners, regardless of the total number of shareholders.	Technically, the same as a regular corporation. By its nature, however, most owners are likely to be active in management.	Usually, all general partners will participate in management. However, other partners may grant management control to one or more partners by agreement. Limited partners, by definition, cannot be active in general management.

EXHIBIT 4 Income Tax Considerations for Comparison of a Regular Corporation, an S Corporation and a Partnership

Factor	*Regular Corporation*	*S Corporation*	*Partnership*
Who pays the tax?	The corporation is taxed on its taxable income whether any is distributed to the shareholders.	The shareholders are taxed on the taxable income of the corporation whether any is distributed to them.	The partners are taxed on the taxable income of the partnership whether any is distributed to them.
Distribution of earnings subsequent to year-end	Taxable to shareholders as ordinary dividends to the extent of earnings and profits.	No tax effect to the shareholders unless the distributions exceeds the Accumulated Adjustments Account and/or tax basis of stock. A distribution in excess of current and cumulative S corporation earnings will be a dividend if the corporation has accumulated earnings and profits.	No tax effect on partners unless *cash* distributions exceed a partner's tax basis in his or her partnership interest.
Net operating loss	Deductible only by the corporation within prescribed carryback and carryover periods.	Deductible by shareholders subject to certain limitations.	Deductible by partners subject to certain limitations.
Salaries paid to owners	Owners are employees. Salaries are taxable to them and deductible by the corporation. Salaries must be reasonable in amount in relation to services rendered.	Same as regular corporation. The question of reasonable compensation may also be important if salaries are used as a device for shifting income among shareholders within a family group.	Partners are not employees. Amounts paid are considered partial distributions of income unless they qualify as guaranteed payments.
Liquidation of the business	Amount received in excess of basis in stock is taxable as capital gain, or ordinary income if the corporation is collapsible.	Same as regular corporation.	Normally, no tax unless cash or equivalent exceeds basis in partnership interest. Excess then taxed as capital gain unless the partnership is collapsible.
Pension or profit-sharing plan	Owners who are employees can be included in a regular, qualified plan.	Owners who are employees can be included in a regular, qualified plan.	Partners may participate only in a qualified self-employed plan.

EXHIBIT 4 *(continued)*

Factor	*Regular Corporation*	*S Corporation*	*Partnership*
Capital gains and losses	Taxed to the corporation; there is no capital gains deduction.	Capital gains and losses flow through to the shareholders as such. Capital gain may be taxed to the corporation in certain cases.	Capital gains and losses flow through to the partners as such.
Tax on transfer of assets to business	Generally, none.	Same as regular corporation.	None.
Special allocation of net income or loss or different types of income and deductions among owners by agreement	Not possible.	Not possible.	Can be done so long as business allocations have substantial economic effect.
Earnings accumulation	May be subject to penalty tax if accumulation is unreasonable.	No limit since all income, whether distributed or not, is taxed to the shareholders.	No limit since all income, whether distributed or not, is taxed to partners.
Passive investment income	May create a personal holding company taxed at penalty rates.	No effect unless the corporation has Subchapter C earnings and profits. Excess passive investment income for three consecutive taxable years may then terminate the election. The corporation might then be a personal holding company.	No effect.
Selection of taxable year	No restriction.	Limited to "permitted year," generally a calendar year with limited exceptions unless consent of commissioner is obtained. Existing fiscal years are grandfathered for S corporations electing *before* October 20, 1982.	Must conform to that of the principal partners, generally the calendar year, unless consent of commission is obtained.

EXHIBIT 4 *(concluded)*

Factor	*Regular Corporation*	*S Corporation*	*Partnership*
Specific dollar limit on certain deductions	Applies at corporate level only.	Generally applies at both the corporate and the shareholder level.	Applied to the partnership and individually to each partner as well.
Sale or liquidation of ownership interest	All capital gain, or all ordinary income, if corporation is collapsible.	Same as regular corporation.	May be part capital gain and part ordinary income.
Charitable contributions	Deductible by the corporation limited to 10 percent of taxable income. Excess may be carried over.	Not deductible by the corporation, but by the shareholders subject to the limitations applicable to individuals.	Not deductible by the partnership, but by the partners subject to the limitations applicable to individuals.
Tax preferences	Applies at corporate level only.	Tax preferences pass through to the shareholders, except for certain capital gains subject to tax under Sec. 1374, and considered in shareholders' computation of Alternative Minimum Taxable Income.	Tax preferences pass through to the partners and are considered in partners' computation of Alternative Minimum Taxable Income.
Investment interest limitation	Not applicable.	All items necessary to the calculation pass through to the shareholders.	All items necessary to the calculation pass through to the partners.
At-risk rules	Not applicable except for certain closely held corporations.	Applicable at the shareholder level.	Applicable at the partner level.
Tax credits	Credited against the corporate tax.	Pass through to the shareholders.	Pass through to the partners.

CHAPTER **4**

Lease Financing

Frank P. Slattery, Jr.
President
Lease Financing Corporation
Radnor, Pa.

Frank P. Slattery, Jr., is president of Lease Financing Corporation, Radnor, Pennsylvania, with which he has been associated in an executive capacity since 1969. He is also director of the Provident National Bank, Philadelphia, Pennsylvania, the American Association of Equipment Lessors, Arlington, Virginia; Greenwich Capital Markets, Greenwich, Connecticut; and Lemans Group, Valley Forge, Pennsylvania. He earned his A.B. from Princeton University, and his LL.B. from the University of Pennsylvania Law School.

Rex H. Anderson, Jr.
Director of Special Projects
Lease Financing Corporation
Radnor, Pa.

Rex H. Anderson, Jr., has been the director of Special Projects, Lease Financing Corporation, since 1983. He was a private consultant from 1980 to 1983, and assistant to the executive vice president, Phoenix Steel Corporation from 1978 to 1979. He received his B.A. from Emory University and his M.B.A. from the University of Pennsylvania Wharton School.

INTRODUCTION

This chapter approaches the subject of equipment lease financing from the perspective of a chief financial officer or a chief executive officer of an emerging and growing business, who may be contemplating the use of leasing either to finance assets that will be used directly in his own business, or to finance the sale of products or equipment that his company manufactures. Leasing is one of a variety of financing vehicles available today to the emerging company, and the objective of this chapter is to provide a broad overview of leasing as a financial tool. This overview will provide the business decision maker with a general guide to the use of lease financing. Economic, accounting, tax, and documentation issues will be covered, as well as the various types and sources of leasing that are currently available in the marketplace today. At the time of the writing of this chapter, we are faced with the prospect of a potential overhaul in the federal income tax system. The result of possible change in the tax law has, to an extent, put the leasing industry in a state of flux. As long as the possibility of a tax law change looms on the horizon, the leasing industry will be operating under conditions of uncertainty that will affect the availability, conditions, and pricing of lease financing.

In the past decade, the leasing industry has grown in size and complexity with the result that there are a wide variety of lease structures and sources of lease financing available. In 1984, the origination of more than $70 billion worth of capital equipment was leased in the United States. Leasing is one of the most important methods of financing capital formation in our economy, and the executive of an emerging company must have a basic understanding of how to employ leasing to maximize the performance of his company. Lease transactions are inherently more complex than many other forms of financing, particularly with respect to tax and accounting issues. As a result, the business executive will often seek the advice of outside tax or legal counsel. These professionals play a very important role in the leasing industry, and this chapter is also designed to highlight the issues and concerns on which they may be called upon to give advice.

WHAT IS A LEASE?

A lease is a device that enables a user of equipment ("lessee") to enjoy virtually all of the benefits of the use of an asset without the transference of the actual ownership of the equipment during the course of the lease term. The owner of the equipment ("lessor") purchases the equipment and maintains ownership and title to it during the course of the lease term but gives up the use of the equipment. The lessee contractually is obligated to make lease payments on a periodic basis to the lessor. The lessee usually has the option at the end of the base lease term of returning the equipment to the lessor, purchasing it at fair market value, or re-leasing it for an additional period of time. The lessor earns a return on the investment in the lease transaction from the lessee's rental payments, the tax benefits that the lessor is entitled to by virtue of being owner of the equipment, and the proceeds of the residual value of the equipment, if any, at the end of the lease.

A True Lease

This type of transaction is commonly referred to as a "true" lease for tax purposes. A wide variety of financing structures are called "leases." However, many of these structures are not true leases since they in fact confer the benefits of ownership to the lessee from the very beginning of the transaction. The Internal Revenue Service (IRS) has issued a somewhat confusing amalgam of revenue rulings and other information that may be used as guidelines for determining whether a lease is a true lease for tax purposes. This chapter will focus primarily on true leases, though mention will be made of other forms of financing that have come to be called leases.

From the lessee's perspective, a true lease will, at a minimum, contain the following characteristics:

1. Title to the asset under lease is not transferred to the lessee at any point in time during the lease term, but title may be conveyed to the lessee at the end of the base lease term for fair market value consideration. Certain lease transactions permit the lessee to purchase the asset for a fixed price at the end of the lease term, and this option may prevent the lease from being characterized as a true lease for tax purposes.
2. The lease term is for a period less than 80 percent of the useful life of the asset.
3. The virtual use of the asset is under the control of the lessee. Certain characteristics, such as the payment of taxes, the maintenance of the equipment, the insurance of the asset, and the care and appearance of the asset, may be, but are not always, the responsibility of the lessee.

This is by no means a comprehensive list of the features of a transaction that the IRS would review. The IRS has outlined many true lease guidelines for the lessor. The lessee may wish to have its tax counsel or accountant review the structure of the lease from the lessor's point of view as a further check on the true lease status of the transaction. One of the prime determinents used by the IRS in analyzing a transaction from the lessor's point of view is whether or not the lessor stands to make a profit from the transaction apart from the tax benefits, and secondly, whether the lessor has a risk of loss in the transaction.

In the ever-changing rules of a true lease, it is necessary that a lessee fully understand the position of both the lessee and lessor. For example, if the investment tax credit is to be passed through to a lessee, and the lease is not a true lease, then it is necessary for the lessee to claim the investment tax credit as owner of the equipment. Additionally, a lessee is often asked to indemnify the lessor as to the availability of tax benefits. If a lease is not a true lease for tax purposes, this may lead to serious financial implications for the lessee.

Since the lessor benefits from tax deductions associated with the ownership of the equipment and from the expectation of realizing the residual value from the equipment at the end of the lease, the lessee can expect that these two benefits will be priced into the lease payments required by the lessor. Therefore, the lessee should expect a stream of lease payments to be less costly when compared to the alternative of purchasing the equipment outright. In effect, the lessor has purchased the tax and residual value benefits of ownership and is providing some or all of those benefits to the lessee.

WHY LEASE?

Leasing is only one of a variety of techniques for financing equipment. There are a number of factors that need to be analyzed in order to determine whether leasing is the proper way to finance a particular asset or group of assets. Clearly, one of the prime motivations for considering leasing is that this device carries a lower cost when compared to other financing techniques. However, there are noneconomic reasons for considering leasing, which can be equally important.

Tax Benefits

In a true lease, the lessee is trading tax benefits in the form of depreciation, the investment tax credit if the asset is new and eligible for it, the interest deduction on the debt incurred to acquire the equipment, and the residual value of the equipment at the end of the lease to the lessor, who is the owner of the equipment, in exchange for the lower lease rental. The value that the lessor places on the tax benefits and residual value is reflected in the lease rate it offers to the lessee. The more highly it values these benefits, the lower the rate. Since most leases are multiyear transactions, the creditworthiness of the user and the ability of the lessee to make lease payments is also considered in the lease rate. However, since a residual value must be brought forward to the present (present value of money), the longer the lease term, the less valuable a future residual value will be to a lessor.

Emerging and growing companies often are not profitable in their early years. Significant funds are being plowed into research and development. Staff and marketing costs are often heavy. Even after the business turns the corner and begins earning a profit, it may still have the benefit of a net operating loss carryforward for federal income tax purposes, which may take several years to use up. In this case, tax benefits in the form of the investment tax credit, depreciation, and interest deductions are not especially valuable to a business, since it is not a federal income tax payer. In this case, such a business can immediately benefit from these tax savings by entering into a lease transaction with an owner (lessor) of the equipment, who can immediately employ these tax benefits to their fullest extent and who will pass these benefits on to the lessee in the form of a lower lease rate. A company that is considering the use of lease financing must therefore make a judgment as to its likely tax liability in the years over which a lease transaction would run. This is often a difficult forecast to make.

Residual Value

The residual value assumed by the lessor in fixing the lease rate will vary widely depending on the asset. Currently, data processing equipment generally retains very little residual value at the end of a five-year lease, whereas certain types of production and transportation equipment, such as machine tools and commercial aircraft, are often worth a substantial percentage of their original value at the end of a lease. Therefore, the type of asset and its anticipated residual value will have an impact on the cost of the lease to the lessee. It is not unusual for a lessee and a lessor to have widely different views with respect to the anticipated residual value of a piece of equipment. If, for example, a lessee expects the equipment to be worth very little at the end of the lease, while the lessor expects it to retain a substantial value and prices this expectation into the lease factor, then this will work to the benefit of the lessee. Of course, expectations can work in an opposite manner as well.

Short-Term Need

A company may have a need for the use of a specific asset for a limited period of time. The leasing industry often can tailor a transaction to meet this kind of a need. A construction company may need certain types of equipment for a year or two, a factory may need a specialized piece of equipment for a long-term contract, after which the equipment will not be required, or a company may not want to lock itself in to certain types of high technology equipment by purchasing it. Short-term leases that are available for many types of assets afford the company the use of the asset, and at the end of the period of use, the company has no further obligation to the lessor other than to return the equipment, although typically the lessee will be required to maintain the equipment and to return it in sound condition, normal wear and tear excepted.

Other Financial Considerations

The mission of any company is to produce a product or provide a service that meets a need in the marketplace. In order to achieve this mission, most companies require productive assets in the form of revenue-producing equipment. The acquisition of this productive equipment is often one of the most significant financial decisions that a young, emerging company must face. Cash can be a young company's most scarce resource and as a result, significant time is often taken by the management and ownership of emerging companies to determine what type of equipment is best suited for the company's needs and, secondly, how best to finance that equipment. Faced with these decisions, it is important for management and shareholders to keep in mind that their firm is not in business to own equipment, but is in business to provide a specific product or service to its marketplace. Leasing has the ability to offer management greater flexibility with respect to the acquisition of income-producing equipment. Leasing can preserve a firm's cash resources, since no down payment is required. A straight debt financing of an asset might require the firm to put up some of its own money to fund the purchase of the asset, along with the funds advanced by the lender, in order to improve the lender's loan-to-collateral ratio. Leasing, however, will not require the lessee to dip into its liquidity in this fashion, since the lessor will advance 100 percent of the asset's price.

If a firm makes the decision to purchase and own its equipment outright, it will be making a significant and potentially long-term commitment of its own funds to the acquisition of that equipment, and to a specific type of technology. Capital budgets must be drawn up to match the equipment purchases with the company's available funds, and board approval is generally required for all major capital equipment acquisitions. The direct acquisition of equipment, however, may lock the company into a technology that could become obsolete. The pace of technological change has been quickening, and the economic life of many types of assets has been growing shorter as technology improves efficiency and productivity. Leasing can furnish a company with the ability to secure the use of income-producing assets for a specific period of time, at the end of which the company can return the assets to the lessor if technological improvements have rendered those assets uneconomical. Lease financing will permit management to change equipment to take advantage of technological change. Outright ownership does not afford this flexibility, since the long-term financial and executive commitments associated with the purchase of equipment create an inherent inertia with respect to replacing it.

Clearly, the lessor who gives the lessee the option to use equipment for a specific period of time or to terminate a lease at various points in time must be compensated for the early termination risk and for the residual risk that is a function of technological change. The lessee, on the other hand, may find that the financial cost of leasing under such circumstances may be equal to the cost associated with debt financing if the asset is acquired outright. However, it must also take into account the reduction in operating or production costs that will result from easily obtaining new equipment incorporating the latest technology.

Leasing furnishes a company with one of the most efficient methods for matching equipment financing with the need to employ the most technologically advanced equipment in order to maintain the status of an efficient producer.

The book accounting treatment for leases from the lessee's perspective is a relatively complex subject and will be treated at further length in another section of this chapter. However, it is important to point out that certain types of leases called *operating* leases may not have to be reported on a company's balance sheet as a liability. The operating lease rentals are expensed and may only need be reported in a footnote. This accounting treatment can permit a company to finance assets without impairing the company's apparent debt-to-equity ratio. This consideration is essentially cosmetic in nature, and any bank or financial institution looking at a company's balance sheet in an effort to determine whether financing should be extended to that company will nevertheless take into account off–balance sheet operating leases in the determination of the company's credit, cash flow, and leverage. The Financial Accounting Standards Board (FASB) is also looking at this area, and it is entirely possible that off–balance sheet financing may soon disappear.

Under certain circumstances, leasing may provide a company access to financing when other types of financing are not available. If a company is struggling or in a turnaround phase, the lessor may be willing to take a credit risk that a commercial bank or finance company may not be so willing to take. Some leasing companies specialize in certain types of assets and are willing to take a credit risk with the knowledge that they understand the market for that asset. If the lessee defaults, the leasing company will be able to place that asset in service somewhere else. Assets that fall into this category might include trucks, railroad equipment, certain types of machine tools, and even commercial aircraft.

Industrial development bonds that have been a popular form of financing, particularly for start-up and growing companies, are often accompanied by a limit as to the amount of additional debt a company can undertake. Typically, though, this limit does not include leasing, and if a company is at or near such a limit, leasing may be the only equipment financing technique available.

TYPES OF LEASES

For years, the leasing industry has suffered from confusion with respect to terminology. *Tax leases, true leases, operating leases, capital leases, direct leases, leveraged leases,* and *single investor leases* are just a few of the many terms used widely in the industry today. Unfortunately, these terms are often used interchangeably, which only adds to the confusion.

Single-Investor Leases

True leases, in which the lessor maintains ownership of the equipment and is entitled to the deduction of the tax benefits associated with that ownership, can be structured as leveraged leases or single-investor leases. The single-investor structure is the simplest of the two forms. In a single-investor lease, the lessor acquires the asset with its own funds and then in turn leases it to the user. Consequently, a single-investor lease involves only two parties, the lessor and the lessee. The single-investor lessor may buy the equipment with its own equity funds, or in turn it may borrow part of the purchase price. That borrowing is not specifically secured by the lease transaction, however, and as a result of this structure, the single-investor lessor is said to have an equity investment in the lease equal to 100 percent of the equipment cost. Single-investor leases are also sometimes referred to as direct leases.

Leveraged Leases

The leveraged lease is a more complicated structure. It involves at least three parties: the lessor, the lessee, and a senior lender. The leveraged lessor purchases the equipment with a combination of its own equity funds and funds borrowed from a senior lender, typically on a nonrecourse basis to the leveraged lessor. The nonrecourse senior lender is generally secured by an assignment of the lease rentals from the lessee and by a first secured position on the asset.

The principal difference, therefore, between the single-investor and the leveraged lease, is the method employed by the lessor to acquire the equipment. In the single-investor lease, the lessor acquires the equipment entirely with its own funds, whereas the leveraged lessor uses a portion of its own funds in the form of equity to acquire the equipment and borrows the balance of equipment cost from a lender. Leveraged leases are more complicated to effect in that more parties are involved. There are more negotiations to undertake, and documentation is somewhat more involved from the lessor's standpoint. Because of their complexity, leveraged leases generally are not available for smaller transactions (under $1 million of equipment cost). However, leveraged leases are commonly used to finance items such as aircraft, railroad equipment, tractor trailer fleets, large pieces of production machinery, and even complete factories or production facilities.

Quasi Leases

Many other types of transactions are called leases but are in fact not true leases as have been defined. These transactions may fall into the category of installment sale agreements, conditional sale agreements, or outright direct equipment financings, even though they may be called leases. These types of transactions may be characterized by, among other things:

1. Transfer of ownership (title) of the asset to the lessee at the end of the lease for a bargain (i.e., less than fair market value) purchase price.
2. Ownership (title) to the asset under lease automatically transferred to the lessee at any time before the expiration of the base lease term for a sum less than the then fair market value of the asset.

3. Other arrangements inconsistent with the rules and regulations of the IRS, such as financial compulsion on the part of the lessee to purchase the equipment at the end of the lease term.

The Financial Accounting Standards Board, in Statement No. 13, has defined a set of standards and guidelines for the book accounting of lease transactions both from the lessee and the lessor perspectives. Another section of this chapter will treat the book accounting of leases in more depth, but it is important to point out here that true leases can be accounted for in two ways on the lessee's books. FASB *No. 13* sets out a series of criteria against which a lease is compared, and depending on the outcome of that comparison, the lessee classifies the lease either as a "capital lease" or as an "operating lease." If the lease meets the capital lease criteria, then the lessee essentially records the lease on his books as if it purchased the property directly. If the lease does not meet the capital lease criteria, then it is de facto an operating lease. Operating lease payments are expensed over time as they are incurred; however, the operating lease obligation is not recorded as a liability on the lessee's books, nor is the leased equipment recorded as an asset by the lessee.

The objective of the company searching for lease financing is to find the best deal. There is no solid rule of thumb to follow with respect to choosing a leveraged or single-investor structure. Oftentimes, the effective cost of financing for a lessee may, depending on market conditions, be lower under leveraged lease financing than under a single-investor lease structure. As indicated, certain large assets are more likely to be financed by leveraged leases. The single-investor structure is very well suited to smaller transactions and is simpler from a documentation and negotiation viewpoint. Just as important as choosing a particular structure for a true lease is the source that a company chooses for lease financing. In a later section we will discuss sources of lease financing, such as finance companies, commercial banks, and independent leasing companies. Finally, the lessee's book accounting of a lease is independent of the structure of the true lease but is, rather, a function of certain criteria established by the FASB.

TAX ASPECTS

Lease financing is largely a creature of the federal income tax laws. In a world without taxes, the benefits to be derived from leasing—both by lessor and lessee—would be diminished. As the tax laws have changed over time, so has the leasing industry. In the past 15 years, the United States has gone through several major tax law changes and, in every case, the leasing industry has found ways to continue to provide benefits to lessors and lessees.

The economic return realized by a lessor on its investment in a lease is a function primarily of three elements: (1) tax benefits, (2) residual expectations, and (3) cash return on its investment. Residual expectations are fundamentally estimates of what an asset would be worth at the end of a specific period of time. Often this estimate, particularly with respect to high technology equipment, is at best a guess. The cash return that a lessor earns on its lease investment is driven largely by the marketplace, which determines pricing and terms of the transaction. Tax benefits, by their very nature, are subject to change and interpretation. In order for a leasing transaction to stand up under IRS scrutiny, the lessor must demonstrate that there is economic substance in the deal apart from the tax benefits.

Fundamentally, the lessee may give up three tax benefits in a lease transaction: (1) investment tax credit, (2) depreciation, and (3) the interest deduction on the debt incurred to acquire the property.

Investment Tax Credit

Sections 38 and 46 through 48 of the Internal Revenue Code deal with the investment tax credit (ITC). Reference is often made in leasing transactions to "new Section 38 property," which refers to that Section of the Code that sets forth the general rule that a credit against federal income tax is available for investments in certain types of property. A wide variety of credits are available, depending on the type of property and the use to which it is to be put. However, for our purposes, most leasing transactions involve tangible personal property in the form of income-producing equipment that, when new, is eligible for a 10 percent investment tax credit. Such property is also often referred to as five-year ACRS property, which means that it can be depreciated over a five-year period under the Accelerated Cost Recovery System established by ERTA (Economic Recovery Tax Act of 1981). Certain types of property are three-year ACRS property, a prime example of which would be certain types of over-the-road tractors. This property is eligible for a maximum investment tax credit of 6 percent. There are several other categories as well.

It is important to remember that although the lessor can utilize the investment tax credit during the first 12 months of the lease transaction, it must recapture a portion of that deduction if it should cease to be owner of the leased asset or the asset should be disposed of during the investment tax credit vesting period. Currently, the 10 percent and 6 percent investment tax credit vests over a five-year period and a three-year period, respectively. As a result, if a lessee defaults in a lease of property eligible for 10 percent tax credit in the third year of the lease and the asset is disposed of, then the lessor must recapture 40 percent of the investment tax credit taken (or 4 percent of the 10 percent credit taken).

Clearly, the investment tax credit is a significant benefit to the lessor since it may be valued in the first year of the transaction. However, portions of the ITC remain at risk until the end of the vesting period.

A lease transaction can be structured such that the lessee obtains the use of the investment tax credit. These transactions are commonly referred to as "ITC pass-throughs," in which full benefit of the credit is available to the lessee, and not to the lessor. The ITC is available to either party, but it is not available in part to the one and in part to the other. It is not uncommon for lessees to request lease rate quotes from lessors both with and without the tax credit priced into the transaction.

Depreciation

ERTA originated the Accelerated Cost Recovery System, which is a system of depreciation of an asset for tax purposes. As indicated above, a large portion of leased equipment falls into either the five-year ACRS category or the three-year ACRS category. From time to time, Congress has changed the depreciation lives of equipment. Consequently, the date on which the item of equipment is accepted may be critical in the depreciable life write-off of the asset.

Interest Deduction

The third tax benefit in a lease is the interest deduction available on the debt incurred to acquire a productive asset for use in a business. The degree to which the lessor benefits from the interest deduction depends in large part on the financing of the lease transaction.

An important element to note is that all of the tax benefits that are available to the lessor would also be available to the lessee if it purchased the equipment directly and financed the purchase with debt. One of the functions of a lease transaction is to efficiently transfer tax benefits from the user of the equipment to the owner of the equipment. Therefore, a lease transaction is more likely to benefit both parties when the transfer of tax benefits occurs between a low-bracket taxpayer (the lessee) and a high-bracket taxpayer (the lessor). In these circumstances, the tax benefits result in immediate benefits to both parties: (1) the lessor is able to reduce his tax liability, and (2) the lessee is able to obtain a lower financing cost for the use of an asset. Of course, it must be remembered that the lease payments made by the lessee are tax deductible, so that the lessee must compare the tax benefits realized from the deduction of the lease payments versus the tax benefits of ownership. In making this after-tax comparison, however, it is also important to keep in mind that the investment tax credit and the ACRS depreciation are heavily front-end loaded in the first two years of the transaction, whereas the deductions of the lease payments are spread out evenly over the course of the lease transaction.

Tax law changes, or more particularly the announcement of a potential tax law change, create uncertainty in the leasing industry. Currently, the industry is operating in such a period, and until or unless a tax law is passed, the leasing marketplace will be forced to operate under greater uncertainty. Will the investment tax credit be repealed? Will the benefits of ACRS depreciation be reduced? At present, the leasing industry is facing these questions. Until these issues are resolved, lessees and lessors cannot accurately quantify the future benefits from leasing transactions. Since tax benefits are important elements in a leasing transaction, many leases typically require a tax indemnity in which the lessee makes certain representations and warranties that the tax benefits which the lessor anticipates are, in fact, available. We will discuss tax indemnifications in more detail in a later section; however, the content of tax indemnities may receive considerable attention when the industry faces a potential change in the tax law. Lessors facing uncertainty with respect to their tax benefits may request tax indemnifications from lessees that are considerably tighter and more comprehensive than absent an impending tax law change. Thus, the question of which party will bear the risk of tax benefits lost as a result of a tax law change often becomes a topic for negotiation.

ECONOMIC ANALYSIS

A firm can employ one of two basic methods for obtaining its equipment. It can purchase its equipment outright and finance the purchase in a wide variety of ways, many of which are described in this book, or it can lease its equipment. Most accounting and finance tax books contain a basic "lease-versus-buy" analysis that compares the after-tax "cost" of leasing versus purchasing (straight debt financing), and this is certainly one way of approaching the two financing alternatives. However, there are other considerations that can be equally as important in the decision-making process.

Present Value

The typical lease-versus-buy analysis computes and compares the present value of the after-tax cash outflows associated with leasing and purchasing. The tax deductions associated with each alternative must be identified, and then the tax rates must be estimated for each year during the term of the financing in order to calculate the value of these tax benefits.

Lease payments are tax deductible, and their after-tax cost is derived by multiplying each lease payment by (1 − the firm's tax rate). If the firm's tax rate is 40 percent and each lease payment is $1,000, then the after-tax cost of each payment is $600. The present value of the after-tax stream of lease payments can be computed using a discount rate equivalent either to the lessee's cost of capital or to the rate at which it could borrow at that point in time.

If the asset is purchased and financed by debt, interest expense associated with the debt incurred to purchase the asset and the depreciation appropriate for the particular asset may be deducted. The sum of these two deductions must then be converted into tax savings by multiplying them by the firm's tax rate. In addition, the asset may also be eligible for the investment tax credit, which is a direct reduction of the company's tax liability in the first tax year the asset is placed in service. Then, a present value of the after-tax stream of cash flows associated with owning the asset can be computed.

Tables can be set up for ease in making these calculations (see Exhibit 1).

The after-tax cash flows in column (2) are then present valued. Note that the lessee's payment for the asset at the end of the lease, should the lessee decide not to return it to the lessor, is made with after-tax dollars and so is not reduced by (1− the tax rate).

Similarly, as illustrated in Exhibit 2, the after-tax cash outflows in column (6) associated with purchasing the asset are present valued and compared with the present value of the leasing after-tax cash outflows. It is important to note that the amount of debt incurred in purchasing the asset will affect the after-tax cost of purchasing. If less than 100 percent debt financing is employed, and the balance of the purchase price is funded from internally generated cash flow or

EXHIBIT 1 Leasing

Payment	(1) *Lease Payment*	(2) *(1 − Tax Rate) × Lease Payment = After-Tax Lease Payment Cost*
1	1	1
.	.	.
.	.	.
.	.	.
.	.	.
n	n	n
	Estimated residual	Estimated residual

EXHIBIT 2 Purchasing

Payment	(1) Debt Service P&I	(2) Interest	(3) Depreciation	(4) ITC	(5) [(Tax Rate) × (2 + 3)] + (4) = Tax Savings	(6) (1 − 5) = After-Tax Cost of Purchasing
1	1	1	1	1	1	1
.	.	.	.	.	.	.
.	.	.	.	.	.	.
.	.	.	.	.	.	.
n	n	n	n	n	n	n
						Estimated salvage value

from working capital lines, then a cost for these funds must be made a part of the calculation of the cost of purchasing the asset.

Internal Rate of Return

Another simpler method of comparing lease-versus-purchase financing is to use a calculator with financial functions to compare the "internal rate of return" for the purchase and lease alternatives. The internal rate of return is that interest rate which discounts the lease payments (including the estimated residual) to the original cost of the equipment. The internal rate of return for the purchase alternative (if 100 percent debt financing is employed) is the interest rate on the debt incurred to acquire the asset. If less than 100 percent debt financing is used, then the purchaser must assign an interest rate to that portion of the funds which are contributed from the lessee's internally generated cash flow or from working capital lines, and blend that rate with the debt rate to determine the internal rate of return associated with ownership. The alternative with the lowest internal rate of return is the cheaper on a pre-tax basis; however, the tax benefits associated with each must be analyzed to determine which is less costly on an after-tax basis.

One of the most important factors in making these comparisons is the estimation of future tax liability that in turn determines the tax rate in future years. Clearly, this is an unknown that can alter the relative attractiveness of leasing versus purchasing, depending on how actual future tax rates compare with those forecasted at the time of the decision to go with one alternative or the other. If a tax-payer has a net operating loss carryforward, then it may be relatively easy to make an accurate estimate of tax liabilities in the near term.

Just as net present value and internal rate of return analysis can be used to compare leasing versus purchasing, so can these methods be used for analyzing and comparing lease costs. Lease proposals generally specify the periodic lease payment as a percentage of the cost of the equipment to be leased. For example, a monthly lease rate factor of 1.7812 percent would convert to a monthly payment of $17, 812 for a piece of equipment costing $1 million. *Implicit rate,* a term widely used, is the rate that discounts the lease payments (excluding residual) to the cost of the equipment.

Example

Lease term:	five years
Lease payments:	monthly in advance
Lease rate factor:	1.7812 percent (of equipment cost)
Discount rate:	12.5 percent
Implicit rate:	2.74 percent (excluding residual)
Net present value:	80 percent (excluding residual)

Note: The discount rate could either be the lessee's present cost of borrowing or its capital cost, or if the lease is structured as a leveraged lease, the discount rate would be the interest rate, if known, on the senior debt. The addition of an estimated residual at the end of the five-year lease term will increase both the implicit rate and the net present value.

Competing lease proposals can be compared on an economic basis using these two methods. One factor that may complicate this analysis is an uneven rent structure. A lessor may structure rents that are lower in earlier years and higher in later years, or vice versa.

Other Economic Factors

There are, however, other economic factors to consider in addition to these two lease-versus-purchase comparison methods. Lease payments for a given asset are almost always lower than the debt service principal and interest payments associated with the purchase of the asset financed 100 percent with debt. For an emerging or growing company, cash is often a scarce resource. Therefore, the lower periodic payments afforded by a lease may ease the pressure on a firm's liquidity.

A traditional lending source may not be willing to lend a young, growing company 100 percent of equipment cost. A loan in an amount equal to the purchase price of an asset secured by that asset may not, in the lender's view, provide sufficient protection in the event of a default. Therefore, the lender may be willing to lend only 70 percent or 80 percent of equipment cost, and the balance of the funds would have to be provided by the user. For a cash-tight growing company, lease financing will permit the firm to have use of the asset without committing substantial funds up front on day one.

SALE/LEASEBACK TRANSACTIONS

A sale/leaseback is a particular type of lease transaction involving equipment that is not new for tax purposes. As such, equipment that is to be subject to a sale/leaseback is not eligible for the investment tax credit. The lease rate associated with a sale/leaseback will be higher than if the asset was eligible for the investment tax credit, since the investment tax credit is absent from the economics of the transaction. Sale/leaseback financings can be accomplished by a single investor lease or leveraged lease. Both are accounted for from a book point of view in essentially the same manner as lease transactions involving new equipment.

A company entering into a sale/leaseback transaction may sell equipment that it already owns to a lessor who, in turn, will lease the equipment back to that company. Alternatively, equipment subject to sale/leaseback may come from another user, be purchased by the lessor, and then be leased to the new user. Oftentimes, especially for older equipment, a lessor entering into a sale/leaseback transaction will require an appraisal of the asset in order to establish tax basis in the asset. A lessor has to be able to demonstrate to the Internal Revenue Service that it paid fair market value for the asset, and an appraisal is an effective means of establishing that value.

In order for a lease to be a true lease for tax purposes, the lease term cannot exceed 80 percent of an asset's useful economic life. Therefore, the lessor will also want to be assured that at least 20 percent of the asset's useful life is remaining at the end of the sale/leaseback term. The lessor may also require that this estimate of remaining useful life be made part of the appraisal. One item for negotiation is the question of which party will bear the cost of the appraisal.

Sale/leasebacks can be an effective form of raising capital for an emerging company or for one requiring cash. The emerging company may have used assets on its balance sheet that have appreciated in value and, as a result of the sale of those assets, will realize book income as well as additional liquidity. Of course, with the book income can also come a tax liability as a result of the sale of the assets to the leasing company.

Sale/leasebacks are becoming more frequently used to finance leveraged buyouts. If most of the assets of a company are being sold pursuant to a sale and leaseback, it is necessary that the bulk sales law, or other laws affecting the disposition of a significant part of the assets of a company, be closely scrutinized. Counsel can provide necessary assistance in this area such that the lessor and lessee can effectuate the necessary advertisements, filings, and other compliance with applicable statutes.

ACCOUNTING FOR LEASES

Guidelines for the book accounting of lease transactions have been established by the Financial Accounting Standards Board in FASB *No. 13.* Lease accounting is relatively complex, and our treatment of the topic will deal only with book accounting from the lessee's point of view. Although FASB *No. 13* is a detailed and complete document on the subject of lease accounting, both lessees and lessors have developed a variety of creative techniques to achieve their desired book accounting treatment for lease transactions. There are more amendments to FASB *No. 13* than any other statement issued by FASB. Hence, the creativity can be judged by the proliferation of such amendments.

Capital Lease versus Operating Lease

Fortunately, lease accounting from the lessee's point of view is simpler than it is from the lessor's perspective. The lessee accounts for a lease transaction on its books in one of two ways. For book purposes, the lessee treats a lease either as a capital lease or as an operating lease. FASB *No. 13* sets forth the following four criteria for distinguishing operating leases from capital leases. If a lease meets any one of them, then it should be classified as a capital lease by the lessee:

a. The lease transfers ownership of the property to the lessee by the end of the lease term . . .
b. The lease contains a bargain purchase option. . . .
c. The lease term . . . is equal to 75 percent or more of the estimated economic life of the leased property. . . . However, if the beginning of the lease term falls within the last 25 percent of the total estimated economic life of the leased property, including earlier years of use, this criterion shall not be used for purposes of classifying the lease.
d. The present value at the beginning of the lease term of the minimum lease payments, . . . excluding that portion of the payments representing executory costs such as insurance, maintenance, and taxes to be paid by the lessor, including any profit thereon, equals or exceeds 90 percent of the excess of the fair value of the leased property . . . to the lessor at the inception of the lease over any related investment tax credit retained by the lessor and expected to be realized by him. However, if the beginning of the lease term falls within the last 25

> percent of the total estimated economic life of the leased property, including earlier years of use, this criterion shall not be used for purposes of classifying the lease. A lessor shall compute the present value of the minimum lease payments using the interest rate implicit in the lease . . . A lessee shall compute the present value of the minimum lease payments using his incremental borrowing rate . . . unless (i) it is practicable for him to learn the implicit rate computed by the lessor and (ii) the implicit rate computed by the lessor is less than the lessee's incremental borrowing rate. If both of those conditions are met, the lessee shall use the implicit rate.[1]

The operation of the fourth criterion can be simplified through an example. Suppose a piece of equipment costs $100 and is eligible for the 10 percent investment tax credit. In order for a lease to qualify as an operating lease, the present value of the lease payments would have to be less than 81 percent of the cost of the equipment. The present value of the lease payments must be less than 90 percent of the cost of the asset less the investment tax credit: [$100 − $10(ITC)] × .90 = $81 or 81 percent. Alternately, if the lessor elected to utilize the 8 percent tax credit instead of the 10 percent tax credit, then the present value of the lease rentals must be less than 82.8 percent of equipment cost in order for the lease to be classified as an operating lease.

If the lease meets any of the four criteria, then it is a capital lease and capital leases are for book purposes, as distinguished from tax purposes, recorded as a purchase of an asset by the lessee. The value of the leased property is booked on the asset side of the balance sheet at the lesser of the fair value of the leased property at the beginning of the lease or the present value of the minimum lease payments. The asset booked as a capital lease is amortized for book purposes according to the depreciation the lessee uses for other assets his company owns. Any residual value assumed by the lessee is deducted from the asset value in determining the periodic deductions. On the other side of the balance sheet, a corresponding liability is recorded.

If the lease is recorded as a capital lease, then the lease payments themselves are recorded for book purposes as each consisting of principal and interest. Just as for an amortizing loan, the earlier payments are more heavily weighted toward interest and later payments are more heavily weighted toward principal. So in short, from a book point of view, capital lease accounting is very similar to the accounting treatment of an outright purchase of an asset.

---

[1] FASB, *Statement of Financial Accounting Standards No. 13*, "Accounting for Leases" (Stamford, Conn., November 1976).

If a lease is treated as an operating lease, the asset and the corresponding liability are not shown on the lessee's books. Rather, each lease payment is expensed in its entirety for book purposes. Therefore, only a single rental is shown each month. However, accounting standards usually dictate that a lessee disclose the future rental payments due on account of those leases that are classified as operating leases. Typically, these disclosures are made in the footnotes to the lessee's financial statements.

Companies that are in developmental or fast-growth stages are generally more concerned with liquidity and cash flow than with the cosmetics of book accounting. However, the ability to employ asset financing that does not appear on the company's financial statements may have some appeal in that it reduces the company's apparent leverage. However, any financial institution that is asked to consider extending credit to a company will in fact look at operating lease obligations disclosed in the footnotes of the company's financial statements and include those obligations in its calculation of the firm's leverage or debt-to-equity ratio.

MECHANICS OF ENTERING INTO A LEASE TRANSACTION

This section deals with some of the mechanical aspects of entering into a lease transaction from the lessee's perspective. Initially, the lessee must select the type of equipment it needs; complete its negotiations with the equipment manufacturer or vendor as to the equipment's configuration, performance, features, delivery, and price; and select a specific leasing company from which it intends to lease the asset. It is important for the lessee to discuss the mechanics of the transaction with the leasing company following some broad guidelines.

Acquiring the Asset

Usually the first event to occur in the consummation of a lease transaction is the acquisition of the asset by the lessor. Installation costs associated with an asset may or may not be financed through the lease transaction—this is an item for negotiation between the lessee and the lessor. For example, leasing companies may be unwilling to finance the cost of software associated with electronic data processing systems or the cost associated with ground preparation for a plant.

The mechanics by which the leasing company acquires the asset are very important for two reasons. First, the leasing company must be certain that it has clear title to the asset, and second, the manner and timing of acquisition of the asset can affect the availability of the investment tax credit.

In general, there are three ways that a lessor can acquire title to the asset:

1. After the equipment is ordered from the manufacturer or vendor on the lessee's purchase order, the purchase order is assigned to the leasing company prior to delivery of the equipment to the lessee's site.
2. The lessor orders the equipment directly on its own purchase order on the lessee's behalf. This assumes that the transaction is entered into prior to shipment of the equipment.
3. The lessor can purchase the equipment directly from the lessee. However, if the lessee has already taken title to the equipment, this can endanger the availability of the investment tax credit to the leasing company. If the lessee purchases the equipment, but does not in turn convey title to the equipment to the leasing company within three months after the equipment is available for first productive use, then the leasing company is not able to take the investment tax credit. This three-month period (which has come to be known as the 90-day window) is of concern only in leasing transactions where the investment tax credit is for the account of the lessor.

Manufacturers' warranties are generally written for the benefit of the owner of the equipment. As a result, though leasing companies often require that the manufacturers' warranties run to their benefit, this should not in any way affect the lessee's ability to assert claims against the manufacturer for its own benefit. In addition, certain manufacturers may issue engineering or safety changes from time to time that should be made to their equipment, generally at the manufacturer's own expense. Lease contracts will typically require that such safety or engineering changes, if offered by the equipment manufacturer, be made. If the lessee fails to have such safety or engineering changes executed, it may be liable to have them performed at the lessee's own expense at a later time, dependent on documentation requirements.

Lease Documentation

Lease documentation differs from secured lending or loan documentation. From the lessee's point of view, single investor lease documentation is somewhat more streamlined than leveraged lease documentation. However, the complexity of leveraged lease documentation is largely transparent to the lessee since the latter is not a party to the documents that are entered into between the lessor and the senior lender.

Lease documentation common to either single-investor or leveraged transactions would, at a minimum, include the following:

1. *Assignment of purchase order:* Depending on the method by which the lessor acquires the equipment to be placed under lease, the lessee may be required to sign an assignment of purchase order form on behalf of the lessor.
2. *Lease:* Lease forms vary widely and can, at their simplest, be only a few pages in length or, for complex transactions such as jumbo jet aircraft financings, may run to several hundred pages. Most leases require lessees to maintain insurance on the leased asset and to keep the asset in good operating condition, normal wear and tear excepted. Lessees generally are also required to pay any taxes (other than income taxes of the lessor) associated with the use of that asset. Certain leases are called "hell or high water" leases in that they require the lessee to make lease payments only as a function of the passage of time. In other words, the lessee has to make the lease payments irrespective of any defenses that it may try asserting against the lessor or an equipment manufacturer or any other third party. Leveraged leases generally are hell or high water leases since the leveraged lessor assigns the lease rentals to his senior lender, who has a first lien on the asset. Most lease contracts contain a clause to the effect that as long as the lessee is performing all of its obligations under the lease, it will be permitted "quiet enjoyment" of the asset from the lessor and its senior lender. In other words, the lessor or senior lender cannot interfere with the lessee's use of the asset so long as the lessee is fulfilling its obligations under the lease contract.
3. The lessee may have to sign other minor documents such as *Secretary's Certificates* or *Incumbency Certificates,* which evidence the authority of the lessee's officers or representatives to enter into the lease transaction.
4. The lessor may require *landlord and mortgagee* waivers to ensure that the asset has not been encumbered by a lien from another financial institution that is already extending credit to the lessee and that has an interest in the real estate on which the equipment will be located.
5. The lessor may require and file *informational financing statements* that will need to be signed by the lessee. The purpose of the statements is to give notice to the lessee's creditors that the lessor is the owner of the equipment subject to the lease, and that the lessee has no ownership rights in the equipment. Therefore the lessee cannot sell the equipment or grant a security interest in the equipment to any other institution or lender.

6. The lessee will subject the equipment to the terms of the lease by signing an *Acceptance Certificate,* which should indicate the date on which the equipment is or was available for first productive use and accepted by the lessee under the lease. The signing of the certificate triggers the lessee's assumption of its obligations under the lease with respect to the accepted equipment.

In addition to these documents, leveraged lease transactions may require that the lessee sign an acknowledgment of the assignment of the lease and the lease rentals by the lessor to a senior lender. The senior lender may in turn, require certain documents to be executed by the lessee. Depending on the size of the transaction and the type of collateral involved, it is possible that there may be many scores of documents. In point of fact, however, the leveraged lease structure does not place any significant additional burdens on the lessee.

Entering into a lease transaction is usually not a complicated procedure from the lessee's point of view, though certainly, the lessee will have his legal counsel involved in the documentation process.

SOURCES OF LEASE FINANCING

The leasing industry has grown dramatically over the past 10 years. There are more lessors active in the marketplace today than there have ever been. While there are always exceptions that fall outside these categories, the majority of leasing companies in the United States can be roughly divided into three very broad categories: (1) financial institutions such as banks, savings and loan associations, and insurance companies, (2) independent leasing companies, and (3) captive leasing companies.

Financial Institutions

For emerging or growing companies seeking lease financing, the first and most logical step would be the firm's lead bank. If the lease transaction is relatively small, once again the company's lead bank may be the best place to start. Most large money center banks have very active leasing operations. These operations may take leasing transactions for the bank's own account to enable the bank to manage its tax base, or they may operate as brokers where the bank will, for a fee, find another lessor to take the transaction. If the transaction is a leveraged lease, the money center bank may commit to be the senior lender in the transaction and then, in turn, find an outside lessor to be the owner or equity participant in the transaction. Typically, money center banks will not become involved in smaller transactions, that is, less than $1 million of cost.

Savings and loan associations and other thrift institutions can invest up to 10 percent of their assets in commercial lending, which may also include leasing. Some S&Ls have been very active lenders in leveraged transactions. However, since the S&L and thrift industry in general has been suffering from depressed profits, these institutions generally do not have the substantial tax base that would enable them to act as direct lessors in transactions.

Some insurance companies will employ leasing to manage their tax position. As a rule, insurance companies typically only become involved in very large transactions, such as project financings, aircraft, ships, and so on. Insurance companies are particularly credit sensitive and, as a result, are not likely candidates to provide lease financing to growing and emerging companies.

Independent Leasing Companies

Most leasing companies in the United States fall into this category. Independent leasing companies do their own marketing for lease transactions and do not rely on the relationship they may have from a parent owner. Independent leasing companies may be privately or publicly owned, or may be subsidiaries of manufacturing, service, or financial corporations. In order for an independent leasing company to act as a principal in a lease transaction, it must, of course, have a tax base. This tax base may arise from the parent corporation that owns the independent leasing company, or the independent may have a tax base in its own right by virtue of having been in the leasing business for a number of years.

Independent leasing companies service the entire spectrum of leasing transactions, from very small, lower middle-market transactions up to the very largest transactions. Some independent leasing companies specialize their services with respect to specific types of equipment. For example, certain independents may handle only car or tractor trailer leases, while others may specialize in data processing, telecommunications, and medical equipment.

Captive Finance Subsidiaries

The function of captive finance subsidiaries is to provide financing for the products or equipment manufactured by their parents. Although captive finance subsidiaries may provide financing for other equipment as well, their main objective is to serve as a marketing aide to the parent corporation by enabling the parent to market its products with financing in place. The distinction, therefore, between an independent leasing company, which is owned by another corporation, and a captive finance subsidiary is based on whether the purpose of the leasing company is to provide financing for the parent company's products, or rather to source leasing transactions in the general financial marketplace. Often captive finance subsidiaries gravitate to other types of leasing and ultimately provide both captive financing and independent financing. Today, more and more manufacturers of income-producing equipment are setting up vendor financing programs that may or may not include leasing. Often this is the easiest method for a lessee to obtain financing for a particular type of equipment.

Lease Brokers

In addition to principals acting in the leasing marketplace, there is also a vital service performed by lease brokers and packagers. Leasing companies that take transactions for their own account are frequently called "principals" or "equity sources," whereas lease brokers and packagers originate lease transactions for the account of others; that is, they do not act directly as lessors. Lease brokers bring together lessees and lessors and, in a sense, act as market makers for lease transactions. The lease broker earns a fee for its services, which may sometimes include a participation in residual proceeds. By virtue of knowledge of the marketplace, a lease broker can often aid the lessee in finding the best source of lease financing for a particular need. Banks, S&Ls, insurance companies, independent leasing companies, and captive finance subsidiaries may, at the same time that they are originating or buying transactions for their own account, act from time to time as lease brokers.

The broker community ranges from one-man operations to the very largest investment banking institutions. For very large or complex transactions, investment banking institutions play an increasing role in bringing equity sources (lessors) together with companies seeking lease financing. The lease broker or packager can play a valuable role in assisting the lessee in finding the right lessor for a particular transaction and in getting the lease transaction closed and documented. Oftentimes lease brokers may undertake an advisory role for one of the participants in a leasing deal, rather than attempting to put the deal together or acting as a participant. Particularly in the larger, more complex transactions, such as project financings, one or more leasing companies may be employed by the participant to act as its adviser(s).

Lastly, leasing companies may set up joint ventures with larger equity sources to create a large de facto leasing company. In particular, highly specialized leasing companies, which may no longer have their own tax base, will arrange with a company having a tax base to obtain transactions, document them, and, in effect, also act as an adviser to the large equity source. This type of role for the traditional leasing company is growing in popularity.

HOW TO APPROACH A LEASING COMPANY

A leasing company has to make a credit decision with respect to a lessee in much the same way that a bank must make a credit judgment on a borrower. Therefore, the most important aspect of approaching a leasing company is to provide it with a complete package of information. At a minimum, this package should contain the following:

1. A complete description of the equipment to be leased, along with a fair price for the equipment. If the equipment takes time to install, for example, a telephone system, then the lessor should be provided with an estimated installation schedule, along with the anticipated fundings required during the installation period. Depending on the nature of the asset and the length of the installation period, the leasing company may provide the lessee with installation or construction financing.
2. The anticipated acceptance date of the equipment should be furnished by the lessee. The acceptance date is the date when the lessee first expects the equipment to be available for productive use.
3. Since young, emerging companies tend to be tougher credits to finance, it is extremely important for such firms to provide historical financial statements for at least the past three years, if they have been in existence that long, and these statements should be audited. Older public and privately owned companies should also make three years of financial statements available.
4. For nonpublic companies and those that have a relatively short historical existence, pro forma financial statements (profit and loss statements, balance sheets, and cash flow forecasts) should be submitted for at least three future years, and the assumptions behind these pro forma statements should be adequately documented.
5. Since the emerging and growing company may not yet have a significant operating history, it is important for the firm to submit a business plan that describes where the firm has been, where it is at present, where it intends to go, and how it intends to get there. Included in the business plan should be detailed resumes and backgrounds of key management personnel, as well as a description of the shareholders of the company.
6. Bank and trade credit references should be supplied.

7. A description should be given as to the utilization and employment of the asset to be leased.

8. The lessee should indicate the desired lease term, and whether the ITC is for its account or that of the lessor.

In short, the prospective lessee needs to submit all the credit information that it would submit to its bank. In addition, since leasing focuses on equipment financing, it is vitally important to supply the lessor with all the information outlined above pertaining to the equipment.

ANALYZING LEASE PROPOSALS

This section is designed to highlight certain terms and conditions that lessees should be aware of when comparing lease proposals.

1. *Is the proposal from a principal or a broker?* At the outset, the most important point to determine is whether the proposal is from a principal, or from a broker who must then attempt to find a lessor. If the proposal is from a principal, then the terms and conditions of the proposal are less likely to change as the transaction moves from the proposal stage to the commitment and closing stages. The terms and conditions submitted by a broker will, of course, be subject to the requirements of the ultimate lessor. It may not always be apparent whether the proposer is acting in the capacity of a broker.

2. *Credit approval.* The proposal should indicate whether it is subject to final credit approval by the lessor. If the proposal is submitted by a financial institution familiar with your company, it may already have granted credit approval to the transaction.

3. *Investment tax credit.* The proposal should clearly indicate whether the ITC is for the account of the lessor or for the account of the lessee. Some proposals will quote alternate lease rate factors dependent on which party will utilize the ITC.

4. *Senior financing.* If the proposal requires a leveraged lease structure, then it may contain a condition that it is subject to the ability of the lessor to raise senior financing. Some leveraged lease proposals will indicate the debt rate assumption that the lessor is making in proposing the lease rate factors. Obviously, if the assumption is incorrect, then the lease rate factor must be changed. In considering a proposal, one must know whether the senior finance rate is available on a best-efforts or a firm basis.

5. *Early termination right.* Some leases contain early termination rights that, if exercised by the lessee, require a lump-sum payment at the time the right is exercised. One of the more common rights of early termination is granted for economic obsolescence.

6. *Equipment delivery flexibility.* Due to the tax-sensitive nature of each lease quote, the lessor's tax year may influence the lease rate factor. For example, a calendar year-end taxpayer for a large transaction would provide a more attractive rate to a user if the equipment was delivered in December rather than in July. Hence, the delivery date of the equipment can be important.

7. *Legal and other fees.* Leveraged lease structures may generate high legal fees, since the documentation is more complex and more parties are involved. The proposal should clearly establish responsibility for these fees. The proposal should also indicate responsibility for debt placement fees, investment bankers' fees, printing costs, and the like.

8. *Satisfactory documentation.* Most lease proposals will indicate that the obligations of the parties to the proposal (the lessee, lessor, and the senior lender) are subject to the preparation and execution of mutually satisfactory documentation. Certainly, the lessee will wish to have the lease documentation reviewed with legal counsel.

9. *Tax indemnification.* Since tax considerations play a very great role in the decisions of the lessor, a lessor generally requires the lessee to indemnify it for loss of tax benefits. Some indemnifications, depending on the complexity of the transaction and the size of the transaction, may run into many pages of documentation. Some indemnifications provide for protection of corporate tax rate, events of recapture, actions on the part of the lessee or the lessor, and the like. It is important to determine the type of tax indemnification to be provided to the lessor. This item probably terminates more lease negotiations than any other single item.

10. *End-of-lease provisions.* At the end of a true lease, the lessee can return the equipment to the lessor, purchase the asset at fair market value, or renew the lease for fair market rental value. If the lessee elects to return the asset to the lessor, the lease documents may require that the lessee bear the costs of packaging and transporting the asset either to the lessor's location or within some radius of the lessee's site. If the lessee elects to purchase or re-lease the asset at the end of the lease, and the lessee and the lessor are unable to come to an agreement as to fair market value, then generally an appraisal process will be called for under the lease documents to determine fair market value.

Lease proposals can range widely in terms of the extent of their detail. The simplest preliminary proposals may be a one-page term sheet highlighting the terms of the proposed transaction. Complete proposals may run to many pages and cover the important terms and conditions of the transaction in some detail.

VENDOR LEASING PROGRAMS

Leasing has been used as a valuable tool to aid equipment manufacturers in the marketing of their products. Producers of data processing equipment, various types of high technology equipment, medical equipment, and transportation equipment are among the types of manufacturers who have benefited from the use of leasing as a sales tool. Vendor financing programs are usually set up by a leasing company for the equipment manufacturer or by its captive finance company. The leasing company provides lease financing to the equipment producer's customers for its products. The equipment producer uses its own marketing force to solicit end users for the equipment. The marketing force in turn offers the leasing company's financing to the end user as a sales tool to close the transaction. For marketing reasons, the leasing company may be transparent in order to preserve the equipment producer's relationships with its customers.

Full-Payout and Operating Lease Programs

Vendor leasing programs have been structured in a wide variety of ways. These programs can be broadly distinguished between "full-payout" programs and short-term operating lease programs. In full-payout programs, the initial lease term for each item financed under the program generates the return required by the lessor, that is, cost of equipment plus cost of financing. In an operating lease program, the initial lease term for the equipment is not sufficient to yield the required return to the lessor. Therefore, the equipment must be re-leased (either with the original lessee, or a subsequent one) or purchased by those lessees at the end of the initial lease term. Operating lease programs almost invariably require that the manufacturer of the equipment remarket off-lease equipment in order to assure the lessor of its expected return. Full-payout programs also may be supported by a remarketing agreement from the equipment manufacturer in the event the lessee defaults and the equipment must be remarketed.

Vendor Credit Supports

In order to induce the lessor to assume the credit risks that are inherent in such a program where each and every credit may not be reviewed by the lessor, vendors may offer a variety of credit supports to the leasing company. Such supports range from direct guarantees for some portion of the equipment's list price to the deferral by the vendor of some portion of his profit for the lessor's protection until the end of the lease term. Residual proceeds from such programs may be used to compensate the vendors for their remarketing efforts or may be used to return that portion of the equipment's purchase price deferred by the vendor or split on some formula mutually satisfactory to the parties.

Such programs are highly dependent on the strength and reputation of the vendor. The lessor must be assured that the vendor has sufficient financial and marketing strength to perform its obligations during the course of the vendor leasing program, which may extend over many years. In addition, the lessor has to be satisfied that the vendor's equipment is technologically competitive and properly constructed. If it is not, lessees, particularly in operating lease programs, may not be willing to renew their leases. As a result, it may be very difficult to find new users for the equipment when the initial lease terms expire. Therefore, in operating lease programs, the lessor is taking an equipment risk as well as a credit risk and must be assured that the vendor will continue to provide service for its products, maintain the products, and control the remarketing of its products.

Vendor programs have been used fairly extensively in the data processing, transportation, medical, and high tech industries. Companies that are bringing such products to market may find vendor financing a very attractive tool to aid in achieving their business plans. However, a smaller company will have more difficulty attracting vendor financing than an established firm for the reasons already mentioned.

CREATIVE APPROACHES TO LEASE FINANCING

As the leasing market has grown and become more complex in recent years, a variety of innovative approaches to lease financing have been developed. Some of these innovative approaches are particularly applicable and beneficial to the growing and emerging company. Many of these approaches have been designed to contend with the problem of extending lease financing to difficult credits. Some other techniques have been developed for tailoring lease payments to the cash flow needs or seasonality in a lessee's business. A few of these creative approaches are outlined below:

Supplier Financing

Some equipment suppliers are willing to offer long-term financing in order to aid the sale of their products. Foreign manufacturers of equipment are often able to offer U.S. purchasers extended payment terms, sometimes up to five years, in connection with export/import type credit insurance or guarantees offered by their respective countries to stimulate exports. Supplier credits of this nature can be an important factor in assisting a foreign equipment producer to enter the U.S. market. This type of financing can lend itself particularly well to the leveraged lease structure whereby a lessor will combine the financing offered by the manufacturer with the lessor's own equity in order to purchase the equipment and lease it to a user in the United States.

In today's marketplace, the ability to offer financing together with the equipment is becoming an important, and sometimes necessary, marketing tool. Therefore, it is increasingly common for certain equipment suppliers to offer some level of credit support to institutions providing financing for the purchase or lease of their equipment to the end user. This credit support can take the form of direct recourse for some portion of the purchase price if the lessee defaults on the lease, or a buy-back agreement whereby during the course of the lease transaction the equipment supplier will agree to buy the equipment back at stated values at various points in time in the event of a default by the lessee. The equipment supplier may offer the lessor a remarketing agreement under which the equipment manufacturer will use its best efforts to find a new user for the equipment if the lessee defaults.

Government Financing

Although government financing programs are shrinking today, there are still programs available that can particularly benefit the growing and emerging company that may not yet have a credit record sufficient to attract needed capital. Urban Development Action Grants (UDAG) are still available in many qualified locations. UDAGs, which often carry below-market interest rates and very attractive payment terms, may be employed as the senior debt in a leveraged lease. Government programs may vary from locale to locale, and these should be investigated to see whether they can be made part of a leveraged lease transaction. State and local governments and authorities often provide assistance to new companies relocating to their area or to newly emerging companies. These government-assisted types of financing programs may be employed in leases as well.

Venture Leasing

In the last few years, the market for venture capital has been active, and an offshoot of this activity has been the development of venture leasing. Venture leasing generally involves the lease of equipment to companies still largely dependent on venture capital for their funding needs. Such firms may be just beginning to bring a product to market and are still a year or two away from establishing a positive cash flow. These companies are unable to attract institutional or traditional bank financing and must rely on venture capital or quasi-equity investment until they emerge into a positive profit and cash flow posture. Under these circumstances, a lessor may view the investment in a lease as a venture capital investment in the user. Instead of supplying capital directly to the firm to be used for general corporate purposes, it is supplying equity capital in the form of a purchase of equipment that will then be leased to the company.

The venture lessor, like the traditional venture capitalist, will require a greater return or an upside potential in the company's future. Therefore, the lease rate will reflect the risk assumed by the lessor in the transaction and the lessor may require an equity "kicker" over and above the obligation of the lessee to make lease payments. Such a "kicker" could come in the form of warrants or stock options to compensate the lessor for taking a risk now in return for the opportunity to participate in the company's future.

Variable Lease Payments

Leases have been structured to tailor the lease payments to the lessee's cash flow position at various points in time. For example, the lease payments associated with a very large productive asset might be a function of the number of units processed through that piece of equipment by the lessee during a given period of time. A formula based on production gives the lessor an upside opportunity for a more rapid return on his investment if the lessee's business performs well, and on the downside, affords the lessee protection from severe constraints on his cash flow during slow times. Such arrangements, where lease payments are a function of production, are often referred to as "tolling" transactions. In a similar manner, lease payments can be structured to meet the seasonal cash flow needs of certain businesses. It is not uncommon, for instance, to find lease payments in the agricultural industry timed to meet with the positive cash flow cycles in the farming or food-production businesses.

Residual Value Insurance

Some insurance companies have been willing to write a policy that provides a sum certain on specific dates for the valuation of residuals. In other words, the policy might indicate that locomotives would have a value equal to 25 percent of their original cost after 12 years. In that manner, a lessor could be assured that it would receive the 25 percent of value on a date certain. The lessor could then factor this amount into the lease rate factor provided to the lessee. This lessens or eliminates the risk of equipment obsolescence.

These techniques can be used in combination with each other to benefit the lessee, not only with the potential for a lower lease rate, but also by the fact that they may help it secure financing that would not otherwise be available.

CONCLUSION

Because of the intermix of taxes, economics, and sometimes complex documentation, leasing has been considered difficult to understand and often arcane. In fact, it is just the opposite. Today, more than $70 billion of capital expenditures each year find their way into the leasing market, and each year the total of equipment financed through combinations of leases increases. There is no reason to expect that this trend will decrease.

Tax laws will change, leasing techniques will change, participants will change. Nonetheless, leasing is the predominant method of equipment financing in the United States. It behooves each company to consider seriously the employment of leasing for the acquisition of its capital equipment.

CHAPTER 5

Government-Assisted Financing

Frank S. Swain
Chief Counsel for Advocacy
U.S. Small Business Administration
Washington, D.C.

Frank S. Swain, chief counsel for the Office of Advocacy of the Small Business Administration, has played an active role on key issues affecting small business. Since his nomination by President Reagan in August 1981, Mr. Swain has supported small business within the federal government, before Congress, in the media, and in front of countless groups nationwide. Under his leadership, the Office of Advocacy is a central focus for small business concerns with respect to the public policies that affect the nation's entrepreneurs.

Walter H. Plosila
Deputy Secretary
Technology and Policy Development
Pennsylvania Department of Commerce
Harrisburg, Pa.

Walter H. Plosila served for four years as the director of the Governor's Office of Policy and Planning for Governor Dick Thornburgh. Prior to this appointment he was director of research for the Pennsylvania House of Representatives, associate state planning director, State of Kansas, management consultant for Westinghouse Electric Corporation and UNCO, Inc., and held positions in the United States Congress and the federal executive branch.

PART A Federal Programs*

INTRODUCTION

For the past several years, the federal government has been attempting to reduce its role in the credit and capital markets. To some degree the private sector and the state and local governments have stepped up their financial outreach to start-up, young growth firms and existing small businesses. Despite the current congressional and administration reexamination of the vast array of federal assistance programs that have proliferated over the past 40 years, the government still plays a significant role in helping small businesses.

The federal government plays an environmental role in ensuring small business access to capital. That is, the economy should be expanding so that demand for small business products and services can sustain debt costs and stimulate equity investments. The cost of money and real interest rates must be affordable, the tax system cannot be confiscatory, and the investment climate must be positive. Lenders and investors need to feel they can work with entrepreneurs to encourage successful businesses and sound investments.

No measure exists of how much money is invested annually in U.S. small businesses. A rough estimate would be more than $100 billion per year in net loans and equity. Even in the boom days of federal financing programs, the few billion dollars per year provided through federal agencies represented only a small proportion of that total.

Today, the approach of the federal government to small business financing is focused mostly on managing a growing economy. Those programs specifically intended to assist individual businesses are being targeted and focused so that their cost to the taxpayer is less and their impact on the economy is apparent.

---

* Part A was written by Frank Swain.

The nature of government in the American economy continues to undergo significant changes that are affecting virtually every level of our society today. A national policy shift to a more market-oriented approach in recent years is recasting the role government is expected to play in the nation's economic growth. These changes are by no means final and are still subject to the usual economic and political processes. It is impossible, therefore, to predict exactly what will happen to the financial stimulus programs now being administered by the federal government.

This chapter examines federal financing initiatives in economic development, small business, and research and development. Section 1 discusses specific small business financing programs; Section 2 highlights economic development initiatives predominantly undertaken by the Economic Development Administration of the Department of Commerce (EDA), the Department of Housing and Urban Development (HUD), and the Farmers Home Administration (FmHA); and Section 3 details primary federal research and development efforts.

SMALL BUSINESS FINANCING

Small Business Administration

The Small Business Administration (SBA) is the only federal agency specifically charged with assisting small businesses. The SBA helps people start and stay in business and obtain federal procurement contracts, and it serves as a strong advocate for the nation's small business community. Its programs assist start-up and ongoing businesses. Aspiring entrepreneurs with adequate collateral and business savvy are good candidates for SBA start-up financing. Traditionally, more than half of its loans have been for less than $50,000, meaning much of the SBA's financial assistance goes to young and newly formed businesses.

In fiscal year 1985, 19,540 direct and guaranteed loans were provided to small businesses for a total of $3.1 billion. The majority of these financings were SBA guarantees of private sector loans. These 7(a) loans—named after the authorizing section of the Small Business Act of 1953—can be used for business construction, expansion, or conversion, for purchase of machinery, equipment, facilities, supplies, or materials, and for working capital.

Applicants must be of good character and know how to run a successful business. They should have enough equity in their firm so that, with an SBA loan, they can run their business operations on a sound financial basis, with reasonable assurance that the loan will be repaid on schedule. These factors are important. Approval of the loan application is based on the likelihood of financial success of the enterprise, not on industrial policy or political factors.

Over the years, the SBA's role has shifted from a direct lender to a guarantor of institutional loans. Under its loan guarantee program, participating financial institutions set the borrowing terms and the interest rate, which cannot exceed two and three quarters percentage points over the New York prime rate. The bank and borrower then apply to the SBA for a guarantee, which can provide up to an 80 percent guarantee on these loans. Current law for most business loans places a $500,000 ceiling on the total amount SBA may guarantee per transaction. The typical SBA guarantee is for about $150,000 with a 7- to 10-year term.

SBA's lending programs are available to all applicants and are not targeted by race or gender. In 1985, for example, 7.5 percent of the loan guarantees went to women-owned firms, 10.7 percent to minority-owned firms, and 22.8 percent to veteran-owned firms.

Delegation of Authority to Financial Institutions

To reduce paperwork and processing time, the SBA now relies more on banks and other financial institutions to evaluate and service individual loans. Two SBA programs augment this effort: the Certified Lenders Program and the Preferred Lenders Program.

In the Certified Lenders Program, certain financial institutions and lenders—about 500 around the country with a history of a positive relationship with the SBA—are certified by the SBA. If participating certified lenders approve a small business loan application and submit it to the local SBA office for concurrence, the SBA has pledged to decide on the application within three working days.

The Preferred Lenders Program delegates more authority to banks and other financial institutions. Those lenders designated by the agency are responsible for making and servicing the loan using SBA's guarantee authority and guidelines. In return for this delegated authority the bank accepts an SBA guarantee of only 75 percent of the principal of the loan. SBA District offices can provide the names of local lending institutions that are Certified or Preferred SBA lenders.

Secondary Market for Small Business Loans

With increased financial services competition, many financial institutions now see small business as a profitable market. Additionally, guaranteed SBA loans become valuable investment and liquidity instruments for financial institutions.

The Small Business Secondary Market Improvements Act of 1984 encourages financial institutions to expand credit availability to small firms by increasing the number of loans they underwrite. The act authorizes the issue of certificates backed by SBA-guaranteed loans, which are assembled into large dollar pools for resale. This law enables institutional investors to purchase large portions of these guaranteed loans, which are fully backed by the U.S. government.

The act represents a major step toward meeting the liquidity needs of financial institutions that, by making loans under SBA's guarantee authority, have the potential to recycle more funds to small firms. This law creates a convenient intermediary tool that encourages pension funds and other large institutional investors seeking sound investments to expand credit availability for small businesses.

ESOTs

An amendment to the original SBA law allows, for the first time, SBA-guaranteed funds to be used to transfer the ownership of a small firm to its employees. Under this program, loans used to finance employee acquisition of stock under an Employees' Stock Option Trust (ESOTs) may be guaranteed under SBA regulations. While only a few of these guarantees have been made by SBA, it is an important breakthrough for those employees seeking equity in their employer's firm. The SBA can guarantee loans for purchases of a small firm's shares of up to $500,000, with a maximum term of 25 years. ESOT loan and guarantee applications must be made by financial institutions according to Section 7(a) provisions of the Small Business Act. Information on this program is available at the nearest SBA District Office.

Export Financing

For many small firms, world markets offer opportunities for export sales. Under its Export Revolving Lines of Credit, the SBA provides working capital to small exporters. According to an agreement between the SBA and the Export/Import Bank (EXIM), guaranteed loans of up to $500,000 may be used with bank-provided revolving credit lines for the working capital needs of small exporters. This guarantee can be combined with the EXIM's working capital loan guarantee program, which places no minimum or maximum limit on the amount of the loan guarantee. From $200,000 to $1 million in export assistance may be provided under the SBA/EXIM Bank agreement.

These funds may be used to purchase goods intended for export, component parts of goods for export, and material and/or labor used in producing export goods or services. These funds also can be used for foreign business development such as marketing, travel expenses, trade fair participation, or other such promotional activities. A guarantee usually covers up to 90 percent of the loan's principal and interest and may be collateralized. The amount of interest charged may not exceed the prevailing prime rate plus two and one quarter percentage points.

Interested small businesses or banks should contact the local SBA office or the EXIM Bank in Washington, D.C., to obtain further details on this new federal outreach effort to promote exports.

Venture Capital Financing

A significant law fostering equity growth in emerging businesses is the Small Business Investment Act of 1958. This act created small business investment companies (SBICs)—privately owned and operated investment firms that are licensed, regulated, and financed by the SBA to provide long-term capital to small firms. SBICs have set financial and legal precedents that support today's $14 billion venture capital industry. There are approximately 525 SBICs and 301(d) licensees; the latter were specifically created to assist businesses owned by socially or economically disadvantaged persons.

Forming an SBIC gives the investor leverage, provided by the government, of three or even four times the private invested capital. SBIC investment in small firms generally must be for at least five years and may be equity (common or preferred stock), loans, a hybrid debt instrument with potential equity rights, or a combination of all three instruments. SBICs are located in nearly 50 states and have resources exceeding $2 billion. More than $500 million was invested by SBICs in small firms in 1984. The average SBIC investment in a company in 1984 was $129,000. SBICs may be owned by individuals, partnerships, banks, or other corporations. The publication, *Directory of Operating SBICs,* is available from the SBA and highlights the locations and principals of each licensee by state of operation.

Surety Bond Guarantee Program

The SBA can guarantee bonds issued by a qualified surety for contracts up to $1 million for qualified small business contractors required to have a bid, performance, or payment bond in order to obtain a contract. This requirement applies to firms in construction, repair, maintenance, service, supply, and janitorial work. The SBA underwrote nearly $1 billion in surety bonds in 1985, working through about 50 surety companies.

Handicapped Assistance Loan Program

Individuals with a certified physical handicap may qualify for direct SBA loans under the Handicapped Assistance Loan Program. These loans can be made directly by the SBA, at an interest rate pegged to the federal funds rate, or may be guaranteed. In fiscal year 1985, 253 loans were made with this program, in an average amount of $96,000.

Overseas Private Investment Corporation

The Overseas Private Investment Corporation (OPIC) extends loans and loan guarantees to small American companies operating in underdeveloped nations. Small firms that adopt foreign investment as part of their growth strategy are eligible to receive investment counseling as well as financial assistance.

ECONOMIC DEVELOPMENT

When a business leaves the early development stage and expands its operations, for example, building a factory or searching for long-term financing for equipment, it often has difficulty obtaining longer term, 10- to 25-year financing. This problem is compounded even further if the factories or buildings are part of rural or urban depressed areas, where it is especially difficult to obtain traditional, private sector financing. In those areas there has been a serious lack of financing for small business expansion, land acquisition, and building construction, and for renovation and the purchase of equipment. The Economic Development Agency, Housing and Urban Development, Small Business Administration, and Farmers Home Administration, individually and together, have administered programs that address this perceived capital gap, often by working through state and local government and private sector initiatives.

Economic Development Administration

The Economic Development Administration (EDA), a part of the Department of Commerce, works with local development corporations and businesses that create or retain permanent jobs and expand or establish plants in economically distressed or redeveloped areas.

The EDA provides loan guarantees to eligible businesses of all sizes for the purchase of fixed assets and/or for working capital purposes. For every $10,000 in guaranteed loans, at least one job must be created. The loan must be secured with a maximum guarantee of 80 percent of cost and may range from $550,000 to $10 million. Examples of EDA assistance include loans to companies hurt by imports, and high technology companies unable to find financing in the start-up phase. Like the SBA, the EDA is a lender of last resort. The total of EDA guarantees was $230 million in 1985, and that will certainly decrease in 1986, depending on final budget decisions by Congress and the administration.

The EDA also provides grants to universities that dedicate their resources to economic and business development by providing management and technical assistance to small business in economically distressed areas. Regional Commerce Department offices have information on EDA programs.

Housing and Urban Development Agency

HUD's Urban Development Action Grant (UDAG) program makes grants to help local governments experiencing severe economic distress. Grant funds must create jobs, leverage private investment, and create public/private participation. Local communities may use these business development funds to assist private business by direct loans, convertible debt, and "equity-type" financings. Individuals must apply directly to the appropriate agencies of the local governments for assistance. The governments and small businesses then apply to HUD and compete with other cities for available funds.

UDAG funds can be used for any project that spurs new private sector development: site clearance and improvements; infrastructure development or rehabilitation; purchase of buildings that have been idle for more than six months; construction or renovation of commercial, industrial, or residential structures; and machinery and equipment with useful life longer than five years. Since April 1978, $3.9 billion has been awarded in UDAG funds. These HUD awards have attracted additional funding: $23.5 billion in private capital; $1.4 billion in state and local funds; and $500 million in additional federal money, for a total investment of $29.3 billion. Five hundred new permanent jobs were created, and UDAG funding has been instrumental in retaining 122,000 existing jobs. Since the inception of the program, 1,108 cities have received UDAG funds for 2,573 projects.

Certified Development Company

The Certified Development Company (503 development company or CDC) program, enacted in July 1980, is a partnership of private lending institutions, local governments, local business concerns, and community groups. Using long-term, fixed asset financing, the CDC program helps communities expand their employment and economic base by stimulating small business growth and modernization within a specific geographic area.

Since the program began, 548 CDCs have been certified—at least 1 in every state—and more than 4,000 loans have been approved, totaling over $800 million. The most active CDCs are located in several states, including California, Ohio, Missouri, Texas, Massachusetts, Michigan, New York, and Washington.

Operating as a nonprofit or for-profit stock corporation, a CDC may operate on a local, regional, or statewide level. Under the program, private lenders can provide long-term funds (up to 25 years) for new business expansion and revitalization. The CDC may also own and lease property to small firms.

The 503 corporation must inject an amount equal to 10 percent of each project's cost. At least 50 percent of the project's financing must come from nonfederal sources. There is a $500,000 limit on SBA-guaranteed debentures, the proceeds of which are loaned to the small business in exchange for a second mortgage, which is assigned to the SBA.

A Certified Development Company directory is available from local SBA offices that lists names and telephone numbers of local CDCs.

Small Business Revitalization

Since 1982, about 30 states have become part of the Small Business Revitalization (SBR) Program, a federal, state, and private sector partnership. Developed by HUD under a technical assistance grant, the SBR combines limited local financing resources with HUD/SBA economic development programs (e.g., HUD's Urban Development Action Grants and SBA's Certified Development Company 503 loans). This jointly funded program provides long-term, fixed rate debt capital to small businesses that may want to expand or modernize.

The initial four-year goals of the SBR program were to create 300,000 new permanent private sector jobs, locate $5 billion in new private sector capital investment, and create a Small Business Investment/Jobs Creation system in each state. By the end of 1984, SBR efforts had resulted in loans totaling more than $1 billion for approximately 800 businesses and industrial projects, creating more than 50,000 permanent jobs. Local SBA and HUD offices can provide more details on this program.

Farmers Home Administration

The Farmers Home Administration (FmHA) provides guaranteed and insured loan assistance to farmers, ranchers, and aquaculture operators to cover losses resulting from major and/or natural disasters. Assistance must result in tangible benefits to the communities where the businesses are located.

The FmHA may make loans to individuals, organizations, or companies. To be eligible, FmHA applicants must demonstrate that credit is unavailable from other sources under reasonable terms and conditions. The Business and Industry Loan Program is the exception to this requirement. Applicants in that program must indicate how many jobs the loans will help create or how the financing will benefit the community.

Guarantees by the FmHA encourage banks to make more loans than they might otherwise make. Lenders may charge whatever fixed or variable rate borrowers will accept. Under a guarantee, a 1 percent fee is charged. Working capital loans may be repaid within 7 years, machinery and equipment loans in up to 15 years, and borrowers may take up to 30 years to repay loans made for land, building, and permanent-fixture purchases.

As soon as a bank agrees to extend a FmHA-guaranteed loan, the borrower and the bank then draft a letter of intent briefly describing the general nature of the business and the purposes of the loan. In the next step, the FmHA determines the eligibility of the business for a loan. If eligible for FmHA assistance, the applicant then submits a personal history, balance sheet, profit and loss data, cash flow statements, and three-year financial projections. Detailed information regarding FmHA programs is available from local USDA offices or by contacting the national office.

RESEARCH AND DEVELOPMENT FUNDING

Funding for private sector prototype development and feasibility analysis for innovative ideas has been difficult. In recent years, federal research and development programs have backed about 45 to 50 percent of the R&D in the United States—almost $45 billion was distributed among different government agencies in fiscal year 1984.

For many reasons, private firms tend to underinvest in R&D, especially in those activities without a clear and immediate commercial potential. Private firms pursue innovations because they either will reduce production costs (e.g., process innovations) or open new markets (e.g., product innovations). The prospect of increased profits also stimulates this process. Yet the private sector carries out most of the development work necessary to complement government-sponsored research. Even large amounts of government funds spent on worthwhile civilian research projects will have no impact unless the results lead to commercial innovations by private companies or some other worthwhile endeavor.

Small Business Innovation Research Program

The Small Business Innovation Research (SBIR) program was enacted in July 1982 to bridge a serious gap in the R&D funding cycle for new, technology-based businesses. The enabling statute requires each federal agency with an R&D budget of $100 million or more—for any fiscal year—to establish an SBIR program and to set aside a small portion (1 to 1.25 percent) of these funds for small R&D firms.

Responding to R&D topics developed by participating agencies, small firms with the best proposals receive awards averaging up to $50,000 for a first phase, which determines the scientific and technical worth of the ideas. The most promising ideas are backed by subsequent awards, which average up to $500,000 for a second phase to further develop the proposed ideas.

The criteria for funding include the scientific and technical merit as well as the feasibility of the proposal, which was demonstrated during the first phase. When two or more proposals are evaluated as having almost equal merit, special consideration is given to proposals with nonfederal capital commitments for the third and final phase. The third phase involves the use of nonfederal capital sources and may result in follow-on production contracts with a federal agency for products or services for government use.

Each federal agency —such as the Department of Defense or the Department of Education—solicits proposals to meet its own requirements at different times of the year. The SBA serves as a coordinating and marketing agent for these SBIR federal activities and maintains information on SBIR presolicitation announcements for each agency.

If a client small firm (fewer than 500 employees) is in its earliest development stage and is working on some technological innovation, this source of funding for prototype development may be one of the few private or government sources available for such a high-risk effort. Many states, realizing this limitation, have begun modeling their own R&D programs after the federal SBIR program.

In fiscal year 1983, the first year for this federal program, small firms were awarded approximately $44.5 million. By 1984, the dollar value of the program trebled to $112 million. To facilitate the commercialization of new innovations, the SBA created a cross-referenced, automated data base to provide SBIR participants with a list of interested investors.

The seed money provided by SBIR can be the bridge to private sector financing and subsequent commercial funding by traditional financial institutions. Additional information on this program is available from SBA's office of Innovation Research and Technology in Washington, D.C., and from local SBA offices. It is important to become acquainted with individual agency SBIR personnel and the technical requirements needed to prepare an acceptable solicitation.

Department of Energy

The Department of Energy (DOE) sponsors two programs that support start-up businesses. The first is run by DOE together with the National Bureau of Standards (NBS) of the U.S. Department of Commerce. The NBS screens the proposals, sending the best qualified to the DOE for a final decision. The DOE also funds energy-related inventions.

The program offers one-time assistance to qualified inventions. This aid, negotiated directly with the inventor or small businessperson, usually amounts to one year of financial and technical backing, provided without cost to the recipient. Eligible entrepreneurs, in effect, can wind up with the equivalent of a one-year stipend from the government. Grants so far have averaged $70,000. Those applicants who do not receive grants get a written evaluation of their inventions.

Inventions are evaluated on three criteria:

1. Is the invention technically competent and unique?
2. Will it save a significant amount of energy? Is it a new source of energy?
3. Can it be successfully developed commercially if given appropriate government assistance?

Strict confidence regarding the ideas and proposals is maintained, and the inventors retain the patent rights resulting from research with government funds. The NBS receives more proposals than it can fund, but if the proposal makes it to the DOE, chances of its being approved are better than 50 percent. Contact the Energy-Related Inventions Program, Department of Energy, Washington, D.C. 20585.

Entrepreneurs with an idea for using energy sources—as opposed to an invention—should investigate the DOE's second program under the Office of Energy Utilization Research programs. This program makes grants of up to $10,000 to develop ideas ranging from new concepts of energy sources to the new application of existing procedures or systems. Awards of up to $50,000 can transform a technological concept into a potentially successful commercial application. Grant decisions are made by selection panels in each DOE regional office. Contact the Office of Energy Utilization Research, at the Department of Energy for more information.

Research grant funds also are available from the DOE for individual inventions and small business owners to explore ways of increasing energy efficiency. No limits are set on the size of these grants. For additional information, contact the Innovative Concepts Program, at the Department of Energy.

It is important for the entrepreneur to realize that the role and size of government-backed programs are subject to constant debate and change. In a free market, opportunities to do business and raise capital must be found primarily within the private sector.

PART B State and Local Programs*

INTRODUCTION

Justice Brandeis once wrote that states played a significant role in our federal system of government as "laboratories of democracy," testing and trying out various approaches to problem solving addressed to each jurisdiction's needs. Brandeis's dictum is still applicable in the 1980s, as states and localities apply a broad range of development finance tools. In the past five years, states and localities have undertaken a whole host of approaches to address the needs of their firms and industries.

While it is nearly impossible to describe all the various types of programs and services to emerging and growing firms available from the 50 states and 80,000 local governments in this country, this chapter will explore some generic programs and use one state—the Commonwealth of Pennsylvania—to illustrate programs likely to be found in other jurisdictions. Pennsylvania's economic development strategy has been described by one national observer of state and local governments as "state of the art" among the industrial states, so using the Commonwealth as the illustrative example is likely to cover most types of development finance programs available. However, the reader should contact his or her own state and local development agency to determine which specific finance programs are available.

* Part B was written by Walter H. Plosila.

NEW STATE DEVELOPMENT FINANCE STRATEGIES

During the 1950s and 1960s, states and localities had a limited set of programs of financial assistance available to business firms. What programs were available generally were limited to long-term debt programs providing below-market interest for fixed assets, particularly land and buildings. The advent of the industrial development or revenue bond (IDB) program during this period was part of this historic trend. These programs focused mainly on manufacturing, most particularly on durable manufacturing, consistent with the economic base of the country at the time. In the 1970s, IDB and other programs were expanded in some jurisdictions to include the commercial and retail sectors. In addition, in the late 1970s some states with substantial revenue enhancements, for example, Alaska, with its development of oil reserves, created new quasi-public vehicles to serve as equity investors in job creation ventures. Since that time, the entire field of development finance at the state and local levels has seen an explosion in the number and types of programs ranging from working capital funds to employee-ownership assistance to applied research and development aid and venture capital.

The emergence of an entire new range of development finance programs by state and local governments in the late 1970s and early 1980s was due to several underlying events. First, due to the pioneering work of David Birch at MIT, and others, increased recognition was given to the role of small firms in the job generation process.[1] States and localities have responded by reorienting existing programs and developing new programs for small and emerging businesses. Second, some fundamental transitions were occurring in the nation's economy, with clerk rather than laborer becoming the largest single occupational group in the work force. Heavy industry was seeing its traditional markets served by new, lighter weight products, and the closed American economy was opened up for worldwide competition. Third, a resurgence in the American entrepreneurial spirit was kindled, in part from real world successes in the computer hardware and software industry, but also due to federal tax law changes in capital gains as well as other factors.

These changes in the underlying economy of the country and state strategic reviews and analyses of the factors contributing to economic growth and job generation led a number of states and localities to focus more of their resources on small firms, particularly start-up

[1] David Birch, *The Job Generation Process* (Cambridge, Mass.: MIT Program on Neighborhood and Regional Change, 1979).

firms and entrepreneurial firms, and growth sectors of their economies. A number of state and local leaders redirected the focus of their economic development strategies away from "smoke-stack chasing" (that is, trying to move a manufacturing firm from one location to another through tax abatements, environmental downgrading, and other means) to one focused more on "homegrown" approaches to economic development. This focus at the state and local level has had two emphases. First, it has focused state financial and other assistance on existing firms, attempting to have them stay and expand, rather than close, the more likely scenario, or in rarer cases, relocate. Second, it has emphasized assistance to small start-up firms, because of the recognition in many jurisdictions that this is where most job growth will come. According to some observers, 90 percent of a given jurisdiction's job growth is likely to come from start-up and growing small firms and existing firms staying and expanding. Only 10 percent will come from investment from without, for example, foreign investment and relocations.[2]

CLASSIFICATION OF GOVERNMENT FINANCE PROGRAMS

To discuss government financing programs, we have classified state development finance assistance tools into the following categories:

- Debt financing programs.
- Grants.
- Export development.
- Research and development.
- Venture capital.
- Employment and training programs.
- Other assistance.

The remainder of this chapter will focus on each of these areas in detail, outlining examples of programs available to assist emerging and growing firms.

In addition to these direct assistance programs, most states have a number of tax incentives. These incentives will not be covered here, given the extreme variation among the states in their tax codes and, correspondingly, the benefits of various incentives. If you want specific information on tax incentives among the states and localities, you should contact the respective developmental or taxing office of the jurisdiction in which you wish to locate.

---

[2] Alan S. Gregerman, "Competitive Advantage: Framing a Strategy to Support High-Growth Firms," *Commentary*, Summer 1984, p. 19.

DEBT FINANCING PROGRAMS

Direct Loan Programs

Debt financing programs probably are the oldest types of public financial assistance to industry. Rarely, however, do these programs provide all the financing necessary to consummate a deal. Indeed, bank and other third-party financing is usually involved. States and localities finance these debt financing programs though a number of sources: annual general fund appropriations, issuance of revenue bonds, use of federal funds to capitalize a fund, and so on. In many cases these direct capital infusions are part of an effort to sustain a long-term revolving loan fund that eventually may reach several hundred million dollars in size.

The governmental role in these programs is not to compete with the private sector but to provide gap financing to meet that share of project costs that cannot be obtained from conventional funding sources, or whose conventional interest costs are so prohibitive as to not permit the project to go forward. State or local financing in these cases generally can serve as a catalyst to allow the project to go forward, with some degree of public subsidy of interest costs.

Thirty-seven of the 50 states have some form of direct public loan program.[3] Many local governments also have established such programs. In many cases direct loan programs have as their targets specific sectors of the economy, for example, manufacturing; specific types of industry, such as R&D; and specific areas of the state or community, such as state enterprise zones or distressed areas. In addition to general loan programs, some states and localities have specific programs to serve minority businesses.

Examples of such direct loan programs can be found throughout the country. They cover a wide variety of targets: Connecticut has a Small Contractors Revolving Loan Fund; Hawaii has two funds for Large and Small Fishing Vessels; and Louisiana has an Agricultural Plant Purchase, Improvement, and Contruction program for agricultural plants.

Another example of a state with a comprehensive array of programs is Minnesota. It has the Minnesota Small Business Development Loan program, which assists small businesses expanding in the state. The loans are offered below market and are fixed rate with a term of up to 20 years. Size of the loans range from $250,000 to $1 million. The purpose of this program is to meet the particular needs of small

---

[3] "19th Annual Report: the Fifty Legislative Climates," *Industrial Development*, January–February 1985, pp. 52–57.

firms, which existing financial markets have trouble meeting. A second Minnesota vehicle is the Minnesota Fund, which provides direct loans at fixed rates on fixed assets to assist small businesses wanting to expand in the state. The maximum loan is $250,000, not to exceed 20 percent of total project costs. Interest rates are negotiated, and maximum terms are 15 years for land and buildings and 7 years for machinery.

Other states having small business development loan assistance programs include California, Hawaii, Maryland, Ohio, and Vermont. A number of other states have programs of loan assistance available to both small and large firms, not specifically to serve only start-up and growing firms.

Pennsylvania has three direct loan programs—the Pennsylvania Industrial Development Authority, the Pennsylvania Capital Loan Fund, and the Pennsylvania Minority Business Development Authority. These programs all include among their eligible clientele, growing and emerging firms.

Pennsylvania Industrial Development Authority. The Pennsylvania Industrial Development Authority (PIDA) was established in 1956 and is the oldest authority of its type in the country. Originally established to help assist larger manufacturing firms, the authority's mission and focus have changed during the 1980s to focus on small businesses, distressed areas, and growth firms. Firms eligible for assistance from this program include manufacturing and industrial firms, research and development, agribusinesses, warehouse and terminal facilities, office buildings used as national or regional headquarters, and computer or clerical operations. Corporate headquarters and clerical operations centers were added to the definition of eligibility in 1980 legislation. Commercial, mercantile, and retail firms are not eligible to participate in this program.

PIDA is limited to the financing of land and buildings or their acquisition for the purpose of increasing employment in the state. PIDA funds three types of activities. The most traditional type is an industrial development project, in which a private manufacturing, R&D, or other eligible industry wishes to buy land and erect a building on such land. PIDA financing can help finance the acquisition costs of the land and costs of construction, but it cannot be used to purchase inventory, operating capital, machinery and equipment, and related installation and maintenance costs. PIDA can be used in conjunction with the Revenue Bond and Mortgage Program (see below), where PIDA funds the land and building costs and the Revenue Bond program funds machinery and equipment.

The minimum-sized project PIDA will consider is $200,000, and the minimum size of the firm must be at least 25 employees after completion of the project. PIDA loans may be made only to and through a local industrial development agency (IDC), which in turn arranges for the selling or leasing of the project to the responsible buyer or tenant.

In addition to industrial development projects, PIDA will also finance industrial park projects. The types of firms and/or tenants that may reside in an industrial park funded through PIDA are not limited to those eligible for an industrial development project. Consequently, commercial and retail firms can reside or be tenants within an industrial park receiving PIDA assistance. Finally, PIDA also funds multiple-tenant building projects. These are facilities occupied by two or more industrial, manufacturing, or R&D enterprises. In such cases, the local industrial development agency must maintain ownership of the facility, but may lease the management of the facility to someone else. This aspect of the PIDA program permits funding of small business incubators as well (see below).

PIDA's participation in an individual deal varies by size of firm. The participation rate is adjusted annually by the state PIDA board within the constraints of its statute. For 1985, PIDA participation rates varied from 40 to 70 percent of project costs for a small firm (less than 50 employees), and 30 to 60 percent for a large firm, depending on the degree of unemployment. Interest rates for PIDA loans are from 4.5 percent for those counties with unemployment above 10 percent, to 10.5 percent interest rate for those counties with unemployment under 6 percent. These interest rates are fixed for the term of the loan.

In recent years, PIDA has further focused its funds on small and growing firms by adopting policies against providing loans to large, financially sound companies (that is, with net worth of $50 million or more), unless the area for the investment has high unemployment, the project will create a substantial number of jobs, the costs per PIDA job are low, the firm is an advanced technology firm, or the state is in serious competition with other states for the project.

PIDA loans are secured by first or second mortgages on the project. The term of PIDA projects is generally 10 to 15 years. By board policy the maximum PIDA loan has been set at $1 million in counties with unemployment of more than 10 percent, and $500,000 in counties with unemployment below 10 percent, to handle the demand for the program and assure maximum amount of funds are available for small firms. PIDA assistance should not exceed $15,000 per new job to be created within three years. Should the recipient of a PIDA loan not employ the projected number of new hires after three years, the interest rate on a PIDA loan can rise to 12.5 percent, provided the lack of hiring was not due to unforeseen circumstances.

In most instances a PIDA project involves the sale of a project from a local industrial development agency to a responsible buyer through an installment sales agreement. PIDA will not engage in refinancing of an asset owned by the responsible buyer. In all cases, to initiate a PIDA project a firm must go through a local industrial development corporation.

Advanced technology firms and firms located in the state's enterprise zone areas are eligible for the maximum state participation in a loan. Depending on the unemployment rate in an area, the state's participation could be as high as 70 percent. In addition, advanced technology firms receive disbursement of funds within four months, while other types of firms on average receive disbursement within six to nine months.

The adoption of new policies for PIDA in the early 1980s has resulted in significant changes in types of firms funded. In 1984, half of the PIDA loans made and nearly 30 percent of the funds went to firms with less than 50 employees; 82 percent of the funds went to counties with unemployment above 10 percent; and 21 percent of the PIDA cash flow ($60 million in 1984) went to advanced technology firms.

Pennsylvania Capital Loan Fund. The second Pennsylvania direct loan program is the Pennsylvania Capital Loan fund. Begun in 1982 with federal funds, the program serves as a vehicle to fill the financing gaps that conventional financing cannot meet. It was designed to assist in the start-up and expansion of small industries in the state, most particularly projects that increase exports from the state, decrease imports into the state, and create new jobs. Originally funded with monies from the Federal Appalachian Regional Commission (ARC) and the Federal Economic Development Administration (EDA), the fund now receives both an annual appropriation from the Pennsylvania General Assembly and $15 million from the state's $190 million economic development bond issue, passed in 1984.

The Pennsylvania Capital Loan Fund provides a maximum loan of $50,000 or 20 percent of project costs with state funds. Federal funds in the Capital Loan Fund can be combined with state funds for higher loan amounts up to $100,000. Generally the program works in conjunction with industrial revenue bonds, the U.S. Small Business Administration 503 Certified Development Corporation program, and the Pennsylvania Industrial Development Authority program.

The program is administered through an area loan organization that may be a local development district, an industrial development corporation, or other nonprofit economic development organization as certified or designated by the Secretary of Commerce, that possesses an acceptable local loan review committee, professional staff support, and such other qualifications as necessary to administer the program. Seven local development districts and 14 local industrial development corporations currently administer the program throughout the Commonwealth. The state loans the funds to the area loan organization that, in turn, actually makes the loan to the firm.

Funds may be used for land, buildings, equipment and machinery, and working capital. Working capital loans must be secured by inventory and accounts receivable. Small business enterprises with less than 50 employees are the only eligible firms to receive state funds. Federal funds within the Capital Loan Fund can be used to assist firms of larger size but generally not more than 250 employees. Federal EDA funds have as a target distressed areas and advanced technology firms. ARC funds must be used as part of the energy cost activities of a firm. To apply for funds, firms must be for-profit manufacturing, industrial, or export service-related businesses. Mercantile and service-related businesses are not eligible unless they are determined to be advanced technology or computer-related businesses that will increase Pennsylvania's national or international market share. A firm must create at least one new full-time equivalent job within three years following disbursement of the loan for every $15,000 in loan proceeds.

The term of loans for machinery and equipment and working capital cannot exceed five years, and terms for purchase of buildings and land and renovations shall not exceed 10 years with state funds. Those projects using federal funds in the Capital Loan Fund may receive longer terms to match terms of other public financing. Interest rates are set by the local area loan organization in cases of ARC funds (usually 50 percent of prime); for EDA funds the interest rates are set at four points below the U.S. Treasury rate for comparable maturities in effect at the time of loan approval. Loans using state funds have interest rates set by the local area loan organization, but they can be no lower than 5 percent.

Loans cannot be used to refinance existing debts or for payments of obligations incurred prior to loan approval. Loan funds cannot be used to assist in the relocation of a business either within the Commonwealth or from another state into the Commonwealth except for those funded with state funds. In such instances they can assist in relocation only if it will result in at least a 25 percent increase in net employment for the firm.

The purpose of the Capital Loan Fund is not to supplant funding that is otherwise available from private sector sources on commercially reasonable terms. The local area loan review committees contain a number of representatives of local financial institutions. Their involvement in the program has already resulted in a reexamination of their loan practices, as they recognize that they were rejecting deals that should have been approved.

Capital loans are secured by lien positions in collateral at the highest level of priority that can accommodate the borrower's ability to raise sufficient debt and equity capital. If an applicant fails to create the number of new full-time equivalent jobs within three years, as specified in its application to the area loan organization, the interest rate will increase to 2 percent above the current prime interest rate for the remainder of the loan, except if the failure was due to circumstances outside the control of the loan recipient.

Pennsylvania Minority Business Development Authority. The third direct loan program is the Pennsylvania Minority Business Development Authority. Similar in operation to the Pennsylvania Capital Loan Fund in purpose and intent, by law it is limited to assisting minority-owned enterprises. The maximum loan it can provide is $100,000, except for advanced technology firms or firms located in enterprise development areas, which can receive $200,000 maximum. Terms and interest are similar to the Capital Loan Fund. Loans are generally for working capital, purchasing machinery, and purchasing equipment. Eligibility is broader to include almost all types of service industries except taverns, restaurants, and bars. Applications in this program are made directly to the Pennsylvania Minority Business Development Authority, whose board makes the final approvals on loan applications. Of the total costs, 25 percent must come from the applicant.

In addition to loan assistance, the authority implements new programs to provide interim working capital financing for minority contractors doing business with state government to increase their share of such contracts. It also provides for a 90 percent guarantee on bid and performance bonds needed to obtain a state contract. The authority also has a technical assistance program to provide counseling and management assistance to potential applicants and current recipients of direct loans.

Employee-Ownership Program. A fourth direct loan program, recently enacted in Pennsylvania, is an Employee-Ownership Program. This program provides three types of state financing. First, it provides loans for feasibility studies of situations where a plant's employees wish to buy a facility but need expert help to determine if it is financially feasible. These loans cover up to 50 percent of total project costs or $100,000, whichever is less. Second, it provides professional services loans up to $100,000 should a feasibility study determine an Employee Stock Ownership Plan (ESOP) might be successful. Professional services help can be used to put together the necessary documentation to implement an ESOP. Such services might also be used to improve the profitability or productivity of the existing company. Third, it provides up to $1.5 million or 25 percent of total project costs as loan assistance to ESOP buyouts. Funds may be used for acquiring common stock of the existing enterprise; acquiring, rehabilitating, or improving land, buildings, machinery, and equipment; and working capital necessary for the operation of the enterprise. Loans may be made to an employee stock ownership trust to acquire common stock of an existing enterprise. The terms, conditions, and the like are subject to negotiation on a case by case basis with term length up to 20 years. The loan interest rate is pegged to the costs of the state borrowing. Applications for this program are made generally through the same local agency responsible for the Capital Loan Fund.

PIDA, Capital Loan, and Minority Business Programs in Pennsylvania are similar to those in a number of other states, with some exceptions. Pennsylvania's programs of low-interest financing have increasingly had as their targets advanced technology firms and firms locating in state enterprise development areas. The programs generally operate through local units, providing a decentralized approach to the delivery of these direct loan programs. A number of other states either have or are in the process of establishing new direct loan programs or redirecting their targets similar to Pennsylvania.

Questions to ask your state or local development officials include:

- What is the interest subsidy, if any?
- How favorable are the loan terms? Is fixed rate or some other terms used?
- Is the program generally used in conjunction with other programs? If so, what are these and where do I get information on them?
- Who is the applicant for the funds?
- What types of firms are eligible or not eligible?
- Are there any special incentives for advanced technology, small business, or growth firms?
- What types of collateral are accepted, and how flexible is the jurisdiction in requiring this?

Loan Guarantee Programs

In addition to direct loan programs, at least 14 states have loan guarantee programs. Loan guarantees are a form of insurance that reduces a financial institutions' risk in a given deal since government backing of part of the debt assures the financial institution of repayment in cases of default. To operate such programs, states generally establish a reserve fund to cover cases of default of loan guarantees. States undertaking such programs feel they have a greater multiplier impact, enabling them to support many more deals with the same dollars as in a direct loan program. This assumes, of course, that no major defaults that both wipe out the reserve fund and require general government support occur. Guarantees can be as high as 90 percent but are generally less.

There are a number of other variants on these loan and loan guarantee programs that will not be covered in detail here, but include:

- Mortgage insurance.
- Interest-only loans.
- Principal reduction payment–only loans.
- Companion loans.
- Reserve and linked deposits.

Finally, a number of states have established business development credit corporations (BDCs) that pool resources of various financial institutions, utilities, and others to make more risky debt or equity investments than traditional financial institutions will make on their own. This is a form of loan pooling and is found in at least 19 states. While these organizations are privately funded and organized, they usually receive a state charter through passage of state legislation. Applicants are usually smaller firms unable to get financing through their local financial institution. Eligibility, terms and conditions, interest rates, and so on vary considerably among the various states.

Tax-Exempt Financing

Industrial development bonds (IDBs) represent another source of financing. These are tax-exempt bonds or mortgages, not subject to federal taxation, permitting the issuer to charge an interest rate 70 to 90 percent of prime. They are a major source of low-cost debt to firms throughout the country. States vary in how they administer these programs. In some states applications can be made directly to the state, in others only through a local agency, and in still others through both sources. Approval processes are usually spelled out in state law, but such programs have increasingly been put under additional federal restrictions. The "small issues" portion of an IDB program is the one of primary interest to small and growing businesses. This permits a firm to use up to $10 million in tax-exempt financing for land, buildings, and equipment and machinery. In 1984, Congress passed legislation terminating the small issue IDB program in 1986, except for manufacturing facilities whose termination date is 1988. In addition, any one firm now has a dollar ceiling on outstanding IDBs nationwide of no more than $40 million.

As was stated previously, all 50 states have some sort of IDB program, with 45 of these issuing such bonds through some local entity. Generally, industrial and commercial projects are eligible for financing. Because of federal legislation passed in 1984 establishing a state volume cap of $150 per capita, states and localities are attempting to establish additional criteria for use of these limited funds.

In Pennsylvania, the IDB program is called the Revenue Bond and Mortgage Program. At one time Pennsylvania's program was the largest in the country, approaching 25 percent of the total volume, but more recently it has been around 9 percent. The Pennsylvania program is handled through local industrial development authorities who approve applications for tax-exempt financing subject to approval of the State. Approximately 90 percent of Pennsylvania's activity does not involve the bond financing side; rather, local financial institutions provide mortgage financing at a tax-exempt rate. For 1985, Pennsylvania has eliminated commercial projects, except in economically distressed areas, from eligibility for the program.

Loans under this program are made through local industrial development authorities who use private sector lenders such as banks, insurance companies, individuals, and public bond issues. Financing can be up to 100 percent, and eligible cost items include construction of facilities, expansion or purchase of existing structures with substantial rehabilitation, and machinery and equipment when part of the building project. The minimum total project costs for commercial facilities is $200,000, and 20 jobs must be created or preserved. Industrial projects require $100,000 and five jobs.

GRANT ASSISTANCE

States and localities have a number of grant programs available to assist in economic development. Traditionally, these have focused on site development and preparation, but in recent years the types and variety of state grant assistance have expanded considerably.

Infrastructure

States and localities provide a wide range of programs, among them to: help get water and sewer services to a site; build access roads to industrial parks; help demolish or clear a site; build bridges; help finance speculative buildings for future tenants; and carry out land banking—holding sites for future development.

States that provide site preparation grants include Alabama, which provides up to $100,000 to improve the sites for future industrial tenants; Indiana, which funds local public infrastructure; and New Jersey, which undertakes similar activities. Land banking is generally done at the local level and involves purchasing land, making public infrastructure improvements, and then selling the improved land for development with the proceeds of the sale placed back into the land-bank fund for additional projects. The Massachusetts State Land Bank is an example of a state agency that assists communities in converting surplus government property to private use, restores historic buildings, acquires and improves blighted residential property, and so on.

Pennsylvania has several programs to meet the infrastructure needs of firms. The site development grant program provides grants to improve access roads, water and sewer lines, and other programs of assistance to a firm in locating at a particular site. The grants can be as high as $100,000 in distressed areas and require a private sector commitment to locate or expand. Improvements can be made only on public property. In addition to this program, the Commonwealth provides $50,000–$75,000 grants to communities with populations of 12,500 or less for community facilities projects such as water supply systems.

The Commonwealth's Business Infrastructure Development program provides $16 million a year in loans and grants for infrastructure. Funds are used to install specific infrastructure improvements necessary to complement industrial investment by private companies, which increases the state's share of domestic and international commerce and creates net new jobs. While private firms cannot apply directly for assistance under this program, they can receive benefits through a local government or other applicant. The program has three components: (1) no-interest loans as high as $1.5 million for improvements on publicly owned property; (2) grants for improvements on publicly owned property up to $500,000 in distressed areas; and (3) low-interest loans to private firms for improvements on private property. Eligible businesses that can participate in the program include agricultural, industrial, manufacturing, and R&D enterprises. Eligible infrastructure improvements include drainage systems, energy facilities, fire and safety facilities, sewer systems, transportation facilities, waste disposal facilities, and water supply systems. Funds can be used for construction, expansion, improvement, rehabilitation, or repair. Private matching is required, but can include any investments by private firms on their land, buildings, and depreciable fixed assets. Matching private investment is on a sliding scale. Any individual project must create at least 10 net new jobs within three years and at least 1 net new job for each $15,000 in loan or grant assistance received. Similar to the Pennsylvania Capital Loan Fund, the Business Infrastructure Development program is not designed to encourage the relocation of firms from one part of the state to another. Distressed areas can receive up to one $500,000 grant per year from this program.

Particularly at later stages of maturity, when seeking to secure their own facilities, small and growing firms may find such grant programs of assistance. Related programs undertaken by nearly half the states are state enterprise development programs. These programs target state resources and those of the community on a particular distressed area, with the intent of influencing private sector investments to be made in these areas. In some states, tax incentives and other benefits are provided. Pennsylvania currently has 12 state-designated enterprise zones that do not receive extra tax advantages but do receive priority in state grant and loan programs, all of which have special provisions for applications from enterprise areas.

Small Business Incubators

The increased recognition of the role small business plays in job generation has led to an increased effort by states and localities to provide assistance so as to reduce the "death rate" of small firms and increase their "birth rate." Studies suggest that somewhere between 50 and 80 percent of all small firms disappear within five years.[4] While some are acquired or merged, in many cases they simply go out of business. In reviewing this situation, states and localities have determined that additional assistance and services to such firms might enable them to become the giants of tomorrow.

Small business incubators are being developed by a number of states and localities to assist in the birth and development of new firms. Incubators provide a cloistered environment in which start-up firms can begin, sharing experiences with other firms in similar situations, but also receiving help from the incubator staff and others on how to run a business. Incubators generally provide three types of assistance. First, they provide low-cost space. Second, they provide not only shared space and reduce the costs of receptionist, computer use, conference room, and so on, but they also provide management and financial assistance services to tenants. Third, incubators are selective in whom they accept, focusing on those that otherwise could not start up on their own in regular commercial-industrial space. They have exit policies so that after a certain amount of time, the firm leaves, whether or not it has made it, to free up space for new tenants.

A number of states and localities are undertaking efforts to establish incubators, including Michigan, Illinois, Missouri, Kansas, Ohio, and North Carolina. Pennsylvania already has 23 incubators in operation, the largest number of any state in the country.

The range of financial help in Pennsylvania, both to developers of incubators and to their tenants, is illustrative of the types of programs and activities that might be found elsewhere. Pennsylvania has a $17 million Small Business Incubator Loan program available to private and public applicants. It provides up to $650,000 or 50 per-

---

[4] David Birch, "Matters of Fact," *Inc.*, April 1985, p. 32.

cent of total project costs, for acquisition and rehabilitation of facilities as well as equipment and furnishing. The Pennsylvania Industrial Development Authority can also be used to finance the land and building costs of incubators. Current incubators in Pennsylvania include several vacant school buildings, an auto repair shop, a former toy factory, a former zipper plant, and a former post office. The state's policy favors rehabilitation of older buildings.

In addition, there is funding through the State's Ben Franklin Partnership program, on a matching basis, for feasibility studies to determine whether a community has a supply of entrepreneurs, volunteers, other services for tenants, and types of buildings amenable to development as incubators. Pennsylvania has already funded approximately 20 incubator feasibility studies.

The Ben Franklin Partnership also provides funds, on a matching basis, through its four Advanced Technology Centers, for services such as management assistance and government financing help to incubator tenants. These may be through the state's 13 Small Business Development Centers, through the local development districts, through community volunteers such as attorneys and accountants, and through the staff of the incubator.

Additionally, the Pennsylvania Capital Loan Fund and the Seed Venture Capital Fund (see below) can provide debt and equity help to tenants of the incubator.

Small business incubators represent another grant and loan tool to assist in creating an entrepreneurial environment in a community. Some are composed mainly of product development firms and are closely tied to universities. Others are of a light manufacturing type, located in former manufacturing facilities. An emerging or growing small business may find such an environment conducive to its early efforts to get underway, providing access to services otherwise not available and permitting it to share common problems and experiences with other entrepreneurs in similar circumstances.

Questions you should ask your state and local development offices include:

- What kinds of programs are available for small firms?
- What services are available for a start-up firm?
- What types of grants are available to meet my infrastructure, start-up, and other needs? Where do I go to apply for these funds? What are the restrictions?

EXPORT DEVELOPMENT FINANCE

As the nation's economy becomes increasingly intertwined in the world's economy, a number of states have recognized the increased need to improve their industries' abilities to participate in this international trade. Several states have established programs modeled on the U.S. Export-Import Bank, providing financing assistance for the export of goods and services from their states. In addition, there has been increased recognition that the Export-Import Bank's portfolio needs to show increased use by small and medium-sized firms, since larger firms tend to be the bank's current major users. State export development programs are generally geared to increase the involvement of small and medium-sized firms in U.S. Export-Import Bank programs.

Fourteen states have passed programs of financial assistance for export. Their funds have been capitalized with state appropriations, with bond issues, and with cash deposits in state banks as sources of loans. All these programs are directed at small and medium-sized firms that lack the capacity or resources to secure financial support from commercial banks or federal sources. The programs may also include counseling assistance, either direct loans or loan guarantees, export credit insurance, and technical assistance in securing additional financial and other Export-Import Bank assistance.

A large number of states have also established overseas offices or representation. Pennsylvania, for example, has four representatives abroad. Not only do these representatives try to encourage foreign investment within the Commonwealth, but they also attempt to promote Pennsylvania goods and services for export. Pennsylvania and other states' offices particularly focus on small and medium-sized firms that do not have the full-time staff and expertise necessary to enter new foreign markets.

Questions you should ask your state and local development officials include:

- What financing assistance is available for exporting?
- What types of counseling and other technical assistance is available so I can learn more about the opportunities and problems of exporting?
- Where and how do I go about getting help from any representatives our state or city has working abroad?

RESEARCH AND DEVELOPMENT

Technological innovation will be critical to our country's ability to compete in the international marketplace. With 90 percent of our knowledge in the basic sciences generated only since 1950, it is likely that scientific discoveries will have a greater impact than ever before on what we make, how we make it, and where we make it. In recent years, states have taken a leadership role in building bridges between their private sectors and their higher education institutions, recognizing the importance of R&D to product development and innovation. Increased emphasis is being placed by the states on ways to aid the commercialization process, to provide entrepreneurial support, and to build on the assets of universities in an effort to diversify their economic bases.

Some states are approaching these goals by building "centers of excellence" within their research universities, which will provide equipment, personnel, and knowledge that can be tapped by the private sector for problem-solving pursuits. Other states are creating new research institutes associated with both the universities and the private sector, such as the Microelectronics Center in North Carolina. Other states are funding applied research and development projects between their colleges and universities and the private sector. Some states are providing funds to supplement the amount their small firms obtain under the Federal Small Business Innovation Research program, which requires each federal agency to set aside some of its R&D funds for competitive bid by and allocation to small firms.

Pennsylvania has a comprehensive set of technological innovation programs which may provide examples of some of the types of programs, found in other states. Through its 15-member Ben Franklin Partnership Board, five programs to support state technological innovation are being administered: (1) Challenge Grants to fund four Advanced Technology Centers throughout the Commonwealth; (2) Small Business Research Seed Grants; (3) a Small Business Incubator Loan program; (4) a Seed Venture Capital Fund; and (5) an Engineering Equipment Grant program. The Incubator Loan Program was discussed elsewhere, and the Seed Venture Capital Fund will be discussed later in this chapter.

The Challenge Grant program funds four Advanced Technology Centers throughout the state. These four centers undertake three functions: (1) joint R&D with the private sector, (2) education and training, and (3) entrepreneurial development. The centers are organized locally and include business, labor, academic, and other representation through local policy boards. The four centers compete annually for funds from the state that are allocated on the basis of equity, quality and quantity of matching funds, and performance. Each center must have a minimum of $1 of match for every $1 of state expenditures.

Growing and emerging businesses are a vital part of the program. The Ben Franklin Partnership Challenge Grant provides the underwriting of a significant sum of the research and product development work of such firms. Each of the four centers must focus its R&D agenda on four areas. Provided these areas fit the needs of a small firm, for example, computers and robotics at Carnegie-Mellon/University of Pittsburgh, sensors at the University of Pennsylvania, biotechnology at Penn State University, and CAD/CAM (Computer-Aided Design/Computer-Aided Manufacturing) at Lehigh University, then the small firm develops a proposal with a faculty member at one of the state's colleges and universities, committing some of its staff and funds to the effort. Provided the proposal survives quality reviews on a competitive basis, the project can then be funded. The firm and the colleges and universities work out provisions as to patents or new technologies: The program is flexible, even permitting transfer of patent ownership or exclusive licensing. R&D-funded projects range from application of technology to traditional industries, such as machine shops, to development of new products and establishing of new firms on the leading edge of technological innovation.

In the education and training area, research universities and other colleges and universities work hand in hand to assure that the curriculum and faculty are teaching courses and programs that will be needed by firms in the future. Projects range from provision of degrees and course work to firms by 28 colleges and universities within one research park, to linking five community colleges to a research university's equipment by computer terminal to teach technical programs needed by the private sector but unaffordable if each community college had to buy the equipment and develop the education program on its own.

In the entrepreneurial development area, small and growing firms have access not only to small business incubator space supported by the Ben Franklin Partnership but also to assistance in the development of business plans, management, technical, and a range of other services. Many small and emerging firms have found this to be the first access point to the program, using this assistance to chart their future plans and determine what types of assistance, both governmental and nongovernmental, they need.

The Ben Franklin Partnership program in 1984–85 had $18 million in state funds, matched by $55 million in private sector and other matching support. This $73 million program was the largest state technological innovation program on an annual basis, and the most leveraged. It has already assisted 124 new firms to become established and another 89 firms to expand in less than two years of operation. In addition, it has attracted $15 million in venture capital to its projects. Over 100 of the state's colleges and universities are involved, and a majority of the firms involved have less than 50 employees.

In addition to the Challenge Grant program, Pennsylvania also has a Small Business Research Seed Grant program that provides direct state grants of up to $35,000 for R&D by private firms. Firms must have fewer than 250 employees, with a preference shown to those with less than 50 employees. In 1984, the state awarded $550,000 to 17 firms. The eligible areas for work include nine growth areas identified as having maximum growth opportunities in the state, such as computers, robotics, and CAD/CAM. The program does not require any matching, and while university involvement in a project is encouraged, it is not required. This program, modeled after the Federal Small Business Innovation Research Act, has encouraged a number of small firms to also work with one or more of the four Ben Franklin Advanced Technology Centers.

A related program is Pennsylvania's PennTAP program, located at Penn State University, which provides informational assistance to firms on the latest scientific advancements and developments, permitting both existing and new firms to find quick answers to complex problems. This technology transfer service saves firms considerable time and money they would otherwise spend on literature review and searching.

Aspects of Pennsylvania's efforts in R&D have some counterparts elsewhere, such as Ohio's Thomas Alva Edison Partnership Program. New Jersey and New York also have Advanced Technology Center programs. Other university-industry matching grant programs are found in California, with its MICRO program, Michigan, Missouri, Indiana, and Virginia, to name just a few. Thirty-five states have some sort of state technological innovation program, and many of these are geared to the emerging or growing small business. The programs generally can be divided into industrial affiliate programs, sponsored research programs, research parks, and centers of excellence. Some states, like Pennsylvania, combine all these elements.

Questions to ask your state and local developmental officials include:

- What programs are available to underwrite applied research and development costs?
- What role does the university have? Does it work jointly with the private sector or, basically, does it use the program to fund university R&D?
- What entrepreneur assistance is available in starting up a new firm?

VENTURE CAPITAL

Venture capital has become of great interest to states and localities as their policies have given increased priority to emerging and growing businesses. In many cases, such firms do not have a product ready for manufacture, need "patient monies" to further develop the product, and have no ready source of informal venture capital such as friends, neighbors, or family.

While the country as a whole has seen a dramatic increase in venture funds available, their disbursements have been concentrated in three or four locations throughout the country. Three states accounted for over 50 percent of all venture capital in 1982.[5] States and localities have now started to undertake a number of new catalyst or facilitator roles to assist in both early and later stage venture capital financing.

The Massachusetts Technology Development Corporation serves as a quasi-public agency to directly provide venture capital to early-stage, high-risk, technology-based companies in that state. Its investments to date have leveraged nearly seven times its $3.4 million in public investments. Funding primarily is given to technology firms that have been unable to secure adequate funding from conventional sources. They also help entrepreneurs package their proposals for presentation to venture capital and other investors. Another example of a direct state role in venture capital is the Minnesota Seed Capital Fund, which provides early-stage financing to firms offering significant job creation potential.

Other states have sought to stimulate the growth and development of in-state private venture capital. Iowa has created the Iowa Venture Capital Fund and a product development fund, the former using tax credits and the latter using a small amount of state funds. The Connecticut Product Development Corporation has been in operation for more than a decade. It provides existing manufacturers with financial help up to 60 percent of the costs of new product development. Indiana's Corporation for Innovation Development also receives assistance through incentives in the state's tax code.

A number of states have encouraged their pension funds to devote part of their assets to venture capital. This includes Michigan, Ohio, New York, and several other states. The Michigan Fund has available over $400 million for venture capital and makes investments in the form of stock or convertible debentures up to 40 percent of the total funds raised by an individual firm.

State government involvement in the traditionally private venture capital market has increased significantly in the 1980s. Pennsylvania is no exception. Currently its two state pension funds are investing up to 1 percent of their assets, or $100 million, in venture capital firms in Pennsylvania. In addition, the state has established a Seed Venture Capital Program whereby $3 million in state funds are in-

---

[5] *Technology and Growth: State Initiatives in Technological Innovation* (Washington, D.C.: Final Report of the Task Force on Technological Innovation, National Governors' Association, October 1983).

vested on a one to three matching fund basis, with private venture capital funds to create four regional seed venture capital funds in the Commonwealth. This initial $3 million state investment will have attracted $20 million in private investment for early-stage start-up firms. Two of these funds are already in operation having obtained private financial support from utilities, banks, apparel and technology manufacturers, and others. The seed portion of this fund will invest in early-stage start-up firms in the $50,000–$250,000 equity range. Preference is to be given to firms in the state's incubators. It is also expected that a number of spin-offs of the state's Ben Franklin Partnership R&D work will receive initial financing from this effort.

Questions to ask your state or local development office include:

- What state or local supported venture capital funds are in business in my area?
- What financial assistance is available for early-stage equity financing? How do I access it?
- Is there a state or local program that will underwrite my product development costs?

EMPLOYMENT AND TRAINING

Work Force Needs

Increased attention has been given by states and localities to the need for a skilled and trained work force. States throughout the country have increased their minimum high school graduation requirements, including major increases in minimum number of courses in science and math; improved certification and induction standards for future teachers; and increased funding support for basic education.

But because much of the work force over the next 15 years is already working today, it is likely that additional assistance in the area of adult training and retraining will become even more essential. One way to address this problem is through use of customized job training programs, now offered by 32 states. Initially established in South and North Carolina, the general thrust of these programs is to tailor the training to the needs of the firm rather than to take the normal approach of offering the same formal course work year after year, hoping that graduates will find jobs upon graduation and that the private sector will be satisfied with the type of classroom training provided.

Customized Job Training Programs

Of particular interest to new and emerging firms is that these customized job training programs will generally cover the costs of supplies and materials used in the course and the instructors' time, including instructors employed by the firm, and require only that trainees who qualify upon completion of the training be hired by the firm.

Georgia's Quick Start program is aimed at employees of new and expanding companies with industry-specific training prior to plant start-up. This program involves setting up a training program near the new plant site, drawing on the state's own equipment holdings and instructional expertise. The program designs training materials, supplies the instructional facility, and pays the instructors—in most cases company personnel—at no cost to the company. Indiana's Training for Profit program provides assistance to new or expanding industries for training, retraining, and upgrading the skills of potential employees. The California Worksite Education and Training Act (CWETA) is particularly directed at upgrading existing employees' skills. A considerable portion of the training is conducted at the work site immediately after work hours. The Massachusetts Bay State Skills Corporation is a quasi-public state entity that provides training programs for occupations in high demand by industries. Fifty percent of the training cost must come from the private sector.

Pennsylvania also has a customized job training program that to date has assisted 12,000 participants in industries ranging from software development to steel. The program is delivered through local vocational technical schools or community colleges and can be provided both on- and off-site as determined by the firm. To receive upgrading, a firm must show substantial new capital investment. Contact for the program is made through the local education agencies.

Questions to ask your state or local development officials include:

- What assistance is available in finding qualified workers?
- Do you have a customized job training program? How do I apply? What are the conditions and restrictions?

OTHER ASSISTANCE

The above material has focused heavily on financial assistance available from state and local governments. However, there are a number of other activities that involve nonfinancial government aid which are important to emerging and growing companies.

Costs of doing businesses in a state or locality are important factors to a firm. Accessibility and responsiveness of the government unit, a flexible regulatory attitude and environment, and stability and predictability in taxation are all important. For example, in Pennsylvania, the state had no increase in business taxes from 1979 to 1985. In fact, it decreased overall business tax levels. In addition, the state established a Small Business Action Center that provides a "one-stop shop" to find out what permits, forms, and the like are needed from state government to start up in the Commonwealth, and also provides a 48-hour turnaround on any problems one might have with any state department or agency. Small and growing firms should determine if a similar center exists in their town or state.

In many cases, counseling assistance can help a small firm save time and money. Pennsylvania provides this type of counseling assistance through 13 Small Business Development Centers located throughout the state. Similar programs exist in other states.

Through Pennsylvania's seven local development districts, a set of services to the private sector is provided, including help in starting up a small business incubator, providing one-to-one assistance to private firms in obtaining federal procurement awards, packaging of the various loan and grant programs described above, and building private-public partnerships to address other problems. Few states have an integrated delivery system at the local level to provide such services.

CONCLUSION

The needs of the emerging and growing business will vary greatly. Programs of financial aid and assistance also vary among the states and localities of this nation. This chapter provides both generic information on types of programs that might be of assistance to you and examples of programs currently in place. While not all states and localities will have the complete array of programs that Pennsylvania has, it is likely that any locality will have some of them.

In determining what assistance government can be to you, please keep in mind that development finance tools are designed to serve a variety of users. For example, the Pennsylvania programs described herein, in essence, result in the state being able to provide help to a firm, at whatever stage of maturity it may be. You need to assess where you are now and where you plan to be. Then determine what programs and services apply to you.

If you are at an early stage of development—with an idea, a general plan—then programs such as applied R&D, seed capital equity finance, and other grant assistance may be most appropriate. If you have developed a prototype and are ready to move into production, then debt financing for working capital and equipment along with product development financial help may be appropriate. If you have had early success in production and now wish to move into your own facility, then debt financing for land and buildings and for additional equipment may be of most interest to you. And if you are an existing firm, growing or moving into new product lines, that new activity can be thought of just as if it were a new firm, following the sequence above in seeking the appropriate governmental financial assistance.

REFERENCES

The Federal Role in State Industrial Development Programs. Washington, D.C.: Congressional Budget Office, July 1984.

HAMILTON, WILLIAM; LARRY LEDEBUR; and DEBORAH MATZ. *Industrial Incentives: Public Promotion of Private Enterprise.* Washington: Aslan Press, 1984.

PEIRCE, NEAL R.; JERRY HAGSTROM; and CAROL STEINBACH. *Economic Development: The Challenge of the 1980s.* Washington, D.C.: Council of State Planning Agencies, 1979.

Technology and Growth: State Initiatives in Technological Innovation. Washington, D.C.: Final Report of the Task Force on Technological Innovation, National Governors' Association, October 1983.

VAUGHAN, ROGER, *State Tax Policy and the Development of Small and New Business.* Washington, D.C.: Coalition of Northeastern Governors Policy Research Center, May 1983.

CHAPTER 6

Industrial Development Bond Financing

WHAT IS IT?
HOW DO I GET FINANCING?
WHAT ARE THE FEDERAL TAX LAW RESTRICTIONS?
WHO BUYS TAX-EXEMPT BONDS?
WHAT STRUCTURES ARE AVAILABLE IN TODAY'S MARKET?
CREDIT ENHANCEMENT AND LIQUIDITY SUPPORT
COSTS OF ISSUANCE AND TIMING
WHAT ABOUT THE DOLLAR LIMITS?
SUMMARY

Charles R. Ellinwood
Vice President
Kidder, Peabody & Co.
New York, N.Y.

Charles R. Ellinwood is a vice president and shareholder of the Corporate Services Group, a unit of the Public Finance Department at Kidder, Peabody in New York. Since joining the firm in 1977, Mr. Ellinwood has had primary responsibility for over $4 billion in Kidder, Peabody managed financings. He has had extensive experience in several areas of revenue bond financing, including pollution control, water and sewer systems, colleges, public power systems, and industrial development bond projects.

A graduate of Villanova University (A.B.), Mr. Ellinwood received his M.B.A. in Finance from Boston College.

Robert S. Price
Partner
Saul, Ewing, Remick & Saul
Philadelphia, Pa.

Robert S. Price received his A.B. degree from Kenyon College in 1958 and his LL.B. from Yale Law School in 1961. Since his graduation, he has practiced law in Philadelphia, specializing in taxation, employee benefits, and tax-exempt financing. He is a partner in Saul, Ewing, Remick & Saul and has written on a number of subjects in his fields of expertise, including *The ABC's of Industrial Development Bonds,* fourth ed., Packard Press, 1985.

WHAT IS IT?

Industrial development bond financing is a technique whereby a state or local government allows a private user to benefit from that government's status as a tax-exempt entity and its ability to issue debt obligations at tax-exempt rates. As the ultimate recipient of the proceeds of such debt obligations (or bonds), the private user benefits because the interest on the obligations is tax-exempt and therefore bears a lower interest rate than comparable taxable financing. This "conduit" financing technique has been known for approximately 50 years, but only in the last 10–15 years has it become available to private users in almost every state.

Depending on the many factors that make up the market, especially supply and demand and the length of maturity, the tax exemption typically reduces a private user's interest cost by two to four percentage points over taxable obligations. In addition, today's financing structures in the tax-exempt market will permit a private user, assuming adequate credit rating and/or credit enhancement, to obtain access to virtually any point along the yield curve from one day to 40 years.

While in certain cases state or local governments themselves may issue tax-exempt obligations for private purposes, local law may prohibit a state or local government from issuing its obligations directly for private benefit. In that event, the obligations are usually issued by authorities or agencies that act "on behalf of" those governments. Occasionally, the obligations are issued by nonprofit corporations that act on behalf of those governments, though this type of financing is subject to restrictions that confine its use to special situations.

After issuance, a variety of devices may be employed to transfer the proceeds of the obligations from the issuer to the private user. The particular mechanism that is used will depend on local law, custom, and the security requirements of the buyers of the obligations. In a typical format, the authority that issues the obligations uses the proceeds to build or buy the facility for the private user and, simultaneously with the issuance of the obligations, enters into an installment sale or lease-purchase agreement with the private user. This agreement gives the private user the right to use the facility in return for its commitment to pay the debt service on the obligations plus the fees and costs of the authority. An alternative method is to issue the obligations and lend the proceeds of the issue directly to the private user, who then builds or buys the facility.

HOW DO I GET FINANCING?

Initially, local and state law determine whether a project will qualify for tax-exempt financing. Historically, the technique was first developed in the South to attract industry. A town in Mississippi, for example, would build a carpet mill to the specifications of a northern manufacturer. It would issue tax-exempt obligations to pay for the mill and then sell the mill to the manufacturer, who would agree to pay principal and interest on the obligations. If the town agreed to use its own credit to guarantee the obligations, they were often called industrial development bonds. When only the mill property, the installment sale/lease purchase agreement or the manufacturer's own guarantee (but not the town's credit) were security for the repayment of the obligations, they were called industrial revenue bonds. Over the years, this distinction has become blurred and the two terms—revenue bonds and development bonds—are now used interchangeably whether or not there is a government guarantee. However, the historical origins of the technique have, in some states, survived to limit what they will finance.

While the original purpose of industrial development bond financing was to attract new industry to a state, in time this purpose was expanded to help existing industry add facilities. It was further expanded in some states to help existing industry survive by enabling new owners to purchase existing facilities that would otherwise be closed. In some states, it was also recognized that commercial, nonindustrial expansion was equally desirable. However, where commercial projects are permitted, a multitude of local distinctions are often drawn as to what are acceptable commercial facilities. For example, some jurisdictions will not permit the financing of warehouses or office buildings where the tenants will be doctors, lawyers, or other professionals. Some vary the distinctions, depending on where the facilities will be located, the number of jobs to be created or saved, and the minority or other employees to be hired. These distinctions reflect local priorities. Most states and localities now have industrial development agencies or authorities that are fully knowledgeable about what they can finance. You should consult with your local issuer to best ascertain what is able to be financed in your state under its law.

WHAT ARE THE FEDERAL TAX LAW RESTRICTIONS?

For purposes of this description, we will assume that your state will finance anything that is permitted to be financed under the federal tax laws. Under those laws, most projects will have to be financed under what is known as the "small issue" exception of Section 103(b)(6) of the Internal Revenue Code. This exception limits the size of the projects it will finance to $10 million or less. We will discuss this dollar limitation later. However, at this point it is appropriate to note that financing for any *commercial* small issue project will not be permitted after December 31, 1986, and for any *industrial* small issue project after December 31, 1988. As this chapter is being written, Congress is the scene of conflicting attempts to both repeal these dates and to revise the various limitations discussed in the next half-dozen paragraphs.

In addition to the current federal limitations on the overall size of the project, there are certain other restrictions: No more than 25 percent of the proceeds of a small-issue industrial development bond may be used to provide a facility the primary purpose of which is retail food and beverage service, automobile sales or service, or the provision of recreation or entertainment. Furthermore, no portion of the proceeds may be used to provide any private or commercial golf course, country club, massage parlor, tennis club, skating facility (including roller skating, skateboarding, and ice skating), racquet sports facility (including handball or racquet court), hot tub facility, suntan facility, racetrack, airplane, skybox, or other private luxury box, any health club facility, any facility primarily used for gambling, or any store the principal business of which is the sale of alcoholic beverages for consumption off-premises.

While these specific federal limitations are unlikely to curtail many projects, two other federal limitations may. First, you may not use, directly or indirectly, any portion of the proceeds of an issue to acquire land for farming purposes. In addition, less than 25 percent of the proceeds may be used to acquire land for other than farming purposes and less than 50 percent for land for an industrial park. In practice, this limitation has rarely been a problem since the cost of land for an industrial facility is seldom near 25 percent. It has occasionally presented a problem for commercial facilities in large cities, unless the project has equity that may be allocated to the cost of land. Usually, the principal problem has been to prove that you met this limitation, either through allocations made in the documents or in accordance with relative fair market values per an appraisal. The second limitation requires that you not use any portion of the proceeds of an issue to buy used property. However, there are exceptions to this limitation that can be best explained by the following example.

Assume that you will buy a used shoe factory building for $500,000, containing a shoe manufacturing line that will cost $250,000. The property has a dock or an adjacent river that will cost $50,000 and a crane on that dock which will cost $25,000. You can use tax-exempt obligations proceeds to buy the building and the integrated shoemaking machinery for a total cost of $750,000, provided that you spend at least $112,500 (15 percent of $750,000) to rehabilitate the building and/or the machinery. This $112,500 can also be paid for out of the proceeds of the obligations, but doesn't have to be; you may use other funds. You can also buy the $50,000 dock with proceeds of the bonds, if you spend at least 100 percent (another $50,000) to fix it up. You can't spend any proceeds of the obligations to buy the crane, but you can rehabilitate it with those proceeds if you wish. Exactly what constitutes a good rehabilitation cost is subject to very technical rules. Basically, you cannot add to the building but have to fix up what you have. However, you have two years from the later of the date on which you bought the property, or the obligations were issued, to make the expenditures.

Congress also imposed four other limitations on the issuance of industrial development bonds that should trouble your bond counsel and your accountant more than they will trouble you, but you should know about them. First, before the obligations can be sold at all, you will have to get an "allocation of volume cap" from your state. In 1984, Congress imposed a cap on the total volume of private purpose financing. Each state is permitted to issue only a limited amount of most types of tax-exempt private purpose obligations each year. Generally, the available amount per state is calculated by multiplying its population by $150 ($100 after 1986). Your state will have to allocate some of this volume cap to you before your obligations may be issued.

Second, you will have to have a so-called TEFRA hearing. TEFRA is the name of the act of Congress that imposed this requirement. The issuer will advertise at least 14 days before the hearing that your obligations are to be issued. A hearing will be held to give the general public a chance to voice its objections prior to project approval. Unless your project is controversial, the hearing and approval will be no problem; you need only make sure that the proper notice was given and the proper approval was received. The issuer will also have to file Form 8038 with the IRS, and may also have to make the $10 million election discussed below. The election has to be made *before* the obligations are issued.

Third, you will have to rebate your arbitrage "profit" to Uncle Sam—if you have one. This problem will not occur if your tax-exempt obligations are sold to a bank or other financial institution and the funds for your project are advanced to you as you need them. However, if the way your obligations are sold makes all of the funds available to you on the day the obligations are issued, and they are invested until you need them, the possibility of rebatable arbitrage arises. Arbitrage profits are defined as the earnings on acquired nonpurpose obligations (such as certificates of deposit or Treasury bills) in excess of the earnings the investment in those obligations would have generated had those earnings been restricted to the bond yield (what you are paying on your tax-exempt bonds), plus all earnings on the reinvestment of such excess earnings.

For example, if you pay 8 percent for the money you get from the sale of the obligations and invest that money at an average of 9 percent during the first year until it is used up, the 1 percent arbitrage profit has to be rebated to the U.S. Treasury, plus whatever other interest income is earned on the 1 percent, regardless of the rate. This requirement will not apply if you spend all of the proceeds of the obligations within six months of the issue.

The chief problem with this requirement is not that you will have a great deal to pay to Uncle Sam but rather the difficulty you will have figuring out exactly what you owe. Since the tax exemption of the obligations depends on your compliance (although an innocent error will be forgiven), you must do your best to get it right. The help of a good, knowledgeable CPA will be a necessity. One way people have been avoiding this problem is by investing the proceeds of their obligations in other tax-exempt paper until the proceeds are needed. If you do that, you don't have to make the rebate.

The fourth limitation is that you must use at least 90 percent of the proceeds of the obligations to acquire land or "property of a character subject to the allowance for depreciation." You can't use proceeds for working capital or property that would be amortized, such as certain leasehold improvements. In testing whether you will meet this limit, you eliminate the "neutral costs." These are generally the costs of preparing and marketing the obligations, such as bond counsel fees and underwriter's discount on a public issue. Once neutral costs have been eliminated, 90 percent of what remains must be used for "good" costs—land or depreciable property. Interest payable during construction is probably a good cost that qualifies for the 90 percent. Warning: Congress is now considering increasing this percentage).

The major danger here is that you may have spent a good bit of your own money (or money borrowed at taxable rates) on the project before your obligations have been sold. To the extent that proceeds of the obligations then pay you back, they are restoring your working capital rather than buying the land or depreciable property. You can, however, avoid this trap if you get an "inducement resolution" from the issuer early in the planning stages of your project. This resolution will loosely commit the issuer to your project. You will thereafter be able to sell your obligations when the market seems best to you, provided that you do so within a year after the project is completed.

WHO BUYS TAX-EXEMPT BONDS?

The tax-exempt bond market has experienced radical change during the past few years. The days of a predictable market and "vanilla" financing structures have been replaced with an extremely volatile market, a wide variety of structures (especially in the short-term area), and the ever-expanding role of third-party guarantors. In addition, the buyer profile has dramatically changed from institutional to individual.

Since the mid-1950s, three categories of investors have dominated the tax-exempt bond market: property and casualty insurance companies, banks, and individual investors. Property and casualty insurance companies typically buy bonds maturing in the 20- to 30-year range and, during the height of their activity in the late 1970s, were responsible for approximately 24 percent of all new issue tax-exempt bond purchases. Commercial banks generally buy bonds maturing in the 1- to 10-year range and at one time accounted for 43 percent of new issue purchases. Individual participation in the tax-exempt market is manifested through true individual purchases or purchases of units in tax-exempt bond funds. The bond funds vary from short-term, open-ended, managed funds to long-term (30-year), closed-end funds or unit investment trusts. At any point in time, demand from each of these buying groups can vary from substantial to virtually nonexistent. For example, in 1980, property and casualty insurance companies and banks together purchased approximately 87 percent of all new issue tax-exempt bonds, with individuals accounting for the balance. By contrast, in 1984, these two groups combined for only 17 percent of new issue purchases, with individuals responsible for 83 percent. This dramatic change in institutional purchases occurred because both the insurance industry and the commercial banking industry suffered downturns in profitability during the early 1980s, which reduced the attractiveness of tax-exempt obligations to them. The reduction in demand has been compounded by new federal tax laws that restrict the ability of financial institutions to deduct a portion of the interest they pay on their borrowings to finance their inventory of tax-exempt obligations.

WHAT STRUCTURES ARE AVAILABLE IN TODAY'S MARKET?

The change in buying patterns that began in 1980 was also partly responsible for higher tax-exempt interest rates and, consequently, a variety of new financing structures. With the withdrawal of the banks and insurance companies, a tremendous burden was placed on the individual purchaser to absorb an ever-increasing amount of tax-exempt bonds. In addition, a substantial amount of industrial development bonds, which had hither to been purchased directly by banks, were now forced into the public market, adding more pressure to supply. This supply/demand imbalance, when coupled with the devastating inflation of that time, pushed interest rates to record highs. As with all fixed income securities, interest rates in the tax-exempt market increased to compensate creditors for the added inflation rate risk. An unfortunate result of high, long-term interest rates was severe erosion in bond values. Bonds that had traded near par for years were suddenly worth 60 to 70 cents on the dollar. This was most disconcerting to individual investors, who became as concerned about preservation of capital as return on investment.

This development had a negative effect on the long-term market and forced issuers and their bankers to reevaluate the viability of traditional structures. Most tax-exempt bond issues were historically structured to include serial bonds for the first few years, with one or more term maturities on the long end (20–30 years). In the early 1980s, with banks and insurance companies out of the market and interest rates rising in all markets, the tax-exempt yield curve became more steeply sloped. This had the predictable result of causing borrowers to move to the short end of the yield curve, either to shorter term paper or to the various forms of adjustable rate tender securities (tender bonds or "put" bonds). The latter are securities with long-term nominal maturities and put features that allow the investor, on an agreed date or dates (the put dates), to tender the bond back to the issuer's remarketing agent for purchase at par. Since this put at par provides the economic equivalent of a maturity date, these bonds bear interest at rates that approximate those of tax-exempt notes with an equivalent maturity. Thus, a bond with an annual put right bears a one-year interest rate.

Adjustable rate tender securities usually have the additional advantage of being convertible to a fixed rate for the remainder of their maturity on certain specified dates (often at any time). The issuer can thereby obtain the rates available on the short end of the yield curve while waiting for general rate levels to drop, at which point it can convert to a long-term, fixed rate security. As long as the weighted interest cost on the bonds over the life of the issue is less than the long-term rate at the time of the issuance, the issuer realizes savings vis-à-vis the long-term bond option. The issuer analyzes this risk through breakeven analysis (Exhibit 1). The break-even rate is that rate at which the issuer is indifferent between having issued a long-

EXHIBIT 1 Annual Tender Bond Converted to a Long Bond (break-even rates over time)

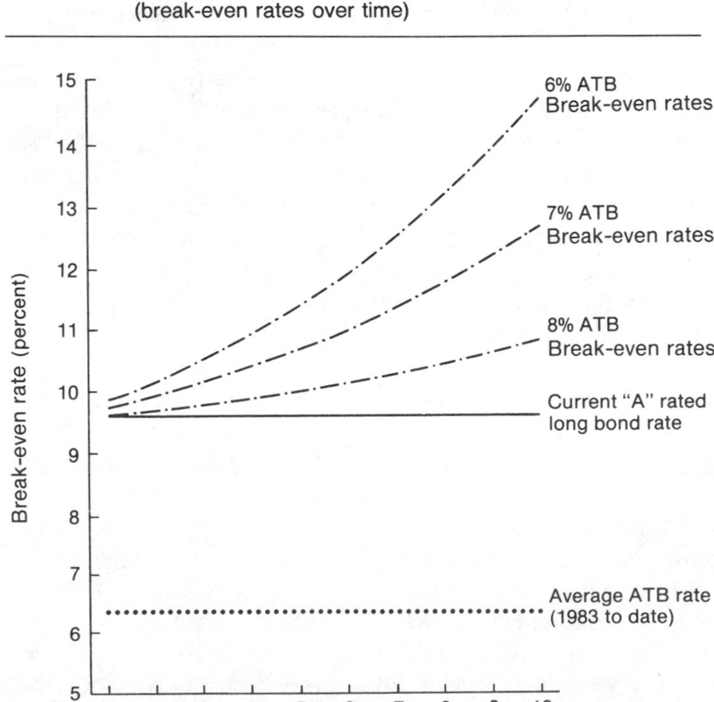

term, fixed rate bond at the outset versus having issued an adjustable rate tender security and then converting to a long-term bond at a future time.

Investor preference has also shifted to shorter term securities. Many individuals and banks prefer short-term or serial maturities and their increased participation has increased demand at this end of the yield curve. This trend has contributed to the growth of tax-exempt money market funds (Exhibit 2), which act as intermediaries for individual and corporate investment in short-term (less than one year) tax-exempt obligations. The tax-exempt money market fund demand and the desire of borrowers to access the low-cost money at the short end of the yield curve via adjustable rate tender obligations

EXHIBIT 2 Growth of Tax-Exempt Money Market Funds (net assets at end of month)

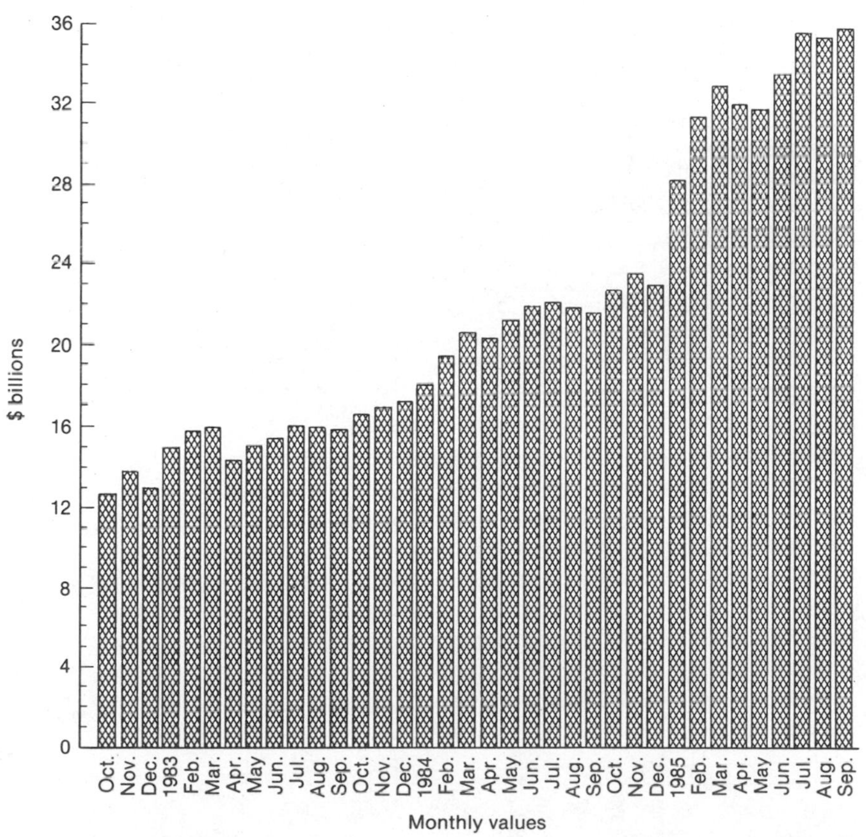

SOURCE: Donoghue's *Money Fund Report.*

have reinforced each other. Adjustable rate tender obligations provide a product to meet the growing demand on the part of the funds for short-term paper, while the money market funds provide a growing pool of capital that issuers need in order to successfully access savings offered at the short end of the yield curve (Exhibit 3).

Although put bonds were first introduced for hospital financings in the mid-1970s, the structure was popularized in the form of "low floaters" in 1982. Low floaters were issued as long-term bonds with an interest rate that changed every 30 days pursuant to a predetermined index, with an investor put option every 30 days. The obligations could be converted to long-term, fixed rate obligations at the borrower's option. Since 1982, this structure has evolved to the point where a

EXHIBIT 3 Basis Point Spread (bond buyer 30-year revenue bond index versus 30-day floating rate demand note interest rates)

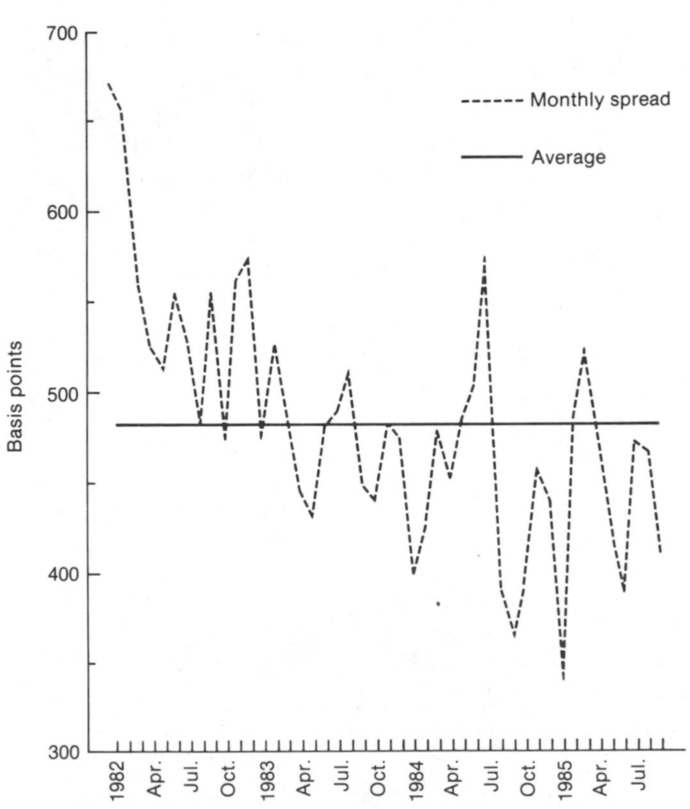

SOURCES: *The Bond Buyer* and Kidder, Peabody Municipal Bond Dept.

borrower can structure a transaction to provide for a variety of interest rate periods from one day to 40 years. Financings in today's market have interest rate periods and corresponding put provisions of one day, seven days, 30 days, six months, one year, three years, five years, and so on. Some structures offer a tax-exempt commercial paper option as well. (Though of all the possible variations, the commercial paper option seems to cause the Internal Revenue Service the most distress.) This type of structure is known by a number of different names, including adjustable rate tender securities, flexibonds and multiple-mode demand bonds.

The pricing mechanisms to determine the new interest rates for these structures have also evolved during the past few years' in an attempt to achieve a true market interest rate at the time of remarketing. The following mechanisms reflect the growing confidence of bond-counsel in the belief that they will not cause the remarketing to be treated as a reissuance:

1. *Indexing agent*—An independent third party like J. J. Kenny, a municipal bond broker, would devise an index based on municipal securities of comparable credit rating and maturity. The index would then be the new interest rate on the bonds for the subsequent interest rate period.
2. *Indexing agent with collar*—Later financings still provided for an index, but allowed the remarketing agent (usually the original underwriter of the bonds) to remarket the bonds at a rate slightly above or below the index subject to a predetermined collar (e.g. 90–110 percent).
3. *Remarketing agent serves as indexing agent*—Under this structure, the remarketing agent also serves as indexing agent and, as such, formulates an index based on comparable securities and then remarkets the bonds at par.
4. *Remarketing without index*—Some transactions have been structured to allow remarketing agents to simply remarket the bonds at that rate which, in their judgment, is necessary to sell the bonds at a purchase price equal to par, without referring to any index.

Issuers also have the option under these structures to convert the bonds from a floating rate to a long-term, fixed interest rate. Conversion to a long-term bond is accomplished by giving notice to current bondholders of the decision to convert to a fixed interest rate. Since the issuer will be accessing a totally different market upon conversion, there is usually a mandatory redemption of all bonds, with the exception of bondholders who wish to retain their bonds as long-term obligations. Again, both Congress and the Internal Revenue Service are reviewing their positions on these obligations. Because of the efficiency of such obligations, it is hoped that Congress and the IRS will take a favorable view toward them, but there is no guarantee that they will.

As Exhibit 4 indicates, adjustable rate tender obligations have experienced explosive growth in the past two years, and this growth is expected to continue. These vehicles make sense for many issuers, but not for all, and it should be clearly understood that there are risks inherent in these financings. First, many bond counsel firms have reservations as to whether adjustable rate tender securities can satisfy the legal requirement that each rate adjustment does not constitute the reissuance of a new bond. Even if such concerns are overcome, short-term financing is not a replacement for sound budgetary practices and long-term financing. Becoming overly dependent on floating rate debt can adversely affect an issuer's credit ratings. Issuers should not focus solely on the low-interest rates available in the short-term

EXHIBIT 4 Volume of Long-Term versus Short-Term Financings, 1980–1984

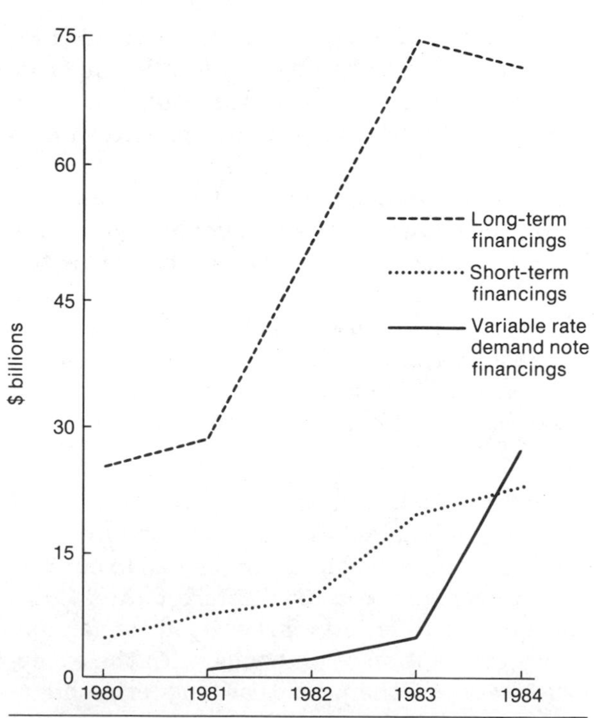

SOURCE: Securities Data Company (Municipal Data System).

market, but rather on the level of interest rates in general. Issuers should take advantage of long-term rates when they are reasonable by historical standards and they can secure permanent financing at a relatively attractive rate.

CREDIT ENHANCEMENT AND LIQUIDITY SUPPORT

A common problem for some companies is the inability to access the public market because the company is not rated. A way to overcome this is to secure some form of credit enhancement or liquidity support for an issue. This, too, has been an area of phenomenal growth in the tax-exempt market. In 1981, $10 billion in tax-exempt obligations were issued with some form of financial guarantee, while in 1984 almost $45 billion came to market with credit/liquidity support (Exhibit 5). This is in large measure attributable to growth in the aforemen-

EXHIBIT 5 Volume of Tax-Exempt Issues with Financial Guarantees

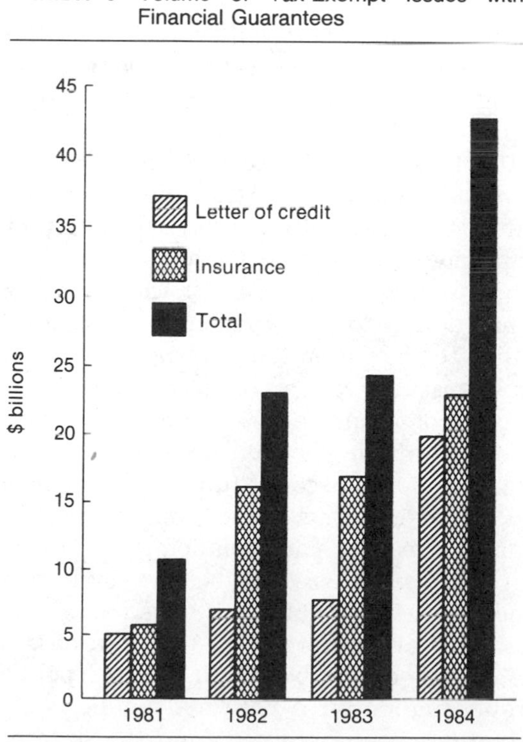

SOURCE: Securities Data Company (Municipal Data System).

tioned adjustable rate tender securities area, which requires credit and liquidity support due to the investor put option. The credit and liquidity support in the short-term market is accomplished primarily through bank letters of credit from large, rated banks, which permit the obligations to be sold in the public market. Credit support in the long-term market is secured primarily through municipal bond insurance which is offered by companies that specialize in this area, such as AMBAC, MBIA, FGIC and BIG. Both letters of credit and municipal bond insurance guarantee the timely payment of principal and interest should project revenues not be sufficient to pay debt service on the obligations. Credit supports are justified when the present value of the interest savings resulting from the higher ratings outweigh the cost of the guarantee. Letter of credit fees are usually payable annually based on principal amount while municipal bond insurance premiums are payable on a one time, upfront format based on total debt service over the life of the issue.

COSTS OF ISSUANCE AND TIMING

Regarding costs of issuance and timing, there will be a substantial difference between a public issue and a privately placed bank issue. Industrial development bonds that are purchased directly by banks are usually quickly and easily issued once the bank's commitment is made. Interest rates in the private bank market are generally slightly higher than in the public market, but the financing costs are lower. Conversely, the interest rate available in the public market is usually more favorable, although financing costs are higher. The key determinant in selecting a market is the size of the financing and your bank's willingness and ability to book the loan. As a general rule, financings below $2 million to $3 million tend to border on being prohibitively expensive as public issues from a true interest cost perspective (interest rate plus costs of issuance). You should evaluate both alternatives, however, before making a final decision. Costs of issuance for a public issue include bond discount (underwriter's fee), bond counsel, issuer counsel, trustee, rating agency, authority fees, printing, and other miscellaneous fees. If your financing has credit enhancement and/or liquidity support, there will be fees for letters of credit, bond insurance, and counsel associated with the bank and/or insurer. Total costs of issuance are generally in the area of two to three percent of the par amount of the bonds for a rated public issue and could be considerably higher for a nonrated public issue. Once an inducement resolution has been obtained from the state or

Week 1:	Structure decision
Weeks 2–3:	Document preparation
Weeks 4–5:	Working group meetings to finalize documentation
Week 6:	Apply for ratings
Week 7:	Print and mail preliminary official statement
Week 8:	Market bonds; execute purchase contract; print final official statement
Week 11:	Close

local government issuing the bonds, the normal timetable calls for a closing within 10 to 12 weeks. A typical timetable is shown above.

WHAT ABOUT THE DOLLAR LIMITS?

We have been describing the small issue limitation in this chapter. If your project is for certain other types of activities, for example, residential rental property, sports facilities, convention or trade show facilities, airports, docks, wharves, parking, solid waste disposal facilities, or air or water pollution control facilities, there are other rules that may apply. However, most emerging and growing businesses will be looking to the small issue exemption.

The small issue exemption permits tax-exempt obligations to be issued for your project for almost any purpose (except for the few forbidden purposes described earlier) up to $1 million. If the issuer so elects before the obligations are issued, the exempt amount may be increased to $10 million. However, the $10 million amount is not computed only on the size of the issue of obligations. It also limits the size of your project, regardless of how you finance the part not paid for out of the obligations. Complicated rules exist to make sure that these limits are not exceeded.

First, whether the issue is up to $1 million or up to $10 million, you have to take into account certain prior tax-exempt issues, to the extent they are still outstanding. Those are issues for facilities located in the same political unit (your county or your city) that are used by the same principal user, or a related person. You, as the owner of the project, will be a principal user, and so will anyone who uses more than 10 percent of the facility financed by the obligations.

For example, if your project is in a city and you financed another project in that same city with an earlier tax-exempt obligation, and you or a related person will use both projects, you have to aggregate the earlier tax-exempt obligations with the obligations for this project in counting whether you meet the dollar limit. This will be the case even when you don't use both projects but another principal user (someone who uses more than 10 percent of a facility) does use both. For example, assume your project is an office building and a tenant occupies 30 percent of your project. If that same tenant occupies all of a building elsewhere in the city that was built with earlier-issued tax-exempt bonds, you have to aggregate those other bonds with your new obligations.

Second, if you elect the up to $10 million limit (but not if you use only the up to $1 million limit), you have to include not just certain prior issues, but also certain other capital expenditures. These include expenditures that were paid or were incurred *other* than with bond proceeds, during a six-year period that begins three years before the date your bonds are issued and ends three years after that date. The includable capital expenditures were paid with respect to facilities in the same political unit, where the principal user of the facilities is the same person, or two or more related persons. The expenditures had to be chargeable to the capital account (or could have been capitalized under some provision of the Internal Revenue Code).

For example, if you built a building two years ago with your own money for $6 million and you now want to expand it with a $3 million issue of tax-exempt obligations, you will have $9 million expenditures for purposes of this limitation when your obligations are issued. If, in the next three years, you have capital (or capitalizable) expenditures on that building of $1,001,000, the limit will be exceeded and your obligations will become taxable from the day you exceed the $10 million.

These rules are obviously extremely complicated, and there are a number of surprising inclusions and exclusions in computing the $10 million. Perhaps the most useful exclusion is one for leased personal property, which need not be aggregated. Great care must be taken to comply with these rules because, as noted above, if the $10 million limitation is exceeded at any time during the period, the obligations thereafter lose their tax exemption.

Another dollar limitation—added by the Deficit Reduction Act of 1984—may sink your project if you are not careful. It provides that you may not issue a tax-exempt small issue if any principal user of the facility to be financed thereby will be a beneficiary of more than $40 million in tax-exempt financings, counting issues anywhere in the United States. This rule was intended to prevent large companies from benefiting further from small issues around the country.

SUMMARY

Industrial development bonds have been an attractive financing tool for the emerging and growing business. The cost of capital is relatively low, and there are many financing structures available to meet a company's needs and objectives. However, their use is subject to many pitfalls due to the complexity of the rules. A company should proceed into this maze of rules only with the most skilled bond lawyers, accountants, and financial advisers. The potential savings involved can have a substantial effect on the financial success of a project, as well as the financial health of a company.

CHAPTER 7

Venture Capital Financing

Frederick R. Adler
Managing General Partner
Adler & Company
New York, N.Y.

Frederick R. Adler is managing general partner of Adler & Company, which manages or advises six venture capital funds and Adler family venture investments having aggregate assets in excess of $300 million. He is also a senior partner of the New York City and Los Angeles law firm of Reavis & McGrath.

Mr. Adler entered venture capital in 1968 and has emphasized start-up and very early-stage investments, which account for approximately 85 percent of his portfolio. As to his publicly owned companies, he is a founder and director (chairman of Executive Committee) of Data General Corporation (computer manufacturer), a founder and director (chairman) of Bio-Technology General Corp. (molecular biology), a founder and director (chairman) of Daisy Systems, Corp. (computer-aided engineering), a director (chairman) of Life Technologies, Inc. (clinical microbiology), a director (chairman of Executive Committee) of MicroPro International Corp. (microcomputer software), a director of Scitex Corporation Ltd. (computer-aided graphics), and a director of Optrotech Ltd. (electric-optical inspection and design equipment).

Stanley E. Pratt
Chairman
Venture Economics, Inc.
Wellesley Hills, Mass.

Stanley E. Pratt, chairman of Venture Economics, Inc., Wellesley Hills, Massachusetts, is recognized as a leading authority on the venture capital industry. He is publisher of *Venture Capital Journal,* which has been reporting and analyzing business development investing since 1961, and is editor of the ninth edition of *Pratt's Guide to Venture Capital Sources.* He is also a noted consultant and spokesman for the venture capital industry, providing data and testimony for government agencies as well as background for the national media, in which he is quoted extensively.

Alan B. Miller
President and Board Chairman
Universal Health Services, Inc.
King of Prussia, Pa.

Alan B. Miller, president and board chairman of Universal Health Services, Inc. (UHS), of King of Prussia, Pennsylvania, a hospital management company with 1985 revenues in excess of $500 million, started the company in 1979 with an important assist from the venture capital community. Mr. Miller, former chairman and president of American Medicorp, Inc., a hospital management company acquired by Humana, Inc. in an unfriendly takeover, raised $1 million from each of three venture partners after he and his management team of six individuals put up $1 million of their own capital. Starting with the acquisition of a single hospital, UHS has grown dramatically in six years. The company presently owns, manages, or has under development, 44 acute care and psychiatric hospitals in the United States and England. It has also diversified into other areas of health care service, including physical rehabilitation and addictive disease facilities, medical equipment sales and rental, and a full line of health insurance products.

PART A What Venture Capitalists Look For*

WHAT IS VENTURE CAPITAL?

Classic modern venture capital involves the professional investing of risk capital in an enterprise in which the venture investor shares ownership as well as board of directors–level management responsibilities with the founding management team. Investments are usually targeted at companies that attempt to satisfy significant and rapidly growing needs for products or services. Venture capitalists provide seed and start-up financing as well as later rounds of private expansion funding to companies that they believe have demonstrated viability but that do not yet have access to public debt and equity markets or bank lines.

The close relationship between venture capitalists and entrepreneurial management teams differentiates venture investors from the broad spectrum of traditional investment institutions. The role of the venture capitalist, in terms of active, ongoing involvement undertaken to add value to the investment and long-term investment commitment, is quite different from that of most money management institutions, who prefer to make passive investments.

---

* Part A was written by Frederick R. Adler.

While the great bulk of such investing in the last 25 years has been in high technology areas, principally microelectronics and, more recently, in biotechnology, large sums have also been invested in more mundane areas such as food (e.g., the creation of frozen orange juice in the 1940s), magazines, movies, hospitals and alternative forms of medical care, retailing, and so on.

FINANCING STAGES

Early-Stage Financing

Early-stage financing usually takes the form of seed or start-up financing. Seed financing provides a relatively small amount of capital to an entrepreneur to prove a concept. Although product development may occur, initial marketing is rarely involved. Start-up financing provides funds for product development and initial marketing efforts. Recipients of start-up funding are often in the process of being organized or may have been in business a short time; generally, however, the product has been test marketed but not yet sold commercially. Most companies receiving money at this stage have assembled key management, prepared a business plan, completed marketing studies, and prepared themselves to begin commercial manufacturing and sales. Other early-stage financings include companies that are already developed and are selling products.

Expansion Financing

More relevant to ongoing companies is expansion-stage financing, which is also provided by venture capitalists. In second-stage financing, working capital is provided for the initial expansion of a company that is already producing and shipping, and has growing accounts receivable and inventories. Although revenues are growing, such companies often have not yet reached the break-even point. Third-stage financing is provided for major expansion of a company in which sales volume is increasing, and which, in most cases, is operating at the break-even point or a profit. Such funds are utilized for further plant expansion, marketing, working capital, or development of an improved product. The last level, or what we call bridge financing, may also be provided for companies expecting to go public within six months to a year. According to the *Venture Capital Journal* (May 1985), 46 percent of all venture capital investments made in 1984 were seed, start-up, and other early-stage financings, while 43 percent of all investments were made in expansion financings. Within the subcategory of expansion financings, approximately 29 percent were made in second-stage financings, while 14 percent were invested in later-stage financings. The remaining 11 percent of venture capital investments were made in leveraged buyouts, acquisitions, and other forms of investments.

VENTURE CAPITAL FIRMS

Independent Private Firms

The principal institutional source of venture capital is independent private venture capital firms. Such firms generally consist of professional partnerships funded by pension funds, major corporations, individuals and families, endowments and foundations, insurance companies, and foreign investors. There are currently approximately 270 such firms in the United States that invest equity in the full range of investment opportunities from start-ups to more mature companies and management/leveraged buyouts. Examining the structure of a venture capital organization can help in understanding how such organizations operate.

Adler & Company, for example, manages funds with approximately $200 million of contributed capital. About $60 million represents investors from France, Switzerland, the United Kingdom, and the Middle East. The United States' portion includes major pension funds, insurance companies, individual corporations, and wealthy families. Adler & Company is structured as a limited partnership so that no corporate taxes are paid.

Including myself, there are 9 full-time professional managers, 3 in the California office, and 6 in the New York office. To search out new investments and to monitor prior commitments, all of our venture managers travel a great deal. Thus, in 1984, I traveled more than 125,000 miles.

Our partnerships were established in 1978 as the successor of a business that I started in 1968 and managed alone for 10 years. Some of the now public companies for which I, and later my partnership, have been responsible include Data General Corp. (1968, computers, recent annual sales of $1.15 billion); Intersil, Inc. (1970, semiconductors, sold to General Electric when annual sales were over $100 million); Scitex Corporation Ltd. (1978, computer-based publishing equipment, recent sales of $140 million); Applied Materials, Inc. (1968, semiconductor production of equipment, with 1984 annual sales of $168 million—although I left in 1977); Daisy Systems, Corp. (1980, computer-aided engineering, recent annual sales exceeding $125 million); Fibronics International, Inc. (1977, fiber-optics communication equipment, recent annual sales of $13 million); MicroPro International Corp. (1981, word processing software, annualized sales exceeding $40 million); Optrotech Ltd. (1981, electro-optical systems for printed circuit board design and inspection, annual sales rate of approximately $11 million); Ungermann-Bass, Inc. (1979, local area networks for communications, annualized sales of about $52 million); Bio-Technology General Corp. (1980, genetic engineering, sales presently minimal); and Life Technologies, Inc. (1982, biotechnology, with annualized sales of approximately $85 million).

At present, we have nearly 60 investments in technology companies, with board membership in 32. To assist us in monitoring the activities of the companies in which we invest, portfolio companies submit detailed monthly reports to their boards of directors and to us. These reports are tailored for each company by our firms and go far beyond what is normally available to most investors or even to boards of directors. We request, and usually obtain, financial information by department, (e.g., sales, engineering, manufacturing) and include unedited discussions of past and expected performance by each department manager, including planned versus actual results, key issues, problems, goals, and time-specific milestones, with an overview by the president and chief financial officer. Because managers know these written reports will be reviewed and discussed on an ongoing basis, they tend to be factual and accurate, and history cannot be rewritten. Perhaps more important, this reporting process becomes a significant management tool for maintaining strategic focus and setting operational priorities. In addition, the board, as well as the venture manager, is thereby better able to provide assistance in planning, personnel development, marketing strategy and tactics, supplier relationships, and future financing requirements.

Corporate Venture Capital

Many financial institutions have separate subsidiaries to invest in business development situations that do not meet the parent's traditional standard investment or loan criteria. In addition, venture capital divisions have been founded by large industrial corporations such as GE and Xerox Corporation. The industrial subsidiaries using corporate funds function much like venture capital partnerships, but in addition to the normal motives, frequently operate as a "window on technology" for the parent industrial corporation. The unit therefore acquires equity holdings in a number of different companies, usually where the products, market, or technology is related to the corporation's operations, or where the business is of interest as a diversification opportunity. The better corporate venture funds are set up as separate profit centers, targeted at good returns, with management receiving a profit override. Where this has not been done, high turnover of venture managers has been prevalent and returns have been below par.

HOW VENTURE CAPITAL WORKS

At Adler & Company, we use five guidelines to investigate a possible investment. First, we have to see a large long-term profit potential. Forecastable market growth over an extended period is the key. Strong industry growth prospects are essential except when the product offers major productivity or cost savings in an existing mature market. One caveat: There are plenty of attractive businesses in markets of $10 million or more, and while individual entrepreneurs can earn a great deal of money in those businesses, venture investors do not. For a company to be an attractive investment vehicle for outside investors, it must have a potential that is significantly greater. Therefore, it does not usually pay to invest time and energy in companies unless the company can be expected to have sales of $50 million in five years, with a return on invested capital targeted at yielding 10 to 1 within seven years, although actual returns will average less. This requires gaining a large share in a substantial market or creating products of value in a rapidly growing industry. Strategic positioning is critical since building and maintaining a significant competitive advantage is the only method of reducing the risks inherent when smaller-sized companies compete with larger, well-financed, established companies.

Second, does the potential investee company have the right technology? Uniqueness or long lead time is important—technology moves rapidly and large, well-financed competitors can catch up on easily replicable technology, then use their better distribution channels to dominate small competitors.

Third, venture capitalists look for a market that allows a high level of profitability. This means that there is a strong likelihood of achieving a high positive cash flow from operations in a reasonable time frame. Cash is the lifeblood of any company. Companies that cannot generate cash suffer from anemia, cannot grow, and eventually die. It is therefore important to choose a market that is unlikely to experience severe and prolonged price competition before the company becomes well established. Timing is key. Venture capitalists prefer to back companies that sell in existing and growing markets. Conversely, enterprises that must build primary demand through a long educational process will run out of money. A company facing this problem can be described as the technological early bird that starves to death waiting for the worm.

Fourth is management. Venture capitalists look for the best available managers, preferably those who have substantial experience, or reasonable experience and great potential for growth. All venture capitalists hope for projects staffed with well-rounded teams of managers with proven track records, but because of the risk element, will usually settle for a very strong leader, first-rate engineers, and a generally young team overall. The potential for growth can take many forms: It not only involves a basic competence, but it also requires a willingness to talk, listen, and learn. In most successful investments, venture capital groups have a very close working relationship, both financially and operationally, with management. Senior management in venture enterprises tend to operate in a very open-minded, flexible, questioning fashion in order to obtain everyone's views. Exploring alternatives, "truth seeking," and brainstorming on key decisions with a high caliber team leads to better management decisions.

My firm has five characteristics in mind when we evaluate a venture manager. The first characteristic is judgment, the ability to think things through objectively and accurately. Second is aggressiveness, that is, determination, courage, and a refusal to accept defeat. Third, sincerity: A person who is not sincere with others is unlikely to be honest with himself. Fourth, experience: If you know the road, you can travel it faster and more safely than someone who doesn't. And finally, something that is difficult to define, but is best described as charisma: It is the strength of character necessary to attract and hold good people. The importance of the management team is most evident when a company is in trouble. At such a time, the problems are just too much for one or even two managers.

Under the fifth investigative guideline, active venture funds ask what they can bring to the investment. Of course, money is one essential element, but venture capitalists find that providing a great deal more than just money helps earn a greater return on investment. They provide assistance in securing sales, particularly in Europe; help in obtaining bank and other financing; help in finding personnel, including, where appropriate, additional management; setting up specialized reporting systems; assisting in strategic planning, including preparing market and technical data; generally through active participation on the board of directors. Although all venture firms make some purely passive investments, companies that use their venture investors the most tend to do the best. Again a caveat: Venture firms prefer to avoid getting involved in day-to-day operations, that is a poor use of time. On those occasions when they have done so, it is usually because management can't handle the job.

EXAMPLES OF THE VENTURE CAPITAL PROCESS

The following examples illustrate the venture capital process.

Data General Corporation

In 1967, it seemed clear that the advent of complex semiconductors was changing the face of the world, and that usage of small computers was increasing rapidly. In early 1968, a group of young engineers from Digital Equipment Corp., accompanied by a young regional sales manager from Fairchild Semiconductor Corp., asked me to join them in starting a brand new computer systems company—structuring it, raising funds, and being part of its team. The reasons the proposal was accepted were as follows:

1. The proposing group had enormous *drive,* a desire to make it work, and were willing and able to work long hours to do so.
2. They had similar *experience.* They had designed 8-bit computers and were taking the next step toward a more complex computer—a 16-bit, small computer with large computer architecture.
3. The sales and marketing man *had a successful track record* of selling to the computer industry and understood it well.
4. They were *committed.* They were willing to quit their jobs and invest a portion of their assets to build a major enterprise.
5. They were a *team.* They wanted to work together toward a common goal—the building of a major company.
6. They wanted to *reduce risks* involved in starting the company. They targeted something totally feasible rather than a machine either totally beyond the market's or their own capabilities.
7. Because they were using a new, just-designed family of more complex integrated circuits (medium-scale integration), they would have a substantial *time-performance lead* over potential competitors.
8. They believed in *substance,* not form. Money was a vehicle to reach an objective; *spending* money was not the objective. *Making* money by creating a major company was to be the proof of success.

Five of us started the company. We put in $50,000 in April of 1968. We raised $750,000 privately in June of 1968. We became a publicly traded company in 1969, and were listed on the New York Stock Exchange in 1973. Two founders took their profits and left. Three of us remain. The company grew rapidly. When it had problems, we simply worked harder to solve them. Data General now employs approximately 16,500 people, and had revenues of more than $1 billion last year.

Daisy Systems, Corp.

In September of 1980, a young engineering manager at Intel, a leading semiconductor manufacturer, proposed a new concept, a computer-based graphics workstation with application software aimed at helping improve the productivity of integrated circuit designers. Before he and his partner had approached me, they had been turned down by a number of venture capitalists.

As the president of a semiconductor company, Intersil, Inc., in 1975 and 1976, I had experienced firsthand, the shortage of fine circuit designers and understood the need for such a product. This belief was confirmed by the engineering people at Data General, by a leading academic expert in digital electronics, and by friendly engineering managers at various semiconductor companies. The need was there, the feasibility seemed likely, the lead time against competitors seemed impressive.

Checks on the two managers indicated that they were drivers—focused, ambitious perfectionists, who worked interminable hours—managers who picked the best engineers for their teams and were reputed to be very, very smart.

Their business plan, while ambitious, was realistic and well planned. Their proposed team members appeared first rate. Before the company went public in 1983, a total of $8 million had been invested, more than 10 times the initial amount of Data General. Today, the founders are multimillionaires. The Adler Group—my investors and my family—made over $140 million on less than $3 million. Daisy created a new industry (computer-aided engineering), gave jobs to almost 1,000 employees, and has an annualized sales rate of about $150 million.

Life Technologies, Inc.

Problems may be profitable—particularly when they are not yours. By 1981, a total of $15 million had been invested in an early-stage biotechnology company called Bethesda Research Laboratories (BRL) that made products for research laboratories. BRL tried to expand too fast and in too many directions.

In 1982, BRL ran out of cash, losing over $1 million per month. In February, we were brought in. Money was raised, the chief executive was changed, 300 of the 550 employees were let go, sales offices were closed, unprofitable and weak product areas were cut out, and assets were deployed to areas of strength. In about six months the company was at break-even point, and by December 1982 it was profitable.

In September of 1983, BRL merged with GIBCO, a division of Dexter Chemical, to form Life Technologies, and I became chairman. Both companies were reorganized, divisions were sold off, and additional scientists and new technologies were employed.

By late 1985, the combined company had about $23 million in cash, no debt, exciting new products, was very profitable, and employed 650 people. It is expected that the company will have a public stock offering in 1986. The investors who almost lost their money will end up making a profit. Even the entrepreneur who started the company and who was fired has become a multimillionaire.

DEALING WITH VENTURE CAPITALISTS

In deciding to approach a venture capital firm for funding, you should carefully consider which firms to contact. You should inquire about the reputation and integrity of the venture capitalists. Ask their portfolio company presidents for references. Do the partners have much relevant experience? Is the fund nearly fully invested? Can the fund provide continued expansion financing? What size investments does the firm make? In what types of businesses and at what stages of development has the firm made prior investments? What are current preferences, if any, in terms of industry or geographic location? These types of questions can help determine the fit between your company and a venture capital firm.

Approaching a venture capitalist is perhaps best accomplished through an introduction from an individual or organization with whom the venture capitalist is well acquainted. This could be someone who had brought them investments in the past, managers already operating within portfolio companies, or bankers or lawyers associated with them. Without a personal introduction, you should send a brief letter that summarizes your business plan and follow this up with a phone call. If a venture capitalist is interested in the potential investment, more information can be provided as needed.

THE BUSINESS PLAN

The heart of the presentation to any venture capital firm is the actual written proposal. The ideal proposal includes a business plan and a market analysis, with a full explanation of how and why the plan will work. It should discuss the problems—every company has or will have problems—and tell how they will be overcome. A proposal should be an analytical operational plan, not a sales pitch.

Most initial proposals are poorly constructed and poorly written. Sometimes entrepreneurs send proposals consisting of one-page cover letters attached to a copy of a patent. Some proposals look like the *Encyclopaedia Brittanica,* with endless but often meaningless statistical tables and graphs. Both types end up in wastepaper baskets.

The ideal proposal should generally include a one- or two-page summary of the plan that highlights its important features and opportunities, in order to catch the venture capitalist's attention. The summary should contain very brief statements about:

- The company's proposed activities, management, and performance.
- The distinguishing features of the products or service and the business strategy.
- The attractiveness of the market.
- A summary of financial projections, including the amount of money being sought and for what purpose.

The proposal itself should be concise and contain the following:

1. The short summary described above.
2. A description of the present stage of development, if any. In other words, trace the history of the business: when it was formed, how its products were chosen, and what roles each of the principals played. Describe any early problems and setbacks and what is being done to avoid their recurrence.
3. A description of the product or service being offered, including distinctive advantages of the products and services as well as the disadvantages. To whom will it sell and what is the cost justification for purchasing it? What is the nature and current condition of the industry? What are the important trends? An in-depth market analysis, citing support for figures, is usually very effective.
4. The main corporate objectives—what is to be achieved in the market and why, particularly sales and profitability goals.
5. The corporate/market strategy—how will it be implemented and how will it enable the company to build a lasting competitive edge?
6. The most significant risks that the company faces.
7. Lists of the names of all close competitor firms or products with a summary of their strengths and weaknesses both on an absolute basis and relative to the proposed new products. The same for probable future competitors. In doing so, pricing or anticipated selling prices for each product in the projected line should be compared to prices of competitive products on a performance basis.

8. Existing or potential customers, who have expressed an interest in the proposed products or who have rejected such interest.
9. A summary of the functional specifications of each product with a physical representation, if possible.
10. The key technologies and skills required to develop and manufacture the products, with an indication of products in which leading-edge technologies are involved, the problems anticipated, and how they may be overcome. Patents and any other proprietary rights.
11. The alternative sales channels or other distribution modes in detail.
12. Any after-market service operation and any major problems.
13. Cost-volume information with full breakdowns for material, labor, factory burden, and so on.
14. The manufacturing processes and facilities needed and the types and quantities of capital equipment needed, with costs and timing of purchase or lease.
15. A three-year, full cash flow chart, including monthly cash flow for the first year and quarterly cash flow for the other two years. If possible, investment should be related to achievement of stated goals, including, when the company reaches positive cash flow. Labor and plant space requirements over the three-year period (by month and quarter as above).
16. Pro forma balance sheets for the current and two prior years, if applicable, and five years of annual projections.
17. Profit and loss statements for the current and two prior years, if applicable, and five years of pro forma projections. Also include best case, worst case, and expected revenue projections.
18. A summary of the proposed deal.
19. Resumes of all key people with the percentage of insider shares owned by each, proposed or current salary, and salary at last independent job.

In short, the best proposals give precise information and are concise and candid about the company's problems as well as its successes.

After a plan is submitted, the venture capital firm will do a "due diligence" investigation if it is seriously interested in considering a proposal. This investigation includes an analysis of product, technical and marketing considerations, a review of the financial plan and a check on the background and potential of the management team. Many venture firms retain a number of consultants in a variety of fields for this purpose. Often, during the "due diligence" process, the plan goes through iterations encouraged by the venture capitalist to make it more realistic and achievable. The process may seem long and difficult, but it is one of the most valuable services a venture capitalist can offer to the would-be entrepreneur.

SUMMARY

Largely because of venture capital's well-publicized association with the technology revolution of recent years, the venture capitalist occasionally (particularly when the stock market is up) seems to have become a new kind of folk hero. Venture capitalists have been credited with playing the catalystic role of awakening the entrepreneurial instincts of scientists and engineers from large corporations and academic institutions, who have left those jobs and founded large numbers of leading-edge companies that have achieved great stock market valuations.

All this is a bit overdone. Basically, a venture capitalist is simply someone who invests his own and others' money in a business with growth potential and, hopefully, outstanding management. The venture capitalist is interested in protecting the investment, so the ultimate goal is to get managers to manage better. Venture capitalists by staying close to and informed about their investments become backboards for ideas, they help managers become their own management consultants, and if they improve efficiency just a small amount, the returns will be even greater. The venture capitalist is a participatory investor, unlike the investment banker or ordinary shareholder. When he does a good job, profits go up and losses go down. When he does a bad job, he bears the loss.

PART B Overview of Venture Capital*

INTRODUCTION

Venture capital has received enormous attention in the last few years and is now recognized as an important factor in our nation's business development and revitalization process. Entrepreneurs' interest has been spurred by the success of role model companies that were developed with venture capital financing, for example, Apple Computer, Federal Express, and Lotus Development. The reduction of the capital gains tax in 1978, together with the institutional investor's search for high-potential investment rewards, led to a rapid increase in the

* Part B was written by Stanley E. Pratt.

amount of venture capital available. Entrepreneurs, seeing both opportunities and the resources needed to capitalize upon them, ushered in the 1980s with a burst of activity.

For most of the 1970s, venture capital had been a low-profile activity showing virtually no growth for seven years. Compared with the providers of other forms of financing described in this book, venture capital has only recently become recognized as a distinct profession, and it is important to delineate venture capitalist roles and methods of operation.

Venture capital is seen by many as the early-stage financing of new and young companies seeking to grow rapidly. This is true for many venture capitalists, and for some it is the sole or principal focus of their activities. The venture capital industry, however, and most of its firms, provide a wide range of development financing for viable, private companies that are not yet at the stage where they can attract funding from credit-oriented institutions like insurance companies and banks, or conventional stock market equity investors. Venture capitalists may even participate in the public stock market where their support of management can have an impact on the building of greater future value for the business.

The characteristics of venture capital, be it for early- or expansion-stage companies, are:

- Equity participation directly through the purchase of shares, or indirectly via warrants, options, and convertible debentures.
- Involvement of the venture investor in a partnership relationship with the management, thereby adding value—bringing more than money—to the business.
- Long-term (five- to seven-year) orientation with capital gains from the building of additional value being the main objective.

The equity interests help to bring about the needed partnership, sharing the common objectives of ownership, between entrepreneurs and venture capitalists. The venture capitalist also needs the unlimited upside potential, but limited downside risk, of equity ownership. In a venture portfolio, a few big winners that return many times the investment can offset many disappointments that only lose the actual amount of the capital invested. This important dynamic of venture capital funds enables investors to seek significant investment returns from a number of high-risk opportunities where the chances are far greater for losers than winners.

The value added is what really differentiates venture capital from traditional investment and makes it truly "the business of developing businesses." Venture capitalists should not run businesses, but should provide real assistance and support for the management team. The experience of the venture investor who has worked with numerous new business developments can often be a critical factor for success. Building a business is always a difficult task, and the ongoing involvement of a committed team is a key facilitator.

The building of real and lasting values requires dedication and hard work over a long period. While most of the traditional investment markets are dominated by a trading mentality for short-term profits, successful venture capital investments must be driven by a long-term orientation. Stock market investors consider six months long term, and are often driven by quarterly, monthly, and even daily performance. Venture capitalists generally identify their bad investments within three years, but their winners can often take five to seven years to emerge as proven successes. Building takes time, but the rewards from long-term development generally eclipse short-term, often illusory, profits.

In this chapter, the focus is on professional venture capitalists who spend all or most of their time on managing venture investments and who have the experience and expertise as well as the financial resources needed to contribute to the growth of companies that they back. It should be noted, however, that some individuals investing informally can and do play a supportive role and are particularly important as providers of seed capital to back an idea before a formal business can be identified.

Since the venture capital profession is growing so rapidly, it is now more important than ever for entrepreneurs to select their backers as carefully as possible, paying particular attention to expected future relationships. Those who have founded and built extraordinarily successful new businesses with venture capital often stress that who your backers are is far more important than the precise terms on which they invest, especially in the early stages. The entrepreneur must examine the venture investor just as carefully as the venture capitalist examines a new opportunity. Different venture firms have different skills, and a five- to seven-year productive relationship requires personal chemistry from day one. The partnership selection process is a very critical first step in successful business development.

WHEN TO CONSIDER VENTURE CAPITAL

Basically, venture capital should be considered when the rapid growth to a substantial-sized business (annual sales of $30 million and up) is both contemplated and credible. Such growth will require significant amounts of capital investment, often in several rounds of financing. Debt or loan capital is not generally appropriate either because it cannot be obtained on the basis of the guarantees that the founders can give, or will prove to be too great a burden on the venture. What is needed is equity capital as well as support and guidance to achieve ambitious objectives. When the resources of the founding management team are not adequate to meet the requirements, this equity capital will often be sought from venture capitalists. If the business is at an early stage, it is particularly important that the venture capitalists chosen can provide the needed business development skills and experience to supplement and enhance the management team's own capabilities.

WHAT ENTREPRENEURS AND VENTURE CAPITALISTS EXPECT FROM ONE ANOTHER

Having decided that venture capital investment fits your corporate objectives and makes sense for your company financially, you should ponder its implications for you and your management team. Consider what you can expect of the venture capitalists and what they will expect of you.

In addition to providing the risk capital you need in the form of equity and/or equity-linked subordinated debt, venture capitalists should be able to provide introductions to and credibility with potential customers and suppliers. They should also help find and screen additional members of your management team, and support this effort with their expertise and experience. When you confront a problem, they should be ready to share their experience with similar problems in other ventures that they have backed. This will require unique commitment, and the results of past involvements of the venture capitalists should be carefully examined. This applies, particularly, to ongoing requirements for additional capital after the initial investment: Once they have a stake in the future of your company, the venture capitalists' interest in its continued growth will be equal to yours. You should expect them to focus on the needs of the company. While these may not always coincide with your own needs as manager, they should coincide with yours as shareholder. These nonfinancial contributions by venture capitalists are made as partners, not as service providers—there is normally no fee involved; the rewards come from the building of equity value.

For their part, the venture capitalists will want a significant participation in the equity of your company, through which they hope to realize a profit within five to seven years by selling all or part of their equity interests. If you have no intention of ever going public or being acquired, you will find it hard to raise substantial amounts of venture capital.

The venture capitalists will want to be convinced that you view your relationship with them as a partnership. They may want to serve on your board or nominate someone with experience in your industry to do so. They will make their decision to invest because they believe that you and your management team can build a company rapidly and successfully. They will expect you to make the decisions, having consulted with them on issues of strategic importance. In the ordinary course of business, they will expect open discussion of concerns and problems. Forewarning will enable them to assist and support you while surprises will endanger productive working relationships.

Given the nature of these expectations, it is clearly important to find the right venture capitalist. Make sure that good personal chemistry exists—that you respect *and* like each other. You are likely to go through some tough times and be together for many years before success overshadows prior problems.

HOW TO CHOOSE VENTURE CAPITALISTS

In times when venture capital is hard to raise, even well-qualified managements with unusually exciting opportunities can find it tempting to view all dollars alike. You will do better if you establish some criteria and make that extra effort needed to find the right investor with whom you can work closely and effectively. The first criterion to be considered is their ability to provide adequate amounts of capital, alone or through a syndicate. Past performance, alone, is no proof of this. You need to know that they are currently liquid and actively investing and in a position to support a multiyear development program.

Second, a venture investor willing and capable of assuming substantial involvement and/or principal monitoring responsibilities should be located close to your business, if possible. Syndicate members of an investor group from out of town like to have a respected local venture capitalist assist you in the development of your business.

Third, your potential partner should have an interest in and a good knowledge of your industry, since this will not only facilitate the evaluation of your proposal more rapidly but also contribute, subsequently, to the growth of your business. Relate your needs to the specific skills, expertise, and experience of the potential venture capitalist.

Fourth, you should establish that your lead venture investor has a good reputation in the venture capital community. Do other venture capital firms work well with the group you are considering? Does the firm have a reputation for fair and prompt dealing and for taking the time to work closely with portfolio companies? Some venture investors have large funds, but if they are almost fully invested, their attention may be focused on the investments they have already made and they may not be able to devote the time needed to evaluate and support yours.

Finally, there is the most important issue of all, personal chemistry. You need to develop a real sense that you can get on with the venture capitalists with whom you are dealing, since this will greatly ease your way through the difficulties that you inevitably encounter subsequent to the investment.

HOW TO DEAL WITH VENTURE CAPITALISTS

The first word that the venture capitalist hears of your venture should ideally be from someone whom the venture capitalist already knows. The best reference is from an entrepreneur with whom the venture capitalist has a good working relationship. You should speak with your banker, lawyer, accountant, and any existing private investors, and ask them if they know venture capitalists likely to be interested. These advisers can help refine your choice and, hopefully, make an introduction. The best number of venture capitalists to approach, initially, is around five or six. This enables you to get started with a reasonable number, without appearing to be shopping around. It also avoids the problem of approaching just one or two, learning two or three weeks later that neither are interested, and then having to start all over again with the next two or three venture capitalists.

The best way to use the introduction is to call the venture capitalist directly, mentioning the name of the introducer and then following it up with your business plan, reiterating the name of the introducer. Venture capitalists prefer to work with the management team that will be responsible for the business development, even from the beginning. The venture capitalist may know your accountants or lawyers very well, but will wonder if having them make the initial presentation reflects a lack of confidence on your part in being able to attract and stimulate their attention.

The written business plan that you send to the venture capitalist should spell out the potential of the business and the capabilities of the team you have assembled or are putting together to realize that potential. A description of the management team and its relationship to, and delineation of, a clear market niche opportunity are the most critical points to be covered in the business plan. You may have heard that there are three factors to consider in real estate investments: location, location, and location. In venture capital there are five principal factors:

Management
Management
Management
Market Niche
Product or Service

Entrepreneurs often tend to overemphasize the product in business plans in the expectation that the world will beat a path to the door with a better mousetrap. To attract venture capital, you must demonstrate your ability to build a business, not just a product.

It is particularly important that you show that you and your team understand the marketplace in which you plan to establish your business. You must be able to demonstrate your ability to develop and execute a plan of action for building your business. The business plan provides you with an opportunity to display your team's skills and outline your tactics and strategies. Though you may use help from outsiders in developing the plan, it is important that it is fundamentally your own and that it be thought through and personally completed by you and your team. By all means, have the outsiders suggest what should be in the plan, if you have not had the experience of putting one together before, but resist offers to have sections of the plan written by outsiders or your financials prepared by your accountant. These advisers should be the critics of what you do. The plan must be your own responsibility and must be a reflection of what you honestly believe can be accomplished.

It is important that you present an achievable set of expectations, particularly in early revenue projections. These should be directly linked to the data you present on existing or future market needs so that the venture capitalist can see and, more importantly, believe that there is an opportunity to build a business in the niche you have identified and delineated. Once these projections have been made, you should be prepared to alter them if the venture capitalist can convince you that they are unrealistic. Avoid indicating lack of confidence by being too flexible and quick to change, but equally, do not be inflexible and stubborn.

In dealing with a venture capitalist, you should be prepared for at least a three- to six-month period between the first contact and a final investment. During this time of what may be termed a courtship or an investigation you should carefully track your own performance and that of the venture capitalist. If you are responsive to his requests in a timely manner and he does not reciprocate, this may indicate his relative lack of interest in your venture compared with others he is considering. You can, within a week or two, expect to know whether or not any one firm is seriously interested. Although the investigation can at times be wearying, the checking of the management, the analysis of the market, the technical and product considerations, and the financial implications do require significant time. It is much better that it be done thoroughly at the outset than have surprises develop later. If the venture capitalist spots a flaw in your plan, it is much better to correct it initially than to run into a problem in the marketplace later. The process of investigation can be hastened if the data you present in your business plan are fully substantiated.

While this is going on, you, the entrepreneur, should be conducting a complete investigation of the venture capitalists showing interest in the venture, particularly contacting the managements of other companies in which they have invested. It is important not to talk just to those who are the jewels in the venture capitalist's crown but also to those with whom there have been difficulties. You should know how the venture capitalist behaves when the going gets rough. Most important of all, you need to develop a sense of whether there will be mutual trust between you and the venture capitalist and whether you can work effectively together over an extended period, through thick and thin.

In setting out to establish a relationship with a venture capitalist, it is important to start as you mean to carry on. Be yourself, not as you think the venture capitalist wants you to be. Long-term relationships must be built upon solid foundations.

In the negotiating phase, it is important that decisions be taken by you and your management team. Your attorneys, accountants, and other advisers can certainly help in developing your preliminary positions and also in reviewing any proposals that the venture capitalist makes. But it is not a good idea to rely on them in meetings with investors. It is, at this point, that the future expectations of the business, as set out in the business plan, are tested. The venture capitalist's view of the value of the business three to five years out and the entrepreneur's view are unlikely to be the same, but there must be a willingness to work together to achieve mutual understanding and compromise.

The matter of valuing a new business is an important issue in the negotiations. Entrepreneurs should understand that valuations at any point in time are markedly influenced by external market conditions that may have little relationship to the ultimate worth of the company. For example, euphoric times produce unrealistically high valuations in the heated competition for opportunities. Subsequently, the pendulum will swing too far back toward low valuations in depressed market conditions. It is important that entrepreneurs understand these cycles in order to establish reasonable expectations. The critical first step is to complete the first financing, rather than to get that extra few points in the initial price of your shares. Pricing is not as important in early-stage financings, when returns are expected to be many times cost, as it will be in later stages, when potential return may be a lower increment.

Another important issue that will come up in negotiations is the difference between ownership and control. Here the venture capitalist's intention is that the management team it backs normally controls the business and the venture capitalist should play a supportive role. In situations where the initial risks are very high, or where the amount of capital is very significant, the ownership interest needed to attract investment may require more than a majority of the equity. In these cases, the investment will often be split between several venture capitalists, and over time, with additional financings, the interests of each single investor will usually be reduced. In any event, management will normally control the day-to-day operations, a function that most venture capitalists seek to avoid. There have been numerous cases when venture capitalists have introduced programs, such as stock options or warrant plans, to increase the ownership interests of a management team during, and even after, successful developments. The bottom line to remember is that, very often, a smaller piece of a larger pie is far more rewarding than a larger piece of a smaller pie—and that it is critical to get the pie made in the first place.

If the business deviates significantly from plan, the venture capitalist as an owner of a minority equity interest or his representatives on the board of directors will generally want the authority to change the management. You should make sure that you accept the possibility, even in the event of great success, that you and/or members of your team may have to play different and less crucial roles in later years.

The entrepreneur should expect that capital committed by the venture capitalist will be made available in a series of stages dependent on the progress of the business. The rounds of financing concept has enabled the development of many businesses where the capital required was obviously too great to risk prior to the attainment of specific objectives. In some cases a large amount of initial financing would result in an investor-owner position that would not leave enough incentive for the management team. By staging the investment to be provided, hopefully at increased valuations with each round, the investor is able to limit the early risk exposure and the management team can retain greater ownership through successful development.

Once an investment has been made, it is important that the entrepreneur and the venture capitalist immediately devote enough time to develop a close working relationship. With early-stage businesses, this could involve meeting as frequently as once a week. With established ventures, the meetings might only be quarterly. In all cases there will be substantial time spent on the phone between meetings, and there will be many informal discussions and meetings.

DEVELOPMENT AND STRUCTURE OF THE VENTURE CAPITAL INDUSTRY

In going through the process of choosing and dealing with venture capitalists, you should develop some understanding of how the profession is organized.

The industry had its origins with individuals and families investing informally. Some of these families, such as the Rockefellers and the Whitneys, formalized their activities, creating a private company or limited partnership, and putting their investments under professional management. The first manifestation of venture capital from institutional investors, the dominant sector of our nation's capital markets, was American Research and Development Corporation, founded in 1946. The next major development was the creation of the Small Business Investment Companies under the Small Business Investment Act of 1958, which led to a rapid expansion of the venture industry and the introduction of many new firms. Though many of these federally licensed leveraged vehicles did not survive the tests of time, those that did played an important role in the evolution of the venture industry. The other principal category of venture investor includes subsidiaries of financial and industrial corporations, whose involvement has varied in both nature and extent over the past 20 years.

Independent Private Firms

As the industry has evolved, independent private firms have become the dominant category. At the end of 1984, 271 of these firms managed $11.8 billion of the 509 professional venture capital firms with $16.3 billion. Most of these firms are organized and operate as partnerships, with a limited life of 7 to 12 years. This enables the professional venture capitalists who manage them to have a relatively long-term orientation while providing a return to investors within a reasonable time period. The investors' capital is locked in for long enough to allow the ventures in their portfolio to develop. The funds are not expected to pay interest or declare dividends. The investors are willing to commit their capital for this period in the hope that it will be returned with very significant profits when the fund is liquidated. Since liquidity is a prerequisite to achieving investment returns, venture capitalists must plan to sell or exit from their investments during this 7- to 12-year period.

The limited partners of these partnerships include pension funds, corporations, wealthy families and individuals, endowments, foundations, insurance companies, and foreign investors. The managing partners of these partnerships are the professional venture capitalists, providing a conduit through which passive investors can participate in the financing of new and young companies. The size of these funds generally range from $10 million to $75 million, though some are over $100 million and some specialized early-stage funds are under $10 million. They normally make 10 to 15 new commitments a year, ranging from $100,000 to several million per company.

Small Business Investment Companies (SBICs)

SBICs are licensed by the federal government to specialize in small business investment. While there were 391 SBICs at the end of 1984, only 143 of them are so-called venture SBICs and invest as part of the venture capital industry. The others are classified as lenders that make loans to small businesses that are normally not perceived to have the potential to become major enterprises. The venture capital SBICs have private capital of $500,000 to $10 million that can generally be leveraged with government guaranteed loans providing up to four times the private capital.

The venture SBICs operate in a manner very similar to the independent private firms in the sense that they invest in both early- and expansion-stage financings. There is, however, a greater diversity among SBICs, since they are a source of financing for the more moderate growth business. These may often involve less risk and greater predictability and are therefore appropriate for financings where subordinated debt is involved. SBICs often require income in the form of interest as well as planned debt reduction, in order to service their own debt payments.

Minority groups and U.S. military Vietnam veterans can raise capital from a special class of SBICs, called MESBICs (Minority Enterprise Small Business Investment Companies). They operate like SBICs, but their investments are focused toward the needs of the minority entrepreneur.

Corporate Venture Capital Subsidiaries

By the end of 1984, there were some 95 venture capital firms handling almost $2.9 billion that were subsidiaries of larger corporations. These break into two categories, 51 corporate subsidiaries of financial organizations, and 44 corporate subsidiaries of industrial corporations.

Most of the financial subsidiary venture capitalists are part of commercial bank holding companies that have set up separate groups

EXHIBIT 1 Types of Venture Capital Firms at 1984 Year-End

	Number of Firms	*Amount (millions)*
Independent private funds	271	$11,800
SBICs exclusive of nonventure capital–related funds	143	1,638
Corporate, financial, industrial, and non-SBIC public funds	95	2,870
	509	$16,308

SOURCE: Venture Economics, Inc.

(often in addition to an SBIC) to make business development investments. These subsidiaries are often called 5 percent funds since their capital is limited to 5 percent of the parent's capital and they may not own more than 5 percent of the voting stock of an investee. This latter restriction is often overcome by the use of preferred stock and warrants that do not give the investor voting rights. These groups generally invest in expansion financings and management buyouts rather than start-up and early-stage developments. Their commitments normally range from $1 million to $5 million with no particular industry focus.

Industrial corporate subsidiaries are often looking to achieve more than a financial return through their venture capital investment activities. They often look to invest in businesses related to the operations of the parent—be it technologies deemed of interest or products that could be sold through the parent's market and distribution channels.

In the late 1960s and early 1970s, direct investment by industrial corporations was popular, in order to view the "window of technology." Today, however, corporate investors realize that it is necessary for the small business to be independently profitable. Consequently, corporate investors seek investment success as a principal objective and often invest alongside private partnerships.

Industrial corporate venture capital groups will invest in both early-stage operations, where technology assistance can be crucial, and later-stage development, where market and distribution channels can assist the young business.

Exhibit 1 indicates the relative size of the three segments described above.

Geographic Location of Venture Capital

The geographic spread of venture capital resources in the United States at year-end 1984 is illustrated in Exhibit 2.

EXHIBIT 2 Distribution of Industry Resources by Leading States at 1984 Year-End

	Capital (millions)		*Offices*	
		Percent of Total		*Percent of Total*
California	$5,296	32%	173	27%
New York	3,262	20	95	15
Massachusetts	2,054	13	60	9
Illinois	863	5	23	4
Connecticut	794	5	21	3
Texas	775	5	54	9
Minnesota	380	2	15	2
Maryland	342	2	9	1
Pennsylvania	305	2	15	2
New Jersey	285	2	12	2
Ohio	256	2	15	2

SOURCE: Venture Economics, Inc. (Wellesley Hills, Mass.).

While it is clear that the three leading states—California, New York, and Massachusetts—dominate as sources of venture capital, in recent years there has been a definite dispersion of venture capital availability throughout the country. In 1984, venture capital investment in areas outside the three leading states was greater than the entire industry's investment activity in 1980. In addition, the funds located in the three leading states with 65 percent of the capital are increasingly investing more capital outside their home state. In 1985, it was clear that venture capitalists were broadening their investments beyond the technology orientation of the past few years. This should lead toward increased activity from business development outside the traditional East Coast and West Coast orientation.

Technological and Industry Focus of Venture Capital

One of the most prevelant misconceptions about venture capital is that venture capitalists only invest in high technology. In fact, most venture capital investments are in applications of existing technology to develop products and services that meet clearly defined market needs. To be successful, developing businesses must focus on market factors rather than products. Studies by Venture Economics, Inc. have shown that the most important single factor in venture capital investments is that the products or services are related to productivity increase. This is easy to understand if you consider that a product or service that saves the end user money or makes the end user more efficient—a simple definition of productivity increase—is obviously the easiest product or service to market.

Venture capitalists seldom finance research and development, but rather the building of the capability to produce and sell new products with clear market niches. In 1983, a number of venture capitalists overlooked the importance of market niches and financed too many "me-too" products such as microcomputers and disk drives. Entrepreneurs, however, should not be misled by that activity, and should concentrate on market niche factors in their search for financing.

As the transition of our society from an industrial base to an information base accelerates, venture capitalists will be investing in an even wider spectrum of industries. Service businesses and consumer-related products and services are attracting greater shares of professional venture capital investment. As this industry view broadens, it is clear that the geographic locations of businesses backed by venture capital will also expand.

Specialization and Cooperation

It is important that entrepreneurs understand how venture capitalists work together to support the development of new businesses. Venture capitalists specialize by industry, by stage (seed, start-up, expansion, or buyout), or by geographic location. The cooperation takes the form of the sharing of specific expertise and resources. This is generally accomplished through a syndicate process whereby different venture capital firms can be brought together to focus their particular skills in a given financing. These syndications will designate lead investors who work directly with the entrepreneur.

A way of determining how to locate venture capital firms with different foci and expertise is to consult *Pratt's Guide to Venture Capital Sources*, (10th edition) published by Venture Economics, Inc., Wellesley Hills, Massachusetts, which shows the project preferences of venture capital firms in terms of stage, geography, and industry. In addition, the *Guide* identifies the venture capitalists and shows the amount of capital under management as well as some indication as to the extent of the firm's recent venture investment activity.

TIMING AND TRENDS

When considering the feasibility of raising venture capital, it is important to note the current trends in venture investing that may influence your chances for success. For example, in 1981, professional venture capitalists sought out start-up and early-stage opportunities when other investors were making later-stage venture investments. In 1984 and 1985, many established venture capital firms were concentrating on current portfolio companies, and much of the start-up financing came from venture capitalists specializing in early-stage investments. In 1985, many venture capitalists, learning from prior mistakes with "me-too" investments, were placing particular emphasis on unique market niches. The applications software industry, which until a year ago was much favored by venture capitalists, is an example of how particular types of ventures can become more difficult to finance in a short period of time.

While investment decisions were often reached very quickly in 1983, the subsequent difficulties of many companies financed at that time have influenced venture capitalists to be more selective and take the time to conduct in-depth analysis. By 1985, the time to complete financings was back up to three to six months versus two to three months in 1983. If capital is currently required in too short a period of time, this may indicate difficulties and might block the ability to attract long-term financing. Remember that venture capital is a long-term process, and taking the time to locate and attract the right investor is most often a very worthwhile investment.

SUMMARY

Venture capital is now recognized as a critical segment of the business development process. While entrepreneurs, the individuals that accept the enormous demands and risks of managing new businesses, are the key component, a working partnership with venture capitalists can often mean the difference between success and failure.

This partnership must be entered into with a long-term view, recognizing that new business development is never easy and that there will be many traps, pitfalls, and frustrations along the way. The common objective of both the entrepreneur and the venture capitalist must be to create and build lasting value.

To justify the very intensive development process, professional venture capitalists seek major growth opportunities. While the focus in the early 1980s was apparently almost exclusively on high technology, this is really quite misleading. Most successful developments with venture capital have been applications of existing technology for products and services that fulfill market needs. The most important common factor for success is productivity increase, products or services that save money for the end user or make him more efficient.

The availability of venture capital has grown dramatically in the early 1980s, but so had the demand for it. The process of making venture capital investment is highly selective, with less than 5 percent of the opportunities reviewed by venture capitalists actually funded. To underscore the difficulties, it should be noted that most of the businesses that do achieve financing will not turn out to be successful investments for the investor.

The megatrends that are transforming the U.S. and even the world economy from an industrial base to an information base are creating and stimulating new opportunities for entrepreneurs. The 1980s will go down in history as the decade of entrepreneurship. The opportunities are increasing in diversity and are spreading geographically into new national and even international areas.

There will always be economic cycles that will influence venture capital and the business development process. But most short-term cycles bring new opportunities for long-term development. If entrepreneurs and their venture capitalists have truly long-term views, the time to begin is usually now. The rewards for successful new business development can be exceptional, both in terms of material wealth created and of personal satisfaction. Those who decide to join the turbulent and demanding world of venture development need and deserve congratulations, condolences, and good luck.

PART C Using Venture Capital*

THE ENTREPRENEUR–VENTURE CAPITALIST RELATIONSHIP

From the very outset of any quest for venture funding, it is important to understand the often symbiotic relationship that exists between entrepreneur and venture capitalist. The extent to which that relationship works can be an important determinant of the success of entrepreneurial aspirations. The relationship forms an equation to which the entrepreneur brings an idea and the management skills and commitment to propel it along the road to success. The venture capitalist contributes not only the financial fuel to keep the enterprise rolling, but may lend a great deal of business savvy to complement the entrepreneur's strengths and energy. In the lexicon of today, it is crucial for the entrepreneur to understand where the venture capitalist "is coming from" so as to establish the most productive relationship. As contrasted with investment in the public marketplace, private venture capitalists are more likely "active" rather than "passive" investors, committed to the successful development of the business they are un-

* Part C was written by Alan B. Miller.

derwriting. Unlike public investors operating within the liquidity of a public marketplace, they can't simply walk away from an investment should problems arise. Of course, the public marketplace is often a later step along the road for a venture investor, taken after initial performance has demonstrated the prospects for success.

FINDING THE APPROPRIATE VENTURE CAPITALIST

The venture marketplace is oriented toward start-up and early-stage financing, that all-important and risky commitment to a new enterprise. But even within the parameters of early-stage financing, there exists a range of stages at which different venture firms specialize and participate. One firm might specialize in seed financing, another in research and development financing, still others in start-up or first-stage financing. As companies grow and mature, other stages of financing will attract still other venture firms. It is important for the entrepreneur to research the venture community carefully in the interest of saving time and avoiding frustration. Identify which firms tend to specialize in which business sectors, and at what stage of a company's developmental needs they are likely to participate.

Venture firm directories provide a valuable resource for investigation and screening of firms that may meet your particular needs. Research will reveal what firms are active in what business sectors, and at what level of commitment. Further investigation will provide a more detailed profile of these firms, including geographic preferences that may influence their investment decisions, and at what stage of business development they are likely to participate. Select likely prospects and approach them individually. The venture community is a small one, and firms will look askance at deals they suspect are shopworn and have been rejected within their fraternity.

Our thinking at Universal Health Services in seeking out the most appropriate venture firm for our needs was based on our original strategy of developing a national company rapidly, primarily by acquisition. We did not intend to acquire a single hospital, digest it for a year, and then acquire another, a timetable that would have given us no more than 10 or 20 hospitals over a 20-year period. Our plans were far more ambitious and projected growth at a far more accelerated rate. We had the confidence and experience to move more rapidly as a result of having managed a large and successful national company. From the outset, therefore, we sought large venture groups with extensive resources and the ability to invest more and more capital as needed.

Large venture groups are like any other substantial investor. Once they have made a credit analysis and taken the time to assess management, its reputation, and business plan, they want to make a meaningful investment, not nickels and dimes. They only have a finite number of situations they can investigate and negotiate, and when they find the right situation, they want to make a sizable investment. We wanted a group that could put up substantial equity, so we went to a venture subsidiary of a major money center bank which, in 1978, was the largest venture capital source available. We were fortunate in that the venture community was not that large at the time. It has since expanded and many, many firms now seek promising investment opportunities.

WHAT VENTURE CAPITALISTS LOOK FOR

You and Your Management Team

On a personal level, it's important for the entrepreneur to determine if he truly possesses the entrepreneurial characteristics necessary to succeed, as well as the characteristics and attributes the venture capitalist is looking for. It is generally agreed that the venture capitalist regards the entrepreneur and his management team as the most important elements of a new business proposal. A class A entrepreneur with a class B idea is preferred to a class B entrepreneur with a class A idea. Teams, not one-man bands, are also important. Every enterprise has its guiding light, but the venturists want to see strong capabilities across a broad range of management skills. Tough introspection is necessary to determine if you possess the characteristics of a successful entrepreneur.

Many attributes are intangible and your assessment must be objective and candid. Examine your drive and energy level, your self-confidence, your ability to set challenging yet realistic goals, and your commitment to stay the course over a period of difficult developmental years. Are you a problem solver? Can you learn from failure and use criticism constructively? As the impetus behind an enterprise, can you attract the individuals necessary to complement your skills, and can you delegate responsibility and inspire a true team effort?

If your goal is to build a multimillion dollar business, and venture capitalists are not interested in ideas of limited potential, you must attract a management team with the proven ability to perform such critical functions as marketing and sales, operations, engineering, finance, management and administration, and other specialities that your business may require. Venture capitalists look for teams of individuals with strong credentials in all of the requisite skill areas. Too often teams are comprised of college buddies or co-workers in the office or lab. These are people you know well, but they may not have the range of talents to direct diversified functions in a rapidly expanding business. Teams comprised only of fellow marketing types, technicians, engineers, or family members will wave a red flag in the face of the venture capitalist.

At the founding of Universal Health Services, we were already successful hospital managers with an outstanding record. It's much easier to secure financing if you have a proven record for success in your business. In addition to our track record, and the individual abilities of our management group of six, we were also prepared to invest, in total, $1 million. The personal investment of officers of a new business is a commitment that impresses venture firms and demonstrates tangible evidence of confidence. For our first-stage financing we put up $1 million and our venture partners—subsidiaries of three major banks—put up over $3 million, approximately $1 million each. Later we got a $20 million line from a major money center bank; but one of the key elements in the foundation of the business was the $1 million of personal finances that we put at risk. We put ourselves on the line and were recognized as having a great deal at stake.

The bank, Manufacturers Hanover Trust, which had been our lead bank at the previous business and had monitored our activities very closely over a period of years, came on board as a result of their confidence in our future, and the fact that we had already generated $4 million in equity. They knew that we would have to expand it as we spent their funds. In essence, they had a cushion. To reiterate, we achieved our objectives by building one block on top of another. The key blocks were management, personal investment, the business opportunity, and the financial resources we attracted.

Our management capabilities were well documented, and when the venture partners saw our financial commitment they became believers. They knew we had made a substantial amount of money from the American Medicorp sale and were concerned that we might dabble in the new venture. But the money we were willing to lay on the line converted any concern to confidence.

The subsequent bank loan was strictly secured, with availability determined by the value of our hospital acquisitions. When we had a hospital to acquire, the bank would extend financing toward that acquisition on a formula based on the collateral value of the asset. The loan was certainly not a blind pool without accountability.

Market Potential and Market Niche

Venture firms are looking for companies that have been conceived to fill demonstrable needs. Regardless of the business sector, or grade

A versus grade B considerations, all companies ultimately financed by venture firms share a number of characteristics. They demonstrate a potential for growth in the 30 to 50 percent range per annum, at least in the initial stages. Good management is the most vital ingredient. However, a growth market must be evident to provide the environment in which good management can excel. The market should also be of sufficient size to support growth potential of $100 million in five years. Market size and a strongly demonstrated product need are both prerequisites for venture attention. It's a rare situation in which a venture firm will support a product in search of a market.

In addition to overall market potential, a business seeking venture support should demonstrate the capacity to secure a niche within that market and vigorously exploit it. Every business should strive to dominate a market niche by competing more effectively within that niche than anyone else. Look at the automotive industry. There are literally hundreds of parts manufacturers that are successful because they have identified their niche and consolidated their hold on it. In seeking venture funding it is also important to demonstrate a potential for high gross profit margins in your business sector. Wide margins can compensate for a myriad of errors or miscalculations in the launching and nurturing of a new business. Finally, visibility in the marketplace is an asset. From day one, venture capitalists are assessing the opportunity to cash in on their investment by selling privately or going public, and the potential for recognition is a quality that does not escape their attention. Certainly, a management team with a record of note is desirable because it can be expected to provide an attractive public vehicle, should the venture prove at all successful. This is what the investors really are seeking.

Specific venture capital firms tend to concentrate on specific industry sectors, having acquired a knowledge that enables them to analyze proposals and make financing determinations based on experience and contacts within the industry. During the early to mid-1980s, such sectors as data communications, computer software and peripherals, communications, and medical and health-related areas were commanding the largest investment percentages, both in terms of the number of investments and the dollar amounts. In future years, the glamour areas may be robotics, genetic engineering, or a field yet unknown. Today, much venture money has been redirected to leveraged buyout opportunities. Technology-related companies with the capability to produce products cheaper and perhaps better than competition are always likely to attract venture interest. Industries that are not "hot" will find venture dollars harder to come by, although the recognition of grade A entrepreneurs in grade B business opportunities is often sufficient to generate interest.

In seeking venture financing, it is important to remember the discouraging statistics of ventures funded versus applicants, and to present yourself in the most professional manner possible with all prerequisite information for funding clearly enumerated. Probably 60 percent of all proposals that cross the desk of a venture capitalist are rejected after the most perfunctory scan. Another 25 percent are reviewed for a short time and rejected. The remaining 15 percent are investigated in depth, whereupon two thirds are turned down because of deficiencies in the business plan or management team. Negotiations are pursued with the remaining 5 percent, of which 3 percent come to terms with the investor group and are funded. Those are the odds you are up against, and in view of your 3-in-100 chance, it behooves you to approach the objective with a clear understanding of what a venture capitalist wants to see, and a business plan that indicates and addresses all such areas. Put yourself in the position of the investor and ask if your business plan responds to every question and concern he may have. This exercise will also serve as a further opportunity for you to assess the viability of your idea and fine-tune it where necessary. Remember, while the venture capitalist wants to see a business plan with a high return, you have to deliver, so don't be unrealistic.

Contacting the Venture Capitalist

Ideally, introduction to the prospective venture firms you have selected should be made through a banker, lawyer, or accountant who has had some association with the firm. Consultants to entrepreneurs also exist, but investors will ultimately decide if they want to invest in you and your management team, and reliance on an intermediary to represent you can have negative implications. An intermediary is prone to oversell, and his involvement may raise questions about management's ability to represent itself. In the absence of a personal introduction, a letter summarizing your objectives should be followed by a telephone call.

DEVELOPING A BUSINESS PLAN

Once you have generated initial interest from a venture firm, your business plan becomes the single most important element in your efforts to continue the momentum that you hope will culminate in a deal. Your written business plan, plus your accompanying verbal presentation of its highlights, provides prospective investors with the information and firsthand perspective on which decisions can be made. While an overly optimistic plan is subject to skepticism, a plan that errs on the side of understatement will not generate much excitement either. Do present positive but realistic projections of your business expectations. A shortcoming of many presentations is the failure to articulate the basic need for a product amid a glowing description of what the product is. A description of the most unique widget in the world won't impress a venture capitalist if that description is not accompanied by well-documented research demonstrating why the widget will be purchased and by whom. Your presentation should not be a flashy sales pitch so much as a thoughtful discussion, warts and all, about your service and product, and its potential. The venture group you are petitioning may well become your partner for an extended period of time, and the extent to which your presentation is given in a professional and effective manner will go a long way toward determining the tenor of that relationship.

Anybody who has been in a business that was professionally run should be able to develop an effective business plan. The difficulty seems to be that inventors, scientists, or other entrepreneurs are typically not experienced with the discipline of formulating the sort of business plan that venture capitalists demand. A business plan should be a comprehensive road map showing how a new business intends to get from the start-up point to a destination further down the pike. It should incorporate detailed market research, competitor assessment, cash needs, projected sales, and eventual profitability. Entrepreneurs may have great ideas, high energy levels, and the capacity for hard work, but they often lack a formalized approach to going about business. They are the "doers," and ultimately the doers of this world are the ones who get things done. However, doers are typically not writers of business plans. Much of their intellect is instinctive and may be correct, but an institutional investor needs to see a disciplined exposition of the business and its prospects. Doers are people of action who go out and seize an opportunity, and operate the business with a strong sense of intuition. Their priorities are in the area of generating clients, building the machinery, and working out production and distribution challenges. These individuals are often living hand to mouth, in a highly competitive environment, and simply don't take the time for comprehensive forward planning. That is often the Achilles heel in their efforts to secure venture capital.

On the other hand, an individual with a promising idea coming out of a more formal business background is more likely to make the very important commitment to the development of a thorough business plan. I had the advantage of being oriented to planning from my early business career at Young & Rubicam, an international advertising agency. Our planning included the development of a comprehensive assessment of the product, its need in the marketplace, and its unique selling advantages. We determined what we were going to say, where we were going to say it—television, print, or radio—when and how often, and how much money we were going to spend. The plan included market share projections several years down the road, advertising as a percentage of sales, and many other projections of critical interest to the client.

I also served as an army officer and was well indoctrinated in the concept of the "five-paragraph field order," a planning guideline that covered every major aspect of a military operation, including the mission, the units involved, where they were going, the formation, the transportation, the equipment, the timing—every nitty-gritty detail involved. Therefore, having personally emerged from a formal business background, and having a diversified background in planning, I was able to convey our strategy and financial needs in an effective manner to the venture capitalists. It also helps to be a logical thinker.

Historical Background

Your business plan should be well organized and comprehensive, addressing all issues of relevance. Put yourself in the shoes of the prospective investor and ask yourself if all questions you might have about the business have been answered, or at least addressed. A logical starting point would be a discussion of the historical and present perspective of your industry. Provide a broadbrush overview and then position your business and the niche it is intended to fill. Describe your product or service, the opportunities you foresee, and the capabilities you can marshal to achieve your marketing objectives. If your company is already operating but requires expansion capital, review its history, financial performance to date, and outlook. Don't whitewash any problems incurred along the way—these will only come to light later and prove an embarrassment.

Positioning Your Product or Service

Starting with the basic question of what is to be sold to whom, embark on a comprehensive description of the projected operation of your business, identifying your objectives, how you intend to achieve them, at what cost, and over what time frame. Questions that any potential investor might have should be foreseen and addressed. Such questions might relate to your product's salability, your customer profile, the competition, its profitability, your competitive advantages, and market potential. Is your business a recognized growth industry? Investors would want to see detailed projections on the dollars required to compete, how they would be spent, and the time frame for all activities, including product development, marketing, manufacturing, distribution, and sales.

In evaluating your industry, include as much competitive information as you can secure, including performance figures and forecasts of all major players. Identify competitors who have recently entered or exited your marketplace and why. Discussion of the competitive advantages of your product or service, and how it will capture market share in a competitive environment, can be accompanied by photographs, diagrams, and other visual schematics. Do you envision your operation as a single product or service firm, or do you foresee opportunity to build and develop a family of mutually reinforcing entities? If expansion into complementary operations has downstream revenue potential, discuss that opportunity. Investors are always interested in your potential to generate return on investment, and even if diversification is premature at the time of your existing capital needs, it demonstrates your vision and ability to recognize business potential. Remember that most venture investments are made with the understanding that a commitment of at least five years is necessary to generate acceptable returns.

Don't paint an unrealistically rosy picture of your business sector and the niche you intend to fill. If the venture firm looking at you is not expert in your business, it will bring in consultants who are. Any attempt to pull the wool over your investors' eyes will not remain undetected and will reflect adversely on your overall reliability. Identify the downside risks of your venture and any untested areas of marketing and production that you want to initiate. If you address all of the tough issues, and come up with uncertainties in any area, you will have to ask yourself if they result from lack of research or available data, or if your venture is somehow flawed.

Some venture firms will not even meet with a prospective entrepreneur without first reviewing his business plan. In this case the plan is your one shot for financing. In all cases it is a vitally important document that should be well prepared and persuasive. It should not be skimpy, nor should it be a tome of endless minutia. Fifty pages is a realistic rule of thumb for most businesses. Your plan should also encompass the economic and financial climate of your business sector, the outlook for the near and long-term future, and how you intend to respond to conditions on the horizon. If your product is spawned by a high tech environment, where ongoing innovation is a competitive necessity, describe your flexibility and other applications your product can fulfill. If you foresee regulation or deregulation pressures, technology changes, or other factors that would enhance your viability, incorporate them into your business plan.

In my area of endeavor—hospital ownership and management—

we had prospered in an environment in which dramatic changes were evolving that could make us even more successful in the future, or undermine profitability. At the time we were seeking venture capital, the government was seriously considering hospital cost containment legislation that would cap reimbursements for medicare patients. The government would no longer reimburse hospitals for health care services, regardless of price.

The emphasis was dramatically shifting to cost containment and efficiency of operation across a broad front of hospital operations. Pressure was being applied to get patients in and out speedily to avoid incurring costs above and beyond reimbursement levels. As we have now witnessed, an array of stand-alone surgicenters and other alternative health care services have sprung up to compete for what was once traditional hospital business. We foresaw this coming, and based on our experience in the assessment of hospital operations over many years, we recognized the fact that many institutions were ill prepared to compete in a new environment of cost containment pressure and increasing competition. Hospital administrators were not always experienced business managers supported by sophisticated information processing systems taking advantage of economies of scale. We foresaw an accelerating trend away from stand-alone institutions and toward merger, to help spread costs, acquire marketing muscle, and avoid competitive duplication of service. Many hospitals, especially the urban not-for-profits, that could not achieve the necessary reorganization and restructuring to compete, would not survive.

In short, tumultuous change often begets opportunity, and we stressed the opportunity in the decade ahead to acquire hospitals and put them on a positive financial footing through astute fiscal and business management. The national health care climate, and the increasing opportunities it presented, were important to the outlook of our business, and an area we emphasized in the development of our business plan. No business is an island unto itself, uninfluenced by economic and financial crosscurrents, and outside influences that have an impact on business prospects should be an integral part of any business plan.

Painstaking preparation of your business plan may often result in revisions to certain aspects of your original strategy. In our case, it led to the revision to certain details of our long-range intention to complement basic, acute-care hospital operations with the development of new lines of business. We recognized increasing opportunity in the field of psychiatric care, and we saw additional opportunity in such areas as addictive disease and physical rehabilitation facilities. We have since expanded into all of these areas, but it was during the preparation of our business plan that we developed implementation strategies and timetables for these new lines of business. Planning is a difficult process, but I can assure you that it's a lot less costly than making adjustments further down the road that could have been avoided.

Market Research

Having described and positioned your product or service, its anticipated demand, and your talent to build and manage the business, it is important to analyze the market research you have undertaken to support sales projections. Because it is your sales that will greatly determine the budgeting and financial requirements of all aspects of your operation, your market research must be solid and presented in a compelling fashion. This important section of your business plan is one in which most entrepreneurs are deficient. Identify your customers, where they are located, and just why they are customers or prospective customers. Discuss the strategy to be employed in selling these customers. Cite specific customer reactions, positive and negative, and discuss your efforts to convert negatives to positives. Identify the size of your market and factors within the market that will support your expectations. But don't overestimate the breadth of your market. If independent venture group research reveals diminished potential, your credibility will suffer. By the same token, don't underestimate competition. Tables, graphs, and charts are often useful ways to present trends, comparisons, market share data, financial projections, and other important areas of information. At minimum, it shows that you are thoughtful and logical.

Product Pricing

Product pricing is a vitally important consideration and one in which entrepreneurs tend to sell themselves short. A superior product should command a greater, not lesser price, than a competitive product. Contention that a superior product should be sold for less to gain market share might be viewed as a commentary on the new organization's lack of confidence and salesmanship as much as an attempt to gain market share. Low prices mean low margins, a dangerous situation in a start-up business where any number of developmental and production costs might run over budget and further squeeze narrow margins. Pricing policy is a make-or-break aspect of any business, and investors will demand every assurance that your price is on target to achieve sales and profit projections.

Sales Strategy Implementation

Sales strategy implementation is another crucial link in the chain, and one that investors will analyze closely. Your business plan should spell out the mechanics of your sales operation, including use of your own sales force, representatives, distributors, or a combination thereof. Include a discussion of salaries, commissions, percentages to wholesalers and retailers, quotas, and bonuses in conjunction with sales strategy. Promotion costs as a percentage of sales should be projected, along with breakouts for advertising, PR, trade shows, direct mail, or any other promotional expenditures.

Operations

Operations should also be a key section in your business plan, encompassing a comprehensive overview of facilities requirements, equipment, materials acquisition, and labor. Investors will certainly want every assurance that you have the internal capabilities to produce the product, or the expertise to deliver the service, at levels sufficient to achieve sales and profit projections. If your business depends on production at high volume, for example, you must also demonstrate your capacity to deliver your product to customers, retailers, or wholesalers. If yours is a service business, proximity to your customer base would be considered advantageous.

Our aspiration at Universal Health Services was to acquire hospital properties wherever opportunities presented themselves that met our performance criteria, regardless of geographical location. Because hospital management demands extremely close day-by-day supervision, we took particular pains in our business plan to describe how we intended to keep on top of changing situations that were distant from our suburban Philadelphia headquarters. In addition to a highly refined management reporting system, we demonstrated our planned computer capabilities—among the most sophisticated in the business—that would enable us to monitor a vast spectrum of operational and financial results, and respond to aberrations, within extremely tight time frames.

If you are a manufacturing operation planning to utilize subcontractors and suppliers, support this strategy with information identifying your resources and their reliability. Play the devil's advocate and identify contingencies for worst-case scenarios. The extent to which you can anticipate and respond to tough "what if" questions from potential investors, the higher your credibility will rise in their eyes. If you are a high tech business, and anticipate the need for training to upgrade the skill level of your local labor pool, explain how this will be financed and how you will be able to produce a competitive product within your production time frame.

Management Team Resumes

A great many of these questions will relate to the responsibilities of various members of your management team. The capacity of top management to perform and supervise all of the tasks necessary for a successful start-up or expansion is perhaps the single most important assessment that prospective investors will make. It's imperative, therefore, to present your management team in terms of their capacity to provide the specific knowledge and leadership required for the task. Any instance in which specific past experience and responsibility relates directly to the challenge at hand is a plus in reinforcing your capability to succeed. Complete resumes for each member of management should be attached describing their backgrounds in key areas of marketing, finance, and operations. In addition, identify board members describing their areas of individual experience and expertise that could benefit the company.

Executive Compensation

Considerable thought should also be given to executive compensation, bearing in mind that investors are more impressed by commitment than personal aggrandizement. Salary levels for a start-up operation in excess of previous earnings might raise justifiable questions about commitment. An incentive program, however, with bonuses for performance above projections, would be more palatable. Investment in the business by individual officers, such as the $1 million we put up to launch Universal Health Services, is another positive indication of confidence and commitment. Be sure to plan and operate a lean organization—no corporate jets, please!

Start-Up or Expansion Schedule

Having discussed all of the key components of your business, it is valuable to bring them into closer focus through the projection of a start-up or expansion schedule, with costs and revenues anticipated at each juncture. Investors will be better able to understand the sequence of needs and the interrelationship of all of the management talents previously described. When timetables and deadlines are brought into sharp focus, investors will have a better grasp of your financial requirements as well as your ability to plan and initiate.

If you are successfully funded, the schedule will also provide the means for investors to monitor your progress and determine if you are on course and on schedule. Projections should be realistic and potential problem areas identified. The minimization of adverse surprises should be an underlying objective of your relationship with your investors. Situations can certainly occur that are outside of your control, such as competitive developments, legislation, new technology, raw material shortcomings, labor problems, and the like, and they should be identified and perhaps assigned degrees of probability.

Financial Plan

Accompanying your detailed scheduling projections should be an equally detailed financial plan, providing a framework for understanding your capital needs projected several years forward. The basic elements of your financial plan would include profit and loss forecasts, cash flow projections, and balance sheets at time of start-up, after six months, and then annually for the number of years your plan extends. Normally, P&L forecasts are projected three years forward, with a monthly breakout for each item the first year, followed by quarterly breakouts for the next two years. In addition to projecting sales, operating, and profit forecasts in chart form, you should incorporate a written description of your assumptions whenever further explanation might be helpful. Assumptions such as those for bad debt provision would provide further clarification of your projections.

Like your P&L forecasts, cash flow forecasts should also extend three years, on a monthly basis for the first year, and quarterly thereafter. This forecast can be more important than profit forecasts because it identifies the amounts and timing of cash inflows and outflows. Projected levels of sales, and the timing of expenditures, provide the investor with a clearer understanding of the scheduling of additional financing requirements. This forecast should also take into account peaks and valleys of a business affected by seasonal or cyclical factors, as well as supplier cash demands and other situations having an impact on cash flow.

Summary

Your business plan should close with a summary section encapsulating the highlights of your plan in just a few pages. It should summarize your cash flow projections and the timing and extent of financing you will require to support your start-up or expansion plans. Identify the type of offering you have in mind, the unit price, and the quantity you intend to sell. Also provide the percentage of the company that investors of the immediate offering will hold when the deal is consummated, or after stock conversion and purchase rights have been exercised. A listing of current shareholders and shares held by each should be provided, as well as the number of shares that will remain authorized but not issued after the offering.

Your summary will serve as an introductory overview for the venture capitalist and, in many cases, the basis on which he will decide if he will pursue your proposal further. Write your summary last, not first, so that it will better reflect the key elements of your ultimate business plan, which will almost certainly undergo revisions as it is developed. It would be a mistake simply to expand a summary to create a business plan.

Although I have dwelled on the importance of a comprehensive and compelling business plan in the pursuit of venture financing, supported by a superior management team, I want to reiterate that a superior business plan cannot overcome basic deficiencies in the viability of the business itself.

If initial response to your overture is positive, be aware that considerable time is required by venture groups to complete investigations and commit to an investment. Six months is a normal time frame, and entrepreneurs who require survival funding sooner are usually viewed as deficient planners by the firms they are soliciting. Rather than react to prolonged investigation as an annoyance, the entrepreneur should welcome it as an opportunity to refine and improve aspects of his strategic planning. Examination by the venture group will dwell on management capabilities, product analysis, production and marketing planning, and financial analysis. Concurrently, the entrepreneur should undertake his own assessment of the venture firm, focusing on the personal expertise it can bring to bear and its investment history. It might be revealing for the entrepreneur to interview other businesses in which the venture group has invested to learn how the investors reacted to both successful and not so successful performance.

The entrepreneur should be well aware before venture funding is even considered of the rate of return demanded by the investor. Venture capitalists who underwrite start-ups or initial stage financing are generally looking for compound returns of 40 to 50 percent on investment annually. A 44 percent compounded annual rate of return, before tax, would triple an investment in three years. A 40 percent return, over a four-year period, will increase the original investment fourfold. Second-stage investors are generally looking for a 30 to 40 percent annual return, while third-stage investors want an annual return of 25 to 30 percent. Other factors the entrepreneur must realize will influence the investor's attitude on pricing include the desire for a "fudge factor" to hedge against errant projections. Venture capitalists, mindful of the likelihood of additional funding needs within the same round of financing, are inclined to build room into pricing for more dilution. If you anticipate additional needs for capital, be sure the venture group has the capability to support you, should you be highly successful.

NEGOTIATING THE VALUE OF THE INVESTMENT

Once the entrepreneur passes muster, negotiations will ensue to draw up the usually complex arrangements and conditions of the investment. Compromise is frequently necessary to resolve all of the issues of negotiation, and it is important for both sides to leave the table feeling that a fair and realistic deal has been struck, encompassing objectives that are both challenging and achievable. Mutual enthusiasm and satisfaction from the outset is vital to a productive working partnership between investor and entrepreneur as the challenges of a new business are tackled.

In negotiating pricing for your shares, it is helpful to recognize the difference between the perspective of entrepreneurs and that of the venture community. Entrepreneurs are optimists and feel that their companies are worth more than investors' assessments, and that investors should have to pay a high price to participate in such an opportunity. The investor, however, based on his experience, knows that many obstacles arise to foil the achievement of sales and earnings objectives.

Pricing actually describes the total return to be generated over the life of an investment, including current interest and dividends and capital gains. From the standpoint of the entrepreneur, there are a number of considerations that influence the share pricing determination. How much of his own money can he afford, what is the company's profit potential, and within what time frame? How much additional equity financing is needed? How will the company's stock likely be priced in the public marketplace? What price-earnings ratio will it command when investors want to liquidate?

Venture capitalists approach the challenge of valuation analytically, assessing diverse companies, both small and large, within a given industry to identify key operating statistics that may prevail. These include sales, operating costs, profits and margins, overhead and administrative expenses, and ratios of net profit to sales, return on equity, and long-term debt. Price-earnings ratios would also be examined to gain insight into receptivity in the public marketplace. As an entrepreneur, it is important to understand the priorities of the venture position. The venture capitalist has invested in your enterprise in the face of considerable risk, on the expectation of generating a high rate of return on that investment. By the same token, he has built in procedures for recovering his investment if the business does not meet projections. The investor will normally require that three options be written into the purchase agreement: (1) the right to sell his stock when opportunity arises, (2) the right to a senior position if the enterprise is sold or liquidated, and (3) the right to more shares if projections are not attained. The more ownership the owner wishes to retain, the more liquidity options he will have to relinquish.

In negotiating with venture firms you, the entrepreneur, are at a disadvantage because they do this all the time and you don't. You're the operator of a business and your energies are focused on running that business: You might not know all of the ins and outs of raising capital. At Universal, we were knowledgeable about finance and how to go about working with bankers, but the venture game is entirely different. Venturers succeed in great measure on their ability to negotiate and cut the most advantageous deal. However, in a capital-rich venture environment, which was the case in the early 1980s, an entrepreneur could play one venture firm against another, as much capital chased too few good business opportunities. Where business prospects were considered particularly promising, one could shop around among venture firms, and negotiate from a position of strength.

In our case, alternatives were somewhat limited since we wanted the top venture investors, who were subsidiaries of major banks. They had the deep pockets that would be required. These top venture groups share the same investment goals and philosophies as we do and are looking for the same levels of return. Often, if you're able to attract one venture firm, that firm will bring additional partners into the deal. You don't have to try to round up the requisite number of partners yourself. In our case, our initial group attracted two other groups, and all three put up $1 million apiece. Most venture firms tend to give out financing with an eye dropper, in relatively miniscule amounts. The $1 million we got from each of our three partners was substantial. The nature of our business, hospital acquisition, is unusually capital intensive; we needed the big dollars. Most entrepreneurs who invent things or develop new services don't require massive infusions of capital as we did.

Before pursuing the venture capital route, you should have developed a strategy determining just what you are willing to give up and at what price. The ideal situation, of course, is to start a company, build it with your own resources, and retain full ownership. If it's successful and you have 100 percent ownership, that's ideal. It is possible to start a business, husband capital, build sales, and eventually go public. You would not need the venture people at all. But if you are not satisfied with slower growth, or need a critical mass to succeed, the venture community may be the best or only avenue.

You don't have to be overly sophisticated financially to deal successfully in the venture marketplace. If you have a highly promising invention or a sound business service concept, you can locate a financial adviser who knows his way around the venture community. It's like working with a real estate broker when buying a property. When you're negotiating with venture operators, you've got to be knowledgeable about their modus operandi, their philosophy, their objectives, and the way they make their money.

The trick is to give away as little of the company as possible in the initial round of financing on the theory that as you mature and become more successful, the shares will be worth more. It is also important to give away only what is required to secure only the essential financing, because in dealing with a capital intensive business you will have to give up more of the company in exchange for capital. The investors understand this, and if they like the company they will try to acquire as much of it as they can. The negotiations are usually very intense. Remember, this is their best suit.

When venture people put equity into your company, equity means ownership. They are risk takers trading for an equity stake. They want to invest, see that investment grow, and then get out at a high return. Even before you might fail to perform to high expectations, they have assumed the business is salable. If you, the entrepreneur, can't expand effectively or can't ship enough or whatever the difficulty might be, the investors know your company might be attractive to a well-established company in the business. If the investors don't have the personnel or specific expertise to help you, they'll bring in professional managers from the outside. And if their gunslingers can't clean up the business, they'll sell it and you. They'll have a list of major corporations in the field they'll call on and arrange a sale. And selling is something they can do very well! They can be sharks, and they love to tell war stories about how well they've done, or how they've thrown out this investor or taken over that company. A lot of it is exaggeration, sort of like the tales we hear from fishermen or golfers, but some stories are all too true.

OWNERSHIP VERSUS CONTROL

Entrepreneurs should understand the distinction between ownership and control. The entrepreneur normally maintains control of the business and exercises the leadership and decision-making responsibilities necessary to carry out the objectives of the business plan. In this regard, the role of the venture capitalist is supportive as he offers counsel and business expertise as needed. However, if management comes up short, and projections are not met, the investor, like any owner, can exercise his authority to affect change. Working through the company's board of directors, the venture group can exercise its powers and votes to initiate change.

If everything goes well and there are no problems, the investors will sit tight. Eventually they will be bought out, as the company has a public offering and everyone will be happy. If things go badly, however, they have the right to get more active and exercise more control. They can vote new people on the board and ultimately replace the president. They will step in and work with management if problems arise, and you'll see a flurry of involvement. They are knowledgeable about dealing with your banks to forestall bankruptcy. If you miss a dividend payment, they may give you 30 or 60 days to rectify the situation. In three months, however, they may exercise the right to convert shares into more voting control.

STRUCTURING THE INVESTMENT

Common stock is the instrument most frequently used to strike the balance between liquidity and control in the venture purchase of an ownership position in a private or public company. It carries voting rights and can pay dividends, although in liquidation, common stockholders are last. The balance sheet is more appealing to other creditors if the venture investment is in the form of common stock or its equivalents, instead of straight debt.

Convertible preferred stock may provide shareholders with the ability to effect changes in the capital structure of the company, and would reward shareholders with proceeds of sales or mergers ahead of compensation to shareholders of common stock. This instrument equates to equity and, if properly structured, can assure the venture capitalist of seniority in a merger or liquidation, as well as the authorization to affect management decisions.

Subordinated debt, convertible or with warrants, is issued when the investor demands the security and yield of a debt instrument, but the company does not want to restrict its ability to borrow from banks. Bankers view subordinated debt as equity if it does not dominate the capital structure. Here the investor can accelerate repayment if the entrepreneur defaults on the loan, as well as exercise leverage to influence management decisions.

Selection of the most advantageous instrument or combination for a given venture investment is determined by a number of factors, including the existing capital structure and the amount of ownership that can be purchased with each instrument. An investor is not likely to accept convertible preferred if a company has already sold several such series. He will probably insist that all preferred be converted into common so that he can invest in a new class of preferred. Or, he may accept the capitalization but invest with subordinated debt to retain a senior position over previous investors.

The structuring of an investment is influenced by a host of considerations. Although common stock is the instrument most frequently employed, there is always the possibility that a company may remain static. If such a company is not a candidate for going public or selling out to another company, it would be difficult for the venture capitalists to recover an investment held in straight common stock. Sale of the company would be the only recourse for the investor, a move that might be strongly opposed by management. Some investors are reluctant to make an outright purchase of stock in situations in which management has controlling interest or can block a sale or merger. To resolve issues of both liquidity and capital protection, investors may minimize common stock holdings, investing more heavily in debentures or convertible preferred stock, thereby providing some income and protection in the event of a business decline.

The issue of control is often a determinant of structuring. Although most businessmen want to control their own businesses, there is often a concern by investors that management of emerging businesses may lack the necessary experience to respond to all contingencies. A loan agreement, or preferred stock indenture, would provide management the flexibility to operate the business while giving the investor the authority to intervene if problems arise.

A successful venture capital environment requires a favorable capital gains tax to attract high-risk involvement and a strong stock market. The stock market is the ultimate way for the investor to get out. Venture firms can't raise money in a period when the stock market is anemic. In the absence of investment capital, the new issues market obviously suffers. It's harder for these companies, that might have been venture capital deals in a better environment, to get into the market. If underwriters bring these companies out, and people are not willing to pay high valuations for them, it's difficult for venture group investors to recoup. If you, the entrepreneur, have to buy out your venture investors in the absence of a public issue, you may well impair the soundness of the company. If you have to use your investors' capital to buy them out, you're not getting any benefit from that capital in the marketplace. That's an expensive way to go.

In a more desirable scenario, a company would sell a piece of the equity to a venture group. Call it round one. As it requires additional cash to generate additional business, it would sell another piece of the company, at a higher value but still at wholesale. Now we have a sizable company and are ready to go retail. The company has been in business usually three years at the minimum. It selects an underwriter, who places a sizable valuation on the company and takes it public. It has management, a track record, and has generated earnings. It is sold to the public at 20 times earnings and has negotiated with the venture participants as to how much of their investment they can sell in the initial public offering. If everything goes according to script, the venture group would have bought in at an initial low level, then again, and perhaps a third time in subsequent rounds. On that initial public issue the venture people might elect to sell a portion of their holdings and management might do the same. Later, the venture investors might sell in the open market.

Interestingly, one of our original venture group at Universal Health Services has never sold a share of the company. When they came in, shares were valued at $1. They have since split and been traded at a high of $29. In fact, they've done better than 29:1 because their initial investment was not all common, but preferred stock that paid a dividend.

Universal Health Services had its initial public issue in July of 1981, less than two years after its founding. The company was fortunate to have its securities underwritten by a group headed by Merrill Lynch. The company sold 1 million common shares at $10 each, which placed a valuation on the company of approximately $40 million at that time. All proceeds went to the company, as management and the venture capitalists refrained from participating in the sale.

The company has completed four additional financings, it sold another 1 million shares in July of 1982 at $9.50, and later that year sold 575,000 at 16⅞. In April 1983, it sold $110 million of convertible subordinated debentures (convertible at 25⅛), and in July of 1985 sold 2 million shares at 17⅞. The market value of the company, with 20 million total shares outstanding, is approximately $350 million. Universal Health Services was highly successful in its business, which made for an unusually good investment.

CONCLUSION

Despite my characterization of the rapacious nature of some venture investors, and reference to their "war stories," it is important to recognize the often invaluable role a venture partner can perform in the development of a fledgling business. Remember, the venture capitalist is intent on generating a return five times or more on his investment and assuring the liquidity of his shares. For this reason, he will often assume a very positive role and work long and hard with the entrepreneur to protect and nurture his stake in the business. This relationship can be of major benefit to the entrepreneur who can tap investor expertise in every area of the business. Often, the venture capitalist is willing to roll up his sleeves and work side by side with company management in resolving problems related to planning, finance, personnel, suppliers, manufacturing, or any squeaky wheel that needs oiling.

The term *value added* is often heard in discussions of the relationship between venture partners and entrepreneurs. Essentially, it describes the contribution a venture firm can make to a new business start-up or expansion, in addition to cold cash. Start-up operations often need help in areas where they cannot afford in-house expertise. Most venture firms invest in specific business sectors in which they have developed considerable knowledge. Through their analysis of many existing and prospective businesses in a given industry, the venturists have developed reliable contacts and informational networks.

Investors with solid reputations in your industry can be instrumental in executive recruitment, negotiations with suppliers, sales, and any number of operational tasks. Commentary by a respected venture capital firm about why it invested in a company can overcome a great deal of uncertainty about the company. Your venture partner can also be helpful in the development of market criteria, especially related to a start-up in an emerging business sector where operating characteristics are not so well known or easily researched. Assumptions related to various costs and margins, the aging of receivables, and other characteristics of the business may not be readily available through normal channels.

Another valuable function that outside investors can perform is acting as a sounding board. During the intensity of new business development, important fresh perspectives can be gained by going outside of the immediate circle of your management group.

As I suggested in my opening sentence, the relationship between entrepreneur and venture capitalist is symbiotic, which by definition should be mutually beneficial.

CHAPTER 8

Corporate Joint Ventures

Raymond H. Kraftson
Vice President and General Counsel
Safeguard Scientifics, Inc.
King of Prussia, Pa.

Raymond H. Kraftson was admitted to the Virginia bar in 1967, the Pennsylvania bar in 1970, and the Missouri bar in 1971. He graduated from the University of Pennsylvania (B.A., 1962) and the College of William and Mary (J.D., 1967), managing editor, College of William and Mary Law Review, 1966–1967, and W.A.R. Goodwin Scholar. He is a member of the Philadelphia and American Bar Associations (member, section on corporation banking and business law) and the American Corporate Counsel Association.

Richard J. Giacco
Assistant General Counsel
Safeguard Scientifics, Inc.
King of Prussia, Pa.

Richard J. Giacco has been assistant general counsel of Safeguard Scientifics, Inc., since late 1984. Previously an associate with Morris, Nichols, Arsht & Tunnell in Wilmington, Delaware, he is a graduate of Delaware Law School (J.D., 1980) and the University of Virginia (B.A., 1976).

INTRODUCTION

A good working business definition of a joint venture is the pursuit by two (or more) parties of a profit-oriented project within a specific time frame. It is a flexible relationship that allows the venture partners to define the venture project, and to agree up front on the respective contributions necessary to make the venture project succeed. In our experience, the contributions should always include varying degrees of active participation by both parties.

ACTIVE PARTICIPATION

The feature of active participation distinguishes the joint venture partner who supplies capital from the venture capitalist. The activities of a venture capitalist are generally limited to providing capital in exchange for convertible debt or equity, receiving financial statements on a periodic basis, and then, at some critical point, deciding how to realize the best return on its investment. Frequently, the only active involvement beyond board-of-directors participation in the business occurs when things go sour, at which point the venture capitalist commonly has the right to step in and attempt to remedy the problems or otherwise salvage the investment.

The joint venture partner, however, will want the right to participate to some negotiated degree in the business of the joint venture.

This desire to participate is not based on a fear of bad judgment by the entrepreneur, but on the philosophy that each venture partner will benefit from the strengths of the other and that the mutual consideration of key issues provides a better forum for analysis than consideration by an entrepreneur alone. In addition, the joint venture partner is generally willing to share the risks of the venture project in exchange for his participation.

ADVANTAGES

Sharing of risks and combined input on key issues are two advantages of the joint venture relationship. Another advantage, which is also the best reason to consider a joint venture, is the combination of complementary strengths that occurs in a well-conceived joint venture. Common examples are combinations of the technological know-how of an entrepreneur with the managerial abilities of an experienced venture partner, or the market-ready product developed by an entrepreneur with the national marketing and distribution abilities of an established venture partner. An illustration of the mutual benefits derived from combining strengths was a joint venture corporation known as KSG Industries. In the late 1970s, Safeguard Scientifics, Inc. decided that in order to begin heading toward its new corporate strategy and to raise cash for other ventures, it would reduce its 100 percent interest in a manufacturing subsidiary that produced engine parts for the automotive aftermarket. At the same time, a major West German auto parts manufacturer was planning its entry into the American market with products based on its newly developed diesel piston technology. Industry economics indicated that the product line should be manufactured in the United States. After extensive negotiations, it was agreed that Safeguard would combine its production facilities, access to national distribution, marketing channels, and management skills with the new technology and management skills of the West German manufacturer. The result was KSG, a joint venture company with a technological edge that positioned it for market advantage. In addition, Safeguard received the cash it had sought for new ventures, and the West German manufacturer established an American presence at a fraction of the cost of proceeding on its own. The arrangement was formalized in a comprehensive and intricate joint venture agreement outlined at the end of this chapter.

Flexibility is an additional advantage of the joint venture concept. Most issues are open to negotiation between prospective partners. In financial terms, the attractiveness of flexibility to entrepreneurs is evident when joint venture capital is compared to the inherent rigidity of commercial loans, the traditional capital source of growing small businesses. While a commercial loan will allow the entrepreneur to retain exclusive management of the business (within the restraints referred to in the loan agreement as "negative covenants" and as long as the business does not run into serious problems), the lender will usually require unsecured liquid assets as collateral and the personal guarantee of the loan by the entrepreneur. These requirements eliminate a lot of entrepreneurial businesses. Frequently, a small business will have already pledged all of its assets to position itself for further growth. Also, even if unsecured assets are available, they may not be sufficiently liquid. For example, from the lender's perspective, a standard industrial drill press is considerably easier to sell, and sell quickly, when a default occurs than highly specialized computer software. Personal guarantees are another drawback. While an entrepreneur invariably has faith in the prospect of the ultimate success of his business, he or she may be unwilling or unable to risk losing the family home and hearth because the business fails for unforeseen or insurmountable problems. There is also the very practical consideration of whether the debt service burden of the commercial loan (generally higher than venture partner loans) will break the growing business in the event of a economic downturn or other temporary adverse developments.

Commercial loan requirements are rarely present in the financial arrangements of the joint venture. Since the primary concern of the venture partner in contributing the capital is to help the venture project succeed rather than to protect a loan, there is no interest in unnecessarily restricting the venture partner. Safeguard's experience with Chesco/Nichols, a real estate development joint venture, provides a relevant example. Our venture partners are two individuals who had the experience, ambition, and all other essentials, except adequate capital, to succeed in a highly competitive market. Due to the speculative nature of the business and lack of sufficient collateral, a commercial loan was not a viable option. Safeguard realized their potential and agreed to participate in and provide the initial capital for a joint venture. A Safeguard-guaranteed line of credit was also set in place to provide the joint venture with additional working capital if required. The joint venture agreement was structured to allow our venture partners to make major decisions quickly, which both sides agreed was an essential to letting the venture succeed in the fast-paced real estate development business. To date, this joint venture has performed well beyond Safeguard's original expectations, in significant part because the primary concern has been to let our venture partners focus their talents on operating the business, relatively free of cumbersome financial requirements.

DISADVANTAGES

On the negative side, a joint venture relationship includes a number of features that entrepreneurs may find objectionable. The venture partner making a capital contribution is generally going to expect to be able to participate in at least major business decisions, requiring the entrepreneurs to work with others on an equal footing, and to have decisions discussed, questioned, or overruled. For example, an entrepreneur may be willing to concede that while he has exceptional marketing talents, neither he nor anyone else in his company has the very different talent of managing a business on a daily basis. His prospective venture partner will likely want to bring a talented manager into the joint venture business as a condition to supplying capital, and generally, a talented manager will not accept that position unless his decisions on operations are final. Conflicts in this situation are likely unless the entrepreneur and the manager understand the extent of their authority from the beginning. To avoid unnecessary conflicts, and to protect the venture partners' expectations over control of various types of business decisions, the authority and responsibilities of the entrepreneur and all other key people should be specified up front in the joint venture agreement, associated employment agreements, or in corporate bylaw provisions.

The venture partner will also expect to own a share of the venture project, receive a share in the future, or some combination of the two. To the entrepreneur putting his business into the joint venture, this translates into selling a share of the business. While an entrepreneur's concern about sharing equity can be addressed in buy-back provisions that allow the repurchase of the venture partner's equity in certain circumstances, as well as in the dissolution provisions of the joint venture agreement, it is unlikely that a venture partner will agree to a buy-back option in a good prospect absent a substantial premium payment. If an entrepreneur regards these features as unacceptable, particularly in regard to relinquishment of equity, a joint venture relationship is inappropriate.

NEGOTIATING THE VENTURE

The Written Business Plan

Once an entrepreneur decides that a joint venture may be a desirable vehicle, he should prepare for discussions and negotiations with prospective venture partners. The first step is to formulate a written business plan. The plan should describe the business, its results to date, the results the entrepreneur expects to produce through the joint venture, the requirements to produce those results, ownership interests, and the return the venture partner can expect to receive for its capital and other contributions. It should be readily understandable and as free of technical terms as possible. In addition, since the plan may also serve as the basis for evaluating performance criteria under the joint venture agreement, and therefore affect the rights of the entrepreneur in respect to the business, realism is advisable.

The next step is to develop an oral presentation based on the business plan. It is a good idea in this preparation to "change hats" and try to anticipate the questions a reasonable investor would ask about the business.

The remaining preparation is to locate likely venture partners. While initial contacts with most of our venture partners have come through trusted mutual business associates, general information on prospects is available from numerous sources, ranging from commercial bankers and attorneys, to new and small business publications, to computerized information exchanges. There are no hard and fast rules in this area, but common sense dictates that an entrepreneur examine a number of sources. With general information in hand, the entrepreneur can target prospective venture partners that may be interested in his business plan and then make contact, send the written business plan, and set up initial meetings.

In these meetings, it is important that the entrepreneur have a firm grasp of his requirements for control, the respective responsibilities of the venture partners, and the division of profits and losses of the joint ventures. Special consideration should also be given to what set of circumstances will end or "unwind" the joint venture, because more problems occur at termination than at any other stage. It's important to understand who can dissolve the venture, under what set of circumstances, and who gets what from the joint venture business upon dissolution.

The venture partner may make proposals for supplying management or technical assistance as a condition to capital contribution, if he thinks they are necessary to make the venture succeed. The parties should also decide on ground rules for the day-to-day operation of the venture project and which factors will warrant a change in the business plan. Finally, since he will have to get along with his venture partners, the entrepreneur should satisfy himself that they are sufficiently ethical and candid. Similarly, a regular part of early "due diligence" on prospective partners may include background and credit references checks, so the entrepreneur should put any potential problems on the table first.

The Term Sheet

When the entrepreneur is reasonably satisfied with a proposed deal, the prospective venture partners should reduce the proposal to a "term sheet." The term sheet is clearly drafted to serve as a non-binding working document to clear up any basic misunderstandings early and streamline further negotiations. The term sheet should also specify the further steps necessary to enter into the joint venture agreement.

While the term sheet is under negotiation, the venture partner will talk to the entrepreneurs' employees, business associates, and lenders. The entrepreneur should talk to other entrepreneurs who have similar relationships with the venture partner. And, once the term sheet is finalized, attorneys for both sides will discuss and negotiate the various joint venture documents. The venture partner's accountants will examine the entrepreneur's financial statements. At this stage the entrepreneur frequently will have to make a number of decisions on issues neither contemplated nor discussed in the earlier negotiations. The willingness of the venture partner to make reasonable accommodations for the important concerns of the entrepreneur, and vice versa, provides a good litmus test for their future working relationship.

Due Diligence Examinations

Assuming all issues are resolved, the prospective venture partners will execute a binding agreement to establish the joint venture, on a closing date after certain contingencies are satisfied. The venture partner will want to examine the books of the small business closely and conduct other "due diligence" examinations. These commonly involve reviews of open and threatened litigation, product warranty claims, labor relations, tax returns, compliance with antitrust, environmental and other regulations, patents, open quotations, and other matters significant to the operation of the business. The entrepreneur should require an appropriate confidentiality agreement before this review. Once the examinations are completed, and any issues that arise in the process are resolved, the closing takes place and the joint venture business can begin.

CASE HISTORIES

The preceding covers the main points for consideration of the joint venture by the entrepreneur. However, because few joint ventures are identically structured, the following examples have been provided to demonstrate the diversity possible in such a relationship and to illuminate some of the prior points.

Novell, Inc.

Following an unsuccessful attempt to break into the business microcomputer hardware market, Safeguard took a relatively large write-off in 1982 and was faced with a number of undesirable options for the future of its major computer subsidiary. Prior to a final decision, Safeguard was introduced to Raymond Noorda, an entrepreneur with an extensive background in executive management and computer technology. He had determined that a high-growth opportunity existed in developing and marketing "local area networking" devices to link microcomputers and peripheral equipment in various configurations. The initial components of a local area network product line were among the assets of this subsidiary. Four young software entrepreneurs who had developed this product line for the subsidiary agreed to sell it in exchange for equity in a new joint venture corporation, Novell, Inc. Safeguard contributed the assets of its microcomputer subsidiary, worth a little over $1 million. Noorda made a significant cash contribution, but, more importantly, he and the software group agreed to develop the product to a marketable stage. Noorda became chief executive officer. For its contributions, Safeguard received just over 50 percent of the common stock of Novell, and Noorda and the software group received a substantial percentage of the remaining common stock. All stock issued to key employees was subject to vesting restrictions. Two of the three corporate directors were Safeguard executives, but the day-to-day operating decisions were left to Noorda and his management team.

The goal was to develop and market the networking software as quickly as possible under stringent quality standards, and to do so on a profitable basis. Novell met the goal by late 1983. The venture partners then decided that Novell was ready to go public, and in early 1985, Safeguard offered its shareholders exclusive rights to purchase approximately one half of its Novell common stock.

The offering was well received. Based on the market price of those shares six months later, that one fourth of Novell stock was valued at $28 million, an impressive result considering the entire company was valued at about $1 million less than three years earlier. More importantly, the venture goals were accomplished. Novell has proven to be a leader in its market, and Safeguard was able to give its shareholders the opportunity to take part in that success.

Machine Vision International Corporation

Although not initially structured as joint venture for a number of reasons, Safeguard's relationship with Machine Vision International Corporation provides a good example of the match of complementary strengths desired in a joint venture. Machine Vision develops and manufactures computer vision systems that serve as the "eyes" for industrial robots and inspection systems. Its basic vision system had been developed by Dr. Stanley Sternberg, who later developed a management staff to develop and market the system. After receiving an initial infusion of capital through a private placement of stock, Machine Vision decided that significant additional capital would be needed not only to increase production and sales of its first-generation systems, but also to fund the internal research and development efforts necessary to develop second-generation products and to maintain a competitive edge in a young and fluid industry.

Safeguard initially provided two sources of capital, combining a purchase of Machine Vision stock with a guarantee of a revolving commercial loan. In return for the guarantee, Machine Vision provided Safeguard with a series of options to purchase additional stock at set prices, exercisable before the earlier of an initial public offering of stock or certain outside dates. Because Safeguard was satisfied with the overall quality and balance of Machine Vision's management, it was satisfied to limit its participation to a seat on a board with a majority of outside directors.

The initial capital contributions of Safeguard helped Machine Vision meet its goal of developing its basic second-generation products. The next steps, which included intensification of marketing efforts and broadening the applications of its products, required further capital. The hesitation of purchasers to commit to large orders during the infancy of the industry, high unit cost, and necessary but significant research and development expenses made additional outside funds mandatory. A commercial loan was unavailable because of the company's failure to produce profits and for a number of the restrictions referred to earlier in this chapter.

At this juncture, Safeguard was able to contribute its understanding, heightened by the Novell public offering, of public equity markets. First, it headed a private placement of stock. It also suggested the sale of Machine Vision stock exclusively to Safeguard's shareholders as a capital-raising device. The intention was to provide Machine Vision with additional capital without the increased debt service or other restrictions tied to commercial loans, and to provide Safeguard shareholders exclusive rights to invest in registered stock of Machine Vision. The transaction was completed successfully in the time frame agreed upon, with net proceeds to Machine Vision exceeding expectations.

Center Core

Our experience with Center Core demonstrates how missing pieces that frustrate the growth of a small business with a winning product can be provided by a joint venture partner. Our entrepreneurial partner, Michael Martin, ran a company that manufactured office furniture with a design concept keyed to the rapidly increasing business use of microcomputer terminals and electronic communication devices. The furniture facilitated the economical use of that equipment and required significantly less floor space than conventional office furniture. It was also attractive, well made, and reasonably priced. As a result, it was a readily marketable product that, when promoted by the considerable talents of Martin and his staff, sold well.

However, the business was not set to take full advantage of the strong sales. It needed an experienced executive manager and a support staff to integrate all operations of the company so that, for example, products could be delivered as promised on a consistent basis. Another missing element was a national distribution system to facilitate market penetration across the country. The last requirement was additional capital to increase production and marketing capabilities.

Martin was cognizant of what the business needed and began looking for a venture partner. Safeguard was introduced to Martin through a mutual business associate, and negotiations led to the formation of Center Core. Safeguard contributed needed capital and bought the assets of Martin's business, using them as the basis for the new corporation in which both venture partners held equity positions. Safeguard conditioned its participation on bringing in a top manager, George Mitchell, to run the business on a daily basis. This allowed Martin to concentrate on his strengths in design and marketing, which has provided a significant dividend to the growth of the company. Safeguard also worked with the company in setting up a distribution system that has allowed Center Core to grow from a regional to a national presence.

OUTLINE OF A JOINT VENTURE AGREEMENT

The following is an outline of key provisions of the joint venture agreement between a Safeguard Scientifics subsidiary (SAC), and a subsidiary of a West German auto parts manufacturer (MGC), resulting in KSG, a jointly owned company.

Article I

1.1. *Formation of holding company.* KSG Industries, Inc. (KSG) to be established as a Delaware corporation.

2.2. *Organization of holding company.* KSG to hold stock of two operating subsidiaries; the first (SEPI), to continue line of engine parts developed by SAC, and the second (MGKS) to develop product line based on diesel piston technology.

Article II

2.1 *SAC subscription.* SAC to receive 50 percent of KSG common stock at closing in exchange for 100 percent of SEPI stock.

2.2 *MGC subscription.* MGC to receive *(a)* 50 percent of KSG common stock and *(b)* 100 percent of KSG cumulative preferred stock. Dividend rate below market. Preferred to be redeemable by KSG at any time, and by MGC after 15 years.

2.3 *MGC subscription price.* MGC to pay cash for common and preferred shares.

2.4 *State blue sky exemption.* Venture partners acknowledge restrictions on KSG shares under applicable state law.

2.5 *Investment representations.* Venture partners acknowledge KSG shares are not registered under federal securities laws, and their acquisition is for investment purposes only.

Article III

3.1 *Payment of SAC loans.* At closing, KSG to direct SEPI to repay preexisting loans from SAC.

3.2 *Subordinated loan.* MGC to make subordinated loan to KSG at closing, with graduated principal repayments.

Article IV

4.1 *Instruments to be delivered at closing.* Outlines responsibilities for delivery of stock certificates, property, officer, and director resignations, and so on, at closing.

4.2 *Damage limitation.* Either party liable to the other for withdrawal before closing only for expenses.

Article V—Representations and Warranties

SAC and SEPI and MGC represent and warrant to each other a number of points in respect to their organization, capital, financial statements, the existence of undisclosed liabilities, litigation, contracts and insurance, and awareness of adverse events.

Article VI—Conduct of SEPI Business

SEPI and SAC agree to not change capital structure, not transfer any shares, and to conduct business normally prior to closing.

Article VII—General Conditions Precedent to Closing

7.1 *Representations and warranties.* Those made in Article V of the agreement to be true as of date of closing.

7.2 *Bank loan agreement.* SAC signs agreement to arrange commercial loan for KSG.

7.3 *Management agreement.* SAC signs agreement to provide management services for KSG.

7.4 *Phase 1 plan.* SAC and MGC to have agreed to initial business plan for Schmidt subsidiary.

7.5 *No damage to business.* SEPI's business shall not be threatened by force majeure.

Article VIII—Actions to Be Taken at or after Closing

8.1 *Formation of MGKS.* MGKS to be incorporated and established by KSG by time of closing.

8.2 *Preparation of postclosing financial statement.* Financial statements for SEPI to be updated with possible adjustment to amount of repaid SAC loan. Any disagreement to be settled by arbitration submission to CPA.

Article IX—Conduct of Business of KSG and its Subsidiaries

9.1 *Restrictions on corporate action—equal ownership of KSG common stock.* No major corporate or other business decision to be made without mutual consent.

9.2 *Restrictions on corporate action if MGC acquires 60 percent or more of KSG common stock.* Restrictions on corporate and business decisions when Metall assumes majority shareholder status.

9.3 *Annual profit plan.* KSG to prepare an annual profit plan.

9.4 *Transactions with affiliates.* Establishes arbitration mechanism for prospective disputes between SAC, MGC, SEPI, MGKS, and their affiliates.

Article X—Restrictions on Transfer of KSG Stock

10.1 *General restriction.* For first 15 years, no transfers permitted, except for MGC Call and SAC Put.

10.2 *Call option.* After first 7 years but before 16th year, MGC has right to buy from SAC up to 60 percent of SAC's KSG shares (or 30 percent overall), subject to maximum purchase of 10 percent (overall) in any year.

10.3 *Put option.* SAC has right, after initial exercise of MGC call option, to require MGC to buy all or any of its KSG shares (in 10 percent blocks).

10.4 *Value of common stock.* Agreed to valuation of KSG stock on exercise of Put and Call, determined by relative earnings of SEPI and MGKS but with minimum specified value. Call requires cash payment, Put requires one half cash, one half notes.

10.5 *Rights of first refusal.* After expiration of Call and Put, if SAC and MGC remain equal owners, each to have corresponding right of first refusal on proposed sale of KSG stock.

10.6 *MGC right of first refusal.* After expiration of Call and Put, if MGC 60 percent or greater shareholders, it has right of first refusal on proposed sale of KSG shares by SAC. No restrictions on MGC as long as 51 percent of KSG retained. Below that level, sale only of *(a)* all shares or *(b)* sale leaving MGC at least 31 percent. SAC to have right to "piggy-back" its shares on sale of all of MGC's KSG shares.

Article XII—Phase 2 Plan for MGKS

12.1 MGC to submit Phase 2 plan when it desires to expand business of MGKS beyond Phase 1 plan before seventh year. Plan to include financing, production, time proposals, projections of sales, net earnings and cash flow requirements, consequence of expansion on other business, and commitment to provide equipment and machinery.

12.2 If plan not accepted by KSG within specified time, MGC to have right to dissolve joint venture. *(a)* KSG to sell MGKS stock to MGC for equity, MGC to pay MGKS debt to KSG., and *(b)* SAC to buy MGC's KSG common and preferred stock for original purchase price. Parent of SAC to guarantee $5 million subordinated loan.

Miscellaneous

Access. Sets out the venture partners rights and obligations with respect to inspection of SEPI and KSG.

Specific performance. Acknowledgment that damages for breach of agreement are inadequate and allowing specific performance.

CHAPTER 9

Going Public

Alfred R. Berkeley III
Managing Director
Alex. Brown & Sons, Incorporated
Baltimore, Md. 21202

Alfred R. Berkeley III is a managing director of Alex. Brown & Sons, Incorporated. He specializes in the in-depth research of public companies in the computer services industry. He has also played a role in the firm's efforts to manage or comanage public offerings for a number of these companies. He also manages Alex. Brown & Sons' internal data processing and telecommunications departments.

Mr. Berkeley is past chairman of the financial analysts committee of the Association of Data Processing Service Organizations (ADAPSO), a member of the National Computer Graphics Association, the Information Industry Association, the Baltimore Security

Analysts Society, the Data Processing Management Association (DPMA), and the Videotext Industry Association.

Business managers must make two basic decisions: Which businesses should they pursue, and which sources of capital should they use to finance those pursuits? Both decisions affect the value of an enterprise: Hard-earned capital can be frittered away on ill-conceived businesses, and hard-won businesses can be lost through financial blunders. The fundamental premise of this discussion is that managers can enhance the value of an enterprise by financing it properly. It is trite, but true: There are three games in life—games of chance, games of skill, and games of strategy. We are constantly amazed by managers who leave virtually nothing to chance except finances. Few develop financing strategies worthy of their technical, production, and marketing strategies. Often, more time is spent, more tactics developed, more strategies discussed on the company's fringe benefit plan than on how to properly finance the enterprise. Managers pursue investment opportunities aggressively, but wait passively for chance encounters with investment bankers who happen to show some interest in the company's financing decisions.

Investors speak from the perspective of earning a return on capital appropriate to the risks they perceive in a business. The manager's perspective is from the opposite direction: He must ensure that the business activity employing capital is able to return enough cash fast enough to cover the cost of that capital. A well-developed financing strategy matches the risks associated with different sources of capital to the returns in the business activity employing the capital. Timing is an important element in the equation.

Developing a financial strategy requires expert advice and a keen awareness of the sources of capital. Financing decisions come in several basic flavors:

- Internally generated funds or outside capital.
- If outside capital is sought, debt or equity.

Internally generated funds are often insufficient to maintain market share and profitability in fast-growth markets. Most businesses need to supplement internally generated funds with outside capital, and most use a mix of debt and equity.

Equity is permanent capital. It can be used to finance both high-risk and low-risk activities. Equity alone should be used to finance high-risk activities such as research and development of new products for new markets. Equity is, by definition, risk money.

Debt, on the other hand, must be repaid. It should be used to finance low-risk activities. Timing is important. Debt that must be repaid in the short term should be used to finance activities that will return cash before the debt becomes due. Short-term debt is often used appropriately to finance receivables and projects with short-term cash requirements. Debt that may be repaid in the long term is used appropriately to finance long-term assets. Equipment leases and mortgages are common examples.

The inability to repay debt can cripple and destroy the enterprise. Companies financed entirely with equity rarely face insolvency. The risk of insolvency is reduced when the company increases its equity. It is the public's willingness to provide risk money that attracts so many companies to public equity offerings.

In an economy as robust as ours, active markets have emerged for virtually every sort of debt. Mortgages, loans secured by equipment, loans secured by receivables, various types of leases, commercial paper, even personal guarantees constitute a spectrum of debt instruments. But at some point, the lender and the borrower alike become uncomfortable. The need for more equity—more risk money—becomes apparent. Again, a spectrum of sources has emerged in our economy. Detailed discussions of private sources of capital, particularly venture capital, are presented elsewhere in this book. Although equity is only a piece of a company's total financial structure, and although going public is only one of several ways to raise equity, going public is typically so significant an event in a company's life cycle that it merits an extensive, focused discussion.

Going public allows the business to sell equity to the public. The first offering a company makes to the public is an initial public offering (an "IPO," or a "new issue," in the jargon of Wall Street). The new issues market is a distinct segment of the equities market. Most entrepreneurs are aware of the cycles of new issue activity, but the *whys, whens,* and *hows* of going public remain mysterious to them.

WHY GO PUBLIC?

The most powerful force in economics is the cumulative effect of individual consumer's decisions to buy or to bypass a vendor's product. The second most powerful force is the cumulative effect of investors voting with their wallets to fund or ignore an industry or a company. Companies attracting investor interest have no practical limits to growth. Companies attracting investor interest will have capital to attract talent, develop new products, build plants, and advertise their wares. Companies coming to the public market are playing in the biggest of leagues, and they are playing for keeps with real money. In the hands of talented people, capital is the ultimate competitive weapon.

Going public is appropriately viewed as part of a process of building value, market presence, and scale operations. *The central reason to go public is to gain a competitive advantage* (or remove a competitive disadvantage) by lowering the cost of capital, enhancing corporate visibility, and increasing the sense of permanence in the eyes of customers, competitors, suppliers, and employees.

It is difficult to overestimate the competitive advantages of access to public funding. The genius of capitalism lies in its ability to tap the savings of millions of ordinary citizens, each risking a modest amount. Extraordinary amounts can be marshaled for promising businesses. Only the public markets are large enough to supply the equity a truly large enterprise needs. Unlike some capital markets, where share prices are kept so high as to preclude purchases by ordinary citizens, American markets are characterized by low per share prices. The public participates directly, as individual investors, and indirectly, through mutual funds, pension funds, and insurance pools. As a result, the public markets are large and generally quite liquid.

There are ancillary and corollary reasons for going public as well, including publicly traded stock for acquisitions, meaningful value in stock option plans to motivate employees, and liquidity for shareholders, including founders.

WHEN TO GO PUBLIC

In theory, companies can go public at any time. They need only register the appropriate documents with the Securities and Exchange Commission, or satisfy one of the exemptions to the registration requirements. In reality, companies must find buyers for their shares on mutually acceptable terms. There are clearly cycles at work in the new issues market, and company life-cycle issues to consider as well. The state of the new issues market is frequently a matter of concern to entrepreneurs and often is discussed in the financial press. In reality, it is far less relevant to the question of when to go public than the state of the company's own development. Nonetheless, the new issues cycle deserves comment.

The New Issues Cycle

Since the tulip mania of 1637, Western financial markets have seen periods of speculative excess followed by periods of financial collapse to one degree or another. The new issues market of 1983 was such a period of speculative excess. In periods of excessive speculation, the market becomes confusing. In the frenzy of greed that characterizes speculative bubbles, hundreds of companies go public that would not have found buyers in less speculative periods. Truly promising growth companies, *which are able to find buyers for their shares in any market,* are suddenly accompanied by second- and third-rate companies of no investment merit whatsoever. These companies have neither the business prospects nor the managerial attitudes to merit the public investors' trust.

In the early stages of a speculative market, first the financial press and then the popular press are filled with articles on issues that rise quickly to large premiums above their offering prices. Naive writers dignify poorly managed companies with poor prospects by indiscriminate comparisons to well-managed companies with excellent prospects. Speculation feeds on itself as shares of weak companies are bid to excessive prices. Buyers and sellers alike seem to be winners in this environment. Even discriminating investors play, knowing that, as in a game of musical chairs, the music will stop.

The subtle changes that occur as the speculative fever grows are not understood by the indiscriminate buyer. As the speculative fever grows, not only do the characters of the companies offering shares change, but also the characteristics of the public offerings themselves.

In order to understand the changes, the reader must have a baseline, a frame of reference. In the new issues market, the baseline format is the "emerging growth company." Typically, this is a company with $15 million–$30 million in revenues, three or more years of audited operating history, roughly 10 percent after-tax (fully-taxed) earnings, and a full team of experienced managers. The company typically has a leadership position in a market that promises fast growth for a considerable time. The company reinvests heavily to stay competitive. Typically, the company is selling equity at 12–18 times anticipated earnings per share. Usually a total of $15 million–$25 million is being raised. Some shares may be offered for selling shareholders, but most of the proceeds of the offering will go into the company's accounts. Typically, the offering is registered under an SEC Form S-1, a well-known underwriter is leading a syndicate of Wall Street firms, and the offering is available to citizens of most states.

Why is this the base case? Because the emerging growth company is able to raise capital, that is, to find buyers on mutually acceptable terms, in any market. Such companies are able to find capital bacause, contrary to popular opinion, Wall Street is not a monolithic market. Quite the contrary, the financial markets are extremely splintered and specialized. Some investors focus on bonds, some on high-dividend common stocks, some on convertibles, and some on emerging growth companies. There are as many niches as there are types of securities, types of industries. Why? Because investors seek a competitive advantage by developing expert knowledge in a particular field. Knowledge is money on Wall Street.

A significant number of investors have focused on the emerging growth company as an investment vehicle. Initial public offerings are the first chance most of these investors have to participate in a company's growth. These investors have become quite expert in knowing what to look for in new issues. The characteristics described below have been hammered out on the anvil of experience.

- Revenues show that there are arms-length, marketplace transactions taking place, enough transactions to show that real buyers will spend real money in significant amounts to buy the company's product.
- Sufficient earnings show that the company can be profitable, that it has enough profit to reinvest in staying competitive, and that it can afford the not inconsiderable costs of being public.
- A management team is in place that is capable of running a larger business and capable of carrying on if any one manager were missing.
- The offering is large enough to permit reasonable daily trading volumes in the stock. The ability to sell in an orderly way becomes as important as the ability to buy.

The emerging growth company's public offering provides sharp contrasts to those of companies that emerge like 17-year locusts as the speculative fever swells. Weaker and weaker companies begin to register offerings. Revenues drop sharply and operating histories contract. Eventually, companies with no revenues and no operating histories offer shares.

At the same time, the characteristics of the offerings themselves change. Hybrid securities emerge that raise money for the company and offer various "kickers" designed to attract speculators. Warrants are included with shares to create "units" offerings. Most importantly, the price per share or per unit drops precipitously. The "penny stock" offering emerges, appealing blatantly to the speculator. The penny stock and units offerings differ from the emerging growth market in several important ways. Not only are they structured and priced to appeal to a constituency of speculators, but also they typically involve larger fees ("spreads" in the financial vernacular) to the underwriters. Offerings are often done on a "best efforts," as opposed to an "underwritten" basis. In the wisdom of Wall Street, "stocks are sold, not bought," and larger fees tend to focus the brokers' attention. (Penny stocks and units offerings virtually disappear when fear displaces greed after a speculative bubble breaks.) Investment banking firms that have not been active in the new issues market emerge leading syndicates of small firms. To the uninitiated, all these offerings appear similar. To the professional investor, they mark the peak of speculative fervor and foreshadow the end of the new issues cycle.

During a period of rising speculation, companies can sell shares at unusually high prices. For this reason, many companies feel that they should sell shares only during speculative bubbles. In fact, there is virtually nothing that an individual company can do to affect the overall emotion of the new issues market. There is, on the other hand, a great deal a company can do to influence the prices at which it can sell shares *relative to the prices of other companies.* Management can influence how high the boat rides in the water, but not the level of the tides. If a speculative mood exists when a company raises equity, so much the better for the company. But the existence or absence of a speculative mood is a minor factor in the decision to tap the public markets.

Company Life Cycle

Far more relevant than the new issues cycle is the company's own life cycle, its need for equity capital, and, specifically, the appropriateness of raising equity from the public. The key point here is that the question of when to raise equity is quite different from the question of when to go public.

Companies typically raise equity when they cannot or will not increase their debt: cannot, because lenders and creditors do not like the company's ability to service more debt; and will not, when management perceives debt as too risky or too expensive. Debt becomes too risky when management forecasts an inability to maintain comfortable reserves and still meet debt payment schedules. Debt becomes too expensive when interest expense exceeds marginal returns on employed capital. Whatever the reason, private companies often desire to raise equity to strengthen their financial position. At this point, it is important to understand the differences between a private offering (a "private placement") and a public offering.

The distinction is an important one *regardless* of whether the public offering is an available option or not. In other words, there are times in the speculative cycle when public money is available to virtually any company. The smart ones look beyond the issues of availability and examine the question of appropriateness. The smart manager will do this even though there appears to be a penalty to ignoring the public market. In a speculative market, public monies are available at very favorable rates. Companies can participate in speculative markets perfectly legally. Why would any one in their right mind sell shares for less?

The reason that thoughtful companies often raise equity privately despite the availability of "cheaper" public money has to be understood within the context of total costs. In simplest terms, going public is more than an event; it is part of a process. Going public leads to being public, and being public adds yet additional considerations for the manager to juggle in the high wire balancing act that is chief executive management. Whether a company is public or private, management must balance the interests of owners, customers, and employees. Being public subjects the company to "life in a fishbowl," and carries the burden of a massive moral responsibility to the public shareholder. The expectations of public shareholders are often out of step with the realities of small company performance. The liquidity of the public market encourages money managers to set unrealistic goals for companies—uninterrupted quarter-to-quarter growth that defies business cycles and product life cycles. Earnings reports issued quarterly become a report card that enormously—and erroneously—oversimplifies the company's performance and, by implication, management's competence. Stocks that fail to deliver are sold mercilessly. To the company, the public market can become a nameless, faceless tyrant.

Significant practical problems can emerge. Life in a fishbowl opens the company's books to competitors and customers alike. Shares selling below book value or below any sensible appraisal of value can damage the company's reputation, make stock incentive plans difficult, preclude raising additional equity, and make acquisitions for stock too expensive. In a worst case, the company may bear all the costs of being public—legal, accounting, and managerial—and receive virtually none of the benefits. Coming public too early in a company's development complicates the already difficult process of growth.

Private buyers, unlike public buyers, often have expectations more in line with the realities of the company's likely performance. Detailed discussions of the role and expectations of the venture capital community are included elsewhere in this book. Another significant source of private capital is the corporate investor. Corporations make direct investments in promising companies every day. Contrary to the conventional wisdom, not all corporate investors want to take control of the smaller companies in which they invest. Many are interested in minority positions.

The point is that going public is more often than not the wrong decision, particularly for companies that have meager revenues and limited operating histories. *Public offerings should occur only if there is a reasonable expectation that the company can meet the public market's needs for consistent, predictable returns on investment.*

HOW TO GO PUBLIC

If a company is going public for the right reasons (as a result of a well thought out financing strategy that will enhance the company's value and improve its competitive position) and if it is going public at the right time in its development (when it has reasonable chances of meeting the public's expectations for consistent, predictable returns), then the logical next issue is how to go public.

It is not our purpose to treat in one chapter what is well covered in excellent legal texts and in rather comprehensive booklets from the major accounting firms. These sources catalog the various methods of registering shares and the exemptions from registration. What is important is to know that there are several ways to go public, each with different disclosure requirements, some with specific requirements regarding the financial resources of purchasers, all with different registration requirements. The highly visible public offerings of most well-managed companies are known as underwritten offerings. A syndicate of underwriters actually buys all the shares from the company and resells them to the public. It is the most complex form of offering, with the most complete disclosure of corporate information. It uses SEC Form S-1 as its registration form. The current discussion presumes this type of underwriting.

In this chapter we will not focus on the mechanics of going public, but rather on the planning process that will make the mechanics go smoothly. Even when a sensible financial strategy is developed, proper execution often remains elusive. Going public successfully is, more than anything, a team effort. Assembling the team early and working toward a planned offering will prevent common mistakes and costly delays. At the very least, the team will involve:

- The company's management.
- The company's SEC counsel.
- The company's auditors.
- The lead underwriter.
- The underwriters' counsel.
- The financial printer.

The company considering a public offering has a lot within its control. These items fall into three broad categories:

- Results.
- Records.
- Relationships.

Additionally, the company needs to understand the needs of various participants in the process:

- The buyers' expectations.
- The regulators' needs.
- The underwriters' needs.

Some sophistication about the state of the market and the company's relative strengths and weaknesses is helpful too:

- How does the company compare to comparable companies in revenues, profitability, and growth?
- What are the current values of comparable companies?

What You Control

Results. Detailed planning will allow the company to control its financial results to make revenue and earnings growth as consistent and predictable as possible. A "model" company might have:

- $10 million or more in revenues.
- 10 percent after-tax (fully-taxed) margins.
- 10 percent minimum reinvestment in R&D.
- 20 percent growth in revenues and earnings.

The higher the recurring revenue content of the business, the better. Conservative revenue recognition is a strength. Development should generally be expensed.

Records. The SEC requires three years' audited financial records. Prudent planning would have the company in a position to register shares at any time. This means audits prepared each year.

Additionally, depending on the company's business, the SEC requires specific accounting methods. These requirements should be reflected in the company's statements. For example, software development houses generally must expense some expenditures and capitalize others, and purchased software must generally be amortized over five years or less.

Careful planning will also eliminate self-dealing. For example, purchases of goods or services by the company from principal owners requires lengthy disclosure to the public. So do loans to officers and employees. Careful planning can generally eliminate these transactions by finding alternative means to accomplish the same goals.

Expert professional advice from qualified legal counsel, accountants, and underwriters will simplify the process of identifying potential problems. For example, being classified as a personal holding company can have disastrous implications. Hence the importance placed on developing relationships with such experts early.

Relationships. Companies are often shocked at the number and complexity of issues to be dealt with while preparing an offering. Going public is no time to be training any of the participants involved. For this reason, managers must make hard-nosed assessments of the experience and capabilities of their traditional advisers, and make changes if necessary. For example, securities law is a complex, specialized niche of the law. Companies need experienced, expert counsel in these matters. It is not appropriate for the faithful company counsel to brush up on his securities law and represent the company in registering a public offering. Registrants should retain experienced SEC counsel for the task.

Likewise, use a nationally recognized accounting firm. Investors do care which accounting firm signs your statements. They want the comfort that comes from a firm's being large enough to resign your account if all the details are not proper. Conversely, you want an accountant with detailed experience of SEC accounting interpretations. Most local accountants are tax, not securities oriented.

Carefully developed relationships with investment bankers will serve two purposes. First, the company will be able to tap the expertise of the firm's corporate finance department regarding its financial strategy and the technical concerns of an offering. Second, the investment bank will begin to introduce the company to selected institutional investors. The investment business is, like any other business, ultimately a business of personal relationships. Sophisticated investors are interested in knowing about private companies that might come public. Knowledge of the company's business and management over a long period decreases the investors' anxiety over a new issue. Investment banks specializing in the company's area of expertise have many opportunities to introduce private companies to prospective investors.

The well-prepared company can take advantage of opportunities to offer stock quickly. Poorly prepared companies may find that it takes months to develop just the accounting records required by law. In the course of a few months, the market's appetite for public offerings can change dramatically. Furthermore, the very process of planning and preparation will alert a company to coming capital needs. As the old adage says, its far easier (and cheaper) to raise money before you need it than when you have to have it.

Expectations of Various Participants

While a public offering typically appears to be a crisp transaction, in reality, every offering is a series of compromises. Offerings are successful when the needs of all participants are balanced. Companies typically understand their own needs. They can accomplish the compromises that let an offering succeed by understanding the expectations of the other participants: buyers, regulators, and investment bankers.

Buyers' Expectations. At the very price the company feels that the stock is attractive to sell, the investor must think it is attractive to buy. To the investor, a public offering means a chance to buy into a promising business. The investor needs a reasonable return for the risk he incurs. Experience indicates that small companies are considerably more risky than larger companies, and consequently, the investor needs the opportunity for a larger return. During the marketing phase of a public offering, which occurs between the time the company files a preliminary prospectus with the Securities and Exchange Commission and the time the registration statement becomes effective, the market forms expectations about the company's earnings prospects. Companies are expected to meet the market's expectations. The investor wants no surprises.

Regulators' Expectations. Most publications about going public contain detailed discussions of the *process* by which registration statements are developed and the *contents* of registration statements required by regulation. In other words, there are many sources for entrepreneurs to read about the *what* but not the *why* of the process, the *quantity,* if you will, but not the *quality.* We intend to provide a brief review of the requirements (see The Registration Statement at the end of this chapter) but to emphasize a more detailed discussion of the interactions among buyers, sellers, regulators, and underwriters.

Federal and state regulators expect specific information. The Securities Act of 1933 is part of the country's legislative response to various abuses in common practice before that time. It regulates the disclosure required for securities offered and sold in interstate commerce. It contains both civil and criminal penalties for noncompliance. The 1933 Act provides for certain simplified registration requirements and exemptions from registration, depending upon:

1. The size of the offerings.
2. The number of purchasers.
3. The financial qualifications of the purchasers.
4. The type of organization issuing securities.
5. The length of time the organization has been an SEC registrant.

These simplified requirements and exemptions are mentioned only to inform the reader that they exist. This discussion focuses on the "full-blown" (SEC Form S-1) underwriting. This form requires the most extensive disclosure.

Excellent publications are available from most of the Big Eight accounting firms. Ernst & Whinney's *Deciding to Go Public* and Deloitte Haskins & Sells' *Strategies For Going Public* are typical. The letter of the law is available from any lawyer's library or directly from the Securities and Exchange Commission.

The relevant point is that preparing a registration statement to conform to the law's requirements is a team effort. The company's management, its attorneys, and its accountants work with the underwriters and the underwriters' attorneys to complete the task. The process often takes months of intensive effort.

The Securities and Exchange Commission's Division of Corporate Finance has primary responsibility, through the registration process, to require issuers to provide full, fair, and accurate disclosure of the character of securities sold in interstate commerce. The commission does not approve or disapprove any security. It does not pass judgment on any issue, and no endorsement of the investment merits of any issue or of the veracity of statements made in the registration statement are implied when the commission allows a registration statement to become effective. Every prospectus bears a notice to this effect: "These securities have not been approved or disapproved by the Securities and Exchange Commission, nor has the Commission passed upon the accuracy or adequacy of this prospectus. Any representation to the contrary is a criminal offense."

It is the company's responsibility to provide full, accurate, and fair information about the company and the securities being issued. Extensive guidance on what must be included in the registration statement is included in various SEC publications. Regulation S-X prescribes the form, content, and periods of coverage for financial statements. Regulation S-K prescribes nonfinancial subjects to be disclosed. Regulation C prescribes paper size, number of copies, and the like. *Staff Accounting Bulletins* publish SEC interpretations and practices. Financial reporting releases elaborate on certain requirements in Regulation S-X and certain accounting practices. SEC Form S-1 is used by registrants for whom no other form is authorized or required. There is absolutely no magic to any of these requirements. The regulations are clear and detailed. Anyone can write for them and read them. However, they are extremely complex, and it is important to use experienced SEC counsel.

The regulations reflect the Security and Exchange Commission's cumulative experience (over 52 years). The genius of the federal approach is that it requires full disclosure but assumes that an informed buyer can balance risks and rewards.

Most states regulate the issuance of securities, and some make judgments as to the investment merits of an issue. Underwriters' attorneys typically navigate these shallows for the offering—another good reason to use experienced underwriters.

The Underwriter's Needs. An underwriter's ability to place a company's shares depends on its reputation with investors. Its reputation depends on its previous offerings. Every underwriter has sponsored some companies that have had difficulties, but the better underwriters are known to investors for bringing to market high-quality companies that perform as anticipated.

In an effort to reduce its risks, an underwriter will develop detailed knowledge of a particular industry or group of industries. This focused knowledge not only allows the firm to discover promising companies within an industry, but also to understand the competitive dynamics at work among them.

There are economies of scale and learning curve effects at work in investment banking. Financial analysts at an investment banking firm can afford to delve deeply into an industry because they can market their investment insights to many investors. No one investor can afford to dig so deeply. If a company falls within one of the underwriter's areas of specialization, the company can receive extraordinary benefits from that underwriter's sponsorship. Investors rely on an investment banking firm's reputation and specialized knowledge. The underwriter's prior experience has enabled him to identify buyers interested in companies similar to the one being offered.

Economically, investment bankers need a flow of offerings within their areas of specialization. They simply cannot afford to do the due diligence or offer research coverage on stand-alone companies. Companies are well served to use investment bankers experienced in their industry.

Investment bankers posture their businesses many ways. Some are trading houses; some offer diversified financial services. The investment banks that are best known in the new issues market typically posture their business to be profitable through a combination of underwriting fees and brokerage profits. They need to make active, profitable trading markets in the stocks they underwrite. Companies need a number of over-the-counter market makers to provide liquidity to their shares. Companies typically use two managers (co-managers) for public offerings. This virtually guarantees the company research coverage and market making from two firms. The lead manager is usually the investment bank with the most experience in the company's industry. The lead manager, called the "book-running manager," will use its experience in selling shares of related companies to identify likely buyers.

Companies should pay particular attention to the investment banker's commitments to emerging growth companies in general and to the company's industry in particular. What level of staffing does the investment bank commit to researching the industry? How many analysts does it have, and what is their experience? After a company is public, the sponsorship of the company's shares shifts from the investment banking department to the research department and the trading desk. The research analysts will variously offer buy, sell, and hold recommendations, based on their *independent* assessment of the company's prospects relative to other stocks. Managers should recognize the analyst's goal for what it is: to make money for investors. Similarly, traders are in business to trade, regardless of the price of the shares. Managements need to understand these crosscurrents.

Costs. Underwriting costs are often misunderstood by smaller companies. Underwriting costs, called "spreads," are composed of several elements that have been hammered out over the years. They balance the risks that underwriters and their brokers take with the company's need to have a successful placement. New issues compete with existing shares for the investor's attention. Fees paid to brokers on new issues are considerably higher than fees paid on trades of existing shares. Higher fees are needed to justify the broker's perceived risk in recommending a new, untried issue to his clients. A group of brokerage firms assembled to market the stock is called the "selling group." The portion of the spread that goes to the selling group is called the "selling concession."

Another part of the fee is the underwriting fee that goes to the underwriting group. The underwriting group is the syndicate of investment banking firms that band together to share the risk of purchasing the shares from the company and reselling them to the public. A brokerage firm may be in the selling group without undertaking the risks of being in the underwriting group.

The third part of the underwriting spread is the management fee. This goes to the managers of the underwriting group, to cover the costs of their expertise.

In total, underwriting costs average between 7 percent and 8 percent on most initial public offerings for emerging growth stocks. This fee structure has evolved over the years to balance the company's needs and the underwriter's needs.

Time. In addition to the management time needed to develop the company's financial records and registration statements, the underwriters will also need a substantial amount of management time for due diligence and for marketing the offering. Due diligence is the double checking of the company's claims to ensure that investors reading the prospectus are receiving full, fair, and accurate disclosure of problems and risks, as well as opportunities. The company typically provides the managing underwriter with unlimited access to its books and records, officers, accountants, and lawyers. Underwriters typically contact customers and suppliers, on a confidential basis, to verify management's claims. The managing underwriters will also need about two weeks of management's time to market the offering. This is the "road show," typically a blitz to major money centers to talk directly with major institutional investors. The underwriter's research analysts will also expect management to meet with them, with institutional clients, and with brokers several times per year.

Underwriting Agreement. To provide a significant incentive to full and fair disclosure, the company and the underwriters enter into a contract, called the underwriting agreement, which, in addition to setting the exact terms of the purchase and the price, provides the underwriter with indemnification by the company and by selling shareholders as to the varacity of their statements.

Pricing

Pricing is a subject of acute interest to companies. While it appears that the investment bankers mysteriously set a price, in reality the preliminary prices on a prospectus are developed by comparing the company's earnings to the earnings and then the prices of companies with comparable growth and prospects.

The final price is determined by the market in a completely unmysterious manner. The book-running manager's syndicate department has direct conversations with its counterparts at other underwriters and with its own sales force to determine how many shares are spoken for at what prices. The syndicate management function is particularly important for the company to understand. It is pointless to try to second guess the syndicate manager, who is the only person in the entire process that has a complete picture of the demand for an issue.

In summary, if a company has a well thought out financing strategy that will enhance its value and improve its competitive position, and if the company has reasonable chances of meeting the public's expectations of consistent, predictable returns on investment, it should have no trouble assembling a team of experienced, legal, accounting, and underwriting experts. This team will enable the company to achieve the results, create the records, and establish the relationships needed for a successful public offering. Every offering is a balance of competing interests. Companies are well served to learn the needs and expectations of the investors, the regulators, and the underwriters.

Going public is the gateway to being public. Virtually any investment banking firm can float an offering for a good company. After the offering, however, the abilities of various underwriters to support and sponsor a company in the market vary tremendously. Support is key in over-the-counter market making and in research coverage.

Managers can create incremental value for shareholders by carefully thought out and well-executed financing strategies. Capital in the hands of talented people is the ultimate competitive weapon.

THE REGISTRATION STATEMENT

In general, a registration statement includes two parts. Part I is the prospectus and is used by the underwriter in discussions with investors. Part II contains additional information of importance to the transaction but typically of marginal interest to investors.

Part I: Prospectus

Outside front cover
- Name of company.
- Type, quantity, and description of securities offered.
- Offering price, underwriter's discount, proceeds to company.
- Date.
- Proceeds to selling shareholders (if appropriate).
- Managing underwriter's name.

Inside front cover
- Table of contents.
- Price stabilization.
- Dealer's requirements to deliver prospectus.

Summary of Prospectus
- Company's business.
- Securities offered.
- Use of proceeds.
- Selected financial information.

The company
- Detailed background on company.
- Location of offices.
- Description of primary business.

Risk factors
- This section is typically not required for companies with established records and promising prospects.

Use of proceeds

Dilution to prospective purchasers
- Due to significant differences between prices paid for shares by earlier investors and current investors, significant dilution can exist for new purchases. This must be disclosed.

Dividend policy
- Does the company pay or intend to pay dividends?

Capitalization
- The company's debt and equity before and after the offering.

Selected financial data
  The last five years' financials plus interim quarterly results since last year-end.
Management discussion and analysis
  Typically covers last three years and recent interim periods.
  Provides investors with ability to evaluate cash flow from operations and other sources.
  Management must address significant issues having an impact on operations and risks that may affect future operations.
The business
  The last five years' development of the business.
  Major products or services offered.
  Geographic breakdown of sales, profits, and assets.
  Industry segment breakdown for sales, profits, and assets.
  Announced new products or services.
  Sources of raw materials.
  Patent, trademark, copyright, trade secrets, license, and franchise information.
  Seasonal nature of business.
  Dependence on a few customers.
  Backlogs, government contracts.
  Competitive characteristics of business.
  Research and development expenditures.
  Number of employees, union relationships.
  Export sales.
  Environmental laws.
  Working capital practices, inventory levels, credit terms extended.
  Material legal proceedings.
Management and certain shareholders
  Officers, directors, and major shareholders—their compensation, share ownership, and business experience.
  Loans to management, directors, and major shareholders, and their immediate families.
Description of securities
Underwriters
  Underwriter's obligation to and material relationships with the company and any indemnification by the company.
  Members of the underwriting group.
Legal opinions, experts, and additional information
  Attorney's opinion on the validity of the securities offered.
  Accountants and other experts relied on in preparation of the document.
  Availability of information in Part II, filed with SEC.
Financial statement
  Audited balance sheets as of end of last two fiscal years.
  Audited income statements, changes in financial position, and shareholders' equity for each of the last three fiscal years.
  Interim financial statement if anticipated effective date is more than 134 days after fiscal year-end.

Part II: Other Issues

Part II, filed with the SEC, but not included in the Prospectus, is prepared in the "item and answer" format.

Expenses of issuance and distribution

Indemnification of officers and directors acting for the company

Sales by the company of unregistered securities within the last three years

Selected financial schedules

Various exhibits
  Underwriting agreement, articles of incorporation, by-laws, material contracts, pension plans, stock option plans, consents of experts used in preparation of registration statements.

CHAPTER 10

Mergers and Acquisitions

Application to Earnings
Restatement Requirements
Loss Avoidance
Disclosure Requirements
ACCOUNTING FOR DIVESTITURES
ACCOUNTING FOR THE DISPOSAL OF A SEGMENT OF A BUSINESS
Disposition in Form Only
Disclosure Requirements
Expenses Related to a Divestiture

Peter Sears
Vice President
Business Investments
SmithKline Beckman Corporation
Philadelphia, Pa.

Peter Sears is vice president, Business Investments, of SmithKline Beckman Corporation, the $3 billion Philadelphia-based health care concern. In his present role, he is responsible for managing his company's $50 million venture capital and direct investment fund. Prior to July, 1985, he was vice president, Corporate Development, responsible for the corporation's acquisition planning and market analysis functions.

Mr. Sears joined SmithKline in 1963 as an attorney in the Law Department. He was appointed assistant counsel and assistant secretary in 1971 and general manager for SmithKline operations in Japan in 1973. He was vice president and area director, Canada and Asia/Pacific for Menley & James Laboratories—International from October 1975 until his appointment as director, corporate development, in November 1977, and vice president, corporate development, 1980. He has actively participated in more than 50 acquisitions, divestitures, and joint ventures, including the building of SmithKline Bio-Science Laboratories over 17 years, the acquisitions of Allergan Pharmaceuticals in 1980 and Beckman Instruments in 1982, and the joint venture with Fujisawa in Japan in the mid 1970s.

Peter E. Berger
Partner
Arthur Andersen & Co.
New York, N.Y.

Peter Berger is a financial consulting partner with Arthur Andersen & Co. He is a graduate of Boston University and the Columbia University Graduate School of Business. He has served as the audit engagement manager for several of Arthur Andersen's largest multinational clients, including ITT, Colt Industries, Inc, and International Paper Company. In addition, Mr. Berger consults frequently with investment and commercial banking institutions such as Smith Barney, Donaldson Lufkin Jenrette, Salomon Bros., and Bankers Trust Company, on leasing arrangements, alternative financing techniques, and mergers and acquisitions.

Mr. Berger is a member of the American Institute of Certified Public Accountants, and is currently serving on the Financial Accounting Standards Committee and has been a member of the SEC Practice Committee of the New York State Society of Certified Public Accountants.

PART A The Business Aspects of Mergers and Acquisitions*

RATIONALE FOR THINKING OF A MERGER AS A SOURCE OF CAPITAL

Why is there a discussion of mergers and acquisitions in a book related to raising capital? Perhaps this chapter would better be entitled "When all else fails," or "Is there life after death?" Of course it depends on

* Part A was written by Peter Sears.

whether a company is a seller or a buyer. In the case of a buyer, an acquisition can be used as a source of capital if the buyer is among one of the more aggressive concerns. In fact, the aborted 1985 merger between Hospital Corporation of America and American Hospital Supply Corporation, programmed to be the largest deal in the history of the health care industry, was billed by some investment analysts as an acquisition by HCA to take advantage of the unused borrowing capacity of AHSC. Perhaps that is why it failed.

The purchase of a company in order to convert its assets to cash, either through stripping or gaining debt capacity, is a business for only the best trained acquirers. The process of stripping a business requires a deft touch, lest the buyer cut into the acquired company's ability to conduct its business competitively. The process of gaining additional debt capacity can run into trouble if the acquired company hits a down cycle and cannot produce enough income to service the debt. Therefore, it seems inappropriate to dwell on buying to raise cash in the context of this book, which is designed to offer a basic reference for more orthodox methods of securing capital.

From the seller's standpoint, a merger does appear to be a last resort for raising capital, even though there can be several legitimate reasons for going this route. Furthermore, some of the reasons for *not* selling one's business to raise capital are weak.

The reason most often cited against this approach is that upon completion of a merger, independence is lost. However independence is a state of mind as much as anything else. Most former owners who carry on in the management ranks of their companies after a merger are inclined to interpret any suggested change of methods coming from the new partner as evidence of the loss of independence. And yet, when the company stood alone, were there not more serious impediments to independent action? A few questions may serve to illustrate the point:

- Did the lack of capital prevent the company from building that new plant?
- Did management hunger for additional economic power to hold off competitors?
- Did the bank ever apply pressure to keep current assets under good control?
- Did investment analysts plague the management with embarrassing questions?
- Had the pressure from investors ever been a cause for imprudent accounting?
- Did that venture capitalist sitting on the board make noises about selling out if the company didn't do things his way?
- Did family squabbles disrupt operations?

- Was the mixing of business and personal activities causing the owner/manager to squirm at income tax audit time?

A typical owner/manager of an independent company has felt a reasonable number of these pressures from time to time. Each one of them limits a company's freedom to act. Working with a merger partner will free a previously independent company from numerous pressures, as it will undoubtedly create new ones. What is lost in a merger is not independence, but the appearance of independence, which in itself can be of critical importance to an owner/manager.

There are steps that can be taken in the merger process that limit the damage done by the loss of the appearance of independence. For example, Emerson Electric subordinates its corporate name to the name of acquired companies in the marketplace. Customers and the general public rarely know that an acquisition has occurred. Another example is Johnson & Johnson, which assures each operating center of continuation of titles and boards of directors. "The leader of a Johnson & Johnson company is known in his community as the president, not a subordinate in a long chain of command," is a proud claim of that great organization.

If an owner/manager of an independent company can get past the psychological barrier to merger as a source of capital, then the question becomes one of quality of money. All sources of capital put conditions on the use of it. Some conditions are more palatable to the manager of a business than are others. Some conditions are financial, such as interest and repayment schedules; some are operational, such as the installation of a new board member, or the requirement for comprehensive communications to those who advance the money. The merger as a source has to be measured against other sources, such as lending institutions, venture capitalists, and the public market, in light of the conditions attached. Each source has its own profile with respect to the above factors:

Lending Institutions. Lending institutions more often than not are paid to protect assets, not risk them. Therefore, while the abundance of available capital is great, the near term cost of capital and the restrictions on assets and behavior can be a burden. Furthermore, younger companies with thin asset bases can rarely qualify for the quantity of capital needed to make them really grow. Growth eats cash—and that can be frightening to a banker. Between the cost of the cash and dealing with the lending institution's desire for security, an emerging company may find this source of capital as the least desirable qualitatively. Nonetheless, a bank can be paid off and then told to go away—something that doesn't easily happen with other capital sources.

Venture Capital. Venture capitalists love growth, and they are willing to sacrifice the security of collateral for the right to participate in above-average growth opportunities. However, the economics of their business requires that they demand a huge "equity risk premium." An equity risk premium is simply a reasonable chance at earning an extraordinarily high annual return on the initial investment. Venture capitalists promise their backers a rate of return in the 30–40 percent range. This means that successes and failures in their portfolios have to produce this kind of return on average. An owner/manager of a business seeking venture money must be confident of bettering a 40 percent annual growth rate year after year, or else the venture money will cost too much of his company. Furthermore, venture capitalists can be terribly intrusive when times are bad and can sell a company out when times are good. The objective of a venture capitalist is to go from "Green to Green"—take money, invest it, and then convert it to more money. The relationship is rarely a long-standing one.

The Public Market. The public market includes everyone else, from family and friends of an entrepreneur, to institutional investors, to your Aunt Minnie. On theoretical terms, the cost of money obtained from the public ought not to be substantially different from the cost of money obtained at a bank. In reality, there are times when tapping the public market is nothing but thievery, and there are other times that the public market won't buy gold at 10 cents an ounce. Timing is the key. When a company's timing is right, money can be acquired cheaply with very few strings attached. When timing is poor, no money is available. If timing is too good for the company from the quality of money standpoint, managers are asking for difficult times at future shareholder meetings. Public markets are vehicles for institutional investors today. Institutional investors engage spies called Investment Analysts, whose job it is to predict the performance of a public company. The institutional investors make the lives of these spies difficult if there are untoward events within a subject company. Therefore, the spies who survive in their field have come to learn how to ask the most difficult and embarrassing questions of managements and measure the responses with sophisticated critical judgment. The process of dealing with the investment community, when looked at in economic terms, has to be considered a time-consuming diversion for operating managers.

The Merger Market. The merger market is a blend of the three other markets, and an acquiring company with a lot of capital works like the other markets: Like the bank, the assets of the business become, for all intents and purposes, the property of the supplier of funds; like the venture capitalists, the acquiring company expects to stimulate and benefit from the growth of the acquired business; and like the public market, money is probably cheaper than from other sources, and its availability may be influenced by the business cycle. The advantage of the merger market is that the terms for acquiring the capital can be negotiated to a much greater extent than with other financial institutions.

There are also significant differences between the merger market as a source of capital and the other sources, and these differences need some analysis:

- In the merger market, both the owners <u>and</u> the company are looking for capital. In other capital sourcing markets, the interests of the owners are normally subordinated to the financial interests of the company. In the merger market, the owners normally subordinate the financial interests of the company to their own.
- In the merger market, the economic ties between owners and company are weakened, if not broken.
- In the merger market, the buyer adopts as his own, the capital needs and interests of the company.

These three differences create a natural tension between the buyer and company on the one side, and the owner/seller on the other. The cause of this tension needs further elaboration.

In the ideal merger (there is no such thing in fact), the buyer has made a rational decision to buy something rather than to build. That decision is capable of being measured in economic terms. The present cost of building a business is X, the present cost of buying the same business is Y. Most buyers concede a higher risk in building than buying—that too can be quantified. A merger makes sense when Y is lower than X.

However, Y is made up of more than just the purchase price. It includes a calculation of the present cost of resources needed first to strengthen the acquired company and then to make it grow. So Y is the sum of the purchase price, and postmerger capital, which is the present value of future support of the company. Buyers recognize that postmerger capital should probably be a constant. Without it, a company cannot grow, or even hold its own in a competitive marketplace. The purchase price is the variable. If the purchase price is kept low, the buyer has a cushion for postmerger capital. If the price is too high, the rational buyer will conclude that the cost of buying and building (Y) has exceeded the cost of building from scratch (X) and will choose the latter course.

A typical owner/seller will fail to give credit to such rationality in a buyer (often with considerable justification). However, a well-prepared buyer will set a limit on the investment and will negotiate to limit the purchase price and maximize his freedom to invest post-merger capital in the business.

This is a significant factor for an owner/manager who views the merger as a source of capital for his business rather than himself. If the owner/manager is more concerned about personal wealth than business growth, he will make the task of securing future capital for the business more difficult. If the owner/manager is truly motivated to regard the merger as a capital source for the business, he may be sacrificing the interests of other, more passive owners of the business, but he will normally find the merger partner one of the most accommodating sources of business capital imaginable.

What does postmerger capital cost within a larger organization? In some companies it costs what the market charges, and in others it is free. The answer depends on the free cash flow profile of the buyer and the management accounting system that the merged company employs.

A typical active buyer of companies has found itself in a market with slowing growth and is looking for diversification that will enable it to grow faster. Assuming the buyer's base business is healthy, the slowing growth trend of the base business is likely to free up cash that doesn't have to be reinvested. In searching for a merger partner, an enlightened manager of a selling company will look for this kind of opportunity.

A large company with numerous operating divisions employs accounting systems that incorporate features specifically designed to measure managerial performance. Since most large companies manage corporate cash and taxes centrally, an operating division is measured most often by its earnings performance before taxes and interest, or under a system that imputes taxes and interest. In either event, the operating unit is relieved of the burden of raising capital and paying the government its due. This frees up the time of the division management to devote to the task of making and selling products. Any manager of an independent company seeking capital will testify to the fact that raising capital can indeed be frustrating and time-consuming. The extra time that membership in a larger organization frees up is well appreciated by those who have chosen the merger route to financial support.

In summary, while the merger is not immediately thought of as part of the capital market, there are valid reasons for it to be considered that way. The "independent" company may be shy about following a merger path, but close analysis of what independence actually is will reveal it to be more a state of mind than anything else. An owner/manager who puts the progress of his company ahead of personal gain goes a long way toward simplifying the merger process and aligning his interests with those of the merger partner. Once on board, the merged company may come to find the new partner surprisingly generous compared to the cold outside world.

THE PROCESS OF FINDING A MERGER PARTNER

The Investor Chain

This is at work in the United States today, the institutionalization of the process of financing and developing young companies. A typical young company today moves through several stages of ownership in fairly rapid time: conception stage, with ownership restricted to founders' friends and kin; venture stage, with ownership expanded to professional manager/investors; mezzanine stage, when larger financial institutions play a role in getting the company ready for public ownership; IPO stage, when certain select clients of the underwriter invest; broad public ownership stage, where the shares leak out to a larger investing populace; and merger stage, when all the chips are cashed in. Sometimes companies skip a stage or two, and some hold the line at one stage for a long time, but the progression is now quite normal for successful young companies.

Ideally, each shift in the ownership comes about because of the need to fund a growing business in increasing amounts. Each level of investor expects to earn a return. The rate of return expectations decline as the business matures and the associated risk diminishes; nonetheless, the smooth operation of the process depends on the realistic expectation for profit of the next level of investor. An enlightened manager of a business should understand this process. This should govern the manager's timing in moving from one level to another. The manager who waits too long, milking his business rather than letting it grow, as well as the manager who squeezes too hard in negotiations and leaves nothing on the table for the next group of owners, had both better be of a mind to retire. Doing violence to the process invites retribution.

Therefore, the skilled manager will start planning to develop the next owner group early. He must ask the question, "What will make the company attractive for the next class of owner?"

A good financial profile is what one thinks of as most important, and no doubt it tends to add to the luster of a company, but sophisticated investors look for much more. Good historic financial performance says a lot about how the company has been managed, but it says far too little about the future.

What is more important is how the company has planned its future growth. The intelligent investor, be it a venture capitalist, an underwriter, or a merger partner, will investigate the following areas:

New Products. What steps has the company taken to be innovative? Is there a stream of new products for the future? What resources have been employed to develop new products? Do new products fulfill unmet market needs? Does the management pay close attention to the product development process? Are there skilled people employed in product development?

Markets. At what level of maturity are the served markets? Did the company employ a niche strategy, and if so, are the niches in fact blind alleys? Are the markets cyclical? What is the structure of the markets, and how strong is the competition? Is the company giving away market share?

Organization. Has the management of the company anticipated growth through the hiring of good people? Has there been adequate delegation of authority? Does the company tolerate dead wood? Is the management team compatible? Is the work force motivated?

Plant. Does the company adequately support its investment in plant? Has the company been too extravagant or too tight? Does the company support unnecessary or less efficient production activities?

Planning. Does the company embrace a planning process? Is it reliable? Does the work force participate in planning? Are plans strategic?

A company that flunks this test is bound to suffer. Either (1) the investor will be driven to other investment options, (2) the investor will lower the price he is willing to pay to reflect the company's weaknesses, or (3) the investor will effect dramatic change in the company once the investment is made. An investor who doesn't do at least one of those three things will lose his money.

The manager who plans to move to the next level of financial support should look inward first and try to satisfy the questions shown above. Studies have shown that the greatest hurdle that young companies have to overcome before becoming attractive to investors is in the area of new product development. Young companies grow rapidly to fill a niche, and then cannot determine what to do next. The time of management is so taken up with early growth, that consideration of future growth is postponed.

The Role of the Planning Process

A good planning process in place will offer managers insights about investor expectations. While volumes have been written about corporate planning, a few rules will suffice here:

Planning Is Empirical. Early attempts at planning will produce undue optimism and pessimism. The key is improvement of reliability of plans from year to year, not what one plan may itself say.

Planning Is an Iterative Process. It doesn't happen all at once, or just once a year. A series of planning dialogues throughout an organization improve the process.

Planning Is Communal. The best plans come from far down the organizational ladder, not from the top. People at the top set objectives: The organization lays the plans to meet the objectives.

Planning Promotes Corporate Growth. When managers set objectives, corporate growth is the ultimate guiding influence. This is because no company can stay in one place for very long—it will either grow or decline—and because growth both requires and attracts investment capital. In setting objectives, managers must fashion their companies in such a way as to attract investment capital.

Most planning programs begin with a statement of what a company is. This is referred to as a charter statement. The charter statement performs two functions. It sets the tone of the company, and declares what businesses the company is *not* in. For example, "We are a specialty chemicals company, we engage in research to produce high-value-added products to serve users in the building materials industry."

This charter statement declares with some specificity what industry the company participates in. It suggests something about life within the company, the research emphasis denoting a long-term view and the need for high gross margins to support sophisticated marketing efforts. It also says that low-margin commodity chemicals are to be eschewed along with every other business foreign to the company.

Now the company is in a position to see more clearly what it is about the business that will attract investment. The company may conclude that the business is in an attractive sector of the economy. What this means essentially is that it is easier to grow in a growing market than in a mature one. The company then has to measure itself against competitors for investment dollars within the industry. "We expect to enjoy the best margins, the best growth rate, and the best ROI in our industry, in that order."

The company has thereby determined that good margins allow the company to invest in more research per sales dollar than others, and that leads to higher growth. The company has also determined that it can be a little more lax about plant and working capital investments so long as it leads to product superiority and the high margins.

Now the company is in a position to make comparisons as an investor might. How does the company stack up today against its chief competitors? If an investor chooses to move into the industry, will the company be at the top or bottom of the list?

If the company is not at the top, it will be able to measure what it takes to reach the top. Suppose the favored competitor is growing 5 percent faster. The company can calculate how wide the gap will become over time. It may also be able to determine what resources it needs to close the gap. Such resources may include cash to build new plant, an improved international organization, a sales force, an upgraded research team, or perhaps new blood in management ranks.

The strategic plan of the corporation can then be directed toward improved performance to strengthen the company competitively. It is at this point that the merger option should be considered along with other ways to gain needed resources.

The advantage of merger versus other methods of obtaining resources is that it is fast. Sometimes, the marketplace demands rapid action to secure a strategic position. Sometimes it doesn't matter and a company can obtain resources piecemeal and at leisure.

It really shouldn't matter which of the parties to the merger ends up playing the dominant role. What matters is that the combined entity itself is stronger and attracts investors in turn. This idea is anathema to most managers, but is nonetheless a fact of life.

What is important is that the other party to a transaction possesses the needed resources. For example, two companies with high levels of capital intensity and growth may need cash more than anything—but they don't need one another. In fact, they could very well compound one another's problems.

So now, the process of choosing a merger partner is beginning to take shape. The objective of the corporation is to create value for investors—not only existing ones, but those who are better able to help the company grow. The process began with the establishment of a strategic plan that not only forecast the future sales and profits of the company, but also determined how the company was going to conduct its affairs in a manner most attractive to investors. The plan determined the resources at hand to accomplish the objective, as well as the resources that would be needed. It is now time to search for needed resources through the merger process.

Finding the Right Partner

If a company is going to be sold to gain a sustainable source of capital for growth, then the process of finding a merger partner seems at first to be simple. There are data bases available that display financial histories of all major companies in exquisite detail. Just find the company with the most ample free cash flow, visit its president, and offer your company at a fair price. If the first company says no, then move to the company with the second most ample free cash flow, visit the president, and offer the company at a fair price.

This approach is not only simple, its logic is undeniable—and yet companies don't behave this way for a variety of reasons, good and bad.

The good reasons

- Choosing a partner on financial grounds alone will do little to assure compatibility (more about this later).
- After the first few solicitations, word gets out that the company is for sale, employees become restive, and competitors use the information with valued customers to the company's detriment.
- Historic free cash flow and future free cash flow are different. A buyer's future investment aims and requirements must be examined before future free cash flow can be ascertained.
- Experienced buyers assume that companies that are obviously for sale are for sale because of a flaw. Therefore, any quoted price will be assumed to be excessive.

The bad reasons

- People don't like the word *no* and will go to great lengths to avoid hearing it. Since a direct solicitation stands a better chance of yielding a *no* answer than no solicitation at all, it is better not to ask.
- It is bad etiquette to approach a total stranger with such a monumental proposition.
- This is a business for professionals, so a trained intermediary ought to be employed to pop the question.

In other words, there is much to be said for a direct solicitation so long as the seller does his homework and handles the price issue with some skill. Use of an intermediary out of shyness is the wrong reason to do so, while use of an intermediary to protect security may be wise.

Doing One's Homework

Since the orientation of this chapter is the merger as a method of tapping a financial resource, it may be incorrectly inferred that gaining access to funds should be a primary reason for merging. Far from it—most mergers occur for a complicated set of reasons. A rational process of choosing a merger partner should sort out and prioritize those reasons. One merger partner will be better for a company than most others, and a choice between candidates will have to occur.

Benjamin Franklin, proof positive that America was born in the Age of Reason, used to list pros and cons before making a key decision. If the pros outweighed the cons, he proceeded. The same technique should not lose currency when it comes to selection of a merger partner, although the process of selection from among several alternatives requires a more elaborate methodology. A matrix evaluation method provides a satisfactory way of sorting through the pros and cons of any number of prospective partners.

Step 1. List and give numerical weight to needs as shown in Exhibit 1.

Step 2. Score merger partners according to fulfillment of needs as shown in Exhibit 2.

Each item of the evaluation list for companies matches up with an item on the needs list.

Step 3. Score a prospective merger partner, giving a score of 1 to 10 by category. If particular item is an unknown, give it a score of 5, and vow to revaluate the subject when more information is at hand.

EXHIBIT 1 Weighted Needs of Seller

Needs	*Weight (1–10)*
Need investment money	10
Need to move quickly	8
Need partner that understands the business	7
Need stronger sales force	7
Need international network	7
Need pool of younger managers	5
Need to keep company whole to reassure customers	8
Need to reward shareholders with handsome price	9
Need job security for top managers	4
Need to save face among friends	2

EXHIBIT 2 Potential Merger Partner Scores

Fulfillment	*Score (1–10)*
Company has ample cash resources	________
Company has experience in mergers and is quick	________
Company is in the business	________
Company can deploy sales force in support	________
Company well established internationally	________
Company hires well, has managerial pool	________
Company allows merger partner to stay independent	________
Company pays well for high-quality acquisitions	________
Company protects managers of merger partner	________
A spot on the board is feasible	________

Step 4. Multiply the score of the company in each category by the weight given on the corresponding needs list.

Step 5. Add the results. This renders a composite score for a company, and it can be compared to composite scores for others. Six, or a dozen, or a hundred companies can be evaluated this way, and their ranking will be determined by their composite scores.

It is difficult to perform such a qualitative analysis with great precision. Information about some companies will be better than about others. However, experience with this method shows that it takes a significant revaluation of a company to move it a great distance in a ranking. Cream tends to rise to the top and stay there.

The matrix evaluation method may seem a little intimidating to some because the amount of investigation needed to make an informed evaluation of candidates is so extensive. To some, it may appear insurmountable because the information required may not appear to be publicly available. In recent years, alumni of intelligence agencies have reported that the lion's share of intelligence is gathered from public sources. That may provide some reassurance. There are numerous sources of information about potential merger partners that should give one confidence that the matrix can be developed thoroughly. Some sources are obvious, and others not quite so obvious:

Business Literature. The articles published in a decade on any major company can fill volumes. While the information is usually transitory in nature, it can offer valuable insights into methods of doing business. Local newspapers, particularly away from major cities, devote significant space to key regional companies. Investment analysts publish high-quality research on companies of interest. Market research firms publish multiclient studies on companies and markets and encourage the commissioning of more detailed analyses. Finally, business school students and faculty like to produce studies on individual companies. These studies usually sit unread in university files.

Investment Seminars. Numerous entrepreneurs and financial advisers conduct meetings at which companies and markets are featured. These meetings offer the attendees a good chance to meet the managements of such companies and to hear them talk about themselves.

The SEC. All companies traded publicly in the United States must make extensive filings with the Securities and Exchange Commission. This material only begins with the 10-K. There are numerous supplemental filings made on a quarterly and an events basis, together with backup schedules that yield information in excruciating detail.

Other Federal Agencies. The Departments of Commerce, Labor, and Agriculture; the Federal Trade Commission; the Patent Office; and a variety of dedicated regulatory bodies receive numerous filings both company and industry related. Congress itself has studied most industries at one time or another and has published extensive studies. A consulting company called Washington Researchers specializes in instructing companies about commercial intelligence utilizing our nation's capital as a prime resource.

Court Cases. Litigation in which a company is a party will tell a lot about how a company behaves, and the background documentation to a court opinion can offer substantial data on company practices as well as insights into the personalities of key managers.

Computer Data Bases. Financial data is available in abundance, going back decades. The time-sharing services that access the data also provide programs for manipulation of the data to yield custom-made analyses for subscribers. In addition, there are extensive time-sharing stock ownership and trading data sources available.

Trade Associations. Trade associations will often gather statistics from members in support of a position on legislation or regulatory change. They also may produce public relations data of value. Trade associations will also invite speakers from companies to speak at meetings and conventions, and invitations to sit in on speeches are often easily obtained. Professional and scientific societies are another important related source.

Trade Shows. Trade shows will yield up-to-date information on products and competitive performance, and may give some clues about products in the development pipeline.

Directories. There are directories available that list managements and their educational and work histories. There are numerous product directories and catalogs available.

The issue is often not whether there is enough information available on companies, but rather whether there is time enough to sift through that which is available.

Once a comprehensive number of companies has been evaluated this way, the process of identification of the best partner may well be complete. No doubt there may be some wild cards that would be great merger partners but are and will remain undiscovered. The only way to enhance one's ability to find the wild cards is to advertise the sale of one's company, thereby drawing out such candidates. As noted, this may be an undesirable step because of potential damage to work force and customer relationships.

The Tie-In between Evaluation and the Selling Message

It is now time to develop approaches to the lead candidates and to perfect the selling message. The merger process is usually a two-way sale, in which the burden of persuasion normally rests upon the party making the initial approach. It takes the attractiveness and guile of a Cleopatra to shift the burden once the initial contact is made. Few companies have the ability to work things that way. Therefore, it pays a company well to assume the burden and develop the most powerful selling points that it can. Fortunately, the matrix methodology used to identify good merger partners also provides a list of points that can be employed in the sales message.

There are three elements of a good selling message:

- Flattery: You have what we don't and never will by ourselves. (The matrix provides a list of the needs that are met by the particular candidate.)
- Fit: Our two companies are well matched. (The matrix provides a list of what the company has to offer that the other party probably desires.)
- Appeal to Greed: The combination will make a lot of money for you. (The matrix may give clues about synergies in the merger that would immediately improve the buyer's ROI (return on investment).)

Sophisticated buyers are usually well tuned to sales approaches and are turned off by hyperbole. The best selling messages are clearly but modestly stated. Facts and figures do much of the selling when put forth in a quiet, nonpromotional way. Again, the matrix method provides the outline for illustration of pertinent facts and figures.

Direct versus Indirect Solicitation

Buyers like to take the measurement of sellers. The question is when that should take place. Sellers seeking out buyers will often hire an intermediary to make the contact in order to solicit initial interest. The desire of the seller to assure security is the primary motivating factor in using a third party for the initial approach. While this is a legitimate purpose, it is not without its risks:

The negatives

- If the intermediary is unknown to the buyer, the solicitation will receive less attention than a direct call. Companies that are active acquirers receive scores of solicitations and sometimes have difficulty differentiating the strong from the weak ones.
- Intermediaries cannot possibly know the business of the seller as well as the seller does. This lack of knowledge is readily discerned by the buyer and can get in the way of the delivery of an effective sales message. The buyer will often be persuaded by the confidence and purpose conveyed by a seller in a direct encounter, whereas that will be lacking in most intermediaries.
- An intermediary may promise confidentiality to the seller at the outset of a relationship, but using one can also, after a series of dismissals from potential buyers, lengthen the list of solicitees. Sooner or later this will break security and cause the harm that the seller initially sought to avoid.

The positives

- Intermediaries, especially the ones who work particular industries, make it their business to be informed about what larger firms are seeking as acquisitions. They can fit two pieces of a puzzle together and save buyer and seller time and money.
- Skilled intermediaries know how to read responses of the parties. Sometimes an initial no means maybe, and more often yes means maybe too.
- Intermediaries can disguise the eagerness of the seller, at least for a while. This may have positive implications on the price paid in an acquisition.
- Intermediaries can really earn their fees when negotiations are under way. Sellers are notably sensitive about their businesses

during this time, for the tone of a negotiation offers a clue about future relationships between buyer and seller's management. Buyers are facing substantial risks when sponsoring an acquisition and can find it easier sometimes to turn away from the risks. An effective intermediary can manage the relationship from the outset to avoid skittishness.

It all comes down to the question of who the intermediary happens to be. The good ones can do a great job, and the poor ones can ruin everything. The industry is populated by professionals, incompetents, and, in some cases, rascals. Sometimes it is difficult for a seller to distinguish between them. Sellers will rarely sell more than once in a lifetime, whereas buyers have much more experience. There are a few basic rules that buyers should follow in dealing with intermediaries that may help sellers as well.

Do:

- Learn who are the best in the industry. Best doesn't necessarily mean volume of deals as it does a reputation for good communication and character. The financial press is filled with advertisements about transactions and who advised whom. It is a place to start. If solicited by an intermediary, ask for references. The good ones will gladly supply a list of satisfied clients.
- Go to one or two established merger courses. For example, Northwestern University and New York Management, Inc. both sponsor management seminars on the subject that have run regularly for several years. The subject of dealing with intermediaries will come up. Other companies will share their views. Don't worry about revealing selling intentions; sellers and buyers cannot be easily differentiated at such sessions unless they want to be.
- Join the Association for Corporate Growth. This is an association of more than 2,500 executives dedicated to the acquisition business—some on the industrial side, some on the service side. There are active chapters in most of the major cities of the United States, as well as in Canada and the United Kingdom. It holds numerous local meetings featuring CEOs and planning executives from across industry, as well as a well-attended annual convention every spring. The contacts made within the association will shed light on the use of intermediaries.
- Know the legal obligations running between client and finders and brokers. Basically, a finder is not required to act in the interest of one party, whereas a broker always does. In some jurisdictions, the production of a willing buyer alone, even if no transaction results, could trigger a fee obligation. In some jurisdictions, a brokerage contract must be in writing, in others

it need only be verbal. Some obligations expire after a fixed period of time, others run on and on.

- Learn the ins and outs of various compensation schemes. Some compensation arrangements based entirely on the completion of a deal look cheap at the outset but end up buying low-quality effort. Others may look expensive but buy valuable time and attention of professionals. Remember that intermediaries have to eat, too. Much of the trade quotes something called the Lehman Formula, which is a contingent fee based on a purchase price. Usually, the rate of compensation declines as the price goes up, but the total dollars to be paid can be considerable. There are numerous variations to the Lehman Formula, some of which are more suitable to buyers than sellers. Sellers might even want to reverse the Lehman Formula, giving an increasing percentage to the intermediary who secures an extraordinarily good price. However, sophisticated buyers know how the fee systems work, know that it ultimately gets paid by the buyer in one form or another, and that in a pinch, the buyer can condition his offer on a reduction of the fee.

Don't:

- Express any intention to sell the business, or even to consider the sale of a business, to an unknown inquirer. The trade abounds with what are known as "Ham and Eggs" people, who solicit a sale on scanty information, and who represent no one at the outset. It is true that management must be careful legally about closing off bona fide offers to acquire a business. The decision to respond to such an offer is most properly left to boards of directors, the elected fiduciaries of the shareholders. Managements and boards are entitled to have the basis to make reasonably informed judgments before declaring their intentions. Hypothetical questions do not offer enough for that process to occur properly.
- Make verbal commitments to unknown intermediaries. See an attorney before engaging anyone. Make sure the full dimension of the relationship is in writing.
- Be fooled by the elegance of investment bankers. Good manners can effectively disguise mean intentions. Wall Street has become very competitive in the merger business, and sometimes companies can get hurt in the competitive battle. Merger departments develop shopping lists for potential buyers based on slim information and sometimes on pure inspired speculation. A company that gives a hint of availability will rapidly become shopworn.
- Ask the family attorney or small town banker to help find a buyer. While such people can be entirely trustworthy, and offer

meaningful assurances on confidentiality, chances are they don't know the brokerage business well enough to get the best value. An accountant is marginally better. Some accounting firms have developed a substantial merger practice, but not all of them.

The ideal intermediary is a professional broker or investment banker who enjoys an impeccable reputation for fair dealing; who communicates well; who obeys instructions; who takes the time to understand the seller's business, motivation, strengths, and weaknesses; who will patiently hear the seller's ideas about the ideal buyer; and who is willing to commit the time and effort to do a responsible job. Anyone less than ideal can spoil the seller's business.

The seller striking out on his own because of the inability to find the right representative has lost only a little ground, provided he has done his homework assiduously. Buyers are complemented by sellers who know them well. Furthermore, sellers don't always have to propose merger at the beginning of a relationship. Buyers will often engage in exploratory talks with prospective sellers in order to get to know the other party to a transaction better. The business result may end up short of a merger, but be productive for both parties. In today's world, potential buyers are frequently advocating "Elephant and Flea" arrangements, wherein the buyer acquires a small amount of equity of the seller in exchange for, or in conjunction with, the granting of product or distribution rights. The characterization stems from the realization of both parties that the two parties may share the same bed so long as the elephant promises not to roll over and crush the flea. There is no reason why the process cannot be put to work for the seller as well as the buyer. A license, a distributorship, a product development collaboration, or a minority investment, may be an important way to begin the relationship.

When and What to Quote as the Price

Sellers have difficulty coming to grips with a fair price for their businesses. They may have greater difficulty handling the price issue during merger discussions. Again, homework is necessary before anyone can arrive at a decent price intelligently.

Most skillful buyers understand in advance what they can afford to pay for a particular business opportunity. With the growth of microcomputers and fancy financial software, buyers are able to construct economic models that assess the value of all investment opportunities. These models provide a vehicle for reducing to a present value the future cash flow streams of a potential acquiree.

Buyers apply a discount to future cash flow streams to derive a present value. This is called the discounted cash flow method of valuation. The discount rate applied is referred to as a hurdle rate. Hurdle rates are dictated by three factors: (1) anticipated sales and profit growth of the buyer's business, (2) anticipated incremental capital intensity of the business, and (3) anticipated dividend and debt policies of the business. Each of these factors directly influences the others. Capital produces growth, and the lack of it retards growth. Sales growth eats up working capital and from time to time requires capital for plant construction. Dividends disperse capital. Profits and debt produce capital. A buyer has to keep all these elements in proper balance. A hurdle rate is merely a statement of what kind of return a company must receive on its investments in the aggregate in order to sustain these elements in proper balance. A hurdle rate is not selected arbitrarily based on money market standards, it is arithmetically derived.

The formula below offers an estimate of the maximum sustainable growth of a company employing the factors stated above. The ROE in the formula can be interpreted as the corporation's hurdle rate. Try out this formula by comparing a corporation's stated growth objectives with its financial history in order to determine where the gaps lie between what the corporation wants to do and its financial resources to carry out its plans:

$$\text{MSG} = \text{ROE} \times \text{Ret. Rt.} + [\text{Ret. Rt.} \times (\text{ROE} - \text{I}) \times \text{D/E}]$$

where

MSG = Maximum sustainable growth
ROE = Return on equity
Ret. Rt. = Retention rate, or 100 percent minus the percentage of net earnings paid out in dividends. (Note that the first part of the formula, ROE × Ret. Rt. is the baseline for estimating a company's ability to finance its growth and is referred to as the reinvestment rate.)
I = After-tax interest rate on debt
D/E = Ratio of debt to equity

The factor with the greatest amount of leverage in this formula is ROE. A company that can improve its ROE most dramatically improves its ability to finance growth. Adherence to high hurdle rate standards offers the best chance for a company to improve ROE. A company that fails to adhere to hurdle rate standards will ultimately stop growing and will stop creating value for shareholders. Such a company will ultimately be forced to take drastic action down the road. A seller who is merging to raise capital for a business is better off dealing with a company that takes its hurdle rates seriously. Again, the tension between owners and managers of the seller may manifest itself.

Of what use is anticipation of the buyer's hurdle rate to the seller? The ideal merger negotiation is the development of a joint business plan. The seller superimposes his projections on the buyer's company. The parties then look for opportunities to effect growth that neither could do alone, and for opportunities to save money. The incremental benefit of the joint plan over what the buyer would do on its own is the basis for calculating a purchase price. The future cash flow stream attributable to the incremental benefit can then be discounted back to a present value using the hurdle rate as the discount factor. The present value is probably what the buyer is willing to pay.

This process is not unlike what an independent company does when applying for a loan. The company expects to derive an incremental benefit over and above the cost of the money. If the cost of the money is so high that no incremental benefit is derived, then the loan is not worth it. So it is with purchase prices.

By understanding what motivates the buyer, the seller can help the buyer visualize benefits from the merger that may not be readily apparent. The merger negotiation can follow a reasoned course, and differences of opinion can be objectively addressed. However, there are two important warnings to heed.

1. Using the superimposition of business plans to derive a value in a merger means that companies that can afford to pay more for an acquisition are those that can best effect integration of the merging companies. This means the loss of autonomy and jobs to a greater extent than in a merger with a buyer who is diversifying.

2. A cash flow projection for a going concern has to have a finite end, yet businesses theoretically go on forever. To be correct, people who use the discounted cash flow valuation method attach at the end of the period examined a terminal value (sometimes referred to as a residual value). Opinions differ on how terminal values are conceived. Some prefer to use a net book value figure that is somewhat akin to salvage, others apply a mathematical formula that simulates an infinite cash flow stream, others use a price earnings multiplier that approximates the stock market on the theory that a business that is acquired can be sold in the same way. The problem is, and it is a big problem, fast-growing businesses will often show negative cash flow until their growth slows. Therefore, valuation techniques will yield present values that are totally dependent on terminal value assumptions. The parties to a merger negotiation will remain calm through the business planning phase and then get hot under the collar during the process of selection of an appropriate terminal value.

When approaching a prospective buyer, a seller should be equipped with the following minimum facts:

- The historic growth rate of sales and profits of the buyer for its key business segments over the last 2, 5, and 10 years.
- An objective assessment of the rates of growth of the buyer's markets.
- An historic analysis of the capital intensity of the buyer's business, expressed as a ratio of incremental capital employed to incremental sales, year by year, for 10 years. It would help if capital employed is itemized for the purpose of revealing changes in asset management policies on the working capital side, and plant aging on the fixed asset side.
- An understanding of buyer's announced growth objectives, dividend policies, and historic debt-equity trends.

Armed with this information, the seller will have a baseline against which the representations of the buyer can be measured, will know pretty much whether the buyer will have the money to invest in the seller's business over the long haul, will be able to calculate the hurdle rate needed for the buyer to make good on promises of growth, and may even be able to discern what the combination of buyer's and seller's businesses will have to yield in order to justify a satisfactory price.

A company with regular sales and profit growth of 10 percent annually, incremental capital employed to incremental sales of 50 percent, net margins of 6 percent, and a dividend payout policy of 30 percent of net earnings is just about at a break-even point in net cash flow after dividends. A seller aware of this profile will know that any acquisition by the buyer will largely have to be self-financing—or the buyer will have to demonstrate through some change in business how new cash flow will be generated. A seller will also realize that the buyer would have to stretch to maintain its historic growth rate. The buyer's profile suggests a return on equity of 12 percent, and with a dividend rate of 30 percent, the reinvestment rate is 8.4 percent. The company would probably have to improve margins or increase debt in order to meet the 10 percent growth objective.

Suppose a seller who is merging to raise capital engages in a negotiation with such a buyer. The more the seller demands in purchase price, the bigger the hole he is digging for the resulting combined entity. Even if the seller bargains for the buyer's stock there is a problem, because the additional dividend load could jeopardize the financial health of the buyer. The least harmful effect that the transaction would have on the combined entity is to slow the growth of the companies in order to minimize working capital and new fixed asset requirements. This is called milking the business. A business without serious competitors can be milked. Milking a business with such competitors around will destroy the business.

It is important that sellers looking for the merger as a source of capital seek out companies with high ROEs and modest growth expectations. Such companies will have the lower hurdle rates and can spare the cash to support the growth of the acquired company. Since a company with a low hurdle rate gives future cash a higher value than a company with a high one, companies with low hurdle rates can afford to pay more up front.

Exhibit 3 below shows the value of $10 million received five years out, discounted back to a present value, using a variety of discount rates:

EXHIBIT 3 Present Value by Discount Rate (of $10 million received five years out)

Discount Rate (percent)	*Present Value (millions)*
5%	$7.8
10	6.2
15	5.0
20	4.0
25	3.3

Were one to adhere to hurdle rate analysis, it would appear that the acceptance by a seller of a price from a buyer with a 5 percent hurdle rate would yield a price nearly 2.4 times higher than one from a buyer with a 25 percent hurdle rate, unless of course the buyer is offering stock as the medium of exchange.

Where stock is offered for a company, and the seller either wants or is compelled to hold the stock for a period of time, a low hurdle rate for a buyer suggests strongly that the buyer is not acting in the interest of his shareholders, and that should diminish the value of the stock over time. A stockholder would be far better off trading his holdings for bonds than investing in a company whose own investment standards are for returns far below money market rates.

Normally, sellers take stock in an acquisition for one of two reasons—either to be assured of power in the combined entity, wherein the seller probably intends to hold the stock for a substantial period, or to defer the impact of taxes on the transaction. With capital gains taxes being in the 20 percent range today, the second reason has less significance to a seller's decision to take stock. Furthermore, a premium price for cash versus stock is not unheard of in acquisition negotiations and can cover at least some of the taxes required to be paid. Therefore, unless the seller really is going for power in the combined entity, it is far preferable for the seller to take cash from companies with low hurdle rate expectations. In dealing with companies with high hurdle rates, the seller has to make a careful assessment of the quality of the management of the buyer, and the price the stock is realizing on the market.

Good management presumably will make investments pay according to hurdle rate expectations, and therefore their stocks will continue to be premium priced. A seller may then see his own purchase price enhanced with improved performance of the combined entity.

A seller that is equipped with these concepts will be much better prepared to deal with a price issue than one who uses extraneous information to set a price.

One of the poorest methods of setting prices in a deal, and one that the investment banking community persists in employing, is to look at what one considers comparable transactions. The question is asked: What recent deals have taken place within a particular industry, and what ratios do those deals reflect, that is, price-earnings, price-to-book value of acquired net assets, price-to-sales?

These comparisons are improper because:

- There is no such thing as a characteristic earnings profile of a company or an industry. One glance at the stock pages shows the highest P-E ratios apply to the companies with the weakest earnings. Within a given industry over time, the range of profitability is wide. Market leaders tend to be more profitable than weaker players. An acquisition of a market leader ought to carry a higher P-E than an acquisition of a company with a lower market share. Since the term leader generally refers to only one company, there is no room for a comparison.
- The investment standards of one buyer versus another may be entirely different. As seen above, a difference in hurdle rates can make a substantial difference in prices paid.
- The medium of payment varies from one deal to the next. For example, the exchange of stock in a transaction is a two-way, not a one-way valuation. Use of certain hybrid securities and deferred payment mechanisms may also obfuscate the comparison.
- The truly representational samplings are insufficient in number, and in order to build the number, the comparative tables usually reflect a drift into other industries.
- Net book values may not reflect true asset values. Several large-

scale transactions in the oil industry, for example, place more importance on the market value of oil reserves than the value placed on such reserves on company books. Companies with large and long-standing real estate holdings may have a wealth of unrecorded assets. On the other hand, in spite of valiant efforts by accountants to be correct, some corporate assets on books may be overvalued, inventories of companies in fast-moving industries being one of the larger problem categories. In some cases, liabilities are substantially understated—for example, unfunded health care obligations to retirees.

- In some industries, particularly those in rapidly growing markets, the price-to-book ratio is excessive and therefore meaningless. Once a price goes above twice book value, the reason for making the ratio becomes absurd.
- Price-to-sales ratios are meaningful only to the buyer who knows better what to do with a sales base than a seller. Otherwise, sales can be bought in any business—usually at the expense of earnings.

Buyers are both embarrassed and irritated when confronted with comparative deals in a price negotiation. Often the seller will select the highest prices paid and ignore the lower ones. The buyer is then forced to downgrade the seller's company or disparage the recklessness of some other buyer. Neither response moves the discussion forward. It is like a man telling his fiancée that the honeymoon will be at the Jersey Shore instead of Bali (where Jerry took Susie) because Susie was prettier, Jerry was dumber, or both. It is far smoother to base discussions on the long-range plans of the marriage.

THE QUESTION OF FIT

Today, there is great popularity in examining the "corporate culture." It has been perceived that successful companies develop distinct ways of looking at their businesses, communicating, and otherwise behaving. Corporate culture can be evidenced by the product development and pricing strategies pursued, by the way meetings are conducted, or by the dress and language of the CEO. In the case of mergers, it is a given that the two parties to a merger will have distinct cultures. However, there are some cultural differences that will have a more profound effect on the merger than others. These differences are economic in cause but are manifested by the clash of broader value systems in their effect. Sometimes, these economic causes are not revealed to the merger partners in time to avoid spoiling the relationship. To be forewarned that such differences exist and are profound will at least allow parties to seek ways in advance to accommodate one another.

Perception of Risk

Businesspeople take risks. Great businesses take great risks. However, the process of risk taking becomes so much a part of everyday life in an enterprise that the parties become insensitive to the magnitude of the risks taken. Consider the aggregate risks of public utilities in investing in atomic power plants. Not only have they made enormous capital expenditures, but also they have faced substantial regulatory and public relations hurdles in moving new plants on stream. In the meantime, the capital remains unutilized—burning money instead of fuel, as it were. The pharmaceutical industry takes big risks in investing in research and development. Years can pass and hundreds of millions can be paid without a major product emerging—or in some cases, a product can reach the market, succeed for a while, and then fail because of an untoward side effect.

Two companies that take different kinds of risk can fail to reach an understanding about each other. If each is unaccustomed to the other's form of risk taking, the novice will be wary of the boldness of the professional. What the novice sees is real; what the professional sees may in fact be distorted by complacency, but is nonetheless an essential part of doing business. It is when the novice has operating control of a merged company that the differences in view can create operating difficulties for the professional.

The Pace of Decisions

Some businesses enjoy long product life cycles. In the chemical business, patents and substantial plant investments result in product selections that offer a good chance of serving a market for a long time. In the electronics business, the pace of change can be quite rapid, and product offerings can be technically obsolete even before they are introduced. In a long product life-cycle business, there is a tendency to do exquisitely detailed planning and budgeting. In short life-cycle businesses, response time is the key to success. Again, if one style of operations is superimposed upon the other, the decisions made may end up being either rash, when the fast-moving business is on top, or sluggish, when the slow-moving business prevails.

Cycles

Some businesses are subject to cycles. For example, businesses that serve the cattle industry must contend with a seven-year cycle. First, the cattle population grows, margins narrow, and cattlemen cut back on supplies. Then, the herds shrink, margins climb, and supplies are again affordable. Some businesses have no cycles at all. Consumer disposables are reasonably cycle free. A business that must deal with cycles will make judgments about where and when to cut back on operations, and when to move forward, whereas a cycle-free business will exercise unsophisticated judgment on such questions. If the cycle-free business is making the decisions for the cyclical company, it probably will be hurt more than necessary during bad times, and reluctant to gear up as a recovery approaches.

Debt Service

Companies that use debt leverage to progress have come to learn that there are some businesses that must be avoided. They like prosaic businesses, and they avoid high technology firms whenever they can. Even though high tech firms can produce substantial value added and hence superior growth and margins, their vulnerability is a changing marketplace and the specialization of their managers. A company that loses a key scientist or engineer in a high tech business can rapidly lose its ability to respond to change. Profits can disappear overnight. Yet, the interest on debt has to be paid.

The two parties to a merger should spend a substantial amount of time addressing those cultural differences that have a profound effect on their respective partner's ability to function effectively in the marketplace. The result of those discussions should be the development of an administrative process that takes into account what behavior is needed to serve a market. A research intensive company cannot be pressured to make premature decisions about research projects, a company that relies on heavy consumer advertising to sell its products should not be needled continuously about waste, a fixed asset–intensive company cannot be told to rely on subcontracting, and a company in a fast-moving market cannot be told to wait until the annual budget review for a decision.

Not only should the parties have a complete intellectual understanding of one another's requirements, but they should "internalize" them, to borrow the psychologist's term. The only way the internalization can successfully occur is when the parties have learned to trust one another. The establishment of a relationship of trust in a merger is indeed delicate. The euphoria of the deal will often lead to excessive mutual expectations and a subsequent disillusionment destructive of trust. Hard bargaining, on the other extreme, can create suspicion that can last well into the relationship.

The best approach to walking the fine line between the two is if both parties bring to the merger talks well-developed business plans, created not for the purpose of the merger, but for the future progress of each of the business units. Plans that are developed this way are easy to spot, and they offer a basis for a thorough understanding of one another's business, and ultimate trust.

What about businesses that enjoy essentially the same economic styles, in that they serve the same marketplace with similar products? In such cases, it is important for the parties to discuss differences in much greater detail. More often than not, differences down the road between partners relate to perceptions of what the customer expects. The price-quality trade-off is the source of the most dangerous form of disagreement. A move by one partner in the direction of the other after the merger may have a profound effect on the image of the company.

DUE DILIGENCE

After the parties have fallen in love, the engagement ring has been delivered, and the bans have been published, the merger partners enter one of the more trying phases of their relationship—the due diligence exercise.

The term derives from court cases that arose in the 1960s accusing accountants and attorneys of doing a poor job of examining companies prior to public offering. There is a standard of conduct imposed upon professional advisers to exercise their best skills in making sure that there are no undue surprises to those who are parting with their money.

Independent underwriters, attorneys, and accountants who have experience with the due diligence process are well aware of their responsibilities and do not take umbrage at embarrassing questions. In fact, in the due diligence process between two publicly traded companies about to merge, the advisers seem to fall over one another in making full disclosures about their clients. They all are well aware of the dangers of withholding or distorting important information.

The hard part of the due diligence exercise rests on the shoulders of inexperienced managers witnessing the process as it unfolds. Managers must above all bring a sense of perspective about the process that the advisers may lack at a time when all the joy of the merger announcement has been washed over with reports of problems.

It is important to recognize the following truths about due diligence:

- All companies have flaws. Some parts of companies will be performing exceedingly well, and others will look like disaster areas.

The test is not whether a company is facing problems, but how it is facing them. If a company has a weak division, what decisions has it made to correct it? Who within the organization is addressing problems, and what experience do the people have in fixing difficulties?

- Attorneys know the law, but may not know economics. Some know how to extract disclosures, but not how to interpret them. Both parties to a transaction should, in fairness, allow themselves time to review the business implications of negative disclosures. To let these disclosures get pressed against a deadline is asking for trouble down the road.
- Accountants love crises. Given the choice between stress and boredom, they will take stress every time. A manager has to measure the financial implications of a problem and discourage dramatizations from members of the profession.
- Accountants and attorneys are not actuaries. Some of the most profound issues in mergers are based on actuarial assumptions. It is important to get good advice from wage and benefit professionals.
- Accountants and attorneys who are not tax specialists generally know enough about taxes to be dangerous. The second most profound category of problems in mergers is the field of taxes. Companies can ruin their tax situations by making simple mistakes in day-to-day operations. It takes tax specialists to examine not only tax returns, but business conduct in support of tax-minimization assumptions.
- Accountants and attorneys are not marketing people. Companies make very big decisions about products and markets. A carefully constructed program of talking to customers, and in some cases competitors, provides important insights that merger partners need.
- Due diligence experts are not management psychologists. The way a problem is resolved during a due diligence phase, when the parties to a transaction are under considerable stress, will offer clues about the future relationship of managers as partners. The use of experts to sort out problems in their respective fields is intelligent. The use of experts to sort out other problems may create unnecessary hostility.

POSTMERGER EVALUATION

It serves the interests of both parties to a merger to engage in a process of soul searching some time after the merger is complete—the posthoneymoon phase.

Some companies engage consultants whose job it is to assess the working relationships between management groups. Such people normally have psychology backgrounds and do an excellent job at differentiating real from imagined problems of organization and communication. They also bring the perspective of dealing with similar types of problems with other companies. This has the cathartic effect of reassuring managements that problems may not be merely the clash of personalities.

In addition, it is wise during the process of self-examination to determine the business assumptions that were the foundation of the merger on both sides of the transaction. In some cases, the business assumptions were valid at the time, but the parties became slaves to them rather than adjust to new economic conditions. In other cases, the assumptions were euphoric, and never should have been made in the first place. Dealing with such a situation effectively requires the parties to consider the expense of the merger as sunk cost, and move constructively to new ground. And—in a very few cases—the assumptions were modest. The parties are enjoying a happy and mutually rewarding relationship. An examination of what went right can't hurt either.

PART B The Accounting Considerations of Mergers and Acquisitions*

INTRODUCTION

This chapter primarily discusses the required accounting for business combinations. In addition, equity investments and divestiture accounting are discussed.

Business combinations involve two principal accounting issues—

* Part B was written by Peter E. Berger.

the determination of the method to be used to give effect to the combination and how to apply that method.

Two basic methods are used to account for business combinations—pooling-of-interests and purchase accounting. The two methods are not viewed as alternatives for a given business combination; One of the two will be the only one appropriate for the circumstances.

In the purchase method, the combination is viewed as one company acquiring another, and the required accounting closely parallels that used in the purchase of assets in the ordinary course of business. The purchase price of the acquired company is allocated to the net assets obtained. A difference between the cost of an acquired company and the sum of the fair values of tangible and identifiable intangible assets, less liabilities, is recorded as goodwill (the "residual"). The incomes of the entities are combined only for periods after the acquisition date, with the income of the acquired company adjusted to recognize depreciation on the revised net asset values.

In the pooling-of-interests method, the transaction is viewed as a merger (pooling) of the ownership interests into a single entity as though such entity and its combined shareholder groups had always existed. The assets and liabilities of the constituent companies are carried forward at their previously recorded or historical amounts and the incomes of the enterprises, before and after the date of the transaction, are combined with change.

APB (Accounting Principals Board) *Opinion Nos. 16, 17,* and *18* specify the accounting practices to be followed in accounting for mergers and acquisitions.

APB Opinion No. 16 provides specific guidelines to be used when accounting for a business combination as a purchase or a pooling-of-interests.

APB Opinion No. 17 specifies the accounting required for goodwill arising in a business combination accounted for as a purchase, as well as the accounting required for other acquired intangibles. In particular, *APB Opinion No. 17* requires that goodwill and other acquired intangibles be amortized over a period not in excess of 40 years and not be written off in the period of acquisition.

APB Opinion Nos. 16 and *17* were adopted amid much controversy. The accounting issues in these areas had been under consideration for many years and debate on them had been lengthy and heated. The resulting opinions reflect numerous compromises. For example, *APB Opinion No. 16* created numerous arbitrary rules to be met if the pooling-of-interest method is to be used. Accordingly, these rules have become extremely difficult to implement. Of course, in recent years, purchase transactions have become more prevalent, and related purchase price allocation issues have arisen.

In addition to the arbitrariness of the opinions, the Security and

Exchange Commission (SEC) has been quite restrictive concerning the use of pooling-of-interests accounting for a business combination. The SEC staff often interprets the pooling rules literally, but emphasizes substance over form in other cases. This results in further confusion over the accounting rules and frequently requires extensive consultation regarding the appropriate accounting with accounting advisers and the SEC.

The following discussion summarizes the major requirements of *APB Opinion Nos. 16, 17,* and *18;* however, the actual *opinions* should be referred to with respect to specific transactions, and professional advice should be sought. Subsequent sections discuss certain *special application problems.*

PURCHASE ACCOUNTING RULES

Accounting for a business combination by the purchase method follows accounting principles normally applicable under historical cost accounting. It applies whether the acquisition involves an entire entity or a portion of an entity; whether stock is acquired or assets are purchased; and whether the consideration given is in the form of cash, other assets, debt, equity securities (unless pooling-of-interest conditions are met), or a combination of these forms.

There are three basic steps in applying the purchase method:

1. Determining the acquirer.
2. Determining the cost or purchase price of the acquired company.
3. Recording the assets acquired and the liabilities assumed (or allocating the purchase price).

Determining the Acquirer

When nonstock consideration (e.g., cash, other assets, or debt) is offered, the offerer is clearly the acquirer. When stock is issued, regardless of the extent, the acquirer is usually evident from the facts and circumstances.

If not clearly evident, the general presumption should be that the acquirer is the one whose shareholders end up owning the majority of the voting control of the combined enterprise. This may not be the case, however, if, for example, voting restrictions are imposed on the "majority's" stock. If the Board of Directors and management of the combined entity are from the "minority"; if the market value of the shares issued to the minority is greater than that of the shares issued or retained by the majority; or if the assets, revenues, and earnings of the company previously owned by the minority are greater than those of the company owned by the majority; then the acquiring company may not be the one whose shareholders own the majority stock.

Careful consideration of the above should be given to situations where an acquisition is to be made of a target of comparable size. The determination of the acquirer can have a dramatic effect on the resultant financial reporting, particularly if the market value of one of the companies is substantially below its book value, the market value of the other company is substantially in excess of its book value, or the relative price/earnings multiples of the two companies is significantly different. Careful structuring of the transaction could eliminate all or a portion of the "step-up" in value (discussed below) or of the recorded goodwill and, accordingly, could reduce the impact of the related amortization on earnings if the target is deemed to be the acquirer for accounting purposes.

If a new corporation is formed to issue stock to effect a business combination to be accounted for as a purchase, one of the existing companies should be deemed the acquirer based on an evaluation of the facts described above. SEC Staff Accounting Bulletin No. 24 discussed this problem in more detail.

Determining the Cost of the Acquired Company

The second step under the purchase method is determining the cost of the acquired company. This determination should be made as of the date the business combination is consummated. This is normally the date assets are received and other assets are given or securities are issued. However, it also is acceptable to use an earlier date if the terms of the combination are fixed and if effective control was obtained by the acquirer at that date. This, however, requires adjusting the cost of the acquired company and recognizing income related to the acquired company as of the earlier date. To compensate for recognizing income before consideration is transferred, interest on the consideration given should be imputed for the period from the transfer date to the control date.

The cost of the acquired company generally should be measured by the fair value of the consideration surrendered. When equity securities are issued, their fair value should be based on current market prices. However, when the securities carry restrictions, their value generally is less than the market price—sometimes substantially less. In other situations, a thin market for the securities may exist or individual blocks may be significant in relation to normal trading, in which case discounts from quoted market price also may be appropriate. In such situations and when no market exists, reputable investment bankers or others experienced in such valuations may be engaged to help determine the fair value.

In rare cases, when the fair value of the consideration issued is not clearly evident, the cost of the acquisition should be determined by valuing the acquired net assets; Goodwill would not be recognized in such instances unless its separate value were clearly evident.

A purchase agreement may provide for the issuance of additional shares of a security or the transfer of cash or other consideration contingent upon specified events or transactions in the future. For example, additional consideration may be contingent upon maintaining or achieving specified earnings levels in future periods, or may be contingent upon the market price of a specified security issued to effect a business combination.

Contingent consideration, which is determinable beyond a reasonable doubt, should be recorded at the acquisition date and included in the cost of the target entity. Contingent consideration not determinable beyond a reasonable doubt should be included in the cost of the acquired entity when the contingency is resolved. This normally creates additional goodwill which should be accounted for prospectively, not retroactively.

Only in rare instances are contingencies based on earnings determinable beyond a reasonable doubt. Accordingly, this value is usually included in the purchase price at the acquisition date unless immaterial. There need not be symmetry of determination of purchase price between buyer and seller. This is because the seller need only apply a "probable and estimable" test compared to the higher threshold of "beyond a reasonable doubt" for the buyer.

If the purchase agreement provides for a market price guarantee through the issuance of additional securities, the cost initially recorded for the acquired entity should be the greater of (1) the guaranteed amount of the consideration, or (2) the fair value of the securities originally issued. This amount should be recorded when the combination is consummated. Any additional consideration given at a later date should not affect the acquisition cost, but should be treated as an adjustment to paid-in capital or debt discount/premium accounts, where appropriate.

Direct acquisition costs (finder's and investment banking fees, legal and accounting fees, etc.) are considered part of the cost of an acquisition and must be included as part of the cost assigned to the acquired assets. Indirect costs (generally expenses incurred internally by an acquiring company) must be expensed.

Recording the Assets Acquired and the Liabilities Assumed

The third step under the purchase method is allocating the acquisition cost.

In order to assign the purchase cost to individual assets acquired

in a purchase transaction, all tangible and intangible assets must be identified and individually valued. This indentification process should also include consideration of overfunded pension plans and other unrecorded assets and liabilities. Similarly, unrecorded pension liabilities (the excess of the actuarially computed value of vested plan benefits over the assets of the pension fund) and post-employment benefits need to be considered and recorded as liabilities, if applicable. The purchase cost plus the fair value of liabilities assumed or incurred must then be allocated to the acquired assets based on their individual fair values.

If the aggregate purchase cost exceeds the total fair value of the identifiable assets acquired, less liabilities assumed, that excess or "residual" amount must be allocated to goodwill. If there is an excess of fair value of assets acquired over the purchase cost, the values assigned to noncurrent assets (such as land, buildings, machinery and equipment, intangible and other assets, but excluding long-term investments in marketable securities) must be reduced proportionately to a basis of zero, if necessary, before recording negative goodwill. If an excess of fair value over cost still exists after reducing the basis of noncurrent assets to zero, it should be assigned to negative goodwill. Negative goodwill normally should be amortized in the same manner as goodwill.

In many cases, the final amounts assigned to individual assets will differ for accounting and tax purposes due to the differing valuation and allocation practices that are prescribed for each purpose. In these instances, the resulting allocation differences must be considered an inherent part of the accounting valuation process. For example, if an amount allocated to a particular asset for accounting purposes is greater than the tax-basis allocation, the final value to be used for accounting purposes must be reduced in recognition of the lower tax value of that asset or tax effect of that difference. This is accomplished by reducing the accounting cost allocated to the asset by the effective loss of tax benefit resulting from the lower tax valuation (commonly referred to as "tax effecting" the difference). Generally, the amount of the reduction is assigned to goodwill or noncurrent assets.

When measuring the impact of tax effects assigned to individual assets and liabilities, the timing of the tax effects may be important in certain cases. (Accordingly, discounting of the tax effects, while not common in practice, may be acceptable in certain instances.) The tax rate to be used should be based on the tax attributes of the target, not the acquirer.

Liabilities assumed should be recorded at the present value of amounts to be paid, determined by using appropriate current interest

rates. This may result in the creation of debt discount. Recording such a discount reduces the amount assigned to goodwill, if any, or other noncurrent assets by a corresponding amount. This generally has a negative effect on reported earnings in the initial years after the combination, since debt discount must be amortized by charges to earnings over the term of the related debt, and that term is frequently shorter than the period for goodwill, in particular, but also for other noncurrent assets.

Unresolved contingencies (other than contingent considerations) may exist at the date of acquisition ("preacquisition contingencies"). Such contingencies include such things as unsettled litigation, contractual disputes, renegotiations proceedings, and contested tax assessments. The fair value of any preacquisition contingency should be included in the allocation of the purchase price when determinable (i.e., "probable" and "estimable"). However, if this determination is made beyond one year from the acquisition date, the difference between the estimate used in allocating the purchase price and the actual amount of the contingency should be included in net income in that period. Because of this requirement, care should be taken in identifying and estimating the impact of contingent matters.

Changes in other estimates used in allocating the purchase price should normally also be included in net income if they occur after a reasonable period of time (the "allocation period" which normally extends to one year after the date of acquisition).

Unused investment tax credits acquired may not be recognized as an asset at the acquisition date. Instead, in the period in which they are utilized, they should be recorded as an adjustment to goodwill.

Net operating loss carryforwards (NOLs) acquired are normally not recognized at the acquisition date, unless realization is assured beyond a reasonable doubt. This will rarely occur. Subsequent realization of NOLs that were unrecorded at the acquisition date should be recorded as a retroactive adjustment of goodwill if the impact of doing so is material. Otherwise, the goodwill adjustment should be computed prospectively, which is usually the case.

Amortization of Goodwill and Other Intangibles Required

Goodwill and other intangibles must be amortized over a period not in excess of 40 years. They cannot be written off in the period of acquisition. Intangibles should be amortized over their estimated useful life if less than 40 years. Legal and regulatory aspects, contractual provisions, renewal provisions, competition, obsolescence, and so on should be considered in establishing the amortization period, and a periodic review of the amortization period should be made to determine if later events warrant revision in the original amortization period established. The straight-line method of amortization normally is required.

The trend toward very large purchase combinations involving significant premiums over net tangible asset value has caused acquirers to become more aggressive in identifying short-lived, tax-deductible intangibles. However, for accounting purposes acquirer's prefer to either assign such premiums to nondeductible goodwill, the amortization of which over 40 years does not as adversely impact future earnings, or to amortize the identified intangibles over a longer period for accounting than tax purposes. Thus, an inherent conflict exists between tax and accounting objectives. The general presumption should be that identified intangibles have comparable lives for both financial reporting and tax purposes, unless statutory requirements or other such facts and circumstances justify differences.

Disclosure Requirements

Complete details of a purchase transaction should be disclosed, and summary pro forma results of operations should be shown for the current period (and the prior period if comparative statements are issued) as though the companies had combined at the beginning of the period.

Other Purchase Accounting Issues

Acquisitions of Minority Interests. Acquisitions of minority interests (pooling-of-interests) should be accounted for under the purchase method. The consideration paid should be allocated as previously discussed.

Push-down Accounting. When substantially all of the common stock of a company is acquired in one or a series of purchase transactions, the SEC generally requires that the purchase price be "pushed down" to the acquired company's (subsidiary) financial statements if those statements are included in a SEC filing (e.g., an initial public offering).

Push-down accounting reflects the allocation of purchase price adjustments to assets and liabilities in the financial statements of the acquired (subsidiary) entity. No retained earnings are carried forward by the acquired entity after applying push-down accounting. Acquisition debt of the acquirer is normally not pushed down and, therefore, the net effect of pushing down the purchase accounting adjustments is reflected in the equity of the acquired company.

When push-down accounting is required in an SEC filing, the reporting requirements for the initial period(s) following the acquisition normally include both the historical financial statements through the acquisition date as well as those reflected on a "pushed-down" basis.

POOLING-OF-INTERESTS

The pooling-of-interests method is applicable to a business combination in which the ownership interests of two or more companies are united or combined by an exchange of solely the majority class of voting securities. Since the transaction occurs solely among the shareholders, neither assets nor liabilities are added or withdrawn from the companies themselves and, consequently, no revaluation of the assets or liabilities of either company is reflected in the combined financial statements. Historical financial statements of companies qualifying for this accounting treatment are combined as though the two companies had always been commonly owned. Shareholders prospectively share risks and rewards in the company as they previously did in the separate companies. The pooling accounting concept is applicable to business combinations involving partnerships or proprietorships, as well as corporations.

A pooling of interests is usually preferred when the purchase price exceeds the historical carrying amount of the net assets acquired since in a pooling the excess of the fair market value over the historical carrying amount of the assets acquired does not have to be recorded. Consequently, the surviving company can continue to amortize the historical cost amounts without recognizing and depreciating or amortizing fixed assets and goodwill.

The other critical difference between pooling and purchase accounting is that in pooling accounting the surviving company reports the results of operations of both businesses combined for all periods presented in its consolidated financial statements, including preacquisition periods. In contrast, purchase accounting permits the results of operations of the acquired company to be included in the surviving company's financial statements only from the date of acquisition.

Pooling Accounting Rules

As discussed above, *APB Opinion No. 16* sanctions the use of both purchase and pooling-of-interests accounting but not as alternatives in any given business combination. Detailed conditions, rules or criteria must be met if a business combination is to be eligible for pooling accounting. If these conditions are not met, the acquisition must be accounted for as a purchase. These conditions are extremely technical and the discussion below is an attempt only to capture the flavor of the rules. The spirit of these rules is to prevent the use of pooling-of-interests in any case not involving a merging of the respective shareholder interest. For example, the use of cash, alterations of equity interests, redemptions, changes in the merged entities and similar actions change the shareholder groups in some way and prevent such a true merging of interests.

Conditions for Pooling

The conditions necessary to record a business combination as a pooling-of-interests can be classified as (1) preacquisition attributes, (2) combining attributes, and (3) post-combination attributes.

Preacquisition Attributes. There are four preacquisition attributes that must be met in order to qualify the transaction for pooling-of-interests accounting:

1. Neither of the companies can have been owned over 50 percent by another company within two years before the pooling is initiated. Exceptions to this rule include a new company incorporated within the two-year period that is not a successor to another company and a subsidiary or division being divested to comply with an order from a governmental authority.
2. Each of the combining companies must be independent of the other. Neither may hold more than 10 percent of the voting common stock of the other at initiation of the pooling.
3. Neither of the companies involved in the pooling can "alter the equity interests" of their voting common stock or of their relative shareholder interests in contemplation of the combination, either within two years before the plan is initiated or between the dates the combination is initiated and consummated. Any such alteration is presumed to be in contemplation of the business combination and precludes pooling. Changes in contemplation of effecting the combination may include distributions to stockholders or additional issuance, exchange, or retirement of securities. Normal dividends are not considered changes. Generally, if a company sells a significant portion of its assets prior to combination, it will not qualify for pooling accounting; likewise, a spinoff of assets would disqualify pooling since this would constitute a change in equity interests. The SEC has concluded that sales of a significant portion of a compa-

ny's assets (i.e., spinoffs) occurring six–nine months prior to initiation of a pooling are presumed to be in contemplation of the combination.

In some situations factual evidence may support a contention that the "alterations" were not in contemplation of a business combination and, accordingly, do not preclude pooling accounting. Such factual evidence must be clear; the closer the alteration is to the initiation of the combination, the more difficult it is for any factual evidence to be persuasive.

4. In the absence of persuasive evidence to the contrary, it is presumed that all Treasury shares acquired within two years of a business combination and between initiation and consummation of the transaction were made in contemplation of the business combination and, accordingly, pooling is prohibited. This prevents the indirect use of cash through acquisition of treasury shares just before and during the combination. Additionally, significant greenmail transactions normally preclude pooling accounting.

   The SEC has issued detailed rules (*Accounting Series Release Nos. 146* and *146A*) that must be met to provide "persuasive evidence" that Treasury shares were not acquired in contemplation of the combination. Exceptions to the rule include normal acquisitions to support option plans, stock purchase plans, or convertible securities; these shares must be acquired in a systematic manner over the two-year period, however. In addition, exceptions include purchases made under agreements related to a shareholder's death, settlement of lawsuits or other contractual obligations.

   In view of these requirements, companies must use care when establishing stock reacquisition plans. Plans established to reduce capitalization, forestall later dilution of earnings per share, utilize available cash, buy shares at times when the stock market price is depressed, or defend against takeovers—as is often done in today's environment—will not meet the specified conditions.

   "Tainted" shares are cured automatically two years after their acquisition. Tainted shares can also be cured through sale in the marketplace or through use of such shares in an unrelated business combination accounted for under the purchase method.

Combining Attributes. There are four combining attributes that must be met in order to qualify for pooling-of-interests accounting:

1. The acquisition must be effected in a single transaction or in accordance with a specified plan within one year of the plan's initiation. The period may be longer than one year if the delay in completing the transaction is beyond the control of the companies because of litigation or proceedings of a governmental authority. A substantive change in the terms of a merger agreement is considered a new plan and, accordingly, a new one-year term applies.
2. The acquiring corporation can issue only common stock with rights identical to those of the majority of its outstanding voting common stock in exchange for substantially all the voting common stock of the acquired company. Substantially all the voting common stock means 90 percent or more, and no pro rata distribution of cash is permitted. Cash may be used to purchase fractional shares or shares held by dissenting stockholders, however, providing the 90 percent test is met. If the company to be acquired has outstanding equity or debt securities other than voting common stock, the acquiring company normally can exchange cash, substantially identical securities or its common stock for those securities or retire the securities for cash or debt. Warrants, options, and securities deemed "voting common stock" must be exchanged for common stock or comparable securities.
3. Each individual common stockholder who exchanges his stock must receive a voting common stock interest exactly in proportion to his relative voting common stock interest before the combination.
4. *APB Opinion No. 16* requires purchase accounting when an earnings or market-price contingency agreement is present in a business combination. However, the opinion does not prohibit certain types of contingency agreements in a pooling as long as they relate to a condition at consummation and not a post-combination contingency, e.g., are not in effect earnings or market-price contingency agreements. The most common types of contingency agreements not prohibited in a pooling are those related to specific contingencies, such as litigation and income tax disputes and "general management representations," which are present in nearly all business combinations. In general, contingency agreements related to specific contingencies may extend for the period during which the underlying contingencies are unresolved, while general management representation contingency arrangements should normally not extend beyond one year.

Post-combination Attributes. There must be no planned transactions on the part of the combining companies to (1) agree, directly or indirectly, to retire or reacquire any of the common stock issued; (2) enter into any financial arrangements for the benefit of stockholders of the acquired company that in effect negate the pro rata exchange of equity securities, such as a guarantee of loans secured by stock issued in the acquisition; or (3) intend or plan to dispose of a significant part of the assets of the combined companies within two years of the combination, other than by disposals in the ordinary course of business or in order to eliminate duplicate facilities or excess capacity of the acquired company (elimination of the acquirer's duplicate facilities will invalidate the pooling). Treasury stock transactions can occur subsequent to combination. However, to avoid the presumption that these transactions are considered "planned transactions" a waiting period of six months is suggested.

Other. If the sum of (1) intercorporate investments (up to 10% normally allowed), (2) "tainted" Treasury shares (expressed in equivalent shares of the acquired company), (3) shares acquired for cash (dissenter or fractional shares) and (4) minority interests of the acquired company remaining after the combination, exceeds 10% of the voting common stock of the acquiring company, pooling accounting is precluded.

Recording Poolings

In a pooling, the historical carrying amounts of the net assets of both entities must be carried forward without change. Adjustments to conform the accounting practices of the combining entities are acceptable if these changes would otherwise have been appropriate for the separate entity; these adjustments should be made retroactively.

The shareholders' equity accounts of the separate entities should be combined with the retained earnings totaling the aggregate retained earnings of both companies. When the par or stated value of the shares issued is less than the par or stated value of the acquired entity's stock, the difference should be assigned to additional paid-in capital. When the par or stated value of the shares issued exceeds that of the acquired company's stock, the excess should be assigned first, to reduce or eliminate any additional paid-in capital of the acquired entity; second, to reduce or eliminate any additional paid-in capital of the issuing company to the extent permitted by law; and, third, to reduce retained earnings.

A pooling-of-interests should be recorded as of the date the combination is consummated. That date usually is the date of the legal closing of the transaction. A combination consummated after year-end but before the annual financial statements are issued should not be reflected in the earlier year's annual financial statements.

The combined entity should report results of operations for the period in which the combination occurs as though the entities had been combined as of the beginning of the period. Financial statements presented for prior periods should be restated on a combined basis as if the entities had always been one enterprise. However, if the operations acquired are immaterial, prior periods do not have to be restated.

Costs incurred to effect a pooling-of-interests—such as registration fees, costs of furnishing information to stockholders, and legal, finders' and consultants' fees—should be charged to income. Costs incurred to integrate the continuing operations and to eliminate or mitigate existing inefficiencies should be charged to expense as they are incurred.

Disclosure Requirements

APB Opinion No. 16 provides for significant disclosures relating to pooling combinations. Among other requirements, revenue, extraordinary items and net income of each company should be disclosed separately for the period from the beginning of the year to the date of combination. A reconciliation of revenue and earnings previously reported by the acquiring corporation to the restated combined amounts currently presented in financial statements and summaries should be provided.

THE EQUITY METHOD OF ACCOUNTING

Application of Opinion

APB Opinion No. 18 applies to investments in corporate joint ventures, investments of 20–50 percent in the common stock of an investee company (foreign or domestic), and investments reported in parent company financial statements when such statements are prepared for issuance to stockholders as the financial statements of the primary reporting entity. The *Opinion* does not apply to investments in common stock held by investment companies registered under the Investment Company Act of 1940 or by nonbusiness entities such as estate, trusts, or individuals.

Criteria for Use of the Equity Method of Accounting

To apply the equity method of accounting to 20 percent—50 percent investments in the common stock of investee companies (consolidation is generally required when an investment exceeds 50 percent), the investor must be able to exercise "significant influence" over operating and financial policies of the investee. Ability to exercise that influence may be indicated in several ways, such as representation on the board of directors, participation in policy-making processes, material intercompany transactions, interchange of managerial personnel, or technological dependency. Another important consideration is the extent of ownership by an investor in relation to the concentration of other shareholders, but substantial or majority ownership by another party of the investee's voting stock does not necessarily preclude the investor's ability to exercise significant influence.

To achieve a reasonable degree of uniformity in application, the *opinion* states that investments from 20 percent—50 percent in the voting stock of an investee are presumed, in the absence of evidence to the contrary, to indicate that an investor has the ability to exercise significant influence over such investee. An investor's voting stock interest percentage in an investee must be based on currently outstanding securities that have present voting privileges. Potential voting privileges that may become available to holders of an investee's securities normally should be disregarded.

Equity Method as Applied to Carrying Amount

When the equity method of accounting is used, investments in common stock of an investee should be shown in the investor's balance sheet at cost plus the investor's share of the investee's undistributed earnings since the date the investment was made. Any loss in value of an equity investment that is considered permanent or that results in other than a temporary market decline should be recognized in the same way as a loss in value of other long-term assets and noncurrent investments.

The difference between the cost of an investment and the amount of the underlying equity in net assets of an investee should be accounted for as if the investee were a consolidated subsidiary. Normally, this difference will affect the determination of the amount of the investor's share of earnings or losses of an investee as if the investee were a consolidated subsidiary. If the investor is unable to relate the difference to specific accounts of the investee, the difference should be considered goodwill and amortized over a period not to exceed 40 years in accordance with *APB Opinion No. 17.*

Equity Method as Applied to Earnings

The investor's share of earnings or losses of an investee should ordinarily be shown in the income statement as a single amount, except for extraordinary items. The investor's share of extraordinary items reported by an investee should be classified separately by the investor in a similar manner, unless it is immaterial in the income statement of the investor. Dividends and intercompany profits and losses between the investor and investee should be eliminated. In determining the earnings per share of the investor, consideration must be given to the effect of common stock equivalents of the investee.

In computing its tax provision, the investor should include deferred taxes (at ordinary or capital gains rates depending on the expected form of realization) on the undistributed portion of the investee's earnings as well as current taxes, where applicable, on the portion distributed through dividends.

Gains or losses on the sale of an investee's stock by an investor should be reported as the difference at the time of sale between the selling price and the carrying amount applicable to the investment sold. A sale of additional shares by the equity investee can be treated by the investor as either a capital transaction or the gain/loss can be recognized as if the shares had been sold.

Restatement Requirements

An investment in voting stock of an investee carried on the equity basis may fall below the 20 percent level of ownership. In this case, or if for any other reason an investment no longer qualifies for the equity method, an investor should discontinue accruing his share of an investee's earnings or losses. Investment accounts should not be adjusted retroactively under these circumstances; however, dividends received by the investor in subsequent periods that exceed its share of earnings for those periods should be applied as a reduction of the carrying amount of the investment.

An investment that was previously accounted for under the cost method that currently qualifies for the equity method should be adjusted retroactively. The investment balance, results of operations (current and prior periods presented), and retained earnings of the investor should be adjusted retroactively in a manner consistent with the accounting for a step-by-step acquisition of a subsidiary.

Loss Avoidance

The SEC has recently focused on situations in which an investor corporation's ownership interest does not meet the specific requirements to record such investment under the equity method (for example, if the investment is not in common stock but is in convertible debt or convertible preferred stock). In these situations, the SEC is concerned about the failure to record losses that are incurred by an unconsolidated entity, such as when a transaction is structured to avoid start-up losses that would be recorded on the books of the investor corporation were it not for the form of the initial investment.

Initial investments that are in the form of convertible debt or preferred stock that on an if-converted basis give the investor corporation sufficient common stock to apply the equity method should be carefully reviewed. The SEC staff believes that such transactions should be accounted for according to their substance rather than a blind reliance on the form of the investment.

Disclosure Requirements

Investments accounted for on the equity basis are subject to significant disclosure requirements. *APB Opinion No. 18* should be consulted for the details of these disclosures.

ACCOUNTING FOR DIVESTITURES

The accounting method for divestitures in the financial statements of the divesting company depends on whether the unit being divested qualifies as "a segment of a business."

If a divestiture qualifies as a segment of a business, the results of operations of the divested entity should be retroactively deconsolidated and reported separately from income from continuing operations as a component of income before extraordinary items.

If the divestiture does not qualify as a segment of a business, the results of operations and assets and liabilities are still deconsolidated, but prospectively rather than retroactively. In addition, results of these operations cannot be reported separately as a discontinued business. Instead, they must be reported as part of income from continuing operations. If material, such results of operations should be disclosed separately as a component of income from continuing operations, e.g., as gain/loss on the sale of a business.

ACCOUNTING FOR THE DISPOSAL OF A SEGMENT OF A BUSINESS

APB Opinion No. 30 provides specific guidelines for accounting and reporting the effects of the disposal of a segment of a business. A "segment of a business" refers to a component of an entity whose activities represent a separate major line of business or class of customer. A segment may be in the form of a subsidiary, a division or a department, provided that its assets, results of operations, and activities can be clearly distinguished, physically and operationally, and for financial reporting purposes, from other assets, results of operations, and activities of the entity. Operations of a segment that have been or will be sold or discontinued should be retroactively "deconsolidated" and reported separately from "income from continuing operations" on the face of the income statement as a "discontinued business" component of "income before extraordinary items." For example:

Income from continuing operations before income taxes	$	
Provision for income taxes	______	
Income from continuing operations		$
Discontinued operations (Note):		
Income (loss) from operations of discontinued Division X (less applicable income taxes of $)	$	
Loss on disposal of Division X, including provision of $ for operating losses during phaseout period (less applicable income taxes of $)	______	______
Net income		$

The assets and liabilities of the divestiture should also be deconsolidated and reported net in one or several summary lines in the balance sheet.

The actual or estimated gain or loss from disposal of a segment should be included in the reported results of operations of the segment in the year in which the divestiture plan is adopted.

Dispositions in Form Only

Discontinued operations treatment should not be applied to the disposition of an operation when the risks of ownership have not in substance been transferred. This may be the case when (1) there is continuing involvement by the seller after disposal; (2) the principal consideration is debt of the buyer with repayment dependent on the success of future operations; or (3) significant debt or other performance guarantees are made by the seller. Although losses on such disposals should be recognized, gains should generally not be recognized until the uncertainty concerning realization of the gain has been removed, at which time discontinued operations treatment should be applied.

Disclosure Requirements

APB Opinion No. 30 provides for significant disclosures relating to the disposal of a segment of a business. The disclosure requirements include the identity of the segment, expected disposal date, manner of disposal, a description of any remaining assets and liabilities of the segment at the balance sheet date, income taxes applicable to the results of discontinued operations and the gain or loss and any proceeds expected from the disposal of the segment as of the balance sheet date.

Expenses Related to a Divestiture

Under the provisions of *APB Opinion No. 30,* costs and expenses directly associated with the decision to dispose of a segment, which may include severance pay, additional pension costs, employee pension expenses, and so on, must be charged to income, as part of the results of operations of the discontinued business.

CHAPTER **11**

Divestitures

Arnold S. Hoffman
Managing Director
Shearson Lehman Brothers, Inc.
Philadelphia, PA

Arnold S. Hoffman is a managing director of Shearson Lehman Brothers Inc. and president of Financo, Inc., a Philadelphia based subsidiary specializing in merger, acquisition and divestiture services. Mr. Hoffman joined Financo in 1977 and brings over 20 years of hands-on operating experience and a variety of business and executive disciplines to the firm, which was acquired by Shearson Lehman Brothers in October 1985.

Paul R. Van Wyck
Vice President
The Chase Manhattan Corporation
New York, N.Y.

Paul R. Van Wyck has been vice president and deputy director, Corporate Development, at the Chase Manhattan Bank for the past 10 years. During this period, he has managed a number of acquisitions and divestitures. Prior to joining Chase in 1973 as director of International Planning, Mr. Van Wyck held corporate development and general management positions with a major U.S. airline. He has also served as an international management consultant after beginning his business career as a commercial banker. He holds an undergraduate degree from Duke University and an MBA in finance from New York University Graduate School of Business.

Roger Mulvihill
Partner
Olwine, Connelly, Chase, O'Donnell & Weyher
New York, N.Y.

Roger Mulvihill is a partner in the New York law firm of Olwine, Connelly, Chase, O'Donnell & Weyher. He is a graduate of Georgetown University and Yale Law School and holds a masters degree in law from New York University. He is member of the American Bar Association, the New York State Bar Association, and the Association of the Bar of the City of New York. Mr. Mulvihill has lectured on a variety of legal subjects at conferences sponsored by the Practicing Law Institute, The Wharton School, New York University, and others.

PART A Raising Capital through Divestiture*

INTRODUCTION

Divestiture can offer management a unique tool for raising capital. While the concept of divestiture (or sell-off, as it is often called) is

* Part A was written by Arnold S. Hoffman.

not entirely new, only since the early 1970s has it become an accepted practice for the astute operator. A successful sell-off of a company, division, or product line not only produces cash for the corporate treasury without equity dilution, but in those cases where the sale is of a troubled unit, it improves the overall performance of a company by directly eliminating losses and allowing management to focus quality time on more profitable business segments.

In the 1960s, the goal of the management of most conglomerates was to build a multimarket company that could profitably withstand changes in the economic cycle. In concept, the more widely diversified a company, the better able it is to take advantage of both up and down economic cycles. In practice, most management groups found themselves spending an inordinate amount of time trying to turn around losers and having almost no time available to expand and improve healthy operations. This caused considerable concern to most companies from a strategic viewpoint, since management was always putting out fires but was never able to rebuild after the damage. In the late 60s the issue was not which companies were acquired and how they fit in with existing operations, but rather how many companies could be acquired and how big volume and profits could grow.

By the early 1970s it became apparent that conglomerates would have to develop a portfolio management strategy. The goal of these organizations could no longer be pure expansion through acquisitions, but would have to include spinning off or selling divisions or product lines that either did not fit long-term strategy, had no growth potential, or were damaging the other operations of the company. In the days of active acquisitions, most managers of conglomerates felt that selling off a unit or two was a sign of failure in their aggressive buying programs and felt a deep concern that a selected divestiture program would result in a lower stock price. In order to avoid risking a reversal of the upward trend in stock prices, they patched, fixed, regrouped, restocked, and retooled, but despite these efforts, often failed to turn around and solve their problems.

Though conglomerates in general realized divestiture in concept was needed as an additional management tool, it was not until the mid-70s that certain managers defied accepted practice and began to restructure their companies. To everyone's surprise, the stock market welcomed restructuring by divestiture, and those managements that pursued this course were looked upon as properly serving their shareholders. Divestiture is now an accepted and welcomed management tool and should be utilized on a regular basis in reviewing an organization's business units.

An ongoing task of management now involves recognizing the need that exists within a company to redirect a portion of its portfolio of assets in order to take advantage of the opportunities that might exist if this redirection were to include the sale of a division or product line. In order to ensure its effectiveness over time, the practice of systematizing management's review of its company's portfolio is critical.

Divestiture cannot only cure a failing situation and offer a good profit opportunity, but a timely sell-off, whether planned or forced, does in fact put capital into a company's treasury without dilution of equity. The following factors, some of which are internal, some external, should be considered as management reviews its company's holdings to determine whether divestiture opportunities exist and, in the case of a losing situation, whether divestment is mandatory to help redirect a company toward a new course that is consistent with long-term strategy.

DIVESTMENT DECISION CONSIDERATIONS

Exhibit 1 provides an overview of a number of the factors that come into play in making divestment decisions. These factors are grouped under three general categories: (1) opportunistic, (2) planned, and (3) forced. The opportunistic considerations in column 1 are totally optional and are meant to be implemented in a reactive manner. An example might involve profit motivation. A division that was operating successfully receives an unsolicited cash bid from a suitor that translates into an extraordinary profit, and while there may be no immediate use for the cash, the profits from selling off this division are such that management cannot in good conscience turn down the offer. This consideration is slightly different from profit motivation in column 2, planned considerations. Under this scenario, a company may have a profitable, well-run division, but may decide to divest in order to raise the necessary capital to invest in something new, or if there is concern about the division's long-term future. While in both instances profit motivation is the same, it is clearly different circumstances that lead to the divestiture decision.

Another example of the fine line between these categories is shown in column 2, the planned sell-off scenario, when the seller recovers some capital. Clearly this consideration refers to a faltering situation wherein, as a result of an ongoing portfolio review, the division is sold off in time to "recover some capital." Conversely, under column 3, the forced scenario, the extent of capital recovered would generally be much less, since a forced liquidation of assets would probably occur only after a greater erosion of assets than if a divestiture were implemented as part of an ongoing planning review.

While there is understandably some overlap between the three

EXHIBIT 1 Divestiture Considerations

Categories	*(1) Opportunistic*	*(2) Planned*	*(3) Forced*
Economic		Never be a factor at any investment level	
		Continual failure to meet goals	
	Tax considerations	Tax considerations	Tax considerations
		Shrinking margins	
	Better alternative use of capital	Better alternative use of capital	
	Profit motivation	Profit motivation	
		Marginally profitable	
		Recover some capital	Recover some capital
		Unprofitable division	Unprofitable division
		Liquidity problems	Liquidity problems
Psychological		Eliminate psychological effect of a loser	
		Bad apple theory	
Operational		Lack of intercompany synergy	
		Labor considerations	Labor considerations
		Competitive reasons	Competitive reasons
		Management deficiencies	
		Concentration of management efforts	Concentration of management efforts
		Eliminate inefficiencies	
Strategic		Change in corporate goals	
		Change in corporate image	
		Technological reasons	Technological reasons
	Poor business fit	Poor business fit	Poor business fit
		Market saturation	
	Takeover defense	Takeover defense	Takeover defense
Governmental		Government-directed divestitures	Government-directed divestitures

NOTE: Some considerations may fall under more than one category. For example, Shrinking margins and Better alternative use of capital may also be strategic considerations.

basic scenarios that trigger or motivate a divestiture, there is also interchangeability among the individual factors.

In order to simplify the use of these factors, they can be easily divided into five categories: (1) economic, (2) psychological, (3) operational, (4) strategic, and (5) governmental or legislative. Naturally, many of these subjects overlap, but they have been split into the above categories in an attempt to isolate their primary meaning in relation to the overall divestment or spin-off situation.

Economic

Never Be a Factor at Any Investment Level. In many situations, the market the company is dealing in is too narrow. Regardless of the dollars and corporate muscle put into the particular division, it will be impossible for management to realize an adequate return. It is the old case of throwing good money after bad, and generally occurs in situations where the company is faced with impossible goals of achieving market share in the face of competition that is either too well entrenched, tough, or numerous to make it worth investment at any particular dollar level. RCA Corporation faced this situation when it abandoned its mainframe computer business after attempting to compete directly with IBM.

Continual Failure to Meet Goals. The frustration faced by most corporate managers when a division continually fails to make quarterly or yearly projections is an excellent rationale for divesting. Patience with meeting predefined or predetermined goals is certainly a virtue. However, continual losses or continuing shortfalls from overestimating the potential of a division can be very costly to any company.

Tax Considerations. Tax considerations as a justification for divestment come into frequent play, given the complexities of our tax laws. A company can often take advantage of changes in the tax law by selling a division or product line at an opportune time, and deriving the benefits from losses or other quirks allowed by the existing tax laws. This rationale is somewhat unique in that tax laws continually change, and therefore divestment should be considered on a regular basis, as an opportunity that can quickly be lost by a change in law. As an example, when net operating losses (NOLs) could easily be sold and utilized by the acquirer, many companies took advantage of this temporary tax benefit by selling loss-plagued divisions.

Shrinking Margins. Reduced profit margins should be reviewed in all divisions and product lines and are often the primary reason for a divestiture. Typical of companies that have run large divestiture programs because of shrinking margins are G. D. Searle and American Can. While the divestment programs for both of these companies were part and parcel of a strategic plan, the short-term reason for initiating them was the continual softening in the profit margins of the divisions the companies sold.

Better Alternate Use of Capital. Here again is a combined economic and strategic reason for considering divestment. This factor should be a key to the rationale for beginning any divestment program. The list of companies that have begun divestment programs to make better use of capital reads from A to Z in corporate America. Companies that have used in-depth divestment programs to reinvest proceeds into other areas of existing businesses or into new acquisitions have been extremely satisfied.

Profits. Profits are still the ultimate motivator. Lack of profits, on the other hand, is the most noted and visible reason for corporations to begin divestment programs. The marginally profitable divisions, those divisions not in line with the financial performance of other divisions in the company, are certainly divestment targets. Unless they satisfy some strategic requirement, such as a research and development unit, divisions that continue to be unprofitable and lose money year in and year out certainly should be divested. A corporation exists at the pleasure of its stockholders, and for the most part, the best way to satisfy stockholders is to perform well and produce generous profits. Divisions and product lines that erode profits and cannot be restructured and reshaped to turn a substantial and acceptable return on investment within the range of the corporation's goals should be prime candidates for divestiture.

Psychological

Eliminate Psychological Effect of a Loser. No one wants to be associated with a loser. Nothing is more depressing psychologically than to know that you are working for or are associated with a company that is losing money and has very little future ahead of it. The effects of a loser can be as contagious as the effects of a winner, and having a losing company over a long term is something that every management should try to avoid. If it cannot be fixed, sell it.

Bad Apple Theory. Unfortunately, losers have a way of creating other losers. The faster a company gets rid of a loss division, the better off all its other divisions will be. Employees have a difficult time understanding the rationale of trying desperately to turn around an operation year after year. Losers should be eliminated quickly before they infect the company's management teams at its other, more profitable divisions.

Operational

Lack of Intercompany Synergy. Prime targets for sell-offs are product lines or divisions that were originally acquired or begun in order to add synergy to the company's other divisions, but failed to do so. In cases where one plus one equals two rather than three, these operations should be considered divestment candidates. If management is not able to consolidate operations to increase profitability, then liquidation or divestment is an alternative.

Labor Considerations. In many cases, companies are divested because of unusual labor situations. These situations might consist of labor unrest in a particular plant, the lack of an adequately skilled labor pool, or outside economic and political factors causing a shortage of labor at competitive prices. If the situation cannot be remedied by moving or consolidating the operation, divestiture might be an alternative.

Competitive Reasons. Certainly competition is the basis of a capitalistic system. However, when competition is intense, and the competition is of a nature that it is so large and effective that it is impossible to compete, withdrawing from a market can be accomplished by divesting an ongoing division. International Harvester has recently been involved in several markets where the competition was too intense, much larger, and more able to compete in terms of productivity, research and development, and new facilities. Instead of remaining in these market segments as an ineffective also-ran, management chose to sell off one of its staple old businesses to a larger, more financially capable company. Separating emotions from reality in terms of competitive ability is often the key to properly making this decision.

Management Deficiencies. Oftentimes, for one reason or another, a company has not been able to put together the right management team to run a division. This problem does not generally speak well of management's ability to recruit, hire, and even provide, internally, the proper management to run its companies, and if the situation exists and cannot be corrected, divestitures should be considered. An example of a divestment yet to happen for this reason is Mobil Oil Corporation's Montgomery Ward & Co. division.

Concentration of Management Efforts. Perhaps the key element underlying all of the operational factors is the need to focus management's efforts where they will be most productive for the company. It is often hard to measure the total losses absorbed by a corporation when one or several of its divisions are losing money and management has to concentrate its efforts on trying to turn around the losers. When problem divisions are divested quickly, management has ample time to return to its normal and important functions of promoting the solid and strategically important units of its company.

Eliminate Inefficiencies. Many companies will operate marginal divisions indefinitely as long as these units do not encounter significant losses. However, marginally profitable units tend to get caught in the trap where management will starve them for growth capital. Over a period of time those units become more inefficient and less competitive and eventually begin to lose important money. It is mandatory to spot these trends early and to try to sell these units before they become big losers and start gathering significant downward momentum. If divestiture can be accomplished within a reasonable time frame, not only are future losses eliminated, but the sale of the unit will inject more capital into the corporate treasury than if the sell-off was delayed too long. Many times, these situations occur in vertically integrated firms, where various operations can no longer be conducted efficiently. Ford Motor Corporation's divestiture of its basic steel operations is an excellent example.

Strategic

Change in Corporate Goals. This factor is probably the most visible reason for companies to begin divestment programs. Oftentimes a company's motivation to divest itself of bad divisions, or any division, is masked by the statement that the corporation is changing its strategic goals and wishes to divest one or several of its divisions. Perhaps the best example of a total commitment to a change in corporate strategic goals was Gould Inc.'s efforts several years ago to get out of the electrical equipment and equipment-support business and upgrade technologically into the electronics business. Over several years, the company divested all of its more technologically mundane divisions and used those funds to acquire companies in the electronics business, thereby moving several steps up the technological ladder. In beginning a divestment program as a result of a change in corporate strategy, the key to the divestments is not only getting out of the businesses that are not wanted, but estimating and projecting how much capital will be raised by selling off these divisions and how much this capital will assist in either acquiring or starting up new ventures that are more in line with newly stated corporate strategic goals.

Change in Corporate Image. In addition to the change in corporate goals mentioned above, some companies feel that in order to effect a "new" image, certain divisions must be divested. While the divestments are not necessarily segments that are failing, or even segments that have limited long-term potential, the businesses might be in areas that are not to the liking of management. For example, Gulf & Western has been involved in a total restructuring and has utilized divestiture of several of its large divisions to move out of mundane manufacturing areas and become more visible in the fast-moving, aggressive financial and entertainment businesses.

Technological Reasons. Many companies have begun divestment programs to technologically upgrade operations. Litton Industries goes through a continual year-to-year upgrading of its companies, regardless of profitability, to maximize the potential of growth companies in higher and higher technological areas. On the other hand, companies downgrade technologically when they are not able to adapt to the fast-moving nature of technology-oriented businesses. Many companies that have decided to withdraw from the high tech areas have retreated to their core businesses and have used divestment strategies to accomplish these goals. Warner Communications, with the sale of its Atari division, provides an excellent example.

Poor Business Fit. Many times, divisions make no sense at all strategically and just do not fit with other divisions of the company. Acquiring companies sometimes use strange rationale for justifying an acquisition, and oftentimes the new management that inherits these businesses take the course of divesting quickly. One of the first management initiatives of Western Union Telegraph Co.'s newly appointed chairman was the divestiture of E. F. Johnson Company, an operation that fit only marginally with Western Union's core business.

Market Saturation. From a strategic standpoint, a division or product line in which the investment required to maintain market share is greater than the cash it generates is a divestiture candidate. This situation is simply a case of a cash cow becoming a dog.

Takeover Defense. In the recent wave of takeovers, divestitures have become one of a number of key defense mechanisms. Typical of these maneuvers is the sale of a "Crown Jewel" to deter an aggressive takeover artist from going forward with his plans. An example of the use of this tactic was Brunswick Corporation's sale of its medical division, the best operating division of the company, to American Home Products in order to stave off an unsolicited takeover attempt by Whitaker Corporation. Shortly after that event took place, Whitaker withdrew its takeover bid for the company. Divestment has become a classic takeover defense mechanism in the last couple of years and has been used successfully to thwart many of these bids.

Governmental

Government-Directed Divestitures. These often occur as a result of major mergers or acquisitions where the merger of two like companies creates antitrust problems. In order to avoid antitrust litigation on the part of the government, the companies are either directed to, or voluntarily, divest certain divisions. The rash of oil combinations that has taken place over the last few years has resulted in major oil companies selling off large parts of their merged companies. The Gulf/Standard Oil of California, and Texaco/Getty transactions are good examples of government-directed divestitures.

As a result of government-enacted environmental laws and practices, companies are forced to evaluate offending operations, and in many cases, either decide to sell a plant, convert to an alternate method of operation, or shut down the offending operation to meet government regulations.

While the above is a fairly comprehensive listing of the factors to be considered when making divestment plans, there are obviously other factors that may come into play. Outside pressure from stockholders, the economic conditions at any given time, and political considerations can certainly have a direct bearing on divestment strategy. Any combination of the factors described above plus these additional macroconsiderations should be reviewed before the divestment decision is made.

IMPLEMENTING A DIVESTMENT PROGRAM

Choose In-House Staff or Outside Professionals

Once the decision has been made that divestiture is necessary to stop losses, to raise additional capital, to strategically redirect a company's focus, or to accommodate a multitude of other reasons, implementing that strategy becomes paramount. A company can choose either to handle the divestitures in-house or to retain an outside professional. This decision depends on the size, structure, and workload of each particular case and relationships with the outside investment banking community. Larger companies that have corporate planning or development departments, or a large financial staff, have the ability to accomplish these divestitures internally. Medium to smaller-sized companies or, in some cases, large corporations that are overloaded in certain administrative areas, may want to retain outsiders to do their divestiture work.

There are a number of alternatives available to companies that prefer to take advantage of outside professionals. There are several independent merger, acquisition, and divestiture firms with the needed expertise that have had excellent results in directing effective divestiture programs. Most of the large regional and national investment banking firms have either special departments or considerable expertise in assisting companies with a total divestment program or with particular individual divestitures as they arise. Both methods, either the use of in-house staff or retaining professional help, have been utilized successfully by many companies. If a company has an active mergers and acquisitions department that is constantly in the mergers and acquisitions marketplace, handling divestments on an in-house basis can make sense. However, if a company is not familiar with the process, and would have to find someone to assign to a particular program or project regarding divestitures, it should strongly consider the use of outside professional help to implement divestment plans. In addition to investment bankers and independent business brokers, many large national accounting firms, management consulting firms, and even some banking institutions perform divestment services. It is best to retain a professional who is knowledgeable about divestitures in general and preferably one who is knowledgeable about the industry within which the division operates.

Retain Key Management Personnel and Current Course

Generally, there are two major items to keep in mind while doing either a divestiture or a spin-off of an operation. The first is to keep key management in place throughout the divestment cycle. It is imperative that the chief executive officer and the chief financial officer of the company or department that is being divested stay on board throughout the entire divestment process. As incentives to these individuals, bonuses upon sale can be promised, and employment contracts should be entered into to prevent them from leaving during this period. Stable management often is critical to getting the divestiture accomplished properly and can provide great comfort to the employees and also to the potential buyers as a source of knowledge and, particularly, the continuity so much needed during the transition process from one corporation to another. It is most difficult to keep divestiture plans private, as much as management might try, and therefore the presence of the CEO and the CFO are key to the success of any divestiture program undertaken. If they leave or are dismissed before the divestiture is complete, the process becomes traumatic to the unit and could cause irreparable damage.

Secondly, corporate management must continue to operate the divestiture candidate in the normal course of business as though the decision to divest had not been made. Decisions cannot be made based on projecting what a new owner would want, but on what current management believes is the correct course.

Prepare a Selling Memorandum

Once the decision to divest has been made, the actual divestment process in either case is started by the preparation of a complete selling memorandum describing the company. This memorandum is usually written either by internal staff or by an outside professional. Those topics discussed are company motivation for the sale; the company history; its present condition; its future potential; its product line (if it is a manufacturing facility); its service capability (if it is in the service business); its people, plant facility, physical facilities, and real estate; and a comprehensive financial overview of the company. The financial presentation should consist of a three- to five-year profit and loss statement, a current balance sheet, cash flow projections, and a short-range forecast.

Target Potential Buyers

In-house staff or outside counsel will then develop a list of target buyers to consider. At this point a decision must be made whether to directly market the company through a negotiated basis or to effect an auction. This choice is an individual decision and depends on the inherent characteristics of the business being sold, how quickly management would like to dispose of the company, and what effect a wide open, broad-range marketing thrust will have on the continuity of the business. Again, these are decisions that have to be made and evaluated with each individual divestiture. There is no basic formula to do a divestiture. Each one has to be handled like any other major business decision, on an individual basis, where all the facts and circumstances are weighed before making a decision on how to proceed.

Negotiated Format. Under the negotiated format, companies are contacted directly on a controlled basis—perhaps three to five companies at a time. The essence of a negotiated divestiture is the proper targeting of prospective buyers so as to enter into substantive negotiations with a qualified buyer until a satisfactory agreement can be reached. If it becomes obvious that an agreement cannot be reached, the seller must quickly move to another viable buyer. A negotiated sale is employed when management wants to maintain secrecy, keep employment unrest to a minimum, avoid a competitive reaction, and control the market reception.

Auction. An alternative method of selling a company is the use of an auction. This tool has evolved during the past few years and is used very effectively with high-visibility companies. The M&A (Merger and Acquisition) auction is generally limited to divestitures of divisions of public companies, both large and small. Like any other methodology employed in the sale of a business, there are a number of factors in utilizing this technique of which sellers should be aware before committing to its use. In theory, the auction offers the following advantages to the seller: (1) efficacy, (2) simplicity, (3) control, and (4) visibility.

Efficacy. The auction is able to draw the greatest number of interested parties into the activity within the shortest time span, at the lowest possible selling cost, and with minimal business interruption.

Simplicity. The process eliminates the slower, more complicated method of seeking a buyer by approaching selected target buyers as stated above.

Control. By virtue of the nature of an auction (take it or leave it), the seller can better control the momentum of the particular transaction. Time deadlines are set early, and if the seller meets its target for the dissemination of information to the buyers (the confidential memorandum as discussed above), he can control the timing and response in a competitive atmosphere, which eliminates bidder delays. The bidder either responds on time or loses not only the investment opportunity, but the time, effort, and dollars he has put forth to examine this opportunity.

Visibility. Companies committed to a specific divestiture often go "public," which generally opens up the market potential and allows the seller to reach the largest buyer universe within the shortest period of time.

While the seller seeks to reach the greatest number of people in the shortest time frame, it sometimes reaches too many potential buyers, including a combination of real players and casual opportunists as well as competitors whose motives may be clouded by the process. The sheer volume of interested parties can lead to the virtual elimination of one of the primary motives for using the M&A auction—speed. Unfortunately, it is difficult to limit early participants and maintain the aura of a true auction process. Indiscreet control of the number of bidders tends to destroy the whole process and ultimately leads to an arm's-length negotiation with several bidders. This process is time-consuming and difficult to orchestrate without turning off bidders who originally would not have made the investment in due diligence if they knew a protracted negotiated auction was going to take place. The M&A auction also eliminates buyers who will not come to the table at all without having an exclusive (30/45/60-day) period to negotiate a purchase.

Further complicating the bid process is the complexity of trying to negotiate a "purchase agreement" before the business issues are resolved. While business issues seem to be consistent from buyer to buyer in the main, the legal issues tend to reflect the individual style of each buyer's attorney, which creates a complex of legal questions that ultimately requires writing individual contracts with each prospective buyer. These negotiations slow the process down to a crawl while drastically increasing legal costs. The promise of speed and simplicity sometimes backfires by using the M&A auction and instead becomes a nightmare of accommodation to each buyer's individual goals.

There are also other serious negatives associated with the process: (1) secrecy, (2) employee unrest, (3) competitive reaction, and (4) market perception.

Secrecy. Surely a company with technical and proprietary information to protect will find it almost impossible to use the M&A auction as a means of divesting a division, since full disclosure to all interested parties is a must in effectively utilizing this process.

Employee Unrest. All divestitures cause both management and labor force unrest by virtue of the cloud of uncertainty hanging over the business. Many times, key players panic and leave the company or attempt to hold up the new owners for lucrative contracts that can cause a buyer to pass. The constant presence of strangers in offices and plants slows productivity, engenders low morale, and often causes negative feedback that can severely damage the process by raising a caution flag to the buyer interested in retaining management and maintaining normal relations with all other employees.

Competitive Reaction. Competitors usually have a field day when they find out about a public divestiture. Furthermore, if the seller runs a fair M&A auction, it will usually get a large number of competitors at its doorstep to take a look. As mentioned before, their motives are not always the same as those of other buyers, yet in many cases where the M&A auction has been successful, a direct competitor has often been the successful high bidder. It is still difficult to properly orchestrate the selling of a division to a direct competitor, and it always causes great consternation and unrest during the process. Not only do competitors get to look into the bowels of a company but they will have that advantage over the new owner, if not a competitor, which may leave the auction buyer queasy enough to drop out or pass on the auction situation as a matter of policy.

Market Perception. If the divestment decision is correct for the parent, the perception of the market should be positive. For the most part, especially during the past five to eight years, selling of divisions has been a strategy usually welcomed by the investment community. On the other hand, the perception within the specific industry in which the divestiture candidate operates can be cause for concern. Customers worry about maintaining an uninterrupted flow of products or services during the process, and begin to look at the competition as an alternative, since they are never sure who will eventually buy the division and how the new owner's policy and philosophy will affect their past relationship.

SUMMARY

Divestiture, as with any major corporation decisions, can result from a multitude of factors. As a management tool, it is somewhat unique in its implications and far-reaching effects. Though it should not be used cavalierly, or viewed as a universal elixir for what ails a company, management should not avoid divestiture when its appropriate use can benefit the corporation and its stockholders. In conclusion, the following short poem might sum up the essentials of this chapter.

> Buyers are winners, the track record shows
> They flash brilliance with numbers in charts and cash flows
> The target once landed is turned over to staff
> The brilliance may fade which is no cause to laugh
> Some fight it with money and people and such
> Some look for a saviour with a magical touch
> When momentum heads south you must face up to the test
> If you can't solve your problem, it's time to divest.

—By Arnold S. Hoffman

PART B Divestiture Techniques*

The decision to divest a business, like the decision to acquire one, represents a very significant strategic action and critical corporate undertaking. Acquisitions and divestitures derive from fundamental

* Part B was written by Paul R. Van Wyck. Some of this material was drawn from the *Acquisition and Divestiture Guide* of the corporate development department of the Chase Manhattan Bank.

decisions about the future strategic direction of the corporation. For the emerging, growth-oriented corporation, the acquisition or divestiture of a business may well be the single most critical event in determining the future success or failure of the enterprise. While acquisitions are almost always exciting corporate events, surrounded by much glamour, divestitures very often take place in a much more subdued environment.

Acquisitions bring with them a sense of accomplishment and positive corporate visibility along with great expectations of future growth, profits, and size. While these expectations do not always work out, everyone in the acquiring corporation wants to be part of the triumph, and few corporate resources are spared in assuring that the transaction is professionally managed and staffed.

Divestitures, on the other hand, are often corporate events with which few in the corporation wish to be associated and for which the primary objective often tends to be getting the transaction consummated as quickly as possible. While the corporate psychologist may find the attitudinal difference between the manner in which acquisitions and divestitures are approached quite understandable, the management, directors, and stockholders of the corporation should not. The thesis here is very simple. In order to maximize the benefits or minimize the losses associated with a divestiture, these transactions must be professionally managed and supported in the corporation with the same type and level of commitment given acquisitions. Like acquisitions, divestitures are not business-as-usual transactions. They require not only professional management but also specialized functional skills and experienced negotiating capability. These skills should be brought together in a dedicated team and, where necessary, supplemented with outside professional advisers.

Part B of this chapter addresses the steps required to complete a successful divestiture. These steps include:

- Assembling the divestiture team.
- Preparing the divestiture.
- Valuing the business.
- The selling process.

ASSEMBLING THE DIVESTITURE TEAM

Divesting a business requires a team of functional experts under the direction of an experienced project manager. Selection of the project manager is the first and one of the most important actions taken after reaching the decision to divest. In addition to general project management skills, the project manager must be knowledgeable in the tasks and techniques necessary to consummate a successful divestiture. Within the corporation, people with these types of skills most often reside in the corporate development function. Those corporations that do not have a formal corporate development activity may find qualified divestiture managers within the financial, legal, or corporate planning organizations. Even in those instances where the corporation elects to engage an investment banker or some other intermediary to assist in the divestiture, the appointment of an internal project manager and core team is absolutely critical.

The project manager's first task is to assemble the core team. While the makeup of the core team will vary depending on the specific nature of the divestiture, it generally includes someone extremely knowledgeable about the business being sold and someone from the corporate financial function. Where practical, a member of the corporate legal staff should be closely associated with the activities of the core team from the very beginning of the project. This will facilitate the preparation of the offering memorandum, the negotiations, and the writing of the letter of intent and definitive purchase agreement. The core team will also need assistance from time to time during the project from other functional areas of the corporation. These often include the tax department, human resources, corporate communications, and the corporate controller.

Having assembled the core team, the project manager should draw up a definitive project plan and obtain approval of the approach to be utilized from corporate management. The project plan will include:

1. Identification of the core team and supplementary internal resource requirements.
2. The specific tasks to be performed and the responsibilities of each project participant.
3. Identification of outside resource requirements such as investment bankers, their specific tasks, and the anticipated costs of these services.
4. The timetable for each major phase of the project.
5. An overall project budget.

A critical element in assembling the project team and preparing the project plan is the decision regarding the use of outside resources. Some corporations may not have the breadth of resources and talent internally to effect a successful divestiture. These types of organizations often turn to investment bankers, outside law firms, or other intermediaries for professional assistance. This is a perfectly appropriate decision because, as indicated earlier, selling a business is a highly specialized activity. In addition to providing the necessary professional expertise that may be lacking in the selling corporation, investment bankers can be particularly helpful in a number of other areas important to a successful divestiture. These are:

1. Identification of potential purchasers.
2. Approaching potential purchasers on an anonymous basis.
3. Assisting in the structuring of the deal.
4. Assisting in the negotiating process.

The process of engaging outside resources must be carefully planned and executed. Both investment bankers and outside law firms receive substantial compensation for their services. While these services are generally worth their cost, it is important to be very specific as to the services to be rendered and the billing methodology to be used. For divestitures, like acquisitions, investment bankers generally bill on the basis of a percentage of the selling price. Before engaging an investment banker, it is worthwhile to do some research on deals of comparable size and complexity as preparation for discussions of the fee arrangements. Investment banking fees are negotiable even with those firms that profess to have policy-directed fee structures. Since fees for deals of this type are generally based on a percentage of the price, small deals are by definition less attractive to the most senior people in the firm than are large deals. Therefore, part of the negotiations in engaging an investment banker should include a discussion of specifically who in the firm will be assigned to the project. The well-known investment banking firms all have very talented young people, but experience can be worth substantial dollars in the ultimate price received for the business being sold. Therefore, when engaging an investment banker, it is important to get the best talent available in the firm assigned to the project.

Outside law firms generally bill on the basis of time and expenses. Here again the best law firms have large numbers of very bright young lawyers, and as with the investment bankers, these people are often assigned to the smaller deals. While this will save some money since the billing rates for these people are considerably lower than those of the partners, the value of experience should not be underestimated. The real value of the larger law firms is in the breadth of legal specialization available. Divestitures often involve technical legal issues ranging from tax matters to complex licensing agreements. It is always comforting for the selling corporation to know that the lawyer preparing the contracts of sale has, at his or her disposal for consultation, lawyers with specialized knowledge in almost every aspect of the law.

PREPARING THE DIVESTITURE

One of the earliest tasks for the project team is to determine exactly what is to be sold. No two divestitures are exactly the same. Some divestitures involve the sale of assets, others the sale of legal corporate entities. For example, the sale of a division of a company or part of a division usually results in the transaction taking the form of an asset sale. There are cases where for tax, legal, or other reasons the selling company may find it beneficial to package the assets being sold within a legal corporate entity prior to sale. In those cases where an existing corporate entity is to be sold, the selling corporation may find the marketability and, therefore, the financial return on the divestiture to be better if the transaction is converted into a sale of assets. When determining specifically what is to be sold, there are tax and legal as well as business implications to be considered from both the buyer's and seller's perspective.

In addition to the form of the transaction, there are a number of other issues to be considered in preparing the divestiture. The cleanest divestitures are those involving totally stand-alone businesses that after the sale have no ongoing relationship with the selling corporation. However, often divestitures do involve some sort of continuing business relationship. The selling corporation may be a supplier of products and or services to the business being sold. These may be critical to the future success of the business and the purchaser will expect to negotiate a service agreement as part of the transaction. In other instances, there may be marketing or distribution dependencies between the selling corporation and the business being divested. Here again, the purchaser will want to develop operationally viable and economically feasible agency agreements as part of the transaction. These types of interdependencies must be carefully analyzed at the outset of the divestiture project. Failure to understand them and to prepare for their resolution as part of the overall transaction can often cause major problems in completing the divestiture successfully. Discovery of critical interdependencies late in the negotiating process can, at a minimum, seriously impact the selling price or deal structure, and may cause the buyer to walk away from the deal.

Another important matter in preparing the divestiture is the resolution of management and human resources issues. These aspects of a divestiture may affect the nature, timing, and valuation of the business. If key members of management are critical to the future success of the business or if staff expertise is a valuable asset of the enterprise, these people must be retained and motivated to assure a successful sale. The needs and desires of these people must be understood and dealt with early in the divestiture process. In some instances, special compensation and employment contracts are useful tools to be considered in order to assure management and staff cooperation in the divestiture process. The manner in which employees are handled can affect the price a buyer is willing to pay for a business and the net value of the deal to the seller.

The major effort in preparing the divestiture is the gathering of the data and information necessary to present the business to prospective purchasers. This data-gathering exercise serves several purposes. It will enable the selling corporation to make some of the policy-type decisions identified above. It is the basis on which the initial selling document or offering memorandum is developed and it is the foundation for the business reviews that will be held with serious prospective buyers later in the selling process. In this regard, it has been observed that often as a result of preparing a business for sale, the project team ends up knowing more about the business being sold than either the management of the business or the selling corporation. This is simply another way of saying that successful divestitures depend on careful preparation and intimate knowledge of the business being sold.

In order to address the types of data and information that must be gathered in preparing a divestiture, it may be helpful to look at these requirements in the context of a typical offering memorandum. While all divestitures do not require the preparation of a formal offering memorandum, the data and information necessary to start the selling process tend to be the same. The decision whether or not to prepare a formal offering memorandum is generally driven by the type of selling process elected. If the business being sold is to be offered to a number of potential buyers, either sequentially or on a competitive bidding basis, a formal offering memorandum is essential. In those instances where the selling corporation has a high degree of confidence that it knows the buyer and that the deal will be done with that one party, the formality of an offering memorandum may not be necessary; however, the same level of information will have to be made available to the prospective buyer.

One final comment is in order before moving to the contents of a typical offering memorandum. The offering memorandum must provide a sufficient level of detail for prospective buyers to determine if they are seriously interested in acquiring the business. Its contents must be accurate in every respect. Errors or misstatements about the business that appear in an offering memorandum will almost without exception be identified by prospective buyers during the negotiating process or later during due dilegence. This can cause serious difficulties in consummating the transaction and may cause discussions to be terminated completely. Although anything short of complete accuracy in an offering memorandum puts the transaction at risk and should be avoided, this document from the sellers perspective should be viewed, and therefore prepared, as a selling tool. It should emphasize the strengths of the business and position these, where possible, in the context of the strategies or potential strategies of prospective buyers.

CONTENTS OF THE OFFERING MEMORANDUM

Executive Summary. This is one of the most important parts of the document. In addition to summarizing the key points about the business, including specifically what is for sale and the reasons the business is being offered for sale, it should stress the strengths and advantages of the business. This is the key selling chapter of the document.

Buyer Procedure. This section lays out the rules of the sale as set by the selling corporation. It indicates if competitive bidding or another process is being used. It sets the dates for indications of serious interest and for initial bid submission. It stipulates when and where detailed business reviews will be held, and it sets the date for submission of final bids. It describes the methods of payment that the seller will accept as well as outlining both acceptable and unacceptable deal structures. Finally, it indicates specifically who at the selling corporation prospective purchasers are authorized to contact.

Background. This section introduces the business by providing a historical perspective and by highlighting key events in its evolution to date.

Important elements of this section are:

- The history of the business, date of founding or acquisition, identification of minority stockholders, if any.
- Past and current strategic objectives.
- Background on why the business is being sold.
- Summary financial history.
- Geographic locations, legal entities, and states of incorporation.
- Organization chart.
- Background on key officers and employees.

The Market. This chapter presents a comprehensive picture of the industry in which the business participates and provides information that emphasizes the strengths of the business being sold. This is done using the following types of data and information:

- Market size, major products/services, historic growth rates.
- Industry's current position in its life cycle.
- Product/Service life-cycle position.

- Projected growth rate of market and major segments.
- Barriers to entry.
- Importance of product/service to customers.
- Purchase frequency.
- Customer concentration.
- Market saturation.
- Market share of business being sold.
- Major competitors and their market shares.
- Market strengths and weaknesses.
- Domestic and international factors.
- Product/service analysis by major competitors.

Products/Services. In describing the products/services of the business being offered for sale, the following types of information are helpful to prospective buyers:

- Quality objectives.
- Pricing policies and schedules.
- Technical specifications of the product/service.
- Operating and/or production processes.
- Descriptions of differentiating features.
- Customer profiles by product/service.
- Customer turnover by product/service.
- Trademarks and patents.
- New product development history and current activities.

Facilities and Fixed Assets. Specific lists of facilities and fixed assets to be included as part of the sale should be shown on separate exhibits. Facilities and fixed assets are broken down in terms of owned versus leased, by location, and by key activities. Contractual obligations are indicated. An analysis of the adequacy of both facilities and equipment for future growth is included.

Systems and Operations. Complete descriptions of the systems and operations of the business are included. Those systems and operations capabilities to be included as part of the sale are separated from any not included in the sale. This section addresses the adequacy of the systems and operations included as part of the sale for both current and future production and delivery of the product/service.

Organization, Management, and Personnel. This section describes the key human resource elements of the contemplated transaction. Where management and/or personnel are believed critical to the business, this is so stated. The numbers and categories of employees to be made available are listed. All employee benefits are described.

Key Financial Information. Prospective purchasers will expect to receive sufficient financial information necessary to make a preliminary judgment as to their interest in acquiring the business. Generally, a five-year financial history of the business is provided. Often this five-year history is shown in pro forma terms in order to accurately reflect the specific nature of the business being sold. Items that are often left out of the profit and loss statement include intercompany charges for services that the selling corporation no longer intends to provide, overhead allocations from the selling corporation, and federal and state taxes. Prospective purchasers are advised of these adjustments and instructed to insert their own estimates of these expenses when valuing the business. Similar adjustments are often made to the balance sheet, again to reflect specifically what is being sold.

Listed below are the types of data and information that might be included:

- Balance sheet and income statement (past five years).
- Revenue analysis.
  - By product or service.
    - By customer.
    - By geography.
    - By month.
    - By location.
  - Seasonality factors.
  - Sales policies.
- Expense analysis.
  - By business segment.
  - By product or service.
  - Fixed versus variable cost.
  - Break-even levels.
  - Growth rates for major expense items.
- Other specific financial items.
  - Loans or other financial assets.
  - Receivables analysis (turnover, bad debts).
  - Prepaid expenses and deferred charges.
  - Purchase Contracts.

VALUING THE BUSINESS

Prospective purchasers can be expected to utilize one or more of several basic valuation techniques in developing their offering price for the business. The divestiture team should conduct a similar analysis. This effort will serve a number of purposes. First, it will provide the selling corporation with an estimate of the market value of the business.

Second, it will assist in the identification of prospective buyers. Third, in those instances where more than one offer is received, it will assist in comparing the values of the different offers. Finally, it will provide the foundation for negotiating the price later in the selling process.

Some of the basic valuation methodologies that might be used are:

1. Book value: The accounting value of the items on the balance sheet.
2. Comparables: Public market values and price earnings multiples of similar firms, or prices paid for recent acquisitions of similar firms.
3. Discounted cash flow (net present value): The after-tax cash flows discounted at a risk-adjusted cost of capital results in a net present value.
4. Payback: The length of time necessary to generate cash flows equal to the purchase price.
5. Replacement cost: Estimated cost of replicating the business on a de novo basis.

It is important to recognize that these are basic valuation methodologies and that they must be modified to reflect the special circumstances of each prospective purchaser. For example, different prospective buyers will assume different purchase price adjustments. These include the method of acquisition (tax free or taxable), purchase price allocation assumptions, tax assumptions, and the application of accounting policies. These adjustments can have a very significant impact on the valuation of the business and on the price a purchaser is willing to pay. Furthermore, the price that a prospective purchaser is willing to pay will be affected by considerations of market forces, competition, and the effect of the acquisition on the buyers' base business. Prospective purchasers will evaluate the impact of the acquisition on current and future earnings, return on investment, financing capability, and balance sheet considerations.

The valuation and pricing of a business are not, therefore, precise activities. The outcome of these activities is influenced by business, market, financial, and other assumptions. Successful divestitures often depend on the seller's knowledge and understanding of these as they apply to specific purchasers.

THE SELLING PROCESS

There are four key elements of the selling process: (1) identification of prospective buyers, (2) selection of the type of selling process to be utilized, (3) business reviews, and (4) negotiating the transaction and closing the deal.

Identifying Potential Buyers

The selling process begins when the project team starts to identify potential buyers. Prior to this step, the decision to divest, the organization of the project team, and the preliminary work in preparing the divestiture have all been activities internal to the selling corporation. The identification of potential buyers is the beginning of the external process that hopefully will lead to the successful consummation of the divestiture transaction.

At this stage in the divestiture process, the decision to engage or not to engage an investment banker or other intermediary is often considered or reconsidered. The decision to use an intermediary to identify prospective buyers is often made based on the selling corporation's experience with divestitures, the confidence it has in its divestiture team, and the knowledge it has in-house regarding potentially interested buyers. As indicated earlier, investment bankers can be helpful in identifying prospective buyers. They know the types of businesses their clients are seeking to acquire, they often know the kinds of businesses their competitors are seeking, and they have the capability to identify potential acquirers who have not been active in the market, but for whom a particular business may be a good strategic fit. Since, almost without exception, selling corporations do not enjoy the prospect of having the business they are divesting characterized as having been widely "shopped," investment bankers can also often qualify potential leads anonymously.

Potential buyers can be identified by evaluating the assets of the business being sold and matching these against the strategies or apparent strategies of others. Often it is possible to consider the assets of the business to be sold and to create a strategic rationale for the acquisition of these assets by another company. In other words, as part of the selling process, it may be possible to create the strategy for the potential acquirer by demonstrating that a good strategic fit does exist between the business being sold and other things a particular company may be doing or planning to do.

Potential buyers tend to fall into several general categories:

Competitors. Direct competitors are the most obvious potential buyers. They have the most to gain and, therefore, they are generally in a position to pay the highest price. For potential buyers who are direct competitors, the acquisition will increase market share, provide both marketing and operational economies of scale, and should result in a significant increase in earnings. If the business being sold is operating at a loss or break-even point, selling to a competitor may be the only viable option since only a competitor has the leverage to turn the business around quickly.

While a direct competitor can be expected to pay the best price for a business for the reasons summarized above, there are some definite disadvantages in selling to a competitor. The direct competitor will usually plan to reduce the expense base of the business being acquired by combining the acquisition with his current business. Therefore, the residual costs of the divestiture to the selling corporation can be very high and must be factored against the selling price to determine the net value of the deal. If the form of the transaction is the sale of assets, the selling corporation is often left with significant shutdown costs in the form of personnel severance, lease obligations, and the need to sell fixed assets at below book value. If the form of the transaction is a stock sale, these same costs can be left with the selling corporation or, if the entity is to be sold intact to a competitor, the purchase price can be significantly reduced in anticipation of these costs by the buyer.

Companies in Similar Types of Businesses. These types of potential buyers tend to have some of the characteristics of direct competitors, but not all. The trick here is to identify companies that might see marketing leverage or operational synergies that could be gained through the acquisition. The following are some examples of these types of potential buyers.

Buyers Who Want to Broaden Their Product Lines. If the business being divested is a provider of specialized information based on a proprietary data base, potential buyers may be other information companies who provide data base services and see the benefits of adding the information service of the company being sold to their product line. In this example, the buyer is able to broaden his product line and possibly leverage his existing distribution system.

Buyers Looking for Operational Economies of Scale. If the business being sold is a transaction processing organization, it is often productive to look for potential buyers who are also transaction processors. The acquisition may enable the acquiring company to achieve operational economies of scale and will generally fit with the management style and culture of these types of acquirers.

In attempting to identify these types of potential buyers, it is important to understand their strategies and views of their business without judging their correctness. In other words, the selling corporation should not disregard potential buyers by imposing its own strategic or operational philosophy while screening them. In the second example above, the selling corporation may see no operational efficiencies and may even see risks in combining two different transaction processing activities, and therefore eliminate a particular potential buyer from consideration. That same potential buyer may see the situation quite differently, and therefore may be willing to pay handsomely for the business.

Suppliers and Customers. Depending on the nature of the business being sold, both suppliers to that business and customers of the business may be potential buyers. Good candidates in both these categories are relatively easy to identify and assess since the business being sold has had an association with them.

Others. Companies seeking diversification, holding companies, investment groups, and venture capitalists all may be potential buyers. These types of buyers are often more difficult to identify and screen. They are generally identified by the management or directors of the selling corporation who have personal knowledge of the investment objectives of certain of these types of organizations. Investment bankers and business brokers are other sources of information on these types of buyers. Often the management of the business being sold will identify and introduce these types of buyers as part of a management buyout plan.

Selecting the Selling Process

There are basically four different methods of selling a business. Each has its advantages and disadvantages. The selection of the process to be utilized depends largely on the nature of the business being sold and the objectives of the selling corporation. The four methods are:

- Competitive bidding.
- Sequential selling.
- One buyer.
- Going public.

Competitive Bidding. In most instances this process, if managed correctly, will produce the highest price and best deal structure for the selling corporation. By definition, it suggests that more than one prospective purchaser has been identified. This process is usually most effective when 5 to 10 potential buyers have been identified and when diverse strategic objectives are present in the potential buyer list. The process begins when the divestiture manager contacts each identified prospective purchaser to determine if there is initial interest. Those indicating interest are then requested to sign a confidentiality letter prior to receiving a copy of the offering memorandum. As indicated earlier, the offering memorandum will state the rules to be followed by potential bidders, including the date for preliminary bids, and the individual at the selling corporation to be contacted for any necessary clarification prior to the bid date.

To maximize the effectiveness of competitive bidding, the selling corporation must carefully control the process and information flow. Upon receipt of preliminary bids, the prospective buyer list will usually be reduced. Some may not bid at all. Others may bid low or present an apparently unacceptable deal structure. In any event, all bidders should be contacted in order to clarify their bids and their bidding philosophies. At this point, it is important to understand that the highest bidder may not be the winner and that the lower bids may not be losers. It is, however, necessary to determine which are the serious bidders and which are not. Those considered serious should then be scheduled for business reviews (see below).

Final bids are generally scheduled for receipt a short time after the completion of the business reviews. Upon receiving the final bids, the project team will conduct what is often referred to as an apples-to-apples analysis. This is the process in which the similarities and differences in the bids are identified, and it is the basis on which the apparent winner is selected. This is the most critical point in the use of competitive bidding from the selling corporation's perspective. It is at this point that the project manager notifies the bidders of the results. This should be done in reverse order, that is, from the least attractive bid to the most attractive. Often during this process, when a bidder is advised that his bid has been unsuccessful, he will ask what it will take to win. These discussions can result in the revision of one or more bids and often lead to a transaction considerably more attractive than any of the so-called final bids.

The potential disadvantages of utilizing competitive bidding generally derive from the unlikely possibility of an unsuccessful sale. If the business, for whatever reason, is not sold, the use of competitive bidding can impair the value and near term viability of the business. Customers see a lack of commitment to the business on the part of the selling corporation. Employees feel that lack of commitment as well. Competitors turn this to their advantage. If a competitor has been a prospective buyer, it will have gained significant knowledge about the business that can be used against that business in the marketplace. Unsuccessful divestitures, in general, usually result from poor initial planning of the divestiture or, in some cases, from badly managed selling processes.

Sequential Selling. Having identified prospective purchasers, the selling corporation can elect to offer the business to what is believed to be the most likely potential buyer and, if unsuccessful, move down the preestablished priority list. If successful with the first potential buyer, this is obviously a much easier process to manage than competitive bidding. However, the price and deal structure that is negotiated will have no market frame of reference. The seller will never know if a better deal could have been made with someone else. If the primary objective is to get out of the business, with price and deal structure secondary, this is an acceptable selling method. Should the preestablished priority list prove faulty, requiring the business to be offered to a number of prospective purchasers in sequence, the business will quickly become known as one that has been "shopped" and rejected, and its value potentially impaired.

One Buyer. If, in the identification of prospective buyers, only one candidate can be identified, the seller will be in a position with little negotiating leverage. Even in those instances where the selling corporation has been approached on numerous occasions by the apparent single buyer, the seller's negotiating position will be weak, and therefore the resulting transaction most probably will not meet all of the seller's objectives. In those instances where there is a known anxious buyer, the seller should carefully consider the value this buyer sees in the business and attempt to identify others who might see it as well. If successful, a one-buyer divestiture might be turned into a competitive bidding transaction, thereby shifting the negotiating leverage away from the anxious buyer. The result will be significantly better price and terms than could have been expected in a one-buyer transaction.

Going Public. Taking a division or a subsidiary public as a means of divesting that business is considerably different than selling an entity through a private transaction. First, the entity to be sold must have an established history of profits and growth or at least a proprietary product or service on which a public market price can be based. Second, market conditions must be favorable in terms of an appetite for initial public offerings and for those in the industry in which the proposed new issue operates. Unlike private transactions, even the most sophisticated selling corporations require the assistance of investment bankers when contemplating the divestiture of a business through an initial public offering.

Business Reviews

Where the selling process involves the use of competitive bidding, business reviews are held for all prospective buyers who are considered serious after receipt of initial bids and clarifying discussions. In a sequential sale, a business review is held only for the top-priority prospective buyer, and no one else, unless discussions with that buyer are terminated, in which case the process is started over with the next potential buyer on the priority list. The same is true in a one-buyer transaction; however, in this instance, should discussions terminate, the selling corporation's only alternatives are to keep the business or, as mentioned earlier, perhaps try to turn it into a competitive bidding deal by finding other prospective buyers who can be shown the value of the business originally only seen by the one buyer.

During the business reviews, which generally last one or two days, prospective buyers are given detailed presentations on all aspects of the business. It is during the business reviews that prospective buyers are able to meet the key members of management of the business being sold and to obtain a level of detail about the business that reaches well below the general type of information contained in the offering memorandum. Also, during the business reviews, prospective purchasers are often given the opportunity to visit the company's facilities.

The primary purpose of business reviews is to provide prospective purchasers with sufficient information necessary for the preparation of firm offers for the business. In those instances, where the selling process utilized is competitive bidding, prospective purchasers will often want to significantly refine their initial bid after the business reviews. This will enable the selling corporation to better understand the offers and will facilitate the selection of the winning bidder. If the process being utilized is sequential selling, the business reviews will either reinforce the interest of the priority purchaser, thereby significantly increasing the probability of consummating the transaction with that party, or they will result in less interest, causing the selling corporation to consider moving to the next potential purchaser on the priority list. In a one-buyer type selling process, the business reviews will tend to blend with the negotiating process. While the same, detailed level of information will be provided in this instance, since both parties are generally aware that there is only one potential purchaser, the information exchange will invariably combine discussions of the deal structure and purchase price.

Negotiating and Closing the Transaction

Negotiating and closing a divestiture transaction requires a diverse set of skills and very thorough preparation. Facts and information alone are not sufficient. The chief negotiator must be a consummate actor, and the other members of the negotiating team must know their roles. Good negotiators know when to be tough and when to give on a specific point. Furthermore, they know how to effectively link negotiating points so that if they must retreat from a position on one point they can maintain or improve their position on another. Even in those rare instances where businesses almost sell themselves, the objective of good negotiators is to maximize price and optimize the deal structure.

Preparing for Negotiations. As stated above, the chief negotiator must be an accomplished actor, and the other members of the negotiating team must know their roles. Like successful plays, effective negotiations require a good script, trained players, and sufficient rehearsal. Prior to beginning negotiations, the negotiating team should identify all major points to be discussed. Each of these points should be carefully evaluated in the context of the overall objective of the divestiture. For each negotiating point, the team should prepare its opening position, preferred position, fallback position, and the deal breakers. While the negotiations will generally be led by the chief negotiator, other members of the team may be assigned to take the lead on specific points. This should be determined in advance. It is also helpful sometimes to designate a "hero" and a "villain." There will certainly be some difficult points during the negotiations. Often a position on a point can be preserved if it can be made to appear that while one member of the team is working toward a compromise, another member of the team is very unhappy. For this technique to be effective, the point being negotiated must have been established as a critical one and the individual playing the villain must have been positioned as a person of sufficient authority to upset the deal.

Prior to beginning negotiations, and where possible, it is often helpful to role-play the forthcoming negotiations. This will often identify weaknesses in the positions established for each point and will enable the members of the negotiating team to polish their roles.

Conducting the Negotiations. Actual negotiations usually take place in several steps. The first step usually deals with reaching an agreement in principle. This is the process where the seller and the buyer meet to discuss and negotiate each of the key points of the transaction as they see them. In some cases, this process results in what is simply a term sheet to be used as the basis for negotiation and preparation of the definitive purchase agreement. In other cases, the parties may agree to sign a formal agreement in principle once all major points are believed to have been resolved.

Due Diligence Examinations. Having reached and documented agreement on the major points of the transaction, the purchaser will expect to conduct a due diligence examination of the business. This requires the seller to make available to the purchaser all appropriate books, records, and facilities of the business for verification of financial statements and other information. Any misrepresentations discovered by the purchaser can void the agreement or cause renegotiation of price and deal structure.

The due diligence inspection will include examination and verification of:

Accounting records.
Physical inventory.
Accounts receivable.
Current liabilities and long-term obligations.
Contracts.
Systems and operations.
Insurance coverage.
Contingent liabilities and litigation.
Employment contracts.
Other pertinent issues.

Upon completion of the due diligence examination, negotiations will address the resolution of any issues that may have arisen as a result of that process.

The Purchase Agreement. The next step in the conduct of negotiations is the preparation of the definitive purchase agreement and any supplementary agreements that may be required. The extent and depth of negotiations required to finalize the purchase agreement will generally depend on the level of detail included in the agreement in principle and the extent to which major new issues have developed as part of the due diligence examination. If few or no major new business issues are outstanding at this point in the process, negotiation of the definitive purchase agreement will tend to focus on legal matters.

The final step is the actual preparation of the definitive purchase agreement and any necessary supplementary agreements. These agreements generally go through numerous drafts and revisions prior to the closing. If the divestiture was planned well by the selling corporation and the business issues were negotiated in good faith by both parties, the preparation of agreements and closing documents will be greatly facilitated.

Closing the Transaction. The actual closing should be nothing more than the signing of agreements, the exchanging of the proceeds of the transaction, and perhaps a glass of champagne to celebrate a successful deal for both buyer and seller. A word of caution, however, is in order. The best way to state this caution is to quote Yogi Berra, who is reputed to have said, "It ain't over 'til it's over." Stated in more traditional terms, a seller can never relax until the documents are signed and proceeds change hands. A high confidence level after reaching an agreement in principle is a sure prescription for disaster. A comfortable feeling about the last draft of the purchase agreement can bring great disappointment, and insufficient attention to detail in preparing the closing documents can result in a deferred closing or no closing at all.

SUMMARY

The decision to divest a business represents a significant strategic action and critical corporate undertaking. While divesting a business is one of a number of alternative methods of raising capital, it is one of the most complex, and therefore requires specialized skills and professional management. Divestitures are not business-as-usual transactions. They should not be undertaken by, or assigned to, individuals with little or no experience in successfully completing transactions of this type. Successful divestitures are those that are carefully planned, cleverly sold, and competently negotiated.

PART C Legal Aspects of Corporate Divestitures*

Divestiture projects have been staple fare in Fortune 500 strategic planning departments for many years, and this interest has been heightened by the recent wave of hostile takeovers that have forced managements to maximize asset values. Little attention, though, has been paid to divestiture strategies for emerging companies, yet these firms are often under acute pressure to realize the most from limited resources. An emerging company may seek to sell a subsidiary or division to raise funds for more immediate or favorable projects, or divestiture may be contemplated because the targeted operations, though promising, would require an investment commitment that

* Part C was written by Roger Mulvihill.

would detract from the company's primary objectives. In another variation, the emerging company might retain a minority interest in the divested subsidiary or division, which will now be funded by the buyer, in order to reap a benefit from an opportunity it could not have exploited alone. Finally, emerging companies might implement, in appropriate cases, a divestiture strategy that has attracted favorable attention in other quarters—the corporate spin-off. Although the spin-off of a subsidiary or a division does not raise any funds for the corporate coffers, it could improve the divesting parent's balance sheet by relieving it of subsidiary debt. If the parent is publicly held, the spin-off could also create additional value for stockholders by creating another public company that might enjoy a higher market valuation alone than as a unit of the parent. Corporate spin-offs have also been utilized as a means of tying managerial equity incentives (such as stock options and stock appreciation programs) more directly to the performance of the subsidiary or division.

Each of these corporate divestiture strategies raises a host of tax, accounting, and legal issues. The purpose Part C of this chapter is to provide an overview of these issues from the perspective of the emerging company, particularly from the point of view of the manager or professional without extensive experience with divestitures. While volumes can—and have—been written on the technical nuances of corporate divestitures, this material attempts to minimize technical discussions except where necessary to understand the issue under consideration. As in other complex corporate transactions, the emerging company will wish to consult experienced accounting and legal advisers in structuring and implementing any corporate divestiture program.

ANTITRUST CONSIDERATIONS

Federal antitrust laws may pose one of the first serious hurdles for a planned divestiture. Often the most likely purchasers for a subsidiary or division will be firms with a substantial presence in the same industry. These firms, which know the business and may be able to realize substantial economies of scale not available to other purchasers, are frequently able to offer the most attractive purchase terms. The federal antitrust laws, however, may disqualify them.

Setting the Stage

Section 7 of the Clayton Act is the principal federal antitrust statute applicable to divestitures. Somewhat cavalierly, the statute purports to prohibit any acquisition "where in any line of commerce or any activity affecting commerce in any section of the country, the effect of such acquisition may be substantially to lessen competition or tend to create a monopoly."

The courts have struggled for years with this discouragingly vague standard. Eventually, prospective acquisitions came to be analyzed in terms of whether a particular acquisition was horizontal (between competitors), vertical (between companies having a supplier-customer relationship), or conglomerate (all others).

In a series of 12 cases starting in the 1960s, the United States Supreme Court fashioned an analytical framework for viewing acquisitions from the perspective of the federal antitrust laws. In this analysis, the Court was significantly influenced by the legislative history of the Clayton Act, which it thought showed a clear congressional concern with possible trends toward concentration in industries. In Congress' view, as the Court saw it, an economy consisting of industries with numerous small firms was important to preserve. A critical aspect of this analytical framework was the evaluation of the effect of an acquisition on competition by defining a product market (the "in any line of commerce" language of the statute) and a geographic market (the "in any section of the country" language). Under this approach, the government and, ultimately, the courts were encouraged to identify well-defined submarkets, for example, a relatively narrow product line or relatively circumscribed geographic area, in which the anticompetitive market effects of a proposed acquisition could be measured. The boundaries of these submarkets, fairly subjective under the best of circumstances, became the battleground over which lawyers, economists, and other combatants struggled in complex litigation proceedings, for the definition of the product and geographic submarkets, narrower or more expansive, would often dictate the outcome of the litigation.

Various other antitrust theories were also adopted or developed by the Supreme Court during this period. While the degree of concentration in appropriate submarkets was the touchstone in analyzing horizontal mergers, the primary analysis in vertical mergers (i.e., supplier-customer acquisitions) was thought to be the foreclosure of competitors of either party from a segment of the market otherwise open to them. Conglomerate mergers were found unlawful where they facilitated reciprocal buying practices, entrenched a dominant firm, or eliminated potential or actual competitors.

Though not models of consistency, the Supreme Court cases through the 1960s and early 1970s, in the view of many, betrayed distinct antimerger leanings. In one oft-quoted remark, Justice Potter Stewart said that the only consistency in any of these cases was that the government always won.

In the mid 1970s, the Supreme Court in several cases tempered its earlier antitrust rulings. Among other things, the Court evidenced a greater willingness to consider the specific factors of a given case in assessing the effect on competition. Thus, defendants were permitted to demonstrate that other factors would suggest an absence of reduced competition (such as the financial weakness of one party), even though the government could demonstrate, in a manner that might have carried the day under earlier decisions, that a significant degree of concentration existed in certain markets and that market shares would increase as a result of the merger.

Merger Guidelines

As the reader might suspect, predicting the likelihood of a government challenge to any particular merger was a little like reading tea leaves, only less scientific. In 1968, at the urging of various interested groups, the Justice Department issued guidelines outlining the standards employed by the department in reviewing mergers under the Clayton Act. In the eyes of many economists these guidelines were flawed, particularly in overemphasizing market structure by looking primarily at the combined market shares of the top four firms. In June 1982, the department issued new guidelines (further refined in June 1984) that addressed some of these concerns. The Federal Trade Commission, which shares antitrust enforcement responsibilities with the Justice Department, adopted an analytical approach similar to that set forth in the guidelines.

The guidelines are important on a very practical level. Few parties to a divestiture transaction are willing to slug it out with the government in court over a period of years in an effort to prove that a proposed business combination is, in fact, in compliance with the federal antitrust laws. Accordingly, the determination of the parties with respect to the likelihood of a governmental challenge, as judged in the light of the guidelines, frequently becomes the critical element in determining whether divestiture negotiations with a particular party will be pursued. Of course, a favorable judgment that a proposed sale is unlikely to provoke a governmental challenge, even if correct, would not preclude a competitor from challenging the combination in court, but even here the guidelines could influence any ultimate judicial determination.

The stated purpose of the new guidelines is "to reflect the current emphasis—both in the antitrust division of the Justice Department and in the courts—on the need for economic evidence of harm or potential harm to competition before a merger will be challenged." The fundamental theme of the guidelines is to focus on the creation of "market power," defined as the ability of one or more firms to profitably maintain prices above competitive levels for a significant period of time. A market for this purpose is defined as "a product or group of products and a geographic area in which it is sold such that a hypothetical, profit-maximizing firm, not subject to price regulation, that was the only present and future seller of those products in that area would impose a small but significant nontransitory increase in price above prevailing or likely future levels." In this connection, the guidelines contemplate a price increase of 5 percent for one year, but larger or smaller price increases could also be hypothesized under appropriate circumstances. If the price increase results in such a shift to other products or to producers in other geographic areas that the increase could not be maintained, these other products or other producers will be taken into account and the 5 percent price increase revaluated until the relevant markets have been identified.

Having identified the product and geographic markets, the Justice Department, in proposed horizontal mergers, would then turn to a new analytical tool to judge the market concentration after the merger—the Herfendall-Hirschorn Index (HHI). The HHI is determined by adding the squares of the individual market shares of all firms in the market (not merely the top four as in the case of the 1968 guidelines). For example:

Firms	*Market Share (percent)*	*HHI*	
1	30	30 × 30 =	900
2	25	25 × 25 =	625
3	20	20 × 20 =	400
4	15	15 × 15 =	225
5	10	10 × 10 =	100
	100%	=	2,250

In addition, the department will review the increase in concentration resulting from the acquisition, determined simply by multiplying the market shares of the merging firms and doubling the product.

In general, the department will not challenge a horizontal merger if the postmerger HHI is below 1,000. These markets are considered unconcentrated and market power too diffused to raise serious anticompetitive concerns. If the postmerger HHI is between 1,000 and 1,800 (i.e., a modestly concentrated market), the department would then look at the increase in concentration resulting from the acquisition, as noted above. If the HHI increase is less than 100 points, a challenge is again unlikely; if over 100, a challenge is probable, unless the factors noted below would lead to a different conclusion.

Finally, if the postmerger HHI in a horizontal acquisition is above 1,800 (i.e., a highly concentrated market), the department will again look at the increase in concentration as measured by the HHI. If less than 50 points, no challenge is likely; if over 50, and particularly if over 100, look out. They're probably drafting the complaint as you sit in your lawyer's office. The department is also likely to challenge a merger of any firm with a 1 percent market share or more with a leading firm whose market share is 35 percent or more.

In evaluating horizontal mergers under the guidelines, the Justice Department will also consider other factors, including changing market conditions that might invalidate historical share data, ease of entry into the market, financial condition of the firms in the market, degree of actual competition between merging firms, questionable or anticompetitive market practices in the past, and efficiencies resulting from the merger if established by clear and convincing evidence.

Vertical mergers (between suppliers and customers) will be reviewed under the merger guidelines in terms of the likelihood of three possible anticompetitive effects: (1) raising barriers to entry such as requiring new entrants to integrate vertically themselves; (2) facilitating collusion; and (3) in the case of regulated utilities, circumventing rate regulation. In general, the standards for challenging vertical mergers, which are set forth in some detail in the guidelines, are more relaxed than under the 1968 guidelines.

In conglomerate mergers, the standards have also been relaxed. The department is generally unlikely to challenge conglomerate mergers if the acquired firm's HHI is below 1,800, if there is relatively easy entry to the market by possible competitors, or if the acquired firm has a market share of 5 percent or less. The department will also consider efficiencies resulting from the business combination in determining whether or not to mount a challenge.

The Failing Firm Defense

A likely candidate for divestiture will often be a subsidiary or division that is not performing up to earlier expectations, frequently because of an inability of the parent company to commit necessary resources. The subsidiary or division may be salable, perhaps even at an attractive price in the light of its untapped promise, but struggling financially at the moment. A sale to a competitor, which would otherwise raise serious antitrust obstacles under the guidelines, might nevertheless be justified under a concept called the "failing firm" defense. In general, the Justice Department will consider the possible failure of the division or subsidiary as an important consideration in weighing the anticompetitive effects of a merger if the proponents of the business combination can establish that the division or subsidiary would be liquidated in the near future if not sold, and that they have made unsuccessful, good faith efforts to obtain an acquisition offer from a competitively preferable purchaser. However, the department is likely to strictly construe this defense in any given case.

Premerger Notification

The Hart-Scott-Rodino Antitrust Improvements Act was enacted by Congress in 1976 to provide the Justice Department and Federal Trade Commission with information and additional time in which to review certain proposed business combinations before consummation. The act does not alter the substantive law of antitrust, but it does assure that the antitrust authorities will focus on the legality of any proposed divestiture transaction that meets the thresholds for reporting contemplated by the act. So much for the layman's hope, forlorn in most cases anyway, that his deal will slip through the cracks.

The act applies to business combinations (including divestitures) that satisfy two criteria: (1) the size of party test and (2) the size of transaction test. Under the size of party test, the acquired firm must have at least $10 million in annual net sales or total assets if it is engaged in manufacturing, or at least $10 million in total assets if not engaged in manufacturing, and the acquiring person must have at least $100 million in total assets or annual net sales. Alternatively, the size of party test could be satisfied if the acquired firm had annual net sales or total assets of at least $100 million and the acquiring firm had annual net sales or total assets of at least $10 million.

The size of transaction test will be satisfied if the acquirer purchases at least $15 million of the acquired firm's assets or at least $15 million of the acquired firm's voting securities. If the acquirer gains control of the acquired firm, as is normally the case in a divestiture, the size of transaction test will be satisfied if the acquired firm has at least $25 million in annual net sales or total assets, regardless of the amount of the transaction. While various exemptions from the reporting requirements are available (such as ordinary course of business transactions, limited acquisitions for investment purposes, intracorporate transactions), they are not likely to be applicable to divestitures.

If the size of party and size of transaction tests are satisfied with respect to any proposed divestiture, both the acquirer and the divesting company must file various information with the antitrust division and the FTC on a premerger notification form and then delay consummation of the transaction for a specified waiting period. The required information includes a description of the acquisition, financial data, areas of competition, and supplier relationships. The information in the premerger notification is confidential and exempt from disclosures normally required under the Freedom of Information Act, but not disclosures required pursuant to administrative or judicial proceedings. The waiting period begins on receipt by the government of the notification form and runs for 30 days. If the government requests additional information during the waiting period, it can be extended for up to an additional 20 days from the date of submission of this additional information, but further extensions may be granted only by a federal court.

Flunking the Guidelines

After reviewing the guidelines and huddling with your antitrust advisers, hopefully it will be clear enough that a proposed divestiture will not pose a serious antitrust problem. But what if it does?

The next step is a meeting with the antitrust authorities, which may occur either before or after the premerger notification filing, if required. The purpose of this meeting is to persuade the Justice Department or FTC that other factors should override apparently unsatisfactory HHI scores, such as changing market conditions, unusual efficiencies resulting from the combination, or even failing company issues if relevant. The key here is thorough preparation and some confidence that the antitrust authorities, in the course of their own informal discussions with customers, suppliers, competitors, and others, will be able to confirm your assertions.

If the authorities remain unpersuaded, the buyer may be able to avoid antitrust hurdles by agreeing to dispose of operations in areas or lines of business that are particularly troublesome. In recent years, the Justice Department and FTC have permitted numerous combinations subject to an agreement by the buyer to restructure its business to meet specific antitrust objections within a reasonable period of time. All of this, of course, will impose an additional cost, one way or the other, on the buyer who will inevitably seek comfort in a reduced purchase price.

FEDERAL INCOME TAX ISSUES

The treatment of any proposed corporate divestiture under federal income tax laws typically has an important influence on the structure and other economic terms of the transaction. It is important for the divesting corporation to understand the tax impact of various divestiture alternatives, both from its own point of view as a seller of a corporate asset and from the perspective of the buyer. In a spin-off transaction, the divesting corporation must also consider the tax effect of the divestiture on its own stockholders. Since tax reform is in the wind, various proposals are afoot which could significantly affect corporate divestitures. It is not possible to predict which, if any, of these proposals will actually be adopted, and this tax discussion will therefore focus on current tax principles.

Although it goes downhill rapidly from there, the Internal Revenue Code starts with a simple proposition. All transactions are fully taxable, unless the transaction can fit within one of several narrowly defined tax-free exceptions. If taxable, the analysis then shifts to the character of gain, whether capital gain or ordinary, and the timing of its recognition for tax purposes. Because additional tax concepts come into play, the taxation of spin-offs will be dealt with separately.

Taxable Divestitures

The emerging corporation that wishes to sell one of its operations or lines of business could structure that divestiture as the sale of the assets of that business or the sale of the stock of the subsidiary that holds those assets. Typically, the divesting corporation would receive cash or, if necessary to assist the buyer in financing the acquisition, a combination of cash and notes or possibly other securities. These other securities may include the buyer's preferred or common stock.

Whether the divestiture transaction is actually structured as a sale of assets or of subsidiary's stock will be worked out in the negotiations and will be influenced by a number of factors. These would include the buyer's degree of comfort, or lack of comfort, over the possibility of unknown liabilities of the acquired business, which can more readily be avoided in an asset sale; the sheer size and geographical disparity of the acquired business; the nonassignable character of important contracts or franchises that might make an asset transaction impractical; and the tax considerations noted below.

From the divesting company's perspective, the typical divestiture will be taxable whether the transaction is structured as a sale of assets or a subsidiary's stock. The seller's desire for cash or at least short-term notes for most of the purchase price usually precludes the use of various tax-free reorganization provisions. The objective of the divesting corporation, then, is to structure the divestiture in such a way as to minimize the tax bite.

In a taxable divestiture, the amount of the divesting company's gain will be calculated by determining the amount received by the seller and subtracting the tax basis in the subsidiary stock or assets sold by the seller. Securities of the buyer received by the seller are valued at fair market value, except for debt instruments, which are generally valued at their face amounts. In a sale of the assets of a business, the amount received by the seller is deemed to include any liabilities assumed by the buyer, such as the obligation to pay various trade payables or other liabilities of the acquired business. The seller's tax basis in the transferred assets is calculated by determining the seller's original cost and deducting any depreciation taken by the seller for tax purposes.

Assuming that this exercise results in a taxable gain to the divesting corporation, the next task is to determine whether that gain is capital or ordinary in nature. Corporate sellers generally prefer to have all gain treated as capital gain because of the favorable (28 percent) tax rate on the sale of capital assets held for more than six months, as opposed to the ordinary income corporate tax rate of 46 percent. However, there is an important catch here. If the divesting corporation is selling assets (and not the stock of a subsidiary) and if a portion of the transferred assets has been depreciated for tax purposes, the gain on those depreciated assets will be treated as ordinary income to the extent of prior tax depreciation deductions taken by the seller (so-called recapture taxes). The sale of assets that have been held for less than five years may also give rise to the recapture of previously claimed investment tax credits. Moreover, assets held for sale to customers in the ordinary course of business, like inventory, would be taxed at ordinary income rates in an asset sale.

With this tax treatment in mind, the divesting corporation will typically seek to structure the divestiture as a sale of stock, rather than assets. Since the stock itself is almost always a capital asset, the seller will generally be entitled to capital gain treatment on the entire sale and will not be subject to any recapture tax liability at ordinary income rates.

However, the buyer may be less than enthusiastic over this suggestion. As mentioned earlier, the purchase of stock would automatically bring with it all the liabilities of the acquired subsidiary, both known and unknown. Moreover, a stock purchase now subjects the buyer to any recapture tax exposure since the only way the buyer can apply the purchase price to the underlying acquired assets (and not merely to the purchased stock) is to elect to "step up" the tax basis of those assets under to Section 338 of the Internal Revenue Code. The step-up will be important to the buyer, particularly if the purchase price substantially exceeds the historical tax basis of the acquired assets, but the cost of this election can be steep. Now the buyer is subject to the recapture taxes rather than the seller.

If the buyer insists on an asset deal, the divesting corporation can still seek to minimize its tax bill by allocating the purchase price in ways favorable to it. In practice this means allocating as much of the purchase price as possible to assets that are capital in nature, like goodwill or know-how, and as little as possible to assets that would result in recapture or other ordinary income taxes. Again, the buyer objects. In order to maximize its ongoing tax deductions after the closing, it wants to allocate much of the purchase price to assets that are deductible, depreciable, or amortizable over relatively short periods—such as inventory, machinery, and equipment—the very assets likely to expose the seller to ordinary income treatment.

Like many other areas in the divestiture negotiations, there may not be a perfectly happy solution for both buyer and seller. The Internal Revenue Service requires that the purchase price be allocated to the transferred assets, including intangible assets like goodwill, in accordance with their respective fair market values. In the light of the usual adversarial relationship between buyer and seller, the IRS will normally accept the allocations set forth in the divestiture contract, unless the allocations suggest an absence of arm's-length bargaining. This might occur if the seller is relatively indifferent to the tax effect of the allocations, such as where the seller has a large net operating loss carryforward.

If the allocation negotiations bog down, it is common practice to adjust the purchase price for the tax concessions or benefits accruing to one side or the other. If an IRS challenge is a realistic possibility, the parties may also obtain independent appraisals to support their positions.

Once it is determined that there will be a gain to the seller, and the nature of that gain (whether capital or ordinary) is decided, it is then important to determine when the gain will be recognized. As a general rule, gain or loss in a divestiture will be recognized by the seller for tax purposes in the same year in which the transaction occurs. However, the installment sale rules are an important exception, since gain under these provisions may be recognized only when cash or other property is actually received by the seller, except for depreciation recapture income, which is still recognized in the year of sale. Thus the seller can defer paying the tax man on most of the gain, at least for a while. To qualify for an installment sale, the seller must receive at least one payment of the purchase price after the close of the taxable year in which the divestiture occurs.

Tax-Free Divestitures

Under the tax code, a variety of corporate reorganization transactions, including corporate divestitures, might be structured in such a way as to avoid any tax to the divesting corporation. However, a common theme running through these tax-free reorganizations is that the seller receive most of the purchase price in stock of the buyer, although one variation would permit the seller under some circumstances to receive up to 50 percent of the purchase price in the form of cash or other nonstock consideration (so-called boot) with only the boot being taxable. From the perspective of the emerging company seeking to raise additional capital, a tax-free divestiture may be of largely academic interest since the seller will wish to maximize its cash from the transaction and not simply invest in the buyer's stock. If the buyer's stock has a ready market value, the seller might raise additional capital by pledging the stock to a bank or other lender, thus generating funds while avoiding, at least for the moment, any tax on the divestiture. While this approach might be feasible under some circumstances, there are a number of limiting factors. First, if the buyer's stock trades in the market, it is probably a margin security. Under the present federal margin rules, a lender will not be able to advance more than 50 percent of the market value of the stock. Second, the federal securities laws place significant, though not insurmountable, restrictions on the resale of the buyer's securities, which may discourage a lender from extending the maximum permitted credit or, perhaps, from loaning against the buyer's stock at all. Finally, the seller under these circumstances continues to be exposed to the risks of the buyer's business. The emerging company usually feels it already has more than enough risk in its own business.

The tax-free reorganization provisions are as complex as anything in the tax code and are, in the light of their limited usefulness in emerging company divestitures, beyond the scope of this discussion. Each form of reorganization (such as statutory mergers, subsidiary and reverse subsidiary mergers, sale of assets, or stock for stock exchanges) has its own requirements. Some of the more important elements are noted below.

Statutory Mergers (Type A Reorganizations). In a statutory merger, one company is merged into another under state law and upon the effectiveness of the merger, the assets and liabilities of the acquired company automatically become assets and liabilities of the surviving corporation by operation of law. For tax purposes, an essential requirement of a tax-free reorganization, including a statutory merger, is a sufficient "continuity of interest" (i.e., the seller must obtain a sufficient stock position in the buyer as a result of the transaction). If all of the consideration paid by the acquirer is in stock of the buyer, then the continuity of interest requirement has obviously been satisfied and no gain or loss is recognized by the divesting corporation. In a statutory merger up to 50 percent of the consideration may be nonstock consideration, or boot, and the transaction will still be regarded as a valid tax-free reorganization (i.e., only the boot portion of the purchase price is taxable). Anything over 50 percent, however, will raise a question as to whether the continuity of interest requirement has been met.

Several tax-free variations on the statutory merger are popular—the so-called triangular subsidiary mergers. In the forward subsidiary merger, the buyer organizes a subsidiary into which the company to be acquired (i.e., the subsidiary of the seller) is merged, and stock (and possibly boot) of the buyer is distributed to the seller. The new subsidiary creates a liability shield for the buyer between the acquired company's operations and its own. Assuming the continuity of interest rules noted above have been satisfied, the stock received by the seller is tax free. In another twist, the newly created subsidiary of the buyer may be merged into the company to be acquired in a so-called reverse subsidiary merger. Here the buyer is trying to maintain the continuing separate existence of the acquired company, usually to avoid losing a nontransferable franchise or contract right. If the continuity of interest requirements are met and the seller exchanges at least 80 percent of the stock of its subsidiary for voting stock of the buyer, the reverse subsidiary merger will be tax free.

Stock for Stock (Type B Reorganizations). The buyer issues its stock to the seller in exchange for the stock of the subsidiary to be acquired. In order to be tax free, at least 80 percent of the stock (generally both voting and nonvoting) of the subsidiary must be owned by the buyer after the exchange and the seller must receive only voting stock of the buyer. Any boot will disqualify the reorganization.

Acquisition of Assets (Type C Reorganizations). The buyer issues its stock to the seller in exchange for the assets of a preexisting subsidiary of the seller. In order for this transaction to be tax free, the buyer must exchange solely its voting stock for substantially all of the assets of the subsidiary, although up to 20 percent of the fair market value of the acquired assets may be purchased for nonstock consideration. As a general rule, the assumption by the buyer of various liabilities of the acquired business will not be regarded as nonstock consideration for this purpose so that the buyer may, and usually does, agree to assume such liabilities without jeopardizing the tax-free nature of the acquisition. The "substantially all the assets" test would be met if at least 90 percent of the net value of the subsidiary's assets and 70 percent of the gross value were acquired.

As a general rule, the tax attributes of the acquired company will be carried over to the buyer in a tax-free reorganization. Accordingly, the buyer will take over the acquired company's tax basis in its stock or assets and will not recognize any gain or loss in the issuance of its stock in the transaction. Tax attributes that would carry over would include the acquired company's earnings and profits and, subject to various limitations, tax credits and net operating losses.

Net Operating Losses

One of the more valuable characteristics of a subsidiary that an emerging company may wish to dispose of is its tax loss carryforward. This is particularly true of a relatively new operation that shows considerable promise but is outside the primary area of focus of the emerging company. The operating loss will be of interest to the buyer if it can be used to offset the buyer's taxable income from other sources.

In the early 1950s, the IRS became suspicious of the growing traffic in tax loss companies, and in 1954 Congress passed legislation that significantly restricted a seller's ability to pass along the tax losses in one of its subsidiaries to a buyer. In the Tax Reform Act of 1976, Congress adopted even more restrictive provisions, but under a storm of protest repeatedly postponed the effective date. If ever adopted, the 1976 revisions would significantly reduce the value of tax losses in the circumstances of divestitures.

Given their complexity, it is difficult to summarize the pre-1976 rules (i.e., the "current" rules). In general, they provide that if 50 percent or more of a corporation's stock is purchased in a taxable transaction within a two-year period, and if the acquired company does not continue to carry on substantially the same trade or business, then the net operating losses of the acquired company are lost forever. Under the "current" rules, if the transaction is tax free, stockholders of the divested corporation (i.e., the emerging company) must receive at least 20 percent of the fair market value of the stock of the buyer. If the stockholders receive less, the net operating loss carryforward is reduced by 5 percent for each percentage point below 20 percent.

If the acquired company remains a separate entity, net operating loss carryforwards may only be utilized by the buyer to offset postacquisition taxable income of the acquired company, not the taxable income from its other operations. As a result, buyers frequently contribute profitable operations or assets to the newly acquired company. As in most other areas of the tax law, any such asset redeployments must have a valid business purpose other than outmaneuvering the tax man.

Spin-Offs

As noted earlier, there may be valid business reasons for an emerging company to distribute the stock of a subsidiary to its stockholders (i.e., a spin-off) rather than sell the subsidiary. If at all possible, the divesting corporation will wish to effect the spin-off on a tax-free basis; indeed, the possibility of any tax liability to either the corporation or its stockholders may effectively eliminate the spin-off as an alternative divestiture transaction.

The requirements for a tax-free spin-off are set forth in Section 355 of the IRS Code, as embellished by IRS rulings and court cases. In view of the complexities arising from sometimes conflicting interpretations of an ambiguous provision, it is common practice to seek a private letter ruling before proceeding with a spin-off under Section 355.

The following five requirements must be satisfied for a tax-free spin-off:

Distribution of Stock Constituting Control. The divesting company must distribute to its stockholders enough stock of its subsidiary to constitute control of the subsidiary. For this purpose, control is generally defined as the ownership of at least 80 percent of the subsidiary's voting stock and at least 80 percent of the aggregate number of shares of all classes of nonvoting stock of the subsidiary. Note that this provision restricts a public parent company's ability to retain a large block (over 20 percent) in order to benefit from an expected increase in the market value of the subsidiary's stock once the shares are in the hands of public stockholders. Indeed, if the parent retains any stock of the subsidiary, it must satisfy the IRS that the retention is not pursuant to a plan of tax avoidance.

An Active Business. Both the divesting company and the subsidiary must be engaged in the active conduct of a trade or business during the five-year period ending on the date of the distribution. While the trade or business cannot be one that was acquired in a taxable transaction during the five-year period, the parent could incorporate a division that meets the five-year test in order to effect the spin-off. What is or is not the "active conduct of a trade or business" has given rise to numerous rulings and cases. Like many concepts in the tax law, it doesn't necessarily mean what it seems to say.

Business Purpose. The distribution must be carried out for real and substantial nontax reasons germane to the business of the parent corporation. Although the proposed IRS regulations do not specifically cite the various business reasons mentioned earlier for a spin-off by an emerging company, they seem consistent with the spirit of the regulations.

The Device Test. The spin-off cannot be used principally as a device for the distribution of earnings of the parent or subsidiary. Among other things, the prearranged sale of the spun-off stock could be evidence, in the view of the IRS, that the spin-off was really for the purpose of distributing dividend income to the parent's stockholders at capital gains rates. So might placing liquid assets in the subsidiary beyond its reasonable needs or even postdistribution transactions between the parent and subsidiary that suggest that business is being conducted as usual.

Continuity of Interest. There must be a continuity of interest in the subsidiary on the part of the parent company's stockholders after the distribution. Again, this is a somewhat hazy concept, but generally it contemplates that most of the stockholders of the subsidiary remain such for a decent interval.

What if a purported tax-free spin-off fails to satisfy the exacting requirements of Section 355? The consequences are not very pleasant, again emphasizing the desirability of a private letter ruling from the IRS before the spin-off. The nonqualifying spin-off is treated like a dividend to the divesting company's stockholders to the extent of the parent's earnings and profits. Moreover, taxable gain may be recognized by the distributing corporation measured by the excess of the fair market value of the subsidiary's stock over the parent's tax basis in that stock.

ACCOUNTING CONSIDERATIONS

From the perspective of the divesting corporation, the accounting considerations in a sale of a subsidiary or division are relatively straightforward. Under *APB Opinion No. 30,* the results of operations of a segment of the business that has been or will be divested would be reported as a discontinued operation before extraordinary items in the income statement. The income taxes applicable to the discontinued operation and the gain or loss from the sale would be shown separately on the face of the income statement or in related notes, and the revenues applicable to this segment would be separately disclosed in the footnotes. A segment of a business for purposes of *APB Opinion No. 30* is a component of the business whose activities constitute a separate major line of business or class of customers that can be clearly distinguished physically, operationally, and for financial reporting purposes.

APB Opinion No. 30 would also govern the accounting treatment of most spin-offs from the point of view of the divesting corporation. However, in a spin-off, another rule, *APB Opinion No. 29,* will also come into play. This rule basically provides that if the aggregate fair value of the spun-off stock (i.e., the fair value of the subsidiary's net assets) is equal to or greater than its book value, no gain is recognized by the distributing corporation and the parent's investment in the subsidiary is no longer reflected in its accounts. However, if the fair market value of the subsidiary's stock is less than the parent company's book value, the divesting corporation must recognize a loss measured by the difference between book value and fair market value. The requirement of recognizing these losses can be a significant deterrent to a contemplated spin-off transaction, particularly for emerging companies whose historic investment in a promising line of business may be significantly higher than its demonstrable fair market value at the time of divestiture.

If the accounting treatment of divestitures from the selling company's perspective is relatively straightforward, the view from the buyer's side can be distinctly unsettling. The choice of accounting principles can have a significant impact on the buyer's financial statements after the acquisition, and in business combinations the buyer's problems have a way of becoming the seller's as well.

The principal accounting problem from the buyer's point of view is the adverse impact of "purchase," as opposed to "pooling," accounting on its financial statements. In a pooling, the separate stockholder interests of the buyer and the acquired company are combined and the separate recorded amounts for assets and liabilities of the two companies are added together and carried forward. In a purchase, on the other hand, the buyer is deemed to have acquired (not merely combined with) the other company and a new basis of accounting is accordingly established for the individual assets and liabilities of the acquired company based on their respective fair values at the date of acquisition.

A number of important accounting consequences to the buyer flow from this distinction. One of the most important is the treatment of goodwill. In many acquisitions, the negotiated purchase price will exceed the current fair value of the acquired company's assets. Usually with the enthusiastic encouragement of the seller, the buyer will perceive values in the acquisition that cannot be measured solely by the demonstrable value of specific assets. In a pooling this premium is ignored, since the historic carrying values of the constituent company's assets and liabilities are merely combined. The result from an accounting point of view is generally lower reported depreciation and amortization expense in future periods, thus permitting the buyer to report higher ongoing earnings. In a purchase, though, the carrying values of the acquired company are adjusted to current fair value, with the result that the premium will be recognized as goodwill and amortized against income over a period of up to 40 years, and the buyer will otherwise report higher depreciation and amortization expense in future periods. And, in case that's not bad enough, the buyer will generally not receive any tax benefit from the goodwill amortization since the federal taxing authorities do not recognize goodwill amortization as a deduction for tax purposes.

Unfortunately, the more favorable pooling accounting seldom will be available to the buyer in a divestiture situation since 1 of the 12 pooling requirements is that neither of the combining companies may be subsidiaries or divisions of another corporation within two years prior to the initiation of the divestiture transaction. Faced with the prospect of purchase accounting, the buyer will seek to minimize any undesirable consequences to its financial statements by allocating as much of the purchase price as possible to the acquired assets, thus minimizing any premium or goodwill element in the transaction. If the amount of the goodwill amortization in future years still remains a problem, buyers have been known to attempt to reduce the purchase price or seek other concessions from the seller to compensate for the accounting impact. One variation on this theme can occur when the purchase price is less than the fair value of the acquired assets, such as may occur where the seller disposes of a business at a loss. Here the buyer may be able to recognize "negative goodwill" so that any remaining bargain element in the purchase, after first reducing the carrying values of long-term assets, flows through the income statement, in effect, as additional earnings over a period of up to 40 years.

The buyer's allocation process itself can be quite complex. It involves identifying the aggregate cost of the acquisition to the buyer, which in addition to the more evident elements of the purchase price, such as cash or securities paid by the buyer, could include the present value of any liabilities assumed by the buyer, direct expenses of the acquisition (such as professional and finders' fees), and any contingent consideration (such as payments based on future earnings, if reasonably determinable). The total acquisition cost is then assigned to the assets acquired and the liabilities assumed on the basis of their respective fair values. In the case of certain assets, these values will be further adjusted if the tax basis of that asset to the acquirer is different than its fair value to reflect that the normal tax benefit will not be available through the depreciation of that asset.

The allocation process is also of more than passing interest to the divesting corporation. As we noted earlier, the allocation of the purchase price to certain assets (inventory, depreciable property subject to recapture, covenants not to compete, etc.) can subject the buyer's gain to taxation at ordinary income rates, while allocations to other assets will have more favorable capital gain treatment. Indeed, the seller would like a large chunk of the purchase price allocated to goodwill, the quintessential capital asset. Because of the sensitivity of this issue to both sides, many acquisition agreements provide for specific allocations of the purchase price, usually after a certain amount of bloodletting at the negotiating table. The buyer, and less frequently the seller, may also obtain independent appraisals that hopefully confirm the legitimacy of the allocations for accounting and tax purposes.

Several other accounting issues may also be important in divestitures. While a seller may prefer an all-cash transaction in the light of its financing objectives, the commercial realities may require that a portion of the purchase price be in the form of the buyer's securities. Under equity accounting principles *(APB Opinion No. 18),* the seller may include a pro rata portion of the buyer's earnings in its own income statement if the seller receives sufficient common stock of the buyer to exercise a "significant influence" (generally thought to be between 20 and 50 percent of the outstanding voting common stock). Accordingly, if the seller has confidence in the buyer's prospects, it may improve its own financial statements in future periods by taking back some stock of the buyer. Of course, if the seller's optimism in the buyer turns out to be misplaced, it works the other way as well.

If the buyer is a public company, or has near term ambitions in that direction, the acquisition of a division of the seller that will constitute a material portion of the buyer's ongoing business may pose another accounting problem. The seller typically will not have prepared separate audited financial statements for the division, but the accounting rules of the Securities and Exchange Commission require that companies seeking to raise funds publicly prepare and file audited financial information. This financial information includes data regarding significant acquired businesses for prior periods ranging from six months to three years, depending on the materiality of the acquired operations. The buyer will be concerned that a material acquisition could close off the public markets to it if the requisite audited financial information is not available. And this information is not always easy to come by, since many divesting companies will not have maintained adequate financial reporting systems along divisional lines. In some cases, if the division's operations are not material to the divesting company (although material to the buyer), the seller's auditors may never have set foot on divisional premises, observed its inventories, and so on. In the typical case, the seller should gird for a determined push by the buyer to require reconstructed audited financials for the division or, more realistically, a concession on the purchase price.

OTHER LEGAL CONSIDERATIONS

Divestitures raise a number of other legal issues of varying degrees of complexity.

Securities Laws

Under the federal securities laws, it is axiomatic that any sale of securities, including sales in the context of a business combination, will require registration of the securities with the Securities and Exchange Commission, unless an exemption from registration is available. The transfer of a subsidiary's stock to the buyer by the divesting corporation would probably be regarded as a sale for this purpose, as would the issuance by the buyer of any of its securities (e.g., preferred or common stock, or promissory notes) to the seller as part of the purchase price. Registration of these securities with the SEC can be an expensive and time-consuming process, however, so both buyer and seller often rely on the private offering exemption from registration. This exemption is based on the notion that an informed recipient of securities is able to judge the risks involved in acquiring the securities in question (the so-called sophistication standard) and is not involved in a widespread distribution of those securities to others. This latter requirement is reflected in fairly stringent restrictions on the public resale of the securities without registration, including a two-year holding period.

These resale limitations will not pose serious difficulties for the buyer since it is not likely to attempt a public redistribution of the stock of the newly acquired company anyway. However, the divesting corporation that has taken back a publicly held buyer's securities as part of the purchase price is in a much different position. The resale limitations of the private placement exemption, particularly the two-year holding period, can significantly reduce the value of the buyer's securities, both in terms of resale and as collateral for borrowing purposes. A practical compromise here is to permit the buyer to rely on the private offering exemption in the acquisition transaction, but to afford the seller extensive registration rights in the acquisition agreement to cover later resales.

Spin-offs also raise federal securities law issues. If the divesting corporation is publicly held, the distribution of the subsidiary's stock to its stockholders is likely to result in an active trading market for the subsidiary shares. Indeed, one of the benefits of the spin-off is the creation of such a market. Because this trading market may otherwise have little information about the newly spun-off subsidiary, the

SEC generally insists that the subsidiary's shares be registered before the spin-off. One potentially troublesome aspect of registration, however, is the requirement of audited financial statements for the subsidiary for the three years preceding the spin-off. As noted before, the divesting corporation will seldom have separated audited subsidiary statements already on hand, and the expense of preparing such statements on a retroactive basis can be sobering.

State Law Issues

The board of directors of the divesting corporation will be required to approve any divestiture transaction, usually by at least a majority vote of directors constituting a quorum. While unanimous consent is seldom required under state law, the fact that some directors dissented may be a disclosure matter (particularly if stockholders will vote on the transaction) and may raise questions as to the desirability or propriety of the transaction. As a result, the management of the divesting corporation typically devotes considerable effort to structuring a transaction that will obtain at least the grudging support of all of its directors.

As a general rule, directors have the benefit of the so-called business judgment rule when considering divestiture transactions. Under this rule, the directors are presumed to have acted in good faith and in the best interests of the corporation even if their decisions later turn out to be incorrect. Of course, the business judgment rule does not protect the director against his own fraudulent conduct or self-dealing.

What about stockholder approval? If the divesting corporation is publicly held, a stockholder approval requirement will necessitate calling and holding a stockholders' meeting, including the preparation of appropriate proxy materials that are reviewed by the SEC. Moreover, under most state corporate laws, stockholders who dissent from certain asset sale transactions are entitled to appraisal rights, which means they may demand to be paid the fair value of their shares in cash. Too many appraisal claims may doom a proposed transaction, particularly one designed to raise additional funds for the corporation.

Under most state laws, stockholder approval will be required for the sale of all or substantially all the assets of the divesting corporation. In the context of divestitures, the sale of a division or a subsidiary would both be viewed as the sale of an asset for purposes of this requirement. On the other hand, a spin-off would normally not be regarded as a sale so that the stockholder approval requirement would not come into play.

While the standard for triggering a stockholder vote (i.e., the sale of all or substantially all the assets) does not appear very restrictive in the context of divestitures, various state court interpretations have focused on both the quantitative and qualitative aspects of the asset sale. As a result, it is necessary to analyze the proportion of the seller's assets represented by the proposed divestiture, as well as the contribution of those assets to the seller's overall revenues and operations. Although there are no hard and fast rules, the sale of assets representing less than 25 percent of the fair value of the divesting corporation's total assets would probably not require stockholder approval, while the sale of over 75 percent no doubt would. In the middle ground (i.e., between 25 and 75 percent), qualitative factors, such as the contribution to earnings of the divested assets and the effect on the seller's future operations, will be important.

More complex rules come into play if the divestiture will involve the sale of a division or subsidiary to a purchasing group that includes officers or directors of the seller or large stockholders. Since corporate insiders might be on both sides of the bargaining table in these conflict-of-interest transactions, the legal rules require that the insiders be prepared to prove, if challenged by minority stockholders, that the transaction is fair and reasonable to the corporation and its stockholders. Since this standard is hardly a model of clarity, it is common practice to incorporate a variety of procedural safeguards that tend to reinforce management's assertions of fairness. Thus, stockholder approval is sometimes sought even if not technically required under state law, or large stockholders who are interested in the transaction may refrain from voting or commit to vote their shares for or against the divestiture proposal in the same proportions as public stockholders. It is also common practice to obtain an opinion of independent investment bankers on the fairness of the transaction to the seller from a financial point of view and to have the transaction approved by the disinterested directors of the seller. In some cases, sellers have appointed committees of outside directors to actually negotiate the terms of the divestiture with the interested parties.

Contract Issues

A divestiture structured as a spin-off does not typically involve an adversarial relationship, so that management is more or less free within the applicable technical parameters to design the transaction in any way that makes the most sense. A divestiture in the form of a sale of a division or subsidiary, however, will involve a third-party purchaser whose needs may not mesh comfortably with those of the divesting corporation. Nowhere is this more evident than in the negotiation of the acquisition contract itself, particularly the provisions dealing with various representations and warranties of the seller concerning the company being divested. These provisions will form the backbone of any effort by the buyer to recover all or a portion of the purchase price if the acquired business turns out to have various undisclosed blemishes. On the other hand, the seller will not (and should not) be placed in the position of a guarantor of the future success of the divested company.

Although there are a number of potentially troublesome representation and warranty issues in divestitures, the following seem to crop up most often:

Unaudited Financial Statements. The buyer will wish assurances that the financial statements furnished to it concerning the acquired business are substantially accurate and correct and that they were prepared in accordance with generally accepted accounting principles, consistently applied.

In many cases, the divesting corporation will not have audited financial statements available for a subsidiary or division and, while confident that the unaudited statements are generally a fair presentation of the acquired company's operations, may not be very confident that they satisfy all the exacting requirements of generally accepted accounting principles. The seller would no doubt prefer to deal with this issue by limiting its representation to what it knows (i.e., that it believes the unaudited statements are materially accurate, not that they necessarily are), but this formulation does little for the buyer if the statements are seriously inaccurate. Sometimes, though not often, the buyer's own due diligence investigation will confirm the essential integrity of the statements to the point where the buyer feels comfortable with a qualified representation. More often the seller will be required to give an unqualified representation, but the parties will agree that the seller has no liability for breach unless the buyer's after-tax damage exceeds a negotiated figure (a "basket").

Compliance with Laws: Full Disclosure. The buyer will wish to have assurances that the divested business is not in violation of any laws (e.g., environmental statutes, pension regulations, occupational health and safety rules, and many more), which would materially and adversely affect the acquired business. A variation on this representation would also require assurances from the seller that the buyer has been told everything of importance concerning the acquired business (i.e., a full-disclosure representation).

From the buyer's perspective, of course, it seems reasonable enough to ask the seller to confirm that it is not in material violation of laws or to confirm that the seller does not know of some important negative fact about the acquired business. On the other hand, the seller will be concerned that an unscrupulous buyer may use the sweeping nature of these assurances to claim an adjustment to the purchase price for alleged breaches that are largely theoretical in nature.

In practice, these representations are among the most difficult to deal with in the acquisition contract. The buyer will try to hold out for unqualified coverage with, possibly, a "basket" to spare the seller from numerous small claims. The seller will encourage the buyer to make his own investigation, but in the end it often comes down to a balancing of the attractiveness of the deal against the risk of later damage claims.

Assignment of Contracts. The buyer will want confirmation that all the important contracts of the acquired business will be properly transferred to the buyer. Many contracts prohibit assignment without the consent of the other party, and the buyer will quite naturally ask for assurances that all necessary consents have been obtained. However, an important asset of the business may be a favorable contract with a nonassignment clause, so that any attempt to solicit a consent would lead to a renegotiation of the contract. If the assets to be sold are already in a subsidiary of the seller, one way around this problem is to merge a newly created subsidiary of the buyer into the subsidiary to be acquired (a so-called reverse subsidiary merger), since in the metaphysics of state corporate law, the acquired subsidiary is the surviving corporation and nothing has been assigned. If this doesn't work, there may be no alternative but to go to the third party with hat in hand.

Contingent Liabilities. Balance sheets and footnotes, even audited ones, do not necessarily tell the whole liability story. At any given point there may exist significant contingent liabilities that are not reflected on the acquired company's balance sheet, usually because management is not yet aware of their existence. The fact that the seller does not know of a contingent liability is of little comfort to the buyer, however, and it usually insists on a broad representation to the effect that the acquired company has no material liabilities other than those disclosed in the acquisition contract.

Although a company could be exposed to contingent claims from many quarters, the most dangerous area is typically product liability claims. These may arise many years after the product was sold and under some circumstances may even follow the sale of the business into the hands of successor purchasers who expressly decline to assume any product liabilities. The buyer is not likely to yield on fairly comprehensive protection against contingent liabilities, so much of the negotiation on this issue centers on how long the representation will survive, that is, the point in time when a contingent claim, if asserted, will no longer entitle the buyer to recourse against the seller. Of course, there is no magic period for survival and, at least for product liability claims, the determination of an appropriate period will be influenced by the nature of the product and its claim history. If the exposure to the seller under the representation is substantial, sellers sometimes carry insurance against this risk well beyond the sale of the divested business.

CHAPTER 12

Leveraged Buyouts

John G. Quigley
General Partner
Adler & Shaykin
New York, N.Y.

John G. Quigley is a general partner of Adler & Shaykin, a $125 million management leveraged buyout fund. Adler & Shaykin acts as the equity partner and sponsor of management groups in buyout transactions. Prior to joining Adler & Shaykin, Mr. Quigley was an attorney with the law firm of Kirkland & Ellis in Chicago. At Kirkland & Ellis he was involved in a corporate legal practice that emphasized leveraged buyout transactions, venture capital investments, and the formation of a wide variety of private equity investment funds.

Mr. Quigley is a graduate of Georgetown University (A.B. 1976, *summa cum laude*), Stanford Law School (J.D. 1980) and Stanford Graduate School of Business (M.B.A. 1980; Baker Scholar), and a member of the board of directors of Ecolaire Incorporated and The Sun-Times Company.

William R. Klaus
Partner
Pepper, Hamilton & Scheetz
Philadelphia, Pa.

William R. Klaus is a partner in the law firm of Pepper, Hamilton & Scheetz, where he has practiced law in its Philadelphia office for 33 years. At Pepper, he serves as chairman of its corporate group, while his principal area of practice is general corporate law and finance, with emphasis on international practice, leveraged buyouts, other forms of venture capital acquisitions, and the formation and operation of funds related thereto.

A graduate of Temple University Law School (LL.B. 1951), an honorary fellow of the faculty of the Law School of the University of Pennsylvania, he serves as a director of Fidelcor, Inc., Fidelity Bank, and of Westmoreland Coal Company.

PART A Explanation of Management Leveraged Buyouts*

INTRODUCTION

Few subjects have received as much recent attention in the business and legal communities as management leveraged buyouts. Buyouts have been utilized during the past few years for the acquisition of companies ranging from small, privately held operations to multibillion dollar, publicly held enterprises. In terms of both dollar value and number of transactions, leveraged buyouts have become an acceptable and important means of effecting changes of corporate ownership.

---

* Part A was written by John G. Quigley, who wishes to thank his partner Leonard P. Shaykin for his valuable input.

The quick rise to popularity of management leveraged buyouts has been accompanied by a combination of fascination and apprehension. The financial press often seems to oscillate between the polar extremes of breathtaking instant wealth for all leveraged buyout participants or, conversely, impending financial disaster that will eclipse the banking community's current troubled loan portfolio to South America. Somewhere between these polar extremes lies a calm equatorial island of truth concerning the phenomenon of leveraged buyouts. It is this island that we will attempt to explore.

The objective of this article is twofold. First, we will address a number of fundamental questions such as the following:

- What is a management leveraged buyout?
- Under what circumstances is a leveraged buyout a viable alternative?
- What are the criteria for a successful buyout? Or, put another way, what do institutional lenders and investors look for in a buyout presented to them?
- How are the transactions financed?
- What are the current trends in the leveraged buyout marketplace?

Second, we will set forth a description of certain legal issues relevant to the structuring and consummation of these acquisitions. There are few, if any, types of transactions that involve the interplay of so many legal areas—corporate and shareholder taxation, state corporate law, securities law, debtor-creditor rights, executive compensation and others—as leveraged buyouts. To do justice to the full range of complex legal questions that can be involved in putting a deal together and the creative responses devised by the attorneys who work on these transactions is obviously beyond the scope of this chapter. Our focus will be a practical one, with the aim of familiarizing the reader with the key substantive legal issues and the transactional context in which they arise.

WHAT IS A MANAGEMENT LEVERAGED BUYOUT?

A management leveraged buyout refers to the acquisition of an existing company by a new corporation that is formed by the acquirer for that sole purpose, funded using a high proportion of institutional debt, and in which management participates in the equity ownership. The company being acquired may previously have been privately or publicly held, or have been a subsidiary or division of a larger company. The critical elements of this type of transaction are as follows:

Financial Leverage. The amount of leverage employed in a management leveraged buyout depends in large measure on the nature of the business acquired and the confidence that the acquirer and the lending institutions have in the company's ability to generate cash, or in its underlying assets, as assurance of its ability to meet debt service obligations in a timely fashion. Depending on these factors, the debt-to-equity ratio of an acquired company immediately after consummation of the transaction can be as low as 3:1 or as high as 20:1.

Management Ownership of Equity. The single most important factor in the success of this type of investment is the quality, commitment, and ongoing performance of the management team. (It is this fact that leads experienced participants in the field to prefer to refer to the transaction as *management* leveraged buyouts, and not the more widely used sobriquet of LBO!) As a result, it will normally be the case that the management of the company will purchase a meaningful equity position in the company established for the acquisition.

Establishment of Goals Shared by All Participants. The objective in a management leveraged buyout is to create a capital structure in which all parties to the acquisition—management, investors, and lenders—play a constructive role in the future success of the company. To further this objective, lending institutions in the transactions may be given an opportunity to participate with management and investors in the equity of the company. All parties will be focused on a common set of operating and financial goals. In all cases, these goals will be aimed at building the fundamental underlying value of the company.

Potential for Substantial Equity Appreciation. As a result of the substantial leverage employed, the total common stock portion of the investment is created at an extremely low valuation relative to both the underlying asset values and historical earnings level of the acquired company. The common stock offers potential for significant appreciation over time as debt is repaid, particularly when the debt repayment is accompanied by improved results of operations. The objective is to create high-equity returns by imposing financial leverage on companies with relatively low business risk characteristics.

Management leveraged buyouts are popular, in large measure, because it has been demonstrated that through a properly crafted capital structure, and with the full participation of management and the lending institutions, substantial long-term equity values can be achieved.

TYPES OF TRANSACTIONS

Companies acquired in management leveraged buyout transactions typically fall into three general categories.

- Publicly traded companies, in which case the management leveraged buyout constitutes a "going-private" transaction.
- Divisions or subsidiaries of larger corporations, in which case the management leveraged buyout creates an independent and free-standing enterprise.
- Privately held companies, in which case the management leveraged buyout is essentially a recapitalization designed to effect a partial or complete change in ownership of the equity of the company.

Each type of management leveraged buyout, though similar in execution, solves quite different business problems.

Publicly Held Companies

In the case of publicly held companies, management leveraged buyouts are increasingly employed as a desirable response to the fact that the securities markets quite often do not reflect a company's intrinsic value. Many public companies, simply because they are public, are being managed with an eye toward short-term earnings-per-share considerations, and not for the purpose of achieving long-term, return-on-capital, cash flow, and return-on-assets goals. Because some companies have fallen into the trap of being managed for the short term, or are followed by analysts concerned primarily with quarterly earnings estimates and not intrinsic value, the securities markets eventually undervalue them on a long-term fundamental basis. When this occurs for any extended period, it often leads to dissatisfaction among the public stockholders over their inability to realize the value of their investment, a situation, that can result in a hostile or unfriendly takeover attempt by sophisticated market investors who understand fundamental corporate value. Under these circumstances, the management leveraged buyout is becoming a preferred and acceptable defense to unwelcome overtures and a desirable means for maximization of shareholder wealth.

A management leveraged buyout allows the management and directors of a publicly held company to regain control of their own destinies and remain independent by going private. Management is freed to focus on the proper direction of the business outside the spotlight of a public forum. The public shareholders of the company are provided with a cash price for their shares, generally at a substantial premium over the public market, and more closely in line with the real value of their security holdings. Finally, a buyout provides the proper incentive for the company's management, through meaningful equity participation, to build the real, long-term value of the business, for themselves and their investors.

Exhibit 1 shows the accelerating trend toward going-private transactions. Note that the 1984 increase in the acquisition of publicly traded companies was entirely attributable to transactions of this type.

Division and Subsidiaries

Management leveraged buyouts have also proved to be quite effective and efficient solutions for larger public or private companies that wish to divest themselves, generally for strategic reasons, of profitable divisions or subsidiaries. In these instances, a management leveraged buyout allows the parent company to realize a full price, often completely in cash, for the unwanted division or subsidiary, without selling to a current competitor. At the same time it creates an atmosphere of goodwill throughout the parent when the division's or subsidiary's operating executives are allowed to purchase the business under their management. In divestitures such as these, a management leveraged buyout allows a parent company to conduct its divisional or subsidiary

EXHIBIT 1 Going Private: 1979–1984

	Number of Transactions		
Year	*Total Public Takeovers*	*Going Private*	*Percent of Public Takeovers*
1979	248	16	6.4%
1980	173	13	7.5
1981	168	17	10.1
1982	180	31	17.2
1983	190	36	19.0
1984	211	57	27.0

	Aggregate Dollars Paid			
			Purchase Price (millions)	
Year	*Total Value Paid (millions)*	*Number of $100 Millions–Plus Deals*	*Average*	*Median*
1979	$ 636.0	1	$ 39.8	$ 7.9
1980	967.4	3	74.4	25.3
1981	2,338.5	4	137.6	41.1
1982	2,836.7	11	91.5	29.6
1983	7,145.4	14	198.5	77.8
1984	10,805.9	26	415.6	66.9

SOURCE: W. T. Grimm & Co.

sale discreetly, with a minimum of management disruption, and achieve for itself a full-cash price. Many divisions and subsidiaries are being sold in this fashion in the current marketplace. An investor group that includes management is now considered a prime candidate to be the purchaser.

The dramatic growth of management leveraged buyouts of divisions and subsidiaries is demonstrated in Exhibit 2.

Privately Held Companies

Owners of privately held companies who wish to sell are generally faced with a difficult choice: either they can go public, in which case they will generally dispose of only a small portion of their closely held stock position in cash at the initial public offering (the remainder being subject to future sales in an ever-changing public market environment), or they can sell to another, generally larger, corporation, often a competitor. In many instances, especially after years of competition, this latter alternative is anathema to an owner-manager. In the case of such a privately held company, a management leveraged buyout provides the owner-manager with an opportunity to keep his company independent and also pass on an equity stake in his business to loyal and competent operating management. At the same time,

EXHIBIT 2 Unit Management Buyouts: 1979–1984

	Number of Transactions		
Year	*Divestitures*	*Management Buyouts*	*Percent of Total Divestitures*
1979	752	59	7.9%
1980	666	47	7.1
1981	830	83	10.0
1982	875	115	13.1
1983	932	139	14.9
1984	900	122	13.6

	Aggregate Dollars Paid			
Year	*Management Buyouts*	*Number Disclosing Price*	*Tabulation of Prices (millions)*	*Average Price (millions)*
1979	59	14	$ 46.7	$ 3.3
1980	47	15	363.3	24.2
1981	83	30	484.1	16.1
1982	115	41	1,361.1	33.2
1983	139	51	2,499.4	49.0
1984	122	42	3,833.4	91.3

SOURCE: W. T. Grimm & Co.

an owner-manager can realize, in cash, for himself, his family, and his investors, a full price for his business. In consequence, management leveraged buyouts are particularly attractive solutions for the sale of privately held companies.

INVESTMENT IN MANAGEMENT LEVERAGED BUYOUTS

Criteria for Investment

Management leveraged buyouts are particularly appropriate for companies having the characteristics identified below.

Business Characteristics

- Companies with strong, seasoned operating management at virtually all key levels in the organization.
- Companies whose management, as a group, is willing to commit its own capital to purchase equity, as partners.
- Companies that enjoy strong market niche positions with distinct and identifiable competitive advantages, such as being a low-cost producer or having proprietary products or favorable distribution channels.
- Companies with the prospect of real unit growth in their base businesses during the investment period in markets that are growing.
- Companies whose products will not be subject to significant technological changes and companies whose technologies can be enhanced through further acquisition, consolidation, or strategic R&D refocusing.

Financial Characteristics

- Companies with a substantial and sustainable revenue base and a consistent history of profitability and strong, predictable cash flow.
- Companies with a low debt-to-equity ratio before the transaction and capable of sustaining significant additional leverage in the new capital structure.
- Companies whose asset base (real estate and fixed plant and equipment) is carried on the balance sheet at substantially less than its fair market value, or with unnecessary assets that can be sold after the acquisition with the proceeds of such sales available to immediately retire debt.
- Companies whose purchase price is generally in line with industry and market averages and that will not generate, postacquisition, significant balance sheet goodwill after asset revaluation.

- Companies whose unfunded pension costs, exposure to potential litigation, or other contingent liabilities are minimal.

The effort to determine whether these criteria are met is not insignificant in a well-conceived transaction. In all investment situations that are seriously pursued by Adler & Shaykin, for instance, a rigorous and thorough due diligence analysis will be performed, including analysis of market position and potential, revenue stability and growth potential, sensitivity of margins to economic and competitive shifts or changes in technology, assessment of ongoing capital requirements, depth of management capabilities, reputation with customers, salability of excess assets, and exposure to large or contingent liabilities of a product, tax, or pension-related nature. Closing audits and appraisals will typically be conducted, and consultants will be utilized in cases where a major business or market question exists.

While the list of criteria may appear lengthy, in the final analysis there is one consideration that overrides all others: quality management. Leveraged buyouts are uniquely driven by management. Contrary to what is so often said and written on the subject, leveraged buyouts are not driven by lots of undervalued assets in a company, by high or low interest rates, or by the relative price of the stock market. It is management, finally, not assets, not cash flow, not earnings per share, that gets financed. The reasons are apparent: good management won't pay too much for a business; good management won't leverage a business enterprise beyond its capability to retire the debt; good management won't set sail in a leaky boat across an ocean. To extend the analogy, bad management doesn't know that it is sailing in a leaky boat and probably doesn't know what it takes to cross an ocean. The criteria for investment largely reduce to this: Acquisitions should only be pursued based on the fundamental underlying strength of the business being acquired and the quality and commitment of the management team.

The Purchase Price

Once it has been determined that a particular transaction involves the acquisition of a fundamentally sound business with strong and committed management, the remaining issue to be addressed is that of the purchase price. A transaction must be fairly priced to truly work as a management leveraged buyout; otherwise, the company will not be able to adequately meet its debt service obligations, and the investors are unlikely to realize their target rates of return. This is the so-called "good company/bad investment" syndrome that is the lament of all buyout investors.

There are a myriad of rules of thumb that are utilized in valuing a business to assess whether or not it can be acquired via a management leveraged buyout (e.g., avoid paying a significant premium over book value, or more than six times operating income). Particular valuation indexes are used for specific industries, such as broadcasting properties (a multiple of cash flow), soft drink bottlers (a price-per-beverage case sold), and health maintenance organizations (an amount per subscriber), to name a few. These rules of thumb should be referred to, if for no other reason than that the financial institutions reviewing the transaction will undoubtedly make reference to them. Yet religious adherence to any such tests is likely to result in letting potentially excellent transactions slip away, particularly given the keen competition for deals that exists today and the deep pockets of corporate acquirers who may covet the target company.

The success of a management leveraged buyout is largely dependent on the creation of a capital structure that does not overtax the earning power of the acquired company. The purchase price is a critical part of the equation. The transactions are most effective when both buyer and seller recognize each other's objectives and constraints in negotiating a fair and financeable price. Creativity and determination are the key elements in fashioning a doable deal.

FINANCING MANAGEMENT LEVERAGED BUYOUTS

Leveraged Capital Structure: Layers, Players, and Rules

A leveraged buyout is the acquisition of a business by its management utilizing large amounts of debt of various kinds relative to the equity. Because of the leverage involved in these transactions, they require a significant amount of financial tailoring to design appropriate and acceptable instruments for the various lenders and equity participants. The primary categories of lenders and equity participants typically involved are as follows:

Senior Lenders. These will be the banks, insurance companies, and asset-based lenders that provide the majority of the financing. Their major concern will be twofold: First, does the company to be acquired have the cash flow to service and retire the acquisition indebtedness? Second, is the value of the assets of the acquired company close (if not at least equal) to the amount of their loan? The more aggressive lenders will finance a transaction if the first of these concerns is adequately addressed and will tolerate some shortfall with regard to asset coverage. However, as a result of recent tightening by the banking regulators concerned about the upsurge in leveraged acquisition financing, many senior lenders have come to require a "second way out," thereby entailing that both criteria are met in any situation that they finance.

Mezzanine Lenders. These are the insurance companies, pension funds, bank holding company subsidiaries, and other purchasers of high-yield debt securities, as well as the mezzanine investment funds that have been growing in popularity and prominence during the past year or so. These lenders will typically receive subordinated debentures (and preferred stock, in certain instances), generally coupled with an equity interest in the company. The combination of a high coupon rate and an equity kicker is designed to produce a return that will compensate the mezzanine lender for the added risk that is undertaken by making a loan that is not supported by the asset values of the company and that is subordinated to the rights of the senior lender to share in the collateral.

Equity Investors. Equity will be invested in a management leveraged buyout by buyout equity funds, venture capital pools (which are increasingly focusing on this area), and management. (In addition, as mentioned above, the lenders may receive an equity interest in the company.) It is this equity position that is totally at risk in the transaction and is usually structured not to receive any current return. This increased risk is to be compensated for through increased returns. A central concern of the equity investor—particularly when the investor does not have control of the company—is the establishment of an "exit" that provides a clear method to dispose of his stock (via a public offering, sale of the company, or repurchase by the company).

Knowing how to give each layer of debt and equity the proper rights and remedies relative to their contribution to the financial structure, and further, how to give the proper return for the risk to each layer of the financing, requires a certain amount of diplomatic financial engineering. This aspect of arranging the financing—"properly spreading the pain"—is essential to make the deal work. Structuring the financing to satisfy the participants' various objectives is the key.

Management's Equity Participation

The proper structuring of management's equity participation is central to consummation of a management leveraged buyout. While the dollar amount contributed by management may not represent a significant portion of the financing, the manner in which it is invested and structured is critical. Various devices are utilized to deal with the fact that many management groups will not have adequate funds to purchase the share of equity that they are to receive in the transaction (e.g., payment through delivery of promissory notes, or utilization of incentive stock option plans). It is typically the case that a meaningful portion of management's equity be subject to a performance vesting or "earn-out" schedule that essentially requires that various financial goals (e.g., operating income or debt reduction) be attained in order for management to receive its full share of the equity. Establishment of a performance vesting schedule goes a long way toward making the lenders and other investors in the transaction know that management is committed to attaining the various goals set forth in the game plan to which all participants have agreed.

Enhancement of Cash Flow

Part of the planning of an acquisition through a management leveraged buyout will include development of a business plan that demonstrates the manner in which cash flow can and will be enhanced. The following questions are illustrative of those that need to be addressed:

Tax Planning. Can the company create additional depreciation and amortization deductions that will allow it to shelter more of its taxable income by writing up the tax basis of its assets to their fair value? What is the up-front recapture cost associated with doing so? Can and should the company's inventory method be changed? Its fiscal year?

Working Capital. What is the company's net investment in working capital, and how does this change over an annual cycle? Can it be improved through requiring faster payment of receivables, or by stretching payables, without unduly damaging the company's relationships with its customers and suppliers?

Capital Expenditures. What capital expenditures are essential during the first few years subsequent to the closing? What expenditures are desirable but not essential? What is the trade-off between capital expenditure levels and sales and earnings growth? How much of a time lag is there between these variables?

Real Estate. Does the company have significant real estate assets? Can these be financed through a sale/leaseback arrangement in a manner that improves the overall financing package for the acquisition?

Underutilized Assets. Are there underutilized or nonperforming assets that can be identified and sold?

ROLE OF THE DEAL SPONSOR

The critical role of the firm that serves as the deal sponsor and lead investor in a management leveraged buyout is understood more clearly when one considers the life cycle that these transactions typically proceed through. This life cycle consists of several stages that begin with the identification of an acquisition candidate, proceed through the arrangement of financing and closing of the deal, and end several years after the closing with the disposition of the investment. The involvement of a firm with the resources, talents, and experience necessary to successfully handle all stages of this life cycle can often be the difference that determines success or failure of a transaction. The critical functions conducted by the deal sponsor during this life cycle are the following:

Facilitation

The deal sponsor will facilitate the execution of these complex financial transactions and take the financial risk should the transaction fall apart. Basically, a leveraged buyout firm takes responsibility for pricing the transaction, structuring it, organizing and conducting the legal and accounting due diligence, identifying the appropriate lenders, presenting the company in a clear and concise fashion, arbitrating the differences between the various lenders—the "spreading the pain" function referred to earlier—that leads, of course, finally, to raising all of the funds necessary to accomplish the transaction.

Equity Partner to Management

What the deal sponsor is looking for and what all the financial institutions are looking for, is a management that understands the business it is in, that has made money in the business consistently over time, and has done this with integrity as a strong and a fair competitor. Once such a situation has been located in a business with the proper characteristics, the leveraged buyout firm also provides the equity necessary to close the transaction as partners with the backers of management. There is a duty to ensure that the management's ownership incentive is as substantial as is merited and properly structured.

Monitoring as Fiduciary for Financial Institutions

Once the transaction is closed, the leveraged buyout firm monitors the progress of the company for its own account and as a fiduciary for the accounts of the other financial institutions involved to be sure that the company is on plan. An active monitoring program requiring a significant amount of focused attention, especially in the early years, is critical in a management leveraged buyout. The deal sponsor will monitor the attainment of the various objectives that will have been developed prior to closing—earnings and sales growth, improved margins, debt reduction, and current asset management to name a few—that are essential for success.

Realization upon Investment

Finally, usually after four to seven years (depending on market conditions and the shareholders' objectives), comes the liquidation of the investment through either a direct sale or public offering. The buyout firm, being in close touch with prices being paid for businesses and conditions in the initial public offering market, will take the lead in getting the stockholders to realize their return.

The intention of quality management buyout funds is not to run or manage an acquired business. The intention is to simply finance, to provide the equity for, and to facilitate the acquisition of businesses on behalf of quality management teams. Quality deal-sponsoring firms have that skill and knowledge of the market, as well as benign, nonintrusive capital, and they stay involved.

RECENT DEVELOPMENTS IN THE BUYOUT MARKETPLACE

As management leveraged buyouts have come to be widely viewed as legitimate solutions to a broad range of business problems, the marketplace for these transactions has continued to evolve in an exciting fashion. A number of recent developments and trends in this marketplace are noteworthy.

Availability of Financing. The amount of financing available for management leveraged buyouts has grown at a rapid pace as the number of participants in the market has broadened and their experience has grown. Many large money center banks—and a good number of regional banks—have established specialized lending teams to finance these transactions. An increasing number of both large and small insurance companies, pension and endowment funds, and venture capital funds have committed a significant portion of their portfolios to this area. The amount of equity available has similarly grown quite rapidly.

Availability of Candidates. The confluence of a number of forces has resulted in the generation of a substantial number of acquisition candidates that are attractive as management leveraged buyouts. Notable trends include the following:

- The continuing deconglomeration of large U.S. businesses.
- The large number of acquisition candidates resulting from the restructurings and government-mandated divestitures that accompany the type of major corporate combinations that have been occurring with increasing frequency.
- Widespread acceptance of the management leveraged buyout as an acceptable defense to unwanted takeover overtures.

Each of these forces, coupled with the day-to-day strategic operating decisions of management, and management's natural desire to participate in the equity of the businesses they are running, will continue to generate a substantial number of acquisition and divestiture candidates, many of which will be especially attractive as management leveraged buyouts.

Competition for Transactions/Growth of Large Funds. The growth of the marketplace for management leveraged buyouts has been accompanied by a concomitant growth in the number of firms competing for transactions. The market is rapidly evolving toward one in which only a select number of credible, well-capitalized firms will be able to compete successfully for the most appealing large acquisition candidates and to be shown such opportunities on an exclusive basis. The ability to assess a potential transaction decisively, act with speed once an investment decision has been made, and commit substantial debt and equity capital is crucial. This will be increasingly evidenced by the formation of ever-larger equity pools and, perhaps more significantly, mezzanine funds such as the major partnership presently being formed by Adler & Shaykin and The Equitable Life Assurance Society of the United States, which will be devoted to the subordinated debt portion of these transactions.

The "Junk Bond" Marketplace. The market for high-yield noninvestment-grade debt securities is growing in breadth and size at an explosive pace as investors are recognizing the superior rates of return that these instruments provide. Virtually every major Wall Street firm is in the midst of attempting to increase its presence in this marketplace. This development bodes well for those who may wish to utilize this form of financing as a part of a management leveraged buyout.

Corporate Partners. There are an increasing number of major corporations that wish to have as their financial partner an experienced leveraged buyout firm, with the major corporation and buyout firm jointly acquiring a business (keeping the acquisition debt off the corporation's consolidated balance sheet) or with the major corporation selling 50 percent or more of a business to the buyout firm (thus raising cash and moving the business off its consolidated balance sheet).

Retention of Equity Interest by Sellers. It is likely that an increasing number of transactions will feature a structure in which the sellers retain an equity interest in the acquisition company, either through an investment in its common stock or the receipt of warrants for a portion of the common stock. This will be done for a variety of reasons, not the least of which is the desire on the part of sellers to not be embarrassed by future successes enjoyed by companies that they sold. This feature is likely to become particularly evident in the public arena, where the offer of cash plus warrants to the selling public shareholders in a going private transaction helps to alleviate some of the concerns that the company's board may have regarding management's having structured a bargain purchase for themselves.

PART B Legal Aspects of Management Leveraged Buyouts*

INTRODUCTION

Any comprehensive discussion of the laws and related lore applicable to leveraged buyouts would necessarily embrace all of the tax, corporate, and regulatory issues found in a "normal" or unleveraged business acquisition or merger. The solicitations of prospective investors to obtain the capital that may be needed for equity investments may be regulated by federal and state laws relating to the registration and sale of securities. Federal premerger clearance under the Hart

* Part B was written by William R. Klaus.

Scott Rodino Antitrust Improvements Act may be required.[1] The negotiation of senior and intermediate debt structures are advanced exercises in banking law, while tax and accounting considerations figure heavily in the structuring of the acquisition of a controlling interest in a going business—to say nothing of ERISA (Employment Retirement Income Security Act), labor law, environmental regulation, and general business and corporate law required in evaluating the target and crafting the appropriate purchase and related agreements. Space does not permit treatment of all such issues in a single chapter, and the reader is referred particularly to Chapter 10, Mergers and Acquisitions, and to almost every other chapter in this book. Indeed, so many aspects of corporate and commercial law and government regulation are involved that we limit this discussion to aspects that are peculiar to the leveraged buyout as opposed to other forms of mergers and acquisitions.

The term *leveraged buyout* (LBO) is a misnomer, a buzz word. There have always been business entities bought out or purchased with borrowed money (leveraged). Banks have always loaned to finance business acquisitions, particularly if the customer already sported good financials. The real differences are not so readily apparent. Today's classic LBO is characterized by three significant idiosyncracies:

1. The growth of specialized investment pools of venture capital administered by highly skilled entrepreneurs who invest other peoples' (and their own) money in the acquired business, usually in cooperation with an existing management group who will also take equity interests and continue to operate the business.
2. The legal structuring of the transaction so that the target company ends up with the acquisition debt, amortizable from the earnings of the business, thus avoiding the need to upstream earnings in the form of taxable dividends to the investors to service the acquisition debt.
3. The pledge of the assets of the target, and its earning stream, as collateral security for a significant portion of the acquisition debt, the proceeds of which flow to the sellers.

REPRESENTATIVE STRUCTURE OF A LEVERAGED BUYOUT

The Acquiring Corporation

A new corporation ("Newco") is formed and funded with such equity as is deemed requisite for the surviving company. The capitalization

---

[1] 15 U.S.C.A. §§1 (note), 8 (note), 12, 15c–15g, 16, 18a, 26, 66, 1311–1314; 18 U.S.C.A. §1505; 28 U.S.C.A. §1407.

required is often dictated by the acquisition lenders, by tax and liability consequences of "thin" incorporation, and by the excess of the total cost of closing over available debt-source funds. It is most important that sufficient amounts of equity be available to ensure the success of the ongoing business.

A shareholder agreement, negotiated at this time, should embody the deal struck with the investor group that includes the buyout fund, if one is present, any other initial investors, and the management group that will own shares (often on easy-term loans made to them by other investors or under stock option earn-outs based on future performance). The shareholders' agreement should also regulate and restrict the sale of the shares except within the shareholder group and regulate the rights of the shareholders in the event of further issuance of securities. The sharing of obligations on guarantees, powers of management, rights to the registration of shares, the composition of the board of directors and management team, voting rights and restrictions, and other control features are included either here or in related agreements.

Borrowing (the Leverage)

Senior indebtedness is arranged for the acquisition of the target company, and its assets are pledged to secure the loan that will be used to pay the purchase price. Any necessary additional cash may be provided by loans from a mezzanine source, which will lend funds subordinated to the senior debt, or unsecured and usually with warrants, for the acquisition of stock at the original issue price as the reward for the higher risk of subordination. Borrowings are arranged for closing date and occur simultaneously with the acquisition transaction.

Merger and Closing

There are numerous alternatives to the following procedure, depending on the facts of the transaction and tax and corporate considerations. However, in order to provide an example, the following would be a typical transaction. At a simultaneous closing where no money or documents are finally exchanged until the closing agenda is completed satisfactorily to all parties:

1. Newco gives a demand note to the sellers in exchange for the stock of the target company.[2]
2. The loans are made, security is pledged, and the proceeds of loan are delivered to the target.

---

[2] *Target* is used throughout to designate the business being acquired.

3. Newco is merged into the target, and the new board of directors thus takes control of the target.
4. The requisite portion of the loan proceeds now in the hands of the merged company goes to the sellers in payment of the purchase price. Or if target is to be kept as a subsidiary of Newco, the loan proceeds must be dividended up to Newco, a step that must be made in accordance with applicable state corporation laws that govern limits on dividend payments.
5. As the closing ends, the transaction is complete, the investor group owns the target, and the target owns the debt. Transactions involving the purchase of assets rather than stock will take a slightly different form, with differing tax and legal ramifications to both buyer and seller.

REPRESENTATIVE DOCUMENTATION

This section summarizes the documentation that could be utilized to effect the above-described acquisition. For purposes of the discussion set forth below, it is assumed that the buyout is structured as the purchase of all of the capital stock of a corporation from its principal shareholder.

Letter of Intent

As in most acquisitions, it is customary to proceed from a Letter of Intent, outlining the basic terms of the agreement as to price or pricing formula, timing, format, and other key points including a due diligence examination period. The letter should state that it is not legally binding and is subject to the subsequent execution of a definitive purchase agreement and related documents between the parties. Often the offering group will negotiate for a fee to be paid them if competing bidders later acquire the company at a higher price. A "standstill" should be agreed upon whereby the seller agrees not to negotiate with other bidders for a specified period while the buyer pursues due diligence investigations. After the letter is executed, the buyer's team of lawyers and accountants investigates the general legal and financial health of the target and begins negotiation of the basic purchase agreement. In addition to the usual acquisition audit, the accountants should prepare realistic pro forma balance sheets and cash flow statements as of the closing date demonstrating the present and future solvency of the company even with the acquisition debt in place. Counsel's opinion as to the absence of a "fraudulent conveyance," discussed later in greater detail, must necessarily rely on the accountant's calculations.

Stock Purchase Agreement

The sale of the shares of the capital stock of the target to the purchaser is effected pursuant to the terms of a stock purchase agreement, which will set forth the purchase price, method of payment and representations, warranties, and convenants of both buyer and seller.

Formulas for fixing the purchase price may take innumerable forms and may include cash or debt instruments, or both. The purchase price for the shares or assets could, for example, be five times the average after-tax profits of the operating entity for three consecutive fiscal years of the company, commencing with the third fiscal year prior to that in which the acquisition is to be effected. Whether to acquire stock or assets is a legal and tax issue discussed generally in the tax discussion that follows but involves the same considerations that are present in any acquisition.

The past financial performance of the target is an important factor in the determination of the purchase price and a gauge from which the buyer hopefully can predict whether or not the investment will be successful. For this reason, the seller should be required to make comprehensive representations and warranties with respect to the financial and operating condition of the company. These provisions generally include, inter alia, the seller's representations with respect to (1) the accuracy of the audited financial statements of the target; (2) the absence of any material adverse change in the financial condition of the target since the date of the financial statements; (3) the absence of any existing or threatened litigation against the target or of labor strife or environmental problems; (4) the target's possession of all of the permits, licenses, and government approvals necessary to conduct its business; and (5) noncompetition by the seller or its shareholders if such may affect the target's future performance.

Special attention in the representations and warranties may be given to the application of pension fund law, the so-called ERISA rules, to an acquisition. These are extremely complex, particularly where multiemployer pension funds are involved and a participating division of the seller corporation is the target. Divisional financial statements also can be troublesome to construct and may require special expertise, especially where the division's numbers were previously part of a larger whole.

Trouble often can arise in negotiation with the seller regarding various warranties, including those mentioned above. Managers, who are now part of the acquisition group and who are most familiar with the business, are often said by the seller to have a more intimate knowledge of the affairs of the target than the seller. This is often true when the seller has not actively participated in the operation of the target and has relied on existing management to run the business and provide the dividends. In such instances, the seller will seek to limit his warranties to his "knowledge" of specific warranted events, leaving the investors to deal with representations from the surviving management group as to the accuracy of the representations and warranties. The other investors are justified in requiring the management group to warrant those things regarding the ongoing business that the sellers are unwilling to warrant and in no event should go forward unless there is complete confidence in the management group, with or without warranties.

Loan Agreements

Senior Debt. The loan agreement evidencing the senior secured acquisition loan employed in a leveraged buyout contains the same standard terms and conditions as those used in a standard asset-based loan, only usually more strict and protective of the bank's interests. When marketable shares of Newco or of the target are given as collateral, or publicly issued shares are involved, the margin restrictions of Regulation U of the Federal Reserve Board may come into play. Care should be taken in structuring and negotiating the lending component of the transaction to minimize the legal dangers inherent in the transaction that may affect the enforceability of the lender's security interests in the assets. These issues are discussed in detail below.

Present in many acquisitions is a target with one or more operating subsidiaries, which entities hold a significant portion of the assets of the target. The lender often will require the pledge of such assets for the target's debt, or a guarantee of the debt by the subsidiaries. Such "upstream guarantees" may constitute a fraudulent conveyance as to the subsidiary's creditors unless there is some significant consideration given in return. Courts have rather consistently held that as between such lender and creditors of the subsidiary, the latter would prevail in the event of the insolvency of the target.[3] A possible mechanism to protect against this would be to take guarantees and collateral, therefore, only to the extent it can be demonstrated by separate financial analysis that the subsidiary's net worth is capable of supporting the guarantee at the time it is given. Adjustment to the scope of the guarantee can be made in the future as net worth increases or decreases.

Subordinated Debt. The glue in most leveraged buyouts is the unsecured, subordinated debt that fills in the gap between the equity that

---

[3] See *Taylor* v. *Standard Gas & Electric Co.*, 306 U.S. 307 (1939).

the investors are willing or able to invest and the acquisition loan that the banks or other lenders can justify lending on a secured basis. Although banks are cautiously becoming cash flow lenders, lending not only against the market value of tangible assets but also against expected earnings, there is seemingly always a gap between the equity and senior debt that must be filled with what has come to be known as mezzanine debt. Mezzanine lenders, often funds, some off shore and established specifically for this purpose, are willing to subordinate their interests to those of the senior bank or banks, taking a second position in mortgages and security interests in property, or even going unsecured, in return for high-interest returns and an opportunity to share in the future success of the business through "equity kickers" such as warrants to purchase shares at a later date, or debt instruments convertible to the company's stock. Such securities, their complexities, and their forms are discussed in other chapters of this book.

Guarantees

In order to induce the lender to enter into the loan agreement, it is sometimes necessary for the investors in Newco to guarantee the acquisition loan. The acquiring investors (but usually not the funds) may be willing to provide such a guarantee. The terms of the guarantee will provide that, if the target ever does not pay its loan obligations, the lender may seek enforcement of its rights under the loan agreement directly against the investors without first exhausting all of its remedies against the borrower. An indirect form of guarantee whereby the payments on the guarantee are made to the target as a contribution to its capital, affording the target sufficient cash to pay its loan obligations, is more beneficial to the guarantor and the target than a direct repayment to the lender. Care must be exercised to assure that any payment under the guarantee qualifies as a business loss deduction.

Employment Agreements

The employment agreements will generally provide that the former managers of the target company will continue to serve as officers of the company for a specified number of years after the closing date of the acquisition. In consideration of the performance of their duties, the management group will usually be entitled to receive a salary and incentive bonuses, and, more importantly, may be required or given the opportunity to acquire an equity position in Newco. The investment can be made initially or "earned out" over a period of years based on formulas designed to reward the managers' efforts in contributing to profits. Twenty percent of the equity ultimately in the hands of the management group is not uncommon. Often these interests are funded by the investor group by personal loans to such managers, on most favorable terms, that is, low-interest charges, or less than full payback if the endeavor is not successful. Options to purchase shares are subject to the rules of Section 83 of the Internal Revenue Code of 1954, amended in 1984.

SECURITIES LAWS CONSIDERATIONS

The federal securities laws have an impact on leveraged buyouts in several different ways, depending largely on structural considerations such as the nature of the entity being acquired, the relationship of the acquirer and its affiliates to the target, and the consideration offered to selling shareholders. The most common type of large leveraged buyout is one in which, by obtaining outside financing, investors and a management group of an existing company or division acquire its stock for cash. As to acquisitions of publicly held target companies, the applicable securities law considerations center on Section 13(e) of the Securities Exchange Act of 1934 (the 1934 act) and the "going private" rules adopted under that section. Other transactions that may be part of a leveraged buyout, such as a tender offer made by unaffiliated persons, involve other sections of, and rules under, the 1934 act.

Section 13(e) generally applies to purchases of the equity securities of a public company if the company files reports with the Securities and Exchange Commission (SEC) under the 1934 act. That section prohibits the company or its affiliates from violating SEC rules relating to "fraudulent, deceptive, or manipulative" acts or practices. Rule 13e-3 applies to purchases, tender offers, or proxy solicitations by the company or its affiliates of, or with respect to, its equity securities, if the transaction has the effect of either permitting the company not to make public periodic reports or causing the equity securities to be delisted from an exchange or no longer quoted on NASDAQ. In addition to general prohibitions against misleading disclosures and fraudulent activities, Rule 13E-3 requires filing of a Rule 13E-3 Transaction Statement on Schedule 13E-3 with the SEC, disclosure to the company's shareholders of specified information, and the taking of other action. Generally speaking, the required disclosures are extensive and include all plans, arrangements, or understandings relating to the business and operations of the issuer, and all compensation (cash or otherwise) that a management group may receive as a result of the transaction.

The 13(e) going private rules are directed at publicly held companies. However, the rules developed in this area may well be applied by analogy to any acquisition where sellers, subsequent to the closing, allege that the buyers, armed with insider information or because of manipulative practices, misled sellers as to the fair price of the business. Care must be exercised to be certain that management, prior to the offer to purchase, has not "rigged" the company to appear less profitable to its owners, who, by reason of age, education, or other impairment of intimate knowledge of the target, including a passive investor status, are not in a position to understand the true value of the target.

There can be a general problem of overreaching if defensive structures designed to discourage other bidders are created by management within the company. Also, by investing heavily in capital goods, management can, by prior design, depress current profits and enhance future income, lucrative contracts can be postponed, inventory costing can be altered, expenses can be prepaid, and income can be deferred. It seems clear that the disclosures required under the regulations for Section 13(e) would set the standard of "fairness" for disclosures required in private transactions as well. For counsel for the acquirer, the disclosure requirements become a convenient checklist of items that should be made clear to uninformed sellers.

In addition, other provisions of federal securities laws may apply. Of particular note, civil and criminal liability can arise under SEC Rule 10b-5, which applies to all purchases and sales of securities, including the securities of nonpublic or private companies, and which requires disclosure of all material facts relating to the transaction and prevents the use of deceptive or manipulative devices. Also, if a shareholder vote is required (as with a merger with a public company or the sale of a substantial part of a public company's assets), preparation of an extensive proxy statement will be necessary. Furthermore, if as part of the leveraged buyout, debt financing that constitutes a security is used or equity securities are issued, the issuer of the debt or equity securities must comply with the registration and antifraud provisions of the Securities Act of 1933 (the 1933 act) in connection with issuance of the securities. Although most typical buyout transactions will be eligible for the "private placement" or Regulation D exemptions from the 1933 act registration requirements, care must be taken to ensure that the investor sophistication, financial wherewithal, and disclosure requirements of those exemptions are met.

Lastly, one area of frequently overlooked possible difficulty involves *state* securities laws (blue sky laws). This large body of concurrent (but frequently inconsistent) law and regulation often has an impact on the structure, planning, and implementation of a leveraged buyout, including state antitakeover laws that frequently are designed to impede any hostile takeovers. Although much of state antitakeover legislation has been invalidated on constitutional grounds, new "third generation" laws disguised as corporation law amendments have been enacted in several states and have not had judicial scrutiny. The issuance of the equity securities to investors, management personnel, and others in a typical leveraged buyout usually requires registration or availability of an exemption from registration (such as a state exemption that coordinates with the SEC's Regulation D) in one or more of the states involved. Because of the lack of uniformity in the blue sky laws and regulations, leveraged buyouts frequently need to be structured to comply with one or more of these state regulatory laws.

CREDITORS' RIGHTS—THE FRAUDULENT CONVEYANCE

One of the most significant obstacles to the successful leveraged buyout is the set of laws designed to protect creditors from the removal of the assets of a debtor corporation out of their reach. Commercial lending and dealings on open account by suppliers and others are often based on disseminated financial information disclosing a free asset base on which credit is extended. Suddenly, the company changes hands. The old owners are gone and, with them, the value of the assets, now taken as security for the acquisition debt and blanketed by security interests and mortgages, while the proceeds of the loan have disappeared into the pockets of the selling shareholders.

The protection of such existing creditors or innocent new creditors has received sharp attention from the courts, which have generally treated buyouts with great suspicion, as the general framework of our commercial laws is designed to protect the creditor over the interests of shareholders. Because this is one of the most troublesome, as well as the most distinctive, issues in this area of practice, we shall discuss it in some detail.

At the outset, the most straightforward way to deal with the problem is to fund the acquiring entity with sufficient funds to pay off not only the selling shareholders but also all existing creditors, establishing a two-tier senior loan, a term loan to fund the acquisition price, and a revolving credit to meet existing debt as it matures, and to finance new operating credit needs. Still, it may be impossible to fund in advance all contingent debts such as those pursuant to guarantees, unmatured notes, tort, or other litigated claims, including those not yet identified.

If existing creditors remain after closing with either vested or contingent interests, they are protected initially by the state's Bulk Sales Act as embodied in Article 6 of the Uniform Commercial Code

(UCC), with which compliance must be assured or appropriately avoided, and, more importantly, by state and federal statutes prohibiting "fraudulent conveyances," that is, Section 548 of the Bankruptcy Code and the Uniform Fraudulent Conveyance Act (the UFCA), which has been adopted in 25 states. If the target goes into bankruptcy proceedings, the lender's lien may be avoided and the debt owed to the lender by the target may even be subordinated or disallowed entirely if the transaction is found to have been a "fraudulent conveyance," unless the lender is deemed to have made its loan "in good faith" within the meaning of Section 548(c) of the Bankruptcy Code.

Both Section 548 of the Bankruptcy Code and the UFCA contain two provisions prohibiting intentional fraud and two provisions prohibiting technical fraud. The major difference between the statutes is the limitations period, which for Bankruptcy Code Section 548 is one year and for the UFAC is longer, for example, six years under New York's enactment of the UFCA. Therefore, a bankruptcy trustee may use Section 548 to attack a transaction that occurred no more than one year before bankruptcy, whereas a bankruptcy trustee may use the UFCA (through his state law "avoiding powers" under Section 544 of the Bankruptcy Code) to attack a transaction that occurred no more than six years before bankruptcy, under, New York law, for example.

Bankruptcy Code Section 548(a) provides for the avoidance of fraudulent transfers, and Section 548(c) provides for the protection of entities that lend on a secured basis in transactions that are later held to be fraudulent conveyances, so long as the loan is made "for value and in good faith." Bankruptcy Code Sections, 548(a) and (c) provide as follows:

§548. Fraudulent transfers and obligations

(a) The trustee may avoid any transfer of an interest of the debtor in property, or any obligation occurred by the debtor, that was made or incurred on or within one year before the date of the filing of the petition, if the debtor—

(1) made such transfer or incurred such obligation with actual intent to hinder, delay, or defraud any entity to which the debtor was or became, on or after the date that such transfer occurred or such obligation was incurred, indebted; or

(2) (A) received less than a reasonably equivalent value in exchange for such transfer or obligation; and

(B) (i) was insolvent on the date that such transfer was made or such obligation was incurred, or became insolvent as a result of such transfer or obligation; or

(ii) was engaged in business or a transaction, or was about to engage in business or a transaction, for which any property remaining with the debtor was an unreasonably small capital; or

(iii) intended to incur, or believed that the debtor would incur, debts that would be beyond the debtor's ability to pay as such debts matured.

* * * * *

(c) Except to the extent that a transfer or obligation voidable under this section is voidable under section 544, 545, or 547 of this title, a transferee or obligee of such a transfer or obligation that takes for value and in good faith has a lien on or may retain any interest transferred, or may enforce any obligation incurred, as the case may be, to the extent that such transferee or obligee gave value to the debtor in exchange for such transfer or obligation.

Note that two of the provisions of Section 548(a) require a finding of intentional conduct, that is, Section 548(a)(1): "with actual *intent* to hinder, delay, or defraud (creditors)"; and Section 548(a)(2)(B)(iii): "*intended* to incur."

Intent is not an element of the other two provisions relating to fraudulent conveyances, although a common element is the receipt of "less than a reasonably equivalent value" in exchange for the pledge of assets and debt. Assuming the common element of "less than a reasonably equivalent value" exists, then there will be a fraudulent conveyance if the target company (i) was insolvent or became insolvent as a result of the conveyance, or (ii) was left with an unreasonably small capital for the business in which it was engaged.

If a fraudulent conveyance exists, the lender may nevertheless be saved by Section 548(c) if it acted in "good faith," but even then only to the extent that the lender gave value. Good faith means not only honesty in fact but also lack of knowledge, or reason to know, of facts that should have caused the lender to inquire further into the transaction. In other words, in connection with the loan, the lender should exercise a certain amount of due diligence and document its files in three major areas: (1) did the target receive a reasonably equivalent value in exchange for the lien and debt instrument given to the lender, (2) was the target insolvent, or rendered insolvent, by the transaction, and (3) did the target have sufficient capital to continue to engage in its business and to pay its debts as they matured in the future?

With respect to the first inquiry, what constitutes "reasonably equivalent value" is open to question. However, a simple secured loan may not in and of itself be sufficient. The leading case of *U.S.* v. *Gleneagles Investment Co., Inc.*, 565 F.Supp. 556 (M.D. Pa. 1983), indicates that the lender must not limit its inquiry to that portion of the overall transaction with which the lender is immediately involved, but rather must be aware of the intended disposition of the loan proceeds by the target company. In *Gleneagles*, the target was found to have received from the lender less than reasonably equivalent value in exchange for the mortgage granted, because in the second step of the transaction, the target company took a major portion of the loan proceeds and paid it to the selling stockholders, to the detriment of the target company and its creditors.

The *Gleneagles* decision should be studied by all who are involved in leveraged buyouts. Its general holdings and expressed rationale define the serious task of counsel and accountants for all concerned parties, because a faux pas could interfere with or destroy the standing of any one or more of the various participants in the investor group or among the holders. Yet *Gleneagles* is a "hard" case, a seemingly blatant case of overreaching, fraud, and manipulation. The record indicates that the target could not have been expected to develop the cash flow necessary to pay all of its debt, was at the brink of insolvency at the time of the transaction, and that the very purpose of the transaction may have been to defraud creditors.

The selling shareholders in *Gleneagles* were required to disgorge the proceeds of the sale, that is, the loan proceeds, to the bankrupt estate, the lenders' mortgages were voided, and the sale transaction was unravelled. *Gleneagles* must be addressed directly and distinguished effectively from every transaction to assure that its sting will not be felt.

In a case under the provisions of Article 9 of the UCC, *In Re Terminal Moving and Storage Co., Inc.,* 631 F.2d 547 (8th Cir. 1980), the court, in upholding a security interest given pursuant to the UCC, held that the "value" required by Section 203(1)(b) of the Code to be given in order for a security interest to be binding, was value given by the lender, although that value was received not by the corporation granting the security interest but by its sole shareholder.

Prior to closing, the lender should inquire into the solvency of the target company on and after the transfer date. However the Bankruptcy Code definition of *insolvent* for the purpose of Section 548 is a balance sheet type of definition, as opposed to a cash flow type of definition. The balance sheet to be examined will be different from a balance sheet prepared in accordance with generally accepted accounting principles because, inter alia, the liability side of the balance sheet will now sweep in all contingent, unliquidated, unmatured, and disputed claims against the target, including conditional liability on instruments of guarantee and potential tort or product liability claims. Bankruptcy Code Section 101(29) defines insolvent as an entity (other than a partnership) whose "financial condition [is] such that the sum of such entity's debts is greater than all of such entity's property, at a fair valuation," exclusive of property transferred with intent to hinder, delay, or defraud creditors and certain exempt property. The lender and also the buyer should view with healthy skepticism the numbers presented to it by the target and should charge their own independent auditors and appraisers with responsibility for the preparation of a pro forma balance sheet for the target company (taking into account the amortization of the acquisition debt), to be reasonably certain that the target will remain solvent for the foreseeable postclosing future. Based on these accountants' reports, the lender must be assured of solvency at the time of closing.

Prior to closing, the lender should also have its auditors prepare a cash flow analysis of the postclosing target to determine that it will be able to pay its debts as they mature for at least two years after closing. The chief financial officer of the target should certify, in writing, the accuracy of the figures relating to accountants' analysis of the target's solvency and ability to pay postclosing debts.

In conclusion, although leveraged buyouts may take many forms, the end result should not put money into the hands of selling stockholders to the detriment of the creditors of the target company. A lender would be well advised to conduct a thorough preclosing review of the target and document its files to the effect that the lender gave value to the debtor, acted in good faith, and had a basis to believe that the debtor was solvent and was able to pay its debts as they matured after the closing.

TAX CONSIDERATION[4]

Stock Acquisition

In the typical stock acquisition, Newco is formed and funded by the investor group. Newco then purchases the target's stock directly from the selling shareholders for cash or notes. In some instances, Newco may form a subsidiary and merge the subsidiary into the target for cash or notes. If such consideration is distributed to the sellers in the merger, the subsidiary will be disregarded and the merger treated

[4] In May 1985, President Reagan released a report that contains proposals for far-reaching fundamental changes in the existing federal income tax system. In December, the House of Representatives passed H.R. 3838, known as the "Tax Reform Act." The Senate Finance Committee is currently drafting its version of a tax reform bill and expects to have a bill through the House-Senate Conference Committee to send to the president as early as late summer 1986. Various provisions of H.R. 3838, if enacted, may adversely affect the economics of acquisitions effected through the leveraged buyout technique, particularly in relation to the elimination of opportunities to use stepped-up bases as discussed below.

as a purchase by Newco of sellers' stock (Rev. Rul. 73-427, 1973-2 C.B. 301). If the target's cash or notes are used, the subsidiary also will be disregarded and the merger will be treated as a redemption by the target of its stock (Rev. Rul 78-250, 1978-1 C.B. 83). So long as the notes of Newco or the target are not readily tradable, use of notes will permit sellers to qualify for installment method treatment of the sale. Finally, if Newco stock is used as part of the consideration to the sellers but the transaction does not qualify for treatment as a reorganization or a Section 351 transfer, the sellers will be taxed based on the fair market value of the Newco stock received.[5]

The cash consideration received by the sellers should qualify for capital gain treatment, if the target's stock is a capital asset in the sellers' hands. This is true even if Newco later makes a Section 338 election to step up the basis of the target's assets, or if the target is immediately liquidated by Newco. To the extent that the sellers receive part of the purchase price in the target's or Newco's notes, pursuant to Section 453, the shareholder will be taxed on the installment method unless he elects otherwise. Under Section 453(f), however, installment treatment is not available to the extent that the notes received are obligations of a third party, payable on demand, or readily tradable on an established securities market.

The tax treatment of Newco and the target depends on whether a Section 338 election is made. If no such election is made, the target will become Newco's subsidiary and will retain its historic tax basis in its assets and other tax attributes. If a Section 338 election is made by the 15th day of the ninth month after Newco purchased 80 percent control of the target, the target will be treated as having sold all of its assets to Newco. The target generally recognizes no gain or loss on the deemed sale, but will recognize recapture of investment tax credits, accelerated cost recovery, LIFO reserves, DISC income, and so on. Newco will be treated as purchasing the target's assets, and will acquire basis in those assets equal to the sum of the target's liabilities and the price Newco paid for target's stock. The target's tax attributes, such as net operating losses, will be extinguished. There is no requirement under Section 338 that the target be liquidated in order to make the election effective. If the target is liquidated by Newco after the acquisition pursuant to a plan of liquidation, or if the target is merged upstream into Newco, the liquidation will be tax free under Section 332 and Newco will take a carryover basis in the target's assets.

---

[5] All references in this part are to the Internal Revenue Code of 1954 as amended.

Purchase of Assets

In the typical asset acquisition, the target transfers all of its assets to Newco or its subsidiary in exchange for cash and/or notes of Newco or its subsidiary. The target remains in existence as a shell holding the proceeds. Thereafter, the target usually liquidates and distributes the cash and notes to its shareholders. In some cases, it may be more practical for the target to merge into Newco or its subsidiary in a state law merger; the target's shareholders would receive cash and/or notes in return for their stock. This merger transaction will be viewed by the IRS if the target had sold its assets to Newco or its subsidiary and then made a Section 337 liquidation.[6]

If the target/seller does not liquidate, the target will recognize various types of recapture. The target's gain (other than recapture gain and gain attributable to inventory) will be treated as capital gain or Section 1231 gain. If the target's shareholders are elderly and will benefit substantially from a stepped-up basis for their stock when they die, and if the gain on the asset sale is not extremely large, it may be worthwhile to keep the target/seller alive as a personal holding company, an "S corporation," or a regulated investment company. In any event, the target generally can use the installment method for recognizing gains to the extent that it receives notes as consideration. The installment method is not available, however, to the extent the notes are allocable to loss assets, sales of inventory that do not qualify under Section 453A, or depreciation recapture.

If the target adopts a Section 337 plan of liquidation, completes the liquidation within 12 months after the plan's adoption, and does not violate the liquidation-reincorporation doctrine, then it generally will not recognize gain (other than recapture) on the transaction. Under Section 331, its shareholders generally will recognize capital gain on the liquidation. Section 337 treatment is not available if it is an 80 percent or more owned subsidiary of another corporation, unless the parent also is liquidating. Pursuant to the Installment Sales Revision Act of 1980, installment treatment is available to its shareholders, where it sells its assets to Newco for its installment obligations, which the target/seller then distributes to its shareholders in a Section 337 liquidation.[7] If a Section 337 liquidation is employed, Newco will acquire a basis in the target's assets equal to the amount paid plus any liabilities assumed.

---

[6] Rev. Rul. 69-6, 1969-1 C.B. 104.

[7] Section 453(h).

Imputed Interest

Any debt obligations received by the target's shareholders, or charged in relation to management loans, must bear interest at an effective rate of at least 110 percent of the applicable federal rate (compounded semiannually) in order to avoid the imputed interest rules of Sections 483 and 1274. The applicable federal rate is published monthly by the IRS. To the extent that the obligations do not bear interest at 110 percent of the applicable federal rate, interest will be imputed at 120 percent of the applicable federal rate. There are a number of exceptions, however, applicable to transactions involving less than $2.8 million of debt obligations. These imputed interest rules are intricate, and Congress has revised the law in this area several times in the last year.

Section 83

Pursuant to Section 83, if the fair market value (FMV) of property (such as Newco's stock) received in connection with the performance of services exceeds the amount of consideration paid therefor, the person performing services (the employee) will realize ordinary income in an amount equal to such excess on the date that the property is transferred to him. For purposes of Section 83, FMV is determined without regard to lapse restrictions (such as investment letter restrictions).[8] If the property is subject to a substantial risk of forfeiture when received by the employee, however, no income will be realized until the substantial risk of forfeiture lapses. At the time that the risk of forfeiture lapses, the excess of FMV (measured at the time of the lapse) over consideration paid will be taxable income to the employee.

If the employee files an election under Section 83(b) within 30 days after receiving property that is subject to a substantial risk of forfeiture, the excess of FMV (at the time of receiving the property) over consideration paid will constitute ordinary income when the property is received, notwithstanding the substantial risk of forfeiture. The employee would then realize no additional income when the substantial risk of forfeiture lapses, so that any appreciation element would not be taxed until the property is sold or otherwise disposed of.

Debt versus Equity: "Thin" Incorporation

The characterization of securities issued in connection with a leveraged buyout is significant to both the issuer and the recipient. If found to be equity, not only can a debt instrument be rendered a nullity for

[8] Treas. Reg. §1.83-5(c), Example 3.

creditor status purposes but interest payments deductible by the target become nondeductible "dividends" to the recipient instead of "principal payments." In 1980, the Treasury released a draft of extremely complex legislative regulations under Section 385, which attempted to define debt versus equity. The regulations were withdrawn in 1983, but the Treasury has announced that it intends to publish another set of regulations on this subject. For the time being, therefore, characterization as debt or equity will be determined in accordance with existing case law and IRS rulings. In addressing the thin incorporation issue, the acquirer should ensure that the surviving company will have (1) a material amount of equity (certainly enough to purchase the "core assets"); (2) a realistic debt structure (the payment of the acquisition debt should be feasible); (3) straightforward debt structures (avoid hybrid securities); (4) collateral sufficient to reinforce the concept that the debt is real debt, not equity; (5) proper corporate formalities; and (6) guaranteed loans only when necessary. These factors will also be helpful in avoiding the fraudulent conveyance issue.

REDUCING CAPITAL REQUIREMENTS

Often the acquisition group is hard-pressed to raise the necessary equity for the transaction. It may be useful to examine the possible sources of equity available other than through the usual venture capital or leveraged buyout funds.

Employee Stock Ownership Plans

Federal tax law provides a structure for the formation of a trust (an ESOP) by the target's employee group for the purpose of acquiring and owning, on behalf of all employees, shares of the employer corporation. By prearrangement, the acquirers can sell shares of the newly acquired target to the ESOP using monies borrowed by the trust separately for the purchase price. The loan is then repaid by contributions on behalf of the employees made to the ESOP annually from the profits of the employer, which payments are deductible to the employer. Although the route may seem a veritable panacea, it is fraught with difficulty, not only legal but also practical in nature. The trust is regulated by the restrictive and complex ERISA rules and, if nothing else, presents the owner with a new and unpredictable partner in the business.[9]

---

[9] The Department of Labor's Office of Pension and Welfare Benefit Programs has stated that it will issue guidelines for companies putting together ESOP deals. The guidelines will be used to determine what price per share an ESOP should pay for stock and what percentage of equity it ought to receive. See *Business Week,* October 21, 1985, pp. 40–41.

Net Operating Loss Partnerships

When the target is predicted to throw off large cash profits, companies in possession of net operating losses may be interested in joining as a partner in the acquisition group, consolidating the target for tax purposes, and applying the profits against its net operating losses while using the actual cash flow to amortize the acquisition debt. As might be expected, excessive manipulation of such transactions will be viewed with great suspicion by the Internal Revenue Service and should be undertaken only with the most sophisticated tax advice.

"Junk Bonds" of Target

Where the market exists, it may be possible to supplement other debt funding with the issue of debt securities of the target, immediately following closing, in the so-called junk bond (noninvestment grade/high-return) market.[10]

CONCLUSION

As is readily apparent from the above discussion, there are few, if any, types of transactions that involve the interplay of so many legal areas—corporate and shareholder taxation, state corporate law, securities law, debtor-creditor rights, executive compensation, and others—as leveraged buyouts. To do justice to the full range of complex legal questions that can be involved in putting a deal together and the creative responses devised by the attorneys who work on these transactions is obviously beyond the scope of this chapter. Our focus has been a practical one, with the aim of familiarizing the reader with the key substantive legal issues and the transactional context in which they arise.

---

[10] On January 10, 1986, the Board of Governors of the Federal Reserve System promulgated an interpretation which subjects debt securities issued by a shell corporation to Regulation G and presumes such securities to be "indirectly secured" by the stock to be acquired. The interpretation is directed to impede the use of junk bonds in unfriendly situations, and may have broader meaning depending on the takeover structure being used. 51 Fed. Reg. 1771 (1986).

CHAPTER 13

Asset-Based Financing

Frank J. Medeiros
Department Executive
Marine Midland Business Credit
Wilmington, Del.

Frank J. Medeiros is a department executive with Marine Midland Business Credit, the asset-based lending unit of Marine Midland Bank. Marine Midland Business Credit provides financing to manufacturers, wholesalers, and service companies through a national network of regional offices throughout the United States. Mr. Medeiros is also a member of the Executive Committee of the National Commercial Finance Association and chairman of the Committee on Legislation and Regulation.

Mr. Medeiros began his career with Commercial Credit Business Loans, Inc., later acquired by Marine Midland Business Credit, in 1962. He began as an account supervisor in Los Angeles, was named regional credit manager in Atlanta in 1965, regional vice president in Dallas in 1971, group vice president in Baltimore in 1976, and executive vice president in 1981. He received a B.S. in Business from Southern Massachusetts University in 1961.

George D. Caffrey
Vice President
Marine Midland Bank, N.A.
New York, N.Y.

George D. Caffrey is currently vice president, Wholesale Marketing and Planning, for Marine Midland Bank in New York City. He has previously held senior credit and marketing management positions with Commercial Credit and General Electric Credit Corporation. A graduate of both Holy Cross College and Johns Hopkins University, Mr. Caffrey has lectured on issues related to the asset-based lending industry.

INTRODUCTION

Asset-based lending is a form of financing that has experienced tremendous growth and popularity in recent years. It has provided funds to entrepreneurs and big businesses alike. It has enabled businesses to sell subsidiaries, troubled companies to a return to health, and individuals to purchase companies with limited personal investment. If it sounds intriguing, it is.

This form of financing has existed since the early 1900s. Small to medium-sized businesses that required funds to run their day-to-day operations were often funded by an asset-based lender. Until recently, asset-based financing was commonly called commercial finance. The commercial finance or asset-based lender would advance funds against the assets of a business. Most frequently, these assets would consist of accounts receivable. The lender would evaluate the borrower's accounts receivable and determine how much he was willing to lend against each account. The borrowing company could then get immediate cash instead of having to wait for his accounts receivable to be paid. Although it did not dramatically affect the business's balance sheet, asset-based lending provided a valuable cash flow resource, allowing the business to operate on a day-to-day basis.

Collections were used to pay down the loan balance. However, as new accounts receivable were generated by the business, these receivables generated new cash. Thus the loan balance might never actually be paid off. This self-renewing attribute of asset-based lending generated the terms *evergreen* loan or *revolving* loan to describe this kind of financing.

For many years, the industry was dominated by a few independent finance companies lending primarily to small and medium-sized businesses that could not obtain unsecured bank financing or required more cash than banks were willing to lend on an unsecured basis. For this reason, the commercial finance lender was often perceived as the lender of last resort.

Over time, inventory became acceptable collateral. Loan values were established against collateral to provide more cash to borrowers. The marketplace, however, continued to be dominated by independent finance companies servicing generally smaller businesses.

During the 1960s, banks noticed the potential for asset growth and profitability in this form of lending and entered asset-based lending in a big way. Today, the vast majority of asset-based lenders are banks or bank subsidiaries. Nearly all major money center banks and many regional banks participate in this industry.

This competitive explosion created many changes in the asset-based lending industry. Bankers approached the asset-based financing market differently from finance companies. Asset-based finance was no longer perceived as last resort financing for small to medium-sized businesses: It became a product that could fit the needs of any size company. Finally, other products and services were packaged with asset-based lending, for example, letters of credit, short-term unsecured loans, leases, and so on.

Today's asset-based lender is a new breed. His marketplace is wide open and he has greater flexibility in structuring transactions. Almost daily accounts in the *The Wall Street Journal* show asset-based financing used for nine-figure (or more) transactions, but the product's fundamentals remain the same.

INDICATIONS FOR USING ASSET-BASED FINANCING

The most common business conditions that indicate the use of asset-based lending are:

1. High growth.
2. Seasonality.
3. Acquisition financing.
4. Turnaround situations.

Generally, each situation requires more funds than would be available on an unsecured basis. The growth company's current assets, that is, receivables and inventories, do not turn quickly enough to provide the cash flow necessary to support significant growth. The seasonal business's cash flow is irregular, which again dictates converting assets—in this case receivables or inventories—into cash to carry the business through slow periods.

While acquisition financing has been part of asset-based lending for many years, the number and size of these transactions has grown exponentially over the last decade. In acquisition financing, the company's assets are used to collateralize a loan. That loan, in turn, is used to purchase the company. Finally, turnaround situations are candidates for asset-based lending if the borrower's business plan is realistic and presents a high probability of success.

In each of these cases it is likely that an unsecured lender would be unable either to make the loan or to completely satisfy the cash needs of the client. Clearly there are many other reasons for using asset-based lending, but these are the most frequent situations in which asset-based lending is the preferred alternative.

CREDIT EVALUATION

Unlike most other forms of lending, an asset-based lender reviews available collateral before evaluating the overall financial strength of the borrowers. This is not to say that cash flow analysis, management capabilities, industry trends, and so on are not key features in the asset-based lender's evaluation of the loan, but evaluation of collateral is the initial step in determining if the loan is feasible.

Credit evaluation varies with the lending institution's preference for either cash flow or collateral coverage. Thus, the potential borrower should review his own balance sheet to determine if his needs are realistically supported by the assets and/or cash flow of the company. Before this review, the potential borrower must reevaluate his concept of the value of his assets. He must answer two questions that the lender will ask. First, is this asset of tangible value that can be readily liquidated? Second, does the book value shown on the balance sheet reflect that liquidation value? The answer to the first question is frequently no, and the answer to the second is almost universally no.

Assets such as prepaid expenses and leasehold improvements have no value to a third party and, therefore , are unacceptable as collateral. Other assets, such as specialized machinery or investments in other privately held companies, are not easily liquidated by the lender and, therefore, are usually not acceptable. After striking these items from the balance sheet, the potential borrower is left with tangible, liquidatable assets. These assets are usually accounts receivable, inventory, real estate, buildings, machinery and equipment, and stock.

Each tangible collateral type is then reviewed to determine an acceptable loan amount. The initial step consists of reviewing the current assets, specifically accounts receivable and inventories.

Evaluation of accounts receivable begins with establishing the overall quality of the receivables. Long past-due accounts, for example, will be considered ineligible as collateral. Therefore, the book value of receivables at any time will usually be greater than the amount of receivables the asset-based lender finds acceptable.

Following this, the lender will determine an advance rate—usually by reviewing the returns, credits, and other allowances, and expressing that as a percentage of the total receivables. For example, if 5 percent of a business's receivables are usually not collected because of returns, credits, or other such items, then the lender will not lend 100 percent against these receivables. The lender will advance less than 95 percent. To summarize lending on receivables, the lender will establish what accounts receivable are acceptable and lend something less than 100 percent against those receivables.

Similarly, inventory is evaluated from a liquidation perspective, including the costs associated with a liquidation. In most instances, raw materials and finished goods can be resold by the lender to a third party in the event of a default. (There are exceptions, such as goods made exclusively for one buyer, or potentially obsolete high tech equipment.) Work in process, however, cannot be resold and is usually excluded as acceptable collateral. Because inventory is more difficult to monitor—it can become obsolete and requires considerable effort to dispose of in the event of liquidation—lenders typically advance 50 percent or less against acceptable types of inventories.

These two current asset items are at the core of the revolving asset-based loan, and the more comfortable the lender becomes with the ability to liquidate these current assets quickly in the event of default, the greater the amount that will be made available to the borrower.

Other tangible fixed assets are frequently used to provide additional funds. Almost always, these additional funds are provided on a term loan, rather than a revolving loan basis. Once again, the key is to establish the liquidation value of these assets.

Outside Appraisers

Usually, outside appraisers acceptable to the lender will be brought in to evaluate these assets. Generally speaking, the lender will require a forced sale appraisal to evaluate machinery and equipment. The "forced sale" or "liquidation value" is typically lower—sometimes substantially lower—than fair market appraisal. In fact, the lender is attempting to establish the minimum amount a sale of machinery and equipment can generate under the most adverse conditions, that is, a forced sale at an auction. Because his determination is inexact, the lender often advances less than 100 percent against this forced sale amount.

Real property, such as land, buildings, or manufacturing facilities, is subject to similar appraisal techniques. Advance rates vary depending on the perceived salability of the assets. For example, a multipurpose warehouse facility in an urban area will provide a greater advance rate than a single purpose manufacturing facility in a remote location.

Finally, negotiable securities can be pledged to the lender. The stronger the security, the higher the advance.

To summarize, the lender will establish an asset value based on a realistic liquidation amount and lend an amount less than 100 percent against these values.

Other Considerations

There are, however, four points that should give the borrower solace. First, for an asset-rich company, the asset-based lender can almost always lend greater amounts than can an unsecured lender. Second, the liquidation value of depreciated assets and real estate carried on the books at cost can be higher than the book value of those assets. Third, the establishment of advance rates lends a permanence to the lending arrangement. The lender cannot arbitrarily reduce the loan amount or cancel the loan agreement before its specified termination date.

Finally, disregard all of the preceding discussions of evaluating collateral, since more and more lenders are disregarding them as well. Seriously, many lenders determine funding needs of the borrower and create a loan structure to provide that amount. Lenders will sometimes advance against work in process inventories. "Soft assets" such as franchise rights and royalties may have lending value under certain circumstances. Previously unheard of advance rates against equipment or machinery are being granted to "make the deal work." And lenders who are not very willing to stretch their normal advance guidelines may, under the right circumstances, lend some amount on an "unsecured basis." Much of this flexibility is due to the influx of banks into the asset-based lending arena, which has changed the nature of the product.

UNSECURED VERSUS SECURED BORROWERS

Most borrowers, unsecured and secured, must provide periodic financial information to the lender. The secured lender will require additional information on the assets used as collateral. The purpose of this is twofold: One is to provide collateral justification for additional advances, and the other is to assure the lender that the collateral is still there. For example, the lender will require an accounts receivable aging. The lender will analyze the receivables, determine which accounts are acceptable, and establish a new loan availability amount. The borrower will then either have additional amounts available to be borrowed or (and this is rare) be required to pay down the principal amount due on the loan. Similar requirements will be made to report and evaluate inventory levels.

Beyond requiring additional reporting, a lender will periodically audit the borrower. The checks and procedures followed by the asset-based lending auditor are virtually the same as those used by an outside auditor in establishing the accuracy and reasonableness of company assets. This process is intended to assure the asset-based lender of the accuracy of the reports being provided by the borrower and the quality of the collateral.

Naturally, this additional reporting has a price. More people are required to monitor and evaluate an asset-based loan than an unsecured loan of comparable size. Therefore, a price differential is charged to the borrower. Although in recent years this differential has been reduced, it is foolish to assume it will ever disappear.

INTEREST RATES AND FEES

Typically, these loans are priced on a variable rate basis with a benchmark interest rate used in the calculation. More often than not, this benchmark is the prevailing prime rate, but it may be Libor (London interbank offered rate), CD rates, or something else.

A typical interest rate would be expressed as prime plus X percent per annum. This X percent varies dramatically depending on the quality and size of the loan, the market's competitiveness, and the lender's own internal requirement at the time.

There are often a number of fees and other charges attached to the loan. Some of these are:

Audit fees: A fixed charge for each audit performed during the year.

Wire charges: A fixed amount charged for each additional advance.

Collection of float days: A specified number of days before the principal loan is credited.

With the explosion of leveraged buyouts, success fees or warrants have come into vogue. As the lender perceives himself as putting up the bulk of funds to acquire a company, he demands some share (in the reward) should the acquired company be successful.

INCREASED ATTENTION PAID TO ASSET-BASED FINANCING

As previously mentioned, there has been an accelerated interest in asset-based lending over the last decade by the commercial banking community. There are a number of reasons for this. Some key reasons are:

1. Commercial finance, or asset-based lending divisions, provide banks with the source of growth that compensates for slower growth in more traditional markets.
2. Return on assets are often more attractive in asset-based lending than with other forms of lending.
3. Out-of-state commercial lending offices could position banks for interstate banking—when and if this occurs.
4. The client base is broadened by offering an additional financial product.

The booming participation by commercial banks in asset-based financing is borne out by membership statistics of the National Commercial Finance Association—the industry's trade association. In 1972, a mere 27 percent of NCFA's membership was composed of banks or bank affiliates. Today those groups comprise 75 percent of the membership.

Generally, a potential borrower does not have far to go to find an asset-based lender. In all likelihood, several banks in his community will offer this product. Additionally, major banks have established loan production offices in many cities throughout the United States.

However, to determine which institution to approach for this form of financing, the borrower should evaluate his own needs. The market can be broadly divided into three ranges: extremely large transactions over $50 million; transactions between $2 million and $50 million; and transactions that fall below $2 million. The reason for classifying the borrower's needs is that those ranges provide the borrower with several competitors who can book the type of transaction he needs. Also, it provides the type of lender who can fund the transaction quickly and easily.

For the extremely large transaction—$50 million and greater—the borrower is best served by one of the money center banks such as Bankers Trust, Citibank, Manufacturers Hanover, Marine Midland, or a large independent such as General Electric Credit Corporation. This type of institution has the resources, experience, and desire to book this size transaction. While regional banks may consider these transactions desirable, their lending limits and lack of experience in this arena could cause delays and ultimately fail to produce the most satisfactory results.

The second classification of needs is between the $2 million to $50 million mark. These loans see the most competition, as both national large banks and most regional banks, as well as independent finance companies, desire to participate in this end of the market. Thus the competition is fierce for this type of business, and the borrower has a myriad of opportunities open to him.

Last are transactions below $2 million. These transactions are typically funded by smaller regional or local banks and some small independents. Due to the costs involved in handling these types of loans, there are fewer lenders interested in this end of the market.

INDUSTRY TRENDS

Asset-based lending services are now offered by almost all money center and regional banks and in some instances by single unit "neighborhood" banks. Unlike factoring, whose services have never expanded beyond its initial user market, asset-based lending has exploded into almost all market segments. This asset-based lending explosion will continue, with emphasis on service industries and helping rebuild the so-called rust belt.

The dramatic need for plant investment that helped fuel the initial growth years in the industry will resurface in the form of plant modernization as the need for the United States to remain a producer as well as a provider of services becomes more evident.

The premise that there will be an increasing demand for asset-based lending services over the next decade is almost universally embraced. However, one unknown is how the asset-based lending industry will shape itself in order to fulfill the projected increased need for its services.

One possibility is that the traditional barriers between asset-based financing and unsecured financing will begin to break down. Evidencing this trend is the acquisition financing arena where unsecured senior debt is frequently being offered along with asset-based financing. The potential synergy between these different divisions of the banks could accelerate this process.

This movement may result in asset-based lending becoming a product along with the other products and services provided by commercial lenders.

The knowledge and skills required to successfully compete in the asset-based lending industry will continue to require a degree of specialization by lenders. However, these developments will broaden the availability of the product. Ultimately, this will benefit both lending institutions and borrowers.

Chapter **14**

Long-Term Borrowing

Leonard E. Meads
Vice President, Corporate Finance
Drexel Burnham Lambert Incorporated
New York, NY

Leonard E. Meads is a vice president in the corporate finance department of Drexel Burnham Lambert Incorporated, which he joined in 1977. He specialized in financing oil and gas and other energy-related companies until 1985, when he became involved in the application of options theory to corporate finance. His financing experience includes initial public offerings; offerings of straight debt, convertible debt, debt combined with warrants and common stock, and oil indexed notes; common stock offerings; and exchange offers. A holder of a B.A. and M.B.A. from U.C.L.A. and a J.D. *cum laude* from the University of San Diego, he is a member of the State Bar of California.

Long-term borrowing is a major method of financing for corporations. There are three major sources of long-term debt financing: (1) commercial bank term loans, (2) the private placement market, and (3) the public debt market. The first two of these are covered elsewhere in this book. We will concentrate here on borrowing in the public market. We will review some basic definitions; explore the factors that affect the cost of debt capital; learn some of the things a company can do to lower its cost of capital; examine the trade-offs between cost, flexibility, and risk; and, finally, go through the process of an underwritten public debt offering.

THE PUBLIC DEBT MARKET

The public debt market is open to emerging companies even if their debt is rated below "investment grade." Investment grade is commonly defined as a rating of Baa or better by Moody's Investors Service, or BBB or better by Standard & Poor's. (These are the largest nationally recognized rating agencies.) About 85 percent of all public companies in the United States would receive a noninvestment grade rating on their debt if they were to apply for a rating.

The ability of such companies to tap the public debt market is a recent development. Before the late 1970s, access was limited largely to investment grade issues. Since 1977, a new segment of the bond market—the "high-yield bond market"—has opened for emerging companies whose size or lack of history bars them from investment grade status but that nevertheless have good prospects. From only $1 billion of new issues offered in 1977, the high-yield market has exploded to $15 billion offered in 1984. Looking at all outstanding straight public corporate bonds, not just new issues, we find the high-yield segment accounts for approximately 14 percent of the total $425 billion market.

Prior to the establishment of this market, companies that could not issue investment grade debt had to rely mainly on bank financing. The private placement market was, and still is, dominated by institutional investors who preferred investment grade issues. Bank term loans and private placements typically have stricter provisions and shorter maturities than those for public debt, thus making them less flexible. The ability of a company to borrow in the public bond market now allows it to stabilize its balance sheet at a known cost for a longer period under more flexible terms. Therefore, the emergence of a new issues market for high-yield debt is a major innovation that benefits corporate America.

DEFINITIONS

Now let's cover some definitions and concepts.

Short-term debt is any interest-bearing obligation that matures in one year or less. The one-year cutoff is a strict accounting definition.

Long-term debt is any interest-bearing obligation that matures in more than one year, that is, not short-term debt. The accounting definition time limit differs from the financial use of the phrase that means debt that matures in more than 10 years.

Intermediate-term debt is a financial concept that refers to debt that lies between short-term and long-term debt. Usually, it applies to debt maturing in more than 1 year but no more than 10. Because it is a subset of long-term debt in the accounting sense, it will be considered here as long-term debt unless specifically noted otherwise.

A *straight bond* or *straight debt* is a debt instrument that is not convertible in another security.

A *convertible bond* or *convertible debt* is a debt instrument that is convertible at the investor's option into the common shares of the company that issued the bond. The number of shares received on conversion is determined by dividing the bond's principal amount by the conversion price per share, which is typically set by adding a "conversion premium" to the market price per share existing at the time the bonds are initially sold.

The *principal amount* of a debt instrument, for example, a bond, is the dollar amount to be paid by the borrower to the investor at maturity. A bond usually has a principal amount of $1,000.

The *face amount* or *face value* is the same as the principal amount.

The *coupon rate* is the annual percentage rate of interest on a bond's face amount paid periodically in cash or other consideration to the investor during the bond's life. It is a "nominal" rate; that is, it does not show the effect of compounding due to payments that are made more frequently than annually.

The *coupon payment* is the dollar amount of interest on a bond paid periodically in cash or other consideration to the investor during the bond's life. It is computed by multiplying the coupon rate by the principal amount and dividing by the number of payments made during one year. Coupon payments are generally made semiannually on a bond. For example, a bond with a face amount of $1,000 and a coupon rate of 12 percent payable semiannually would have a coupon payment of $60 twice a year.

The *cost of capital* is the return demanded by the market to make an investment, whether equity or debt. It is the investor's marginal opportunity cost of not investing in another asset having the same risk.

The *cost of debt capital* is the risk-adjusted cost that a company must pay for borrowed funds. It is expressed in terms of an annual rate of interest.

The *price* of a straight bond is the present value of the future coupon and principal payments using the cost of debt capital as the discount rate. The price of a bond having conversion or option features is the sum of the price of the bond without the features plus the present value of those features. The price of a bond is generally quoted as a percentage of the principal amount. For example, if the $1,000 face bond from our example above has a value of $900, it will be quoted as 90.

The *yield to maturity* is the internal rate of return on a bond if held from purchase until maturity. Given a bond's price, coupon rate, number of coupon payments in a year, the maturity, and face amount, the yield to maturity can be computed in the same way an internal rate of return on a project is computed. The yield to maturity is the geometric average cost of debt capital for the bond if held to maturity. As an example, let's take another look at our example bond. We know its price is 90 ($900), it pays a 12 percent coupon semiannually, and it has a $1,000 face. If its remaining maturity from today is 15 years, the yield to maturity is 13.58 percent.

The *current yield* is the annual coupon payment divided by the current price of the bond. Our example bond has a current yield of 13.33 percent. This comes from multiplying the $1,000 face by the 12 percent coupon rate to get the annual coupon payment of $120, and then dividing that by the current price of $900. Note the current yield is not the same as the yield to maturity. Current yield is not a good indicator of the cost of debt capital except for a bond with no maturity.

COST OF CAPITAL VERSUS RISK

The goal of long-term borrowing is to obtain the desired amount of funds at the lowest cost of capital and lowest risk to the borrower.

The company's cost and risk in raising capital are related to the investor's risk and return involved in making the investment. We therefore need to examine the matter from the viewpoint of both the company and the investor.

From the viewpoint of a company needing capital, the lowest risk capital is equity, because no fixed cash outlays are required. However, equity presents the highest risk to the investor. Common stock, the most common form of equity, is a residual claim on the company's earnings and assets. The investor in common stock stands last in line behind all others in getting a share of the profits. Dividends may or may not be paid, and even if paid in one period, can be cut off the next. The last spot in line also holds true in bankruptcy, where the common stockholder may lose everything. Because equity is the investor's riskiest investment, the required rate of return is the highest. And since the investor's required rate of return is the company's cost of capital, the least risky capital to the company will be the most expensive.

The opposite holds true for debt. Debt is more risky to the company because of the fixed obligations, but less risky to the investor because of those obligations and the higher claim in bankruptcy. The lower risk to the investor means a lower required rate of return, and therefore a lower cost of capital to the company.

As a general rule, the cost of capital is an increasing function of the risk to the investor. This means that debt will generally be cheaper than equity. However, since debt is more risky for the company, an issuer must trade off cost versus risk in deciding how to finance.

The concept of a security as a claim on a company's earnings and assets is important. We have just seen that debt and equity securities can be thought of as different types of claims, and that the character of the claims determines the cost of capital of the security. The claims concept is also useful as a framework for thinking about a company's financing needs and how best to satisfy them. It allows for innovation and tailoring, which may be obscured using traditional notions of debt and equity. We may be able to create securities that are legally and structurally different but economically similar, for example, the synthetic convertible bond discussed below. We will also be able to make a better estimate of the cost of capital involved.

GENERAL FACTORS AFFECTING THE COST OF DEBT CAPITAL

Term Structure

Maturity affects the cost of debt. The *term structure* of interest rates can be seen by looking at the interest rate required by the market on bonds differing only in maturity. A plot of yields to maturity (on the vertical axis) versus years to maturity (on the horizontal axis) shows this relationship graphically. The line that best fits the different points is called a *yield curve*.

An *upward* sloping yield curve, sometimes referred to as a *normal* or *positive* yield curve, shows short-term rates lower than longer rates. The opposite is true for a *downward, inverted,* or *negative* yield curve. A *flat* yield curve results from no difference in required yield regardless of maturity. All of these curves or combinations of them can be observed at one time or another.

There are two major theories out of many that attempt to explain the term structure. The *expectations* theory is that a long-term rate is an average of the current short-term rate and future short-term rates expected to exist during the life of the long-term period in question. The *liquidity preference* theory says that because the risk of change in the value of principal increases as maturity increases, investors prefer to lend short and must be paid a risk (liquidity) premium to loan long. Evidence suggests that a combination of the two theories offers the best explanation.

For an issuer, the term structure means it will often need to pay more to borrow on a long-term basis. The company will have to reconcile the higher rate with the lower risk to it (as opposed to the investor) provided by long-term financing.

Default Risk

The risk of default in the payment of interest or principal to the investor affects the cost of capital. The greater the risk, the higher the cost. The *risk structure* of interest rates is the relationship between the risk and the required yield, holding all other factors constant. Like the term structure, the relationship can be shown graphically by plotting yields on the vertical axis and risk on the horizontal axis.

The rating agencies assign a rating to a security as an indicator of the credit risk of that security. The rating is based on the agency's analysis of qualitative and quantitative factors concerning the issuer and the terms of the security. Generally, higher rated, lower risk bonds require lower yields than lower rated, higher risk bonds. The rating is given to the specific security, not to the company. Therefore, a company may have different bonds outstanding having different ratings. (The rating process is described below in the discussion of a public offering.)

Factors affecting default risk of a bond may be separated into two groups. The first, and more important, relates to the company's ability to pay. The second involves the quality of the claim, that is, the terms of the specific security and its relationship to other securities that have been or may be sold by the company.

A company's operating and financial risks and opportunities are analyzed by investors and rating agencies to determine the ability of the company to make the obligated payments. The question is, Does the company have the earning power and assets necessary to service the debt?

The risk of a security depends not only on the company's ability to generate funds, but also on the quality of the security's claim on those funds. The quality of the claim derives from the contract terms and covenants concerning the security.

The *bond indenture* is the contract between the issuing company and a trustee for the benefit of the bondholders that states the bond's claim on the company's earnings and assets in relation to other obligations of the company. It contains *covenants* that are promises by the company to do or not do certain things.

The more important terms and covenants concern the principal amount of the issue, the interest rate, the maturity, the ranking of the bonds relative to other claims, any collateral, the company's redemption of the bonds on a mandatory basis through a sinking fund or at its option through a call feature, any limitations on the ability to refinance the issue, any restrictions on dividends or incurrence of other debt, and any requirements to maintain or meet certain financial tests. We will examine here the provisions regarding ranking, collateral, sinking fund, dividend restrictions, and incurrence and maintenance tests. Later we will look at call and refinancing (also known as refunding) provisions.

The *ranking* of a bond is its relative claim versus others. The higher the ranking, the higher the claim on the earnings and assets of the issuing company. The higher the claim, the lower the risk and the lower the cost of capital. Bonds are typically classified as either *senior* debt or *subordinated* debt. As their names imply, senior debt is higher ranking than a subordinated obligation. Senior debt has precedence in the payment of interest and principal, and has a prior claim in bankruptcy. A *senior subordinated* bond is a subordinated bond that is senior to other subordinated issues sold by the company.

A *secured* bond is less risky for the investor and thus less costly than *unsecured* debt because the issuing company has set aside specific assets as collateral for the payment of interest and principal. Examples of secured debt are mortgage bonds and collateral trust certificates.

A *debenture* is an unsecured bond that is a general obligation of the company. Since the claim is only on the general earnings and assets of the issuer, it has a higher cost of capital than a secured bond. Debentures may be senior or subordinated.

A *sinking fund* is the mandatory redemption by the issuer at specified dates prior to final maturity of a portion of the total face amount of bonds originally issued. The timing and size of the payments vary with different issues. However, sinking fund payments are generally made annually beginning several years after issuance, and then continue until final maturity. The size of each payment is typically a fixed percentage of the total principal amount of the issue. The company may satisfy the requirement using cash or, often, bonds of the issue purchased in the open market or redeemed through an optional redemption provision.

A sinking fund has different and opposite effects. It can lower default risk while increasing the investor's price risk.

The common reason for a sinking fund is that partial retirement of the bonds prior to maturity may reduce the risk of default on the repayment of principal. It also makes the average life, that is, average maturity, of the issue shorter than the final maturity. This may be desirable to the investor depending on his desired holding period.

On the other hand, the sinking fund's effect on price may favor the company to the bondholder's detriment. The redemption price of a sinking fund payment is generally the face amount of the bond, that is, a price of 100. If the bond's market price is less than 100 at the sinking fund date, the investor would gain from having his bond redeemed at 100. However, the ability to use purchased bonds as payment gives the company the benefit of a decline in the bond's price since it will buy bonds in the market at less than 100 to satisfy the sinking fund requirement. If the bond's market price at the time of redemption is higher than 100, the company will redeem at 100 and the investor will suffer a loss if he paid more. (This risk is similar to the call risk that is discussed below. However, since the sinking fund schedule is known, the investor can adjust for it more easily.)

A bond that has no sinking fund is said to have a *bullet* maturity.

The company may also be given the ability to *double up* its sinking fund payment. This option to double gives the company the right to make an additional redemption equal in size and price to the corresponding mandatory sinking fund payment. This right is useful when the company may call the bonds pursuant to the optional call provision (see discussion below) but must pay a call price that is higher than the concurrent sinking fund price.

A *dividend restriction* prohibits the company from making any cash dividend or distribution on its capital stock or otherwise acquiring the stock if the bonds are in default or if a dividend test is not met. Dividend tests vary depending on the perceived default risk. A common test would allow dividends that, when added to all other dividends paid after the bonds' issuance, do not exceed the sum of (1) a specified percentage of the company's net income earned after a specified date (generally the end of a fiscal reporting period just prior to the offering date), (2) proceeds from the sale of capital stock made after the issuance of the bonds, and (3) a cash basket of a fixed dollar amount. The size of the cash basket also depends on the particular case, but a rule of thumb would be the greater of 10 percent of the company's net worth or two years of cash dividend payments.

Dividend restrictions are commonly imposed on issuers. Without them, issuers could take the equity out from under the bondholders and thereby substantially increase the risk of default.

Incurrence tests prohibit the issuer from doing something unless a test is met. Although a dividend restriction is a type of incurrence test, it is usually considered separately. Those described next are some of the more common ones.

A *limitation on indebtedness* is a typical incurrence test. For example, the incurrence of subsequent debt might be restricted if it caused the company's ratio of total debt to capital to exceed a specified limit. Suppose a company had $80 million of total capital, including $20 million of debt in the form of bonds. Its debt-to-capital ratio is 25 percent. Also assume there is a covenant in the indenture covering the $20 million of outstanding bonds prohibiting the incurrence of new debt if it would mean a debt-to-capital ratio greater than 30 percent. Now assume the company wants to issue new bonds for $10 million. New total debt would be $30 million and new total capital $90 million. The new debt-to-capital ratio would be 33 percent, which exceeds the incurrence test maximum of 30 percent. Thus, the company could not issue $10 million of new debt. (Of course, it could sell up to $5.7 million, which just meets the test.)

A *limitation on secured debt, limitation on liens,* or *negative pledge* is a covenant typically seen in unsecured senior debt indentures that prohibits the incurrence of secured debt unless the unsecured bonds are then made equally secure. Secured debt already outstanding at the time the unsecured bonds are issued is generally exempted.

A *maintenance test* requires the company to meet a test, either at all times or at certain dates. Failure to do so would constitute an event of default.

A *net worth maintenance test* requires a company to have a specified level of net worth.

A *security maintenance test* requires that sufficient collateral be maintained to secure the bonds sold, if they are secured bonds.

Noninvestment grade senior and secured debt issues, and some senior subordinated ones, generally contain the restrictive covenants of incurrence and maintenance tests. They protect the bondholder by limiting the amount and quality of other claims on the company's earnings and assets. They limit leverage by holding down the level of debt and keeping up the level of equity. For secured debt, they ensure that collateral is there if needed.

Call Risk

A company is generally given the option to *call* an issue before maturity (as distinguished from a sinking fund, which is a mandatory redemption). This optional redemption feature increases the company's flexibility since it can call the bonds when interest rates have declined and refinance at a lower rate. It is particularly valuable for bonds issued during a period of high rates that are expected to fall. The value to the company, however, is a reduction in the bond's value to the investor. This is clear since the economic gain to the company in calling the bonds is a loss to the bondholders.

To mitigate the company's advantage in having a call on the bonds, *call premium* and *call protection* features are normally provided for the investor. The price and terms of a call vary.

The *call price* paid by the company to redeem the bonds typically starts at the principal amount plus a premium in the first year of the bond's life equal to the coupon rate. The premium will continue over several years but will scale down over time to zero. The call premium protects the investor because the company will not call the bonds if the call price exceeds the market price even though interest rates have fallen. Of course, the company is free to buy bonds in the market.

In addition, the indenture will usually have either a *noncall* or a *nonrefunding* provision as call protection. Noncall means the company is prohibited from calling the bonds for a specified period of years. Nonrefunding prevents the company, for a given number of years, from using borrowed funds for the redemption if the funds have a lower cost than the bonds to be called. Nonrefunding is more flexible from the company's viewpoint since it can still call during the nonrefunding period if it does not use borrowed funds or if for some reason it wants to use borrowed funds having the same or a higher cost. If a bond has both noncall and nonrefunding provisions, the nonrefunding period will be the longer.

Call protection provisions most often apply only in the early years of a bond's life, for example, for the first five years for straight debt. However, longer periods, even to maturity, are not unusual for straight bonds. On the other hand, call protection provisions may be absent in issues that provide a much larger than normal call premium, for example, if the bonds were sold at a significant discount but are callable at face. Call protection for convertible bonds generally runs only for the first two or three years, since the investor has some protection from his ability to convert into the underlying common shares.

As an example of call terms, let's take a 20-year maturity bond with a 12 percent coupon that is noncallable for the first three years.

A standard call price would be 112 (100 percent of face amount plus a call premium equal to the coupon of 12 percent) in the first year of the bond's life if it were callable then. The premium would be reduced on a straight line basis over 10 years, that is, by 1.2 percent per year, to zero at the end of the 10th year. In the first year that a call is permitted, that is, in the fourth year of the bond's life, the premium would be 8.4 percent (12 percent minus three years' reduction of 1.2 percent per year) and the call price 108.4. In the 11th year of life and thereafter, the premium would be zero and the call price 100.

AFTER–TAX COST OF DEBT CAPITAL

The after-tax cost of debt capital is the company's primary concern, since it is the actual cost of borrowing. The tax deductibility of interest expense lowers the cost of debt capital. The after-tax cost of debt capital to the company is:

$$\text{Pretax cost} \times (1 - \text{Marginal tax rate})$$

with the marginal tax rate expressed as a decimal. The less tax the company pays, the less valuable the tax benefit in lowering borrowing costs. The tax shield for interest payments is a powerful incentive to use debt financing. It enhances the cost advantage of debt relative to equity. It also implies that a company should maximize the interest component of the investor's total return, as we shall see in a discussion below on convertible debt.

WHAT'S A COMPANY TO DO?

We now know a lot about the investor's risk, but what does it all mean to a company that wants to borrow money? What does the issuer really need to do, and what can it do, to lower its cost of capital commensurate with the risks to the company? And what about flexibility, which is especially important to a growing company?

As we shall see, a company can affect its cost of debt capital through the terms of the debt issued, but its responses are limited and involve trade-offs among cost, risk, and flexibility.

One important determinant of a company's cost of debt capital is the term structure of interest rates. Unfortunately, a company cannot change the yield curve, only adapt to it. It can decide what maturity to use, and therefore what yield it must pay, for its debt. If there is an upward sloping yield curve, the advantages of certainty of coupon rate and a distant repayment schedule for long-term debt must be weighed against a higher cost. The decision can be especially difficult

if the slope is steep. It may be that the best solution is to choose the maturity dictated by operational considerations and pay whatever is required. However, the alternatives are not limited to a long-term bond with a fixed rate or short-term bank borrowing. For example, an intermediate-term, fixed rate issue or some form of variable rate debt may be attractive.

Variable rate debt or *floating rate debt* is debt that pays interest at a rate that changes over time, generally determined with reference to one or more base rates. If the company is willing to take the interest rate risk, it may issue intermediate- or long-term debt with a variable rate. The variable rate paid in any period would be based on a formula pegged to one or more indexes appropriate for that length period. For example, a rate reset quarterly could be the higher of (1) the three-month U.S. Treasury bill rate plus a spread, or (2) the London interbank offered rate (Libor) plus a spread. Variable rate, long-term debt has the advantage of a longer maturity than bank loans, but the rate mechanism is a double-edged sword. With a positive yield curve, there is an advantage in paying a short rate. However, there is a risk that short rates will increase and exceed what the company would have paid in a fixed rate.

An *extendable note* is a type of variable rate instrument that also has a variable maturity. The rate is reset periodically, usually at intervals of one year or more. Whenever the rate is reset, the investor either rejects the new rate by demanding redemption of the note, or does nothing and thereby accepts the rate and extends the debt's maturity to the next redetermination date. A significant disadvantage to the issuer is the uncertainty of the size and timing of redemptions.

An *exchangeable variable rate note* is designed to deal with a positive yield curve. It is an intermediate-term note, typically subordinated (though it need not be), that pays a fixed "teaser" rate for one or two quarters from issuance, then a variable rate. The variable rate notes are exchangeable at the company's election into fixed rate notes during a designated exchange period, usually four to six years from issuance. After that period, they will either remain outstanding or must be exchanged, depending on the terms of the particular offering. The fixed rate notes generally have a five- or six-year maturity from the exchange date, but some have a fixed maturity date regardless of the exchange date. Quarterly fixed interest is based on a formula, typically a spread above or multiple of an intermediate-term U.S. Treasury rate existing at the time of exchange.

The exchangeable variable rate note gives the company great flexibility. It takes advantage of an upward sloping yield curve by paying short rates on intermediate-term debt. It also gives the issuer the ability to fix the rate later when desired and without the cost of refinancing. As with other variable rate instruments, the risk of rising short rates must be considered a disadvantage. However, the ability to fix the rate allows the company to move swiftly if need be in the face of rising short rates.

A company must also adapt to the risk structure of interest rates. At the time of an offering, it cannot manipulate its ability to pay, so its cost of debt will rest in a set range. A company can maneuver in the range by using the terms and covenants of the issue.

Ranking and security of a bond are the most important terms concerning default risk that affect the cost of debt. Either can lower the required yield, but at the expense of flexibility.

A company can lower its cost by issuing senior rather than subordinated debt. The difference in yield varies and depends on such factors as the relative significance of the ranking for a particular company and the general risk structure of interest rates. For example, if a company's senior debt is ranked BB versus B for subordinated debt, it will see a greater difference than another company whose senior bonds are A while its subordinated debt is A−. Also, the general interest rate levels and spreads based on ranking expand and contract over time so that there may be more or less room for a difference at a given time.

Similarly, secured debt will lower the cost of debt capital because the collateral reduces the investor's risk. However, the collateral must be truly valuable independent of the issuer. Investors do not want to own the collateral. They want its value. If there is a default and the collateral is seized, the investors will want to sell those assets as quickly as possible at the highest price possible. This means that the assets must have a ready market with substantial and easily determinable resale value before investors will give much credit to the issuer for securing its bonds.

The ability of a company to issue secured debt may be limited by lack of "good" assets, the prior use of assets to secure existing debt, or a negative pledge in an existing indenture. Bank loan agreements often require security or a negative pledge, thereby tying up a company's assets.

Flexibility is something we need to consider in talking about senior or secured versus subordinated debt. Companies, especially emerging companies, need financial flexibility. Lack of it is a risk to the company. But noninvestment grade senior and secured debt come with a host of terms and covenants that limit a company's maneuverability. In contrast, subordinated debt has fewer and milder requirements that permit more flexibility. The chief difference is the universal use of incurrence and maintenance tests with senior and secured debt but their absence in almost all subordinated issues. Moreover, a company's bank may be willing to loan more if subordinated debt is placed underneath, since it is "quasi equity" relative to the bank's position. Of course, the subordinated bondholder's claim on the company's earnings and assets is more risky, so the required yield is higher. Despite the higher interest cost of subordinated debt, the freedom it provides causes emerging companies to use subordinated debentures more often than senior or secured bonds. On the other hand, companies that do not need the flexibility or whose highest priority is minimizing the cost of capital may prefer senior or secured debt.

A company cannot significantly change sinking fund, dividend restriction, and call protection provisions required by the market, and therefore cannot significantly affect its cost of debt capital through these terms. The terms tend to be more standardized and changes are used to fine-tune the transaction. In other words, a general yield quote for a proposed debt issue implicitly assumes a certain standard that these provisions must meet. Any significant deviation in the company's favor may cause outright rejection of the offering, not just an increase in rate. In some cases, the market may require stronger provisions just to maintain the original quote. On the other hand, a company may not be able to significantly reduce the rate by enhancing terms already deemed adequate.

ALTERNATIVES WHEN DEBT SERVICE CAPACITY IS LIMITED

A problem arises when debt service capacity appears inadequate for the amount of financing the company requires if it uses straight debt sold at face value. In that case, the company must decide whether the main concern is default on interest or on principal, and if the risks are confined to a certain period. If the problem is primarily an inability to make cash interest payments, or if the inability to pay interest or principal is expected to be remedied in the near future, then there are ways to solve the problem. Securities can often be issued whose requirements match the expected debt service capability. Examples are discount bonds, bond units, convertible and synthetic convertible bonds, and commodity-indexed bonds. These alternatives can be very costly. Therefore, the company must weigh the benefits of raising the funds needed against the possibly higher overall cost of capital that would be paid.

One way to match debt service capacity with requirements is to reduce the coupon, though not the cost of capital. Reducing the coupon rate reduces periodic cash interest payments. This reduces the risk of default on interest payments. However, the bondholder still requires the same cost of debt capital so the difference between the coupon and the required yield is paid to the bondholder at maturity. This increases the risk of default in the repayment of principal. However, the expectation is that by the maturity date the company will be in a stronger financial condition and will have little difficulty in repaying.

The reduction is accomplished by issuing the bond at a discount, that is, selling it in the offering at a price lower than the principal amount. The offering price will be the present value of the future coupon and principal payments using the market-required yield as the rate to discount to present value. For example, assume a company must pay a market rate of 14 percent. If it issues a $1,000 face bond maturing in 20 years that pays a coupon rate of 10 percent per year (semiannual payment basis), the market value (and offering price) of the bond is only $733.37. The difference between the face amount and the price is the *original issue discount* or OID. OID is the amount of interest that will be owed by the maturity date but not paid until then. The company effectively borrows the price paid at the market rate. In our example, it borrows $733.37 at 14 percent. Only 10 percent is paid periodically in cash while the rest is deferred until maturity. The company borrows less initially, but increases the borrowing over time as the accrued but unpaid interest mounts.

A *zero coupon bond* is a discount bond that pays no current coupon.

The effective interest paid on a discount bond, that is, the market rate of interest, is generally a tax-deductible expense of the issuer and taxable as ordinary income to the investor despite the fact that some or all (in the case of a zero coupon bond) of the interest is not paid currently in cash. This is an incentive for companies to issue bonds with as great a discount as possible. However, investors will have a disincentive to buy unless they pay little or no income tax. This is because they need to pay taxes currently, but the cash interest paid, and thus the cash available to make the tax payments, declines as the discount increases.

Investors will buy discount bonds to the extent they want to minimize reinvestment risk, that is, the risk that the coupon payments cannot be reinvested at the same rate as on the original bond. A discount bond reduces this risk because the portion of the interest not paid is compounded at the original market rate. A zero coupon bond completely eliminates the reinvestment risk.

Bonds are sold at a discount usually in one of four situations: (1) to reduce the coupon to match the issuer's interest service capability, (2) to reduce the coupon for cosmetic reasons, for example, the company does not want to show a higher coupon although it is capable of paying it, (3) to satisfy market demand for discount issues which occurs from time to time and lowers the required yield below that for issues priced at the face amount, and (4) to fine-tune the pricing of an issue, for example, selling at a slight discount to avoid a coupon with a nonstandard fraction due to the required market rate.

There may be only a small difference in the proceeds that can be raised using a bond sold at a discount versus one sold at face for a given level of interest service capacity. If the company in our example can pay only $100 of cash interest per bond per year, a 14 percent coupon bond sold at face would raise $714.29. Thus, a bond sold alone at a discount may not solve the issuer's problem of raising enough proceeds.

Bonds can be issued at a discount either alone or in a *unit* with other securities. Two types of units frequently offered are those with common shares and those with warrants. Such units lower default risk through a combination of reducing the coupon rate and simultaneously selling equity or equity-related securities. Shortly after the offering, a unit is normally "broken" or "stripped" to allow the individual securities within the unit to trade separately.

Units offerings are used to increase the amount of cash proceeds raised in the financing and to increase the equity capital below the debt. If the bond in our example above is sold alone, the company would receive $733.37, and repay $1,000 of principal in 20 years. Suppose the company needs more proceeds but does not or cannot issue more bonds. Assuming the company's common shares had a price per share of $26⅝, we could put 10 shares in a unit with one bond and sell the unit for $1,000. (The resulting yield is 13.99 percent. If exactly 14 percent is needed, we would sell the unit for $999.62.) At maturity, $1,000 of principal would still be repaid, but the company keeps the $266.25 paid for the common shares in the unit. The result is that the company has increased the proceeds by selling some equity along with the debt in a unit. The added equity also reduces default risk although the effect may be small in many cases. (If a large equity infusion is desired, for example, to maintain the company's debt-to-capital ratio or to mitigate the increased leverage resulting from offering new bonds, a separate parallel offering of equity can be made simultaneously with the debt offering.)

The relationship among the bond's price, coupon, and yield is the key in a unit offering. The market-required yield remains constant while coupon and price, and thus the discount from face, are adjusted. The lower the coupon, the lower the price and the greater the discount. As the bond price decreases, the value of the other securities in the unit must be increased in order to sell the unit for $1,000. (Most units are offered at or close to $1,000, but any price may be used.) This means more securities of a single type or more than one type of additional securities must be included in the unit. For example, value could be added by increasing the number of common shares or including warrants along with the shares.

The cost of capital of the unit may be greater than that of the bond alone depending on the other securities in the unit. The unit's cost of capital is the weighted average cost of capital for the components of the unit, weighted by the relative value of each component in the unit. In our example above, the value of the debt accounted for about 73 percent of the unit's value while the common shares contributed about 27 percent. We said the cost of debt capital was 14 percent. Since the cost of equity capital will almost always exceed the cost of debt, let's assume that the cost of common equity here is 20 percent. The unit's pre-tax weighted average cost of capital is then equal to 15.6 percent. The computation is:

$$\begin{aligned}&(73\% \text{ value due to bond} \times 14\% \text{ cost of debt capital})\\ +&(27\% \text{ value due to common shares} \times 20\% \text{ cost of equity capital})\end{aligned}$$

The after-tax cost is 10.9 percent, assuming a 46 percent tax rate. (Note that the use of a cost of capital for equity eliminates the need to struggle with dilution since it permits the direct comparison of cost versus expected returns from capital projects.)

Convertible bonds are often used to lower the coupon rate. Because they are the subject of a separate chapter, we will limit our discussion here to their cost of capital. These bonds are normally offered at their face amount with a coupon lower than that for straight debt, but with the bondholder having the option to convert the bond into common shares of the issuer. A convertible bond is therefore a mix of claims on the earnings and assets of the issuer.

Economically, a convertible bond is an inseparable unit consisting of a straight bond sold at a discount plus a call option written by the issuer on its common stock. The value of the debt component is a function of the straight debt yield since that is the rate required by the market no matter how the straight debt component is disguised. The value of the option makes up the difference between the face amount offering price and the value of the debt component. Unlike a true unit composed of legally distinct securities, the two "securities" in a convertible bond are not separable because, legally, a convertible bond is a single security, that is, a bond that has a conversion feature.

Since a convertible bond is economically a unit, we can analyze its cost of capital as we did for a true unit. The cost of capital for a convertible bond is the weighted average of the cost of capital for the straight debt component and the cost of capital for the option, weighted by the respective values for each component relative to the offering price. Because a call option on common shares is riskier than the shares themselves, the call's cost of capital will be greater than that for common equity. This means that the cost of capital for a convertible bond will exceed that for straight debt in virtually every case. This contradicts the common misconception that convertible debt is cheaper than straight debt because of the lower coupon.

Although the cost of convertible debt is higher than for straight debt, this doesn't mean convertible bonds should not be used. They are very useful in reducing cash interest service requirements. It simply must be recognized that the lower interest service comes at a price.

Traditionally, convertible bonds have been offered in a low-coupon, low-conversion premium form. The coupon would be set as low as possible commensurate with a conversion premium of about 15 to 20 percent. Within the last few years, the high-premium convertible has appeared with a higher coupon to compensate for a higher conversion premium often in the 30 to 35 percent range. Does it make a difference which is used?

A lower coupon clearly reduces the debt service requirement and thus default risk compared with a higher coupon. If the main consideration is minimizing cash interest payments, it makes sense to use the low-premium convertible. However, a high-premium convertible will have a lower cost of capital, other things being equal. Therefore, if there is sufficient debt capacity to service the higher coupon, it should be preferred. Of course, in any specific case or market, there may be a distinct market preference for one type over the other, which changes the analysis. Debt buyers will prefer high-premium convertibles because they pay a higher coupon, whereas equity buyers like low-premium convertibles since they are close to being common stock with a good "dividend" in the coupon.

The cost of convertible debt decreases as the coupon increases, assuming that the cost of straight debt is unaffected by the increased debt service requirement. As the coupon increases, the value of the straight debt component increases and the value needed in the option decreases. Since the relative weight of the values shifts toward the straight debt, its normally lower cost of capital increases in importance in the weighted average cost. In other words, the higher the coupon, the more the convertible looks like straight debt and costs like it.

The tax deductibility of interest expense also implies that a company can lower its after-tax cost of convertible debt by paying a higher coupon. As more of the cost arises from interest expense, the tax benefit from deductibility rises.

A *synthetic convertible bond* is a unit composed of a straight bond and warrants for the purchase of the issuer's common stock. It demonstrates the economic reality of a normal convertible bond. Most units are offered at a price equal to the face amount of the bond, normally $1,000, but many are offered at a lower price. The bond's coupon rate is lower than normal, which produces a bond discount. The value attributable to the warrants makes up the difference between the unit's offering price and the value of the bond. The exercise price of the warrant is equivalent to the conversion price of a convertible bond. In lieu of cash, the "usable" bond may be used at face value to pay the exercise price of the warrant. The number of warrants included in the unit can be varied for a particular issue so that not all the bonds are needed to exercise all the warrants. The warrants generally have a shorter life than the bond, for example, 5-year warrants with a 10-year bond in the unit.

Synthetic convertibles offer greater flexibility to the company than a regular convertible bond because of the ability to adjust the number of attached warrants. Marketability is also enhanced since the bond and the warrants can be stripped apart after the offering and sold to investors who prefer one or the other. Accounting treatment is also more favorable. The bond in the unit will be shown net of OID, and the warrants will increase equity. In contrast, the face amount of a convertible bond will appear as debt. Most importantly, a synthetic has a lower after-tax cost because the entire effective interest on the discount bond is deductible, not just the coupon as for a regular convertible.

Commodity-indexed bonds are related to convertible bonds. Essentially, they are bonds that are convertible into the value of a specified quantity of a commodity rather than a number of shares of common stock of the issuer. Such bonds have used gold, silver, and crude oil as indexes. Like a convertible bond, the coupon can be lowered because of the value in the option feature. These bonds are primarily useful to companies that own the indexed commodity.

We now know something about the cost of debt capital and what affects it, and how a company can trade off cost, flexibility, and risk in issuing new debt. But how does a company actually do an issue?

THE PUBLIC OFFERING PROCESS

The Investment Banker

Companies generally use an investment banking firm to tap the long-term debt markets, both public and private. Investment bankers are financial intermediaries who, among other things, specialize in channeling funds from long-term investors to companies that need long-term financing. They increase the efficiency and reduce the cost of finding money due to their knowledge of the markets, their knowledge of and relationships with investors and rating agencies, and their expertise and experience in the mechanics of raising funds. Additionally, the investment banker's financial expertise can aid the company in choosing the right instrument in the right market to optimize the company's capital structure at the lowest cost.

The term *investment banker* refers to both the firm and the individual banker working in the firm's corporate finance or investment banking department, depending on the context.

Types of Offerings

In a public offering, the investment banker usually acts as a principal by being an underwriter on a *firm commitment underwriting* basis. This means that the underwriter promises to buy all of the securities offered by the issuer if it decides to buy any of them, subject to certain conditions, as specified in the underwriting agreement. The *underwriting agreement* is the contract between the company and the underwriter that states their respective rights and obligations. Because the underwriter buys the bonds from the company, it takes the risk of reselling them to the public. The issuer gets a known price and shifts the market risk to the underwriter. The underwriter also assumes the risk of underwriter's liability, that is, liability to the investor under the securities laws if the offering documents fail to meet the required standard of disclosure. To compensate for these risks and the effort and expense involved in preparing and marketing the offering, the underwriter purchases the securities from the company at a discount from the public offering price and then resells them to the public at the public offering price. This discount is the *underwriting discount* or *gross spread.*

In contrast to acting as a principal by being an underwriter, an investment banker acts only as an agent, not an underwriter, in a *best-efforts* offering. The investment banker does not promise to buy any securities. Rather, it promises to use its best efforts to sell the issue. This is similar to the agency role assumed in a private placement. A fee is paid to the investment banker only to the extent that bonds are sold. Best-efforts public offerings are rarely done by major investment banking firms. They are more often used in very risky transactions by smaller, regional investment bankers.

Starting the Process

A public offering is a complex procedure. The process can take a few weeks to many months, but averages two to three months. At the start, the company should make a judgment that such a financing is desirable. It should then contact one or more investment bankers to get an opinion as to the advisability and feasibility of the financing. This sequence is often reversed, with the investment banker approaching the company first with an idea for a financing. This is more common where a relationship already exists, but it also occurs where there was no prior contact.

The investment banker will make a preliminary judgment based on information provided by the company and current market conditions. The response to the company may be oral or in writing. A written proposal might be a letter or a term sheet listing the proposed terms of the offering, including a range of market rates, call and sinking fund provisions, and significant covenants for the bonds. More elaborate proposals often include other comparative data on the company and the market.

If the response is favorable and the company decides to proceed, it retains the investment banker to act as *managing underwriter* of the offering. If several investment bankers have been approached, the company generally chooses one of these. More than one manager can be selected if special circumstances warrant, but in that case one of them must be designated as the *lead* or *book-running* manager in overall control, with the others being comanagers.

Additionally, the company must retain several other professionals. Attorneys skilled in securities law, the company's auditors and, in some cases, other experts such as independent appraisers or petroleum engineers are needed to help prepare the registration statement for the issue. The managing underwriter will retain separate attorneys to act as underwriter's counsel. In addition, the company must select someone, usually a commercial bank, to act as trustee under the trust indenture covering the bonds to be issued, and must choose a financial printer for the documents.

An organizational meeting of the company's management, company's counsel, the auditors, the managing underwriter's representatives, and underwriter's counsel will be held soon after the decision to proceed. Matters to be covered are the timetable for the offering, determining the timing and responsibilities for the preparation of needed documents, scheduling "due diligence" meetings and visits, and any other significant topic that might affect the offering.

The Registration Statement

The *registration statement* is the disclosure document regarding the securities offered that must be filed with the U.S. Securities and Exchange Commission (SEC). All information that is material to an investor's decision to purchase the securities must be disclosed within the borders of the registration statement or incorporated therein by reference to other documents on file with the SEC. Such information includes a description of the offering, the securities offered, the company and its business, and financial data. The *prospectus* that is distributed to the public in connection with the offering is the part of the registration statement that contains the most important information, including that referred to above.

The registration statement is the company's document, even though others participate in its preparation. It is critical that a company's board of directors and management be totally candid and careful in the preparation of this document. Federal and state securities laws require that there be no misstatement of material fact or omission of a material fact in the registration statement. Failure to meet this standard could result in significant legal and regulatory penalties. Usually, there is no problem in knowing what to disclose. However, gray areas do appear. In such situations, it is best to discuss the question with the attorneys, investment banker, and if appropriate, the auditors or other experts involved. A decision can then be made on how to handle the issue.

Due Diligence

Due diligence is the investigation of the company undertaken by the underwriter and the attorneys for both the underwriter and company. Its purpose is to learn everything material about a company, its business, operations, financial status, plans, people, competitive position, and reputation. Historical, current, and future periods will be examined. Background checks on key personnel are common. Facilities will be inspected, and third-party suppliers and customers will be queried. Nonpublic information will be kept strictly confidential.

Although a company may view due diligence as a nuisance at best, or unwarranted prying at worst, it serves many important functions. For the company, it provides a discipline to organize its thoughts about itself that will be useful during the marketing of the issue. It can also reveal aspects of the company and its information system that were not fully appreciated before and that may need improvement. For the investment banker, it provides insights into the company and its future. This knowledge of strengths and weaknesses allows the banker to better advise the company on financial strategy in general and this offering in particular. It also permits the banker to make meaningful comments on the adequacy of disclosure in the registration statement. Further, because the prospectus is the primary selling as well as disclosure document, the banker can ensure that the company's strong points are appropriately highlighted.

Most importantly, due diligence provides the legal basis for a defense by directors and officers of the company, and by the underwriters, to a suit alleging violations of federal and state disclosure requirements. A director or officer who signs the registration statement, and any underwriter, may successfully defend against liability for misstatements or omissions of material fact in the registration statement if he can establish he exercised due diligence in its preparation. In contrast, the company remains strictly liable for damages so suffered by a purchaser.

Document Drafting and Review

Document drafting and review are major activities. The drafting process can take a few days to several months, depending on the form of registration statement and other documents required, the availability of information, the complexity of the disclosure, the drafting abilities of the parties, and turnaround time between drafts. The usual time is several weeks. Company's counsel is primarily responsible for maintaining the registration statement and documents related to the company. Underwriter's counsel will generally prepare the underwriting papers, the trust indenture covering the bonds, and blue sky documents required by securities regulatory agencies in the states where the bonds will be sold. The auditor will check the accuracy of the financial data and draft the "cold comfort" letter required for the underwriter. The company's management and the investment bankers will help in the editing of all documents to ensure full disclosure and as positive a presentation as possible in the prospectus.

Drafting of documents generally begins right after the organizational meeting. First drafts are circulated for review and comment by all parties. The initial all-hands drafting session is held a few days later to discuss the drafts and incorporate comments and changes. Revised drafts will then be prepared and circulated, followed by another drafting session to discuss comments and make changes. This process goes on until all documents are ready to be filed with the SEC.

It is important for company personnel to understand the extreme importance of due diligence and the drafting processes that generally overlap. Drafting sessions often involve due diligence, since noncompany people need to understand the facts in order to help prepare the prospectus. It is common for the company's management to feel that a first draft of the registration statement explains everything perfectly, and they may get exasperated by the long drafting sessions and possibly lengthy period until filing. However, experienced managers know that they understand the company better than anyone else, and they subconsciously "fill in the blanks" in a text that is unclear to others. The investment banker is especially eager to make the prospectus as clear as possible, because it will be read by potential investors who know nothing about the company. Thus, it is imperative that senior management be available to provide the facts and to participate in the drafting process as much as possible. Patience is the key.

Initial Filing with the SEC

When the documents are ready and market conditions acceptable, the initial filing of the registration statement and other documents in the filing package is made with the SEC in Washington, D.C., along with a check for the filing fee. The documents are subject to review by the SEC's Division of Corporation Finance, which will decide whether or not to make a review. If it does review, it may make comments and request additions and deletions, especially in the prospectus, and may request supplemental information that need not appear in the publicly distributed documents.

The registration statement as originally filed contains the preliminary prospectus, which is also called the *red herring* because of the disclaimer legend printed in red ink along the left border of the front cover. The preliminary prospectus is the most important document in marketing the offering since it is distributed to the public as the primary source of information about the offering and the issuer.

Post Filing

Marketing. Filing with the SEC triggers marketing activity, which is strictly prohibited before filing. The managing underwriter has the major role here. The skilled investment banker starts a carefully orchestrated marketing process upon filing that should build to a climax with a successful offering that makes both the issuer and the investors happy.

Marketing involves contacting potential investors, providing them with the preliminary prospectus, explaining the merits of the company and the offering, and convincing them that it is a sound investment that they should buy. The process begins internally with the investment bankers discussing the offering with their marketing and/or trading department personnel. Given the "story" by the corporate finance people, the marketing personnel will conduct the actual marketing to investors. Corporate finance will provide any necessary support and act as liaison between the company and marketing people.

The investment banker will generally organize a "roadshow" that consists of a series of meetings over one or two weeks in various cities where significant potential investors reside. Each meeting consists of a formal presentation by the company's senior management, followed by a question and answer period. The audience for a bond issue will usually be composed of representatives of institutional investors, since these are the major bond buyers. Institutional investors include mutual funds, private investment companies and money managers, banks, savings and loans, pension funds, insurance companies, and educational and religious institutions. One-on-one meetings may also be held. All of these meetings are important in exposing the company to investors that may supply substantial funds not only for the current offering but for future ones as well. Good impressions made in these face-to-face meetings can clinch a deal.

The managing underwriter will also begin the formation of an underwriting syndicate if one is to be used. An *underwriting syndicate* is a collection of different investment banking firms, each of which will underwrite the issue by purchasing a portion of it from the company on a several, not joint, legal basis, then selling the bonds to the public. The traditional use of a syndicate began to fade in 1982, and today most debt offerings are done by the managing underwriter without a syndicate. The investment banker will decide whether to use a syndicate based on market conditions, the size of the issue, the perceived underwriting risks, the desired breadth of distribution, and the expected reception of the issue by the market. The managing firm's syndicate department will form the syndicate and may also form a *selling group* of firms not in the syndicate to help sell the issue.

If an underwriting syndicate is used, each member will be given the opportunity to perform its own due diligence at an underwriters' information (or due diligence) meeting. This will be arranged by the managing underwriter and is generally held in New York.

Rating Agencies. The investment banker will generally arrange a meeting in New York between the company and one or both of the two biggest rating agencies—Moody's Investors Service, Inc. and Standard & Poor's Corp. (The other rating agencies are Fitch Investors Service, Inc.; Duff & Phelps Inc.; and McCarthy, Crisanti & Maffei, Inc.) These meetings are vital because the rating of an issue can affect the market's demand for the issue and the interest rate required. The better the rating, the lower the rate. The issuer will prepare a written presentation with the investment banker's advice. The presentation generally includes historical and projected financial data, comparisons with comparable companies, analysis of future capital expenditures, and other factors that may be important for the particular issue, including possible financing alternatives. This will be sent prior to the meeting along with the preliminary prospectus and other information requested by the agencies. The meeting consists of an oral presentation by senior management on the company's operating and financial plans and policies, and other key points that may affect the rating.

Many factors, qualitative and quantitative, influence the rating of an issue. The agencies look at the company's industry, its relative position in its industry, and its management and accounting quality. Financial factors include earnings protection, leverage and asset protection, adequacy of cash flow, and financial flexibility. The terms of the issue are also examined, for example, its ranking and protective covenants. The mix of and relative weight given to different factors depends on the specific situation. Since there is no set formula, it is not possible to predict with total certainty what rating will be given. However, the investment banker will ordinarily tell the company from the outset what he thinks the rating might be.

The rating agencies will usually notify the company through the investment banker of the proposed rating for the issue. Notification generally comes before the offering date. If the company disagrees with the rating, it can ask for a reconsideration based on new or additional information.

Listing. If the bonds are to be listed on an exchange, the listing application will be made by the company. Bonds are often listed to enhance their marketability and liquidity. The investment banker will make a recommendation whether to list.

State Requirements. In addition to filing with the SEC, the issue must be filed with the securities regulatory authorities in the states where the securities may be sold. This requirement applies to sales to the public but excludes sales to institutional investors. These state blue sky authorities generally follow a different philosophy about securities regulation than does the SEC. Federal securities law under the Securities Act of 1933 is based on the concept of *full disclosure.* As long as the investor is apprised of all material facts, it is up to him to make the investment decision for better or worse. Most states adhere to the concept of *merit.* In effect, the state decides whether an offering is good or bad. If the merit standard is not met, the state will not allow the securities to be sold to the public, even with full disclosure.

States also regulate investments by fiduciaries within their purview, including mutual savings banks, savings and loans, and insurance companies. Only securities in companies that meet certain statutory criteria are eligible for investment by these particular institutional investors. Thrift institutions generally may only purchase investment grade securities. However, some states allow a "basket" exception, that is, a purchase from a limited pool of funds. Insurance companies must ordinarily follow a fixed charge coverage test, and most states permit basket purchases. Underwriter's counsel will prepare a legal investment survey detailing the eligibility of the offered bonds in each state.

Underwriter's counsel will prepare and file the necessary blue sky documents given a list from the managing underwriter of those jurisdictions in which the offering will be marketed. The company, however, will pay the appropriate filing fees and the fees of underwriter's counsel for this activity.

NASD. Unless the company already has outstanding straight debt or preferred stock with an investment grade rating, the managing underwriter must file the offering with the National Association of Securities Dealers, Inc. (NASD). The NASD reviews the terms and arrangements of the proposed underwriting and distribution of the issue to determine whether they are fair and reasonable. The company pays the filing fee.

Timing. The timing of the receipt of comments from the SEC is important to the marketing effort. The issue cannot be sold until the SEC declares the registration statement effective. However, marketing occurs prior to effectiveness and is designed to produce the maximum impact by the effective date. By this technique, the underwriter learns what the market demand will be for the offering and at what price. The company will therefore know how successful or not its offering will be. It will know whether to proceed, delay, or cancel the proposed offering before the actual sale takes place.

What about the firm commitment underwriting agreement? Doesn't this allow the company to shift the risk of sale to the underwriter? Yes, but only after it is executed and becomes effective. To minimize its risk, the underwriter will not execute the underwriting agreement until just before the effectiveness of the registration statement. Therefore, if it feels the offering will go badly, it will decline even if the company wants to proceed. However, such disagreements are rare so late in the process.

The SEC will be told the desired offering date, and the SEC staff will indicate if it is possible for them to respond accordingly. Marketing efforts and the roadshow schedule will be keyed off of the anticipated time of receipt of the SEC comments, in order to create maximum demand.

Final Filing and Offering

Document Changes. When SEC comments are received, they are reviewed by the drafting group in order to make appropriate responses.

A telephonic conference call with the staff is usually held to go over the company's proposed responses. Some comments will result in changes in the registration statement, either additions or deletions. Comments with which the company, counsel, the underwriter, or the auditors disagree may be discussed. Such disputed comments may or may not result in changes, depending on the outcome of the discussions. Some comments may be requests to supply the SEC with additional information but with no need to make changes in the documents.

In addition to changes made in response to SEC comments, changes must be made in the documents to reflect the current state of the company and the offering. Any new material fact must be disclosed, and any outdated material fact must be corrected or eliminated. Also, with feedback from marketing, adjustments may be made in the terms of the issue. For example, the initial filing will often indicate an amount to be raised that is on the low end of a range the company wants. If marketing reveals strong demand, the offering size can be increased.

Significant changes are generally shown to the SEC prior to refiling. This is especially true if there is a chance the staff will have further comments. Changes are shown by letter or printer's proof page. At times the changes will be shown by a new filing of an amended registration statement that is not meant to be the final one. The method of response depends on the significance and extent of the changes as well as the staff's desire.

A similar process may be undergone to satisfy the state blue sky commissions. Usually, all such issues with the state authorities can be resolved satisfactorily. However, there may be instances that cannot be resolved, and in such cases the offering cannot be made in that jurisdiction. The managing underwriter will advise the company how significant the impact would be of losing the ability to sell the bonds in that state or states. It would be unusual for an offering to be canceled due to the lack of clearance by blue sky authorities in a few states.

When all documents are in final form, no further comments are expected from the SEC, clearance is received from the state regulatory bodies and NASD (if necessary), and marketing is completed with good demand for the issue, then the offering is ready to be made.

Pricing. A pricing meeting is held by the managing underwriter and the company at which the investment banker tells the company the size of the offering, the price terms, and the gross spread at which the underwriter or syndicate will purchase the issue. The meeting is generally held after the market's close on the day before the offering date. There may be some negotiation, but often there is little. This is because the investment banker usually keeps the company continually informed about the anticipated terms based on the marketing effort so the company will not be surprised. Thus, the company will have a good idea what the terms will be and whether or not they will be acceptable before going into the pricing meeting.

Once the terms are agreed upon, they are put into the final registration statement, underwriting agreement, and other documents as necessary. The final registration statement is also called the pricing amendment, since changes to the registration statement are filed by amending the original, and this final amendment contains the price terms.

Final Filing. The final documents, including letters from the company and managing underwriter requesting acceleration of the effectiveness of the registration statement, are then filed with the SEC. The preparation of the filing package is done overnight so a courier can file the package with the SEC in Washington when the doors open the morning after pricing. The goal is to have the SEC declare the registration statement effective before the market opens. This minimizes market risk. Close coordination and cooperation with the SEC staff is essential. In general, the staff will be both sensitive and accommodating, assuming that their earlier comments and requests have been satisfactorily addressed. If all is in order after the review of the final documents, the SEC will declare the registration statement to be effective. The SEC does not approve it.

Signing and Offering. On the morning the final registration statement is filed, but before its effectiveness, the company and the managing underwriter will sign the underwriting agreement. If there is an underwriting syndicate, the manager signs on behalf of each member. (The rights and obligations between the managing underwriter and the underwriters in the syndicate are contained in the *agreement among underwriters.* The issuer is not a party to this contract.) The underwriting agreement becomes effective when the issuer notifies the underwriter that the SEC has declared the registration statement effective.

When the registration statement becomes effective, the sole underwriter or syndicate can legally sell the bonds. If all goes well, the issue will be all sold within minutes or a few hours at most. The syndicate, if there is one, will be terminated. A purchase confirmation and final prospectus is sent to all buyers.

If an *overallotment option* exists, the managing underwriter may exercise it during the specified period, usually within 30 days of the offering date. This option, also called a *green shoe,* is common in stock offerings but is used only occasionally for debt issues. It gives the underwriter the ability to purchase more bonds from the company on the same terms as for the original amount. The overallotment may be up to 15 percent of the original amount sold.

Closing

Closing occurs in five business days after the offering date. If all closing conditions are met, the company and managing underwriter execute the necessary closing documents. The underwriter then hands the company a check for the purchase price (public offering price minus the underwriting discount) and takes receipt of the bonds. Standard practice is for the check to be in next-day funds. The offering is now completed.

PUBLIC OFFERING TRANSACTION COSTS

The transaction costs to the issuer of an underwritten public offering are the underwriting discount, out-of-pocket expenses, and management time.

The Underwriting Discount. The underwriting discount is the largest explicit cost. It compensates the investment banker for the effort and expense of orchestrating the offering, for assuming the underwriter's risk of market loss and potential legal liability, and for selling the security (no sales commission is charged to the investor). If the offering is done with a syndicate, the gross spread is usually divided as follows: about 20 percent of the discount to the managing underwriter, about 20 percent to the syndicate members (including the manager), subdivided among them in proportion to the amount each underwrote, and about 60 percent to the firm that sells the security.

The discount varies largely based on the effort and difficulty in selling the issue and the risks involved. Selling effort and risk are intertwined—a riskier security is harder to market than a less risky one. Factors such as the bond's rating, the type of security offered, and the size of the offering are good indicators but may not totally explain the gross spread in a specific case.

A bond's rating is the best single predictor of the underwriting discount. The gross spread will be higher for lower rated bonds than for higher rated debt. For example, in the five years of 1980 through 1984, the average gross spread for industrial straight debt issues (excluding units) rated B+ to B− was 3.30 percent, while the average for issues rated A+ to A− was 0.88 percent. (The underwriting discount is generally expressed as a percentage of the principal amount of bonds offered. The figures here are adjusted for the offering price to eliminate any distortion due to issues sold at a discount.)

Out-of-Pocket Expenses. Out-of-pocket expenses are composed of several items:

1. SEC filing fee.
2. NASD filing fee.
3. Blue sky fees and expenses including legal investment expenses.
4. Legal fees and expenses.
5. Accountants' fees and expenses.
6. Trustee's fees and expenses.
7. Printing and engraving.
8. Miscellaneous.

The size of each of the above expenses and their total vary greatly from one offering to the next. The biggest expenses are usually printing and professional fees for attorneys and accountants. For the five years 1980 through 1984, industrial straight debt issues (including units) rated BB+ to B− (noninvestment grade) incurred an average out-of-pocket expense of $372,000, with a range from $32,000 to $2 million. About two thirds of the issues had expenses from $100,000 to $400,000.

Management Time. The cost of management time is significant. Senior management will be deeply involved in the offering, and many others in the company will be involved in the backup work needed to ensure accuracy of the registration statement.

SUMMARY

Long-term debt is a major component of corporate financing. The public bond market generally allows a company to borrow on more favorable terms than those available from bank term loans or private placements. Since the late 1970s, the high-yield bond market has been open to companies whose debt is not investment grade.

The pre-tax cost of debt capital is the pre-tax, risk-adjusted rate of return required by the market. To understand the cost of debt capital, we looked at the investor's risk. The greater the risk, the higher the required return. Investor risk appears in the term structure of interest rates, which shows the relationship between maturities and yields, and the risk structure, which relates default risks and yields. Default risk concerns the issuer's ability to pay, and the terms and covenants pertaining to a particular debt issue. Call risk also arises from the indenture terms and involves the possible early repayment of the bonds to the investor's detriment.

The after-tax cost of debt capital is lower than the pre-tax cost due to the tax deductibility of interest expense.

A company can affect its cost of debt capital through the terms of the debt issued, but its responses are limited and involve trade-offs among cost, risk, and flexibility. Emerging companies usually use subordinated debt, instead of senior or secured debt, despite its higher cost, because of the greater flexibility available.

If the company's debt capacity is insufficient to service the amount of debt it needs to raise, it may still be able to get the funds it requires by offering bonds at a discount, selling units of bonds plus common shares or other securities, selling regular convertible bonds or synthetic convertible bonds or, for a few companies, commodity-indexed bonds.

Companies generally use an investment banker to raise funds in the long-term debt markets. The investment banker normally acts as an underwriter in a public offering.

A public offering of securities is a complex process that averages two to three months in length and requires compliance with federal and state securities laws. The registration statement, which includes the prospectus, is the key document. There must be no misstatement or omission of material fact in it. Failure to meet the required standard of disclosure can result in severe legal penalties.

When the documents are ready and market conditions are acceptable, the initial filing is made, and the managing underwriter will start marketing, including a roadshow for investors and meetings with the rating agencies. A syndicate will be formed if desirable. Upon completion of marketing and responding to SEC comments, the issue is priced and the documents are refiled with the SEC. The underwriting agreement is then signed. After the SEC declares the final registration statement effective, the offering is made.

The transaction costs of a public offering are the underwriting discount, the out-of-pocket expenses, and management time.

CHAPTER **15**

Finance Company Borrowing

Edward J. Roncoroni, Jr.
Vice President
Beneficial Business Credit Corp.
Allentown, Pa.

Edward J. Roncoroni is a vice president of Beneficial Business Credit Corp. one of the nation's largest providers of credit to small and growing business institutions. Prior to joining Beneficial, Mr. Roncoroni gained credit-lending experience as vice president for Girard Investment Company, where he worked for 12 years. He graduated *cum laude* from Marywood College in Pennsylvania with a B.S. degree in Business, and served in the U.S. Army National Guard.

INTRODUCTION

Ask anyone over a certain age about finance companies, and you can be pretty sure you're going to hear stories about people sneaking up side stairs to second-floor loan offices, so no one would know they had been forced to turn to the "lenders of last resort." You may hear, as well, speculations about stratospheric interest rates or aggressive collection officers. And the final comment will probably be, "But, of course, no one *we* know ever went *there.*"

Even back in the days of the Great Depression, the old loan company image wasn't entirely justified. But today, two generations later, it bears no resemblance at all to reality. Finance companies are listed on the New York Stock Exchange alongside the largest banks, savings and loans, insurance companies, and stock brokerages. Finance companies operate in the same commercial and business districts that those companies do. And, far from loaning money only to down-and-outers who have no place else to turn, finance companies provide mainstream financial services to good credit risks throughout the social and economic spectrum. For example, Beneficial Corporation (the parent of Beneficial Business Credit) represents both the nation's largest holder of residential second mortgages and the nation's largest issue of Gold MasterCards.

Finance companies are also an important source of credit for small and growing businesses. For many of those businesses—particularly those that are just starting out or just beginning their first major expansion—finance companies can in fact be the best available source of needed credit. Any businessman seeking capital should explore the full range of financing alternatives available to him, definitely including a stop at a major finance company.

FINANCE COMPANIES VERSUS BANKS

A finance company's business is quite straightforward. It borrows money, from the public or from other sources, and then lends it out to individuals or to businesses. Out of the difference between the interest it receives from its borrowers and the interest it pays to its lenders, it pays its operating costs (and the cost of any bad loans it makes) and keeps the rest as profit.

By comparison, a bank, for the most part, depends on funds that are deposited with it by its customers. Those deposits can be withdrawn, often without much notice, so that banks don't always have funds to lend, especially to such high-risk borrowers as small businesses. Since banks are also using other people's money that has been left with them for safekeeping, they are subject to strict rules about how that money can be used. Those rules can in turn affect the availability of funds for small business borrowers.

In effect, a finance company almost always has money to lend to small borrowers. If all its funds have been lent and a worthy applicant appears, the finance company can usually borrow more money in order to serve that applicant. A bank sometimes has money to lend to small borrowers—but not always. If its deposits decline, a bank won't have money to lend; or if demand from high-quality borrowers is strong, there may not be enough money to serve smaller, riskier borrowers as well.

Finance companies can also be more flexible than banks. In order to comply with banking regulations and to protect the interests of their depositors, banks have evolved strict criteria for the distribution of their loan portfolios (commercial, business, mortgage, personal, auto, etc.), for the sizes and terms of the loans they grant, and for the measures of creditworthiness that they apply to their loan applicants. As a result, if you are turned down by one bank, there's a fair chance that you will be turned down by all of them. Finance companies also have to comply with certain regulations, but, generally speaking, they have a lot more freedom—and a lot more incentive—to try to find a workable loan arrangement, even if the application doesn't meet the banks' well-established yardsticks.

Finance companies can also be more knowledgeable than banks. The loan officers at finance companies specialize in lending money to individuals and small businesses. Money and service are a finance company's only products. A good finance company loan officer can draw on a substantial body of small business experience both before a loan is negotiated and later, when the business is in operation after the loan has been made. At banks, however, the on-and-off nature of small business lending, the needs of larger borrowers, and the multiplicity of services provided to customers may all lead to a more limited level of small business expertise.

These statements are, of course, generalizations. There are banks that do a consistently superb job with small business lending, just as there are small businesses that have had bad experiences with finance companies. On balance, though, I believe that consistent availability of funds, flexibility, and small business expertise are valid competitive selling points for the finance companies.

These selling points do have a price tag. While banks usually pay no interest to their checking account depositors, and only minimal amounts to their passbook savings depositors, finance companies have to borrow all their funds at competitive rates. On an identical loan approved by both a bank and a finance company, the bank will frequently be able to offer a lower interest rate to the borrower. Note the word *frequently,* however: A smart borrower will check both sources before committing himself to either one.

There are more kinds of credit risks than there is room to list them. Most of them, I have found, can be divided into three groups, according to the "stoplight theory" of loan desirability. The first group consists of loans to large corporations, partnerships, and individuals with a substantial net worth. These are the best borrowers—people who don't need the money, as the old saying goes. The loans would be rated A+ or A, or perhaps B+, and any lender would give them a green light.

At the other end of the spectrum are the borrowers with low income, minimal net worth, limited assets, and slow to poor credit ratings. Loans to these borrowers would be rated C– or worse, and any lender would give them a red light.

In between lie the loans that would get an amber light—a caution light. These loans would be rated B or C, with more emphasis on B than on C. In this category are the classic middle-American borrowers—people and businesses with small net worth, moderate assets, good credit, and average income. Most of the loan applicants rejected by banks fall into this category (the red light borrowers are less likely to apply). But these people are good potential borrowers for a finance company—they are creditworthy, and they are willing to pay the high initial cost of capital to launch their businesses or make them grow. Most major finance companies, like my own, have instituted a business or commercial loan department to provide funds for these fledgling businesses.

WHAT A FINANCE COMPANY CAN OFFER

There is no such thing as a typical finance company loan. Just like the businesses they serve, these loans come in every conceivable size, shape, and description. The following, therefore, are offered primarily as general guidelines.

Size of Loan. A recent survey of business loan activities at major finance companies indicated that the minimum loan obtainable was $10,000, and the maximum was $5 million. In practice, however, the vast majority of these loans fall between $50,000 and $1 million. The top and bottom limits vary from company to company, so it's usually wise to shop for available amounts at the beginning of the search for financing. Also, the limits have increased sharply in recent years in response to inflationary pressures and the escalation of real estate values, and will most likely continue to do so in the years to come.

Term of Loan. Finance companies usually do not make many business loans with a term shorter than 1 year or longer than 15 years. Most loans fall into the two-year to five-year time span, but terms vary primarily with the nature of the business and the ability of the borrower to repay the loan. Real estate loans, obviously, tend to have longer terms.

Interest Rates. Finance companies prefer to make loans with floating interest rates that vary in relation to the prevailing "bank reference rate," as the prime rate is called in the industry. The normal minimum interest rate is currently three points above the reference, or prime, rate; an exceptional lower rate might occur if a loan combined top creditworthiness with little risk and minimal account servicing requirements. Conversely, as creditworthiness declines and risk and service requirements increase, so will the interest rate. Fixed rate loans are now rare at finance companies and would probably command an interest rate three to six points above prime (higher than the floating rates, because future changes in the lender's cost of funds cannot be passed on to the borrower).

WHAT DOES A FINANCE COMPANY LOOK FOR?

Every finance company has its own formulas and yardsticks for determining the quality of a loan application. In the end, they all boil down to the same traditional Three Cs of Lending: Credit—Does the borrower have a history of paying his major credit obligations according to terms (on time)? Collateral—What is the realizable value of the assets that will be used to secure the loan? Cash—Will the borrower's cash flow be sufficient to service the debt he is taking on? To these basic variables, we generally add a fourth C in the case of small and starting-up businesses: Competence—Does the borrower have the managerial experience and ability to run his business successfully?

There's an important point to be made here. Legally, a small business loan may be made to a corporation, a Subchapter S corporation, a general partnership, a limited partnership, a sole proprietorship, or an individual person. Each of these business forms, however, ultimately represents one or two or a small group of individuals. It is those individuals that a finance company is going to want to scrutinize carefully in a small business loan situation. Their personal credit histories will indicate how the business might be expected to meet its obligations; their homes or other assets may secure the business loans; and their abilities will determine whether the business generates enough cash to service the loans. With this point in mind, let's consider each of these in more detail.

Credit

There are many types of credit, ranging from 30-day purchase agreements to long-term financial obligations. Not everyone repays every loan precisely according to terms. In determining the quality of your credit, it is important to know which credit obligations carry the most weight.

The single most important credit reference is the home mortgage. Not only is it the financial obligation nearest in size to a business loan, but a finance company will often request a second lien on the borrower's personal residence as collateral for the loan. If a mortgage is delinquent, a lender would not be interested in a second mortgage that might at some point require him to step in and cure the first mortgage in order to protect his own interests. Any mortgage that is past due is considered a bad reference. If the delinquency is due to explainable temporary circumstances, however, and if the mortgage is usually paid on time, the delinquency might be overlooked.

Installment loans, which are usually for personal goods or automobiles, come next on the credit reference list. Credit cards are a more abused form of credit; some slowness is common, and an account 30 or 60 days past due would not necessarily disqualify a loan if mortgages and larger obligations were paid as agreed. Bills for services rendered, such as from doctors or tradesmen, do not reflect on term and installment decisions. This does not mean that certain kinds of credit are not important—any weakness in your past credit performance is a reflection on your future creditworthiness. However, if there are weaknesses in your credit record, those weaknesses will most affect your chances for loan approval if they involve your service of mortgages or other large installment obligations.

It is now often possible for individuals to examine their credit standing at the large credit rating bureaus. Before applying for a large loan, it's often a good idea to do this and to correct any erroneous information that may have become part of your file. A typical credit report will list basic information about the individual, followed by the names of each of his creditors, the date on which credit was established with them, the maximum amount of that credit, the current outstanding balance, and the rating of the account. A rating of CURR (for current), AA (as agreed), or EX (excellent) is highly desirable. Other acceptable terms are very good, satisfactory, or good. An indication of 30 days (meaning it takes that long to pay your obligations) would be a problem if applied to a mortgage, but less so if applied to a department store account. Indications of 60 days or 90 days would be a greater cause of concern, and so would the word *collection*, showing that your account had been turned over to a collection agency due to your nonpayment.

When a small business has established a track record of its own, the credit performance of the business will be taken into account along with that of the principals. Better Business Bureau reports can help to establish the viability of the business and its products, while reports from Dun & Bradstreet can provide basic financial and credit data.

Accounts payable are another important credit indicator. If they are not being satisfied according to terms (usually 30 to 60 days), or if they are growing in relation to the size of the business, the creditworthiness of the business is open to question. Accounts receivable are usually given similar scrutiny. Without the cash generated by collection of receivables, a business may have trouble meeting its obligations. If those receivables remain outstanding longer than the normal 30 to 60 days, or if they grow too large in relation to the business, the company's creditworthiness is again in doubt.

Collateral

Loans to small and growing businesses are, for the most part, risky loans. For every reason imaginable, a proportion of new and expanding businesses fail. As a result, finance companies rarely make business loans on an unsecured basis. The required collateral can consist of the assets of the business—inventory, plant and equipment, or receivables—or it can consist of real estate, either owned by the business itself or by the owners of the business. In either case, the key question for the lender is liquidity: If the business goes bad, can the collateral be readily liquidated to pay off the loan?

Inventories. When inventories are used as collateral for a loan, a specified current inventory is secured; as portions of that inventory are sold, the loan must be reduced by an amount equal to the cost of the units sold. For example, a $50,000 loan is secured by 10 lots of men's suits. Each lot contains 50 suits and has a cost value of $5,000. The manufacturer sells four lots of suits, with a cost value of $20,000 (presumably, the sale generates additional revenue beyond that cost figure). On completion of the sale, the manufacturer pays $20,000 to the lender and reduces the principal amount of the loan to $30,000. This doesn't take interest charges into consideration—they are discussed elsewhere.

Inventories used as collateral are viewed in terms of their liquidation value. There are three generally accepted types of liquidation. First is "under the hammer" liquidation, which means that the passage of time would seriously reduce the value of the collateral (e.g., swimsuits). Second is orderly liquidation, which normally takes place within a six-month period (e.g., electronic equipment). Third is in-place liquidation, in which the inventory is included in the sale of the business (e.g., furniture manufacturing). Each of these forms of liquidation implies a different value for the inventory in question. (Alternatively, in classic management text analysis, finished goods are the most desirable inventory collateral, work-in-progress is the least desirable, and raw materials the most widely variable, depending on their nature).

Plant and Equipment. Machinery and office equipment can be used as collateral for a business loan. Their value is established in part by an extensive valuation performed by a qualified appraiser. Depreciation and useful life are taken into account when determining the value of such assets, but the single most important factor is liquidation value. Liquidation is defined as the worth of security under stress conditions (or, in layman's terms, How much can you get for it if you have to sell in a hurry?). This type of financing is secured by a security agreement and by forms called UCC-1s, which provide detailed descriptions of each item, right down to the serial number.

Receivables. Financing based on receivables involves a complete audit of all customer accounts by a representative of the lender. This analysis includes a check of the financial condition of the customer. A lock box arrangement is normally established with a local bank, to provide the lender with control of incoming receivables. Receivables-based financing normally carries a higher rate of interest than other asset-based financing. This is not due to the risk so much as it is to the amount of service that is required for the lender to handle the account.

This form of financing could comprise either a direct loan or a line of credit. The line of credit, in which portions of the maximum sum approved are taken by the borrower as needed, will usually carry a slightly higher interest rate (due to higher bookkeeping charges), but may still be less expensive to the borrower in terms of total cost. For example, a $100,000 loan at 10 percent for 90 days would cost the borrower $2,500 in interest. But a $100,000 line of credit, with an interest rate of 11 percent, and an average daily balance of $90,000 for the same 90 days, would cost the borrower $2,475 in interest. The point of this exercise is that a businessman borrowing against receivables should consider the nature and timing of his cash flows before deciding which form of financing to employ.

Other types of collateral are stocks and bonds, certificates of deposit, savings accounts, and other securities of a readily negotiable or redeemable nature. These assets are virtually equivalent to cash, and loans are usually made for up to 90 percent of their face value. This formula allows for accrued interest and the legal fees and other costs associated with collection if the loan falls into default. This type of loan is not frequently submitted to a finance company, since these assets are usually highly acceptable to a bank as security for a loan.

Real Estate. The primary collateral used by finance companies is real estate. Its value is readily quantifiable, and it is not subject to erosion if the business itself is poorly managed. It also does not require an ongoing relationship, such as checking or savings accounts, and does not require audits of inventory, monitoring of receivables, or the like.

The types of real estate that are normally eligible for use as collateral include: residential buildings, both owner-occupied and nonowner occupied; income-producing properties, such as duplexes, apartment houses, office buildings, and shopping centers; and commercial retail buildings, which are highly marketable if located in good commercial areas.

Less desirable are: single purpose properties, such as gasoline stations and hospitals (though these examples have acquired additional marketability recently through transformation to convenience stores and nursing homes, respectively); industrial and manufacturing properties, because they are usually built to the specifications of a single type of business, which limits their resalability; and vacant land, which requires additional money for improvements if resale is necessary.

A piece of real estate is never collateralized at its full market value. A series of formulas known as Lendable Equity Formulas are used to determine how much money can be lent against any one piece of property. The following are the most common of these formulas:

- For residential, owner-occupied property, the percentage is 80 percent of the appraised fair market value, up to a maximum appraised value of $200,000, less the first mortgage balance. Thus, a house appraised at $100,000 would have a maximum loan value of $80,000. If the first mortgage balance was $40,000, the lendable equity would be $40,000.
- For residential, owner-occupied property with an appraised value between $200,000 and $500,000, the percentage drops to 75 percent in determining the maximum loan value, and to 70 percent for residential property with an appraised value in excess of $500,000. Once again, the first mortgage balance must be subtracted to determine the actual lendable equity.

- For residential property that is not owner occupied, the percentages used to determine maximum loan value drops by 5 percent in each bracket, to 75 percent on property appraised at $200,000 and below, 70 percent on property appraised between $200,001 and $500,000, and 65 percent on property appraised above $500,000. As before, the first mortgage balance must be subtracted to arrive at the lendable equity.

Cash

The third of the finance company Cs is cash, or more broadly, expected cash flow generation needed to service the loan. No matter what a borrower's past credit history, and no matter how solid his collateral, if the cash flow isn't there, the loan is not going to be repaid without foreclosure. All this does not prevent finance companies from seeing their share of true Pollyannas—borrowers who won't be able to meet their interest payments even if their own personal projections all come true.

Business borrowers coming to a finance company in search of capital should bring with them several pertinent documents: balance sheets, income statements, and cash flow statements for the business for the past three to five years; financial projections for the business for the life of the loan being sought; and income tax returns for the business for the last three to five years—and for the owners as well, if their income, assets, or net worth will be required to secure the loan. Granted, businesses that are seeking start-up capital, and those in their first year or two of operation, will not have all of these materials. Nevertheless, it is important to provide the lender with as much relevant documentation as possible. Note also that the less documentation that exists for the business, the more documentation will be required for the individuals behind the business, since it will be their income and assets that will create the basis for the loan if it cannot be supported on pure business data.

When examining the balance sheet of an applicant business, finance company analysts generally look first to what is called the "acid test" ratio. It is a fundamental barometer of a business' ability to pay its bills. The business' cash and current accounts receivable are added together, and the total is divided by current liabilities. Other current assets, such as inventories, are excluded, since it might take a considerable period of time to convert them to cash, and the purpose of the test is to determine if the business could pay its bills within 30 days from its existing resources. (This is not a perfect test: Knowing that his business was facing disaster, an unscrupulous businessman could convert these highly liquid assets to cash and then divert the cash to purposes other than paying off current liabilities.)

Many finance companies require an acid test ratio of 1.2:1 or greater in order to approve a loan. In some cases, a lending institution's policies will require a higher ratio, such as 1.5:1. At the other extreme, it is extremely rare for a lender to consider a loan when the acid test ratio is less than 1:1. Exhibit 1 shows two examples of acid test ratios:

EXHIBIT 1 Acceptable and Unacceptable Acid Test Ratios

	Acceptable	*Unacceptable*
Cash (in bank)	$ 20,000	$ 20,000
Current receivables	190,000	190,000
Total current assets	210,000	210,000
Current liabilities	170,000	240,000
Excess/(deficit)	$ 40,000	$ (30,000)
Acid test ratio	1.2:1	0.9:1

This test carries a lot of weight in short-term financing, which tends to increase current liabilities. The owner of a company could argue that he must use all his cash to increase inventories, thereby generating sales revenue and ultimately profit. But if his cash will not support his short-term obligations, he may never reach the point of seeing those profits.

A second key yardstick examined by finance company analysts is working capital—the difference between current assets (cash and equivalents, receivables and inventories) and current liabilities. This is the money that the business has available for its operation and growth. All too often, new and struggling businesses fail because their working capital is inadequate for their needs.

The ability of an individual or a sole proprietorship to service debt is normally substantiated by Schedule C of current federal income tax returns, coupled with personal or business financial statements. The acid test can be applied. However, when dealing with individuals, net income is often given more weight than an acid test ratio.

Business properties, or income-producing properties, usually show cash available on Schedule E of their current federal income tax returns. This figure can be substantiated by an appraisal of the company ledger, which would show rentals and expenses. Exhibit 2 shows an example that would be an acceptable substantiation of ability to service debt:

EXHIBIT 2 Income-Producing Property with Adequate Cash Available

Gross income	$50,000
Vacancy factor (5 percent)	2,500
Effective gross income (EGI)	47,500
Expenses	21,000
Net operating income (NOI)	26,500
First mortgage	9,500
Second mortgage	8,000
Acid test ratio	1.2:1

Gross income is all rents, income, and other charges. Vacancy factor varies from place to place and can be supplied by local realtors or appraisers. Expenses include all costs related to operation of the property (the type of lease can be important here). NOI is the residue of money remaining to service financial obligations and provide profit to the owners. To determine the ratio, add operating expenses to mortgage service costs, and divide that total into the EGI. In this case:

$$\$21{,}000 + \$9{,}500 + \$8{,}000 = \$38{,}500$$

That sum divided into $47,500 yields 1.23, a ratio sufficient to justify consideration of the loan.

Negative incomes or ratios below the minimum of 1.1:1 can be waived if a statement is submitted showing that the individuals involved will realize compensating tax advantages. For example, individuals in the 50 percent tax bracket may be able to reduce tax liability by showing a loss in rental properties.

The last and hardest substantiation is the pro forma profit and loss statement, which is a projection of the business's expected results after receiving the loan for which it is applying. The borrower would not be applying for the loan unless he were convinced his venture would succeed; therefore, his projections are bound to be positive. There are scores of factors that analysts look for when examining pro forma projections, but the single overriding theme is this: Are these projections realistic? Can they be achieved? If they are too grandiose, they are going to be reviewed unfavorably, and the loan's chances of approval will diminish correspondingly.

Competence

If a borrower's projections are realistic, that is still no guarantee that he is capable of making them come true. One of the many judgment factors in lending is the assessment of management competence. If the business has been in existence for some time, its actual performance over a three- to five-year period will provide a good indication of the job its managers can be expected to do in the future.

When a business is just starting up, or when it is in its first year of operation, there is no suitable track record to scrutinize. Instead, the track record of the owner/managers must be examined. In general, a loan applicant who wants to start a new business should be able to show that he has three to five years of experience in a managerial role in a similar business, and that he has been successful in that role.

Once a loan has been made, particularly to a new or expanding business, most finance companies will make periodic reviews of the financial condition of the business. If trouble is brewing, the time to head it off is early—not when it becomes so severe that the business cannot meet its payment schedule.

These financial reviews will focus on liquidity and the operating factors that contribute to it. Here, the extensive experience that finance companies have with small businesses can be valuable to a borrower, because the reviewer may be able to spot warning signs that have indicated future problems in many other, similar situations. Staff may be too high; inventories may be out of line with sales; collection of receivables may be too slow—these and many other problems can be identified (and remedies suggested) by an effective finance company situation review.

TYPICAL FINANCE COMPANY BUSINESS LOANS

From the finance company viewpoint, business loans can be made to corporations, to partnerships, or to individuals, and in varying forms within each of these categories. Each type of borrower requires different documentation in order to complete the loan. The following examples will serve to illustrate both the kinds of business loans that a finance company will make, and also the documents involved.

Corporation Loans

A loan to a corporation normally involves these documents: a promissory note, a standard document that sets forth terms, interest rates, prepayment penalties or premiums, legal remedies, and so on, in accordance with state law; an affidavit of business use, in which the president and secretary of the corporation state that the loan proceeds are to be used for the business purposes of the corporation; a corporate resolution to borrow, or loan resolution, which authorizes certain individuals to borrow money on behalf of the corporation and certifies that the resolution is in accordance with the bylaws of the corporation; and a continuing absolute unconditional guarantee of payment, in which individuals (usually the owners) guarantee that the corporation's obligations will be met, using their own assets and income as security, if necessary. Other documentation is related to the specific nature of the loan transaction and could include mortgages, real estate security agreements, and UCC-1s encumbering tangible assets such as machinery. Three examples follow:

Example 1. An individual formed a corporation to purchase a local strip shopping center in Pennsylvania. The purchase price of $350,000 represented a distress price, since the previous owner had failed to maintain the center and vacancies were high. The new owner spent a year upgrading the property and built occupancy up to 95 percent, attracting a state agency, a department store, and an Italian restaurant as new tenants. The short-term bank loans that had financed the improvements came due, and the corporation sought to restructure its finances so that rental income would service the debt. The physical improvements and higher rental income justified a $425,000 loan.

Example 2. A husband and wife contracted to purchase a restaurant in Philadelphia. Since a liquor license was to be pledged for security, and a Pennsylvania liquor license is deemed a privilege that cannot be encumbered, the couple formed a corporation to operate the business. The couple, as individuals, owned the property and derived rent from the corporation. As officers of the corporation, they also signed an undated resignation and corporate stock pledge agreement. This would have made it possible for the lender to take over and operate the corporation in the event of a default, while waiting for the liquor license situation to be resolved. Additional real estate security was pledged to make possible a loan of $250,000.

Example 3. A Subchapter S corporation in New Jersey sought $180,000 to purchase inventory at off-season discount rates. But there were no receivables available for security and the firm's financial statements were not acceptable to local bank financing. A finance company made the loan, using a first mortgage position on the commercial property owned by the individuals who owned the Subchapter S corporation.

Partnership Loans

Partnership agreements are so incredibly varied in their provisions that it is very difficult to generalize about either the nature of the partnerships or the loan agreements made to them. The documentation involved in a partnership loan will certainly include a promissory note, an affidavit of business use, and a continuing guarantee, as did the corporation loan mentioned earlier. In addition, there will be additional information patterned to the specific nature of the partnership and to the specific loan transaction.

The promissory note will be executed by the general partner on behalf of the limited partners, in the case of a limited partnership, or by all the partners, if all share responsibility for the partnership. For this reason, it is essential that the complete partnership agreement accompany all loan requests.

Many partnerships that seek finance company business loans involve real estate holdings. Though the individual partners may have substantial net worth, the assets of the partnerships are normally limited to the investment, and a mortgage is thus required to secure an equity position in the real estate for the lender. Most mortgages are standard in form and can be interchanged between corporations, partnerships, and individuals, so that further explanation is not needed here.

A rent roll reflecting all current tenant rentals (plus copies of leases) is also important, since rental income must service the loan and since real estate financing can also involve an assignment of rents. This assignment can be either conditional or unconditional. The former is preferable, since a default on the part of the borrower is necessary before the lender can take control of rent collection. Conversely, in the case of an unconditional assignment, the borrower can lose control of rent collection even when no default is involved. This means more expense for the lender (and thus more cost to the borrower) as well as possible loss of management control of the borrower's operations.

Sole Proprietorship Loans

Here, again, the basic documentation remains the same—a promissory note, an affidavit of business use, a continuing guarantee, and, in most cases, a mortgage securing an interest in the borrowers' business or residential real estate. The first three documents here are essentially similar to those employed in the case of a corporation.

Example 1. A franchise store operated by a husband and wife needed to renovate its building and update its fixtures in order to meet the terms of the franchise, at a cost of $75,000. A second mortgage on the couple's home enabled the loan to be approved.

Example 2. A husband and wife needed $165,000 to complete the purchase of an apartment complex they had bought three years ago under a lease agreement. Schedule E of their income tax returns showed that since the purchase, they had upgraded appliances and fixtures and completed all deferred maintenance that had been neglected by the previous owner. The complex had a live-in manager and most tenants had lived there for several years. An analysis of the rent rolls showed sufficient income was generated to pay all operating expenses and mortgage payments. The loan was granted, using a first mortgage on the complex, coupled with a conditional assignment of rents and a security agreement perfected by a UCC-1.

Individual Loans

This type of loan usually parallels the sole proprietorship loan, with the proceeds often used for start-up or expansion situations. This is a risky loan, and one that finance companies are more likely to take on than banks. Because the risk factor is high, higher interest rates are often applicable.

Example. An individual owned and operated an economy store in a small town for 35 years. The store depended on steelworker trade, and when the steel industry went into recession, the owner was forced to obtain short-term loans from several financial institutions. To consolidate those loans and to create a payment schedule that her store could support, a finance company extended to her a $15,000 loan, secured by a security agreement and UCC-1 on inventory and equipment, along with a personal guarantee backed by a mortgage on the store property.

Construction Loans

These are short-term commitments, designed to finance construction of business property and to be paid in full when construction is complete and the business is in operation. They can be made to corporations, partnerships, sole proprietorships, or individuals, and they are good, profitable loans in today's marketplace.

In addition to the basic documents required by other types of loan (promissory note, mortgage, assignment of rents, security agreement, UCC-1, corporate resolution, and continuing guarantee), several other documents are necessitated by the specific nature of this loan.

A building loan agreement sets forth the terms of the loan, including the size, timing, and conditions of disbursements and repayments. The first disbursement is usually made when all documents have been submitted or executed, and subsequent disbursements occur as specific milestones in the construction process are reached. This agreement spells out in some detail what the borrowers and their contractors and suppliers can, cannot, and must do in the course of construction, as well as what will occur if default takes place during construction. Also included is a construction cost control, including an approved budget.

A construction mortgage and an assignment of rents are combined into a single document, providing the lender with the protection of an equity interest in the real estate and rental income to service the loan. An architect's consent and agreement specifies that no material changes in the building will be made from the approved plans without the lender's consent, and that the architect will notify the lender if he finds any deviations from those plans as construction proceeds. A contractor's consent and agreement parallels the architect's consent, but also states that the contractor will use the disbursements to actually build the building, as agreed.

The final document, no less important than its predecessors, is a loan commitment. Since the construction loan is designed to be repaid when the building is complete, the borrower will need funds with which to repay the loan. (On the other hand, with the building completed, he will then have a tangible asset against which he can borrow.) The loan commitment can come from the construction lender, or from any other lender, and will normally be mortgage backed.

Example. Two brothers successfully operated a Chinese restaurant for 10 years under a lease agreement. But rentals rose sharply, and the business began to outgrow its quarters. There were no suitable buildings in the immediate area, so the brothers decided to purchase an adjacent parcel of land and build their own, larger restaurant. To augment their income, they decided to add two retail spaces adjoining the restaurant. The entire cost of construction was estimated to be $600,000, including satisfaction of a first mortgage on the parcel of land. The down payment necessary to satisfy the lender's requirements was 25 percent, or $150,000, which the brothers covered by executing second mortgages on their personal residences.

Real Estate Syndications

Syndication financings have become popular in the last 20 years, in large measure because of their tax shelter aspects. There are numerous forms of syndication but, in general, finance companies limit themselves to real estate syndications. Whenever a financial institution provides funds to a limited partnership for real estate that is being syndicated, the key is to be sure that the property being acquired is not overvalued. This is important, because the limited partners are primarily investing for tax advantages and not for real estate ownership. Once it has been determined that the purchase price is in line with real value of the property, normal loan-to-value ratios can be applied to a syndicated property.

In addition to the normal loan documentation (such as promissory note, affidavit of business use, continuing guarantee, and copies of partnership agreements), the syndication aspect of the transaction will require an agreement, a tax opinion, pro forma financial statements, compliance and shelter information, appraisals of the property, and good standing and lien certificates on the corporate general partner.

Example 1. An attorney practicing in a state capital had the opportunity to purchase an office building in a suburban area for a price of $2 million. An assumable first mortgage made through a local industrial authority was in place in the amount of $1 million. Because of the equity building on the property, and to take advantage of the assumable first mortgage at a low rate, an additional $1 million of capital was needed to effect the purchase. Since the attorney did not have that amount of capital available (and would not have wanted to invest it all in one property if it had been available), he formed a limited partnership of 20 investors, who put up $25,000 apiece to raise $500,000, or 25 percent of the purchase price. He therefore needed an additional $500,000 to buy out the equity building, which was acquired in the secondary market from a financial institution. Because of the equity contributions of the investors and the rental income available from the building's tenancy, a finance company was willing to loan the $500,000, secured by a second mortgage on the property. The total encumbrance-to-value was 75 percent of the purchase price, which is an acceptable leverage factor for this type of financing.

Example 2. A group of chefs needed $1 million to purchase a dilapidated waterfront restaurant in New York. The chefs were world renowned, but they had limited capital to invest. A limited partnership was therefore formed through a local attorney, and a local "money broker" was enlisted to obtain financing. A total of 10 investors were found to put up a total of $1 million in the form of notes, guarantees, and letters of credit. At this point, all the ingredients were available, except that the money was not in cash. The money broker therefore prepared a package of financial information on the project and the investors and submitted it to an insurance company with an A+ rating from A. M. Best Co. After careful review, the insurance company agreed to insure the individuals. The insurance company issued a policy guaranteeing principal and interest, and a finance company purchased the investor's notes, backed by a surety bond, from the limited partnership.

Participation Loans

A participation loan is nothing more than a loan that involves several different lenders. Any of the loans discussed up to this point can be structured as participation loans. They are important as a loan category because today's financial market is seeing far larger loan requests than it did in the past. Since banks and other lending institutions have limits placed on their lending, either by regulation or by internal policy, larger loans would have to be declined, regardless of their quality, if other participants could not be found.

The only additional documentation for a participation loan, other than that mentioned earlier, is a participation agreement between the lead financial institution and the other participants. This agreement establishes the relationship between the various participants, including the principal amount that each will provide and the resultant payments that each will receive. The lead lender is usually the original financial institution contacted by the borrowers; in most cases, the lead lender takes the largest portion of the loan and handles the servicing of the loan.

Example. A movie theatre chain was in need of $14 million for expansion and also wanted to consolidate $10 million in existing mortgages. The finance company originally contacted was interested in the loan, but company policy prevented it from loaning more than $9 million. It therefore contacted other lenders and was able to bring two local banks, one savings and loan, and two other financial institutions into the project, allowing the lead financial institution to approve the request.

FINANCE COMPANY TERMS AND INTEREST RATES

In recent years, the American consumer has become accustomed to easy comparison of various financing alternatives as a result of consumer lending laws that require disclosure of actual APRs (annual percentage rates), which reflect finance charges that are associated with consumer loans. Veteran business borrowers have long performed a similar calculation through the use of discounting to compare various cash flows. But for the individual just venturing into the business loan arena for the first time, caution is in order. APR disclosure generally is not required for business loans, and it may take some work to figure out and compare the actual cost of various financing alternatives.

For example, a 25-year loan with a nominal interest rate of 10 percent and a term of 25 years with a 5-year call (balloon payment) might also carry an origination fee of three points. This would increase the yield to the lender to 10.8 percent (the general rule of thumb is that one point equals 0.25 percent added to the interest rate on loans with a balloon payment of 5 years and an amortization period of 15 to 25 years).

Term or amortization is another consideration that reflects on the desirability of a loan. A borrower should be careful here, since an increase in the term of the loan may not always be best for the borrower. Consider, as an example, a $50,000 loan with an interest rate of 12.5 percent. Should the borrower opt for a term of 20, 25, or 30 years? The monthly payments would be, respectively, $568.07, $548.18, and $533.63. But the total finance charges over the life of the loan would be, respectively, $86,336.87, $113,553.12, and $142,106.40.

The moral of this comparison: If the small difference in monthly payments genuinely makes a difference to the health or survival of the business, then a longer term loan should be chosen. If not, then it may well serve the business best to select the shorter term loan. (Note also that these figures are based on fully-amortized loans. However, the balloon payment is considerably higher in longer amortizations, which would have an adverse effect at the time of expiration.)

Finance companies in general charge floating rates, but will often offer fixed rates as well. A fixed rate ranging from 3 to 6 percent above the prime rate or bank reference rate is ordinary and should not be construed as high. Fixed rates are generally higher than floating rates, but they do have the value of constancy and predictability, which can be meaningful to some borrowers, particularly those whose budgets allow little margin for error or adjustment to change.

Floating rates can be applied to all kinds of loans. The three basic formats used by finance companies are (1) the revolving commercial loan, (2) the closed-end commercial loan, and (3) the construction loan. All three carry interest rates tied to the prime, or bank reference, rate. A construction loan will usually be based on a rate 2 percent above the reference rate, while a closed-end commercial loan will carry a rate 1.5 to 5 percent above the reference rate.

These reference rates fluctuate constantly in accordance with changes in the demand and supply of money. They can be adjusted daily, weekly, monthly, quarterly, or yearly, with quarterly adjustment as the most common formulation. The adjustment is within limits, though—most loans have a floor and a ceiling (the lowest and highest rates that can be used in calculation of the applicable interest rate).

A FINAL NOTE

Finance companies are, in one sense, a lot like gophers. Those creatures lead risky lives and, as a result, spend huge amounts of time digging escape tunnels from their burrows. But unless they are threatened, they always enter and leave through the visible "front door" to their burrow.

Similarly, finance companies operate at the risky end of the lending spectrum. When they make a loan, they build in a lot of protection for themselves, just in case the risk turns sour on them. But they, too, would rather go in and out through the front door. Their profit, in the end, comes from making successful loans. That's why, for the right borrower, they are a valuable source of capital for today's small, growing businesses.

CHAPTER **16**

Real Estate Financing

INTRODUCTION
BORROWER/USER VERSUS LENDER/PROVIDER
COMPETITIVE MARKET FACTORS
COMMERCIAL BANKS
  Construction/Development Loans
  Business Loans
  Residential Loans
  Mortgage Warehouse Loans
SAVINGS AND LOAN ASSOCIATIONS
  Regulatory Changes
  Land Acquisition and Construction Loans
  Direct Joint Ventures
  Direct Development and Syndications
  Other Approaches
LIFE INSURANCE COMPANIES
  Changing to Short-Term Commitments
  Equity Participation
PENSION FUNDS
  Commingled Funds
REAL ESTATE INVESTMENT TRUSTS
FOREIGN INVESTORS
SELLER FINANCING
MORTGAGE COMPANIES
SALE/LEASEBACKS
SUMMARY
REFERENCES

Frederick Blumberg
Partner
Pepper, Hamilton & Scheetz
Philadelphia, Pa.

Frederick Blumberg is a partner in the firm Pepper, Hamilton & Scheetz, and heads the firm's national real estate group. He has been engaged in the private practice of real estate law for over 30 years and has represented numerous developers, builders, syndicators, lenders, landlords, and major space users. He is a graduate of Cornell University and Harvard Law School.

Jack E. Salmon
Manager
Arthur Andersen & Co.
Philadelphia, Pa.

Jack E. Salmon is an experienced real estate consultant in the Philadelphia Office of Arthur Andersen & Co. Since joining the firm in 1976, he has specialized in accounting and audit consulting services to a variety of real estate clients. His clients include nationally known developers, syndicators, property managers, and an REIT. He has significant SEC experience and has been active in prospective financial statements and limited partnership offerings.

Mr. Salmon has developed several training seminars within the firm pertaining to real estate. He graduated from Pennsylvania State University. Mr. Salmon is a CPA and an active member of the AICPA, PICPA, National Association of Accountants, Real Estate Securities and Syndication Institute, and other civic groups.

INTRODUCTION

Raising capital in the current real estate industry involves traditional and creative financing techniques. A real estate transaction results from an exchange of economic resources between a seller, a buyer, and, usually, a financial entity. Numerous variations can occur depending on each participant's objectives. At times a seller may provide financing as a means of realizing an ongoing economic return in excess of the gain on sale during tight money markets, or to facilitate a transaction when third-party financing is not readily available at reasonable rates. The buyer may intend to occupy, hold for appreciation, or lease back the property to the seller. The financing party may also have an ownership or profit sharing interest in the property. The financing entities may be commercial banks, savings and loan associations, pension funds, or life insurance companies. The funds may be raised through mortgages, sale/leasebacks, joint ventures, partnerships, or real estate investment trusts. The variety of entities and objectives creates the opportunity for diverse methods of raising capital.

BORROWER/USER VERSUS LENDER/PROVIDER

The following discussion will explain how to take advantage of real estate as both a resource and a target for raising capital. Two perspectives will serve as a framework—the borrower/user and the lender/provider of capital. The borrower/user is product oriented as owner, lessor, trustee, developer, syndicator, or property manager. Borrowers desire control of the project and seek economic reward through appreciation, cash flow, tax benefits, and management. They take the ownership risk, especially in highly leveraged positions that require minimal levels of owner's capital. For example, a syndicator has a low degree of financial capital at risk in a leveraged real estate limited partnership funded by investors' capital contributions. However, the syndicator usually receives a disproportionate share of the cash gain on sale or refinancing.

A lender/provider delivers a service and participates in real estate in a manner that protects against the downside risk of direct ownership, especially by lending, in most instances, no more than 80 percent of the value of the real estate taken as security. Lenders expect an immediate economic return relative to their financial risk position. Real estate typically holds its value or increases in value, thereby minimizing the lender's risk of losing capital. If the lender can also share in the long-term appreciation from a gain on sale, it has achieved a win/win situation—current market rates of return and the long-term upside participation/reward. The equity kicker and shared appreciation mortgage are two examples of this concept. However, in those instances, the lender is usually advancing more than 80 percent of the value of the real estate and is therefore assuming a higher than usual risk.

COMPETITIVE MARKET FACTORS

Success in today's highly competitive real estate market requires a good understanding of the competitive market positions of industry participants. As with most industries, real estate has historical cyclical trends. An overall trend is that real estate will hold or appreciate in value over time, given that it is a limited resource.

A useful framework for understanding real estate financing is the product life cycle. Real estate lending differs depending on which segment best reflects the current status of the project. The three segments are (1) acquisition, development, or improvement financing; (2) construction financing; and (3) permanent financing. The inherent risk characteristics are different in each segment and the sources of capital vary accordingly.

Successful financing strategies have anticipated the investment goals of equity and financial participants in advance of their broad acceptance. Participating as an equity partner has been a key step in this process.

The construction industry has experienced shorter cycles of investment favor. This phase of real estate financing is recognized today as the most complex and risky in the development process. No one wants to merely warehouse land, even if it is improved with roads and necessary utilities. It is still nonincome producing and hence creates a negative return in the short run. Construction lending was relatively risk free in the early 1960s as the general U.S. economy was in a period of strong growth, labor was relatively inexpensive, market demand for new construction was high, and interest rates were stable. This changed as the economy softened, but was primarily affected by an ever-increasing cost of labor. Construction projects became a more risky investment for lenders. The result was a continuing shrinkage in new construction activity. One outcome was the emphasis on smaller housing, such as apartments followed by condominiums. Another outcome was the shift to commercial and industrial development as opposed to residential development, which led to rehabilitation of existing structures as opposed to new construction. During these changes, construction lenders became familiar with participation in the development activity via equity kickers.

The allure of equity participation in real estate for small investors helped foster the birth of the real estate investment trust, or REIT. REITs were established in 1960 as a result of changes in the tax laws. They provide an opportunity for investors in public and private trusts to participate in the equity returns of real estate, including cash flow and appreciation. This investor interest spurred construction activity at a rate greater than the demand for commercial, industrial, and residential real estate. As interest rates rose in the early 1970s, the highly leveraged REITs, especially the mortgage REITs, became increasingly susceptible to a negative spread between their investment or interest income and their debt service and dividend requirements. The mortgage REITs were, in many instances, receiving fixed interest income while their debt service cost was escalating based on a spiral increase in the prime rate. At first, dividends suffered, and, thereafter, such an economic squeeze led to a near collapse of the mortgage REIT industry. Coupled with the effects of the oil crisis on the economy in the mid 1970s, construction activity in office buildings, especially in the Sun Belt area, went through several boom and bust cycles in a short period of time. This overcrowding of existing projects resulted in an opportunity for the next wave of real estate financing through joint venture participation projects by institutional investors.

The institutional investors had the staying power to weather the cyclical booms and busts in construction activity. They purchased real estate at reasonable prices and generated a steady earnings stream from operating quality real estate. Many institutional investors were able to create secondary earnings streams as a result of creative financing techniques, such as sale/leaseback, participation mortgages, and joint venture participations in real estate. Similarly to the construction industry, real estate investors had the safety net of continuing inflation, which assured such institutions that they would recapture their initial capital investment.

By the early 1980s, the market was primed for another style of real estate investment. This change was also predicated by repetitive changes in the tax law to accelerate deductibility of depreciation and to encourage investment in real estate. Tax shelters through limited partnerships became big business. Public syndicators attracted upwards of $4 billion annually in real estate capital. The private syndication market was a multiple of two or three times that much as a result of investors looking for the "two-to-one" (ratio of tax deductions to cash investment) or even greater tax shelter.

The limited partnership structure has many advantages in raising equity. It permits a large number of investors to invest relatively small amounts of capital in significant real estate without the risk of personal liability. This structure results in tax benefits of depreciation and the conversion of ordinary income into capital gains at a much lower marginal tax rate. Most importantly, the limited partnership can obtain a high level of financial leverage by pledging the partnership interest and underlying assets as collateral for a loan. An objective is for this debt to be nonrecourse, since it is then includable in the partner's basis for determining tax losses: hence, the ability to deduct more than the cash investment of a limited partner. The privately syndicated partnerships have the added advantage of having the equity funded in stages, typically over 3 to 5 years, to further minimize the after-tax cash invested.

During this period, real estate values were bid up dramatically as syndications were being formed overnight to purchase and resell real estate to a hungry investment community. The economics of real estate acquisition, management, and disposition became very strained. Several high-flying investment portfolios may yet suffer as a result of the overpayments by purchasers of real estate during this period, coupled with high leverage. The threat of tax law changes has dampened the marketability of public and private syndication programs. Hopefully, the age-old adage that real estate will continue to go up in value over time still holds true for the thousands of investors who currently participate as limited partners in real estate shelter programs. Even if many of the tax proposals that are detrimental to tax shelters are enacted, decreased construction activity could increase the demand for existing real estate, thereby increasing the value of existing equity investments.

Where do we go from here? Since it is likely that history will repeat itself, it is not implausible to reconsider the real estate financing techniques started in the early 1960s as precursors of the next techniques. Some of the signs are already there. For example, the REIT industry is making a rebound, and new REITs are emerging at a record pace. This format may prove to validate the original concept of equity participation by individual investors. The hybrid REITs and finite life REITs of today, however, have benefited from the lesson of the equity REITs of the 1970s. They now participate on upside appreciation and have variable returns based on interest rate changes in the debt markets. It seems likely that the industry will rebound since several early REITs survived even in the down times because of good management and proper analysis of real estate trends. Moreover, the concept of a finite-life REIT cures certain structural defects in marketing of an equity REIT. A finite-life REIT must be liquidated within a predictable range of years. This has resulted in these REITs selling at a small or no discount from the value of the underlying real estate. This eliminates a real flaw in that industry and should protect investors from the arbitrageurs that preyed on REITs with undervalued securities. Many REITs are having their securities listed on national exchanges, thereby making these investments readily salable, which is rarely the case with limited partnership interests.

An important question in today's real estate market is, Whose money are we using to acquire, hold, develop, and generate an economic return on real estate? Most real estate experts agree that financial leverage is the key determinant to achieving success in real estate. This means using "other people's money" but retaining a participation in the appreciation of the real estate. This permits participants to obtain the highest rate of return for their efforts. However, some participants firmly believe that by investing their own capital, they are more diligent and, accordingly, more responsive and therefore more likely to achieve success. Even developers and property managers can readily appreciate the advantage of investing money in a transaction in return for services and fees generated through acquisition, development, and management of real estate held for their own account. Additionally, the relationship between the nominal and real cost of debt and the expected yield on the property must be considered.

Given the competing factors of risk and reward, it is helpful to understand how certain financial concepts affect decision making. Both borrower and lender need to measure the economic aspects of operational real estate. Two common concepts—leverage and internal rate of return—are described below. To illustrate the effects of leverage on an investor, consider the following facts and the example shown in Exhibit 1:

Purchase price:	$2,000,000
Land allocation:	10% (nondepreciable asset)
Depreciation period:	18 years
Marginal tax rate:	50%
Interest rate:	10%
Yield through rental income:	12%

EXHIBIT 1 Annual After-Tax Cash Effects

	(A) Without Leverage	*(B) With 50 Percent Leverage*	*(C) With 90 Percent Leverage*
Investment	$2,000,000	$2,000,000	$2,000,000
Loan	–0–	1,000,000	1,800,000
Net cash invested	$2,000,000	$1,000,000	$ 200,000

If we assume that any unused cash can be reinvested at 8 percent tax free, the taxable income and cash effect of leveraging are as shown in Exhibit 2.

Regardless of whose money is used in making the investment in real estate, and whether there is leverage or not, most participants would agree that they are seeking economic reward. Economic reward is typically measured by internal rates of return on a pre-tax and after-tax basis. Exhibit 3 is an example of an internal rate of return calculation, using the same purchasing facts as in Exhibits 1 and 2.

This example demonstrates how an investor can evaluate an investment in comparison to alternate investments. It also reflects the

EXHIBIT 2 Taxable Income and Cash Effects of Leveraging

	A *Without leverage*	B *With 50 Percent Leverage*	C *With 90 Percent Leverage*
Interest income (tax free)	$ -0-	$ 80,000	$ 144,000
Interest expense	-0-	(100,000)	(180,000)
Depreciation expense*	(100,000)	(100,000)	(100,000)
Net taxable income	(100,000)	(200,000)	(280,000)
Tax effect	50,000	100,000	140,000
Net income	(50,000)	(100,000)	(140,000)
Add			
Depreciation (noncash)	100,000	100,000	100,000
Income that is nontaxable	—	80,000	144,000
Net cash flow	$ 50,000	$ 80,000	$ 104,000

* $2,000,000 − 10% = $1,800,000/18 years = $100,000.

favorable impact of leveraging in real estate. In addition to the quantitative measure, it is important to determine the quality of these returns in terms of duration and likelihood.

By defining the competitive market position of each party in the real estate transaction, we can better understand our perspective in participating in real estate. By definition, a competitive market environment implies that someone will gain at someone else's expense. The degree by which you succeed can be measured and depends on your expectations of economic risk and reward. Let us return to the discussion of borrower/user and lender/provider in the real estate capital markets to help answer this question for ourselves.

Perhaps it is helpful to identify sources of raising capital by relative rankings. The rankings in Exhibit 4 are meant to indicate a general trend from A (most likely source) to C (least likely source) within each major segment of the product life cycle.

The remaining discussion will further describe the financing characteristics of these providers as they affect borrowers.

EXHIBIT 3 Internal Rate of Return

	A *Without Leverage*	B *With 50 Percent Leverage*	C *With 90 Percent Leverage*
Net cash flow after tax	$ 50,000	$ 80,000	$ 104,000
Cash invested	2,000,000	2,000,000	2,000,000
Internal rate of return	2.5%	4.0%	5.2%

EXHIBIT 4 Ranked Sources of Capital

	Product Life Cycle		
Providers	*Acquisition and Improvement*	*Development*	*Permanent*
Commercial banks	A*	B	A
Savings and loans	A	A	C
Life insurance companies	A	B	A
Pension funds	C	C	A
REITs	B	C	A
Foreign investors	C	C	A
Sellers	B	C	A
Syndication	A	A	C
Mortgage companies	C	C	A
Sale/leaseback	A	C	C

* A = Most likely source; C = Least likely source.

COMMERCIAL BANKS

Commercial banks have long been a large, diversified source of funds for real estate financing. The banking industry's desire for a high return on its assets coupled with a strong commitment to the community it serves has made real estate lending an integral part of commercial banking. The major categories of real estate loans entered into by commercial banks are construction/development, business, and residential loans.

Construction/Development Loans

"Without the necessary experience and skill, financing construction can be one of the riskiest lending activities of a commercial bank."[1] Construction lending is done by both large and small commercial banks. However, because of the highly specialized nature of construction lending, large banks are much more active than smaller community banks. Although community banks tend to stay within the boundaries of their local banking environment, they can become involved in large projects through loan participations with large banks. Participations are an effective tool to channel excess funds to areas with a high loan demand and to distribute the loan risk among several institutions rather than only one.

A construction loan is typically extended to the developer of a project for the purpose of financing the actual construction of the building. Construction loans typically run from two to three years

[1] *The Real Estate Handbook,* p. 665.

in length or less, with the funds being advanced as progress payments based on the amount of construction completed less a retainage until the final draw. Interest charges generally float with a specified market interest rate. "When the project is completed, the funds advanced through the construction loan are repaid to the commercial bank, generally by the long-term lender."[2] The long-term lender supplies the permanent mortgage money for the completed property and is typically an insurance company or a pension fund.

However, in recent years, the traditional roles in construction financing have become somewhat blurred. Interest rate fluctuations, coupled with the changes brought on by the deregulation of the financial service industry, have many institutional investors turning away from long-term mortgages. The former separation between construction and long-term financing is also breaking down. A host of institutional lenders (e.g., insurance companies, savings and loan associations, pension funds, and syndications) are providing a combination of construction and mortgage financing. Creative approaches include forming joint ventures with developers and equity participations in property income and/or appreciation.

To combat the increased competition, commercial banks are supplementing their construction loans with "mini-perm" features. "Whereas banks used to avoid making uncovered construction loans, they will now write intermediate-term loans (mini-perms) against their own construction loans."[3] Developers are being offered these financing packages under a variety of reasonably priced methods. The intermediate financing serves to "take out" the construction loan for a short term to allow the developer to find alternative financing.

To further compete with the deregulated S&Ls in the area of construction/development financing, commercial banks are seeking the ability to take equity positions in real estate. Currently, some state-chartered California commercial banks are allowed a limited degree of equity financing. Though most small community banks fall within the federal (Federal Reserve's Regulation Y, which prohibits bank holding companies from equity participations) and state guidelines, they have been successful in many joint ventures with real estate developers.

Business Loans

Business loans extended by commercial banks can take many forms. One of the most common types of business loans is the financing of

---

[2] *The Real Estate Handbook,* p. 665.

[3] George A. Smith, "Market Is Best Served by Financing Variety," *National Real Estate Investor,* p. 84.

an industrial property. "Financing industrial property is more complex than financing residential or commercial property. In this type of financing, judging the mortgage pattern calls for special knowledge of industrial location and industrial technology and for a more intensive review of borrower credit."[4]

An industrial loan extended by a commercial bank can be of two basic types: (1) a conventional mortgage, which in certain instances may be tax free; or (2) a direct commercial loan. Whereas a mortgage may be secured solely by the value of the property, a direct loan is secured by both the property and the credit of the borrower. Because of the nature of an industrial property, its alternative use value is more restricted than a commercial property. Because of the limited alternative use of industrial property, the bank will sometimes require additional security in the form of the borrower's guarantee of the debt or assignment of additional assets to secure the loan.

Commercial banks are a major source of shopping center financing. Unlike other mortgages extended by banks where the appraised value of the property is the key factor, a detailed financial analysis of future cash receipts and disbursements is needed to adequately assess the credit. In many cases, the credit is enhanced when major lead or anchor tenants enjoy a national reputation (e.g., Sears Roebuck & Co., J. C. Penney Company, Inc., K mart Corp., or Wal-Mart Stores, Inc.). "Shopping center analysis is unusually complex; the economics of retailing, forecasting techniques, and mortgage finance are part of the typical analysis. Shopping center financing may vary significantly from conventional, first-mortgage financing depending upon the outcome of the bank's analysis of the project."[5] Oftentimes, a financial projection of operating results is prepared to depict the sources and uses of cash flow for debt service and as a return for investors.

Residential Loans

In addition to savings and loan associations and mutual savings banks, commercial banks continue to be a major supplier of residential mortgage funds. "Commercial banks recognize that residential home mortgages are a major means of meeting community needs. For most community banks, the residential home mortgage is the most important type of real estate lending. The four main types of residential loans extended by commercial banks are: conventional loans, FHA loans, VA loans, and construction loans."[6]

---

[4] *The Real Estate Handbook,* p. 669.

[5] *The Real Estate Handbook,* p. 670.

[6] *The Real Estate Handbook,* p. 668.

A conventional real estate loan is any loan secured by real estate that the lender makes without benefit of government insurance or guarantee. Conventional loans include those insured by private insuring agencies where the loan-to-value ratio exceeds the limitations set by banking laws or policies. An FHA real estate loan is any loan secured by residential real estate in which the lender is insured by the Federal Housing Administration (FHA). The borrower, the property, and the loan must comply with requirements that have been established by the FHA. A VA real estate loan is any loan secured by real estate and made to an eligible veteran in which a portion of the loan is guaranteed by the Veterans Administration (VA). The veteran, the property, and the loan must meet the requirements of the VA. A real estate construction loan is any loan secured by real estate on which partial disbursements are made during the construction period. Such a loan may be arranged on a long-term conventional basis, on an FHA or a VA basis, or on a short-term loan basis.[7]

Mortgage Warehouse Loans

Commercial banks also indirectly serve as a source for residential mortgage bankers. These warehouse loans are extended to the mortgage banker to facilitate the origination of mortgages prior to the sale and distribution to permanent investors. The proceeds of the sale from permanent investors are used to pay off the warehouse loans.

Mortgage warehouse loans are typically in the form of a line of credit with the bank. But the warehouse loans are additional security. There are two general types of warehousing loans that are made directly to mortgage bankers: (1) the committed technical, and (2) the uncommitted technical. The more common type is the committed technical warehousing loan. With this type of warehouse loan, the funds are loaned to the mortgage banker for the origination of a number of mortgages, of which he has a prior commitment from an investor to purchase the mortgages when completed. With an uncommitted technical warehousing loan, there is no prior commitment from a permanent investor to take up the loans from the mortgage banker. The amount of the warehousing loan is usually based on the amount of the investor's commitment.

SAVINGS AND LOAN ASSOCIATIONS

Savings and Loan Associations (S&Ls) have traditionally been one of the largest sources of residential mortgage funds, along with commercial banks and mutual savings banks. S&Ls were founded on the principle of promoting thrift among the working class in order to

---

[7] *The Real Estate Handbook,* pp. 668–69.

build a capital base to finance the purchase of the family home. To accomplish this goal, S&Ls acquired funds, mostly in the form of savings deposit accounts. These funds were then extended to the public in the form of long-term, fixed rate mortgage loans.

The S&L industry remained essentially unchanged until the late 1970s. The volatile economic environment of the 1970s had a damaging effect on the thrift industry. The higher interest rates common in the inflationary period of the late 1970s caused a dramatic increase in the cost of funds. S&L earnings began to plummet.

> The Federal Home Loan Bank Board (FHLBB) reported in its 1981 Annual Report that the net worth of the nation's federally insured S&Ls declined by roughly $5 billion in 1981 compared with a $667 million increase in 1980. The drop in net income was due, in part, to the fact that the average portfolio yield of mortgages held by S&Ls was only about 9 percent. The mortgages held by S&Ls are almost entirely long term and fixed rate, and were made in periods of much lower interest rates than the current market rates. Against this were the liabilities of S&Ls, the majority of which were tied to current market rates.[8]

In general, the negative spread earned on their mortgage portfolio, coupled with the regulatory restraints limiting the S&Ls' ability to diversify their asset base, resulted in lower and, in some cases, negative earnings to the S&Ls.

The troubles of the S&Ls were further magnified by a dramatic increase in deposit growth. "The 1981 gain of $13.3 billion in deposits was one third as large as the 1980 gain, and was the smallest gain since 1970. Withdrawals exceeded deposits by $26 billion in 1981, while in 1980 S&Ls showed a net gain in deposits of $10.7 billion."[9] The decreasing earnings of S&Ls and strong competition from money market mutual funds caused a great deal of the stagnation in deposit growth. As a result of the losses in net income and reduced cash flow, S&Ls began to merge or collapse at an unprecedented rate.

Regulatory Changes

In response to the trouble experienced in the thrift industry, legislation was enacted to enable the S&Ls to successfully adapt to the changing economic scene. In particular:

> The provision of the Depositing Institution Deregulation and Monetary Control Act of 1980 and the Garn–St. Germain Depository Institutions Act of 1982 empowered federally chartered thrifts to engage in a variety of activities that had previously been prohibited. Generally, the acts en-

[8] *Real Estate Investor's Deskbook* (1983 Supplement), p. 55-2.

[9] *Real Estate Investor's Deskbook* (1983 Supplement), pp. 55-2–55-3.

able thrift institutions to invest in nonresidential real estate. Although there are still some limitations on savings and loan activities in commercial real estate and real estate development, these institutions may now participate in such development in a variety of ways.[10]

The regulatory changes have resulted in a steady rise in deposits and real estate investment by S&Ls. The largest concentration of real estate loans made by S&Ls have been to developers for land acquisition and construction loans. S&Ls are moving into territories that had previously been the property of commercial banks. As more S&Ls gain experience in the real estate field, developers are turning to them as a viable source for financing. S&Ls are developing a mixture of creative financing methods involving the formation of joint ventures with developers and equity participations in the projects. In fact, the relationship between S&Ls and developers has been so successful that it has become common for some developers to acquire an S&L to provide financing for their projects or the projects of other developers.

Land Acquisition and Construction Loans

Land acquisition and construction loans are entered into with developers by some of the larger S&Ls. Larger institutions are involved in these loans because "in many states a thrift may not lend to a single borrower an amount that is greater than its equity base."[11] Among some of the financing structures adopted by S&Ls for these loans are: equity participation loans, profit participation agreements, and direct joint ventures. Under an equity participation loan, the S&L forms a service corporation subsidiary that enters into a joint venture, or limited partnership, with a real estate developer.

> The developer is the general partner, and the service corporation is the limited partner. The S&L, through its service corporation subsidiary, limits its liability to its nominal contribution to the joint venture, such as $1,000. The S&L extends a loan to the partnership and takes a first lien position on the property. In many cases, the partnership makes no payments to the S&L, either on the principal of the loan or the interest, until the project is complete. When the partnership sells the project, and when the partnership receives the proceeds of the sale, it pays off the loan plus the accrued interest. The developer and the service corporation then divide (usually equally) the difference between the final selling price and the total cost of the project.[12]

---

[10] John Crockett, Clifford Fry, and Paul Horwitz, "Are S&L Participations in Real Estate Ventures Too Risky?" *Real Estate Review,* Summer 1985, pp. 54–55.

[11] N. Christopher Cheatham, "Gap Financing: An Opportunity for Venturesome Thrift Institutions," *Real Estate Review,* Summer 1985, p. 50.

[12] "Are S&L Participations," p. 55.

Some large S&Ls resist the joint venture concept because they fear potential legal liability, despite their position as limited partners.

> Instead, they participate in the profits of some of the projects they finance by attaching profit participation agreements to standard loans. The S&Ls' profit share varies from 5 to 50 percent. The greater the financial contribution of the developer to the project, the smaller is the S&Ls' share in the profits. In some arrangements, the S&L shares in the project's operating cash flow; in others, it shares in the realized increase in the project's value at the time of sale. The loan terms always provide that principal and interest must be paid in full before calculation and payment of any profit.[13]

Significant controversy now surrounds the acquisition, development, and construction (ADC) loans. The ADC loans typically have equity features that enable the lender to share in operations or receive other benefits beyond the stated interest terms. The economic nature of these loans is under review by regulatory, tax, and accounting authorities in an attempt to standardize their treatment.

Direct Joint Ventures

Another financing technique for an S&L is a direct joint venture with a developer. In some instances, the S&L will not advance funds to the joint venture directly but will guarantee the repayment of a loan from an interim lender, typically a commercial bank. The S&L will actively seek a buyer for the property during the construction period and will offer the extended financing to the buyer. Profits from the sale of the property are divided evenly between the developer and the S&L.

Direct Development and Syndications

In addition to joint ventures, some larger S&Ls are also expanding into direct development and syndications. As with joint ventures, most direct-development projects are single-family homes, apartments, and condominiums. Very few commercial and industrial products are currently being developed by S&Ls. Syndications represent an area into which S&Ls will rapidly expand. Following a familiar pattern, S&Ls tend to limit their syndications to multifamily apartments. Little syndication is being done in commercial and industrial properties. Despite the thrift's access to a large potential customer base, most S&L syndications tend to be private placements made through brokerage houses.

---

[13] "Are S&L Participations," p. 56.

Other Approaches

Bow Ties and Mini-Perms. In addition to the various types of equity transactions entered into by S&Ls, other creative approaches include "bow ties" and "mini-perms." A bow tie arrangement is designed to protect both borrower and lender against volatile interest rates. Regardless of the stated interest rate in the documentation, which is usually the ceiling rate supportable by the cash flow from the property, an additional amount may be payable. An accrual rate may rise above the ceiling (usually tied to prime or a federal treasury rate), and the excess interest will be added as a balloon payment to the principal at maturity. A mini-perm is a short-term construction takeout loan to finance the project until the developer can obtain longer-term financing.

Smaller S&Ls. Smaller S&Ls can become involved in financing real estate development through the participation of loans with other thrifts. Smaller thrifts are sometimes found to utilize loan participation because they are restricted from lending to one borrower an amount in excess of their equity base. However, several problems are common with participations. A thrift can issue a commitment to a developer that is subject to sale of participation interests. Such an arrangement may not be considered adequate to a developer, especially if time is a crucial factor. An alternative is for a thrift to attempt to sell participations on an "if transacted" basis. This approach tends to be quite time-consuming, and most thrifts are reluctant to indicate interest in a transaction that has not yet been closed. A small thrift also has the option of purchasing a participation in an origination of a large institution. However, many thrifts are unreceptive to this approach because it lacks the prestige of origination and does not give the institution a community presence.

Gap Loans. An attractive alternative for some S&Ls, both large and small, who desire to be involved in real estate financing is a "gap loan." A gap loan is extended by the S&L to the developer to cover the difference, or gap, between the bank construction loan and the total cost of the project. The gap loan is priced considerably above prime, with an origination fee and a participation in net profits. The loan is secured by a second lien on the property. The package also includes an intermediate takeout loan with a much higher participation in net profits. The major advantage to the developer is that he obtains 100 percent financing and does not need to either invest his funds or bring in a partner, although he does sacrifice a percentage of his profits. Gap financing is a further example of the increasing role of S&Ls in real estate development. In addition to the gap loan, some S&Ls are beginning to package permanent takeout loans along with the initial construction financing. The permanent financing was heretofore the exclusive role of an insurance company or a pension fund.

In addition to opening the doors for commercial real estate lending, the recent legislation also served to strengthen the S&Ls' position in the residential mortgage industry. The use of sophisticated new products such as adjusted rate mortgages (ARMs), shared appreciation mortgages (SAMs), and equity CDs has significantly aided S&Ls to more effectively match their asset yields with their cost of funds.

LIFE INSURANCE COMPANIES

Life insurance companies have long been a large provider of real estate financing to both residential and commercial properties. Traditionally, life insurance companies were able to accurately project cash inflows from premiums and outflows from benefit payments. As such, a life insurance company has a large source of funds available for investment. Though popular in the past, residential mortgages have fallen out of favor with insurance companies because their fixed rates, long terms, and state usury ceilings make them a poor hedge against inflation. The life insurance company's role in the residential mortgage market has been filled by "GNMA and conventional mortgage-backed securities, which are sold mostly to institutional investors."[14] The lack of residential mortgages limited the insurance company's investment choices to real estate, corporate bonds, and private debt placements. Prevailing interest rates are the major determinant of what investment vehicle is chosen. However, in recent years, the use of joint ventures between insurance companies and developers has added the use of equity participations to enhance the return on investment for the insurance companies. The use of such creative financing approaches has made real estate an attractive investment for insurance companies.

Changing to Short-Term Commitments

Until recently, the bulk of real estate loans extended by life insurance companies were takeout loans to developers. The takeout loan would serve as the long-term financing of a property and allow a developer to pay off, or "takeout," the construction debt. These long-term or permanent mortgages would typically range from 25 to 30 years at a fixed rate. However, the volatile economy of the early 1980s has

---

[14] *Real Estate Investor's Deskbook,* p. 5-5.

changed much of the traditional structures of real estate lending. High interest rates and extensive deregulation of the financial service industry has forced insurance companies to alter their real estate lending philosophy. No longer are life insurers willing to extend commitments for long-term mortgages of 20–30 years. The old time barriers between construction and permanent financing have fallen. Today, some major insurers are forming their own construction lending departments and are providing both construction and takeout financing (on a short-term basis). In general, insurance companies are seeking to keep their mortgage investments short, instead of investing in the traditional long-term mortgages.

The reasons for keeping short terms are obvious in an environment of rising interest rates. Insurance companies do not want to get tied into a particular rate for a long period of time. Another factor influencing insurance companies is the projected outflow of their funds. Whereas, previously, most cash outflows were well into the future (thus allowing for investment in long-term mortgages), the influx of pension funds in the late 1970s and early 1980s resulted in the establishment of a short-term investment instrument. This instrument, called a "guaranteed investment contract" (GIC), provides for a stated principal and interest payment to the investor. The maturity on the GICs is typically five years. Thus, insurance companies found themselves in the same position as banks and S&Ls, namely, with the challenge of matching assets and liabilities by maturity while at the same time earning a spread on their funds. Insurance companies more and more came into competition with other financial institutions in search of a quality real estate investment that meets their particular needs.

Equity Participation

To meet the challenge, insurance companies have adopted a series of creative approaches to financing also being used by other institutions. Most mortgages being entered into have some form of equity participation such as convertible debts and participating mortgages. In addition, many insurance companies are entering into joint ventures with developers. Many of these deals involve no debt; they are done on an all-equity basis. Another thrust toward equities is the popularity of syndications. Most of the large life insurance companies have either divisions or affiliations with syndicators, or are in the process of buying or starting a syndication company of their own.

In general, the mortgage must be a first lien on the property, and title must be good and marketable and insurable on such a basis. Most life insurance company lenders require the assignment of important leases to the lender as additional security. Fire and other hazard insurance in amounts acceptable to the lender must also be provided. Another consideration is that the property must meet all local environmental and zoning requirements.

Some creative approaches are often used in financing arrangements with life insurance companies. Life insurance company lenders may be willing to advance funds well in excess of the normal loan-to-value ratio of 75 to 80 percent if the property is leased on a net basis to a tenant with strong credit. The credit of the borrower must be strong enough to qualify him for an unsecured debenture borrowing from the insurance company.

In recent years, insurance companies have reduced their level of investment in the real estate market. Policy loans and terminations are draining company assets, and insurers are turning to short-term investments as a source of liquidity. Another factor contributing to the declining presence of life insurance companies in the real estate market is increased competition from S&Ls. Thrift institutions are becoming increasingly involved in real estate financing, from origination of construction loans to the formation of joint ventures with developers.

Insurance companies are still active in current real estate transactions, primarily through their management of commingled pension funds. Acting in fiduciary capacity for the funds they manage, large insurance companies such as Prudential Life and The Equitable Life Assurance Society of the United States provide a wealth of experience and talent in the acquisition and management of properties.

PENSION FUNDS

A pension fund receives contributions from corporations, government agencies, unions, and workers for the eventual repayment to former employees in the form of retirement benefits. The manager of the pension fund will usually entrust the funds to a trustee to convert the funds into earning assets. The return on the assets should be sufficient to guarantee payment of future benefits to retirees without risking the loss of the assets. The trustee of the pension plan has a fiduciary responsibility to safeguard the prudent investment of the plan's assets.

"The asset and liability structure of pension funds is somewhat similar to that of life insurance companies in that the inflow of funds is continuous and stable and payment of obligations are actually determinable. Consequently, pension funds would seem to be a logical source of long-term real estate loans."[15] However, pension funds have pre-

[15] *Real Estate Investor's Deskbook,* p. 5-16.

dominately invested in stocks and bonds over the years. Pension trustees have had little or no experience in real estate dealings. They have had neither the staff nor the expertise to purchase, manage, and sell real estate.

In the 1970s, the pension funds began to look toward real estate as a viable investment alternative. The high inflation of the period caused a deflation of the total return on most investment instruments. As pension trustees began to look for investments that would serve as a secure hedge against inflation, real estate investment became more attractive. Foreign pension funds recognized this strategy and have maintained a substantial portion of their portfolios in real estate investments. U.S. pension funds conversely have typically maintained three to five percent of their funds in real estate. In addition, the passage of the Employee Retirement Income Security Act of 1974 (ERISA) served as a further incentive of real estate lending. ERISA admonished trustees for concentrating their investment in stocks and bonds, and encouraged pension funds to diversify their asset base. This was interpreted to mean that some portion of pension assets should be invested in real estate.

Commingled Funds

The majority of pension fund investments have been through commingled funds managed by life insurance companies or commercial bank trust departments. Some of the large commingled funds are managed by the "Prudential Life Insurance Company of America, The Equitable Life Insurance Society of America, and the First National Bank of Chicago."[16] The pension funds turned to the insurance companies and banks because they possessed the technical expertise that was lacking in the pension funds.

In general, the commingled funds seek to purchase income-producing properties of four types: (1) office buildings, (2) industrial buildings, (3) shopping centers, and (4) apartment buildings. Prior to 1981, commingled funds sought to purchase properties free of all mortgage encumbrances so as to avoid payment of the unrelated business income tax (UBIT).

> Until 1981, a pension fund that bought real estate that was in part financed by a mortgage had to treat a portion of the income from the real estate as unrelated business income and pay a tax on it. The theory was that to the extent the pension fund was using borrowed money rather than its own cash, it could unfairly compete with other purchases of real estate if the rental income generated from the use of the borrowed

[16] *The Real Estate Handbook,* p. 703.

funds was tax free. As a result of this rule, pension funds almost always limited their real estate investments to all-cash deals.[17]

The tax law was changed at the end of 1980 to permit qualified pension and profit sharing plans to invest in certain debt-financed real estate without becoming subject to the unrelated business income tax. Some pension managers may have hesitated to invest in leveraged real estate not only because of the potential tax burden but because such investments might not have been considered prudent. The exemption created by the new law implicitly approves debt-financed real estate as a prudent investment for fiduciaries such as pension funds.[18]

A combination of the change in the tax laws and a greater amount of hands-on experience in real estate has led some pension funds to become more creative in real estate investments. Some of the approaches adopted by the funds now include debt financing with equity kickers and convertible debt.

REAL ESTATE INVESTMENT TRUSTS

A real estate investment trust (REIT):

> is a vehicle that pools the capital of a large number of individual investors and the issuance of debt, and then either invests the capital in the ownership of real estate (equity trust) or lends the capital to real estate borrowers on the security of mortgages (mortgage trust). Today, most REITs are a combination of equities and mortgages. REITs were first authorized in 1960 by an amendment to the Internal Revenue Code; they are creatures of the tax law and must comply with specified conditions in order to retain their special tax status. This special status enables a REIT to distribute its income to its shareholders (at least 95 percent without the REIT itself paying any federal income tax. If a REIT fails to comply with the requirements set in the tax code, it becomes taxable on its income as if it were a regular business corporation.[19]

REITs are involved in most types of real estate financing, both equity and mortgage financing.

REIT property holdings center on such structures as apartment houses, shopping centers, office buildings, warehouses, and light industrial centers. In evaluating possible investments, REITs look for high rental income as well as appreciation of property values or possibilities for increased future rental income. REIT property holdings tend to be on a long-term basis. This is because a trust which buys and sells property in a short

---

[17] *Real Estate Investor's Deskbook,* p. 5-18.

[18] *Real Estate Investor's Deskbook,* p. 5-19.

[19] *Real Estate Investor's Deskbook,* pp. 5-10–5-11, 5-15.

period is subject to 100 percent tax on any gain as opposed to long-term capital gains tax.[20]

> REIT[s] may acquire property through several methods. They may purchase existing improved properties for their portfolios; they may hire independent contractors to construct improvements on land that they own; or they may invest in a joint venture with developers. In a joint venture, the REIT typically becomes a passive partner, with the developer supplying most of the capital for the project. Another popular combination is for a REIT to own the land under buildings owned by others. The REIT leases the land to the building owner on a long-term basis.[21]

Of all the mortgage lending done by REITs, construction lending has remained the most common. Some REITs offer a package of construction and standby financing. In addition, REIT construction loans are made where there is no permanent commitment available to handle the long-term financing. Some REITs are attracted to this type of deal because they can price the construction loan at a higher rate due to the increased risk, plus offer a standby commitment, at a fee, to finance the project until permanent funding can be obtained. Among the other financing arrangements offered by REITs are: wraparound mortgages, sale/leasebacks and second mortgages with equity kickers for developers, and warehouse financing for mortgage bankers.

According to the REIT Report, 1984 was a year of exceptional growth for the REIT industry in that its assets increased 25 percent from $7.6 billion to $9.5 billion. The total number of qualified REITs increased nearly 10 percent from 115 to 126. In addition, 10 public offerings were registered totaling $449 million. As of April 1985, 15 companies filed registrations totaling $1.5 billion in initial public offerings. Moreover, existing REITs have reentered the capital markets. With the advent of the Treasury tax proposals, investors are now considering liquidity, income, and growth, rather than the losses generated by tax shelters.

The new generation of REITs has brought an innovation in the form of finite-life trusts. These trusts have specific life spans, with a specific liquidation date such as 5 years, but not more than 10–15 years. This perceived ability to assure a predictable time for the return of investment is intended to reduce the disparity between the market price of the REIT shares and the underlying value of its real estate assets. Moreover, a new style of mortgage REIT has been gaining popularity. These mortgage REITs include many of the equity features formerly reserved to equity REITs. These REITs seek equity enhancement rights in the underlying real property such as participating in

---

[20] *The Real Estate Handbook,* p. 689.

[21] *The Real Estate Handbook,* p. 693.

the appreciation of property and in cash proceeds, and acquiring a portion of gross income generated by the property above a certain amount, conversion rights, and options to purchase. It is, therefore, obvious that the mortgage REITs are attempting to obtain a bundle of equity rights.

FOREIGN INVESTORS

Foreign investment in real estate continues to grow as a source of real estate capital in the United States. Foreign investment in general has been on the upswing in recent years. The United States presents an attractive economic environment for investment because of its stable government, more reasonable inflation rates, and limited legal restrictions on foreign investment.

Real estate, in particular, has been viewed by foreign investors as an attractive investment. Real estate's popularity is due, in part, to the universality of its nature. In addition, the U.S. real estate climate offers the foreign investor a number of features that may not be available in his native country, such as an established and predictable legal framework for real estate ownership, abundant mortgage financing, investment appreciation, and experienced property management.

Foreign investors tend to concentrate on existing commercial and industrial property in or near major U.S. cities, Raw land and development projects are not as attractive to the foreign investor due to the inherent risks involved as well as the logistical problem of physically overseeing the project. Residential properties are also frequently avoided because of continuing management problems and the possible threat of tenant strikes or rent control. "Shopping centers and office buildings are the most favored form of investment by foreigners, particularly if a large percentage of space is anchored by Triple A tenants. Industrial buildings with similar high-quality-credit tenants may also be considered, although they do not possess the image quality of shopping centers and office buildings."[22]

Other guidelines followed by foreign investors include a preference for high-quality buildings in the best locations. Foreigners also avoid properties subject to long-term leases. These policies are followed so as to maximize rental income and secure a hedge against inflation.

Some of the newest sources of foreign capital include "banks, pension funds, investment groups, and private individuals. Few work directly in the domestic marketplace, choosing instead to deal with

---

[22] *Real Estate Investor's Deskbook,* p. 5-22.

money center bank trust departments, their own representatives, or domestic representatives under foreign names."[23]

SELLER FINANCING

Seller financing is usually accomplished through the issuance of a purchase-money mortgage. "In a purchase-money transaction, the seller accepts, in lieu of cash, the buyer's note for the unpaid price secured by a mortgage on the property being sold. Not only does this provide immediate financing for the buyer, but it also creates a simultaneous investment for the seller secured by property with which he is intimately familiar."[24] In addition, the return to the seller is often at a higher rate than would be otherwise available.

Not only can purchase-money mortgages take the place of an institutional first mortgage, they can also be extended to the buyer for additional financing in the form of a junior mortgage. In such cases, a second mortgage is advanced to make up the difference between the seller's equity in the property and the buyer's available cash, and purchase-money second mortgages are also used by syndicators when acquiring properties for syndication. A syndicator may issue a second mortgage, at a moderate rate of interest, to lower the initial outlay of cash for the purchase of the property. This will result in additional interest payments to the seller and a high rate of return for the syndicator's cash investment.

The specific terms of the mortgage can be treated in a great many ways to make the deal attractive to both parties. Among the major considerations are: the loan-to-value ratio, the interest rate, the mortgage terms, a prepayment option, and a right to assign the mortgage. The seller will want the buyer to invest as much cash as possible in order to keep the loan-to-value ratio down. The buyer will attempt to minimize his cash investment to about 10 percent. The interest rate will be a strong indication of the relative bargaining strengths of the two parties. An anxious seller may be willing to settle for a below-market rate or vice versa. However, recent proposed regulations pertaining to original issue discount could limit the use of these creative interest features, since the tax code provides for a minimum taxable income even if the required payment rate is lower.

The mortgage term can be a point of contention because a seller is typically not willing to wait 20–25 years for his money, but the buyer cannot afford costly monthly payments based on a short-term amortization schedule. A possible solution may be a balloon mortgage,

---

[23] *Real Estate Investor's Deskbook* (1983 supplement), p. 55-13.

[24] *Real Estate Investor's Deskbook,* p. 6-88.

with monthly payments geared to a long term but with a short-term maturity. Consequently, at maturity there will be a large unpaid balance (the balloon).

Prepayment terms are usually desired by both parties, since the seller may want his money back to pursue other ventures, and the buyer wants to be free to arrange more favorable institutional financing when it becomes available.

The right to assign the mortgage can be an important consideration, depending on the buyer's plans concerning the property. If the buyer desires to resell the property in the near future, the right of assignment of the mortgage obligation is crucial to any subsequent sale. Likewise, the seller will typically require that his consent is needed for any subsequent sales, pending an analysis of the new buyer's credit standing and the availability of better terms.

A creative approach to seller financing has been developed called the hypothecation loan. The purpose of a hypothecation loan is to help the seller maximize cash from the real estate transaction in which he takes back paper from the buyer. The hypothecation loan provides the seller with a source of cash without triggering a taxable gain.

> Here is an example of a hypothecation loan. Assume you have sold a property worth $1 million with a $400,000 first mortgage. You carried back $300,000 in a second deed of trust payable in seven years, interest only, at 10 percent. The annual payment due you on the loan is $30,000. You should be able to borrow at least 50 percent of the $300,000 second (or $150,000 at, say, 15 percent) by making an absolute assignment of the note to a bank.
>
> Most banks would regard this as an extremely secure loan. If you do not pay the $150,000, the bank can assume your position in the second deed of trust. It can, in the case of subsequent problems, foreclose on the property on which the debt-to-value ratio is only 70 percent. Furthermore, the bank's debt coverage on the $150,000 loan is excellent. Because you are collecting $30,000 on the note and only paying $22,500 to the bank, the bank's coverage is roughly 1.3 to 1. Most banks making such loans would prefer to have a rate that floats up or down with the prime rate or some other index. But they will usually negotiate a floor and a ceiling so that your rate cannot, for example, go any higher than 18 percent or lower than 12 percent.[25]

MORTGAGE COMPANIES

Mortgage companies have served as a significant intermediary of the mortgage market since the mid 1940s. Mortgage companies are a

---

[25] Daniel A. Blumberg, "Real Estate Financing: Hypothecation Loans Secured by Purchase Money Mortgages," *Real Estate Review,* Summer 1983, p. 12.

unique entity within the financial services industry. "Unlike mortgage brokers, mortgage companies originate loans with their own funds and credit resources. Unlike other financial institutions, they sell the mortgage loans they originate to other investors and they service the loans for those investors. As a group, mortgage companies are the most diversified of all the financial institutions that serve the real estate market. Most mortgage bankers are active in a variety of other functions related to real estate."[26] In addition to the origination, sale, and servicing of residential mortgages, mortgage companies provide insurance, purchase land, extend development/construction loans, and perform property management.

The number of mortgage companies has been small as compared to other financial institutions. As with the financial services industry in general, the number of mortgage companies has dwindled as a result of mergers and acquisitions. A relatively small number of firms account for a major share of the mortgage banking business.

Mortgage companies must first obtain funds before they can originate and sell packages of mortgage loans to investors. The concept of obtaining funds to extend to borrowers prior to the sale of loans (and receipt of proceeds on the sale) is known as "warehousing." It is essential to their business that mortgage bankers obtain sources of short-term credit in order to fund their mortgage originations. Commercial banks have historically filled this role by extending "warehousing loans" (e.g., lines of credit) to the mortgage companies.

> Banks have been willing to establish lines of credit for mortgage companies because: (1) mortgage companies usually have commitments from permanent investors to purchase the loans in inventory and the construction loans that they are funding; (2) the single-family mortgages in inventory are mostly insured or guaranteed by the government; (3) single-family loans are usually rolled over by 90 to 120 days; and (4) single-family construction loans also roll over fairly quickly since repayments to disbursements average 85 to 90 percent each year.[27]

Since the cost of warehousing lines fluctuates with the bank prime rate, mortgage companies sought to reduce the cost of their borrowings by expanding their short-term borrowing options. "Many mortgage companies issue commercial paper, either through their parent holding companies, which are financially stronger, or in their own names, but backed by lines of credit from their commercial banks. Large issues of GNMA securities also obtain funds by arranging repurchase agreements in which they sell GNMA securities to investment bankers and buy the securities back 60 to 90 days later at a higher price,

---

[26] *The Real Estate Handbook,* pp. 717–718.

[27] *The Real Estate Handbook,* p. 722.

usually a half point or more higher."[28] Though mortgage companies are involved in a wide range of real estate activities, the major thrust of their lending operations remains the single-family home.

SALE/LEASEBACKS

"In a sale/leaseback, the real property is sold to a buyer who simultaneously enters into a long-term lease of the property with the seller. Thus, the seller-lessee remains in possession of the property and pays a net rental to the buyer-lessor, with the seller-lessee responsible for payment of all operating expenses, insurance, and real estate taxes."[29]

In a sale/leaseback of both the land and buildings, the seller-lessee obtains most of the burdens and benefits of ownership and also converts its investment into cash. However, the seller-lessee also loses the right to take depreciation deductions or share in the future appreciation of the property. In a sale/leaseback of land only, the seller-lessee pays ground rental for the land but retains the depreciation deductions and appreciation. A sale/leaseback of just the buildings is advantageous from the buyer's perspective since his aim is to obtain the depreciation deductions.

Most sale/leaseback transactions occur between a corporation (owner/seller/lessee) and a prospective buyer (e.g., syndication, pension fund, or insurance company). Sale/leasebacks will take many different forms and involve different players, depending on each player's financial position. For example, a pension plan would be more interested in a transaction offering strong appreciation versus high depreciation deductions, because of its tax-free status, whereas a syndicator would be more attracted to the tax benefits derived from high depreciation and interest deductions.

Several examples of sale/leaseback transactions are presented in syndicated partnerships. Wal-Mart Stores, Inc. and K mart Corp. have successfully financed the capital expansion of their shopping centers by entering into long-term operating leases. The capital outlays are "off balance sheet" and typically are owned by syndicated partnerships. The credit of the anchor is used to obtain stable, fixed rate financing. Similarly, hospitals are having their medical office buildings and life care facilities syndicated to tax-sensitive investors. In many cases, an accrual basis, nontax-sensitive entity (e.g., a pension fund) plays an integral intermediate-financing function. These and other creative structures need to be discussed with the appropriate legal, tax, and financial consultants early on in arranging financing.

---

[28] *The Real Estate Handbook,* pp. 722–723.

[29] *Real Estate Investor's Deskbook,* p. 9-56.

SUMMARY

The ability to successfully raise capital in real estate requires skill and creativity. We have presented various sources and techniques available in today's highly competitive market. By developing the appropriate quantitative analysis of the "target project," you can apply such measures against a lender's current guidelines. This process often results in prospective financial statements that depict the product life cycle of acquisition, development, and permanent investment. The legal and tax structuring of the financing transactions requires creative professional advice from lawyers and accountants.

The qualitative factors of the borrower's reputation, track record, appraisal values, and prior performance of the real estate all lend a high degree of value to the anticipated transaction. Lenders often help such borrowers develop a structure when some of the quantitative measures indicate risk. However, the "best real estate deal available" will not be financed if the borrower is severely lacking in these qualitative factors.

Real estate presents many avenues for raising capital. Hopefully, this discussion will help outline alternatives and simplify the challenges in raising capital in today's dynamic real estate environment.

REFERENCES

BLUMBERG, DANIEL A. "Real Estate Financing: Hypothecation Loans Secured by Purchase Money Mortgages." *Real Estate Review,* Summer 1983, pp. 12–13.

"Both Banks and Public Can Profit by Well-Managed Equity Investment." *ABA Banking Journal,* May 1984, pp. 238, 242, 247.

CHEATHAM, N. CHRISTOPHER. "Gap Financing: An Opportunity for Venturesome Thrift Institutions." *Real Estate Review,* Summer 1985, pp. 49–53.

CHRISTENSEN, DAVID T. and CHRISTOPHER B. FEINBERGER. "Mortgage Lenders Broaden Their Real Estate Horizons." *Savings Institutions,* December 1984, pp. 94–98.

COCKER, STEVE. "California Banks Move Cautiously into Real Estate Equity Investment." *ABA Banking Journal,* pp. 213–18.

CROCKETT, JOHN; CLIFFORD FRY; and PAUL HORWITZ. "Are S&L Participations in Real Estate Ventures Too Risky?" *Real Estate Review,* Summer 1985, pp. 54–59.

DERREN, RONALD. "Though a Lot of Cash Is Chasing Major Deals, Most Financiers Want to Be the Developer's Partner." *National Real Estate Investor,* October 1984, pp. 65–92.

EVANS, RICHARD. "The Return of the REIT." *Euromoney,* October 1984, pp. 357–62.

FEINBERGER, CHRISTOPHER B. "Real Estate Investment Becomes Renewing Solution as Deregulation, Competition Strain S&L Industry." *National Real Estate Investor,* May 1985, pp. 86, 90, 92, 264.

"Is the Syndications Boom a Blessing in Disguise for Pension Funds?" *Institutional Investor,* November 1983, pp. 237–43.

KOLMAN, JOE. "The Boom in Real Estate Development Funds." *Institutional Investor,* November 1984, pp. 165–72.

The Real Estate Handbook.

Real Estate Investor's Deskbook.

Real Estate Investor's Deskbook. (1983 Supplement).

SMITH, GEORGE A. "Market Is Best Secured by Financing Variety." *National Real Estate Investor,* February 1985, pp. 84, 722.

THOMPSON, BOYCE. "Builders Sound Off on Banks in Real Estate." *Professional Builder,* July 1984, pp. 34–39, 44.

________. "Builders Weigh S&L Start-Up. *Professional Builder,* August 1984, pp. 54, 57.

CHAPTER **17**

Financing Corporate Construction Projects

Benjamin V. Lambert
President and Chief Executive Officer
Eastdil Realty, Inc.
New York, N.Y.

Benjamin V. Lambert is the founder of Eastdil, a real estate investment banking firm, and has been its president and chief executive officer since it was formed in 1967. Mr. Lambert is widely known in real estate circles and is a director of Hilton Hotels Corporation and the Irvine Company, and serves as a trustee of Wells Fargo Mortgage and Equity Trust. He is also a member of the Investment Advisory Council to the Comptroller of the City of New York.

Kenneth G. Walker
Executive Vice President
Lazard Frères Property Investment Co.
New York, N.Y.

Kenneth G. Walker became executive vice president of Lazard Frères Property Investment Company, a wholly owned real estate investment banking subsidiary of Lazard Frères & Co., in April 1985. Prior thereto, Mr. Walker was both a principal of Condren, Walker & Co., Incorporated, a small investment banking firm specializing in leveraged lease financing, and a consultant to the real estate investment banking group of E. F. Hutton & Co. From September 1976 until August 1979, Mr. Walker was president of Eastdil Credit, Inc., which was an Eastdil Realty subsidiary specializing in corporate real estate finance.

CHOOSING THE FORM OF FINANCING

This chapter is presented in the context of a corporate construction project. The first half deals with corporate objectives; the second, with implementation of those objectives.

Depending on the financial strength of the corporation, many alternative financing possibilities present themselves to those contemplating construction. A major corporation that has access to capital markets, both public and private, may avail itself of the opportunity to obtain the funds to pay for the project out of the proceeds of a large general purpose financing, for example, a common stock offering or a publicly offered debenture issue. Alternatively, many companies choose to relate the financing directly to the particular project, property, or building itself. This latter approach can be generally defined as "secured financing."

In the context of this chapter we shall emphasize the more specific secured financing approach. Adopting this course of action provides access to a broader range of funding sources and, additionally, offers those seeking financing the ability to tailor the transaction to maximize their particular strengths. These strengths can generally be described as "credit" strengths (those relating to credit stature or borrowing capacity) or "real estate" strengths (those related to the basic economic value of the property). Financing is often based on varying combinations of credit and real estate strengths.

Even though a method of financing is applicable to a specific situation, the overall impact of that form of financing on the company must be assessed. Each of the questions that follow should be raised and evaluated in order to choose a course of financing action most consistent with the company's overall objectives, requirements, and capacities.

1. Should corporate credit be committed to the financing?
2. What percentage of financing should be sought?
3. For how long a term should the financing extend?
4. How will the company's tax posture affect the financing decision?
5. What are the company's objectives in terms of earnings to be reported to shareholders?
6. At what point should the permanent financing market be approached?
7. Are governmental programs available that can aid or lower the cost of financing?
8. What is company policy toward covenants or restrictions pertaining to financial ratios or operations?
9. How does the company wish to have the financing reflected on its balance sheet?

CORPORATE CREDIT

The question of dedication of corporate credit turns on the credit standing of a company. If a company is publicly held and is well known to public and private investing and/or lending sources, and if its debt obligations are rated by well-known rating services such as Moody's Investors Service or Standard & Poor's, then the cost of borrowing can be readily estimated. This can be done by reviewing prevailing money market costs for similarly rated companies.

Depending on the nature of the property and the borrower's ability to repay, a company has the flexibility to approach real estate–oriented or credit-oriented lenders. In many institutions, particularly insurance companies, the separation of lending operations into a bond department and a mortgage department bears witness to this distinction. Bond departments, by and large, lend with primary emphasis on the credit of the borrower, while mortgage departments look to the collateral protection of the property and its inherent economic value as real estate. Lenders can probably derive a higher return on their money if the loan is not a credit-oriented loan. Historically, interest rates have generally been higher in situations where financing is associated solely with property value (mortgage rates) than the alternative involving a corporate obligation (credit rates).

The major consideration to focus on in determining whether to utilize corporate credit in real estate financing situations is that fixed assets such as buildings provide one of the few situations where financing can be accomplished without necessarily requiring credit support. Therefore, if corporate credit is not required, even though the cost may be slightly higher, the use of mortgage financing can preserve corporate credit for other purposes, and thereby preserve and augment overall borrowing capacity.

PERCENTAGE OF FINANCING

Generally speaking, full-cost financing (100 percent) is available only where the full credit backing of a company is dedicated. If the loan is to be based on property value alone, lesser percentages apply. In many cases this becomes a function of legal lending limits as prescribed under state laws governing insurance company investment policy and the like. Typically, a loan amount in such a situation is equal to approximately 75 percent of the cost of a property.

If a property such as an office building or distribution facility is general purpose in nature, and is well located, it will command a higher percentage loan in the absence of credit backing.

To the extent that the property is a special purpose property or poorly located, a lesser percentage of cost will be obtainable. If full recovery of cost is sought in financing situations of this type, consideration must be given to the probability that credit support will be required.

LENGTH OF FINANCING TERM

A basic philosophy concerning this issue involves the concept of "matching" the term of the financing to the life of the asset. If the credit of the borrower is unavailable, or if the creditworthiness of the borrower is questionable, the physical security of the underlying asset must be relied on. Consequently, its remaining life has an obvious effect on the ability of the lending institution to recover the balance of its loan.

It is in planning the variety of financing needs of a company that the matching concept has its principal application. It is clear that unless each segment of a business is appropriately financed, overall financial needs will be affected. Working capital cannot be tied up in a building or project without considering the possibility of disrupting the availability of these funds for day-to-day operations. Revolving bank lines or similar arrangements that make funds available to be drawn on as needed are much more suitable for short-term funding needs.

Long-term borrowing is usually the appropriate form for financing most types of building projects. Debt service charges can be a major element in the profitability and cash flow of a business operation. The longer the financing term extends, the smaller the charge is to annual operating costs.

TAX POSTURE

As this is written, the prospect of tax simplification and/or reform once again overshadows the real estate marketplace. Changes in tax law that have been suggested may well shift the scales of economic balance with respect to many areas touched upon in this chapter, as well as financing techniques as they are currently employed.

Financing decisions will often turn on a company's tax posture. A capital intensive company already may have tax deductions available that are substantial enough to render possible additional deductions of marginal use. Here, lease financing can be an attractive alternative. By lease financing, a borrower or lessee company may, in effect, "trade" tax benefits it cannot otherwise utilize to a tax-oriented lessor who is able to take advantage of these tax deductions. The benefit of such a trade to the lessee company is a lower effective interest cost (as measured by the interest rate implicit in the rentals payable under the lease) than the comparable interest cost available in conventional debt financing. This can be achieved because the lessor will typically require less in the way of a cash return on his investment because of the tax benefits available in the form of depreciation deductions, interest deductions (if the lessor finances his purchase of the property), and possibly investment credit for equipment.

Another situation suggesting lease financing is one where a company has a tax loss carryforward from previous operations so that tax deductions attendant to ownership cannot be utilized. Here, imaginative financing possibilities present themselves. For example, other assets of the company, perhaps properties substantially older, which have been written down for tax purposes, could be sold and re-leased back at prices equal to their current market values. The gain realized by the sale and leaseback of the older properties could be absorbed by the tax loss carryforward, and the funds derived from the sale could be used to pay for the new project.

Clearly, heavy emphasis must be placed on the analysis of the after-tax cash flow effect of the financing decision. Sophisticated computer techniques have been developed to assist in such an analysis and should be considered if internal programs are unavailable.

REPORTED EARNINGS

Where a company is publicly owned, management must carefully consider the impact that the form of financing will have on future income statements to be reported to shareholders. In large measure this turns on the philosophy and objectives of a company and whether or not management is "earnings-per-share" oriented or "after-tax cash flow" oriented. Due to differences between financial and tax reporting, the approach that seems best from an after-tax cash flow point of view may not be consistent with an attempt to show higher earnings per share.

In today's corporate environment of growth through acquisition, where multiples of earnings often play such an important part in setting values for companies, in many cases the effect on reported earnings may well be the most important aspect of a long-term financing decision. This may also be an important and forward-looking decision for a small or privately held company that is contemplating the possibility of being acquired or of going public.

In many cases (obviously subject to an evaluation of the facts in any specific case) lease financing initially will have a favorable impact on reported earnings when compared to the alternative of ownership and related direct debt financing. This is due to the fact that the combination of interest on indebtedness and depreciation charges relating to ownership of a property will usually be higher in the early years of a financing transaction than the comparable rental charge to earnings in a lease financing of similar term. In later years, this result will be reversed, and the charges to earnings will be greater in the lease situation. An argument advanced in support of the acceptability of this heavier impact in later years is that it will be more than offset by the overall continued growth of the earnings of the company.

TIMING OF PERMANENT FINANCING

In any construction situation of a magnitude that involves a considerable length of construction time, the following questions need to be answered:

1. When do we attempt to tie down permanent financing?
2. Is now the best time or should we wait?
3. Are interest rates likely to come down and present a better opportunity for financing in the future?

A small company with limited financial resources may have no choice as to timing due to the fact that a long-term financing commitment must be in place in order to obtain construction financing. On the other hand, a major corporation active on a continuous basis in capital markets has greater access to long-term and short-term financing and hence more latitude in responding to the above questions. Conceivably, construction could be financed out of pocket while long-term money market conditions are evaluated.

Prognosticating financial rates and markets is, at best, a guessing game, albeit an educated one. A general rule that should be followed is that the market should be approached when a company needs to know that the project is financed. Knowing that funding is committed may make a narrow band of interest rate savings a quibble if a situation should arise similar to the 1974 "credit crunch," where companies of less than the highest quality credit ratings found that money was not available at any price.

GOVERNMENTAL PROGRAMS

A myriad of programs at federal, state, and local governmental levels are available from time to time. To attempt to detail present programs in this chapter would be impossible, especially as, given the nature of the political bodies involved, these programs are constantly changing. Decisions pertaining to location and financing should be made only after a careful evaluation of inducements that may be available. The need to attract industry, eliminate urban blight, create jobs, and so on dictates continuous governmental review of financing and other assistance, such as real estate tax abatement, to companies considering constructing new facilities.

Many governmental programs are in a stage of development where, as a practical matter, they may be subject to negotiation to fit the framework and objectives of the company contemplating a new facility. This is not to suggest that assistance programs are not properly organized, but is indicative of the fact that in many cases, there is effort by the agencies to attempt to recognize and accommodate market factors and trends that affect financing in order to achieve their desired goals.

A current major inducement relates to the expansion of the limitation on the amount subject to tax-exempt financing under industrial development enabling legislation. This amount was increased from

$5 million to $10 million, and local governments have in many cases been expansive in defining the types of facilities that qualify for these industrial development bonds. Obviously, the savings in the use of tax-exempt financing can be substantial.

Due, then, to the fluid state of these programs and the political factors and changes in tax policy or law that effect them, they must be evaluated on an ad hoc basis, dependent on the particular project and the potential sites under consideration.

COVENANTS AND RESTRICTIONS

In many cases, both in bank lending transactions and in long-term private or public financing arrangements, protective requirements relating to the borrower's operations are written into the documentation by the lender. Typically, these provisions monitor a company's growth and set requirements and obligations on the part of the borrower, based on such things as working capital, cash flow coverage of debt service, ratios of equity to debt, and the encumbrance of assets, both those existing at the time of the financing and assets subsequently acquired. A borrower must approach these restrictions cautiously, for the desire to fund a current project should not be accommodated at the expense of future growth and flexibility. For example, if future lease financing is limited because of loan covenants, the flexibility to gain access to this source of funding could be precluded even if future money market conditions or tax considerations suggest lease financing as an attractive approach in a given situation. A company may find itself "hamstrung" by existing covenants at a time when expansion and growth are dictated.

The foregoing is not intended to suggest that it is inappropriate to insist upon these covenants. Rather it is intended to suggest that the borrower weigh carefully the restrictive covenants' potential effect on its future growth and available financing alternatives that do not require these types of covenants.

Using assets as a base under a secured financing approach is a method that may enable a company to avoid restrictive covenants that could come back to inhibit a desired future project or group of projects. The "restrictions" that would apply when a particular property is financed run directly to the facility itself in terms of maintenance, disposal, intended use, and so on.

The flexibility to finance properties on an individual basis may also result in a leverage capacity where, so to speak, the sum of the parts is greater than the whole. It may be possible that a greater aggregate financing capacity can be arranged utilizing secured financing.

BALANCE SHEET TREATMENT

Historically, in the evaluation of lease financing as one of the major methods of indirectly financing corporate growth, the single most important motivating factor was the ability to achieve "off-balance-sheet" financing. For many years, controversy raged over how leasing should be treated on financial statements. Lease financing supporters contended that leasing effectively expanded a company's capacity to leverage itself (in part due to the uncertainty about accounting treatment). In November of 1976, the Financial Accounting Standards Board promulgated its *Statement of Financial Accounting Standards No. 13,* entitled "Accounting for Leases," commonly referred to as *FASB Statement No. 13.* This complex statement sets forth the criteria on which a determination is to be made as to whether or not leases are required to be capitalized on the financial statements of the lessee. *Capitalization* means that leases so classified must be included as long-term debt in the liability section of the corporate balance sheet. Alternatively, if a lease is not capitalized by reason of qualifying as an operating lease under *FASB Statement No. 13,* this fact must be set forth in footnotes to the corporate financial statement. These footnotes essentially require explanation of the dollar amounts of minimum lease commitments over a period of years.

This footnote treatment is an objective for many companies for a variety of reasons. For example, it may be that under existing loan agreements where there are covenants that affect the ability to raise additional debt, this debt will be set forth in terms that are rigidly defined. Consequently, it may be that in order to avoid violation of the covenant, a lease that need not be capitalized would have to be structured in order to accomplish financing of the property. Another example might involve the precise definition of debt as it would be applied in analysis by rating services in determining a company's quality rating on its debt issues. Opponents of lease financing argue that the machinations involved in structuring these transactions represent nothing more than a triumph of form over substance. Their contention, in many cases correct, is that many lending institutions treat leases in any event as debt. Nevertheless, the fact remains that in many circumstances, a company's particular objectives or requirements will dictate that lease financing on an off-balance-sheet basis is the best method to pursue.

Under *FASB Statement No. 13,* if a lease meets any one of the following tests, it will be classified as a capital lease on the financial statements of the lessee:

1. The lease transfers ownership of the property to the lessee by the end of the lease term.

2. The lease contains an option to purchase the property at a bargain price.
3. The lease term is equal to 75 percent or more of the estimated economic life of the property.
4. The present value of the total minimum lease payments, as defined, equals 90 percent or more of the fair value, as defined, of the leased property.

The provisions of *FASB Statement No. 13* are complex. A thorough analysis should be made by responsible corporate financial officers, and concurred in by the company's auditors, if balance sheet treatment is critical to a decision on how financing is to be best accomplished.

CATEGORIES OF FINANCING

Stated in its simplest terms, the types of financing that can be accomplished on a "secured" basis fall into two general categories: direct financing and indirect financing. Direct financing in turn breaks down into two further categories: "bond" or credit-oriented financing, and "mortgage" or real estate–oriented financing. Reference to the terms *bond* or *mortgage* financing loosely derives from whether or not a transaction qualifies for the bond department of an insurance company or its mortgage department. As mentioned earlier, the bond department historically has been the place where the credit of a company is the prime factor involved in a financing, whereas in the mortgage department, economic or collateral value of the property itself is emphasized. In practical application, this discussion is not limited to insurance companies, and the distinctions drawn generally can be expanded to the entire universe of real estate capital sources.

Indirect financing can, to a large degree, be lumped into the category of lease financing. This type of financing is referred to in a number of ways, for example, as sale/leasebacks or third-party leases, but in a true literal sense, the correct term of reference is lease financing. For example, only an existing property can properly be the subject of a *sale/leaseback,* since that term would not apply to a new property that may never be owned by the lessee in the first place. In referring to lease financing as a category of indirect financing, the essential distinction is that the property be owned for tax purposes by the lessor, which also means that at the end of the lease term the property is owned by the lessor in a very real sense, and cannot be the subject of any nominal rights to recapture or control the property if the transaction is to meet the objectives originally bargained for.

In the descriptive outlines that follow we will touch upon the most pertinent terms and conditions that apply to the types of financing referred to above. In most cases, under the major headings listed, there is a further breakdown as to typical distinguishing features between bond and mortgage transactions.

Bond or Mortgage Financing (Direct)

Basic Formats. *Bond Financing.* Here, typical formats involve either a direct obligation of the issuing company, or the creation of a nominally capitalized special purpose subsidiary to be the issuer. In the latter case, the issuer would be a subsidiary whose obligations would be secured by an absolutely net lease (commonly called "hell or high water" or "bond net") of the properties to the parent company, and additionally by first mortgage security on the subject property or properties. This type of structure is referred to, among other things, as "captive" lease financing, to be distinguished from third-party or "arm's-length" lease financing, which is described below. The essential difference is that the user or occupant corporation retains ownership and control of the properties through outright ownership of the issuing corporation or, if the ownership is vested in a third party (used sometimes for convenience), through options to acquire ownership of the issuing company for nominal consideration. This is a structure that is used in many cases simply to isolate the financing and to effectively give the backing of the credit of the company involved, in cases where it is preferable, for a variety of possible reasons, not to issue additional direct debt.

In cases where there are no problems with issuing direct debt, the form of the debt obligation issued would be a full-faith and credit obligation of the company that again would be additionally secured by a mortgage on the property involved. As mentioned earlier, and notwithstanding the full-faith and credit nature of the undertaking to repay, restrictive covenants on the operations of the obligor company would not typically be involved.

Mortgage Financing. Mortgage obligations may be structured similarly to the above with the major distinction being that the full faith and credit of the corporation involved would not be dedicated to repayment of the indebtedness. If the debt were issued directly to the company, it would be on a nonrecourse basis, which means that the ability of the lender to look for repayment of his loan in the event of a default situation would be limited to the value of the property involved. If the indebtedness were that of a subsidiary or affiliated company and a lease were involved, the lease would not necessarily be a so-called hell or high water lease and accordingly could be terminated in various circumstances by the lessee, again with the result that should such circumstances arise, the lender would have to look solely to the property.

Principal Amount. *Bond Financing.* Depending on the credit standing of the company, 100 percent financing is typically available. This would be true whether or not a direct debt obligation was involved or the captive subsidiary approach were used.

Mortgage Financing. In this case, since the credit of the borrower is not involved, a much closer look will be taken by the lender at the pure "real estate" economic value of the property. Dependent on the outcome of the evaluation, the lender will advance a percentage of the cost of the facility, clearly less than 100 percent, and more likely in the range of, say, 60 to 80 percent, depending, of course, on all relevant factors to be considered. Among the principal relevant factors would be whether or not the property or properties were special purpose by reason of use or size, location, and so on.

Interest Rate. *Bond Financing.* It is obvious that interest rates will be set in the context of market conditions at the time a financing commitment is sought. For larger, readily identifiable companies, the interest rate will be determined based on that company's credit standing as viewed in traditional public and/or private placement markets. Historically, there has tended to be a slightly higher interest rate required on private secured financing of this type, typically in the range of from ¼ of 1 percent to ½ of 1 percent over a company's public market borrowing rate. For example, if a company was rated single A by the two major rating agencies, that is, Moody's or Standard & Poor's, and could borrow in the public markets at, say, 12 percent, then in the private market the cost might have been 12¼ percent to 12½ percent. However, there have been periods when the spread between these rates tended to be narrow and at times nonexistent. Indeed, at certain points, slightly better rates prevailed in private markets.

Mortgage Financing. Mortgage rates have historically tended to be higher than bond rates and to some extent have been somewhat insensitive to credit strength, since reliance, for security of loan purposes, has been on the property itself rather than the credit of the user. For companies with better credit ratings, it generally makes sense to play to credit strength on a recourse basis in order to achieve the lowest possible rate. More recently, there have been times when mortgage rates have been lower than bond rates. Given the variety of ways in which lenders now fund themselves and the impact that it may have on their objectives in putting money out, both methods of financing discussed here should be carefully compared in light of prevailing market conditions.

Term. *Bond Financing.* In bond financing a typical term would be from 10 to 15 years. Longer terms may be available, but seeking a longer term limits the institutions that are able to consider the transaction. Moreover, there is a distinct correlation between term and the credit quality of the borrower. Pressing for a longer term could also have an impact on the interest rate negotiation.

Mortgage Financing. Mortgage terms tend to be longer, and it is not unusual to have a repayment schedule extend for 25 to 30 years. In most cases, however, the stated term for establishing debt service payments is illusory, due to options that the lender reserves to have the loan mature at the end of 10 or 15 years, or to renegotiate rates at those times.

Loan Repayment. *Bond and Mortgage Financing.* Loans made in connection with financing projects of the type we are discussing, whether they be bond or mortgage type loans, typically involve debt service using a so-called constant payment schedule. The amount of the debt service payment is established through the use of compound interest tables that establish the level constant periodic payment necessary to pay interest on and amortize the loan over the term of the financing. For example, if we were talking about a 25-year financing term and an interest rate of 12 percent, which was to be serviced by monthly payments, each monthly payment would be in an amount equal to approximately 1.0532 percent of the amount of the loan (or approximately 12.64 percent on an annual basis). The same type of computation of payment would be applicable even if the periodic payment was quarterly or semiannual.

Variations in structure, of course, are negotiable in particular circumstances, and obviously subject to market conditions. For example, it may be possible to arrange during part of the term of the loan for interest only to be payable so that the principal balance is standing for some period of time. This has the effect of increasing succeeding payments due over the balance of the term necessary to amortize the loan.

In many cases it is possible to arrange for repayment of less than the full amount of the loan so that at maturity there is a remaining balance, or so-called balloon payment, due. This payment, of course, must be satisfied at that time, but it has the effect of reducing the carrying costs over the term of the financing.

Optional Redemption Features. *Bond and Mortgage Financing.* Optional redemption provisions cover the rights of the borrower to prepay the loan in the event of certain contingencies. Typically, if events such as destruction occur as a result of fire or other casualty, or if a building or a significant portion of it is taken under governmental condemnation authority, it is permissible to pay off the outstanding loan balance at the time of occurrence without any premium for so doing. The single most important prepayment provision in most loans has to do with the borrower's ability to take advantage of the availability of lower interest rates in a future money market environment. The lender, of course, wants protection against just such an eventuality for two reasons: First, the lender loses a loan with an attractive rate; and second, the funds he receives as a result of having the loan prepaid must be reinvested in a market where rates available are lower than the rate on the prepaid loan. Usually, the borrower must agree that a purely optional prepayment right cannot be invoked until a predetermined period of years has elapsed in the term of the loan. This period is generally referred to as the "noncall" or "lockup" period and is negotiable in the context of the interest rate and original term of the loan. A 10-year noncall period is not unusual for a 25-year or even a 20-year loan. A shorter term loan of, say, 10 or 15 years, would likely be noncallable for life.

To the extent that there are differences between bond and mortgage financing in this regard, they tend to show up in the length of the noncall period and in the premium that is payable after the noncall period has expired. Mortgage noncall periods are typically shorter. This is probably attributable to the less intense focus on credit and the overall impact credit has on the negotiation of terms. In bond financing, it is typical for the premium in the first year in which prepayment is permissible to be in a percentage equal to the amount determined by reducing the original interest cost ratably over the life of the loan. For example, if the original interest rate was 12 percent, then over a 25-year term the premium would reduce each year by .48 percent. Thus, if there is a 10-year lockup period, the premium applicable in year 11 would be equal to 7.2 percent. In most mortgage situations, the premium that applies in the first year after the noncall period is a standard 5 to 7 percent that thereafter ratably reduces over the balance of the loan term.

Timing. *Bond Financing.* In a bond financing situation, commitments can usually be obtained quite promptly, assuming that the credit standing of the borrower is strong and easily understood. Typically, from the time of submission of a specific presentation of a proposed financing and its terms and conditions, a response can be obtained within a matter of weeks or even, in a situation that must be treated expeditiously, a matter of days. It is largely a function of the negotiation of interest rate. From the point of initial presentation to the signing of a commitment, the time involved could be as little as 30 to 60 days.

Mortgage Financing. Subject to exceptions with particular institutions, the mortgage application and approval procedure is generally more formal and cumbersome. The particular property or properties involved must be subjected to a complete evaluation and appraisal in order to determine basic acceptability as collateral and to determine the percentage of the loan. Interest rate certitude is not achieved until this information has been gathered and submitted in the form of an application so that it can be presented to the appropriate approval committee. In many cases, several months pass while this process is in the works, and the borrower has no assurance that the rate submitted will be the rate approved in the event that money markets have moved away in the interim. In bond financing there is a tacit understanding that the submission rate (the rate suggested in the light of market conditions at the point in time that the transaction is initially submitted) will be the rate at which the transaction will be consummated. It is generally understood that subsequent documentation procedures are based on an agreement that the rate is set.

In General. The foregoing described distinguishing features between bond financing and mortgage financing. In the context of a specific financing proposal and/or the documentation of a commitment, the following additional terms and conditions will normally be required. Here, there is a commonality of requirements for both bond and mortgage financing:

1. The lender is to be furnished with satisfactory title insurance.
2. The building and improvements being financed are satisfactorily completed and are free of liens.
3. A survey of the property will be required.
4. Depending on the credit strength of the issuer, evidence of appropriate insurance coverage for the full insurable value of the improvements with standard mortgagee clauses will be required.
5. An opinion of the lender's counsel will be required to the effect that all of the obligations undertaken by the borrower are valid and enforceable and have been duly authorized and executed.
6. A certificate will be required setting forth in reasonable detail the exact cost of the property and a breakdown of the makeup of the cost.
7. Typically it is appropriate for the borrower to pay all costs in connection with documentation and consummation of the trans-

action, including title insurance premiums, recording fees and taxes, counsel fees, the costs of engineering reports, and so on. It is safe to say that virtually all transaction costs are for the account of the borrower including the payment of any brokerage or investment banking fees for arranging the financing.

8. Commitment fees may or may not be payable in connection with forward commitments. Historically, forward commitments of six months or more have involved commitment or standby fees. More recently, forward commitments have become less commonplace because of interest rate volatility.

Lease Financing (Indirect)

Advantages. The following represent advantages of and reasons for consideration of lease financing:

1. The possibility of doing off-balance-sheet financing.
2. The avoidance of restrictive covenants.
3. The affording of the opportunity to transfer the tax benefits associated with ownership to the lessor in order to enable the lessee to obtain a lower effective money cost (particularly applicable in a situation where the lessee is unable to fully utilize tax benefits itself).
4. The provision of access to alternative funding sources in situations where a company may wish to preserve its traditional sources of funds for other financing requirements.
5. The benefit (generally) from a reported earnings point of view for the near term.
6. The opportunity to obtain 100 percent financing.
7. The ability to achieve off-balance-sheet financing for nonrevenue-producing assets, which certain real estate assets may be.
8. The provision for longer term financing at what are essentially fixed rates.

Disadvantages. The disadvantages that are most often noted by companies that are disinclined to consider lease financing are:

1. Property residual values are lost at the end of the term of the lease.
2. If a company is able to use the tax benefits of ownership itself, suggested interest cost savings in lease financing may be largely offset.
3. Changes in the future could result in loss of flexibility if they

prevent the utilization or operation of particular properties or projects to their maximum advantage.

Major Terms and Conditions. The outline below summarizes major terms and conditions that a prospective lessee must evaluate.

Term. Lease financings typically involve basic terms of from 20 to 30 years. Shorter lease periods would not make sense where one is using lease financing as a method of long-term financing. The exception is when the lessee, for operating reasons, wants to retain the flexibility of discontinuing the use of the property at some point in time, for example, after 10 years. Here, however, we are assuming that the building in question would be used for a longer period of time, and since the lessee is giving up residual value, it makes sense to have the lease extend for a 25- to 30-year period since this basic period will essentially amortize the cost of the facility. If its continued use is contemplated, the renewal rents payable will effectively increase the cost of this method of financing. On the other hand, if lease financing is to be utilized principally to accomplish off-balance-sheet treatment, then it is probable that a shorter term lease, in the range of 20 to 25 years, would achieve this objective. This is principally due to the fact that the present value calculations that are made to determine whether or not the rentals, when discounted, are equal to less than 90 percent of the value of the property, will work out to a higher present value the longer the term of the lease. Longer lease terms make it more difficult to have this calculation work out so that the lease will not be a capital lease.

Lessor's Purchase Price. The price paid by the purchaser/lessor to acquire the property will generally be equal to 100 percent of the cost of the property. Indeed, if the credit strength of the lessee is significant, even slightly more than 100 percent financing may be possible. However, to have the lessor purchase for an amount in excess of 100 percent of certifiable cost raises tax considerations in that any gain on the sale might be considered to be a taxable event to the lessee. For weaker credit companies, 100 percent financing is achievable because of the combination of debt and equity sources of funds: In many cases this will provide their only means of obtaining full financing. An equity investor who is looking for a "hard" investment in something like real estate and who knows that he will own the residual value may be willing, or indeed prefer, to put up anywhere from 20 to 40 percent of the cost. This has the effect of facilitating mortgage financing, since the ratio of the loan is obviously smaller than if the lender were asked to fund 100 percent of the purchase price.

Lease Rentals. In today's marketplace, unless you are dealing with a very weak credit situation, lease financing will generally provide a savings in interest cost versus the lessee company's so-called incremental borrowing rate. This incremental borrowing rate refers to the rate that would be available to the company in question in a conventional financing and would be the debt rate appropriate, if ownership were involved, in a bond financing or mortgage financing as referred to above. The saving in rate is usually referred to as a so-called spread or discount from the debt rate and can be explained as follows: Assume that in acquiring a property, the lessor in today's marketplace is able to arrange financing, based on the credit of the lessee, at an interest cost of 12 percent to be repaid over 25-year term. Given such an assumption, a typical lease quote that would be available to the lessee would be structured so that the schedule of rental payments, from the lessee's point of view, would be equivalent to amortizing the purchase price of the property over 25 years at an effective interest rate in the range of from 9½ to 10½ percent. The difference between this effective rate and the borrowing rate of 12 percent would thus be 150 to 250 basis points in interest cost and so the spread would be quoted as discounting the borrowing rate by 1½ to 2½ percent. Lease rental structures and quotations have been subjected to very rapid change and have become markedly more complex as this type of financing experienced dramatic growth in recent years. There is great pricing sensitivity to changes in tax law and debt structuring, and it would be fair to describe lease financing as being in a continuously evolving status.

Renewal Rents. Renewal rent provisions in lease financing have recently undergone significant changes. In the past it was usual for renewal rents to be nominal as compared to the basic term rents. Annual renewal rents in the amounts from 1 to 3 percent of the original property cost were fairly typical and option periods were set forth in 5- or ten-year increments beyond the basic lease term for as long as 30 to 50 years. This was largely due to the fact that purchasers at those points in time were almost exclusively tax-oriented individuals, and the tax laws were such that transactions were favorable based on tax savings alone. Great attention was not paid to residuals. With the continuous scrutiny of tax shelter investments by the Internal Revenue Service and with the concurrent scrutiny of balance sheet treatment by the accounting profession, these nominal options have disappeared and are not presently available to lessees. Moreover, the spectrum of investors interested in this type of transaction, including pension funds and offshore investors, are now looking at this type of transaction in a completely different way. They look to significant residual values. The ravages of inflation in past years have made them extremely conscious of fixed future options to renew leases. Consequently, in today's market the general rule is that renewal rents parallel the basic term rents and do not extend as fixed rents for much beyond a total of 40 to 50 years (including the basic term). Where a lessor suggests that renewal rents be reduced, accounting advice should be sought, for most accounting firms tend to view reduced rents as bargain rents. This would result in lease capitalization under *FASB Statement No. 13.*

Purchase Options. If the "true lease" nature of a transaction is to be sustained, fixed price purchase options cannot be granted to the lessee. In general, purchase options should be stated in terms of fair market value of the property when the options are exercisable (which is typically at the end of the basic lease term). Fixed options would raise many of the questions referred to in the discussion of renewal rents. The most essential issue that a company must face in considering lease financing is the fact that if the lease is properly structured, the company must give up residual value. From an operating point of view, the right to continue to use the property is provided through renewal rents, but from a purely financial point of view, the residuals are surrendered. This, however, is sometimes an illusory problem, for as a practical matter, if the company is operating in a building or facility and anticipates that it will continue to do so for a long period of time, then "residual values" cannot be realized in the sense of a cash sale for the very reason that they are continuing to be utilized. If that is the case, then on a present value basis the incremental effect on interest cost of renewal rents that are so far out in the future is not significant. It should also be noted that the "fair market value" of the property would effectively be limited by the alternative right of the lessee to renew the lease.

SUMMARY COMMENT

It should be apparent that money market conditions, tax laws, and accounting regulations are always subject to change, and the nature of the changes could obviously have an impact on some of the conclusions and/or considerations discussed in this chapter. The point to be remembered is that the asset involved is open to a variety of financing structures and a variety of sources of funding. The corporate construction project thus provides unique flexibility and a particular opportunity to employ the most effective financing techniques achievable under whatever overall conditions apply at a given point in time.

CHAPTER **18**

Convertibles and Warrants

Stephen L. Schechter
General Partner
Wertheim & Co.
New York, N.Y.

Stephen L. Schechter is a general partner of the investment banking firm of Wertheim & Co. He joined Wertheim in 1975 as a vice president in the corporate finance department where he now heads the private placement and lease financing areas. One of his prime responsibilities is advising emerging growth companies on capital-raising alternatives and capital structures. Over his 23 years on Wall Street, he has been involved in all aspects of convertible, warrant, and equity-linked financings and has assisted numerous companies in achieving their financial goals and objectives. His department works with both institutional investors and corporate clients to optimize the money-raising ability of the corporation while minimizing its costs.

One of the most flexible ways of raising capital is through the issuance of convertible debt or convertible preferred stock, or debt or preferred stock with a warrant feature attached.

First, let us define the security in its simplest form. It is a note or preferred stock with a stated maturity, yield, and negative covenants as found in any other note or preferred stock *except* that the holder has the right under the terms of the issue to convert or exchange the note or preferred share for common stock for a specific amount of shares per note or preferred share. This, in effect, gives the holder of a convertible both the yield or income feature of a senior security, and the capital gains potential of the underlying equity. For this "double play," the buyer, as a rule, will take a lower yield than he would expect to receive on an equivalent straight (nonconvertible) issue, and would be willing to have his security convertible, if publicly traded, at a premium above the current share price, or if private, at a negotiated conversion value substantially in excess of the underlying equity valuation. Almost as important, the buyer, because of the equity component, would be willing to accept a junior or subordinated feature as part of the debt security and would agree to liberal restrictive covenants so as to give the issuing company maximum corporate flexibility and to achieve a greater potential return on his underlying equity security.

A warrant is the right to acquire a security at a specific price for a given period of time. In the main context of this chapter, a warrant will be used for the acquisition of common stock, but other forms will be touched on later.

THE MAGNITUDE OF THE MARKET

In 1985, there were 167 offerings of convertible debt public issues amounted to over $10.2 billion, and private placements reported by investment bankers totaled 30 issues and over $260 million. However, I believe the private market to be more than double that amount due to directly placed and unreported issues. In addition, if one adds in convertible preferreds and issues with warrants, the domestic market easily absorbed over $12.5 billion in 1985 alone. These figures do not touch public and private Eurodollars so the true size of this market may well be running at $6 billion plus per year. At present, the New York Stock Exchange has 291 listed convertible debt issues and the American Stock exchange has 78. With another 228 issues traded OTC, and some others traded on regional exchanges, the publicly traded convertible debt market in the United States exceeds 600 issues.

In spite of these impressive numbers, one must put convertible debt in proper perspective. In 1985, total nongovernment domestic straight debt issues issued publicly were just over 900 offering and $100 billion. The reported private market showed just under 1700 placements and over $61 billion. In terms of total dollar volume, convertibles represented approximately 6 percent of the dollar volume of the domestic debt market.

More and more companies, both public and private, are looking at convertibles as an attractive financing vehicle. Today, aside from the historical buyers—insurance companies, pension funds, and trust departments—special mutual funds have been formed just for convertibles, and there is substantial individual awareness and demand for issues with both a yield and equity component. It is my belief that this demand will continue to increase, and I envision the convertible market expanding to $10 billion per year by the end of this decade.

ADVANTAGES AND USES OF CONVERTIBLES

One of the most logical and frequently asked questions from a chief executive officer or chief financial officer is, Why issue a convertible or warrant-linked security instead of straight debt or straight equity? The answer to this question is not as simple as it sounds, as no two financings are alike, and each issue must be tailored to the needs and desires of the individual corporate issuer. However, there are certain answers that are applicable to all.

Yield

The coupon or dividend on a convertible or equity-linked security will be lower than on comparable maturity senior debt or nonequity-linked debt. A good example here is the Zayre Corp.'s $75 million public issue of 7¼ percent convertible subordinated debentures, due in the year 2010, issued July 19, 1985. On that day, comparable maturity U.S. Treasury issues were yielding 10.60 percent and Zayre, as an A rated company, would have expected to pay at least 115 basis points over the comparable Treasury. Therefore, by issuing a convertible, Zayre saved 4.5 percent or $3,375,000 per year in interest expense on this borrowing. Zayre, the discount department store and specialty retailer, by giving the holder a long call on underlying equity, issued debt at an interest rate that was unattainable from any other source at that time.

Maturity

As a rule, because of the equity feature, investors are willing to accept a longer maturity on equity-linked financings than straight issues. The reason for this is the purchaser's desire to have the longest possible call on the company's common stock. He is prepared to trade off a long maturity for the potential equity return.

Covenants and Subordination

Any company that has ever borrowed money from a bank or an insurance company is familiar with the term *negative covenants.* These are the restrictions and conditions under which a company must live during the term of the loan. Covenants such as permitted senior debt, capital expenditures, limitations on working capital, current ratio, and net worth maintenance are substantially reduced, and in the case of public issues, usually eliminated. The reason for this is the purchaser is prepared to trade off covenant protection for the underlying equity "kicker" or play. Additionally, in the opinion of most investment bankers, because of the conversion or warrant, the subordination feature and the relaxation of negative covenants, which permit greater leverage and more corporate flexibility, are probably the most important reasons for issuing a convertible or warrant.

Leverage

Senior lenders, particularly banks and private placement lenders, will, in most cases, treat convertible subordinated debt or subordinated debt with warrants as part of the company's capital base in determining senior borrowing capacity. An excellent example of this is Eaton Financial Corporation, a nationwide leasing company, that in three equity-linked private placements—two subordinated notes with warrants, and one convertible subordinated note—increased its capital base by $19 million. Since Eaton's loan agreements permit senior debt up to 87.5 percent of total capitalization, these issues effectively increased Eaton's senior borrowing capacity by $133 million.

Premium

One of the most attractive features of a convertible or warrant issue is that the purchaser is willing to accept a substantial premium above the current stock price for the long-term right to acquire the common stock while still having a current yield. In the case of the earlier mentioned Zayre issue, it was convertible at $70.40 per share on a day that the stock closed at $55 per share, or a premium of 28 percent. Up until this issue, the highest Zayre common stock traded was 57⅝. In the case of Eaton's private placements, a premium of 125 percent over a 10-day trading period was used to determine the conversion and warrant strike prices on its two most recent issues. Again, prices were above the highest price the company's shares had ever traded prior to the issues.

Call Feature

One of the objectives a company has in issuing convertibles is that when the underlying shares go up, they can call or optionally redeem the issue. If the call price, at the time of the call, is well below the dollar amount of the market value of the common stock, the bond holder will convert into common stock rather than take cash at the lower dollar amount. This way the company increases its equity, reduces its debt, and improves its capitalization, all through a feature placed in the issue when it was originally sold. On public issues the issuer, as a rule, can redeem the convertibles at par plus its coupon at any time if the underlying common stock sells above 140 or 150 percent of the conversion price, usually for a 20-trading-day period. This is one of the nice features of a convertible, where financial flexibility really rests with the issuer. In the private placement market, it is common to have callable warrants. This feature is very attractive for all parties, as it locks in a yield for the holder and conversely permits the issuer to force holders to exercise the warrants earlier than they would normally like to do.

Dilution Minimization and Limits on Equity

Public or private common stock offerings are done at the current market price, or in some cases even a slight discount. However, with a warrant or convertible issued at a premium, such premium translates to less equity given up per dollar received. Again, this is a very attractive feature, especially when founder/management is concerned about personal equity holdings and dilution. The use of warrants with debt has another advantage to management: With warrants, a company can issue less shares underlying the debt than with a convertible. Eaton Financial Corp. issued only 400,000 warrants at $10.19, or an equity cover of 40.76 percent, on a $10 million subordinated note issue. In both of these cases, while a higher coupon was required for both issues versus a convertible, a substantial amount of dilution was avoided in two companies with exciting growth prospects.

Value-Setting for Public Offering

One of the most common uses of private convertibles is to determine a value of a private company with the intent of going public in the not too distant future. Companies have been known to issue different series of convertibles over a few years prior to going public, with each issue being priced at a premium above the previous one. An example of this is the National Guardian Corporation, which on April 2, 1984, in a private placement, sold 996,514 shares of straight common stock at $5.75 per share. On April 13, 1984, it issued, in a private placement, $8 million of 10 percent cumulative convertible preferred stock at $6.25 per share. A year later, May 1985, National Guardian issued another private placement, this time $15 million of 9.5 percent convertible subordinated notes that were convertible at $9 per share. On July 19, 1985, National Guardian went public on a 3 million share offering at $12 per share.

Acquisition Financing

Whether a company is public or private, the use of convertibles or warrants for acquisition financings is one of the most common uses of this type of security. Many companies overextend their senior debt capacity to do an acquisition, and either cannot or will not issue common stock in order to make the acquisition, because in the opinion of management the shares are undervalued in the marketplace vis-à-vis the postacquisition projected values. Usually, a public convertible offering is out of the question because the SEC filing requirements do not permit projections and pro forma management discussions. Therefore, in this case, a private placement of convertibles or notes with warrants increases total borrowings, reduces senior borrowings, values common stock at a premium, and takes into account the pro forma earnings and debt service capacity, since projections can be made in a private placement.

Two excellent examples of this use are Malrite Communications Group, Inc. and SunMedia Corp. First, Malrite, in 1983, agreed to acquire WXIX–TV, Channel 19 in Cincinnati, Ohio, for an acquisition cost of $45 million. At that time, Malrite was not yet public, and had a net worth of approximately $14 million. However, broadcasters, of which Malrite was a strong one, are valued on a multiple of operating cash flow, and in many cases, projected and pro forma operating cash flow, which would have placed a valuation on Malrite after the

WXIX–TV acquisition in the $90 million range. Malrite, with its investment banker, structured the acquisition financing as follows: The seller, Metromedia, Inc., took back $6.5 million of subordinated notes, and the remaining $38.5 million was paid in cash through $28.5 million of senior bank borrowings under the company's $40 million, 10-year revolving credit/term loan facility, and $10 million from the private placement of 10 percent convertible subordinated debt with two institutional lenders. The private placement had a maturity of 15 years and was convertible at $11.726 per share for a pro forma equity valuation of over $92 million. Malrite went public less than two months after the closing of the private placement, issuing 1,850,000 shares of common stock at $12 per share.

SunMedia Corp., a private company, was formed in early 1986 to acquire the common stock of ComCorp, Inc. and Gowe Printing Co. from the Gillett Group, Inc. in a management buyout transaction for approximately $29 million.

ComCorp, Inc., based in Cleveland, Ohio, is the parent company of Sun Newspapers, one of the nation's largest fully-paid suburban newspaper groups, with 18 weekly newspapers covering 62 communities in a geographic ring around metropolitan Cleveland and a total combined circulation of approximately 224,000. Gowe Printing Co. is one of the largest full-service commercial printers in Ohio. Problem: SunMedia had an excellent operating history with pre-interest profits of $5.8 million in 1985 but tangible assets of slightly over $18 million; how does one structure a transaction of this type?

As SunMedia's investment bankers, we proposed a financing structure that would keep the senior debt ratios in line with Ba-type credits, give the company additional funds for capital expenditures, and provide a subordinated capital base with a sufficient equity component to induce institutional investors to take a meaningful subordinated position. The proposed structure consisted of $20 million of 10-year senior notes, $10.5 million of 12-year subordinated notes, and $1.0 million of a cumulative convertible preferred stock which was attached as a unit to the subordinated debt. The preferred was convertible into just under 50 percent of the common stock of SunMedia. In effect, the subordinated lender is putting up $11.5 million for his equity play while being junior to $20 million of fixed-rate senior debt. What makes a structure like this work are the following primary facts:

1. SunMedia's strong operating cash flow covers all interest expenses over 2.3 times and;
2. The senior lender is looking at a capital base below him in excess of $12 million versus his $20 million position.
3. Most important, because of the convertible preferred, the subor-

dinated holder is looking for a dramatic equity return when SunMedia goes public in the next few years.

The result is a management group with minimal capital whose members have the opportunity to fulfill a lifetime dream to become owners of their company and participate in its growth and development as owners rather than employees.

Make an Undoable Financing Doable

In this example, a company (to remain unnamed) was heavily leveraged with a minimum capital base, and its senior lender, a bank, wanted to be paid down. The company tried to place $15 million of senior notes with insurance companies to no avail, but when warrants were added to the notes, the issue was oversubscribed to $20 million, with institutions who rejected the earlier-offered straight debt issue. This is one of the more important uses of warrants, even though in this case management is really admitting that it is in an overleveraged position.

Foreign Securities

The capital markets in the United States are the largest and most sophisticated in the world, and more and more foreign corporations are turning to them for debt and equity through direct issues and America Depository Receipts (ADRs). Inevitably following these issues are convertibles and warrants. As early as the 1960s, Japanese companies were issuing convertibles in the U.S. market. A good example of this was in 1967, when Komatsu Manufacturing Co., Ltd. issued $15 million of 7¼ percent convertible debentures that were convertible into common stock of the Japanese company for ADRs representing 50 shares of common stock, at a conversion price of 134.2 yen or, at that time, $0.37, which translates to $18.64 per ADR. While all this may be confusing to a layman, what it did was give the holder not just a call on Komatsu, a manufacturer of machine tools and industrial and construction vehicles, but an additional opportunity to benefit from any positive moves of the yen versus the dollar.

An interesting problem was brought to my firm in 1984. How can Electra Investment Trust plc raise additional capital for portfolio expansion without dilution? Electra, one of the best performing closed end investment trusts listed on the London Stock Exchange with assets over £ 250 million was already borrowing under its lines of credit in both sterling and dollars, but with its shares selling at 115 pence against a net asset value of 143 pence, a rights offering would be too costly, and their U.K. merchant bankers could not come up with a creative solution. We proposed a private placement of $40 million, seven-year notes with warrants above net asset value rather than above the lower current share price, and the issue would be priced on year-end March 1985 net asset value. The issue closed, in June 1985, with a 100 percent warrant cover on the notes, but with an exercise price of 174 pence, 5 pence over net asset value, and a premium of 40 percent over the current market price. The reason for this high premium was twofold; First, a seven-year warrant on the closed-end trust with the highest five-year return on assets for large trust; and second, the holders have the right to use the notes to exercise the warrants at $1.233 per pound for the life of the issue. Therefore, if the pound goes above $1.233, the holders get an even greater return due to the dollar/pound warrant play.

Commodity Indexing

In the first issue of its kind, in April 1980, Sunshine Mining Company issued $25 million of 8.5 percent silver-indexed bonds, which were effectively convertible into 50 ounces of silver per $1,000 bond, a premium of 25 percent above the spot price on the day of issue. What was unique, aside from the indexing, was the fact that Sunshine could deliver, at its option, 50 ounces of silver per $1,000 bond to holders electing to accept such delivery in satisfaction of the indexed principal amount. The issue was oversubscribed, and Sunshine issued another $25 million in December 1980, and $30 million in February 1983. The success here was not due to Sunshine's record—the company had lost money in 1980, 1981, and 1982—but due to the upside play on silver. In fact, even though silver was down 12 percent from the 1980 prices, the first two issues were selling at a premium of 8.5 to 10.5 percent respectively above par when the 1983 issue was sold. The excitement of the call on the silver outweighed, in the eyes of the investors, the negative performance of Sunshine. In the past few years, other companies have discussed issuing gold or oil-indexed issues, but to my knowledge, none of the issues have been sold publicly, even though over the past few years both commodities have demonstrated exciting price moves.

Convertible Preferred

A question commonly asked investment bankers is, Why not issue a convertible preferred instead of a debenture? The answer is not as simple as it seems on the surface. Theoretically, a corporate buyer in a 46 percent marginal income tax bracket could buy a preferred issue and the dividend would qualify from the 85 percent dividend exclusion, which means an 8 percent convertible preferred would have an equivalent bond yield of approximately 13.25 percent. The question here should be, How does the issue effect the issuer? First, if we assume all the features discussed in this chapter are similar for a debt or preferred convertible, let us focus on the differences.

The preferred dividend is an after-tax charge and may have a negative offset on earnings per share versus a tax-deductible interest payment on a debt issue. A convertible preferred could be used effectively for a broadcaster, airline, or a company in a low- or nontax situation, such as a company with a Puerto Rican or foreign manufacturing subsidiary, where tax incentives benefit an issuer manufacturing in a tax-free zone. Many companies have excellent prospects and projections and may have substantial ITC (investment tax credit), depreciation, or tax loss carryforwards, so again, a convertible preferred is both appropriate and attractive. There are also some situations where senior lenders say debt is debt and the only way to increase leverage is to utilize a preferred vehicle rather than a convertible debt issue.

Preferreds have another inherent advantage over debt: In order to have an 85 percent dividend exclusion, the issue must not have debt features, so preferreds do not have acceleration rights in default, and a covenant default on a preferred issue would not trigger a cross default on senior debt, which could be the case with a subordinated debt issue.

Two examples of proper uses of convertible preferreds are the 1981 issue by Forest Laboratories Inc., and the 1985 issue by JAG Communications Inc. These examples are valid uses of preferred stock for growth companies where convertible debt or debt with warrants just would not work.

Forest Laboratories Inc., for the five years ending March 31, 1980, had a five-year up record in revenues and a four-year down record in net income, with a loss in 1979, and finally a $1.3 million income from continuing operations in fiscal year 1981. Due to tax loss carryforwards and manufacturing in Puerto Rico, this manufacturer of ethical specialty and generic drug products projected it would not be a tax payer until fiscal 1984. INA, an insurance company that was a 46 percent marginal rate tax payer, stepped up and bought the $4 million, 11 percent convertible preferreds with a conversion premium of 25 percent at $20 per share. This made sense to all parties, as the 11 percent rate was below Forest's incremental borrowing cost, and INA was getting a very attractive return with a strong equity play.

JAG Communications Inc., in 1985, owned four top-rated radio stations, and wanted to acquire WFOG–FM in Norfolk, Virginia, as well as WLPM–AM in Suffolk, Virginia, an affiliated company. Pro forma for the acquisitions JAG would have had a net worth of $1.8 million and $15.5 million in borrowings if it could have found a lender to make the loan. In addition, because of depreciation and interest expense, JAG would not have been a tax payer for approximately three years. A $10.5 million senior-financing loan was obtainable, but that left a $5 million shortfall. With less than $2 million in equity, on an equity basis management would have had to give up over 70 percent of the company to do the deal. We proposed a convertible preferred issue that was bought by a trust company for a managed account, which valued the equity not at $1.8 million, but at $12.5 million, based on the projected broadcast operating profits and a current return of 10 percent on the issue.

WARRANT ALTERNATIVES

Briefly, I will attempt to enumerate additional positives and some negatives of warrants, as well as some other interesting features.

The most important feature of a warrant is that when it is exercised, the company gets an infusion of new money that can be used for any corporate purpose, including retiring debt. This feature of unexpected new money at a time when the stock moves up may cause a company to postpone a common stock offering and let its stock go higher due to more demand and no new stock, other than that from the warrant being exercised coming into the market.

Warrants can be callable, that is, the warrant may be redeemed by the issuer for a specific dollar amount. The advantage here is when the common stock moves up and the warrant is "in the money," that is, when the shares trade above the exercise price, the warrant may be called and the holder would exercise his warrant rather than receive a lesser amount in cash.

Warrants may be detached from the debt issue and two separate markets would exist: the debt that is a yield security, and the warrant that is the equity security. By issuing a unit and later splitting it into its components, the issuer would be appealing to two different markets with one issue.

Warrants may have adjustments in their exercise price over time. The longer they are out and unexercised, the higher the exercise price, for example, a step-up every two years of $1 in exercise price on a 10-year warrant.

Warrants may be exercised by the use of cash or, in some cases, by the debt they were issued with, at par, as a cash equivalent. The advantage here is that the debt would be extinguished when the warrants are exercised. The obvious disadvantage is that cash does not come in at the time of exercise. This feature, which costs a company nothing at the time of issue, creates a potential arbitrage situation in the future that could cause debt to be extinguished and common stock to be issued because of changes in the interest rate market, rather than the company's equity prospects.

Lastly, in the past few years, warrants have been linked to debt securities to acquire other debt securities, giving the holder an attractive interest rate play for a specific period of time. The quid pro quo is that the issuer gets a lower coupon (yield) on his initial issue because, in effect, the buyer is paying a premium for the issue because of the warrant feature.

THE OTHER SIDE OF THE COIN

One of the most memorable comments I ever heard about a convertible goes something like this: "It is the ultimate security . . . it has all the disadvantages of both debt and equity." In my opinion this is a great exaggeration, as I have previously noted the many uses and advantages of convertibles and warrants, but in all fairness, like every other security, convertibles and warrants do have some disadvantages.

The minor ones are that you must maintain sufficient authorized but unissued stock to cover the underlying shares, which is a slight increase in expenses. If the issue is public, there are the additional expenses of a new security as well as rating agency expenses, if appropriate.

The major disadvantages are that you are paying a coupon or dividend above the common dividend as a trade-off for the conversion premium. A default of any type on a convertible could trigger a cross default on senior debt. With private convertibles, registration rights and the expenses of a registration statement must be granted to the holder.

However, the worst disadvantage, unlike with common stock or straight debt, is something called an antidilution provision. What this means in its simplest form is that if there is a 2:1 stock split, the conversion price is halved and, in effect, you get the same bond convertible into twice the amount of shares, which is both fair and appropriate. Where this gets complicated, especially in private placements, is when you start getting into subsequent stock issues above or below market or worse, conversion price on the old issue. Worse still is the future issue of a new class of convertible or warrant where the language in the note agreement may run for several pages to describe the circumstances under which an adjustment in conversion price is required. In all fairness, this most negative of negatives can be handled quite easily by a company's lawyers and investment bankers prior to an issue being sold so that all aspects of this are covered to the issuer's satisfaction.

CONCLUSION

In conclusion, convertibles and warrants are a valuable financing tool for any company. They provide a flexible security that by its nature can be tailored to meet the issuer's needs and requirements. They can be issued in all types and sizes and, unlike common stock or straight debt, can be the security that is almost "all things to all people." They can be issued publicly or privately, and they are the one form of security that provides both the issuer and the holder with very attractive features.

There can be no question that this one form of financing alternative answers many questions for an emerging growth company and in most cases will assist it in achieving its growth potential with the maximum dollars at minimal cost.

CHAPTER **19**

ESOP Financing

Fred E. Newberg
President and Chief Executive Officer
Butcher Capital Markets, Inc.
Philadelphia, Pa.

Fred E. Newberg is president and chief executive officer of Butcher Capital Markets, Inc., a subsidiary of Butcher and Company Inc. He is also a director and executive vice president of the holding company. Mr. Newberg is an attorney, a certified public accountant, a member of state and federal accounting and bar associations, and an allied member of the New York Stock Exchange. His responsibilities include the coordinating of all of the group's corporate finance, energy, and health care activities. He is actively involved in the structuring of ESOP financings for private, closely held, and public corporations.

Michael J. Mufson
Managing Director, Corporate Finance
Butcher & Singer Inc.
Philadelphia, Pa.

Michael J. Mufson, managing director, Corporate Finance, joined Butcher & Singer in August 1981. Presently, his emphasis is on public offerings, mergers and acquisitions, and valuations. Mr. Mufson also provides general corporate financial consulting to the firm's clients.

Prior to joining the firm, he spent four years with Arthur Young and Company's National Management Consulting Group. Mr. Mufson graduated from George Washington University in 1976 with a B.A. degree in accounting, and in 1977 with an M.B.A. degree in finance. He is also a certified public accountant.

Research Associate: **Romi Lamba**

INTRODUCTION

The Employee Stock Ownership Plan (ESOP) has become a much discussed and utilized financing vehicle for a host of corporate finance transactions. The purpose of this chapter is to present the fundamentals of an ESOP and raise the reader's cognizance as to how this cost-effective financing can be explored in a number of situations. Although ESOPs touch on a number of disciplines, including accounting, investment banking, securities law, labor management, tax law, and other legal areas, we will attempt to discuss the fundamental issues from an investment banking, tax, and accounting viewpoint.

An ESOP is a qualified employee benefit plan designed to invest primarily in employer securities. ESOPs were traditionally created to give workers a major stockholding in their company, hence enhancing worker productivity, improving labor-management relations, and ultimately increasing profitability. In recent years, however, ESOPs have gained popularity as effective financing vehicles for corporate growth, raising capital, increasing cash flow, acquisitions and divestitures, and as defensive measures against unwanted takeovers.

An ESOP is a form of a stock bonus plan, or a combination of a stock bonus plan and a qualified money purchase plan, holding mainly employer's common stock and other marketable securities. Stock can be accumulated (1) through annual tax-deductible contributions in stock by the company, or (2) through money borrowed from a financial institution (a "leveraged" ESOP) or the employer itself to purchase either newly issued shares from the company or stock from existing shareholders.

Although there are several types of ESOPs, leveraged ESOPs are used to raise capital for general corporate purposes, finance corporate divestitures, and finance leveraged buyouts (LBOs). The remainder of this chapter will discuss primarily the uses and various aspects of leveraged ESOPs.

Salient tax advantages of ESOP financing include:

- Employer contributions to ESOPs of up to 25 percent of its compensation (payroll) will generally be deductible.
- Interest received by the ESOP lender is tax-exempt up to 50 percent.
- Dividends paid by an ESOP to its participants are generally tax-deductible.

These and other tax advantages allow ESOPs to borrow funds at a lower after-tax cost of capital than other types of financing, resulting in savings in after-tax cash flow.

BACKGROUND

Recent encouraging legislation has fueled the growth of ESOPs from less than 1,000 plans in existence in 1974 to over 10,000 plans in 1985. The Employee Retirement Income Security Act of 1974 (ERISA) was the first major step toward formally defining and establishing guidelines for ESOPs. The decade-long efforts of Senator Russell B. Long (D-La.) to strengthen ESOP legislation resulted in further reformulations, including the creation of TRASOPs—tax reduction ESOPs—in 1975 and significant changes under the Revenue Act of 1978.

In 1981, under the Economic Recovery Tax Act (ERTA), ESOPs were made substantially more attractive to companies as the tax-deductible limits of employer contributions were raised from 15 percent to 25 percent of compensation. As an incentive to financial institutions, the 1984 tax law allowed lenders to exclude from their taxable income 50 percent of the interest they receive on loans to ESOPs. In the past year, several banks have structured deals to share this benefit with ESOP borrowers, lending at rates below prime.

The present ESOP tax laws encourage the establishment and use of ESOPs both as an employee benefit and a financing vehicle, and the legislation's effect is evidenced in the growing number and uses of ESOPs across the country.

FINANCIAL STRUCTURE

Illustrated below are the steps involved in a typical leveraged ESOP transaction. The many variations in the use of an ESOP are described in greater detail in the next section; the diagram below highlights the key features common to most leveraged ESOPs.

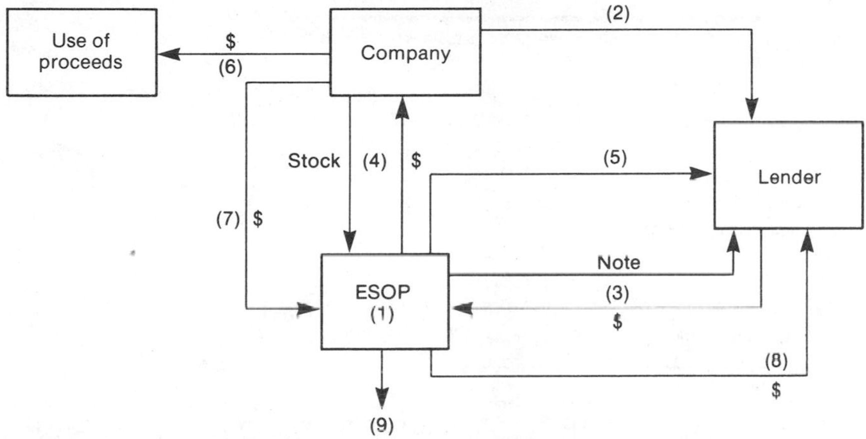

1. The company establishes a leveraged ESOP.
2. The company agrees to make contributions sufficient to service the ESOP's debt and to guarantee the ESOP loan.
3. ESOP borrows the money (to purchase employer securities) from a bank or other lender; the lender receives ESOP note.
4. The company sells stock to ESOP for loan proceeds (cash).
5. ESOP pledges stock to secure note from lender.
6. The company uses proceeds of ESOP financing for corporate growth, an acquisition, purchase of a shareholder's interest, or a leveraged buyout of the company.
7. The company makes annual tax-deductible (up to specified limits) contributions in cash to ESOP in the amount needed to repay loan interest and principal.
8. ESOP services debt.
9. As principal of the note is amortized, ESOP stock equivalent to principal repayment is allocated to employees on a pro rata basis.

The chief advantage of leveraged ESOP financing over regular debt financing is its unique ability to deduct both principal and interest payments. If the ESOP lender shares its 50 percent tax exemption on interest received by charging the ESOP a lower lending rate, the cost of ESOP financing is further reduced.

The after-tax cash savings of leveraged ESOPs are illustrated in Exhibit 1. A company in the 50 percent tax bracket wishes to raise capital of $1 million. A bank will lend it $1 million, the principal payable in 10 equal annual installments of $100,000 each, at an interest rate of 10 percent a year. The interest over the term of the note will total $550,000.

EXHIBIT 1 After-Tax Cash Savings of a Leveraged ESOP

	Direct Loan	*Leveraged ESOP*
Payment over 10 years		
Principal	$1,000,000	$1,000,000
Interest	550,000	550,000
Total payments	$1,550,000	$1,550,000
Tax savings—50 percent		
Principal	—	$ 500,000
Interest	275,000	$ 275,000
Total tax savings	$ 275,000	$ 775,000
After-tax cash cost	$1,275,000	$ 775,000

If the bank lends the $1 million to the ESOP at only 8 percent, versus 10 percent for regular debt financing, since 50 percent of the interest income is exempt from tax, the ESOPs after-tax cash cost would be $720,000, an additional savings of $55,000.

Although ESOP financing results in a lower after-tax cost to the company than debt financing, if new stock is sold to the leveraged ESOP, the company's book value and earnings are diluted on a per share basis. A leveraged ESOP financing transaction is, in effect, a combination of debt and equity financing. While the company does initially receive fair market value for its shares, it must repay the entire amount to the ESOP in future contributions. The net effect to the company is a tax deduction on the shares' fair market value ($500,000 in the above example) and an additional savings in interest costs, if applicable.

In a buyout situation, the tax advantages inherent to ESOPs allow the management buying group to value the acquisition (employer company) using pre-tax dollars. In this way, management and employees can bid more aggressively than third parties, since their effective cost of borrowing is significantly lower.

USES OF LEVERAGED ESOPs

The ESOP financing structure described above is generally used for raising capital to fund corporate growth or to increase the company's working capital. Slight variations in the transaction procedure permit the substitution of ESOP financing for most cases of conventional debt financing at a lower after-tax cash cost. Described below are other typical uses of leveraged ESOPs. Leveraged ESOPs are best suited to companies with large payrolls, allowing them to benefit from deductibility of principal to the fullest extent (up to 25 percent of payroll).

Acquisitions

The steps involved in using a leveraged ESOP to acquire another company are:

1. Acquiring (employer) company creates a leveraged ESOP.
2. ESOP borrows sufficient funds from a bank or other third-party lender to buy the stock of the target company from shareholders of the target.
3. ESOP buys the stock of the target company and exchanges this stock for stock of the employer/acquiring company; or ESOP buys stock of employer company, which uses cash proceeds to purchase target company.
4. The employer company guarantees the ESOP loan and makes annual cash contributions to the ESOP to repay the loan principal and interest until the loan is amortized.

Divestitures

An ESOP "spin-off" of an employer company's subsidiary involves the following:

1. The employer corporation creates a subsidiary corporation, which in turn creates a leveraged ESOP.
2. ESOP borrows funds guaranteed by the employer company from a lender.
3. ESOP acquires the assets to be divested and contemporaneously exchanges the assets for the newly formed corporation's stock; or ESOP purchases the stock of the newly formed company, which then uses those funds to purchase divested assets.
4. The new company makes annual contributions to the ESOP to amortize the loans.

In both ESOP-financed acquisitions and divestitures the tax advantages are the same as already described in the preceding section.

Purchasing Shareholders' Interest or Leveraged Buyout

In order to purchase the shares held by a large shareholder of a closely held corporation, the ESOP can borrow funds with which to buy the shareholder's stock. The shareholder sells his stock to the ESOP at a "fair market value," and the employer company makes annual contributions to the ESOP to amortize the loan.

The ESOP-financed purchase of the employer company by key employees—a management buyout—enables the key employees to gain control of the corporation with a relatively small personal equity investment, and the selling shareholders to receive fair market value for their stock. An ESOP-based leveraged buyout usually takes the following form:

1. Employer company to be acquired by management creates leveraged ESOP.
2. Management buys a small part (normally less than 15 percent) of the company's stock from existing shareholders.
3. ESOP borrows sufficient funds, guaranteed by the company, to buy the remaining company stock from existing shareholders.
4. ESOP purchases the remaining shares of the corporation.
5. Acquired company makes annual cash contributions to the ESOP until the loan is amortized.

In this way, management gains control since they directly own the corporation's stock, even though it is a minority interest. In addition, as the loan is amortized and ESOP stock is distributed to employees, the participating officers increase their holdings.

Additional considerations of "going private" through ESOP financing are presented in a later section of this chapter.

ESOP REQUIREMENTS

The loan made by a financial institution to the ESOP is required to meet certain IRS requirements. Listed below are the most relevant requirements to qualify as an "exempt" loan for an ESOP:

1. Primary benefit requirement—the loan must be for the benefit of the employees who are ESOP participants.
2. Net effect on assets—at the time that a loan is made, the interest rate for the loan and price of the securities acquired with the loan proceeds should be such that assets are not drained off.
3. Use of loan proceeds—must be used to purchase employer securities. Hence, an ESOP cannot purchase and hold assets.
4. Liability and collateral of an ESOP loan—the loan must be without recourse against the ESOP. Only assets of an ESOP

financed by the loan may be given as collateral on the loan, which would be the underlying securities of the employer.

5. Reasonable rate of interest.
6. Distribution to participants—stock must be distributed to participants upon termination of employment, retirement, or the like.
   a. Right of first refusal—employer securities acquired with proceeds may be subject to right of first refusal if the stock is not publicly traded. Such rights may only be exercised in favor of the employer.
   b. Put option—upon a distribution, the ESOP participant has the right to put the stock to the employer in certain circumstances.

Other requirements for an ESOP include voting rights intent and related party transactions.

Voting Rights Intent. The ESOP must meet certain IRS requirements regarding voting rights intent. IRS requirements dictate that if an employer has a registration-type class of securities, such as common or preferred stock, each participant is entitled to direct the plan as to the manner in which employer securities are entitled to vote. If the employer does not have a registration-type class of securities, the requirements for voting are those with respect to a corporate matter, which must be decided by more than a majority vote of outstanding common shares voted.

Related Party Transaction. The Internal Revenue Code prohibits transactions between certain parties. A relevant prohibition is direct or indirect sale of leasing of any property between the plan and a family member of a person exercising control over the plan.

"GOING PRIVATE" CONSIDERATIONS

Mergers effected by majority or controlling shareholders in which minority shareholders are squeezed out raise the spectre of "going private" concerns. There are very few corporate transactions that are more fraught with conflict of interest than the going private transaction. Since the controlling shareholders will be benefiting most from the proposed ESOP purchase, and will continue its domination of the board, fiduciary concerns are heightened. The basic objective in structuring such a transaction is to overcome its inherent conflict of interest. The fairness of price requirement is also important because an ESOP will be involved in the transaction. The regulations governing the going private transactions have three requirements that should guide its structuring:

1. Neutralized voting of insiders.
2. Fairness of price.
3. Transaction fairness.

Neutralized Voting

Such a requirement places the decision-making responsibility on outside shareholders to decide their own fate. Two techniques employed in such transactions are: (1) insiders agree to vote shares in favor of the transaction only if a majority of shares voted by outside shareholders vote in favor of the transaction, and (2) inside shareholders vote for the transaction in the same proportion as outside shareholders for and against. The objective in structuring the voting should present the larger voting requirement to maintain a squeaky-clean transaction.

Fairness of Price

This is the most pertinent element in the transaction, and preliminary evaluation should commence immediately prior to expending many legal and accounting professional hours. To promote an arm's-length determination, certain procedures are utilized to determine a fair price and to demonstrate fairness of the transaction.

Conducting the Transaction Fairly

To meet this important requirement of insuring an honest effort to determine a fair and equitable price, and generally promote and demonstrate fairness, the following techniques are employed:

1. Involvement of independent board members in price determination.
2. Outside board members should engage an investment banking firm to conduct the valuation and promote fairness to the board and management.
3. The outside directors should consider the advisability of its own legal counsel or the financial adviser using its counsel for the benefit of the outside directors.

CASE STUDY

XYZ Corporation is a privately held family business whose major stockholders wish to divest their holdings to the highest bidder. XYZ's management group is extremely interested in using this opportunity to acquire XYZ, and have engaged an investment banker to advise them on the acquisition.

XYZ has sales of close to $300 million, with encouraging growth prospects. Sales projections through 1990 are presented in Exhibits 2 and 3. XYZ's management group has heard a lot about LBOs and is interested in a 100 percent LBO with no equity required up front. The investment bankers think they can arrange the financing necessary, but have just completed a leveraged ESOP deal, which they think will work well here.

Management has reason to believe two competing purchasing groups are going to offer approximately 10 times earnings, or a purchase price between $40 million and $43 million, for XYZ. They have asked their investment bankers to examine the impact of an LBO on XYZ's financial statements, using realistic projections supplied by management themselves, and a purchase price of $45 million.

The investment bankers have prepared two comparative sets of projections—case A, a 100 percent leveraged buyout, and case B, a 100 percent leveraged ESOP buyout—both borrowing the $45 million at 14 percent, principal payable over 10 years. See tables beginning on page 564.

The investment bankers are strongly recommending leveraged ESOP financing for a number of reasons:

- Although earnings per share are reduced (both because the principal is tax deductible on the income statement and because the shares outstanding increase as annual ESOP contributions are made), the cash flow in the leveraged ESOP case is significantly higher than for the straight LBO.
- The higher cash flows in the ESOP case, resulting from a lower effective after-tax borrowing rate, will allow management to bid a higher purchase price, if necessary, at the same after-tax cash cost as LBO straight debt financing.
- The 50 percent exclusion accruable on interest received on ESOP loans for lenders will probably allow management to borrow at a rate lower than 14 percent, further reducing the effective cost of borrowing, increasing cash flow, and enabling management to bid more aggressively than the competing groups at a lower cost.

In addition, the investment bankers pointed out other salient features of ESOP financing: how contributed capital increases as the loan is paid back by XYZ in the amount of principal repaid; the fact that management will receive ESOP shares in proportion to their share of total XYZ compensation; and that dividends paid out by the ESOP in future years (when cash flow is positive) are tax deductible.

EXHIBIT 2 Case A: Combined Statement for a 100 Percent Leveraged Buyout (in thousands)

Projected Income Statements	*1984*	*1985*	*1986*	*1987*	*1988*	*1989*	*1990*
Sales	$279,750	$307,725	$338,498	$372,347	$409,582	$450,540	$495,594
Cost of goods sold	203,354	223,283	245,164	269,191	295,571	324,537	356,342
Gross profit	$ 76,396	$ 84,442	$ 93,333	$103,157	$114,011	$126,003	$139,252
Depreciation of fixed assets	1,988	2,655	3,055	3,455	3,855	2,764	2,664
Selling, general and administrative expense	65,796	72,376	79,613	87,574	96,332	105,965	116,562
Operating income	$ 8,612	$ 9,412	$ 10,665	$ 12,128	$ 13,824	$ 17,274	$ 20,027
Interest expense (excluding financing)	573	578	586	579	593	617	648
Interest expense (income) on cash balance		33	210	376	524	643	670
Financing expense (interest for LBO; principal and interest for ESOP)	–0–	6,336	6,266	6,126	5,846	5,426	4,964
Adjusted pre-tax income	8,040	2,465	3,603	5,847	6,861	10,588	13,745
Taxes	3,859	1,183	1,729	2,422	3,293	5,082	6,598
Goodwill amortization	–0–	221	221	221	221	221	221
Net income	$ 4,181	$ 1,061	$ 1,653	$ 2,483	$ 3,347	$ 5,285	$ 6,927
Earnings per share	$1.85	$8.47	$0.73	$1.86	$1.48	$2.33	$3.06
Projected Cash Flow Statements	*1984*	*1985*	*1986*	*1987*	*1988*	*1989*	*1990*
Net income before taxes	$ 8,040	$ 2,465	$ 3,603	$ 5,047	$ 6,861	$ 10,588	$ 13,745
Income taxes	3,859	1,183	1,729	2,422	3,293	5,882	6,598
Net income (after goodwill)	$ 4,181	$ 1,061	$ 1,653	$ 2,483	$ 3,347	$ 5,285	$ 6,927
Add: inventory write-up	–0–						
Add: goodwill amortization	–0–	221	221	221	221	221	221
Add: depreciation of fixed assets	1,988	2,655	3,055	3,455	3,855	2,764	2,664
Less: nonfinancing debt service	380	388	514	332	266	250	250
Less: financing debt service	–0–	500	1,800	2,800	3,800	3,380	3,630
Less: capital expenditures	3,000	3,800	3,800	3,800	3,800	3,800	3,800
Less: dividends	–0–	–0–	–0–	–0–	–0–	–0–	–0–
Add: change in working capital	($1,845)	($1,985)	($2,184)	($2,482)	($2,642)	($2,986)	($3,197)
Cash flow	$ 1,823	($1,857)	($1,778)	($1,655)	($1,486)	($1,187)	($226)

Projected Balance Sheets	January 1 1985	December 31 1985	1986	1987	1988	1989	1990
Assets							
Current assets:							
Cash	$ 1,523	($334)	($2,103)	($3,758)	($5,244)	($6,431)	($6,697)
Securities	4,000	4,000	4,000	4,000	4,000	4,000	4,000
Accounts receivable	4,957	5,453	5,998	6,598	7,258	7,983	8,782
Inventory	25,863	27,569	30,326	33,359	36,695	40,364	44,401
Inventory write-up	–0–						
Other	1,800	1,800	1,800	1,800	1,800	1,800	1,800
Total current assets	$ 36,543	$ 37,688	$ 39,221	$ 41,198	$ 43,708	$ 46,916	$ 51,485
Net fixed assets	12,921	15,267	15,212	14,758	13,983	14,139	14,476
Fixed asset write-up	2,000						
Goodwill	8,836	8,615	8,395	8,174	7,953	7,732	7,511
Other	300	300	300	300	300	300	300
Total assets	$ 60,601	$ 61,871	$ 63,128	$ 64,430	$ 65,864	$ 69,087	$ 73,772
Liabilities and shareholders' equity							
Current liabilities:							
Accounts payable	$ 5,685	$ 6,166	$ 6,782	$ 7,460	$ 8,206	$ 9,027	$ 9,930
Accrued expenses	4,564	5,020	5,522	6,075	6,682	7,350	8,085
Current portion (long-term Debt. outs)	388	514	332	266	250	250	250
Current portion (financing debt)	500	1,000	2,800	3,800	3,300	3,630	3,993
Other	2,447	2,447	2,447	2,447	2,447	2,447	2,447
Total current liabilities	$ 13,424	$ 15,147	$ 17,883	$ 19,248	$ 20,885	$ 22,784	$ 24,705
Long-term debt (outstanding)	2,418	1,904	1,572	1,306	1,856	806	556
Long-term debt (financing)	44,759	43,759	41,759	38,759	35,459	31,829	27,836
Stockholders' equity:							
Contributed capital	–0–	–0–	–0–	–0–	–0–	–0–	–0–
Retained earnings	–0–	1,061	2,713	5,117	8,463	13,748	20,675
Total stockholders' equity	–0–	$ 1,061	$ 2,713	$ 5,117	$ 8,463	$ 13,748	$ 20,675
Total liabilities and shareholders' equity	$ 60,601	$ 61,870	$ 63,128	$ 64,429	$ 65,864	$ 69,887	$ 73,771

EXHIBIT 3 Case B: Combined Statement for a 100 Percent Leveraged ESOP Buyout (in thousands)

Projected Income Statements	*1984*	*1985*	*1986*	*1987*	*1988*	*1989*	*1990*
Sales	$279,750	$307,725	$338,498	$372,347	$409,582	$450,540	$495,594
Cost of goods sold	203,354	223,283	245,164	269,191	295,571	324,537	356,342
Gross profit	$ 76,396	$ 84,442	$ 93,333	$103,157	$114,011	$126,003	$139,252
Depreciation of fixed assets	1,988	2,655	3,055	3,455	3,855	2,764	2,664
Selling, General and Administrative expense	65,796	72,376	79,613	87,574	96,332	105,965	116,562
Operating income	$ 8,612	$ 9,412	$ 10,665	$ 12,128	$ 13,824	$ 17,274	$ 20,827
Interest expense (excluding financing)	573	578	586	579	593	617	648
Interest expense (income) on cash balance		8	133	193	180	112	(74)
Financing expense (interest for LBO; principal and interest for ESOP)	–0–	6,836	7,266	8,126	8,846	8,726	8,594
Adjusted pre-tax income	8,040	1,990	2,680	3,230	4,205	7,819	10,859
Taxes	3,859	955	1,286	1,550	2,019	3,753	5,212
Goodwill amortization	–0–	221	221	221	221	221	221
Net income	$ 4,181	$ 814	$ 1,173	$ 1,458	$ 1,966	$ 3,845	$ 5,426
Earnings per share	$1.85	$0.36	$0.52	$0.64	$0.87	$1.70	$2.40
Projected Cash Flow Statements	*1984*	*1985*	*1986*	*1987*	*1988*	*1989*	*1990*
Net income before taxes	$ 8,040	$ 1,990	$ 2,680	$ 3,230	$ 4,285	$ 7,819	$ 10,859
Income taxes	3,859	955	1,286	1,550	2,019	3,753	5,212
Net income (after goodwill)	$ 4,181	$ 814	$ 1,173	$ 1,458	$ 1,966	$ 3,845	$ 5,426
Add: inventory write-up	–0–						
Add: goodwill amortization	–0–	221	221	221	221	221	221
Add: depreciation of fixed assets	1,988	2,655	3,055	3,455	3,855	2,764	2,664
Less: nonfinancing debt service	300	308	514	332	266	250	250
Less: financing debt service	–0–	–0–	–0–	–0–	–0–	–0–	–0–
Less: capital expenditures	3,000	3,000	3,000	3,000	3,000	3,000	3,000
Less: dividends	–0–	–0–	–0–	–0–	–0–	–0–	–0–
Add: change in working capital	(1,845)	(1,985)	(2,184)	(2,482)	(2,642)	(2,906)	(3,197)
Cash flow	$ 1,023	($1,608)	($1,249)	($600)	$133	$673	$1,863

Projected Balance Sheets	*January 1 1985*	*December 31 1985*	*1986*	*1987*	*1988*	*1989*	*1990*
Assets							
Current assets:							
Cash	$1,523	($80)	($1,330)	($1,930)	($1,797)	($1,124)	$740
Securities	4,000	4,000	4,000	4,000	4,000	4,000	4,000
Accounts receivable	4,957	5,453	5,998	6,598	7,258	7,983	8,782
Inventory	25,063	27,569	30,326	33,359	36,695	40,364	44,401
Inventory write-up	–0–						
Other	1,000	1,000	1,000	1,000	1,000	1,000	1,000
Total current assets	$ 36,543	$ 37,942	$ 39,994	$ 43,027	$ 47,156	$ 52,224	$ 58,922
Net fixed assets	12,921	15,267	15,212	14,758	13,903	14,139	14,476
Fixed asset write-up	2,000						
Goodwill	8,836	8,615	8,395	8,174	7,953	7,732	7,511
Other	300	300	300	300	300	300	300
Total assets	$ 60,601	$ 62,124	$ 63,901	$ 66,258	$ 69,311	$ 74,395	$ 81,288
Liabilities and shareholders' equity							
Current liabilities:							
Accounts payable	$ 5,685	$ 6,163	$ 6,782	$ 7,460	$ 8,206	$ 9,027	$ 9,930
Accrued expenses	4,564	5,020	5,522	6,075	6,682	7,350	8,885
Current portion (long-term Debt Outs)	388	514	332	266	250	250	250
Current portion (financing debt)	580	1,000	2,000	3,000	3,380	3,630	3,993
Other	2,447	2,447	2,447	2,447	2,447	2,447	2,447
Total current liabilities	$ 13,424	$ 15,147	$ 17,083	$ 19,248	$ 20,885	$ 22,704	$ 24,705
Long-term debt (outstanding)	2,418	1,904	1,572	1,386	1,056	806	556
Long-term debt (financing)	44,759	43,759	41,759	38,759	35,459	31,829	27,836
Stockholders' equity:							
Contributed capital	–0–	500	1,500	3,500	6,500	9,800	13,430
Retained earnings	–0–	814	1,987	3,445	5,411	9,256	14,681
Total stockholders' equity	–0–	$ 1,314	$ 3,487	$ 6,945	$ 11,911	$ 19,056	$ 28,111
Total liabilities and shareholders' equity	$ 60,601	$ 62,124	$ 63,901	$ 66,258	$ 69,311	$ 74,395	$ 81,288

XYZ's management was impressed by this argument and decided to bid for the company using a leveraged ESOP.

ADVANTAGES AND DISADVANTAGES OF ESOP FINANCING

The main advantages of ESOP financing result directly from the tax benefits already mentioned. For the most part, ESOPs work well in closely held private companies, where minimizing taxes and maximizing cash flow are greater priorities than increasing earnings per share. Since ESOPs dilute ownership and reported earnings, their use in a public corporation as a financial instrument is offset by management concerns regarding dilution.

In the case of subsidiary spin-offs, ESOPs enable employees to aggressively purchase the entity and minimize the loss of value inherent upon a sale to a third party. The ESOP spin-off is a powerful incentive to existing management and employees, resulting from the cost advantage to both the selling parent and the division.

Recently, ESOPs have gained popularity as handy tools with which to fend off a hostile takeover. A leveraged ESOP acts as an in-house "White Knight," allowing management to finance an LBO at a lower cost than the party trying to take over the company. Such ESOPs, called Management Entrenchment Stock Ownership Plans (MESOPs) by observers, have come under heavy criticism for abusing the original intentions of ESOP tax advantages, that is, to confer equity ownership on workers, increasing productivity.

Disadvantages of ESOP financing include the cumbersome and expensive nature of administering these plans. The plan must be formalized, trustees employed to administer the plan's accounts, and valuations performed. The size of the financing involved must be substantial enough to make the ESOP costs and management attention worthwhile.

Presented below is an ESOP checklist that highlights certain factors essential to successful ESOP financing.

- Extreme caution must be taken in selecting the plan administrator.
- ESOPs are best suited to companies with large payrolls, since loan principal deductibility is limited to 25 percent of employee compensation.
- The stock valuations necessary for ESOPs in privately held companies should be performed by reputable investment bankers or other generally recognized valuation experts.
- The plan must clarify what ex-employees may do with their por-

tion of distributed company stock (i.e., use put option, hold stock, or sell to third party).

- If ex-employees sell to third parties, management's control may be diluted. This can be minimized if rights of first refusal are implemented.
- The composition and liquidity of the ESOP fund must be balanced to cover ex-employees' put options.
- The financial reporting implications of establishing an ESOP must be understood, including the requirement that the employer company report guaranteed ESOP loans as liabilities (reducing the shareholder's equity by a corresponding amount).
- The potential "dilution" effects of ESOPs must be considered.
- The company must be able to maintain large ongoing annual cash contributions until the ESOP loan is amortized.

CHAPTER 20

Letter of Credit Financing

Scott A. Beaumont
Executive Vice President
The Eagle's Eye, Inc.
Malvern, Pa.

Scott Beaumont is the executive vice president and general manager of The Eagle's Eye, Inc., a position he has held since 1980. The Eagle's Eye, Inc. designs, manufactures, and markets high-quality sportswear and apparel. The company has overseas affiliates and deals extensively with both international and domestic letters of credit.

Prior to his work with The Eagle's Eye, Inc., Mr. Beaumont served as a general management consultant with Touche Ross & Co. Mr. Beaumont is a graduate of the Harvard Graduate School of Business Administration and of Dickinson College.

Letter of credit financing is an inexpensive way for the emerging and growing business to expand its trade credit. Since trade credit is probably the most simple, direct, and cost-efficient financing for an emerging business, any method that enhances its availability deserves attention.

A letter of credit is a letter from the buyer's bank to the seller, promising payment to the seller when the terms and conditions of the letter are met. The terms and conditions may be as simple as submitting an invoice for merchandise shipped to the buyer. In general, letters of credit assure that the seller will be paid and that the buyer will receive merchandise in a timely fashion.

The economic substance of a letter of credit transaction is that the buyer's bank knows much more about the creditworthiness of the buyer than the seller knows. The bank substitutes its own credit standing for that of the buyer, and the seller subsequently offers more generous trade credit to the buyer than it would without the letter of credit. This is how letter of credit financing expands the availability of trade credit.

Letter of credit financing is most applicable to emerging growth businesses that have not yet developed a payment history with the trade, and to international transactions. In each case, the seller has minimal information regarding the solvency of the buyer, and is often reluctant to offer trade credit without a letter of credit from the buyer's bank. Letters of credit are widely used in international business, but they tend to be overlooked as a financing tool for the small, developing domestic business. This is primarily because their effectiveness and simplicity are not well understood.

In the ensuing discussion, domestic letters of credit and their practical applications are described. This is followed by a review of international letters of credit.

DOMESTIC LETTERS OF CREDIT

Consider an emerging medical technology company that manufactures diagnostic equipment for hospitals. The company has recently received firm customer orders for its equipment. It now must purchase $35,000 worth of microprocessors, which are components for the equipment, to manufacture the equipment to fulfill the orders. The supplier of microprocessors will not accept the $35,000 purchase order without a prepayment of $30,000, because the new medical technology company has virtually no revenue, a weak balance sheet, and no payment history or trade terms with any vendors in the industry. How can the medical technology company obtain the microprocessors without issuing a prepayment of $30,000 to the supplier?

The medical technology company asks the supplier if it will accept the order if the medical technology company's bank issues a standby letter of credit to the supplier. The supplier agrees, accepts the purchase order, and issues trade credit of up to 45 days. If the buyer does not pay the invoice within 45 days, the supplier draws on the standby letter of credit and the bank pays the supplier. The bank then receives $35,000 in cash or notes from the buyer. This process is illustrated in Exhibit 1.

The bank is willing to open the standby letter of credit; it has faith in the creditworthiness of the medical technology company because of the confirmed sales order backlog. The bank will also earn a fee for minimal risk. The buyer is willing to open the letter of credit because it expands the availability of trade credit at a much lower cost than borrowing the money to prepay the vendor. The supplier accepts the letter of credit because it can accept a purchase order with a virtual certainty of being paid.

Mechanics and Terminology

Domestic letters of credit are simple to establish and to use. Emerging companies should encourage their vendors to accept letters of credit. The credit department of the vendor may not have had experience with a letter of credit and may not consider it as a financing option before asking a customer for a prepayment. The buyer can inform the seller of the benefits of a letter of credit. Similarly, the bank of the emerging company may not think to suggest letter of credit financing to the emerging company. This frequently occurs when the account officer does not have specific letter of credit experience.

Assume that the medical technology company's bank on the example above is The National Bank. A typical example of a domestic standby letter of credit is shown in Exhibit 2. This letter includes four key features that letters of credit must have. They are:

- A conspicuous title stating that it is a letter of credit.
- A specified aggregate amount.
- An expiration date.
- The terms and conditions of payment.

The letter in Exhibit 2 is entitled an "Irrevocable Letter of Credit." An irrevocable letter of credit may not be revoked by the applicant. Although a letter of credit may be either revocable or irrevocable, virtually all are irrevocable because a supplier who is reluctant to grant trade credit is also generally reluctant to accept a revocable letter of credit. The title does not need to indicate that the letter is domestic or standby. If the letter is between a buyer and seller in the same country, it is domestic. If the terms of the letter specify that invoices are first sent to the buyer, but if they remain unpaid within the agreed upon terms then a draft is presented to the bank for payment, then the letter is a standby letter. This is the most common case for a domestic letter of credit.

EXHIBIT 1 Participants and Steps in a Domestic Standby Letter of Credit Transaction

Buyer	Seller
(Letter of credit applicant)	(Letter of credit beneficiary)
(Medical Technology Company, in example)	(Microprocessor Company, in example)

Buyer's bank
(Issuing bank)
(National Bank, in example)

Steps

1. Buyer places purchase order for $35,000 with seller.
2. Seller does not accept purchase order on account, because seller will not issue $35,000 of trade credit to buyer.
3. Buyer asks seller if it will accept a standby letter of credit; seller agrees and offers trade credit.
4. Buyer applies to buyer's bank for a standby letter of credit for $35,000, in favor of the seller.
5. Buyer's bank opens a $35,000 standby letter of credit in favor of the seller.
6. Seller ships and invoices $35,000 of merchandise to the buyer, with the invoice payable in 45 days.
7. Invoice is unpaid after 45 days; seller submits a draft to the buyer's bank for $35,000, accompanied by a copy of the invoice and a signed statement indicating that the funds are due.
8. Buyer's bank issues a bank check to the seller upon receipt of draft.
9. Buyer's bank receives $35,000 in cash or notes from the buyer.

EXHIBIT 2 Domestic Standby Letter of Credit

THE NATIONAL BANK

June 4, 1985

IRREVOCABLE LETTER OF CREDIT NO. 9999

(Seller's name and address)

Gentlemen:

We hereby authorize you to draw on The National Bank for the account of (buyer's name and address), up to the aggregate amount of $35,000, available by your drafts at sight.

The drafts drawn under this credit are to be endorsed thereon and shall state on their face that they are drawn under The National Bank, Letter of Credit No. 9999, dated June 4, 1985. The drafts presented for payment under this Letter of Credit must be accompanied by (1) a copy of the signed Commercial Invoice(s) and (2) your signed statement certifying that "the funds drawn hereunder are due you on account of (buyer's name and address) failure to pay, within terms quoted therein, the invoice(s) issued to them by (seller's name). Demand for payment has been made and the funds have not been forthcoming from (buyer's name) or any other source."

Documents must be delivered to The National Bank, (bank's address), and drafts must be drawn and negotiated not later than (expiration date of Letter of Credit).

Except so far as otherwise expressly stated, this credit is subject to the Uniform Customs and Practice for Documentary Credits, 1974 Revision, International Chamber of Commerce Publication No. 490.

We hereby agree with drawers, endorsers, and bona fide holders of the bills drawn in compliance with the terms of this credit that the bills shall be duly honored upon presentation at The National Bank.

Very truly yours,

THE NATIONAL BANK

By: ______________________________

John Doe
Senior Vice President

EXHIBIT 3 Example of Completed Draft

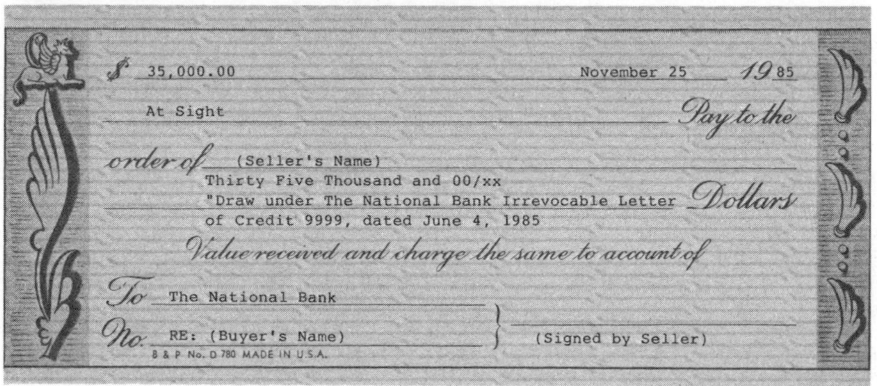
$ 35,000.00 November 25 1985

At Sight Pay to the

order of (Seller's Name)

Thirty Five Thousand and 00/xx

"Draw under The National Bank Irrevocable Letter Dollars

of Credit 9999, dated June 4, 1985

Value received and charge the same to account of

To The National Bank

No. RE: (Buyer's Name) (Signed by Seller)

B & P No. D 780 MADE IN U.S.A.

The letter shown in Exhibit 2 is also a "documentary" letter of credit. This means that the bank's obligation to pay arises only upon presentation of a draft and other documents as specified in the letter of credit. The bank is not obligated to determine the suitability of the merchandise shipped. Most letters of credit are documentary. A nondocumentary letter of credit is called a "clean" letter, because it is clean of documents. An example of a clean letter of credit is a letter of credit issued by a company in lieu of a performance bond.[1]

With a standby letter of credit, the seller first invoices the buyer. If the buyer pays within terms, the seller does not draw on the letter and the letter expires at the expiration date. If the buyer does not pay within terms, the seller draws on the letter by presenting the bank with a draft and other documents, such as the invoice and a statement indicating that the invoice is past due. A draft is a form that resembles a check and is available at a local stationery store. An example of a completed draft for the scenario described above is presented in Exhibit 3. Upon receipt of the draft and other necessary documentation, the bank issues a bank check to the seller, who is the beneficiary.

In this case, the drafts are payable on sight. This means that the bank issues the beneficiary a check immediately. Occasionally, letters of credit are structured with time draft payments rather than sight drafts. In such a case, the bank issues the beneficiary a banker's acceptance with a specified maturity date rather than a check. The

---

[1] This example is used in James McNeill Stancill, "Domestic Uses of Letters of Credit," *Harvard Business Review,* September–October 1979, pp. 198–202.

beneficiary typically cashes the acceptance at an acceptance broker for a discount. Time drafts occur less frequently than sight drafts because sellers typically won't agree to too many delays in receiving their money.

Benefits

The primary benefit of letter of credit financing is that the buyer obtains trade credit that otherwise would not have been available. In the case of the medical technology company and the microprocessor supplier, the buyer saves $900 by issuing a standby letter of credit rather than borrowing the money to issue the prepayment to the supplier. These savings come from the expanded availability of trade credit to the buyer. A domestic letter of credit costs the applicant approximately 1.5 percent of the principal amount of the letter, which in this case is $525. If the buyer had borrowed the $30,000 prepayment for three months, and had forgone the 45 days of trade credit on the $35,000, the buyer would have incurred interest charges of $1,425, assuming an interest rate of 1 percent per month.

The buyer has also developed a more meaningful credit history with the trade by paying on a standby letter of credit than through a prepayment. A vendor is seldom able to evaluate the creditworthiness of accounts with prepayments.

It is highly recommended that emerging growth companies establish standby letters of credit with their top three or four suppliers for the first one or two years of development. This has the following advantages:

- It substantially increases the likelihood of uninterrupted supply from key vendors.
- It obtains trade credit inexpensively.
- It builds a payment history for sizable sums with key suppliers who can be used as trade credit references to obtain additional trade credit from other vendors. Generous trade credit is an exceptionally valuable financing device for the emerging company, and often tends not to be as readily available as desired in the early years.

The standby letter of credit provides other advantages. A standby letter of credit is a contingent liability. Accordingly, it is not recorded as a liability on the applicant's balance sheet; it is merely a footnote as a commitment. A letter of credit is off-balance-sheet financing and has a much more favorable impact than short-term debt on a company's debt-to-equity ratio, current ratio, and working capital. The contingent liability aspect of a standby letter of credit also makes it more attractive to a bank. This is because contingent liabilities aren't part of the calculations of a bank's reserve requirements. Consequently, for a bank, letters of credit are less expensive than a loan.

A domestic letter of credit is so simple that it can be handled by virtually any bank between nearly all potential buyers and sellers. Domestic letters of credit are underutilized as a financing instrument because many banks, suppliers, and buyers simply don't think to use them. The manager of an emerging growth company can realize several benefits with the initiation and encouragement of more widespread use of domestic letters of credit.

INTERNATIONAL LETTERS OF CREDIT

Letters of credit are widely used in international transactions. This is because the exporter usually has no way of assessing the creditworthiness of the importer. Since the exporter wants either a prepayment or a high certainty of payment and the importer wants some terms, an international letter of credit is frequently the solution. International letters of credit have many similar characteristics to domestic letters; but because, typically, different currencies and specific exportation or importation regulations are involved, they are usually more complex than domestic letters of credit.

A basic understanding of international letters of credit can provide the manager of an emerging company with a higher comfort level in the attempt at some overseas resourcing. The manager of an emerging company should consider overseas resourcing as a competitive edge. Overseas resourcing can have an enormously favorable impact on a company's cost structure. The following discussion describes the participants, steps, and typical terms in an international letter of credit transaction, and provides practical tips.

Participants and Steps

The key participants in an international letter of credit transaction are the importer, the exporter, the issuing bank, the advising bank, and the negotiating bank. The importer submits a purchase order to the exporter, which the exporter accepts, subject to letter of credit financing. The importer applies to the importer's bank for a letter of credit in favor of the exporter. The importer's bank, also known as the issuing bank, issues a letter of credit in favor of the exporter. An advising bank informs the exporter that the credit has been issued. An advising bank is reasonably local to the exporter, and generally has a reasonably direct relationship with the issuing bank.

The exporter sometimes uses the letter of credit to obtain local

EXHIBIT 4 Participants and Steps in an International Letter of Credit Transaction

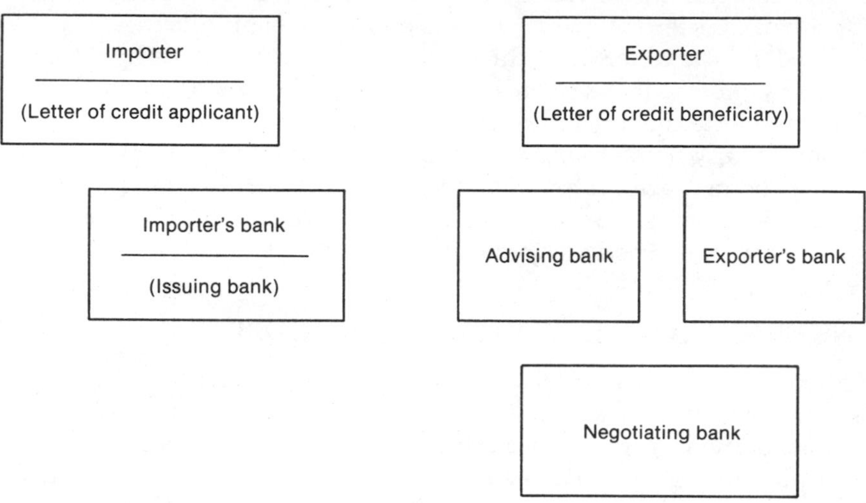

Steps

1. Exporter accepts purchase order from importer, subject to establishment of letter of credit.
2. Importer applies for letter of credit with importer's bank.
3. Importer's bank issues a letter of credit in favor of the exporter.
4. The advising bank notifies the exporter that the letter of credit has been opened in favor of the exporter.
5. The exporter sometimes uses the letter of credit to obtain local financing for the purchase of materials necessary to manufacture and ship the merchandise.
6. The exporter ships the merchandise to the importer.
7. The exporter presents necessary documents to the negotiating bank to negotiate payment on the letter.
8. The negotiating bank presents documents to the issuing bank.
9. Assuming there are no discrepancies, the issuing bank pays the negotiating bank and the negotiating bank pays the exporter.
10. The issuing bank receives cash or notes from the importer.

trade credit for the materials needed to manufacture the merchandise for shipment. The exporter ships the merchandise to the importer and presents documents for payment to a negotiating bank. The negotiating bank obtains payment for the exporter against the credit. The negotiating bank may be the exporter's usual bank, it may be the advising bank, or it may be both. The negotiating bank submits a draft and documents to the issuing bank. Assuming that there are no discrepancies, the issuing bank pays the negotiating bank, which pays the exporter. The issuing bank also receives cash or notes from the importer. These participants and steps are shown in Exhibit 4.

Sometimes the exporter includes a confirming bank in the transaction. A confirming bank is a bank local to the exporter whose creditworthiness the exporter trusts. This is done in cases when the exporter is unsure of the creditworthiness of the issuing bank. The confirming bank will honor the letter of credit if the issuing bank fails. Any fees to the confirming bank are typically paid by the exporter.

Typical Terms

The typical terms and conditions to draw on an international letter of credit are more complex than a domestic letter of credit. The typical terms and conditions include:

- The commercial invoice from the exporter to the importer.
- An inspection certificate signed by an agent of the importer.
- An export license.
- An ocean bill of lading or an airway bill issued by the carrier.
- An insurance certificate for the merchandise.

The terms and conditions are more stringent for an international letter of credit because, typically, the letter of credit is drawn on before the importer receives the merchandise. This is because transit time may be six weeks.

If the documents are not in order, there is a discrepancy. If there is a discrepancy, the issuing bank must obtain the approval from the applicant before paying the draft. Discrepancies are almost always resolved.

Most international letters of credit are set up between the applicant and the beneficiary. Variations include transferable letters of credit and back-to-back letters of credit. A transferable letter of credit enables the beneficiary to transfer the credit to another beneficiary. This is typically used in countries that have strict control over foreign exchange. The importer deals directly with a governmental agency that transfers the letter to the manufacturer. The governmental agency monitors the transactions to ensure that the country is earning all possible foreign exchange on the transaction.

A back-to-back letter of credit is a letter issued from the applicant to the beneficiary: the beneficiary uses the original letter of credit to secure and open a new letter of credit between the beneficiary and a third party. This typically occurs when an importer deals with an agent, and the agent does not want to reveal to the importer the source of supply of the merchandise.

Practical Tips

The costs of an international letter of credit vary widely and depend primarily on the relationship between the applicant and the issuing bank. The components and general ranges of the charges are as follows:

Bank commission:	⅛–¾ percent of principal amount
Opening charge:	$30–$50
Amendment charge:	$15–$50 per amendment
Cabling charge:	$10–$30

When selecting a bank to issue international letters of credit, choose a bank that has a large number of correspondent banks local to the exporter. A correspondent bank is a bank that keeps an active account with the issuing bank. The advantage of a correspondent banking relationship is that funds can move much more quickly because the correspondents merely debit and credit each other's accounts, rather than actually moving and clearing international currencies. If the issuing bank has a large correspondent network, there is a greater likelihood that the exporter's bank is a part of it, or has a relationship with another bank that is part of the issuing bank's correspondent network. This improves the timeliness of notifying the exporter that the letter of credit is issued and improves the timeliness of the exporter receiving payment. Both of these events improve the overall relationship between the exporter and the importer. Recall, the exporter will not begin producing for the importer until the exporter is notified that the letter of credit is issued. Otherwise, the exporter would accept the importer's purchase order on open account. Timely notification is required to assure timely delivery of merchandise.

To obtain particularly favorable letter of credit terms from the issuing bank, the importer should seek an issuing bank that has an overseas subsidiary bank local to the exporter. The importer can usually assign the exporter to use this bank as the negotiating bank. Recall that a negotiating bank provides two major services to the exporter: it arranges for payment of the letter of credit, and it exchanges the payment into local currency. The majority of letters of credit with a U.S. company as the importer are issued in U.S. dollars. The exporter wants payment in local currency, so a foreign exchange transaction must take place. The negotiating bank performs this transaction and makes money on the exchange.

The advantage of an issuing bank with an overseas subsidiary local to the exporter becomes clear. The importer can assign the exporter to use the subsidiary as the negotiating bank. The exporter has an incentive to agree to this because payment is received quickly. The negotiating bank is earning more money because it has more clients conducting foreign exchange transactions, and it has leads on prospective new customers locally. The importer therefore becomes a valued customer to the issuing bank because the importer enables the bank to make money on both sides of the ocean. This puts the importer in an excellent position to negotiate hard for rate reductions on letter of credit charges.

The manager of the emerging company has so many concerns that overseas resourcing may not seriously be considered as an option. This can result in forgone opportunity. It is well beyond the scope of this discussion to describe overseas resourcing techniques. However, as a start, contact an import agent based in a major U.S. city and determine if the agent may be able to reduce cost through overseas resourcing. This can be accomplished relatively easily.

As the manager of the emerging company gains experience in resourcing, more of the tasks will be done directly instead of through an import agent. One of the first tasks to perform directly rather than through an import agent is the clearance of merchandise through U.S. Customs, and the direct payment of duties, freight, and customs brokerage fees. This reduces letter of credit requirements by approximately 30 percent. If an import agent clears the goods and pays all duties, freight, and brokerage charges, as well as paying the exporter, then the letter of credit is typically opened in favor of the agent and includes the amount for duties, freight, and brokerage charges. If the importer clears the merchandise through U.S. customs, which is really done by a customs broker on behalf of the importer, then the importer pays the duty, freight, and brokerage charges directly upon clearance. This eliminates the need to establish letters of credit for these amounts, and thereby reduces total letter of credit requirements.

CONCLUSION

Letter of credit financing is an inexpensive way for the emerging company to expand its available trade credit. Trade credit is such an inexpensive financing mechanism that companies should increase its use at every opportunity. Letter of credit financing also facilitates the majority of international transactions. Letter of credit financing, particularly domestically, is relatively simple. It is underutilized as a financing tool because it is not well understood. The manager of the emerging company who encourages more frequent use of letter of credit financing can significantly increase the sources of inexpensive financing for the company.

CHAPTER 21

Commercial Paper

Robert F. Murphy*
Chairman of the Board
General Motors Acceptance Corporation and
Motors Insurance Corporation

Robert F. Murphy is chairman of the board of General Motors Acceptance Corporation and chairman of the board of its insurance subsidiary, Motors Insurance Corporation. In 1949, Mr. Murphy received his B.S. degree from Columbia University and joined GMAC as a member of the financial staff. Since then, he has served in numerous supervisory and managerial positions covering a broad spectrum of the company's activities. Mr. Murphy was elected to his current posi-

* Mr. Murphy acknowledges the assistance of Thomas A. Cover of GMAC in preparing this chapter.

tions on January 1, 1986. He is a member of the Consumer Advisory Council of the Federal Reserve Board, a member of the Mortgage Roundtable of the National Association of Home Builders, and a trustee of the Mortgage and Realty Trust.

INTRODUCTION

Commercial paper is a short-term unsecured promissory note with a fixed maturity. Issued primarily by large, well-known corporations, commercial paper is usually sold as an alternative to short-term bank credit. In this chapter, we will examine the commercial paper market with the primary emphasis on factors of interest to a prospective commercial paper issuer.

NUTSHELL OVERVIEW

Today, there are approximately 1,400 issuers of commercial paper in the United States. While the ranks of these firms are dominated by large, well-known issuers, smaller and lesser known firms have been able to enter the market through the use of various credit substitution and enhancement techniques. Commercial paper is sold primarily to large institutional investors such as money market funds, insurance companies, bank trust departments, and pension funds. Public offerings of commercial paper are exempt from the registration and prospectus requirements of the Securities Exchange Commission if the proceeds are used to finance current transactions and have a maturity no longer than 270 days. Most commercial paper is issued with a maturity less than 30 days. Commercial paper is sold either directly by the issuer (only about 80 of the largest issuers who are continuously in the market do so today), or through dealers (for those issuing smaller amounts or with seasonal needs). While highly rated commercial paper generally sells at rates below the bank prime rate, there are many associated costs such as rating agency fees, selling expenses (dealer or internal sales staff), and expenses related to maintaining backup bank lines of credit (e.g., compensating balances or straight fees). Rates on commercial paper are also a function of the issuer's creditworthiness, use of the market, and yields on alternative investments. Rates tend to move with and at varying margins (risk premiums) above Treasury securities of comparable maturity, recognizing the increased credit risk and lower liquidity of commercial paper as compared to government backed securities.

Commercial paper may be sold on either a discount or an interest-bearing basis, computed for the actual number of days to maturity on a 360-day basis. Yields are identical regardless of the basis. Commercial paper is typically issued in bearer form, but may be issued in registered form. Payment at maturity is effected by presentment to the bank shown as the paying agent on the face of the note. Trading is usually for New York delivery with same day settlement in federal funds, but delivery can be made at other money centers by using one of two methods. First, a due bill with notes payable to the investor may be shipped to the place of settlement to redeem the due bill. Alternatively, a local bank may be designated as the paying agent. The minimum denomination is usually $100,000, but some issuers will sell smaller denominations. Typical transactions are for millions of dollars. For many issuing firms, commercial paper is an efficient alternative to short-term bank credit.

HISTORY

Since its earliest days, the commercial paper market has been dynamic, not static. Changes in the environment affecting both issuers and investors have had an impact on the market in many ways. A brief look at the history of the commercial paper market, and some of the environmental factors that have affected its development, should provide a prospective participant with a basic understanding of the market's strengths and weaknesses.

The market for commercial paper is rooted in colonial times and predates the development of a banking system in the United States. The forerunner of commercial paper was a bill of exchange, which was an order written by a seller containing a buyer's promise to pay the seller a fixed sum on a certain date. Bills of exchange were used to facilitate trade financing in the early 18th century by providing the buyer of goods with short-term credit from the date of delivery to a predetermined payment date. Typically, the amount of the bill was equal to the purchase price of the goods. Prior to the Civil War, bills of exchange were issued in the name of both the buyer (issuer) and seller (drawee) of the goods. If the bill was sold to a third party and the buyer/issuer defaulted, the third party holder could collect from the seller/drawee. Unlike today's commercial paper issuers, the buyers of goods needing bill of exchange financing were inferior credit risks, and the cost of this type of credit was high relative to bank financing. However, banks, brokers, and entrepreneurs began discounting bills of exchange for sellers. After the Civil War, it became customary for bills of exchange to be issued in round lot denominations unrelated to the price of a shipment of goods. Also, they were issued only in the name of the buyer/issuer and were not supported by the credit of the seller.

The development of a national market for commercial paper in the late 19th and early 20th centuries was primarily the result of the decentralized banking system's inability to easily respond to regional credit needs and to exploit the interest rate differentials that were a consequence of varying regional demand for credit and supply of funds. Commercial paper served as a mechanism to permit both borrowers and investors to take advantage of these regional variations. A borrower located in an area of relatively high interest rates could sell its commercial paper to a bank or other investor located in an area of relatively low interest rates, thereby obtaining credit for a lower price. Conversely, this disintermediation process benefited banks and other investors in relatively low-rate areas by permitting them to easily invest in relatively high-rate areas. Commercial banks quickly became the principal buyers of commercial paper because the paper enhanced portfolio diversification, was considered highly liquid, and served as a secondary reserve asset. By 1914, some commercial paper was eligible for discount by the Federal Reserve.

By 1920, there were over 4,000 issuers of commercial paper active in the market and all commercial paper was sold by the more than 30 dealers who were servicing this business. Most of the funds raised in the market were used to meet issuers' seasonal peak demands for short-term credit. However, with the growth of consumer demand for automobiles and other durable goods, finance companies became the major borrowers in the commercial paper market. In 1920, General Motors Acceptance Corporation (GMAC) became the first issuer to bypass the dealers and sell its paper direct to investors. In the 1930s, C.I.T. Financial Corporation and Commercial Credit Corporation joined GMAC as direct issuers. While GMAC and other early finance company direct issuers concentrated their commercial paper sales to banks, they eventually expanded the market to appeal to the nonbank investor by tailoring denominations and maturities to meet individual and other institutional investor requirements.

Throughout the Great Depression, as the demand for business fell, so did the number of issuers and dollar volume of commercial paper. With few exceptions, trends in the commercial paper market have followed trends in the overall economy. There was a resurgence of the market following World War II. At the end of 1945, commercial paper outstanding totaled a mere $200 million. However the market experienced relatively steady growth, so that by the end of 1959, commercial paper outstanding totaled $3.7 billion. The market changed significantly during this period. Directly placed commercial paper, primarily issued by the largest finance companies, accounted for the largest share of total commercial paper outstanding. The role of banks as the major investors in the market declined as Treasury securities became a more significant secondary reserve asset. Nonfinancial firms also became significant buyers of commercial paper.

The commercial paper market continued to grow through most of the 1960s as the overall demand for credit increased. Twice during the decade the market was dramatically affected by tight markets for bank credit.

In 1966, as the general level of free market interest rates rose above Regulation Q ceilings on bank certificates of deposit (CDs), it became difficult for banks to raise sufficient funds to meet the demand for credit. Many banks encouraged their most creditworthy customers to issue commercial paper backed by bank credit lines, thereby introducing many new issuers to the commercial paper market. This scenario with intense demand for credit occurred again in 1969. This time, instead of sending many of their best customers to the commercial paper market, many bank holding companies issued commercial paper and used the proceeds to purchase their subsidiaries' loan portfolios. This action fueled the rapid growth of bank-related commercial paper. At the end of 1969, bank-related paper outstanding totaled \$4.3 billion, which grew to \$7.8 billion by July 1970, just prior to corrective action by the Federal Reserve System. In addition to liberalizing the Regulation Q ceilings on short-term, large denomination CDs, the Federal Reserve imposed a reserve requirement on funds channeled to a member bank by a bank holding company or any of its subsidiaries or affiliates. These actions resulted in a decline in bank-related commercial paper outstanding to \$2.3 billion by the end of 1970. Bank holding companies still raise substantial funds in the commercial paper market, but generally use the proceeds to fund nonbank-related activities such as leasing, and sales finance subsidiary operations.

Since the outset, the commercial paper market has been dominated by issuers of the highest credit standing and there have been few defaults. For example, in the 1960s, only a handful of issuers (five) defaulted on their obligations and none of those defaults resulted in significant losses or market disruption. However, in 1970, Penn Central defaulted on \$82 million of commercial paper outstandings, creating widespread disruption in the commercial paper market. The largest and best known issuers had little difficulty in weathering the temporary loss of confidence and were able to roll over their maturities as they came due, but many were forced to pay higher rates. However, due to the combination of higher interest rates on commercial paper and roll-over difficulties, many lesser rated issuers turned to banks to meet their short-term credit needs. To reduce this market disruption, the Federal Reserve System modified its discount policy and removed the Regulation Q ceilings on large denomination CDs with maturities from 30 to 89 days, so that issuing companies could utilize their backup credit lines to cover their maturities.

The environment of the 1970s and early 1980s created more change in the market. The wage and price controls of the early 1970s caused a shift from commercial paper to bank credit for many issuers. On October 15, 1971, the Committee on Interest and Dividends (CID) imposed "voluntary" restraints on administered interest rates such as prime. The result was to artificially hold the prime rate below market rates, thereby creating a shift of demand in favor of bank credit. By April 1973, in order to reduce some of the pressure on banks, the CID created a dual prime rate with one of the rates designed to reflect market rates for loans to large businesses. By the end of the year, the CID controls were removed and there was a natural shift back to the commercial paper market for many issuers. During the decade, the market for some issuers also was affected by the oil embargo and its effect on utility companies, as well as the losses experienced by many real estate investment trusts (REITs). The inflationary environment of the late 1970s and early 1980s also contributed to the growth of the commercial paper market. During this period of sharply rising interest rates, many corporations facing unusually high long term borrowing rates opted to alter their debt mix by relying to a greater than normal degree on short-term credit, much of which was raised in the commercial paper market. This was further fueled by the relatively depressed state of the capital markets, making new equity issues uneconomic. From the perspective of investors, the depressed equity market coupled with continually escalating interest rates pushed investors to short-term instruments, especially commercial paper. Overall, the commercial paper market has grown with the economy and adapted to its ever-changing environment. Clearly, it is most affected by the relative cost of substitute credit and yields available to investors on alternative investments as well as the market's overall confidence in the creditworthiness of commercial paper issuers.

INVESTORS

Investors in commercial paper are primarily large institutions such as money market funds, insurance companies, bank trust departments, state and local governments, and private and government pension funds. While the vast majority of transactions with institutional investors are in large denominations, some issuers will sell commercial paper in denominations as small as $25,000, which opens the market to smaller investors. While the mix of investors changes over time, all are concerned with the issuer's creditworthiness and are attracted by the flexibility to tailor maturities to meet their particular requirements.

Today, money market funds are probably the single largest class of investor. Commercial paper meets the primary objective of these funds to invest for specific short-term periods with minimal credit risk. By investing in money market funds and other pooling arrangements, small investors have access to the higher short-term returns offered to large institutional investors, as well as reduced risk through diversification.

RATINGS

With increasing numbers of companies issuing commercial paper, ratings by recognized credit rating agencies have become increasingly important to both commercial paper investors and issuers. For the investor, ratings reduce research time and expense. For the issuer, high ratings promote the marketability of the issuer's commercial paper. Since the Penn Central default of 1970, ratings have become more widespread, rating standards have been tightened, and it has become difficult to sell low-rated or unrated commercial paper.

Issuers bear the expense of having their commercial paper rated, which may cost between $10,000 and $50,000 annually. Although a seeming conflict of interest, issuers depend on the validity of ratings to preserve investor confidence in the market generally, and their issues in particular. In other words, the value of ratings to the issuer is a function of their value to the investor. If ratings were subject to abuse by issuers, their value would diminish and the efficiency of the commercial paper market would be seriously impaired. Of course, the rating agencies are diligent in their efforts to accurately rate commercial paper. While each rating agency sets its own standards, all are based on a thorough review of the issuer's management record, industry trends, the issuer's position in its industry, balance sheet and earnings trends, with a particular emphasis on the issuer's projected ability to liquidate its maturing commercial paper.

Virtually all commercial paper issuers obtain at least one rating and most issuers obtain two. There are many nationally recognized statistical rating organizations, but the two primary rating companies are Moody's Investors Service and Standard & Poor's Corporation. From the highest to lowest quality, commercial paper is rated Prime-1 (P-1), Prime-2 (P-2), or Prime-3 (P-3) by Moody's; and A-1, A-2, or A-3 by Standard & Poor's. Only commercial paper of the two highest ratings (i.e., P-1 or P-2) is generally readily acceptable in the market. The highest rating is most sought after because there can be a quality spread in rates, which is particularly pronounced during times of market stress. Generally, there is a correlation between the commercial paper and long-term debt ratings of individual issuers. Also, when issuers have rated long-term debt outstanding, the issuer's commercial paper rates are usually, but not always, affected by the bond's rating.

BACKUP LINES

In order to reduce the risk of an issuer not being able to roll over or otherwise liquidate maturing commercial paper, issuers generally back all, or a high portion of, their outstanding commercial paper with bank credit lines. This is an important consideration since major issuers have billions of dollars maturing weekly. While some issuers are in the market only to meet seasonal needs and will liquidate maturities with funds generated from their operations, most issuers sell new commercial paper to liquidate current maturities. This roll-over risk for both issuer and investor is reduced by having alternative backup funding sources available.

The amount of credit line backing required is a function of the issuer's strength, position in the market, and investor demand. While most issuers maintain 100 percent coverage, some of the largest and strongest issuers maintain much less coverage. Some issuers, particularly those with seasonal or cyclical borrowings needs, may maintain a credit line of a constant dollar amount, which results in being over lined when commercial paper outstandings are low and underlined when outstandings peak.

Various types of credit lines are used by issuers to back up their commercial paper outstandings. A full description of all the possibilities is beyond the scope of this chapter, but typical arrangements include swing lines that permit the issuer to borrow on one day and repay on the next or to take down advances against the line which are converted to term notes with a specific maturity. In addition to the interest expense on actual borrowings, costs associated with backup credit lines can include compensating balances and commitment fees.

DEALER-PLACED COMMERCIAL PAPER

Dealers sell commercial paper for more than 1,300 of the approximately 1,400 current issuers representing about one half of all dollar volume. Approximately one half of the issuers using dealers to place their paper are industrial companies, with financial institutions, utility companies, and others representing the remainder. Because the short-term credit requirements of many nonfinancial companies are seasonal or cyclical, they have little incentive to maintain a permanent commercial paper sales staff in house. Typically, the dealer's commission is one eighth of 1 percent of the face value of the notes sold, or $125,000 per $100 million. There are several principal dealers of commercial paper operating in the market today.

Issuers using dealers to place their commercial paper sales advise their dealers daily of their sales objectives for dollar volume and mix of maturities. Most issuers rely on their dealer to set rates, while other issuers retain control of this function. When a dealer assumes the responsibility of establishing rates for the issuer it serves, it may also assume the obligation to position (hold for its own account) any commercial paper left unsold at the rates it established. In this situation, the dealer is attempting to balance the competitive pressure to establish the lowest possible rates to retain its issuer's business, against the need to avoid possible losses from the carry expenses resulting from taking a position in the issuer's underpriced commercial paper.

Because of the short-term nature of commercial paper, together with investors' ability to select a specific maturity, requests for repurchase occur infrequently. However, if an investor in dealer-placed paper needs to liquidate prior to maturity, most dealers will bid on commercial paper sold by them at the market rate for paper of similar quality and maturity. Due to the limited need for repurchase and the fact that most issuers place their commercial paper through a single dealer, the secondary market for this type of commercial paper is relatively small.

DIRECTLY PLACED COMMERCIAL PAPER

While less than 100 of the market's 1,400 issuers sell commercial paper directly to investors, their volume accounts for approximately one half of the dollar value of all commercial paper outstanding. Most of these issuers are large financial companies such as GMAC, Sears Roebuck Acceptance Corporation, and Ford Motor Credit Company. The principal benefit for issuers who sell their commercial paper on a direct basis is the ability to avoid the dealer's commission, typically one eighth of 1 percent. The offsetting burden is the expense of maintaining an in-house sales staff.

Direct issuers of commercial paper determine their borrowing needs by dollar amount and maturities spread daily. Rates estimated to generate targeted sales objectives are posted on Telerate, communicated directly to key investors, and some of the largest issuers post rates with bank money centers. While banks are prohibited from underwriting securities (which the Supreme Court recently decided includes commercial paper) by the Glass Stegall Act, they may arrange purchases on behalf of their customers. The issuer closely monitors sales throughout the day and adjust posted rates as needed to meet the day's sales objectives. For example, if sales of a certain maturity are slow, the rate may be increased to attract purchasers, or if the sales objective for a particular maturity has been met, the rate for that maturity can be lowered (priced off the market) to discourage additional sales. The vast majority of commercial paper sales occur before 12 noon each business day.

Many direct issuers will repurchase their commercial paper, but requests are relatively infrequent. Unlike dealer-placed commercial paper, there is significant trading in the secondary market of the commercial paper of the largest issuers. While the secondary market is not large or as well developed as the market for Treasury securities, the volume of the largest issuers' paper outstanding is substantial enough to support secondary trading. Also, some issuers have encouraged the development of a secondary market to further expand the number of investors active in the market generally.

Bank trust departments purchase a substantial volume of commercial paper and a particular bank's holdings of the commercial paper of a single issuer may remain relatively constant over time. Many direct issuers establish master note arrangements with their "regular" bank trust department investors. Under a master note, the commercial paper issuer typically pays a rate related to its posted commercial paper rates, and the amount outstanding may vary daily depending on the needs of the trust department. The rate may also be based on a formula, but regardless of the method used to establish the rate, the principal objective is to provide the bank with a return greater than it would yield on alternative short maturity market instruments and to offer a more convenient and effective investment medium, which recognizes that the trust department's total investment is likely to change little from day to day. Master notes provide bank trust departments with a very convenient method of aggregating small sums from individual trusts for short-term investment at attractive returns.

CREDIT SUBSTITUTION AND ENHANCEMENT

Through various support arrangements, some smaller and lesser known firms that could not issue highly rated commercial paper on their own have been able to enter the commercial paper market. For example, a letter of credit from a commercial bank, or surety bond, can be attached to the commercial paper with the effect of substituting the bank's, or surety's, credit standing for that of the issuer. While the reduced credit risk will result in access to the market of lower rates to the issuer, the issuer must pay a fee for the letter of credit, which typically ranges from one fourth to three fourths of 1 percent.

Of course, the bank or other surety must be confident of the issuer's ability to liquidate commercial paper as it matures. Letter of credit paper is similar to bankers' acceptance financing, except that the issuance of commercial paper is unrelated to a shipment of goods. Letter of credit paper is generally associated with lesser known firms engaged in such diverse businesses as leasing and powerplant construction, but has been used by other well known "regular" issuers facing difficulty selling their commercial paper at a satisfactory price in the market after a ratings downgrade.

Credit enhancement through collateralization or asset-backed programs has enabled some issuers to enter the commercial paper market. While such issues represent a very small percentage of the market, there has been a steady stream of structured deals in recent years designed to improve investor safety through collateralization. For example, one dealer has designed a program for thrift institutions based on collateralization with U.S. Treasury issues. Similar programs have been structured using such nonfinancial assets as vehicle lease agreements as collateral. Credit risk is reduced and market acceptance increased through overcollateralization. Typically, a separate entity is created to serve as the actual issuer of the commercial paper, and a trustee holds the collateral and is obligated to liquidate the collateral and redeem the commercial paper in the event of default. Also, it is common for a commercial bank to commit a credit line to help ensure timely payment of maturing commercial paper before the collateral is liquidated. Potential issuers of collateralized commercial paper weigh the costs associated with such an issue against the benefits of the lower financing rates to be achieved.

RECENT DEVELOPMENTS

Commercial paper dealers are continually seeking to develop innovative uses of commercial paper to expand the market for their services. For example, an outgrowth of credit enhancement has been cooperative issuance, or the pooling together of lesser known and smaller organizations, to form a front company to issue commercial paper. The participants support the issue by providing a pro-rata or other formula-based share of the issue's collateral (e.g., letter of credit or surety bond). The separate entity created to issue the commercial paper operates as a flowthrough funding source designed to minimize bankruptcy and other credit risks for the investors. Cooperative ventures can be based on some commonality of business interests (e.g., auto rental company franchisees), or for no other reason than to raise short-term working capital for a number of unrelated businesses.

Commercial paper has been used to generate foreign exchange and to facilitate currency conversion, as well as interest rate swaps.

For example, if a foreign subsidiary of a U.S. corporation needs short-term funds, it can raise money in its local market, or issue commercial paper in the U.S. market (which is usually supported by its U.S. parent). If the foreign subsidiary borrows in the U.S. market, it can arrange to obtain the currency it needs in an integrated conversion transaction. Of course, the choice of where to borrow will be primarily dictated by the relative cost of credit between the markets open to the issuer.

Interest rate swaps emerged in 1981 as a method for transaction participants to exchange interest payments to achieve borrowing cost and debt structure efficiencies. While some corporate borrowers have relatively easy access to favorably priced long-term fixed rate debt, but have a need for variable rate credit, other corporate borrowers have relatively easy access to favorably priced short-term variable rate debt (e.g., commercial paper), but have a need for fixed rate credit. In a typical transaction, these two types of borrowers would swap interest payments, but not the underlying debt obligations. Interest rate swaps have grown in popularity and provide participants with greater flexibility to efficiently meet internal cost of funds objectives.

Relatively recent entries to the commercial paper market has been made by issuers in Europe, foreign bank holding companies, and municipal borrowers. While the European commercial paper market has developed slowly (current outstandings are approximately $10 billion compared to over $250 billion in the United States), many U.S. dealers purchase European issues for resale in the United States. Much of this volume is sold through the U.S. subsidiaries of foreign companies. The decision to utilize the market in this fashion can be affected by restraints on the outflow of capital (e.g., the previous Interest Equalization Tax). Foreign bank holding companies sell commercial paper through U.S.-based subsidiaries with a parent company guarantee. This market becomes active whenever Eurodollar borrowing rates are greater than financing rates in the United States. Municipal commercial paper is a relatively undeveloped market. However, it permits municipal issuers to borrow at the base of the yield curve instead of at the higher rates associated with longer term issues. Many state and local governments have not been able to participate in the market due to the lack of enabling legislation. Municipal commercial paper is also known as short-term revenue bonds, or short-term interim certificates.

CONCLUSION

The commercial paper market provides many corporations with a flexible and attractive alternative to short-term bank financing. Commercial paper has been a desirable investment for many investors because of its low credit risk, flexible maturities, and competitive yield. While the market is dominated by large, well-known issuers, smaller firms have been able to enter the market through various credit enhancement techniques. Although no one can predict the future of the market with any certainty, it is likely that, based on the market's history of adapting to its environment, commercial paper will continue to be used to meet a large share of the nation's short-term commercial credit requirements for the foreseeable future.

REFERENCES

ABKEN, PETER A. in *Instruments of the Money Market,* ed. TIMOTHY Q. COOK and BRUCE J. SUMMERS. Richmond, Va.: Federal Reserve Bank of Richmond, 1981.

GREEF, ALBERT O. *The Commercial Paper House in the United States.* Cambridge, Mass.: Harvard Univ. Press, 1938.

HURLEY, EVELYN M. "The Commercial Paper Market." *Federal Reserve Bulletin,* June 1977.

STIGUM, MARCIA. *The Money Market.* Homewood, Ill: Dow Jones-Irwin, 1983.

WEINSTEIN, GRACE W. "Commercial Paper: The Booming Short-Term Market." *Fortune,* June 1985.

CHAPTER 22

Selling the Business

Philip J. Kendall
Chairman
Packard Press Corporation
Philadelphia, Pa.

Philip J. Kendall is currently chairman of the board and CEO of Packard Press Corporation. He is also a member of the board of directors and the executive committee of BASIX Corporation and Automatic Toll Systems, Inc.

One of the most challenging—and traumatic—decisions any entrepreneur can make is to sell his or her business. I can speak from experience. Over the last 20 years I've sold the same business twice. (I repurchased my company two years after selling it the first time.) I can assure you that it's a decision that should never be taken lightly.

Most entrepreneurs spend a lifetime building their businesses.

They pour years of energy and personal resources into something that becomes almost like a child. Even the consideration of selling such a part of themselves is uncomfortable, if not distasteful.

Selling is a decision that many avoid altogether. There are two basic reasons for this, both of which relate to the role of the entrepreneur after the sale. In some cases the sale marks the end of his or her association with the business. To put the future of this lifelong project into someone else's hands is incredibly traumatic.

In many cases, though, the sale represents a change in ownership but not in management. While the former owner is still directing the company the fear of the unknown comes into play. What is going to happen to me and my business once it is actually sold? What surprises are in store? I, for one, do not like surprises. Not in business, anyway. The best way to avoid unforeseen problems or catastrophes (under either scenario) is to follow a carefully developed plan of action.

Most successful businesses did not get that way by accident. A great deal of thought, planning, and execution is necessary before success is achieved. Business planning is also a key requirement for selling a business. Such a plan should establish objectives which, along with the strategies for achieving them, will be very important in negotiating the value of the enterprise to its future owner. In addition, the plan should include any personal objectives that you may wish to accomplish by selling the company.

Many complex elements need to be factored into the selling plan. Some of the most obvious are related to the legal and financial considerations that are involved in any transfer of ownership. But these are by no means the only factors that should be considered. In many cases, the legal and financial points may actually prove to be of lesser importance when compared to other salient issues.

Personally, I have always given a great deal of consideration to my potential business partners. I am a strong believer in forming alliances with individuals who can be of mutual benefit. There is a popular buzzword that is often used in this context: *synergism*. Synergism occurs when two entities, acting together, produce a greater result than the sum of their individual efforts. When two people or two organizations come together to produce a result that they could not have achieved alone, then we see synergy at work.

These are but a few of the issues that you should consider in developing your plan. If you make a rational plan and schedule for the selling of your business, you will be doing yourself a big favor. Naturally, few business deals progress exactly according to the predetermined plan. But by having such a plan in hand, you can ensure that, at the very least, your selling program starts off in the right direction. Assuming that your plan and schedule is well considered and that it allows for flexibility, you can use it to control whatever variations and adjustments prove necessary during the selling process.

WHY SELL?

Why do people choose to sell their businesses? Any number of reasons are evident, ranging from capital problems to the need for a new challenge.

Sometimes it's simply a lack of the capital needed to grow. Perhaps a business needs the infusion of additional financing from external sources in order to maintain or expand its market share. Many entrepreneurs find that they lack the financial muscle to take an idea from its conceptual stage to market rollout. In addition, the high cost of equipment can sometimes create the need for capital that the entrepreneur simply cannot raise.

Sometimes it's a lack of foresight. The founder and/or owner may fail to properly groom a successor. Or the owner may find that existing levels of management are incapable of meeting new technical, financial, or marketing challenges. The choice may be one of selling out or, ultimately, seeing the business slide into mediocrity.

Sometimes it's a question of proper estate planning. For example, private companies often lack a basis for valuation and liquidation for tax purposes. Selling the company can establish this basis and provide more advantageous tax treatment. The sale can also assist the owner in providing his or her heirs with the liquid funds which will be necessary to pay estate taxes.

Sometimes an owner may decide to sell his or her company after only a few years in business. These generally younger entrepreneurs often enjoy the benefit of a fairly rapid return on their investment while at the same time securing the financing to start the cycle again with a new venture. The recent explosion of entrepreneurial start-ups and venture capital investments seems to indicate that sales for this reason are becoming a more common phenomenon.

These are only a few of the more general reasons why people sell. If you are trying to decide whether or not to sell your business, it's time to develop a good, solid plan of attack. My advice is to begin by looking at three key areas: personal objectives, business considerations, and potential buyers.

KNOW THYSELF

As an entrepreneur you are involved in an enterprise that is uniquely your own. In many ways it is an expression of your values and personal philosophy of life. It will be these values and philosophy that will guide you in developing your plan and determining your future steps.

As obvious as it sounds, your first requirement must be a clear understanding of your particular needs and objectives. These needs and objectives are not limited solely to financial or business considerations. Personal considerations, including matters of family, can play a paramount role in any decision to sell your business.

For example, many entrepreneurs have sold their businesses mainly for some additional breathing space—to give themselves more leisure time, more time to "stop and smell the roses." Many of these individuals found that their perspective on life had changed as they reached the age of 45 or 50. They found that, having invested a significant portion of their lives in building something, they really wanted to savor some of the returns that their investment had earned. Since they weren't ready to retire to some Florida beach the sale of their business allowed them the best of both worlds—a continuing involvement in the business and the financial resources to do what they wanted. Still others found that selling the business gave them the personal liquidity that they required.

Family considerations can frequently be an important factor in the decision to sell. Understanding what your business means to your family—both positively and negatively—is an important issue to confront. For many, owning and operating a business can be an all-consuming passion. Many examples exist of people who have sold their businesses largely because the business had become a major problem for their marriages. For some, the day-to-day management of a growing enterprise simply consumed too much time and thus threatened their marriage.

Other company owners, especially those involved in family-owned enterprises, viewed selling the business as a means of eliminating much of the business-related family squabbling that had arisen during the company's growth. Thus the need to understand yourself, your family, and its makeup is critical. Your family makeup is usually an important influence on your own makeup. Give special consideration to the needs and feelings of your spouse and children: Will there be someone who might assume your role in the future? Also, you shold ask yourself what you hope to accomplish over the next 15 to 20 years, as well as where you hope to be at each 5-year interval.

There are any number of personal reasons why someone may choose to sell a company. Before making a decision of such great importance you must have a clear idea what your personal objectives are and how selling your business will help to attain those objectives.

BUSINESS REASONS FOR SELLING

There can be any number of business-related reasons why you may find it appropriate to sell your enterprise. Many times, a principal stockholder or partner feels that selling the business is the best way to solve serious problems of capital structure, liquidity, or even managerial competence. You may be considering the possibility of adding a new partner. In such cases it is generally in everyone's best interest to dissolve the current company and form a new one. Or, you may be locked into a partnership where your partner is playing a passive role and wants to terminate his ownership. Often, it is difficult to finance the buyout from current earnings—particularly for a small company which should be retaining its earnings to finance growth. In any case, significant changes in management organization may create an opportune time for expansion through infusion of outside capital. Acquisition by another company could be the element that makes the necessary difference.

While the need for money is often a key factor, sometimes selling the business is a solution, but not to the problem that exists. Careful analysis may reveal that some alternative solution may be possible. For example, financial problems can be solved by making a public offering or a private placement, renegotiating short- and long-term debt financing, or acquiring a profitable subsidiary. Sometimes the problem is with the management or ownership structure; thus, replacing specific members of management or eliminating a troublesome stockholder may be the solution. You should always explore other possibilities before assuming that money is the problem.

Money was definitely a key factor for me, particularly in 1977 when I sold my company, Packard Press, for the second time. (I had previously repurchased the company.) At that time, Packard Press faced a situation common to many companies that are ultimately sold. We were a growing company with a solid track record and a good marketing program in place. However, we didn't have sufficient capital to grow and expand as rapidly as I would have liked. This growth capital was provided by our new owner, BASIX Corporation. Through the combination of our expertise and BASIX's capital Packard Press has grown from $8 million in sales to over $50 million, with no end in sight. Using their financial muscle and our management skill, along with a diversified product mix, Packard Press now can compete head to head with any and all financial printers in the country. In fact, we're the fastest-growing and one of the largest financial printers in the United States.

PREPARING FOR THE SALE

Once you've accepted that selling your company is a prudent decision you should begin putting your financial and operating house in order. Naturally your company's financial history will give any potential buyer a fairly clear idea of what your company is worth. Arthur H. Rosenbloom, a leading expert in the field of mergers and acquisitions, explained it this way: "No amount of explanation, financial reconstruction, or contingent earnout design will completely explain apparently lackluster historic performance."[1] Obviously, the historical, financial, and operational record of your business will directly affect its ultimate purchase price.

As you begin to put together the deal, be confident and candid in making your presentations. Make sure that these presentations are based on verifiable facts and past history. Using phrases such as "could have," or "should have," or "can be done in the future" only discount your credibility and the future potential of your company. Also, remember that the acquiring company typically looks at the worst possible scenario. What's its downside risk? Like the Miranda warning in criminal cases, anything you say can and will be used against you.

Audited financial statements can be a major asset to you and a boon to the attractive buyer. These statements can be of inestimable value since they can be independently verified. Typically, five years of such statements are sufficient. As you and a potential buyer are bargaining over a fair and acceptable price for the company, these financial records establish the credibility of your business capabilities. Showing the kind of proof represented by five years of audited financial statements can eliminate a lot of questions and suspicion on part of the potential buyer—factors that might lead to doubts about your company's future benefits to the buyer. Therefore, if you don't already have audited statements, you should have them prepared. While a potential buyer may have an audit performed anyway, your volunteering of these important records can reduce the buyer's anxiety and can establish you as a fair-minded individual who is interested only in open, ethical business dealings.

Net operating losses (NOL) can play a major part in any acquisition or merger. However, the NOL may be the acquiring company's or yours. If your company happens to be in an NOL position, you should take great care in presenting it. Although the acquiring company may be able to use your losses to offset some of its own tax liabilities, it may look with disfavor upon acquiring the current management (in your company) that produced those losses. On the other hand, if the acquiring company has NOLs of its own, it may seek a profitable acquisition to apply the losses to.

Your accountant will be a vital member of your sales team. He

---

[1] Arthur H. Rosenbloom, "Selling Your Business—Making the Best Deal," *Cashflow,* July/August 1980.

or she can provide critical advice on how to structure your financial presentation to gain maximum advantage. If properly challenged, your accountant may be able to suggest several alternative methods of accounting that improve your financial picture according to generally accepted accounting principles (GAAP) standards. Any improvement in your company's net income and retained earnings (equity) will translate into an enhanced purchase price. Such changes can also result in a much cleaner and healthier balance sheet with fewer explanations required. However, before manipulating your revenue figures, make sure you obtain competent, accurate professional advice from your accountant, outside consultant, or both.[2]

At the same time that you are tending to your revenue figures, you should eliminate unnecessary, nonproductive company costs—luxury items such as private planes or club memberships. In addition, you should restructure and consolidate any existing financing agreements that are made through small and complex loan arrangements and that are secured by multiple assets and leases and/or personal assets. Also, try to do away with any contingent liabilities and buy out any minority interests that may exist.[3] These actions will help reduce the complexity of any arrangements that must be made for the possible sale of your business.

LOOKING FOR A BUYER

Once you decide to sell your business, you must find a buyer. Since many owners remain with the company after the sale, the mesh of personalities between those selling and those buying is of critical importance. As part of your plan for selling your business you should include the most desirable characteristics that the ideal candidate should have.

The first barrier that you'll have to overcome is fear: What will this unknown suitor be like? It is not easy to face the possibility that someone else will have the final say on many matters that were once your exclusive province.

From my own standpoint, this is why I was attracted to BASIX Corporation. One of the key operating philosophies at BASIX is to let the management of each subsidiary run the business. The top management at BASIX is comfortable filling the role of venture capitalist. They are willing to provide funding and counsel wherever needed,

---

[2] Bertram Frankenberger, Jr., "Painting a Clear Picture of the Acquisition," in *Handbook of Mergers, Acquisitions* and *Buyouts,* ed. S. J. Lee and Robert Colman (Englewood Cliffs, N.J.: Prentice-Hall, 1973).

[3] Arthur H. Rosenbloom, "How to Determine the Value of a Business: A Case Study," *The Practical Accountant,* March 1983.

but they maintain a loose hold on the reins of day-to-day decision making. As a result, I'm fairly free to make the decisions necessary to keep Packard Press effective and profitable.

Another primary consideration is the ability of the acquirer to contribute. Many other authors have analyzed and explained how a company grows and meets new challenges at different levels of operation. At each level there is a plateau that is reached after which, unless certain hurdles are overcome, the growth of the company is stymied.

My situation was similar before I sold Packard Press to BASIX. I found that once I reached approximately $8 million in sales I needed to be able to draw upon additional advice and counsel from time to time. With BASIX, I found the sounding board that I was looking for. In the past it seemed as if I had made all the decisions by myself. When you're faced with a tough decision, it can be comforting to know that you have others with whom you can consult, and who, in turn, can make available a network of contacts who've faced similar problems.

One of the best ways of locating a potential buyer is to examine other companies that are active in the acquisition business, and to speak with the presidents and managers of companies that have been recently acquired. You can gain important insights by talking to these key officials about the nature of each potential buyer and how your company will be affected if acquired by that buyer. Remember, these key officials have just gone through the acquisition process and should be very familiar with the way it works.

During merger negotiations, you will want to meet and get to know as many key people from the potential acquiring company as possible. This early process of establishing rapport is particularly important since you and the suitor are inclined to be on your best behavior. Both companies are trying to present themselves as the ideal marriage partner. Unfortunately, reality often compares unfavorably with the images projected. Unless each partner has a fairly clear idea of how the other will behave during the marriage, any number of unpleasant surprises may result.

The more information and knowledge you have, the less likely it is that those surprises will occur. The dialogue that you establish with the people from the other company will help you determine a number of critical factors: whether or not the philosophies of the two companies are compatible; whether one company's management style will be a significant problem to the other; and whether or not you are really going to enjoy working closely with the people of the acquiring company.

Remember that the organization that you've built over the years has developed its own cohesiveness and way of doing things. Any sudden, drastic changes (such as the introduction of new control modes or the revision of established procedures) that are undertaken without discussion with your key people or prior notice will certainly undermine their morale. The bonds of loyalty that have developed over the years will vanish and your company will become just another place to work. Your subordinates will realize that loyalty does not pay, that investing themselves in a company is a mistake, and that they should not tie themselves to one particular president or organization. Keeping your people abreast of events as they occur will make it less likely that you'll lose them at a time when you need them the most.

Bringing your own staff into the negotiation process at an early stage is a positive motivating force. Your people have a tremendous stake in the future of the company, and their enthusiasm will be important to that future. I believe that letting them know what's going on is not only ethical but also will lessen their sense of foreboding.

Nonmanagement employees have a stake in the acquisition process, too. Try to maintain open channels of communication with them. Special luncheon programs, for example, can provide employees with an effective means of expressing their fears and concerns to senior management. By developing these avenues of information, you and your key management can gain better insights into the problems that might be involved in a potential merger or acquisition.

Bringing your management team into the negotiation process enables your people to prove that they are a vital part of your company's operation. By proving their current worth to the company, they will also be proving their future worth to the acquiring company. At the same time, officials of the acquiring company will have an ideal chance to assuage any additional fears that your people might have. Thus, by extending the feeling-out process to these management levels at an early time, you can help alleviate many of the misunderstandings and much lack of communication that might otherwise occur.

HOW MUCH IS YOUR BUSINESS REALLY WORTH?

You've completed your inventory of needs and those of your company, and you've begun to line up potential buyers. Now is the time to establish a realistic selling price. My advice on this is straightforward: price to sell. Don't use the selling process merely as a way of ascertaining the value of your company. If self-gratification is what you are really interested in, do yourself and any potential buyer a favor by contacting a good valuation company.

One thing you never want to lose sight of is what the person on the other side of the table wants to see. When the potential acquirer is a public company an earnings trend is key. Sometimes this earnings trend can work to your advantage in that you end up having a share in the profits through an earnout. (With an earnout you receive a cash payment at the time of the sale with the remaining payments tied to future profit or return levels of the company.) Thus, while the purchaser gets the earnings to report, you still get an ample share of the earnings as part of your compensation package. The stumbling block is: How much are you willing to settle for versus how much is the buyer willing to offer?

Different industries have different ways of measuring financial worth. However, a variety of benchmarks are used to establish a fair market value for your business. One of the most common formulas is a multiple of earnings. Depending on the size of your company and the ability to project future earnings growth, a multiple ranging from 5 to 15 times net earnings is not unreasonable.

Another barometer in determining a purchase price is the ratio of pre-tax profits to sales. Typically, this ratio should be in the neighborhood of 10 to 15 percent for a healthy printing company. This ratio can vary significantly, depending on the nature of the business in which the company is engaged.

There are many other means that are commonly used by potential investors or buyers to judge the future potential of your company: net book value, comparison of profit margins, working capital ratios, the amount of common and preferred stock to total capital investments, rates of return on common stock and invested capital, payback analysis, discounted cash flow, and valuation of assets. To gain a complete understanding of these terms and procedures (and to protect yourself when negotiations begin) I suggest you make use of your advisers and consultants. They can give you valuable and unbiased advice on what the fair market price of your business should be.

NEGOTIATING THE FINANCIAL ASPECTS OF THE DEAL

Perhaps the most important part of the merger/acquisition process is the financial negotiations stage. Of course, this depends on the relative importance that you happen to place on money. If you are like most of us, the question of how much you'll receive for a lifetime of love, labor, and devotion—your business—will be of paramount importance.

Selling a business is a process consisting of a series of steps. Each step is not only unique and important in its own right, but influences each of the steps that follow. You must be very careful to carry each step through to completion and not look too far ahead. Also, you must make allowance for the completion of each successive step and commit the necessary time. If things are to be done well, you have to allow enough time to do each step correctly.

This is particularly true during financial negotiations. If you've reached this stage, you can be fairly certain that the potential buyer is very interested in acquiring your company. You can sense that the reward you've been striving for is almost within your reach.

Reaching this stage is similar to the position of a baseball team that has won the pennant and is about to play in the World Series. Many teams subconsciously relax at this point and fail to achieve the greatness that winning the World Series implies. Winning the divisional pennant is only a step in the process of winning the championship. You, too, must remember that there are still games left to be played—and won—before you have achieved your goal. In other words, be patient and maintain your focus.

I have found that the advice of professional consultants can be of inestimable value during this phase of the selling process. Before sitting down with any merger/acquisition candidate, you should conduct brainstorming sessions with your key outside consultants such as your lawyers, accountants, underwriters, investment bankers, or any others who may play a significant role in the eventual success of the transaction. Strategy sessions before actual negotiations begin will help ensure that you have developed the most appropriate means for attaining your objectives.

Experienced attorneys who specialize in buying and selling businesses can provide valuable advice on how to structure the terms of the sale. Letters of intent, covenants, warrantees and representations, considerations, and other legal instruments are often used to more clearly define specific terms that are being negotiated. The timely input of an experienced lawyer can significantly enhance the effectiveness of these legal instruments. With the proper advice, sellers can often create favorable positions in such areas as escrow terms, indemnification, purchase price allocation, registration rights, timing, allocation of expenses to various parties, and closing conditions.

Investment bankers help by offering timely financial advice and by arranging contacts with potential buyers who might not otherwise have shown an interest in purchasing the enterprise. In addition, investment bankers can lend greater credibility to the buyer's negotiating posture while providing a more objective rationale for certain prices that might otherwise seem oppressively high.

Frequently, your advisers and consultants bring a level of experience that you don't possess. You may be dealing with a buyer who has been through the acquisition wars many more times than you. Since there is little likelihood that you will have mastered all of the legal, financial, and tax ramifications of your business deal, your advisers will be an important resource.

But again, I offer a word of caution. You must maintain control over the entire selling process. You must provide the leadership that ensures that negotiations are carried through to completion. It is no one else's company but yours. What happens in the future to the company, and to you, will largely depend on decisions made during this phase of the negotiations. Never forget that responsibility for making key decisions is *yours;* it's a responsibility that can never be abdicated.

As CEO you are used to rendering a decision based on alternatives prepared by your staff. In the same way you can use your skilled advisers to help screen potential problems as they develop. You should have them doing such things as shortening and simplifying the selling procedure, and arranging compromises when negotiations reach an impasse. You might consider using one of your advisers as the "bad cop" who makes the tough demands while you play the role of the conciliatory "good cop."

This can be especially important if you will be staying with the company in some capacity after the sale. Selling the company is only the beginning of the partnership between you and the buyer. If you are the one who is fighting for the best deal, you are certainly going to be remembered later on. You and the buyer may find it difficult to work together in the future if the past is too burdened with contentious comments and forced decisions.

ADDITIONAL CONSIDERATIONS DURING NEGOTIATIONS

Do not be greedy; don't go for the last dollar. Small items can often be deal breakers. Don't let the small things create major stumbling blocks.

If stock is to be conveyed as part of the transaction, make certain that what you are receiving is not "watered down." You should insist that at some point the stock can be converted into hard cash. True value, not diluted worth, is your goal. This is where your financial advisers must show their mettle. Many deals have been struck where a person went to bed a millionaire only to find that the night (and dubious circumstances) had wiped them out. If you are part of a consolidated group of companies, an adverse problem unrelated to your business but affecting another subsidiary of the parent could significantly influence the price of the parent company's stock.

FUTURE MANAGEMENT ISSUES

For the most part, the company that acquires yours is going to insist on more than absentee management. You should agree, in advance, on what is to happen after the buyer has taken control of the corporation. Continuing management is usually a must.

In addition, you will need to determine your future scope of authority and postmerger reporting functions and requirements. These agreements should be formalized in both the agreement of sale and in a management contract. Also, it is critical to know in advance how finances will be controlled, monitored, and reported. As I've discussed, a reason for selling may be the need for additional capital. Finding that you must perform feats of financial wizardry will certainly not be a pleasant surprise.

One of the unpleasant consequences of going from being a private to a public company is the reporting requirements. In the past, you might have made decisions that would have paid off in 2, 3, 5, or 10 years, and you would have fitted these decisions into your personal program as you deemed appropriate. But now, as a public company, you find yourself up against a quarterly benchmark, where earnings must be reported to support the parent's stock price. Consequently, the types of decisions that you make and the results that are expected of you are on a more immediate basis. The result is that long-term plans are sometimes relegated to the back seat. Also, the timing and content of financial reporting can be rather burdensome. In the past you might have prepared complete financial statements on a quarterly or annual basis. Now you need a support staff capable of producing statements on a monthly basis.

The operational and marketing areas of the contemplated deal warrant special review and consideration. Depending on the company with whom you intend to merge, there might be other opportunities to expand on a national basis or into other closely aligned product lines. These opportunities may be a vital consideration for the acquiring company, so now is an ideal time for you to consider them as well.

These types of issues should be raised, questions should be asked, and investigations should be conducted prior to the culmination of the sale. There should never be an excuse for a misunderstanding on such fundamental points. They should be negotiated in good faith and clearly spelled out in the acquisition agreement. In essence, you should do your best to be aware of not only the various aspects of the new environment in which you will be operating, but also how that environment will affect the needs and perspectives of other parties.

CONCLUSION

Naturally, not every merger or acquisition will be as successful as the one between Packard Press and BASIX Corporation. Most mergers and acquisitions are no doubt undertaken in the hope that the eventual outcome will be mutually beneficial to the parties involved. But statistics indicate that good intentions are not enough.

Nearly one out of three acquisitions is eventually undone. According to W. T. Grimm & Co., a merger and acquisition specialist, the number of divestitures during the past five years has increased 35 percent.[4] That figure represents approximately 900 divestitures, worth approximately $30 billion. Figures such as these have not cooled the ardor of corporate America for acquisitions. One need only read the newspaper (and not just the business pages anymore) to see reports of the latest megamerger. The actions of America's giants are shared by other companies, large and small. According to statistics released by *Business Week* magazine for 1984, more than 2,500 deals were consummated, for a combined worth of $122 billion.

Why do one out of three acquisitions eventually turn sour? A large portion of the blame involves such things as lack of efficient planning, lack of foresight, incompatible management philosophies, misplaced expectations by either buyer or seller (or both), and for a failure to follow through on policies that would more effectively meld the two companies together once the marriage takes place.

How can you create the circumstances that make your corporate marriage one of the successes? It's imperative that you "know thyself" well before even contemplating any kind of agreement. Once you decide that some action is necessary, work out an overall strategy and determine what you want to do and how you'll do it.

If selling is the right course of action for you, make sure that you have consulted with everyone who can make a contribution to your decision-making process, including outside consultants and any other people you know who might have gone through a similar process. Make sure that your company is correctly postured, that you have adequate financial statements, and that you have ongoing marketing and operational plans already in place.

Next, establish what you feel are fair parameters in determining the price that someone should pay for your company. Don't put your company on the market merely to find out what someone may be willing to pay for it. Clarify and consolidate any outstanding debts or obligations your company might have, and try to simplify the acqui-

[4] "Do Mergers Really Work?" *Business Week,* June 3, 1985, p. 88.

sition process as much as possible by eliminating stumbling blocks such as complicated accounting methods or minority interests that you may be able to buy back.

Keep in mind the concept of synergy when searching for the best partner. That is vitally important. Determine what your needs are, from both a personal and business standpoint, and figure out how these needs can best be met by an outside buyer. Ascertain the benefits that a particular buyer can bring to your organization and vice versa.

Be confident and candid in making your presentation. Show that you are in control of your organization and that you know where you are today and where you will be in the future. Also, demonstrate your understanding of the potential buyer's needs and how your company will fit into his or her corporate organization. Above all, make sure all your evidence and conclusions are logical and based on verifiable facts.

Make sure you have conducted a thorough investigation of your future partner. Failure by one party to fully investigate the business of the other is one of the most common causes of failed corporate marriages. At the same time, consider how your organization and that of the acquiring company will fit together. Your negotiations with the seller should clearly delineate where your company will stand within the structure of the acquiring corporation, as well as your own role in planning, administration, operations, and marketing for your soon-to-be-sold business.

Finally, make sure that your personal objectives and those of the potential acquirer are compatible. The idea is not just to get married but to build a relationship that lasts. Often, this is not the easiest thing to do.

Establishing a carefully thought-out plan for the acquisition process, then adhering to that plan, can eliminate many of the pitfalls that characterize so many of the more publicized business mergers and acquisitions that have failed. The battlefield is strewn with the corpses of those who made an effort but failed to carry the day. Planning, persistence, and determination—and a dose of luck—will carry you to the same success in selling your business as you had in creating it.

CHAPTER 23

Raising Foreign Capital

Jacques T. L. Delacave
Chairman
Abbeyside Group plc
London, England

Jacques T. L. Delacave is chairman of the Abbeyside Group plc, which provides corporate financial services in the United Kingdom to domestic and foreign companies, concentrating on smaller entities or transactions. Before coming to Alva he was with the Banque de Bruxelles, Brussels (1959–1964), Citibank, Brussels and Geneva (1964–1973), and Bank Brussels Lambert (United Kingdom, 1974–1983).

Mr. Delacave is a director of a number of other companies in the United Kingdom, Europe, and the United States, and is also involved in many civic and educational organizations. He graduated from Trinity College, Cambridge (1956, B.A., Economics), Albert Ludwig Universitäit Freiburg-Breisgau (1958, Dr. rer. Pol.), and Columbia University (1959, M.B.A.).

INTRODUCTION

The topic of attracting foreign investors to finance emerging and growing businesses needs a restricting definition, as it is an almost endless subject. First, assuming that only the requirements of emerging and growing businesses in the United States are being considered (excluding the rather special case of real estate finance), and also only from a European standpoint, then the one common characteristic often encountered in attempts to raise finance seems to be the misguided feeling that if lenders or investors cannot be found in the United States, there may be someone overseas who could be persuaded to support a project rejected closer to home. This may be an extreme way of representing the situation, and indeed some such attempts have been successful, but for the purposes of this survey, it is assumed that any project for which foreign finance is considered will also have viability within the U.S. financial market. Projects will be presented differently from the conventional U.S. format and, indeed, terms and conditions will vary from U.S. practice, particularly in elaborating legal documentation. In general, the discussion will be centered on the requirements of the smaller company; the "household" name can easily make use of sophisticated and extensive sources of capital and finance in Europe and find comparatively attractive terms. This is especially the case for multinational corporations whose needs for finance cover activities in many countries and in many different currencies.

The smaller company will not have found it easy to gain access to conventional channels and sources of finance. The past, however, is not necessarily a good pointer to the future. There have been considerable changes in financial markets, and some far-reaching and fundamental modifications are being implemented now. This is particularly true of the most important market in Europe, the London market. In comparison with other European countries, London is the most active point of encounter for both British and overseas institutions and private investors with borrowers. Until recently, London operated on a basis that had been evolved over a period of time, and which, at the risk of oversimplification, can be broken down into three investor/lender categories: first, the banks providing both sterling and currency loans; second, institutions such as insurance companies or pension funds and individuals providing both equity and investment in securities; and third, certain intermediaries whose roles were historically defined, such as discount houses that trade essentially fixed interest securities and intermediate between banking institutions and the Bank of England. The equity market has been in the hands of stockbrokers who always acted as agents and of jobbers who "made" markets by carrying positions as principals. Finally, the merchant banks have provided a broad range of services and are certainly for all major transactions the introducers of proposals to the market.

Two new markets have recently been established: the Unlisted Securities Market (USM), and the Over-the-Counter market, which provides varying degrees of scope and liquidity. This structure is now being substantially altered by the introduction of free commissions for the stockbrokers who will also be able to make markets as principals. Capital requirements for brokers will rise so that the rules that prevented ownership of stockbrokers other than by the partners active in the business have been lifted, and a number of amalgamations have been announced comprising major banks or institutions with stockbrokers and jobbers. At the same time, changes have been announced in the area of control and the outcome is far from clear, although the tradition in London of self-regulation has deep roots and hopefully can prove to be successful in the future to avoid the need for more formal regulatory structures. The consequence of maintaining the character of London will be to protect its advantages of flexibility, cost effectiveness, and simplicity over other centers.

Again, running the risk of excessive oversimplification, most of the changes that have taken place in other European countries have either been to improve the systems and procedures from an internal point of view, or in cases such as Switzerland, for the international market, but basically reserved for the major foreign borrowers or issuers. This is the main reason for concentrating on the United Kingdom—other markets have not been reviewed as extensively in this context.

Nevertheless, there are important aspects of financing, such as the incidence of tax, that will be very relevant. For instance, the Luxembourg market is particularly attractive to holding companies whose earnings come essentially from capital gains on securities. More important, however, is the incidence of tax from the point of view of the investor in a U.S.-structured proposal. This aspect is much too complex to be reviewed at all correctly here but three main points have to be made. First, the partnership formula so often used advantageously in the United States is generally not applicable for a European investor. Second, there are major differences depending on the sources of income, interest, dividends, and capital gains, not to mention royalties. Finally, the legal and tax solution will nearly always depend on the activity itself and the nationality of the participants. These aspects should be kept in mind whenever the details of a transaction are being studied, even though they cannot be reviewed meaningfully here.

There are a number of sources of information for all markets. For instance, most of the large public accounting firms produce up-to-date information in English on financial structures in Europe and indeed will cover such specific aspects as new issues or listings on stock markets. Stockbrokers, banks, and other official institutions also provide readily available information and advice on these matters, country by country, so that it is thought unnecessary to give here any particular references.

USES OF FINANCE

It may be tautological to suggest that emerging companies raise finance to fund their growth, but it is often very difficult to determine precisely why a prospective borrower would wish to access a foreign market. Essentially, in this context, it will be assumed that the company will wish to fund activities "onshore" in the United States and is indeed a U.S. corporation. It is, however, useful to consider two other purposes—funding activities outside of the United States, and financing imports. As we are considering corporations that will tend to be relatively small and not generally well known, the proposal will be essentially evaluated in terms of the U.S. corporation itself. But if the planned activities were to be in Europe, then the matter could be quite different, as each country has its own policy to support investment and development, particularly in areas designated for this purpose. At the same time, the nature of the activity itself, for instance the prospect of job creation, will weigh much more heavily in the balance for granting aid and general support than pure financial parameters relating to the parent company. Information on these programs and on the sources of finance are readily available, particularly from major commercial banks in each country.

The other consideration is that if the U.S. corporation is funding purchases for, say, investment purposes, some of this finance can be provided in Europe if the goods are manufactured there. Depending very much on the goods themselves—and essentially they should be investment "hardware," although "software" or engineering and design can be part of the package—loans attractively priced can be provided by commercial banks with the support of public insurance programs, similar but often more generous than those of the Exim (Export-Import) Bank in the United States. In several instances, this has been found to be an attractive alternative to local purchase and competitive in terms of cost to the borrower: Indeed, there have been occasions when the products without the financial package were more expensive out of the United States but became more competitive when the cost of financing was added. To a certain extent, the balance sheet strain may also well be less than by conventional borrowing methods, and certainly more attractive if equity has to be increased to maintain borrowing ratios. It is also clear that these are not the only considerations in making choices for investment or equipment, but it remains an opportunity for a U.S. firm to obtain financial support from Europe. Again, the major commercial and merchant banks maintain specialized departments to cover this area in each of the countries.

Returning, therefore, to the smaller U.S. corporation wishing to raise finance in Europe for use in the United States, there is little conventional finance that commercial banks can offer that could not be provided by their branches, affiliates, or correspondents in the United States. Focusing on the use of funds, it is easy to understand that bank finance will essentially be required to bridge a mismatch in timing between cash flows and be either self-liquidating or, if for a longer term, will depend on profitability and also security. Even superficial supervision of a smaller project poses nearly insurmountable problems, so that such a proposal has little chance of success.

Turning to the longer term, there are a number of instances where funding can be structured on a secured basis, and this can often be the case, for instance, in the "take and carry" contracts of the petroleum industry, but can also encompass leasing transactions. If either the contracts or the equipment concern Europe, then there is good reason for commercial lenders to look seriously at the proposals. If this is not the case, the major hurdle is to convince Europeans of the reason why these requirements are not covered by U.S. sources.

When considering the possibility of funding outside of the United States, it is therefore probably not appropriate to present transactions that normally would fall into the domain of commercial banking in the United States.

The conclusion from this is that a successful approach to the European market is likely to be centered on equity or long-term finance. Consequently, the focus has to be on profitability and cash flow for debt service rather than the ability of the ongoing business to provide a self-liquidating situation. It is therefore in conjunction with the shareholder capitalization of the equity of the business that foreign source funding has to be considered. One of the most important criteria has to be that the balance sheet ratios be appropriate for the activity concerned—and therefore satisfactory to the lenders of the shorter term facilities—and that either the cost of notes or convertible instruments or the price at which equity can be issued are competitive with other sources of finance.

This is not the place to review in detail the criteria that have to be used, nor to attempt to define in general what must be largely variable from case to case. For the purposes of discussing the availability of funds in Europe for smaller U.S. growth corporations, it has to be stressed that even if there are exceptions that can always arise and serve as examples, activities in the United States will only attract longer term finance on equity. Fundamentally therefore, the questions will involve the viability of the project, the prospects and the management of the U.S. corporation, but also, as always, the attraction of a proposal will be related to a certain extent to the form in which it is made and how the message is conveyed. In this context, as will be discussed later, the personality of the "introducer" and presenter is going to be of crucial importance.

SOURCES OF FINANCE

Quoted Securities

As in most markets in the world, there are major categories of lenders and investors with their own specific requirements and characteristics. The first division arises from the very existence of a market; in the stock markets, whether they be individual or institutional, investors make purchases of securities subject to set rules and regulations that tend to make the investment "vehicle" the same for all concerned.

Individuals. Individuals, including private holding companies, trusts, and so on, will in all countries participate in the quoted markets, but their representation has decreased in favor of institutions. In the United Kingdom, for instance, regulations and tax advantages have favored pension funds and made them one of the determining factors in these markets. Moreover, when considering individuals as a group, it must be stressed that, especially in countries like Switzerland and Luxembourg, decisions are vested in the hands of portfolio managers who specialize in this work and whose action is similar to that of institutions. As in the United States, the smaller portfolios have tended to be handled in the mutual fund type of structure—in the United Kingdom, unit trusts really correspond to open-ended mutual funds. This segment of the investor market is essentially determined by the ability of the company offering securities to obtain a quotation or listing. Since in nearly all cases of smaller non-European corporations, a full listing on the main markets will not be available—requirements of size, capitalization, and records (often over five years of consolidated accounts are needed)—the focus has to be on unlisted security markets, in London, the Unlisted Securities Market (USM) or the Over-The-Counter market.

Clearly, requirements are less stringent, but at the same time, the scope and liquidity of the markets are also considerably more limited. The individual investor participating in this area will therefore concentrate on performance and the prospects of the issuing company. In this context, the introducing institution, be it a broker or a merchant bank (or both together), will play a very important role in the appeal for the investment.

Institutions. By far the most important lenders for quoted securities are institutions. In a market such as London, but also on the Continent of Europe, pension funds, insurance companies, and closed-end investment companies have gained in importance and now constitute by far the largest segment. In the United Kingdom, single pension funds for nationalized industries manage assets that often represent several billion pounds sterling. Regulations that determine their investment policies concern either the type of security—sometimes the sector of activity—the country of origin, and the tax position of the investment. In the United Kingdom, for instance, some of the funds will derive a benefit from receiving income without a tax deduction, as their status does not provide a tax base against which a credit can be taken; others do not bear tax on the capital gains that are realized, and their respective investment criteria will of course reflect this situation.

Two main points need to be stressed to explain why it is really not appropriate to try to describe in detail the position of the different institutions—even if they were to remain unchanged for any significant periods of time—and the various aspects of their investment operations. The first is that in the case of quoted securities, an intermediary such as a stockbroker will always have to be involved and, as discussed below, will handle the negotiations with the stock exchanges and with regulatory authorities as may be appropriate, will be fully cognizant of the requirements of the institutions as these are their major clients, and will advise on the structure of the issue to meet their criteria.

The second point is that, generally speaking, the institutions do not welcome direct approaches but will refer them to their normal appointed channels, and this is, of course, particularly true of securities quoted on exchanges. The largest amongst them will, of course, have their own operations in the United States, covering certain sectors if of specific interest, such as the petroleum industry. The point of contact can therefore be either in the United Kingdom or the United States, but clearance by the U.S. entity is often required. Lastly in this context, and again especially when dealing with the largest institutions, the management function is clearly divided between U.K. or European investments and U.S. securities, the latter often being handled directly in the United States.

When considering an approach to the institutional sector in any of the European countries and recognizing the advantage of a quotation, then a stockbroker and a bank would be consulted to check whether the status of the U.S. corporation, and its ability to make available to the U.K. or European market shares or bonds, enable them to constitute a group of investors sufficiently wide to provide a real base for market transactions. In this context, it should be mentioned that the over-the-counter markets are not at all as developed as in the United States so that, generally speaking, institutions or portfolio managers seeking liquidity will not consider such issues as meeting their criteria.

Nonquoted Securities

When considering the nonquoted area, the requirements of individual investors or lenders become much more prominent in determining the format of the securities and the conditions pertaining thereto and, consequently, the participants are less easy to categorize. This will have particular bearing on the methods adopted to raise finance.

Individuals. Normally, the investor who would be interested in unquoted situations is likely to be either in the high net worth category or to operate through private investment companies. As will be discussed below, regulatory requirements as enforced in the United States for private placements are not applicable in Europe, even though care must be exercised not to contravene the laws on the distribution of securities that are enacted in each of the European countries.

Quite clearly, as is the case for venture capital in the United States, negotiations will become much more direct and involve terms and conditions particular to the investor as well as to the corporation raising funds. In some cases, it will be more attractive to create interest-bearing securities, convertible or with detachable warrants, for the investor. It is also clear that in this case, a direct approach can be made to the investor, or the intermediary need not be an institutional entity, as there will not be, at this stage, a requirement for a full prospectus (as will be discussed below).

However, it is also a much harder group of investors to approach systematically because of the great variety of sources. Undoubtedly, in a city such as London, most investors seeking opportunities to acquire participations in U.S. corporations will be represented, but it remains very hard to find a way of ensuring an adequate coverage and it very often becomes a matter of personal contacts. This, of course, is extremely time-consuming. Even if this difficulty is recognized, there is no doubt that as this is a most important source of finance for the U.S. growth company, it must be overcome. But there are also common characteristics that have to be underlined in the transactions that are effected by this group of investors. The European group might seek, if not control, at least a significant and dominating position, thus excluding other major participants. Such would be the case, for instance, of "congeneric" activities giving the investor a position in the U.S. market. Alternatively, and this is by far the most frequent case, the European investor will wish to be in a syndicate with other U.S. investors, and indeed prefers to be in a senior position so that, in case of a failure to meet expectations, he would be repaid before the U.S. partners. Apart from real estate or other transactions that are easy to structure in this way, this is quite difficult to implement, but remains a major consideration for non-U.S. investors. In certain cases, solutions have been found so that U.S. investors benefited from tax advantages on depreciation through limited partnerships whilst the non-U.S. investor acquired interest-bearing securities that might have a senior position. Again, this depends entirely on the issuer, the investor, and the company concerned, and not one particular formula can be generally applicable.

When considering approaching this group of investors, such matters as board representation, cooperation in Europe itself, and technological transfers have all to be taken into account as these will have great importance in the attractiveness of the proposal to an individual investor.

Institutions. Investing institutions generally have some ability to invest in unquoted securities, although this segment is restricted and much smaller than the quoted portion of their portfolios. On the whole, and excluding here venture capital organizations, the institutions do not wish to play an active role in the management of the companies in which they invest, so that transactions proposed to them are usually of a syndicated nature both in the United States and Europe. In this context, one of the most useful approaches is to involve what might be called a "technological" partner. Thus, a significant part of the investment is acquired, often on special conditions, by an entity that is involved in the field concerned and that will play an active role in supervision, management, and so on, and that therefore will give the investing institutions the confirmation that their research has been correct and that experts in the field are prepared to back the project.

The most important fact to keep in mind when considering attracting European institutions to acquire unquoted securities is that, irrespective of the promise of great growth or return on a current basis—and many are keen to see an interest paid to help carry the investment—the real concern is how the investment will be finally sold. Whilst it is true that most investments of this nature are finally the object of "trade sales," that is, sold to corporations in the field of activity of the issuer, it is essential to have a program, and the institutions will be looking for some commitment from the majority owners to accept a quotation within a reasonable period of time to give liquidity to their investment. This may be achieved by quoting the securities of the corporation in the United States or in Europe or by reversing into a suitable vehicle, but whatever program is adopted, the outcome must be that the investing institution can look forward to selling its participation at a profit.

In many cases, and because of the difficulties posed in monitoring such investments, institutions have been led to concentrate their participations in specialized vehicles, themselves quoted or not, that will then carry out the analysis, implementation, and monitoring on behalf of their sponsors. Generally speaking, all of these entities will be in contact with intermediaries such as brokers and banks who will tend to channel to them opportunities that correspond to their requirements. One of the main factors to be considered is that there is usually much less difficulty when making contact with institutions for an attractive proposition to raise enough funding at the outset, rather than having to go back later because the original issue was not sufficient to cover the needs of the business. Moreover, funds available for smaller company U.S. transactions are quite restricted in Europe, and, with the growth of European "venture capital," U.S. issues will face greater competition. Nevertheless, the awareness of investment opportunities in this sector will offset the limiting factors in the future.

Operating Companies. As mentioned above, there is a definite place for companies in the same field of activity taking an interest in the U.S. smaller growth corporation. Needless to say, their investment may not be welcome as it is often linked to giving the European company substantial control or ownership. Nevertheless, this is not always the case, and a number of examples exist where a minority participation is taken by an industrial or commercial company, often for purposes of diversification. In some cases, shares have been swapped and have been accompanied by "vendor" placing so that cash can be made available to the issuer.

The rapid development of technology has led many substantial companies to dedicate some funds to acquiring minority participations in smaller companies to achieve a form of diversification that cannot be effected otherwise. In order to identify potential investors, the U.S. corporation should research its area of activity as it is usually in the best position to know and select the right partners. In some cases, however, major corporations have joined forces with financial intermediaries to ensure that proposals are made to them as early as possible to give them first choice of opportunities in their field of activity or interest.

The smaller U.S. growth corporation will find a syndicate of investing institutions and a minority technological partner a very favorable solution for the future, especially if linked to U.S. investors of repute. If business plans once implemented prove up to expectations, then future quotation on, say, the London market would be achieved in the most advantageous conditions, giving access to wide funding and preserving control and independence to a large extent. The question must, however, be asked as to why a U.S. corporation would go through all these steps to raise funds that, in theory at least, should easily and speedily be financed in the United States. The answer might, of course, be the desire of the U.S. owners to develop activities in Europe and other countries, but the answer can often be one of cost and ease of implementation.

METHODS AND PROCEDURES

When approaching foreign investors, it was seen that in most cases, if not in every case, it will be necessary to retain an intermediary. London has, of course, the advantage of language, but in all European countries, institutions are used to handling business matters in English, so that this should not create too great a concern. Nevertheless, the most active and broad-based financial center remains London, particularly for the purposes of quoting smaller companies. To a certain extent, it could be argued that the first approach should be made to the London market, using it thereafter as a stepping stone to other markets. This would clearly not always be the best policy; private investment companies in France, portfolio managers in Switzerland, or possible market introductions in Luxembourg or the Netherlands would not necessarily be best served by concentrating only on London. However, it is true that in the majority of cases, the smaller U.S. growth corporation will find both a wide source of professional advice and a depth of contacts that may serve its needs without reference to other markets.

Recently, as mentioned above, the reorganization that has been taking place in the U.K. financial markets has, to a certain extent, brought it closer to its European counterparts. Thus, commercial banks are now active in what used to be the merchant banking domain—indeed several merchant banks are now subsidiaries or affiliates of major commercial banks—and both domestic and other commercial institutions such as the large U.S. banks offer their clients a full range of services that will even encompass stock brokerage services.

The problem faced by the smaller U.S. corporation is that, on the whole, these institutions, while extremely well placed in the market, and having substantial funds under management, tend to concentrate on large transactions and are expensive. In the case of an introduction to the Unlisted Securities Market, this has tended to favor issues sponsored by stockbrokers only. As a number of stockbrokers are now linked with larger groups, if the need arises to call on other professionals, they can do so without difficulty. Depending on whether the U.S. corporation is intending to raise equity or bonds through a private placement or through a public issue, the choice of the intermediary will be different. Moreover, if the intention is to approach private groups or technological partners, a different approach may still be required.

Considering potential intermediaries, it is clear that if a public issue of over £2 million is being considered and is fairly complex, retaining both a substantial U.S. bank established in London and familiar with the issuer and a stockbroker will be the right way to handle the offering, on the assumption that the bank also can provide merchant banking services. It will be advantageous to retain one of the major international firms of accountants to provide the necessary support.

If a small private placement for a special situation is being considered for, let us say, \$200,000 or \$300,000, then direct contact with potential investors is all that should be required. And indeed, varying the factors, any combination of the groupings above can be imagined.

Before turning to the costs involved in such transactions, it is important to note that there are no requirements really equivalent to the disclosure requirements of the 10-K or 10-Q regulations in the United States, nor are there rules similar to those pertaining to the means and personality of the investors, especially when risky issues are concerned. However, unless a recognized intermediary handles the proposal, only very few documents can be shown to potential investors and, as a rule, only to professional investors such as institutions or managers of funds. In the case of a private placement, whether proposed by a licensed intermediary or not, a relatively simple document can be drawn up, incorporating the business plan, financials, and any other relevant information concerning the requirements of the company.

If a public issue is being envisaged in the United Kingdom, the statutory requirements are very simple—the essential difference between a public and private placement being the number of documents that are circulated—and is of course considerably simpler than the U.S. counterpart. Indeed, further reporting requirements are also straightforward and the costs involved are commensurately low.

It is often assumed that the costs of an issue on the Unlisted Securities Market will vary between £150,000 and £300,000, but this will depend on a variety of factors. Take, for instance, the publication of a prospectus in the financial press, that may, on its own, account for some £100,000. The expenses will also be very dependent on whether the securities are sold as an offer for sale or more simply as a placement. (As a comparison, a full listing may engender expenses twice as high as those for the USM, but as the amount of money to be raised is usually much more substantial, the percentage cost may well not be markedly different).

The expenses that will, in all likelihood, have to be taken into account, can include the "sponsor's fee," that is, the merchant bank's or the stockbroker's fee. In the latter's case, this is different from the fee to cover the expenses of placing the issue. These expenses tend to be considerably lower than those prevalent in the United States, perhaps because until now operating costs have been lower in Europe and also because the institutional investors are closely monitoring the cost of investment. Nevertheless, there has been a trend toward increasing expenses as regulations have been introduced that place a greater load on the sponsor. It is clear that a public issue as an offer for sale will involve more work and therefore higher fees than a private placing.

The fees that will vary most, of course, are those to the professional advisers, such as the reporting accountants who may, in some cases, be required to produce a "long form" report for the sponsors, and what is sometimes described as a businessman's review of the offering document. The tax advisers' and legal fees are likely to be much lower than in a comparable U.S. issue—again because the requirements governing the issue are much less complex—but they are still not an insignificant amount. In this context, it is essential to appoint legal advisers who are especially active in city business and who have a strong U.S. connection; this means that a leading city firm will probably be chosen and its remuneration will reflect its position. Finally, a number of other costs have to be met, such as printing, stock exchange, registrar, and receiving banker's fees.

The problem that has to be faced in attempting to discuss this subject, apart from the fact that it encompasses such a wide field, is that it is difficult to establish rules that will apply generally, as every transaction is likely to have its own characteristics. There is, however, one aspect that is common to all markets, not only in Britain but in Europe as a whole, and that is the time taken to raise funds. It is generally the impression that, in the United States, a powerful investment banker will be able to syndicate a transaction on the telephone. Of course, this is not the normal experience when raising venture capital, but generally speaking, the reaction time in Europe tends to be slower.

As the corporation being considered and aiming to attract foreign investors is unlikely to be familiar to the market, a more substantial education will have to be achieved. This may, of course, entail visits by the proposed sponsor if a U.K. placement or issue is being considered. The same is true of other markets if an introduction to an exchange is in question, although for the reasons discussed, this will not be the most likely approach. The choice of the sponsor can be made in such a wide variety of ways—personal connections, recommendation from banks, or professional advisers—that it is very difficult to give any set method of approach. In markets such as London, there are a great number of intermediaries ranging from the representatives of the largest organizations to individuals specializing in arranging contacts. It is the luck of the draw which will determine the smaller corporation's course in this respect. When, however, the final choice is made, it is particularly important for such companies that the sponsorship of their issue—and, of course, included in this is professional advisers—be of a proper caliber. In making such a determination, it is also crucial to understand that the largest firm is by no means necessarily the most appropriate; smaller corporate issues can find rather more dedicated support from organizations that themselves are neither too large nor too small, and whose clientele is perhaps more attuned to such investments. Recently, for instance, regional brokers have introduced smaller U.S. issues to the USM.

However, it is a mistake to assume that once the appointments are made, matters will proceed very rapidly. In some cases, a number of potential investors will be contacted, and then information meetings held to introduce the proposals and to familiarize their management with the issuer. But generally, a one-on-one approach is preferable—if only because one negative reaction can sometimes swing a number of potentially interested investors away from a transaction. The consequence of this is that much more time is required on the part of management to present their issue and the corporate plans. And this is, of course, multiplied if several countries are being covered. There are indeed organizations that will arrange appointments, visits, presentations, and so on to help corporations inform the investment community of their plans, covering all of the important centers, but this is appropriate only for larger projects, as costs mount rapidly. It is difficult to predict the time taken, but let us say that, as a rule, funds will not successfully be raised in less than 90 days, once the selection and appointment of advisers has been made, and it may, of course, take considerably longer.

This raises the question of the most appropriate date on which to make an offer for sale and since, in principle, we are not concerned with issues over £3 million in the United Kingdom or issues that would fall under similar rules in other countries such as Switzerland, and that would require Central Bank approval and an "impact" date in the queue established to regulate access to the markets, the important factor is more that of the financial year of the issuer. There is a growing feeling that once a corporation has published its financials—and in Europe this occurs with much longer delays than in the United States—it is difficult for prospective investors to ascertain the position without obtaining details of up-to-date trading and makes the forecasts rather more difficult to evaluate. This has prompted sponsors to make offers one or two months before the end of the year, knowing that the audited accounts that will follow are very likely to confirm management forecasts—so that, for a corporation whose year ends in December, the time to come to market may be in November. This concept is not necessarily shared by all and is more important for securities to be listed than for private placements or for over-the-counter dealings.

The last aspect to be considered in the context of foreign participations in smaller U.S. growth corporations is the ability to raise more funds from the same or similar sources and the liquidity of the markets.

In many cases, an initial funding exercise has to be followed by further calls for support, either because growth has overtaken expectations or because hopes have not become reality. In the case of a private placement, where by definition only a small number of investors are involved, it will be relatively simple to make contact through the broker or intermediary who had sponsored the issue and to negotiate the necessary assistance. But, as in other cases, it should not be felt that this will be any easier, any less expensive, or any more welcome in Europe than it would be in the United States. The only difference may stem from the unwillingness of European investors to take a managerial role in a difficult situation in the United States, which may make their support more complex and difficult to obtain.

In the case of an offer for sale and a listed security, only the circumstances can determine possibilities. The ideal outlook is to see a USM company proceed to a full listing and raise more funds in that way as a result of successful growth and profitability. And it does take time.

The liquidity aspect is much more complex, but if a grading is to be given, excluding obviously private placements of unquoted paper, the USM gives some liquidity but, generally speaking, any disposal of blocks of shares will, in most cases, not be absorbed by the market without severe price adjustments. Consequently, disposals have to be arranged by the broker whose role in this area is of the greatest importance. Of course, this also goes for the acquisition of shares. It reflects on the ability to use the price of a share as a benchmark for merger or other similar transactions and is therefore not dissimilar to an OTC pricing in the United States. It may be rather extreme to say that the USM is very liquid when comparing it to the over-the-counter market in the United Kingdom; the OTC market does provide funding for companies and there are, of course, transactions in the securities introduced to that market, and a number of houses deal and maintain positions. Nevertheless, the overall liquidity provided by this market is limited and price volatility reflects this situation.

As can therefore be seen from this short description, there are a number of different sources of funds available in Europe, some more sophisticated but providing larger amounts for the bigger transactions as well as effective liquidity, some smaller and giving no access to liquidity, some found through markets such as the London market, some in all European countries, and indeed benefiting from sources even outside of Europe. In all cases, the regulatory requirements are much simpler than in the United States, the role of the lawyers therefore more limited and less costly, and even in the case of quotation on European markets, the disclosure and submissions are considerably less complex and extensive. Therefore, both in terms of expense and implementation, a European source of funds will compare favorably with one in the United States.

This may, however, not be the case in terms of time taken to raise funds, which, as mentioned, will be longer in most cases. If the original assumption of the viability of the project in the United States is taken into account, then the decision to tap European sources will be based essentially on the cost advantage and on the relative ease of implementation.

CONCLUSION

To conclude this short review, the first point that has to be stressed is that a smaller U.S. growth company must have good U.S. sponsorship and be able to demonstrate the ability to attract investors to its proposal. Undoubtedly, the first question that will always be asked is, Why should an American corporation come to Europe? The presumption too often will be that the funds cannot be raised in the United States and so there must be a "catch." Moreover, even if the costs of raising finance are lower in Europe, generally funding will not be much less expensive on a current basis, so that some convincing explanation must be given, such as developments in Europe, relationships with European firms, imports from Europe, or particular characteristics of the transaction.

It has been assumed that the European markets as a whole will be better approached by smaller U.S. companies through the London market, as most important factors and participants will be represented in London, and that all professional services can also be retained there.

This concept may be unduly chauvinistic, and arguments can be validly made that certain transactions are better handled directly in other markets, but this will depend so much on each and every individual proposal that it is difficult to make any general statement and, also, it is likely that in such cases professionals in London will be able to give the proper advice and contacts to approach a suitable market.

In all cases, but particularly in the United Kingdom, the choice of a sponsor or introducer is of the greatest importance: There are a wide variety of institutions and individuals specializing in raising finance or counseling borrowers, and obviously not all can perform the same duties. The more senior the broker or merchant bank, the larger the transaction has to be in order to be commercially viable. Smaller private placements can often be successfully undertaken by smaller firms that may not even be principally established in the main centers.

The time taken to implement an issue on a market such as the USM or similar markets in Europe will tend to be longer than in the United States, and for the moment, the high-yield bond that is so prevalent in United States financing is not yet available. There is, however, good reason to believe that this is one of the developments that will take place in the future as investors become more attuned to the needs of growth companies internationally. Most of the major investment banks are established in Europe and have been originating new formulas to finance companies worldwide. Even if the greatest efforts have been made for large transactions, initiatives by houses such as Drexel Burnham Lambert will favor such methods to give the advantages of equity to investors whilst providing a carrying yield.

Finally, even though there are substantial funds that can be tapped outside of the United States, both private and institutional, the success of such an approach must, to a large extent, be a function of the patronage that the U.S. company can obtain locally. The growth of venture capital and the development of direct representation of institutions and banks in the United States will make it even more important to show that the approach is reasonably made and is not the result of difficulties encountered in funding transactions in the United States. Therefore, when considering attracting foreign investors, the first place to start is at home.

CHAPTER 24

Futures, Options, and Swaps

Gail Gordon
Vice President
Wertheim & Co., Inc.
New York, N.Y.

Gail Gordon is a vice president in the financial instruments department of Wertheim & Co., Inc. She is primarily engaged in creating and implementing hedge strategies for institutional clients. Ms. Gordon devotes a great deal of her time to writing and speaking on aspects of institutional use of financial futures. In 1985, Dow Jones-Irwin published her *Financial Futures and Investment Strategy,* coauthored with Arthur L. Rebell. Ms. Gordon oversees the futures and options on futures trading at Wertheim on a daily basis.

Arthur L. Rebell
General Partner
Wertheim & Co.
New York, N.Y.

Arthur L. Rebell is a general partner of Wertheim & Co. After practicing law with Cahill, Gordon and Reindel, he joined Wertheim's research department in 1968, where he specialized in problems relating to energy. He became coordinator of the energy division of the corporate finance department and later returned to the research department as its director. In 1979, Mr. Rebell established Wertheim's financial instruments department. The department works with institutions, regulators, attorneys, and accountants to foster an understanding of applications for financial futures and options as tools for prudent institutional money management. Mr. Rebell coauthored the Dow Jones-Irwin publication *Financial Futures and Investment Strategy* with Gail Gordon.

INTRODUCTION

The increased price volatility of the financial markets and the historically high level of interest rates over the past decade have revealed the sensitivity of corporate balance sheets to interest rate exposure. Additionally, in periods of high volatility, certain borrowers may not have access to the capital markets. Interest rate volatility, provoked by factors beyond the control of financial managers, only underlines the fact that money is a commodity whose price and availability fluctuate in a similar fashion to oil, wheat, or soybeans. The users of this commodity in the form of short-term credit lines or funded debt should manage their risk exposure just as an oil producer or grain processor does.

In response to this heightened volatility, a number of new risk management tools have been developed. Exchange-traded futures contracts based on financial instruments and interest rate options allow the risks of interest rate fluctuations to be transferred from a hedger to a speculator who chooses to assume it. The more recently developed market in interest rate swaps provides a mechanism, through the banking and brokerage community, to alter the nature of debt financing by allowing fixed and floating rate borrowers to trade off their obligations. Essentially, all of these instruments allow the corporate financial manager to separate the timing of an interest rate decision from its implementation.

The utilization of these tools, which complement traditional financing techniques, presents new challenges to the corporate manager. The goal of this chapter is to describe these innovations and outline some financing problems where futures, swaps, or options can be used effectively to solve corporate financing problems. Risk management is an art as well as a science, and understanding these techniques often points up some of the inherent risks in traditional financing decisions.

The following two situations present basic problems faced by corporations where these risk transfer techniques might be used. They point out that the choice to do nothing, inertia speculation, can have a significant impact on a corporation's financial standing. These two examples will be followed by a basic description of futures, options, and swaps, and by an analysis of how these techniques might be implemented in these particular situations.

Variable Debt Example. A rapidly growing designer, manufacturer, and distributor of computer software has recently completed an acquisition of a company that will enable it to enlarge its market territory and product diversification. The software company completed the acquisition, using bank borrowing at 2 percent over the 90-day Libor (London Inter-Bank Offering Rate) rate. The $7 million loan is quite substantial to the company and represents the best terms that could be secured today. The company's cash flow projections for the next few years indicate that, particularly during the first two years, cash will be tight. The company's management doesn't want to be totally subject to the vicissitudes of short-term rates, which it now feels are near a cyclical low point. Yet, due to its highly leveraged balance sheet, it cannot secure a five-year loan. Even if the longer term funding was available, the company couldn't afford the relatively higher five-year rate. This implies that some level of rate speculation was inherent in the acquisition. The risk of a spike-up in short-term rates today is seen as more serious than the risk of higher rates three years from today, at which point the company's financial condition will be stronger and it may be able to refinance its acquisition with longer term debt. The use of risk transfer vehicles will permit the software company to enlarge the scope of its choices and to create a more tailored risk program.

Term Financing Example. A design and manufacturing company that sells relatively standard items of women's apparel to major chain stores has grown rapidly during the past few years, but still has restricted access to public financial markets. Consequently, this company has substantial short-term variable rate debt. However, the company feels that it must have more funded debt on its balance sheet. Given its recent growth, the company could finalize a 10-year private placement with an insurance company. Management feels that interest rates are cyclically high and would prefer to wait until rates come down, recognizing the corresponding risk of a rate increase. If that should happen, then management would find itself faced with a dual problem. Not only will rates be higher on its future funded debt as well as seasonal borrowings, but the possibility exists that the higher rates will be accompanied by pressure on credit availability in general. In that case, a company that is a more marginal borrower might find the private placement market closed to it, or at best, a wider spread between its rate and rates available to prime credits.

Consequently, the company is faced with two unattractive choices. It can doubly speculate on rates and the corporation's ability to fund debt, or it can accept the 10-year private placement now at today's rates. The use of futures, options, and swaps will permit the company to design a program to benefit from a rate decline without the balance sheet risk associated with being completely out of the long-term financing market. These tools will allow the company to accept a 10-year fixed rate with the possibility of having variable rates for some shorter portion thereof. In other words it can tailor a program that permits it to reduce its risk from the ultimate one of not taking any funded debt, to one that is more tailored to its needs, expectations, and financial capabilities.

Each company needs to decide how to handle its market exposure, given available alternatives. Whether to follow a strategy employing these instruments, or to simply do nothing, will affect the degree to which the company is speculating on rates. A simple test of whether an activity is speculative is to analyze the extent to which it increases or reduces existing risk. In the case of the apparel manufacturer, the company faces an existing risk in its requirement to fund out its longer term growth at the present time. A strategy that permits it to approach that goal, by definition, reduces the inherent risk and would be deemed to be hedging. To the extent that the company does not fund out at the cost available today but chooses to keep some of the risk, that would be deemed speculative. In the same way, the software design company has a variable rate loan on which it can lock in a rate for a period of time coexistent with its maximum risk, and partially hedge its exposure. In both cases, *the analysis of the existing risk and the degree to which the risk is acceptable and perhaps desirable in the scope of the company's activities will be the key to the company's strategy.*

Set forth below is a description of the classes of tools available for designing such strategies. This general discussion is followed by an explanation of the use of these finance tools in the two situations outlined.

FUTURES AND OPTIONS

A futures contract is an obligation to make or take delivery, at a price established today, of a set amount of an underlying commodity, whether that commodity is a Treasury bond, a silver bar, or a bushel of corn. Contract positions must be closed out by either an offsetting transaction or by delivery, although only a very small percentage of contracts are actually closed out by delivery. Delivery is at a point or over a span of time established by the exchange that sponsors the contract. Because a contract position, if not offset, can result in a long (purchase) or short (sale) position in an actual commodity, the contract price reflects any price changes in the spot market.[1] Generally, by being long or short, a futures contract trader stands to gain or lose to the extent that the market price of the underlying commodity changes from the price level at which the contract position was established.

The most recent innovation in the futures area is the futures option.[2] These options represent the right to buy or sell a futures contract at a specified price within a designated time. The price of this right is the option premium. Unlike a futures position whose price moves in line with the market price change of the underlying interest rate instrument, the change in option value is determined by the market's volatility and option terms. The option buyer's risk is limited to the premium amount paid. The option seller, who receives the premium, risks an adverse market move and can only benefit to the extent of the premium received. Delivery is satisfied by the assignment of a futures contract position, rather than by the underlying cash instrument. These instruments can provide hedgers with a complementary tool for protecting rate exposure at an identifiable cost.

---

[1] The market for the actual commodity on which a futures contract is based is called the commodity's "spot" or "cash" market. This is a source of some confusion when applied to financial instruments, where the term *cash* also denotes short-term investments. For the purpose of this chapter, the phrase *cash market* applies to the market for the commodity on which the future contract is written.

[2] Options based on fixed income securities are also available, however this chapter will focus on options written on futures.

Interest Rate Futures

Six contracts have come to constitute the interest rate–related segment of the futures market. These contracts are based on long-term Treasury bonds (CBT); 10-year Treasury notes (CBT); GNMA–CDRs (CBT); 90-day Treasury bills (IMM); domestic certificates of deposit (IMM); and Eurodollar time deposits (IMM).[3] Options on futures are available for the Treasury note, Treasury bond, and Eurodollar contracts. The contracts that provide the best liquidity are the Treasury bond contract, reflecting long-term interest rates, and the Eurodollar contract, which is priced in line with short-term rates (i.e., Libor).

The economic purpose of any futures market is to provide a tool to transfer the price risk of a commodity from hedgers to speculators. The ease of trading and a high degree of leverage lends speculative appeal to these markets. Because of the method of trading and the ability of speculators to easily enter financial markets, volume in a contract will often be greater than the volume of trading among investors in the underlying instrument. Commodity prices can often fluctuate widely due to the effect of unpredictable events on supply and demand conditions. This potential variability creates a real planning problem for businesses that use commodities in production, forcing them to rely on instruments such as futures to protect their costs and manage their expected returns. Since a futures transaction is comparable to a purchase or sale of a commodity for delivery at some later date, futures provide the ability to protect against changing market values without owning the underlying commodity.

As an example, Eastman Kodak wants to maintain its prices for silver-based photographic products for the next six months, but is concerned that silver prices could rise, increasing the firm's production cost. To hedge against the potential cost increase, Eastman Kodak can buy silver contracts. If silver prices do, in fact, increase by $1 per ounce, the futures contract will appreciate by a like amount. Kodak can sell (offset) its contract position and use the gain to counter the higher cost of silver. Likewise, should prices decline, the loss the firm would incur in selling its commodity contract would be recovered by a lower cost of physical acquisition. Regardless of the change in silver prices, the company's cost for silver will approximate the cost of silver at the time the futures contract position was initiated. Kodak could take delivery of silver against its contract, but that would be unnecessary. Hedgers, dealing in futures to offset price volatility they already face, can control their costs by buying and selling futures, and there

[3] The designations CBT and IMM refer to the Chicago Board of Trade and the International Monetary Market, respectively.

is a minimum need for using the contract to take delivery. The delivery provision is there to ensure that the price of the contract will follow that of the physical commodity.

Trading futures and options on futures for this purpose offers several benfits.

Homogeneity and Liquidity. The standardization of contracts creates interchangeable instruments. This brings about a level of participation that gives the markets their liquidity. Trading can be undertaken with ease and with little impact on the market as a whole.

Low Cost. Futures are a low-cost alternative. Trading in this market is often less complicated because there is no physical transfer of assets.

Investor Anonymity. The position of an investor trading in the futures market is not obvious to other traders, nor need his purposes be known. Thus, trading in this market can be done with a degree of anonymity not possible in the cash market.

The obvious link between the price of a financial futures contract and the level of interest rates is that a financial asset, such as a Treasury bond or Treasury bill, is deliverable to satisfy the terms of financial futures contracts. A financial futures price will move in line with its underlying instrument, creating an important tool for the money manager. However, in concept and design, financial futures are closer to commodity futures than to their respective cash instruments. For the money manager used to dealing with actual bonds or bank lines of credit, some adjustment to the characteristics and procedures of the contract market is necessary.

All financial futures contracts have certain features in common, among them the contract cycle. These futures trade on a March quarterly cycle, which means that contracts are written to expire in March, June, September, and December. Most financial futures have at least four traded contracts outstanding, covering a period of one year. Some have as many as 11 contract months trading, representing commitments deferred for as long as three years. The liquidity of the various markets and the ability to create arbitrage positions influence the number of contract months traded.[4] At some point during each contract month, trading in the contract that is about to expire stops, and a price is determined for settlement of the contract. For those

---

[4] Due to this arbitrage process and the concentration of speculative interest in the more current contracts, those with more time to expiration do not trade as actively as the front-month contracts. However, hedgers who intend to maintain a contract position over time can use the deferred-month contracts as part of their strategy.

traders holding open positions, delivery of a cash instrument, or cash settlement in the case of Eurodollars, takes place.[5]

The expiration price of a futures contract is determined by the cash market value of a deliverable security, either through delivery or exchange assignment (i.e., cash settlement). Prior to expiration, the daily *settlement price* ("settle") is determined by the closing price range of the actual trades as they occur in the pit. The exchange assigns a single price from this range on the front contract for a given future. Most exchanges then establish the settlement price for back-month contracts, based on the closing price of the front contract and prevailing price spread between the first or second contract and the more distant contract months. These price levels are used to calculate the daily cash adjustments.

Trading and Margin

The futures market is characterized by a daily cash settlement procedure that is integral to maintaining the trading system. Each transaction calls for a good faith deposit, known as initial margin, to be posted with a broker. The minimum amount of initial margin required is set by the exchange, based on the price volatility of the underlying commodity, but represents a small percentage of the underlying commodity cash value. The value of a contract position is marked to market daily and these changes are settled in cash on a daily basis. For example, if contract prices increase, the longs (contract purchaser) would receive cash equal to the value of gains, while the shorts (contract sellers) would have to pay funds equal to the value of losses. This procedure, known as variation margin, keeps the value of each market participant's position current and contributes to the credit of the futures market. Initial margin ensures that participants will pay variation margin deficits.

As an example, suppose an investor has sold a Treasury bond contract at a price of 70 and the next day the market value increased to 71. The investor would receive a margin call from his broker requiring him to deposit $1,000 in his margin account. Posting variation margin ensures that adverse market moves will be covered by the seller in this case. Exhibit 1 illustrates how the system works.

The procedure also sharply limits credit risk, because any differential between the market value and the transaction price has been paid.

The system expedites accounting for an exchange. The change

---

[5] Some contracts, such as those for Treasury bonds, can be delivered into throughout the delivery month.

EXHIBIT 1 Trading and Margin System

	Participants		
	A	*B*	*C*
	Buys contract at 70	Sells contract at 70	
Market moves up to 71, value of move is $1,000	Receives $1,000	Pays $1,000, Buys contract at 71	Sells contract at 71
Market moves up to 72, value of move is $1,000	Receives $1,000		Pays $1,000

in the market from day to day determines how much cash must change hands between shorts and longs. The exchange simply calculates the net short or net long position established, and credits or debits accordingly. Brokers, in turn, effect the transfer of funds among their individual accounts.

If an investor cannot meet a margin call, the broker can liquidate that investor's contract position and apply the initial margin to any losses incurred.

The term *margin* is really a misnomer as applied to the futures market. For stocks and bonds, margin is a loan representing part of the value required to buy an instrument. Because it is a loan, it involves interest and other costs. In futures, initial margin is no more than a deposit of collateral, the purpose of which is to ensure that price changes in an underlying contract can be met. Variation margin is a daily accounting and settlement of gains and losses. In neither case is there any borrowing: There is no "buying on margin," and for a hedger, for whom the value of the cash position is matched by the value of the instruments underlying the futures contract position, there is no leverage.

The two contracts that are most often used for managing interest rate exposure are based on the Eurodollar time deposits and long-term Treasury bonds. These contracts are briefly described in order to follow through with the hedge strategy examples.

Eurodollar Contract

The Eurodollar futures contract is based on a $1 million par value 90-day Eurodollar time deposit. These securities represent dollar deposits held in offshore banks. The offered side of the Eurodollar time deposit market is quoted as the London Inter-Bank Offering Rate (Libor), which has become an accepted base rate for commercial loans. Unlike the prime rate, a domestic bank's base loan rate that is changed periodically at the direction of the bank, Libor is a market-oriented rate changing daily in line with the supply and demand for funds. The Eurodollar contract was designed to be a perfect hedge vehicle for floating rate debt pegged to the Libor rate.

Introduced by the IMM (the International Monetary Market) in 1981, this contract was the first to use the cash settlement provision. Physical delivery of a Eurodollar time deposit would have been a costly and cumbersome process. However, cash settlement enforces the same pricing discipline onto the contract. The expiration price is settled on the last trading day by determining the cash market rate for a 90-day Euro time deposit from a five-dealer survey, and creating an average rate to be used as the settlement value. Prior to this, the contract's daily settlement price was determined by the last trade.

This contract gained liquidity gradually, and it now forms the basis for most trading done in short-term instruments. By early 1985, the number of Eurodollar contracts traded per day eclipsed the Treasury bill and certificate of deposit (CD) contracts. Volume in this market averages 30,000 contracts per day, equivalent to $30 billion in the underlying asset. Eurodollar contracts are listed quarterly covering a two-year period of time. Though liquidity is greatest in the front contracts, deferred-month contracts that are useful to hedgers can be positioned. The contract's final settlement date is the second London business day before the third Wednesday of each delivery month.

The contract's price is quoted using an index. A quote of 91.50 indicates that the 90-day Eurodollar rate for the period covered by the contract is trading at an 8.5 percent rate.

$$100 - \text{Index level} = \text{Eurodollar rate}$$
$$100 - 91.50 = 8.50$$

A rise in the index indicates a decline in rate. This inverse relationship causes the index to move like the dollar price of a bond or Eurodollar time deposit. An increase in the index results in gains for the long position and losses for the short, whereas a decrease in the index results in gains for the short and losses for the long. The minimum price change for the contract is 1 basis point, referred to as an "01." The value of an 01 is equal to $25.

$$1{,}000{,}000 \times .0001 \times 90/360 = \$25$$

If the Eurodollar contract price changed by 10 basis points, from 91.50 to 91.60, the long's profit would equal $250 per contract.

Consider someone who borrows $1 million for 90 days. In the event that rates were to rise by 10 basis points, that person would incur an additional cost of $250 over the 90-day period because of the rise in rates. If he went short one contract, the nature of the margin mechanism would mean that if the Eurodollar contract price fell in line with the cash or underlying market, the futures market would return to the investor $250, thereby offsetting the higher cost incurred on his loan.

The difference between the rate in the cash market and the rate at which the future contract sells is a function of the time until delivery. Although this can be a complicated subject, for the purpose of this chapter suffice it to say that when one chooses to enter into a long or short contract in the Eurodollar futures market, the price that one is securing is the price prevailing in the futures market at the time of entry, and not the cash market price.

Suppose the current Eurodollar rate for a September 1985 contract was 9 percent, and at the present time the Eurodollar rate was 8.75 percent. By going short one futures contract, one would be securing the rate of 9 percent for the period from September forward three months through December on $1 million.[6] If the Eurodollar rate (i.e., Libor) is greater than 9 percent, the gain on the futures position would offset the higher interest cost. Of course, if market rates improve, the lower interest to be paid would offset the loss on the futures position.[7] In either case, the net interest is known within a few basis points when the hedge is initiated. The Eurodollar contract, because of its liquidity, is often used to hedge short-term debt pegged to rates other than Libor, such as the prime rate. This type of hedge presents the possibility of basis risk, meaning that the prime rate, which is an administered rate, may change differently than Libor. The decision to hedge in this case would call for an analysis of the spread relationship between prime and Eurodollar rates.

Treasury Bond Contract

The Treasury bond contract, traded on the Chicago Board of Trade (CBT), is the focus of speculative, hedge, and arbitrage activity related to the volatility of long-term interest rates. Introduced in 1976, the bond contract quickly gained liquidity and is currently the most actively traded futures contract. This contract trades in excess of 200,000

---

[6] If one closes out a hedge prior to the expiration of a contract, the rate realized would be adjusted by a differential in the cash futures spread. While beyond the scope of this chapter, the yield curve effect on Eurodollar prices can be calculated and this analysis can be used to derive an estimated hedge rate.

[7] One is also affected by the cost or earnings on the variation margin balance. In most applications of this chapter this is not significant, and this consideration is not dealt with extensively.

per day, equal to $20 billion of the underlying securities. The extensive arbitrage activity and known trading characteristics of the contract allow for a fairly predictable relationship to the price of the underlying security.

The contract is written on a Treasury bond with $100,000 principal value, a nominal 8 percent coupon, and 15 years or more to first call date. It is an agreement to make or take delivery of a Treasury bond with the appropriate maturity at a specified price within a specified period of time. Whereas many bonds qualify as deliverable, only a limited number are likely to be delivered. Under almost all conditions, bonds with longer maturities—25 to 30 years—are delivered. Contracts terminate on a March quarterly cycle (March, June, September, December), with 11 of them outstanding at any given time. The bond contract trades in 32nds of a point. One point is valued at $1,000, with $\frac{1}{32}$ worth $31.25.[8]

The hallmark of the Treasury bond future is its delivery process. The short has the choice of which bond to deliver. The bond that is the most advantageous to deliver, based on relative market prices, is referred to as the "cheapest to deliver." Futures prices will move up and down in line with the price change of that cash bond. However, the contract is based on an 8 percent coupon, and a factor adjustment is needed to equate the prices of the contract with all the potentially deliverable bonds. This factor is a function of the contract date, the bond coupon, and first call, or, in the case of noncallable bonds, maturity date. What is important to hedgers looking to protect their cost on long-term debt issuance is that the price activity of the futures contract is predictable relative to the price activity of the Treasury market. The hedger can then assess the potential debt cost under various market conditions and interest rate levels (i.e., Treasury yields) and work to model a protective strategy using futures.

As an example of this factor adjustment, assume that the Treasury 10⅜ percent due 11–15–2012/07 was the cheapest-to-deliver bond against the December 1985 bond futures contract. The factor for this bond, which equates its price to a bond with an 8 percent coupon and the same first call date as that to be delivered, is 1.2427. Since this 10⅜ percent bond is expected to be most deliverable, the price action of the contract will respond to the price change of this bond, such that a 1 point change in the bond price would result in a .8047

---

[8] A 10-year Treasury note contract is also traded on the Chicago Board of Trade. This contract is modeled after the bond future, and the same type of analysis will apply to hedge strategies implemented using this contract. The note future doesn't trade as much volume as the bond but may be a better match for the hedger protecting the cost of intermediate-term debt.

point change in the future. (This fraction is: 1 divided by 1.2427). This relationship occurs since if one were to deliver in December when the bond contract was priced at 75, the amount received for the 10⅜ percent would equal 75 × 1.2427, or 93.2025.

Prior to the delivery period the price of the futures contract will not necessarily equal the value of the bond expected to be delivered. The differential between the price of the bond (adjusted to its futures equivalent value) and the price of the contract is determined primarily by the spread between long-term bond rates and short-term financing rates.[9]

A fully hedged position is comparable to an agreement to sell bonds at some future date but at today's price. The owner of the bond collects the bond coupon over this period of time, but having effectively sold the principal position, there is no risk due to changes in market level. The convergence of the cash futures spread adjusts the yield on a hedged portfolio to reflect the bond's remaining price volatility of the portfolio, which is in line with an instrument of much shorter maturity.

For example, the owner of a 14 percent bond could sell that bond today for 100, at a time when the return on a one-year investment is 10 percent. He would therefore earn 4 percent less on the principal position by selling the bond and investing the proceeds for one year. Alternatively, the bond could be sold for delivery in one year and the original bond owner would receive the coupon income over that period of time. The buyer will earn the one-year rate on the funds set aside for this purchase, but will face all the price risk associated with the longer maturity instrument. Therefore, the forward purchaser would not be willing to pay the current price of 100 for the bond, but would require a discount to make up for the difference between the income on the 14 percent coupon and the 10 percent one-year investment. In this case the forward buyer would be willing to make the trade if the bond price was below 96. As long as the original bond owner could get a price of 96 or better for the forward sale, his realized return would exceed the 10 percent available on one-year investments, and he would willingly sell forward. A futures contract is comparable to this type of forward agreement to buy or sell at a later date at a price established today. Arbitrage activity will force the future price to reflect the difference between short- and long-term yields.

---

[9] The futures equivalent value is the price of the cheapest-to-deliver cash bond divided by the appropriate delivery factor.

Options on Futures

Options on futures combine the limited risk inherent in listed options with the homogeneity and infinite supply of futures.[10] An option contract represents the right to benefit from a market change, rather than an obligation or forward commitment as with a future contract. For an option buyer, options on futures represent a risk/reward vehicle similar to an insurance policy. An option is exercised at the discretion of the buyer. If the market moves against the option position, the buyer will allow the option to expire worthless. Exchange-traded options are available on Treasury bond, Treasury note, and Eurodollar contracts.[11] Options on futures only cover a nine-month time period: Therefore, options are written on the first three outstanding futures contracts. Trading liquidity is heavily skewed to the lead contract month.

Options are classified as puts and calls. The purchaser of a put option has the right to sell the underlying futures contract at a specified price over the life of the option and will benefit if rates increase. The purchaser of a call option has the right to buy the underlying futures contract also at a specified price during the life of the option and will benefit if rates decrease. The specific price at which the future will be bought or sold is the *strike price.* The amount paid for the option is called the *premium.* The amount of money that could be made by exercising that option at current market levels represents the *intrinsic value* of the option. Option pricing is a function of the intrinsic value of the contract and the *time value* (premium minus intrinsic value). Time value reflects the perceived volatility of the underlying market and the time remaining until the option's expiration date. Because an option involves time value, which by definition will be zero at expiration, it is known as a *wasting asset.* An option that has intrinsic value is termed *in the money,* an option with a price that is solely time value is known as *out of the money,* and an option whose strike is equal to the market price of the contract is considered *at the money.* Futures, by contrast, are not a wasting asset, since they represent a forward delivery mechanism that can be continued at a cost related to the yield curve differential.

Suppose a December 74 call on a bond contract was purchased

---

[10] Options written directly on specific fixed income securities are also available. These are traded on the over-the-counter market with less liquidity but perhaps more flexibility than options on futures.

[11] The requirements of each option contract are not explained herein. However these specifications should be understood before using these instruments within a hedge strategy.

at $2\frac{30}{64}$ when the December contract was valued at $75\frac{16}{32}$.[12] This option has an intrinsic value of $1\frac{32}{64}$.

$$\text{Contract value} - \text{Strike price} = \text{Intrinsic value}$$

$$75\frac{16}{32} - 74 = 1\frac{32}{64}$$

The intrinsic value is less than the premium paid and the difference is referred to as the time value.

$$\text{Premium} - \text{Intrinsic value} = \text{Time value}$$

$$2\frac{30}{64} - 1\frac{32}{64} = \frac{62}{64}$$

If the price of the underlying bond future remained constant at $75\frac{16}{32}$, the time value would diminish, reaching zero at expiration of the option, leaving only the intrinsic value of the option upon exercise. The buyer of this option at $2\frac{30}{64}$ needs bond prices to increase in order to profit from this position. Specifically, if the market went above $76\frac{15}{32}$, this option would show a profit for the buyer and the $\frac{62}{64}$ previously representing time value would have become intrinsic value. A hedger, taking on long-term debt while expecting market rates to decline, may use calls to benefit from declining rates and offset the higher cost debt.

The Eurodollar futures option follows the pricing of that contract. The strike price is set to the index price of the Eurodollar future. The option premium is quoted in basis points, with each 01 valued at $25. The hedger of a Libor-based credit line might use Eurodollar puts as a way of capping their interest rate exposure at a defined cost. For example, while the current base 90-day Eurodollar rate is 8 percent, a borrower wishes to protect against rates going above 9 percent. This would be equivalent to a price of 91.00 on the Eurodollar contract. An out-of-the-money put on the Eurodollar contract at 91.00 is comparable to a short position and will have intrinsic value if rates rise above 9 percent. The price of this option to expire in approximately three and a half months may be .28, or $700 per million to be hedged. If the rate rises above 9.28 (a Eurodollar contract price of 90.72), the hedger's put value will offset the higher cost. Had the hedger chosen to sell futures, the .28 basis point premium cost would not have been incurred. However, if rates had declined from the level at which the

---

[12] Options on bond futures trade in 64ths of a point (valued at $15.63), compared with 32nds of a point for the underlying contract. The dollar cost of this option is $2,468.75.

hedge was put on the mark-to-market on the future contract would have offset the lower interest cost of the loan.[13]

In deciding on the purchase of an option, the length of time left until expiration and the strike price of the option are important considerations. Premium costs are typically higher on options, with more time remaining until expiration. With time, there is greater opportunity for the market to move in the right direction—for the option to become profitable. In addition, those options with strike prices in the money will command higher dollar premiums than those trading out of the money.[14]

INTEREST RATE SWAPS

Interest rate swaps have been gaining acceptance as an effective tool for managing interest rate exposure. The market has grown geometrically, and currently the size of the swap market is estimated to be in excess of $80 billion. By matching borrowers and lenders with varied credit standing and unique needs, lower cost liabilities and/or assets with higher returns may be created. The swap market is unregulated and swap terms are not fully standardized, allowing parties to the swap to design agreements for their particular needs.[15] Originally available to large corporations and financial intermediaries, the size of the average agreement's principal amount base (i.e., notional amount) has decreased as the swap market has broadened.

An interest rate swap is a contractual agreement, sometimes made directly between two corporate entities but more generally through a financial intermediary, to exchange the interest payments on loans of differing terms. In effect, the swap agreement is a means by which a fixed rate can be exchanged for a floating rate, or the character of floating rate debt may be changed by the parties to the swap without involving the original lenders. The swap agreement itself focuses on the exchange of cash flow to pay the debt service of a principal amount and is not an exchange of the principal commitment.

A bank might have issued variable rate loans based on the six-month Libor rate, but funded them with fixed rate three-year CDs

---

[13] The issue of convergence and the pricing of futures contracts would be important in selecting the appropriate options strike price for a specific time period.

[14] However, if the market remains unchanged over the duration of the option's life, the buyer of the in-the-money option will recapture its intrinsic value upon expiration. The time value or extrinsic value, which may be equated to the cost of an insurance policy, is relatively higher on the out-of-the money position.

[15] There is currently an effort among financial institutions to standardize some of the provisions and documentation for interest rate swaps.

paying interest semiannually, creating a mismatch between its assets and liabilities. The bank's profit spread would be under pressure if rates decline, since the loan proceeds decrease while the CD payout remains constant. If the bank felt that rates would decline, it might look to better match its liability to its asset with a swap that could transform its three-year fixed rate payout to a variable rate consistent with its loan portfolio. The other party to this swap might be a corporation financing an asset for three years at a rate based on 200 basis points above a floating six-month Libor rate. An increase in rates would be to this company's detriment. A direct interest rate swap could solve each party's financing problem.

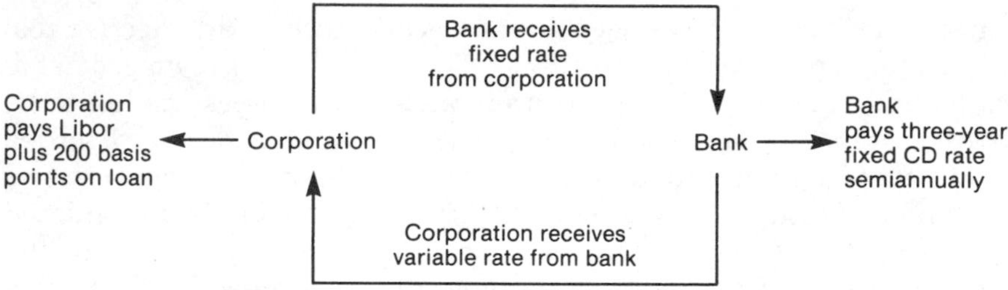

Under the swap agreement the bank receives semiannual payments at a fixed three-year rate, determined at the time of the swap, from the corporation. These payments offset the bank's commitment to pay interest on its three-year CD portfolio. In return, the bank's payment to the corporation is determined semiannually, based on the six-month Libor rate. The corporation applies these proceeds toward interest payments on its bank loan at the same six-month Libor rate plus 200 basis points. The credit spread is paid by the corporation to the bank financing the asset purchase. In this simple example the nature of the parties' obligations are matched off so that the corporation has transformed its floating rate loan to a fixed rate loan and the bank has created a variable rate liability to match its variable rate asset.

For example (see Exhibit 2), assume the current Libor rate is 8.25 percent. The corporate swap counterparty agrees to pay the bank 9.5 percent fixed semiannually for the next three years. This is equal to the rate that the bank has agreed to pay on its three-year CDs.
The bank's fixed rate cost is effectively canceled out, but in return, the bank will pay to the corporation an amount determined by the six-month Libor rate. The bank's liability cost will have become variable, matching its asset basis.

The corporation's goal is to establish a fixed rate loan. Its net

EXHIBIT 2 Interest Rate Swap

	Current Rates			
	Corporation		*Bank*	
	Pay (percent)	*Receive (percent)*	*Pay (percent)*	*Receive (percent)*
Swap—fixed	9.50			9.50
Swap—variable Libor		8.25	8.25	
Original loan cost	10.25			
Original fixed CD			9.50	
	19.75	8.25	17.75	9.50
Net cost:	11.50		8.25	
	Libor Rises 100 Basis Points			
	Corporation		*Bank*	
	Pay (percent)	*Receive (percent)*	*Pay (percent)*	*Receive (percent)*
Swap—fixed	9.50			9.50
Swap—variable Libor		9.25	9.25	
Original loan cost	11.25			
Original fixed CD			9.50	
	20.75	9.25	18.75	9.50
Net cost:	11.50		9.25	

cost of money for this period, after the swap, will be 11.5 percent, the 9.5 percent paid to the bank counterparty plus the 200 basis points paid to the lender bank, regardless of any change in interest rates. For example, if the current period six-month Libor rate is 8.25 percent, the bank counterparty pays interest to the corporation at this rate. The corporation then pays its loan interest at 10.25 percent. If Libor increases by 100 basis points in the next semiannual period, the bank counterparty will pay the corporation interest based on a 9.25 percent Libor rate. The corporation will then pay its 11.25 percent on the loan. Despite the increase in rates, the corporation will pay the bank counterparty based on the 9.50 percent originally agreed.

Swaps can be designed to cover a number of different rates (prime, Libor, or commercial paper) and time periods. Therefore, the swap agreement can be tailored to each parties' needs. This can create a lack of liquidity that can limit a party's flexibility at a later date. For example, if in a year the bank's variable rate loan is paid down, shifting the overall asset and liability balance, then the bank might wish to end its obligation to pay out Libor under the swap agreement. In order to do this, the bank would find a reverse swap that would offset its floating rate exposure.

The swap market is currently unregulated. Therefore, a key issue is the credit standing of each counterparty.

ACCOUNTING AND TAX CONSIDERATIONS

Since futures, options, and swaps are fairly new, accounting and tax treatment is still evolving and should be examined before evaluating any transaction. Treatment of futures and option transactions is currently more defined than is that for swaps.

In general, for accounting purposes, if a futures or options transaction is a valid hedge, any gain or loss on these transactions can be rolled into the cost basis of the item hedged and amortized over its life. Certain balance sheet disclosures may also be required. For tax purposes, if a transaction is a hedge, the gain or loss is not reported until the futures or options contract has been closed out. The gain or loss can then be recognized as an offset to the business purpose of hedge (i.e., as a reduction of interest expense). However, this must be done at the time the position is closed out. Tax accruals in line with accounting treatment are not permitted. Hedges are specifically defined for tax purposes and do not always follow accounting definitions. For example, a capital asset position offset by short futures, even if a hedge for accounting purposes, would not be a hedge for tax purposes. If a future or option on future position is not a hedge, for tax purposes, recognition of gain or loss is required either when the position is closed out or based on the market value at the end of the tax accounting period, even if the future position is maintained. Any such gains or losses on future positions will be treated as 60 percent long-term gain/loss and 40 percent short-term gain/loss, regardless of holding period and regardless of whether the position is a long or a short.[16]

Swaps are currently being reviewed. Presently not all swaps result in balance sheet disclosures. A failure to disclose can result in a distorted balance sheet picture. The difference in interest cost between the original rate and the net rate after a swap will be recognized each period. While this clearly should be recognized as an adjustment to interest income, in some cases the swap receipts or payments have come into "other income," distorting interest presentations. Therefore, it would not be surprising to see more disclosure required in the near future.

Tax treatment of swaps is fairly clear, as most companies will merely recognize the actual net interest expense incurred during any taxable year.

VARIABLE RATE DEBT HEDGE

A rapidly growing software company recently financed an important acquisition by taking down a $7 million loan at 2 percent over the

---

[16] While this is generally true, certain straddle rules may be applicable.

EXHIBIT 3 Projected Flow of Funds Statement (in millions)

	1986	*1987*	*1988*
Funds from operation	$2.00	$2.25	$2.50
Interest on bank loan at 10 percent	(.70)	(.60)	(.50)
Net available cash	1.30	1.65	2.00
Paydown of bank debt	1.00	1.00	1.00
Net cash	.30	.65	1.00

EXHIBIT 4 Pro Forma Capitalization (in millions)

	1985	*1986*	*1987*	*1988*
Long-term debt	$7.00	$6.00	$5.00	$ 4.00
Equity	1.50	2.80	4.45	6.45
Total	$8.50	$8.80	$9.45	$10.45
Equity as percentage of capitalization	17.6%	31.8%	47.1%	61.7%

90-day Libor rate. The loan may be prepaid at any time, but it does require a $1 million principal reduction each year. This results in a substantial cash burden. The company would prefer a longer term fixed rate loan, but due to the leveraged nature of the company's balance sheet, this is not presently available. Therefore, the company needs to examine the means and cost of protecting itself against a sharp increase in short-term interest rates during the next two years when its cash flow requirements are tight.

The company has made two sets of projections that are reproduced below. Exhibit 3 shows projected flow of funds from operations, and Exhibit 4 shows projected capitalization. The exhibit tables are based on the following assumptions:

1. Funds from operations reflect income available after all charges other than servicing bank debt are made.
2. Due to a tax loss carryforward, no income tax will be payable during the relevant period.
3. Extra cash that is generated is required for expanding working capital.
4. The 90-day Libor rate remains at 8 percent for the three-year period, and the company's interest cost remains at 10 percent.

If the company could borrow for five years, the fixed rate would be 14 percent. Under this rate assumption the company's projected 1986 net available cash from operations would be reduced from $1.3 million to approximately $1.02 million. However, the $1 million amortization of loan principal may be avoided. This would be preferable despite the pressure on earnings. At the present time, this term funding alternative is not available to the company.

The flow of funds (Exhibit 3) and capitalization (Exhibit 4) analyses show that if the software company can work its way through 1986 and 1987, its projected debt-to-equity ratio will improve dramatically: from 17.6 percent equity at the end of 1985 to a projected 61.7 percent at the end of 1988. With this improvement, the company would have the financial standing to refund the $5 million outstanding debt and relieve its cash flow strain by funding out for a longer term.

This analysis ignores the risk the software company faces by assuming a constant 10 percent interest rate. If interest rates move up as the economy weakens, the company could find its funds from operations being reduced while interest expense increases. Suppose Libor went back to the 20 percent level it reached several years ago; the company's interest expense would then be 22 percent. The resulting 1986 interest charge of $1.54 million would reduce net available cash from $1.3 million to $460,000. Clearly, this would not be enough to reduce the bank debt even if earnings did hold up during the economic downturn. It might be difficult for the company to reduce its working capital needs quickly in this environment since collections may be slower than anticipated and inventories higher than desired. With only $1.5 million in equity at the beginning of this period, the company does not have the borrowing flexibility that it would like.

However, by the end of 1987, the company's debt will have been reduced to $5 million, and a 22 percent interest rate in 1988 will only cost $1.1 million. As a result, assuming all else equal, cash flow would only be reduced to $1.4 million, still enough money to pay down debt and provide a retained earnings cushion in the event profits fall or working capital requirements are temporarily increased. At the end of 1987, the firm's equity of $4.45 million will be much stronger.

The real problem that the company faces is protecting itself against a sharp rate increase during the highly vulnerable first two years so that it will be in a position to consider its alternatives thereafter. In order to set a strategy for this period of time, the company focuses primarily on the Eurodollar future and the associated options. The software company is looking to reduce existing interest rate risk, recognizing that to the extent that rates are not hedged, it is speculating.[17]

---

[17] Some situations contain an element of inherent hedging. If one postulates that short-term interest rates increase over time with increasing inflation, then to the extent that a firm's profit margin is expected to expand with inflation, the higher interest cost will be absorbed into higher gross margins. For a company in a vulnerable position over a short period of time, this "inherent hedge" analysis may be difficult.

EXHIBIT 5 Hedge Position Initiated September 1985

Contract Month	*Eurodollar Contract Price*	*Yield (percent)*	*Out-standing Loan (millions)*	*Short Contract Position in Contract Month*	*Total Short Contract Position*
December 85	91.80	8.20%	$7	7	52
March 86	91.38	8.62	7	7	45
June 86	90.95	9.05	7	7	38
September 86	90.56	9.44	7	7	31
December 86	90.21	9.79	6	6	24
March 87	89.89	10.11	6	6	18
June 87	89.59	10.41	6	6	12
September 87	89.21	10.79	6	6	6

Weighted Libor average	9.49%*
Credit spread	2.00%
Estimated hedged cost	11.49%

* The cost of the first quarter (September to December) is the actual three-month Libor rate; by including this 8 percent rate, the average base-hedged rate is reduced to 9.31 percent.

Using Eurodollar Futures. The software company initiates its hedge in September 1985, after completing its acquisition, and faces market levels shown in Exhibit 5. The actual first quarter interest cost will be based on an existing 8 percent Libor. In order to hedge the remaining period, the company would sell a strip of Eurodollar contracts from December 1985 through September 1987.[18]

The strip requires that for every $1 million principal outstanding, one contract per quarter be sold. While contracts are closed out quarterly, enough contracts, 52 in total, must be sold at the beginning of the hedge to cover the base loan amount outstanding in each quarter. Initially, a total of 28 contracts covering the $7 million principal outstanding the first year and 24 contracts covering the $6 million principal outstanding the second year would have been sold. The short position would be reduced by seven contracts per quarter in the first year and six contracts per quarter in the second.

The hedged rate calculated as the two-year average on the Eurodollar futures contract equals 9.49 percent. The company then adds on the 200 basis point credit spread paid to its bank for an effective hedge cost of 11.49 percent for the two-year period from December 1985 through December 1987. The base rate achieved by hedging for the two years is 149 basis points over the current 8 percent Libor. This cost need be compared with the risk of rates increasing over the period as well as the cost of fixed rate two-year funds, if available.

[18] An alternative strategy is to sell all front-month contracts and roll the position as each contract month expires. This leaves the company subject to changes in the yield curve.

EXHIBIT 6 Pro Forma Projected Flow of Funds and Capitalization Hedged Interest Cost (in millions)

	1986	*1987*
Funds from operations	$2.000	$2.250
Interest on loan	.804	.689
Net available cash	1.196	1.561
Paydown of debt	1.000	1.000
Net free cash	.196	.561
Long-term debt	6.000	5.000
Equity	2.696	4.142
Total Debt and Equity	8.696	9.142
Equity as percentage of capitalization	31%	45.3%

Exhibit 6 describes the company's flow of funds and capitalization given the hedged interest cost of 11.49 percent.

The first and second years' hedged interest cost of $894,000 and $689,400 compare with $700,000 or $600,000 originally projected. However, if the software company could have obtained a five-year loan at 14 percent, it would have resulted in an annual interest cost of approximately $980,000. Of course, that higher cost, longer term loan would mean that the company would not be exposed on its post-1987 position. The savings on the hedged two-year rate over the five-year, 14 percent loan rate can be used to offset the risk of higher rates when refinancing the $5 million balance of the loan for the three-year period commencing at the end of 1987.

With a futures hedge, the rate at which the Eurodollar contract was sold will equal the base loan cost for that calendar quarter covered by that contract. This net cost is determined by offsetting the actual Libor rate paid with the variation margin debit or credit from the contract position for that quarter. The first quarter's fixed base loan cost is 8 percent, based on the 90-day Libor rate assumed in September. In September, when the hedge was initiated, the December 1985 Eurodollar contract was priced at 91.80, equivalent to an 8.2 percent, 90-day Libor rate, for the December quarter, and a 10.2 percent actual cost after including the credit premium. The loan reset date, in this case, is assumed to be the same as the expiration date on the December contract.[19]

It must be noted that the forward rate for 90-day Libor, as seen in the price of the December futures contract, is 20 basis points higher

[19] This assumption simplifies the potential timing mismatches. If the loan reset date is not the same as the contract expiration date, that must be taken into account in creating the hedge strategy.

than the current quarter's Libor rate. This is due to the positive yield curve. The company's effective hedge cost will be higher than the 90-day Libor and will approximate a two-year Libor rate.

Assume that on December 16, 1985, Libor rates and, consequently, the base rate on the software company's loan has risen by 100 basis points. The interest actually due on its loan for the quarter beginning December 16 will be $17,500 more than for the September quarter. Upon expiration, the December contract price settled at 91.00, equivalent to the dealer survey of a 9 percent, 90-day Libor rate. The gain on the short position that is closed out on December 16 is $14,000.[20] The company's gross interest cost for the quarter at 11 percent (9 percent Libor plus 200 basis points) is $192,500: The net interest cost of $178,500 thus creates an annualized loan rate of 10.2 percent, as projected. The $14,000 profit is fixed when the contract position expires by cash settlement or is closed out by purchasing seven December 85 contracts. The gain or loss on the futures position that offsets the higher or lower quarterly Libor rate would have been received through the variation margin mechanism.

The beginning short position of 52 contracts requires an initial margin deposit of approximately $52,000, which can be met by a deposit of Treasury bills with a broker. During the period of time when 52 contracts are in place, the entire change in the value of the contracts will be reflected in money received or paid to the exchange as variation margin. For example, suppose yields should decline 100 basis points on the first day that the contracts are sold. This would represent a margin call of $2,500 per contract—a total call of $130,000. Should that same rate decline occur in the beginning of the second year, when only 24 contracts are in place, the requirements would be reduced to $60,000.

While the variation margin process does entail a cost or return from this cash disbursement or receipt, the more important consideration in this case is its impact on corporate cash flow. Although any amounts paid into the futures market are eventually recouped through lower interest charges, over the next two years the immediate effect of this timing imbalance and the ability to meet the potential margin calls is critical. During the first year, when the size of the short contract position is greatest, cash flow requirements are more often critical.

Using Eurodollar Options. One solution to the potential variation margin financing might be to use options during the first few quarters

---

[20] The contracts were sold at 91.80 and covered at 91.00, resulting in a gain of 80 basis points, valued at $25 per basis points. The profit is $2,000 per contract. To hedge a $7 million loan for this 90-day period, seven contracts were sold.

EXHIBIT 7 Eurodollar Put Options

		December Cost		*March Cost*	
Strike Price	*Libor Rate*	*Basis Points*	*Dollars*	*Basis Points*	*Dollars*
91.00	9.00	.38	950	.68	1,700
91.50	8.50	.59	1,475	.94	2,350
92.00	8.00	.86	2,150	1.07	2,675

and futures for later periods. Set forth in Exhibit 7 are prices that existed for Eurodollar put options at the time of the transaction. A short contract position for each quarter could be replaced by the purchase of a comparable number of Eurodollar puts.[21]

The company can evaluate its decision to use options based on the risk it perceives for the next few quarters. In order to minimize the immediate option premium expense, the company could choose to insure against a significant increase in rates by purchasing puts with out-of-the-money strike prices. For example, after evaluating the impact of a 100 basis point increase in Libor on its projected flow of funds, management might decide to face the potential cost of a 9 percent Libor rate but choose to protect itself against rates increasing above a 9 percent base. The 91.00 put strike is equivalent to a 9 percent Libor rate.

If rates increase to 10 percent, the expiration value of the December and March options will equal 1.00 point, or $2,500 per option, the equivalent to a 100 basis point increase in the base borrowing cost for three months on $1 million. The advantage of an option is that if rates go down to 7 percent, the resulting lower interest cost on the loan will accrue to the company and the put option will be left to expire worthless. With futures, the hedged borrowing rate would have been locked in. Puts, however, carry a premium cost that futures do not.

The actual cost of insuring the loan for the six-month period covered by the December and March contracts is a function of the size of the loan and the put premium. The software company would purchase seven December and seven March puts, as an alternative to selling futures contracts. The cost of protecting these two periods

---

[21] This assumes that the options will be held until expiration, at which time they are priced on their intrinsic value. Prior to the expiration, option prices change in some proportion to the price of the underlying instruments. This factor is referred to as the delta. If a future price changed by 1 point and the related option by .5 point, the option's delta would be .5. The delta is a function of volatility, time to expiration, and the market price of the future. If one is considering terminating a hedge sooner than the option's expiration, a delta weighting must be considered.

against a rate increase over 9 percent would be $6,650 ($950 times seven puts) and $11,900, respectively, or a total cost of $18,550. The maximum base rates would then be 9.38 percent and 9.68 percent, but the company would not benefit by lower rates unless the Libor rate went below 7.62 percent or 7.32 percent for the two periods, respectively.

The alternative hedge cost of protecting from the 8 percent level is represented by the relatively higher prices of the December and March 92.00 puts. The effective maximum base loan rate for the December and March quarters would be 8.86 percent and 9.07 percent, respectively. This rate is higher than the average hedged rate using futures since the company would still benefit if rates decline. However, 90-day Libor would have to decline to 7.14 percent by December and to 6.93 percent by March for the company to fully recoup the put premium paid for 92.00 puts.

Option strategies can be implemented for longer periods of time by rolling into new contract months as they are listed. The longer term strategy costs may be defined within broad parameters by estimating the cost of the roll under different circumstances. The immediate outlay for a fully hedged option program for a two-year period would generally be prohibitive to the company in a tight cash position. However, the options alternative increases the company's interest rate risk management capability to allow for more certain loan pricing for a period of time.

Using Interest Rate Swaps. A third alternative may be interest rate swaps. Due to the company's relatively weak credit standing, it is unlikely that it could be party to an interest rate swap for five years. A swap might be more viable in two years when the company has only $5 million outstanding debt and is in a stronger fiscal position. However, an illustration of the theory behind a swap transaction may be viewed in terms of changing the company's first two years of floating rate debt into a fixed rate.

The company would enter into an arrangement, probably with a bank acting as principal, whereby the company would agree to pay a fixed rate for a period, for example two years, receiving from the counterparty income at a variable rate. This does not involve any exchange of principal, but rather only a quarterly exchange of interest payments based on different rates. Each quarter, the company will pay to the intermediary bank a fixed rate of interest negotiated at the time the swap was initiated, and receive from them a variable rate payment designed to offset any change in the company's borrowing cost. In this case, the company might agree to receive the 90-day Libor rate, currently 8 percent, and in return pay a fixed rate, which might

EXHIBIT 8 An Interest Rate Swap at Different Libor Rates

	Pay (percent)		*Receive (percent)*
Libor at 8 percent			
Libor + 2 percent	10.00	Libor Swap	8.00
Fixed rate	9.50		
	19.50		8.00
Net cost	11.50		
Libor at 10 percent			
Libor + 2 percent	12.00	Libor Swap	10.00
Fixed rate	9.50		
	21.50		10.00
Net cost	11.50		

approximate 9.5 percent for two years. Actually the interest amount exchanged is the difference between the fixed and floating rate payment, in this case equivalent to 150 basis points. Thereafter, if the Libor rate were to go up, the company's swap receipts would increase accordingly. This would be offset by the higher interest payment payable on the software company's outstanding debt. Exhibit 8 indicates how the swap transaction results in a net fixed rate of 11.50 percent, regardless of changes in rates after the swap is agreed to.

If the Libor rate went from 8 percent to 10 percent, then the company's primary loan rate would have risen from 10 percent to 12 percent. However, this would be offset by the increased swap payment that the company would receive. But since the fixed rate swap of 9.5 percent stays the same, it can be seen that the company will still have a 11.5 percent cost.

The software company has to review its alternatives.

Do Nothing. Inertia speculation represents the highest risk, since the company is betting that the general level of rates will stay low and that it will benefit from the steepness of the short-term yield curve.

Sell Futures. A pure hedge will neutralize the rate risk but will involve variation margin cash flow considerations. This strategy is easily entered into and at any time easily reversed if the company feels that the risk of higher rates over the remaining life of the loan has diminished.

Buy Put Options. This is a relatively high fixed cost alternative that with availability of various strike prices, allows the company

EXHIBIT 9 Apparel Company Balance Sheet before Financing (in millions)

Current assets	$15	Current liabilities	$17
Noncurrent assets	17	Noncurrent liabilities	2
		Equity	13
	32		32
Current ratio	.88		
Capitalization			
Debt	13%		
Equity	87%		

to protect against specific rate increases for a defined period of time while maintaining the potential benefit of a rate decline.

Interest Rate Swap. As with a futures hedge, the swap will give the company an effective fixed rate for the duration of the agreement. The credit consideration and ability to directly match loan terms can be evaluated relative to the flexibility of futures. Ultimately the all-in cost of the swap would be compared to the hedged rate from futures.

TERM FINANCING HEDGE

A woman's apparel manufacturing company specializes in selling relatively standard items to major chain stores. During the past few years the company has grown rapidly. As can be seen from Exhibit 9, current assets are now $15 million and current liabilities are $17 million. The current ratio of .88 is very unattractive, particularly for a company needing to finance seasonal inventory. On the other hand, noncurrent assets have grown to $17 million and noncurrent liabilities are only $2 million. Not surprisingly, the company is constantly facing cash flow pressure. However, its growth in equity would permit the company to borrow long term from a financial institution such as an insurance company.

The pro forma analysis shown in Exhibit 10 indicates what the company's balance sheet would look like following a $10 million, 10-year private placement. This financing will permit the company to continue to grow through bank borrowings and reduce its cash flow pressure. Consequently, the company will be in a much stronger position should business turn down or opportunities for further growth continue. The company could presently take down a 10-year loan at 15 percent. If interest rates rise or the apparel company's business position deteriorates, its opportunity for funding debt might diminish. The company's management prefers not to lock in the current rate available and has decided to speculate rather than accept a 15 percent

EXHIBIT 10 Apparel Company Balance Sheet after Financing (in millions)

Current assets	$15	Current liabilities	$ 7
Noncurrent assets	17	Long-term debt	12
		Equity	13
	32		32
Current ratio	2.14		
Capitalization			
Debt	48%		
Equity	52%		

interest rate for 10 years. However, the company wants to be assured that in the event of an increase in rates, it will still be able to secure longer term debt.

The company, therefore, is seeking to fund its debt today but wishes to separate that basic financing decision from the acceptance of current market rates. In addition, it wants the flexibility to change its strategy and not continue to speculate without the time delays inherent in placing debt. In this case, the company may choose to segment its risk by employing a strategy to benefit from declining rates over the next five years, in line with a more conservative outlook. Through the use of futures, options, or swaps it can tailor its risk within more tolerable limits.[22]

Using Interest Rate Swaps. As was noted earlier, an interest rate swap involves no exchange of principal, but rather permits a company to exchange interest rate payment obligations. This allows a company to take advantage of the best credit terms available while managing its rate exposure. The apparel company has sufficient credit standing to get a private placement, and it could probably secure a matching interest rates swap. The swap will be positioned to transform the 10-year fixed rate into floating rate debt until the maturity of the swap agreement.

Suppose the apparel company believes that rates will be lower than today and wishes to take advantage of that during the next five-year period. The company is willing to live with the 15 percent rate for the second five years of the loan. The 10-year fixed rate negotiated for the private placement is 4.5 percent over the 10-year Treasury rate. Assume that the company enters into a five-year interest rate swap. It agrees to receive a fixed rate based on the current five-year

[22] As has been true throughout this chapter, options refer to the exchange-traded options on futures contracts. There is a market for over-the-counter options on specific government securities that in some cases could also be used in this application. The basic theory and strategy are comparable for either type of option.

EXHIBIT 11 Apparel Company Interest Rate Swap (Libor at 8 percent)

	Pay (percent)		Receive (percent)
Private placement	15	Fixed rate swap	10.5
Libor swap	8		
	23		10.5
Net cost:	12.5		

Treasury rate of 10.5 percent and to pay a variable rate based on the current 8 percent Libor rate. As can be seen from Exhibit 11, the company will reduce its interest cost for the first quarter from 15 percent to 12.5 percent.

In effect, the company is moving along the yield curve in order to achieve a lower financing rate. This reflects a move to shorter maturities and to a variable cost base. Suppose that the Libor rate goes to 7 percent as in Exhibit 12, the company's interest cost will be reduced to 11.5 percent for the quarter.

It is possible that the interest cost resulting from the swap will be more than the company would incur on a variable rate short-term loan, since the credit spread inherent in the 10-year loan may be greater than that for a shorter term loan. However, a bank loan with a variable rate might have a repayment structure different from that for a term loan. Flexibility has been gained by taking a 10-year loan and creating out of it two five-year loans. Depending on the company's long-term projection for interest rates, the variable segment could have been set for two or four years, as swap markets are fairly flexible.

Once the interest rate swap has been entered into, its effect can be reversed by offsetting swaps. Suppose a year has gone by and both market levels and the yield curve have changed so that the four-year Treasury rate and the 90-day Libor rate are both 13 percent. The company could enter into another swap to effectively fix its rates at the new level for the four years remaining on the original swap. This layering is described by Exhibit 13.

EXHIBIT 12 Apparel Company Interest Rate Swap (Libor at 7 percent)

	Pay (percent)		Receive (percent)
Private placement	15	Fixed rate swap	10.5
Libor swap	7		
	22		10.5
Net cost:	11.5		

EXHIBIT 13 Apparel Company Interest Rate Swap
(Libor and four-year treasury rate at 13 percent)

	Pay (percent)		Receive (percent)
Private placement	15		
Libor (swap 1)	13	Fixed rate (swap 1)	10.5
Fixed rate (swap 2)	13	Libor (swap 2)	13.0
	41		23.5
Net cost:	17.5		

The company's net rate for the period has risen to 17.5 percent, 250 basis points greater than its original 15 percent fixed cost, because the yield curve worked against it in a rising rate environment. The point is simply that once one enters into a swap, one can usually change positions as markets change. Sometimes swaps can be offset with the same dealer and sometimes additional swaps have to be layered on, to achieve desired positions.

Using Treasury Bond Futures. The apparel company could also follow strategies that use financial futures or options. In a futures strategy, the company could buy the intermediate-term 10-year note contract or the longer term Treasury bond contract. The advantage of the note contract is that its duration comes closer to the 10-year obligation being hedged. However, for reasons based on liquidity and contract technicalities, we are assuming that the apparel company is willing to take the risk of a divergence between the 30-year and 10-year Treasury rates and use the long-term bond contract.

The futures market permits the company to create a floating rate loan out of its fixed rate loan for all or part of its obligation and for whatever period of time it remains in the long futures position. The company will fix its long-term rate at the time it closes out its contract position. A futures transaction does not require involvement of banks or other third parties. Consequently, if this company would have difficulty with the swap market, it could always use the futures market. Since futures are a regulated market with a controlled margin mechanism, less of a credit exposure may exist.

In order to design its financial futures strategy, the company would first estimate its interest cost for a given change in Treasury bond yields. For example, the company would estimate what its interest cost would be if its loan had been secured at a time when 30-year Treasury bond yields were 100 basis points lower than today.[23] The

[23] This assumes that the spread between 10-year and 30-year rates remains constant.

resulting present value of the interest savings over the life of the loan is the amount that the company will look to earn through the futures position. The expected gain on the futures is determined by evaluating the change in contract price given the 100 basis point decline in Treasury yields. The goal of this analysis is to determine the number of contracts required to generate the interest payment savings the company would have achieved had it waited to take down the loan and had rates declined.

Assume that the apparel company actually borrows for 10 years at 15 percent, with the total principal payable in 10 years, but wishes to be in a position to fully benefit from lower 10-year rates. The semiannual interest cost on a $1 million loan at 15 percent is $75,000. If the loan rate declines to 14 percent, the semiannual cost would be $70,000, a $5,000 saving per semiannual period. A 15 percent, 10-year bond priced to yield 14 percent would sell for $105,297. This implies that a $1 million, 15 percent loan has a value of $1,052,970 at 14 percent. Alternatively, $52,970 invested at 14 percent, compounded semiannually for 10 years would generate the $5,000 differential per period. The objective of the futures hedge, therefore, would be to provide $52,970 today, the same value as if the company's loan cost declined by 100 basis points.

The company must estimate the relative change in the yield on its 10-year loan compared to the change of the 30-year Treasury bond, which is the cheapest-to-deliver bond, determining the pricing for the futures contract. Assume that the 10⅜ percent of 11-15-12 is currently the cheapest-to-deliver bond and that a 100 basis point decline in the company's 10-year loan rate would be matched by a 90 basis point decline in the yield of this Treasury bond. The 10⅜ percent current price of $101,109 results in a 10.25 percent yield to maturity. At a yield to maturity of 9.35 percent, the Treasury bond price would equal $110,005 and the future equivalent value of the December 85 contract will increase by 7.16 from 81.36 to 88.52.[24] Each December bond future would show a gain of $7,160, and a total long position of 7.40 contracts would produce the desired interest saving amount per million dollars.

The actual price of the Treasury bond futures would differ from the futures equivalent value due to convergence, which was discussed earlier in the chapter. This yield curve effect, in this case a gain, shows up in the difference between the actual change in the future's contract price and the change in futures equivalent value. Since the

---

[24] This value is calculated as the price of the deliverable bond divided by the appropriate pricing factor. The December 1985 factor for the 10⅜ percent of 11-15-12 is 1.2427. The bond price of $101,109 divided by 1.2427, results in a futures equivalent value of 81.36. A bond price of $110,005 would result in a futures equivalent of 88.52.

long futures position will reflect the volatility of the 30-year bond rate, the gains on convergence will produce quarterly income in line with the difference between short-term and long-term bond yields. The importance of the convergence value amortized over the life of the loan would depend on how long the hedge is maintained.

A futures position can be maintained indefinitely by a technique known as rolling. The cost of the roll is the price differential, (i.e., spread) between contract months. Prior to the last trading day, the December 85 contract can be sold and the March 86 contract bought as a simultaneous transaction, the only question being the yield curve impact built into that roll. This, too, reflects the convergence gain or loss on a futures position.

The company would have to recognize its obligation to post initial margin and variation margin, as cited in the previous example. However, by being long Treasury bond futures it has the flexibility to close out all or part of its position any time that would create lower interest rates, or should it begin to see that rates are going against it, to sell out all or part of the position, thereby limiting the cost.

One big difference from the interest rate swaps alternative is that with the Treasury bond futures, the entire present value of the change in interest rates is captured in the initial move of the futures. The change in yield of 90 basis points would result in close to a 5 percent change in the asset value. With the interest rate swap, the differential comes into the income statement over a period of time. To the extent that cash flow is a consideration, futures present the possibility of having to take down additional loans to pay variation margin if rates rise, or if rates decline and the debt is repayable without penalty, it could provide the opportunity to repay part of the debt early.

Using Treasury Bond Options. The final alternative the apparel company might consider is using bond futures options. A call option position would be profitable if rates decline enough to recoup the option premium paid. If rates increase, no incremental cost would be incurred. Listed options are available for the front three futures contracts, generally covering a nine-month period. Hedging strategies covering longer time periods can be enacted for an incremental time premium by rolling options. The option hedge would be set up in the same fashion as the futures hedge. In order to hedge the principal effect of an interest rate change over three months for $10 million, one would buy 771 December 85 Treasury bond options. The strategy is set up based on the call options value at expiration so each futures contract is replaced by one call, which would provide enough money to be the equivalent of a 14 percent issuance.[25] This assumes that the options will be held until expiration, at which time they are priced on their intrinsic value. Prior to the expiration, option prices change in some proportion to the price of the underlying instruments. This factor is referred to as the delta. If a future price changed by 1 point and the related option by .5 point, the option's delta would be .5. The delta is a function of volatility, time to expiration, and the market price of the future. If one is considering terminating a hedge sooner than the option expiration, a delta weighting must be considered.

An important aspect in setting up the option hedge is selecting the strike price. Any strike and its coincident premium represents a trade-off between intrinsic value and out-of-pocket expense. An in-the-money call would represent the lowest option (time value) cost if rates decline, but would result in the highest expense if rates rise. Suppose the future was $77^{16}/_{32}$ and the 76 call was priced at $1^{52}/_{64}$, the $1,812.50 represents a $312.50 time value and $1,500 in-the-money value. If the future rose to $84^{16}/_{32}$ at expiration, the call would be worth $8,500. The net profit on the call would be $6,687.50, which is only $312.50 less than the value of the 7-point futures price increase. However, if the contract price is below the strike price, at expiration the entire option premium is lost.

The out-of-the-money 78 call would have cost $^{45}/_{64}$, the $703.13 representing only time value. As was true in the prior example, by choosing a higher strike price, and only receiving the benefit of a price increase above the 78 level, if rates increase a higher total intrinsic cost would evolve, but lower total dollar outlay would be involved. Consequently, the amount at risk would be reduced. Each three-month period that one chooses to protect oneself with options adds to the cost, but a six- or nine-month cost is usually less pro rata, that is, per day, than the three-month option cost. For example, a six-month option would be an acceptable plan should one feel that interest rates are apt to go down during the next six months, but if they didn't, one would need to be prepared to be at the 15 percent rate during the balance of the 10 years.

Option purchases, therefore, provide fixed maximum cost hedges and do not subject one either to the risks involved in changing variable rates of the future or swap markets, or to the consequences of variation margin moves experienced in futures. However, the cost of options must be taken into account.

These strategies can be integrated to create any risk/reward pro-

---

[25] Since the option on futures stops before the futures expire, some minor adjustments may be desired.

file. One could buy calls for a six-month period with the idea of doing a swap if rates, in fact, declined. Or, one could do a five-year swap and buy options to try to protect against a rate increase for a defined time period.

This chapter has attempted to introduce the reader to certain tools that have been created to provide alternatives in today's complex markets. These tools do not make financing difficult, they are merely the reflection of the variables of the marketplace. To ignore these or similar techniques is to leave oneself open to the whims of the market—that perhaps being the greatest form of speculation. While this chapter has attempted to provide an introduction to these techniques, it has, of necessity, been general, and the advice of those skilled in the use of futures, options, and swaps should be sought.

CHAPTER EIGHTEEN

Khoy-Tsahl, 1877

OR THE *NEE-ME-POO* THESE WERE THE FIRST DAYS OF THE SEASON WHEN the blue-backed salmon made its mating run in Wallowa Lake. The meat of those strong fighting fish was red and sweet. Every bit as sweet as were these days now that they had the *suapies* on the run.

After they had ambushed the two Shadows and fought the rest of the soldiers all the way back to their burrows on Cottonwood Creek, Yellow Wolf proudly rode into the village singing an echo of his medicine song. This echo, as his people called it, was a peculiarly intoned melody that announced to the camp that the singer had met and killed an enemy. Oh, how the young women looked at him then! It had been a good night of dancing, singing, and celebrating with those soft-eyed ones who peered at him from beneath thick lashes in the firelight.

Early this morning, the older women and men were up before dawn, preparing for another day's march across the Camas Prairie. This time they were packing for the short journey that would bring them to *Piswah Ilppilp Pah*, or the Place of Red Rocks, a good campsite in the canyon that would take them down to the Clearwater.

As Yellow Wolf crawled on hands and knees from his brush shelter into the bright light, gazing around at the bustle of activity, *Weesculatat* rode up, calling out, "You, young fighter—come with me this morning!"

He ground his knuckles into his red eyes sleepily. "I was awake too long last night."

"I have a ride for you," offered this warrior, who was also called *Mimpow Owyeen*, or Wounded Mouth. "If you want to come with me."

Running his tongue around inside his mouth, Yellow Wolf did not think his belly was particularly hungry for breakfast. He squinted up at the older man, a father whose son was a Christian living on the reservation. "All right. Where do you want to ride this morning?"

"We will call out some other young men," *Weesculatat* replied. "No older fighters—just young men like you. And we will go ride over to see who we might find along the Shadow road out on the prairie. There might be some horses, or rifles, maybe some fighting, too, if we catch anyone out."

By the time *Weesculatat* and Yellow Wolf had moved through camp, calling out to other young men still a little groggy from their long night's celebration, two-times-ten riders were strung out in a crude V that passed right on by the soldier camp.

"See down the road!" *Weesculatat* shouted, waving the arm that he pointed south across the prairie. The older man announced, "We have two in the hand!"

Yipping like playful coyote pups setting off to chase and harass a jackrabbit across a grassy meadow, a handful of the young warriors kicked their ponies into a gallop, reining for the pair of *suapies*.

"You aren't going, Yellow Wolf?" *Weesculatat* asked.

"No," and he shook his head as the pair of distant horsemen spurred their horses into a terrified sprint, both men lying low in the saddle and whipping their animals without mercy. "There are already enough to see to those unlucky soldiers. I killed two of my own yesterday."

"This will be great fun to watch," *Weesculatat* said as Yellow Wolf turned on the back of his pony to peer across the great heaving expanse of the prairie.

Surely there had to be a better game than this. What with all those Shadows holed up in the two settlements nearby, with so many *suapies* hunkered down in their gopher burrows on the Cottonwood, there had to be better sport for a real fighting man than wiping out two lonely mail carriers caught unawares and in the open.

It wasn't long before the soldier chief sent out some men who halted their horses, aimed their rifles toward the six warriors closing the gap on the two horsemen, and fired three volleys.

It was easy to see how the soldiers aimed over the heads of those two oncoming riders so their bullets would land in front of the charging warriors. *Weesculatat* and the five others were just breaking off their chase when the breath caught in Yellow Wolf's chest.

"Now that's what I call a challenge for a fighting man!" he suddenly announced with a shrill cry, every muscle in his body tensing with anticipation. "See who is coming now!"

At the far sweep of grassy prairie, more riders just made their appearance, advancing from the southeast.

"Are they more *suapies?*" asked *Weesculatat.*

"I don't think so," Yellow Wolf replied, one hand tensing on the reins, the other gripping the hardwood carbine he had captured at the White Bird fight. "None of them are dressed the same, and they are coming from the Shadow settlements."

"*Hi-yiii!*" the older warrior shrieked exuberantly. "Yes, this is far better for a fighting man!"

Two Moons reined up beside *Ollokot* in a cloud of dust their horses kicked up with their hooves. "String out!" Two Moons ordered loudly to the rest, all five-times-ten of the young men arrayed along the white man's road. "String out and make a broad line!"

Yellow Wolf agreed, "Yes—we will charge into them and break them up!"

By the time Two Moons and *Ollokot* got their fifty-plus warriors started off the road and onto the long sweep of rolling grassland, Yellow Wolf began to quickly tally the enemy. There were three fingers less than two-times-ten. It would be interesting to see when the Shadows reined up in a hurry as they spotted the warriors, turned around, and fled back for their settlement barricades. But . . . the horsemen kept coming! Instead of halting and wheeling about on their heels, the white men began to spread out, just as *Ollokot*'s warriors were doing in a wide front.

"What trick do you think they are up to?" *Weesculatat* asked.

Yellow Wolf quickly looked over his shoulder, seeing how the mail carriers were just then reaching the soldiers sent out to rescue them and all were retreating to the rifle pits dug around the white man's buildings raised at Cottonwood. Still, there weren't any soldiers coming out to show themselves and lay down a cover fire to protect this bigger group of Shadows.

"I don't think they have a trick to play on us at all," Yellow Wolf said as he saw how the horseman in the center was waving and wildly gesturing while the entire line of white men suddenly kicked their horses into a frenzied sprint. "They are going to try to beat us to the soldiers' gopher burrows."

Weesculatat flicked a look over his shoulder as their ponies lunged into a low, grassy swale. "It is a long way to race us to safety!"

Yellow Wolf quickly glanced at the distance. Many, many bullet flights to the hollows. If the soldiers did not come out to lay down some cover, *Ollokot*'s war party could stop the outnumbered Shadows and cut them up one at a time.

Faint sounds erupted from the throats of those white horsemen as they raced closer and closer, heading on a collision course with the wide band of warriors. Then the first of their guns popped, a puff of smoke appearing at the muzzle of a belt gun, a gray mist whipped away behind the rider. Others fired, and Yellow Wolf heard the first snarl of a bullet as it sang past him. On either side of him, those who had firearms put them to use—more for noise and bluster than to do any good atop a racing horse.

Yellow Wolf hoped the others would not use up too much of their hard-won ammunition in such frivolous sport. They would need those bullets when the tough killing began. Better to save their cartridges until they were sure of hitting a target—

Yelling at the top of his lungs, Yellow Wolf swung his *koplutz,* that short hardwood war club, at the closest Shadow the moment both lines converged on the slope leading out of that low, grassy swale. In an instant the white men were beyond them, through the warriors and on their way to the soldier hollows.

Immediately all the warriors swung their ponies around in broad, sweeping curves, each rider leaning hard to the inside as he brought his horse tearing in an arch that nearly toppled a handful of the Nez Perce as they barely avoided colliding with one another. With yips and howls and screeches, too, they were after the galloping Shadows in a heartbeat, racing after the rumps of those fleeing horses, making as much noise as they could.

Yellow Wolf's throat was a little sore by the time he saw the first of the white men's horses stumble and pitch its rider into the grass. Another horseman quickly reined aside and took the dismounted Shadow up behind him.

"Yes!" *Weesculatat* cried. "Aim for their horses! Aim for their horses!"

"Put them on foot!" came the order from Two Moons.

Almost immediately another Shadow horse stumbled; then it kicked and bucked, throwing its rider clear before it settled onto the ground.

Up ahead of the white men, one of them had reached the top of a low hill where he threw himself out of the saddle and was waving with an arm that brandished a repeater. Yellow Wolf had a lever-action carbine like that in his mother's lodge. But she was with Looking Glass's people. How he wished he had that repeater now instead of this single-shot *suapie* gun.

One by one the rest of the white men were leaping off their horses around that first man, two of them lunging up on foot, their horses already down in the swale behind them.

"*Yi-yi-yiiii!*" Yellow Wolf yipped, his blood running hot.

Hot because they had the Shadows stopped on the brow of that low hill and the white men were going no farther. If those few horsemen had kept on riding, chances were very good most of them could have made it on into the soldier burrows.

But, as it was, *Ollokot*'s warriors could now take their time and have some fun wiping out these foolish whites.

SINCE PUTTING MOUNT Idaho behind them, Lieutenant Lew Wilmot and the other volunteers who rode with Captain D. B. Randall had done their best to save the strength of their horses. While he knew every man around him wanted nothing less than to gallop full-out for that soldier camp at Cottonwood Station, they nonetheless reined in their mounts as they descended to the rolling prairie. No more than a fast walk. Save the horses' strength for when it was really needed.

But the endurance of the animals beneath them wasn't the only worry troubling Wilmot. As he looked around him, Lew quickly tallied the odds against this band of civilians if they did have to make a running fight of it. He himself had been up against it with the Indians more than once, but . . . besides Randall and three more, none of the other twelve had ever found themselves in an Indian fight.

As he looked around at the group tightly bunched behind their leaders, Lew realized there wasn't a good shot among them. Make no mistake, he thought: The odds were in favor of the Nez Perce who had cleaned up every command sent against them so far.

"You see the smoke, D. B.?" Wilmot asked. He had just spotted the signal fires burning atop Cottonwood Butte, which straddled the divide.

"Seen it a minute ago," Randall said. "Likely that's them Injuns talking about those soldiers down below 'em."

Lew was still brooding on the uncertain odds stacked against them if they ran into trouble after covering some two-thirds of the distance to Norton's ranch—when Wilmot's eyes caught some distant movement on the sweep of prairie far off in their advance, a little to their right.

"D. B., you look at all that ahead of us; I think we need to hold up a minute," Lew suggested to the man riding just ahead of him.

"All right," Randall agreed. "Give us a minute to figger out what all this is."

"Lookit all them horses!" Ben Evans cried behind him.

The herd slowly undulating off the last slope of the divide and pouring onto the prairie was impressive in size, to say the least. But it wasn't those Nez Perce horses that held Lew Wilmot's attention. It was those fighting men who suddenly popped up, right out of the low swale about halfway between Randall's volunteers and their village on the move.

"Here, Lew! Look for your own self."

Turning, Wilmot found James Cearly handing him a small looking glass. Lew quickly twisted the outer section until the distant figures slipped into focus. Then he twisted it back, taking the advancing horsemen out of focus as he concentrated on the distant forms among the structures that were Cottonwood Station. The house, barn, and outbuildings appeared clearly, and all those soldiers rising out of their rifle pits, too, at least a hundred of them, watching, what was about to happen. Watching, and waiting.

"Have a look, D. B." Wilmot jabbed the spyglass at Randall. "We don't stand a chance of getting to Cottonwood now."

As their leader was studying the distance, most of the untried men behind Wilmot were shifting nervously in their saddles, an uneasy banter and hollow bravado coming over them as they stared at the distant line of more than a hundred-fifty warriors just then stringing itself into a wide but uneven V, its long side adhering to the Mount Idaho Road, the other angling across the pitch and heave of the Camas Prairie itself.

"While we still got time, we oughtta turn around for the barricades," Lew proposed.

"No!" James Cearly screeched like a bull calf with its bangers tangled in some cat claw.

"I ain't never been yeller!" cried Frank A. Fenn,* elected sergeant of their volunteer company just that morning.

"If we ride back to our families now, nobody's gonna say we was yellow," Wilmot protested, refusing to listen to their angry protests. "Besides, that village is headed in the direction of our towns. Don't you boys figger we oughtta protect our families?"

"G'won back now if you don't wanna get in on the fighting, Lew," Cearly snapped, edging his horse up on the other side of Randall's.

Even young Alonzo B. Leland, the Lewiston *Teller* editor's son, refused to consider retreat while they still had the chance. "Captain Randall, you can lead the rest of us through to the soldiers. I know you can."

"That's right, Captain!" Cearly agreed boldly. "If anybody can get us through, you can."

Lew pleaded one more time, "We've all got families to protect—"

But Randall sternly interrupted, "Helping them soldiers stop those Injuns is the best way I know of protecting our families back at Mount Idaho."

His eyes darting across the rolling sea of tall grass, Wilmot grabbed Randall's elbow with one hand, pointing with his right arm. "Lookit that hill way off there to the left. We got time to make it there. That's the kind of place

***Cries from the Earth*, vol. 14, the *Plainsmen* series.

where we can make a stand, D. B. Just tall enough, let the Indians attack us there, we can wait for the soldiers to come out and drive 'em off—"

"No," Randall growled, his eyes squinting testily. "I'll get everyone through to Cottonwood like I promised." Then he turned away from Lew, looking at James Cearly. "Jim—I think it's time you took over for Lew. I need someone I can count on behind me, so you're lieutenant of this outfit now."

Most of the group hooted and hollered like schoolboys on a summer's lark down to the fishing hole. Wilmot quickly glanced around at them—looking into those eager faces, realizing there wasn't a single one of them who knew what they were about to plunge themselves into.

Suddenly he scolded himself for even caring about these men whom he had known—well, *thought* he knew—friends who were turning their backs on him and the loved ones all them had left behind in Mount Idaho to wait and wonder.

The wide formation of distant warriors disappeared down the slope as the Nez Perce dropped into the low swale of Shebang Creek. They were getting closer and closer yet still approaching at an easy pace. So there had to be enough time to get to the top of that low hill nearby—

Right now it didn't matter who the hell was lieutenant or sergeant . . . or even the goddamned captain. Gulping, Wilmot vowed to try to convince them all one last time.

"D. B., it's better we have us some high ground 'stead of getting caught out—"

"Lew," Randall interrupted, flinging Wilmot's hand off his arm, "if you wanna go back, I said you can go. Me and the rest of the boys have started for Cottonwood and we are going."

Wilmot's horse seemed to sense the tension and sidestepped. Lew leaned over, grabbing for Randall's wrist again. Nearly breathless, he pleaded, "D. B., you know I ain't going back 'less the rest of you go. These here fellas brung near all the guns in Mount Idaho with 'em when we rode out. And now there's enough Injuns between us and Norton's place to have us outnumbered ten-to-one."

"C'mon, Captain!" Fenn shouted. "Let's ride right through those sons-abitches!"

Emboldened by the confidence in the others, Randall shook off Wilmot's hand again. Smiling like it was all a joke, he said, "Well now, Lew—if you're afraid of all them Injuns, why don't you climb up here behind me on my horse?"

The instant laughter was cruel and metallic, sharp-edged, as it fell about Wilmot. There were muted murmurs from some of the others who suddenly voiced criticism against him and Ready for running to Grangeville when the Nortons and Chamberlins were fighting off a brutal attack. Their laughter, even at his expense, showed just how little they understood what they were confronting as the warriors reappeared out of another low swale, closer still.

"D. B.," Wilmot said with a sigh and rocked back in his saddle, fighting down the frustration threatening to overwhelm him, "this is too goddamned serious a situation for you to be making a joke of. I can stand to ride with you if the rest are going. But lookit them warriors now—I still think the best thing is for us to get back to the barricades before it's too late."

Instead of answering, Randall jabbed his heels into his horse and reined away. Caught by surprise, the rest quickly put their mounts into motion, yipping and cheering as they lumbered past Wilmot. Lew quickly sawed the reins around and kicked his horse into a lope to catch up with the other fifteen men who were riding at the rear of D. B. Randall's mount. They had their noses bravely pointed for Cottonwood Station.

Trouble was, a hundred or more warriors stood between them and there.

The half-naked horsemen had emerged out of the swale and put Shebang Creek behind them when they stopped, arrayed in a half-mile-long line that stretched across the road, covering the movement of their women and children and that huge herd of horses. Some of them still sat atop their ponies, while a number of them dismounted and stood alongside their animals, all of them waiting as the small band of white men drew closer and closer.

By now Wilmot could hear a little of the distant yelps and songs from those warriors. Some of them were anxiously shaking their weapons. *Hell, yes,* he thought. They'd be worked up for a fight. *There's enough of the red bastards right out there to chew us up and spit us out in the time a man takes to piss.*

But . . . still . . . those Indians were just sitting there on their ponies.

After weeks of unseasonably cool and rainy weather, the summer sun felt very, very hot on the back of Lew Wilmot's neck. Cold sweat dribbled down his backbone.

Those goddamned Injuns weren't making a move.

Just . . . waiting.

CHAPTER NINETEEN

JULY 5, 1877

EW WILMOT COULDN'T TAKE THE SILENCE ANYMORE. NOT THE WAY THEY just kept riding, riding, riding toward that broad V of the Nez Perce that surely outnumbered them by more than ten-to-one . . . none of Randall's men saying one goddamned word.

"D. B.!" Lew shouted into the dry, hot breeze of that midsummer day. "What the hell you propose to do? Just keep on aiming straight for them warriors?"

"Shuddup, Wilmot!" James L. Cearly growled like a half-sick yard dog.

"I'm fixing to charge the Indians!" Randall announced suddenly before anyone else had a chance to speak. He turned slightly in his saddle, flinging his voice behind him so that all could hear. "We'll charge the Indians!"

They hooped and hollered with that news.

But in the midst of the noise, Lew prodded their leader. "We gotta have some idea what every one of us is gonna do, Captain. What are your orders if someone's shot, or a horse goes down under one of the boys?"

Randall's eyes glared at Wilmot a moment, angry at being questioned. Then their leader said, "Any one of us is shot, or killed, or if their horse goes down—it's every other man's job to stop and pick up that man!"

That edgy bravado of his caused a wild cheer to erupt from the fourteen who were bunched behind Wilmot, Randall, and Cearly.

Moments had passed, mere heartbeats and yards gobbled up and gone, when D. B. Randall bellowed a raspy cry that was immediately answered from all their throats. Something wild and feral that swelled around their tiny group as they kicked their horses into an uneven gallop down the long, low slope of the rumpled prairie.

By then they were so close to that line of warriors that Lew could almost make out the eyes of the enemy—maybe even close enough to read some of the confusion on the faces of those Nez Perce who had no earthly idea why such a pitifully small bunch of white men would be riding straight-out for an overwhelming number of warriors.

"We got 'em!" Cearly shrieked, almost in glee. "By God, D. B.—we got 'em!"

Wilmot was screeching and hollering with the rest as the seventeen charged across that last hundred yards.

The nervous Indian ponies fought their handlers. A few of the Nez Perce rifles popped, but from where Lew sat, he didn't see anyone get hit or their horses falter with the enemy gunfire.

Ten more yards—

Some of the warrior ponies bolted away from the line as the white men slammed against the wide array of Nez Perce.

Jerking his head around, Wilmot peered over his shoulder at the Indians suddenly behind them, realizing he hadn't taken a breath in the last few moments. He dragged the hot morning's air into his lungs and hurrahed right along with the rest of them. They had made it through the enemy and were on their way for the rifle pits at Cottonwood! A little more than three miles to go. That was all!

Then the bullet snarled past his left elbow.

Wilmot twisted with a jerk and looked over his shoulder again. They were coming now. Make no mistake about that. Those warriors had whipped around, regrouped, and were on their way. Not a one of them left standing on foot any longer. Had to be more than a hundred-twenty of them all told. Not just full of false bluster now—but every last one of them angry as spit-on hens as they swarmed like summer wasps after the fleeing white men.

Off to his left, just ahead, Frank D. Vansise's horse crumpled clumsily, pitching its rider ahead into the tall grass. Vansise rolled off his shoulder, hunched over as he frantically searched the grass for his rifle.

"Henry!" Lew hollered at his friend who was coming up behind him. He reined up, levered a shell into the chamber of his saddle carbine, and brought it to his shoulder. "Get Frank! Pull 'im up behind you!"

He fired at the closest warrior, watching the rider immediately drop to the side of his pony, out of sight.

As Vansise's horse keeled over onto its side, neck thrusting as it tried to rise one last time, Henry C. Johnson, who lived close to the White Bird divide, reined up in a whirl, holding down a hand and kicking his boot out of a stirrup. Vansise grabbed the offered hand, hurtling off the ground to plop behind Johnson as Henry wrenched his horse around and both men kicked the animal into an ungainly, lumbering gallop.

Wilmot levered another cartridge into the chamber, expelling the hot copper cylinder, its shiny glitter spinning into the tall green grass beside his horse.

By now more and more of the civilians were strung out to the left of Wilmot, following Randall and Cearly into a wide depression between three low hills after Wilmot stopped to cover the rescue of Vansise. At the moment Lew yanked the reins aside to turn around and light out, more warriors burst over the edge of the prairie; tall grass split in waves as their ponies heaved in the race. But instead of following Randall as the others were, Wilmot turned slightly to the right, away from the distant rifle pits at Cottonwood.

There was no way they were going to make it to the soldiers anyway, Lew reflected. Randall and the other followers—now they were making directly for the ranch. But that would take them over ground where they wouldn't have a single advantage against the warriors . . . especially if the Indians kept picking off a horse here, dropping a rider there.

"Cearly!"

Wilmot heard Randall's anguished cry just before he fired the next shot, holding on a Nez Perce pony. He jerked aside without waiting to see if the pony fell, finding D. B. Randall was rolling onto his knees, hollering for James Cearly, who was hauling back on his reins that very moment. Randall vaulted onto his feet and scrambled for his downed horse. It lay thrashing in the grass at the bottom of that low swale, legs beginning to slow the moment he reached the animal and yanked his carbine from the saddle boot.

Spinning on his heel, Randall started hollering into the dry, hot air.

"Boys! Don't run! Don't run! Let's fight 'em! We can fight 'em here!"

Lew Wilmot turned his back on Randall, reining his horse around savagely, kicking its flanks with his boot heels, pushing it up the easy slope to the crest of that low hill. It wasn't much, save for being the highest thing in this part of the prairie now. The only knob where they could take refuge, maybe make a stand. Everything else was out of the range of possibility now, like those hills Lew had wanted them to light out for minutes ago. No way to reach them or those soldier rifle pits, either. Just this bare, grassy knob still some two miles from Cottonwood.*

Right where he felt like an inflamed boil sticking up on the rounded ass of the world. Up here where they could be easily seen by the enemy, at least the remains of Randall's brave volunteers could command a good field of fire—

"D. B.!" Wilmot shouted as loud as his raw throat would allow while he kicked his right foot free of the stirrup and spun out of the saddle to land on that leg.

Lew fired three rapid shots with his repeater, hot copper cartridges spinning, spinning, spinning out of the weapon in a jagged arc as they tumbled through shafts of bright, brilliant sunshine.

"Eph! Cash! All of you—get over here! C'mon! C'mon, now!"

Ephraim J. Brunker was the first to join Lew on the low rise. Then Cassius M. Day. Charley Case and Pete Bremen rode up together, as lathered as their horses. Lew was among them immediately, darting here and there as he shouted for them to dismount, grab their weapons and cartridges loose, then free the horses.

"Let 'em go!" Cash Day agreed. "Maybeso the Injuns chase off after 'em!"

D. H. Howser lumbered up, wobbling in the saddle, clutching his side. "I been hit."

"Git 'im down!" Brunker bawled.

They dragged Howser to the ground. Someone slapped the frightened horse on the rump and sent it clattering off, stirrups flapping crazily.

"George!" Lew hollered at Riggins the moment the man hit the ground on his feet. "Grab up D. H. there and get him over to that rail fence yonder. Stay with 'im and you watch that right flank!"

---

*One and one-half miles southeast of the present-day community of Cottonwood, Idaho, and one-third of a mile east of the memorial and sign located off U. S. 95.

Riggins glanced over his shoulder to a spot at the side of the rise where Wilmot was pointing, nodded, then sank to one knee beside Houser. "Let's go, D. H. We got a li'l walking to do."

"Cash Day!" Wilmot called out. Day fired a shot and turned before Lew continued, "Get on over to our left! You cover that side!"

Day wagged with his rifle in agreement and rose to a crouch, all hunched over as he shuffled through the tall grass in the direction opposite to that taken by Riggins and Houser.

"Where you want me, Lew?" Ben Evans shouted as he leaped off the wide back of the wagon horse a few yards down the slope from Wilmot.

Lew watched the draft animal lumber away, racing for the end of the Indian line as the warriors fully encircled their knoll. "Stay down there at the bottom, Ben!" he hollered. "You'll be out of sight where you can pick 'em off when they come by you 'cross the bottom!"

Evans shook his carbine and scurried down the slope, where he plopped to his belly, disappearing in the tall grass.

"Where's D. B.?" Bremen asked.

Quickly looking around, Lew spotted Randall hunkered down between the legs of his horse. Nearby sat James Buchanan, slowly firing his carbine as he squatted in the grass, his legs crossed and drawn up under his elbows for a proper shooting rest.

The two of them might do well enough, Wilmot thought. *Well enough to hold the bastards back for as long as it will take for the soldiers to come out and drive them off us.*

But the next time Lew Wilmot turned to gaze over his shoulder at Cottonwood Station some two miles distant, he was baffled why there weren't any figures clambering out of their rifle pits, much less mounted up and riding out on horseback.

A few minutes later Charley Case grumbled, "How long you figger we're gonna be till them soldiers come get us, Lew?"

Wilmot shook his head. "Don't know, Charley. From the looks of things, we may damn well be on our own out here."

FOR THE LAST two days George Shearer had put up with these goddamned Yankee soldiers hunkering down at Cottonwood Station, refusing to lay into the red bastards. But being forced to sit here and watch while his friends were jumped as they were riding to Norton's ranch was simply more than the Southern fighting man could take.

Besides the hundred-and-twenty-some soldiers Captain David Perry commanded, there was a bevy of civilian packers and a handful of volunteers who had shown up to add their weapons to the fight by the time those two couriers had raced into Norton's ranch earlier that morning. In something less than thirty hours, the men Captain Whipple had dispatched made it over to Howard's command across the Salmon River and back again.

To Shearer's way of thinking, there was more than enough men to take on those warriors in a stand-up, head-to-head fight. The odds were all but even!

So why hadn't Perry sent out some men to rescue the civilians when he had ordered Captain Winters's detachment to rescue those two couriers?

The first answer Perry gave the astonished volunteer was, "I'm not all that sure those are civilians. The warriors could be clever enough to wear some clothing taken from a settler's farm—arranging a ruse or decoy to lure some of my men to their deaths."

But when the shooting got closer and the civilians hunkered down on that slight rise with more than a hundred-fifty horsemen swirling around them, it was all the proof anyone needed that those weren't warriors dressed up like white men!

Yet did that blue-belly Perry send help out then? Hell no!

To Shearer the only excuse could be that those men weren't soldiers.

On top of everything else, George knew Perry had to be dwelling on that trouncing he had suffered at White Bird Canyon three weeks ago, able to think of little else!

That wasn't to say all the officers were duplicitous cowards to Shearer's way of thinking. Why, Lieutenant Edwin H. Shelton had even stepped right up to Perry and volunteered to lead a detail that he would take across that narrow strip of ground left open by the hostiles. But the commander was having nothing of it.

"It's too late to do any good," Perry equivocated by the time he got around to giving Shelton an answer. "They cannot last much longer—those men should have known better than to travel that road, as dangerous as it is."

"We owe it to them to try, Colonel," Shelton begged.

"If I did send any relief," Perry refused, "it might well sacrifice our position here."

"Here?" Shearer echoed, a heavy dose of sarcasm mixing with his Southern accent.

Perry wheeled on the civilian near his elbow. "We have a great store of arms and ammunition here. I fear that the moment I would start a detail to help the civilians on that hill, the enemy would rush in here and overrun what men I would leave behind. And all those weapons would fall into the hands of the Nez Perce. Supplies meant for General Howard's column—"

"Bullshit, Colonel," Shearer drawled. "It's a goddamned shame and an outrage to allow those men—those brave men—to remain out there and perish without you making an effort to save them!"

Perry was clearly growing red, about ready to burst, when one of his officers stepped in front of Shearer to plead their case.

"Let me ask for volunteers, Colonel," Henry Winters begged, having finally worked up the nerve to question the battalion commander. "I won't take so many men that you'll be in danger of being overwhelmed. Give me the chance to show that I can force the Indians to break off their attack simply by us starting out of here—"

"No, Captain," Perry snapped, clearly irritated with this proposal by a fellow of the same rank.

To George's way of thinking, Perry was already frustrated and angry by all those pulling and prodding him to put together a rescue.

"It's simply too late," Perry continued.

In exasperation, Shearer was turning away from the group as some of the bystanders grumbled. One of the men in the ranks grabbed the civilian's arm and spoke up, none too quietly.

"Shearer," growled Sergeant Bernard Simpson a little too loudly to be under his breath, "you civilians damn well don't need to come to the First Cavalry for any assistance—since you won't be getting any!"

"Who said that?" Perry demanded.

Not one of those officers and enlisted who stood nearby dared admit a thing or betray their compatriot from L Company.

When no one answered, Perry snapped, "I'll court-martial the next man who questions my authority or my decisions!"

"I'm volunteering to take any of your soldiers with me," Shearer spoke as he stepped up. "After all, they're my friends. Those civilians are our own home guards—"

"Request denied," Perry shot back. "I'm not letting go of a man to a lost cause."

"Goddamn it, you puffed up blue-belly martinet!" Shearer roared, wagging a finger in Perry's face for a moment, then flinging his arm out in the direction of the skirmish. "You hear that gunfire? See that gunsmoke? That fight ain't over!"

"I'll ride with you," Sergeant Simpson volunteered, stepping forward now. This soldier from L Company, First U. S. Cavalry, turned to Perry. "With all due respect, Colonel—I was the one who made the comment 'bout the civilians not getting any help from the First Cavalry."

Perry's eyes narrowed menacingly. "Sergeant?"

"Yes, sir, I owe up to it."

Perry fumed a moment as if searching for what to say, then turned to Whipple. "Captain, place this man under arrest for insubordination!"

"Colonel?" Simpson grumbled. "Let us go and fight. I joined the army to fight our enemies . . . not each other!"

"Colonel Perry," Stephen Whipple pleaded as he pushed Simpson aside, "I wish you would reconsider about the sergeant."

"The man will stay under arrest," Perry shot back. "Nor will I have you questioning my authority either!"

"Not about the sergeant, sir," Whipple said, stepping up to stand directly in front of Perry. "I'm asking you to reconsider sending a relief party while there's still men to save."

Shearer watched as Perry chewed on his lower lip for a long, breathless moment. Then it all came at a gush.

"Very well. Captain Winters!"

"Sir?"

"You'll accompany Captain Whipple and his gun crew—prepare a relief party." Whipple saluted. "How many men, sir?"

"Two companies," Perry ordered.

"I request to go along," Lieutenant Shelton offered.

Winters waved him on as both captains turned away from Perry. Shearer was lunging right in front of Whipple after a few steps, causing the officer to draw up short.

"I'm going, too," George volunteered. "I'll bring some friends with me."

"The more the merrier, as they say, Mr. Shearer," Whipple growled as he brushed by the civilian. "The more the merrier."

CHAPTER TWENTY

JULY 5, 1877

WHEN GEORGE SHEARER TURNED AROUND TO FETCH HIS HORSE, HE RAN right into a friend, Paul Guiterman, who already had the reins to their animals in his hands.

"I figger they're 'bout out of cartridges, George," the stocky civilian declared. "And it's gonna take some before these soldiers are saddled up to ride out."

Shearer studied the look on his friend's face a moment before saying, "Maybeso we ought'n give it a try on our own?"

"I was hoping you was thinking same as me," Guiterman admitted. "I stuffed ever' bullet I could in our saddlebags."

Shearer grinned at the man as he grabbed his reins and stuffed a boot into the stirrup. "Sure you was a Yankee during the war, Paul?"

"I was Union down to my soles, you ol' Reb." Guiterman swung up. "But I can still give one hell of a Rebel yell."

As Shearer jabbed his heels into the horse's ribs, he said, "Better unlimber your tongue—'cause them Injuns just opened up a nice li'l road for us to sashay right on through!"

LEW WILMOT WASN'T sure if his eyes or his ears were deceiving him. But—gloree! It looked as if two riders were sprinting their horses right through a narrow gap the warriors had left open between the soldiers' camp at Cottonwood and the knoll where D. B. Randall's "Brave Seventeen" were fighting for their lives.

"Lew! By God, here we come!"

Wilmot blinked, and blinked again, not sure what was happening when dim, distant figures emerged from Norton's ranch and started wriggling their way. The way his eyes were swimming with moisture and the sting of sweat, the man wasn't sure just what he saw. All through the fight, Lew couldn't get the image of that pink, wrinkled, bawling baby boy of his out of his mind. Now as he dragged the back of a hand under his runny nose, Wilmot realized he just might see Louisa and the girls again. Just might get himself a chance to watch that boy rise up to manhood, too.

It was George Shearer hollering at him as the pair of riders approached—that slow-talking, hard-drinking Southern-born transplant who claimed he had served on the staff of no less than Robert E. Lee himself—and Paul Guiterman, both of them yanking back on their reins, horse hooves skidding, stirring dust into the golden air, sweat slinging off the animals and men alike as a few of Randall's men came lumbering out of the grass the moment Shearer and Guiterman stuffed their hands into those saddlebags and started tossing out boxes of ammunition.

".45-70?" a man asked.

"Here you go," Shearer replied, tossing him a carton of twenty as the Nez Perce bullets sang around them.

"Any .44?"

"I brung some," Guiterman declared.

"Where's ever'one else?" Shearer asked as he knelt beside Wilmot.

Lew was concentrating on holding the warriors back a good distance, where he knew the Indians weren't all that sharp with their rifles. "You're looking at us."

"How many was comin'?"

"Seventeen."

"Shit," Shearer murmured. "Hope like hell we can hold 'em a li'l longer, Lew. Them blue-bellies sure do know how to dillydally when it suits 'em."

"Dillydally?"

"We finally shamed that Colonel Perry into sending you some relief."

Wilmot felt the smile grow from within. "You mean you ain't the only relief that's coming, George?"

"Lookee there now, you side-talking cuss you," Shearer said, slapping Wilmot on the shoulder and pointing. "There come your soldiers now!"

"Wh-where you going?" Lew asked as George Shearer leaped to his feet and lunged toward his ground-hobbled horse.

"Them Yankee blues gonna be all day getting here," Shearer grumbled as he flung himself up onto the horse's back. "I'm fixin' to go nudge 'em to come a li'l faster, is all. Gimme some cover fire whilst I ride outta here, will you, Lew?"

Wilmot levered and fired, levered and fired again, over and over, then flicked a glance at that narrow gauntlet Shearer was racing through for a second time.

Beyond the lone rider, the soldiers were throwing out an overly wide, skimpy line of skirmishers as they began their two-mile advance on that low knoll east of the road ranch. As the wide advance of fifteen foot soldiers emerged from the mouth of the ravine known as Cottonwood Canyon, Randall's survivors could next spot about twice that many soldiers marching behind them in a much tighter formation. With his small looking glass Lew was able to see that they were accompanied by a Gatling gun. As this unit began to make its crossing behind the fifteen skirmishers, about twenty more soldiers, all mounted, shuffled into view and began to cut obliquely across the skirmishers' path—

Of a sudden, the hiss of one last bullet from the Nez Perce quickly reminded Lew Wilmot that the enemy still had them all but encircled. But as he turtled his head into his shoulders and peered around at the naked horsemen, he found the warriors drawing back. While the skirmishers plodded on at an angle that would eventually put them in the Indians' front some distance from the knoll, the larger unit of foot soldiers and those eighteen horse soldiers kept on for the besieged civilians.

In the middistance Wilmot could make out a few shouts and screams from the hostiles as they pranced about, shaking their bows and carbines at the soldiers. But the fighting was over.

"What you figger they're telling us?" Henry Johnson asked.

Lew sighed. "Saying there's gonna be another day, another fight, and a lot more killing before this war's ever settled."

"Lew!"

Wilmot whirled at the cry of his name. "George!" he cried, his throat sore and raspy from overuse. "By damn—you hurried them Yankee soldiers, you ol' Reb you!"

Shading his eyes in the bright afternoon sun as he peered up at Shearer as the man came skidding to a halt again on the sweeping slope of their knoll, Lew suddenly realized just how many hours they had managed to hold off those one hundred fifty warriors. "Get down off that horse!" he yelled at Shearer, starting toward his friend, his thoughts thickened with hope—

He was surprised when he heard a rifleshot from close by, watched the bullet wing Shearer's horse across the withers. The animal began to buck and dance as the civilian struggled to bring the mount under control. Blood seeped down its neck.

"George, by God—get down outta that saddle!"

Vaulting from the back of the wounded horse, Shearer lunged toward Wilmot as a squad of soldiers started loping for the Indian sniper's position. The two friends shook and pounded backs; then Shearer stepped back as a few of the other survivors stomped up at the same moment the first of the cavalry were reaching the hilltop.

His eyes darting about, Shearer asked, "Where's D. B.?"

Wilmot turned on his heel. Pointing, he exclaimed, "Randall was down there, last I saw of him. There! That's his horse on the ground!"

The two were off in a sprint, down the slope to the grassy swale where Lew had watched D. B. Randall's horse crumple to the ground early in the seige. As he raced closer and closer, Wilmot spotted the back of Randall's head resting against the animal's motionless front flank. D. B. was reclining back in the tangle of the horse's legs as Wilmot leaped around the rear hooves and slid to a stop. His breath caught when he saw the dark, shiny smear that covered the whole of his friend's chest, like he'd spilled an entire bowl of blackberry preserves on himself at breakfast that morning—

"D. B.!"

The eyes fluttered slightly, eventually opening halfway. "That you? That Lew Wilmot?"

He held his face down close. "It's over, D. B. Gonna get you to some help now." And laid his palm against the wet, sticky, black stain on that shirt.

"I'm mortal hurt, Lew"—then he coughed, wet and long. "I ain't goin' nowhere now. This gonna be where I die." The eyes seemed to widen perceptibly as Lew moved over Randall, making some shade for the wounded man's face. "Got any water?"

He quickly glanced up at Shearer. "George? You get a canteen for D. B.?"

When the water came, Randall drank a little, then coughed some more, bringing up gouts of blood, almost like he was heaving from a terrible stomach wound as well. When he finally caught his breath and had licked some blood from his bottom lip, D. B. Randall looked up at the two civilians.

His eyes fluttered as he asked, "Tell . . . tell my wife—"

Then the eyelids didn't tremble anymore. They simply stopped moving. For a long time Wilmot and Shearer squatted there by their forty-four-year-old friend. Probably to be sure before Wilmot gently eased the eyelids back down and rose to his feet, watching the approach of an empty lumber wagon rattling toward the bottom of the slope.

James Cearly came up. "D. B.?"

Lew nodded. "He's dead."

"Ben, too."

"Where?" Shearer asked.

Cearly pointed. "No more'n three other boys wounded."*

"That's all?" George Shearer asked, his voice rising a pitch in amazement.

Wilmot looked around them, counting five dead horses, their big carcasses scattered from the long depression to the top of the low rise where he had started their stand.

"We held 'em off, by Jupiter!" Cash Day exclaimed. "Can't believe it's over."

"It ain't over for none of us," Lew declared sourly. "This is far from over—"

"You civilians get your dead and wounded loaded up in that wagon!" announced one of the mounted soldiers Wilmot recognized as the officer called Winters. "I'm moving my forces back to Camp Rains."

"Camp Rains?" Lew repeated, looking at Shearer.

The civilian nodded. "They named their bivouac at Norton's place after the dead officer what led his scouting party into an ambush couple days back. Ain't that just like a Yankee soldier's way of things? Givin' honor to that dead Lieutenant Rains who got hisself killed and ever'body else with him?"

DURING ALL THAT fighting, Yellow Wolf wondered why the soldiers refused to budge from their squirrel holes they had dug. Instead of coming out to save all the Shadows, for the longest time they instead chose to merely watch the skirmishing from long distance. No matter; it was a glorious fight while it lasted. Lots of riding past the Shadow guns at a gallop, some of the men crawling on their bellies through the tall grass to get close enough to the white men to see faces clearly.

That's when Yellow Wolf and his friend *Wemastahtus* recognized one of the young Shadows.

"He is Charley Crooks?" asked *Wemastahtus* in a whisper after they had all stared in amazement.

---

*Charles Johnson, Alonzo B. Leland, and D. H. Howser (who subsequently died of his wounds).

"No," Yellow Wolf replied. "That Charley was at the fight in *Lahmotta.* This is another Charley, son of a settler who raises his horses at the bottom of the hills, this side of the White Bird Hill."

"John-son?" *Wemastahtus* asked.

With a nod, Yellow Wolf said, "I think it is John-son's boy, the one called Charley." He held his head up slightly and yelled at the others his announcement: "John-son's boy, Charley . . . he is here with the other Shadows. He's a friend, so do not hurt him! We should do him no harm!"

"Who is this?" shouted *Weesculatat,* that older warrior who had urged Yellow Wolf to come along for the fight. His pony pranced up, boldly making a target of its rider.

"A Shadow friend of ours!" Yellow Wolf shouted, waving his arm emphatically for *Weesculatat* to dismount. "Get down! This Shadow who was a friend is shooting right at us!"

A bullet suddenly sang through the grass between the pair hiding in the grass, a bullet from John-son's location. *Weesculatat* dropped to the ground, kneeling as he held onto the long single rein knotted around his pony's lower jaw.

"See, *Weesculatat?* This Charley John-son is shooting at us now!" *Wemastahtus* cried.

"I cannot see this friend of yours," *Weesculatat* said as he turned, studying the white men scattered across the slope. "Which one is he?"

A bullet from one of the white man guns struck the older man's horse, causing the frightened animal to rear and hop in pain and fear. *Weesculatat* bolted to his feet, yanking on the long rein, doing what he could to gain control of the frightened animal as Shadow bullets snarled around them.

"Get down!" Yellow Wolf shouted as he started to reach up an arm to pull *Weesculatat* down.

But the older warrior was twisted away by the spooked pony—

Yellow Wolf flinched the instant he heard the slap of lead against flesh. *Weesculatat* let out a little groan as he collapsed forward into the grass, clutching at his knee. Blood was seeping between the fingers of both hands, but he was an older man, a proven warrior who had control of his voice, so he did not cry out when he was hit by Charley John-son's bullet.

Instead, he looked up at the other two and said, "Time for us to go from here."

"I can help you," Yellow Wolf offered.

"I think I can make it on my own, brother," *Weesculatat* explained, using that familial term to honor a friend.

The moment Yellow Wolf turned his head to look back at the young white man who was shooting at them, the older warrior pushed himself up from the grass. A puff of smoke immediately spurted from the muzzle of John-son's gun and another bullet hit *Weesculatat,* this time in the back, throwing him facedown into the grass but not blowing out a hole in his bare chest.

"This Charley John-son," Yellow Wolf yelped in confusion. "I thought he and his father were our friends!"

As *Wemastahtus* started to crawl toward *Weesculatat,* more bullets snarled into the grass and he stopped where he lay. He and Yellow Wolf could both hear the older man's loud breathing, coming hard and wet.

"I will come get you!" Yellow Wolf said. "Wait for me to come!"

"N-no," *Weesculatat* replied, his voice no longer strong as it had been only moments ago. "I can still get away on my own. The bullet did not come out . . ."

Weesculatat slowly rose to his hands and knees in the grass, his head slung loosely between his shoulders like that of a weary dog as he wobbled, eventually pulling himself up to a squatting position, where he looked down at his chest again.

Then he turned to peer back at the two warriors nearby. "See, the bullet that hit me in the back did not come out—"

Another shot from John-son's gun slammed into *Weesculatat* from the side, driving him off his knees, where he skidded in the grass a foot, then lay still, gasping louder and louder, his fingers clawing up a handful of the green shafts.

He was barely breathing when Yellow Wolf reached him. Three bullets. The first would have made him lame, if only he had stayed low. It made Yellow Wolf angry in his belly, very mad to think that an old friend of theirs had done this to *Weesculatat*. Yellow Wolf knew most of the other young men had refrained from shooting at this Charley John-son because his family were old friends of the Non-Treaty bands. But—hard as it was for Yellow Wolf to consider—maybe no white man would ever be a friend to the *Nee-Me-Poo* again.

Not long after Yellow Wolf reached the older warrior, many of Two Moon's warriors started to drift back toward their herd and migrating village, breaking off the surround in favor of putting themselves between the white men and their families once more. He could not blame the others—none of them had any idea when the soldiers would emerge from their hollows or what they would do when they got brave enough to make a fight of it while the camp was in the open and vulnerable.

The other warriors under *Ollokot* did what they could to keep lots of pressure on the outnumbered Shadows with their loud guns—repeating weapons the warriors respected, like the rifle Yellow Wolf himself owned, a lever-action carbine his mother held in safekeeping for him back in Looking Glass's village. More than the single-shot soldier guns, these warriors had a healthy respect for the Shadows' rapid-firing repeaters.

Into the afternoon *Ollokot*'s men wondered if the *suapies* would ever emerge from their hollows. That did not happen until the sun was halfway down in the sky toward its evening set. And then they came out in that opening made when Two Moon's fighters drifted away, soldiers advancing with a big, many-noises gun that rumbled right in the front of some walking soldiers.

"Let us quit for a while!" *Ollokot* shouted as he raced past on his horse, the fringes sewn at the heels of his moccasins flying in the hot breeze like the mane and tail of his pony.

His first horse had been shot out from under him in the early stages of the fight, but his youngest wife, known as *Aihits Palojami*, known as Fair Land, had been watching from a nearby hilltop and quickly brought him another good fighting horse as the bullets landed around them both.

Two others came to join Yellow Wolf and *Wemastahtus*, helping to drag *Weesculatat* back from danger. In a grassy depression they laid the older man over the back of a horse and started with him to the village that would be making camp this afternoon in the canyon of the Cottonwood at *Piswah Ilppilp Pah*, the Place of Red Rocks. Another man had been wounded, but not nearly as bad. *Sewattis Hihhih*, the warrior known as White Cloud, was a half brother of Two Moons. A man of short stature, White Cloud was nonetheless a very brave fighter, shot from his pony during a daring charge on the Shadows.

Despite the rescue of those white men by the *suapies*, the fighting chiefs had accomplished what they had set out to do. If that small war party of Shadows had reached the soldier camp that afternoon, the chances were good the white men would have believed themselves strong enough to leave their camp and venture onto the prairie, where they would have attacked the village then migrating to Cottonwood Creek. The women and children would have been threatened, havoc caused by the Shadows.

As it was, the young men had prevented any interruption in the camp's march. The white survivors of the fight limped back with the soldiers to their hollows, and the village was able to reach *Piswah Ilppilp Pah* without any trouble. Now the mouth of the Cottonwood at the Clearwater was no more than a matter of two marches, three at the most, away. They were not running. No, they were in full control now. Cut-Off Arm and his big army were many days and far, far away across a turbulent river. The warriors had neutralized the only possible threat from the burrow soldiers and now were in the clear.

Over there in the canyons of the Clearwater, the Non-Treaty bands would take refuge with Looking Glass's people—themselves fleeing a band of soldiers. The night they had crossed the Salmon and were camped at *Aipadass*, word had come that the *suapies* had attacked the old peace talker, Looking Glass! Now even he was ready to join the other war chiefs and drive the Shadows from the land of the *Nee-Me-Poo* for all time.

Yellow Wolf felt strong in his heart.

Because of what the fighting men had accomplished that day, those *suapies* entrenched far up the Cottonwood would not dare leave their burrows to follow the village. And Cut-Off Arm was still far, far away on the other side of the Salmon, mired down in mud with his "day-after-tomorrow army."

CHAPTER TWENTY-ONE

JULY 5–7, 1877

BY TELEGRAPH

General Grant Leaves England for the Continent.

Later Dispatches from the
Oregon Indian War.

OREGON.

Latest from the Indian War.
PORTLAND, July 5.— A courier arrived at Lewiston, July 2d, from Kamia, says Colonel Whipple and his command had an engagement with the Looking-glass band on Clear Water, to-day. Four Indians were killed and left on the field dead. Many others were wounded. The squaws and children took to the river and several were drowned. The fighting was still going on when the courier left. Looking-glass's band is estimated by scouts to number about 400. At three o'clock this morning a courier arrived, having left General Howard's camp on the night of the 29th. The troops had made a crossing that day, and scouts who had been out on the hills found stock but no Indians. The latter are believed to have gone down toward the mouth of the Salmon, and to be making for Gray's crossing on the Salmon, thence crossing on Snake river at the mouth of the Grande Ronde. Dispatches were forwarded to Walla Walla, to be telegraphed, so as to apprise persons in Grande Ronde and Wallowapays.

HIS FIRST LOOK AT A NEZ PERCE HAD BEEN FROM SOMEWHAT OF A DIStance: across the Salmon River that is, back there days and many, many miles ago, just before General Oliver Otis Howard had somehow willed his army column to this western side of the furious and foamy Salmon River.

An Easterner by birth and Harvard graduate by way of laurels, Thomas

A. Sutherland had done a bit of traveling in Europe and the Middle East through the aid of some family money before he ended up in Portland, Oregon, working as an ill-paid stringer for the *Standard*. The very afternoon the newsroom was first abuzz with reports of the Nez Perce outbreak, the twenty-seven-year-old had abandoned everything else and marched into his editor's office, applying for this opportunity to march into the field when the army set off on its campaign to punish the hostiles, just as the army always had.

"Newsmen have always been along with the principal officer," he had declared boldly.

"And who would that be now?" he was asked.

"Why, I suppose it would be Howard himself. A general, one-armed, lost it in the Civil War, you see. I've looked up what I can on him. General Oliver Otis Howard—I shall attach myself to him."

"Just the way Mark Kellogg attached himself to Custer, will you?"

Sutherland had immediately reacted to the reference. He felt his face drain of blood as he remembered how Kellogg had gone in with Custer at the death. Two days later they had found the civilian's body among the butchered and mutilated dead.

"I don't think that has any way of happening," he retorted, tugging at his collar in the editor's steamy third-floor office. "Those were the mighty Sioux, after all. Crazy Horse, Sitting Bull—those Sioux. But these . . . these are the . . . well, they're just Nez Perce, sir."

"Very well," his editor had agreed. "I'll grant you a month's leave with the same rate of pay. Send in your dispatches by courier or telegraph if you can, but I'm not going to pay for anything extravagant from you, young man."

His heart leaped in his chest. "No, sir. Nothing extravagant at all!"

Thomas Sutherland wasn't dull-witted, either. He promptly sprinted down to the telegraph office and fired off several telegrams he sent speeding all the way across the continent, paying for the lofty charges out of his own pocket on the speculation that one of the newspapers would bite. Three days later, as he was making his final preparations to embark for Lewiston, Idaho, that very afternoon, Sutherland had received word from not only the San Francisco *Chronicle* but no less than the New York *Herald* itself! Why, he'd have eyes from coast to coast reading his copy written at the front.

He reached Lewiston the following evening, finding the town patrolled by eighty armed men under torchlight, ever watchful of any dark-skinned intruder. In the saddle before dawn the following morning, pulling his packhorse, Sutherland was bound for Fort Lapwai and points south where he could track down Howard's column.

While he soon found out he wasn't the only correspondent hurrying to the front, he alone enjoyed the élan and prestige of arriving with credentials from two of the most prestigious papers in the entire country.

"My editors wanted to assure themselves of a firsthand account for their readers on both coasts," he had explained when first introduced to the general commanding.

Clearly, such status was not lost on the famous one-armed Union general and survivor of the scandals in the Freedmen's Bureau. Since that first day, the twenty-ninth of June, Sutherland had been messing with Howard and the general's staff.

"Extend young Sutherland here every courtesy," Howard had told his headquarters staff and the officer corps that night before they made their first attempt to cross the Salmon after the Nez Perce. "See that he is not wanting for the details that will tell his readers just what a noble effort this army and its campaign is all about."

Not that there weren't times when Sutherland didn't wonder just what he had bitten off, slogging up the narrow trail toward the Seven Devils area, high into a country where nothing but grass grew and even the mules had trouble staying upright. The soldiers lost a few of the overburdened ones careening down the side of the Salmon River canyon, tumbling some two thousand feet to a rocky death below. Cold and wet nights, when it alternated between rain and snow, followed by foggy, drizzly days. And when the sun came out the men became even more miserable when their dampened clothing gave each one of them a steam bath in the saddle!

But there were small victories as well, like the discovery two days ago of those caches left behind by the fleeing hostiles at Canoe Encampment some eight miles below Pittsburgh Landing on the Snake River—proof, so the officers claimed, that Joseph's Indians had grown desperate and were fully on the run now.

Still, it had been many days now since the army had struggled across the Salmon into this unforgiving wilderness, and the best scouting reports said the enemy was miles ahead of them. Then as the correspondent rode with Howard's advance on the afternoon of the fifth, word sent with friendly trackers from Captain Whipple at Cottonwood relayed how Joseph's hostiles had recrossed the river up ahead at a place called Craig Billy Crossing, putting not only distance but also days between them and the army in striking across the Camas Prairie.

Sutherland could read the utter frustration and seething anger on the general's face as they descended to the mouth of Billy Creek—a canyon so narrow the command had to work their way down single-file—and these officers, proven veterans of the Civil War, all studied the snow-swollen torrent that was the Salmon River . . . wondering how the Nez Perce had gotten their horse herd across, how they had managed to negotiate their women and children and camp equipage across that river racing more than seven miles per hour, foaming and tumbling like a caldron. Wondering, Sutherland knew, how they themselves were now going to effect this army's crossing, too.

That's when Christian tracker James Reuben demonstrated how Joseph's people had reached the far side by swimming his horse into the frothy current to the north bank, then returning in due fashion. But when one of the white scouts, Frank Parker, bravely attempted the same feat, he got no farther than a few yards from the shore before the mighty current made him think retreat was a far better choice. Then Reuben instructed Howard in the old craft of constructing bull boats—but this column had few buffalo hides!

After sending two volunteers, Jack Carleton and "Laughing" Williams, upstream to commandeer some boats the command could use in ferrying men and supplies across the Salmon, Howard learned that the pair of scouts had located a boat—but in coming downstream to Billy Creek they had encountered a series of turbulent rapids, capsized, and barely escaped the river with their lives.

That's when Second Lieutenant Harrison G. Otis, artilleryman, was bold enough to point out the poor cabin standing nearby and asked one of the interpreters to see if any of the friendlies along knew what the white owner's name was.

"Why is that of any import to our crossing?" asked the general's young aide, Lieutenant C. E. S. Wood.

"Because," Otis suggested, "we could ask of the owner to disassemble it and construct a raft."

"Capital idea, sir!" Howard roared, slapping his one glove against that left thigh in exuberance.

As it turned out, the poor hovel didn't belong to a white homesteader at all.

"His name is Luke Billy?" Howard repeated as Sutherland wet the end of his pencil on the tip of his tongue and scratched down the pertinent details in his small leather-bound field ledger.

"That's what the white men call him," Ad Chapman said, waving up one of the trackers from Lapwai. "He's a friendly himself."

"This one?" Howard asked. When the interpreter nodded, he continued, "Ask him if we can dismantle his cabin—use it for a raft to cross the river here and pursue the Joseph bands."

Without delay, Luke Billy readily agreed and even helped the young Otis and his soldiers tear down the roof and walls of his poor house here at the mouth of Billy Creek. At the same time, the cavalry was collecting all their lariats, those three-fifths-inch ropes each man was assigned to picket his mount each night, used in erecting company rows in bivouac. The logs proved to be no skimpy planks. Instead, they were at least a foot thick, measuring a foot wide by some forty feet in length. The sweating, bare-backed enlisted men hauled the rain-soaked timbers down to the bank of the Salmon, where the engineers and artillery officers took over, supervising the assembly of that huge raft on which General Oliver Otis Howard's fortunes would soon sail some two hundred yards across the white-capped, wind-whipped surface of the Salmon, so he could continue his dogged pursuit of Joseph and his bloodstained henchmen.

God knows Howard had the manpower and the resources coming to crush the upstart rebels . . . if only the army could only get the hostiles to stop and fight. It seemed that not only the division commander, McDowell, but also the leaders of the army itself in Washington wanted to snuff out this little fire, and as quickly as possible.

To Sutherland's way of thinking, despite the general's numerous setbacks, Howard simply refused to regard the Nez Perce as a serious threat. What he was fearful of more than anything else was the possibility that Joseph's hostiles would form a junction with the Indians south in the valley of the Weiser River, or with the noisy renegades along the Columbia River, even the small bands of Spokanes and other inconsequential tribes to the north and northwest who, while they were no danger of and by themselves, could make for a lot of trouble when confederated under Chief Joseph's bloody outlaw banner.

"You do realize there are some twelve thousand Indians residing in the Northwest, Mr. Sutherland," the general declared. "If Joseph is able to score a decisive victory over our forces, why, the disaffected among those tribes would likely swell the ranks of Joseph's fighting men. Instead of us having to fight hundreds, my army would be pitted against thousands! I simply must stop them and stamp out this fire in the next few days."

So as his troops sweated and groused constructing their huge raft of hewn timbers that fifth day of July, Howard disclosed to Sutherland the details of just what plans he had put into operation to counter such threats of a full-scale territorial outbreak.

"Counting what I presently have in this column, and what is already on its way to me," Howard explained, "I'll soon have ten companies of cavalry—six hundred and seventeen men. In addition, Mr. Sutherland, I'll lead six companies of infantry, one hundred and seventy-seven men. Add to that five companies of artillery, more than one hundred and sixty-six men, and your final tally shows that I'll presently be leading an army of more than nine hundred and sixty soldiers drawn from two departments of the army. Once we catch up to the Non-Treaty bands, you can plainly see why this war will be brought to a swift and dramatic conclusion."

"How long do you believe that will take, General?" he had asked while the raft took shape.

"No more than a matter of days," Howard proposed. "Tell your readers, east and west, that we'll have this outbreak over within a matter of days."

Taking what ropes they hadn't used in constructing the bulky raft, the soldiers tied the lariats end-to-end, fastening one end to the rivercraft, the other wrapped around a stout tree so that a gang of some two dozen soldiers could belay the raft into the river—hoping the men on the craft could get drift close enough to the opposite shore that a soldier could plunge into the current with a section of rope over his shoulder and make it to the north bank, where he would secure the line to another tree. Whereupon Howard would have his ferryboat!

Despite their best efforts to construct that raft, Howard's men were stymied by the full fury of the Salmon on the morning of the sixth.

While Lieutenant Otis's crew prepared to launch their raft, Lieutenant Parnell of the First U. S. Cavalry and fifteen selected men stripped naked, mounted bareback, and attempted to force the horse herd across the river. After losing more than a dozen to the Salmon, the sixteen soldiers admitted defeat and turned back to the south bank. Then came the most stinging disappointment of all.

The unimaginable power of that river was simply too much for that raft the soldiers constructed on the south bank. It came apart in the torrential current, ropes splitting and hewn timbers creaking as they were ground into nothing more than children's jackstraws by this mighty western river. Otis, his men, and matériel were all tossed into the frothy current and hurtled downstream more than four miles until they could struggle to one shore or the other. The tossing timbers of Luke Billy's dismantled cabin tumbled on, making for a junction with the Snake . . . and Lieutenant Otis fondly went down in campaign legend as "Crusoe."

Indeed, some of the young man's fellow officers quickly made up a campaign ditty, sung to the tune of "Turn Back the Pharaoh's Army":

"The raft went down the river, hal-le-lu!"

Despite those grand attempts at good humor, Sutherland watched how that string of defeats registered on Howard's bearded face. Hell, he felt the frustration take root in himself—realizing how these unschooled warrior bands had outwitted West Point's finest graduates and methodologies at every turn!

Perhaps most depressing to the general was the news brought to him here at Craig Billy Crossing by those two Christian trackers James Reuben and Captain John Levi, a report that the hostiles were in the neighborhood of Norton's ranch, where Captain David Perry had established a base of operations on the Camas Prairie. What few depressing details Sutherland overheard quickly proved that Perry's soldiers were not up to the task of stopping Joseph's devils as the Non-Treaty bands pressed on east for the Clearwater, where they would likely join forces with the Looking Glass village Captain Whipple had failed to neutralize.

After watching his cavalry's failure in their attempt to swim their horses across on the afternoon of the sixth, followed by the disintegration of Lieutenant Otis's raft on the seventh, Howard had had himself enough of this northern crossing. The shortest line that would carry him to the seat of the conflicts was to turn back upstream.

Ordering the destruction of some twenty ponies the Non-Treaties had abandoned on the south bank before their crossing, the general gave the command for a countermarch. Noisy, none-too-quiet grumbling reigned as soldiers who had just spent the last five days in this Salmon River wilderness were now told to retrace their steps back through those same hills to that crossing opposite the mouth of White Bird Creek . . . where they had first attempted to tackle this river back on the twenty-ninth of June!

"The Non-Treaties have no intention of surrendering anytime soon, Mr. Sutherland," explained young Lieutenant Wood in confidence the following evening, 7 July, when they were camped nearly opposite Rocky Canyon, close by the traditional Nez Perce gathering ground.

Having left orders for his infantry to come on with all possible speed, Howard had pushed ahead with his cavalry—accomplishing that retrograde march in something less than two days! Sutherland asked, "The general doesn't believe Joseph and his outlaws are running?"

Wood shook his head. "First came word of the defeat of Lieutenant Rains and his scouting detail, and now friendlies have brought us news of Colonel Perry's skirmishes with the hostiles around his Cottonwood bivouac. General Howard isn't waiting until first light to dispatch help: He's sending McConville's and Hunter's volunteer companies across the river here at Rocky Canyon to make their way to Colonel Perry's troops at Camp Rains."

"The general shouldn't be angry with himself," Sutherland observed.

Wood asked, "Why shouldn't he be upset with these setbacks? We're still more than a day from reaching our crossing at White Bird Creek and Joseph's henchmen are roaming at will!"

"But Howard's demonstration on this side of the Salmon has had a great effect on the hostiles, Lieutenant," Thomas argued. "By getting this great army over here and keeping them in motion, he prevented Joseph from leading his hostiles south and west back to the naturally fortified country of his Wallowa homeland. Now he can't reach those impregnable valleys with his herds of cattle and horses to hold out against five or six times his number of fighting men. Don't you see?"

Wood's brow knit in consternation. "See what?"

Thomas had warmed to his argument. "Now Joseph and the other renegade chiefs have been forced out onto the open ground of the Camas Prairie—where they have no cover. In sending those volunteer companies across the river, General Howard is executing a bold maneuver. If all the civilians now holed up at Grangeville and Mount Idaho can be united with Colonel Perry, surely they can stop the enemy village and turn it back on General Howard . . . if not annihilate the renegades outright by themselves."

CHAPTER TWENTY-TWO

JULY 8, 1877

BY TELEGRAPH

Several Stores and Contents
Burned at Pueblo.

General Grant Quietly Arrives
at Brussels.

OREGON.

Later from the Indian War.

SAN FRANCISCO, July 6.—A dispatch to the Portland News from General Howard's camp, on the Salmon River, up to June 30th, says: Five Indians passed along Bald Mountain, opposite camp on the 29th, in full view of the soldiers. General Howard is hurrying with all possible dispatch in order to pursue or find the direction taken by the Indians. If the trail indicates that Joseph intends escaping to the buffalo country, General Howard will immediately retrace his steps to Lewiston, and endeavor to head him off by way of Harmon's creek. Captain Conneville, of the Lewiston volunteers, starts to-day to skirmish the country in the vicinity of Slate creek to find the direction Joseph has taken. The Malbar Indians, in Baker county, Oregon, are restless, and fears are entertained that they will effect a junction with the hostiles. The squaw men say that Joseph has gone toward Spokane river mill, and taken up his position in impassable gulches and canons, intending to stay and fight it out in Walowa valley. The opinion at headquarters is that he will strike for the buffalo country. Joseph has now a day and a half start on the troops. General Howard has telegraphed for a regiment of regulars, which it is understood can get here in ten days from Omaha,

Nebraska. He has now about 500 men, three howitzers, and two Gatling guns.

THE LAST THREE DAYS SINCE THAT FIGHT ON THE KNOLL AND THE ARMY'S shilly-shallying in sending out a rescue from Cottonwood had been little more than an angry blur for Lew Wilmot.

A little while after the survivors reached Norton's ranch with their dead and wounded packed in that lumber wagon, D. H. Howser died from his injuries.

Fires were refed near twilight, not long before more than sixty civilians galloped in from the southwest, just after 6:00 P.M. It was a happy reunion for both groups: Perry's soldiers were relieved for the reinforcements who had just managed to reach them after leaving Howard's column on the far side of the Salmon, and the citizens were gratified to reach the security of the army bivouac after a narrow escape with an Indian ambush in Rocky Canyon.

Finding that the leader of the Idaho volunteers was an acquaintance from Lewiston, Edward McConville—a Civil War veteran and a steady hand who ofttimes put Wilmot up when he and Pete Ready came north to pick up supplies at that Snake riverport town, it turned out to be a happy, and intriguing, reunion.

"Tell me what happened out there today," Ed had asked that evening of the fifth as he settled onto his haunches beside Wilmot's fire.

"Ain't so much what happened out there on the prairie," Lew disclosed, "as it was what *didn't* happen right here in the soldier camp."

Then Wilmot let fly with the whole story, not dismissing a single detail about the fight that had done nothing to improve the strained, prickly relations between the army and the local civilians. Even George Shearer showed up to fill in some gaps in the story by divulging those arguments he had heard between officers, the temporary arrest of Sergeant Simpson for disorderly conduct, and Shearer's own dash to reach the volunteers ahead of the wary soldiers.

"That war party was already pulling off when the soldiers decided to come rescue us," Wilmot sneered. "Wasn't any fight left in the Injuns by then—so it was safe for them soldiers to come out to help us."

"I'll bet some of the same bunch pulled off you came to lay an ambush for us," McConville disclosed. "You 'member which way they rode away from your hill?"

Wilmot shook his head. "Can't say as I do. Just glad to see 'em go! Why, you figger your outfit was jumped by the same Injuns killed Randall and Ben Evans?"

"Had to be the same li'l red bastards," George Shearer declared bitterly. Earlier that evening he had been elected as "major" of McConville's militia.

"I'd lay a month's wages they was the same redskins," McConville asserted, then went on to tell how General Howard had ordered his bunch and William Hunter's civilians to go to Whipple's aid.

To reach the army's camp at Cottonwood, the volunteers had stripped naked to swim their horses across the Salmon just above the mouth of Rocky

Canyon. But that was only the beginning of their adventurous ride. Because that route offered the fastest journey out of the Salmon River breaks, all sixty-seven riders hurriedly redressed in their clothes and started into the narrowing canyon, repeatedly peering up at those walls towering some two thousand feet over their heads. Every man was understandably on edge, wary of ambush and knowing just how vulnerable they were. . . . The whole bunch nearly jumped out of their skins when they spotted a dozen warriors when they popped into sight about two hundred yards up the trail.

"Some of the fellas were more'n ready for a fight by then," McConville confessed. "No matter it was only a handful of the redskins."

But cooler heads prevailed and both leaders decided they had to get themselves out of that canyon. After all, their argument went, those had to be decoys, nothing less than tempting bait a larger war party was dangling out to draw the white men farther and farther into the ever-narrowing canyon.

"So we backtracked a ways and somehow managed to scramble up the side on a deer trail to reach the prairie," McConville declared. "Once we were all together on top, we lit out east for Johnson's ranch, then come round the head of the canyon, making for Cottonwood on the run."

"You see anything more of them Injuns as you come in?" Shearer asked.

The leader wagged his head. "Nothing but some smoke signals on Craig's Mountain, and a big dust cloud off the far side of Camas Prairie."

"Over toward the South Fork?" Wilmot asked.

McConville nodded. "Yep—there's no doubt that village is making for the Clearwater."

Shearer proposed, "Don't you fellas think the army would appreciate knowing where the Injuns are camped once the red bastards make theirselves to home on the South Fork?"

"Damn fine idea, George," McConville said, a twinkle coming to his eye. "What say we head back to Mount Idaho? That's where we can rest up a day or so, while we remount our outfit on some fresh horses. We can cull what we need outta that herd you run off from Looking Glass's camp."

"Once we got horses, then what?" Wilmot asked.

McConville grinned. "We have ourselves a little look-see over toward the Clearwater."

The next morning, 6 July, McConville's volunteers had escorted Randall's dead and wounded, along with most of the survivors, out of Cottonwood Station, bound for Mount Idaho. About the same time, Captain Whipple's men mounted up to ride west with Assistant Surgeon William R. Hall, assigned to retrieve the bodies of Lieutenant Rains's doomed detail. This burial detail had Perry's orders to inter the remains of the ten soldiers, which had been lying out in the hot sun for several days where they had fallen near the boulders. The officer's body would be placed in a crudely fashioned coffin and brought back to Norton's ranch for a decent Christian burial, complete with military honors.

For his part, over the last three days Lew Wilmot had stewed in his own juices, growing all the angrier, and resolved to confront General Oliver Otis Howard with the cowardice and dereliction of duty perpetrated by his subordinate Captain David Perry. Especially after Lew and his friends had laid poor Ben Evans in the ground, then held a burial for D. B. Randall with full Masonic rites in Mount Idaho's little cemetery—a quiet, shady place tucked back among some peaceful pines. Just the sort of place where Lew could get to brooding on his dead friends, all the while nursing his loathing for the man who had delayed and deliberated before sending the civilians any assistance.

As for David Perry, the captain went on with his prosecution of the war: loading up those supplies he had transported down from Fort Lapwai, then led his entire command out of their Cottonwood bivouac on the night of 8 July, after a courier brought word that Howard's advance was approaching Grangeville, exactly where the army had started out on their merry chase thirteen days before!

Earlier that Sunday, McConville had come looking for Lew at Wilmot's tiny home in Mount Idaho. "We're leaving, Lew. Give the family your farewell."

After warmly embracing Louisa and his four children, Wilmot followed his friend into the shadows between some ramshackle buildings.

"There's much afoot, Lew" Ed McConville said as they stood watching three soldiers slowly walk past the nearby barricades. "I've been doing a lot of thinking and talking with some of the men while you been to see your family, Lew."

"What's this got to do with?"

McConville took a deep breath. "I don't figger the army means to do much fighting."

Wilmot snorted, his gall rising again just to think about how the soldiers were far, far better at sitting on their hands than they ever were at fighting. "Howard or Perry, they're the same when it comes to catching the Nez Perce: always a day late and a dollar short."

McConville nodded. "These officers can bumfuggle all they want, but they're never gonna catch up to the Injuns. Why, Frank Fenn and I went to talk with Howard himself when he was sitting on his thumbs at Craig Billy Crossing."

"What'd you tell him?"

"It's what I showed him," McConville explained. "That's a narrow ford, Lew. A few of his men could've defended that crossing if he'd sent some cavalry ahead—or sent word to Whipple for him to get soldiers over from Cottonwood to block the road."

"I don't figger Howard listened to you."

"Oh, he listened to our suggestions politely enough," McConville replied. "Then told us that he believed himself fully competent to manage his own campaign!"

"So what you figure to do now on your own?"

"We've rode down to the mouth of the White Bird late yesterday, where Howard gave our battalion some ammunition since I told him we was going to find out where them hostiles are for him. You wanna come on a little ride with me?"

"Ride? Where?"

"We're gonna cover some ground before nightfall and maybe do a little fighting on our own by morning. It's for certain this army doesn't wanna rub up against the Injuns." Then McConville reached out to grab Wilmot's forearm. "That's why I wanted you to get said what needed saying to Louisa and the young'uns now."

"Just you and me going on this ride?"

"The whole outfit," McConville declared. "Now we got seventy-five ready to ride out tonight, my boys from Lewiston, your bunch from Mount Idaho, along with Hunters's men from over at Dayton—they throwed in with us at Rocky Canyon for the rest of the war. Hunter and Jim Cearly just come back in. From the sounds of things, Joseph's can muster more'n three hundred fighting men. We gotta go find that camp."

"Where you figger on looking?"

McConville said, "Forks of the Clearwater. Wanna get that far north before first light."

Wilmot grinned in the shadows. "Sounds like a fine plan, Captain McConville."

"That's another thing, Lieutenant Wilmot." McConville cleared his throat self-consciously. "I ain't a captain no more."

"Shit—don't tell me someone else is boss of this outfit now!" Wilmot groaned, his belly turning a flop with disappointment. "Not that goddamned Cearly who wanted to take over Randall's bunch when D. B. was killed?"

"Naw," and McConville shook his head. "Way things turned out when we was planning our scout this afternoon, the whole bunch elected Hunter as their lieutenant colonel, and voted me to serve as their colonel."

"*C-colonel* are you now?" Wilmot shrieked with joy, slapping McConville on the back as they turned and stomped away, past the tangle of barricades erected at the end of the street, approaching that large cluster of horsemen gathered back near the shadows cast by a grove of pines.

As they stopped among the others and George Shearer handed them both the reins to their horses, Lew looked over the more than seventy men who stood at the ready beside their fresh mounts selected from that herd taken from Looking Glass's band seven days before, every grim-faced volunteer bristling with weapons and eager for this scout to find the enemy village.

Wilmot smiled in the morning light as he turned to their leader just then swinging into the saddle and said, "All right, *Colonel* McConville. Let's go put our noses on the scent and scare us up some Nez Perce."

AS THEY HAD crossed the Camas Prairie, war parties from the Non-Treaty bands fanned out to search each settler's homestead. Knowing full well that every Shadow family had already scurried toward the towns where they had erected their barricades, the warriors tore through every room in every building, looking for anything of value to them or in trade with the white men for ammunition. The rest they destroyed or burned. Shore Crossing's party left each structure they came across no more than a smoking ruin when they mounted up and rode on to find the next farm dotting the lonely prairie.

If the Shadows had attempted to force the *Nee-Me-Poo* off their ancestral lands, then his warriors were going to see that those Shadows had little to return to once the Non-Treaty bands had cut a swath of destruction through central Idaho. Maybe then, their leaders hoped, the white men would clear out and allow the *Nee-Me-Poo* to live unmolested and in peace once more.

Following the narrow canyon of the Cottonwood east to its junction with the South Fork of the Clearwater—at the traditional camping place called *Pitayiwahwih**—the fighting bands were reunited with Looking Glass's Alpowai, who had at first refused to join with White Bird and *Toohoolhoolzote* at *Tepahlewam*. Now two days** after the fighting bands' skirmish with the Shadows on a low hill, the Non-Treaties set up a large camp erected for the most part on a wide plot of flat ground stretching down the west bank of the narrow river, just upstream from the mouth of the Cottonwood. A handful of families chose to erect their lodges on the narrow strip of ground between the east bank of the Clearwater and the high, steep bluffs that protected the valley. The village numbered a minimum of 750 women and children and boasted of more than two hundred fighting men.

That night, a furious and resentful Looking Glass called a gathering of the leaders so that he could speak to those men he had disdained and rebuked the last time they gathered.

"Six days ago my camp was attacked by soldiers," he told those faces lit by leaping flames. "I tried to surrender in every way I could. My horses, lodges, and everything I had was taken away from me by the soldiers we have done so much for. But I know better."

Looking Glass waited for the grunts of approval to fade, then continued, "Now, my people, as long as I live I will never make peace with the treacherous Shadows. I did everything I knew to preserve their friendship and be friends with the white man. What more could I have done?"

Again he waited while the approval became noisier. His eyes narrowing with menace, Looking Glass said, "It was because I was a good friend of theirs that I was attacked. The soldier chief who came to my camp may say it was a mistake what he did. But that is a lie. He is a dog, and I have been treated worse than a dog by him! He lies if he says he did not know it was *my* camp. I stand before you tonight to say I am ready for war!"

Every war chief and fighting man was suddenly on his feet, for this was a great reunion of the warrior bands who had never buckled under to the treaty.

His strong voice becoming a powerful roar, Looking Glass harangued the crowd, "Come on and let us attack the soldiers at Cottonwood. Many a man dies for his dear native land and we might as well die in battle as any other way!"

The clamor raised from all the war cries and wolf yelping made the hair bristle on Shore Crossing's forearms. Now they had the strength of a man's

---

*Literally meaning "mouth of the canyon," a few miles above the present-day town of Stites, Idaho. In the historic literature, this Nez Perce term is sometimes rendered *Peeta Auuwa*.

**July 7, 1877.

fist, with all five fingers tightly united into action: White Bird, *Toohoolhoolzote*, Joseph, along with *Huishuishkute*, known as Bald or Shorn Head, the Palouse leader . . . and finally Looking Glass.

Three of these other chiefs came forward one-by-one to call for an all-out fight against the treacherous Shadows. Only Joseph did not step into the firelight and add his voice to the call for total resistance.

The following day was one of nothing but relaxation for the warriors who lay about in camp while many of the Non-Treaty people journeyed north to Kamiah to attend Dreamer services that Christian morning.* From this camp a few raiding parties came and went, striking the nearby farms of Lawyer's reservation Indians—driving off their stock of horses and cattle. Scouts, too, rode in and out of camp, slipping onto Camas Prairie to watch for movements of the *suapies* and the civilians venturing out from their fortified settlements. The chiefs needed to know if Cut-Off Arm would come traipsing after them again after they had embarrassed him across the Salmon.

They didn't have long to wait for an answer.

But this time the *Nee-Me-Poo* were completely surprised that it wasn't soldiers who came looking for them.

*Sunday, July 8, 1877.

CHAPTER TWENTY-THREE

July 9, 1877

BY TELEGRAPH

Incoherent Accounts of the Indian War.

Hard to Tell What the Hostiles are Doing.

OREGON.

Latest from the Indian War.

SAN FRANCISCO, July 7.—A special dispatch from Lewiston, July 4, via Walla the 6th, says Colonel Whipple's command, with volunteers under N. B. Randall, came across Looking Glass' band at Clear Creek at 7 a.m. The Indians told the colonel that they were prepared to fight, and opened the ball by the first shot. When the order was given to commence firing the Indians soon broke for the hills and places of shelter. It is not known how many were killed or wounded, as they scampered in all directions. The command captured the Indian camp, burned all their provisions and plunder, and took about a thousand Indian horses, which they brought here. No citizens or soldiers were killed or wounded. The command returned last night . . .

News received at department headquarters from Gen. Sully, commanding at Lewiston, says Col. Perry with thirty men, on his way to Cottonwood, was attacked by hostiles. Lieut. Rainez and ten soldiers and two civilians were killed. Col. Whipple joined Col. Perry, and drove the Indians off. The fight is still going on. Maj. Jackson's company of first cavalry, which left Fort Vancouver yesterday morning, will arrive at Lewiston tomorrow at noon. The following dispatch comes from Walluwa. It was probably received by the steamer Tennie, which arrived at headquarters Thursday night. They say that Joseph decoyed

Gen. Howard across the Salmon river, and then Joseph recrossed the river and got on the Cottonwood between Howard and Lapwai, within thirty miles of Lewiston . . .

Fort Lapwai
July 9, 1877

Dear Mamma,

I must send you a note this morning or you will be anxious about us. We are all alive and well, though all very anxious and in confusion. If you were not so far away, I would come home at once, but I can't bear to think of leaving John and going so far from him. I am thinking seriously of going down to Portland on the next boat and waiting there until things are settled. This post is in such confusion and excitement continually that I feel my strength departing, though I do so want to be a strong woman and able for whatever happens.

There have been so many alarms of Indian attacks, and so many horrible stories are continually being brought in that John says he wants to send us away. This matter may be settled in a few days, and I will not make up my mind what I will do until we hear further.

Our trouble is not enough troops. Another regiment is expected here in this Department at once, but what is a regiment these days? The companies are so small that it only means a hundred or so men after all. Joseph has had strong reinforcements and he has managed so wonderfully that he has been successful everywhere. Another fine young officer, such a nice fellow, has been killed, and we have lost about fifty men. It is time the tide turned!

. . . I will write a longer and more connected letter next mail. We are all right here. Don't be alarmed about us. It is only the worry and anxiety that Doctor wants to save me by sending me away. I don't think I will leave Lapwai, not unless the troubles increase. We all join in love.

Your loving daughter,
Emily F.

HE LOUD REPORT OF THAT SINGLE GUNSHOT SNAPPED LEW WILMOT awake.

"Shit," someone nearby whimpered in the dark. "I-I didn't mean to—"

In a blur, McConville loomed over John Atkinson, wrenching the volunteer's .50-caliber Springfield rifle from his hands. "Keep your eyes open now, boys," the leader growled. "I expect some company to show up real soon."

Wilmot swallowed hard as he swiveled the lever down and opened the action on his big needle-gun. He had a reputation as being the best shot on the Camas Prairie. And now that this poor daisy from Hunter's bunch had just announced to the whole canyon that they were there . . . Lew Wilmot was going to have to prove just how good a shot he was, all over again.

By midday on the eighth, McConville's seventy-five volunteers had crossed the open, rolling land to reach the canyon of the Cottonwood, following the creek until dark, when they decided they could go no farther and went into a cold camp. McConville's subordinate "Captain" Benjamin F. Morris divided the men into two watches, then put out the first round of pickets while the others tried to catch a little sleep right where they had landed when they came out of the saddles. Lew tried but could not do anything but listen to the sounds of the night, thinking about his three daughters and that brand-new baby boy.

Them and poor George Hunter—who lay back in Loyal P. Brown's hotel turned hospital after he had been shot in the shoulder by another volunteer from Dayton in Washington Territory, Eugene Talmadge Wilson, climaxing a quick, hot argument reaching the boiling point after a long-simmering feud the two had carried with them into the Nez Perce War. Wilson was under arrest back in Mount Idaho.

Wilmot wondered why a man like Wilson had failed to realize there were more than enough warriors to go around when he got mad enough he had to shoot George Hunter. A few of Hunter's friends had been understandably edgy as they lit out on their scout, and Wilson's friends were even standoffish by the time they made camp night before last.

Just as Wilmot was dozing off in the dark, one of the pickets from the first watch clambered back into camp to announce that he had discovered that they were less than a mile from the Nez Perce village located at the mouth of the Cottonwood. McConville picked John McPherson to carry word back to Howard that night, since the general was expected in Grangeville before morning.

"You might figger to send another rider or two off with the same news," Lew suggested in the dark as the anxious men settled down to await the dawn.

"Think McPherson might get jumped?"

Wilmot nodded in the starshine. "They're bound to have scouts and outriders sniffing around."

"Then why the hell haven't they found us?" James Cearly goaded in a whisper.

Before Wilmot could snap, McConville said, "Unless you two figger out a way to get along, I'm gonna order you both back to Mount Idaho."

Wilmot was just waiting for McConville to take a breath. "Colonel—"

"Your arguing likely gonna cost the lives of some of these men," McConville interrupted. "Either you get along, or you get out."

Lew looked at Cearly's face, waiting for the other man to make the first move . . . then said, "All right, Colonel. I can get along with any man if I'm given half a chance."

"Me, too," Cearly replied, holding his hand out. "Besides, we're gonna need to have the best shot on Camas Prairie with us if we run into trouble tomorrow."

"All right," McConville said as he settled on his haunches. "I'm gonna send out two more men with orders to get word to Howard."

After George Riggins and P. C. Malin were on their way, each taking a different route back to Mount Idaho, McConville dispatched E. J. Bunker and nine other men toward a high hill figured to be halfway between their bivouac and the enemy camp.

"Bunker, you and your men are under orders to hold that hill at all hazards. Be sure you give the alarm at the first approach of Indians."

Hours later, McConville crawled back to where Wilmot was resting, propped against a tree. He signaled Lew to follow him and together they crabbed over to where James Cearly was dozing.

"We got about an hour or so left till first light," McConville whispered. "I want the both of you to have a look at that camp. Close as you can. Count the lodges; see the strength of those Injuns. Then get back here afore sunup."

The two of them had gotten well within a half-mile of the village before they decided they had little time to beat a retreat back to the bivouac.

Wilmot had reported upon their return, "We counted seventy-two tepees, Colonel. From what we could see in the dark, we counted more than one hundred and fifty of their ponies staked right in camp."

"It look to you that all the bands were there?"

Cearly nodded. "We waited till the first light started to show across the Clearwater—just to be sure we had counted everything we could see."

"We headed back when the herder boys crossed the river toward a few other lodges and their ponies," Lew explained.

McConville called the rest of the men together that dawn, and they discussed their options. Couriers were already on their way to the soldiers, although a significant number of the volunteers doubted Howard and Perry would ever have the will to prosecute this war the way it should have been fought from the very beginning. In fact, many of the volunteers from Mount Idaho even feared the murdering redskins would either get away with their crimes completely or come slinking back to Howard for a compromise and protection from the outraged citizens. To their way of thinking, General O. O. Howard had proven he would make a better missionary than an Indian fighter. At the end of their long, angry discussions, however, they decided to wait and see what the soldiers would do, what word might come back from Howard.

"We'll wait out the day right here," their leader told them. "If we haven't heard from the general by nightfall, I'll send out another dispatch with news on the strength of the camp. When Howard gets here, we'll join in the attack."

They had waited out the morning, then midday as the sun rose higher and hotter, making Lew all the sleepier as the insects buzzed and droned around their faces. He had just been drifting off when that gun belonging to one of Hunter's men tumbled from its stand against a tree and discharged.

They were in the soup now!

"Bring the water!" Wilmot was yelling as he clambered to his feet.

"Where we going?" one of the Dayton volunteers demanded.

Lew pointed at the hill.* "There—where the colonel sent Bunker and his men."

"T-that's *toward* the Injuns!" another Dayton man whined.

"But it's the highest hill we can reach in this country before the Injuns get to us," McConville snarled. "Now do what Wilmot told you: get your canteens filled at the creek and push on for that hill—on the double!"

Those who had brass kettles along filled them with water, making the sprint for that hill an interesting one as they attempted to keep as much water from sloshing out of the vessels as possible as they covered that broken ground and deadfall. By the time the first of them reached Bunker's position, they found those ten guards already prying stones out of the ground with their belt knives and dragging up downed trees to throw up some sort of breastworks.

Lew nodded as he rode up and spun to the ground, pitching his two canteens into the pile McConville was supervising at the center of the scene. It was a good spot; that much was for sure. Nearly flat on top, the crest was as good as anyplace to make a last stand.

"A damn sight better'n that grassy rise on the Camas Prairie," Lew muttered under his breath as he turned his horse among the others and started toward the breastworks, where all of McConville's volunteers were feverishly scratching at the ground, digging rifle pits with their belt knives or tin cups. Anything that could move some dirt.

It wasn't many minutes before some two dozen horsemen appeared, the first to come investigate. Lew had to give the Nez Perce credit for being smart bastards. They could see the white men had a decided advantage on top of their hill. The warriors didn't make a charge or press an attack. Instead, they seemed content with surrounding the knoll with more than a hundred fighting men, occasionally firing an ill-placed shot and constantly hurling oaths at the volunteers. Into that long, hot afternoon and evening, it was a long-distance scrap, if anything.

Then darkness fell and they were all reminded to be extra cautious about making any noise. Their ears were going to have to warn them if any warriors were sneaking up on their fortifications. Besides, there weren't many of them even trying at some sleep, not the way the volunteers shivered with the cold in their sweat-dampened clothes, none of them having blankets along.

A little after 11:00 P.M., while the second watch was on duty, the hillside below them fell quiet for the longest time . . . until the clatter of hooves shattered the starlight.

"They charging?" some man shrieked in terror.

"No, goddammit!" came a growl from the other side of the hilltop as the hammer of hoofbeats faded. "The red pricks just run off our horses!"

"We're staying put for sure now!" Cearly grumbled.

Wilmot nodded. "I wasn't planning on going nowhere anyway."

---

*"Misery Hill" (sometimes called Camp Misery) is located on present-day Doty Ridge.

Not long after midnight the warriors burst forth with a litany of unearthly war cries and screeches, accompanied by the calls of wild birds, the howl of a prairie wolf, and the scream of the mountain panther. It had lasted for the better part of an hour when, from all sides, the warriors opened up a sudden and frightening gunfire. Tongues of yellow and red jetted from the muzzles of their rifles, many of which had been stolen from the dead in White Bird Canyon.

"Just stay down!" McConville hollered.

"You heard the colonel!" Wilmot shouted. "Keep your heads down and they won't have nothing to hit!"

After listening to some steady, sustained fire coming from one of the rifle pits, Wilmot crawled over to find a volunteer firing into the black of night.

"Elias," Lew whispered, "just what the blazes you shooting at?"

Nonplussed, Elias Darr looked over his shoulder and replied, "I-I don't know, Lew. It's so goddamned dark I can't see a blamed thing . . . but I thought it was a good idea to keep the ark amoving."

With a smile, Wilmot put his hand on his friend's shoulder. "Elias, I figger an even better idea is to save your ammunition for morning, when we might need to move the ark even more."

Some sporadic harassing fire from the enemy was kept up on into the blackening of night as the moon fell. Then as first light started to bloom, the firing died away and the hillside fell quiet again. Afraid of drawing a bullet, the volunteers maintained an uneasy silence.

"Hey, you fellas!" a voice cried from down the hillside, heavy with Nez Perce accent.

The volunteers fell silent, watchful and wary of some trick.

Finally one of them hollered, "What you want, you red nigger?"

"We going to breakfast allee same Hotel de France!" the voice called out, referring to one of the best hotels in Lewiston. "You fellas come over and eat with us!"

Wilmot couldn't help it. He started snorting with laughter at the image that created in his head—this band of grubby civilian horsemen setting down for breakfast in the dining room of that fancy hotel with some painted, half-naked Non-Treaty savages.

As a lark, Lew sang out, "No—I got a better idea, fellas. You boys come on in here and have breakfast with us! C'mon now."

For a moment it was deathly quiet; then the voice came again from the timber, "I no think so, fellas. You ain't got nothing to eat much!"

McConville chuckled, grinning at Wilmot. "Leastways they got that right, Lew. We don't have much at all in the way of hold-out food!"

An hour later, as his pocket watch was nearing 7:00 A.M., several of the men on the other side of the breastworks called out a warning.

"They're coming at us now, for God's sake!"

Bunker was pointing as Wilmot came loping over. Down near the base of the hill in the summer sunlight they could see at least a hundred of the warriors lining up in a broad front, as if preparing to make a massed charge on foot.

"Hold your fire until you see the color of the paint on their faces!" Wilmot ordered.

"That's right," McConville agreed. "Make every bullet count!"

Then as the volunteers were hunkering down behind the rocks and deadfall, preparing to sell their lives dearly in those shallow rifle pits, a pair of Nez Perce rode up to the warrior lines, waving and gesturing. In seconds that line of chargers dispersed, turning away to fetch up their ponies lazily grazing in the grassy swales below the hill. One by one and in pairs the warriors mounted up and started away, heading back in the direction of their camp.

Finally, McConville asked, "Hey, Lew—you think they pulled off for good? Or is this a trick?"

He wagged his head. "I dunno, Colonel. Just when a fella thinks he's got these Nez Perce figgered out, that's when they'll up and surprise him—catch 'im in a trap . . . and kill 'im."

CHAPTER TWENTY-FOUR

July 9–10, 1877

BY TELEGRAPH

More Dispatches From the Front—
Serious State of Affairs.

WASHINGTON, July 7.—The following telegram from Gen. McDowell, commanding the military department of the Pacific, was received at the war department this morning:

SAN FRANCISCO, July 5.—*Adjutant General, Washington.*—The following telegrams, both from Lewiston, have just been received from my aide-de-camp I had sent up to Gen. Howard's command. The first telegram, July 4th, says: No news direct from Gen. Howard since the first. The Klamath company is expected to-morrow. Shall go with it. Captain Whipple's detachment struck a band of Nez Perces, under Looking Glass, at Kawais, Sunday, and inflicted severe punishment, capturing a large amount of stock. Indian Inspector Watkins, who has recently been with Gen. Howard, writes from Lapwai this afternoon, to Gen. Sully here, that this success, and Gen. Howard's vigorous action are producing marked results. Looking Glass wishes to come in with his band. Watkins states that Joseph has crossed the Salmon and is making east for the Bitter Rock country, with General Howard at his heels and Whipple barring the way, but Joseph thus harassed is on the point of breaking up. There are no signs of the other Indians taking a hand.

The second dispatch is dated the 5th, and says the following was received from Captain Perry, dated 9 a.m., and that the Cottonwood Indians have been around us all day in force and very demonstrative. It is unsafe to send anything to him until the Klamath company arrives. He urges that it be sent to his command with all dispatch. Information just up by boat postpones the arrival of that company a day or two. Still no news from Howard. It is probable his courier has been intercepted. A citizen from Colville just in represents the situation on the Spokanes as most threatening. General Sully, who is here, shares in his apprehensions. It seems there is ample ground for General Howard's application for more troops.

Signed KEELER,
Aide de Camp.

Instead of sending the infantry as directed I have determined to send it as General Howard desired, that is by rail to San Francisco and by steamer to Portland, thence by boats to Lewiston. The troops en route to Boize City, Idaho, will be sufficient, I believe, for that district, which can be more readily reinforced than that of Columbia. I have ordered all the troops from Fort Yuma, two companies to Boize, and have broken up Camp Independence and sent the company to the same destination.

MCDOWELL, Major General.

AVE YOURSELF A LOOK, COLONEL."

Wilmot handed his looking glass to Ed McConville. It was no more than a heartbeat before the civilian commander took the long brass tube from his eye. "That for sure looks like a band of volunteers coming our way, Lew."

"And that war party headed for them?"

McConville half-grinned. "You think you can come up with some way to help those fellas afore that war party rides 'em down?"

Wilmot stood at the edge of the breastworks. "Can you spare twenty men?"

"Surely. That'll even up the odds something nicely," McConville declared, then called for volunteers to accompany Lew Wilmot as he went to spoil the war party's ambush of those horsemen headed for their hilltop fortress.

What with the Nez Perce running off all their good horses just before midnight, those twenty-one men had nothing more than a dozen poor and played-out horses the Nez Perce considered unfit to ride. Instead, Lew and the others vaulted over their low rock-and-log walls and started down the southern slope on foot, ever watchful that they themselves weren't being lured into a trap by the wily Nez Perce who had disappeared into a ravine that would eventually carry them onto the prairie near the oncoming white riders.

By the time those civilian horsemen were a half-mile away from Wilmot's volunteers, the Indians put in a show just off to the riders' left. . . . But it was only a matter of heartbeats until Lew had his twenty spread out five feet apart and kneeling down to take steady aim at the enemy advancing on the horsemen, thereby springing a surprise on those who had hoped to spring a surprise of their own.

Beneath an intermittent shower of bullets and epithets from the chagrined warriors, the riders continued on their advance until they approached Wilmot's footmen.

"By the glory of ol' Jupiter hisself!" roared George Shearer. "If that ain't Lew Wilmot!"

He loped up close to his friend as the horsemen swirled around those twenty men on foot, every one of them huzzahing and congratulating one another on their rescue.

"Seeing your face here must mean the soldiers are right behind you!" Wilmot bellowed as they shook.

Shearer stopped pumping his friend's arm, his face draining of joy. "No, Lew. There ain't no soldiers comin' behind us."

"N-no soldiers? Didn't Howard get to Grangeville after we left on the eighth?"

The Southerner nodded. "Says he ain't marchin' till he gets all his men up from their mess gettin' across the Salmon."

It wasn't good news, not good news at all, they carried back to those breastworks. Instead of learning they had only to wait a matter of hours for the arrival of Howard's column, McConville's volunteers could come to no other conclusion but that they had been abandoned by the army.

For some of those men, like Lew Wilmot, it felt as if they had been discarded and left to the Nez Perce all over again.

"Lew, I want you and Penny to pick the two best horses George's men rode in here," McConville ordered.

"You best be sending me with a message for Howard," Wilmot said. "And your dispatch better say something about soldiers sitting on their asses while civilians are fighting this goddamned war for 'em."

McConville shrugged it off. "The two of you will carry word to Howard all right," he told them both, "but rather than infuriate that pompous ol' Bible-thumper, I'll inform him of our dire situation and only *request* reinforcements."

After darkness had fully swallowed the valley of the Clearwater, Lew Wilmot and Benjamin Penny led those two strong horses out of the breastworks and down the bare slope, making for the closest patch of timber. There they would wait for a few minutes, listening to every night sound, before they finally mounted up and dared to ride into the open beneath that blackened banner of starry sky.

Heart thumping, Wilmot finally nudged Ben Penny with a tap on the shoulder, and they both mounted up. Without a word exchanged between them, the horsemen quickly shook hands, reined about, and put their heels to their mounts, leaping out of the timber onto the barren ground where a few hours earlier a swarm of warriors had been waving blankets and hollering for white blood.

Lew couldn't recall if he had remembered to breathe that first mile or not. But by the time he figured they had come a half-dozen miles on the backs of those racing horses, Lew Wilmot had indeed begun to breathe easier and finally started thinking about Louisa and those children as the animal rocked beneath him in the dark. Closer and closer, with every lunge of those powerful legs. With every mile, he was leaving that enemy village and those miserable breastworks farther and farther behind.

"You see that?" Penny asked more than five harrowing hours later. It might be the dim flicker of a fire. And from the outline of the stars to the south it appeared that was the heights rising above Mount Idaho just ahead . . . but the fire lay to the southeast instead of the south. Unless he'd gotten turned around. Another glow appeared now as they rounded the brow of a low hill. Then within another mile and a broad sweep of prairie more than a hundred watch fires lay in the distance.

"That can't be Grangeville!" Wilmot cried, his voice raspy with disuse.

Benjamin Penny exclaimed, "What the hell are them fires?"

"That has to be Howard's camp. And those are his soldiers."

His eyes stung, too. They had made their escape.

The sky was graying in the east by the time the two horsemen guided their lathered animals across the South Fork of the Clearwater on the Jackson Bridge and reined into that great encampment spread near the gutted, looted ruin of the Walls ranch.*

"Who goes there!" a cry came out of the dawn's murky light.

"We're looking for General Howard!"

The guards and curious soldiers formed a cordon, refusing to allow the civilians through.

"Who's asking?"

"We need to speak with the general," Wilmot said, trying hard to keep his anger from boiling. He shook an arm to the north. "There's more'n eighty men fighting for their lives off yonder! We've found the goddamned village for you! Why don't you soldiers get up off your rumps and come fight the redskins with us?"

"I'll take you to General Howard," a voice announced as a young officer pushed his way through the older enlisted men.

The officer asked the civilians to dismount and turn over their horses to a saddler sergeant before the three set off down a row of company tents where morning fires were being coaxed back into life and sleepy, trail-weary men were slowly getting onto their feet, rubbing knuckles into gritty eyes.

"I should be ready to move on the morrow," General Oliver Otis Howard told the civilians after he had listened to their story and told them he was aware of McConville's plight from an earlier messenger. "Until then, I can't advise engaging the Nez Perce."

"Right now, right here," Wilmot said with no little exasperation, "you've got twice as many soldiers as they got warriors!"

"Good sir, I will not be dissuaded by you from my campaign," Howard snipped. "I think it goes without question that I know more about such things than either of you, or Captain McConville."

"He's a colonel now," Lew said.

"A . . . *colonel* you say," Howard replied with the hint of a grin as two of his

*Just outside the present-day community of Harpster, Idaho.

aides turned aside with contemptuous smiles on their faces. "Please tell Colonel McConville that he and his battalion are in this kettle of fish because he did not seek out my advice or attempt to work in concert with me."

"I think the entire battalion volunteered to go on our mission because your officers and this damned army haven't done anything but eat tack soup for more'n two weeks!" Wilmot exploded, watching a sudden look of shock cross Howard's face. Instantly he figured he was better off not shaming this soldier. "The Nez Perce are making fools of your officers, General."

"I got here as quickly as I could, sir," a voice announced as it came up behind Wilmot and Penny.

Lew turned to see Captain David Perry stepping up beside Howard.

"Are you gentlemen acquainted with Colonel Perry, commander of my cavalry battalion?"

"Yeah, I know him," Wilmot answered. "Last run onto him at Cottonwood."

Howard turned slightly, speaking to Perry. "These men have just come in from McConville's volunteers, with another request for us to go to their assistance."

The captain said, "You explained to them that we'll be waiting until we have our entire infantry and artillery wings reunited with us, General?"

"I can see the color of this horse!" Wilmot roared. "You fellas are just like all them Union generals was in the war: waiting till you got more soldiers than the enemy before you'll think of budging—"

As two of the general's aides stepped forward, Howard said, "This interview is over."

"Over?" Wilmot snapped. "I was figuring I might be able to talk sense to you, General Howard. But I can see how this Cottonwood coward has poisoned your mind!"

"Coward?" Perry growled.

"That's what you are when you didn't come to the aid of our civilians last Thursday."

"You're accusing me of cowardice?"

"I haven't seen a goddamned thing to make me change my opinion of you."

"You're nothing less than a low-class liar, mister!" Perry snapped. "Fabrications and nothing but half-truths, General."

Wilmot snorted, "What lies, Perry?"

"You just told the general I never came to your aid," Perry retorted. "I did send out the cavalry and infantry both, and a fieldpiece under Lieutenant Shelton, too!"

"Not till you were shamed into it!" Wilmot said forcefully, but to Howard instead of speaking to Perry. "Then George Shearer led your men out to our position on his own—alone!"

"I have no control over the actions of civilians," Perry snarled, whirling on Howard. "I had an entire train of supplies and ammunition destined for you, which I had to protect, General. I could not chance that train falling into enemy hands because of their diversionary tactic—"

"The only reason you sent help was you were shamed by your own officers into sending us some relief!" Wilmot's voice rose a notch higher.

"Get out of here now!" Perry shouted, his face flushing. "Your very presence in this army camp fills me with contempt!"

"C-contempt?" Wilmot echoed loudly with a snort. "You ain't got one-half the contempt for me that I hold for you—so I will leave your goddamned camp!"

Twisting around on his heel, Wilmot was brushing past Penny when Howard bellowed, "Stop where you are! Arrest that man!"

Flicking a glance over his shoulder, Lew saw several of the general's staff lunge for him. On instinct he bolted into a run, but he got no more than three long steps before he found himself in the arms of a pair of armed guards. And both men were a lot beefier than rail-thin Lew Wilmot. They manhandled him back to Howard, his toes barely dragging the ground.

"Perry—when you die, you're gonna be turned away from the gates of both Heaven and Hell!" Lew growled as the soldiers clamped down all the harder on his arms and removed his pistol from its holster. "When you die and your body's gonna be laying out on the prairie . . . the coyote's gonna tuck his tail between his legs and sneak off. The buzzard will fly away from your stinking carcass, and even the little worm that would delight to worry the carcass of a lowly dog will crawl away from yours in disgust—"

"Mr. Wilmot!" the general shouted, red-faced. "It makes my blood boil to hear a civilian blaspheme an officer!"

Struggling between the two large men who imprisoned him, Wilmot said, "Not half as much as it makes my blood boil for this coward to tell me right to my face that I lied!"

The general took a deep breath, staring at the graying sky for a long moment as if attempting to regain his composure. "Why don't you calm yourself, and we'll put this entire affair behind us. I would rather you serve as a guide for us, to show my column where that Indian camp is, instead of placing you under arrest."

Wilmot stared hard at Perry, then turned his withering gaze on Howard. "No, because you're both cut of the same cloth. I ain't gonna guide for either one of you. Hell, I prefer fighting alongside the Indians now to fighting for your officers!"

Howard jutted his bearded chin angrily. "Take this civilian to the officer of the day and tell him I've placed him under arrest."

"What for?" Wilmot snarled as the guards uprooted him off his feet once more.

"I don't have to have a reason right now, Mr. Wilmot," Howard said. Then, looking at one of the guards, he added, "Have the officer of the day put him in shackles until tomorrow when we're ready to march. That should give you enough time to cool down and reconsider your contempt for the officers who are here prosecuting this campaign . . . so you civilians can live in peace on what was once Nez Perce land."

"Is that it, General?" Wilmot shouted over his shoulder. "You and your soldiers don't wanna fight no war to protect your own goddamned citizens?"

Howard took two steps following the guards who had a firm grip on their prisoner and said, "Sometimes, Mr. Wilmot, in this dirty little war, I wonder who really needs protecting from whom. If it isn't the Nez Perce who need our protection from the likes of you!"

CHAPTER TWENTY-FIVE

July 11, 1877

BY TELEGRAPH

More of the Mexican Border Troubles.

The Administration Strongly Favoring Invasion.

No Satisfactory News From General Howard.

OREGON.

Latest from the Indian War.

SAN FRANCISCO, July 9.—A press dispatch from Portland has the following from Lewiston, under date of the 6th, via Walla Walla, 9th: Left Horse-shoe bend and came down Salmon river near its junction with the Snake, leaving Howard in force up the river. A courier express is just in from Colonel Perry who was en route for Howard with a pack train, and an escort of thirty men, says he was attacked on the 4th and ten soldiers and two citizens killed. Captain Whipple, in command at Cottonwood, came to the rescue and repulsed the Indians. The latter are in force around Colonel Perry and Captain Whipple who have only force enough for defence. The route is unsafe to Cottonwood. It is a bold stroke of Joseph and his band, and it is reported by signal to the Indians north and east, and stirs them up to the offensive . . . The Indians have destroyed some fields and gardens and rifled some dwellings. News here this morning indicates a purpose to meet or act with those on the Spokane and such a move will imperil all the upper settlements on the Palouse. It is evident that a volunteer cavalry in large force ought to be put in the field to reinforce General Howard and stop this uprising before it assumes larger and more definite proportions.

Fort Lapwai
July 11, 1877

Dear Mamma,

. . . Everything here has been in such confusion that I believe my mind is in the same condition. I can't tell you, or expect you to imagine, what a horrible time we have had and the unsettled state of everything for the last few weeks. I shall be so thankful when it is all over and we can go to sleep at night without imagining that we will be awakened by hearing Indian yells before morning.

You probably see by the papers what Mr. Joseph is doing. He is the smartest Indian I ever heard of, and does the most daring and impudent things. The command under General Howard in the field is so small that scarcely anything more can be done than to protect settlements. The country all about this region is so particularly adapted to Indian fighting that Joseph has every advantage and would have, even if the soldiers outnumbered him three to one. We know that Joseph's force numbers over two hundred, and we think it may be much more, as it is thought that there are a great many Indians who have joined him lately. No one has any doubts but that a few more successes for his band will bring to him all the Non-Treaty Indians in this Department, and there are hundreds and hundreds of them, different tribes all scattered along the Columbia River. Another regiment of infantry will be here within three weeks, but what Joseph and White Bird will do in those three weeks, no one knows. At first the idea was that Joseph (Indian like) was getting out of the road and making for the buffalo country. There was great fear that he would get off, but it was soon discovered that he had no idea of getting away, and that he was quietly doing all the mischief he could, and reinforcing his band, and preparing for a fight with the soldiers. He says he can whip them. I do hope there won't be a chance for him to try until more troops get here.

Companies of volunteers are gathering from all around, and they will help to swell the number. Colonel Perry was here for three or four days last week. He came in to escort a packtrain for supplies.

. . . Some of the stories of the poor people who have suffered so much make your blood run cold. There was something dreadfully touching to me in the defense that the Norton family made. They were among the first of the settlers molested . . .*

We are uneasy today about a packtrain of arms and ammunition that left here yesterday with an escort of one company of cavalry

**Cries from the Earth*, vol. 14, the *Plainsmen* series.

(50 men) and about 20 Indian scouts. They feared an attack, as the Indians know of the train, and we heard they were going to jump it.

Your loving daughter,
Emily F.

IS CHRISTIAN NAME WAS JOE ALBERT.

Painful as it was for his traditional parents, in recent years young Joe had moved his own family onto the reservation and became one of the peaceful Treaty Indians who lived and farmed near Lapwai.

When trouble broke out with the Non-Treaty bands of White Bird, *Toohoolhoolzote*, and Joseph's *Wallowa*, Joe Albert answered the one-armed soldier chief's call for scouts to lead the *suapies* to find those bad warriors who had murdered many Shadow settlers and burned their farms. Joe led the soldiers into the valley of *Lahmotta*, where a few of *Ollokot*'s warriors turned the frightened, spooked soldiers around and sent them fleeing.

Rather than kill them—as they had done with any *suapie* they found alive on the battlefield—*Ollokot*'s warriors captured three of those Christian trackers scouting for the army. Although many of the young men had screamed for their blood and the women heaped scorn upon the trio, the chiefs decided they would release the three, once the prisoners had vowed to never again raise arms against the Non-Treaty bands or help the soldiers in what everyone believed would be a quick little war.

"If we catch you again, then we will whip you with hazel switches."

Which was a punishment much worse than death itself.

After Robinson Minthon declared he wanted to stay with the White Bird band, the other two vowed they would return home to wives and children, even though both had relations among the Non-Treaties. And since the pair had their soldier horses taken from them, the young warrior Yellow Wolf gave *Yuwishakaikt* a pony to ride, while a kind woman took pity upon Joe Albert. She gave him one of her old travois horses for his ride north.

Still nursing the invisible wounds his pride had suffered by the time he reached Lapwai, Albert eagerly enlisted to work for Cut-Off Arm when he went to punish the warring *Nee-Me-Poo*—despite his promise to the Non-Treaty chiefs . . . even though the white men were often slow on the back trail and sometimes, to Joe's way of thinking, might even be a little frightened of confronting the warriors again. Yet he stayed with the *suapies*, even when they were turned back by the river and forced to return to the mouth of White Bird Creek.

As they plodded slowly up the steep canyon, it was immediately apparent how the heavy rains had been suffered upon the land while Cut-Off Arm's soldiers were on the west side of the Salmon: washing away what skimpy soil the soldiers had scraped over the battle dead. But Cut-Off Arm did not stop to rebury his dead. It was nearing sundown and they still had many miles to go before the advance soldiers reached the settlement called

Grangeville. The first of the officers and soldiers did not drop from their horses until the great darkness at the middle of night.

Then Cut-Off Arm had them on the march again at dawn . . . halting and going into camp after crossing the old mining bridge that spanned the South Fork of the Clearwater. From the many charred and splintered timbers it was plain the warrior bands had attempted—but failed—to destroy the bridge. To Joe, it was a sure sign the Non-Treaties were planning to stay in this part of the country.

The soldiers had laid in camp through the next day,* waiting for more troops, which did not reach them until late in the afternoon. At long last, in this camp scattered below the bluffs on the east side of the South Fork, Cut-Off Arm now had all his *suapies* ready to go in search of battle.

Joe Albert had been ready for some time. Now, after so long a wait, the soldiers would strike the offending warriors, punish them and their women, too; then everything would return to normal once more. When that end to the troubles came, Joe could again visit his father and mother—both Dreamers —without being shamed by so many in the Non-Treaty camp that he had chosen to become a Christian. It should not take long—just one good fight.

After all, Cut-Off Arm had enough soldiers now. One of the scouts who talked the Shadow tongue made marks on the ground for those scouts who did not know the white man's talk. Each mark counted for ten *suapies*, mule packers, or the civilians who traipsed along with the soldiers. One mark after another, after another, until there were fifty scratches on the ground to signify all the white men who would attack the warrior bands. White Bird, *Toohoolhoolzote*, Joseph, and even Looking Glass did not stand any chance of getting away now.

They would hang in the white man way of retribution for having a hand in killing all those Shadow women and children. War was not supposed to be fought against the wives and little ones. But the bad warriors had mixed whiskey and gunpowder, then done very, very bad things, sometimes terrible things, to the women and children. As it was explained in the white man's Book of Heaven, the time had come that these evil ones should pay for their sins.

At dawn the following morning, Cut-Off Arm started north along the South Fork, his long, long column strung out on the broken pine-dotted ridge that rose more than eight hundred feet above the river below. Many steep ravines and coulees made it impossible for the column to travel anywhere near the edge of the bluff. Instead, the soldiers had to make ever-widening detours to skirt around the heads of the deep ravines. The sun rose high and hot that morning as the *Nee-Me-Poo* scouts made fewer and fewer trips to the very edge of the ridge to look down at the river searching for the Non-Treaty village.

Since no one among the Shadows knew for sure where the camp lay, Cut-Off Arm was depending upon his trackers to find it for him while the bluffs rose higher and higher on that east side of the river, eventually more than a thousand feet above the South Fork. And the ravines grew steeper, deeper,

*Tuesday, July 10, 1877.

and darker too, each one requiring a longer detour for the grumbling soldiers. The sun was nearing its zenith, burning in the sky after so many, many days of cold, rainy weather. Joe was sweating heavily in his wool soldier jacket and broad-brimmed black cavalry hat. He wondered when Cut-Off Arm would allow the column a midday halt to rest the horses and catch a nap under a little shade—

Suddenly the white men were shouting, cheering, excitedly forming up, shuffling this way and that. So much noise—

"They found the camp!" came the cry in the middle of all that pandemonium. One of the other two Treaty scouts was shouting as the pair came galloping back from the front of the march.

"Narrow-Eye Chapman found the camp!" announced the other, shaking his soldier rifle in the air. "It is back upstream a ways! Just above the mouth of the Cottonwood!"

Racing their ponies through the shifting masses of white men, sprinting across the bluff, Joe and the others stopped at the pine-covered edge of the ridge and gazed down into the narrow valley of the Clearwater. There, off to their left a long ways, lay the camp of the Non-Treaty bands.

"The soldiers almost missed them!" Captain John said.

"Nearly passed them by!"

Then Joe observed, "They are still a long way back—too far to attack from here."

"I think the *suapies* will have to find a way down to the valley to make their fight," James Reuben said.

"If they don't, then the Non-Treaties will get away before the soldiers can capture the village," Albert declared.

"They're not going to wait to find a way down!" Captain John said. "Look!"

When they turned, looking through the trees, the scouts watched some of the *suapies* hustling one of the two wagon guns through the patchy evergreens and right up to the edge of the bluff, where they were hollering at one another. Farther away at the edge of the ridge, Cut-Off Arm and his soldier chiefs stopped their horses at the edge and peered down as the wagon gun belched its first charge. It made a lot of noise, but no damage, as the shot landed in the river far short of its mark—for the village stood a long, long way upstream.

The *suapies* around the wagon gun shouted at one another again and went about their crazy business with the weapon, swabbing and reloading it for a second charge. Which landed a little closer this time. A little better with the third shot . . . but it was soon clear to Joe Albert that the wagon gun would never come close to those Non-Treaty lodges.

But as he peered down into the valley, through the drifting shreds of dirty cannon smoke, Albert could see that—even while the huge black balls had failed to reach the camp—the noise of the gun and the explosion of those charges was not lost on the warrior bands. The camp was aswirl of motion: men and women racing about on horses and on foot, bathers leaping out of the river, children darting among the lodges, arms flailing in terror.

Riders bristling with weapons appeared at the edges of camp, near the

Cottonwood and on the bank of the Clearwater. It appeared they were prepared to fight . . . if they could only find their invisible enemy.

Of a sudden, in the midst of all that blur and dust and panic gripping the village down below, Joe was struck with an instant horror—wondering just where his father was.

CHAPTER TWENTY-SIX

Khoy-Tsahl, 1877

ELLOW WOLF HAD NOT BEEN THIS HAPPY IN A LONG, LONG TIME. TWO days ago Looking Glass's Alpowai band had rejoined the Non-Treaties, and for the first time since this war began, Yellow Wolf was reunited with his mother, *Yiyik Wasumwah.*

Her cheeks were wet as she held her son's face between her hands, chattering like a happy, happy jay. Then she would lay her cheek against his bare chest and hug him, sighing all the while. After a moment, she would again hold his face in her hands and stare up at her son, telling him how tall he looked, young warrior that he was now.

"He killed four *suapies* at *Lahmotta!*" Five Wounds had announced as he came riding by in that happy rejoining of the people.

"Yes," agreed Rainbow. "Yellow Wolf is a true guardian of the *Nee-Me-Poo!*"

Staring into his mother's eyes, he asked, "Where is *Tommimo?*"

Yellow Wolf's stepfather was three-quarters French and had been raised a member of Joseph's *Wallowa*, but for the past few winters they had lived with Yellow Wolf's mother's people, the Alpowai who farmed on the Clearwater.

She looked at the ground a minute, her face gone tense. He knew his mother was fighting some angry tears.

So he had dared to ask, "He . . . he wasn't killed by the soldiers?"

"No," she replied. "He was not here. *Tommimo* had gone to the Shadow town by the Snake River,* to trade some horses. Others have brought news that my husband has been arrested and won't be coming back until this war is over."

Then she had turned away and scurried back to that bundle of what few belongings she had managed to carry away from the village when the soldiers and Shadows struck Looking Glass. She pulled out a long scrap of blanket and laid it across her arms as if presenting it to him. Yellow Wolf's fingers had gripped the blanket wrap, the hot blood pounding in his ears blotting out the noisy celebration swirling around them.

It was his repeater!

"You have not needed to shoot it, Mother?"

She shook her head. "No, but I protected it for you, knowing one day you

---

*Lewiston, Idaho.

would come back and—if I saved anything from the soldiers—I wanted to protect this rifle for you, Son."

Quickly Yellow Wolf wrapped her close in one arm. His mother knew how to use the gun if she needed to against any soldiers or band of Shadows—a good shooter, she was. And his mother was a strong woman, too, capable of riding any wild pony. In the *Illahe*, the buffalo country near the *E-sue-gha* far to the east, he had watched her bring down buffalo with a big rifle. This woman would not tremble even at the sudden appearance of a grizzly bear.

Yellow Wolf knew he was his mother's son!

And now he had a sixteen-shot carbine for the war—no more would he have to use the one-shot soldier gun, condemned to searching out soldier bullets for it.

That night they had camped near the Middle Fork, farther north and close to Kamiah where many of the Non-Treaties went on Sunday morning for their special services. It was the next morning when riders came galloping back to report that they were being watched by some Shadows.

"*Suapies*?"

"No, not soldiers. But a lot of Shadows."

By the time the young men under *Ollokot*, Five Wounds, and Rainbow had returned with their weapons and their red blankets, the whites had scurried to the top of a large hill Yellow Wolf's people called *Possossona*. At this place known as Water Passing, the Shadows were throwing up rock barricades they could hide behind. But the white men were unable to hold onto their horses that night after it grew very dark.

It was a good thing, too, this taking of the horses, because they had found that most of them belonged to Looking Glass's people.

"These were taken by those Shadows when they came with the soldiers to drive us from our camp!"

"Good," *Ollokot* had said to the Alpowai. "Now we've taken them back and the Shadows can walk on their sore feet if they want to return to their hollows or towns."

They kept four-times-ten of the ponies they had run off from Shadows, then led the rest—those they did not want—onto the Camas Prairie and scattered them far from the Shadow strongholds.

For another day they kept up a little sporadic fire at the whites, just enough to force the Shadows down behind their rock and tree barricades. Even though there had been a lot of shooting, only one warrior was injured: his right trigger finger shot off while he was leading away a pair of Looking Glass's horses the Shadows stole. In all the excitement, *Paktilek* had not realized he was hit until he noticed that the mane of the horse he was riding was wet and sticky with blood. A big ring on another finger was badly dented. It had saved the rest of his hand!

That next morning the chiefs decided it would be better to march upstream a ways.

Toohoolhoolzote said, "If the Shadows have found us here, then the soldiers will be the next to come."

"Yes," agreed White Bird. "We should take our families and lodges away from this place and deeper into the canyon of the Clearwater."

Looking Glass suggested, "We will be safe at *Pitayiwahwih;* there is room enough for us all to camp there."

Away they marched from those Shadows hunkered down in their hollows, just the way the soldiers had been kept in their holes at the far side of the Camas Prairie for many days. Why wouldn't the Shadows and *suapies* learn that whenever they attempted to attack the Non-Treaty bands they were always struck back with an even stronger blow?

Now this morning in that new camp the sun had been long in creeping over the lip of the tall, rocky bluffs just east of the river. Many of the young men slept in after singing, dancing, and courting late into the night. And when they did arise, there was nothing much to do. Already they had lost interest in keeping a close guard on those hill-bound Shadows downstream, and the *suapies* were still far away at the settlements. . . . So this would be a day to relax, here in this most beautiful of settings.

Through this narrow canyon the South Fork of the Clearwater flowed strong and clean, braced on the east by sheer cliffs rising more than a thousand feet in height, while to the west rose irregular bluffs. Both walls were inscribed with deep ravines climbing up to grassy rolling plateau. For much of the morning the canyon remained in shadow. Here summer days reigned.

For Yellow Wolf, it seemed as if the war was holding its breath. Camp would not be moved this day, the sun would be hot, so now had come the time to celebrate—even though there was no more whiskey in the camps. They would hold horse races and games of chance. There would be time for bathing in the cold river, or trying to talk to that young woman in White Bird's band, the pretty one Yellow Wolf had had his eye on for weeks now. At dusk, some of the older men would put out the call when it came time for the *timei*—a special race held but once every summer—when each contestant announced to the whole village the name of the young woman whose hand he would be racing for.

Perhaps she would see in him something worthy, although he was hawk-nosed and snake-eyed, his skin the color of an old saddle many times sweated on. No, Yellow Wolf had not the beautiful burnished copper skin of most *Wallowa*. He was not a handsome man like Shore Crossing or *Ollokot,* but in the last few weeks he had won a reputation as a fighter and man of integrity—one who would provide for and protect a woman and the children to come of their union.

Yellow Wolf had been sitting on his pony, watching some of the horse races on the long flat above the village, when his friend *Wemastahtus* came up and said with much excitement, "Yesterday a soldier was killed below here. I found him this morning."

"I want to see him."

Wemastahtus led Yellow Wolf several miles to the spot on down the Clearwater toward Kamiah. The body was lying in some brush by the side of the river trail, almost as if the man were asleep, except that a cloud of flies tormented his eyes, nostrils, and his slack mouth, too, with their black, buzzing fury. The man had a lot of bushy hair on his upper lip that ran down to the bottom of his chin.

"Maybe he ran away from the army," *Wemastahtus* suggested.

"No," Yellow Wolf said, "I think he ran away from the Shadows pinned down at *Possossona*."

His curiosity sated, Yellow Wolf now wanted to find the young woman with the big eyes. He loped back, reaching the lower end of the village, knowing the chances were good she would take her younger sisters and a brother down to the river to watch the children while they bathed and splashed in the water, now that the sun was high overhead. The best place to tell her his soft words would be in the cool shade of those big cottonwoods here in the quiet of this midday heat, with nothing but the gurgle of the Clearwater—

That loud boom echoed off the canyon wall, then died as the shattering noise was swallowed by the low hills west of the river.

At first, every motion stopped, every voice stilled—the air itself suspended in stunned and stupefied silence. Then, as the loud roar faded, Yellow Wolf heard again the buzz of the flies and other wingeds here along the shady bank. A heartbeat later, the first woman's scream split the dry, hot air.

Her cry was quickly taken up by a hundred more—women and children all, scrambling out of the water as a second dull *whoosh* whistled down the canyon and ended with a terrifying blast that shook the birds out of the nearby trees. Such a *whoosh-boom* could be nothing but a two-shoots wagon gun: roaring once when it was fired, roaring a second time when its round charge exploded on the far bank, well short of camp.

Men were shouting now, war leaders exhorting others to grab up their weapons. A young man was riding down the opposite side of the river, waving a blanket back and forth, back and forth over his head in warning.

Yellow Wolf gazed into the young woman's frightened eyes a moment as she held out her hand. Yellow Wolf touched it for but a moment, feeling her long, slim, cool fingers—

"Yellow Wolf!"

He whirled around, finding *Wemastahtus* on the low bluff just above him. Then he turned for one last look at the young woman, her eyes full of fury and fight, eyes telling him what her lips did not need to say.

"I am coming!" he yelled at *Wemastahtus*, not taking his eyes off her just yet. "We have an enemy to fight today!"

Her face softened for him but a moment before he turned away, scrambling up the slope.

"*Toohoolhoolzote* is already rushing to the bank with a few of his men," *Wemastahtus* announced as they raced their ponies through the camp, heading for the lodge of Yellow Wolf's mother. "I think that old war man wants to be the first to sneak up behind the soldiers!"

Stripped to nothing but his breechclout like the other warriors rushing past them, Yellow Wolf ducked back out of the lodge with one cartridge belt buckled around his waist, slipping a second belt over his left shoulder. Now with his sixteen-shot repeater in hand as he went into battle for the first time in many weeks, Yellow Wolf snatched the long lead rope from his friend, then leaped onto the pony's narrow back. Together they raced to the closest ford just upstream from camp, finding *Toohoolhoolzote* and a few others had already reached the far side—more than twenty, these first to answer the old warrior's call to action, all of them pitching across the river, racing to throw their bodies between their families and the attacking soldiers.

Behind them on the west bank the chiefs were shouting their orders to the rest—by this date in their war with the soldiers and Shadows numbering close to three hundred men of fighting age. Quickly they split all those remaining warriors in two groups, both of which would remain behind to protect the camp. One started to stream toward the north, the direction from which the cannon fire had come, where that group of Shadows might still be pinned down on their hilltop. The other group raced to the south, the direction where they had believed Cut-Off Arm was still camped with his soldiers. And those boys too young to fight drove more than two thousand ponies up the gentle slope west of the village, reaching the top of the plateau, where the herd would be safe from the army's loud guns.

"*Koklinikse!*" *Toohoolhoolzote* bellowed his scolding command at those who swarmed onto the east bank behind him. "Move faster! Faster!"

Slinging water as they came out of the Clearwater, the first of these most eager of the young men reined their horses into the timber dotting the sharp side of the bluff. Yellow Wolf's strong pony quickly vaulted him into the lead, clawing its way into one of the two jagged ravines* that carried the defenders in an ascent to the top of the ridge some nine hundred to a thousand feet above the river. Both hearts beat fast, lungs gasping hungrily for air, as man and horse lunged to the top—a leap at a time—the hoofbeats and war cries of the others right on their tail.

Slipping from the mouth of the rugged right-hand ravine, Yellow Wolf yanked back on the reins of his heaving pony. To his left a dark swarm of soldiers covered the ridge top and prairie to the north of him. They were scurrying around, some headed this way and others headed that way, not seeing him or the first warriors to bristle up on his sides. *Suapies* running in all directions, forming up then breaking apart as they moved here and there—a strange preparation for a fight.

As his pony caught its wind, Yellow Wolf watched a stream of soldiers break off and start down another wide ravine leading to the river below. "Can't you see the soldiers!" he screamed at those who had rushed to the top right behind him. "They're going to attack our camp! Come on now—we must get up close and do some shooting at them!"

Without waiting for a word or sign of agreement from the others, Yellow Wolf jabbed his bare heels into the ribs of the animal and shot away, sprinting across that broad flat south of the massing soldiers. A wide canyon suddenly separated the young men from those white enemies. Leaning far back on his horse's spine, Yellow Wolf urged the horse down the steep wall of the ravine, then rocked forward as the pony clawed its way up the far side, until he found himself in rifle range of the *suapies*. Now these first warriors had

---

*The two ravines taken by *Toohoolhoolzote*'s warriors extend east away from the river on either side of a geographical feature that today is called Dizzy Head.

placed their bodies between the soldiers and the spring. The white men would have no water today!

"Tie your horses here!" growled the deep bullfrog bass of old *Toohoolhoolzote* as his exhausted pony lunged out of the wide cleft in the ridge and hoof-slid into a thick stand of trees.

As one the two dozen followed the war chief into a small copse of tall pines, leaped to the ground, and tied off their horses, out of danger from soldier bullets. At the edge of those trees the old chief's young fighters could see how Cut-Off Arm's soldiers would soon be making for the edge of the bluff . . . and from there they could descend into the valley and attack their village.

"Come, all you young men!" *Toohoolhoolzote* cheered. "*Eeh-heh!* We have to stop those soldiers from reaching our camp!"

"*Amtiz!*" Yellow Wolf yelled. "Let's go! We must throw our bodies between the end of this ridge and those soldier guns!"

"BLESSED MARY AND Joseph!" he growled as the firing grew hotter and the Indians stopped their advance dead in its tracks.

First Sergeant Michael McCarthy wasn't sure just how many of those redskins they were confronting at the edge of the bluff, but he was sure it had to be at least a hundred!

At least, that's how many warriors Perry's cavalry battalion believed had stopped them cold in the valley of the White Bird last month, a little less than the size of the attacking force that flung itself at Perry's Cottonwood bivouac and somewhere close to the same number of horsemen who had jumped the seventeen civilians racing for Norton's ranch. So it made perfect sense a hundred or more of the Nez Perce fighting men must have rushed up the draws to reach this ridge-top prairie, where they managed to stall Howard's advance in a matter of minutes.

Surely the general and his officers could repulse this handful of troublesome snipers, having some 450 men at their command after Howard had waited to gather all his troops and all those supplies before setting off across the corner of the Camas Prairie after the hostiles!

On the eighth of July Howard's advance had recrossed the Salmon at the mouth of the White Bird. Pushing on with H and I Companies of the First U. S. Cavalry, the general's men passed by those shallow graves, a few of which were marked by hats suspended at the tops of short sticks, most of the skimpy dirt having settled into the depressions, what with the heavy rains. By midnight they rendezvoused with Perry's battalion in Grangeville, learning that the Nez Perce were camped on the South Fork of the Clearwater. On the outskirts of town, Howard established what he christened Camp Randall, in honor of the civilian who gave his life in this struggle back on the fifth of July.

Just after dawn that Monday morning, Perry pushed on for the Clearwater with his four companies of cavalry, crossing to the east side of the South Fork on the Jackson Bridge, which some Nez Perce raiding party had attempted to torch in recent days. The horse soldiers went into camp on the long slope behind the burned-out buildings of Thelbert Walls's ranch.

Meanwhile, it took part of the eighth and most of the ninth of the month for Miles's infantry and Miller's artillery batteries to ferry themselves across the mighty Salmon—having virtually run out of supplies by the time they established their wretched bivouac at the mouth of the White Bird: without food or tents or dry blankets. Finally, early on the morning of the tenth, Captain Miles of the Twenty-first Infantry led in his battalion of eight footsore companies. Every man jack of them bailed out of the wagons Howard had sent down to the Salmon for them, collapsing into the grass at Camp Randall, where they promptly fell asleep, knowing it wouldn't be long before they would be ordered back on the road to catch up to the cavalry once more.

Over on the South Fork at Walls's ranch, in those first dim shadows at daylight on the tenth, one of the cavalry pickets opened fire on another guard, making for a brief but lively exchange until the camp discovered they were shooting at themselves and things quieted down once again while they waited out the day and those wagons filled with foot soldiers. They finally rumbled across the bridge and into the midst of the burned-out ranch just before 8:00 P.M. Told to quickly build their fires, choke down their supper, then climb into their blankets, Howard's command learned they would be marching on the enemy at first light.

By 7:30 A.M. on the eleventh, Howard gave the honor of the lead for the day to Trimble's H Company, this time behind a local guide, James T. Silverwood, and a contingent of Nez Perce scouts under Ad Chapman. Behind the rest of Perry's cavalry battalion came the infantry, then the pack train, along with a few horses detached from the main body, while the artillery brought up the rear. A few miles out of Walls's place, the advance ran across a small bunch of mares and their foals, horses that Chapman identified as having been stolen from his ranch. To the army's way of thinking, that was a clue they might be closing on the enemy. Trimble put out skirmishers and they resumed their march.

In short order, they were climbing a thousand or more feet to reach the high ground between the South and Middle Forks along a well-used mining road, forced to inch back farther and farther from the edge of the bluff where they had hoped to keep an eye trained along the Clearwater for signs of the enemy village or war parties. Hour after hour that clear, breezy morning, the ravines grew deeper, scarring the landscape of the plateau, each one more choked with brush and boulders than the last.

As the sun rose higher, and hotter, too, talk was Howard had designs on trapping the enemy between their column and McConville's gutsy volunteers who had gone out days ago to locate the village and were known to be under seige somewhere north of the advancing soldiers.

Captain Joel G. Trimble's H Company was about a half-mile in the vanguard, just emerging from a forested area onto more open prairie, where clumps of brush and small stands of trees made for a thick fringe on either side of the rolling grassland. Three of the civilian scouts in the lead came racing past, on their way to Howard with a report that they had just spotted some Nez Perce herders driving stock over the edge of the bluffs toward the Clearwater below.

Within minutes Howard ordered the artillery to the edge of the bluff and his vanguard to about-face. Far in the lead, McCarthy's H Company was marching slowly, deliberately watchful, when they heard that first distant cannonshot off to the south. Trimble halted his skirmishers and sent a courier back to headquarters to learn what had developed. In minutes the order came racing back that they were to turn about and support the pack train. After all, it contained the many thousands of rounds of ammunition—just what the Nez Perce would covet most.

Dashing up on the double, McCarthy's men found Captain George B. Rodney's D Battery of the Fourth U. S. Artillery—assigned that morning to protect the pack train—taking some harassing fire. Already one of the packers had been killed. As McCarthy's H Company came to their assistance, another packer was struck in the head, dead before he flopped to the ground. There followed a sudden rush of motion on the far side of the frightened packers and their bawling mules when the pack train suddenly split in the middle and a handful of mounted warriors belched through the widening gap, waving blankets at the terrified mules.

Through the heroic efforts of both companies, only one of the mules galloped off behind the raiders. But that mule was carrying two large crates filled with ammunition for the twelve-pounder, a mountain howitzer.

One thing was for certain, McCarthy thought. These sure as hell weren't reservation Injuns!

In a moment more both Rodney and Trimble were shouting orders for their officers to prevent a repeat of that sudden, frightening rush by the red horsemen on their small ponies, warriors who seemed to appear one minute and be gone the next. Dismounting their cavalrymen, Rodney formed his troopers into a column of fours on the prairie side of the bawling, braying, anxious mules, while Trimble likewise formed him men up on the bluff side of the pack train before they started the mules back to the south, carrying that valuable ammunition to the rest of the command.

McCarthy hadn't really noticed the terrain as they marched north, figuring he had been half-dozing there with the rocking of the saddle, the heat and intensity of the sun at its midday strongest. Now as they steered the pack train around the head of a deep ravine, the sergeant saw how this patch of ridge-top prairie was cordoned off north and south by a pair of rugged ravines less than a mile apart. Thick brush not only lined both gulches, but tall trees shaded the sides of those ravines—which meant the enemy had ample cover on three sides of this field where Howard was just now setting up an extensive perimeter: north and south, as well as to the west, along the edge of the ridge itself.

Escorting the pack train around the head of a deep ravine and into a slight depression at the center of that crude semicircle some seven hundred yards across, which the deploying troops had established on the grassy flat, Trimble and Rodney brought the balky mules to a halt near the head of that ravine, where Howard and his staff were just then establishing their headquarters. It was plain to see that their delay in getting the pack train and their companies around that wide ravine had allowed the Nez Perce those critical minutes they needed to establish themselves in the shady timber on both sides of the draw.

Trimble must have realized the threat those snipers represented to the mule train, for he gave the order for his men to leave their horses with holders and follow him to the edge of the timber, where they were suffering the hottest battering at the hands of an unknown number of Nez Perce snipers. They dodged around a number of small boulders and a few sparse trees, grinding to a halt in the tall grass just then going to seed and turning brown with the first real heat of the summer.

And realized there were even more warriors popping onto the grassy plateau from a second ravine. Now Trimble's H Company was pinned down, taking a deadly cross fire.

It was enough to send a shiver down his spine and cause goose bumps to sprout on McCarthy's arms—the war cries of those savages, the braying of the frightened mules Rodney's men were fighting behind them, the yells and cheers of his fellow soldiers, the harsh orders shouted by the officers, all of it mixed with the unsteady racket of Springfield and carbine fire as well as the unfamiliar *clack-clack* of the two Gatlings as they were brought into the fray.

For a moment he considered hurrying in a crouch to the right so he might reach the edge of the bluff and have himself a look down at the enemy camp, maybe even watch for McConville's civilians when they made their appearance. That would throw the village into an uproar, McCarthy thought. To find themselves between the soldiers on one side and that citizen battalion on the other! Any time now, McConville's volunteers would be riding into this fray from the north.

McCarthy quickly turned and gazed over his shoulder at the sky, feeling just how hot the sun was that seared its heat through his wool jacket and gray undershirt. He inched his head up but a moment, looking around the prairie—a mile in any direction now was commanded by General Howard's army.

Already McCarthy's throat was parched, his tongue pasty against the roof of his mouth.

The sergeant wondered if there was any water within the sound of his voice. Hell, if they had any water within the army's perimeter.

CHAPTER TWENTY-SEVEN

July 11, 1877

BY TELEGRAPH

Particulars of the Indian War
in Oregon.

Russians Abandoning the
Seige of Kars.

OREGON.

The Indian War—Details of the Late
Fight, and List of the Killed and
Wounded.

SAN FRANCISCO, July 10.—Dispatches from Lewiston, via Portland, give the details of encounters with the Indians on the 3d, 4th, and 5th inst., near the Cottonwood. Tuesday, Colonel Whipple sent out Foster and Blewett scouting for Indians in the direction of General Howard's camp on Salmon river. They had not gone far when they met three or four Indians, who ran them back toward camp. Foster reached camp, and Whipple ordered the command in readiness to move. Meantime, Lieutenant Raines and his men rode over the first rise this side of the Cottonwood and down into the ravine where the road crosses before the ascent of Craig's mountain, and were attacked before Whipple could get to them, after he heard the firing. Raines and his whole party were killed, including Foster. Whipple's command came forward and formed in line of battle on the east side of the ravine, and the Indians on the west, all on open ground, about one thousand yards apart, and only the ravine between them. Here they remained menacing each other for about two hours, till darkness came. Whipple retired to his camp, and the Indians passed over to a point on the Cottonwood trail to Craig's crossing. No more was done that night. Next Morning Whipple with his men started this way to meet Colonel Perry, who was expected with a supply train from Lopway, and kept out his skirmish lines along the route. They met Colonel Perry with his train near Board house and escorted him to camp. Baird and two men arrived from Mount Idaho soon after, and about 5 p.m. the rifle-pits were placed in position.

The Indians made several attempts to storm the rifle-pits, but were kept at a distance. About 9 p.m. the firing ceased for the night. On the morning of the 5th two couriers arrived from General Howard, chased into camp by the Indians. Soon after they moved their camp, with about sixteen hundred head of stock, across the prairie in the direction of the Cottonwood. No move was made to intercept them. Soon after, Captain Randall and sixteen volunteers from Mount Idaho approached. About one hundred Indians intercepted them at the junction of the Elk City trail with the stage road. At this crisis, being seen from Perry's position on the hill at the rifle-pits, the Colonel was urged to go with troops to their rescue, to which he replied it was no use, they were gone, and he would not order a rescue. The volunteers say that their captain, seeing his position, ordered them to charge and break the line of Indians, dash over toward the creek bottom, dismount, and return the fire, and hold their position, partly under cover of a small hill, until the force at Cottonwood could reach them. The command was no sooner given than Captain Randall and his sixteen men made a charge, broke through the Indian line, reached the position named, dismounted, and returned the fire. In the charge Captain Randall was mortally wounded, Benjamin Evans killed, and three others wounded. They fought there for nearly an hour, and kept the Indians at bay. In about half an hour after, it was known that the Indians had the volunteers in a tight place. Colonel Perry gave orders for fifty men to go to their relief. It was quickly obeyed, and they were relieved in about an hour after the charge. No pursuit of the Indians was ordered, but a retreat was made to camp and no pursuit had been made since, up to the time of Morrill's leaving on the night of the 6th. The volunteers say they know they killed several Indians and wounded many others, as they saw the Indians packing off their dead and wounded the same night. McConville, with a volunteer force, has arrived at Cottonwood from Howard's command. On the 6th a detachment of seventy-five men, under McConville, was sent as an escort to a wagon carrying the killed and wounded to Fort Idaho. Morrill says that Randall, after he was mortally wounded,

> had got into position, sat up on the ground, and fired many shots at the Indians, the last not more than five minutes before he fell back dead. Not one of the seventeen faltered in the least, or showed the white feather, though hard pressed by 100 Indians, nor did one of them seek to run for Cottonwood after they had broken the Indian lines, but strictly obeyed orders to hold their ground . . .
>
> When Baird and Morrill left, he Indians were in full possession of Comas Prairie except for Mount Idaho, Grangeville and the camp at Cottonwood. Yesterday several fires were seen in different directions, some about three miles from the creek, and appearance was that houses, barns and hay stacks were burning. From Lapwai it is reported that the Indians crossed Clearwater yesterday at 11 a.m. near Komia, with their stock. Settlers are being plundered and robbed on Cow creek, on the Colville and Walla Walla road. Forty to sixty volunteers have gone from Walla Walla to the scene of the difficulty.

OU'RE A DAMN FOOL TO THINK YOU'RE GONNA WALK ALL THE WAY BACK to Mount Idaho on foot!" Edward McConville growled.

George Shearer finished tucking his pants into the tops of his tall boots, then straightened before he spoke.

"Colonel McConville. It's past noon and I don't figger we're gonna see a sign of any relief party sent out by that goddamned one-armed Yankee general. Anyone wants to walk out of here is more'n welcome to join me."

They had waited for the better part of a day and a half after Lew Wilmot and Benjamin Penny rode off with a second plea to Howard. As the hours passed, day becoming night, then night seeping into day once again, more and more it appeared that there was only one thing to think: Wilmot and Penny had been jumped and butchered by some roving war party haunting this rim of the Camas Prairie. Over time, George grew angrier and angrier, brooding how he had lost another friend. Lew Wilmot—lying dead and flyblown out there on the rolling prairie.

By noon of this eleventh day of July, Shearer had decided he had had enough.

"You're like to g-get picked off out there!" warned Ben Morris.

"Better'n dying in here from hunger or thirst," Shearer had snapped.

McConville wondered, "What of the Injuns?"

George shrugged and asked, "What Injuns? We ain't seen nary a one since early yestiddy, Ed. I'm gonna take the chance I can make it on shank's mare all the way in to Mount Idaho."

He was the first to clamber over the low rock wall they had piled up for breastworks. A half-dozen of the men were right on his heels when he stopped and looked back at the rest.

"Well, you boys comin' or ain'cha?"

That did it for most of the eighty-some men who stood arrayed across the flat top of that hill. They immediately bolted over the rock and timber barricades, gaping with grins as wide as if they were embarking on a spring social.

Shearer started down the slope at the head of the bunch. After less than fifteen yards, he stopped and went to his knee, scooping up a handful of empty cartridges left by the warriors who had kept them under seige. His eyes slowly climbed back up the hill to their breastworks for a moment, as he realized just how close the enemy had come to overrunning them. Then he spotted Ed McConville standing stoic and unmoving behind their low barricades.

Getting to his feet with a sigh, Shearer turned away and continued down the hill. In less than a minute Bunker loped up to his elbow.

"E. J., g'won an' sneak a look back—tell me if the colonel's coming," George whispered. Bunker turned his head and glanced back while he kept scooting on down the hill with George at the point of that arrow-shaped formation of white footmen. "Ed's coming. He's all the way back there . . . but he's coming."

"Good," Shearer whispered with a deep sigh, picking up the pace a little now. They had a long, long way to walk if they were going to make it to the settlements by morning. "I was afraid to go off an' leave the man all on his lonesome, standing back there on principle an' nothin' else if them red savages was to come back for us."

NOT LONG AFTER *Toohoolhoolzote*'s small band of warriors had stopped the soldiers and forced them to take cover in the tall grass on that dusty plateau,* *Ollokot*, Rainbow, and Five Wounds came bounding up the north ravine and burst into the middle of the white man's pack train—waving blankets, firing pistols, and yelling like demons.

It was a pretty charge, Yellow Wolf had to admit. A rush into and on through the soldiers that he wished he himself had been part of. As it was, the fighting men around him had their hands full once the *suapies* stopped, turned around, then spread out in a great circle with their baggage and animals protected at its center. The few guns carried by those first warriors had forced more than ten times their number to hunker down in the grass without giving a fight!

It was the old war chief, *Toohoolhoolzote*, who had killed the first soldier with his ancient muzzleloader. Then he quickly reloaded as the rest of his war starters crawled up behind him in the timber, and the chief killed a second soldier. The swelling puff of muzzle smoke from his old gun betrayed his position and brought a shower of bullets his way . . . but none found *Toohoolhoolzote*.

"Come, young ones; come!" he cried again and again, goading his war-

*This battle site, located on private land, stands on what is today called Battle Ridge, just above the present-day community of Stites, Idaho.

riors into daring to pit themselves against unimaginable odds. "Let's show these soldiers how to fight: rock-to-rock, tree-to-tree! If they gain any ground on us, let them leave blood on every step!"

Eeh-heh! The old fighter's *wyakin* was mighty strong that day!

As the soldiers began to fire wildly at the shadows in the timber, random bullets began to fall among their ponies. The horses grew scared, making noise and stomping around where they were tied, drawing even more soldier bullets.

"Four of you, go back to the ponies and take them to a safer place," *Toohoolhoolzote* ordered, then named the four young men he selected for this task. "I am afraid they will break loose; then we will not have them when we need them in the fight."

Right after this, their old leader and the two-times-ten set up a hot fire into the soldier lines. Then from two directions, more soldiers came in at a run, diving into the tall grass once they found themselves within range of the *Nee-Me-Poo* rifles. As Yellow Wolf watched and the sun started to slowly slip off midsky, the *suapies* massed, beginning a gradual movement against the timber from which the young riflemen had poured the first fire at the white men.

Back, back, back the soldiers pushed, slowly gaining ground . . . but only one hand span at a time. Although they now outnumbered the young warriors some twenty-to-one, the *suapies* paid for that ground with some blood and plenty of sweat under the broiling sun. Although *Toohoolhoolzote* and the other fighters rallied one another with cheers of encouragement, the pressure finally became too much and the old chief gave the order to leave the timber and slip down into the edge of the ravine. The instant the soldiers found the warriors were no longer keeping them pinned down, their fighting chiefs ordered them to make a charge.

On they plunged toward the timber. *Toohoolhoolzote* stopped and whirled around in a fury, kneeling as he aimed his old one-shoot muzzleloader. It hissed and the round lead ball found its mark, driving a soldier backward off his feet at the same moment the squat warrior scrambled to his feet and joined the others in running from that timber where the bullets buzzed like angry bees, smacking the trunks of trees, zinging through branches—

Suddenly Yellow Wolf slammed his bare feet to a halt. He had forgotten his horse! All of them had forgotten their ponies!

Wheeling about, he squatted and peered off to where the horse holders had taken their animals. The four were nowhere to be seen! They had abandoned the ponies as soon as the firing grew too intense even for *Toohoolhoolzote*. And the rest of the fighters were scampering behind the old chief toward another patch of timber west of the *suapies*.

Yellow Wolf felt the anger rising in him like a fever. The holders had abandoned their horses, and the others had abandoned him. That was a good horse and he wanted it back, even though the soldiers approached the edge of that narrow patch of timber. It was a disgrace for a fighting man to lose his horse to the enemy in battle.

Death while recapturing one's horse would be preferable to leaving the fight without the animal!

At first he started to creep through the trees; then he realized he wasn't going to get there in time to rescue the pony if he did not run. The young warrior took off at a sprint, jumping low rocks and dodging around the pines until he reached the animal, yanked its lead rope loose, and hurled himself onto its back—no matter the whine and whiz of bullets coming into that stand of trees.

Yelling at the top of his lungs, Yellow Wolf did his best to drive off the other horses, sweeping those that would be herded before him as he pressed low against his pony's neck and followed the route taken by *Toohoolhoolzote*. Bullets sang past, striking the ground and singing off the rocks, smacking trees, as the horse carried him down one side of the wide ravine and desperately clawed its way up the steep side onto the plateau once more. He recalled the words of his uncle, Old Yellow Wolf: "If you go to war and get shot, do not cry!"

Just remembering that admonition helped him be brave. Better to die with his horse than to turn away from the fight without it.

In heartbeats the snarling of the bullets was fading behind him. The crack of rifles no more thundered about his ears. He had reached the timber on the south side of the saddle. Dismounting, he tied off his strong brown horse, letting it regain its wind and graze while he started toward the sound of firing on that south side of the fight. Near a copse of trees he came upon a stand of large boulders where many men—mostly older—had gathered to talk about the fighting, make plans, and catch their wind, too. To the *Nee-Me-Poo* this was a "smoking lodge," where older warriors whose day had come and gone now passed their pipes around while discussing the fight others were making against the soldiers.

The sting of the tobacco smoke stung his nose and made his eyes water as he hurried past. Yellow Wolf never had smoked. He did not like it, and it made his head sick when he smelled others burning tobacco. Moving into a lope, the young warrior hurried to the east where the sound of gunfire was the heaviest.

At the edge of the timber he noticed how many of the finest warriors were flat on their bellies behind low boulders they had pushed before them, right out of the timber and into the tall grass, sneaking up on the soldier lines. They had good guns to use against the *suapies* this day! In little time they had captured more than three times the number of his fingers in new firearms from those soldiers dead or frightened and fleeing from White Bird Canyon. And the warriors took a dozen more from the men they ambushed some distance away from the soldier burrow holes at Cottonwood. This meant that now a good deal more than half of the *Nee-Me-Poo* warriors had guns to carry into this hot fight with Cut-Off Arm's men.

Many of those guns had been used most effectively against four, even five times their number, stopping the soldiers in their tracks and forcing them into that protective square while the rest of the warriors rushed out of the valley—once everyone realized the village would not be threatened—and climbed to the plateau to join the fight. Cut-Off Arm must surely be hiding somewhere in the middle of his *suapies*, concealed among the horses and mules at the center of the square in a low depression where he would be safe.

There was no manhood in having others do your fighting for you like that!

The young warrior spotted his uncle, Old Yellow Wolf, lying in the middle of those veteran fighters where the noise was the loudest and the shooting the hottest, firing his soldier gun at the enemy. Beside him lay another old fighter who refused to go to the smoking lodge. Fire Body, called *Otstotpoo*, had killed the first soldier at the White Bird Canyon fight—his bullet hitting a man who blew on a brass horn.* *Tomyunmene* was on Yellow Wolf's uncle's left side. The faces of all three were flecked with bloody scratches caused by flying rock chips as soldier bullets careened off the boulders they lay behind to take their shots.

This had to be the most exposed part of the entire line of these patriots fighting for their country!

Yellow Wolf plopped on his belly as the bullets hissed around him. There were no trees or shade here to hide within. Only these low boulders.

"I see that hat again!" Fire Body announced in a raspy whisper.

"Can you hit it?"

"I did twice before!" the veteran warrior answered Old Yellow Wolf.

He took careful aim through the long sight attached to the top of the rifle barrel and squeezed the trigger.

Tomyunmene shouted, "You took off that Shadow's hat!"

"Three times now!" Old Yellow Wolf cried, slapping his bare thigh in joy as his nephew crawled up beside him and took a place behind the low boulders.

"Welcome, young one!" cried *Howwallits*, the one called Mean Man, sometimes referred to as Mean Person. "I see you brought your rifle today. You will see lots of game to hunt out there in the grass. Look carefully and you won't fail to find yourself a target—"

A bullet smacked the edge of the rock to Yellow Wolf's left, knocking off a large chunk, then ricochetting off to strike his uncle just above the eye, driving the older man's head backward. Old Yellow Wolf grunted as he flopped onto his side . . . then lay still.

"Uncle! Uncle!" Yellow Wolf shouted far too loudly as he brushed the bright, gleaming blood from the older man's face.

Bullets immediately followed the noise, forcing the warriors to hug the ground for a few moments.

When the soldier fire lessened, Mean Person suggested, "See if breath comes from his mouth, or the nose."

Yellow Wolf laid his ear against his uncle's face, trying to hear the movement of air. But with so much yelling coming from both sides of the fight, he could not tell.

**Cries from the Earth*, vol. 14, the *Plainsmen* series.

"Lay your head over his heart," Fire Body ordered. "Press your ear tightly and feel for the life."

After what felt like a long, long time, his uncle's chest moved a little, and Yellow Wolf believed he heard a little flutter of the old man's heart.

With great joy, he shouted, "I think my uncle will live again!"*

---

*For the Nez Perce warriors, being unconscious is considered the same as death, and when a man comes to, he is said to "return to life" or be "getting life again."

CHAPTER TWENTY-EIGHT

JULY 11, 1877

THEY HAD BEEN FIGHTING THESE REDSKINS FOR MORE THAN THREE HOURS by the time Howard ordered Captain Evan Miles to take some of his infantry in a charge on the ravine lying at the northern extreme of the battlefield—a patch of grassy prairie that extended a scant mile and a half wide north to south and a couple of miles long east to west—where the troops, both foot and horse, were forced to fight in the open, their only protection the tall grass just starting to turn with these last few days of searing heat.

While the first few weeks of this campaign, indeed the beginning of summer itself, had been cool and rainy at best, the past handful of days had turned unmercifully hot as storm clouds disappeared from the sky and the sun reemerged with a vengeance—seeming to burn like fire right through an enlisted man's flannel and wool.

First Sergeant Michael McCarthy had first unbuttoned his tunic, praying to the Virgin Mary for a breath of air to stir; just a little breeze it could be. Then he had pulled off the tunic completely, stripped down to his sweat-drenched gray undershirt like most of the other men in Trimble's H Company.

He and the rest, too, were all beginning to dwell more and more on the subject of water. Was there a pond of it back in that center of their perimeter with the supplies? Or would there be a cool spring or gurgling creek somewhere in those trees currently held by the enemy? Where in blazes would his next drink of water come from?

Miles's attack on the northern ravine had been so successful that by 3:30 P.M. Howard had ordered Captain Marcus P. Miller to take his artillerymen and launch the same offensive against the timber west of their enclosure. Breveted a colonel during the Civil War, Miller was an 1858 graduate of the U. S. Military Academy and a workhorse who had spent his entire career in the Fourth U. S. Artillery. Having fought at Antietam, Fredericksburg, and Chancellorsville, he came west to battle Captain Jack's Modocs. It was Miller's leadership of an artillery battery that rescued the survivors of Canby's peace commission after the general was brutally assassinated.*

But today Miller's charge bogged down when the resistance proved fierce

---

**Devil's Backbone,* vol. 5, the *Plainsmen* series.

and the warriors would not be moved. The rest of that afternoon and into the long summer evening, the battle settled into a sniping match between the two sides as both the Nez Perce and the soldiers devoted time between shots to scratching at the hot dirt, attempting to hollow out a shallow rifle pit—the infantry using their trowel bayonets, the cavalry having to plow with their belt knives and scrape with tin cups.

With the sun having slid off midsky, the hottest part of the day had come as it slowly sank to the west, baking this plateau of drying grass and parched soldiers.

The hottest fighting of the battle was yet to begin.

FROM TIME TO time the *suapies* turned their big-throated gun on the timber where so many of the warriors had taken up positions after they rode up from the valley floor. Most of the time the noisy charges overshot the horsemen who had followed *Ollokot* out of the village, but every now and then an explosion showered the men with dirt and tree branches or wounded some horses.

"We must take that big gun!" *Ollokot* exhorted the men from the many bands who had shown up to fight on this west side of the ridge.

Their first three charges at the gun emplacement and those soldiers hunkered down there were as unsuccessful as the quick dash they had made among the pack train earlier that afternoon. Each time *Ollokot*'s warriors were driven back . . . but each time his men managed to get a little closer, a little closer to the big-throated gun. Withdrawing with his warriors, *Ollokot* vowed with the failure of each charge that their next attempt would bring them success. But a fourth and fifth assault only got them to within two long horse lengths of the weapon.

A final attempt might just force the soldiers back enough that *Ollokot*'s warriors could seize the powerful weapon, when they could turn and use it upon the soldier lines.

As he dashed back and forth along his wavering lines of naked warriors, *Ollokot* watched a soldier crawl out through the tall, dry grass until he lay directly beneath the cannon. From that position the *suapie* could load the weapon without exposing himself any more than he had to. As the white man started to slide backward in the grass, *Ollokot* realized the soldier was about to fire the gun. And had to be stopped before he touched fire to the back of the long weapon.

"Come on, all you men who would rather die than give up your country!" *Ollokot* cried, streaming out in front. "Do this for the graves of your ancestors! Do this for the weak and the small ones! Do this so your children will live free!"

In a screeching red wave they broke from the shadows, swarming across the tall grass as the soldiers immediately began to fall back. Of a sudden there was a soldier chief among the *suapies*, then a second, both of them yelling their orders, mingled perhaps with their own encouragement. The fleeing soldiers stopped, turned, and started back toward the gun. On either side of it they were thick as summer wasps now.

Closer and closer both sides advanced, the bullets like clouds of noisome flies, the gunsmoke gagging the fighters. Three arm lengths, no more, *Ollokot*'s warriors got away from the gun and those soldiers protecting it with their bodies. Three arm lengths: close enough to stare into the sweating faces of those frightened soldiers. Three arm lengths and both lines were preparing to fight by hand . . .

When the first of the warriors fell and two of his companions started pulling him back.

A soldier collapsed, close enough that *Ollokot* recognized some of the Shadow words the man shouted in pain. Others dragged him back from the fighting.

Too many of the warriors were backing up instead of following their leader into the breach.

The soldier guns were too intense that final charge. Three arm lengths . . . close enough for this war chief, brother of the Wallamwatkin leader Joseph, to see that the soldiers would not prevail. Yes, they would fight to protect their little square of ground—but they would not succeed in attacking the village of women and children.

The warriors had stopped Cut-Off Arm in his tracks.

EVEN BEFORE THE Non-Treaty bands migrated upriver to this camp at the mouth of the Cottonwood, every day saw a great number of Treaty people coming in from Lapwai, especially from Kamiah, to join the disaffected ones. With that string of successes in those early weeks of their war against the Shadows and *suapies*, many of the once-steadfast Christians and old Chief Lawyer's Treaty supporters had begun to waver in their loyalties.

Indeed, over the last few days the desertions had become so apparent that the government agent named Monteith had threatened banishment and exile to *Eeikish Pah*, the Hot Place,* for all those he caught supporting the hostiles. Why was it still so hard for the white men to see that things were not black or white, that you stood squarely on one side of this agony or the other?

And why did the Shadows fail to realize that many of the Treaty people had family among those bands now taking a stand against the government?

In this distinction, Joe Albert was not alone.

This young warrior named *Elaskolatat* was only one of many who had answered Chief James Reuben's call for volunteers to scout for and guide the soldiers in their chase after the Non-Treaty bands. . . . Although Joe Albert had family among those fleeing camps.

To his way of thinking, this reality was nothing of great note, because there had always been, and always would be, a great measure of tribal pride, if not outright solidarity—no matter if a man were Christian or Dreamer, no matter if his heart came down on the side of the struggling soldiers or those victorious warriors. It was the white man—his ways, his words, and those land-stealing treaties—who had caused the fractures in ages-old loyalties. The Shadows and their soldiers were to blame for chipping away at the cohesiveness of Albert's people.

And now that these Non-Treaty bands were steadily giving back to the

---

*Indian Territory.

Shadows a small dose of the pain that had been inflicted upon all of the *Nee-Me-Poo* over many years, even those who made their home near Lapwai or over at Kamiah could take some degree of satisfaction. Perhaps Albert, like others, hoped the old ways of their people would not be crushed by the white man. Hoped that now, in this season of *Khoy Tsahl*, these Non-Treaty bands would somehow hold the strong white culture at bay . . . if only for a few more winters, a few more joyous summers.

As the summer had warmed, Joe Albert gradually found himself losing what hope he still clung to that his people could be healed. The fractures went deep—especially in his own family—for his own parents were with these Non-Treaty bands camped below on the Clearwater. His father, *Weesculatat*, was a veteran warrior, who had steadfastly refused to give himself over to the white man. Father and son had argued many times, but in the end Joe had walked his own road and converted to the Christian faith, while *Weesculatat* had stayed with the Dreamers.

When Cut-Off Arm first ordered his soldiers to bombard the Non-Treaty village down below in the valley of the South Fork, Albert felt his heart rise to his throat in fear. Not for himself, but for his relations. His parents surely had to be among those scurrying among the lodges at this moment, herding ponies out of the camp, streaming off toward the western plateau. But it wasn't long before he found himself able to think of little else but this dirty fight, what with the Non-Treaty snipers firing from the timber, shouting encouragement to one another as the few pinned down the many—

Of a sudden the hot air caught in his chest, burnt gunpowder stinging his nostrils as he listened intently. It was a *Nee-Me-Poo* voice he thought he recognized as it cheered the others each time a *suapie* was hit or encouraged the Non-Treaties to inch a little closer to the soldier corral.

"*Pahkatos Owyeen!*" Albert cried out from behind the low shelter he had constructed of thin rock slabs like the soldiers around him.

Of a sudden, most of the Non-Treaty voices fell silent, and their guns ceased roaring, too.

"Five Wounds! Answer me! It is your friend!"

"Who calls me?" came the loud demand from the timber. "Who dares call me a friend when he lies among the soldiers come to kill my people?"

"*Elaskolatat* is my name!" Joe shouted.

From the timber a new voice asked, "The son of *Weesculatat?*"

Albert recognized that throat, too. It was Rainbow, the best friend of Five Wounds. "Is that *Wahchumyus?*"

"Yes—you are really *Elaskolatat?*"

Just then a bearded soldier crawled up and tugged roughly on Joe Albert's elbow. "Tell them redskins now's their chance to give up peaceable, or we'll chew 'em up with lead the way we're gonna do to their village and their relations. You tell 'em that now!" Albert's eyes narrowed at the harsh look crusted on the soldier's face. He had no intention of saying anything of the kind. Instead, he turned back to face the timber and shouted in his native tongue, "I am *Elaskolatat!* Son of *Weesculatat!*"

"Why have you have brought these soldiers to attack our camp?" Five Wounds asked.

"They would have come anyway, even if I did not bring them here," Joe Albert explained what he knew to be the truth, listening to the rustle of talk and unconnected words drifting in from the timber where the snipers lay.

"*Elaskolatat*, your father—"

"My father?" Albert interrupted. "Is he with you? Father? Father, talk to me yourself!"

Rainbow spoke now. "*Weesculatat* is not here."

"Then it's as I feared," Joe said. "He is down in the village, protecting my mother?"

"Your father is no longer with us."

His heart leaped to his throat. Joe struggled to holler, "N-no longer with you? He has given up your fight and taken my mother into Lapwai . . . or even Kamiah?"

"No," Five Wounds said with such sadness from the shadowy timber.

His next words were even more disembodied than before. Almost as if each one were a ghost by itself, drifting out of the shadowed place into the bright sunlight where it refused to take form, dissipating slowly as Joe Albert attempted to wrap his mind around it. "*Weesculatat* was killed by the white men a few days ago. Near Cottonwood Creek."

"D-dead?"

Now a new voice shouted from the trees. *Ollokot* said, "*Uataska*, it is true. He is the first warrior killed in this war against the Shadows. A brave man. Be proud of your father, *Elaskolatat!* In all our fights, he is the only man to die, and he died a courageous warrior—"

"My father was killed by soldiers?"

"No!" Five Wounds cried. "By a band of white men—"

"He's dead?" Joe croaked, disbelieving. "Really dead?"

"Your mother is grieving in the old way, the *timnenekt*," Rainbow explained. "Days ago, over the place where they buried him at *Piswah Ilp-pilp Pah*, the *tewats* said their prayers over him—"

Leaping to his feet, unmindful that he wore a soldier coat, Albert roared with an unspeakable pain shooting through his heart, pounding his breast in anguish. "Ahhhhhgh!"

"Get down! Get down, you stupid Injun!"

The soldiers around him tried to pull Joe Albert down as a few of the Non-Treaty guns instantly opened fire again . . . but *Ollokot*, Rainbow, and Five Wounds shouted to all the rest, screaming that they must not fire at this old friend of theirs who had lost his father to the Shadows.

Joe was standing exposed in the bright afternoon light, the *suapies* sprawled in the grass behind their skimpy breastworks, three of them dragging at him with their hands, shouting at him to get down, get down. "Get down or you'll be killed!"

"In the name of *Hunyewat*, our Creator!"

With half a breath caught in the back of his throat, *Elaskolatat* leaped over one of those clawing for him and took off at a dead run . . . leaving Joe Albert behind—racing headlong to reclaim himself. To reclaim *Elaskolatat.*

Son of *Weesculatat*—the first hero of the Non-Treaty war against the Shadows.

Of a sudden his chest was filled by the hot afternoon air buzzing with shouts and bullets. He was screaming in horror, shrieking in pain, shouting in fury, his heart pounding as he sprinted for the timber.

"Don't shoot him!" Rainbow cried, lunging to the very edge of the trees. "He is one of ours!"

With one hand still clutching his soldier rifle, *Elaskolatat* flapped the sleeve of his soldier blouse from his free arm, then slapped the rifle into the other hand and struggled to shed himself of the white man's dark blue coat from that last arm. A few soldiers were getting to their feet back at their lines now, more of them kneeling behind their rocks, too—all of them growling and shrieking, shooting not at the snipers in the trees, but shooting at the runaway tracker.

He could hear the bullets whistle past him as he raced ahead for the trees. And there at the edge of the tree line some of the warrior faces suddenly took shape as the bravest of the brave stepped into the light, showing themselves to the enemy, and began to lay down a murderous cover fire for this returning son of *Weesculatat*.

Midway between the two lines of shouting, shooting enemies, *Elaskolatat* finally flung the soldier blouse from his wrist and sent it pinwheeling into the air.

He left it settling behind him in the tall grass and dust. Left those soldiers and his Treaty friends behind.

"*Imene kaizi yeu yeu, Hunyewat!*" he roared as he neared the Non-Treaty warriors. "Thank thee, O my Creator!"

The moment he reached the timber, *Elaskolatat* sprinted into the welcoming arms of the war leaders. So many hands pounding him on the back, tongues wagging, until he stopped in front of *Ollokot*.

"Your tears tell me you never really left your father's people," the *Wallowa* war chief said.

Elaskolatat raised a finger and touched his cheek, finding it wet with his tears. "My eyes bleed for my father's spirit," he told the warriors in that copse of timber. "And my heart tells me I must now lead you against those *suapies* who killed him!"

Without waiting for any of them to join him, the young warrior whirled on his heel and let out a shriek.

"*Kiuala piyakasiusa!*" he raised his voice to the hot summer sky, his *simiakia*, his personal warrior spirit, on fire. "It is time to fight!"

Shaking his rifle, *Elaskolatat* burst into a sprint, heading back for the soldier lines across the hot, grassy no-man's-land.

But this time, he was firing at the *suapies*, leading more than ten of the others in a sudden, surprising charge against the enemies who had murdered his father at Cottonwood.

Elaskolatat had come home to his father's people.

IN THE LAST, lingering light of that long, hot day, Lieutenant C. E. S. Wood took out the narrow ledger and dug the pencil from his pocket. Lying on his stomach in the grass there at the edge of headquarters, the young officer scratched at the page, making nothing more than notes really, impressions perhaps—on that day's fierce fighting:

> July 11 Advance on Indians Engage them at about 11:30 A.M., we occupy a rolling broken plateau they the rocks and wooded ravines. Howitzers open fire. Skirmishing, sharpshooting, Famous Hat knocked off three times. The sergt & Mcanuly shot. Charge by line in front of me. Firing until after dark. Indians in ravines after horses. Caring for the wounded. No food no drink no clothing. All day without water. Night in the trenches preparing for an attack at dawn. Anxious times. Sound of Indian dancing and wailing. Williams and Bancroft wounded. I, lost on the picket line.

The lieutenant put the pencil between his teeth and bit down hard, feeling the wood give way. He did not want to break it, only stifle his scream. Frustration, anger, disappointment . . . and maybe a little fear. That, too.

He wrote a bit more:

> Warriors continually pressed upon us, their brown naked bodies flying from shelter to shelter. Their yells were incessant as they cheered each other on or signalled a successful shot. Some even wore tufts of grass tied to their heads as they crawled about for a better position, would shoot, then move on to another likely spot.

For a moment the lieutenant remembered how he had seen the war chief he was convinced was none other than Joseph himself.

> Saw him everywhere along the line; running from point to point, he directed the flanking movements and the charges. It was his long fierce calls which sometimes we heard loudly in front of us, and sometimes faintly resounding from the distant rocks.

On all sides of him in the dark he could make out the men grumbling about their thirst and talking incessantly about water, some thanking God for the evening breeze and a little respite from the heat, others saying it was going to get downright cold and they'd all be freezing by morning.

And the wounded. How they groaned and cried out piteously, begging for water, pleading for the surgeon to see to them next, one man asking his fellows to kill him so he would be out of all the ache and pain he could no longer stand it was so monstrous—

Wood clenched his teeth together to keep from screaming himself. If this was Indian fighting, he wasn't sure this army had anything to be proud of.

And he didn't know if he wanted anything more of Indian fighting.

CHAPTER TWENTY-NINE

JULY 11, 1877

CORRESPONDENT THOMAS SUTHERLAND FOUND IT IMPOSSIBLE TO SLEEP that night as the temperature sank and the wind came up atop that barren plateau where the men huddled in the cold, cursing their sweat-dampened clothing that now had them chilled to the bone. As the cold, humid air settled to the ground around their rifle pits, the dew soaked their uniforms, making the men even more miserable.

A few of the wounded men whimpered, and some screamed as the surgeons continued to work over them with the probes and the saws, despite the dark that smothered everything but the sounds of suffering. One of them cried out for his mother just before he died. Sutherland had never heard of such a thing before. Then an old gray-bearded infantryman told him it happened all the time.

"Hundreds of times, fact be," the soldier said beneath the dim starshine. "Back to the war, heard more men beg for their mammas than I ever wanna hear again."

The thought made Sutherland even colder, so chilled to the marrow that he wondered if he would ever be warm again.

Off and on he wrote in his journal, long handwritten pages covered by his tight scrawl, from which he would compose his newspaper dispatches:

> Although we outnumbered the Indians . . . we fought to a great disadvantage. The redskins were in a fortified canyon, shooting from the brow of a hill, through the grass, and from behind trees and rocks, while our men were obliged to approach them along an open and treeless prairie. At times a redskin would show his head, or jump up and down, throwing his arms about wildly, and then pitch himself like a dead man flat upon the grass, and these were the only chances our men had to fire . . .
>
> During the early part of the fight an Indian with a telescopic rifle was picking off our men at long range with unpleasant rapidity (evidently mistaking me for an officer the way his shots fell around me), when one of Lieutenant Humphrey's men "drew a bead" on the rascal . . .

> Desultory shooting is kept up, with intervals of sharp firing, for seven hours . . . Wishing to enjoy all the experiences of a soldier, I took a rifle and crept out to the front line of pickets prepared to take notes and scalps. My solicitude in the former direction was nearly nipped in the bud, for the moment I inquisitively popped up my head, a whine and thud of bullets in my proximity and a very peremptory order to "lie down, you d——d fool," taught me that hugging mother earth with my teeth in the dirt was the only attitude to assume while in that vicinity.

He sighed, vividly recalling just how deadly the enemy fire had become as the temperature rose and the sun slowly sank for the west. That experience was something Sutherland knew he never would forget:

> At one point of the line, one man, raising his head too high, was shot through the brain; another soldier, lying on his back and trying to get the last few drops of warm water from his canteen, was robbed of the water by a bullet taking off the canteen's neck while it was at his lips.

Sutherland brooded on how Private Francis Winters, serving with Captain S. P. Jocelyn's B Company of the Twenty-first, had his black felt hat shot off three times; then spare minutes later a fourth bullet clipped his ammunition belt as if it had been cut with a knife. The same bullet severely wounded him in the hip.

For some seven hours the battle never cooled as the Nez Perce pinned down Howard's army on three sides, despite how the Gatling guns and two howitzers raked the Indian positions.

Crawling up to the west side of the line late in the afternoon, the correspondent had watched Captain Eugene A. Bancroft, M Battery of the Fourth U. S. Artillery, leap to his feet for but an instant—saying he intended to survey that part of the battlefield where the Nez Perce were putting pressure on his howitzer emplacement—and instantly be struck in the left side of the chest.

At another place in the line Sutherland had watched Lieutenant C. A. Williams take a bullet in the hip. As the young officer calmly began to dress his own wound by himself, he accidentally raised one arm too high in the grass and took another bullet, this one shattering his wrist.

Late in the day, Lieutenant Harry Bailey—serving with Jocelyn's B Company of the Twenty-first U. S. Infantry—had come into headquarters, where he blew off a little steam with Sutherland before meeting with Howard's staff among those stacks of pack saddles and apishamores, ammunition and ration cases Trimble's and Rodney's men had piled up at the center of the battlefield, constructing a network of head-high barricades.

"I had a helluva time of it, keeping my men on the firing line this afternoon," Bailey admitted. "As soon as I got some placed at proper intervals and I moved on down the line to instruct others, as many men would run back to their holes or trenches in the rear!"

Grinding a fist in an open palm, Bailey continued, this time telling a story of two officers.

"They were lying behind small head shelters with dusty sweat streaks down their faces, dodging bullets. They yelled at me to get down as I was drawing fire. When two bullets tipped the earth between their heads and my ankles, I dove for cover! After a few minutes of that dangerous give-and-take, I began to realize that a nearby company and my own had mistaken one another for the enemy, Mr. Sutherland! Friendly fire, I'd say!"

"You were drawing fire from another outfit?"

Bailey nodded. "Those damned warriors! They were shooting and whooping so much at us, my company and an artillery battery were distracted enough to start jumping around, bobbing up and down, firing at each other at a lively rate."

"How'd you get it stopped?"

"At first I tried yelling, but the racket of the guns was too much for me, so I ran out between the two lines yelling for all parties to cease fire! 'You're firing into your own men!' "

"You're lucky you weren't hit!" Sutherland snorted.

"Little chance of that," the lieutenant grumbled. "I suppose I'm fortunate that the army can only afford to give each man three cartridges a month for rifle practice."

"Was anyone hurt in that exchange?" the correspondent inquired.

Bailey shrugged. "None of us can ever be certain, and I'm sure no one will ever say a thing about it, but Private Winters claims nothing will ever convince him otherwise but that his dreadful hip wound was caused by a bullet from that artillery battery."

Thinking now about Bailey's powder-blackened, sweat-smeared face, Sutherland shaved a little more off the end of his pencil, sharpening the lead with his small penknife, then licked it and went back to writing, remembering how some companies right at the farthest extent of the firing line had reported they were running low on ammunition earlier that afternoon. When none of the soldiers or officers volunteered to resupply those units,

> Ad Chapman jumped on his spirited horse and with a heavy box of cartridges on his back hip, started at full run amid a shower of balls for the front, where he safely landed his precious burden. Surely this citizen soldier and guide is one of the most intelligent and bravest men in the command.

Then Sutherland's mood darkened a bit again, and he recalled:

> Not long ago Surgeon Sternberg was called at night to go to the fighting line . . . where he found a man

> who was a packer, badly wounded and bleeding profusely. Sternberg feared he could not remove him any distance without danger of great loss of blood. Surgeon instructed his assistant to light a candle and screen it with a blanket, in order to form a shield behind which he could tie the artery. No sooner had the candle been lighted than the bullets came thick and fast at this little mark, and it had to be quickly extinguished.

At times this night could be excruciatingly quiet, eerily so. They could hear the warriors moving about in the timber and brush nearby, scraping rocks atop one another as they fortified their breastworks. At times the sounds of drumming, the shrieks of war dances, and the wails of mourning women drifted up from the river valley encampment somewhere below the bluff.

In such a morose, gothic atmosphere, Sutherland could not help but remember his brief friendship with Sergeant James Workman of the Fourth Artillery and how it had come to such a tragic end in the brilliant glare of a sunny afternoon:

> He was a very intelligent young man, being one of the best Shakespearean scholars and readiest quoters from standard English poets I've ever met. But I think him quite depressed these last few days, weighed down with unspoken troubles and bitter recollections from his past.
>
> During the battle I was shocked, startled when Workman suddenly stood up and charged alone toward the Indians. Almost instantly he fell flat on his face, pierced by Nez Perce bullets on every side. How tragic is his death, but the man seemed fixed upon it, determined to die—

Suddenly in that murky silence of summer night Sutherland was interrupted in his writing when one of the sergeants gruffly reminded his men to get back to work deepening their rifle pits there in the dark beneath the cold pinprick stars, scratching shallow trenches in the barren, rocky soil. Although none of them had eaten since breakfast, come night there wasn't a complaint about food. Only the lack of water.

Thirst had created its own exquisite brand of incomparable torture.

YELLOW WOLF LAY with his cheek against the earth, listening to the sporadic gunfire as the hot afternoon waned, and closed his eyes. So tired was he that the young warrior did not realize he had fallen asleep until he awoke with a start and furtively looked about. The sun was lower, and no one else was around anymore.

He remembered his wounded uncle crawling off earlier, saying he wanted *koos*, so would attempt to reach the spring for a drink. But he had not come back, and the others had crawled away, too. Yellow Wolf could not see another fighting man, only hear the soldiers on their line, dangerously close behind the tall grass. As he was lying there, thinking what to do now that he was alone with the enemy, a voice barked from behind him.

"Why is he lying there? Yellow Wolf must be wounded!"

Then another voice came from a closer point off to his left: "Who are you, lying flat like you are? Soldiers are coming close! Don't you see them?"

Keeping his head low, Yellow Wolf tried to see who had spoken but could not for the grass. In a moment, the same voice whipped his ears again.

"Yellow Wolf! Are you wounded? Why aren't you shooting? Go ahead and kill some soldiers! They are coming close to kill you if you don't defend yourself!"

This time the young warrior raised his head up a little, far enough to see that it was *Wottolen*, the older warrior known as Hair Combed Over Eyes. He was one of the war leaders who commanded some young men at the edge of that bluff. And he was right.

When Yellow Wolf looked, he saw how the soldiers were crawling toward him in the grass, no more than thirty steps from him already, slipping up cautiously like a snake you could not see until it struck.

It made the young man very angry to be left by so many to the soldiers. He did not care if he died; he was going to fight these *suapies* like a man. He had a reputation earned in the White Bird Canyon fight, and he would not lose it here.

Unafraid of the soldiers, Yellow Wolf crawled against two boulders and placed his carbine between them. Quickly levering shells, he fired six shots, stopping most of the soldiers where they were.

As the crack of that last shot faded, he heard heavy breathing behind him and immediately turned. Fire Body was grunting as he dragged his old limbs out of the brush in Yellow Wolf's direction.

"I just heard your bullets, so I realized you were alone, Nephew," Fire Body said while he crawled up on his belly. "We are going to die right here! But remember: Do not shoot the common soldier. Shoot the commander!"*

He understood exactly what the older man said. Fire Body had killed the trumpet soldier at the *Lahmotta* fight and stopped the soldiers from advancing any farther. Now Yellow Wolf looked at the nearby enemy and spotted the commander who knelt behind his soldiers.

Yellow Wolf took aim, and his bullet struck that officer, knocking him back into the grass where others quickly dragged him out of sight. But it was not long before another commander took his place and hollered at the soldiers.

---

*"This characteristic of the Nez Perce's combat methodology was to singularize their performance in subsequent engagements with the army." Jerome A. Greene, *The U. S. Army and the Nee-Me-Poo Crisis of 1877.*

Yellow Wolf shot at him, too. As soon as their second commander was hit, the soldiers promptly began to scoot backward, retreating. He wanted to cheer, for his bravery alone had caused that retreat.

Wottolen pounded a hand on his shoulder. "That was good shooting, Nephew. I think the soldiers know to stay where they are for the rest of the day."

As twilight arrived and it grew darker, the heat escaped the earth and the air grew cold and damp. As the stars came out, only an occasional gunshot was heard.

Through that evening, Yellow Wolf had stayed right where he had been when he shot the two soldier commanders. Even though he began shivering. Dressed only in his breechclout, those two cartridge belts, and that pair of moccasins he had brought with him from the lodge, his body trembled. The night was clear and still. The earth's warmth quickly sucked into the sky. Finally, after moonset, he could not stand the cold any longer and crawled back toward the timber and rocks.

Back at the smoking lodge where the no-fighters had gathered during the afternoon's battle to talk about the fight and other serious matters, Yellow Wolf found no one awake. At least ten men lay asleep, curled up on the ground of the smoking lodge, clutching their legs for warmth. He found that Looking Glass was not among them. Earlier in the day, talk was that the chief made repeated trips down to the village rather than staying put on the fighting lines with his warriors.

Yellow Wolf did not tarry at this place of the no-fighters but crept on for the place where many of the ponies were tethered. He remembered how when the sun was high *Teeweeyownah*, the old warrior called Over the Point, came among the ponies tied in the trees, clearly angry. Here and there this member of White Bird's band had selectively turned some of the horses loose. When those young men finally emerged from the safety of the smoking lodge, they were furious to find their ponies gone.

"Where is my horse!" *Alahmoot* growled. He was called Elm Limb.

Over the Point admitted, "I let them go."

"You have no right to turn our horses loose!" Elm Limb blustered.

"You go too often to camp," the older man explained as more warriors gathered to watch the argument. "We are here to fight."

"I came to fight!"

"No, Elm Limb—you came to smoke and make others think you were fighting," Over the Point protested. "All you young cowards,* I will die soon. But you—you will soon see hardships in bondage to the Shadows. Your freedom will be gone, liberty robbed from you. Our people will be slaves for all days to come. Now, go fight and die for your families!"

Yellow Wolf crabbed into the grove, finding a few ponies still tied there, thinking hard on the old man's strong words. It was hard not to feel deep rage for those who did not help in that first day's fighting, leaving it to the

---

*In Nez Perce culture, cowards or laggards in battle were rarely, if ever, shamed or ostracized.

few who did put their bodies on the line. Even Joseph, the village chief, climbed up to the bluffs to take part in the struggle. Shame was, only half of the men of fighting age showed their faces in the ravines or the snipers' grove: ten-times-ten against four, maybe five, times as many soldiers! *Eeh*, he thought, no matter that the warriors were outnumbered—they still managed to keep all of Cut-Off Arm's *suapies* pinned down without any water!

Suddenly spotting a man lying on the ground, curled up against some brush, Yellow Wolf asked the stranger, "May I sleep with you, on account of the cold?"

"Yes," the man answered. "We can share our heat." As Yellow Wolf knelt beside the man the stranger said, "Yellow Wolf, it is you!"

"Cousin!" Yellow Wolf said with no small joy. His heart was very glad to see *Teminisiki* again. They had known each other from the time when they were both small children just learning to walk.

"There aren't many here now."

"I know," Yellow Wolf replied. "Where did they go?"

"*Ollokot* tried to stop them, telling all the fighters that they should stay and keep the soldiers away from the water."

"Someone told them different?"

Teminisiki nodded in the dark. "Looking Glass. He did not like *Ollokot*'s plan to keep the soldiers from the spring, so most everyone else left for the camp with Looking Glass."

"I am glad you stayed," Yellow Wolf said as he eased himself down to the earth. "It is good to know my cousin is a fighting man."

Just as he was lying down with his back against *Teminisiki*'s, they heard soft footsteps and a woman's voice whispered from the darkness.

"May I stay the rest of the night with you? I have no blanket and I am cold."

Without any hesitation *Teminisiki* said, "Come on! Get in here between us! You will keep warm that way!"

The woman quickly did as he suggested, scooting down between the two young men. As they lay there those first few minutes, Yellow Wolf felt her quivering between them, and it made him all the colder for it. He thought how good a woman felt, with her many curves and soft places. . . . Then he thought of the young woman who had touched his hand as this fight had started that afternoon. How he wanted to find her now—

But suddenly Yellow Wolf remembered what was taught him by the old ones, people who were no longer alive now—the wise warriors who had gone to the buffalo country many times, fighting the Lakota and others in that faraway land.

They had always said: In wartime a man cannot sleep with woman. He might get killed if he does.

"Where are you going, Yellow Wolf?" *Teminisiki* asked as his cousin stiffly got to his feet.

"I will go somewhere else to sleep. You two keep each other warm for tonight."

He went off a little ways and found a low boulder where he could get out of the blustery wind that was growing cold. Whenever the breeze died, he could hear his cousin and the woman talking low. Despite the cold, Yellow Wolf was sure the two of them would couple that night.

But he did not want to take the chance. He wanted instead to believe in the ways of the old ones he had been taught summers ago.

Yellow Wolf shivered all night long, until it grew light enough for the

CHAPTER THIRTY

July 12, 1877

Thursday, July 12, 1877

Mamma,

I wish I could talk to you this morning instead of writing. One of the things I meant to tell you yesterday was the active part the Indian squaws take in these fights our soldiers have had. They follow along after the men, holding fresh horses and bringing water right into the midst of all the commotion. Colonel Perry says that in that fight of White Bird Canyon, he saw one Indian (one buck, as they speak of them here) have as many as three changes of horses brought him by his squaw. See what an advantage that is to them. As soon as their horses are a little blown, they take a fresh one, and our poor soldiers have perhaps ridden theirs fifty or sixty miles before the fight begins. In their efforts to get at the Indians, they do their fighting on their tired animals. Then, in the fight, the soldiers fall scattered in all directions and the bucks can't stop to plunder in the midst of the fight. So, wherever a man falls, they set a squaw to watch him. I do hope their successes are at an end.

We are waiting anxiously for news from General Howard who is about 50 miles away from Lapwai. A young man named Rains was killed last week. It was his first fight. He was a lovely boy. Mrs. Theller felt dreadfully about his death. He was the officer in charge of the party that found and buried Mr. Theller's body. Rains had so marked Theller's grave that he would have no difficulty finding it again, and now we don't know that it can be found. Mrs. Theller is so anxious to have the body. Poor woman . . . it was two weeks after the fight before they were able (from the small number of men and the large number of Indians) to go out to bury the men killed in that first fight, and Mrs. Theller used to say, "If he was only buried. Oh my poor Ned, lying there with his face blackening in the sun."

. . . Last Sunday night, an Indian (friendly) came in and told that he had seen Joseph's men and they were coming to "clean out" the post that night. "Maybe in the night. Maybe in the morning," they said. "Only little bit of soldiers here. Is good time. Plenty

muck-a-muck (food) and plenty gun." The Indian is a reliable one, as the good ones go, so every precaution was taken to guard against the surprise. Everybody at the post slept in one house, and the men slept in the breastworks . . . They did not come, but we have many such alarms . . .

I am so tired of all this excitement, but the children seem to thrive on it. They look neglected but happy as clams at high tide.

Your loving daughter,
Emily F.

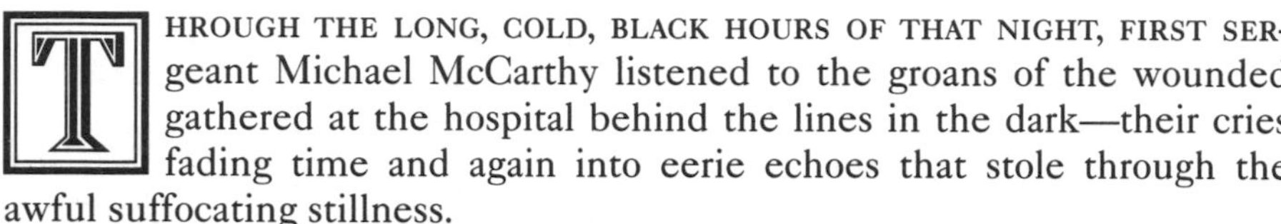

THROUGH THE LONG, COLD, BLACK HOURS OF THAT NIGHT, FIRST SERgeant Michael McCarthy listened to the groans of the wounded gathered at the hospital behind the lines in the dark—their cries fading time and again into eerie echoes that stole through the awful suffocating stillness.

At least the wounded were lucky—they had been picked up off the battlefield and hauled back to the hospital in the wagons, where they lay under awnings erected for shade and waited their turn under the surgeon's knife and saw. The dead, all those dead, still lay where they had fallen.

Those cries of the wounded mingled with the harangues of the enemy chiefs as they exhorted their warriors in the still, gray hours hovering just before first light, while the clear, starry sky gradually faded far to the east.

Yet what nettled him most were the soft, sad whimpers of the women as they keened and mourned for their fallen warriors. Ghostly tatters of their pitiful wails drifted up from the valley below. Enough to make a man give up even the thought of a belly-warming drink . . . if he'd been lucky enough to have himself a flask here on the line this bloody black night.

Hell, to have anything to drink would have been a boon through that first, long day.

When the soldiers went in search of water around midday on the eleventh, a few got close to a spring* tucked up in the head of a timbered draw. But close was all they got. Every time some daring trooper attempted to cross from the cover of trees to the brushy spring, swaybacked under a clattering load of wool-covered canteens, Nez Perce sharpshooters drove him back. It was here that Private Edward Wykoff was killed and another infantryman was wounded. As the hours dragged on and on, their horses and mules suffered every bit as much as the men hunkered down on that thin crescent moon of a battle line.

From time to time the enemy's leaders had signaled an attack or change in strategy to their warriors by emerging on some prominent point where one of them came out, jumping around as he waved a red blanket or circled a pony in some significant manner. At times, McCarthy even spotted blinding flickers of mirrored light and realized some war chief was sending a secret code to his men. Within minutes of every signal, a small group of

*Located in the ravine currently called Anderson Creek.

four, perhaps five, warriors suddenly burst from hiding to make a noisy charge on a weak spot along the line, singing, chanting, screeching all the while. When they tore past his end of the line, it was enough to make even a brave man pucker. After all, Sergeant Michael McCarthy had been left for dead on the White Bird Battlefield. He knew firsthand what fear could do to a man.

And when the momentary terror had passed and the rush was over, it came to the sergeant that the Nez Perce had not dared press their case against the center of Howard's big square. That's when it came to him: how the general had posted his artillery and infantry, with their long-range rifles, at the center of this broad square, positioning the cavalry with their shorter carbines on the two flanks. The goddamned warriors had less respect for the horse soldiers' guns.*

That afternoon as the sun reigned supreme in its sky, McCarthy had stripped out of his dark navy blue fatigue blouse trimmed with tarnished brass buttons, he was sweating so. But now, in the coldest part of the day, he was shivering, his teeth threatening to rattle like ivory dice in a bone cup. He struggled to keep them under control, lest any man mistake the cold for fear.

When darkness fell, orders came round for them to hold their position on the line, the men spaced more than five yards apart, with instructions to improve their defenses by making their breastworks taller where they could find rocks or digging their rifle pits deeper on that part of the line where there were no stones to hunker behind. And McCarthy had his men bunkie-up so one man might try to catch a little shut-eye while the other kept watch.

Twice during the night, H Company had been resupplied with ammunition from the quartermaster's stores. But there was no food for those on the firing line. Didn't matter after awhile: It would've been damned near impossible to swallow the crumbly hardbread and salted beef without some water to wash it down anyway. Earlier in the afternoon as the temperature soared, McCarthy heard of an officer who had been driven so mad from thirst that he had lapped at the muddy water in a grassy mire where the mules and horses had been trampling the ground. By moonrise the man was taken sick, doubled over with terrible cramps at the field hospital back among the pack saddles and apishamores.

Hours of darkness, during which the sergeant and others listened to the sounds of the Nez Perce working on their barricades—rocks scraping together as one was piled on top of the other for the fight they knew was to come with the rising sun. That night General Howard approved a few sorties against the enemy, small squads of soldiers sent out to probe the edges of the timber, hoping to outflank the Nez Perce snipers. Wasn't long before each bunch came crawling back. What with the darkness and getting strung

*At the end of the Nez Perce War, Captain George H. Burton reported: "It is explained by the Indians themselves, who acknowledge freely that they have but little fear of the short gun, in consequence of the short range of the carbine and the difficulty of aiming a piece so light and short with accuracy. . . ."

out far from their lines, the soldiers needed very little excuse to turn back after encountering the first stiff resistance.

A time or two even McCarthy had heard noises from the night that caused him to think the Indians were attempting to penetrate what they hoped would be a weak part of the army's lines through the night.

"Cap'n Trimble says these here Nez Perce are no despicable foe," Lieutenant William Parnell repeated quietly as he eased down beside his sergeant in the cold.

"They've fit us good this second time," McCarthy groaned. He was so thirsty, it even hurt his tongue to wag. "Leastways, we didn't have to run this time, Major."

Parnell nodded. One of the few survivors of the British army's "Charge of the Six Hundred" at Balaklava during the Crimean War, this large man sighed, "The cap'n and me was talking about how these Nez Perce were such pacifists—couldn't be goaded into a fight—before a few of 'em started murdering . . . and now we've seen 'em put a courageous defense of their homeland. This shaped up to be a beautiful battle, didn't it, Sergeant: all of Joseph's reds against all of Howard's soldiers."

"I ain't never heard of no Injuns digging in and holing up the way this bunch has," the Irishman commented. "Always figured they'd be running off once their women and children was safe."

"For a second time, it strikes me these warriors aren't the running kind."

McCarthy studied the big lieutenant in the dark. "You givin' these redskins their due?"

Grudgingly Parnell said, "I told the cap'n there never was a tribe more worthy of my respect, Sergeant."

A rustle of grass and an angry grumble from men disturbed in their sleep caused them both to look over their shoulders. Out of the darkness came the soft clatter of those wool-covered canteens slung around the neck of a young hospital steward.

"Hold up there, bucko." Parnell put out his beefy hand. "Where you think you're off to in the dark?"

With a gulp, the young soldier said, "Surgeon Sternberg sent me, sir. Crawl over to get some water at the spring yonder. The wounded are begging for it something awful."

"The spring's yonder," McCarthy said, pointing with his outstretched arm into the gray light at that ground halfway between the lines.

"T-that far?"

"And them Injuns gonna see you comin' every step of the way," McCarthy advised.

With a rapid, anxious shake of his head, the steward shrank to the ground and groaned, face in his hands. Finally slipping the canteen straps over his head, the soldier turned to his left, finding an open spot behind a low pile of rocks, then crabbed over to join some of McCarthy's men behind the breastworks.

After a few minutes of staring at the foolhardy steward, the sergeant finally asked, "Them wounded the surgeon's working on . . . you say they're really wanting some water in a bad way, are they, soldier?"

With a reluctant nod, the soft-cheeked steward said, "They was begging for water like it was life itself, sir."

Glancing for a moment at the rear of their lines, where Surgeon Sternberg had erected his hospital, McCarthy eventually raised his voice to announce, "I'm asking you weeds for volunteers. Any man of you to crawl to the spring with these here canteens for the wounded?"

He waited a minute more, glancing left and right along the line. "Any one of you—"

"I'll go with you, Sarge."

McCarthy turned back to the left, finding Private Fowler rocking up onto his knees, carbine in hand. For a long moment he measured the young fair-haired soldier, discovering no recklessness, no bravado, about him. The sergeant nodded in appreciation to the blue-eyed youth.

"Awright, you weed. Leave your carbine right there if you want, for you'll need to fill your hands with these goddamned canteens."

"I-I'd just as soon take my rifle with me, Sarge," Charles E. Fowler replied.

"Have it any way you want." McCarthy sighed. "Let's do this."

As they started over the barricade and away from the rifle pits, Parnell's voice boomed behind them.

"Give them brave boys some cover! Any of them bleeming bastards open up on them two, let 'em have it! Watch for the muzzle fire and let the redskins have it!"

Zigging and zagging across the grassy field, McCarthy and Fowler reached the brush-choked spring with a gasp of surprise that they hadn't been hit by those few random shots igniting the waning darkness from the Indian lines. Both collapsed to their bellies and immediately cupped their hands into the cool water, lapping at what little they managed to bring to their lips. One by one they filled the canteens, holding them under the surface of the shallow spring as the air gurgled past the necks.

"We had it easy getting here, you know," the private said softly. "Gonna be weighed down with all this water now getting back out."

McCarthy worried the top back onto the last of his canteens. "I figger we ain't got much a choice, soldier. We stay here—or we run best we can back to the lines."

"I'm f-for running, sir."

"Lead off, soldier. I'll cover your back door."

They hadn't trudged under the weight of those canteens more than twenty yards when the first bullet whistled past, cutting the strap on a canteen Fowler carried. It spun to the grass. The instant the private stopped and stooped to retrieve it, McCarthy lumbered to a halt over him. "G'won! G'won, goddammit! Leave the damn thing!"

As they rocked into a lumbering gait once more, McCarthy could see how Parnell was just getting to his feet above his riflemen, directing fire toward the trees where the Nez Perce marksmen lay hidden. At times in that sprint, the sergeant turned, bringing the carbine to his shoulder, more than relieved he hadn't left his weapon behind. Quickly snapping off a shot at a puff of smoke just then appearing in the distant brush, the sergeant raked open the trapdoor. As the copper cartridge came spinning from the breech, he shoved in a new round.

Whirling around again, he started running, the heavy canteens swinging rhythmically in great arcs from both shoulders. And noticed for the first time how Parnell was still standing, fully exposed as he directed the cover fire. The huge, fleshy lieutenant was waving the two of them on toward the barricades.

With each lunging step, the canteens swung front, then back in opposing arcs that threatened to pull McCarthy off-balance at every stride. An enemy bullet whimpered past just as he reached the breastworks and was dragged down by Parnell and another man. Two others already had Fowler on the ground, patting him over as they searched for wounds, yanking those blessed canteens from his shoulders.

McCarthy clambered to his hands and knees. "Back off, you goddamned weeds!" he roared, kicking at a man who had pulled at a stopper without even taking the canteen from Fowler's neck.

Every one of them froze. Then one of the soldiers said, "Sarge, we just covered your retreat, so I was thinking we all was due a li'l drink of this here water—"

"No, you ain't due no drink till them wounded get theirs," he growled back. "Not till they've had their fill." He knelt beside Fowler. "You think you can get your canteens and mine over to the hospital from here?"

Fowler grinned hugely, his blue eyes sparkling. "Damn right I can, Sergeant."

McCarthy watched the soldier start away, mindful of the uneasy silence that surrounded him. He suddenly called to Fowler, "Say, Private! I'll see to it Cap'n Trimble hears of this."

Fowler stopped, looking back over his shoulder at his first sergeant.

"Fact is, I'll see the cap'n makes you a cawpril for this, soldier. Any private sticks his neck out to make that run you just done for the sake of our wounded . . . least he deserves is a goddamn cawpril's stripes!"

CHAPTER THIRTY-ONE

July 12, 1877

As the darkness had deepened around his lines, General Oliver Otis Howard had learned more and more of the many wild rumors circulating among the men at the front regarding the extent of their casualties. Some were reporting that as many as one in four men had been killed or dragged back to the surgeon's hospital.

That sort of thing was like a smoldering fire to a unit's fighting morale: If you didn't stomp it out right at the start, it could flare up when and where you least expected it. He had seen enough of that sort of reckless, groundless rumor during the recent War of Rebellion.

Howard brushed aside offers to carry word out to the front lines from his aides. Instead, he had announced he was himself going to reassure the troops their casualties were minor in number.

"Besides," he told his staff, "this will give me a chance to reconnoiter our position in relation to the Nez Perce lines."

For more than an hour he had walked the barricades and rifle pits, calmly buoying the men, contradicting the wildfire rumors, and assessing the strengths of his own fortifications while measuring the weaknesses of the enemy. By 4:30 A.M. as the sky grayed, he was back at headquarters among those stacks of pack saddles and crates, blowing on a cup of scalding coffee.

"The men appear exhausted, General," declared First Lieutenant Melville C. Wilkinson.

"Exhausted perhaps, but not discouraged," Howard corrected. Then he glanced at the hospital a moment before continuing, "Our torn and bleeding comrades give us cheer by their brave words spoken, by their silent suffering."

He drank his coffee in silence as this new day came aborning, privately brooding on the failures that had turned what should have been nothing more than a brief flare-up by a few renegades into a full-scale war threatening to spill over the borders of his department.

Perry's singular defeat at the White Bird had convinced Howard that, man for man, these Non-Treaty bands were at the very least the equal of his best soldiers. Since that debacle, he had learned that what the Nez Perce lacked in precision drill and unit discipline they more than made up for in their fighting zeal and the accuracy of their aim. Especially on horseback—something he had never expected to see from mounted warriors. If he were to be successful against such a band of zealots, Otis realized he must be very,

very cautious in not overplaying his hand. Another defeat like Perry's at White Bird would likely bring other disaffected tribes in the Northwest to Joseph's banner.

And that would likely mean the end of Howard's military career, the end of everything he had ever cherished as a fighting man.

Just after dawn Howard made his play for the spring—a force of his men under Captains Miller and Perry finally managing to rout the Nez Perce snipers from the spring and secure the area for his command. Which meant the firing at that end of the battlefield quieted down somewhat and the men could begin taking the first of the horses and mules to the spring in rotation. In the general's most private thoughts, this was the first tangible sign that the tide of this battle might well be turning in his favor. The end might be in sight. He thanked God for that glimmer of hope on the horizon, then ordered that coffee and freshly baked bread be taken out to all the men on the front line.

"They haven't had a meal since their breakfast yesterday," he told aide-de-camp Wilkinson. "Let's feed the men before we see what deviltry this day brings."

But despite all those hopes given birth with that dawn, the firing from both lines steadily increased in tempo and intensity as the air grew hotter. Determined that this would not be his Waterloo, Howard put every available man on the line, ordered to dig in and hold out. Late that second morning, a few Nez Perce horsemen even drove several hundred ponies through the soldier lines in an attempt to cause confusion and disrupt the effectiveness of their fire, perhaps even hoping to stampede the pack animals.

Although the warriors' valiant effort failed and they had already been forced back from the spring where they had caused so many soldier casualties the day before, for some reason the Nez Perce steadfastly persisted on the fringes of the battlefield. Here, then there, they made a rude, noisy appearance on his front. Small groups of them would ride up behind some low elevation in the rolling prairie, leap off their ponies, then quickly fire a few rounds at a weak spot in the soldier line before flinging themselves back atop their horses and racing out of sight. More of them crept forward on their bellies, snaking through the tall grass until within rifle range, whereupon they put their weapons to deadly use—proving just what marksmen they were with those Springfields taken from the White Bird and Rains massacre dead. Some of the more resourceful ones even tied clumps of grass to their heads to better conceal themselves as they made their approach.

And so that morning and early afternoon passed while each side sought desperately to make the jump on the other, wheedling at every little advantage, but with neither the enemy nor Howard's men making any real progress beyond where the lines had remained for the last eight hours.

That was the end of Howard's patience.

Just before two o'clock, the general called Captain Marcus Miller back to headquarters, where he detailed orders for a daring charge. "Colonel, I'm withdrawing your artillerymen from the line and filling that gap with some thinly spread cavalry and infantry," Howard explained.

From his lips the captain tore the short-stemmed pipe he always had clamped between his teeth. "Where are you sending us, sir?"

"You will move your line directly toward the bluff. Your objective will be that shallow ravine I believe is holding most of the warriors. One of the howitzers will be in support."

"Support, General?"

"Lieutenant Otis will be in charge of laying down a harassing fire with the twelve-pounder, to loosen things up in there before your advance; then your men will sweep around the left end of the Nez Perce to take them in the rear."

"Very good, sir," Miller replied, enthused. "With your permission, I'll go begin my withdrawal from the line so we can prepare for our attack."

Howard was squinting into the bright sunlight, watching the right of his line where Rodney's and Trimble's men were deployed, when Lieutenant Wilkinson came huffing up on foot.

"General!" the young officer gasped. "Look there—in the distance, sir!"

Otis quickly put the field glasses to his eyes and adjusted the focus. Beneath that low dust cloud clinging to the ridgeline far to their south he could begin to make out the approach of a blue column.

"Who are they, General?" asked Lieutenant C. E. S. Wood as he came to Howard's elbow.

"That can only be Jackson's cavalrymen," he answered, dread filling him, "bringing in the pack train from Lapwai—"

At the very moment he was about to drop the field glasses from his eyes, something off to the right hooked his attention. His heart sank with the sight.

The enemy had spotted Jackson's company. Howard knew B Troop, First U. S. Cavalry, likely had a complement of no more than forty men along to guard that 120-mule pack train that had been expected to reach his column days ago. The Nez Perce would scatter Jackson's mules and create havoc among the troopers at best. At worst, the warriors would tear through the pack train as they butchered Jackson's undermanned escort.

"Colonel Miller!" he roared, using the officer's brevet rank.

The officer jerked to a halt and turned on his heel as Howard realized just how unusual it was that any of his officers ever heard him raise his voice, much less bellow like that.

Leading his horse, Miller returned. "Sir?"

"Your orders have changed, Colonel," Howard said, shoving the field glasses toward the officer. "Have yourself a look."

As Miller studied that distant detachment advancing beneath the dust cloud, able to see how the warriors were growing agitated with the escort's approach, Howard said, "Your battalion has my orders to do all that's necessary to keep the enemy off that pack train. See that Captain Jackson's men reach the safety of our lines."

"Yes, sir!"

Within minutes Miller was extending his forces to the left of the line, by company-front formation, moving A, D, E, and G Batteries of his Fourth Artillery toward the ridge a mile from Howard's compound—then two miles—

continually keeping themselves between the warriors and the heading that oncoming pack train was taking. The Nez Perce horsemen made a few showy, but ineffectual, charges along Miller's flanks but never got close enough to actually engage the foot soldiers pressing ever on to rendezvous with Jackson's escort.

Howard promptly ordered Rodney's cavalrymen toward the left side of their line, to be position to act as reserves, should Miller require assistance.

It was nearing 3:00 P.M. by the time the pack train neared Howard's lines, with Miller's battalion arrayed entirely on Jackson's left flank. When he had his batteries opposite the end of the jagged ravine along the southern side of the battlefield, the captain gave his order.

"Men!" he roared above the cries of the oncoming warriors and their horses. "Get up and go for them! If we don't do something now, they'll likely kill us all!"

With startling speed, Miller wheeled his artillerymen by the left flank and, as a whole, they bolted into a ragged sprint, racing impetuously for the surprised warriors in the ravine.

As the pack mules and their escort rattled inside Howard's lines, the general immediately threw Captain Rodney's reserves into motion, ordered against the left flank of what would momentarily be a noisy collision.

Just as Howard had gambled, Nez Perce horsemen burst from the ravine, streaming along Miller's front, racing for the soldiers' left, where it was plain they intended to flank those four batteries of artillerymen. But the instant they swept around the back of Miller's artillerymen, the warriors ran right into Rodney's horse soldiers! As the general watched, all but breathless for those few desperate minutes, it seemed the Nez Perce flung every one of their men against that end of his line, attempting to roll it up just as they had done to Perry's battalion at the White Bird.

A fierce, swirling skirmish raised a boiling dust cloud that swallowed both soldier and Indian in the stinging heat of that midafternoon. Moment by moment, the Nez Perce made a most valiant resistance to check Miller's charge, attempting to angle back on Miller's rear when they were caught by surprise between the two forces. Rodney's men had outflanked the flankers and were just beginning to roll up the end of the Nez Perce line when . . . when—the enemy broke!

Only a few horsemen at first. Soon more. Eventually the rest as their entire line gave way, with both Miller's and Rodney's outfits advancing into the onslaught, right on the warriors' tails. Those few who held to the bitter end waited until the soldiers were no farther than twenty yards before they wheeled about and fled.

"To the river!" began the cry from those soldiers experiencing their first success. "To the river!"

Otis knew he must not let Joseph and his warriors escape.

"Captain Winters!" Howard bawled, knowing he had but moments to capitalize on this fracture just opening in the enemy's defenses. "Take two companies of infantry and your dismounted cavalrymen and reinforce Miller! On the double, man! On the double now!"

With Winters on his way toward the retreating tribesmen, Howard next ordered up Jackson's dismounted B Company—weary from its escort duty—to join Trimble's H and advance in double time to support one of the Gatling guns and both howitzers to the edge of the bluff, where the gun crews were to open up a hot fire on the fleeing warriors.

By Jupiter! If this didn't feel a great deal better than had that news of Perry's defeat on the White Bird, than the mucking around back and forth across the Salmon, not to mention those Cottonwood fiascos!

With Joseph on the run now—maybe . . . just maybe, he could end this war in the next two days, three at the most!

ARGHGHGH!

Yellow Wolf hadn't felt anything like the pain piercing his left wrist!

The instant that soldier bullet had smacked him earlier that morning, he had flopped onto the ground, slowly swallowing down the waves of pain, gripping the bloody wound tightly in his right hand. For a long time he lay there, unmoving. When he finally did attempt to raise himself so he could lean back against part of the stone barricades, another soldier bullet slapped the boulder near his cheek. A rock chip gouged the flesh just below his left eye.

Temporarily blinded, he collapsed back into the grass, listening to the increased fury of the *suapie* volleys sent hurling into the timber at the ravine. His cheek felt damp, warm. Yellow Wolf touched it. Blood, streaming down his face from the flesh wound. Closing his right eye momentarily, he realized he couldn't see from the left. He closed them both and worried how this fight would end now.

At dawn, there hadn't been enough warriors to blunt the soldiers' daring charge on the spring. No more than five-times-ten stayed with *Ollokot* now. The rest had long ago retreated back to the village for the night or still slept safely in the smokers' lodge where they held long discussions on what path this struggle should take. Some of the chiefs and older warriors had wanted this to be the last fight against the *suapies*—either defeating the white men in a decisive and pitched battle or being destroyed by Cut-Off Arm. But others still argued for retreat and flight. Looking Glass talked ever stronger about a new life for their people across the mountains.

It turned Yellow Wolf's sour stomach into knots when he thought of so many of fighting age electing not to put their bodies in the struggle . . . while a young man like *Eelahweeman*, called About Asleep—just in his fourteenth summer—bravely carried water up to the hot, thirsty warriors fighting on the ridge top all that first afternoon and again into this second.

Red Thunder was the only brave fighter killed yesterday, shot from his horse during that fierce charge against the mule train as the battle was opened. But it was in that brushy ravine around the spring early this morning that the *Nee-Me-Poo* suffered their heaviest losses. Two veteran warriors gave their lives. *Wayakat*, called Going Across, was killed instantly, and *Yoomstis Kunnin*, known as Grizzly Bear Blanket, received a mortal wound. In addition, *Howwallits*, the one called Mean Man, suffered a slight wound before the warriors were driven back from the water hole.

With things turning out badly as that second day of fighting progressed, the chiefs were already arguing among themselves. *Ollokot* and *Toohoolhoolzote*, Rainbow and Five Wounds, Two Moons and Sun Necklace—too many of their fighting men had refused to add their bodies to this fight. Some had hung back in the village to guard the women and children, but more had simply not advanced to the front to join the fighters. They had tarried at the smoking lodge, safe from the sting of soldier bullets. By the time some of those men on the far right of their defenses spotted the approaching dust cloud, they had been fighting for much of two days. *Ollokot* called for volunteers to follow him as he cut off the arriving Shadows and their long pack train, then rode off to make his noisy charge.

That's when everything went into a blur for Yellow Wolf. Both sides were shooting more furiously as they collided far to the right along the edge of the ridge. In minutes the dust cloud over that part of the fight started rolling in Yellow Wolf's direction. It didn't take him long before he realized why the soldiers were coming on so quickly. There were few warriors to oppose them!

Looking this way and that, he found himself all but alone on this far side of the ravine, where the fighting men were suddenly scrambling to their ponies, pitching them on down the draw for the river below—the *suapies* right on their heels. Glancing a moment into the valley, Yellow Wolf worried about his mother, wondering if she were among those now streaming up the Cottonwood, leaving behind most of their lodgepoles and camp equipment.

Enimkinikai!

Curses to the war chiefs for denying Joseph the opportunity to dismantle the village yesterday! A thousand curses for not allowing the *Wallowa* leader time to have the women prepare to move the village in an orderly retreat rather than this sudden, shocking, and uncoordinated flight—like that of a half-thousand mud sparrows before the night owls' warning screech. Instead of taking all that they owned and slipping away while the warriors had done battle with Cut-Off Arm's soldiers . . . now the families were forced to scramble for their lives, able to take only part of what they owned as they drove their huge pony herds up the steep hillsides west of the South Fork and onto the Camas Prairie once more.

"Nobody here!"

Yellow Wolf heard the voice cry out in his tongue. "Who is that?" he asked.

"*Wottolen*," the disembodied voice replied. "Is that Yellow Wolf?"

"Yes—I thought I was alone!"

"We are. There are but a few of us left now!" *Wottolen* bellowed as he burst into view, leading his pony through the trees. He leaped onto its back and wrenched the animal toward the head of the ravine. "Come, Yellow Wolf! It is time to *quit!*"

He started running on foot, following the older warrior—then suddenly remembered his pony, where he had tied it. Yellow Wolf raced for the tree, relieved to find the animal, and lunged onto its back, doing his best to clutch the reins and his rifle both with his right hand. Down, down, down he put it in motion, flying faster and faster down the ravine toward the river. Cutting left as he reached the valley, the young warrior dashed for the ford. Into the river, each lunging step took him closer and closer to the abandoned village. Up the far bank and into the empty camp.

The first boom of the cannon echoed overhead. Then the shrill whistle of the ball, closer and closer. That shell crashed through an abandoned lodge and exploded in a fury of dirt, flying lodgepoles, and smoke.

As the deafening roar faded, his ears caught the pitiful sound of a woman's cries. The whinny of a frightened horse.

Another boom rattled the valley. He whirled to look at the ridge top, mesmerized by the whining hiss of the oncoming cannonball. It whistled overhead into a patch of ground just beyond the lodges, tearing into their race ground with a loud, dusty explosion that hurtled clods of earth in a hundred directions.

As he kicked his pony into motion again, the woman and her crying horse suddenly appeared between the lodges to his right. She fought the pony as it reared, pawed the air, and landed with a bone-jarring jolt, then pranced and reared again, eyes mooning with terror. It was Joseph's wife, *Ta-ma-al-we-non-my*, the one known as Driven Before a Cold Storm. Her eyes were just as big as the horse's when he chattered to a halt beside her. There was no one else left but the two of them.

"*Heinmot!*" she shrieked his familial name, White Thunder. "My baby! I am worried about my baby!"

"Where?"

"Behind you!"

He whirled his horse to look, but his attention was immediately riveted on the ravine across the river, seeing how the soldiers had begun their descent right on his heels. Tearing his eyes away, Yellow Wolf spotted Joseph's newborn in a *tekash*, its cradle board, propped against a set of bare lodgepoles—where the buffalo-hide cover had been torn away from the graceful spiral of poles. Laying his rifle across the crook of his left elbow and stuffing the reins between his teeth, Yellow Wolf leaned over and seized the top of the *tekash* in his strong hand.

By the time he was bringing the pony around, the woman's horse had settled. She laughed with such unbounded joy as he handed her that bawling child lashed in its cradle board, a daughter, who had been born just as this war ignited against the Shadows.

He ripped the reins from his teeth. "Where is your husband?"

She looked up from the baby's face, saying, "He went ahead, leading the village away to safety as he has done since we left that last happy camp at *Tepahlewam*. I am sure he did not know I would be the last one here with his daughter," her words came breathlessly. "He could not have left us here if he had known. Joseph must think I am the head of the march with the other women and children—"

"Your husband has done what only a great chief would do, woman," Yellow Wolf reminded her. "His duty was to see all the rest of our camp to safety, before seeing only to his own family."

As they brought their ponies around and started away, she dropped her eyes a moment, saying, "For many days now, since the war on us started, my heart wanted Joseph to be something more than a camp chief. Sometimes . . . I secretly hoped he would become one of the fighting chiefs—"

She was interrupted by another loud roar as rocks rained down upon them, limbs from the trees spinning out of the sky.

Yellow Wolf sighed, looking down at the face of Joseph's daughter in that *tekash*. Then he said, "Your husband, our leader, he has always done what he thought best to protect his people—taking charge of the old men, the women and little ones, a sacred duty. I am proud to be part of his family," Yellow Wolf admitted.

She looked at him kindly as their ponies began to clamber into the Cottonwood canyon. "And Joseph is proud of you."

"Your husband, our chief, I have come to think of him as a better warrior than those loud-talkers in the smoking lodge, or those like Looking Glass who slip back to the village." Quickly glancing over his shoulder at the ruins of the village they were leaving behind, Yellow Wolf added, "Joseph is a man who always puts the needs of his people before his own. The same way our warrior chiefs put themselves between our camps and the enemy."

CHAPTER THIRTY-TWO

July 12, 1877

"BOOTS AND SADDLES!" THE SERGEANT BAWLED AT HIS MEN. "*BOOTS AND Saddles*, you godblessit weeds!"

First Sergeant Michael McCarthy hurled his slim frame atop his horse without using the stirrup and yanked back on the reins, immediately bringing the frightened sidestepping horse under control.

Parnell was among them an instant later, Captain Trimble seated on his mount, waiting off to the side as H Troop shuffled into ranks with the other cavalry troops. The mustachioed veteran of the Crimean War bellowed, "On the double, Sergeant! For-r-r-rad!"

With a yelp of his own, McCarthy flung his arm forward, leading them out in a lope after those fleeing warriors skidding, slipping, sailing ass over teakettle down the ravine hundreds of yards ahead of them. But almost as suddenly Parnell hurled his arm upward, halting the column as McCarthy bolted up beside him. He came to a halt beside the large officer, staring down in amazement at the body of a dead Indian—nothing less than gigantic in stature.

"Take a good look at that, you Irishman," declared the lieutenant with the growl of a dog suddenly released from its chain.

The sergeant's eyes poured over the stone breastworks. "Easy to see why we wasn't turning many of 'em into good Injuns this day," McCarthy lamented.

He quickly regarded the tall stacks of rock piled up by the Indians, most of the formations high enough for a man to stand behind as he sniped at the army lines. Many of the stacks even had willow branches poking from their tops—put there so the warriors and their weapons would be concealed from the soldiers.

Of a sudden, behind H Troop arose the noise of a broad front of approaching horsemen. Parnell kicked his horse, ordering, "Let's get this company down to the river!"

At the east bank of the South Fork both Trimble's company and Whipple's men held up, waiting momentarily until Captain David Perry, commander of the cavalry battalion, raced up to the advance and gave the order for those two companies to ford the stream then and there. Like so many of the men milling on the bank, McCarthy, heart pounding, was barely able to wait before crossing in pursuit of the fleeing village, at long last wiping away the stain of the White Bird debacle. Revenge was within reach—

"Cross and hold the village!" Perry declared, his horse backing slightly under the anxiety of its rider.

"*H-hold* the village, Colonel?" Trimble asked.

Perry glared at the captain, his nemesis from the White Bird Canyon debacle. "Yes. *Hold* the village."

"Beggin' your pardon, Colonel," Parnell pleaded. "We ain't never gonna get another chance like this'un to follow up them buggers and tear apart their retreat!"

Perry's withering gaze suddenly pinned Parnell to his saddle. "Your captain has his orders to cross and hold against possible attack, Lieutenant."

Good soldier that he was, Parnell snapped a salute. "Very good, Colonel!"

As Perry ordered, both cavalry companies crossed right there, plunging into the deep, cold water without going in search of a shallow ford. As McCarthy brought his shuddering horse under control, lunging onto the far bank as it flung water from its hide, he glanced up and spotted the last two riders escaping to the top of the far hill just beyond the village. One of the pair carried something bulky in his arms while the other turned to glance over his shoulder before disappearing from sight—

"There's some of 'em still in that creek bottom!" a trooper cried.

McCarthy wheeled his horse, catching the blur of motion as a dozen or more of the warriors took up positions in the trees along Cottonwood Creek, northwest of the village. With the warning, Perry quickly ordered three companies forward at a walk, slowly advancing on the creek, driving the Nez Perce back into the timber. But his charge was so cautious and dilatory that it was plain, even to General Howard, who was crossing the Clearwater at that moment, David Perry never again had any intention of pitching into an enemy so close at hand.

With Jackson's B Troop recalled to the riverbank, Trimble and Whipple deployed their troopers, spreading them on a wide skirmishers' front before they cautiously entered the camp on horseback after warning their men of snipers. The fragrance of cooking meat made McCarthy's mouth water. For more than thirty-six hours Howard's army hadn't eaten anything but bread and spring water. But here, on one fire after another, kettles simmered or meal broiled over low flames—supper already started for the fighting men.

On the far side of the village where both companies were halted and dismounted—with horse holders sent to the rear—the troopers established a skirmish line in the event the enemy decided to double back and make an attack. McCarthy's H Troop discovered a network of extensive log barricades the Nez Perce had constructed. It clearly showed how the war chiefs believed attack would come from that western side of their camp facing the Camas Prairie.

Within minutes the first of the infantry were reaching the far bank, where Jackson's troop was assigned to transport the foot soldiers across the river, riding double on the backs of their horses, then turning around to take up another soldier, one after another.

Already several of the civilians from Mount Idaho and Grangeville and some of the packers were leaping from their horses among the lodges. While some of the men ducked inside to determine what valuables might have been left behind, others yanked the cleaning rods from their rifles and began to probe any likely spot of freshly turned soil.

"What the hell you poking for?" McCarthy asked one dark-faced citizen.

"Caches. Where these red niggers buried the stuff they couldn't take with 'em."

Another volunteer came to a stop nearby, his arms loaded with a blanket and brass kettle, along with an assortment of other goods. "Looks to me them Nez Perce figger to come back for their plunder soon."

"Soon as they get shet of you army boys," the first man commented with a snort, "they'll double round and be back here to dig all this up."

One at a time, or by the handfuls, the treasures emerged from those lodges abandoned beside the South Fork of the Clearwater. A beautiful blue silk dress, which, by tying up the sleeves in the right manner, a woman had cleverly fashioned it into a bag to hold her camas roots. An old-fashioned hoopskirt had been adorned with beads and feathers, reflecting the new owner's tastes. Knives and forks, china plates, much more clothing, all the white man's goods now intermingled with dressed furs, moccasins, feathered headdresses, and more of their dried meat and berries. Some of the packers roared with delight when they ran across jewelry, fine silver tableware, and even small bags filled with gold dust or coins. Ammunition discovered in the lodges indicated many of the warriors were using Henry and Winchester carbines, along with some cartridges for some unknown model of a long-range target or buffalo gun.

But what caught McCarthy's attention was a pair of beaded moccasins sewn for a very small child he spotted near the base of lodge. Right next to them lay some little white girl's rag doll. At a glance it was easy to see that this was not a Nez Perce toy. Side by side these discarded items lay, Indian and white together—

"The general wants it all burned!" Perry shouted as he rode onto the flat, leading some of Howard's headquarters group as more and more infantrymen were "ferried" across the river all around them.

"Give us a little time to get through all this goddamned plunder!" one of the citizens pleaded as he dragged a blanket out of a lodge. On it lay a collection of valuables he was determined to save from the fires.

"Captain Whipple!" Perry shouted. "Give these civilians five more minutes, then put your men to work setting the tepees on fire!"

On all sides of McCarthy the civilians scrambled like ants on a hill a playful child has stirred with his stick—frantic to pull out everything of any value, claiming it for themselves . . . or reclaiming that which it was plain had been stolen from the farms along the Salmon or the ranches dotting the Camas Prairie. *The spoils of war*, Michael thought. *The spoils of a mean, dirty little war.*

In reality, most of what he saw was the few earthly possessions left behind by some dead man or woman now mercifully torn from this veil of tears in that first flurry of brutal and senseless murders.

The sergeant listened as Captain Trimble rode up to Perry, saluted, and asked, "Colonel, when can the men fall out and prepare supper? They haven't eaten much but coffee and a few bites of bread in more than a day and a half now."

"As soon as we have a defensive perimeter established and these lodges burned—just as General Howard ordered," he replied, watching the east bank as more and more of the command streamed down to the riverside from the plateau above.

McCarthy's mouth was already watering, as he thought of the potatoes and bacon back on those pack animals, hot food they could fry up while the coffee was boiling. The first decent meal in days now that they had a firm victory in hand.

His stomach growled in protest. They'd eat till they could eat no more tonight, then set off in the morning, running those fleeing warrior bands into the ground somewhere on the Camas Prairie.

Joseph and Mary—with them Injuns on the run, this war damn near has to be over now!

HE WAS DISGUSTED with the warrior chiefs. Disgusted with the other so-called fighting men, too. Still, Shore Crossing understood why they had decided to leave the soldiers behind and flee the camping place they called *Pitayiwahwih*. After two days of fighting, when no victory was in sight, it was better to leave so that a man could fight another day, in another place.

As the white man's big-throated guns sent the fiery balls into the camp, the women mounted up on their saddle horses and the young boys shooed the herds over the western hills, out of danger. At the edge of the timber west of the camp, Shore Crossing joined one of the knots of warriors waiting in the shadows for the first soldiers to come in pursuit of more than 450 fleeing women and children. But the *suapies* did not come racing in pursuit. It was easy to see how little the soldiers knew about crossing the river. The fast water would delay the white men long enough that the fighting men would not have to keep them busy while the camp escaped up the Cottonwood canyon.

With a struggle the soldiers reached the village, where some of them spotted *Ollokot*'s fighting men in the timber. After making a few shots at the *suapies*, the chiefs gave signals with the wave of an arm. Most of the warriors slipped away through the hills to rejoin the rest of the people already on their way. By the time Shore Crossing and the others caught up to the frantic retreat, White Bird, Looking Glass, and Joseph had restored some sense of order to the line of march. No longer were they in mad retreat. Once more the warriors were positioned along the sides of the column as it emerged onto the edge of the Camas Prairie. As their hearts began to slow and their thoughts were collected, the chiefs, headmen, and warriors began to deliberate their options.

Shore Crossing and the other Red Coats wanted all the young men to follow them and make one last, grand attack on Cut-Off Arm's soldiers. Whoever was whipped, it would be the last fight. But most of the chiefs and warriors said that events did not warrant one last, suicidal fight.

"Why all this war up here? Our camp is not attacked! All can escape without fighting. Why die without cause?"

Which meant that if the chiefs of the Non-Treaty bands were not going to risk their women and children in one last deadly battle, then their only course was to fully commit themselves to a war of retreat and evasion. And that decision left but two options for the leaders.

That night Joseph again proposed, "I want to return my people to the *Wallowa*. That is where we will make our stand, where we can die if we are to be wiped out."

But Looking Glass sneered, arguing, "To march back to that rugged country between the Salmon and the Snake would expose our families to danger on the open ground of the Camas Prairie. The *suapie* fort is on one side, and the Shadow towns are on the other. No. We must stay close by the Clearwater, for here the canyons are deep enough that Cut-Off Arm's men become entangled as they cross back and forth. We can stay out of reach of the white men until we decide what to do, and where to go."

Shore Crossing did not like this Looking Glass. At first the Alpowai chief had turned his back on the warrior bands, calling the fighting men fools for making war and shedding the blood of white men. Then last night, Shore Crossing had seen Looking Glass for what he was. After the darkness deepened and the shooting stopped, the Clearwater chief had slinked back down to camp to eat and sleep—as if no fight was going on above them! To *Wahlitits*, what Looking Glass had done was nothing short of cowardice. The chief was running away from the war.

In the end, the headmen elected to follow Looking Glass's proposal. But this time when they took refuge, they would send out scouts to prowl the surrounding countryside.

"Never again must we allow the white man to slip up on us undetected," Shore Crossing told that large group of chiefs and fighting men.

With a triumphant grin, Looking Glass said, "Perhaps we can leave this war behind here in the Idaho . . . and slip away to the buffalo country, where we will never have to worry again that we will be attacked while our village is sleeping."

There were many, many murmurs of agreement. Shore Crossing had to admit that it sounded seductive, safe, and luring. Could there really be a place where they would no longer be concerned with a blood-hungry army and Shadows crying for vengeance? But . . . was such a choice of running away from the enemy really the sort of decision a fighting man would make?

There on the Cottonwood the head of the march came back around on its tracks, starting east once again, looping for the Clearwater once more. As the sun began to settle atop the far mountains, those in the lead angled north, following the river bluffs downstream. Those warriors riding far out on the flanks stopped on the heights where they could once more look down on what had once been their camp of celebration and joy. The ground of *Pitayiwahwih* crawled with soldiers like a nest of spiders while spires of oily black smoke rose in the hot afternoon air. In huge bonfires the *suapies* were destroying everything the People had left behind. Sadly, the Non-Treaty bands dropped behind the bluffs, continuing downriver for Kamiah, where the Dreamers sometimes visited the Christian Indians who tended their fields there.

If little else was clear, Shore Crossing knew that Cut-Off Arm's soldiers had no intention of chasing them this night. The white men believed they had won a great battle. Even though the *suapies* had managed to kill only four warriors* while three times as many whites were dead, the soldiers would think they had won! Even though the village had escaped, even though the *Nee-Me-Poo* still had their great herds of horses and cattle . . . the white man would make much of that fight on the Clearwater.

From experience, the chiefs knew Cut-Off Arm would make much of a few tired, old horses they had abandoned to the *suapies*. He would make even more of all the lodges the women had been forced to leave behind—even though the women could eventually cut more lodgepoles and the men could hunt more hides, once they were gone to the buffalo country.

So how was it that the white men could turn an ignominious defeat for them into such a glorious victory over the *Nee-Me-Poo?*

"HOW THE HELL old do you think she is, Lieutenant?" Thomas Sutherland asked the general's aide just after sunset.

It was nearing 7:00 P.M. Melville Wilkinson shrugged as General O. O. Howard came up to a stop in that narrow gauntlet made by the Treaty Nez Perce who served as his trackers. The lieutenant whispered to the newsman, "From the looks of her, my guess is she's close to a hundred!"

Sutherland figured that wasn't far off. The old woman had to be no less than ninety, frail and wrinkled and so slow to move that she had been waiting for the soldiers to find her propped against this tree on the outskirts of the abandoned village. While soldiers and civilians alike were gallivanting around camp, showing off their buckskin clothing and moccasins they had saved from the burning lodges, the correspondent had trotted over as soon as he heard the call for some of the Christian Indians to help interpret the gap-toothed woman's garbled talk.

Now that Howard was here, the trackers began to string together broken words in English, a few phrases, for the white men, explaining what she had told them in their native tongue.

"Where is the camp going now?"

She didn't know for sure. Just getting away from the soldiers. They wanted to be left alone, and the chiefs were arguing about how best to leave all the trouble in Idaho behind.

Howard inquired, "What will it take for Joseph to surrender his people and come on the reservation?"

She gazed up at the one-armed general long and steady with her rheumy, watery eyes, then informed the translator that Joseph was not the chief of that village. There were five bands. Five chiefs. And Joseph was too young to be a chief over them all. Older men had the wisdom to assume that sort of

---

*Going Across or *Wayakat*, Grizzly Bear Blanket or *Yoomtis Kuunin*, Red Thunder or *Heinmot Ilppilp*, and Whittling or *Lelooskin*. Both *Wayakat* and *Lelooskin* fell so close to the soldier lines they had to be left where they lay in the retreat from Battle Ridge.

leadership in emergencies such as this. Men like *Toohoolhoolzote*, White Bird, and especially Looking Glass.

"*Toohoolhoolzote*," Howard echoed with an angry growl. "I put that old man in jail months ago. Should have kept him there."

"No, he will never lead the camps," she replied, folding her arthritic hands across her lap. *Toohoolhoolzote* was too unstable, too fiery, too harsh to reign as chief over all the bands together.

"White Bird? If Joseph isn't leading them, is White Bird?"

Again she stared the general in the eye and told the Christian trackers that the only one who seemed to have enough power to hold all five bands in his hand was her chief.

Howard looked quickly at the trackers. "Who the blazes is her chief?"

"Looking Glass."

Sutherland watched Howard wag his head, realizing the general must suddenly be considering how Whipple had botched his mission to arrest the chief and hold him for the duration of the hostilities. Had that sad little debacle been handled better, Howard might well have deprived the warriors' bands of that one chief they were now rallying behind.

"General, sir?"

Howard turned with the rest of them as Lieutenant Parnell rode up on horseback, accompanied by another of the Christian trackers.

"This one just came back from seeing things to the north, General," Parnell explained.

Howard studied him a moment. "Reuben. That's your Christian name?"

"James Reuben," the man said in passable English. "News for you."

"Out with it," Parnell nudged.

"Kamiah," Reuben began. "Warriors go to Kamiah—"

"Seems the hostiles aren't fleeing onto the Camas Prairie like we figured they would when we spotted 'em running west," Parnell declared impatiently. "They're scampering north instead, downriver."

With a lunge, Howard came up to Reuben's knee, staring up at him in the evening twilight. "That's a Christian settlement, isn't it?"

Reuben nodded. "I come back with word of the burning and stealing."

"Joseph's warriors are already destroying Kamiah?" Howard asked.

"They come to cross the river at the Kamiah ford," the tracker explained, his eyes shifting anxiously. "They cross the river there to burn houses of James Lawyer people, or . . . or—"

"Or what?" Howard snapped impatiently.

"Kamiah is the end of the road."

Now Howard grabbed Reuben's reins. "End of what road?"

"End of the Lolo. Kamiah begin the road to the buffalo country."

CHAPTER THIRTY-THREE

July 13, 1877

BY TELEGRAPH

OREGON

Joseph Apparently Getting Away.
SAN FRANCISCO, July 12.—A Portland press dispatch telegram received to-day at military headquarters, dated Cottonwood, July 8, says that all of Joseph's band have crossed the Clear Water, supposed to be heading for the Bitter Root country. Should this be true, the fight will prove a running one. The infantry will prove comparatively non-effective. Decisive work will have to be done by the cavalry.

Fort Lapwai
July 13, 1877

Dear Mamma,

I hurriedly finished up a letter this morning, as John came in and told me a mail would leave in five minutes. I did not say half I wanted to, and I will begin this and write a page a day.

. . . The news we were all expecting from General Howard came. There has been a fight, a very severe one. Our loss was 11 killed and 26 wounded. Two of the officers, Captain Bancroft and Mr. Williams, are wounded. We know both of them well. The Indians must have lost heavily. They make desperate efforts to carry off their dead, and 13 dead Indians were left on the field . . . This is our first good news and we all feel thankful. I hope the end of the war is near, but John and other officers think that after more troops come the Indians will get out of the road, and there will have to be a winter campaign organized to finish them up . . . Two of the medical officers now in the field are not in good health, and I am dreading daily that they will give out and be sent back here to look after the hospital and supplies, and John will be sent out

in their place. In case he should go, he would not like me to stay here, as his movements for the entire campaign would be uncertain . . .

Before I forget it, the jack straws came. The children have had two or three nice plays with them. I meant to speak of these things long ago, but indeed I have forgotten everything I ought to remember for the last month.

Your loving daughter,
Emily F.

IT HAD ALMOST BEEN A MONTH SINCE CAPTAIN CHARLES C. RAWN AND HIS small infantry detachment put Fort Shaw and the Sun River behind them on 9 June. His own I Company, along with Captain William Logan's A Company—a total of forty-five men—had come here to this valley of the five rivers with orders to purchase supplies and hire quartermaster employees, who would help construct a small post* some four miles southwest of Missoula City, Montana Territory. Back in May, Lieutenant General Philip Sheridan requested an allocation of $20,000 from the secretary of war for this post that would police intertribal conflicts over hunting grounds. The citizens on this side of the Bitterroots, on the other hand, wanted Colonel John Gibbon's Seventh U. S. Infantry to make a firm show of protecting the settlements.

After all, from here the Nez Perce War was no more than a mountain range away.

Back in April a large band of Looking Glass's people—returning from a successful buffalo hunt on the northern plains—camped with Chief Charlot's** Flathead, still residing south of their reservation and Missoula City in the Bitterroot valley. For generations it had been a common practice for the Non-Treaty bands to spend a little time with their acquaintances in Montana Territory, both Flathead and white. Later, in mid-June, an additional thirty-some lodges of Nez Perce stopped in the Bitterroot on their way home to Idaho Territory, just about the time the wires began to hum with news that war had broken out. Because a growing number of his citizens were becoming nervous that trouble could boil over into Montana Territory, Governor Benjamin F. Potts began raising hell with the army and officials back in Washington City, asking permission to raise a state militia. He was turned down at the highest levels.

Instead, the army said they had already dispatched this detachment of two companies west to Missoula City, there to establish a presence in the Bitterroot valley, where the Nez Perce were often seen coming and going, as well as trading, during the hunting season.

A Civil War veteran, with sixteen years in the regiment, Captain Rawn didn't know what more he could do to quiet the inflamed passions of the

*This post, officially established on June 25, 1877, was not named a fort until November of that year.

**In Flathead, Charlot means "Little Claw of the Grizzly."

settlers in this country. Upon his arrival, valley locals recommended he place an outpost somewhere up the Lolo Trail because of the threat and the Nez Perce tradition of traveling to and from their home through the Lolo corridor. Rawn agreed, *if* the citizens would provide his detachment with horses. None of the civilians would, so things quieted down somewhat when the locals went back home, grumbling and disgruntled at the army's inaction.

Which gave Rawn the opportunity to pay a call on Peter Ronan, newly appointed agent to the Flathead. Together they had gone to see Chief Charlot, securing his promise that, should the hostiles spill over into Montana, the Flathead would remain neutral but nonetheless provide intelligence of Nez Perce movements to the white man.

"You feel like you can trust this Charlot?" Rawn had asked as they rode back toward the agency.

"I'd like to think I could," Ronan admitted. "But something tells me we'd better keep an eye on him."

"That's exactly what I was thinking," Rawn replied. "There are simply too many of these Flatheads for a right-thinking man not to be wary and mistrustful of them catching this contagion if it spread from Idaho. Something in my gut is telling me I better not be too trusting of that Indian. His eyes shift a little too much."

Maybe it was nothing at all to worry about, but some time back a small band of eleven Nez Perce lodges under Eagle-from-the-Light had already joined Charlot's Flathead, more or less permanently, erecting their camp circle just south of the exit from the Lolo Trail, declaring they wished to stay in Montana despite the fact that Howard and agent John B. Monteith had ordered them back to Idaho and a life on the reservation.

Just last week Eagle-from-the-Light had come to Ronan requesting permission to camp right on the reservation just north of Missoula City itself, in his people's attempt to stay out of trouble should the hostile bands invade Montana Territory. But the Flathead agent refused, saying he did not want to provide a haven for Indians illegally off their reservation. In the end, those eleven lodges stayed where they were near the terminus of the Lolo Trail in the Bitterroot valley.

Even though Governor Potts made his second request of the army to form a citizen militia this very day, the thirteenth of July, for the time being Captain Rawn felt like everything was under control. Word was, General Oliver Otis Howard had a column of some six hundred men, both soldier and civilian, about to crush the upstart Nez Perce. It was an Idaho war. Bred, born, and fanned to a white-hot heat over there in Idaho.

So the kettle would have to boil with a mighty tempest for those troubles to erupt across these mountains.

Despite the constant rains that early summer, Rawn kept on chopping, hauling, and stacking logs as the walls of a few sheds were completed and he surveyed the site for the larger buildings. So much for the unbounded excitement and romance of a frontier officer's life.

AFTER CAPTAIN ROBERT Pollock's men buried the blackened bodies of their twelve* dead comrades in temporary graves at dawn on the battlefield plateau where the soldiers had given their lives, full military honors given over a mass grave dug just behind the field hospital, and Captain Henry Winters's E Troop of the First U. S. Cavalry started Surgeon Sternberg and twenty-seven wounded** for Fort Lapwai in dead-axle wagons and crude travois at 9:00 A.M. that Friday, the thirteenth of July, General O. O. Howard's command set off on that trail leading them down the Clearwater after the retreating Nez Perce.

Marching across the northeastern corner of the Camas Prairie, the column passed by McConville's now-abandoned Misery Hill. By midafternoon they had covered nine miles on the trail to the subagency at Kamiah, located on the north bank of the Middle Fork of the Clearwater. At 3:30 P.M. atop a low rise on the south bank of the river, the general's staff halted to pass around two pair of field glasses, gazing at the well-manicured gardens and the cultivated fields. What drew their attention even more magnetically some three miles away was that sight of the last of the Non-Treaty bands fording the river in their crude buffalo-hide boats shaped like overturned china teacups.†

While he had been congratulating himself for more than a day on the success of the battle, Howard wondered how he was going to follow Joseph and that village across the Clearwater.

When the Kamiah Christians under the leadership of James Lawyer, son of the noted Treaty chief, learned the warrior camp was coming their way, they had the foresight to remove their boats normally kept at the crossing. In addition, they had disabled the cable ferry used with those boats at this crossing. With those actions taken, most of the Lawyer Indians retreated into the hills, unwilling to openly oppose the Non-Treaties. Denied those boats, the warrior bands had resorted to the ancient bullboat, using what few buffalo hides they had managed to take with them in their precipitous retreat from the Clearwater encampment.

Just beyond those last stragglers clambering onto the north bank stood the subagency's buildings, surrounded for the moment by the massive horse herd. A little farther up the hill many of the warriors were already busy erecting some crude breastworks of stone and downed timber.

---

*At this date, one of Howard's men was officially MIA, eventually raising the number to a total of thirteen dead. Almost twenty years after the battle, settlers in the area discovered the remains of a soldier "back of one of the hills near Stites," along with four canteens, some army buttons, and a few silver coins. Could this have been that one soldier listed as missing in action?

**An interesting footnote to this battle's history is the fact that nearly one-half of the casualties, both dead and wounded, were officers, noncoms, and trumpeters—clearly exhibiting the Nez Perce understanding of the army's command structure, which plainly shows they aimed their weapons accordingly.

†The crossing place used July 13, 1877 was adjacent to the geologic feature and cultural artifact called Heart of the Monster, which figures into *Nee-Me-Poo* origin folklore.

Howard's belly burned in frustration. Barely late again! One step behind. Always one step behind Joseph!

"Get Colonel Perry up here on the double!" he ordered C. E. S. Wood, then watched the lieutenant salute and rein about.

In moments, Perry's horse was sliding to a halt before the general.

"Bring Whipple's company and take your cavalry battalion on the double to the right. Stop those Indians from getting away!" the general ordered grimly. "I'll send Wilkinson with a Gatling and limber to support you, then lead the rest myself."

He did not wait for Perry to get his battalion pulled out of column and on its way, content to watch those distant figures finish their crossing, slowly winding away from the east side of the Clearwater. Instead, the general ordered Jackson's B Troop, in the vanguard, to advance on the river crossing as they bore left of Perry's and Whipple's men. Behind Jackson came Miles with his infantry battalion, then Miller's artillery, followed by the rest of the cavalry and pack train. Trimble's H Troop served as rear guard while the column began its descent to the ford.

At the moment Perry's battalion reached the river and wheeled left to return to the main column—which was no more than four hundred yards away—the Nez Perce opened a brisk and concentrated fire on his troopers. It appeared his cavalry had walked right into a well-conceived ambush.

"Order the gallop!" Perry shouted, waving an arm and whipping his horse around as the mounted men began to shoot past him.

But as the bullets sailed around them in the confusion and panic, some of the horses became unmanageable, even wild—rearing and wheeling. Three of the men in the captain's company flung themselves out of their saddles and abandoned their horses, while others dismounted and hung onto their frightened horses, all of them sprinting through a grainfield to the left of their formation, racing back for the main column.

By the time Perry's entire battalion reached Wilkinson's artillerymen at the ford, they had withdrawn from the effective range of those enemy carbines. Already the Gatling guns had been wheeled into position and set up their first distinctive chatter.

"General, sir," said Major Edwin C. Mason as he came to a stop at Howard's elbow, "if I may be so bold as to express my disgust at the lack of . . . of courage shown by Colonel Perry and his cavalry."

"Colonel Mason?" Howard said, his eyebrows narrowing at his newly appointed chief of staff. "What's your complaint?"

"It's clear the Nez Perce hold the colonel's cavalry in profound contempt after the White Bird fiasco. Which is as it should be, General," Mason continued, warmed to his criticism. "The truth is, the First Cavalry is almost useless to you. They cannot fight on horseback, and they *will* not fight on foot!"

Howard seethed, wanting to rebuke Perry then and there for the embarrassing display—but held his tongue, for they had a hot skirmish just getting under way. He had to admit: He was growing disgusted with the captain who had failed him not only at White Bird but again at Cottonwood Station, too, then only the day before when he failed to follow up the fleeing warriors once his men were across the Clearwater.

For some time the warriors kept up their brisk fire, pinning down the soldiers and returning the long-range Gatling and rifle fire from the Springfields. When the noise began to taper off, Howard finally figured out that the warriors were only covering the escape of their families while the Nez Perce streamed out of sight and into the timbered hills, climbing north-northeast.

"Report on casualties, Lieutenant," the general ordered his aide, C. E. S. Wood.

In a matter of minutes, as Howard sat impatient in the saddle, Wood was back.

"No dead. Two men wounded. One in bad shape with a head wound, sir."

Just down the slope from him, Wilkinson's artillery continued to pound those slopes across the river without any effect. After an hour, a disappointed Howard ordered the shelling stopped. With the warriors and their families retreating, it was time for him to begin a crossing. But to do that would require the nonexistent boats of the Lawyer Indians. Complicating matters, the heavy wire cable had been freed from one end of the crossing.

As he was forced to watch the dark figures disappear among the green hillsides, Howard continued to seethe with the failure of his troops. It felt as if he was foiled at every step, kept no more than a narrow river from catching his quarry.

Sending details out to scare up the Christian Indians in hopes of securing their boats and repairing the ferry cable, the general ordered the rest of the command to withdraw a few hundred yards and go into camp for the night.*

That night he would begin laying plans on how he could catch those escaping hostiles between two pincers of his command.

---

*The troops encamped where the Kamiah airport is today.

CHAPTER THIRTY-FOUR

Khoy-Tsahl, 1877

IN THE MIDDLE OF THE NIGHT JOSEPH AND HIS PEOPLE HAD REACHED THE crossing in darkness, finding that Lawyer's people had hidden the boats traditionally kept at the ferry, along with dismantling the ferry's wire cable. Cruel acts to commit against one's people, but Joseph was beginning to understand how those Christians wanted more than anything to stay out of the war. Perhaps more than everything to be seen as not helping their blood relations the Non-Treaties.

Now with the way the warrior bands had been driven away after two days of fighting on the Clearwater and with Lawyer's people doing what they could to blunt the efforts of the Non-Treaty bands to escape, it was clear the tides were shifting in favor of Cut-Off Arm and his soldiers.

No matter they didn't have those boats. As the five camps came to a halt just above the Kamiah settlement, some fell to the side, intending to get a little sleep while the rest started cutting willow or dragging out what they had left in the way of buffalo lodgeskins. But this was not a camp of mourners resigned to running away from a fight with the army. Instead, Joseph saw around him a people enjoying a rising euphoria. For two days they had held off far greater numbers than they were ever able to put into their fight with Cut-Off Arm. And though they had to retreat, they were not fleeing for their lives.

Here, once again, they had the river between them and Cut-Off Arm.

Before marching away from the crossing, the warriors managed to leave the *suapies* with one final indignity as they popped up from cover and fired into the soldiers. As the white men scrambled off their horses and sprinted into the fields, the *Nee-Me-Poo* fighting men hooted and jeered.

On this north side of the Clearwater, maybe they could even choose a place to turn around on their heels and snap back at the army again—if only to show the general that there was clearly enough fight left in the Non-Treaty bands that he had little choice but to offer them favorable terms for their surrender. But . . . Joseph was not leading this camp. For more than a moon now the war chiefs had held the highest favor. Still, after those two long days on the Clearwater, the fighting men were clearly fighting among themselves on what to do, which way to go. There was even growling among the fighting chiefs as Looking Glass snapped at *Toohoolhoolzote,* White Bird sniped at *Huishuishkute.*

Over the last two days he had proposed a dramatic, if not risky, plan.

"I want to take my followers across the Camas Prairie," he had told the gathered chiefs. "From there we will cross the Salmon River, where the Wallamwatkin can make our final stand in our homeland of the *Wallowa* Valley. In a man's own country should he die defending the bones of his relatives. Only in a man's own country can he die with honor defending home and family."

But Looking Glass scorned his heartfelt proposal. "You say you are thinking only of the women and children? To march across the naked extent of the Camas Prairie would put them at great peril, Joseph. On one side stands the *suapie* fort at Lapwai, and on the other side stand the Shadow towns. No, you cannot throw those innocent lives against the very real possibility of death!"

"Then what would you have us do now that we are here at Kamiah," Joseph prodded, "where we get no help from Lawyer's people?"

With a grand smile, Looking Glass told the group, "Because of all those possessions and supplies we had to leave at the Clearwater and because these Kamiah people have run off and won't help us . . . we have but one choice."

"What is that?" White Bird demanded.

"We must go across the mountains to trade with the Shadows who have been our friends for many, many summers." Then he turned his self-assured smirk on Joseph. "Better to go among friends, Joseph—than to risk your people's lives making a suicidal retreat, eh?"

After that rebuke, Joseph thought it best to stay in the background and follow the movements ordered by the others who were swayed by the power of Looking Glass's impassioned oratory. For now—with the army nipping at their heels—he reluctantly decided he could best protect his Wallamwatkin band by staying among the other Non-Treaties as they climbed toward the ancient root-digging meadows at *Weippe* Prairie.*

As he pointed his pony toward the tail end of the retreating families, Joseph longed for an end to this fighting, when he could return to his beloved *Wallowa* valley with his people—there to live out the rest of his days with his wife and newborn daughter. But . . . would the child ever know anything but fighting and running, running and fighting?

BY TELEGRAPH

The Indian War—Reported Defeat of Joseph.

Just in Time to Prevent General Howard's Removal.

Move Against General Howard.

CHICAGO, July 14.—The Times' Washington special says the cabinet yesterday secretly but seriously considered the propriety of displacing Howard and putting Crook in his place. Howard, who has made such a bad mess of the campaign, was sent to that

*Where the Lewis and Clark Corps of Discovery first came across the people they called the *Choppunish*.

> remote country as a sort of punishment after the failure to convict on the court martial for his share in the freedmen's bureau frauds. It is quite possible that he will be removed to-day, as Secretary McCrary, who was absent at yesterday's (Friday's) cabinet meeting returned last night.

"The hostiles aren't moving?" Howard asked James Reuben, one of his most trusted trackers, that evening of the fourteenth.

Howard's command had been resting in their camp beside the Clearwater all day, most of the men taking advantage of the river to bathe and wash their ragged campaign clothing, besides digging some entrenchments in the event the warrior bands revisited the crossing.

The Christian scout shook his head. "Four miles. Maybe five. They stay in camp. No sign they move off."

For a moment Howard studied the tracker's dark eyes. Over time and many muddy miles across the Salmon, he had come to trust this Christian. Reuben was an educated Nez Perce, schooled here on the reservation. But because he was Indian, he was distrusted by the volunteers and settlers. The fact that Reuben carried a better gun than those the army was providing to the civilian militia was just another reason the scout ofttimes appeared haughty to McConville's volunteers. One more thing to hang their hatred on.

Balling his left hand into a fist as he turned from Reuben, the general told his staff, "Now we'll put in motion my plan to lull the hostiles into making a mistake, to catch them between the arms of two forces, compelling them to surrender, or fight to the death."

"But as soon as we set off, General," argued David Perry, "the Nez Perce will just up and run off."

"Not if they believe I'm headed back to Lapwai."

He went on to explain how, come the following morning, he would leave the artillery and infantry at the crossing when he departed with the cavalry, marching downriver on the well-traveled road to Fort Lapwai.

"So they'll believe you've headed back to the post!" Captain Marcus Miller exclaimed.

"After we've put enough distance between that cavalry battalion and this crossing, I will abandon the road, ford the river at a suitable spot James Reuben tells me exists at Dunwell's Ferry,* then move into that broken country, where we'll push ahead with our cavalry on the mining road takes us up the Orofino Creek to Pierce. In that way I can take the hostiles in the rear while Colonel Miller crosses here at Kamiah and pursues the camp, herding the unsuspecting hostiles right into the front ranks of my cavalry near the junction of the Orofino and Lolo Trails."

At six o'clock that rainy morning of the fifteenth Howard rode at the head of four troops—B, F, H, and L—of the First U. S. Cavalry, along with forty volunteers who had arrived the afternoon before under command of Colonel

---

*Near present-day Greer, Idaho.

Edward McConville. To disguise his real purpose, the general climbed up the steep Lapwai–Kamiah Trail,* as if retreating to the army post to gather more supplies—for the benefit of those spies Joseph was sure to have posted. Once out of sight beyond those heights behind his bivouac, Howard cut back cross-country, striking north. They had some twenty miles to wind along the snaking course of the Clearwater before they would reach Dunwell's Ferry but had covered no more than six when Christian scout James Lawyer came dashing up to the column to report that the fighting bands had broken camp in the hills on the far side of the Clearwater and were this morning climbing to the traditional camping ground at *Weippe* Prairie.

"That's at the western end of the Lolo Trail, General," Captain James B. Jackson advised.

"Which makes it good news, gentlemen," Howard enthused. "That means Joseph's warriors are on the way toward us already."

While his officers were making plans to cross then and there, a second Christian courier rode up with even more astounding news for the general.

"Reports from Joseph!" the breathless James Reuben told him. "He wants to talk to you."

"J-joseph . . . wants to parley with me?"

"He sends me to ask what terms for his surrender."

"S-surrender?" Howard echoed, his voice rising noticeably.

"That's the finest news we've had in weeks!" Captain Joel Trimble roared.

Howard took a step closer to Reuben, almost afraid to hope. "Where does Joseph want to talk to me?"

"Kamiah," the tracker explained. "At the crossing."

Without another word to the Indian, the general wheeled on his aides, flush with the excitement of a schoolboy. For a moment his tongue would not work, and he was terrified he would act as if he were a stuttering idiot . . . stammering if not utterly speechless now that he had the end of this war in his grasp. A half-dozen miles back up the Clearwater waited Joseph, the architect of the Non-Treaty resistance, the brilliant tactical mastermind behind their victories at White Bird and Cottonwood, the driving force behind the Nez Perce escape from their battle on the South Fork!

Joseph, the leader of the Dreamer resistance, was asking to come before the one-armed general, hat in hand! What would Sherman and all the rest who had cried for his removal think then!

"This war," he began, not at all surprised to find a lump of unbridled anticipation clogging his throat, "it's all but over, gentlemen. Let's hurry on our back trail to the crossing so that I can accept Joseph's surrender at the Kamiah agency—just as Grant accepted Lee's at McLean's farmhouse!"

While he and Perry's F Company turned around for the crossing, Howard ordered the rest of the cavalry and civilians to continue downriver under Jackson's command to Dunwell's Ferry, where they hoped to get their hands on a boat or two for use in breaching the Clearwater. Although his heart could take wing with hope, his head still told him that he must prepare for

---

*Today's Idaho State Highway 62.

the eventuality that this peace overture would dribble through his fingers. As hard as he might pray to the Almighty, Oliver Otis Howard was nonetheless a practical man who realized the Lord most assuredly helped the man who helped himself.

"His name is *Kulkulsuitim*,"* James Reuben announced later at the crossing, when the nervous-eyed messenger brought his pony onto the south bank of the Clearwater beneath that strip of white cloth he had fluttering at the end of a yard-long stick.

The Indian turned his eyes this way and that as the general gestured Major Edwin C. Mason forward with him and Reuben, signaling the rest of his aides to remain behind at a distance that would not intimidate this nervous courier.

"Be watchful of any false moves on his part, sir," Mason warned as the trio walked on foot to the crossing. "There may be sharpshooters on the far bank waiting for a signal from that Indian soon as he finds out it's you."

"The path to peace is never an easy one, Colonel."

Even before the general, Mason, and their Christian translator came to a halt several yards away, the horseman began talking.

"Says he knows who you are," James Reuben explained, pointing to the general's empty sleeve. "They all know you're the one they call the Cut-Off Arm chief. So he wants to tell you the camps have two white men, captives. Caught them going to Lewiston on business with horses."**

"Forget them for the moment!" Howard snapped, impatient now that the moment was at hand. "This messenger knows why I'm here. When will Joseph come in to talk to me himself?"

"Young Joseph wants to surrender, all right," Reuben said after some brief conversation with *Kulkulsuitim*.

With a quick glance at the heights across the river, the general said, "I suppose the bands are camped somewhere nearby in the hills, but not close enough to make it down here before it grows dark. So, tell this messenger that Joseph can come in with his people tomorrow morning to surrender."

After a moment of translation, Reuben said, "Joseph will try hard to break away from White Bird and Looking Glass. His people have little ammunition and food now. They left much upriver when they made a two-day fight on your soldiers. Says Joseph wanted to surrender to you on last two days, but he was always forced to move with the others."

"Tell him to remind Joseph that I never lied to him. I always spoke the truth."

Then Reuben translated, "How hard will you be?"

"Do you mean what terms I am giving Joseph and his men?" Howard cor-

---

*Even the identity of this messenger is in dispute among the records of that day. Some scholars claim it was a man named *Tamim Tsiya*, while still more say it was definitely a young warrior named No Heart, called *Zya Timenna*.

**William Silverthorne and half-breed Peter Matte, who would claim they were captured on their way to Lewiston to buy horses. Within a week, they would escape and carry some vital news to the soldiers who will be waiting at the eastern end of the Lolo Trail.

rected. "Tell him there are no conditions. Explain that to him—unconditional surrender. They give up their weapons and their ponies to me."

"Then what? What of the chiefs?" the translator posed. "What of the fighting men who made war against your soldiers?"

"The war chiefs are the ones I will arrest," Howard said. "Explain that to him. The bad leaders I want—not the warriors who took their bad advice. Once they have surrendered, I will appoint a court of officers who will try them according to military law—"

From across the Clearwater rang the report of a rifle, its sound magnified as it reverberated from the hills hemming in this gentle crossing. The bullet itself whined past and struck a nearby boulder with a splatter of lead and fractured rock chips.*

"What the devil!" Howard growled, his heart racing.

As he lunged forward, Mason ordered, "Hold that Injun!"

Although the messenger hadn't attempted to flee, Reuben seized the warrior's reins and held the frightened horse. The courier's eyes darted anxiously over those soldiers scurrying about, up and down the bank, responding to that single gunshot. He was jabbering at the translator in a high-pitched voice.

"Says Joseph want to surrender now!" Reuben cried in an excited tone as he tried to keep the horse and rider between himself and that other side of the river, where at least one sniper was hidden. "His people are getting so hungry. Had to leave so much at the Clearwater. The only thing for them to do is to take the women to *Weippe*—"

"They're already on their way to *Weippe?*" Howard shrieked in dismay.

"Yes," Reuben confirmed, "where they wanted to dig some camas to feed the hungry people before they surrender. But even though they are going to *Weippe*, White Bird, *Toohoolhoolzote*, and Looking Glass will not allow him to surrender. They want to make for the buffalo country and do not like Joseph talking peace with you."

"Tell him to remind Joseph that I will be here tomorrow morning to receive him," Howard repeated nervously, "right here in the morning—waiting for him to come down out of the hills. He has my word that he will not be harmed. Have him tell Joseph he will have a fair trial, an army trial. A white man's trial."

As soon as Reuben finished his translation, the messenger turned without another word, tearing his rein from Reuben's grip, and splashed into the river. Howard watched the water flow over the man's thighs, on over the pony's back, and up to the courier's waist as the animal struggled against the current that carried it downstream a quarter of a mile before they clambered onto the north bank, where the man pulled aside his breechclout and slapped a buttock before kicking his animal in its flanks. They quickly disappeared into the timbered hillside.

---

*There is even some broad disagreement on which side of the river this shot was fired and who might have fired it— the Nez Perce on the north side of the Clearwater or one of McConville's citizens on the south side (just as they had started the fight at Looking Glass's camp).

Choosing not to incite himself with that parting vulgarity on the part of the young messenger, Howard turned on his heel, his insides a jumble of excitement and apprehension mixed, troubled by a hint of skepticism. From the bank he hollered up to those officers arrayed on the side of the knoll.

"Colonel Miller! We need to send a courier downriver to Captain Jackson," Howard bellowed. He was clearly fearful of losing the momentum he had just won at the Clearwater with a resounding defeat at *Weippe* Prairie. "The hostiles are marching into the hills for *Weippe*, which will put them in position to wipe out our cavalry battalion. We must recall Jackson before he makes contact."

"I'll start a courier immediately!" Miller shouted as he started to turn away, but was stopped with Howard's next announcement.

Ever the optimist, Howard said, "Colonel, once that rider is on his way to Jackson's battalion I want you to prepare your men to receive the surrender of Joseph and his Nez Perce when they reach us at dawn!"

THAT MORNING THE Non-Treaty bands had awakened in their last camp before reaching the camas grounds of *Weippe* Prairie, a beautiful, extensive meadow where the blue camas flowers extended for as far as the eye could see with a color so vivid it made Yellow Wolf believe he was seeing the sky itself reflected in huge ponds of trapped rainwater. On nearly all sides they were surrounded by timber-blanketed hills, those hills themselves surmounted on the east by snow-mantled mountain peaks.

In the first misty light of dawn Yellow Wolf had watched the older woman lead a pony out of the camp circle. There the mother of *Wayakat* climbed on the animal's back before the woman noticed that he was watching from his mother's blanket shelter.

"Yellow Wolf," she whispered as he approached, his moccasins growing soaked with the heavy dew.

"Where are you going so early?" he asked, looking up at her red, bloodshot, and puffy eyes.

"Now that the *suapies* have left the battlefield on the plateau, I am going to claim the body of my son."

"He was a brave fighter," Yellow Wolf said with admiration. "Your son fell too close to the soldier lines for any of us to get his body for you."

"I do not hold bad feelings for any of you fighting men because my son was left behind when we fled our camp," Going Across explained as she reached down and touched the back of his hand. "But, I need to go bury him now."

"When will you return?"

"By nightfall if I can," she said. "If not, and the camp moves on up the trail to *Weippe*—I will find you."

"Yes," Yellow Wolf said quietly as he took a step back and held his arm up in parting. "I am sure you can find your way."

Late that afternoon just after the Non-Treaties reached the extensive camas digging grounds, a small band of people emerged from the trees at the end of the trail over those mountains. Even from a distance it was easy for Yellow Wolf to recognize that they were *Nee-Me-Poo*— their horse trappings, dressed as they were. Five-times-ten of them, women and children traveling with seventeen warriors under their leader, *Temme Ilppilp*, called Red Heart.

"You have just come from the buffalo country?" asked Looking Glass as the hundreds crowded around the new arrivals, tongues trilling in welcome.

Red Heart's eyes and smile grew big with this unexpected reception here in the meadows of *Weippe*. He gestured toward their numerous travois pulled by trail-weary packhorses. "We have many buffalo robes, yes."

"See?" Looking Glass roared at the crowd pressing in on the newcomers. "What did I tell you? All things are good in the buffalo country!"

Red Heart took the older man's elbow in his hand and said, "Over there in the valley of the Bitterroot River, we have heard talk of your struggles against the army. But—looking at you now—I don't see a people who are at war!"

Looking Glass let his head fall back as he laughed loudly before saying, "We are at war. The *suapies* just can't keep up with our village of women and children!"

But the laughter quickly died as those close around the chiefs realized that Red Heart was not laughing. Yellow Wolf shouldered his way closer to hear all the words.

"The army is chasing you now?" Red Heart asked, his tone heavy with concern.

"Yes!" Looking Glass answered enthusiastically. "But they will never catch us now."

"Then it is as the Shadows in the Bitterroot were saying," Red Heart explained. "They were afraid of us when we marched past their homes and stores this time. Never before were they afraid of *Nee-Me-Poo*, but now these people did not want us to stay long in their country."

"Those settlers in the Bitterroot have nothing to worry about," White Bird vowed.

Red Heart asked the older chief, "If the army is chasing you, where will you go?"

"I told them we should go to the buffalo country, where the animals are fat and we will camp next to our friends, the *E-sue-gha!*" Looking Glass cheered. "Come back with us on the trail over the mountains. It is no longer safe here in the Idaho country for our people."

As he stared at the ground a long moment, it appeared Red Heart already had his mind made up. When he looked at White Bird and the other leaders, he said, "We have already decided: If what we were told was true, we will not join in your fighting. We want to be left alone."

"The soldiers will not leave you alone!" Looking Glass roared angrily.

"Then we will surrender to them and give them our guns," Red Heart countered. "That way they will know we are not part of this war."

"G-give them your guns?" White Bird blustered.

Red Heart wheeled on the old war bird. "Better that than to give them the lives of all these women and children!"

"You are not a man!" Looking Glass bawled with fury. "A man would fight and die for his women and children—"

"I will go surrender with you, Red Heart," a voice suddenly interrupted Looking Glass's tirade.

Yellow Wolf and the rest of the crowd watched a minor leader in the Non-Treaty bands step forward.

"You will abandon this fight?" Looking Glass demanded.

"Yes," Three Feathers answered.

"Don't you remember what Wright did to the Yakima and Cayuse leaders when they surrendered after making a war with the army?"* Looking Glass scoffed.

"Yes," Three Feathers sighed. "Those chiefs were hanged."

"Do you want the same to happen to you?" White Bird chided.

It took a moment before Three Feathers answered, "It is one thing to go east and hunt the buffalo in the land of the *E-sue-gha*. It is another thing entirely to leave our fair land behind for all time."

Toohoolhoolzote asked, "You are not afraid of the white man's ropes?"

"Yes, I am afraid of hanging," Three Feathers replied, "but I will go with Red Heart and surrender my guns so that my families don't have to run anymore. And if I have to die . . . then I prefer to die in my own country. Not in a faraway land of strangers."

---

*Thirty Nez Perce scouts had served with Wright's campaign in 1858 and witnessed the hangings of those Indian leaders. Later, in 1873, Captain Jack and other Modoc leaders had suffered the same fate at the hand of a vengeful government.

CHAPTER THIRTY-FIVE

July 15–16, 1877

Fort Lapwai
July 15, 1877

Dearest Mamma,

This is such a bright Sunday morning. The children look so nicely in their best blue stockings and little brown linens, and they are playing on the porch. This is the first day this summer I have felt like fixing them up from top to toe. Even now I am afraid we will hear something horrible before the day is over and spoil all my pleasant feelings. The Indians (friendly ones) who were in that last fight say that one officer had his leg cut off by the officers in the field, and they describe it so plainly, it must be so. Then from the fact that General Howard named the Camp "Williams," we fear poor Mr. Williams has lost his leg. He is only a young fellow and very fine one . . . Dispatches came in from General Howard yesterday saying the Indians had recrossed the Clearwater River and were making for the mountains with the troops in pursuit. The trail over the mountains, which the Indians are supposed to be making for, leads over into Montana into what they talk about here as the buffalo country, but from a great many things, nearly everybody thinks Joseph doesn't want to get out of the country around here, but is only withdrawing in that direction to prepare for another fight. You never heard of such daring Indians in your life. In this last fight, they charged to within ten feet of the soldiers, and charged up to the artillery and tried to take the guns from the men . . .

My head is full of Indians. It was very warm yesterday, and I baked a cake and churned my butter on a table on my back porch, and I kept one eye and one ear up the ravine watching for Indians all the time. It is a horrible feeling . . .

Everybody here seems to feel a little more cheerful since the last fight . . . It is like the old cry of "Wolf! Wolf!" and when we don't look for it, the wolf comes.

We all join in love and hope to hear soon.

Your affectionate daughter,
Emily FitzGerald

BY TELEGRAPH

A Run on the Savings Banks
of St. Louis.

WASHINGTON.

Dismissal from the Indian Bureau

WASHINGTON, July 14.—L. S. Hayden clerk in the Indian bureau, was to-day dismissed by the secretary of the interior as the first public result of the pending investigation of the allegation of irregularities and fraudulent practices in the Indian service . . . Hayden, according to his own evidence, has accepted money and other things of value from contractors . . .

Better News.

WALLA WALLA, July 14.—*To Gen. McDowell, San Francisco*: Have been with Gen. Howard in the battle of to-day, which he reports in detail. I consider this the most important success. Joseph is in full flight westward. Nothing can surpass the vigor of Gen. Howard's movements.

(Signed) KEELER, A.D.C.

Gen. McDowell says that he thinks this defeat will tend to cause the other Indians to remain peaceable, and may make it unnecessary to act under the president's authority to call out volunteers for temporary service. He will at least defer action till he gets Howard's report.

LATE LAST NIGHT AFTER AGENT JOHN MONTEITH AND INDIAN INSPECTOR Erwin C. Watkins arrived from Lapwai, General Oliver Otis Howard dashed off a short dispatch to be wired to his commander, McDowell, in San Francisco:

CLEARWATER, July 15th

Joseph may make a complete surrender to-morrow morning. My troops will meet him at the ferry. He and his people will be treated with justice. Their conduct to be completely investigated by a court composed of nine of my army, selected by myself. Col. Miller is designated to receive Joseph and his arms.

[signed] O. O. Howard
Brig. Gen. U. S. A.

The following morning, a Monday, the general was up before dawn, composing the congratulatory address one of his aides would read before his troops following their battle on the South Fork of the Clearwater River:

Headquarters Department of the Columbia,
In the Field, Camp McBeth,
Kamiah, I.T., July 16, 1877.

GENERAL FIELD ORDERS NO. 2
The General Commanding has not had time since the battle of the 11th and 12th instants, on the South Fork of the Clearwater, on account of the constancy of the pursuit, to express to the troops engaged his entire satisfaction with the tireless energy of officers and men, that enabled them to concentrate at the right time and place with the promptitude of the first assault; the following up of the first advantage for a mile and a half with inconceivable speed; with the quickness to obey orders; sometimes to anticipate them, which prevented the first flanking charge of the Indians from being successful; then with the persistency of uncovering their barricades and other obstacles, and clearing ravines, both by open charge and gradual approaches under constant fire, thereby making an engagement of unusual obstinacy of seven hours hard fighting; also his satisfaction with the remaining in difficult position and entrenching a long line at night while fatigued, and almost without food and water, till the afternoon of the second day, when the Infantry and Cavalry of the command cheerfully thinned out their lines so as to cover two miles and a half of extent, and to allow the Artillery battalion to turn the enemy's right and enable an approaching train with its escort to come in with safety; then turning briskly upon the foe, the Artillery battalion, by a vigorous assault, sent him in confusion from his works, and commenced the pursuit in which all the troops, including the new arrivals, immediately engaged—through the ravines and rocks and down the most impassible [sic] mountain side to the river; after this crossing, the taking possession of the Indian camp, abandoned and filled with their supplies, and surrounded by their "caches," causing the Indians to fly over the hills in great disorder.

The battle, with its incidents, is one that will enter into history; its results, immediate and remote, will surely bring permanent peace to the Northwest, so that it is with great satisfaction the General can say that not one officer or soldier that came under his eye on that field failed to do his duty, and more gallant conduct he never witnessed in battle. The General feels deeply the loss of the killed, and sympathizes heartily with the wounded, and unites with their friends in their anxiety and sorrow. He mentions no one by name in this order, hoping to do justice to individuals after reports shall be received. The command is indebted to the officers of the staff for their indefatigable work previous to and during the engagement.

With that bit of officiousness put behind him, the general gathered with his headquarters staff on the south bank of the Clearwater, waiting for Joseph to bring his people in to surrender.

"This surrender means nothing short of the end to the war," Howard enthused outwardly, while inside he remained full of doubt.

"We've heard reports from a few Christians that White Bird is driving all those who hoped to surrender before him with the lash," Monteith admitted. "There's some room for error in these rumors, but . . . I feel that if Joseph attempts to surrender, it will lead to an open clash between the Non-Treaty bands."

That's when Watkins declared, "And Agent Monteith doesn't think Joseph will risk such a clash within the Dreamers."

The hours slowly dragged past that morning. The Nez Perce did not show.

His hopes crushed, Howard sensed his anger simmering—figuring that he had been played a fool by Joseph. Not only was the chief a superb military tactician in outmaneuvering Oliver's West Point–trained officers, but Joseph was an unequalled diplomatic strategist in outplaying Howard himself in this ruse* at surrender.

"It was nothing more than a well-manufactured lie designed to hold me in check while he had time to take his hostiles and their livestock toward the terminus of the Lolo Trail," Howard admitted to his staff later that morning as they gathered for officers' call in the shade of some trees.

"Joseph wants to play cat and mouse again with us," Captain David Perry said, "we'll show him the cat can catch that mouse—"

"General Howard! General Howard! Pickets report Indians coming down to the crossing!"

Was it too much to hope?

Howard busted through the circle of officers who barely had time to step aside for him. The moment he had a clear view of the distant hillside, the general stopped in his tracks, staring. A thin column of Indians both on horseback and foot angled down the grassy north slope toward the Kamiah crossing. Not quite a hundred, but close enough from what he could tell. While it was nowhere near all the souls in that hostile camp, it was nonetheless a start. So with Joseph at the head of this first group to surrender, the others would soon see the rightness in giving up and eventually follow their leader in to turn over their weapons and horses.

But by the time the first leaders had their ponies halfway across the Clearwater, Howard was standing at the edge of the river, shifting from foot to foot, bewildered that he did not see Joseph among those riders.

---

*As the years passed, ample evidence came to light to show that Joseph may have indeed been very interested in surrendering to Howard. Years after the war, Lieutenant C. E. S. Wood wrote that he had been told by an unnamed Nez Perce informant, "Joseph wished to surrender rather than leave the country or bring further misery on his people, that, in council, he was overruled by the older chiefs . . . and would not desert the common cause." As late as 1963 Josiah Red Wolf stated, ". . . not only was Joseph hard to persuade to stay in the fight, but he tried to drop out after the [Clearwater battle]."

"Where is Joseph?" he demanded of his translator as James Reuben came up at a lope and dismounted on both feet.

"Joseph isn't with them," Reuben said after he had spoken to the first arrivals. "He is with the others camped back in the hills."

"Joseph is coming down later?"

"No, General. These are the only people surrendering today," Reuben explained. "Their names are Red Heart and Three Feathers. They brought their families in to give up their guns and horses. Don't want to fight the soldiers. No war, so they come in to you."

Bitterly, with more disappointment than he wanted to admit was boiling in his belly, Howard grumbled at his aides, "Take their guns and dismount them. They are my prisoners of war."

He whirled on his heel.

"General," Reuben said, lunging in front of Howard, "these are no fighters. Never fight the army. You can't make them prisoners of war."

He glared at Reuben as he snapped, "I can make any Nez Perce a prisoner of war when I know they've been with the hostiles in their camp. Who's to say they're not spies? Or that they don't mean to kill me if they had the chance? You tell them they are my prisoners!"

Later that morning Second Lieutenant Charles Wood came up to report that Red Heart's people had only two old guns to turn over.

"Were they completely searched?" Howard inquired.

"Yes, General. The translator told me they said more of their people would be coming in later today or tomorrow."

"Joseph?"

Wood shook his head. "The one called Three Feathers said Joseph has been compelled to take his people to the buffalo country with White Bird and Looking Glass. He also claimed he lived on the reservation and has never been—"

"A reservation Indian, is he?" Howard sniffed. "I want them all arrested and taken off to Lapwai under armed escort. They shall remain my prisoners of war until this war is over."*

"I'll see that escort is arranged, sir," Wood replied. "It seems to me that these people showing up to surrender to you is a good sign."

"A good sign?"

"Yes, sir. To me it shows that there is dissension in those warrior bands. I think it bodes well that the war is close to an end, General."

He allowed himself to enjoy a little self-congratulation, at least until midafternoon, when a courier arrived from Fort Lapwai with a leather envelope filled with letters and even a dispatch from division headquarters in Portland. Included was a terse wire from General Irwin McDowell's aide, which read in total:

---

*Which is just what happened. These men in chains, along with their women and children, were herded on foot through scorching heat and choking dust to Fort Lapwai, more than sixty miles away, then on to Lewiston, from there by steamer to Fort Vancouver, where they remained incarcerated behind walls and bars until the end of the Nez Perce War that winter.

> See Associated Press dispatches which state General Howard's removal under consideration by cabinet.

That flimsy was attached to several clippings from recent newspapers, all dealing with stories picked up off the wire from Washington City.

His long string of failures, blunders, and misplaced optimism had gotten him nothing but a blackguard's treatment in the press. All at once, the awful specter of those scandals at the Freedmen's Bureau loomed over him once more like a sword suspended on a very thin thread. Everyone, it seemed, had been calling for his removal, and those cries had found ears all the way to Washington itself.

But, as General McDowell himself wrote in a wire to Howard, with that news of his success in the Clearwater fight Howard himself had reversed all that ill will with one fell swoop:

> To army heads sorely perturbed over Nez Perce successes, your telegrams were welcome news when they reached headquarters a day ago.

Instead of being the one who would have had to remove Howard by order from Washington, General McDowell now relayed his unbounded elation at Howard's turnaround, writing, in part:

> Your dispatch and that of Captain Keeler of your engagement on the eleventh (11th) and twelfth (12) gave us all great pleasure. I immediately repeated them to Washington, to be laid before the Secretary of War and the President. These dispatches came most opportunely, for your enemies had raised a great clamor against you, which, the press reported, had not been without its effect in Washington. They have been silenced, but I think they (like Joseph's band) have been scotched—not killed—and will rise again if they have a chance . . .

"This is great news, General!" Thomas Sutherland exclaimed as he came up to join the headquarters group. "Those wags with their asses plopped down in some comfortable horsehair sofa back in Washington—what do they know of Indian fighting?"

The other officers cheered that approbation.

"It's for sure they haven't been reading any of my dispatches!" Sutherland continued. "If they had, those myopic narrow-sighted imbeciles would know better than to criticize a fighting man in the middle of a fight!"

Howard nodded. "I appreciate your help and understanding, Mr. Sutherland."

"No need to thank me at all, General," the correspondent replied. "Only a blind man couldn't have seen that those two days on the Clearwater were the only fight Joseph's had where his ambition was victory . . . and its plain to see that, ever after, his highest aim will be simply to escape your army."

CHAPTER THIRTY-SIX

Khoy-Tsahl, 1877

I AM NOT AFRAID TO SAY THIS!" WHITE BIRD EXCLAIMED AS THE TWILIGHT deepened, accenting his many wrinkles as the firelight played off his face. "There were too many cowards in our last fight with the *suapies!*"

Toohoolhoolzote grunted his agreement just an arm's length from Yellow Wolf. "There was no convincing them to rejoin us in our fight. Cowards who fled to the smoking lodge. Some cowards slipped back down to the village while the rest of us held the soldiers away from our families!"

Looking Glass bolted to his feet, furious. "Because I came down from the ridge to see that my people were safe, does that make me a coward in your eyes?"

"Did you stay and fight through the cold night?"

Shaking his head, Looking Glass answered White Bird, "You do not understand. My people had been attacked and run off by the soldiers. More than any of you, I did not want to be chased away again, carrying only what we had on our backs." He whirled on the *Wallowa* chief, pointing accusingly. "Joseph should have had the camp packed and ready to go before we were forced to fall back the second day. Joseph should have made more women tear down their lodges and pack their goods so that we would be ready."

Yellow Wolf glanced over at his chief. It was true he had not played a major role in any of the fights against the *suapies* thus far. But Joseph had fought as a warrior with the other fighting men, returning to the camp only when it appeared the soldiers were about to roll over the entrenched warriors. There had been little time for the women to tear down the lodges and pack the travois before the warriors came boiling down to the river.

The sun had finally come out that morning, warming the lush, grassy meadows where the thousands of ponies grazed after the last two days of intermittent rain that made for a muddy, slippery trail ascending from the Kamiah crossing. After breakfast the women scattered to dig what camas the Shadows' hogs hadn't already rooted out of the damp soil. The white men who had settled in the area had always been that way—turning those disgusting animals loose on the *Nee-Me-Poo* digging grounds. Many days ago the settlers fled the *Weippe*, so this morning the young men rode off to torch all the white man's buildings they could find in the area, shooting and butchering what cattle they did not want to steal but refusing to touch one of the white man's hogs. Instead, the warriors killed every one.

Now with the sun's setting, this momentous, solemn council had begun to air all the grievances among the chiefs and to determine the future of the Non-Treaty peoples.

"But instead of talking about what is behind us in the past," Looking Glass growled, "I think we should be talking about what should be for the days ahead."

"I agree," said *Hahtalekin*, known as Red Echo or Red Owl. Earlier that afternoon the Palouse chief had come in with sixteen warriors. "Yesterday is behind us. Now we must think about what to do tomorrow. Where to go."

"Why do you and Looking Glass say we have to go anywhere?" Joseph argued, having been silent for a long time. "Why can't we stay and fight, die if we must, in our own country?"

"Some of our leaders are giving us bad advice," Shore Crossing said as he leaped to his feet near White Bird. "I think we should listen to Looking Glass and go to the buffalo country!"

White Bird shook his head, pointing at the young "Red Coat" warrior from his own band, one of three who had worn their famous red blankets tied at their necks while making the daring charges at *Lahmotta*. "Is this what you want to do now that we are gathered to fight the soldiers? You sons of evil started this war for all the rest of us. No, you are not running away. You will stay with me and Joseph and fight till we kill all the white men, or die like *Nee-Me-Poo* warriors!"

"No, this cannot be so," argued Looking Glass. "Don't we have enough friends and brothers dead already? And still the *suapies* and Shadows come after our trail. They seem like the sands in the riverbed. No matter how bravely we fight them, the more we kill, the more will invade our country."

"Can't we make the best peace we can with Cut-Off Arm?" Joseph pleaded. "Think of our women and children—they will be left widows and orphans if we keep on fighting."

"Surrender?" Looking Glass snorted. "Those of our fighting men the soldiers do not kill in battle Cut-Off Arm will hang."

"This is true," White Bird agreed begrudgingly. "I remember what the *suapies* did to Captain Jack and his Modocs when he surrendered to the Shadows. They died at the end of a rope!"

"If our men are either killed by the soldiers in battle or hanged," Looking Glass argued, "then who will care for our women and children, Joseph? How can you say we should stay when our brothers from Lapwai and Kamiah have turned their backs on us and are helping the Shadows like snakes."

Joseph turned to White Bird, saying, "Perhaps some of the Shadows' wrongs against us have made a few of our young men do bad things. Because of that you are saying we must now give up the land of our fathers and follow Looking Glass into the land of the buffalo far away from the place of our birth?"

"Yes!" Looking Glass cheered. "The white men there are not like the Shadows in this Idaho country. They trade with us. We leave our lodges and poles and many horses with the Shadows and the Flathead every hunting season when we visit them on our way home from the buffalo country. Rainbow and Five Wounds are just back, so they will tell you: The *E-sue-gha* say they are willing to go on the warpath against the white man with us!"

"But what of Cut-Off Arm?" White Bird wondered.

Rainbow stepped forward to say, "If we follow Looking Glass, we will put the Idaho soldiers behind us. Cut-Off Arm will not follow us with his army over the mountains."

"Joseph," White Bird persuaded, apparently won over, "perhaps we can leave the war here. The Shadows will not remain angry with us for long. If some of your people want to come back, they can return to their old homes in a few summers; maybe even by next spring everything will be back to the way it was before."

But the tall chief of the Wallamwatkin band prodded the other leaders by saying, "What are we fighting for? Is it for our lives? No. It is for this land where the bones of our fathers lie buried. I do not want to take my women among strangers. I do not want to die in a faraway land. Some of you tried to say once that I was afraid of the whites. You evil-talkers stay here with me now and you will have plenty of fighting at my side! We will put our women behind us in these mountains and die on our own fighting for them. I would rather do that than run I know not where."

Toohoolhoolzote, that stocky firebrand, now said in a calming tone, "Joseph, I know you think only of the families, those who do no fighting. Now it is time for you to think of the good we will do for them by no longer fighting, by going over the mountains away from the soldiers."

"Joseph?" Looking Glass prodded impatiently.

He wagged his head. "I don't know—"

Suddenly the canny Looking Glass was moving around the circle, gesturing grandly. "The rest of you? Do you want your families to die here like Joseph does? Tell me how many more of your young warriors do you want to bury before you will see we can make a new life for ourselves on the plains of the buffalo country?"

White Bird laid a hand on Joseph's shoulder. In a soft, fatherly voice, he said, "Joseph, we must take our bands across the mountains." Then he promptly turned to the crowd and loudly proclaimed, "I vote with Looking Glass! We take our people east from this trouble."

Looking Glass literally bounded around the fire with youthful exuberance, shouting out a song of victory as he whirled and stomped in the dancing firelight. "To the buffalo country!"

Then more than seven hundred voices—warriors, women, and children, too—were raised to that summer sky, to the very stars hung over that ancient camping ground of *Weippe*.

"To the buffalo country! To the buffalo country! To the buffalo country!"

Fort Lapwai
July 16, 1877

Mamma Dear,

. . . Dispatches from the front have just come in. They say Joseph wants a talk with General Howard. He says he is tired of fighting.

He was drawn into it by White Bird and other chiefs, and he wants to stop. We hear there is great dissatisfaction among the hostiles themselves. The squaws are wanting to know who it was among their men that took the responsibility upon themselves of getting into this war with the Whites. They have lost their homes, their food, their stock, etc. . . .

The artillery companies we were with in Sitka are on their way up here. I will be glad to see our old friends again . . . I shall feel so sorry to see them move on to the front.

They talk of making Lapwai a big four company post with the headquarters of a regiment here, and there is no knowing, even if the war is soon ended, where we will all turn up next spring. Poor Mrs. Boyle says she hopes she won't be left here. She shall have a horror of Lapwai all her life. The Boyles had not been here a week until this trouble began.

Your loving daughter,
Emily FitzGerald

Ad Chapman was ready to ride.

The last four days of sitting around on his thumbs with these soldiers who dillydallied in this direction, them hem-hawed in the other had just about driven him crazy! But late last evening Major Edwin C. Mason, Howard's former inspector general, came round to the bivouac of McConville's volunteers, whistling Chapman up to ride out this morning so he could lead and sometimes translate for the half-dozen Nez Perce trackers the major was taking along under James Reuben.

They weren't all Presbyterians or Catholics, Ad knew. At least one of them, a fella called Horse Blanket, claimed he had no religion of any kind. He hadn't cut his hair like his Christian companions. Chapman knew Horse Blanket kept his hair tucked up under his white man hat.

Chapman was up by three-thirty on the morning of the seventeenth. Mason had the scouting detail moving out less than an hour later when it grew light enough to see the trail as it wound into the hills away from the Kamiah crossing. What with Mason being an infantry commander, Chapman thought it a mite strange that Howard had assigned his newly appointed chief of staff to command a battalion of five companies, both cavalry and a detachment of artillerymen, including their mountain howitzer, along with more than twenty of McConville's citizens, to reconnoiter beyond the junction of the Lolo and Orofino Trails to the *Weippe* Prairie. It had taken the command all of yesterday, the sixteenth, to get itself across the Clearwater—no more than ten soldiers at a time in that single boat they could find and put in service.

Then, too, Chapman thought it strange that General Howard had picked the major to lead this scouting detail, because in the last few weeks Mason hadn't lost an opportunity to show just how much disdain he held for horse soldiers. In fact, it was plain to everyone who had ever listened to the man talk that Mason viewed the fighting abilities of the First Cavalry with nothing less than an undisguised distrust, if not an outright contempt.

Just above the crossing, they entered the timber and began climbing toward *Weippe.* This wasn't like crossing the Camas Prairie, Chapman brooded. Now the column slowed to an agonizing crawl as the trackers up ahead tried to thread their way up a rocky, muddy trail, through the thick stands of windblown trees, over and around centuries of deadfall that lay like stacks of jackstraws a child might toss carelessly upon a thick green carpet where the new day's sun streamed through in broken shafts as it would slash through the slats of a garden fence. After a brief, hard downpour, storm clouds were beginning to break up.

After some twenty miles of tough going, they had stopped for an afternoon halt to blow the horses right after crossing the open meadows at the *Weippe* Prairie. Before thirty minutes had passed, the anxious major had the men hurry through their skimpy lunches of hardtack and bacon, then saddle up once again. On the far side of the soggy meadows they reentered the timber, and less than three hours later they reached a low summit that overlooked Lolo Creek. Here the wind-downed timber, became even more of a nuisance to the civilians and soldiers, but ever more so for the artillerymen struggling to keep up with their howitzer.

Less than a hundred yards below them along the Lolo Trail, another stretch of open meadow beckoned. Beyond it the hoof-pocked path the Nez Perce village had taken now angled into narrow defile, thickly wooded.

At the tree line where they halted on the edge of the meadow, Reuben told Chapman and McConville, "Some scouts watching up there."

"You hear 'em?" Chapman asked. "See 'em maybe?"

The Christian tracker shook his head. "Just feel they're close now."

Anxiety stretched across McConville's features when he told Chapman, "While we wait here for Mason's soldiers to come up, why don't you send the six trackers ahead."

Ad gave his order to Reuben, then watched the trackers cross the open ground and into the trees. It was becoming clear the soldiers coming up behind them were advancing slower than ever.

"Ain't no way in hell that major gonna get us back to Kamiah by nightfall," McConville grumped as they watched the trackers reach the far side of the open meadow,* where they began to penetrate the shadowy timber penetrated by irregular shafts of afternoon sunlight. Chapman wagged his head. "I don't think he figgers to have us back to the crossing at all until he's got some idea how far ahead the war bands got on Howard."

"Hell, it's easy enough to see where the red bastards've been—just lookit the ground!" McConville declared, pointing at the forest floor disturbed by thousands of hooves.

---

*This incident on the western end of the Lolo Trail took place near Musselshell Creek, about three miles from Orofino Creek—where the Idaho gold rush began in 1860.

"But Joseph and the rest are moving faster'n this outfit," Chapman said as Mason and the cavalry came up behind them. He nudged his mount into motion. "From the looks of things they ain't packing many travois poles now to slow 'em up—"

He jerked back on the horse's reins at the shocking nearness of the gunshot, causing the animal beneath him to spin about and fight the bit until he quickly brought it under control. Two more shots rang out, then at least a dozen in quick succession—intermingled with cries and yelps from the timber just beyond the meadow . . . right where the six trackers had just disappeared into the shadows.

First one, then suddenly three, of the scouts burst from the timber, dismounted and without their army carbines, leading their horses with one hand and frantically motioning the white men back, back, back toward the cover of the far trees.

"God-*damn!*" McConville bellowed as he wrenched his horse around, making a dash back for the tree line.

Two other volunteers shot back with McConville, pounding the devil out of their horses for the cloaking shadows and the timber, but Chapman waited a heartbeat longer than the others—watching a horseman bolt away from the trees on the far side of the meadow. There should have been three of them, he thought. As the tracker got halfway across the opening, Chapman could see the rider was wounded, pressing a hand against a shoulder wound, his face as white as riverbank clay as he raced away as another quick rattle of gunfire rocked the woods behind him.

"Chapman!" McConville's cry stabbed out from the shadows. "Get your ass back here!"

Wheeling his horse, he flicked one more look over his shoulder, watching the line of trees for the Christian trackers called Abraham Brooks and John Levi, then jabbed his heels into the horse and raced for the timber. He was reining up beside McConville just as Captain Henry E. Winters was coming forward through the dappled light shafts streaking the forest.

"McConville!" the officer called out. "Colonel Mason sent his order for your volunteers to accompany my men to the front."

"We was *at* the front, Cap'n," McConville snapped. "So we already got us a pretty good idea them trackers run onto some rear guard. You see how they was shot up?"

Winters shook his head. "I only saw one of them wounded—"

"Two of 'em's missing," Chapman interrupted as his horse came to a halt.

Straightening his spine, Winters said, "Be that as it may, we are under the colonel's orders to discover what we're facing. I'll expect you to obey those orders—"

A final gunshot rang out from the trees, its echo swallowed by the hills.

Without waiting for an acknowledgment from McConville, Winters turned in the saddle and hollered, "By fours—horse holders to the rear and remain at the ready! The rest, form a skirmish formation here at the edge of the trees. Five feet apart, five feet and no more!"

Behind Chapman the soldiers were squeaking out of their saddles, attaching the throat latches and passing off three horses to every fourth man, who turned and started them back into the timber away from the attack formation.

"Keep your eyes open, men," Winters reminded. "Don't let us get surprised . . . forward, E Troop. Forward!"

Chapman was willing to let the captain ride across that meadow and into the woods, but he himself left his horse tied at the edge of the trees still dripping with the remnants of the morning's thunderstorm and walked at the middle of that long line of dismounted skirmishers. They had made it no deeper than sixty or seventy yards into the forest cluttered with downfall when a soldier cried out to their right.

"Captain! Captain Winters! Come quick!"

Ordering everyone to halt and hold their positions, Winters turned in the direction of the voice. In twenty-five yards he and Chapman spotted the trio of soldiers clustered together, one of them kneeling over a body.

"You know him?" asked the captain, turning to Chapman.

"Name's Sheared Wolf," Ad replied. "Took the Christian name John Levi."

Winters asked, "He dead?"

"He's done for. Bullet in the head."

At that moment Chapman and the others heard a groan from some nearby shadows.

"Careful, civilian!" Winters advised as Chapman turned aside and bounded off for the sound.

He could hear the others, their feet pounding through the forest behind him, as he approached the body. At least this one was still alive. Chapman dropped to a knee beside the scout.

The eyes fluttered a bit in the dark face gone pale and pasty. He had both hands interlaced over a messy gut wound.

"This one dead?" asked the first soldier to join him.

"No," Ad replied softly, his eyes scanning the forest ahead of them, then glanced over his shoulder to see how Winters was bringing his skirmishers forward through the dense cover. "He may live a little longer."

"Chapman," Abraham Brooks said softly, blood glistening on his lips. "Don't let me die here alone."

"No, I won't let you die here alone, Abraham."

Winters was growling orders at his men, inching his horse this way and that through the tangle of trees and deadfall, the clutter of stumps and the maze of brush, as he fought to keep his men into position to withstand a sudden attack. He came over to Chapman.

"How far before we get out of this tangle and back onto the Lolo Trail?"

Chapman stared up at him, dumbfounded at the question. "This is the Lolo Trail, Cap'n."

For a long moment Winters blinked at Chapman, then gazed around him at the thick timber in which a man could easily lose his direction. "You're telling me the general intends to follow these Indians through this?"

Chapman shrugged and waved two of McConville's civilians over from the line of skirmishers. "There's a dead one back yonder a ways. Go find his horse and tie him over it. This'un—he's called Abraham—we'll make him a travois and get him back to the rest of the soldiers."

"He gonna last long?" one of the civilians asked.

Chapman waited until the tracker's eyes clenched shut with another wave of agony. Then he wagged his head without uttering a sound.

CHAPTER THIRTY-SEVEN

Khoy-Tsahl, 1877

THE VOICE THROUGH THE DARKENED TIMBER AHEAD OF THEM SPOKE WITH the *Nee-Me-Poo* tongue.

It said, "There are fresh tracks—tracks made this morning!"

"Christians?" Yellow Wolf whispered to the man beside him.

The older warrior nodded, his eyes never leaving the trees ahead where the disembodied voices emerged. Here they waited a short distance from the Bent Horn Trail.* These two were among the seventeen who had come down their backtrail, scouting for soldiers and Treaty trackers, stopping only briefly to eat their lunch of dried meat butchered from the white man's cows the warriors had killed on the *Weippe* Prairie two days ago.

Earlier that morning as camp was breaking, Two Moons had come among some of the young men saying, "We cannot remain here, idle. We must meet the soldiers and engage in another battle! They will not stop chasing us. Hear my words! Let our families travel on while the warriors go back to find a suitable place where we can lay for our enemies."

A second voice talked in their language about the pony tracks. Then it advised the other that they should go tell the *suapies* their finding.

That's when the leader of this scouting party spoke loudly enough to be heard by those Christians.

"We are your relations," *Wahchumyus* said. "This war leader called Rainbow declared, 'Your skin, your hair, your bodies—everything you have about you is the same as ours.' "

"Who is that who speaks to us from the shadows?" one of the trackers demanded.

"I am *Wahchumyus*," he answered. "One who knows you by name, Sheared Wolf."

"Show yourself."

Rainbow gestured for his men to advance to the edge of the tiny clearing. It was there they surrounded the five surprised Christians.

"Hello, my brother," Yellow Wolf said to *Seekumses Kunnin*.

"This is your brother?" Rainbow asked.

"Horse Blanket is my half brother," Yellow Wolf explained, never taking his eyes off the older man who stood with the rest of the Christians. "We had the same father."

---

*Perhaps it's named this for the many switchbacks climbing up from Lolo Creek?

"Give us your guns and cartridge belts," Two Moons demanded of the trackers as he stomped up to them.

As the five dropped their soldier guns and unbuckled their belts, Rainbow said, "Do you remember that we caught three of you Treaty men at *Lahmotta*, then set them free with a warning not to lead the soldiers? I see you are not afraid of our warning, Sheared Wolf."

"I broke no promise—"

"The soldiers!" a Christian's voice warned. "They are close on our heels!"

"You brought the soldiers with you?" Rainbow demanded of the Christians. "Your friends, the Americans, have chopped up our native land, spilling on it the blood of your relations! But still you help them against us. Every word you speak and every deed you do is a lie. But I will keep my word to you: the next *Nee-Me-Poo* we capture, we will kill at once. You, Reuben and Sheared Wolf, you are the two we really want—"

"He's running!" someone warned.

The instant Rainbow whirled with the noise of voices and feet pounding on the thick bed of pine needles, Sheared Wolf and Reuben took off at a sprint in a different direction—all five of the Treaty captives were scattering.

Yellow Wolf did not wait for any order from his leader. The Christians were guilty of bringing soldiers down upon their own people. Sheared Wolf could have saved himself if he had agreed to go back to the soldiers and turn them around.

But instead . . .

Yellow Wolf shot the coward in the back as he was fleeing. They all watched Sheared Wolf hurtle forward, flopping to the ground between some mossy deadfall. Another man's bullet hit Reuben as the Christian was vaulting into his saddle and hammering away.

Rainbow stepped deliberated to the wounded tracker rolling onto his back, his eyes flicking over his kinsmen as he coughed up blood from the hole in his chest. Sheared Wolf gazed up at the war party leader with a different look come over his face. Yellow Wolf saw how haunted and afraid was the light behind the eyes.

"S-spare my life, Rainbow," the tracker begged, then coughed up a ball of blood again. "I am badly wounded and have . . . have some news for you."

"I am not interested in your news, Sheared Wolf," he said, stepping up to the tracker's shoulder. "But my news for you and the rest of your kind is that we have spared your lives too often already." He pressed the muzzle of his Henry rifle against the Christian's head. "Now you can go to Heaven to tell your news to all your dead relations."

Sheared Wolf's head barely moved as the bullet crashed into the man's brain. The eyes stayed open, still and lifeless, as Rainbow turned and walked toward the other Treaty men.

"Go on back to the Shadows now," Rainbow said. "If you ever help the soldiers against your people again, you will have a bad end like Sheared Wolf."

"We can keep our horses?" James Reuben asked.

"Go now," Rainbow ordered. "Take your horses and go!"

"What about the other one we shot?" Yellow Wolf asked when the Christians were hurrying away on foot, leading their ponies.

"We will let him go tell the Shadows about us and what we do to those who betray us," Rainbow said.

Two Moon grumbled, "We may as well go on back to our camp and take our families to the buffalo country. No use in staying here any longer now."

"We must get farther back into the trees," Rainbow warned. "The soldiers are close enough I can smell them already."

BY TELEGRAPH

WASHINGTON.

Sitting Bull will Remain North.

WASHINGTON, July 14.—Major Walsh, of the Canada mounted police, visited Sitting Bull near the headwaters of French creek. Sitting Bull said he desired to remain with the Canadians during the summer; that he would do nothing against the law; he came there because he was tired of fighting, and if he could not make a living in Canada he would return to the United States. Spotted Eagle, Rain-in-the-Face, Medicine Bear, and a number of other chiefs of the hostile Sioux, were present, together with two hundred lodges. It is believed there must be some four or five hundred lodges of hostile Sioux now north of the boundary line, numbering at least 1,500 fighting men.

With Lieutenant Albert G. Forse of E Company guarding the rear of their withdrawal, Major Mason stopped his battalion every now and then on their retrograde march for the Clearwater that afternoon of the seventeenth, allowing Ad Chapman a chance to rest his two wounded trackers. While James Reuben welcomed every opportunity to get out of the saddle with his wrist injury, if only for a few minutes before they pushed on, Abraham Brooks's shoulder wound prevented him from moving off his travois.*

At their first stop, after posting some pickets, Mason assigned a few artillerymen to scrape out a shallow hole beside the trail. Here they laid the body of Captain John Levi, then dragged dirt back over the corpse before the battalion moved on into the late-afternoon light.

"Having accomplished all I desired in making this scout," Mason had explained to his officers while the grave was being dug, "I have determined

*Horse Blanket claimed the white men, soldiers and civilians both, abandoned their Nez Perce scouts and he was compelled to carry Brooks with him on his horse, getting soaked with blood during the long ride.

we won't pursue the Indians with my cavalry over a trail plainly impossible to handle a mounted force on."

To Chapman's way of thinking, a double handful of Non-Treaty back-trail scouts had just succeeding in turning back Howard's army of half-a-god-damned-thousand!

As it fell progressively darker that evening, the going got slower and slower. They did not reach Lolo Creek until close to eleven o'clock. The volunteers led them across the stream to a small clearing on a gentle hillside, and Mason's command went into a cold bivouac.

Chapman himself didn't mind in the least. As soon as their wounded guides were made comfortable under a thin blanket, Ad curled up, the reins wrapped around his wrist, while his weary horse cropped at the nearby grass. Chapman figured the animal had to be more hungry than tired—while he himself was more weary than worried about his belly's gnawing emptiness.

Ad drifted off to sleep, thinking how lucky they'd been to lose only one in the ambush. If those warriors who had jumped their trackers had only waited, been patient a little while longer, letting Mason's battalion continue on up the trail into that dense maze of a forest where cavalry simply could not maneuver . . . why, he might well not be curled up here right now, missing the warmth of his wife's body lying next to him in their bed, the coolness of his son's hand clutched in his as the boy learned to ride and to hold a carbine.

A nervous Mason had them up at first light and moving out as soon as it was clear enough to see the trail ahead, moving steadily down the slick, muddy slopes toward the Clearwater crossing. Chapman and his scouts brought the battalion to Howard's camp on the east bank of the river just after the main column had finished taking its breakfast and was preparing to recross to the south bank of the Clearwater in preparation for a march down-river to Lewiston.

As soon as he had turned over both wounded trackers to the army surgeons, Chapman walked into headquarters camp, tied off his horse, then settled on his haunches by the general's low fire. Within moments Howard had his cooks pouring coffee for Major Mason and the civilian, along with starting some bacon and hardtack frying in the grease already hardening on the bottom of the cast-iron skillets.

It had been more than twenty-eight hours since he had eaten last, so that breakfast beside the Clearwater in the shadow of the immense Bitterroot Mountains was just about the best Ad Chapman could remember eating in a long, long time.

Fort Lapwai
July 18, 1877

Dear Sallie,

Mamma said she had sent a letter of mine to you, so I need not explain what a commotion we have been in. This morning our first warriors arrived, the first officers that have come in since the battle of the 11th and 12th, and they brought such good news. We have had, at least I can answer for myself, a very thankful day. Several officers came in early this morning and brought news that the Indians in bands have been giving themselves up for the last two days. Quite a number of Joseph's band came in, and they say Joseph himself wants to come in, but White Bird won't let him. The cavalry are out after those that are still hostile, but our officers think the war is practically over and that there will be no more fighting. They say that the fighting up to now has been horrible. They never saw such desperate fighting as these Indians did.

We are all pretty well but tired, and even though the war may be over, the fuss for this little post will not be. Eleven companies are on their way here from California, will be here this week, and will go into camp until things are settled. A whole regiment of infantry is also on the way. As soon as matters are a little more settled out in the front, General Howard intends leaving the cavalry to follow up the scattered bands out there, and bring the rest of [the] *command in here . . .*

One of the officers, a nice fellow, walks in his sleep. He was unfortunate enough to get up in the night in camp and shoot the picket outside of his tent (one of his own men) and killed him instantly.

. . . Mrs. Perry and Mrs. General Howard are coming to Lapwai tomorrow . . . In a few days all the wounded are to be brought in here, nearly thirty poor fellows. They say there are some awful wounds.

Affectionately,
Emily F.

"You understand your orders, Lieutenant?" Charles Rawn asked the youngest officer in the Seventh Infantry, who stood stiffly beside his horse.

At attention a few yards in front of the four members of his small scouting party, who were already mounted, Second Lieutenant Francis Woodbridge said, "Yes sir, Captain. I'm to look over the trail ascending into the mountains, get up to a point where I can look six or eight miles into Idaho, and determine if the Indians have passed or if they are coming up the far side."

"Very good," Rawn replied. "You have rations for four days, but I am expecting you back on the twenty-first."

"Three days from now."

"That's right, Lieutenant," Rawn emphasized. "It's no more than thirty miles from our end of the trail up to the pass itself. See what you can of the far side—looking for those Nez Perce said to be fleeing from Idaho—then get on back here to help us finish building this post."

Woodbridge saluted and without a word he mounted. Taking up the slack in his reins, the bright-eyed lieutenant, fresh out of West Point, said his farewell: "We'll be back by supper on the twenty-first, Captain."

Rawn watched those five backs disappear through the trees, riding south up the Bitterroot valley where they would reach the end of the Lolo Trail. He sighed, hoping the young lieutenant would not put his small scouting detail in harm's way. He really needed the muscle of those five men if he was going to get these quarters and storehouses finished and sealed off before another Montana winter blew in.

CHAPTER THIRTY-EIGHT

JULY 19–20, 1877

OW THAT HE KNEW WHERE THE NON-TREATIES WERE HEADED, OLIVER O. Howard felt more uncomfortable sitting on the horns of this dilemma than he did sitting in one of those damnable instruments of torture the army called a McClellan saddle!

Once Joseph's warrior bands crossed from Idaho into Montana, they would no longer be Howard's Indians to chase and pacify. Then they would belong to Brigadier General Alfred H. Terry and his Department of Dakota. With the Nez Perce already well started on the Lolo Trail across the Bitterroot, Howard had begun to think it didn't make any sense for him to go traipsing along in their wake—although he had received orders from McDowell that he need not be mindful of division boundaries in pursuit of the Non-Treaty bands.

Through division headquarters in San Francisco, Howard had received General William T. Sherman's instructions to ignore such geographic boundaries on 26 June, and McDowell had again reminded him of Sherman's orders three days ago on 16 July when it appeared Howard was putting an end to his direct pursuit of the hostiles. What gave Oliver pause was the fact that according to settlers in the area and reports from Christian trackers, the terrain of the Lolo Trail was even more rugged than what his men had encountered on the far side of the Salmon River back in June.

At this point, 19 July, Howard was staring at an exhausted command, weary of almost a solid month of campaigning: breaking trail and fighting Indians both. Hacking their way through another two hundred miles of even rougher terrain was far from appealing.

Then there was his guarded concern that if he did follow the retreating Indians, that would leave this region of Idaho devoid of enough soldiers to handle the eventuality of neighboring tribes rising up in revolt. Made bold by the Nez Perce successes, the other tribes in the Northwest had white settlers uneasy for hundreds of square miles. But Howard had more troops on the way: Colonel Frank Wheaton was on his way from Atlanta with infantry, and Major John Green was marching north from Fort Boise with more horse soldiers. They would reach Lapwai within the week. Then, Howard convinced himself, he would feel a lot more secure about pursuing the Nez Perce out of Idaho.

At that point, it didn't take long for him to devise a plan that should carry him over the next several weeks and on to putting an end to this outbreak. He would push downriver for Lapwai, on to Lewiston for resupply. Then he would march his column north for the Mullan Road. Although this route would be more than double the distance of the one-hundred-fifty-mile Lolo Trail, the fact that this freight route extending between Missoula and Spokane Falls was no more than a narrow wagon road did not deter his thinking. The Mullan was undeniably the best means for his command to reach western Montana.

His plan was as ambitious as it was daring—hoping to be in position south of Missoula when the Nez Perce finally debouched from the trail in the Bitterroot valley. Over the last few days Oliver Otis had come to realize he could not afford to rest on the laurels of what he had won at the Battle of the Clearwater. That faint praise sent his way in the Western papers was already beginning to fade. He needed to keep the pressure on if he was going to blunt the criticism coming from both the civilian press and the highest echelons of the army.

In the last month the Nez Perce had killed nearly ninety people and done close to a quarter-million dollars in damage, a monstrous sum in a day and time when the average laborer made no more than seventy-five cents at the end of his dawn-to-dusk workday. To put the very public humiliation of the scandal at the Freedmen's Bureau behind him, to blunt the unseemly reputation he suffered among his army colleagues, Howard had to press forward with his plan without delay.

But, right from the start, the general's hopes began to suffer one wounding after another.

Just yesterday, on the morning of the eighteenth, his men had discovered three Non-Treaty warriors hiding among the ruins of the agency buildings on the east side of the Clearwater. Two of them were wounded, in all likelihood left behind when the rest of the village fled toward *Weippe* Prairie.

After stationing a token force—Throckmorton's battery of artillery, Jocelyn's company of infantry, and Trimble's troop of cavalry—at the Kamiah crossing on the nineteenth and directing McConville's volunteers back upriver to finish destroying the last of the caches at the enemy's Clearwater camp, Howard set off with the rest of his command for Lewiston. He got no farther than the halfway point when a courier reached him with the news that hostiles had doubled back, slipping out of the hills, and had the soldiers pinned down at Kamiah—stealing more than four hundred of the Christian Indians' horses, killing what cattle they could not drive off, and diligently burning houses of Lawyer's Indians.

Leaving his infantry and artillerymen there at Cold Springs, Howard ordered his cavalry back to Kamiah before he and a small headquarters group rode on to Fort Lapwai with Captain David Perry's escort. At the post he intended to make arrangements for the supplies required by the next phase of the war.

When they were finished with their destruction on the Clearwater, McConville's militia was under orders to drive several hundred head of captured ponies past Mount Idaho and Grangeville, into the head of Rocky Canyon, where they were to be slaughtered, in hopes of eliminating any reason the warrior bands might have for returning to central Idaho. That done,

McConville and his men were to station themselves in the area, protecting the settlements should Joseph and his henchmen slip back out of the mountains and make a wide sweep for the Salmon River.

Oliver knew it would be a tiring ride for his old bones, pushing those long hours in the saddle, but three days ago he had received word that his wife would be arriving by steamboat in Lewiston that very night. Oliver managed to make it in time, but when the steamboat was moored at 10:00 P.M. his sweet Lizzie was not on board. However, Mrs. Perry was on board. And upon spotting her husband among those welcomers on the dock, she went into a fit of theatrical hysterics, a display that totally disgusted Howard.

In town for the night, he picked up the first newspapers he had seen in weeks—finding he was under personal assault from the normally conservative San Francisco *Chronicle* to the New York *Herald*. But the sharpest attacks were those of the local papers like the Lewiston *Teller*, whose editor, Alonzo Leland, lost no opportunity to write about how poorly Howard had done with the campaign so far. His brutal words cut Oliver to the marrow.

"The sheep is a very pleasant and amiable animal and has none but sterling qualities," Leland had written in the most recent editorial, perhaps still furious over his own son's reports on the poor showing the army made at Cottonwood, "but we do not expect him to chase wolves and coyotes; we assign the task to the dog—also an amiable brute, but better adapted to the purpose."

Leland broadcast that General Crook was a better man to send against the wolves and coyotes: "He sticks his breeches in his boots, keeps his powder dry, eats hardtack, and goes for 'em. . . . But Howard regards the army as a kind of missionary society for the Indians and holds himself as the head of a kind of red freedman's bureau."

While Crook was a first-class Indian fighter, as proved down in Arizona and during the Sioux campaign, if Howard continued to lead the chase of the Nez Perce, the war would be a six months' campaign, hunting the enemy in the mountains.

Summoning up from inside him his reservoir of fairness in the face of brutal assault, Oliver sighed and folded the paper before handing it off to Lieutenant Charles Wood, his aide-de-camp.

"How wonderfully news can be spread," he began with a cool, even detached, air so unlike what he had boiling inside. "It is like the cloud no bigger than a man's hand, when it leaves us, it is magnified several times before the journals at Lewiston and Walla Walla have put it into type, and by the time it has reached Portland and San Francisco it has become a heavy cloud, overspreading the whole heaven."

"It's those civilian volunteers, General," Major Edwin Mason grumbled. "They play at citizen militia when they're nothing more than a worthless set of trifling rascals! Utterly worthless, a cowardly pack of whelps, sir!"

Captain Birney Keeler jumped in, saying, "Many times I myself have explained to General McDowell how he should not give a grain of credence to any of the civilian accounts of our campaign, sir. Time and again I've informed the division commander that such news reports and editorials are nothing more than wanton, systematic lies. I've even told him that to continue employing civilians of such low character would be worse than useless in ending this war."

"Yes, well," Howard replied to McDowell's aide, sent by the department commander to have a look at the campaign for himself. He cleared his throat of the ball of fury just then rising. "I'd like to put a few of these dishonest enemies attacking me far from their warmth and safety of the rear out on those mountain trails of the Salmon, or march them dawn to dusk and order them to fight under a broiling July sun."

By the following morning, Oliver Otis Howard had changed his mind. It was to be one of the most crucial decisions he made in his life. Turning his back on his initial plan to loop north to the Mullan Road, then sweep down on the Non-Treaty bands emerging from the Lolo Trail just south of Missoula, the general had now committed his men to pursuing the fleeing camp across the Lolo itself. While awaiting his reinforcements in Lewiston, he polished the details of his three-column strategy.

Upon his arrival at Lewiston with his ten companies of the Second Infantry, Colonel Frank Wheaton would start north to the Mullan Road, accompanied by F and H Companies, First Cavalry, along with two companies of mounted volunteers mustered from the eastern regions of Washington Territory. Inspector Erwin Watkins of the Indian Bureau, on the scene with Agent Monteith, had proposed this march of thirty-six officers and 440 enlisted men through the Coeur d'Alene country to blunt any rising zeal the disaffected tribes in the area had for joining up with Joseph's Nez Perce.*

Major John Green, of the First Cavalry, would position his Fort Boise column and some Bannock scouts at Henry Croasdaile's ranch,** located ten miles from Mount Idaho on Cottonwood Creek. With D, E, G, and L Troops of the First Cavalry, along with B and F Companies of the Twelfth Infantry, in addition to those thirty-five Warm Springs trackers, the entire force of twenty-two officers, and 245 enlisted men, Green would be deployed in a central location allowing his men to protect the Camas Prairie settlements and the Kamiah subagency, too, where the major would position an artillery battery and two fieldpieces. From his base of operations Green would dispatch reconnaissance parties to the region of the Salmon and Snake, with orders to capture and arrest any Nez Perce who might possibly be allied with the Non-Treaty bands.

But O. O. Howard had saved the right column for himself. Accompanying him on Joseph's trail would be a battalion of the Fourth Artillery A, C, D, E, G, and L Batteries, commanded by Captain Marcus P. Miller. Under Captain

---

*Wheaton would not reach the theater of operations until July 29, having traveled from Atlanta to Oakland, California, by rail, boarded a steamer to Portland, and traveled by riverboat up the Columbia to Lewiston.

**In August 1877, an officer with the campaign wrote: ". . . The [Non-Treaty] Indians entered the house first and destroyed most of the furniture &c and were followed by the soldiers & volunteers who completed the destruction." From the home of this retired British army officer the Non-Treaty warriors removed many high-powered and explosive bullets, some of which later saw use by the Nez Perce at the Battle of the Big Hole and eventually at the Battle of the Bear's Paw Mountains.

Evan Miles would serve a battalion of foot soldiers: Company H, Eighth Infantry, Company C, Twelfth Infantry—both of which had recently arrived from Fort Yuma along the Mexican border in Arizona Territory—in addition to C, D, E, H, and I Companies of the Twenty-first Infantry, who had already been seeing a lot of service with Howard in the first weeks of this outbreak. Major George B. Sanford was coming up to command the general's horse soldiers: B, C, I, and K Troops of the First Cavalry—all of them fresh companies that had not seen any service so far in the campaign.

Howard wired McDowell: "Will start with the rest of my command through the impenetrable Lolo Pass, and follow Joseph to the very death."

This one-armed general was about to lead forty-seven officers, 540 enlisted men, seventy-four civilian and Indian scouts, as well as some seventy packers for his 350-mule pack train into one of the most far-reaching and inhospitable tracts of wilderness in the United States.

CHAPTER THIRTY-NINE

July 20–21, 1877

BY TELEGRAPH

The St. Louis Bank Panic Subsiding.

The Great Strike on the Baltimore and Ohio road.

OREGON.

Latest From the Indian War.
SAN FRANCISCO, July 18.—A Walla Walla dispatch says the Indians have killed three men and one girl on Cow creek. Old Salty, a Spokane chief, believes fifty of his warriors have gone to join Joseph. They are beyond his control. Col. Green with his column has reached Little Salmon river from the South. A messenger from Smookhalls and Spokane Jerry, non-treaty Spokane chiefs, announces that they desire to remain friendly and go upon a reservation, provided one is set apart for them and food furnished for the winter.

Fort Lapwai
Friday, July 20, 1877

Dear Mamma,

All our troubles are upon us again and worse than ever. I feel even more upset, as John is ordered into the field and I will have to be here alone. He was to have gone with the troop that leaves tonight, but since morning he has been ordered to wait and assist Dr. Sternberg to get the wounded comfortable and then follow with the next detachment. The wounded are being hurried in here. Some will arrive this afternoon, and it is so hot. I never in my life felt such weather. The thermometer in my shady sitting room (the coolest room in the house) stood yesterday at 98 degrees, and that was much less than it was at the hospital and on the porches.

The Indians have gone in full retreat towards the buffalo country. The cavalry went after them nearly a hundred miles and reported them all gone and impossible to follow, from the condition of the country. So General Howard started his command back here, leaving three companies up there to watch the place the Indians ford the river, the ford that leads to the mountains. We knew yesterday that General Howard's command was near Lapwai. In the evening, an officer, who had been sent on in advance, came in and said there were signal fires burning in the mountains. By and by, General Howard himself and some other officer came in, and in a great hurry. A messenger had just reached them from the three companies left to watch the ford saying the Indians were all back. So, of course, everything is in confusion again. General Howard did not wait to rest but started right back, and those poor, tired soldiers have to turn and do it all over . . . I don't know what we will do after John goes. I wish it was over! The confusion, outside of everything else, which is even worse, will set me crazy!

. . . They are going to leave all the Indian prisoners here and double this garrison. With the wounded here, and the Indian prisoners here, and Doctor gone, I think I would like to go, too, but I suppose I had better stay, as I have no friends near I could go to. To board somewhere would be lonely and worse than here . . .

Lots of love to all, and write to me.

Yours affectionately,
Emily FitzGerald

HARLES RAWN WATCHED THE YOUNG FIRST LIEUTENANT STRIDE ACROSS the dry, dusty ground, leading his horse. Just steps behind him followed an enlisted man and a handful of civilians, all of them dismounted, their animals in tow.

"We're ready to ride, Captain."

Rawn sighed. "It shouldn't be hard to find Lieutenant Woodbridge . . . if his men stayed on the trail. I've never been over it myself, but from what these settlers in the valley tell me, it's hard as hell to make a mistake and get off the Lolo."

"We'll find them for you, Captain," promised First Lieutenant Charles A. Coolidge, jabbing his thumb at that small band of civilians who had volunteered to guide the two soldiers up the mountain trail. "We have rations for three days, just as you ordered."

"Scout the trail as far as is prudent. I want you back here by the twenty-fourth, if you've found Woodbridge's party or not. Between his group and yours being gone from the post, I'm feeling a little whittled down—should any of those Nez Perces pop up nearby."

"From everything these civilians have told me about that trail, sir," Coolidge declared, "Joseph's Injuns are going to take a long time getting over the mountains on the Lolo—what with all their women, children, baggage, not to mention that pony herd, too. They aren't going to be making good time up there in those mountains."

Taking a step back, Rawn saluted the lieutenant. "Let's pray those warriors are crawling over the pass real slow. And while we're at it, maybe we should pray young Woodbridge hasn't stumbled into any of them, too."

BY TELEGRAPH

The Railway Strike Spreading
Over the Country.

Trains Moving Under Military
Protection.

Great Activity of Black Hills
Road Agents.

Late War News and General
Intelligence.

CHEYENNE.

The Ready Road-Agents Robbing
Left and Right.
CHEYENNE, July 19.—The coach from Deadwood
was stopped, last night, near Cheyenne river, by
road agents, who robbed the passengers of about $50.
Twelve miles further they were stopped again by four
robbers, who took the passengers' arms and part of
their blankets. The treasure box was opened but
contained no valuables . . .

While Cut-Off Arm attempted to sneak off downriver from the Kamiah crossing so he could slip up behind them, the *Nee-Me-Poo* had decided to follow Looking Glass toward *Moosmoos Illahe*, the buffalo country. For fighting men like Shore Crossing, it was less a matter of possessing any real enthusiasm for this flight over the mountains than it was a matter of there simply being nothing better to do . . . at least for the present.

Indeed, there were many more who felt the frustration he did: warriors who believed that those who wanted to fight the *suapies* should be allowed to stay behind in their own country, there to attack and harass the small groups of soldiers, there to run off horses, mules, and cattle belonging to the Christian Indians at Lapwai and Kamiah, staying behind to slow the army's pursuit to a standstill.

As fierce a fighter as *Ollokot* had been in those early days of the war, at the councils held on the *Weippe* Prairie he had nonetheless joined his older brother, Joseph, in arguing that once the bands had crossed the Lolo and headed south, up the Bitterroot valley, they should recross the mountains into Idaho, circling back to their beloved Salmon and Snake River country.* With every day now, the Frog was sounding more and more like his non-fighting brother, chief of the *Wallowa*.

Since their battle against Cut-Off Arm on the Clearwater, White Bird had begun to advance the possibility of turning north once they had reached the end of the Lolo Trail. There the bands could pass through the country of the friendly Flathead and march for the Old Woman's Country, perhaps even rendezvous with the Lakota expatriates of Chief Buffalo Bull Who Rests on the Ground.**

But in the end, Looking Glass was more persuasive than the others. Why go north when they had friends in the buffalo country, land where they had hunted for many generations with their longtime friends the *E-sue-ghA?* Hadn't several of the leading men—like Looking Glass, Rainbow, and Five Wounds—fought against the Lakota time and again? In fact, at this present time weren't a few of their own young men gone east to the buffalo plains to help the army round up the Lakota?

No, Looking Glass orated, the Old Woman's Country was strange to them; no one he knew had ever been there. Besides, once they had put the Idaho country at their backs, put its soldiers and Shadows behind them, there would be no need to run away to join the Lakota north of the Medicine Line. The *Nee-Me-Poo* would be leaving their war far behind, back there beyond the Bitterroot.

In the end Looking Glass won the day. While *Wottolen* and Two Moons vigorously opposed any alliance with the *E-sue-gha* and Joseph said nothing because he favored returning his people to the *Wallowa* valley, White Bird, *Toohoolhoolzote*, and *Hahtalekin* were unanimous. "All right, Looking Glass—take us to the buffalo country."

The morning of their second day on the Lolo, Rainbow went down their back trail, accompanied by more than three hands of warriors. They were to watch for soldiers. Five of their number had been selected by the chiefs to remain behind near the *Weippe* for three suns. Red Moccasin Tops, White Cloud, and three others were to watch for Cut-Off Arm's men coming up the trail. If, after those three days, they hadn't seen any soldiers following, they were to come on with their good news and reunite with their families. If, however, enemies were sighted, two of their number were to race up the trail with the report so the warriors would have time to prepare a fight to hold the *suapies* on the trail while the families escaped. The last three were to stay and keep watch, staying just ahead of any white or Christian scouts in the process as they fell back.

Riding off in a different direction, Shore Crossing joined Looking Glass's raiding party that swept down on the Kamiah Christians—running off their

---

*Via what is known as the Southern Nez Perce Trail, over Nez Perce Pass, southwest of present-day Darby, Montana.

**Sitting Bull, the spiritual leader of the Hunkpapa Lakota.

horses and cattle, burning a few small buildings, and doing their best to frighten Lawyer's Indians. The warriors were able to scatter and harry those Treaty people just they way they had driven the horses and a few head of cattle* back into the hills while exchanging a few long-range shots with those *suapies* left behind when Cut-Off Arm marched north for Lapwai.

By the time the raiders returned to the Lolo late that afternoon, it amazed Shore Crossing how much ground all those people, a few hundred dogs, and more than two thousand horses had covered in a day. Forced by necessity to stretch itself out for several miles while on the march, the column inched its way deeper and deeper into the wilderness along that tenuous strand of timber-clogged trail taking them ever higher, into ever thicker, mazelike forests. How they were able to accomplish this feat mile after mile, day after day, with women and children, the old and the very young, along with their sick and wounded, too, was nothing short of miraculous to the young warrior.

These Non-Treaty bands were able to march with energy and precision through such impossibly rugged terrain and the clutter of downfall forests because they had two cultural characteristics working for them. The first was that Shore Crossing's people had, for generations beyond count, developed and refined a system of moving people and property, whereby each family unit was responsible to the band by seeing to its own organizing and packing, along with transporting its own members in harmony with the needs of the camp as a whole, day in and day out. The second feature of their success derived from decades of learning to travel through steep mountains and across barren plateaus.

What other people would dare face the terrible ordeal of this trail burdened with their wounded and sick on travois, all those women and children and belongings, not to mention all those thousands of horses? With or without an enemy snarling at your tail, this would be a feat unmatched by any other people. Only the *Nee-Me-Poo* would pit themselves against the Lolo the way they had pitted themselves against the U. S. Army.

Still, for young fighting men like Shore Crossing, the best part of each day's journey was that with Cut-Off Arm sitting on his haunches somewhere near Fort Lapwai, every march put that much more distance between the *Nee-Me-Poo* and the army Looking Glass vowed could never touch them again.

"They are so far behind," Shore Crossing announced when the war party reunited with the village as it was going into camp at the end of that second day on the trail, "we will never have to worry about those soldiers again!"

"Your eyes are half-closed if you think Cut-Off Arm's are the only *suapies*,

---

*Several white ranchers and their hired hands took advantage of the war and its confusion to run off some neighbors' stock for themselves, along with the cattle and horses belonging to the Christian Indians, hoping the blame would fall on the Non-Treaty bands. Nervous settlers raised a protest when Howard prepared to march away from the Camas and Clearwater country—crying that they would be left to the mercy of the savages. Their clamor would cause the general to remain in the area another ten days before Howard was convinced the warrior bands had indeed abandoned Idaho.

Shore Crossing," old *Toohoolhoolzote* warned. "We have seen the soldiers over in buffalo country."

"No," he snorted at the old *tewat*, refusing to be cowed by worry. "We won't have to worry about any of those soldiers or Shadows over there. The Montana people have known us for a long, long time."

"JESUS CHRIST! YOU fellas scared the piss out of me!" one of the pickets hollered from that dark ring of night surrounding their bivouac.

Second Lieutenant Francis Woodbridge nearly leaped out of his skin when that picket suddenly shrieked his high-pitched alarm. The other picket lunged into the dim light thrown off by the low, flickering flames, joining Woodbridge and the other two privates who were scheduled to take their second watch later that night, the twenty-second of July.

"I'll be go to hell!" exclaimed one of those soldiers beside Woodbridge as the picket materialized out of the dark, right behind two young civilians. "They're white fellas!"

"Who the devil was you expecting to come walkin' into your camp, soldier?" one of the strangers growled, his eyes shimmery with relief. "We'd been Looking Glass's red devils sneaking down this trail, you'd never see'd us come up on you the way we done!"

The picket snapped, "I'd shot you in the gut afore you'd got 'nother step—"

"Hold it!" Woodbridge interrupted, then waved the two strangers closer to the light. "C'mon over here and sit yourselves down. Where's your horses?"

"W-we ain't got none," said the sullen, darker-skinned of the two.

"What's your name?"

He looked at the lieutenant, then stared down at the fire and rubbed his hands over it as he said, "Peter Matte."*

"And you?" Woodbridge asked the other stranger, who had been the first to speak to the picket.

"William . . . Bill Silverthorne."

The second picket asked, "You fellas from the Bitterroot?"

Silverthorne flicked a glance his way, saying, "By a damned long way around."

That sounded really odd to the suspicious lieutenant. "What are you two doing out at night on the Lolo Trail, without horses, and you're all the way up here from the Bitterroot to boot?"

"Wasn't my idea to take no trip back over the pass to Montana on foot," Silverthorne snorted. "But we was forced to come with the Injuns."

"Injuns!" one of the privates echoed in a high-pitched whine.

Silverthorne stood up and turned his buttocks to the low fire, rubbing them with his palms as he explained, "Nez Percey, they was. Seven days ago—no, eight days—me and Pete, we was heading to Lewiston to buy us some horses more'n a week back, when a war party of them Nez Percey bucks jumped us on the way to the Clearwater and brung us right on in to

*Recently released from prison after serving a sentence for horse theft.

their camp. Hundreds of 'em was up to the *Weippe* Prairie, camped there digging the roots and hunting. Didn't ever hurt us none—"

"But back at home at Stevensville in the Bitterroot, we both heard how they butchered a lot of white folks over in Idaho not long ago," Matte said.

Woodbridge wagged his head in wonder. "So why'd they let you two go now?"

Silverthorne gazed over at the young lieutenant with undisguised disdain. "The red sonsabitches didn't let us go, for Chrissakes! We slipped away and come on down the trail, making for Missoula City fast as we could."

"How far's we from there now?" Matte asked, the low flames flickering off his dark face.

The lieutenant figured the man for a half-breed, must have some Indian blood in him. "Twenty, maybe twenty-five miles. The pass is only thirty in all—"

"You fellas headed on up the trail tomorrow?" Silverthorne interrupted.

"No, we're on our way back to the post we're building south of Missoula City," Woodbridge explained.

"Awright we go on in with you come morning?"

Woodbridge nodded to Silverthorne. "Sure. We'll ride double or swap off horses. See you get to town."

"We better skeedaddle come morning," Matte said as he glanced around at the dark.

"They find we're missing," Silverthorne said, "they'll come looking, I'll bet. 'Sides, them reds up near the pass anyways."

Woodbridge swallowed. They had covered a lot of ground, crossing over the pass, something on the order of sixty-five miles from Missoula City. "We hadn't seen any sign of the Indians when we stopped up at the top and looked down the west approach."

"Didn't see all of them?" Matte cried, his voice rising two octaves in disbelief.

The lieutenant wagged his head, ready to speak, when Silverthorne blurted out, "Shit, soldier! That bunch of Nez Percey strings out on the trail for better'n two miles, likely more! And that horse herd of theirs! I'll lay a bet there's more'n two thousand, twenty-five hundred of 'em . . . and you say you didn't see anything of 'em when they had us climbing up the other side of the goddamned mountain?"

With a shrug, Woodbridge admitted, "Not a thing. So how far back from here you get away from the Nez Perce? They still on the other side of the pass?"

"*Other* side of the pass?" Silverthorne snorted, waving an arm off into the darkness. "Those red devils is already coming down this side fast as you please, soldier."

Woodbridge stared into the night as if trying hard to listen, hearing nothing more than the crackle of the fire and the pulse of his own blood in his ears. "How far up the trail are they from us here?"

"Six, maybe seven, miles," Silverthorne said. "It's goddamned hard to tell stumbling down the trail on foot in the dark, y'know."

Turning on his heel, the lieutenant waved his two pickets in. "Finish out your last two hours, then come wake me to take over. That way you can get a little sleep in before we ride out soon as it's light."

"Awright we use their blankets?" Matte inquired with a grin.

"Yeah—but don't get too comfortable," Woodbridge advised. "Soon as we can see far enough in front of the horses' noses that we don't stumble over down timber, we're making a run down the trail for Missoula City."

CHAPTER FORTY

Khoy-Tsahl, 1877

BY TELEGRAPH

Late War News and General Intelligence.

OREGON.

Captain Perry and His Men Defended.

SAN FRANCISCO, July 10.—The following has been received here: General McDowell, San Francisco:—Your dispatch of the 10th just received . . . The difficulties of communication have been great. The country from front to rear has until now been infested with hostiles, and couriers and supplies in many instances have failed to get through, though none have been lost. I am not aware of the exact tenor of the reports to which you refer, but I infer that they are principally those reflecting upon General Howard and Captain Perry. I have investigated the most important ones, and find them to be false. The statement in the local papers of the affair at Cottonwood on the 5th, to the effect that seventeen citizens were surrounded by Indians and the troops under Perry refused to go to their relief for an hour and a half, is a wicked falsification. The troops, 113 in number, were themselves outnumbered, environed and attacked by Indians, but nevertheless were sent instantly a mile away to the rescue, which was accomplished within twenty minutes, and not only the life of every man in the command was risked, but the safety of a most important position and a large amount of ammunition and other stores. The accounts as published originated with one Orrin Morrill, of Lewiston, who was at Cottonwood at the time, but who, although armed, remained ensconced in a little fortification there, instead of going with the soldiers to the aid of his imperilled fellow citizens. The other citizens who were present agree with the officers in this statement of facts. The conduct of officers and men has, under the most trying circumstances, been particularly good. They have justified all reasonable expectations. The campaign has been successful. The hostiles have operated skillfully and fought desperately, but they have been defeated and driven from this section with great loss of numbers and supplies. Gen. Howard reports by this courier the events of the last two days and the present situation. The number of killed and wounded on both sides in the action of the 11th and 12th turns out to be larger than at first believed.

KEELER, A.D.C.

OT ONLY DID THE WOMEN HAVE TO COAX THE HORSES OVER, AROUND, AND through a maze of deadfall, but every day that village on the move discovered even more trees blown down by high winds or uprooted by heavy, wet snows the higher they climbed toward the summit of Lolo Pass.

Because of the many outcroppings of sharp rocks, not to mention the neck-wrenching switchbacks as they inched from ridge to ridge, the *Nee-Me-Poo* were unable to use their travois in this flight from war. Instead, the strong young men stumbled along, carrying the litters with their war wounded, carrying those too old and weak. Besides, they simply hadn't dragged that many poles along with them anyway. Those they had managed to dismantle before escaping the Clearwater fight they ended up having to abandon one camp out of *Weippe*, at a place the People named Dead Horse Meadow. It was nothing but a small, elongated patch of meadow ringed by a windbreak of timber. Stacked into the forks of every tree available went the hundreds upon hundreds of peeled, dried lodgepoles the women were leaving behind against the prayers they could one day return to everything they had ever known.

Here in the middle of summer they found the trail little more than a muddy ribbon disappearing through the impenetrable timber that, even at this late season, still shaded deep drifts of soggy, slow-melting snow. Each step upon the saturated ground soon became an ordeal of its own: muddy water gushing into every footprint and hoof hole as the grim, silent procession continued, this march away from everything that had ever been.

Day by day, they were forced to abandon more and more of the poorer horses on the trail—those animals who had stumbled off the rocky path and broken a leg, those with severe, gaping lacerations from shoving through the narrow gaps between boulders and thick timber, along with those growing progressively weaker from what poor forage was available at the infrequent forest glades. The *Nee-Me-Poo* did not have time to stop and tend to their horses now. They pushed on.

Instead of following one ridge all they way to the top, this long-used, traditional trail snaked up and down ever-ascending slopes, a physical necessity that made the journey more taxing than the mere distances on a map would ever indicate. From first light until late afternoon, they put one foot in front of the other and climbed a little more with every step—waiting for that day they would stand at the top and look down on the land of Montana, the buffalo country.

Because of the difficulty of finding one site big enough for all the families, a site that possessed enough grazing for the huge herd and enough water, too, the *Nee-Me-Poo* chiefs usually ordered a string of camps made along the trail rather than the hundreds congregating in one site. These stops were usually at what they called *woutokinwes tahtakkin*, or meadow camps, when they could find them for the night. If not, the column leaders pushed on until they eventually came across a place big enough for their weary people and their exhausted animals. Some of these spots were beautiful, unexpected interludes in the harsh severity of the trail—lush marshlands dotted with shallow ponds of bone-chilling ice melt, their placid surfaces blanketed by pond lilies, each of these tiny meadows ringed by a verdant, chest-high brush, the leaves of which was boiled into a delicious tea.

But many times the People could find nothing better than cramped, waterless sites where the poor horses had nothing more to feed on but the wire grass and dwarf lupine, where the men, women, and children wearily collapsed and slept until it was time to awaken and start out all over again.

It was not an entirely joyful exodus. The People simply made forced marches, went without, and endured in the cause of freedom.

Nonetheless, a couple of days ago when they finally reached the top and everyone paused a few minutes to take in the breathtaking view both ahead of and behind them, there was much cause to celebrate. Many of the women trilled their tongues in joy and the children laughed with unfettered happiness while most of the older men sang their victory songs.

Yes, this, too, had been a battle. But now the long side of the trail lay behind them. From here it would be a quick journey down to the Bitterroot valley. Not only had they won a victory over the Lolo Trail, but this flight meant they had secured a victory over Cut-Off Arm and his soldiers. A victory over the Shadows in Idaho country. A victory that meant they had escaped without any more loss to those who wanted to steal away their long-held way of life.

That was the day, too, when Red Moccasin Tops and his four companions had caught up with the retreating column. This five-man rear guard reported that Cut-Off Arm had given up, marching away from the Kamiah crossing, leaving only a few *suapies* to protect Lawyer's Christians from raiding warriors. What soldiers they hadn't defeated outright they had managed to hold off long enough to exhaust the resolve of Cut-Off Arm. The war was behind them!

So at the top there was much singing, keening, chanting, and prayer giving before they passed over into the Montana buffalo country. Much, much thanksgiving to *Hunyewat*, their Creator, because they had reached a land of plenty and of peace. Truly Cut-Off Arm's war and his angry soldiers were far, far behind them now.

Still, there was another, although less important, reason to celebrate. Just below the pass they would find the lush meadows surrounding those pools of hot water said to possess a magical power to heal and refresh the weary traveler. And here was the first good grass and clear water for their horses encountered since leaving the *Weippe* six camps ago. The People had arrived.

For summers without count, many women returning from the buffalo country had left their lodgepoles here at the hot springs* so they would not have to drag the travois over the roughest part of the crossing from here into Idaho. As the first, eager *Nee-Me-Poo* rushed into these meadows surrounding the steamy pools, those peeled and dried poles stacked in the forks of so many trees stood like a warm and welcoming gesture.

As one of the young warriors riding advance for the village, Yellow Wolf quickly tore off his shirt, moccasins, and breechclout, then eased himself into the hot waters. As more and more of the *Nee-Me-Poo* arrived, singing out with joy as they reached the meadow and selected a camping spot, the men and women, children, too, all stripped off their dusty, trail-sweated clothing and plunged into the life-affirming springs. Yellow Wolf could not remember a finer day since this war had begun.

In fact, Sun Necklace and his son, Red Moccasin Tops, were so relaxed and jovial that they invited their two white captives to strip off their clothes and join them in the pools. The ropes were freed from the prisoners' wrists and ankles, but the pair hesitated to tear off their clothing and sink into the springs like the rest of the *Nee-Me-Poo* were doing all around them—coming and going, yelling, joking, laughing, a raucous cacophony of sounds and a blur of long-denied happiness. Why the Shadow was a man to keep so much of his body covered with clothing in spite of the summer's heat was something Yellow Wolf doubted he would ever sort out. The white man simply thought with a different brain than did his own people! The Shadow looked at things with a different eye, heard with a different set of ears, too, perhaps even tasted life with a foreign tongue as well.

Here in the riding steam of the pools with the sun going down and the sky behind them turning to a brilliant rose, drinking in the fragrance of those many fires where strips of meat sizzled, hearing the soft tinkle of women's laughter and the playful giggles of the many children—Yellow Wolf wondered if he ever would go back to Idaho country now. After all they had gone through, life seemed far better over here on this side of the mountains.

On this eastern slope of the Bitterroot, the *Nee-Me-Poo* would no longer have to worry about Cut-Off Arm and his soldiers, would not have to concern themselves with the angry Shadows who many winters ago had started the conflict by stealing, raping, abusing, and killing their people. Perhaps one day the Idaho men would get over being mad and the *Nee-Me-Poo* could go back home. But for now, this was a good country . . . where they could hunt

*The Lolo Hot Springs made famous by Lewis and Clark on their journey west in 1805.

buffalo, court young women, and sleep till midday if they wanted, because they would not have to look back over their shoulders ever again.

They had left the Idaho country behind. They had put the angry Shadows at their backs, and now they were in a new land—

There arose a sudden commotion as three older warriors raced into the meadow from the east, returning from a scout made on down the trail toward the Bitterroot valley. Yellow Wolf could tell they brought word of something important, something very grave, from the way the trio of riders gestured, pointed, held up their hands to indicate numbers of strangers—and from the way the chiefs and old headmen quickly gathered around those scouts, drawing up close around the three who had arrived with some terrible news like a piece of rawhide shriveling beneath the midsummer sun.

"Where are those two Shadows of yours, Sun Necklace?" someone called out in the middle of the hubbub.

The older man, and his son, too, turned this way and that as they searched the trees on three sides of them.

"Ha!" another man laughed at them. "Did your prisoners get away from you while you were getting your manhood soaked?"

Red Moccasin Tops angrily slapped the surface of the steamy pool as the clamor continued to grow down in the meadow around those three horsemen.

But it was Shore Crossing, his older cousin, who snarled like a dog restrained too long on a short rope, "We will find them for you, Sun Necklace. Your son and I are good at finding runaway Shadows—"

A loud yell arose from many throats in the meadow as more than two hundred men and women cried out in unison—a sound that raised the hair on the back of Yellow Wolf's neck as he stood, the hot water sluicing off his sinewy muscles, down his bony shoulders and boyish hips. Through the midst of the cries and keening, he heard *Ollokot* calling his name as the war chief loped toward him on foot.

"Yellow Wolf!"

"I am ready, *Ollokot*!"

With an impish grin the Wallamwatkin war chief skidded to a halt and peered at this naked young warrior. "You better put on your clothes before you cause a stir among the young women in the camp! I want you to come with me."

"Come? Where?"

"Even though we have left Cut-Off Arm's *suapies* behind," *Ollokot* began as a serious expression came over the *Wallowa* war chief's face. He pointed to the east, in the direction the Lolo Trail took into the Bitterroot valley, then finished, "it seems there are some Montana soldiers waiting down below to make new trouble for us now."

REINFORCEMENTS WERE COMING, but—at best—they were more than a hundred-fifty miles and a week away. Back when the captain in charge of building the army's newest post four miles southwest of Missoula City came asking for volunteers to ride up the Lolo Trail with one of his lieutenants in a search for an overdue reconnaissance party, Chauncey Barbour volunteered right there and then. Even though he was editor of the *Weekly Missoulian*, putting out a newspaper would have to wait, and folks might just have to miss an issue for the first time in many years—because settling these Indian troubles was that much more important.

Besides, those oncoming Nez Perce had made themselves the biggest news of this summer.

Along with a handful of other local citizens, Barbour had climbed toward the pass with Lieutenant Charles Coolidge of A Company, Seventh U. S. Infantry, hoping to run across another officer named Woodbridge. They ended up finding the lieutenant's party coming down the trail, at which point Coolidge's detail turned back for town themselves. Woodbridge's men would spend one more day taking a more leisurely pace down to the valley.

But Woodbridge had hurried back to the unfinished post by midday with two hard-used Bitterroot civilians, both of them reporting to Captain Rawn—along with every one of his quartermaster employees helping in the fort's construction—that the Nez Perce had reached the hot springs!

The warrior bands who had chopped up Perry's First Cavalry at White Bird Canyon, the butchers who had wiped out Rains's eleven-man scouting detail, then went on to play cat and mouse with Randall's seventeen civilians before killing two of them . . . the very same bunch of Joseph's henchmen who had stood off more than half a thousand of General Howard's finest troops were now thundering down the east slope of the Lolo Trail and heading right for the Bitterroot valley!

"I need your help, more than ever," Charles Rawn had proposed to his eager civilians. "I don't think I can stare down seven hundred and fifty Nez Perce with only the thirty-five soldiers I can muster in my command." His intense eyes started to rake over the civilians slowly.

"Count me in, Captain," Chauncey Barbour was the first to declare.

"If any of you volunteer," Rawn offered the rest, "I'll do my best to provide you with ammunition and rations."

"Sounds fair 'nough to me," responded E. A. Kenney.

"I'll go, too," W. J. Stephens said.

Barbour turned around and looked over the group. "Enough of us thrown in with Captain Rawn here, we just might have what we need to keep Joseph's warriors out of the Bitterroot."

More of the civilians started to volunteer then.

Finally, Barbour suggested, "Captain, I figure we ought to ride into town and spread the word. I know we'll enlist more volunteers soon as the folks know what's coming our way."

On 25 July, after only one day of preparation, Rawn left behind a skeleton force of ten men and started his command of twenty-five regulars away from the unfinished walls of his new post, accompanied by more than twenty heavily armed Montana citizens, all of whom had volunteered to stop the Nez Perce from bringing that Idaho war into their valley.

At the mouth of the Lolo they ran into thirty-five civilians from Fort Owens, near Stevensville in the Bitterroot valley. It was here that the nominal commander of that volunteer militia told Rawn he doubted they had enough manpower to turn back the Nez Perce. Refusing to be cowed by civilian naysayers, Rawn told the valley men to go back to their homes and he forged ahead. The thirty-five reluctantly followed.

Sixteen miles from Missoula, only five short miles up Lolo Creek from the mouth of the canyon, the mountainsides narrowed to less than two hundred yards, with a rugged, precipitous wall closing in on the south—both sides of the trail bordered by thick stands of timber, the forest floor cluttered with deadfall.

It was here that the cautious captain's slow-moving skirmish formation took its first fire from a few Nez Perce outriders. Both soldiers and civilians quickly scurried for cover and had themselves a short, ineffectual exchange with those Indian riflemen seen only from the puffs of gunsmoke dotting the canyon vegetation.

"My intentions are to compel the Indians to surrender their arms and ammunition, and to dispute their passage, by force of arms, into the Bitterroot valley," Rawn explained as the Nez Perce fire noticeably trickled off, then—for some reason—disappeared entirely.

"This is the place," Rawn determined as he peered from side to side, studying the site he had chosen, which occupied a bench north of Lolo Creek. "Steep as that slope is, they can't get around us to the south. Even though that north side isn't near so treacherous, I don't think even a mountain goat could pass, much less a tribe of Indians with all their impedimenta. So unless they disarm and dismount, we'll give them a fight right here. Let's dig in."

He now put some his soldiers and volunteers to work scratching out a line of rifle pits in a lazy L shape, one leg stretching to the north from the bench, the other roughly to the west. The rest of his command Rawn ordered to drag up deadfall and to cut down more, all of it to be laid horizontally atop the dirt excavated from those trenches at the rear of the log barricades. To top off their fortifications, the men dropped what is called a head log on top of the walls, shoving a short limb under it at intervals, which opened a space large enough to get the muzzles of their rifles through.

While he got these labors under way, the captain sent local E. A. Kenney to ride on up the trail and attempt some contact with the Nez Perce camp. Early that evening of the twenty-fifth, the scout, who had been elected as "captain" of the Missoula volunteers, returned with an Indian he declared had the Christian name of John Hill.

"This one's been sent to you by Joseph hisself, Captain," Kenney explained.

"Those warriors we skirmished with got back and told him we're here?"

"The whole camp knows," Kenney said. "Four scouts was left behind to keep an eye on us when three of 'em headed back with the news. This fella Hill was one of 'em waiting along the trail to keep an eye on us. When he spotted me coming up the road on my lonesome, he come out of hiding. He led me to their camp this side of the hot springs."

"How far's that?"

"Less'n a handful of miles from here," Kenney answered.

"How many? Two or three?" and Rawn's eyes narrowed, the skin between his eyes wrinkling with worry.

"No more'n that," Kenney said with a shrug, chewing on the side of his lower lip. "Lemme tell you—them chiefs and all their bucks was painted up and ready to wrassle when they surrounded me! I figger they mean to strut and crow up a storm in front of us so we'll just step aside for 'em when they come on down the trail."

The captain asked, "You get a chance to tell the chiefs we're here to turn them back from entering the valley?"

"I told 'em that's why you're digging in here," the civilian sighed. "Explained how folks here in Montana didn't want 'em bringing their Idaho war over here."

"So what'd Joseph have to say for himself?"

"He sent this Injun back with me to ask the soldier chief if you're gonna let his people leave the pass, let them go on by way of Missoula City for the buffalo country."

"That almost sounds like a man who doesn't figure on making trouble," Barbour piped up scornfully.

"How the hell we gonna trust that red son of a bitch after he's been killing men and ruining white women over there in Idaho?" Amos Buck shrieked.

His brother Fred Buck chimed in, "I say we hold this here redskin as our hostage while we explain to the rest of them savages what's gonna happen to 'em if they come on down the trail!"

"Hold on," Rawn soothed, then turned back to Kenney. "Does Joseph sound to be peaceable to you?"

The scout nodded. "The chiefs said they would go their way peacefully if you let 'em pass."

Rawn sighed, studying his boot toes a long time before he looked up at the civilian to say, "All right, Mr. Kenney. We'll hold this Indian here with us for safekeeping while you go back up the road."

"Go back up the road, Captain?"

"I'm sending you to tell Joseph I want to talk with him myself tomorrow," Rawn explained for the hearing of them all. "Tell him to come to our camp in the morning and we'll have a talk about where his people can go now."

CHAPTER FORTY-ONE

JULY 26, 1877

HICH ONE OF THESE IS WHITE BIRD?" CAPTAIN CHARLES C. RAWN quietly asked of volunteer leader E. A. Kenney as the white men brought their horses to a halt a few yards from the two Nez Perce.

"The oldest one there on your left," indicated the civilian as the two chiefs looked over the line of white men.

"Looking Glass is the other," Rawn surmised with much disappointment, glancing at the decorated mirror hanging from the chief's neck. "Which means that Joseph didn't come."

"Right." Kenney pointed beyond the pair. "I figger he's back with the rest of their chiefs—in that group you see waiting at them trees."

"If he's the leader of the whole band of hostiles, do you suppose he sent these two other chiefs out simply to toy with me?"

Kenney didn't speak immediately. Instead, he looked over that group waiting well behind the two delegates, searching for Joseph. Finally he shrugged and said, "Maybe he's over there. Hell, I don't have no idea why Joseph ain't here."

It was late Thursday afternoon, 26 July, when Rawn, accompanied by Captain William Logan, Chief Charlot, and the newly arrived Montana governor, Benjamin F. Potts, along with more than a hundred soldiers and "irregulars," moved out from behind their log-and-pit barricades under a white handkerchief tied to the barrel of a Long-Tom Springfield rifle and rode up the Lolo Trail toward Woodman's Prairie, where Joseph's village was now camped. Upon spotting the big gathering of warriors drawn up on a ridge and displaying themselves in an intimidating manner, the white delegation had stopped just beyond the range of the Nez Perce rifles.

"Let's begin with the point you need to impress upon them about disarming, Captain," prodded Potts, ever the politician.

Over the last few days the governor of Montana Territory had hustled down from Helena by stage. Leading a group of some fifty volunteers from the territorial capital, Potts and his civilians had reached Missoula City a little past three o'clock that very morning. As soon as he had acquired three horses at a livery, Potts and two of his staff immediately led their volunteer brigade south for the Lolo Trail, reaching the barricades just before noon.

Sizing up the situation as only an elected official could, the governor told

Rawn, "It would be madness for us to attack their camp with an inadequate force. The only thing that can be done is to hold these Indians in check until such a force arrives that will compel their surrender."

Hell, that was the same damn thing the army itself was asking the captain to do with his two forlorn, outgunned companies! Hold these savages who had butchered or eluded the best Howard's department could throw at them—and Rawn was expected to nail their moccasins to the ground until help arrived? Even though a hundred more Bitterroot volunteers had drifted in throughout the previous afternoon and that very morning, the captain fretted that he wouldn't have enough men to actually block the Nez Perce if it came to a showdown.

Shit, this was just the sort of assignment that could make a man a hero . . . or a goddamned martyr.

Yesterday afternoon he had written a dispatch to Fort Shaw on the Sun River, addressing it to Colonel Gibbon's aide, Lieutenant Levi F. Burnett.

Up the Lou-Lou Pass
July 25th, 1877
3:00 o'clock P.M.

Am entrenching twenty-five regulars and about fifty volunteers in Lou-Lou canyon. Have promises of more volunteers but am not certain of them. Please send me along more troops. Will go up and see them tomorrow and inform them that unless they disarm and dismount, will give them a fight. White Bird says he will go through peaceably if he can, but will go through. This news is entirely reliable.

The captain was so certain of this development simply because a half-breed named Delaware Jim had brought him word only minutes before he sat down to write out his dispatch.

Having just gotten back from the Nez Perce camp, this mixed-blood Salish, given the right proper and Christian name Jim Simonds, lived with a Nez Perce woman as part of Eagle-from-the-Light's band, who themselves had moved in with Charlot's Flathead people and adopted the Bitterroot south of Missoula City as their own.*

When Chief Charlot had led more than twenty of his fighting men up to the barricades earlier that morning of the twenty-sixth, volunteering to help the soldiers against the Nez Perce, Delaware Jim promptly offered to ride on to the hostiles' camp because he could speak a passable Nez Perce. He had had himself an audience with the venerable old White Bird.

And now Rawn was standing before the chief himself.

"Don't forget what I told you," Potts whispered out of the side of his mouth as the Nez Perce held out their hands and there was a lot of shaking

*Delaware Jim reportedly had scouted for explorer John C. Frémont in the 1840s and had worked in this local area as early as the 1850s as a hunter, guide, and interpreter.

all around. "You must stand fast. Don't budge a single inch on your demands—the safety of our communities depends upon it."

"That's right, Cap'n," Kenney reminded at Rawn's other elbow. "You can't let these here Injuns buffalo you and walk right over the U. S. Army."

"Not like they've done in Idaho," Potts hissed assuredly.

Once the introductory preliminaries were out of the way, Rawn began explaining his demands to the two chiefs, attempting to make his voice strong enough, loud enough, that it would reach the clutter of warriors embraced by the trees in the middistance. Chances were the ringleader himself, Joseph, was among them. If not him, then at the very least every other renegade Nez Perce warrior who wore the blood of innocent white people on his hands.

"By order of the Indian Bureau of the United States of America," Rawn began, pausing for the first time to allow for Delaware Jim's halting translation, "you and your people are hereby ordered to halt, and cease your approach into Montana Territory.

"With the authority of the U. S. Army," he continued, "I order you to surrender your weapons and ammunition immediately. Then your warriors will have to dismount and turn over your horses to me.

"When that is done, then your people can turn around and return to Idaho, where you have been ordered upon your reservation."

"Chiefs says the reservation is not theirs," Delaware Jim interpreted. "That it belongs to Lawyer's people."

"If they have a grievance about their reservation, they should take it up with their agent and the Indian Bureau," Rawn said firmly. "I am a soldier, so I'm here to stop them entering Montana Territory."

The translator did his best to listen to the talk going back and forth between the two chiefs until he finally could tell Rawn, "White Bird says they'll give you their cartridges, but they won't let go none of their guns."

Rawn wagged his head emphatically, uneasiness swelling in him like a hot, festering boil. The tension in the other white men around him had suddenly grown palpable as well. He knew both sides were watching for any sign of treachery. "Tell the chiefs that's not good enough."

"They say what you ask is not something they can decide for themselves," Simonds interpreted. "To give up their guns and horses—that is something every man must decide for himself."

"That means this will take more time?" Rawn asked, a dim flicker of hope warming his breast. "Perhaps a day or two so they can deliberate?"

"Maybe so," Delaware Jim admitted, then listened to more of White Bird's talk.

Rawn drew himself up, feeling a bit more confident that he was not about to be bullied and shoved aside by these Indians. "Tell them they must make their decision no later than midnight."

"The middle of the night?" Potts echoed with disbelief.

Rawn turned slightly and flashed the governor a knowing wink. "And, interpreter—be sure to tell these two chiefs that I'm making them responsible for the actions of their warriors. I don't want any of their young men roaming about or attempting to sneak around our fortified barricades."

The white men waited while those two prickly topics of contention were relayed to the Nez Perce, then for Delaware Jim to absorb what he was told in response to Rawn's stern ultimatums.

"Chiefs vow not to fight the valley settlers, if the white men with you don't shoot at them. The Nez Perce are friends with those white men, and do not wish to have trouble with the settlers in the Bitterroot valley since they have been friends for many years."

Rawn glanced over the faces of those volunteer leaders, studying the effect the chiefs' word had on men like Potts, Kenney, and newspaperman Barbour, too. Then he asked, "What about my soldiers?"

The Salish interpreter said, "White Bird says if your soldiers force them to fight, they will ride over you to get to the buffalo country."

Just then a figure on horseback appeared through the center of those warriors waiting back among the trees. But he did not stop there. The closer he came, the more Rawn found the man remarkably handsome. His approach toward the parley was causing quite a stir among the warriors and headmen.

"Captain Rawn?" whispered William Logan, captain of A Company. "Do you recall how Captain Jack's Modocs ambushed General Canby at the Lava Beds?"*

Rawn tore his attention from that solitary horseman to study the rest of those eighty-some warriors plainly growing more restless, if not belligerent. "I remember, Captain. Send one of the men back to pass word to the non-coms that the units should be ready to advance at once should anything untoward happen up here with us."

Logan turned and whispered to Lieutenant Coolidge, directing the young officer to turn about for the rear.

That's when Rawn peered again at that handsome horseman again and asked, "So who is this coming to our conference?"

"He's the one you been waiting to meet," Kenney said before Delaware Jim could get the words out. "That's Joseph hisself."

When the chief came up to dismount among the others, Looking Glass and White Bird began relating to him what they had discussed with Rawn. In a matter of moments, Joseph made only a simple gesture with his hand to show his token assent to the plans of those other chiefs, but he did not utter a word.

That gave the captain a sudden overwhelming sense of relief: to think that he might be able to stall the hostiles and thereby delay the inevitable clash until either General Howard made it over the Lolo Trail or Colonel Gibbon got down from Fort Shaw with reinforcements. Even with the growing number of civilian riflemen and Charlot's Flatheads augmenting his paltry twenty-five foot soldiers, the captain was not at all eager to plunge headlong into a scrap with some two hundred resolute warriors fresh from Idaho and their stunning battlefield victories scored against numbers far stronger than his.

"So," Rawn sighed, trying to appear as if he were disgruntled with the

---

**Devil's Backbone*, vol. 5, the *Plainsmen* series.

news, "these leaders are telling me they can't make a decision on their own right now?"

"Yes," Delaware Jim replied with some visible measure of his own relief as the three chiefs began to turn away for the trees.

"So they'll let me know by midnight?"

"No," the interpreter admitted as they watched the backs of those three leaders returning to their lines. "But Looking Glass claims they will come back to talk with you again sometime tomorrow morning."

BY TELEGRAPH

The Strike Subsiding—Bummers Still Rioting.

More Indian Massacres in the Black Hills.

BLACK HILLS.

Indians Murdering Near Deadwood—
A General War.

CHEYENNE, July 26.—A dispatch from Deadwood, dated yesterday, says: James Ryan, a resident of Spearfish City, just in, states Lieutenant Lemly, with his company of soldiers augmented by a dozen civilians, left this point Sunday morning with two days' rations, and have not been heard from since . . . Two large bodies of Indians were seen yesterday morning on Red Water, about five miles from Spearfish . . . Intense excitement prevails throughout Deadwood. At short intervals since yesterday morning, horsemen have been arriving from the different towns and hay fields in this vicinity, bringing details of fresh murders and outrages by the savages, who seem to have broken loose from the agencies in large numbers and are infesting the country in all directions . . .

Chauncey Barbour wondered if he should slip Captain Rawn's courier a little hard money to have the man stop by the newspaper office this Saturday morning, where the soldier could pick up some writing tablets to bring back to the barricades the next time one of those privates was sent down the trail to Missoula City with some bit of news or a dispatch for those army commands known to be both west and east of the Bitterroot valley.

For now the newspaperman thought he had enough paper to last him until tomorrow. But if he kept on writing as much as he had put down on paper already, Barbour would run out before morning. There had been more to tell about than there had been Indians to shoot at during these last couple of inconclusive days of this stalemate. With all those hours of nervous waiting, Chauncey had more than enough time to reflect, to interview other volunteers, time enough for all of them—civilian and enlisted man—to argue over just what course they should take.

It was downright intriguing for the newspaperman to watch human nature at work. Despite their extensive fortifications, many of the valley volunteers continued to believe that if the warriors showed up for a fight, it would turn out to be another Custer massacre. John L. Humble, "captain" of volunteers from Corvallis, was clearly the leader of that school of thought.

"Captain Rawn," he said, presenting himself and a delegation before the officer, "it's clear to me there's too many of them for us. Clear, too, it's useless to try fighting them."

"Useless?" Rawn echoed. "But I'm an officer of the U. S. Army. My job is to fight the enemies of my government—"

"You do not have to get yourself killed needlessly," Humble interrupted.

Rawn wagged his head, rain sluicing off the brim of his soggy hat. "I've been sent here with a job to do."

Then Humble said, "I have soldiered, too, Captain. Served in many dirty battles in the Civil War. Union, I was. So I want to remind you—most times it's too damned easy to get into trouble . . . but damned hard to get yourself out once you're in."

"Just what in the blazes are you trying to tell me?" Rawn snapped.

Humble flinched. "I want to tell you that if you are going to fight those Indians, I will take my men and go home."

"If I'm going to f-fight them?" Rawn repeated as if not believing what he had heard. "If you're going to turn tail for home at the sign of a fight . . . then why in hell did you and your men ever come here in the first place?"

Humble wagged his head and turned away. "We're going back to our families."

"The best I can tell you men," Rawn announced, pausing while the Corvallis civilians stopped and turned around, "is that I won't fight them if I can help it."

However, there were many more of the civilians and some soldiers, too, who figured that the simple fact that the Nez Perce hadn't charged down the trail signified that Rawn was striking some sort of deal with the chiefs that would allow them to pass on by without a fight.

Yesterday morning, Territorial Governor Potts had once again come out from Missoula City to visit Rawn's rifle pits after he had issued a general alarm to all the papers in the area, putting out a call to all area citizens to reinforce his local militia.

When the Nez Perce chiefs had refused to put in an appearance by midafternoon yesterday—after telling Delaware Jim they would show up in the morning—Rawn decided to press the issue and called for a hundred mounted men to march out with him again. Some of the Flathead warriors rode along under Charlot. With skirmishers posted on both flanks, the column pushed up the canyon until reaching a knoll less than a half-mile below the Indian camp. Here Rawn halted his irregulars and, this time, sent forward one of the Flathead, a man named Pierre.

"Looking Glass come alone," Pierre had explained in his halting English before the hushed crowd of white men after he had returned a half hour later. "Say you, too, come alone. No guns. No guns on him. No guns for soldier."

That was the longest five-minute round-trip Barbour could remember watching in his life. Maybe not even a full five minutes at that—every second of it spent staring at the backs of Rawn and Pierre, seeing Chief Looking Glass emerge from a group of his warriors at the edge of their village. The three men did not sit atop their horses for long and talk things over. The captain and his interpreter turned around and were back among the irregulars within the span of those same five minutes.

"Well?" Chauncey demanded.

"Yes, Captain," Potts huffed. "Is the fact you've returned so quickly a good sign? Or a portent of trouble?"

With the makings of a shrug, Rawn disclosed, "I don't know for sure. A voice inside is warning me that the Nez Perce are planning an attack. But on the other hand, Looking Glass offered to surrender all the ammunition in his camp, as a guarantee his Indians intend to go through this country peaceably."

"I sure as the devil pray you set that godless red bastard on the right path!" Potts grumbled.

"I think for want of ammunition, or Charlot's threat to fight alongside with us, the Nez Perce are wavering," Rawn declared.

Potts enthused, "Now's the time to hold fast, Captain!"

With a nod of affirmation, the captain continued, "I repeated that nothing short of their unconditional surrender would be accepted by the army. I could tell he didn't like that a wit, gentlemen. Not at all. But, in turn, he could see I was not about to bend like a reed in the wind. So that's when he asked me for another meeting tomorrow morning."

"Tomorrow?" Potts echoed in a higher pitch.

"Perhaps another day will find General Howard's column racing up behind the village," Rawn had asserted hopefully.

"Have you received some news from Idaho I don't know about?" the governor demanded.

"No," the captain admitted. "But, even allowing for the Nez Perce marching a little faster up the Lolo, with General Howard's column coming out of Idaho right behind these hostiles, they shouldn't be but a day, maybe two, behind this camp."

Potts puffed his chest out showily. "So we're going to have to come out here again and beg a goddamned audience with this vermin-infested redskin tomorrow morning?"

Rawn's face had suddenly beamed, as if he were the cat who had cornered the canary. "No, we won't be begging for another meeting, Governor. Before he turned to leave, I told the chief if he wanted to have any further communication with me . . . it would have to be under a flag of truce at our fortified barricades."

"So there's no definite plans to hold another parley?" Barbour inquired.

"Nothing definite," Rawn confessed. "But I did tell him that I had to see him at the rifle pits by noon tomorrow."

Later that Friday evening as a relentless drizzle began, the newspaperman crabbed through the log-and-rifle-pit barricades, making a firm count of the current manpower available to the captain. A day ago, at the height of the scare, Rawn could boast a strong garrison. Including officers and enlisted, civilians, and about eighteen Flathead warriors, Barbour had tallied 216 men ready to deny the Nez Perce passage if and when they pressed the issue a day ago.

But things sometimes have a way of unraveling on a man.

As more and more of the valley volunteers argued over the possibility of the Nez Perce remaining peaceable as they passed through the Bitterroot, small groups of civilians began to slip away just after darkness gripped the canyon. Rumors that Looking Glass had guaranteed not to harm any of the valley residents were good enough for more than half of them.

Throughout that soggy night of 27 July, volunteers continued to saddle up and ride away for their homes. Then, just before dawn, three unarmed Nez Perce approached the breastworks and were taken into custody.

"Tom Hill," one of them gave his name to E. A. Kenney.

Kenney in turn explained to Rawn, "He's kin to John Hill, Cap'n. Part of Poker Joe's band."

With Hill were a half-breed companion named George Amos and an elderly full-blood named *Kannah*.

"The old one's a squaw man," Kenney explained.

"He looks awful Indian to me," Rawn stated. "Where I come from a squaw man is a white fella who marries an Indian squaw."

"In this country, it means half-man, half-woman."*

All three had been visiting the Non-Treaty camp up the Lolo Trail but sneaked out to reach the soldier lines over the objections of their chiefs. Having spent years in the Bitterroot, they admitted not having much stomach for a fight with the white man.**

Still, Rawn's diminishing manpower wasn't the thorniest problem he had to tackle. Come morning, he was about to find out that Looking Glass and his people weren't going to play along with the captain's delaying game any longer.

At 8:00 A.M. on 28 July Pierre had come in from scouting close to the Nez Perce camp with the astounding news that the hostiles were tearing down their lodges and packing up for the trail.

"That could mean that the scouts they surely have posted on their back trail have brought news of Howard's approach!" Rawn cheered. "We'll have to delay them only a little while—until the general's cavalry can race up on their rear."

"It might also mean that Looking Glass has decided not to enter Mon-

---

*A squaw man, as the Nez Perce would put it, is "one who does not have the dignity of a warrior." To their way of thinking, such a person was gender-neutral. In history contemporary to the Nez Perce War, there were two such persons. One had been killed in Lewiston by a miner during the gold rush, and the other died at Kamiah, one of Lawyer's Christians.

**Dawn placed the three under arrest and would take them back with him to the Missoula post where they would remain in custody for the remainder of the war.

tana," Potts conjectured, tugging on his Van Dyke. "They might be pulling back to Idaho after all."

"Either way," Barbour declared aloud as he madly scribbled notes on that pad perched upon his knee, "you've won this bloodless little fray, Captain Rawn!"

Some of the giddy civilians set up a hurraw for the officer, for themselves, and for that day they sent the Nez Perce packing without firing a shot.

But at just past ten o'clock, Chauncey Barbour and the rest were brutally yanked out of their self-congratulatory reverie.

"Injuns! Injuns!"

"I see 'em!"

"Goddamn—lookit all of 'em!"

Barbour brought the looking glasses from his eyes and quietly exclaimed, "The red bastards are slipping right around us!"

CHAPTER FORTY-TWO

JULY 28, 1877

HIS LAKOTA ENEMIES CALLED HIM LIMPING SOLDIER. TO THE CROW scouts who had served him during the Great Sioux War he was known as No Hip.

Since July of 1863 the man had walked with a decided limp, having suffered a debilitating pelvic wound at Gettysburg.

John Gibbon was his name, colonel of the Seventh U. S. Infantry, stationed in the District of Montana.

During the Civil War, General George McClellan, then commander of the Army of the Potomac, had lauded Gibbon's "Iron Brigade" as being the equal of any soldiers in the world. But after he was promoted to brevet major general and transferred to the command of a full division, Gibbon experienced a humiliating defeat at Fredericksburg, suffering 40 percent casualties, including his own severe hand wound. Just hours after the battle, Gibbon shook his bloody fist at the officers and enlisted of his failed command, roaring at them, "I'd rather have one regiment of my old brigade than to have this whole damned division!"

By the end of the war he had been wounded numerous times and was the recipient of no fewer than four brevet promotions. A shining example of the army's old school—dependable, straightforward, not at all full of inflated self-consciousness as were so many of his contemporaries—war hero Gibbon accepted the colonelcy of the Thirty-sixth Infantry, regular army. Five years later he took over the Seventh and moved onto the plains to fight a new enemy.

Sporting a gray-flecked Van Dyke, Gibbon was fifty years old this summer of 1877.

For the last few years his regiment had been headquartered at Fort Shaw, on the Sun River in north central Montana Territory. But Gibbon was also in charge of Fort Ellis at the head of the Gallatin Valley* along with Camp Baker in the valley of the Smith River just east of Helena, the territorial capital, and he also maintained a small detachment at the important steamship terminus of Fort Benton, on the high Missouri River. In addition, Gibbon was overseeing construction of Fort Custer on the Bighorn at the mouth of the Little Bighorn.

While he owed some small measure of allegiance to his departmental

*Near present-day Bozeman, Montana.

commander, General Alfred H. Terry, this Civil War hero of South Mountain, Antietam, Spotsylvania, and Petersburg had long ago given his loyalty to the brash, cocky, hot-tempered little lieutenant general who was not only in command of the entire Division of the Missouri but also the second highest ranking officer in the whole bloody army—Philip H. Sheridan.

Over the past two months this straight-talking hero of Gettysburg had been watching the Idaho situation brew itself into a foul-smelling broth. Knowing firsthand just how nervous a lot the Montana citizenry were, Gibbon was not at all surprised when Governor Benjamin Potts was able to persuade Secretary of War George W. McCrary into sending troops to the western part of the state, hoping to quiet things down a bit earlier that summer. The colonel wrote back to the secretary, in his own inimitable way, questioning that decision made by civilian bureaucrats all the way back in Washington City.

> Your dispatch of yesterday (19) received. Have but sixteen (16) privates for duty, a little better off at Ellis, and I will send all the men that can be spared from there. The force remaining in the District is so small that to scatter it any more than it is now is objectionable.

His polite disagreement with the War Department was barely gathering momentum when the wires buzzed with word from the west that the Nez Perce were indeed headed for Montana. No longer merely a rumor.

That very next day, the twenty-first of July, Sheridan ordered Gibbon into the field with what troops he could muster to stop the Nez Perce. That same afternoon, the colonel sent a wire to Charles Rawn, whom Gibbon had constructing a post near Missoula City, informing the captain that it would be up to him to hold the Nez Perce in check until Gibbon could bring up reinforcements.

On the twenty-second, Gibbon wired Sheridan in Chicago:

> Dispatch of yesterday received. Have ordered one company of infantry from Fort Ellis to Missoula direct. As soon as I can assemble troops here from Camp Baker and Fort Benton, I shall move via Cadotte Pass down the Blackfoot River towards Missoula. Shall probably be able to take nearly one hundred men. The troops being all infantry, these movements will necessarily be very slow and can do little but check the march of the Indians in the passes . . .

Departing Fort Shaw six days later to the music of Professor Mounts's barrel-organ harmonica pumping out "Ten Thousand Miles Away," Colonel John Gibbon had his hundred marching off to the Nez Perce War.

The same morning that dirty little war was spilling over into Montana Territory.

ON THE TWENTY-SECOND of July, General Oliver Otis Howard had returned to Cold Spring on the Camas Prairie from Lewiston, bringing with him those two batteries of artillery culled from the San Francisco area and two companies of infantry from Fort Yuma, Arizona—both commanded by Captain Harry C. Cushing.

Although it had been a crushing disappointment for Howard not to find his wife on that steamboat, there had been a joyous reunion on the docks of Lewiston nonetheless. Coming down the gangway was Cushing's junior officer, a dear and familiar face that brought joy to the old warhorse's heart. The general embraced his eldest son, Second Lieutenant Guy Howard, declaring he would serve out the campaign as one of Howard's aides.

Across the next four days settlers came out from Mount Idaho and Grangeville to visit the army camp at Cold Spring—registering lost cattle and stolen horses with the army, selling beef to Quartermaster Fred H. E. Ebstein, or simply to gawk, talk, and gab. During that time, the general, along with his newly appointed aide-de-camp, Guy Howard and correspondent Thomas Sutherland, reveled in the fishing at this popular resting spot for wayfarers traveling between Kamiah and Lapwai. Here, the correspondent detailed in his journal, the command settled into Camp Alexander near the mouth of Lawyer's Canyon and slowly went about the recuperation and preparation required of them if this army were to successfully pursue the Nez Perce fleeing Idaho.

"This stream would have made Izaak Walton himself brave all the Indians in Christendom for just one day's whipping at it," Sutherland opined.

Howard grinned as if the war were held at bay and far from his mind, happy perhaps just to watch how much his son enjoyed their daily excursions along the leafy banks.

"We've already caught enough fish to drive amateur fly flingers into a hospital with sheer envy!" Sutherland gushed.

Howard's face went grave. A sudden cold dash of realism seemed to mock the newsman's high spirits. The general declared, "I only wish Joseph and his hotbloods could be caught this easily."

Sutherland knew just how much Howard was suffering at the public criticism going the rounds in the national papers. It did not take a phrenologist to diagnose that this beating the general was taking at the hands of the press was the primary, if not the sole, reason for his decision to follow Joseph's war camp himself.

In a dispatch intended for all three of his three newspapers, sent with a mail courier back to Lapwai and beyond, Sutherland wrote:

> General Howard rode into Lapwai that night on special business . . . and returned the next afternoon with the face of his proposed campaign somewhat changed. He had learned at Lapwai that on account of the hounding of several influential papers, the

> Cabinet at Washington had been considering the feasibility of removing him from his command and appointing Crook in his stead. Hearing that the cause of dissatisfaction was want of activity—which is not only baseless but almost ironical, as we have been constantly on the go ever since the troops have been in the field—General Howard resolved to . . . start with the rest of his command through the impenetrable Lolo Pass, and follow Joseph to the very death.

In private circles, Major Edwin Mason was telling others that the plan for the command to take up the chase over the Lolo was his idea, preempted by the general commanding.

"No matter," Mason grumbled to Sutherland, and in a letter to his wife as well, "my plan will tell in the end—if we keep after them we are bound to strike them sometime and somewhere."

On the morning of the twenty-sixth of July, Howard led the short march from Lawyer's Canyon to the subagency at Kamiah, where the command set about the laborious task of crossing the Clearwater with men and matériel, horses and mules, soldiers and packers, along with a contingent of Treaty scouts. The general paid a few of the Treaty men one dollar per head to swim the command's stock over.

Early the next morning, 27 July, Howard dispatched two of McConville's civilians, "Captain" James Cearly and "Sergeant" Joseph Baker—both Mount Idaho volunteers—each to carry a copy of his message for Captain Rawn. Should the pair run into trouble and have to split up, Howard was counting on one of them to make it through to Missoula City. But instead of setting off on the Lolo route Howard had chosen for his column, Cearly and Baker decided they would take what was called the Old Nez Perce Trail. Following the Clearwater to its source in the mountains, they would make their crossing of the southern pass,* then drop into the head of the Bitterroot valley, where they would finally point their noses north for that new army post being raised near Missoula City.

In his dispatch, Howard informed Rawn that the Nez Perce were demoralized, so he believed it wouldn't take much to hold the Non-Treaty bands until the general could come up from the rear to take them in whole:

> If you simply bother them, and keep them back until I can come close in, their destruction or surrender will be sure. We must not let these hostile Indians escape.

On each of those three laborious days of crossing and seeing to a thousand final preparations, Howard received a telegram from General McDowell back in Portland, besides a flurry of frantic messages from Governor

---

*Today's Lost Trail Pass in extreme southwestern Montana.

Potts in Montana Territory, all of them relating the most current revelations about the Indians' movement up the Lolo Trail, clearly intended to nudge the general into starting on his chase. At the bottom of every one of McDowell's wires, the division commander had hand-written the same succinct postscript: "I most strongly encourage your rapid movement up the Lolo Trail."

In the last few weeks Sutherland had come to know Howard as a man who held his emotions close to the vest, rarely allowing anyone to get a glimpse of who he was inside or what turmoil he was going through. All the correspondent could learn was that the general's dispatches back to McDowell remained steadfastly upbeat day after day, repeatedly explaining to his commander and their superiors back east: "In another month I shall surely be able to make clean work of the whole field."

Then early on the morning of the twenty-eighth, just as they were honing the final preparations to depart Kamiah the following day, some fifty packers—who had charge of more than 350 mules for the campaign—went on strike for higher wages.

In a spasm of anger, many of Howard's officers threatened to commandeer the mules and assign their own men to duty as packers. But it did not take long for the general to realize what an impossible struggle greenhorn troops would have with the notoriously testy animals on that impossibly narrow and treacherous wilderness trail over Lolo Pass. Without making the slightest complaint or threatening the civilians with retaliation, Howard gave the Mexican head packer, Louis, and his civilians their due.

As the general walked away from that meeting with his mule skinners, Thomas Sutherland read the expressions of unvarnished satisfaction, happiness, and downright respect for this one-armed officer those half a hundred hard-cases wore on their faces. After those many muddy days tramping through the Seven Devils region of the Salmon River wilderness with this column, the correspondent was already impressed with this outfit of packers. When describing them in several of his dispatches, he referred to them as a splendid class of men physically, with just enough of an accent—since many possessed some degree of Mexican blood—to give proper pronunciation to the word *aparejos* or to swear in a most musical tone. Sutherland marveled how those crude, unlettered, and rough characters were always the first to build their campfires at night and the first to cook their meals. More important for what was yet to come, the packers had never faltered in battle or on long marches demanded of them.

Howard had not only done the just thing in giving those civilians their raise in pay, no matter that to some it seemed like a bold case of highway robbery since they were less than a day from embarking on their journey up the Lolo—Sutherland knew the general had done the right thing.

Now all this column had to do, come dawn, was finally get on the trail of those hostiles once more . . . before the Nez Perce had a chance to scatter all across the buffalo plains of Montana Territory.

Wreaking havoc and murder in their wake.

"DON'T SHOOT! DON'T shoot!" came the cry from that lone stationary horseman who continued to shout at his fighting men as the warriors turned aside, starting up that ridge less than a half-mile from the white man's breastworks.

Captain Charles Rawn focused the field glasses on the Nez Perce riders as Pierre, the Flathead interpreter, quickly translated the horseman's commands for every man, soldier or volunteer, who could easily hear the chief's loud bellow, admonishing his warriors to protectively flank the column of women, children, and old ones.

" 'Don't shoot,' Looking Glass tells them," Pierre explained. " 'Let those white men shoot first!' "

The vanguard of the fighting men had escorted their families and horses laden with baggage to within some eight hundred yards of the fortress before angling away to their left, starting up the ridge rising at the north side of the narrow canyon. For the longest time the white men did nothing but stare, dumbfounded at how they had been caught so flat-footed.

"White Bird told you he didn't wanna fight if he didn't have to," reminded scout E. A. Kenney, breaking the uneasy silence. "I s'pose you can take 'em at their word about it now."

Frustrated to the point of taking a bite out of his soggy slouch hat, Rawn stomped around the rifle pits, angrily keeping his soldiers and what few civilians were left at the barricades ready for an assault, watchful for anything that might prove this to be a ruse meant to conceal an attack by more of their warriors.

The captain hadn't gotten much sleep the night before—what with all the clatter and chatter as more than a hundred of the brave Bitterroot valley volunteers abandoned the barricades and rode off for home. By dawn, the officer found he was left with less than eighty men all told: soldiers, civilians, and Charlot's Flathead, too.

Two hours after getting the report that the Nez Perce were packing up for the trail, those men behind the barricades spotted the first warriors leading the women and children up the narrow ridgeline until they disappeared behind a tall, conical hill, completely hidden from view.

By 11:30 A.M., the captain ordered a mix of forty-five soldiers and civilians to accompany Lieutenant Tom Andrews on a mission downstream, where they were to guard the trail below the barricades and arrest any stragglers they could.

No more than a half hour later, the last of the Nez Perce rear guard had disappeared from sight behind the high timbered ridge north of the barricades.

"Captain Rawn!" came the shout from the rifle pit nearest the steep slope to the north. "The Injuns coming our way! Coming for us!"

With a loud clatter of metal and wood, the squeak of leather, and the pounding of hundreds of feet, the soldiers, civilians, and Flathead warriors streamed toward that section of the barricades. As the men hunkered down in the dapple of overcast sunlight broken by the tall evergreens that towered over the canyon floor, the breastworks bristled with weapons trained on that small group of Nez Perce slowly advancing on the white men.

A civilian announced, "They got women with 'em, too."

"What the hell they doing?" someone asked as the group halted two hundred yards from the muzzles of those rifles.

Before anyone could venture a guess, one of the riders at the front of that group of men, women, and children advanced a few more yards, then stopped before he shouted something in bad English.

"Pierre!" Rawn ordered. "Tell 'im to talk Nez Perce so we can understand him!"

After a brief exchange, the Flathead declared, "Old man's name Amos. Friend of mine. Live for some winters near Missoula with his people. Eight lodges—men and women, children, too. They come surrender to you."

"Surrender?" Rawn asked dubiously. "What the blazes were they doing up here with the hostiles if they've been living friendly near Missoula City?"

Pierre shrugged. "Amos says he heard the Looking Glass people were coming. He was once a Looking Glass Injun. So he took his families up the Lolo to visit old friends. But when he saw there gonna be trouble, Amos want no part of it. Want to come in and give up to you. But Looking Glass and White Bird, they keep warriors close by Amos people so they don't surrender."

"But they're surrendering now?"

"Looking Glass let them go this morning because the village go on by your log soldier fort."

"All right. Captain Logan, go out there with Pierre and a squad of men. Quickly disarm those warriors."

"You want us to dismount them, Captain?" William Logan asked.

"No. Just take their weapons for the time being." Rawn turned to gaze down the valley where the Nez Perce camp was migrating at a leisurely pace. "We'll find out if they're all that friendly soon enough."

Fifteen minutes later the captain was leading out the rest of his force, turning east down Lolo Creek. Instead of hurrying to catch up to the tail of the Indians' march, Rawn had his men cautiously probing forward in a military formation, with flankers to the sides and a number of civilian skirmishers arrayed in advance of the main body.

It wasn't long before those volunteers grew increasingly bold and eased up much too close on the end of the column—where the Nez Perce fighting men suddenly whirled about on their ponies and stopped in their tracks, bringing their weapons up, ready to fire on the white men. For a moment there was an anxious clamor as the civilians skidded to a halt there on the banks of Lolo Creek and turned around, bumping into one another to be the first out of danger and rifle range.

"What the devil's going on?" Rawn bawled at the first of those retreating volunteers galloping back to the main group. "I didn't hear any damn shots—have you been fired on? Did you take any casualties?"

Alfred Cave, a settler from the Bitterroot valley, yanked back on his reins and stopped near the officer, breathlessly explaining, "They made a show to shoot us then and there! Bastards gotta be setting up an ambush for us right ahead, Captain! They was drawing us in closer and closer, just the way they would afore they'd close the trap!"

"Trap?" Rawn echoed skeptically. "How the blazes can those Indians lay a trap for us when we know right where they are?"

Without a word of reply, Cave sheepishly turned aside, rejoining the rest of those who had fled from the advance without uttering a word.

"Mr. Matte!" he called over to the older, French-blood half-breed from the valley.

Alexander Matte moved up on his horse, followed by a half-dozen Flatheads, all of whom wore strips of white cloth around their heads, another strip tied around one upper arm so that, should a fight erupt, soldier and civilian alike would know who was a friendly, who was not.

"Take your trackers and go up the line," Rawn ordered. "Keep your head down and find out if the Nez Perce are laying an ambush for the rest of us."

CHAPTER FORTY-THREE

Khoy-Tsahl, 1877

ITH BRAZEN BRAVADO, THE SOLDIER CHIEF HAD YELLED ANGRILY AT *Ollokot*'s warriors as the horsemen drifted down into the valley of Lolo Creek, ordering the *Nee-Me-Poo* fighting men to dismount, to give up their horses and weapons.

"Is the man crazy with whiskey?" Yellow Wolf asked some of his fellow riders.

Many of them laughed at such Shadow arrogance now that the village had made it all the way around the north side of the *suapies*' log-and-burrow fortress.

Ollokot asserted, "Does this little chief honestly think the *Nee-Me-Poo* would go on to the buffalo country without our horses and rifles?"

"How foolish he is to be a chief for the *suapies* at all!" snarled Shore Crossing. "That one is not even smart enough to be a horse holder for a *Nee-Me-Poo* war party!"

"Even if he had returned our weapons to us after we left the Bitterroot valley as he promised he would do," Yellow Wolf said, fixing his eye on those white men keeping their distance back in the trees, "how can any man actually think we would let him keep our cartridges?"

"Because that's what Looking Glass told the little chief we would do," *Ollokot* argued sourly.

"But Looking Glass said that only to buy us a little time while the women made ready for our trip down to the valley," Red Moccasin Tops spoke up.

Yellow Wolf thought that was a good idea to fool the soldier chief. Any soldier chief.

Like Looking Glass had just done with the little soldier, so, too, *Zya Timenna* had made a prank on Cut-Off Arm back at the Clearwater many suns ago. It was good to laugh after all . . . but—he stopped to think for the first time. Now the *Nee-Me-Poo* had hurt Cut-Off Arm's pride. When you hurt a man's pride, you make him angry.

To fight a stupid soldier was one thing. But to fight a stupid soldier you have made angry was a pony of an entirely different color. Stupidity made a soldier merely a nuisance. But anger could now make Cut-Off Arm a real danger. Yellow Wolf found himself hoping that Howard and his soldiers would indeed remain in Idaho country.

"Perhaps you are right," he said to Red Moccasin Tops. "None of our leaders want us to fight the soldiers in this country, to fight these settlers in the Bitterroot."

"So we let them fire a few shots at us?" Shore Crossing snapped. "To let the Shadows feel some pride in fighting our warriors? I think our chiefs shame us when they even talk of giving up our cartridges to the *suapies!* When they keep us from shooting back at the white men!"

There had been a little gunfire from the fighting men after the *suapies* and Shadows let go with a few arrogant shots. Yellow Wolf knew the white men had aimed their bullets high, none of them made to land anywhere near the column of women and children. Those silly whites fired only to make themselves feel better since they were being made to look the fools!

"Yes—why should we start a little war here in Montana?" Yellow Wolf declared, watching a change come over *Ollokot*'s face of a sudden. "Now that we are safe and getting that much closer to the buffalo country."

This part of his argument made the most sense to Yellow Wolf. After all, why had most of the Shadows chosen to slip away in the dark last night if it wasn't because of the Lolo treaty Looking Glass had struck with the soldier chief? All those white men abandoning their barricades and heading back to their homes just went to prove that the *Nee-Me-Poo* had indeed left the war behind in Idaho country. It was clear the Montana whites did not want to see the army make war on their *Nee-Me-Poo* friends.

Turning his gaze to his war chief, Yellow Wolf continued, "The trek over the Lolo Trail was the hardest part of our journey—but it is behind us now! Why should we start a war, even if it means a little lying to that soldier chief?"

His eyes narrowing with distrust, *Ollokot* declared, "I think Looking Glass will say or do anything—even if it is not the truth—to get this village through to the buffalo country without trouble. His reputation, his very honor, is at stake now."

Yellow Wolf watched *Ollokot* rein away, kicking his pony into a lope, sweeping toward the front of the long column as it neared the mouth of Lolo Creek, where its waters tumbled into the Bitterroot River flowing north through the last miles of that long, narrow valley. Shoulders squared, *Ollokot* was a fighting man by any definition, Yellow Wolf thought. Yet, this *Wallowa* war chief had been forced into a new role of late. Because his older brother had been shamed and shoved aside time after time in the council meetings of the chiefs, *Ollokot* had been compelled to step forward and take up more and more of the duties for the Wallamwatkin as the silenced Joseph slipped further and further into the background. Ever since Looking Glass had consolidated his control over the warrior bands, even Joseph's stature among his own people had been compromised.

Especially when Joseph had lobbied to have the Non-Treaties turn around for the Salmon, where they would make a stand in their own country rather than risking everything they had ever known on a life none of them knew anything about . . . the rest of fighting men voted to leave the traditional *Nee-Me-Poo* homelands under Looking Glass's leadership, to abandon the bones of their ancestors, to leave behind the good memories their children and grandchildren would never share.

But last night a few of the fighting chiefs had begun to mutter among themselves that Looking Glass was wrong to even talk to the little chief about giving up their ponies and guns. When the headmen met to discuss those talks held with the soldiers, Red Moccasin Tops shouted at them.

"I will not lay down my gun! We will not quit fighting! Blood of my people has been shed and I will kill many of the white men before I die! My hands will be stained with the enemy's blood—only then will I die!"

Looking Glass defended himself, "I never meant to let the little chief think we would lay down our guns—"

At the edge of the council Rainbow sat upon his war pony, his rifle braced against his thigh as he declared, "Do not tell me to lay down my gun, Looking Glass! We did not want this war. Cut-Off Arm started it when he showed us the gun at the Lapwai peace talks. We answered his rifle and that answer still stands for me. Some of my people have been killed and I will kill some more of our enemies—then I shall die in battle!"

"Never again will there be any talk of giving up a thing to the white man," Looking Glass had vowed.

Early this morning, Looking Glass and White Bird had ordered their warriors into position along the front of their march, placing their ponies and their bodies between the soldier guns and their own women and children. It took only moments for Joseph to have that camp of women and children, the old, and the wounded ready to turn aside for the sharp ridge where scouts had located a narrow path only mountain goats must have used to cling to the backside of a tall peak.*

Once the fighting men had guided the column back to the Lolo Trail itself, they discovered how the soldier chief had ordered some of his men and the Shadows to press in upon the rear of the *Nee-Me-Poo* march. A few of the older warriors who had been to the buffalo country before recognized some familiar faces among the valley settlers and called out greetings to those they knew, even cracking some jokes back and forth with those Shadows trailing them at a distance while the entire procession slowly paraded toward the mouth of the Lolo. Why, Looking Glass even turned about and rode back to the settlers, doffing his tall beaver-felt top hat with its plume, smiling hugely as he shook a few white hands—reminding the Shadows that his people did not mean to cause trouble as they passed through the valley.

Only one time that morning were the white men foolish enough to get too close upon the column's rear, forcing *Ollokot* to order his young men to wheel about and level their rifles at their pursuers—ready to knock down the first ranks. The warriors all had a good laugh watching those Shadows rein up with surprise, stumbling over one another, barely clinging to their frightened horses, as they turned about in total terror.

---

*This angling, northward movement took them out of Lolo Canyon, over to Sleeman Creek, which they followed until joining Lolo Creek again about two and a half miles west of its junction with the Bitterroot River.

Frightened white settlers such at these posed little threat. Twice already in this war, the *Nee-Me-Poo* had witnessed the Shadows' fighting resolve—once at White Bird Canyon, the second time at Water Passing.* Shadows could make a lot of noise and bluster, but there was little danger when it came down to making a fight of it.

"Perhaps the Shadows needed a little reminding that we do not want to fight them," Yellow Wolf stated to the warrior beside him as they laughed together, watching the white men scurry in retreat, "but that we will fight if pushed to it!"

"The little soldier chief realized we would fight. That's why he made his treaty with Looking Glass," *Wottolen* reminded grimly. "He knew it was far better to let us ride past with our promise not to make trouble than to have a lot of angry warriors turned loose on the Bitterroot valley."

The Non-Treaty bands had successfully scooted around the soldier barricade in a maneuver that had made the *suapie* chief look as much like a fool for failing to hold the *Nee-Me-Poo* back as he was a fool to erect a barricade in the Lolo Canyon to hold them back in the first place.** With Cut-Off Arm, the Book of Heaven chief, still far, far back in Idaho country and the little soldier chief turning aside now so that he no longer followed the camp, from this point on the journey couldn't look brighter!

Now that they had reached the Bitterroot valley, the sun finally came out behind the dissipating clouds, bright and hot, drying the muddy, mucky road so that the traveling was easier on the ponies and those who plodded on foot. In every direction Yellow Wolf chose to look, the sky was big and blue, barely a cloud marring the aching immensity of it. Here they were that much closer to the *E-sue-gha*, longtime friends and allies who would join them not only in the buffalo hunt but also against the army—should those *suapies* ever want to start another war on the *Nee-Me-Poo*.

Once they had climbed the road out of this long, narrow valley and made their way across the heights to the Place of the Ground Squirrels,† they would be within haling distance of the buffalo country!

Eeh-yeh! Already Yellow Wolf could feel the joy of that realization spreading through him like the warmth of the sun, replacing the cold, bone-chilling despair and despondency he had suffered for having to put his *Aihits Palojami*, his fair Fair Land at his back.

He could not remember a finer day than this! Looking Glass had made his Lolo treaty with the little chief and those valley settlers, an agreement that guaranteed the *Nee-Me-Poo* passage up the Bitterroot without either side having to fear attack. And now the *suapies* had marched out of sight to the north, away from the noisy, joyous village that began to celebrate even

---

*McConville's volunteers at Misery Hill.

**Because of this very public fiasco, in the local press Rawn's abandoned log-and-rifle-pit fortress immediately became known as "Fort Fizzle," its army and civilian defenders regarded as cowards afraid to fight, much less die, to halt the Nez Perce invasion of Montana Territory.

†The Big Hole.

before they started to make camp.* The women were trilling, jabbering, laughing—their high voices like happy birds on the wing. The children immediately picked up on the mood: running and shouting and laughing with such great abandon. Which meant the men, like Yellow Wolf, could congratulate themselves on how well they had fought the soldiers in Idaho country, how hard they had worked to get their families over the Lolo, how steadfast they had remained in their pledge not to fight the Shadows in Montana Territory.

Imene kaisi yeu yeu! With the Creator's blessing, there would be no fighting now!

Give great praise to *Hunyewat!* The war was over!

"SHIT! THEM'S THE goddamn Nez Perceys!" exclaimed Henry Buck as he and more than two dozen civilians suddenly found themselves stumbling into the Indian camp after dark that Saturday night after the Indians had slipped around the Lolo barricade.

These twenty-six valley settlers and shopkeepers, who had answered the alarm to bolster Captain Rawn's small detachment of regulars from Missoula City, had remained with Rawn to the last. While most of their compatriots had turned back for their homes in the steady drizzle that fell the night before, most of Buck's friends had stuck it out, even as the Non-Treaty bands scooted right around them slick as a gob of wagon-hub grease.

For most of the day the civilians knew they were some distance behind the slow-moving village, but little had they realized that, when they turned south to ride up the valley of the Bitterroot for their homes near Stevensville, they would end up running right into the Nez Perce camp! Of a sudden these startled white men found themselves among the lodges and willow shelters before they had time to rein up and retreat.

"Shadows!" a Nez Perce voice called out from the hubbub and clamor as the civilians milled about and clattered together, not really knowing which way to turn now that they had stuck their foot right in it.

Voices were calling out to one another, many warriors running up on foot, some racing up on horseback, until what seemed like more than a hundred of them had streamed out of the darkness—converging on the frightened whites from every direction.

"Stop, white men!"

More shouting arose as a handful of faces approached out of what starry light illuminated the valley floor. Closer and closer those new arrivals came, followed by a crowd of warriors, until their red noose came to a halt no more than six feet from the civilians' nervous horses.

"Hello, Boston Men!"

The speaker stepped forward, a figure sporting his famous tall top hat decorated by a showy bird plume attached to the very front, sticking straight up.

---

*That first evening out of the Lolo Canyon, the Nez Perce erected their camp on the McClain ranch, about five miles south of the Lolo's mouth, on Carlton Creek.

It was Looking Glass. Henry didn't know if he should be relieved or even more scared.

"W-we're lost." Buck could think of nothing more to say than the truth. The eyes of all those warriors gleamed in the starshine, measuring him and the rest of the citizens caught in this tightening snare.

The top hat walked closer to Buck's horse, held up his hand as if to shake. Grinned, too. "Me Looking Glass. You?"

"B-buck. Henry Buck," and he held down his hand, thinking it quite odd that this Nez Perce chief would practice such a custom—to shake hands with a white man when the chief should realize that earlier this day these very white men had attempted to bar the Indians' entry into the valley.

"Looking Glass?" Myron Lockwood echoed, sitting on the horse next to Henry's. "Why, I didn't know this was Looking Glass. This here's the chief hisself—the one who come back and shook hands with a few of us this mornin'!"

"I guess he puts great stock in this hand-shaking thing," John Buckhouse said, nervousness cracking in his voice.

"This ol' buck even had his eyes checked up to Missoula City on his way back from the buffalo plains just this past spring," explained Wilson B. Harlan. "Doctor fit him for a pair of glasses, too, Henry."

"We're going home," Buck explained to the chief, speaking his words slowly. He pointed on south up the valley. "Home, there, tonight."

For a long moment Looking Glass turned to peer up the valley, too. "Yes, home." Eventually, he brought his eyes back to Buck and smiled when he said, "You home, no hurt you home now. No war with white valley man here. No war come to Montana buffalo land. No war. You go home all now, too. All white man go home. No war now."

He held up his hand to Buck and they shook again; then the chief moved among the civilians, eagerly shaking every white man's hand. When Looking Glass had greeted all the stunned horsemen he stepped back against that tight ring of warriors.

"No war now, white mans!" he cheered, doffing his tall hat, sweeping it to the south in a grand gesture. "Go home—you no fight. No war for you. No war for us."

"Y-yes. We go home," Buck repeated the chief's broken English, nodding as he urged his horse into motion. "No war. We'll go home because there ain't gonna be no war now."

More than a hundred warriors slowly parted, gradually forming a very long and narrow gauntlet as the white men started away, every one of the Nez Perce silent, glaring.

It wasn't until they were three miles farther south up the Bitterroot that Henry realized how tense his muscles had been, feeling just how tight his ass had been clenched from the moment he realized they had moseyed into that village by mistake. Even though he and his brothers had seen quite a few Nez Perce coming and going through the valley across the years and some had even visited their store in Stevensville on every journey through the Bitterroot, Henry Buck had never seen that many Nez Perce warriors in one place . . . nor that many so goddamned *close*—all of them glaring at him and the others. It was enough to make a man's scalp itch.

Henry Buck decided every fella was granted at least one second chance in life to make up for some stupid, lunkhead blunder. He figured he'd just used up his.

CHAPTER FORTY-FOUR

JULY 29, 1877

Kamiah
Indian Territory
July 29, 1877

My Precious Darling Wife,

Got here today at 10 A.M. without adventure of any sort. It seems a month or longer since I left you. Yet . . . I have, after a fashion, enjoyed this nomad's existence of two days and nights . . .

The troops to go (and with whom my lot is cast) are all across the river, and stores are being crossed over. It looks like a war picture, indeed quite an army, and among them, I am glad to see about 25 Indian scouts who were brought through by Colonel Sanford. By the by, I go with Colonel Sanford . . . 1st Cavalry . . .

I shall mess with Colonel Sanford—

U.S. ARMY SURGEON JOHN FITZGERALD PAUSED, PENSIVELY CHEWING ON the wooden stem of his ink pen as he studiously gazed out upon the noisy clamor of that camp readying itself to follow General Oliver Otis Howard over the Lolo Trail into Montana Territory in pursuit of the escaping Nez Perce murderers and outlaws.

This might well be the last chance FitzGerald had for a long, long time to write Emily from the campaign trail—and know with any certainty that she would get his letter. Why, she might well be reading it by tomorrow afternoon. Each of the many officers had tossed a little something into a pool to entice one of the Christian Indians to ride off to Lapwai with their final messages before embarking on what they knew had to be a short campaign.

The Indian scouts will be in the advance. It is said and believed here that Joseph's Indians are all over in Montana and peacefully disposed among the settlers in that region. Doctor Alexander says that I will be back at my post in 30 days. I hope so, Darling, for I feel that I have been away from you for an age already. I don't see how I can stand it for 30 days. You may rest assured, Darling,

> *that absence for that time, or maybe a week or so longer, is all you have to fear on my account.*

Oh, how to tell her all that he sensed was ready to gush out of him here and now . . . yet how to keep from telling her what he must not let slip in there, even between the lines. He thought at first of somehow preparing her for the eventuality that he might not make it back home, then thought better of that idea and decided not to write anything morose or melancholy—exactly the way a man felt in those hours before riding into battle or setting off on an uncertain campaign.

> *. . . I forgot to tell you our Indians all wear soldier's uniforms with a kind of blue sash of stripes and stars. It looks, in fact, like a piece of old garrison flag. They belong to the Bannock tribe of Indians farther to the south, and they can be depended on . . .*
>
> *I hardly know, Darling, what else to tell you. I suppose we will reach Missoula in a week at farthest. I was going to say you might write me there, but that would not do, as I suppose it would take two weeks for a letter to reach that place via San Francisco. There will be one or more opportunities for you to write me by courier from Lapwai. Take care of yourself and the babies, and wait for me as patiently as you can . . .*

John FitzGerald quickly looked up to see if anyone might be approaching.

Furtively he dabbed his thumb at that errant teardrop soaking into the writing paper, then dragged the back of his hand beneath the end of his nose. This surgeon, husband, and father did not want another man to misread his reluctance to leave his family behind. After all was said and done, this was his calling. He was a soldier. A doctor yes, but a soldier above all.

Jenkins FitzGerald had been an army doctor since the outbreak of rebellion among the Southern states. And this was what a soldier did: go off to war against his nation's enemies.

> *I keep thinking of the long absence from you, my dear wife, but it must be. I suppose there are 30 to 40 more gentlemen in this command who have left their wives and babies, and who, in case of more fighting, will be in far greater danger than your man can possibly be in, but, honestly, I don't think we shall see an Indian hostile. I said to Colonel Miller, "Colonel, what are we all going to do over there?" He replied, "Oh, we will have a big mountain picnic with no Indians to trouble us."*
>
> *. . . We will have some hard marching only, with no fighting of any kind—*

"Dr. John!"

He looked up of a sudden, finding the Indian leading his horse, walking easily toward the cluster of hospital tents and baggage where FitzGerald sat. The dark-skinned Kamiah courier wore a large leather pouch over his left hip, the wide strap looped over his right shoulder. Already there were two other, younger, officers hurrying their envelopes up to the rider. Chances were neither one of them had a wife or children at home, FitzGerald thought as his eyes connected with the Nez Perce courier.

"Dr. John," the Treaty Indian said as he stopped a respectful distance away. "I go soon. Take mail to Lapwai. I go with your letter, yes? Take to Mrs. Doctor."

"Yes," he sighed sadly, then went back to chewing on the wooden stem of his pen, looking over those young men bringing their mail to the courier.

Such young, eager officers would have written home to mothers, perhaps even a sweetheart to whom they had pledged their hearts, planning a distant betrothal when affairs with the Nez Perce were settled.

So . . . until he got back from the far side of the Lolo . . . perhaps the far, far side of the world itself, this last letter to her might well have to be it for a long, long time—

> *Be patient, darling, sensible wife, as you always have been, and 'ere long I will be with you again. My ink is getting low, so goodbye, my honey, and believe me.*
>
> *Ever your faithful,*
> *John*

"And I am especially glad to see you again, *Wa-wook-ke-ya Was Sauw!*" Looking Glass exclaimed as he moved among the small party of men, women, and children, touching hands, pounding backs.

The newcomers had just approached the large *Nee-Me-Poo* camp with their leader, Eagle-from-the-Light, being hailed by many of the Non-Treaty headmen who had come out to greet the new arrivals—six lodges of them, accounting for ten warriors. *Wa-wook-ke ya Was Sauw*, this man called Lean Elk, was one of those fighting men who for the last few winters had paid his allegiance to the Eagle.

Weeks ago when the first flames were fanned in Idaho country, the men of their band had gone together to petition Flathead agent Peter Ronan at the Jocko agency for permission to camp on the reservation north of Missoula City, where they would be far from the danger of being swept up in a war should the Non-Treaty bands cross over the Lolo Trail, as everyone knew they would. For generations the Flathead people had been good friends of the *Nee-Me-Poo*, crossing over the Lolo each year to harvest those salmon doggedly fighting their way from the distant ocean to the high streams that fed the Clearwater River. When Ronan had refused their request, Eagle-from-the-Light kept his small band near Charlot's Flathead, who themselves had steadfastly refused government orders to move north from the Bitterroot valley onto their own reservation.

Then just a few days ago Charlot and some of his fighting men had ridden off to join those soldiers who planned to block the trail—so Eagle and his men decided to find another place to lay back out of sight, somewhere they might let events on the Lolo take their own course. But when the *Nee-Me-Poo* managed to slip around the foolish soldier chief, Eagle's band figured they could no longer ride the fence. Agent Ronan had plainly shown that he did not care to have Eagle's allegiance, so . . . Eagle-from-the-Light, Lean Elk, and the others figured they would feel out the mood of things in that Non-Treaty camp.

This first morning after the debacle up the Lolo Canyon, those ten warriors led their women and children down the Bitterroot valley to find the Non-Treaty village.

"Last time I saw you was in your camp at *Pitayiwahwih* on the Clearwater, Looking Glass," Lean Elk confided to the garrulous chief.

"Yes—just after you cut your leg carving the wood to make another one of your fine saddle frames," Looking Glass replied to the short, stocky half-breed. "Do you still limp like you did when you left to ride back to Montana?"

"I do," Lean Elk explained, patting his thigh. "But the wound is getting better."

Looking Glass snorted with laughter, "I hope you are getting better using a knife, too!"

"It is a good thing he cut his leg," Bird Alighting said with a smile as he came through the crowd. "He cannot race his horse against us until his wound heals!"

Their good-natured ribbing carried the weight of truth to it. Named Joe Hale by the Shadows over in Idaho country, Lean Elk was widely known for his love of gambling, betting on everything from horse races—this past spring he had beaten all the best ponies the Flathead could bring against him—to his favorite card game, poker. In fact, the white man had given Lean Elk a nickname, too, one that stuck to him much better than Joe Hale. *Poker Joe*, it was.

Considered a subchief among Eagle's band—his wife's people—this mixed-blood French-Canadian *métis** of Nez Perce descent was a good Shadow talker, too, able to keep up with most any white man in the white man's difficult tongue. Still, even that did not help Lean Elk when he returned from Idaho to the Bitterroot not long after he had cut his leg while visiting Looking Glass's people on the Clearwater. The deep, nasty gash gave him a decided limp—leading most Shadows to believe that he had been wounded in the fighting between the *Nee-Me-Poo* and the soldiers west of the Bitterroot.

Truth was, Poker Joe had cleared out of that camp, eager to recross the mountains with his family and rejoin Eagle-from-the-Light's band, just two days before the *suapies* attacked Looking Glass's village, driving the Asotin people right into the ranks of those disaffected warriors already creating havoc up and down the Salmon and boiling across the Camas Prairie. Over here in the Bitterroot, Poker Joe and his friends heard delayed reports of all

---

*His father was said to be a Canadian voyageur, once employed by the Hudson's Bay Company of Adventurers.

the fighting on the Cottonwood, as well as that long two-day battle on the Clearwater. While a few of Eagle's young men thought they would like to be a part of the fighting, Lean Elk and most of the others had decided it best they stay out of the troubles and keep their relations with the valley settlers good.

But now that the Non-Treaty bands had come to the banks of the Bitterroot River, Eagle-from-the-Light's people decided they might do well to join up. If all the Shadows in this part of Montana Territory were in an uproar over the Idaho bands, it might be wisest for Eagle's small outgunned group to join up with the hundreds for the safety of their numbers. And if the fighting truly had ended and the war was left behind them back in Idaho—so much the better! Since he, better than most any other *Nee-Me-Poo*, carried in his head all that terrain and geography of the buffalo country, it might just be time for Poker Joe to suggest another hunt on the plains.

Late the following afternoon three more newcomers showed up about the time the village was going into camp, having marched no more than a leisurely handful of the white man's miles that day. That trio of *Nee-Me-Poo* warriors rode among the lodges and celebrants, many of the bands noisily calling out their greetings to the new arrivals who were just returning from the country of the *E-sue-gha*.* For more than a year now, Grizzly Bear Youth and his two companions—*Tepsus*, called Horn Hide Dresser, and a Yakima scout named *Owhi*—had been scouting for the Bear Coat,** the soldier chief who was waging a very telling war on the Lakota from his log fort raised at the mouth of the Tongue River.

That evening, the chiefs called on the three to meet with them in council, seeking to learn more about the best path to take to the buffalo.

"The Bear Coat's fort lies east of the Bighorn," Grizzly Bear Youth explained. "He is the best *suapie* chief I know in tracking down an enemy, no matter how bad the weather."

"Not like Cut-Off Arm, still sitting way back there in Idaho country!" White Bird snorted with a wry laugh. "I think we should rename him Never Going to Fight Until Tomorrow!"

"If you go to *E-sue-gha* country," Grizzly Bear Youth warned grimly as the laughter died, "I think the army will tell the Bear Coat to stop you. I recommend you stay away from that soldier chief at all costs."

Now it was Looking Glass's face that turned grave with worry. "You are warning us we should not go to the land of the *E-sue-gha?*"

Grizzly Bear Youth shook his head. "Go there if you must, but just stay as far away from the Bear Coat as you can. Indeed, we must now stay as far away as we can from any soldiers."

"So where would you have us go?" White Bird demanded impatiently. "If we have been driven out of our own homeland and we are not welcome

---

*The Crow.

**Colonel Nelson A. Miles, Fifth U. S. Infantry, stationed on the Yellowstone River in Montana Territory, serving under Lieutenant G. C. Doane. See *Wolf Mountain Moon*, vol. 12, and *Ashes of Heaven*, vol. 13, the *Plainsmen* series.

to stay here in the Bitterroot valley—if we can't go to live and hunt with the *E-sue-gha*—where are the free *Nee-Me-Poo* to go?"

"To the Old Woman's Country," Grizzly Bear Youth declared with enthusiasm.

"To join up with the Buffalo Bull Who Rests on the Ground?" Looking Glass asked skeptically. "He is an enemy of ours. You yourself have just returned from fighting the Lakota for this Bear Coat. All of you know that I have fought the Lakota more than once. So how can I ever go to the Old Woman's Country to live with such a fierce Lakota leader?"

"He has run away from the army, too!" Grizzly Bear Youth argued. "No different from any of you leaders—even Joseph there. You are running away to the east, leaving the army behind. Buffalo Bull Who Rests on the Ground ran north to get away from the army, just like you have."*

White Bird wagged his head, appearing confused. "Why should we go north like they have?"

"With my own eyes I have seen what the soldiers can do to the mighty Lakota," Grizzly Bear Youth explained. "So I think it is folly to consider that we can continue to fight against the government and its army. For the sake of our families, we should just turn aside and go north as quickly as we can."

"How would we get to this Old Woman's Country from here?" *Toohoolhoolzote* asked.

Grizzly Bear Youth explained, "The shortest way is to turn directly north. March past Missoula City; continue across the Flatheads' reservation. Just beyond it lies the country where the army can bother us no more."

There was some downhearted muttering in the group, men murmuring among themselves in low tones—yanking on the question this way, tugging on it that way, like a woman would stretch a wet piece of rawhide. Poker Joe thought he liked the idea of going north through the Flathead reservation. The Flathead owned many good horses. This past spring he had raced against some of the finest. Perhaps on their way north to the Old Woman's Country, he could adopt some of those Flathead horses for his own, taking them across the Medicine Line to race against the Lakota!

That's when he cleared his throat. The chiefs looked in his direction. Poker Joe was not an important leader like the rest of them, not even as big as Eagle-from-the-Light. But he had something significant that needed saying.

"If you will think about it: These days we have more in *common* with Buffalo Bull Who Rests on the Ground than we have differences with the Lakota."

No one spoke for several minutes. The large fire crackled. Moccasins shuf-

---

*When the Lakota warrior bands considered waging their last great fight against the U. S. Army, they went so far as to invite all of their traditional enemies to a great council that was held in eastern Montana Territory, during the summer of 1875. It is indicative of the esteem the Lakota held for the Nez Perce that the Non-Treaty bands were invited to this council. In the buffalo country at that time, Looking Glass and Eagle-from-the-Light both attended. Even Joseph came from the *Wallowa* to listen to the Lakota proposal of a strategic alliance.

fled. Some bystanders coughed nervously. And women standing in the ring around the seated men hushed the noisy play of small children.

Toohoolhoolzote turned to White Bird. "Who wants to go to the Old Woman's Country?"

Old White Bird immediately raised both his spindly arms in a most dramatic fashion. "I believe it is time to consider a vote."

"To vote on what?" Looking Glass snapped uncertainly, his eyes darting over the others.

"Who agrees with Grizzly Bear Youth that we should march north through the Flathead's reservation?" White Bird proposed. "Start north from here to the Old Woman's Country?"

Poker Joe looked over the six chiefs who were present. White Bird had his arm up even as he asked for the vote. Then Red Echo raised his hand, too. For a long moment, the elderly, white-headed leader of the Salmon River band waited for more to join the two of them, but they were the only votes for turning north.

Looking Glass leaped to his feet and swaggered over to stand behind White Bird's shoulder, looking smug as a sparrow hawk with a fat deer mouse clamped in its beak. "I think these other leaders remember so well how Chief Charlot and his Flathead warriors joined the *suapies* in that silly attempt to bar our way into this valley. Since the Flathead are no longer our friends, to march north through their country now would be very, very dangerous."

"Charlot's Flathead are no danger to us!" Red Echo protested vigorously. "Without many guns and much ammunition, the Flathead need the white men to protect them. They are no threat to us by themselves!"

Looking Glass strenuously shook his head. "I will never trust the Flathead again!"

"So what do you propose?" Rainbow asked.

"Yes," Sun Necklace demanded. "Which way do we go to avoid the soldiers?"

"For many summers I always took the shortest way," Looking Glass explained. "From here we ride north and east, up the Big Blackfoot River, over the pass, and down to the plains at the Sun River."

"But that way is blocked by a *suapie* post,"* Five Wounds argued.

"Or we could go a more southerly route to the Three Forks country and on to the Yellowstone," Looking Glass proposed.

"And that is blocked by the *suapies* at another post,"** protested Rainbow.

"So where would you have us end up, Looking Glass?" Sun Necklace growled. "Right in the jaws of more soldiers?"

"Lean Elk, who knows the way, tells me we are less than five or six easy marches from the head of the Bitterroot valley," Looking Glass explained as Poker Joe nodded. The heads were turning to look at him in a different light now. "Once we get there, we drop over the mountains and are but a few more days from the buffalo country."

---

*Fort Shaw.

**Fort Ellis.

Five Wounds exclaimed, "It's a good way, Lean Elk! Maybe go through the Land of Smokes, out along the Stinking Water River. The road that way is open, with plenty of grass and not many whites, all the way!"

"Yes," Rainbow echoed. "That route avoids the soldier forts and the big mining camps, too!"

Wheeling an arm across the entire assembly, courting not only the handful of other chiefs but more so the audience of hundreds, Looking Glass moved the question, "Who votes for going on to the *E-sue-gha* country with me to hunt buffalo?"

As the Asotin chief's own arm shot into the air, his eyes raked over the group. Rainbow and his spirit brother, Five Wounds, immediately added their illustrious reputations to the vote in favor of the buffalo country.

Now Looking Glass slowly turned to the only chief who had not spoken out his wishes. "Joseph?"

"As before, there is nothing for me to vote on, Looking Glass," the Wallamwatkin chief said.

"Speak your mind, Joseph," White Bird prodded.

"When we were fighting in our homeland, there was a reason for us to fight, and for our men to die," Joseph declared. "But since we have left our country behind, it matters little to me. I am not in favor of taking my people far away to the Old Woman's Country . . . but neither am I in favor of taking my people far away to the land of the *E-sue-gha* to live. We already have a home. We have a country of our own."

"If we go to the land of the *E-sue-gha*, we must all go united," White Bird warned.

"I agree with Joseph," Pile of Clouds suddenly spoke, surprising many in the council. "Why go to the land of the Sparrow Hawk people when we have a home of our own already? The land of the *E-sue-gha* is too open for good fighting—and we will have to fight the Bear Coat's *suapies* there, sooner or later."

"You want us to march back over the Lolo now that we have just arrived here?" Looking Glass asked with a trembling fury, clearly angry with the testing by this young *tewat.*

Pile of Clouds shook his head. "No, we go by the southern pass,* move quickly back to the Salmon River country where we will have the mountains and timber. That is the country good for fighting the soldiers."

Joseph nodded. Many of the others were looking at the *Wallowa* chief now. However, Poker Joe turned to Looking Glass, realizing what the angry Asotin chief must be thinking. Joseph was leader of the largest Non-Treaty band. His reluctance to come east had become like a sharp thorn in the Asotin chief's side.

Looking Glass suddenly loomed over Joseph, asking, "Did you, or did you not, with these other chiefs, elect me for leader through this country?"

"Because you knew this country and the people here," Joseph agreed.

"And did you not promise me that I should have the whole command to do with as I thought best?"

---

*Today's Lost Trail Pass.

"Perhaps the *E-sue-gha* will help us as you say, Looking Glass. But in these two choices that you and White Bird have given us, I have no words," Joseph admitted to that hushed audience. "You know the country and I do not. So I can make no vote—"

Triumphant once more, Looking Glass whirled away from Joseph without even waiting respectfully for the man's words to drift away into silence. His voice thundered over them all.

"To the buffalo country!"

CHAPTER FORTY-FIVE

July 30–August 1, 1877

Fort Lapwai
July 30, 1877

Mamma Dear,

. . . John left on Friday and I am lonely without him, but I would not be any place else than here for anything, as here I can hear from him every time anything goes in or out to General Howard. I heard this morning from Kamiah, and I will enclose John's letter . . .

The Indians, it is supposed, have gone off over that Lolo Trail to Montana. A dispatch from the Governor of Montana says a great number of ponies, women, and children, with a lot of wounded men, had come over the Lolo Trail, and he had not force to stop them. No one knows whether Joseph and his warriors have gone over there too, or whether they just got rid of their families and helpless men so they could make the better fight themselves. General Howard is determined to find them and has formed two columns. The one he commands himself will follow over the trail the Indians took into Montana. The other goes north through the Spokane country and joins General Howard's column sometime in September over at Missoula where General Sherman will meet them. Then, if the trouble is not over, a winter campaign will be organized, but we hope it will be over even before that . . .

Mrs. Hurlbut, the poor little laundress I have mentioned in several of my letters, the one who lost her husband in that first terrible fight, was here staying in my house at nights all that first month. She is expecting daily to have another baby, and she was afraid, in case of an alarm at night, she would not be able to get across the parade to the breastworks. So she asked me if she could bring her children and sleep up with our servant girl, Jennie, which she did until lately, since our fear for the post is over. She is a nice little woman, and her children are as nice as I know. She is left destitute. After her sickness, we will all help her. A purse will be raised to take her back to her friends . . .

Doctor, I expect, is marching up the mountains today, farther and farther away from us. How I hate the army and wish he was out of it! I hope they won't find any Indians, and I hope he will come back to me safe and sound . . . I don't see what they do want with John on that Lolo Trail . . . Sometimes when I think what might happen out there, I get half distracted, but I fight against it and keep my mind occupied with other things, and I plan for John's coming home . . .

All the Indian prisoners are here, some 60 in all. They are horrid looking things, and I wish they would send them away . . . Don't feel anxious about us. I am only anxious for the Doctor. Write soon. Lots of love to all.

Your affectionate daughter,
E.L.F.

BY TELEGRAPH

The Strike Virtually but not Actually Ended.

Chicago and St. Louis Quiet.

Late Washington and Indian Intelligence.

MONTANA.

Looking Glass Marching On.

DEER LODGE, July 30.—Governor Potts returned from Missoula this morning. On Saturday Looking Glass, with three hundred Indians and squaws and some Palouses, passed up a fork around Deep Bitter Root. Some settlers have been in the Indian camp and the Indians assured them that they would pass through the country without destroying property. The citizens therefore did not attempt to fight, and Rawn declined to open fire with his small command of regulars, and there was no pursuit made. On the Governor's arrival he ordered the volunteers who had gone to Bighole to return, the force being insufficient. There will be a party left in Bighole valley to observe and report the actions of the Indians.

TWO DAYS BACK, WITH THE FIRST SHRILL ANNOUNCEMENT THAT THE NEZ Perce caravan was coming their way, Henry Buck ran outside and clambered up on the old fort's fifteen-foot-high sod wall and watched to the west in the direction of the Bitterroot Mountains as the vanguard of the Non-Treaty bands hoved into sight on the flat of the river, just opposite the town of Stevensville. He thought to look down at his pocket watch, making a mental note of the time that warm summer morning, 30 July. Ten A.M.

For years now Henry and his two older brothers, Amos and Fred, had owned and operated the Buck Brothers' General Store in the thriving settlement of Stevensville, several miles south of Missoula City. When the alarm first came that the warrior bands were turning away from McClain's place near the mouth of Lolo Creek, headed their way, panic spread like a prairie fire igniting the Bitterroot valley. Most everyone up and down the river, Henry included, had herded their families into old Fort Owen,* a long-abandoned fur-trading post erected more than twenty years earlier north of the little town—often used in the past as a bastion of safety during raids by the once-troublesome Blackfeet. More recently, the walls had been patched up by valley citizens, who now renamed the place Fort Brave because of the courage its high walls gave those who flocked within its protection during this current Indian scare.

After decades of weathering, the two-foot-thick walls were generally in good shape, except for sections on the north and west walls where the adobe was crumbling. At one time there had been four square bastions, complete with rifle ports, but now there were only two, both at corners of the south wall. As soon as the first alarm was raised weeks ago, the local citizenry promptly went about cutting green sod and repairing the gaps in the aging walls. Benjamin F. Potts's territorial government had seen to it the settlers were armed with a few weapons: obsolete Civil War–vintage muzzleloaders.

Three miles southwest of the fort where more than 260 people had taken refuge when their men marched off to aid Rawn's outmanned soldiers—almost within sight of the sod walls—the Nez Perce went into camp for the night on Silverthorne Creek. Within hailing distance of Charlot's home.

After tossing around how peaceful the Indians appeared to be, Henry and his brothers decided to reload the trade goods in a pair of wagons and return to their store in Stevensville. The threat appeared to be over. The Nez Perce were making good on their promise not to make a lick of trouble while passing up the valley.

Early on the morning of the thirty-first, as the three were restocking their shelves, a handful of Nez Perce women showed up at the doorway to make known their wants through sign and a little halting English. To pay for those desired items, the women made it clear they had government money or gold dust.

---

*Partly reconstructed, between Highway 93 and the present-day community of Stevensville in Ravalli County, twenty-seven miles south of Missoula, Montana. John Owen arrived in the valley in 1850, later buying the place from some Jesuit priests who were giving up their missionary work after witnessing nine years of constant warfare between the Flathead and Blackfeet. By the time of the Nez Perce War, Owen had lost his Shoshone wife, Nancy, drunken himself into madness, and been sent back to his family in Pennsylvania, where he slipped into obscurity.

"Henry, you tell them we'd prefer not to sell to 'em," his older brother Amos instructed from the back of the store.

A few minutes after the youngest Buck brother had declined to sell anything to those squaws, the women were back at the open doorway—this time with three middle-aged, dour-faced warriors. While two of the men stepped inside the store, their rifles cradled across their arms, to look about the place as if to ascertain just how many white men were about, the third came up to the counter where the three brothers nervously awaited trouble.

"Women, have gold for trade, you," he started, his English better than any from the squaws. "Take supplies. Pay gold now."

He patted the front of his cloth shirt, then stuffed a hand down the neck of the garment and pulled out three small leather pouches. One of them clanked with coins, while the other two must certainly be filled with dust.

"We don't want no trouble," Fred, the eldest Buck, declared confidently. "But you go take your business somewheres else."

The warrior measured him for a moment without a change coming over his stoic countenance; then the Indian gazed around the store shelves stocked with goods and said, "We need supplies. Supplies for our trail journey. You have supplies. We have gold. Trade now. If you don't let us buy supplies . . . we take what we need. You decide. Want our gold? Or you want us to take supplies for no gold?"

When the warriors put it that way, the Buck brothers felt they had little choice but to open up a limited trade with the migrating bands. The afternoon the Nez Perce arrived, small-time merchant Jerry Fahy had loaded up a creaky wagon with some sacks of flour and a few other items and rumbled across the river to do a brisk business with the Non-Treaty bands. Flour turned out to be the one item the women wanted most. Shame of it was, the Buck brothers had none on hand at the time. By the next morning the Indians had repaired to a mill near Fort Owen where they traded for all the flour they wanted.

Although Henry and his brothers decided they would trade for cloth and other staples, they steadfastly refused to barter away any powder or ammunition. Word spread quickly among the Non-Treaties, and by that afternoon the Nez Perce were showing up at the store from their nearby camp in clusters of eager shoppers. Still, it wasn't until the morning of 1 August when things got scary, as more than a hundred-fifteen warriors rode into Stevensville together under the leadership of the aging White Bird, all of them bristling with weapons. Henry rushed to the front of the store with his brothers to watch their colorful, noisy arrival. Even though they had spent those anxious minutes passing through the village coming back to Stevensville the night after the Lolo fiasco, Buck doubted he would ever forget the sight of so many fierce young warriors clotting the town's main street.

Wouldn't be able to ever forget their formidable appearance, their stern looks, their sheer swaggering aggressiveness and brazen actions—which all together put the white shopkeepers in town immediately on their guard. Riding their finest ponies—some of which wore the brands of their white

Idaho ranchers—wearing their brightest blankets and showiest buckskins encrusted with beads and quillwork, all of the warriors strutted around with Henry repeating rifles or soldier carbines. In every store they entered, it was clear they had more than enough money to make their purchases as they shuffled through the few shops open that day in Stevensville.

While they came and went from the Buck Brothers' Store, Henry found the men an open and talkative bunch—willing, if not eager, to tell about their tribulations back in Idaho, what tragic events and wrongs had led up to the outbreak on the Salmon River, explaining in honest but graphic terms what depredations and murders they themselves had committed against innocent civilians before the army rode against them in White Bird Canyon. And most all of them spoke in bright and upbeat tones of their current condition, even disclosing where they were headed to make a new life for themselves now that they had left Cut-Off Arm and his army back in Idaho.

From time to time, old White Bird would yell something at one warrior or another from the middle of the street, where the chief maintained a wary vigil atop his pony. But his instructions were always in their native tongue, so it remained a mystery to Henry. White Bird and other older warriors were on guard and at the ready, keeping a watchful eye on some two dozen of Charlot's friendly Flathead, who had slipped into town once word was spread that the Nez Perce had shown up in great numbers. Their chief had ordered them into Stevensville to protect the tribe's white friends from the noisy, bellicose invaders.

Early that Wednesday afternoon, another merchant in town came huffing in the door, announcing that an unscrupulous trader down the street had opened up a whiskey keg and was selling it for a dollar a cup in gold dust or coin.

"Already there's a few of 'em getting real mean-faced and growling like dogs down at Jerry Fahy's place," the man explained to the Buck brothers.

"Fahy can't sell that whiskey to these here Injuns!" yelped Amos. "Henry, you go with him and put a stop to this. Hammer a bung back in that keg and make Fahy see the light!"

By the time young Henry had unknotted the apron from his waist and was stepping out the door, five more citizens were scurrying across the street, streaming right past White Bird himself. On the boardwalk a few yards to the north, about a dozen young warriors were clearly enjoying themselves, weaving side to side and lurching back and forth across the dusty street.

"Henry!" cried Reverend W. T. Flowers, the local Methodist minister, as his group of concerned citizens lumbered to a halt like a flock of chicks around a black-feathered hen. "You know the bartender down at the saloon?"

"Dave Spooner?"

"That's him," the preacher said. "We've just convinced Brother Spooner how wise he would be to cease selling bilious spirits to the redskins."

Henry asked, "Or?"

"Or he might feel the coarse rub of a hemp rope tighten around his neck!" Flowers warned, pantomiming with both hands clasped at his throat. "Now I've heard Fahy is doing a land-office business with a keg of his own. You're coming with us to see an end is made of that liquid evil?"

"I am, Reverend."

Stomping right down the middle of the street, the six of them crammed through Jerry Fahy's open doorway and demanded his whiskey barrel be turned over to them. Inches away, more than a dozen warriors stood in line clutching newly purchased pint tin cups, impatiently waiting their turn at the spigot.

"Why you want my whiskey?" Fahy demanded from behind the counter where he was dispensing the potent amber liquid.

"We're acting before any of these Injuns gets drunk and ready to raise some hair!" the gray-headed minister thundered, sweeping back the long tails of his black wool morning coat.

"You ain't got a leg to stand on, Reverend," the merchant chimed back with a gritty smile. "Begging God's pardon, but I'm just a shopkeeper doing an honest day's business, and I ain't breaking no Sabbath. . . . So I don't reckon it's a damn lick of your business."

"For sure it's my business, too," added one of the other merchants.

Fahy snorted, "By what authority do you fellas think you can come an' take my whiskey?"

Quick as a blink, Preacher Flowers yanked out a single-action army Colt .45-caliber revolver and immediately dragged back the hammer with a click made loud in the sudden silence of that room. Without the slightest hesitation, he shoved the muzzle against the whiskey seller's forehead, pressing it to that spot just above and between the eyes.

The right reverend announced gravely, "By *this* authority!"

"W-what you gonna do with my whiskey, if I give it to you?" Fahy asked, his eyes crossing each time he stared up at the long barrel. "You gonna pay me for it?"

"Not on your life," Flowers sneered. "We're gonna take your keg of evil concoction to Fort Owen for safekeeping until these Indians have departed from our valley."

"You're stealing my business from me!" Fahy squawked.

That's when an emboldened Henry Buck spoke up: "We could just knock a hole in that keg right here, 'stead of keeping it safe for you out at the fort."

"Take it, goddammit!" the merchant spit, unrepentant and taking the Lord's name in vain even before the fire-and-brimstone preacher. "Maybe one of these days the Nez Perce will come to pay a call on you and take what they want without payin'!"

"We're not stealing your whiskey," Henry said as the resealed keg was rolled out the door to a waiting wagon. "We're just borrowing it until this trouble all blows over."

When one of the concerned merchants and the reverend were on their way out to the fort with the trader's keg in the rear of a prairie wagon, Henry started back for the Buck Brothers' Store—only to find even more of the drunken warriors congregating in the street, their voices growing loud enough to wake up the dead. He had to zigzag to make his way across the rutted street, then shove past several inebriated Nez Perce clustered just outside the store's open doors. Henry stepped inside just as his two older brothers reached out from either side of the door and hoisted him toward a rack of hemp rope.

"Get in here so we can lock up!" Amos ordered.

"We're closing?" Henry asked his brothers.

"You see'd it yourself out there," Fred, the eldest, explained. "Better off not dealing with 'em while so many's got a snootful of that whiskey."

Henry proposed, "Maybe we'll wait till the whiskey wears off, then we can open up again—"

His voice dropped off just as he caught a flash of motion out the front window. One of the belligerent warriors he had pushed past at the doorway was dragging his wobbly rifle up, pointing it right through the large plate-glass in the window at Henry, beginning to clumsily drag back the hammer on his weapon.

In a blur of color, one of the Flathead suddenly rushed in from the right, his arm sweeping up, shoving the rifle away from its mark, wrenching the weapon from the Nez Perce.

At least ten of the warrior's friends immediately descended on the scene, along with a half-dozen of Charlot's Flathead. All appeared destined to die in a hail of angry gunfire . . . when White Bird appeared out of nowhere, still mounted on his pony, swinging his elkhorn quirt. Whipping his tribesmen with the long knotted rawhide straps, the chief drove his warriors back.

In a heartbeat the old chief dropped to the street, lunging at the youngster who had prepared to fire at Henry Buck. White Bird cocked his arm into the air. Eight, nine, ten times he savagely lashed the quirt across the offender's face and shoulders, back and arms, raising angry red welts wherever it landed, while the warrior pitifully cried out for his friends to pull the old man off.

When the youngster finally collapsed against the storefront, shielding his face behind a pair of bleeding forearms, White Bird ceased his furious attack, took a step back, and dropped his arm to his side. Then he called out in a loud, sure voice.

Two of the older men pushed their way through the cordon of young warriors, grabbed the offender by his wounded arms, and heaved him onto a nearby pony. Bellowing like a bull, White Bird motioned them in the direction of their camp.

Once the two guards were on the way with their young prisoner, the old chief turned to the rest of the drunken crowd, berating them, waving his quirt in the air threateningly.

As his brothers shoved the bolt through its lock on the double doors, Henry watched the old chief disperse the drunken rowdies and young trouble-makers, driving them off toward their ponies.

Only as the noise died down and the hard-eyed, sullen young men drifted away from the front of the store and out of town* did Henry realize he was trembling like a leaf in a spring gale. Listening to his heart pound in his ears. Remembering how that whiskeyed-up warrior had pointed his rifle at him through the window.

Henry never wanted to be that close to death again, not for a long, long time.

---

*The older men managed to evacuate Stevensville about 3:00 P.M., having spent more than three thousand dollars in gold coin, dust, and paper currency. Out at the Silverthorne camp that night, unscrupulous traders arrived with ammunition and powder to sell to the Non-Treaty bands.

CHAPTER FORTY-SIX

WA-WA-MAI-KHAL, 1877

BY TELEGRAPH

ILLINOIS.

Remains of General Custer at Chicago—Other News Items.
CHICAGO, July 31.—The remains of General Custer arrived here to-day from Fort Lincoln, and were forwarded at 5:15 p.m. by the Michigan Southern railroad, to West Point, where they will be interred in the receiving vault until the funeral in October. The remains of Colonel Cooke, Lieutenant Reilly, and Dr. DeWolf arrived on the same train . . .

IT WAS THOSE MEAN BOYS WHO WERE FOLLOWERS OF OLD TOOHOOLHOOLzote—they were the troublemakers.

They were the ones lapping up a lot of the whiskey and making bold talk about what they would do if Cut-Off Arm and his soldiers ever caught up. These bad ones wanted to have another big fight with the army, even though most of the people believed the fighting was over now that they were in Montana, now that Looking Glass and White Bird had made a pact with the little chief and Shadows in Lolo Canyon, now that they were on the way to a new life in the buffalo country.

So when some hot-blooded young men got together and started talking tough with noplace to go where they could prove just how tough they were, Bird Alighting realized those bad-tempered ones were likely to cause some trouble. With no other way to get the fighting steam out of their systems, the mean boys rode away from the Non-Treaty camp,* itching for something that would break the boredom of camping and marching, camping and marching a little farther each day. Bird Alighting knew that bunch was up to no good the moment they thundered out of camp, most of them red to the gills with some whiskey brought into camp on a trader's wagon come out of Stevensville.

He was certain the swaggering youngsters had let the wolf out to howl by

*By now past Sweathouse Creek, farther up the Bitterroot valley.

the time they came roaring back late that afternoon, leading seven stolen horses.

"Did you kill any Shadows while you were away disobeying me?" Looking Glass shrieked at *Toohoolhoolzote*'s young hotbloods the moment he had them stopped at the southern edge of the village.

"No," one of them replied in a surly manner as their ponies pranced around the chief and some of the older men. "Everyone is gone—so we weren't lucky enough to find any Shadows we could torture and kill!"

The rest in the party laughed along with their brassy leader, then stopped abruptly when Looking Glass hauled the arrogant leader to the ground. He stood over the youth, glaring down at him, trembling as he pointed at the stolen horses.

"Where did you get these Shadow ponies?"

"How do you know they are not my horses?" retorted the leader as he slowly got to his feet, rubbing a scuffed-up shoulder.

Grabbing hold of the callow youth's elbow and wrenching him around, Looking Glass pointed a finger at the picture scar on one horse's rear flank. "Is that a Shadow brand?"

"I-I—"

"Then this is a Shadow horse you stole!" the chief snapped.

"There was no one there to watch over them," the leader explained, turning with an impish grin to the rest of his friends, "so we took them."

Slamming the heel of his palm against the big youngster's chest, Looking Glass knocked the horse thief backward two steps as he thundered, "You have broken my promise to the Shadows!"

"The white men have no need of knowing," *Toohoolhoolzote* said as he stepped up beside the young man.

Looking Glass glared at them both. "It was *my* word," he snarled. "These stupid boys have broken my word not to cause any trouble as we pass through the Bitterroot!"

Taking a meaningful step toward the top-hat chief, the shaman said, "They are only horses—"

"*Toohoolhoolzote*, these are yours," Looking Glass chided, shoving the youngster toward the squat medicine man. "If they were my people, I would lay their backs open with a whip."

That old, square-jawed *tewat* began to speak: "But—"

"But," Looking Glass interrupted, "they are yours to discipline. If this happens again—if any man disobeys my orders against causing trouble—then I will see that he is severely punished and left behind."

Again the old shaman began to speak, but before he could, Looking Glass purposefully turned his back on *Toohoolhoolzote* and stuck his face right in that of the young leader.

"On second thought . . . I will discipline these stupid boys," he growled.

The young horse thief's eyes quickly snapped at *Toohoolhoolzote*, then back to Looking Glass.

"I want all of you to pick out one of your own horses from those you own," Looking Glass ordered, "and if you don't own another, then you will give me the one you are riding at this moment."

"W-what do you want our horses for?" the leader asked.

"You will take me back to where you stole the Shadow horses," Looking Glass declared sharply. "There you will leave your horses in place of the ones you stole."

Bird Alighting and others rode with Looking Glass when the horse thieves led them to the white man's ranch house and corral. The poles the young warriors had removed from a section of the corral lay scattered on the ground; the door to the cabin hung open. Inside they found how the young troublemakers had rooted through it all, breaking and destroying everything they did not want to carry away with them.*

"Build a fire over there," Looking Glass ordered the young thieves.

"Are you going to burn some of this?" the leader demanded, grinning, some haughtiness returning to his voice.

"No, I'm going to find this Shadow's iron marker and you are going to burn his brand into the horses you are giving him," the chief said sourly. "Go build that fire for me, now."

Proof of their raids back in Idaho became evident as some of the Non-Treaty warriors traded off a few horses to ranchers and merchants as they moseyed up the valley at a leisurely, unconcerned pace—animals that bore the brand scars of their Idaho owners. Here as they neared the head of the Bitterroot, Bird Alighting realized why Looking Glass was doing right by this individual settler: Maintaining the goodwill of these Montana Shadows was crucial to the success of a new life outside their ancient homeland.

In fact, if they were to be sure that relations with the white people of Montana did not disintegrate as they had in Idaho country, Looking Glass and the older men had to be constantly vigilant, assuring that the young men did not ride off and do something stupid to reignite the flames of war. In this case, the chiefs were clearly as anxious as the Bitterroot Shadows to avoid trouble.

Every time one of the white men had appeared with a wagonload of trade goods near the camp as the People slowly migrated up the Bitterroot valley, the older men remained close to the visitor so they could assure that the young hotbloods fomented no trouble while the women purchased flour and cloth, and even some cartridges for the guns, although a few of the white men charged as high as one dollar a bullet.

But the *Nee-Me-Poo* had money! Lots of it: the Shadows' paper currency, silver and gold coins from Idaho, and sacks of gold dust earned in trade or taken in those first raids. A dollar a cartridge? That was no problem! After all, each of those bullets would kill a buffalo, making meat and providing another winter robe for the women to tan once they reached the land of their friends the *E-sue-gha*.

---

*Myron Lockwood later put in a claim for $1,600 for the loss of not only some horses and a few cattle but also a supply of flour, all his busted furniture, some harness chopped up, and three of his favorite shirts.

Far up the Bitterroot, where the terrain no longer lay flat, the valley narrowed and the slopes of the Bitterroot and the Sapphires closed in as the village began its ascent toward the nearby passes. But first, the *Nee-Me-Poo* temporarily halted their migration to pay homage at the Medicine Tree,* an ancient and hallowed site for them and the area's Flathead. For generations beyond remembrance the Non-Treaty bands had been coming and going by this spot, migrating between their homes and the buffalo country. Even before the arrival of the first pale-skinned Boston men, they had stopped to make offerings and pray at the base of this tree.

More than eight feet off the ground, embedded at the base of a large branch, hung the bleached skull and horns of a mountain sheep—those bony remains more encircled with every season as the ancient yellow ponderosa pine inexorably grew around that timeworn skull.**

Pausing briefly here in this region cloaked with heavy mystery and sure signs of the supernatural at work, the women came up, dragging young children they hushed as the People crowded around the tree's enormous base. With murmurs of prayers and praise, men and women alike tied offerings of cloth or ribbon, tobacco or strips of buckskin, even some copper-cased cartridges, to the branches and limbs, each item attendant with a special and heartfelt prayer . . . for this was known to the *Nee-Me-Poo* as the wishing tree.

Found along many Indian trails, these renowned "wishing" sites offered a traveler the opportunity to make his or her prayers for success in some current undertaking, be it as innocent as a new love affair or a hunting trip or as serious as a deadly foray against a powerful enemy. Far, far back into the days of the ancient ones, the Non-Treaty bands had believed this sacred tree itself would not only grant the wishes of those women who made their prayers at its base but also give their men the power of mastering horses and killing game for the survival of their people. There were powerful forces at work in this place of great mystery. Now that they were closing on the buffalo country, their prayers to such spirits would be vital to the survival of the bands—

"*Kapsisniyut!*" Lone Bird exclaimed. "This is a bad and evil thing I see!"

Everyone suddenly turned the man's way as he stumbled in approaching the base of the tree, collapsing to his knees—eyes rolling back in their sockets—a long moment while the crowd grew hushed.

Bird Alighting rushed to the man's elbow, supporting this warrior known as *Peopeo Ipsewahk*. As the frightened women pulled their children against

---

*This colossal tree dating back to the 1700s still stands east of U. S. Highway 93 a few miles south of present-day Darby, Montana.

**For many years the local settlers protected this revered religious icon. Some time after the Nez Perce war, the skull was chopped out of the tree by a local lumberjack, roaring drunk at the time. After hearing that irate locals were planning to lynch him for his desecration of this sacred object, the man fled for safer parts. As the tale is told, he had only meant to adorn the wall of his favorite saloon in nearby Skalkaho (present-day Hamilton, Montana).

their legs, everyone inching back to give Lone Bird a broad circle, the warrior's eyes slowly focused on the Medicine Tree's highest branches and he began to explain in a trembling voice.

"I have just had a dream given me while I was awake!" he spoke in a loud voice. "A dream of what is to come," he said a little quieter but even more emphatically. "A great heartbreak, a terrible tragedy, is about to befall us if we tarry too long in making our way into the land of the buffalo! *Koiimzi!* Hurry! We cannot wait; we cannot linger!"

Never before had Bird Alighting heard the slightest fear enter Lone Bird's voice. An icy-cold fingernail scraped itself down his spine.

All too true: They were moving slowly—taking as much as nine days to march the one hundred Shadow miles it would take to get from the mouth of the Lolo Canyon to reach the Big Hole Prairie.

"We are going, Lone Bird," consoled Looking Glass as he stepped to the man's side. "We are marching to the land of the *E-sue-gha*."

Lone Bird reached up to grab the front of Looking Glass's shirt as he leaped to his feet again. "No! I feel the breath of *hattia tinukin*, the death wind, on my neck," he pleaded. "We are taking too long, too long!"

White Bird himself shouldered his way through the fringe of the murmuring crowd and confronted the two men, glaring at Looking Glass with worry graying his wrinkled face. "See, Looking Glass? For the past two days I myself have told you we should leave the lodgepoles behind and hurry, hurry! The women can cut more another place."

"The war is far behind us!" Looking Glass argued, shrugging, his palms to the sky.

"Dragging our lodgepoles is making us too slow!" White Bird snapped.

"But we have children and women, a big herd of horses," the head chief explained.

"Yes!" Lone Bird warned, turning from Looking Glass, his frightened eyes searching out others in the front ranks of that hushed crowd shrinking back from his nightmare vision. "My dream showed me how we are moving too slow. Far too slow . . . on this trail that will bring us death—"

"Just on the other side of these heights is the *Iskumtselakik*,"* Looking Glass scoffed. "And Cut-Off Arm is far, far behind us. Besides, the Shadows of Montana have shown themselves to be our friends. They trade with us; they sell us what we need for our travels. We have left the war far behind us—"

"No! Even as we stand here, the death wind is already coming up behind us!" Lone Bird whirled, pointing down the valley in the direction they had come.

Past the little settlement of Corvallis. On past Stevensville and their big earthen fort. Perhaps even past the mouth of Lolo Creek toward the community of Missoula City itself.

"I have seen the face of death," Lone Bird whispered in the stillness of that hushed assembly, "the death that is already stalking our trail!"

---

*What the *Nee-Me-Poo* called the Place of the Ground Squirrels, the valley of the Big Hole.

Bitter Root Mountains
Camp Spurgin in the Field
August 1, 1877

Darling Wife,

Last night we had rather an unpleasant time, but I was somewhat comforted with your letter of the Saturday after my departure, and was made happy in your saying that you are all well, or were so when I left. I said we had a rather unpleasant night of it, for we went to bed without our tents, and it began to rain about midnight. So I had to get up and make a shelter with a tent fly which I had laid on the ground as a sort of mattress. Doctor Newlands and I were bunking together. However, we finally made it comfortable and rain proof, and then slept on till morning.

Got up at 5 A.M. but did not march until 11 A.M., and then only went 8 miles and made the nicest camp we have yet had in among partially wooded hills, or rather, mountains. We had some fine mountain views yesterday and today. We were so high up that the whole extent of mountainous country was spread around us. Tomorrow we are to march about 18 miles and make camp on the Clearwater River, the same river that runs by the Agency, only we shall find it a mere mountain brook that can be easily forded by the men and horses. I shall think then of my darlings, and make the stream a little mental address about going down to the Lapwai and leaving a message from me to those I so love.

Captain Spurgin, 21st Infantry, caught up with our army last night, and today some beef cattle arrived to serve as food for us all, poor things. We find for the last 3 nights hardly any grass for our horses and pack mules. It is very poor, indeed, and we shall not get any better for 3 or 4 days to come. We are still some 50 miles from the summit of the Bitter Root range of mountains which, you know, is the dividing line between Idaho and Montana Territory. Then we shall have 60 miles more to Missoula. No Indians have been heard of yet, and I suspect that our mountain climbing this week and next will not accomplish any substantial result. The life we lead on such a campaign is very rough, and it would puzzle many to account for the fact that it is, to some extent, enjoyable. Only when the elements frown upon us does it seem discouraging. Last evening and night, and also this morning, everyone looked disgusted with everything, but we made an early and very pleasant camp after a short day's march, and presto, everybody is changed, and a generally cheerful aspect prevails.

I hope, Darling, that this scribble will find you all well. Tell Bert that Papa is coming back to his place at the table and home just as soon as he can. Tell him that when I was riding along in the big woods today, I came upon a poor little Indian pony which had been left behind, and it followed us into camp. If I was only going towards home, I would try and bring it in for him. Tell Bessie, my girl, that Papa yesterday saw a great many beautiful flowers along the way, and they made me think of my little girl. I wish I could send her some fresh ones. As it is, I will put it in for you, Dear, and a sprig of heather in bloom which is all about our camp tonight. I gathered an armful of it to spread my blankets on for my bed tonight. I wish, Darling, you would write—every chance you get. I will endeavor to do the same.

Your loving,
John

Remember me to the Sternbergs and the Boyles.

CHAPTER FORTY-SEVEN

AUGUST 2–7, 1877

BY TELEGRAPH

MONTANA.

Progress of the Indian War.
PORTLAND, July 30.—General Howard is at present at Kamia, awaiting the arrival of Major Sanford, and as soon as that officer joins him, Howard will take all the available forces and push vigorously on after Joseph and White Bird, who have already crossed Bitter Root mountains by way of the Lolo trail. He will go to Missoula as rapidly as his command can move. He will have in the neighborhood of five hundred men. Another force, under command of General Wheaton, will leave Fort Lapwai and pass through the Spokane country over into Montana, through Sahon pass. After crossing the mountains the troops will push down to Missoula, where they will join General Howard. It is expected that Howard's and Wheeler's detachments will reach that point simultaneously.

HE HAD BEEN THE FIRST WHITE MAN TO VIEW THE STRIPPED, BLOATED, mutilated bodies of more than 220 dead soldiers offered up on that hot, grassy ridge beside the Little Bighorn River as if in sacrifice to some heathen deity.

First Lieutenant James H. Bradley was his name. Seventh U. S. Infantry; serving under Colonel John Gibbon out of Fort Shaw on the Sun River in north central Montana Territory.

This past May Bradley had celebrated his thirty-third birthday. Uneventful his life had been until April 1861, when seventeen-year-old Jim left his place of birth—Sandusky County, Ohio—and marched off to war with the Fourteenth Ohio Volunteers. Taken prisoner and held for half a year by the Confederates, he was released in time to serve during the siege of Atlanta. By the time he was discharged at the end of the war he had risen to the rank of sergeant with the Forty-fifth Ohio Volunteers.

The remembrance of those long, deadly days on the outskirts of Atlanta always made the young soldier smile at the ironic twists his life had taken. With Reconstruction under way across the Confederated states, he fell in love with and married a daughter of the Old South, her father, an Atlanta physician—his Miss Mary Beech.

Knowing what little opportunity he had to return home to at the end of the war, Bradley enlisted in the regular army, serving with the Eighteenth U. S. Infantry—which engaged against the Lakota at Crazy Woman's Fork in Dakota Territory during the early days of the Bozeman Road—before he was transferred to the Seventh U. S. Infantry in 1871, along with a promotion to first lieutenant.

The young lieutenant and his wife were soon blessed with the first of two daughters—Bradley called all three his houseful of ladies.

Those who served with him vouchsafed that he was a man absolutely without fear, a true warrior in whom the fighting spirit was aroused in battle. While not as large as many infantrymen of the day, Bradley was lithe and sinewy, ever active and energetic.

Ever since his arrival in Montana Territory, he had endeared himself to many of its earliest pioneers as he tirelessly collected their reminiscences for the possible publication of a book at some future date. In particular, he was fascinated with the early fur trade of the Far West. His collection of narratives was one of the earliest to record the history of Fort Benton and the American Fur Company on the Upper Missouri River. With an insatiable appetite for the history and ethnography of the region, this budding scholar—who was just now joining the ranks of other inquisitive frontier army officers like John G. Bourke and Charles King—hoped his studies would one day provide a comfortable life for him and his Miss Mary and give both their daughters the grand weddings every girl dreams she will have.

But war would remain his chosen profession.

On the evening of 26 June 1876, as he was leading a few Crow scouts and the small advance up the valley where they would eventually discover the grotesque, dismembered bodies of the Custer dead, in some way the lieutenant already sensed what he was about to stumble across. Only a day earlier, he had confided to his journal: "There is not much glory in Indian wars, but it will be worthwhile to have been present at such an affair as this."

He hoped the Seventh Infantry would now have a chance to make a little history—instead of merely witnessing it.

Their colonel commanding had mobilized the Seventh from Camp Baker, Forts Ellis and Shaw, and even out at a tiny way camp pitched beside Dauphin Rapids on the Missouri River to pull together this skimpy force of eight officers and eighty-one* enlisted men.

Gibbon had wired Governor Benjamin F. Potts concerning two possible eventualities, depending upon where the Nez Perce turned once they debouched from the Lolo. If the Non-Treaty bands turned north at the end of the Lolo Trail for the Blackfoot River, Gibbon wanted Potts to have his local militia assist Captain Rawn, who would be forced to follow the Indians

---

*Historians have concluded that Colonel Gibbon was incorrect when he listed seventy-six soldiers on his duty roster for that day.

until the colonel met them somewhere west of Cadotte Pass. But if the hostiles turned south, Potts was to send his volunteers to guard those passes leading into the Big Hole basin, with orders to delay the Non-Treaty bands until Gibbon could catch them from the rear and give a fight.

"Please give instructions," the colonel told the governor, ". . . to have no negotiations whatever with the Indians, and the men should have no hesitancy in shooting down any armed Indians they meet not known to belong to one of the peaceful tribes."

Rendezvousing just west of Cadotte Pass with eight troopers from the Second U. S. Cavalry out of Fort Ellis, they soon met wagons loaded with families and their meager belongings, civilians escaping the western sections of the state. Near New Chicago, several small parties of militia from Pioneer and Deer Lodge, already on the way to the Bitterroot, joined Gibbon's men.

Accompanied by the eight cavalrymen, the colonel himself had pressed ahead of his column for Missoula City with all possible dispatch, reaching the community on 2 August. There he commandeered some wagons to be sent back for his foot soldiers and pack-master Hugh Kirkendall's mule train from Fort Shaw.

Bradley himself reached Captain Rawn's post the next afternoon with the rest of Gibbon's undermanned column. At this early stage of the pursuit, the colonel maintained the optimism that he could overtake the slow-moving village within two days by making long, forced marches.

"I speculated the same thing you did, General," Charles Rawn disclosed to Gibbon, using the colonel's highest brevet rank awarded for gallantry in the Civil War. "Utilizing locals and some of my own men as spies, I've managed to keep an eye on the hostiles, charting their movements every day. We should be able to overhaul them in a matter of days and bring them to a fight."

"They're headed over the mountains by their normal route, Captain?" Bradley asked Rawn.

"They'll have to go through Big Hole Prairie. Two days ago when I wasn't proof certain of when you'd arrive, I wired Governor Potts that I would lead some fifty or sixty regulars in pursuit, knowing full well I'd have to temporize my march so that you or General Howard could catch up before I overtook the rear of the hostile village."

"What do your sources tell you the bands are doing, Captain?" Bradley asked. "Are they moving any faster the closer they get to the head of the valley?"

"No, Lieutenant," Rawn said. "If anything, they appear to dawdle a little more each of the last few days. I've become pretty well satisfied that they will not hurry out of the Bitterroot until they know that one army or the other has arrived to give them chase. Not surprisingly, they have been keeping a watch on us, too, and therefore know everything that's going on with us."

"How many warriors do you estimate are with them at this point?" inquired Bradley, who would be in charge of a small detail of scouts.

Rawn turned to the lieutenant and said, "At least two hundred and fifty."

His eyes squinting with determination and a heap of keen anticipation,

Bradley looked at Colonel Gibbon and declared, "That ought to make for a damn good scrap of it, sir."

BY TELEGRAPH

KANSAS.

An Imposing Military Funeral at Fort Leavenworth. LEAVENWORTH, Ks., August 3.—Yesterday evening the Chicago, Rock Island and Pacific brought the remains of Captains Yates and Custer, Liets. McIntosh, Smith, Calhoun and Worth. The bodies were placed in the Post chapel, and a guard of honor was stationed and remained during the night. This morning a large number of people visited the chapel and viewed the caskets containing the remains of the honored dead . . . The procession was formed, and the remains taken to the cemetery, about one mile distant, upon artillery caissons. Each caisson was drawn by two bay horses. Following each caisson was a horse caparisoned in mourning, and led by a cavalry soldier, according to the custom of the funeral ceremonies for officers in the cavalry service. During the march to the cemetery, minute guns were fired and flags lowered to half-mast . . . Arriving at the Post cemetery, the Episcopal service was read and a salute of three volleys was fired over the graves. The ceremonies were very imposing. All the arrangements were complete and carried out in perfect order. It was estimated that there were nearly three hundred carriages in the procession . . . The fact that the lamented dead had lived at that garrison and were well known and honored by our people created an intense feeling of sympathy among the entire community. Five of the brave soldiers in the army have thus been tenderly placed in their final resting place in the beautiful Leavenworth cemetery with all the honors due to men of noble and daring deeds, and their memory will be cherished by every patriot in the land.

Fort Lapwai
Sunday August 5, 1877

Dear Mamma,

It is doleful living alone this way without John and not knowing when he will come home. I don't know how much longer I can get along . . . We are four ladies at the post now. Dr. Sternberg sent for his wife, and she has arrived.

Yesterday the Indian prisoners were taken away from here down to Vancouver. The squaws seemed to feel awfully about being taken away. Some of them moaned and groaned over it at a great rate. I did feel sort of sorry for them, as parts of all their families are still up here. One poor woman moaned and cried and really looked distressed. Just before she left, she took some ornaments of beads and gave them to the interpreter to give to her little girl who is up somewhere near Kamiah. One old man cut the bead ornaments off his moccasins and left them for his wife.

We have not heard anything from General Howard's command up in the Lolo Trail for a week. I wish we could hear! We have had all sorts of rumors about the Indians, but we don't know anything. I had a note from John written Monday night at their first camp on the Trail. He said it was a hard mountain trail. They had been all day going 15 miles. It is a zigzag, winding, steep trail, in many places impossible for two to walk abreast, with either rocks or a dense pine forest close on all sides.

There are several companies of troops over on the other side in Montana, and we have heard that the Indians were allowed to pass, but we don't think it possible. We also hear the Indians have gotten back on General Howard's rear . . .

Your loving daughter,
Emily F.

Rationed for twenty days, General O. O. Howard's seven-hundred-thirty-man column struck out for the western terminus of the Lolo Trail beneath a steady, cold, depressing rain early that Monday morning, 30 July.

It had taken more than a day to repair the wire cable across the Clearwater, then two more days to slog the entire command across to the north bank. That final day of preparation, the twenty-ninth, was a Sunday. Howard attended a Presbyterian service conducted in both Nez Perce and English by Archie Lawyer, son of the great treaty chief. It was a chance to offer prayers to the Almighty. And that night, their last beside the Kamiah crossing, the general committed his innermost doubts to paper:

> There is a stern reality in going from all that you love into the dread uncertainty of Indian fighting, where the worst form of torture and death might await you. It is very wise and proper to ask God's blessing when about to plunge into the dark clouds of warfare.

In the advance by four o'clock that Monday morning rode twenty-four members of a tribe that was an ancient enemy of the Nez Perce, Bannock scouts, who had arrived on the twenty-eighth from Fort Boise with Major George B. Sanford of the First U. S. Cavalry. Major John Wesley Green, also of the First, would be along soon, temporarily delayed with two infantry companies at the nearby mining community of Florence. Above their traditional leggings of buckskin or antelope hide the Bannock wore army tunics of dark blue, gaily set off with bright sashes of stars and stripes fashioned from old garrison flags. They were led by Buffalo Horn, who, just two days before departing Fort Boise, had returned to his people after serving Colonel Nelson A. Miles during the last skirmishes of the Great Sioux War.* Despite the rain that fell in sheets, Buffalo Horn and his fellow trackers were eager to hunt down the fleeing village filled with their longtime enemies. With the arrival of these Indian scouts, the general dismissed McConville's volunteers mustered from the rural settlements of eastern Washington.

The quartermaster had seen to it the column was supplied with rations for twenty days, along with additional beeves on the hoof. Howard designated Lewiston as the main depot for his army in the field, leaving orders that the general staff was to keep the depot well furnished with at least three months' supplies on hand. Forage would not be carried along, because the general and his officers believed they could obtain what they needed for their stock along the way.

The column's supplies would be transported on the backs of a long train of more than 350 mules, in addition to what mules were needed to carry the dismantled Coehorn mortar** and drag the two Gatling guns and a pair of mountain howitzers over the rugged Lolo Trail. This march would prove itself to be like no other since Hannibal himself had crossed the Alps.

From the Kamiah crossing of the Clearwater, the rain-soaked, slippery trail was an ordeal Howard likened to a monkey climbing a greased rope, as it angled northeast for sixteen miles toward the *Weippe* Prairie—where the soldiers found that the Nez Perce women had dug up much of the lush camas meadows—then would extend almost due east into the Bitterroot Mountains for more than a hundred miles of narrow ridges and harrowing precipices, not to mention boggy mires where man and beast sank to their knees and slapped at blood-devouring mosquitoes or that fallen timber so thick an exasperated Howard believed a man could cross from one side of the Lolo to the other stepping only on downed trees, without his feet once touching the ground.

Eleven years before, at the time of both the Idaho and Montana gold rushes, Congress had funded a party of axmen and former Civil War engi-

---

***Wolf Mountain Moon*, vol. 12, and *Ashes of Heaven*, vol. 13, the *Plainsmen* series.

**A small bronze, twenty-four-pounder, Model 1841, used primarily as a seige or garrison mortar, mounted on a sturdy wooden bed. With a maximum range of 1,200 yards, this fieldpiece, including its bed, weighed about 296 pounds, and was easily transported by a mule. This particular gun had not been used in the Battle of the Clearwater, so I have to presume it arrived with the fresh batteries of the Fourth Artillery from San Francisco.

neers under Wellington Bird and Sewell Truax to survey and build a road over the Bitterroot. It was, by and large, this narrow, primitive "wagon road" that the Nez Perce had started out on a full two weeks before General Howard ever got under way, his column following the same exhausting path toward Montana Territory—fighting their way over and around trees felled by high winds and heavy, wet snowfall, over and across the remnants of once-massive snowdrifts. On either side of the plodding column arose peaks rising more than seven thousand feet high, all still blanketed with a thick mantle of white that day by day became moisture draining into the Middle Fork of the Clearwater on the west, into the Bitterroot River to the east.

So slow was their pace that it did not take long every morning for the entire command to find itself strung out for more than five, sometimes as many as six, miles in length.

"How far ahead of us do you think Joseph's village is now?" Howard once asked Ad Chapman near the end of a day's march.

The civilian had shrugged, clearly unsure of how to answer. "Far enough I fear we won't catch 'em less'n they stay put for a time, General. No man can get so much out of a horse as an Indian can."

Almost from the first day they began to come upon remnants of the Indians' passage: horses abandoned with serious wounds and broken limbs, other ponies already dead and stiffening upon the trail. At many of the tightest switchbacks and where the Nez Perce had forced themselves through tight stands of trees, the soldiers found streaks of blood and bits of horsehide still clinging from the busted branches.

Just behind the Bannock scouts, who ranged far in the lead, a unit of fifty skilled civilian "pioneers" hired by Jack Carleton, a Lewiston timberman, all of whom served under Captain William F. Spurgin of the Twenty first Infantry, labored day after day after day with their axes and two-man crosscuts to chop down and saw their way through that knotty maze of timber slowing the army's progress. When there was time, Spurgin's "skillets," as they were affectionately called by the soldiers, built bridges across rocky chasms and improved portions of the dangerous trail by corduroying with timber or shoring up muddy walls with fragments of rock.

Up every morning with reveille at four. Breakfast by five. On the march no later than six. One long, arduous afternoon as they plodded toward the pass, correspondent Thomas Sutherland reined to the side of the trail to let others pass by while he let his horse catch its breath.

He called out, "General!"

"Yes, Mr. Sutherland?" Howard asked as his horse slowly carried him past the newsman.

"I was wondering if you intended to kill all your men by these hard marches, rather than waiting for them to have the chance to kill Joseph!"

It rained every afternoon, long enough to soak through their woolen garments and make the trail a slippery, mucky, sticky obstacle to be endured. Many evenings when they finally limped into bivouac after 6:00 P.M., the men were mud-caked from chin to toe. But a cheery fire and a little sunshine as that bright orb fell from the undergut of those dark clouds to the west did much to raise any flagging spirits, despite a monotonous diet of salt pork, hardbread, an occasional dollop of potatoes while they lasted, and plenty of coffee to wash it down.

The column ended up losing a little of its crackers and some of its bacon the fourth day out, abandoned along the way with the injured and broken-down mules carrying those packs up the torturous loops of the Lolo Trail.

Not only did the unbelievably rugged terrain hamper the speed of the march, but so did the fact that the men could water only a few of their horses and mules at a time when they ran across those infrequent springs and freshets on their climb toward the Continental Divide. In addition, at one stop after another, the soldiers failed to find enough forage to fill their weakening stock. The Nez Perce herd had grazed nearly all of the coarse, non-nutritious wire grass down to its roots.

That, and the cocky defiance of the hostiles, infuriated Howard to no end. On the fourth day, the Bannocks located a beautifully executed carving of an Indian bow, whittled out of the bark of a dark pine tree growing alongside the trail. The bow and its arrow were pointed to the rear—clearly meant to strike Howard and those soldiers who were following.

That same afternoon the general's advance heard the dim rattle of gunfire up the trail. He and others hurried ahead, fearing the Bannock had been ambushed by a rear guard, but found instead his trackers, scouts, and some of Spurgin's pioneers standing knee-deep in the headwaters of a gushing creek, shooting salmon with their carbines. That night, most of the column had a brief change in diet.

Then on 4 August as the head of the column entered a pretty mountain glade dotted with swampy ponds and the lushest green grass, disappointing news arrived with James Cearly and Joseph Baker, those two Mount Idaho couriers he had sent south over the Old Nez Perce Trail with dispatches for Captain Rawn. They rode up to Howard that Saturday afternoon, accompanied by Wesley Little, who had run across the couriers on the Elk City Road and ended up accompanying the pair all the way to Missoula City.

Rawn, he learned, along with his small force of soldiers and a large contingent of civilian volunteers, had somehow allowed the Nez Perce to get around them and exit the canyon into the Bitterroot valley. In fact, they were reportedly camped near the small community of Corvallis and were likely to move toward Big Hole Prairie on the Elk City Trail. And according to the dispatch brought him from Captain Charles Rawn, Colonel John Gibbon was momentarily expected from Fort Shaw, along with a small force of his Seventh U. S. Infantry.

The captain addressed his note to Howard:

> Start tomorrow to try to delay them, as per your letter and Gen'l. Gibbon's order. Will get volunteers if I can. Have sent word to Gov. Potts, that it appears from information gained from men who know the country, that the Indians intend to go through Big Hole or Elk City trail. By sending his 300 Militia

> ordered mustered in, direct from Deer Lodge to Big
> Hole Prairie, can head them off.

The only bright spot these revelations brought Howard was that, at the very least, now he no longer had to fear that Joseph's warriors would lay an ambush for his column somewhere along the Lolo Trail or fear that the village would double around and sneak back to the Camas Prairie, where they would recommence their deviltry, destruction, and murderous rampage.

Dropped right in his lap at that moment was the justification for splitting his force and attempting a junction with Gibbon. Hope rekindled, the glimmer of victory sprang eternal in his breast. Howard was about to put the frustratingly slow pace of the climb up the west side of the pass behind him.

On the following morning of 5 August, after they had awakened to ice in their water buckets, the general impatiently pushed ahead with his staff, the "skillets," and part of his pack train. Riding out at dawn with them and seventeen of the trackers were Major George B. Sanford's cavalry and Captain Marcus P. Miller's artillery battalion—who were serving as mounted infantrymen—leaving the foot soldiers and most of the pack train to follow behind at its slower pace. With this detached advance of some 192 cavalrymen, thirteen officers, and twenty of the Bannock scouts, in addition to one officer and fifteen artillerymen given charge of both mountain howitzers and that Coehorn mortar, Howard hurried for the summit of the pass, hoping to reach the Bitterroot valley in time to form a junction with Gibbon's undermanned infantry as quickly as possible.

While Joe Baker would continue as a guide for Howard, the general sent Cearly and Little on west to Lapwai, carrying messages for McDowell and Sherman.

The following day, 6 August, this fast-moving advance nooned at Summit Prairie,* where they finally gazed down into Montana Territory. They had crossed from McDowell's Division of the Pacific and entered General Alfred H. Terry's Department of Dakota, part of Philip Sheridan's Division of the Missouri. From here on out Howard was acting upon the direct orders of the commander of the army himself, William Tecumseh Sherman, ordered to forsake all administrative boundaries in running down the Nez Perce to their surrender or to the death.

From there Howard pressed on until they reached the lush meadows that surrounded the numerous hot springs. It was this afternoon of the sixth that Joe Pardee, one of Gibbon's civilian couriers, reached the Idaho column, explaining that the colonel's men had struck south from Missoula City two days before, pressing up the Bitterroot with all possible dispatch. Gibbon was requesting a hundred of Howard's cavalry. That electrifying news, and this beautiful spot with its magically recuperative powers, went far to lifting the spirits of every officer and enlisted man, newly cheered to learn they were closing on the Nez Perce.

---

*Present-day Packer Meadows.

That following morning, the general composed a message for Gibbon that he himself was hurrying ahead with 200 horsemen:

> I shall join you in the shortest possible time. I would not advise you to wait for me before you get to the Indians, then if you can create delay by skirmishing, by parleying, or maneuvering in any way, so that they shall not get away from you, do so by all means if you think best till I can give you the necessary reinforcements. I think however that the Indians are very short of ammunition, and that you can smash them in pieces if you can get an engagement out of them. Your judgment on the spot will be better than mine. I will push forward with all my might.

This same morning he would send his quartermaster, First Lieutenant Robert H. Fletcher, ahead to the Missoula post with frontiersman Pardee, asking that rations and forage for his stock be waiting for him at the mouth of Lolo Creek.

If he hadn't felt McDowell's spur before, General Oliver Otis Howard sensed it cruelly raking his ribs at this moment. He found himself in another commander's department.

Joseph's hostiles were almost within reach.

Now the race was on.

CHAPTER FORTY-EIGHT

AUGUST 4–7, 1877

BY TELEGRAPH

News from the Indian War.

WASHINGTON.

General Sherman's Report: Pittsburgh Wants a Garrison.

WASHINGTON, August 4.—General Sherman, in a letter to the secretary of war, says: "With the new post at the fork of Big and Little Horn rivers and that at the mouth of the Tongue river, occupied by enterprising garrisons, the Sioux Indians can never regain that country, and they can be forced to remain at their agency or take refuge in the British possessions. The country west of the new post has good country and will rapidly fill up with emigrants, who will, in the next ten years, build up a country as strong and as capable of self defense as Colorado. The weather has been as intensely hot as is Texas. I am favorably impressed with the balance of this country on the upper Yellowstone . . .

"IF YOU CAN DO WITHOUT THE SLEEP, SERGEANT," THE GENERAL SAID AS he peered up at the veteran noncommissioned officer, "it will be a feather in your cap to reach General Gibbon that much earlier."

First Sergeant Oliver Sutherland saluted, his backbone snapping rigid there in the saddle as he gazed down at General O. O. Howard. "Sir, I'll do my damnedest to stay bolted to this saddle until I have delivered your dispatch to General Gibbon."

Howard took two steps back, joining the ranks of his headquarters staff and a gaggle of more than a hundred curious soldiers and civilians as Sutherland jabbed the heels of his cavalry boots behind the ribs of that well-fed and watered cavalry mount he would ride on down Lolo Creek, reaching the Bitterroot valley, where he was to chase after the rear of Colonel John Gibbon's pursuit of the fleeing Nez Perce camp.

The general and his advance had been the first to reach the hot springs on the downhill side of the pass, with the rest of the command not trudging in till late that afternoon. Sutherland was amazed at just how fast the men could get shed off their clothing, flinging off their boots and stripping out of greasy sweat-caked trousers to ease themselves down into the steamy pools. After that initial plunge, the soldiers dragged their clothing into the steamy water with them as the sun sank behind the Bitterroot Mountains, doing what they could to scrub weeks of campaigning from their shirts, stockings, and britches, not to mention the frayed and graying underwear. Soon it had all the makings of a laundresses' camp, what with all the wet clothing airing on every bush, hanging from every limb.

It was as Sutherland was dragging his limp, but renewed, body out of the sulphurous waters that a civilian and a Flathead warrior rode into camp. The tall, lanky frontiersman dropped to the ground, announcing that he was carrying a message from Gibbon for the general.

"The Seventh Infantry departed Missoula City on the fourth," Howard told those hundreds who crowded around the two riders from the valley. "He's requested one hundred men to overtake his column before he pitches into the hostiles. I believe I alone can drive my troops more miles in a day than an officer less spurred by a sense of responsibility than myself. Therefore, I resolve to start in the morning with this advance force intact, marching as fast as possible with those two hundred men in hopes of reaching Gibbon before he reaches Joseph's camp."

Suddenly it appeared Howard was struck by a thought that caused a crease of intensity to furrow his brow. The general turned round, spotted the officer he sought in the front ranks of the crowd, and called out, "Captain Jackson, select your best rider! A steady man, one enured to hardship—one who can make the ride without faltering."

"The ride, General?" asked James B. Jackson.

"I want a man I can depend on—no, a man General Gibbon can depend on—to get my message through."

Without a flicker of hesitation, Jackson turned on his heel and quickly located the half-naked Sutherland in the crowd.

"Sergeant Sutherland?"

"I'll be back with my horse inside twenty minutes, Cap'n," he had answered. "No sir, Gen'ral Howard. Beggin' your pardon—I'll be ready to ride in *ten* minutes, sir."

Now he was loping through the gathering darkness, speeding toward the mouth of Lolo Creek beside that taciturn Flathead who had accompanied civilian Joe Pardee to Howard's camp.

The sergeant's real name was Sean Dennis Georghegan. Wasn't all that odd a happenstance for a man to have his name changed once he set foot on the shores of Amerikay. Not long after reaching his adopted homeland, Sutherland had volunteered for the Union Army, rising in rank to serve as a noncom in the Eighteenth Infantry, regulars. Later in that war against the rebellious Southern states, Sutherland was transferred to the Tenth Infantry, where he distinguished himself in battle and rose to become a second lieutenant by the time the cease-fire was called at Appomattox. Rather than return back to the Northeast, Sutherland itched for more travel and adventure. He scratched his itch by enlisting in the postwar First Cavalry and coming west.

An arduous ride awaited the sergeant as both a gathering darkness and an intermittent rain descended upon the two horsemen. But this was just the sort of adventure a hardened boyo like himself had prepared for. Trouble was, the adventure awaiting Oliver Sutherland was not anything like the Irishman had planned.

Upon reaching the mouth of Lolo Creek and the Bitterroot River as first light embraced the western slopes, the Flathead did his best to shrug and gesture, attempting to communicate that he was not going any farther with the soldier. He pointed off to the north, in the direction of Missoula City, and tapped his chest. Then he signed that the Nez Perce and the other soldiers would be found moving off to the south, somewhere *up* the valley.

It was up to Sutherland alone from here on out.

The sun was refusing to blink its one dull eye through the sullen gray clouds overhead, suspended near midsky, when Sutherland realized his horse had been pushed to its limit and was all but done in from the punishment he had given it over the last eighteen grueling hours. Limping along on that exhausted animal with its bloody, spur-riven sides, the sergeant reined up in the yard of the next ranch he came across, hallooing with a voice disused for the better part of a day.

"I'm bearing dispatches from General Howard to General Gibbon," Sutherland croaked.

"Gibbon, you say? Yes, yes—you'll have to ride right smart to catch Gibbon's bunch."

"How long ago they come by?"

The settler considered that at the door of his small barn. "He streamed it by with his men in their wagons day before yestiddy . . . yes, yes. They've got three days on you now."

"Howard's give me authority to get a remount," Sutherland sighed, his body already aching for that hard road yet to come. "Back down the road, I was told this place might have a horse I could ride. Need to swap you a played-out cavalry mount for one what's fresh, mister," he explained while the settler stepped from the double doors of his small barn, shovel in hand, his britches stuffed down in gum boots, busy at mucking out the horse stalls.

After bounding over to quickly inspect the strong but lathered army horse, the civilian looked up and said, "I ain't got but two sorts. One is big and strong, but a mite slow—there's two of 'em pull my plows and wagon. Only other horse I can swap you is a green colt, half-broke by a neighbor cross the valley. I ain't had time to gentle it to the saddle yet. But by damn if you don't look like a spunky feller."

Sutherland ground his teeth on the dilemma, then hurried his decision. Hundreds of men were counting on him. Bringing a rapid conclusion to this Nez Perce war would depend upon his finishing this ride.

"Bring out that green-broke colt. Howard's quartermaster will settle with you when they come through. While you fetch up the colt I'll take my saddle off this'un here," he grumbled, his brogue thick as blood soup. Then as the settler turned away for the paddock behind the barn, the sergeant asked, "You got a saddle blanket I could swap you? This'un's near soaked through."

The two of them managed to drape a dry saddlepad on the back of that wild-eyed colt they had snubbed up to a fencepost, then laid the McClellan saddle across its spine, drawing up the cinch to tighten it down as the horse sidestepped this way, then that, forcing the two men to scurry left, then right, as they finished the job of securing the snaffle-bit over the animal's muzzle.

He tugged the brim of his shapeless rain-soaked campaign hat down on his brow, then stuffed his hand between the buttons of his shirt, fingertips brushing the folded message he had taken from General Howard's own hand—as if to remind him that he alone had been hand-picked for this duty. Shifting his pistol belt nervously as he glanced one last time at the colt's wide, terror-filled eye, Sutherland seized the reins in hand, then slowly poked his foot into the left stirrup.

"When I'm nested down into this here God-blasted army rockin' chair," he told the grim-faced settler, "you free up that knot and step back, real quick."

"You a good horseman, soldier?"

His puckered ass ground down into the saddle and he heeled up the stirrups, tight as he could. Then swallowed. "I'm a horse soldier, mister. Ain't a horse gonna throw this boyo. Now," and he paused, ". . . let 'im go."

And go that horse did let go. Like lightning uncorked.

Screwing up its back, head tucked south and tail tucked north, nearly folding itself in half, that green-broke colt compressed all its energy on a spot centered just beneath that man stuck on its back. The pony flung itself into the air just starting to rain once more with a fine, soaking mist. As it slammed down hard on all four hooves, Sutherland felt his teeth jar, the side of his tongue grazed painfully, some of the pasty hardtack still digesting in his stomach brutally shoved up against his tonsils.

The sting of bile and the pain beneath his ribs robbed him of breath. As he wheezed in shock, the pony beneath him twisted itself in half again, but sideways this time, attempting to hurl the rider off to the left. From the corner of his eye he saw the fence coming up in a blur as the pony's rear flank wheeled round. Suddenly wondering how in Hades he would get the general's message through with a broken leg, on instinct Sutherland hammered the pony's ribs with his boot heels.

Just inches from that crude lodgepole fence, the colt shot away toward the middle of the corral, racing with its head down for three mad leaps, then twisted sideways again, preparing to uncork itself once more. This time the pony shuffled left, then suddenly right, bounding up and down on its forelegs—each jarring descent to the rain-soaked ground hammering his breakfast against the floor of his tonsils, tasting stomach gall each time he landed with a smack in that damned McClellan saddle.

The wind gusted of a sudden, driving a sheet of the fine mist right into his face. Blinking his eyes that fraction of an instant, he opened them to find the colt tucking its head down as it careened toward the lodgepole fence anew but suddenly planted all four hooves, skidding in the drying mud, jerking to a halt as it flung its rear flanks into the air, catapulting the man ass over teakettle like a cork exploding from a bottle of fermented wine.

For a heartbeat Sutherland found himself suspended upside down, peering at the horse through wondering eyes, unable to make out the fence coming up behind him as he completed that graceful arc out of the gray, rainy sky, but having no time at all to realize anything before he collided with the top rail and a rough-hewn post of that paddock fence.

With a shrill wheeze, the air was driven out of his lungs . . . but it wasn't until after he had landed in a heap at the bottom of the fencepost that he realized he was lying in a shallow puddle. Dragging the side of his face out of the caking mud, Sutherland immediately sensed he had broken something deep inside him. The pain was faint-giving, hot and cold at the same time. Starting cold in his lower spine, as it radiated outward through his gut and lower chest, the agony flared with a white-hot fury.

"You hurt, soldier?" the settler asked as he came over and bent at the waist to stare down at the sergeant.

"Get that g-goddamned horse . . . ," he rasped, then gritted his teeth together and clenched his eyes shut while the pain exploded through him, "tied off again afore I shoot it an' you both."

A whitish look of fear crossed the settler's face as he tore his eyes from the old soldier and straightened, shuffling off toward the pony standing motionless, but for its head bobbing, near the barn doors.

Slowly, gingerly, Sutherland dragged an elbow under him, pushing himself up. The toughest part was the searing pain he caused his body as he attempted to rise. But once he was upright, the waves of nausea slowly dissipated. Only when he tried to twist round or slightly rocked side to side did he have to clench his teeth together to swallow down the bitter taste of gall as his stomach sought to hurl itself against the back of his acid-laced tongue.

Just the sort of motion his body would suffer on the back of a horse, any horse—even a plodding plow horse. But . . . Sergeant Oliver Sutherland, Sean Dennis Georghegan, did not have the luxury of time to find a gentle draft horse—

"Your saddle's broke."

He blinked at the settler. Then glared at the pony with a look of pure hate. The McClellan lay across the muddy, hoof-pocked corral, its cinch broken. "Get me one of yours."

"I ain't got but the one—"

"Get me your goddamned saddle!" he snarled. "General Howard will damn well make it right for you when he comes through in a day or so."

"Day or so? You sure the quartermaster gonna make it right by me? Like I said, them other soldiers is three days ahead—"

Sutherland gripped his holster menacingly. "Get that saddle on, or I'll have to shoot you right after I kill the horse."

The frightened settler's Adam's apple bobbed nervously when he turned away from the old soldier, scurrying into the small barn.

In minutes the civilian had that colt snubbed to another post, the blanket dragged out of the mud and draped across the pony's back before he looped the cinch through its ring.

Sutherland moved slowly, each step its own agony, reaching the horse as the settler pulled up on the strap. "Kick the son of a bitch in the belly."

"What?"

"Said: Kick the goddamned horse in the belly," he wheezed. " 'Cause I can't do it my own self. An' when you do kick it, the bastard's gonna take a deep breath—that's when you pull like the devil to get that cinch tight as it'll go."

He watched the doubtful man do exactly as he had ordered—and, sure enough, the pony was forced to exhale, allowing the civilian to yank the cinch even tighter.

"Now, help me up . . . for I fear I might black out to do it my own self."

"You're hurt," the settler said, suddenly realizing what might be the extent of the soldier's injuries. "Maybe you'd be better off to wait out a few hours to see—"

"I ain't got a few hours," Sutherland cut him off. " 'Sides, my muscles only gonna get tighter every minute we stand here jawing. Get me in the goddamned saddle."

They both grunted as together they raised Sutherland into the old saddle. The sergeant's head swam with an inky blackness, and behind his eyelids swirled a cascade of shooting stars. But he managed to push through the faintness—tasting the bile over the extent of his tongue.

"I got a message to take to General Gibbon," Sutherland explained when his eyes opened at last. "Gotta get to him . . . afore he gets to the Nez Perce."

Sergeant Oliver Sutherland . . . once known as Sean Dennis Georghegan, now studied that length of rope as the knot came untied and the settler stepped back against the fence.

But—for some reason this time the pony did not fling itself about wildly. It fought the bit as he yanked its head to the left but it obediently lurched into motion when the sergeant gently tapped his brass spurs into its flanks.

"I was chose for this mission," Sutherland proudly declared to the civilian as he rode out of the yard for the Bitterroot Trail. "So . . . it's up to me."

He grimaced in pain as every hammering step felt like a cold blast of agony from his tailbone all the way up to the crown of his skull. Yanking up a generous dose of double-riveted courage from some secret well, the sergeant pushed on up the valley, the Bitterroot and Sapphire mountain ranges looming higher and higher, closer, too.

And him sittin' on busted j'ints, blackened with a Welsh miner's crop of bruises, perched on top of the most unlikely of trail horses he'd ever dared to ride!

From time to time, Sutherland clenched his eyes shut and reminded himself, muttering under his breath, "It . . . it's up to me. G-gotta find Gibbon's men afore they lay into that camp of murderin' hostiles."

CHAPTER FORTY-NINE

AUGUST 6–7, 1877

Monday, August 6, 1877

Dear Mamma,

It always does seem as if everything goes wrong when the Doctor is away. Both children are just a little sick, just enough to make them fretful and worry me. I was awake with them many times last night. They seem better this morning and are playing, but my one wish is that the war was over and John home again.

Afternoon

Dr. Sternberg just came in to see the children. They are not well, either of them, and it is so hard to have them get this way when John is away . . .

You should see some of the Indian garments that were taken from the camp the day of the battle when the Indians left in such a hurry. They are made of beautifully tanned skin, soft as chamois skin, and cut something like we used to cut our paper dollie dresses. The bottom is fringed, and the body part down to the waist is heavily beaded. You never saw such bead work, and the beads make them so heavy. These, of course, are the costumes for grand occasions. One of them I could not lift. Then they have leggings to match, and if it is a chief or big man, they have an outfit for his horse of the same style. Doctor Sternberg is an enthusiast on the subject of collecting curiosities, and he purchased from the men who had gotten them four or five of these garments. For one he gave ten dollars in coin, and for another with a horse fixing, 25 dollars. So you can see, they must be handsome . . .

Your affectionate daughter,
E. L. FitzGerald

BY TELEGRAPH

THE INDIANS.

Late News from Joseph and His Brethren: They Will Fight.

SAN FRANCISCO, August 4.—A press dispatch from Lewiston, August 1st says: Yesterday Indians Joseph and his family, who have been with the people at Slate Creek all through the Indian troubles, and proved true and faithful to the whites, returned from Kamiah, where they had been sent to ascertain the movements of the hostiles. His squaw says the hostiles at Kamiah told her they were going across the mountains by the Lolo trail, with their stock and families and when they got there in a secure place they would return and fight the soldiers. She also states that before leaving Kamiah they went to a friendly Indian camp and drove off all the young squaws, beat them with clubs and forced them along, and many cattle also. They came back and robbed them of everything they could find, including all their horses of any value. She further states that the hostiles are to be reinforced by other Indians from the other side of the mountains when they return. Her statements are considered reliable by those who have known her. This morning Lieut. Wilmot with thirty men started to go across Salmon river to ascertain if any hostiles remain there. It has been reported for several days that a few had been seen in that direction, and the object is to hunt them out and destroy all their supplies. It is now believed by old acquaintances of Joseph, that he will put away in safety his stores and extra horses, and return to Comas prairie, returning by Elk City over the Pietee trails, which are much more easily traveled. The march will be made in about seven days. He has asserted his determination to burn the grain on the Comas prairie, and then arrange his plans to go to Willowa, and the opinion is prevalent that he will attack, before they break camp. Couriers say the hostiles have Mrs. Manuel with them as the property of a petty chief called Cucasenilo. Her sad story is familiar.

Camp on the East Lolo
20 miles from Missoula
August 7, 1877

Darling,

The last two days we have been in rather a handsome country, i.e., since we struck the eastern Lolo River, which is a tributary of the Bitter Root River. Last night we had the most picturesque camp I have ever seen—a very remarkable spot where there are 4 hot springs. The steam from them this morning rose up as if from a number of steam mills. I bathed my feet in one of them last night and found it as hot as I could bear comfortably. There was good trout fishing in the Lolo nearby, and Colonel Sanford and I got quite a fine string and had them for breakfast. Today we had a long hard march over the hill and got down on the Lolo again this evening for camp—and in a pretty place. Colonel Sanford and I again had some trout fishing.

We are 20 miles from Missoula, but we learn tonight that the Indians are about 60 miles off, and that General Gibbon is after them with about 200 infantry in wagons, and is within 30 miles of them. We are to push on tomorrow with the cavalry, with a view to overtake him.

The Indians were allowed to pass through this valley by the scalawag population that bought their stolen horses. And it is said some of them traded ammunition, powder, etc., to the redskins for their stolen property, gold dust, etc. We hear that several watches have been traded for by citizens of Missoula, and it is possible that Mr. Theller's watch may be recovered. Mr. Fletcher went into Missoula this morning, and Mr. Ebstein is to go in tomorrow, but our command, the cavalry, is to turn off in another direction about 10 miles this side of Missoula tomorrow. The artillery and infantry are nearly two days behind us, but General Howard and staff are now with the cavalry commands. It seems to me that things look as if we should have an end of it all in a few days or weeks, as the Indians will either be whipped or driven across the line into British possessions. The rumor is that Joseph has left White Bird and Looking Glass and is somewhere in the mountains by himself with his band.

Our poor animals are tired and considerably run down. Old Bill is but a shadow of what he was when I left Lapwai.

Well, Darling wife, how are my precious ones? What a happy hub you will have when his "footsteps homeward he hath turned." I hope you are well. I am and have been, and a large part of the time have rather enjoyed this nomadic life. Do you know, or rather, can you realize, that for nearly every morning of this month we have found ice in our wash basins and buckets? It is rather rough on us to be roused out of our warm beds at 3, 4, or 5 A.M. It almost "takes the hair off," as they say.

Your old husband,
John

T TWO O'CLOCK ON THE AFTERNOON OF 4 AUGUST, COLONEL JOHN GIBbon had finally started his column away from the Missoula City post, his infantry rumbling south in those commandeered wagons, hurrying up the valley of the Bitterroot River in pursuit of the Nez Perce village. After pushing hard for more than twenty-five miles, at nine o'clock that night they went into bivouac opposite the community of Stevensville, camping on the southern outskirts of town located on the east side of the river. It was here that he and most of his officers were disgusted to learn for the first time how the civilians of the valley had bartered and traded with the hostiles as the overconfident Nez Perce moseyed south.

No matter, Gibbon thought. His men would put things right.

Including Sergeant Edward Page and those seven Fort Ellis troopers from the Second Cavalry who had joined G Company in its march over from the Galatin Valley, Gibbon was now at the lead of fifteen officers and 146 enlisted men, in addition to a twelve pound mountain howitzer mounted on a prairie carriage he managed to run across and commandeer at Fort Owen.

At dark that first evening of the pursuit, Gibbon rode over to the Flathead camp to have an audience with Charlot. The chief did not even give the officer the courtesy of inviting him into his lodge, much less offering to take part in the normal amenities of the pipe. And when the colonel asked for some Flathead to help H. S. Bostwick scout for his column, Charlot flatly refused.

"The Nez Perce have kept their promise," the chief's interpreter translated Charlot's words. "They did not start trouble in the valley. So I will honor my pledge to stay neutral."

Before departing their bivouac the morning of the fifth, Gibbon received word from Missoula City that as many as 150 civilians were already en route from Bannack City, Montana's first territorial capital, intending to head off the Nez Perce from the east. In addition, he took this opportunity to speak with Father Anthony Ravalli, a Catholic priest who had spent the last forty years ministering to those Flathead in the Bitterroot valley at St. Mary's Mission, erected just outside Stevensville.

"The Nez Perce are a very dangerous lot, Colonel," Ravalli declared dourly.

"That's why I intend to catch them just as soon as we can," Gibbon replied.

"How many soldiers are there with you?" the missionary asked.

Instantly suspicious that the priest might leak word concerning just how few soldiers he did have with him at present, Gibbon considered a small lie the most expedient route to take: "I have just over two hundred, Father."

Ravalli considered that, his brow creasing with worry. "Not enough," he remarked, grim lines crowfooting the corners of his eyes. "The Nez Perce boast of at least two hundred and sixty warriors, Colonel. They enjoy a reputation as splendid shots, besides being well armed and possessing plenty of ammunition."

So much for the priest's blessing.

That Sunday the colonel sent Howard his plea for 200 horsemen with civilian Joe Pardee and one of Charlot's Flathead, clearly not intending to await the reinforcements of that big column then somewhere in the Bitterroot Mountains. After turning those two couriers back for the Lolo, instead of delaying any longer Gibbon pushed his men up the valley, eventually encountering more than seventy-five volunteers from the Bitterroot settlements: a company of thirty-four who had ridden down from Stevensville under the leadership of "Captain" John B. Catlin and another forty-some who had come north from Corvallis under John L. Humble.

Upon catching up to Gibbon's column, Humble spared no effort to explain how he was personally opposed to chasing down the fleeing Nez Perce after reaching a peaceful accord with the Non-Treaty bands at Rawn's barricade. Catlin explained that although he was in favor of giving the Non-Treaty bands a fight, many of his men had their doubts about making war on those Indians who had kept their end of the Lolo agreement, passing peacefully through the Bitterroot.

Not only did many of the volunteers' Southern drawls* make Yankee Gibbon a bit uncomfortable, but the colonel was taken aback, thinking it odd, even a bit amusing, that these men should vacillate in their loyalties the way they had over the past few days: Enthusiastically answering Rawn's call for volunteers when his soldiers headed up the Lolo to erect their barricade at the onset of troubles, those same citizens soon drifting off for their homes—Gibbon now bluntly told these seventy-five-some volunteers they had committed nothing less than outright desertion at the Lolo barricades—when it appeared the Nez Perce had given them a way to avoid a fight; later a few of the more enterprising civilians even pursuing the Nez Perce camp in wagons weighed down with trade goods so they could continue the profitable barter all the way up the Bitterroot valley.

Upon reaching Gibbon's troops, both companies of civilians had begun to grumble and argue with their elected "captains," Catlin, a steady-handed Civil War veteran who himself wanted to throw in with Gibbon's column while his volunteers were something less than enthusiastic, and John Humble, the leader who had openly argued with Captain Rawn's actions just before he and others abandoned the Lolo barricades.

It gave the colonel reason to question the volunteers' steadfastness. He was exasperated to see how these citizens ran hot and cold. Here, a matter of days after the barricade desertions and the scandal of trading with the enemy, these brave civilians were again offering their services to the army?

The colonel was dubious of the Missourians' intentions at best, if not outright scornful of their offer. So when Catlin and Humble formally presented themselves and their men, offering to join Gibbon's column, the colonel wagged his head.

"I prefer not to be encumbered with your company of volunteers," the colonel explained bluntly.

That chilly reception made no difference for the moment. Catlin, Humble,

---

*In his *Tough Trip Through Paradise*, frontiersman Andrew Garcia explained Gibbon's uneasiness: "One side of the Bitter Root valley was settled mostly by Missourians. The other side . . . mostly by Georgeians. So in all this bunch of Jeff Davis's Orphans, it could not be expected that their Civil War record, from a union man's point of view, was good."

and their companies clung to the fringe of the column, refusing to be dissuaded and forced to turn around.

That afternoon of the fifth, the column rumbled past the small community of Corvallis, another fifteen miles up the valley, which boasted about one hundred inhabitants in 1877. When news of the Nez Perce escape from Idaho reached the Bitterroot, valley settlers had hastily built a fortress surrounded by twelve-foot-high sod walls, one-hundred-feet square, with interior rooms constructed of tents and canvas wagon covers, partially partitioned with rough-milled lumber. They named it Fort Skidaddle, since many of its occupants were settlers who had "skidaddled" from their native Missouri after suffering repeated attacks at the hands of Southern partisans before the bombardment of Fort Sumter, as well as harassment from Confederate soldiers during the Civil War.

Not much farther south, Gibbon's forces passed the much tinier settlement of *Skalkaho,** where the eighty-some locals had constructed a small, crude stockade of rough timbers and sloping sod walls no more than five feet high. They christened the shabby affair Fort Run, because that's where their women and children would run in time of an Indian scare. But its sloping sod walls were so short that when the Nez Perce village marched past more than two dozen warriors reined their ponies up to the top and peered down at the frightened families.

That night of the sixth they camped on Sleeping Child Creek, within hailing distance of the fort's walls.

Near noon of the following day, 6 August, after successively passing the ransacked houses belonging to a settler named Landrum, that of Alex Stewart, and even the cabin belonging to valley pioneer Joe Blodgett—who had enlisted at Corvallis as a volunteer and offered Gibbon his trail-scouting skills—the column discovered that volunteer Myron Lockwood's ranch house near the mouth of Rye Creek** had been vandalized worst of all. The structure itself had been gutted, every piece of furniture and china thrown into the yard, where it was broken, every tick, curtain, and pillow slashed with a knife. Lockwood wasn't the only civilian along who furiously gnashed his teeth at the wanton destruction, cussing the Nez Perce raiders in no uncertain terms now—especially when Lockwood discovered the warriors had left seven poor Indian ponies in his pasture to replace seven of his finest horses.

"That bunch of spavined cayuses are all sick and sore-mouthed, just plain used-up comin' over the Lolo!" the civilian yelped to Gibbon.

"I recommend that you file a complaint with Captain Rawn once the two of you return to the valley after we have subdued these predators, Mr. Lockwood." Gibbon brushed aside the vandalism he saw as a minor irritant when compared to the larger goal of stopping murderers, rapists, and thieves. "State the dollar amount of your loss, and I'm sure the Indian Bureau will consider your motion for recompense."

It was here that the volunteers held a heated argument among them-

*"Sleeping Child" in Flathead.

**Approximately four miles south of present-day Darby, Montana

selves on whether to go on or not, because they were low on provisions and many thought it better to return to their homes.

"Gather your volunteers," the colonel told Catlin and Humble. "I'll speak to them myself."

Minutes later when he stepped before the civilians, Gibbon said, "I want to assure you men that my soldiers will share their supplies with you, down to the last ration."

That got some of the heads nodding, a little of the gray worry draining from the faces. Gibbon continued, "And another thing I know I can assure you: We can give you a fight with these Nez Perces."

That singular remark elicited the first cheers and boisterous displays of the march, arising not only among the civilians but from all his soldiers as well.

"I plan to put these Nez Perces afoot," Gibbon explained as the crowd quieted. "So one last thing I can promise you civilians—you'll have all of the hostiles' ponies you can capture."

Setting off from that brief halt, Fort Shaw post guide H. S. Bostwick and local Joe Blodgett led them up toward the low saddle that would eventually carry them over to Ross's Hole.* On their rumbling journey up the twisting, torturous switchbacks in those wagons Gibbon and Kirkendall had commandeered from Missoula City civilians, the colonel and his men were suddenly struck with how the Nez Perce trail up the mountainside lacked a lot of those scars made by travois poles. Indeed, what they had been seeing at each of the enemy's camping grounds over the past two days was that the women weren't pulling along many drags burdened with heavy loads. Instead, the wide areas stripped of trees surrounding each new campground showed that the squaws were cutting down saplings and some lodgepole pine, leaving those temporary poles standing when they moved on come morning.

In the Hole, the colonel called "Captain" John Humble aside, asking him to take some of his locals and scout ahead.

"Scout how far ahead?" Humble sounded dubious.

"As far as is necessary to locate the enemy," Gibbon explained. "When you find them, engage and delay the village until I can catch up with my men."

Humble didn't give it much consideration. He wagged his head. "Don't think it's a good idea, General. Too damned risky."

"You're refusing to go?"

Humble hemmed and hawed, then said, "I'll supply four or five men, and you can furnish the same number of your soldiers. We can scout for the village, then send back a man to tell you where we've found them."

Gibbon was startled. "But you won't engage them, won't hold them till I can catch up with the rest of this command?"

"No, General," Humble eventually admitted. "I refuse to imperil my men on any such risky adventure."

---

*Named for Alexander Ross (of the British Hudson's Bay Company of Adventurers), who first came here to trade with the Indians in the early days of the fur trade.

Fuming, the colonel asked, "Do all your men feel the way you do, Mr. Humble?"

"They elected me as their leader, so I'm speaking for 'em—"

"Let's go have a talk with your . . . your outfit," Gibbon interrupted, turning aside.

He stomped over to the seventy-plus civilians who all got to their feet as the officer approached. Quickly he told the citizens of the conversation he just had about the scouting mission.

"I've been told you men would refuse to be part of such an important scout to find and hold down the enemy."

"General?" Myron Lockwood, the rancher whose house had been looted and stock stolen from his pastures, took a step forward, his eyes glowing with a fierce anger. It was clear he had undergone a change of heart. "I demand to see the color of the feller's hair who refused to go."

Before Gibbon had a chance to speak, John Humble stepped out from behind the colonel to say, "Mr. Lockwood, you better look at my hair. I am that man! If you choose to get into a scrap with those Indians, you will damn well know you have been somewhere!"

"It was you, Humble?" Lockwood took another step toward the man, his hands clenching.

Gibbon quickly moved in front of Humble. "Now's the time for all you men to decide on your own, or together, if you will continue with this army until we run the Nez Perce into the ground."

Those first moments were deathly quiet. Then Humble shuffled off to his horse tied nearby. Slowly, close to forty more civilians wordlessly went to their animals, too.

"Mr. Humble?"

The civilian leader turned before he climbed into the stirrup. "This is as far as I propose to go with your army, General. I am not out to fight women and children." Immediately turning and rising to the saddle, Humble snubbed up his reins and concluded, "I am going home now. Any of you who want to come with me are welcome on the ride back to the Bitterroot. And those of my company who want to go on can throw in with Captain Catlin there."

For a few moments Gibbon watched Humble nervously shift in his saddle. When the man was sure no one else was about to join him, he turned and rode away, leading those forty-some for home.

The colonel waited a minute more, then turned to the thirty-five volunteers who would forge on. He sighed, "Let's get on the move."

As twilight deepened that evening of the seventh, making the narrow trail even more difficult to follow, the colonel ordered that camp be made there and then, just short of the summit of the divide. The site offered the men and stock no water to speak of.

"From the odometer I attached to a wheel on one of the wagons," Gibbon confided to Lieutenant James Bradley and the other officers, "it appears the hostiles are moving at a leisurely pace: no more than twelve to fourteen miles each day at the most."

"It won't take us long to overhaul them at the rate we're covering ground, sir," Bradley declared.

Gibbon looked at his most trusted lieutenant. "I intend to have this column march at least twice that distance every day from here on out until we catch up to the village. If my calculations are correct, we should accomplish that in as many as four days, perhaps no more than three at the most."

"From the summit of the pass ahead," Bradley explained, "we should be able to determine if the Nez Perce have turned south and are making for their homeland beyond the Salmon River Mountains in Idaho—or if they've turned east to the buffalo plains, where they repeatedly told the settlers they were headed."

Gibbon asked, "What's your instincts tell you they're going to do, Mr. Bradley?"

The lieutenant pointed toward the top of the divide. "Colonel—I'll bank a month's pay that Joseph and White Bird will take their families south and skedaddle for those mountains, where we'll have to pay the devil to ever get them out."

CHAPTER FIFTY

Wa-Wa-Mai-Khal, 1877

IT INFURIATED LOOKING GLASS THAT THESE OTHER CHIEFS SHOULD ARGUE with him!

Who were they to carp and snipe at him anyway?

Hadn't they stirred up a hornets' nest all on their own—not listening to him from the very beginning of the troubles? Hadn't he told them they should do as he always had done: Simply stay out of the white man's way?

But when they went ahead with their foolish war, it had been like a kettle of bone soup suspended over a fire grown too hot—it boiled over, scalding Looking Glass's people, too, even though they had done everything they could to stay out of a war started by those who had no experience with war.

Looking Glass knew about war.

But these other chiefs who criticized him? Why, not one of them had fought against the mighty Blackfeet, or the Lakota on the plains of Montana Territory! Not like him, Rainbow, and Five Wounds—experienced war chiefs who regularly traveled to the buffalo country, where they would find themselves squarely in a disputed land, that country where the *E-sue-gha* held forth against stronger, more numerous tribes. No, none of these petty men arguing with him now knew anything of war!

But for some reason they prattled on like they knew everything better than Looking Glass.

Meopkowit! They are fools, he thought as he listened. Wasn't he the one who had led them to that victory after two days on the Clearwater? Wasn't he the one who had held forth and convinced the Non-Treaty bands they should leave Idaho country until the troubles cooled down? Wasn't he the chief who had ordered the raids on Kamiah and that scouting party along their back trail to delay the Treaty band traitors who were scouting for the *suapies?*

And wasn't Looking Glass the supreme chief who had toyed with the little soldier chief at the log barricades while they made ready to slip around the soldiers and Shadows in a maneuver of such genius that tribal historians would be singing his praises for generations to come?

In the end, wasn't it Looking Glass alone who was responsible for bringing the *Nee-Me-Poo* to the *Iskumtselalik Pah*, this Place of the Ground Squirrels,* this afternoon, a beautiful campsite where the People could rest

*In naming this place after a ground squirrel, the Nez Perce more specifically made reference to a smaller animal called a picket pin, due to the fact that when the tiny,

themselves and their horses for a few days,[**] cut lodgepoles, and refresh their spirits before moving on to the buffalo country?

Why did these men of so little courage suddenly screw up enough bravery to dare ask that scouts be sent on their back trail now that they were nearing the western edge of buffalo country? To send back a party of young men simply to assure they were not being followed might well open the way for more stupid, foolish depredations against the settlers in the Bitterroot valley—perhaps even the thoughtless killing of any Shadows those scouts might run across. No, Looking Glass was still fuming at *Toohoolhoolzote*'s young vandals for what they had done to break his word to the white men. He refused to send back any scouts.

"Here we are safe!" he roared back at the *tewat*, Pile of Clouds. "That little chief and his few walking soldiers up at Missoula City are not foolish enough to follow us and make trouble now!"

Looking Glass knew only too well how this respected shaman's premonitions were valued. Pile of Clouds might well start a mindless stampede; then nothing would stop them. So he sneered a little at the taller, younger man. "Maybe you are afraid of those fools we cowered and shamed at the log-and-hole fort?"[†]

"I am not afraid of any Shadow we passed to reach this place," Pile of Clouds answered defensively. "I am only afraid of . . . of—"

"Of *what?*" Looking Glass demanded, smelling the scent of blood from his adversary.

The *tewat* sighed. "I am only afraid of those white men I *cannot* see."

Looking Glass glanced around the crowd, quickly studying the faces of the other leaders; then his eyes narrowed on Pile of Clouds once more. "If you are so frightened, perhaps you should make a *tewat* or chief out of one of your brave fighting men. Then I would have no doubts that I am supported as we take our families into the land of the *E-sue-gha*."

Pile of Clouds blanched at the chief's slur on his courage. "When did you start turning your nose up at another man's medicine?"

Looking Glass scoffed at that transparent boast, "M-medicine?"

"My medicine has told me—not once, but twice!" the shaman asserted, waving his arm back up the hillside they had just descended. "Death is behind us! I am certain of that. We must hurry—there is no time to cut lodgepoles here. We must hurry away!"

Before Looking Glass could respond, even the elderly White Bird spoke of his doubts. "Why do you allow the women time here so they can drag lodgepoles from this place, Looking Glass? We should be hurrying away without lodgepoles!"

---

thin animal stands at watchful attention beside its burrow, it looked just like the wooden picket pin a man would use to anchor his horse.

[**]The Non-Treaty bands arrived in the valley of the Big Hole on the afternoon of August 7, and would stay again the night of the eighth—relaxed and celebratory up to the fateful morning of August 9.

[†]Rawn's Fort Fizzle in the Lolo Canyon.

"We have only arrived at this place," Looking Glass's tone softened, became more fatherly. Better that the Non-Treaty bands see him as a benevolent leader rather than despotic over the other chiefs. "Can't you see that we have left behind the war and the soldiers? Far behind us are the Shadows who wanted to do us great harm. All of that—left behind in Idaho country. There is no cause for alarm. Cut-Off Arm sits on his rump and does nothing. The white men who wished us evil are back there in Idaho country with his army, too."

"We can't wait!" Pile of Clouds repeated. "We must hurry away—"

"No," Looking Glass snapped. "We will stay here so the women can cut poles for the lodges. I will not have us arrive in the land of the *E-sue-gha* looking as if we are some poor relations without lodges!"

Many of the older women murmured their agreement with that on the fringes of that crowd gathering around the headmen.

"Here we will begin to regain our greatness." Looking Glass warmed to his oratory and the support of his people. "Here we will eat from the fat of the land and drink this good water. And here tomorrow night we will celebrate, dance and sing . . . for we have left the war far, far behind us."

Both upstream and down-, the slopes west of camp were thickly timbered. Only the hillside immediately across from the village stood barren of evergreens, covered only by sage and tall grass—except for a pair of immense fir trees that seemed to stand as sentinels near the base of the hillside. It was there the boys herded most of the more than two thousand horses.

Stopping at this traditional camping ground located in the southwestern edge of a narrow valley nestled between high mountain ranges, they did indeed have here everything they needed in a camp while they laid over for a few days to rest and recruit themselves before continuing on to the *E-sue-gha* country. Besides sweet, cool water of both the creek they had followed from the pass down to the valley,* as well as the bigger stream it joined at the bottom of the hillside,** both of which were lined with dense thickets of head-high willow, the People had an abundance of good grass for the horses they had harried through the rigors of that mountain passage. What with the short marches they had been making ever since leaving those recuperative hot springs on this side of the pass, the spirit of every man, woman, and child had been soaring. Couldn't the other chiefs and *tewats* see what the leisurely pace had accomplished? Everyone but those complainers realized in their bones that they had left the fighting behind in Idaho country.

Sensing no threat from those Shadows and *suapies* they had tricked on Lolo Creek, Looking Glass and his leaders did not feel as if they should ring sentries around their camp, especially at night. Oh, they did know that the little soldier chief had spies following them and that some of the Bitterroot

---

*Today's Trail Creek.

**Today's Ruby Creek, which, with Trail Creek, forms the North Fork of the Big Hole River.

settlers were surely keeping an eye on the People's movements from site to site. But no one would be sneaking up on them, because the only Shadows who had worked for the *Nee-Me-Poo*'s destruction were a long, long way behind, back over a tall string of rugged mountains!

Not that they hadn't spotted a white man or two lurking on the hillside, and even the outskirts, of this new camp—spying on the *Nee-Me-Poo*, keeping the little soldier chief informed of everything. Those men seen prowling the fringes of the hills were of little consequence, Looking Glass told the other chiefs. The very fact that there were spies keeping an eye on their village was as good an argument as any that the Shadows did not intend to attack. Only to follow and watch.

So the camp making continued with renewed enthusiasm. Spread out along the east bank of the little river, eighty-nine lodges were eventually raised, their brown cones stark against the blue of that late-summer sky, arrayed in an irregular V formation, its apex pointed downstream, toward the north. Between the camp and the base of that timbered mountainside flowed the wide, deep, gurgling creek where the children went to play, where the women bathed the tiny infants newly born during this difficult passage out of a troubled land, on to a life that now held nothing but promise for the *Nee-Me-Poo*.

With a breast-swelling pride, Looking Glass realized that as the women cut and dried new poles from those forests on the surrounding slopes, this would be one of the largest, happiest gatherings the Non-Treaty bands had experienced in the recent past. As a shaft of bright light suddenly burst upon the meadow, he was forced to squint. The high, thin rain clouds were breaking up. Then he remembered: Over here on this eastern side of the mountains, the sun always shone a little more strongly. There were fewer clouds to mar its intensity than there were on the west side of the Bitterroot range. It gave his heart a strong feeling to look over these seventy-seven lodges who had followed him over from Idaho country, good, too, in gazing upon those twelve lodges under Eagle-from-the-Light who had joined up in the Bitterroot valley.

Besides the women and children who waded across the stream and started up the slopes with their axs to chop down new lodgepoles, other women walked east from camp toward a half-mile of open ground fringed on the east by a low plateau, carrying their fire-hardened digging sticks—there to jab into the earth for the tasty camas roots in that *tegpeem*, an open meadow the *Nee-Me-Poo* called "a flat place of good grass." Riding north and south from camp, small hunting parties of men went in search of deer, elk, and especially antelope that would sizzle over the fires this first night at *Iskumtselalik Pah*. The People did not find antelope west in their old homeland.

Yes—Looking Glass thought—he would have to announce the dance he would hold tomorrow evening after everyone was settled in at this peaceful place. Such festivities would make his people even happier because it would be the first celebration of any kind since the war began and they started on their flight away from their old homeland.

It was about time that the Non-Treaty bands began their new life here in the buffalo country with a grand feast, Looking Glass decided—singing and dancing into the night!

It was here that the *Nee-Me-Poo* could begin to celebrate their victory over the white man!

BY TELEGRAPH

———

A Thrilling Chapter of Secret
Political History.

———

A Chicago Free Love Murderer Acquitted.

———

No more Arms to be Sold to
the Indians.

———

MONTANA.

———

Latest from the Indian War.
HELENA, August 7.—Advices from Missoula, up to August 6, say General Gibbon, with 200 regulars*—infantry, in wagons—left Missoula post to follow the hostiles at 1 p.m. Saturday. He designed making thirty-five miles a day. The hostiles were at Doolittle's ranch on [Sunday] night, seventy-five miles from Missoula and within ten miles of the trail to Ross Hole. Charlos declined to lend his warriors to General Gibbon, but will find the Nez Perces on his own account. The hostiles were moving with more celerity Friday. Stevensville had advices Saturday that 100 or 150 men were coming from Bannock to intercept the Indians. Howard has not heard from Lent, the courier, He had not returned on Sunday and anxiety was felt for him, as two Nez Perces had come over the trail. A considerable number of Missoula county volunteers are prepared to advance, but are independent of the regulars.

"I respectfully request the honor of leading this scout, sir," asked Lieutenant James H. Bradley, the officer who moments ago had suggested just such a reconnaissance to catch up to the hostile village.

"It is yours to lead, without question," Colonel John Gibbon replied that twilight of 7 August. "Mounted, of course. Take Lieutenant Jacobs with

---

*Do you remember this figure? It did not come from the actual number of soldiers Gibbon had along. Instead, this was the exact number he had told Father Anthony Ravalli he had with him back on August 5. The priest must have been the source for this news story!

you, along with sixty picked men—soldiers and volunteers both—and do your best to overhaul the Nez Perce before dawn."

"Once we've made contact, what are your orders?" Bradley inquired.

"Send word back as quickly as possible."

"Am I to engage the Nez Perce, Colonel?"

"By all means. Stampede their horses. Impede their escape." Gibbon ground a fist into an open palm. "Immobilize their village and hinder their retreat until I can come up with the rest of the outfit."

Everything they had seen and heard as they hurried up the Bitterroot valley confirmed that the Nez Perce could boast somewhere in the neighborhood of 250 fighting men.* In addition, Gibbon's men had come to realize the village was moving slowly, unconcerned and perhaps completely unaware that the army was on their back trail . . . and closing fast. The distance from campsite to campsite was extremely short, indicating the village was making only brief migrations each day—perhaps only to find new forage for their horse herd. Gibbon and his officers determined that they could cover twice as much ground as the Nez Perce were each day—perhaps three times more. In that way, the Seventh Infantry and those few Second Cavalry troopers along would catch up to and surprise the enemy in less than half a week.

In fact, right now it appeared the hostiles were no more than a day and a half away! Perhaps as little as one long day's march to bring them to battle.

So now was clearly the time to go in search of the enemy. To account for Joseph's position and his strengths. To determine how best to attack the Non-Treaty stronghold—and send back word to Gibbon once contact had been made.

One thing was for sure as Bradley and First Lieutenant Joshua W. Jacobs led their sixty men into the dim light of dusk, clambering over a maze of downed timber for that two miles up to the summit: the Nez Perce hadn't turned aside with designs on doubling back for Idaho and their old haunts in the Salmon River country. They had clearly bypassed the route they would have taken if they had intended to return to their homeland.** It was abundantly clear that Joseph's warriors and their families had no intention of reclaiming their ancient homes. If Gibbon didn't stop them here and now, the Nez Perce could well be free to scatter, roaming and pillaging at will across Montana Territory—igniting a much farther-reaching war than General O. O. Howard had failed to put out back in Idaho.

Through the night of the seventh and into dawn's earliest light on the eighth of August, Bradley and Jacobs struggled ahead on horseback, a little quicker now that their scouting force could begin to see just where it was going. From the summit of the divide the trail angled down a gentle incline

---

*John Deschamps, a valley volunteer now with Gibbon, had counted 250 guns among the Non-Treaty bands and two-thousand-plus horses in their herd, some of which were fine "American" horses bearing their brands. One of the Nez Perce had tried to interest Deschamps in buying a gold watch with the former owner's name engraved inside, for the paltry sum of thirty dollars!

**Through present-day Nez Perce Pass, in the extreme southwestern corner of Montana.

for about a mile, where it finally reached the headwaters of Trail Creek. From there trail guide Blodgett led them through some increasingly rough country, staying with the banks of that stream, forced to slog through boggy mires where Trail Creek meandered and cross from bank to bank more than fifty times in their descent.

Down, down, down now, accompanied by the first telltale indication of a coming sunrise—descending toward that high mountain valley a few of the Bitterroot civilians along were calling the Big Hole. Still no sign of the village. Not a sound or a smell, much less a sighting of fire smoke or smudge of trail dust rising from the plain below.

"They aren't where we figured we'd discover them," Bradley grumbled in dismay as he threw up his arm and ordered a halt to those soldiers and Catlin's civilians following the two of them.

"We've got to press on till we find them," Jacobs suggested.

"There never was any question of that!" Bradley replied peevishly, then instantly felt bad for snapping. "I figured we'd spot their camp right down there, where you can see the head of that valley. But," and he sighed, "their trail leads around the brow of these heights, angling left instead of dropping directly onto the valley floor. Damn, Jacobs—if we don't find that village soon, it's going to take even longer than we calculated for the rest of Colonel Gibbon's forces to catch up."

Jacobs spoke softly, "Do you think we should give the mounts a brief rest here?"

"No," and Bradley shook his head emphatically. "They'll have plenty of time to rest after we've caught up to the village and run off their horses—"

"L-Lieutenant! Lieutenant Bradley!"

He whirled on his heels, finding John B. Catlin, Joe Blodgett, and a handful of Bitterroot volunteers weaving their horses through the timber in their direction. Bradley brought up his long Springfield rifle, half-expecting there to be bullets accompanying the harried civilians, what with the dire expressions on their flushed and mottled faces.

"The hostiles?" he asked Catlin, lunging out to grab the bridle on the leader's horse.

Catlin gulped breathlessly, "We saw 'em."

A lump of apprehension rose in Bradley's throat. "They see you?"

"Don't think so," Catlin said too quickly. Then his eyes flicked away. "I . . . I dunno. Maybeso."

Letting go of Catlin's bridle, Bradley asked, "You were shot at?"

"No."

"They follow you?"

With a shake of his head, the civilian again answered, "No. If they saw us, they let us go 'thout any trouble."

"How far are they?"

"Not far at all, Lieutenant," Catlin replied with a swallow. Then the Civil War veteran said, "On round the gentle side of this hill, you'll hear voices, laughing, too. And the sound of chopping wood."

"Sergeant Wilson, you and Mr. Catlin see the men have their breakfast now."

"Yes, sir."

Then Bradley looked at Jacobs and Corporal Socrates Drummond. "The two of you, come with me on foot. We'll go see for ourselves."

When they reached the last of the thick timber, the lieutenant halted the pair. Quickly his eyes searched the trees at the edge of the grassy slope.

"Wait right here with our horses and guns, Corporal. The lieutenant and I are going for a climb."

Stripping off his blue wool tunic, the lieutenant then rebuckled his gun belt around his waist, and they started up the tree, hand and foot, slowly working this way and that around the thick trunk until their heads popped above the uppermost branches. It provided a perfect view, placing them atop the emerald evergreen canopy—giving the lieutenants a chance to gaze unimpeded over the entire vista as the narrow valley of the Big Hole stretched away from them some ten miles to the east.

"Jesus," Jacobs whispered.

Not only did the telltale sounds of chopping and women's voices drift up to him from below and far to the left, but he could also see the smudge of smoke from their many fires, the dust from the hooves of the ponies the young men were racing on the flat beyond the village, along with hearing the chatter of those small boys he spotted chasing one another through the horse-high willow growing along the creek that gurgled at the base of the slope right below him. Other youngsters sat atop their ponies, watching over the horse herd. More than a hundred warriors lazed about in the sunny camp. Women pitched tepees here or there; others dragged poles across the creek or prepared a midday meal over their fires.

His mind quickly turning like a steam-driven flywheel, Bradley began calculating the distance he had covered since separating from Gibbon, working over the hours it would take those foot soldiers in their wagons, pulled by the weary teams laboring up the divide, to reach the headwaters of Trail Creek before they could ever begin to work their way down to this spot. Only if those foot soldiers left the wagons behind . . .

"Come on," he whispered to Jacobs.

They scrambled down the limbs like a pair of schoolboys, exuberantly leaping the last five feet to the ground before trudging uphill to Drummond, waving for him to remount and follow rather than chancing any more words on the hillside. Surprise was of the utmost concern now. Surprise—that most fragile of military commodities.

Bradley threaded his way in and out of the trees, climbing slightly, following his own back trail to where he had left Blodgett, Catlin, and his sixty men. And as his horse huffed across the grassy hillside, he began to formulate the terse note he would send back to the colonel somewhere far above them this morning—perhaps still on the other side of the pass as the sun came up bold and brassy, striking the western slopes of the Big Hole. His heart sank as he recognized that it was too late for his small detachment to run off the horse herd and harry the village this day. The others were too far in the rear for that.

They would have to wait now, he would write Gibbon. Wait for the general to bring up his entire column before they would jump the enemy.

When that dispatch was written and the courier on his way, the lieutenant decided he would lead his advance detachment down this trail, to the very edge of that stand of timber where he had spied on the Nez Perce camp.

And there they would lie in wait for the arrival of Colonel John Gibbon—who would lead the rest of the Seventh Infantry when he unleashed all bloody thunder on that unsuspecting village.

CHAPTER FIFTY-ONE

AUGUST 7–8, 1877

AN HOUR BEFORE DAWN ON THE MORNING OF 7 AUGUST, THEIR NINTH day since departing Kamiah Crossing, General Oliver O. Howard had asked the tall frontiersman Joe Pardee to guide his aide-de-camp, First Lieutenant Robert H. Fletcher, and correspondent Thomas Sutherland down the Lolo to the valley below, from there to escort them north to Missoula City as quickly as they could ride without endangering their mounts. Fletcher, acting quartermaster for the column, carried writs to purchase what additional supplies were needed to see Howard's column through to the end of the chase.

At this point, they all had a feeling—admittedly something more than a mere hope—that the campaign was nearing its end.

By 9:00 A.M. when the command reached those log breastworks erected by Captain Charles Rawn's regulars and volunteers, Howard felt unduly disgusted, believing the Nez Perce War should have bloody well ended right there.*

"Over there, General," explained Joe Baker, one of the few citizens who rode at the head of the column, "you can see where Joseph's hostiles turned off to the north and circled around the barricades by going up that ridge."

"Joseph was too smart for them," commented Lieutenant C. E. S. Wood.

"Maybe they believed they could trust Looking Glass," Baker voiced the civilian point of view. "From what I hear, he's always been a good Indian when he's in the Bitterroot country."

Howard squinted beneath the high, intense sunlight, his eyes tracing that narrowing trail as it disappeared up the grassy hillside, looping behind the rounded hills far above Rawn's fortress, beyond the effective range of an army Springfield. *Joseph never should have gotten around them. How in blazes did he do this?* the general brooded, ruminating on just how many times the wily chieftain had outwitted him. Surely that *Wallowa* leader had to be one of the

---

*Even at this early date, the inaction of Rawn's soldiers and the wholesale desertions from the barricades by the valley citizens, along with the fact that the Non-Treaty bands were able to slip around the barricade without so much as an attempt made to stop them, were proving to be fodder for vehement editorials across the region. Rawn's log-and-rifle-pit structure erected across that narrow part of the Lolo Canyon was becoming known as Fort Fizzle.

most talented military strategists Oliver Otis Howard had ever confronted on any battlefield.

"How far to the Bitterroot valley itself?" he asked of those who had joined him during this brief halt at the barricades.

Baker, who had made the crossing between Montana and Idaho territories many times, answered, "Not far, General. A few more miles is all."

Later that afternoon, when they did reach the mouth of Lolo Creek, Howard called for a halt to rest the men and graze the animals while he composed a short dispatch to Colonel Frank Wheaton, to be carried north to the Mullan Road, thence west, by two civilians from Idaho. He ordered the campaign's left column to shorten its daily marches until Wheaton would next hear from Howard about the possibility of returning to Lewiston, Idaho. "You may not be obliged to come through to Montana,"* the general wrote.

Because Division Commander McDowell in Portland had ordered Captain Cushing's and Captain Edward Field's batteries of the Fourth U. S. Artillery back to their stations days before Howard got around to starting east on the Lolo Trail and since Oliver could no longer justify needing the batteries because he was now *behind* the action, he separated those two units from his command at this point in the chase, ordering them on to Deer Lodge, from whence they would march south to reach the railhead at Corrine, Utah. From there they would travel in boxcars back to San Francisco. At the moment, however, both batteries were more than two days behind Howard, along with the infantry still negotiating the Lolo Trail.

Before he was finished composing his dispatch, Quartermaster Fletcher and Sutherland showed up at the head of a string of wagons the lieutenant had commandeered in Missoula City. Howard now had the supplies he hoped would allow him to catch Gibbon, who must surely be closing the gap on the Nez Perce.

"AWAKE! AWAKE! ALL the People must listen to the contents of my shaking heart!"

At the old warrior's cry Yellow Wolf sat upright, the single blanket sliding off his bare shoulder in the dim gray light of dawn. He squinted, blinked, then rubbed his gritty eyes with the heels of both hands. Last night, he and other young men and women had stayed up, dancing, singing, talking of sweet things in their future around the fire until well past the setting of the moon. He had been asleep no more than two hours at the most—

"Awake!" Lone Bird's voice crackled even closer as the old warrior emerged through the nearby lodges, his pony slowly carrying him toward that scattering of blanket bowers where many of the young men slept away from their families now that they were of an age to marry . . . of the age to become fighters.

Kicking the blanket from his legs, Yellow Wolf stood and darted unsteadily toward the brave warrior. Many others were emerging from their

*In fact, Wheaton's left column did not reach Spokane Falls in Washington Territory until August 10.

bowers now to listen to the warrior who had first given them warning at the Medicine Tree.

"I am awake, Lone Bird," Yellow Wolf muttered as he approached the horseman. "What say you now so early on a quiet morning?"

"This quiet will not last, Yellow Wolf!" Lone Bird announced as he eased back on the single buffalo-hair rein tied around his pony's lower jaw. The animal stopped.

More and more people gathered, still half-asleep, a murmur growing like an autumn brook as they emerged from their blankets and robes into the misty morning air, so damp and chill it penetrated to the bone.

Looking Glass suddenly appeared scurrying around the side of a lodge, looking perturbed. "Lone Bird—"

"My shaking heart tells me something, Chief Looking Glass," Lone Bird interrupted. "Listen again to my warning, for my words do not come easy."

"What warning?" demanded *Ollokot* as he pushed through the forming crowd and laid his hand on the older warrior's knee.

"Again I have been told, as I was at the Medicine Tree: The eyes in this heart of mine say trouble and death will overtake us if we make no hurry through this land," Lone Bird pronounced.

Looking Glass snorted a mirthless laugh. "We've heard your foolish talk before!"

"My heart does not regard it as foolish!" Lone Bird snapped. "I have never been one to talk of things that never came true." His eyes turned, glaring into the face of the *Wallowa* war chief. "You know that, *Ollokot.*"

"Yes, I trust the eye of your heart, trust what it can see," *Ollokot* replied, his hand sliding from Lone Bird's knee.

"I cannot smother, I cannot hide, what my heart sees!" Lone Bird announced, his deep voice rattling over them all as if by the same thunder of the white man's throaty cannon. "I am commanded to speak what is revealed to me."

"What would you have us do?" White Bird asked, the crowd parting as he stepped into that tight circle gathered round Lone Bird.

"Let us be gone to the buffalo country, if that is where we are bound, you chiefs," Lone Bird demanded as he tapped his bare heels into the sides of his pony and moved into the crowd. "Let us be gone from this place. As quickly as the women can take down the lodges and pack the travois, let us be gone from the trouble and death that is already nipping at our heels."

For long moments Yellow Wolf watched the old warrior's back as Lone Bird's pony carried him away. That's when he recognized the face of Burning Coals, known as *Semu*, a man rich in horses. "Come," he said, tapping the arm of his friend *Seeyakoon Ilppilp*, the one called Red Spy.

Trotting over to the wealthy man, Yellow Wolf begged, "Burning Coals, please let me and my friend borrow two of your fastest horses—"

"You have horses of your own," Burning Coals responded, gazing down his expansive nose at the young warriors. "Why would I loan you two of mine?"

"Everyone knows you have the finest—the fastest—horses in all the bands," Yellow Wolf praised, hoping the compliment would seal the loan. "I grow concerned by these warnings from Lone Bird's lips."

"He is just a man given to unfounded fears," Burning Coals sneered, waving off argument.

"We should see for ourselves," Red Spy admitted. "Your horses are best for a hard scout up our back trail."

"Scout? Up our back trail?" echoed Burning Coals. "No. I will not let you use up my horses for that. They are too fine for the likes of you and your friends, Yellow Wolf. Go somewhere else to get horses to carry you on your fool's errand!"

"Even *Wottolen*, a man with strong powers, dreamed yesterday of soldiers!" Yellow Wolf argued in disbelief. "Surely you cannot dispute the medicine of *Wottolen!*"

Burning Coals turned away without a word, no more than a smug arrogance on his face as he waddled off.

"Go hunting, Yellow Wolf. There won't be any more fighting. I have seen it."

He twisted suddenly, finding the eyes of White Bull staring into his like two-day-old embers.

"You have seen this in a vision of your own?" Yellow Wolf asked. "A vision as powerful as that of *Wottolen* or Lone Bird?"

This loyal supporter of Looking Glass shook his head. "Fighting is over, young man. The war is done—war is far, far behind us now. Go hunting and think no more of war."

Many of the young men did just that. Quickly their thoughts shifted from making that scout to hunting the swift antelope. Children shuffled off in giddy play. Some of the women went back to their knees, digging the big, shallow pits they would line with heated rocks and grass, before covering the camas roots with more grass and letting them steam overnight. To be good, camas had to bake in the heated ground until the following morning.

As the crowd dispersed, their feet and lower legs kicking up swirls of ground fog here in the bottoms near the twisting creek, Yellow Wolf's gaze was drawn up the hillside, there to the south and west—across the stream, to the patches of dark timber . . . then back along the trail they had followed down from the high pass to reach this campground.

Place of the Ground Squirrels.

Realizing his own heart was sorely troubled. This was not a place of peace any longer. Too many upsetting visions already. As much as he tried to squeeze the dark, somber thoughts out of his mind, one question repeatedly floated to the surface.

If they had actually left the war behind them . . . then what trouble and death could be racing up on their back trail?

AT 5:00 A.M., just as soon as it was light enough to travel that dawn of the eighth, Colonel John Gibbon had stirred his men from their blankets and pushed ahead. Word was they had a little over two miles before reaching the pass. One way or the other—with mountain travel or the possibility of battle—they had a long day ahead of them. But as they put hour after hour behind them, Gibbon's hope that they would be able to launch an attack on the hostile camp this Wednesday faded.

During the first two hours it took to cover no more than a half-mile, the ordeal of wrestling the wagons and their teams over the downed timber, fighting their way up the ungraded slope, was excruciatingly slow. After that, the struggle up the next mile and a half of rugged slope to the top became all but unendurable. His civilian volunteers and soldiers alike stripped off tunics and coats in the high-altitude August heat, sweating as they double-hitched the teams and attached draglines to each of the wagons, so the men themselves could assist the draft animals in yanking one heavy vehicle at a time toward the pass, managing each foot of elevation only under the most extreme exertion. Grunting, sweating, cursing, they purchased another yard of the trail, rarely looking back down the slope to where they had started their climb . . . never, never looking up the hill to where they needed to will these wagons.

It would be small wonder, Gibbon brooded from atop his gray charger, that the Nez Perce didn't hear his army coming—what with all the cussing and pained yelps from both men and draft teams alike.

Just before one o'clock, as the hot sun sulled overhead like a stubborn mule and they reached the high, grassy divide* that meant the trail was all downhill from there on out, one of the advance men hollered that a rider was coming in. Gibbon's heart leaped, wanting to hope—not daring to let that hope show on his face—as he watched the horseman in blue rein up before him, salute, then reach inside his sweat-stained fatigue blouse.

"With Lieutenant Bradley's compliments, sir!"

Snatching the folded paper from the corporal's hand, Gibbon exclaimed, "He's spotted the Indians—this has to mean he's found their camp!"

"Yes, sir," the soldier answered as Gibbon tore open the dispatch and his eyes eagerly raced over Bradley's scrawl.

> Camp . . . horse herd . . . valley . . . will remain in hiding and await your arrival with the command.

His heart rising to his throat, the colonel's eyes misted. He would be the commander in at the kill. Howard was far behind. If any civilians from Bannack or Virginia City were coming west, they were still too damned far away to play any role in the coming fight. Gibbon squinted into the bright sun a moment, measuring what they had left of daylight.

Then he turned back to his company commanders, the half-circle of them like expectant actors awaiting their cue offstage. "We will leave the wagon train here to continue at its own speed."

"You want us to follow your trail, General?" Hugh Kirkendall asked.

Gibbon's eyes found his wagon master. "Yes, you must redouble your efforts to follow along as quickly as the animals and conditions will allow.

---

*Today's aptly named Gibbon Pass.

The rest of us will push forward on foot with all possible dispatch. Bradley's found the village in the valley below us. We must . . . no, we *will* do everything in our power to reach his scouts before dusk."

"An attack at dawn, Colonel?" asked Captain James M. W. Sanno, commander of G Company.

"Yes, Captain," Gibbon said as he stuffed Bradley's note inside his own damp tunic. "We engage Joseph's warriors at first light."

"*TANANISA*!"

Shore Crossing bolted upright as he cursed, shaking like a leaf, sweating as if he had been lying out in the sun instead of sleeping in the shade of his wife's lodge, a gentle breeze wafting beneath the sides of the lodgeskins she had rolled up earlier that morning.

"What is it, my husband?" she asked, settling beside him on the robes.

For a moment he looked at her face, his eyes falling to glance at her swelling breasts, then staring at that rounded mound of a belly beneath her buckskin overshirt. She carried his child inside. In four more moons, no more than that, she would give him his first child.

And for that he resented her. When her time came he would not only be her husband, but he would be a father. He was not old enough to settle down with one woman and to make a family. He wanted other women—especially the sloe-eyed girl who watched him whenever he paraded about the camp or rode up and down the flank of their march coming out of Idaho country. He resented his wife for being here now, for carrying his child, for standing in his way of happiness.

"Leave me be!" he snarled, pushing her aside roughly as he kicked his way off the heavy wool blanket.

He heard her grunt in shock as she tumbled aside and he rose there beside the low fire. Like a quick flare of lightning he whirled on her, pointing his finger at her with an outstretched arm.

"You will be happy one day very soon, woman!" he growled. "I will be dead and you will have all this to yourself!"

"You are all that makes me happy!" she cried to him, both hands held up, imploring him as he escaped through the open doorway.

As he stood there, his eyes adjusting to the bright afternoon light, he looked this way and that, seeing how many cones of lodgepoles stood drying without any hide covers. Then he heard her begin to sob. Shore Crossing stopped, took a deep breath, then steeled his heart. He simply must not let her touch him there. His days were numbered. Perhaps no more than hours now. His dream foretold the coming of the end.

Holding his arms to the sky, Shore Crossing raised his voice to those at the middle of the village.

"My brothers! My sisters! Listen to my dream! Listen to the vision in my heart when I awakened moments ago!"

He waited a few breaths as the murmur grew into a loud cacophony, as footsteps and hoofbeats drew near. Men, women, and children came—like the young babe he would never hold on his lap or bounce on his knee. He resented his wife for getting herself with child . . . because now he would never know if she carried a boy or a girl. If it would survive the coming horror.

An old woman's voice called from the crowd, "What do you have to tell us, *Wahlitits?*"

"Yes, you are a brave fighter," White Bird said as he stepped to the fore of the crowd. "You were one of the Red Coats who started this war, one of the Red Coats who made the bravery runs past the soldiers who came to attack us at Lahmotta in the first battle. Tell us of your dream."

He took a breath. "In the dream that awakened me now, I saw myself killed!"

The crowd went to talking among themselves, a dull roar that seemed to crash about his ears. Some of the chiefs raised their arms, demanding silence from the hundreds.

White Bird prodded, "Continue, Shore Crossing."

"I will be killed soon—I saw this in my dream. For this I do not care. I am willing to die. But, before I am killed, I will kill some soldiers!"

"I will kill some soldiers, too!" cried Red Moccasin Tops, Shore Crossing's best friend, as he lunged through the fringes of the crowd.

Wahlitits laid his hand on his friend's shoulder. Together they had started this war against the Shadows, killing four white men on the Salmon River. Together they had raced back and forth across the front of *suapies* at the White Bird fight.

"I shall not turn back from the death that is coming my way!" Shore Crossing announced in a firm voice, finding that this knowledge that death was coming gave him a peace he had never known before.

"And I shall be at your side when the soldiers come to kill you!" Red Moccasin Tops roared.

As he slowly swept his arm across the gathered hundreds, Shore Crossing's eyes touched one warrior after another, one woman after another . . . until he found his wife's face, her eyes swollen and red from crying.

With his agonized heart swelling in his breast, *Wahlitits* warned, "I tell you this from my dream—there will be tears in many, many eyes . . . for most of us are going to *die!*"

CHAPTER FIFTY-TWO

AUGUST 8–9, 1877

OW COLONEL JOHN GIBBON WISHED BRADLEY HAD REACHED THE NEZ Perce camp before dawn that eighth day of August so the lieutenant could have initiated his preemptory attack and driven off the horse herd.

But from Bradley's report he had found the village situated a bit farther than where they had expected to locate it. Throughout the rest of that afternoon as his column was forced to cross and recross the twisting creek a half a hundred times, struggling through those boggy glades created by the meandering stream, Gibbon formulated his plan of attack—what companies would stand where on the line, who to put in the center with him as they stabbed into the heart of the hostile camp.

No matter what demands the terrain might compel him to make in the way of minor adjustments to his battle plan, the colonel was determined to hold fast to his original strategy. By attacking the very moment there was enough light to make out the lodges and horses he hoped to catch the warriors completely by surprise. Theoretically speaking, his men should be in the village before the enemy could mount any resistance. With their horses driven off and the camp surrounded, the warriors would have no choice but to surrender—rather than risk a slaughter of the innocents.

Gibbon knew those twenty men he left behind with Hugh Kirkendall and the wagons had their work cut out for them. When the iron-tired wheels weren't sinking to the hubs at every swampy crossing, the soldiers were having to muscle those wagons up every grade by double-hitching the teams and utilizing draglines as the twenty assisted the struggling mules. It made him all the more unnerved that the mule-drawn Fort Owen howitzer he had brought along with his advance was encountering the same frustrating delays every step of the way.

Then, near sunset, he caught sight of one of Bradley's men, stationed to watch over the back trail. Not that far on down the slope, the lieutenant's soldiers and civilians lay waiting in the timber.

"How far to the camp?" he asked, his voice breathless with excitement as the lieutenant loped up on foot.

"Five miles, maybe four," Bradley answered. "No more than five, sir."

"Then we'll await the wagon train here," Gibbon explained to the rest of his officers. "Take our supper, then advance within striking distance in the dark. That way we'll be in position come first light."

Just past dark, Kirkendall's wagon train rattled in. Hardtack was distributed among the men and raw bacon for those who wanted it, the soldiers washing their cold supper down with creek water from their canteens because the colonel had forbidden any fires for coffee—no fires for the lighting of pipes. With orders to sleep for the next few hours, the men wrapped themselves in their blankets and settled on the cold ground. John Gibbon was an old war-horse, the affectionate nickname his men of the Iron Brigade had first called him. Because he could sleep on the eve of battle, he was the envy of those who were a bundle of exposed nerves, unable to drift off.

He had graduated from West Point in 1847, a year after the war with Mexico had made heroes of, and bright futures for, the many. Instead, Gibbon tromped off to fight the Seminoles in Florida before he was selected as an instructor of artillery tactics at the military academy. In fact, he had authored the school's new *Artillerist's Manual*, which was finally published in 1863, about the time he was getting himself wounded at Gettysburg—his second of four wounds for that war.

Leaving orders with First Lieutenant Charles A. Woodruff to awaken him at 10:30 P.M., the colonel laid his cheek upon an elbow and for some reason thought back to the final miles on that journey from Fort Shaw to Missoula City. The Nez Perce had gotten around Rawn; Governor Potts was headed home saying the soldiers may no longer be needed; it appeared the crisis in the Bitterroot was over.

That's when the starch had seemed to go out of his men. They had endured a long, hot campaign the previous summer and ended the Great Sioux War a bridesmaid—without firing a shot at the enemy! Ever since they had received word they were moving out, Gibbon's men had known they were going to get in their licks against the Nez Perce. But over the past five days the colonel had kept their minds on the pursuit, put their vision on the horizon—and convinced them the enemy was within reach.

Pretty soon, it reminded him of a pack of hunting dogs howling down a hot trail the way his men were showing their eagerness for this fight.

By blazes—the Seventh wasn't going to be denied *this* fight!

Gibbon was snoring within minutes of closing his eyes.

ARISING IN THE dark, Gibbon gave the command to awaken the men and distribute ninety rounds of ammunition to each soldier for his Long-Tom Springfield rifle—fifty rounds stuffed into the loops of their prairie belts and twenty each in their two leather belt pouches, ofttimes called sewing kits.

"Bring the howitzer and fifteen shots forward at dawn," Gibbon gave the order to the gun crew under sergeants Patrick C. Daly and John W. H. Frederick. "Along with a pack mule carrying those two thousand rounds of extra ammunition for the men."

Everything else—rations, blankets, shelter halves, and more cartridges—would remain behind with Kirkendall's wagons.

Except for the horses of Gibbon and three other men, the animals were left behind with the wagon master, placed in a rope corral beside Placer Creek, a small guard to watch over them until the column's return or Gibbon ordered them forward. When all was in readiness, the colonel gave the command for the heavy wool greatcoats to be left behind at the corral; they would impede a man's movement not only on the nighttime trail ahead but also in the coming battle.

The civilians and those foot soldiers of the Seventh U. S. Infantry stood shivering slightly with the cold in that hour before midnight, 8 August, 18 and 77.

"Lieutenant Bradley," Gibbon said as those around them fell to a hushed silence beneath that starry sky and the nervous soldiers shuffled from foot to foot, "take us to the enemy's doorstep."

They moved out on foot, single-file behind Bradley, Blodgett, Bostwick, and Catlin's thirty-four civilian volunteers from the Bitterroot valley. A total of seventeen officers and 132 enlisted bringing up the rear.

Over the next three miles of sharp-sided ravines and washouts, swampy marshlands of saw grass—where they sank up to their ankles in cold mud and muck—alternating with thick stands of timber, where they stumbled and tripped over fallen and uprooted trees in the dark, broken up by patches of rocky ground strewn with sharp-edged boulders, Gibbon grew more and more anxious. Initially certain the Nez Perce would have sentries posted along their back trail, as his men marched farther without encountering any sign of guards, he became more and more convinced that he was being lured right into a trap.

His eyes straining into the moonless night, ears attuned for any sound that would mean they had been discovered, they crept toward the sleeping camp. On two occasions some of the men at the rear of the column got separated in the dark and mazelike forest, requiring the rest of Gibbon's men to stop and wait for the lost and the laggards to catch up before pressing ahead once more.

Of a sudden the whole sky seemed to open up to them as they emerged from the thick evergreen canopy, finding themselves on a gentle slope overgrown with sage, jack pine, and a fragrant mountain laurel. The heavens ablaze with stars, it was easy for a man to gaze across the full extent of the Big Hole and recognize where the distant, seamless mountains raised their black bulk against the paling horizon.

The grassy hillside where they found themselves was cluttered with little more than a few sagebrush, here above the confluence of two creeks.

"We're very close, Colonel," Bradley whispered, then pointed ahead to the left. "Around the brow of the hill. That's where you should get your first look at the enemy camp."

"You have a staging area in mind, Lieutenant?"

Bradley nodded. "From there we can watch the whole village until it's time to move into position for the attack."

"Show me."

The lieutenant and Fort Shaw post guide H. S. Bostwick led off now, angling left, heading northeast around the sweeping brow of the hill, at the base of which the stream they had just descended joined with Ruby Creek to form the North Fork of the Big Hole. It wasn't but minutes before Bradley and Bostwick suddenly stopped in their tracks.

In a whisper, the lieutenant said, "There they are, sir—look!"

The breath caught in the back of Gibbon's throat as he got his first glimpse of the Nez Perce camp in the valley below: Some of the lodges glowed faintly from within, even more the dull-red reflection of the embers in those abandoned fires still flickering in the open spaces among the lodges.

Gibbon swallowed. "How many are there, Lieutenant?"

Bostwick wagged his head as a dog yapped its warning below. "We never got close enough to count the tepees, Colonel."

Another dog bayed this time, and the faint wail of an infant drifted up the barren hillside to the expectant soldiers.

"Is your staging area close, Lieutenant?" Gibbon asked Bradley.

"On past that point of timber that extends almost down to the edge of the water, Colonel," Bradley explained, pointing.

Gibbon nodded with approval. That dark patch of hogback timber narrowed from a wide V to a point just above the creek. It could well cover most any approach to the village. "What's on the other side of the timber?"

Bostwick said, "If my guess is right, it'll be the ponies."

With a smile, the colonel whispered, "Let's find out if your hunch is good."

Minutes later as they stepped out of the dimly lit timber, Gibbon was startled by the movement of forms on the starlit hillside at their front—fearing they were enemy warriors. After some anxious heartbeats while he sorted out what to do, the colonel realized they had bumped into the Nez Perce herd, right where Lieutenant Bradley had stated it would be.

Which meant that now Gibbon had a new worry, alarmed that the horses would make a great racket, maybe even bolt and stampede, before his men had a chance to direct their movement. But, to his utter surprise, the Nez Perce animals did little more than quietly snuffle and mill about when they winded the approaching white men. Meanwhile, down at the base of the hill, a few of the dogs in camp seemed to understand that warning inherent in the muted whinny of those ponies . . . but while Gibbon and his men held their breath—awaiting some shrill alarm from a camp guard—the dogs below quit barking and the nervous horses shuffled up the hillside, away from the soldiers.

"Bostwick!" he whispered for his post guide, a half-blood Montana Scotsman.

"Colonel?"

"Pick three or four of the citizens, men you can trust," Gibbon ordered. "Start driving this herd back on our trail toward the wagons. I want you to get the ponies out of here before—"

"Not a good idea, sir," Bostwick interrupted grimly, shaking his head in the starlight. "Could be, your surprise will be ruined."

"How?"

"These Nez Perce, they surely got 'em some guards on this hillside," Bostwick explained, "if they don't have guards down watchin' the camp. We go driving off the ponies—we'll be discovered and there'll be trouble, shots fired."

"Which will bring out the whole camp," Gibbon concluded, realizing the man's intuition had to be right. After all, Bostwick had spent his entire life in Indian country.

"Time come soon enough," Bostwick whispered. "We'll have them horses run off for you. But this close to having that camp in your hand, Colonel—you don't want to be discovered now."

"No," and Gibbon wagged his head. "We'll wait out the dawn right here."

"For a man to go on foot is one thing, General," Bostwick whispered. "But you lend me you big gray saddler there, I'll ride down, have a look at the camp."

Gibbon was dubious. "But you just said they'd have camp guards about."

"I'll wrap myself in a blanket," Bostwick explained. "If there's a picket about they won't think nothing of a horseman. A man on foot makes a noise that draws attention—but not a man riding a horse."

"All right," and the colonel passed his post guide the reins to his iron gray gelding. And watched Bostwick disappear into the dim light.

So it was on that grassy sage-covered hillside that Gibbon would halt and hold his men in the dark and the cold.

"Canteens stacked by company," he told his officers.

They would have the tendency to bang and clank against rifle and belt pouch. No worry leaving them here: Soon enough, his men would be in control of that village nestled by a cold, clear gurgling stream.

With this task done, the colonel had his men settle on the cold ground no more than thirty yards directly above the sluggish twisting creek bordered by bristling stands of willow. As the shivering men collapsed around him on the hillside to await the coming of predawn light, the colonel dragged out his big turnip watch from a pocket, remembering he hadn't wound it since the previous morning when they started the wagons up those last two miles to the pass. Turning it just so in the faint starlight, he read that it was a little past 2:00 A.M. Here in this startling quiet, the softest of sounds emerged from the camp below: a horse's snuffle, a babe's cry quickly silenced by a mother's breast, the growl of a dog answering the howl of a coyote somewhere on the mountainside.

In minutes he had his officers together, issuing their orders. Bradley would take Catlin and the volunteers to the extreme left. Logan and Browning positioned on the extreme right flank. With Williams and Rawn serving as reserves right behind them, Captain Richard Comba and Captain Sanno would be in the middle, spearheading the dawn attack.

Once he issued the command to move out, the company commanders would spread their formation roughly as wide as the village itself—which appeared to be a distance of some twelve hundred yards. With his men deployed, the front ranks would ease down to water's edge. The signal to attack would be a single rifleshot, whereupon the men would quickly advance, fire three volleys into the camp, then immediately charge their entire line across the shallow river, certain to enter the village uncontested.

At that moment Gibbon's attention was drawn again to the horse herd. It had been of crucial importance to his plan all along to capture the ponies . . . but—it might be a stupid blunder to awaken the guards who surely must be watching over the horses. Better that they await the moment of attack before moving on the herd, he decided. Then he could seize the ponies at the same time he launched into the village—

"Put out that light!" a voice snapped sharply.

Gibbon wasn't sure who was involved, but there was a scuffle to his left as a few of the shadows quickly lunged toward the man who had just illuminated his face with the flare of a sulphur-headed match. One of the noncoms swung with the back of his hand, knocking both match and the stub of a pipe from the thoughtless soldier's mouth.

As the infantryman shrank back, holding up both hands before him protectively, he muttered, "I fergot, just fergot."

"Just like one of them blokes with Colonel Perry forgot when them horse soldiers was marchin' down White Bird Canyon," the gruff voice of a sergeant growled as he leaned right over the offending soldier, finger jabbing, those gold chevrons shimmering on his arm in the starshine.

"Lemme get my pipe, Sarge," the infantryman begged. "I'll put it in me haversack, straightaway."

"Just be glad I don't tuck you away in me own haversack," the sergeant grumbled. "One lil' slip now—an' our attack won't be no secret no longer."

As the line quieted once more and the forest resumed its night sounds, Gibbon sighed, damp, chill breath smoke slipping from his mouth. Across a deep and willow-choked slough where the meandering creek was backed up, the lodges were arrayed on a line running roughly southwest to northeast. The greater number of the poles were standing near the western end of the camp, off to Gibbon's right. The sky was starting to lighten as post guide Bostwick slid up beside Gibbon and settled to his haunches beside the colonel.

"Won't be long now and you'll see those tepees start to glow like Fourth of July lanterns," Bostwick explained. "That means them squaws are laying firewood on the fires."

"Why is that important to us?" Gibbon asked.

"It means the women are starting to build their breakfast fires, General. Which tells me we ain't been discovered."

"So when the fires flare up, that's a good sign."

Bostwick turned away to gaze into the valley. "It means that village down there will be yours."

A man snored nearby.

Running over the order of battle in his mind once more, Gibbon realized he had done just that hundreds of times since leaving the wagons and horses five miles behind. Everything was ready, he told himself. A flawless plan that would end this Nez Perce war here and now.

All Colonel John Gibbon had to wait on now was the coming of this glorious day.

CHAPTER FIFTY-THREE

Wa-Wa-Mai-Khal, 1877

BY TELEGRAPH

Indian News—Very Serious
Trouble in Texas.

THE INDIANS.

Shooting Match at Fort Hall.
FORT HALL INDIAN AGENCY, August 2.—A band of Indians shot two teamsters at this agency this morning, one seriously and the other slightly, but neither mortally. The shooting was done under the excitement caused by a rumor that hostile Indians were approaching the agency. The shooting was an individual act and condemned by all the Indians in the agency. Agent Donaldson immediately called together the head Indians in council, who condemned the act and sent men in pursuit of the Indians who had fled. They have assured the agent that they shall be caught and brought back and they will guard against any recurrence of the kind. Everything is quiet and peaceful now.

BE CAREFUL, OLD MAN," SHE WHISPERED TO HIM.

Natalekin leaned over in the dark, his cold, stiff joints paining him, and touched her wrinkled face with his fingertips. He could not really see her for the darkness and their fire all but dead now. But he would know the feel of her face anywhere. This would be their fifty-first winter together. Although his rheumy eyes had been growing more and more dim with every summer, *Natalekin* had no doubt he could pick her out of a lodge filled with women.

She patted the back of his hand as she rolled onto her side. He rocked back, slivers of ice stabbing his joints. The damp cold of this Place of the Ground Squirrels had seeped clear down to his marrow. Dragging on the worn, greasy capote, *Natalekin* shuffled around the firepit for that tall, graying triangle that indicated the doorway of their darkened lodge.

Outside at the edge of the brush where he quickly watered the ground, he found that the mist was no longer gray beneath the cover of night. Already that dense fog rising off the creek, clinging to the tall willow, and scudding along the ground between the lodges was beginning to shine with a whitish hue, announcing the coming of first light far to the east behind that barren plateau beyond the camp.

Natalekin heard the old pony snuffle in recognition as he approached, even before he spotted the animal tied there to the fourth stake left of the doorway or it saw him. One cold, throbbing hand followed the picket rope from its jaw down to the stake, untied it clumsily, then took a deep breath. It always hurt to climb atop this steady, old horse. He caught his breath again when he was on its back, letting the waves of cold pain wash through him and out again. A little colder every morning, this agony of growing old become like icy lances stabbing through his joints.

Wiping the hot tears from his eyes at that diminishing pain, *Natalekin* pulled the single rein about and nudged the old pony into motion. He blinked to help clear his foggy eyes of everything that prevented him from seeing what little his old eyes could still see while the animal led him past an old woman trudging between the lodges with her loads of firewood. Three others were already hunched over, starting life anew in cooking pits dug outside their lodges. On down to the shallow creek his old horse led him among the buffalo-hide covers and a few of those tall, bare cones of freshly peeled lodgepoles, stacked in their timeless hourglass shape, drying for their journey to the buffalo country.

At the creek's edge, the horse did not falter as it stepped into the water with a shocking splash to his bare legs. Together they parted the thick, drifting fog bank that seeped along the low, cold, damp places near this north end of the camp, clinging tenaciously to the head-high willow as the pony carried him into the north end of that boggy slough tucked against the base of the nearby hillside where he would find the herd.

Natalekin did not have to awaken so early of a morning just to bring his handful of horses down to water. Chances were they would wander down to the creek on their own, if they hadn't already. But he was an old man and couldn't sleep very well, or very much, anymore. Restless especially when the dark and the damp penetrated his bones with all the more bite. Better to be up and moving about, sensing a little warmth creep back into his body with his spare and economical movements—

Dragging back on that single rein, *Natalekin* halted the horse, letting the quiet, cold water settle around his bare ankles as he stared into the darkness. Then rubbed his dimly seeing, watery eyes with his fingertips. How far away was that?

He squinted, then shifted his head slowly from side to side, attempting to make out the dim forms. These were not horses he saw.

Quickly glancing up the grassy hillside, he could make out no more than the dark squirming of the herd on the slope above. His eyes came back down to the willows ahead. Had some of the horses wandered down into the creek bottom to water or graze on the tall, lush grasses sheltered by the thick banks of willow?

Or was it a prowling coyote? For the past two nights they had bayed and yipped from the hillsides at the camp dogs—

There! Now that was a sound he knew did not belong to a horse. Or a scavaging coyote, either. That breathy rasp, something just sort of a cough. These were not horses. After rubbing his eyes again, he nudged the pony forward another few steps. Ten horse lengths away, no—less than that now. He could see the first three of them. Gradually he made out even more of them, nothing but shapes. Dim figures, man-sized and -shaped, slowly taking form out of the swirling fog snagged above this boggy mire where the creek slowed down and backed itself against the side of the hill.

Perhaps these strangers were those spies the chiefs said were keeping an eye on their camp yesterday. Shadows from the Bitterroot valley who had traded with the Non-Treaty bands, everything from whiskey to bullets. Belief was that such white men had followed the village over the mountains and down to this place—perhaps to do even more trading.

But he did not want them bothering the horses, did not want the strangers to even make an attempt to cut out a few of the *Nee-Me-Poo* ponies they would take back to their towns and ranches in the Bitterroot because the *Nee-Me-Poo* had so many—

Natalekin heard the low voices. Unable to understand any of the words, he could nonetheless understand the harsh tone—like a knife blade grating across a stone—and thereby understood the meaning. These were not spies. Nor were they here to strike up some trading. These Shadows had indeed come to steal.

"Go away!" he called to them as he leaned forward on his pony.

Fuzzy and dreamlike—how he watched the yellow tongues of fire spew from the muzzles of those guns, puffs of gray, gauzy smoke drifting up from the mouths of each one, even before his weakened, arthritic body snapped back, back . . . back again with the terrible impact of each lead bullet.

His eyes were open as he spilled off the back of the pony, feeling the animal twist to the side, rising slightly on its hind legs as its rider tumbled into the waist-deep creek. Flat on his back on the stream bottom, staring up through the dark water. Eyes frozen, staring at the way the fog skimmed along the creek's surface just above him. Hearing the hollow, muted reverberations of those many guns that quickly answered the ones that had killed him. Watching the dark, shadowy figures move past, legs lunging, the water churning with their hurried passage as they advanced on the village. But from here he could do nothing.

Realizing, too, he had no worry about smothering here at the bottom of the creek as the gentle current nudged him slowly around, easing his body downstream. A body that no longer ached.

Natalekin realized he had already begun the journey of death.

First Lieutenant James H. Bradley had brought his left wing of the attack into these tall willows at the bottom of the hill. He commanded no company of his own here; instead, he was the only officer leading both the cavalrymen and Catlin's thirty-four volunteers from the Bitterroot valley. Stepping off the low cutbank, he had quietly plunged into the frigid water that nearly rose to his crotch, so shockingly cold it robbed him of breath for a moment.

The rest came off the bank behind him, stretched out to right and left.

Since witnessing the Custer dead last summer, the lieutenant had been compiling his memoirs of that Great Sioux War. In fact, the day before departing Fort Shaw for the Bitterroot valley, he had completed his remembrances of 26 June 1876—the day before that terrible Tuesday when he had been the first to discover that gruesome field of death.*

But what jarred him now was that he had intended to write another letter to his sweet Miss Mary waiting back at Fort Shaw, some word before he found himself caught up in finding this village. The last he had sent her was written at twilight back on the third of August, from Missoula City before Gibbon decided to march after the Nez Perce with an undermanned force.

> *It has not yet transpired what we are to do, but it is probable we will remain inactive for a few days till Howard comes up from the west side of the mountains and the 2nd Cavalry battalion from the Yellowstone, and then we will push for the Indians.*

Events had a way of catching up a man and hurtling him along with them. Maybe Gibbon was smarting at all the criticism Rawn was taking for his lack of action up the Lolo. That reflected on the Seventh Infantry. Or maybe the colonel was simply tired of all the rumors of his overcaution during the campaign of 1876. For the last year that had reflected on John Gibbon himself.

Bradley was a soldier. A good soldier. Yet the husband and father in him now made him regret not sending a letter back from Stevensville or Corvallis, some word sent with a civilian courier, just a note to tell her where they were going and what they were about.

As James Bradley stepped off the edge of the bank into the cold water, he had a remembrance of how he had ended that letter already on its way to his Miss Mary.

> *Kisses for the babies and love for yourself.*

Most of Catlin's civilians were gathered right behind him at his elbow as they slowly waded toward that last stand of willow shielding them from a certain view of the lodges. Across no more than a half-dozen steps, the water slowly rose past his waist, deeper, too, eventually drenching some of the shorter men clear up to their armpits. They slogged forward at an uneven gait, boots frequently slipping on the uneven creek bottom, shuddering with their cold soaking, parting the stringy mist with each step.

"Hold up!" one of the civilians whispered harshly, and a little too loudly, too, down to his right.

---

*Lieutenant James H. Bradley would not live to complete this vivid chronicle of that war on the northern plains. Ever since, Custer scholars have regretted not having his recollections of the twenty-seventh and the subsequent days of burials, along with the discoveries his advance detail made in the Cheyenne-Sioux village.

Everyone froze.

"One of 'em comin'!" another voice announced.

"How many?"

"See only one," a different voice asserted. "On a horse."

Of a sudden, there he was, taking form behind the gauzy fog. The warrior's pony eased off the far bank into the creek, gingerly picking its way across the rocky bottom, slowly, slowly without the clatter of iron horseshoes. The figure and his horse were swallowed by the dancing mist, then reemerged once more, a few yards closer.

Bradley heard low whispers murmured to his right among the civilians and wanted desperately to call out to them, to order silence. Nothing must spoil their surprise. Catlin's men must goddamn well wait until they heard Gibbon fire that shot announcing their charge into the enemy camp.

Maybe the lone warrior would somehow manage to pass on by them, if the civilians just stayed quiet enough, hunkered down in the willows—let that horseman ease past on his way to the pony herd on the slopes behind them. Then Bradley saw the rider wasn't going to bypass them unawares. The warrior stopped, cocking his head this way, then that.

He'd heard those goddamned volunteers whispering!

Leaning forward, Bradley looked harder than ever, studying the horseman—figuring he really wasn't a warrior at all. Not sitting his pony lithe and agile. It was an old man, nearly white-headed, wrapped in a blanket, maybe a blanket coat.

It surprised the lieutenant when the figure drew one of his legs up, bracing the knee atop the pony's spine, rising and rocking forward as if to have himself a better look at something. Some*thing*? Hell, the old bugger was trying to get a good look at their line! How could he disable the old man without firing a gun—

Suddenly the old man spoke a sharp question, deciding it.

His words were instantly answered, without orders, from the right side of that line Bradley had been leading toward the north end of the village.

Four, five, maybe more guns rattled in volley their low boom muffled slightly by the sodden air. More than one bullet caught the old man, driving him off his horse as it reared slightly—probably hit by bullets, too. The rider sank beneath the surface of the water as the pony wheeled about in fright, scrambling back for the creek bank.

On down to their right, the other units opened up: Logan, Browning, Comba, Sanno. Damn, that old man had robbed Colonel Gibbon of his chance to make the first shot!

"Forrad!" Bradley bellowed to the ranks.

Remembering how the colonel himself had quietly admonished him in the dark that morning, warning him to use great caution going into the tall brush on this far left flank of the line. "Stay with the riverbank as much as possible—where they can't see you so well," Gibbon had asked of him.

The men were starting to talk now, the way a man always would to work himself into the fighting lather.

"Remember your orders!"

They stepped on out of the thick willows, onto some spongy ground there in the slough, seeing how fires instantly brightened in a few of the lodges, shrill voices calling wildly from beyond the gray, swirling mist.

"Hold for my command!"

Another volley roared to their right, from those units positioned farther south along the line of attack.

Screams from the village now. Women's and children's voices—

Quickly interrupted by the ordered third volley from the other companies.

"That's our cue, men!" Bradley bellowed. "Charge!"

With that third wave of rifle fire fading from his ears, Bradley turned to his left slightly as a half-dozen naked figures flitted between the northernmost lodges and those bare skeletons of poles erected on the bank ahead. He raised his right arm, waving to all those around him as their wide front burst from a thick pocket of fog.

"Shoot low!" he hollered a reminder at them as he poked the muzzle of his rifle into some tall brush, taking his first step through the patch of willow. "Shoot low and pay heed to women and children!"

"Hold on, sir!" a voice cried behind him. "Don't go in there—it's sure death!"

The muzzles of those weapons in the village jetted bright flame—

Bradley instantly sensed it like a steam piston slamming into the left side of his chest. No wonder. Here in this brush he was so close to the bank he could make out the fury in the eye of the man who had shot him.

Sitting down in the water as the strength went out of his legs like the gush of a river over a busted dam, the lieutenant found it none too cold now. The creek lapped around his chest, swirled under his armpits, as he sat there, weaving slightly and wondering what had happened to his Springfield. Did he forget it back . . .

He blinked, staring now at the surface of the stream, not sure if the water around him was turning a different color here just before the coming of the sun. Maybe even warming slightly with his flowing blood. But his chest was becoming so heavy he wanted to lie back and sleep. Even right here in the water. After all, it wasn't cold anymore.

The water sucked at him, drawing him back, back so he could sleep just a little.

Eyes closing, he suddenly recognized the top of the timbered hill from his boyhood in Ohio. A few more desperate steps and he found himself on its crest, looking down into a beautiful valley, a wide, beckoning meadow ringed with green, leafy trees barely rustling at the tug of a warm breeze.

The water surrounding him like summer air was cold no longer.

And he heard voices, the chatter of men who hadn't been able to speak for more than a year now. He recognized faces, even though he had never served with any of them. Cavalrymen all. Off to the side somewhere, his ears brought him the music of a fiddle. Some man playing a mighty fine fiddle.

He started to turn that way—then Bradley realized why he heard such music. Knew why he recognized these faces . . . they were Custer's dead, one soldier after another.

The very first time, and the very last, too, he had seen these men, they had been lying upon a bare, stark field of death—bodies stripped of clothing, heads completely scalped, nearly every one of the horse soldiers mutilated: hands, feet, arms, privates hacked off, heads smashed to jelly.

No matter how much he stared at the soldiers now, Bradley could see no signs of mutilation as they turned in his direction and started walking toward him; the first of those two hundred called out to Bradley, welcoming him to Fiddler's Green.

He had made it. Thank God he had made it.

So this was how it was for a soldier to die, he remembered thinking as the first of these heroes came up and put their arms around his shoulders, others pounded him on the back—bringing him along to that green and leafy meadow.

So this . . . is how it feels for a good, good soldier to die.

CHAPTER FIFTY-FOUR

Wa-Wa-Mai-Khal, 1877

SHE WAS THE WIFE OF A GREAT WARRIOR, *WAHLITITS*. THE ONE CALLED Shore Crossing.

After enduring many winters of ridicule and sniping, he had started this war to wash himself clean of the shame of that vow he had made to his father not to take vengeance upon the Shadows. After all the *Nee-me-poo* had endured over the years . . . not to take vengeance?

For some time now she had struggled to understand what made him flirt with other, younger women. Perhaps it was only the pain he tried so hard to hide from everyone but her. Seeking the approval of the younger women to somehow make up for the lack of respect from the older men—warriors they were.

With Red Moccasin Tops her husband had started this war. Swan Necklace came along as their horse holder. Every war party needed at least one horse holder. And when the trio returned to the traditional camp at *Tepahlewam*, they were instantly covered in glory. Shore Crossing was a changed man. No longer did he make courting eyes at the women younger, prettier, than she. Women who still had their flat bellies while hers had begun to swell big and round with Shore Crossing's child.

She had long prayed it would be a son. Not just for her husband, the child's father . . . but for all *Nee-Me-Poo* people. To carry on the bloodline of a great warrior of the People.

From that season of *Hillal*, when Shore Crossing had started the war that would finally throw off that yoke the white man had put upon the *Nee-Me-Poo*, down through *Khoy-Tsahl* and now into the time of *Wa-Wa-Mai-Khal*, these three summer seasons, at long last the People had risen up against an enemy much stronger, far more numerous. Yet their warriors had been victorious in one fight after another against greater foes.

Although the People had been compelled to leave their traditional homelands in Idaho country, she knew they could make a new home with their allies the *E-sue-gha* in the buffalo country. While it would not be the high, green hills she had known since her birth, that new land was where their son would be born in freedom. Perhaps she would name him Buffalo Calf, or Little Buffalo, or something of that sort, to commemorate their coming to the land of the buffalo to escape the war and white men of Idaho country.

The people of Montana country were not angry with them. They had allowed the *Nee-Me-Poo* passage through the Bitterroot valley and over the mountain pass without trouble, once the village had skirted around the small band of soldiers hiding behind their log barricades.

But that next night, Shore Crossing awoke her for the first time with his disturbing dream, seeing himself killed by a soldier's bullet. He was unable to sleep for the rest of the night and told no one else of his frightening vision the next day.

When he finally fell into a troubled sleep the following night, his terrible dream returned. And for every one of the last few nights as the village slowly made its way up the Bitterroot River and down to this Place of the Ground Squirrels.

Here, for the first time in many nights, *Wahlitits* wasn't troubled by the nightmare! Instead, they celebrated with the others their arrival in this country where they could take the time to cut, peel, and cure lodgepoles in the timber above their camp. Last night there had been a lot of gambling by stick or bone around the fires. Dancing, singing, drumming, and laughter. Much, much laughter. They had left the war behind.

Even more important to her, Shore Crossing had finally left his terrifying dream behind. No more would he jerk awake with that vision of a soldier aiming his rifle at him, a powerful bullet taking his life—

That first quick burst of shots awoke her with a start.

She quickly turned to him beneath the buffalo robe beside her. Shore Crossing lay on his back, eyes open and unblinking, staring at the place where the lodgepoles were lashed together with loops of thick rope. She knew he had heard those gunshots, too.

Deliberate in his actions, *Wahlitits* threw back the robe, exposing her, as he reached for his breechclout and leggings.

"No!" she wailed.

He flung her hand off his arm without a word and belted on the breechclout.

Gritting her teeth stoically, she sat up. Over the past few weeks of travel from camp to camp, her once-small breasts had grown heavy atop the swelling mound of her belly. She reached up on the liner rope and took down the cloth skirt and overshirt, quickly pulling them on as Shore Crossing finished tying his leggings to his belt, then quickly knelt to pick up his cartridge belt. Looping it over his forearm, he grabbed his moccasins in hand and took up the carbine he had stolen from the first Shadow he had killed.*

"I want to go with you, *Wahlitits*."

"Yes," he said softly after pausing a moment for reflection at the doorway in the gray light of predawn spreading upon the valley. More gunfire crackled outside, loud, booming volleys of soldier guns. "I want you to come watch a brave man die this morning."

She stifled a wounded cry that fought to free itself from her throat.

---

*Englishman Richard Devine.

He buckled the cartridge belt around his waist, then chambered a cartridge with the gun's lever and quickly ducked from the door.

The instant she followed on his heels, she realized there weren't many husbands and fathers stepping forward to meet the attack. Downstream and up, she heard the soldiers, saw so many of them—more than Shore Crossing could ever stop by himself.

But she knew he had to do what he could.

At the first crackle of gunfire off to their right, her husband seemed to come alive, animated now of a sudden, hearing some other man, another warrior, young or old, crying out his war song, making his stand against the first of those *suapies* in blue slipping out of the whitish mist so cottony it clung to the twisting stream. A lot more soldiers emerged from the brush and willows to their left, wading waist-deep in places as they splashed toward the nearby bank.

"Go with the people to hiding!" he ordered.

"No!" she shrieked, her sob lost in the terrifying racket falling around them.

Bullets began to slap against the new lodgepoles, to thunk through the thick, dampened buffalo hides stretched upon some of the hourglass cones. Lead ricocheted, clanging off iron skillets and brass pots. Favorite war ponies whinnied and cried out humanlike as the bullets struck them, become as thick as wasps on a late-summer day.

"Woman!" Shore Crossing cried out, ripping her attention from the rest of camp and riveting it to him. "See how a brave man dies!"

He fired the carbine at those soldiers no more than twenty feet away now. Striking one of them, driving the white man back into the water.

Quickly levering, Shore Crossing aimed again, fired a second time, and hit another *suapie*.

"Make yourself smaller!" she begged him from the doorway of their lodge.

Ejecting a hot copper cartridge, Shore Crossing did not answer but continued to stand at his full height, turning slightly as he selected another target—

She watched the bullet slam under his chin, driving him off his feet, but as quickly she twisted aside to locate the soldier who had shot him. Wanting so badly to be able to tell her husband who needed killing next.

But when she turned back to her husband, *Wahlitits* was flat on his back, sprawled there near the log he could have taken cover behind, right in front of their lodge.*

Her heart froze a moment as she gazed down at him—struck with the fact that he looked so much the way she had seen him just moments ago: lying so still and unmoving on his back, eyes wide open and staring right up at the sky. . . .

Moving on instinct, she lunged across his body, snatching up the carbine he had dropped. Without thinking of what to do, she pressed the weapon

*Stake No. 10, Big Hole National Battlefield.

against her shoulder, laying her cheek along the stock as she had always seen him do—then found the soldier at the end of the barrel.

The same *suapie* who had killed Shore Crossing.

She pulled the trigger, surprised with the force of the kick against her shoulder as the carbine bucked upward in the air.

Knowing she had to lever another fresh cartridge into the weapon for it to fire another time, she shoved the lever downward, watching the hot, empty casing come spinning out of the action—immediately feeling a tongue of fire course through her upper chest.

Making her feel so heavy she didn't think she could breathe.

Struggling to draw in a breath as she lurched to the side, she felt a second bullet smack into her body, just below her left breast. A third, at the base of her throat. It spun her around violently, flinging her off her feet.

Where she landed, she could almost reach out and touch *Wahlitits* with her fingertips.

It was the greatest struggle of her life—but one that the wife of a great warrior had to make, she told herself with every inch she dragged herself across the grass grown soggy with their blood.

Until she found herself at his side, peered into his wide, staring, glassy eyes one last time—then collapsed across his body . . . her final thought that the bloodline of Eagle Robe and *Wahlitits* was no more.

"GET UNDER THAT buffalo robe and stay there!"

He could tell by the look in his father's eyes that he meant for his son to obey. All little Red Wolf could do was nod his head. No words would come out, he was so frightened.

Although he was tall for his age, this was only his sixth summer. And he was scared to his core. Never had Red Wolf heard such a clatter of gunfire, all the screaming of the women, so much yelling from the men as they darted here and there past his family's small lodge.

"*Suapies!* They have come to kill us!" a voice screamed.

Another warned, "*Suapies* in the river!"

From those first loud shots that brought the whole family awake, Red Wolf looked to others to tell him what to do. First to his mother—but she was busy dragging his younger sister out of the blankets, where the girl had been sleeping beside Red Wolf after the late night of dancing and singing that had followed a long summer day of swimming and watching the young men race their ponies on the bench near camp. His little sister clung to their mother like a plump deer tick not yet ready to drop off its host.

"What of Red Wolf?" his father had asked as he reached the door of their lodge and stopped.

"I cannot take him, too," his mother said. "He would have to hold my hand."

That's when his father dived back into the lodge, knelt, and dragged up the buffalo robe over his six-year-old son. "Stay here until one of us comes back for you. No matter what. Stay under that robe!"

It went dark. He listened as his father dashed away, swallowed by the screams, the gunfire, the terror that had struck their village in the gray light of dawn.

"Do as your father says," his mother's voice came to him muffled by the robe. "One of us will be back for you very soon."

"Good-bye, Red Wolf," his little sister said through the robe.

He did not answer her as he carefully raised the edge of the buffalo hide and peered out at his mother's face one more time before she turned away and squatted through the doorway, that little girl clinging to her back.

The moment they disappeared from view, Red Wolf disobeyed his father and rolled toward the side of the lodge, raising up the edge of the sleeping robe, then tugging at the side of the buffalo hide so he could watch his family make their escape. He did not see his father at all but quickly found his mother racing toward the eastern plateau that stood several short arrow flights from the cluster of lodges.

Strange voices—unfamiliar words—snagged his attention, suddenly yanking his eyes to the left. Red Wolf spotted the first of the strangers standing in the creek: working their rifles, moving forward a few steps, aiming and shooting, then working at their rifles again before they would advance a few more steps.

That one clearly had to be aiming at his mother.

Quickly Red Wolf twisted his head to the right there beneath the edge of the lodgeskins—watching the bullet strike his sister in the back. Watching her spin away and fall, unable to hold onto their mother any longer.

Then he saw the red patch on his mother's bare back as well, the same blood-smeared hole she scratched at with her arm as she stumbled forward a few more steps after losing his sister. Watching his mother pitch onto her face—arms spread wide, legs tangled in each other. She did not move—

A lodgepole just above his head splintered.

On instinct he dropped the edge of the lodgeskins and quickly ducked back under the buffalo robe as his father and mother had instructed. He lay there in the deafening darkness, the suffocating sounds of death all around him—screams of horses, cries of other children he had played with in the creek now possessed by the soldiers, the grunts of those struck by the white man bullets. Crackle of fractured lodgepoles above him as the bullets splintered new wood. Hot lead whining through the air, hissing through one side of the lodgeskins and hissing on out the other side.

He trembled in the darkness. Drawing his legs up fetally. Covering up both ears with his arms, Red Wolf began to cry. Silent sobs as he realized his mother and sister would never come back for him, even though they had promised. Knowing somehow that his father would never return, either. That he was already dead somewhere on that bank of the creek where a few of the first warriors had stepped out to confront the *suapies* emerging from the willows and fog still hugging the ground the way his sister had clung to their mother's back.

No one would be coming back for him now. Little Red Wolf's agonized sobs were drowned out in the darkness that embraced and cradled him.

CHAPTER FIFTY-FIVE

AUGUST 9, 1877

AS THINGS TURNED OUT WHEN THEY INCHED DOWN TO THE CREEK, THE soldiers of William Logan's Company A had the farthest to go in reaching the village the moment those shots rang out.

They had been moving forward in perfect silence. A silence suddenly shattered.

For a heartbeat, the Irish-born captain wasn't certain what to do. He had heard Gibbon's aide-de-camp say the colonel would fire one shot—*one* shot would be his order to commence their three volleys followed by the rush into the enemy village.

But that had been more than one solitary shot.

Nonetheless, Logan could not deny that the battle had been enjoined. Not with that loud, unmistakable roar of voices all the way down the line that extended far to their left, a raucous cheer clear over to where Bradley led his horse soldiers and volunteers, too. Comba and Sanno were bellowing in the thick of it now. It seemed the whole line on their left had taken to yelling as they started forward.

"Volley-fire!" he reminded his company. "Three volleys—low! Fire low into the tepees! Ready . . . aim . . . fire!"

Although some men had instinctively jumped the gun and started for the village, with his loud bellow Logan yanked them to a halt. He ordered the second volley after a few seconds, watching the men palm down the trapdoors on their Springfields and thumb the heavy hammers back into position.

"Aim low! Ready!"

Ahead of them the Nez Perce were breaking from their lodges.

"Aim!"

They'd been caught by surprise. Ripped out of their beds at those first shots, half-clothed. Dazed and terrified, they scattered in half a thousand directions.

"Fire!"

More than fifteen rifles roared again.

"Reload for the third volley!" cried this solid, unflappable twenty-seven-year veteran of both the Mexican War and the rebellion of the Southern states, realizing his voice had risen in pitch. Probably in excitement, knowing that after the third volley his fourteen men and three officers would be pitching into the village.

This warmhearted Irishman well known for his rollicking sense of humor turned and peered momentarily into the camp. Amazed to see so many of the warriors already massing, appearing among the lodges, guns in their hands as they came forward to blunt Logan's attack. A few of the Nez Perce had already begun to kneel or drop to their bellies, carefully aiming their weapons at the fifteen men of Logan's A Company, Seventh U. S. Infantry.

He had to get his men into that camp, drive back those warriors, and put the Indians on the defensive—before the Nez Perce could muster enough fighting men to mount a counterattack.

"Ready!"

Suddenly he thought about his son-in-law, D Company's captain, Richard Comba, another good Irish-born soldier somewhere down the line to his right at this very moment. Regretting how just this past spring they'd both suffered the unexpected death of Logan's daughter, Anna, Comba's wife. And the baby, too. She was the captain's granddaughter, Anna's first child. Born sickly, the little thing hadn't lasted much longer than her mother after a hard and terrible labor.

Logan quickly stuffed his left hand in his pants pocket and fingered the rosary beads that had been his mainstay during those first tragic hours at Fort Shaw this past March. He gripped them tightly in his palm, the crucifix digging into his flesh—

"Aim . . ."

And as he said a prayer for his son-in-law, begging God to remember Comba now in battle before these screaming warriors—

"Fire!"

Captain William Logan turned right, then left, peering down his line. Some of the warriors had jumped over the bank into the creek at the extreme southern end of the village, attempting to take cover and return his company's fire from there. He wasn't sure, but he thought he saw a few women taking refuge there among the fighting men. Logan knew he would have to remind the men to watch for the women.

His company was out in the open now. They had the farthest to go before they punched to the far side of the creek and into the village. The farthest, by bloody damn.

But that was the sort of job the generals always gave to the Irish in this man's army. Cross the open ground where lesser men might shrink from duty. Close on the enemy no matter how they're throwing lead at you. Then seal the damned village tight.

"Reload, goddammit!" he hollered above the racket as they started taking a heavy fire. "Reload!"

On the bank just ahead of them a few young boys appeared with only knives in their hands—dashing headlong into his fifteen. The youngsters slashed, screaming, mouths open like deadly *O*s as the infantrymen clubbed them this way and that instead of wasting bullets on such small defenders.

"Don't shoot the women and the young!" he bawled. "Don't shoot the noncombatants!"

When most of his men had flipped open their trapdoors and the hot, smoking copper cases came spinning out of the chambers to land in the creek, only to stuff fat new shiny cartridges back down into the breeches, their captain knew the time had come to take the village.

He dragged the back of his hand beneath one end of his grand, sweeping, gray-flecked mustache and gave his men their final order.

"Charge, you soldiers! Char—"

The bullet drove him off his feet with a deafening echo in his head.*

Logan lay there on the damp grass, boots tangled in the willow, listening to all their feet pounding on the rocky cutbank as his men carried out the last command he would ever give them.

Ah, now, he thought as he opened his eyes slightly. *This truly is peace.*

Tears slowly drained from Captain William Logan's eyes. There before him swam the face of his beloved Anna. Cradled in one arm was the newborn babe, every bit as lovely as Anna had been on her birthing day.

"Here," Anna said in a whisper as she floated above him, stretching out her empty arm to him while brilliant light tunneled into eternity behind her, "let me help you along, Papa."

HUSIS OWYEEN, CALLED Wounded Head, was not thinking clearly as he burst from the door of his family's small lodge at the southern end of the encampment.

With those first shots he was on his feet, shouting to his wife, *Penahwenonmi,* to get their son out of the lodge to safety. But he himself did not catch up his rifle so that he could fight these attackers. He forgot that soldier gun he had taken from one of the *suapies* who had raided their *Lahmotta* camp. With that gun and the cartridge belt he had taken off the dead soldier, Wounded Head had defended his family and his people in every skirmish that summer.

But this was the first time the soldiers had ever gotten this close to the women and children! To find them almost at their lodge doors, crossing the creek.

"Father!"

He wheeled suddenly, finding his two-year-old son staggering toward him, arms outstretched. Behind the child at the darkened doorway, his wife's frightened face suddenly appeared. Helping Another was screaming for their child—

As he was slammed forward, Wounded Head thought how the feel of that bullet striking the top of his skull, how the very sound of it, must be the same noise a *kopluts,* the short *Nee-Me-Poo* war club, would make in colliding against a man's head. From his first experience, he knew he had been struck a second time in his life by a soldier bullet not strong enough to penetrate his skull.

Stunned, knocked senseless, he lay there, strangely remembering the

*Stake No. 36, Big Hole National Battlefield —although Nez Perce testimony after the battle place the death of an officer wearing "braid and ornaments" at the nearby Stake No. 13.

morning he had taken the soldier rifle in battle—the same day he had saved the life of a white woman on that battlefield,* back in the season of *Hillal*.

Ho! How foolish were those white men to bring along their women merely to warm their blankets when taking to the war trail! But there she was, left completely alone, abandoned in the wake of the soldier retreat up White Bird Hill. Even though neither one could speak the other's language, he convinced her she would be safer with him than on the side of that grassy slope with the many enraged warriors chasing after the fleeing *suapies*.

He started back to the village with his prisoner mounted behind him—no telling how much she might be worth if the *Nee-Me-Poo* had to barter for the return of prisoners when making peace with the Shadows following this fierce and bloody fight. That frightened, blood-splattered, mud-coated white woman might be worth something after all. Besides, he was anxious to show her off to his wife and others. Not only had he taken himself a rifle and bullets, but he had captured himself a prisoner, too!

Then five women had appeared and scolded him for wanting to keep her. That was something the white men did. *Nee-Me-Poo* did not take captives! Besides, she would only bring them trouble if Wounded Head kept her. Finally he was convinced that he should let her go back to the soldiers so the white men wouldn't be angry with the *Nee-Me-Poo* for keeping their woman.

He let her go so the soldiers wouldn't come following the Non-Treaty bands to get their woman back . . . although one of the mean little chiefs had kept his white woman prisoner ever since he stole her from a house on the *Tahmonah*,** that woman with hair the color of honey.

Wounded Head had held out his hand to the woman he was freeing, and they had shaken before she turned to disappear in what brush dotted a crease in the grassy slope. At the time he figured that was what he must do in saving his people from another soldier attack. Give back the woman so the white men won't come looking for her.

As he lay there this morning, unable to move, it was abundantly clear to him that the soldiers had come looking for that honey-haired prisoner they had dragged along with them ever since the first troubles. The *suapies* were here to take her back and exact their revenge on the *Nee-Me-Poo* for stealing her from Idaho country, from her man, from her people.

"Wounded Head!"

Blinking his eyes groggily, he forced them to focus momentarily on his wife, who crouched at the lodge door, pointing frantically.

Helping Another screamed again, "The boy!"

His youngest child was staggering toward the line of soldiers less than an arrow flight away. More than two-times-ten of them, just dropping to their knees, drawing their rifles to their shoulders to fire into the lodges.

No-o-o! his stunned mind cried out, even if his tongue could not make a sound.

But words never did stop a bullet. Lead whined overhead, slapped the

---

*Isabella Benedict in *Cries from the Earth*, vol. 14, the *Plainsmen* series.

**The Salmon River, where Jennet Manuel and her infant son were kidnapped in the outbreak of the Nez Perce War.

lodgepoles, tore through the hide cover, and made his wife scream in terror. Yet in the midst of all that thundering noise, Wounded Head still heard the startled grunt escape his boy's throat as the child was pitched onto the ground no more than three pony lengths away from him. Rolling onto his back, the boy dragged a right hand over one wound, now covered with blood. Then a left hand over another wound. The bullet had gone in one hip, out the other, passing completely through the child's body.

With a shriek Wounded Head had never heard her make, Helping Another sprang to her feet, sprinting for the boy even though she was running toward the soldier guns. Smoke and fog clung low to the ground in riven shreds as she raced into danger, scooped up the child, and turned in retreat, hunched protectively over the boy she cradled in her arms. No more than four steps when a bullet caught her low in the back.

Wounded Head watched how the impact made her stumble as the bullet blew out the front of her chest, just below one breast. She dropped the child, their boy rolling across the trampled grass, crying piteously as he tumbled toward his father.

His wife lay on her belly, barely moving, lips trembling. Wounded Head knew she must be dying.

Their son lay on his back, arms flailing, unable to stand, even to roll over—in great pain.

Still Wounded Head could not move. It was as if the bullet that had struck him just above the brow had taken away all movement from his chin down to his toes. Wounded Head wore the front of his hair in the traditional upsweep of a Dreamer. But what made his different was that it was much longer than Joseph's or *Ollokot*'s. With a thin strip of *hemene*, a piece of hide from a wolf he had used ever since he was a boy, Wounded Head tied up his hair in front—daring any enemy to take it. The wolf had always been his spirit animal.

But now it was only a matter of time until they all would be dead, he decided. Cursing the spirits for this terrible fate: forced to lie pinned to the spot, unable to move, watching as his wife and young son died before his eyes, just beyond his reach. Unable to respond to the boy's calls, to drag his wife to some safe place to die . . . unable to give back hurt for hurt against these soldiers who had come to retake their honey-haired woman and punish the *Nee-Me-Poo* once and for all.

A hard lesson, this pain of watching his family die right before his eyes.

"CLEAR THAT GODDAMN tepee, Private!"

Young Charles Alberts nodded and gulped his reply. "Yes, sir, Sergeant!"

Captain Logan's A Company was spreading out through the south end of the village now, having started to push the Nez Perce out of their lodges after a little trouble stabbing into the camp at first, seeing how the captain was knocked off his feet and killed. But Sergeants John Raferty and Patrick Rogan were taking a few of the men off the firing line as the resistance slowed, sending a few of the privates here and there to check the tepees for any of the enemy who might be hiding inside and capable of doing some sniping.

It was dangerous work, but this San Francisco-born soldier never had been one to shy away from anything that smacked of danger.

Flicking open the trapdoor on his Springfield, the private assured himself that he had a live round in the chamber before he clicked it shut again and pulled the hammer back to full-cock. With the weapon braced against his hip, ready to fire, Alberts stopped just to the side of the loose hide suspended over the tepee door. Using the muzzle of his rifle, the private pushed the door flap away from him, staying well to the side in case one of the occupants fired a weapon at him.

He counted slowly to ten, then snatched a quick peek inside before he jerked his head back again. Not good to give them a target to aim at, he thought. After another quick look into the darkened interior, he felt ready to dive inside himself. In a squat, Alberts stepped through the doorway, stopping immediately inside to let his eyes grow accustomed to the dim light—

Black shadows suddenly tore themselves out of the darkened interior, streaking his way. Two, then three, then more than five of them. Women and children all. His wide, frightened eyes instantly raked them to see if there was a warrior in their number, remembering that Colonel Gibbon had given orders to kill just warriors—women and children only when it was avoidable. But later on in the dark as they had waited out those last hours before launching this attack, word quietly filtered through the units that Gibbon really had no use for any prisoners.

"You fellas know what to do," Sergeant John Raferty told A Company. "When the time comes, the general's counting on you boys all knowing what to do for captives."

Screaming, shrieking, making the hair rise at the back of his neck—the women and children clambered toward him in that heartbeat.

Alberts lurched back, his head and shoulders bumping against the low top of the doorway as he reversed the Springfield in his hands—intending to use it as a club. Even though he was a good soldier who obeyed orders and knew what to do when it came to taking women and children prisoner . . . the private nonetheless would do everything short of giving up his own life to keep from killing one of these innocents.

"None of 'em innocent," an older soldier had grumbled in the darkness just before it got gray enough to move into their final positions. "Squaws and nits—they'll all gut you soon as look at you. Taught that right from the day they was whelped. Ain't no different than the bucks that way. You watch out for 'em, sonny—or they'll slip a knife atween your ribs!"

Before Alberts knew it he was swinging that rifle left and right, back and forth, in a panic, smacking wrists and whacking elbows—knocking their knives and axs out of the way as he stumbled backward through the doorway with the ferocity of their attack.

Kicking out with one boot, he freed his leg from a child attempting to hold him while the women and other children finished his execution. A woman flopped backward, senseless, when his rifle butt collided against her skull. That only emboldened the other two women and the last three children.

Alberts spilled backward, tripping at the lodge door. Dragging up the

Springfield where he lay on his back, he pointed it at the open doorway, ready to fire at the first one of them who came vaulting out with a weapon in her hand.

But for the first heartbeat no one burst from the darkness. Two, then three more heartbeats—not one of his attackers showed her face.

Quickly Private Charles Alberts elbowed his way backward, never taking the muzzle of his rifle from the doorway; then he swallowed hard. Realizing he'd stumbled into a nest of vipers but—for some reason—had just been spared.

"S-sergeant!" he bellowed for Patrick Rogan, managing to catch his breath. "Gimme a hand for God's sake! They amost killed me in there!"

CHAPTER FIFTY-SIX

Wa-Wa-Mai-Khal, 1877

E*LAHWEEMAH* WAS CALLED ABOUT ASLEEP. NOW IN HIS FIFTEENTH SUMmer, he was nearing the age when young men began thinking of those rituals that would lead to full manhood.

Never before in the history of the *Nee-Me-Poo* had the killing of Shadows and *suapies* been part of those rituals.

While part of him was racked with the fright and terror of a child watching the soldier attack on his sleeping camp, another part of him felt the fury of a young warrior throwing himself into battle against the white men who had slithered up on this village, intent upon killing the innocent women and little ones who had never hurt another person in anger.

"Bring your brother!" his mother had yelled at him just before the three of them squirted from their lodge right behind his father.

While the man of the family sprinted off to join *Ollokot*, who stood hollering for others to rally with him near the center of the long, irregular camp, About Asleep's mother pointed to a nearby group of four women, all nearly naked, who were huddled just beneath the creek's sharp cutbank, frantically waving at the others to join them.

"This way!" his mother ordered, unable to pull anything more about her in the instant panic than a leather skirt that she had knotted at her waist. Gripping her oldest son's elbow in one hand, she dragged About Asleep's younger brother along by the wrist while the tiny child sobbed in confusion and fear, bullets striking the lodges all about them, splintering poles.

Together now, the five women and two boys dashed right over the lip of the cutbank and into the shockingly cold water, the leap of each one dispersing a little more of that thick fog clinging to the rippled surface of the creek.

One of the older women pointed out a different direction, saying, "We must take cover beneath those willow!"

Without a word of argument, the seven began wading into the deeper part of the creek, struggling over the slippery rocks and hidden holes to reach the west bank where they could hide beneath the lush overhanging branches.

Just as they were reaching the leafy cover, strange voices speaking the Shadow tongue began crying out both up- and downstream from them. This close to cover, the women did not have a chance to get beneath the long, bobbing branches before three *suapies* appeared, suddenly parting the brush to stand almost directly above the seven cowering *Nee-Me-Poo*.

Unable to comprehend that what he was watching could actually be real, About Asleep saw the first bullet strike the woman beside his mother. She whimpered as if an infant, with that faint cheep of a newborn sage chick when she slipped beneath the water.

The other four women cried hideously at the sight, both in anger and in panic as they bent to scoop her from the water that swirled in this deep eddy, soaking those who wore any covering to their armpits.

A second of the soldier guns fired. About Asleep's own mother jerked, back arching violently; then she eased down into the water, slowly turning around on the surface, her eyes wide but already lifeless.

About Asleep shrieked in terror, his younger brother, too, their voices joining those of the three gray-headed women.

With another gunshot, About Asleep felt the burn along his upper arm, heard the big bullet *ploosh* into the water beside him.

"Come on!" he screamed to his brother, waving desperately for the women to follow before he grabbed the youngster with his other hand.

But the women were not as quick as the youngsters. While About Asleep and his brother lunged out of the water to grab a soldier's ankle, vainly attempting to upset him, the women were paralyzed in fear.

The young soldier easily kicked himself free, then wheeled away into the brush, crying for his companions. About Asleep realized the two of them would never have a better chance of escape.

"Get out of the water!" he ordered his younger brother.

Dragging himself onto the grassy bank among the thickest growth of the willow, About Asleep reached out and pulled his brother into the brush.

Four soldiers suddenly burst through the thick vegetation, their rifles already pointing down at the older women in the creek. Even though those women waved their arms and pleaded for mercy, the bullets erupted from the guns in a fury—driving the victims back, back, back until they slipped lifeless beneath the surface turned white with angry foam, tinged red with the blood of their many wounds.

"Run!" About Asleep shouted at his brother, pushing the youth ahead of him into the leafy brush that whipped and cut and lashed their naked bodies.

Yet About Asleep did not feel the mere touch of a single branch or suffer the clawing of any of the sharp alder limbs.

To stay alive, they had to run far, far from this killing place.

CORPORAL CHARLES N. Loynes quickly looked left, then right. Every other soldier was too consumed with something else to notice what the young corporal had just witnessed, disbelieving. No one else saw it . . . so maybe those women weren't really there.

Loynes blinked his eyes, rubbed them with the heel of his left hand, and looked again.

But there they were, four Nez Perce squaws sliding that buffalo robe over their heads once they had slipped over the creek bank and all were in the water.

Moments ago he had breathlessly watched the four, admiring their courage and amazed at their audacity, as the side of a lodge was split open with a huge butcher knife and the women popped out of that long slit like peas from a crisp pod, dashing for the edge of the stream, one of them dragging a hairy buffalo hide behind her—the sort he knew these Nez Perce curled up in to sleep. Every few seconds Loynes had looked left and right to check if any other soldier in his I Company, even one of the civilians, had spotted what he was watching.

Somehow the four had managed to dash through the fog and gunsmoke unnoticed by anyone but the corporal, who found himself somehow separated from the rest of his unit at this moment—Captain Rawn's own company, men who had watched these same Nez Perce skip right around them on the Lolo. *They're a tricky bunch, these Injuns!*

He immediately scolded himself for not inspecting those women more closely. Since both the bucks and squaws wore their unbound hair long and loose, it was hard for him to remember if all of the four truly were women. Maybe there was a fighting man or two among them. Just fine that the women should make a run of it—but if one or more happened to be a warrior with blood on his hands, then Loynes wouldn't be doing his job as a soldier to clean up this village of rapists, thieves, and murderers. A warrior who would escape death today could well be a warrior who would kill more soldiers, pillage more settler homes, and shame more white women with his evil somewhere on down the line.

With their buffalo robe unfurled upon the surface of the creek he had lost all chance to tell buck from squaw. But he immediately knew how to get himself a good look at the four: Loynes figured he would shoot at the floating robe while the four started downstream past the middle part of the enemy camp.

"What the bloody hell you shootin' at down there, Cawpril?" a voice demanded just after Loynes had pulled the trigger for the first time, standing on the bank overlooking the hide.

"Look!" he exclaimed as Sergeant Michael Hogan stomped over to his elbow and peered at the creek, too. "Watch that robe—there's four of 'em under it!"

"Four?" the sergeant boomed, bringing up his Long-Tom. "Warriors?"

"I think some of 'em are," Loynes answered with a swallow, noticing the edge of the robe rising slightly from the surface of the water as if one of the four were peeking out from under the hide. "Lookee there—them bucks is sneaking in a breath of air!"

"Lemme shoot one of them red bastards when he pops up for a breath," the sergeant growled, shoving his Springfield into the crook of his shoulder.

"I get another shot after you, Sarge."

One after the other, the two soldiers swapped shots at the floating buffalo hide, their bullets piercing the robe here, then there. One time Loynes caught a glimpse of a hand, another time a cheek, and once he saw an eye peer beneath the dark blot of shadow before the robe was dropped onto the surface again. Inching slowly along the brushy bank, both sergeant and corporal followed the floating robe, reloading while they kept a watchful eye locked on the hide—strangely oblivious to the terrible fight raging behind them in the Nez Perce camp.

One at a time, the bodies of the Indians they had killed rose to the surface at the edge of the robe, twisted and rolled gently in the current, then bobbed slowly downstream . . . until there were no more to shoot and the hide finally swerved about and became ensnared on some overhanging willow—now that no one controlled its movements.

"Four more bucks won't be cutting no shakes no more!" Sergeant Hogan exclaimed, immensely proud of himself.

Loynes smiled wanly. "Four . . . four more. That's right, Sarge."

"Won't be jumping no more white women now, Cawpril."

"No, the four bastards gonna feed the coyotes now," Loynes replied, remembering how that eye had peered out at him.

Hogan pounded him on the shoulder. "You helped me make 'em good Injuns!"

The corporal nodded. "Yeah, Sarge. We made all of 'em good Injuns!"

CHAPTER FIFTY-SEVEN

Wa-Wa-Mai-Khal, 1877

TRUCK IN THE HEAD BY A *SUAPIE* BULLET, *HUSIS OWYEEN* HAD NO IDEA HOW long he had lain there, stunned and unable to move, while more wayward bullets hit both his son and wife near their lodge at the southern end of the village.

His muscles not heeding his desperate cries, Wounded Head cursed the spirits for dealing him such an agonizing blow as this—not only having to watch his beloved family die right before his eyes but being unable to go help them. Forced to listen to the boy's whimpers as the child struggled again and again to rise, Wounded Head could see how his son couldn't roll this way or that because of his broken hips.

And Wounded Head was forced to watch the way his wife's hand clawed at the grass at her side for the longest time. It was the only part of her body that moved, all she could do, so badly wounded through the chest was she.

Slowly, with excruciating discomfort, he sensed feeling beginning to return to his body, an icy tingle eventually creeping down his legs, worming its way out through both arms, until all his limbs finally did as he willed them.

Wounded Head sat up in the midst of that yelling and gunfire, the hammer of running feet and the whine of bullets.

"Father!"

Instantly he knew what he must do.

Rocking onto his feet unsteadily, running in a lumbering crouch, Wounded Head clambered toward his son. He paused to scoop the boy's bloody body into his arms, then wheeled about and made for a patch of thick willow on the creekbank. Inside that modest cover, he laid his son upon the ground.

"I'm going back for your mother." And he touched his son's cheek, his fingertips wet with the boy's blood.

The moment he reached *Penahwenonmi*'s side, Wounded Head stretched out upon the ground beside her—the better to appear wounded or dead himself. Carefully he reached out and rolled Helping Another onto her back. A flood of relief washed through him when his wife's eyes fluttered open.

"Th-the boy?"

"He should live," Wounded Head whispered.

"Take good care of him . . . always," she said in a raspy voice pierced with much pain.

"I'm taking you to him now," he vowed.

"No!" she whimpered, tears bubbling from her clenched eyelids. "It hurts too much."

"If I leave you here, surely you will die," he said with a touch of anger at her refusal. "Or the soldiers will find and kill you, maybe even shame you with their lusts before they put a bullet in your head."

Only her eyes moved as she peered at him, each of them with a cheek resting on the ground, their faces only inches apart, noticing his head wound. "You are hurt, too."

"I'm taking you now," he said suddenly, scrambling up to a kneeling position, looping his hands beneath her shoulders, and gripping her armpits.

Whirling her around despite her shrill wail of pain, Wounded Head started backward in an ungainly wobble, making for the brush where he had secreted their son. All around them, on both sides of the creek, the booming of guns and the shouts of fighting men failed to drown out the screeching of those terrified women and children who were unable to escape the village before the soldiers were upon them.

Not far to his left stood the maternity lodge.

Wounded Head wondered if any young mother would still be in there, if one of the aged midwives remained with her. Forced by nature to be giving birth at this hour of travail and horror. It could not be a good omen for the child.

In heartbeats he got his wife inside the concealing brush with the boy. She held out an arm as he gently slid the boy across the blood-soaked grass, nestling their son against his mother.

"Stay here until I—"

"Don't go!" she whimpered in a gush.

"There is a fight," Wounded Head said as he bent over her and kissed her damp cheek. "If the Creator decides that I am to come back for you, I will return when the fighting is over."

"Father?"

"I brought you both here where you will be safe," he told the boy. "And when you cry, do not cry out loud so those soldiers will find you like hungry wolves sneaking through the willow. Bite down on your teeth so they do not hear you cry. I will come back for you when this fight is done."

In a matter of a few breaths he was back beside his lodge, stabbing a slit through the side of the spongy dew-soaked hides. Diving inside, he quickly gathered his soldier rifle and cartridge belt taken from the *suapie* he had killed at the *Lahmotta* fight back in the season of *Hillal*. While he was buckling the belt around his waist, he heard a familiar voice sing out a brave-heart song just beyond the lodge cover—the great warrior Rainbow, calling for the men to rally around him.

"I am here, Rainbow!" he shouted as he crouched from the lodge door and dashed around the side of his home.

Already more than ten warriors stood or knelt around Rainbow as Wounded Head ran up—all of them concentrating their fire on a cluster of soldiers they had pinned down at the edge of the village, on the cutbank where the white men could not gain any more ground. "A Shadow for every bullet!" Rainbow yelled.

Sliding up beside the great warrior, Wounded Head went to one knee and dragged back the hammer on his short soldier carbine. As he sighted along its barrel, Rainbow continued to shout encouragement above them all. His gallant, brave voice suddenly made Wounded Head remember the words known to so many of the *Nee-me-Poo*: this great fighting man's vow.

"*I have the promise given me by the spirits that in any battle I engage in after the sun rises*," Rainbow had told and retold of his powerful vision, that sacred *wyakin* or warrior's medicine, "*I cannot be killed. I can therefore walk among my enemies. I can even face the points of their guns. My body will be no thicker than a hair. The enemies can never hit me with their bullets. But . . . if I fight any battle before the sunrise—I will be killed.*"

The shock of that sudden remembrance shot through him like a bolt of summer lightning, Wounded Head immediately twisted around, peering over his shoulder at that low bench east of the village—terrified to find that, even though it had grown light enough to dispel all the dark, murky vestiges of night, the sun had not yet made its appearance over the edge of the earth.

"Rainbow!" he shrieked in panic, reaching up to seize the great warrior's forearm. "Look! The sun! It hasn't shown its face yet today!"

His cry of encouragement ceased in the middle of a sentence as the war chief turned suddenly, staring in panic over his shoulder at the eastern bench a long, long time. Then the fear faded from his face. Gone was the terror that had clouded his eyes only a moment before. He turned to gaze down at Wounded Head, laying his empty hand on the warrior's shoulder, the look upon his face one of deep calm now.

Rainbow said, "Tell my brother, Five Wounds—that this *is* a good day to die!"

Once more the war chief turned to face the assault, again raising his voice against those four-times-ten he and the few were holding back while the women and children made their escape from the village. Standing unafraid in the midst of the others who knelt or lay on their bellies to make themselves smaller, Rainbow refused to cower in the face of all those bullets.

Of a sudden, no more than four paces from them, a tall soldier leaped from behind some brush. The much shorter Rainbow raised his weapon at the same instant and the two enemies fired together. But the great warrior's action clicked—his carbine was empty. The white man's bullet struck Rainbow squarely in the breast, knocking him backward a wobbly step.

The tall soldier immediately whirled on his heel and dived back into the bushes.

"Rainbow!" Wounded Head shouted, bolting off the ground for the war chief.

As Rainbow collapsed to his knees, then crumpled backward into the grass, that look of calm on his face seemed to grow all the more serene as he cried out to others, "Fight on! Remember always to fight on! You must fight—"

His last words were choked off by a gush of blood.

But before anyone could grieve Rainbow's death rattle, Grizzly Bear

Youth shouted a warning. This warrior named *Hohots Elotoht* lunged to his feet and darted for the tall soldier who reappeared from the bushes with his rifle reloaded. As Grizzly Bear Youth leaped for him, the hammer on the soldier's gun snapped without firing—exactly as Rainbow's had done the instant before he was killed.

Now the two enemies brandished their empty weapons overhead as they raced toward each other—colliding with a crunch of bone, falling to the ground in a heap. It was immediately clear to Wounded Head how much smaller Grizzly Bear Youth was than the bigger white man. In moments the soldier had the warrior pinned to the ground.

As he struggled for his life, Grizzly Bear Youth cried out to his *wyakin* for power to defeat this big enemy!

The warrior was soon answered and managed to somehow drag himself out from under the soldier—yet the white man quickly gripped Grizzley Bear Youth around his neck and began to choke him. At that moment *Lakochets Kunnin* burst from some nearby willow, landing right beside the wrestlers, and fired his carbine into the *suapie*'s side.

It did not take long for the soldier to let go of Grizzly Bear Youth, stumbling backward before he collapsed against the brush and lay perfectly still. Nearby the smaller warrior sank to his knees, clutching his forearm. Blood oozed between his fingers.

"Your bullet broke my arm!" he cried out to *Lakochets Kunnin.*

"Maybe it did," said this warrior called Rattle on Blanket, "but I saved your life!"

While they argued, Wounded Head turned to stare down at the great warrior Rainbow, who had been offering encouragement and hope with his final words, in his last act of defiance . . . even though it was a battle waged before the coming of the sun, before the awakening of his powerful *wyakin*. He had refused to shrink from his duty to his people—

When Wounded Head looked up, none of the other fighters remained. He was alone with the body of Rainbow. The others were scattering this way and that as the soldiers finally began to gain ground, quickly advancing on the spot where Wounded Head knelt over the great warrior's lifeless body.

"If you can be killed," he whispered to Rainbow, starting to weep as he closed the man's blood-splattered eyelids, "then we all can be killed."

HE COULD NOT remember when his head had ever hurt this bad.

Nor could Private George Leher* recall just where he was, what day it might be, or what he was doing flat on his back—finding himself dragged along the wet, soggy grass by the older woman who took shape as he came to and his blurry eyes began to focus.

It took a few moments, this realization did, what with the bullet wound to the head that had knocked him senseless. Struggling to remember how he had come to find himself lying flat on his back, Leher recalled bits of things the way a man might tear up the whole sheet of a memory into tiny pieces of

*Variously spelled Lehr in some of the Big Hole battle literature.

confetti and toss them into the air. A panic gripped him, as he realized he never would get all those pieces back together again, not in the same order, nor with all the details intact. . . .

She gripped him by one heel, tugging him over the ground one yard at a time, his ankle pinned beneath her armpit as she struggled to drag him to the closest tepee, his rifle used as a crutch in her other hand while she lunged forward a few feet, replanted the weapon, and lugged him a little farther.

The numbness he felt radiating through his body from the head wound gave him such panic—just knowing that he was powerless to do a damned thing to save himself for the moment.

That's when he remembered that he had just come out of the water, cold and wet from his midchest down, hearing the enemy's rifles crack all across their front, seeing the enemy flitting here and there, watching a bullet hit Captain Logan himself—when lights suddenly exploded in his head.

Since the old shrew could have finished him off where she found his body if she'd had a knife or ax, she must be dragging him toward the lodge to kill him there.

Leher tried to twist his leg free of her grip.

The woman immediately stopped and peered back at him with an angry face, screeching at him in her strange talk that only made his head hurt even more. She shook his rifle at him menacingly, then turned around and started off again.

This time the private somehow willed his loose leg to coil up, cocking it near his body—then lashed out at her.

His water-soaked boot caught the older woman in the small of the back, sending her sprawling with a yelp of surprise.

His head swam as he slowly rolled onto his hip, spying the rifle lying between them. Rocking forward, he seized it by the butt and began to drag it toward him in his left hand just as she pounced forward and snagged hold of the muzzle.

Back and forth they tussled with it, she gripping the barrel in one hand and swinging her closed fist at his head like a club, forcing him to duck this way, then that, as his right hand crawled up the stock, farther and farther, reaching the wrist, then the trigger guard, finally to yank back the hammer—

When the weapon went off, it blew a bullet through the side of her face as she was leaning away, almost as if she had realized in that final moment what was about to happen to her. The close impact of that bullet striking her in the head drove the woman backward a few feet, her body flopping against the dew-dampened buffalo-hide lodge.

She slowly slid down the tepee, the pulpy side of her head smearing the hide cover with a wide, moist, red track until she came to a rest on the ground, staring at him—her eyes already glazing in death before her silent mouth moved one last time. Then she teetered to the side and fell on her shoulder to budge no more.

With his head still ringing from his own wound, Private George Leher felt along his prairie belt and pulled one of the long copper cartridges from its canvas loop. When he flung up the trapdoor, the extractor shot the empty cartridge from the smoking breech and he jammed home the fresh round.

Snapping down the trapdoor and dragging the hammer back to full-cock, he took a deep sigh and closed his eyes a minute more—relieved that he had possession of his rifle once more. No squaw was going to drag him anywhere. None of these screaming bucks was going to get close enough to finish him off.

He'd just lie there by the side of this lodge and wait until one of Logan's A Company came back to find him . . .

Act like he was dead till someone came along to help.

He clenched his eyes shut a moment longer, praying that next person would be a white man.

CHAPTER FIFTY-EIGHT

Wa-Wa-Mai-Khal, 1877

BY TELEGRAPH

Indian News—Very Serious
Trouble in Texas.

THE INDIANS.

Sitting Bull Heard From.
WASHINGTON, August 8.—A letter from the United States consul at Winnipeg says: Near Sitting Bull's encampment a war party of twenty-seven Sioux robbed the traders of three kegs of powder and one bag of bullets. Besides Sitting Bull's band there is an equal number of Sioux refugees from the Minnesota massacres of '62 and '63, over whom Sitting Bull seems to exercise much influence.

ONE DAY HE ALONE WOULD CARRY HIS ELDERLY UNCLE'S NAME, BUT FOR the present, this ten-year-old was merely known as *Young* White Bird.*

Awakening with the first rattle of gunfire, the youngster was dragged from beneath his sleeping blanket by his mother as his father, Red Elk—a brother to Sun Necklace—dashed from their lodge. Bullets ripped through the lodgeskins, pattering like hailstones and splintering the new poles.

"Come with me, Son! Run, run!"

He followed his mother outside, where they immediately started for the closest protection: a bunching of tall willow some of the charging soldiers had just abandoned as they thrust into the village. Here and there favorite ponies were hitched near the lodges, where they would be close when a man or youngster went to see to the herd. One by one, these animals were being killed on their tethers. As they neared the brush, his mother cried out, shak-

---

*Under tribal practice, he would not actually receive this name until he had reached manhood, at which time he began to tell his remembrances of this Big Hole fight. I was unable to locate any reference to what this child's name was *at the time* of the Nez Perce War.

ing her free hand. It dripped with blood as she held it up for her son to inspect. A bullet had clipped off a finger and the end of her thumb.

Young White Bird was just reaching out to cradle his mother's wounded hand when they both flinched the instant another bullet struck the hands they had joined. His left thumb was severed now, the splintered end of the whitish bone poking out of the raw, bloody stub on his hand.

"We can't stay here!" she cried. "To the water!"

They lunged toward the nearby creek, leaped in, and waded across a narrow tongue to reach a patch of overhanging willow, where they sank to their haunches in the cold water so only their heads would be showing to any soldiers on the riverbanks.

No sooner had they squatted among the branches than a young girl appeared on the bank opposite them. Naked, she jumped into the water and quickly swam toward the willow where Young White Bird and his mother were hiding.

"Come in here with us!" his mother sang out.

The young girl reached them just as three more children, all about Young White Bird's age, appeared at the same spot on the bank and hurtled themselves into the water without hesitation. They floundered and splashed, kicking their way across the languid stream to reach the willow and the three who waited under the branches.

Through the noisy din of battle Young White Bird recognized his uncle's voice, raised loud and strong above the racket of gunfire.

"Why are you young men retreating! Are we going to run to the mountains and let the white men kill our women and children? It is far better that we should be killed fighting!"

His uncle's words gave him a fierce pride.

A soldier suddenly stood on the bank, then disappeared as quickly. The next few minutes were filled with terrifying screams and the shouts of frightened white men, before a different soldier appeared on the opposite bank, looked across the water at that group huddled beneath the willow. He, too, disappeared without taking any action.

The moment he was gone, a young woman of no more than fifteen winters, naked to the waist, bolted over the edge of the bank at full speed as if she were being pursued. She hit the water flat on her belly with a painful smack, immediately churning her arms like wind-driven limbs on a high-mountain aspen during a strong gale.

Young White Bird and his mother reached out to offer their hands to her, pulling the young woman into their temporary shelter just as another girl about his own age crawled to the edge of the bank on her belly, flopped over the precipice, and landed in the water.

"Get her, Son!"

He swam out to retrieve the girl, dragging her back to rejoin his mother.

"See there, how she was wounded in the arm," his mother said, holding the young child's upper arm out of the cold water. The girl winced as he peered at the bullet wound. He could see all the way through the ragged bullet hole—

One of the youngest children shrieked in terror the instant a young woman—old enough to marry and have a child of her own—pitched off the bank into the stream but did not move much to save herself from the water.

"Bring that one to us!" his mother commanded.

Her body was limp as he dragged it, bobbing gently on the current, toward their hiding place.

"Help me place her head on the sandbar so she can breathe," his mother said.

The older girl helped them. She asked, "Will she live?"

Gravely Young White Bird's mother shook her head. "I don't think so. She has a big bullet wound in her chest. But we can help her breathe until she either wakes up or she dies."

He looked at the young woman as she lay in his mother's arms, finding her very pretty. Young White Bird did not remember ever seeing this unconscious one before. He thought she was one of the prettiest young women he had ever seen. Her blood colored the water around her body.

"Soldiers!" one of the children cried out before an older one could get her hand clamped over the child's mouth.

Young White Bird counted seven of the *suapies* spread out on the far bank, all of them training their rifles at the clump of overhanging willow. Just as he was about to yell in protest—to curse the white men for killing women and children—his mother shoved his head under the water.

Sputtering, he leaped back up for air, finding his mother had stepped from beneath the overhanging branches, both arms raised, waving them from side to side, yelling in the white man's tongue.

"Women! Only women and children here! Do not shoot! Only women and children!"

First one, then two more of the soldiers slowly lowered their rifles, talking among themselves. Finally the rest of them took their rifles from their shoulders and quickly backed away from the creek bank.

"You saved our lives," the young woman told his mother when the *suapies* were gone.

Young White Bird's mother wagged her head as she lifted the youngest children onto the grass bank opposite the village.

"Saved your lives only for a little while," she said grimly. "Let's do what we can to save you for good."

HE HAD TO restrain himself to keep from cheering aloud!

Colonel John Gibbon had rarely been this elated before. His men had control of the village about twenty minutes after those first confusing shots rang out. The Nez Perce were on the run, driven from their lodges. And it appeared some of Catlin's civilians had a good chance to capture the horse herd and get it started on their back trail, depriving the warriors of mobility and escape.

Despite the blunder with those opening shots from the overeager volunteers and despite the momentary delays of some units charging across the creek and into the village . . . the surprise had nonetheless been sudden and utterly complete.

The only drawbacks were that their twelve-hundred-yard front had not been long enough to completely encompass the southern end of the village. That and the northern end, too—where the attack completely stalled.

Despite all these failures, the Nez Perce had been caught sleeping!

The men, women, and children, too—all came tumbling from their beds partially dressed, if not naked, ill-prepared to mount a momentary defense. Watching from the side of the hill across the creek, he waited until the bulk of his troops were across the slough before he gave his big gray charger the spur and moved toward the seat of the action. Gibbon hadn't been in the village very long when the first report arrived, accounting the high rate of casualties among his officers.

Lieutenant Bradley was dead almost from those first shots. Captain Logan had also fallen among his men, shot by a woman.

"A woman?" Gibbon had asked for clarification.

"Yes," replied Lieutenant Charles Woodruff, his aide-de-camp, who rode back and forth carrying messages in that first desperate hour. "Seems the women and young boys are fighting as hard as their men, General."

"It's difficult to tell the fighters from the innocents in this melee, Mr. Woodruff," he told the soldier. "Some accidents are unavoidable."

"The women—they're fighting like she-cats on the other end of the village, General."

That caused him to look at the far northern flank of their line, off to the left side of the assault. There on the hillside above Bradley's initial position he had hoped to find the Nez Perce herd under control of Catlin's civilians, perhaps even started away on their back trail already. Instead, some of the volunteers were trading shots with more than a dozen of the half-naked warriors crouched on the fringes of the herd while nervous ponies reared and jostled one another.

He had to find a way to drive off that small band of warriors and seize their herd. Those horses must not fall into the hands of the enemy, now that it was painfully clear his men had failed to seal the trap around the village.

WHEN YELLOW WOLF saw his chief, Joseph of the *Wallowa*, for the first time that terrible morning, the leader was crossing the creek bare-legged with No Heart—both of them barefoot. Joseph had a shirt on, and breechclout, too, but instead of leggings Joseph wore half a blanket belted around his waist as he clambered out of the water, onto the bank, and lunged up the slope toward the horse herd. At first Yellow Wolf thought it might be *Ollokot*—the two looked so similar in many ways—but after a moment he was sure it was Joseph.

After all, going for the horse herd was something a camp chief was sure to do, while staying in the village to fight the soldiers was what a war chief would do. Joseph had gone to secure the herd so the People could make good their escape on this awful morning.

Before everything had come undone in a noisy instant, Yellow Wolf recalled awakening to the sound of a horse crossing the stream. After a long night of singing and dancing, he had gone to sleep in his parents' lodge erected right against the creek bank. At the time he heard the hoofbeats, Yellow Wolf wondered if the man was crossing to his horses on the west side. But later he came to think it must have been one of the white spies: riding his horse close to the sleeping village before the attack was ordered.

At the first shots he had bolted out of his blankets there in his parents' unfinished lodge. They hadn't put up the heavy lodge cover. Instead, they had roped together the cone of freshly peeled poles, then draped part of some old hides over the lower part of the framework to give them a little privacy when they all trudged off to bed after a late night of celebrating their escape from the war in Idaho country.

Sleeping in his parents' dwelling meant Yellow Wolf was caught away from his rifle, too. When the fight started, he had nothing more than a war club handy. Grabbing the *kopluts*, Yellow Wolf dashed into the fray.

A woman stood near the edge of the village, scolding in a shrill voice, "Why aren't you men ready to fight? You sing and dance all night—so you are slow to fight these attackers! Get up and do not run away from this battle!"

Her stinging words made a lot of sense as so many of the young men stumbled from the lodges, rubbing the sleep from their bleary eyes, shaking their groggy heads, ill-prepared to turn away this challenge from the soldiers.

"*Ukeize!*" a woman cursed at Yellow Wolf, reaching out to grab his arm and stop his dash. "Rainbow is dead! Rainbow is dead!"

This is unbelievable, his mind raced. The *Nee-Me-Poo* had three great warriors: *Ollokot*, Rainbow, and Five Wounds. Now one of the bravest was killed!

Sprinting as fast as he could through the first bullets, Yellow Wolf started for the far northern end of camp where Joseph's lodge was standing. Near the middle of camp he encountered *Jeekunkun*, called Dog. This older man was bleeding badly from his head and stumbling along, plainly unable to use the rifle he dragged along the ground.

"Give me your gun!" Yellow Wolf demanded. "You have plenty of bullets on your belt and I have nothing but this *kopluts*. Trade me now so you can get away from danger and see to your wounds!"

"No!" Dog growled angrily, clumsily swinging the rifle's muzzle at Yellow Wolf, forcing the young warrior to back away. "I must keep my gun. I don't want to die with no way to fight back!"

Yellow Wolf pushed on. Close by he came across a younger warrior, this one wounded more severely than Dog. "Red Heart," he called out to *Temme Ilppilp*. "Trade me your carbine so I can fight the soldiers who have hurt you!"

But Red Heart would not let go of his gun even though he had a very serious stomach wound and could not straighten up, as he walked bent over in a crouch.

Of a sudden Yellow Wolf heard some Shadow cursing. A grin began to grow on his face. Creeping around the side of a lodge, he spotted a soldier crawling on his hands and knees, wobbling side to side like a man with too much whiskey in his belly, as he dragged a rifle along. The white man did not hear Yellow Wolf approaching until the last minute, when the soldier looked over his shoulder, eyes growing big as brass *conchos* to find the *kopluts* swinging down at his head. The white man's teeth loosened in his mouth as he fell.

Bending over the dead man, who had blood seeping from both his ear and the splintered bone on the side of his head, a curious Yellow Wolf pushed on the loose teeth with two fingers. All the teeth moved together. He pulled on them, finally freeing those at the upper part of the mouth, then those from the bottom. Now the white man had no teeth and Yellow Wolf had an extra set!

A bullet whined past his head. He scolded himself for being so heedless in his curiosity. Tossing the false teeth into the brush, he swept up the dead man's rifle.

Yellow Wolf now had a soldier gun and a cartridge belt, nearly every one of its loops filled with shiny bullets. He immediately turned to go in search of *Ollokot*.

With bitterness he recalled how the head chiefs had given orders to the bands not to harm any Shadows in Montana as they started away from the Idaho country.

"No white man must be bothered on the other side of the Lolo!" Looking Glass had commanded.

"We will only fight the enemies here in our old homeland," White Bird had emphasized. "Trouble no white people after passing over the mountains. Montana people are not our enemies. Only the Idaho people."

"Do not kill any cattle across the mountains," Looking Glass had warned. "Only if our women and children grow hungry will we take cattle or any food we need to feed our people."

Those were strong laws made by their leaders—laws that must not be broken for the sake of all the *Nee-Me-Poo*, since they were leaving the war behind by crossing the mountains.

Now it was clear the Montana whites did not think the same way as Yellow Wolf's people.

Even though the warriors had taken precautions not to injure any of the soldiers and Shadows at the log barricades, even though the People had been scrupulous in their dealings with the Bitterroot settlers . . . the *Nee-Me-Poo* had been betrayed. At first the angry warriors were confused, baffled how Cut-Off Arm could have gotten his slow-moving soldiers up the trail so fast as to catch them here at the Place of the Ground Squirrels.

Then *Ollokot* startled them all with his assertion right in the midst of the fighting.

"These are not Cut-Off Arm's Idaho soldiers!" the war chief declared. "They are Montana soldiers!"

"The *suapies* who tried to stop us with their log fort on the Lolo?" Yellow Wolf asked as he chambered another round into his soldier gun.

"Yes, those soldiers and settlers, too," *Ollokot* answered angrily as he shook his rifle in the air, leading his band of young men southward toward the brush where they would pitch themselves into a close, hot fight with the double-talking white men.

"And many, many more who have come from far away to catch us sleeping here," *Ollokot* explained. "These soldiers and settlers of Montana betray the trust we put in the people on this side of the mountains!"

CHAPTER FIFTY-NINE

AUGUST 9, 1877

HENRY BUCK HAD BEEN WITH CAPTAIN RAWN AT THAT BARRICADE THE newspapers in the region had already christened Fort Fizzle. Later he and his two brothers had watched the great Nez Perce village drag its horse herd past Fort Owen and go into camp, then mosey into Stevensville the following day for some trading—flour and cloth were all the Buck brothers would sell at their store, even though other merchants had traded whiskey and cartridges.

Well, now them chickens was coming home to roost!

Following in the wake of the Nez Perce, this Colonel Gibbon had taken his pitifully small bunch of soldiers and licked out after the Indians. When the valley's leading citizens issued a call for volunteers, forming militia companies of their own, Henry Buck offered his services to John Catlin of Stevensville. Their bunch caught up with Gibbon's men just shy of Ross's Hole—more than half turning back for home with "Captain" Humble, while the rest ended up pushing over the divide in the advance with Lieutenant Bradley to find this enemy camp.

That march seemed so damned long ago now—thinking how them warriors drank up all that whiskey, every last one of them redskins wearing a full cartridge belt around his waist, the whole of this foolishness made possible by those traders . . . more correct to call them *traitors*, Henry Buck brooded the moment Lieutenant Bradley's charge faltered at the far northern end of the village, positioned at the extreme left of Gibbon's line.

Not one of the men, soldier or civilian, had been told to ask any mercy of, or to give any mercy to, this enemy that had blazed a wide swath of murderous destruction through central Idaho. Now the time had come for those Injuns to pay the piper, the officers had told their men in those last hours before the attack.

"When you get within firing range of the village," explained one of the cavalry sergeants who had crawled over from Bradley's company to relay the message to the volunteers, "fire low into the tepees. That'll scare the bejesus out of 'em, and kill a bunch, too." Then the trooper paused a moment before adding, "The general, Gibbon I mean—ain't said it right out . . . but we all been told he don't want no prisoners."

Some of Catlin's men laughed at that, buoyed up by bravado and feeling this would be a quick, easy fight as they waited restlessly to start the advance.

Then that old man had to show up on his horse and all hell busted loose. Catlin finally barked the order for a half-dozen of them to fire. The ball was opened and Bradley led the whole outfit toward the north end of the camp . . . where things stalled and turned ugly.

"Bradley's dead!"

Another claimed, "Shot in the head!"

And by then, there were a couple of dozen warriors with carbines—not just those old muzzleloaders but good repeaters probably bought off some low-minded trader, if not taken off some white man they'd killed. Those warriors had that north end of things snarled up and bogged down just across the creek. Even before the civilians and soldiers got anywhere close to the village.

Natural was it that those men around Henry Buck drifted to the right, making for the two companies already pressing against the village and having a hot time of it. Hell, so hot a time that Gibbon hadn't held any companies in reserve but ended up throwing every man right into the fray as soon as their advance stalled, his advance moving slower than he had a liking for.

"Give it to 'em!" shouted one of the officers in those companies at the center of the line, prodding his soldiers forward. "Push 'em! Push 'em hard now!"

A sergeant was bellowing, "Shoot low! Shoot low! Into the lodges, boys!"

Henry had levered another round into the chamber of his Winchester carbine and was preparing to fire at a group of warriors making from right to left, frog-hopping from lodge to lodge, when he suddenly realized they weren't warriors at all. A small knot of women and children, all of them running hunched over, arms looped protectively over the little ones.

He gulped a deep breath, glad he hadn't fired—then blinked his eyes, startled.

Right there in the midst of those women and children was a blond woman!* Her waist-length honey-colored hair whipped this way and that. There was no mistaking its color among those squaws and children. She glanced Henry's way, gazing at those soldiers and civilians they were racing past; then she was gone behind another lodge.

"Did you see that?" he asked, turning quickly to the man on his right.

Tom Sherrill was struggling over the action of his rifle, intent on the weapon he held in his hands. "See what, goddammit?"

"N-nothing," Henry murmured and looked back at those lodges where she had disappeared, the open ground between him and the camp littered with a clutter of fog and a little gunsmoke.

Suddenly he caught a glimpse of the group as it reappeared for an instant among more of the stacks of lodgepoles and the last few tepees at the far northern end of the village . . . but he never saw the honey-haired woman again.

Squeezing his eyes shut, then opening them quickly, Henry Buck wondered what the hell a white woman was doing with all them squaws—and dressed just like them, too.

---

*Was this the long-lost Jennet Manuel from the Salmon River valley?

"Give 'em hell, boys!" an officer bawled near his shoulder, moving up behind the volunteers.

"You heard 'im!" Catlin cheered. "Shoot anything what moves afore it shoots you!"

Henry Buck brought that carbine to his shoulder, sighting down the barrel, looking for a target as they continued for the creek bank.

Then he glanced one last time between those northernmost lodges where she had disappeared. Wondering if he really had seen her at all.

HIS UNCLE WAS Joseph, chief of the Wallamwatkin band from the *Wallowa* Valley. *Ollokot*, the great war chief of their people, was his other uncle.

But he wasn't old enough to talk in council or to become a fighting man—not yet he wasn't. Because *Suhm-Keen* was barely ten summers old. He lived with his parents and his father's parents in a small lodge after leaving their old homes west of the mountains to come to the buffalo country. Here at the Place of the Ground Squirrels, their lodge stood in the midst of those erected at the far southern end of camp.

As had been his grandfather's practice for many years now, early every morning, the old man would leave to go check on the horses or walk off by himself to watch the sun come up. That's when his grandmother, *Chee-Nah*, would softly whisper for *Suhm-Keen* to come join her beneath her buffalo robe, where he would drift back to sleep beside her warmth.

Many rifleshots had startled him just as he was drifting back to sleep that morning, curled against her soft bulk. Many horses tied outside the lodges were calling out, neighing in fear. His father grabbed up his rifle and dived out of the door, closely followed by his mother. Now the boy was alone with *Chee-Nah* in the shattered grayness of that dawn yet unborn.

"Grandmother!" he cried when she brushed by his shoulder and started for the door.

"I must see for myself," she said, then knelt at the opening and peered out as bullets came thick, like summer hail rattling on the taut hides.

Chee-Nah had no sooner settled to her haunches when she was driven back into the darkness near the firepit, a soft whimper escaping from her throat.

"You are hurt!" he cried, frightened, as he vaulted to her.

Although blood streamed from the wound in her left shoulder, the old woman firmly grabbed hold of his bare arm and pushed him toward the side of the lodge, where she quickly jabbed a knife through the pliant, fog-dampened buffalo hide.

"Get out, *Suhm-Keen!*" she ordered. "Run to the trees and hide! Run as fast as you can!"

As he stood frozen, staring at the blood oozing from her wound, his grandmother had to nudge him one more time before he turned and did as she instructed. Stretching apart the sides of that slit, he jumped free of the lodge and started running, barefoot and naked but for his little breechclout.

He dived to the left out of a horse's way, then scrambled to the right as two fighting men sprinted around a lodge, headed for the gunfire that was rising steadily, grown almost deafening . . . except for that pounding of his heart. Already there were other children, some younger than *Suhm-Keen*, some older, too, all dashing for the brush on the south where the low plateau bordered the valley. Bullets clipped the branches and rustled leaves on either side of him as he clawed his way up the slope—more frightened than he had ever been.

As the sun had gone down yesterday, he and some other boys had been playing the stick game near a large clump of brush beside the creek. With the coming of darkness, they lit a small fire for light and warmth and continued to play happily. That was when one of his friends noticed two men stepping out of the nearby brush. Both were wrapped in gray blankets up to their noses, not Indian blankets at all. *Suhm-Keen* looked close and could see the men were not Indian. Frightened, the boys ran away.

But rather than alarm the adults, one of the older youngsters said, "Leave it be. Our parents and the chiefs know we are being watched by spies. Leave it be."

"That's right," another boy said. "Awhile ago I saw a Shadow on horseback cross the canyon on the other side of the creek. No one was excited when they talked about it. Some of the adults think he must be a spy. But other men think he is a miner, working his mine somewhere close by. He might have quarreled with other miners and be looking for a new place to stay away from the other Shadows."

When the group came back to their little fire later, the strangers were gone—as if they never had been there. The boys returned to their play, and those two spies were quickly and completely forgotten.

Until now. What if they had reported their news to the chiefs? he wondered. Would it have made any difference? Would the headmen have put out guards to watch for soldiers?

As he fled, *Suhm-Keen* found a depression in the ground not too far from the lodges and sank to his belly in it. Peering over the edge, the boy had watched the madness for the longest time when his attention was caught by one of the *suapies* who limped behind one of the lodges and settled against the buffalo-hide cover with a loud grunt. He took something large and flat from inside his blue shirt, then removed a small twig from somewhere else in his shirt. The youngster was mesmerized, watching the small soldier scratch on the thin, flat object with that twig* while the battle raged on around him.

Not a lot of time passed before the *suapie* was hit by a bullet. His hands flew up—the flat white object flying one way, the small twig sailing in another. *Suhm-Keen* was even more astounded as he watched the white object slowly become many, all of them gradually scudding across the ground like the dance of swirling feathers with each gust of breeze.

---

*It was not until some years later, when *Suhm-Keen* was able to understand that the white man wrote his language down, using a pen and paper, that he was able to explain to others what he had watched the soldier doing in the village that morning. So who was this soldier? Whom was he writing to? Because *Suhm-Keen*'s testimony states that the soldier was already wounded when he got behind the lodge, did the white man sense he was about to die, and was he attempting to write down some last words for his loved ones back home?

Sudden he heard a man's loud voice booming nearby.

"Soldiers are right on us! They are now in our camp! Get away somewhere or you will be killed!"

Breathless, but afraid to stop until he had scrambled to the top, *Suhm-Keen* raced to the base of the plateau and started climbing to the rim. Only then did he turn to glance over his shoulder, surprised to find so many other children right behind him, scratching up the side of the ridge to join him. Then he peered back at the village. Hard as he looked, he could not find his parent's lodge at first, what with the gunsmoke, people scrambling here and there, and the dense ground fog.

He squatted on the rim of the plateau with the other children, watching, listening to the battle as the white-skinned *suapies* entered the village, spreading out to search the lodges. . . .

He managed not to cry until he saw the soldiers start to burn the first of those lodges. That's when *Suhm-Keen* buried his face in his arms, realizing that first one had started to smoke, a greasy black tendril stretching to the sky.

It was the lodge where his grandmother lay bleeding.

AT THIS SIDE of camp where the fiercest fight was raging, Yellow Wolf watched many things that he was certain would stay burned in his memory for as long as he lived.

Somehow through the noisy din of battle he nonetheless heard the cries of a small infant. Turning in a squat to peer over his shoulder, he spotted the tiny child sobbing next to the body of its mother. The woman lay sprawled, blood on her leg and belly—unmoving and clearly dead. Then there was a rush of blurred motion, and a knot of soldiers appeared around the side of a lodge, yelling very loudly. Out of the lodge crouched an old woman, her hands held out in supplication. Yellow Wolf was afraid she was about to be shot. . . .

But instead, one of the *suapies* bent over the bawling infant and picked it up as if he was quite used to holding a baby. He patted its back a few moments, then passed the child to the startled woman and motioned for her to go. She stood there a breathless heartbeat longer, plainly baffled. He motioned again, yelling at her this time, pantomiming for her to run off. The soldiers watched her lunge away, then turned aside to another lodge, their rifles pointed and ready.

This confused Yellow Wolf. Maybe not all Shadows were brutal and without feelings for people they did not understand.

But minutes later, not far away at that same end of camp, he and two others came to the birthing lodge . . . where they discovered the wife of Sun Tied had been shot in her bed. Beside her lay the body of the older midwife, a woman named Granite Crystal, who had helped the young mother deliver a child. She, like the young mother, had been shot.

Clutched in the birth nurse's arms lay the still form of the newborn, its tiny skull brutally crushed with either a boot heel or a rifle butt. In Sun Tied's lodge nearby, Yellow Wolf and his friends found the woman's two older children, both of them shot with soldier bullets.

Looking at those little bodies, he felt the sting of gall rise from his belly, and with it a deep and unsettling anger. While there might well be a few Shadows who could commit acts of kindness and generosity that might come close to rivaling the humanity of the *Nee-Me-Poo*, most white people were simply a dark-hearted race intent upon taking everything they coveted, killing everyone who stood in their way. A black and shadowy race.

Then he remembered *Ollokot*'s words spoken to his warriors after they fled the fight on the Clearwater.

"Fear can be a potent killer in battle—paralyzing those it strikes—but anger is the greatest killer of all," the war chief had declared. "Anger always assures that the warrior consumed with rage will not be thinking clear enough to be wary of every danger."

Sucking in a deep breath as he stared at the bodies of these children, Yellow Wolf vowed he would not let anger eat away at his common sense. No, he vowed to see this day out, alive.

"My brothers—see how they set the first lodge on fire!" he heard *Kowtoliks*[*] shouting, "Make a good resistance! We are here today for that reason!"

Around the young *Kowtoliks*—no more than sixteen summers old—rallied some warriors, their guns firing. They were all whooping together as Yellow Wolf spotted movement from the corner of his eye. He whirled, ready to shoot, when he saw it was a older man emerging from his lodge pitched upriver toward the south end of camp. He had a white King George blanket belted around his waist, covering only his legs, while his upper chest and shoulders were bare.

It was *Pahka Pahtahank*, who was called Five Fogs—a man of middle age who had never learned a thing of the white man's firearms. He was one of the very best among Yellow Wolf's people at using a bow.

Five Fogs held his short, sinew-backed bow at the end of his outstretched arm, firing steadily at the wave of soldiers near the riverbank. Not running away from his home, the warrior stood his ground, methodically shooting one arrow after another at the white men who were aiming their rifles at him. He moved slightly from side to side after every shot, then aimed and freed another arrow. A volley of bullets clattered against the lodge behind him, then a second burst of gunfire. Then a third time after he shifted and loosed two more arrows at the advancing soldiers.

But a fourth, massive volley struck Five Fogs and the brave *Nee-Me-Poo* bowman fell beside the door to his home.[**]

Uttering a quick prayer to *Hunyewat* for the spirit of Five Fogs, Yellow Wolf had just started around a lodge, ready to make for the far end of camp, when he suddenly slid to a halt, unable to believe his eyes!

Not far away a very, very old man sat outside his lodge[†] apparently calm

---

[*]This name has no definitive translation but refers to the hair and bones of human dead that are scattered by wild predators.

[**]Stake No. 50 designates where his lodge stood, and Stake No. 49 shows where this bowman died. His quiver and bow are in the Big Hole National Battlefield collections.

[†]Stake No. 24, Big Hole National Battlefield.

in the midst of the frantic fighting, warriors and soldiers running here and there, horses rearing and racing about, smoke and fog roiling along the ground. Yet this ancient one sat and smoked his pipe as if it were a quiet autumn morning in an abandoned camp.

Wahnistas Aswetesk sat upon a small rug cut from a buffalo robe, his tobacco pouch beside his knee, puffing calmly on his pipe as the first bullets began to fall about him.

Yellow Wolf started for the old one—to drag him to safety—but the fury of the soldier guns drove him back. Instead, he had to take cover beside a lodge, where Yellow Wolf could only watch what he was sure would be a quick and terrible end for the pipe smoker.

The first time a bullet hit the ancient one, his body jerked, but still he did not topple to the side. Two and then a third struck him. He simply did not move to safety or collapse from his terrible wounds. More bullets rattled the lodge cover and poles around him. To Yellow Wolf it sounded like the battering of hailstones—but the ancient one did not budge. As if the bullets were nothing more than harmless drops of rain!

Twenty bullets—a full two-times-ten—must have entered his body as Yellow Wolf counted, amazed.

Then as suddenly as the shooting had converged on the old man, the soldiers moved on past, running into camp, either satisfied they had killed the ancient one or deciding they never would.

When Yellow Wolf slid up beside him and crouched over the wrinkled face, he was surprised to find *Wahnistas* breathing. "Are you alive?"

The creased eyelids fluttered open. "You go fight, young man. Do not worry about an old man like me. I have seen many days and if this is to be my last—then I have had my smoke to the new sun. Go now, and fight for those you can save."

The young warrior said, "You are brave to look at the face of death so calmly—"

"*Eeh-heh*, Yellow Wolf!"

The young man turned to look over his shoulder and spotted *Seeskoomkee* propped against a nearby lodge. This one called No Feet was leaning against some poles to hold himself and his soldier rifle in place while he fired with the one hand left him.

"Do you need my help?" Yellow Wolf yelled at the former slave, who had brought the warning of soldiers advancing the morning the *Nee-Me-Poo* had their first battle with the *suapies* at *Lahmotta*.

"Do you have any bullets for my gun?"

Yellow Wolf saw No Feet was using a lever-action repeater. "I don't have any bullets that will fit your carbine!" he replied.

Seeskoomkee laughed boldly as he pointed at Yellow Wolf's rifle. "I will see what I can do to kill a soldier so you can have more bullets to use!"

"I will kill some soldiers myself."

"There, young man," the old one said, tapping Yellow Wolf on the forearm. "Look there."

When he turned around to see where *Wahnistas* pointed, Yellow Wolf spotted his chief again. Joseph had returned from the horse herd where

Yellow Wolf had first sighted him and No Heart early that morning at the beginning of the fight. Now the chief stood in the midst of some warriors at the center of camp, cradling his two-month-old daughter within one arm while directing action with the other arm.

When he had spotted Joseph on the hillside in those first moments of battle and now, too—neither time was the chief holding a gun. He was not a fighting man, not a fighting chief like his younger brother. Instead, Joseph was assisting the flight of the innocent women and children caught sleeping in the village.

"There, you see, young man?" *Wahnistas* asked. "Do not waste your time here with me! I am old and will die soon. So go give a good fight like our chiefs—save the little ones, and our people, for tomorrow!"

CHAPTER SIXTY

August 9, 1877

By 8:00 A.M. JOHN GIBBON WONDERED IF HE SHOULD HAVE ORDERED HIS men to set fire to the lodges or not.

That simple command ended up taking a good number of his men off the firing line and prevented them from keeping the pressure on the Nez Perce fighting men. But he had already committed his manpower, so he would follow through with his original battle plan . . . even though some doubt still nagged at him—causing him more than a little concern that perhaps he should have pursued the warriors until they were completely driven off, away from the lodges, far enough from his perimeter that they could not cause his lines any real worry.

He had remained on the hillside across the stream from the camp for some time, watching from that elevated vantage point that soon showed him that the attack on the left side of his line had faltered under Bradley. It wasn't until Lieutenant Woodruff galloped up carrying the news that the lieutenant had been killed that Gibbon suffered his first apprehensions, misgivings that he might have blundered in his planning, if not in his plan's execution.

Not until the Nez Perce launched a fierce counterattack, lodge by lodge near the center of the village, did he decide to venture across the boggy slough to get a closer look for himself. No sooner had he emerged near the south end of the camp among the units attempting to set fire to a seventh and eighth lodges than Gibbon realized he made a pretty target of himself perched high upon this nervous horse he was repeatedly having to rein up, as it clearly wanted to bound away, what with all the gunfire and yelling going on around them.

"Horseback's not the healthiest position for a man in battle," he said to his aide-de-camp as he landed on the ground and snubbed up the reins of the nervous animal.

Lieutenant Woodruff turned to say, "While an officer might stay mounted to rally his troops, sir, you can look around you and see your men already have reason enough to fight off the hellions who are trying to make a counterattack of it—"

"General Gibbon!"

He wheeled at the call, finding a sergeant hurrying over.

"General, sir—did you know that your horse is wounded?"

"N-no," he muttered as he went to his knee beside the sergeant, immediately finding the animal's front leg broken. It wobbled nervously on the other three, unable to put any weight on that bleeding leg. "A stray bullet, damn," Gibbon muttered. "Must've happened just now when I entered the village—"

"You're bleeding, too, sir!" Charles Woodruff announced with a little fear in his voice. "My God!"

Peering down at his calf, just above the top of his boot, Gibbon saw how the sky blue of his wool britches was generously stained with a circle of blood surrounding a small black hole. Curiously detached, he bent over to study the wound, amazed that he felt no pain from the wound.

"The bullet came out the back, sir," the sergeant offered.

Woodruff wagged his head. "Maybe even the same bullet hit you somehow came out to break your horse's leg."

"I doubt that," Gibbon replied. "Been a tough angle."

"We don't have a surgeon along," the sergeant said.

"I don't need a doctor, Sergeant," the colonel argued. "I'll walk down here to the stream to wash it out myself, then tend to it better later on in the day when we've tied up everything here."

Waving off Woodruff's offer to help him clamber down the short, but steep, cutbank, Gibbon stood a moment, watching how the sergeants and their details were working over the lodges.

To expose any possible snipers who could be hiding within a lodge, several of the soldiers tore at the buffalo-hide covers while others stood back at the ready, prepared to shoot anyone who might be flushed from within. Now that Gibbon's men were discovering how difficult it was to torch a dew-damp buffalo hide, they were content to throw lariats over the uppermost lodgepoles, toppling the cones with the power of a horse or with a squad of men all pulling together.

Gibbon turned away for the creek bank, even more amazed that the double wounds did not give him any complaint at all. Squatting on the grassy bench next to the stream, he pulled off his boot and stocking, then tugged at the leg of his britches until he could begin to bathe the wounds with the cold water. Some movement at the corner of his eye caught his attention and he looked up—

To find a large number of warriors having crossed the stream opposite the village to the west side, where they were making their way through the brush toward the horses and the timber. Several of the Nez Perce were already skirmishing with a few of Gibbon's men, those warriors succeeding in driving off the herd by waving pieces of blanket at the animals, shooing them north along the grassy hillside, eventually sloping back into the valley once they were away from the soldiers and the fighting.

But even more of the warriors streamed into the trees on the hillside directly above the enemy camp, taking positions above his men at work in the village.

It was not only as clear as the coming sun that his men had just lost any crack at those horses Bostwick hadn't wanted to drive off in the early-morning darkness because of possible horse guards . . . but also clear that some troublesome warriors were about to flank his men—securing the hill behind and above his line, where they could do a lot of damage.

Of a sudden he became of aware of a growing clamor—voices and gunshots quickly and steadily rolling his way from the village he thought his men had secured. Gibbon scrambled up the bank to find the Nez Perce darting this way and that on both sides of his men. Try as they might, his companies hadn't been able to hold the warriors off those units assigned to torch the lodges.

Here and there soldiers were already dragging their wounded comrades back from the firing lines to a safer place. Trouble was, Gibbon was coming to realize, there wasn't much of anyplace safe here in the village now. Not with Joseph's hellions throwing everything they had back against his lines in a fierce concerted counterattack.

It hit the colonel like a bucket of cold water dashed in his face: He had committed a blunder in not pursuing the enemy on out of the valley, driving them far from their homes.

From everything he had ever learned of the Sioux and Cheyenne on the northern plains, once soldiers had them on the run from their camp, once the warriors had their women and children on the way, the fighting men would dissolve and disappear.

Not so these damned Nez Perce. They weren't about to merely cover the retreat of their families, then pull back and disappear themselves. These warriors appeared determined to snatch victory from the jaws of defeat, which Colonel John Gibbon had planned to snap shut on them at dawn. Measured by every axiom and theory taught at the U. S. Military Academy, these unlettered stone-age warriors had turned the tables and were now getting the best of his classically trained officers.

Where was that damned howitzer?

He whirled to the left in frustration and anger, looking most longingly toward the side of the hill where the path out of the timber had carried his units down to this valley. That gun crew should have had the howitzer here by now!

"Lieutenant!" he cried.

Woodruff trotted over to the edge of the cutbank. "General—your leg, it's better?"

"Forget the damned leg," he growled. "Pass the word among the officers. We've got to begin a retreat. Get me Captain Rawn—"

"R-retreat, sir?"

"To that point of timber, across the creek—there!" he said as he pointed. "Rawn's company will lead the file. I tried to hold them in reserve as long as possible, so I Company will form a skirmish line they will hold long enough to get the rest of us through to the hillside. Remind every one of the officers that all dead and wounded must go with us."

"Of course, sir! All dead and wounded."

"Let's make this orderly, Mr. Woodruff. Impress that upon Captain Rawn and the other officers. Orderly. We don't want this to become a . . . ," and

Gibbon paused, having started to say the word *rout*, but instead he finished by declaring, "We want to assure we hold on to our victory we've won here."

FOR AS LONG as they could, the young men around Yellow Wolf and *Kowtoliks* made a furious struggle of it, throwing themselves against the soldiers who were attempting to tear down and burn the lodges.

A woman screamed behind the warriors, a terrified mother—shrieking that she had left her five children beneath buffalo robes in that lodge the *suapies* had just set on fire. Her little ones were being consumed by the flames and there was no way for the men to drive back the soldiers, to get anywhere close to that lodge as the smoke turned black and curled upward in the heavy, damp air. From inside that lodge Yellow Wolf heard the pitiful screams of the helpless ones over the rattle of gunfire.

He vowed to kill as many of these monsters as he could this day, to avenge this terrible, tragic war being made on the women and children.

First one soldier, then a second, and finally a third went down before Yellow Wolf's accuracy with that rifle. Each time he pulled the trigger, he saw a white enemy fall. And when he could, he hurried in to seize the dead man's gun, freeing the cartridge belt from his waist. He passed them and the soldier weapons on to warriors who had no firearms of their own. One by one, those rifles were turned against the Shadows and soldiers. It was for the lives of the women and children that the warriors were fighting, throwing the battle back into the faces of the enemy.

If the *Nee-Me-Poo* were whipped in this fight, it was better to die in the struggle than live on in bondage with freedom gone.

"Look at them now!" Five Wounds roared.

"They are running away from us!" Yellow Wolf shouted in glee as they all leaped to their feet and started rushing after the escaping soldiers.

Many of the white men stumbled in the brush, bumping into each other, tripping over their own feet as they rushed out of the village, down into the creek, then slogged up the other side into the bogs and mire of the slough, desperate to reach that point of timber angling down from the western slope. It was as if the whites refused to put up much resistance—all of them become creatures to be herded by the Nez Perce rushing up from behind.

Upon reaching an open space among the tall willows, Yellow Wolf spotted a lone soldier no more than a few steps away. No one else had spotted that soldier who was moving almost too cautiously, perhaps slowed down by the thick brush or the muddy, foot-sucking mire of the slough.

The *suapie* was so intent on escape that he had not noticed Yellow Wolf, so the warrior decided he would touch this soldier while he lived—a great feat of battle courage.

But suddenly—the soldier must have somehow *felt* Yellow Wolf directly behind him, because the white man whirled without warning, hoisting his gun up to fire. But Yellow Wolf fired first, knocking the soldier down. He did not move as Yellow Wolf came up to stand over him, reloading.

After waiting a moment for any sign of life, he knelt to take the soldier's gun, his belt filled with bullets, and a strange knife, too.* Giving the rifle and most of the ammunition away to a warrior who had none, Yellow Wolf followed after the others who were pursuing those fleeing soldiers. But as he came to the creekbank where the stream made a hard turn to the west, he immediately stopped, jerking up his rifle, pointing it at the soldier who stood at the steep bank, staring directly at him.

But the white man did not fire. He made no movement. No sound of any kind. Ready to pull the trigger, Yellow Wolf advanced cautiously—eventually to realize the soldier was already dead, somehow propped against the bank, standing rigid in death!

"We have them surrounded in the trees!" *Ollokot* hollered from above as Yellow Wolf reached the bottom of the hill.

"They cannot escape?" he asked.

Red Moccasin Tops shook his head. "Warriors stopped them from above—no way for them to get away now!"

Yellow Wolf took a deep sigh, then looked across at the village. He said, "I want to go back to the camp for a while—to see what they did to our homes."

"This is a good thing," Five Wounds said, a grim sadness surrounding him. "When you come back, you tell me what the soldiers have done to our village."

Halfway down to the camp, Yellow Wolf had just emerged from a thick stand of willow when he happened upon the body of a soldier sprawled in the damp grass near the creek bank. Here was another rifle and more cartridges, too!

But as he knelt down to retrieve the weapon off the ground, the soldier came back to life—jerking up an arm, swiping the point of a knife just past the end of Yellow Wolf's nose. As the warrior lunged backward, out of the way of the blade, he dropped his carbine and instinctively lashed out with the *kopluts* that hung from his wrist. In a loud, resounding crack, he connected against the man's head—sending his soldier hat sailing.

Pouncing on the *suapie*, Yellow Wolf finished him off with the man's own knife, the blade that had almost taken off his nose. As he caught his breath there beside the dead man, the warrior noticed another soldier lying in some brush nearby. His eyes were closed—so Yellow Wolf was concerned that this one was also feigning death.

The warrior poked and prodded the body with the muzzle of his rifle to assure himself the soldier was fully unconscious. After digging around in the man's pockets, the warrior opened a leather pouch strapped over the white man's shoulder, finding inside a little of the hard, crunchy bread and some greasy bacon, too. He would take it to eat for his lunch later on that morning. While he thought he should finish off the wounded soldier, Yellow Wolf nonetheless left the man alone and continued on into camp. It was plain from the chest wounds that the soldier couldn't live for much longer.

---

*Later determined to be the soldier's Rice or trowel bayonet, which hung from the belt in a leather scabbard.

"Kill him!" came the shouts from a chorus of throats just beyond a cluster of lodges as Yellow Wolf approached.

He hurried to the scene, where many angry people shoved tightly around Looking Glass and Rattle on Blanket, who together held the arms of a captured Shadow, who, from his clothing, was certainly one of the Bitterroot valley settlers.*

"No!" Looking Glass snapped at the angry crowd as Yellow Wolf shouldered his way to the front of the ring. "Stay back and he will tell us some news!"

"This one was playing dead so he could sneak away!" a woman cried out in anger.

Looking Glass shouted back, "So for being a coward he should die?"

All around them in that smoky village arose the wails of grief mingled with cries of horror, fury, and revenge. It was clear why most in that group wanted to kill this prisoner, now that they had time to extract some exquisite torture from their victim.

"Get him to tell us some news from the army," Looking Glass demanded of Rattle on Blanket. "These soldiers who have followed us here from Idaho country."

After exchanging some Shadow words back and forth, the warrior turned to Looking Glass and said, "This one says these are not Cut-Off Arm's soldiers."

"Who are they?"

"They came from this Montana country, like *Ollokot* believed," Rattle on Blanket explained. "This Shadow tells me news of Cut-Off Arm: that he is following behind us very swiftly. Perhaps even to be here by this afternoon so his soldiers can continue the attack on our camp."

That brought a great and anguished wail from the crowd of women and old men, every person fearful of even more destruction and death.

"We must leave in a hurry!" a woman yelled. "Get away before Cut-Off Arm's soldiers catch us again."

"Looking Glass!" someone accused bitterly. "I thought you told us we would be safe when we left Cut-Off Arm and his soldiers back in Idaho!"

Another angry woman snarled, "Yes, Looking Glass—you said the war was over when we came here to Montana!"

"Look at us now!" screamed a third. "You said we would be safe here—the war over for us—so you forced us to stay in this camp when so many of us wanted to hurry away!"

An old man shrieked at Looking Glass, "Yes—many of us wanted to hurry away, but you would not let us!"

"We still can go to the buffalo country," Looking Glass proposed. "We must gather up all that we have and start out today—"

"This Shadow says there are more Montana settlers waiting for us between here and the buffalo country," Rattle on Blanket interrupted sud-

---

*As best as historians can ascertain, this was Campbell Mitchell, civilian volunteer from Corvallis, Montana.

denly. "He says the settlers from the mining towns are coming to attack us before we can reach the land of the *E-sue-gha*."

"So we will reach the land of the buffalo by another trail," Looking Glass promised, his eyes darting about anxiously like those of a man distrustful of those pressing in around him. "Make another trail of our own if the Shadows try to block us from joining up with our friends."

Rattle on Blanket asked, "What do we do with this one when we leave this camp?"

"Take this Shadow to my lodge," Looking Glass ordered. "I'll keep him there until I want to dig more news out of him."

With both of the prisoner's arms pinned behind him, Rattle on Blanket started the Shadow across the middle of camp. They hadn't gone but a few steps when out of the crowd lunged a woman who stopped them, raising her loud, shrill voice to Looking Glass in complaint.

"Why do you let this Shadow live anymore?" she demanded, jabbing a finger at the chief. "He's told you all he is worth! My brother is already dead by the hands of these strangers. And I watched my children die when the white men set fire to my lodge! Let me kill him myself!"

With that last word of hers, the woman reached up and slapped the Shadow across the face, so hard it immediately raised a bright red mark on his cheek, clearly visible even though the man had not shaved in several days.

His lip curled in instant fury. With his arms pinned behind him, the Shadow lashed out at that woman the only way he could, kicking her savagely in the leg with his muddy boot. She crumpled to the ground, clutching her shin and crying in pain as a warrior jumped from the crowd, shoving his gun against the white man's chest, and pulled the trigger. It was Yellow Wolf's cousin *Otskai*.

"Why did you kill him?" Rattle on Blanket shrieked as his prisoner crumpled to the ground at his feet.

"We can't waste time—we must kill him," *Otskai* sneered, a big and powerfully muscular man. "No use to keep him alive. The difference is, had he been a woman, we would have saved him. Sent him home unhurt. Are not warriors to be fought and killed? Look around you! These babies, our children are killed! Were *they* warriors? These young girls, these young women you see dead all around you. Were these young boys, these old men, were they warriors?"

"They were not warriors," Rattle on Blanket replied. "But does it make you brave to kill an unarmed man?"

"*We* are the warriors!" *Otskai* snorted with scorn. "But these Shadows are not brave men—coming on us while we slept in our beds! And once we had a few rifles in our hands, these cowardly Shadows ran away to the hillside!"

"So must we become as evil as these white men?" Yellow Wolf demanded of his taller cousin.

Whereupon *Otskai* whirled on him, snarling, "My brother, tell me if these Shadows who came with the soldiers are our good friends from the Bitterroot? See how they traded with us for our gold—then sneaked behind us with the soldiers to rub us out. Our promise given in the Bitterroot was good and honorable . . . while their Lolo treaty was a lie made with two tongues! Why should any of us waste time saving this Shadow's life?"

The more Yellow Wolf thought about it, the more he found he could not argue with his cousin. Even though *Otskai* was impulsive and was well known to do the wrong thing at the wrong time, he could never be faulted for his bravery. He never hid from a fight.

At first Yellow Wolf had believed *Otskai*'s act one of crude and bloody impulsiveness, thinking Looking Glass was right—that the Shadow might have told them a little more news about how that "day after tomorrow soldier chief," Cut-Off Arm, was following closely on their heels now.

But the more Yellow Wolf considered it . . . maybe they had already heard everything they needed to know to save themselves.

CHAPTER SIXTY-ONE

AUGUST 9, 1877

BY TELEGRAPH

THE INDIANS.

More About the Indians.
HELENA, August 8.—W. J. McCormick, of Missoula, writes to Governor Potts on the 6th, as follows: A courier arrived from Howard at 6 o'clock this evening. He left Howard Saturday morning last; thinks Howard will camp near the summit between the Lolo and Clearwater to-night. He is distant about fifty miles from the mouth of the Lolo. The courier reports that Joseph, with over one-half of the fighting force has gone to the head of the Bitter-Root valley by the Elk City trail, and will form a junction with Looking Glass and White Bird near Ross Hole. He says Howard has 750 men, and 450 pack mules, and is moving forward as rapidly as possible. Advices from the upper Bitter-Root say the Indians will camp to-night in Ross Hole. Gibbon is following rapidly. Other advices say the Indians were still at Doolittle's sixteen miles above Corvallis, and Gibbon expects to strike them on the morning of the 7th, before they break camp. Couriers say the hostiles have Mrs. Manuel with them as the property of a petty chief called Cucasenilo. Her sad story is familiar.

JOINING THOSE FIRST SOLDIERS AND CATLIN'S VOLUNTEERS IN FLIGHT, Henry Buck scrambled toward the point of timber that stretched down from the western slopes in a narrowing V, a small flat-topped promontory that jutted out from the mountainside, terminating just above the boggy slough they had struggled across in their retreat.

The Nez Perce horse herd was already gone—successfully driven off by a few mounted warriors. Which meant Gibbon had failed to put the hostiles afoot.

And now it looked damned good the army wouldn't end up destroying the village, either. While many of the lodgepole cones had been pulled over, only eight of the damp covers smoldered back there in the enemy camp.

Neither of those failures would have caused a man great consternation, at least to Buck's way of thinking. Henry was certain there wasn't a soldier or a civilian who would fault Gibbon for failing to capture the herd or to hold onto the village long enough to destroy the hostiles' homes and possessions. Not with the way the Nez Perce had surprised every last one of them by striking back with such fury.

So what stuck in Henry's craw so bad was the fact that Gibbon didn't make sure the warriors would give up when they were attacked.

As bullets hissed and whined about the retreating white men like acorns falling on a shake roof in autumn winds—smacking tree limbs and knocking leaves off the surrounding willow, even digging furrows into the ground at their feet or where they planted their hands whenever they stumbled in their race—it was plain as the sun rising at their backs that the Nez Perce had no intention of scooping up their survivors and fleeing the valley.

Isn't that what Indians are supposed to do? his mind burned with the question. *To run away when attacked?*

These . . . these *red bastards aren't about to give up!*

There was a good number of the warriors already on the slope, positioned in the timber, by the time the soldiers started clearing out of the village. That meant the whole of Gibbon's command suddenly found itself caught in a hot little cross fire, strung out in the bottomground between those warriors pushing out of the encampment itself and those warriors tidily ensconced on the western slope above the creek.

No men had a hotter time of it than Captain Charles C. Rawn's I Company, detailed to lead the retreat—which as quickly became both confusing and terrifying to boot, with a little eye-to-eye and hand-to-hand fighting in the brush and tall willows as they vacated the village itself. Skirmishing for the contested ground with their firearms was so close that a few of the men were powder-burned by their enemy's weapons; a warrior's shirt was set on fire with a muzzle blast. Men on both sides fell noisily, calling out, beseeching their friends to help as the tide of battle moved past.

Then men who had started their retreat in two lines, back-to-back, quickly began to drift apart as the fighting grew intense. Ordered to bring out their dead and wounded, many of the soldiers merely stopped long enough to pick up a fallen comrade's rifle so it could be pitched into the deep water in their retreat and kept from falling into the enemy's hands.

With the death of A Company's Captain William Logan, command had fallen to First Lieutenant Charles A. Coolidge, who had begun this Nez Perce War by scouting part of the Lolo Trail. In Gibbon's retreat, Coolidge's men were assigned to close the file.

But just short of the boggy slough, Coolidge dropped before Rawn's advance had even reached the bottom of the hill—wounded through both thighs in the nose-to-nose skirmishing the embattled A Company encountered in covering the rear of the retreat. Once more the command of A Company and responsibility for covering their retreat to the timber was transferred, this time to Second Lieutenant Francis Woodbridge, newly turned twenty-four years old.

Under Gibbon's orders, once the base of the timbered point of land was reached by Rawn's advance, Woodbridge wheeled his men about and anchored them just above the creek—where they were to cover the retreat of the rest of the command scrambling up behind them. Spread out some three to five yards apart, wherever they could find a little cover on the hillside, Rawn's foot soldiers watched the other infantrymen and civilians stream through the wide gaps in their line while they continued to lay down a hot covering fire, until the last man moving out of the slough had been accounted for. Only then did Captain Rawn cry out his order to about-face.

Needing no more prodding than that, I Company bolted to their feet and resumed their retreat up the slope behind the rest.

Henry Buck turned his head quickly, glancing over his shoulder as he made his climb into the timber, hand over foot, slipping and falling, then crabbing back into motion again. He thanked his lucky stars he wasn't one of the stragglers slow in getting out of the village when the red sonsabitches came flooding back in. By that time the aim of those warriors had become deadly. At every crack of a rifle, it seemed, one of the white men fell somewhere in the retreat. Most of the wounded, and even a few of the dead, were promptly scooped up by the wrists or ankles and dragged along—those bleeding and unable to get out on their own begged not to be left behind, terrified those warriors and squaws would get their hands on them.

Just inside the point of timber the first of the soldiers staggered to a breathless halt and started to regroup, many of Catlin's civilians among them. They still were far from being safe. Bullets snarled through the trees, smacking trunks and branches, whining in ricochet as the lead hornets slammed against exposed rocks protruding from the loose soil. Henry's eyes darted about. This spot was about as good as they were going to find on the side of this mountain.

He sucked in a breath and flopped to his belly, clutching his carbine like life itself. Although it seemed like no more than mere minutes to the attackers, Gibbon's assault on, and temporary possession of, the village had lasted a little less two and a half hours.

In bemused exhaustion, Buck watched several weary soldiers lunge right on past him and the others, running still farther up the slope—either terrified of the snipers already at work from the timber around them or frightened of those warriors herding the white men into this surround.

"Don't run, men!" Gibbon shouted as he limped into the timber, dragging his wounded leg, and started to collapse. "If you run away . . . I will be forced to stay right here alone!"

Through their midst sprinted a young corporal, head down and legs churning, huffing up the slope in full panic. "To the top of the hill!" he screamed as he ran. "To the top of the hill or we're lost!"

"Corporal!" Gibbon shouted above the tumult. "By bloody damn, your commanding officer is still alive!"

Henry watched that yank the corporal to a halt, wheeling around, his face flushed as he said, "General! We gotta get these men to the top of the hill! Only safe place—"

"As you were, Corporal!" Gibbon snapped, then turned to the rest, balancing on his one good leg. "This is the place, men. Take cover and dig in!"

From where Gibbon had sunk to the ground in utter exhaustion and pain, the south end of that enemy camp where the colonel had been wounded was no more than a half-mile away.

"Is this our last horse, General?" shrieked Adjutant Woodruff as he lunged up through the timber leading his mount.

"Get on the ground!" Gibbon hollered.

A spray of bullets spit through that stand of timber. The lieutenant instantly flopped to the ground with no more urging. For a few heartbeats it seemed all those men hugging the forest floor were staring at that lone horse among them. It tugged and pulled at the young lieutenant lying on the ground gripping its reins, nearly stepping on several men as it pranced about in fright.

"Sh-should I let go, General?"

"No!" Gibbon replied sternly. "Long as it's alive, we've got a chance to send a courier out on horseback."

After no more than the space of another heartbeat, Captain Rawn lunged into the grove, surrounded by what he had left of his skirmishers, dragging four of their wounded and one dead man slung between a pair of soldiers, the casualty's boots bouncing loosely over the rough ground.

"General Gibbon!" Rawn yelled. "Lieutenant English* is down, sir!"

"Get in here, man! Get in here!" Gibbon hollered in a crimson frustration. "Keep your heads down! Company commanders, spread your men out! Firing lines, dammit! Form a skirmish formation and give them back what they're giving us!"

With agonizing slowness, the soldiers and most of Catlin's volunteers did as Gibbon ordered—what good sense itself dictated. With the soldiers and volunteers bunched up the way they were, the warriors could slip in all the closer on them. So they began to spread out, forming a long irregular corral running, for the most part, up and down the slope, from east to west.

"Dig in!" came the call from one of the captains as the men began moving apart.

"You heard 'im!" a frog-throated sergeant bellowed. "Entrench, you goddamned buckos! Entrench afore they blow your bleeming brains out!"

Those infantrymen equipped with the Rice bayonets tore them out of the leather scabbards hung from their prairie belts and put the small trowels

*William L. English, I Company, Seventh U. S. Infantry.

to work. Those cavalrymen and volunteers who did not have the luxury of such a tool went to work with tin cups, belt knives, even folding pocketknives—anything they could use to scrape away at the loose, flaky surface of the forest floor. A few of the men slashed the wool covers off their canteens and started whittling at the thin bead of solder welding the two halves together. When finally pried apart, a half a canteen made an admirable entrenching tool. Around Henry it appeared about half of the men had started digging, while the other half worked to keep the warriors back from their lines. Looking around at their ragged oval, he thought that those who had been lucky enough to end up behind some downed timber or a tree stump were rich men by any measure.

"You dig," said the soldier beside him. "I'll spell you later."

Buck snapped his pocketknife open and started digging. After a few scrapes with the blade, he pushed the loosened soil away from the hole he had started. More digging, followed by moving another handful of dirt, slowly beginning to build up a low mound in front of the long, shallow trench he was gouging out of the ground. Copying the work of the soldiers who seemed to know what they were doing, no questions asked.

A few of the soldiers and volunteers returned the enemy's fire from time to time—if for no other reason than to keep the warriors honest, holding the enemy back from their ragged perimeter—while the rest continued to dig in for themselves and those wounded who could do nothing as the sun rose higher and the air got hotter. Shafts of hot, steamy light burned through the thick canopy of tree branches.

"What you think of that, Henry Buck?" Luther Johnson called out a few yards away. He was consumed with scratching at a trench using his big belt knife. "You know I dug for gold on this very hillside back in the sixties, the angels' truth it is. Never, Henry Buck, never did I figger I'd be back on this spot one day—not digging a shaft to find some gold . . . but digging a hole to save me life!"

Henry saw how much soil those soldiers moved with their bayonets and realized how pitifully slow he was getting the same job done with his folding knife. But as long as he could dig for a while, then shoot every now and then, Henry Buck figured it would keep his mind off the fact that Gibbon's attackers were now surrounded . . . maybe sixty or more miles from any assistance . . . without food or water . . . cut off from resupplying their ammunition.

"Where's that howitzer?" Gibbon wondered aloud. He slammed a fist into an open palm angrily.

"The gun crew should have had that twelve-pounder here by now," Rawn complained.

"Not just the howitzer," Gibbon muttered with a barely bottled frustration. "We're damn well gonna need those two thousand extra cartridges they were bringing us, too."

WITH LOOKING GLASS slinking back from the front lines, aware of the new anger and undisguised contempt most of the *Nee-Me-Poo* now held for him,

White Bird—oldest chief among the Non-Treaty bands—now assumed the ascendancy. Hard as he was on all the fighting men, he was even more brutal on his own young warriors.

"Ho—Red Moccasin Tops! And you there, Swan Necklace! See how your friend Shore Crossing is already dead!"

Yellow Wolf, like many of the other fighting men, turned his attention away from those soldiers retreating from the village, curious to watch White Bird scold the two surviving members of those first raids along the Salmon River that had ignited this wholesale war.

"Look at these *suapies* and Shadows, Red Moccasin Tops!" the old chief chided the two young men. "Swan Necklace—see how these enemies are not asleep like those you murdered back in Idaho country!"

Lumbering up to the front lines in the village, old White Bird shrieked right into the face of Red Moccasin Tops, "This is battle against an enemy who can defend themselves! Now is the time to show your courage and fight!"

Without a word, but plainly smarting from the chief's public rebuke, both of the young warriors led the charge into the willow, sprinting ahead along the path the retreating soldiers were taking—beginning to lay down a deadly fire into the white men as the soldiers scattered through the brush, racing madly for the hillside across the stream.

"I would like to ride them down on horseback!" Old Yellow Wolf suggested as he came up to grab his nephew's elbow. "Come with me!"

Yellow Wolf agreed. He spotted a brave warrior coming toward the village from the willow. It was *Weyatnahtoo Latat*, the one called Sun Tied. Yellow Wolf's eyes immediately darted to the birthing lodge as he sadly remembered the brutal death he had seen inside earlier that morning, the man's wife and newborn daughter savagely killed.

"Sun Tied!" he called out. "Catch up a horse and come with us to kill the stragglers running for the hillside!"

The warrior looked over the uncle and nephew quickly and agreed with a harsh grin. "A fine idea! We can shoot them like ducks on a pond!"

Three more* joined the trio, and all six sprinted away to locate any ponies still tied to lodges, horses that hadn't been killed or hadn't bolted off with the noise, gunfire, and confusion.

Once they were mounted, the small war party raced their ponies south, to the upper end of camp, heading for a shallow crossing, where they would double back on the other side of the creek and launch their mounted attack on the last of the retreating soldiers—

Yellow Wolf and the other fighters jerked with the loud, shrill whistle as the cannonball hissed overhead on its way toward the village. They waited, watching the last of its flight—fully expecting the ball to explode the way such singing balls had at the Clearwater fight when Cut-Off Arm's soldiers used just such a cannon. As their eyes followed the descent of the

---

**Tenahtahkal Weyun* (Dropping from a Cliff), *Pitpillooheen* (Calf of Leg), and *Ketalkpoosmin* (Stripes Turned Down).

black ball, it landed just beyond the easternmost lodges but failed to detonate.

Sun Tied turned, a smile widening on his powder-grimed face. "Yellow Wolf—I would like to see these soldiers who have brought this big gun that shoots twice. Maybe we can capture it for ourselves."

"*Eeh-heh!*" Yellow Wolf exclaimed, spotting the puff of powdersmoke clinging to the hillside. "We must do everything we can to keep any more of the big bullets from reaching our village!"

The six set off at a gallop, their horses splashing across the shallow ford and onto the grassy slope, angling southwest as they climbed toward that place where he had seen the curl of gray gunsmoke.

A second roar belched from the wide throat of that cannon on the hill as the horsemen entered the timber just north of the big gun's position. Ahead through the labyrinth of trees, Yellow Wolf spied the six mules and the big gun's wagon those mules were hitched to. He and Sun Tied immediately reined to the right, moving uphill through the trees to come around on the soldiers, when a single shot rang out from the forest, followed by a rattle of gunfire from those huddled around the cannon.

Someone was shooting at the *suapies* from above, and the soldiers were firing back.

Then Yellow Wolf heard gunfire coming from the direction his uncle had taken to launch his attack. That meant they had the soldiers wrapped up on three sides now! As he and Sun Tied reined their horses to the left and started downhill toward the gun crew, Yellow Wolf watched two of the *suapies* bolt from the ground and take off at a dead run into the trees. He fired his rifle at the pair, the exact moment one of the frightened mules reared in its harness—a soldier clinging to its back. The bullet struck the mule and it crumpled on all fours, crying out almost humanlike in its noisy bawl.

As the animal fell, it caught the soldier beneath it, pinning the man's legs beneath its heavy bulk while the mule shuddered, dying slowly.

Quickly dismounting so that he would do better with his aim, Yellow Bird sighted another warrior on the far side of the white men. *Seeyakoon Ilppilp*, known as Red Spy, was the one making things hot for the *suapies* from above. The moment one of the cannon men popped up to make a shot, Red Spy was already aiming and fired his gun. His bullet struck the soldier in the back and he crumpled over the gun's wagon, then slumped to the ground.

In the next heartbeat, Dropping from a Cliff fired at the other lead mule. The animal kicked twice, then went down in a heap. That's when Stripes Turned Down stepped from the edge of the trees and bravely aimed his rifle at the last of the handful of soldiers still huddled around their gun. His bullet struck one of them, causing the rest to suddenly bolt, turning tail and dashing into the timber, heading up the hill, away from their back trail.

Earth Blanket, the one named *Wattes Kunnin*, surprised Yellow Wolf by bursting into the clearing from the southwestern side of the hill, his face flushed with excitement. He did not carry a firearm in his hands.

"Where is your rifle, Earth Blanket?" Yellow Wolf asked.

"I have none!"

"You do now," and Yellow Wolf pointed to those rifles abandoned by the fleeing soldiers.

With a big gulp of air, the breathless Earth Blanket nodded, saying, "I came to tell you of more soldiers coming!"

Sun Tied looked at Yellow Wolf and asked, "Could it be Cut-Off Arm and his *suapies?*"

"No," and Earth Blanket wagged his head. He was a half-Umatilla who had been born on White Bird Creek but had nonetheless joined Joseph's *Wallowa* band. "Only the fingers on my two hands, maybe less. All but one riding horses. That black-painted Shadow man walking on foot is leading a mule—and it carries a heavy load: four boxes on its back."

"Four boxes?" Old Yellow Wolf repeated. "Those boxes must hold something very, very important for that mule to have so many soldiers to tend to it!"

"Come with me to see what surprise we can make of this!" Sun Tied suggested.

"Horses and guns!" shouted Dropping from a Cliff in excitement.

At the same time they sighted the oncoming riders and the black-skinned man on foot with his single pack mule, Yellow Wolf also spotted his mother's brother, *Espowyes*, called Light in the Mountain, another relation of Joseph of the Wallamwatkin band. He was without a horse, crouched near the side of the trail where he was about to ambush the *suapies*.

Light in the Mountain stood and fired at the lead soldier who held the rope to the pack mule in his hand. When the bullet whistled past him, the soldier jerked backward, twisting to the side in his saddle, immediately freeing the rope as he spurred his horse in the flanks and reined it back up the trail.

Instantly Yellow Wolf and the others kicked their horses into a gallop, every one of them yelling his loudest, their shrill war cries ricocheting off the side of the mountain. As that lead soldier wheeled and bolted his way back up the trail, the rest of the *suapies* scattered like a flock of frightened quail, turning to flee in a wild dash to safety.

"Cut those ropes!" Sun Tied ordered.

The four boxes clattered to the shady ground as Light in the Mountain crouched over the first one and hollered, "Bring me a rock for my hand!"

Slamming the rock down on the wooden crate again and again, he finally succeeded in busting it open about the time more of their number started work on the other three crates. Inside were small boxes made of hard paper. And inside each one stood as many bullets as Yellow Wolf had ever seen on a cartridge belt!

Old Yellow Wolf laid his hand on the young man's shoulder. "Nephew, come with me."

"You want the soldiers who got away from us?" he asked.

His uncle nodded. "I think we might find out where those soldiers are running to."

"Maybe they will have more bullets for our guns?" Yellow Wolf asked as they caught up their ponies and mounted.

With a grin, the uncle said, "And if the spirits are smiling on us . . . we will get ourselves a look at Cut-Off Arm's soldiers coming up the other side of this mountain."

CHAPTER SIXTY-TWO

AUGUST 9, 1877

HE COULD HEAR THE MUFFLED HOOFBEATS COMING IN THAT EAR PRESSED against the forest floor. Even more of the red buggers come to join in the god-blamed slaughter.

In panic, Private John O. Bennett took another deep breath and heaved with his free leg, giving all he had to shove it against the ribs of the dying mule, desperate to pull the pinned leg free before those horsemen, or those working in on foot, got close enough to finish him off. Grunting again, straining harder this time, Bennett threw every bit of his dwindling reserves into his task—heart thumping, breathing short and ragged, his eyes ever darting about, ears attuned to every little sound that thundered out of the shadowy timber.

It wasn't as if John O. Bennett were a stranger to fighting; no stranger to tough scrapes was he. Why, he'd even be celebrating his fifty-seventh birthday this fall if he ever got his leg out from under this damned mule. If, that is, the critter hadn't broken any of his bones when it collapsed with him under it.

Bennett clenched his eyes shut, of a sudden praying that God with His limitless grace would move the damned mule so he could make a run of it, just to have a chance . . . rather than be trapped here when the red bastards showed up.

He'd marched into Mexico with Kearney's frontier army back in '46, no mere lad at twenty-five. Dragoons, they were called in those days. Then he had served out another entire war in Union Blue. While there were some who craved the stripes of corporal or sergeant—Bennett had tried them both—private had a much nicer ring to it these days of what he had figured would be his last enlistment. B Company, Seventh U. S. Infantry.

Last summer he'd been with his captain, James H. Bradley, that hot afternoon they spyglassed the carcasses of man and beast on the distant hillside overlooking what few burial lodges the Sioux and Cheyenne had left behind at the Little Bighorn.

Old enough to be the lieutenant's father, how Bennett had wanted to march into battle with Bradley again that morning—good man that the lieutenant was and all—but Bradley had other ideas for the aging private who vividly personified "an Old Army soldier."

"You know how General Gibbon feels about you, Private."

He had smiled at Bradley. "You always did know how to make this old man blush now, sir."

"Gibbon calls you his 'brave old John Bennett,' " Bradley had repeated. "So we want you to stay and give the two sergeants a steady hand."

"They ain't young whips, are they, Lieutenant?"

Bradley had shaken his head. "No. Daly and Frederick. Both old salts."

"Not near as old as me."

The lieutenant had grinned. "No man's a fighting man like you, Private Bennett. With you along, we know the gun will get down there when we need it to open up on 'em come morning."

Minutes later Bradley was leading the rest of Gibbon's boys away, leaving that mountain howitzer and its six-man gun crew to nurse the balky six-mule team down the trail behind a civilian who would scout ahead and pick a way down to some spot overlooking the village, where they could put the fieldpiece into action. Wouldn't that make them Nez Perce scamper and prance!

At the wagon train in those final minutes before Joe Blodgett started them down the creek, Lieutenant Jacobs's Negro manservant, William Woodcock, decided he'd come along, too, rather than waiting back with the train guard on the mountainside.* Woodcock figured he would carry his master's double-barreled shotgun along for some proper protection since he was going on foot, leading a packhorse burdened with a quarter of a ton of rifle ammunition.

Bennett climbed up on the off-hand lead mule and they rumbled out of the wagon camp, the twelve-pounder on its prairie carriage, its long, wheeled caisson attached, following Sergeant John W. H. Frederick, a thirty-year veteran of both the Civil War and the Seventh Infantry with a record marked "*most exceptional*"—the only man in the crew with any artillery experience—and Sergeant Patrick C. Daly, a forty-four-year-old emigrant from county Limerick, Ireland. After three long enlistments in the Seventh Infantry, his was an excellent duty record as well.

The rest of the detail consisted of Corporal Robert E. Sale, a twenty-nine-year-old recruit with an extreme devotion to duty; Private Malcolm McGregor, a thirty-one-year-old emigrant from Glasgow, Scotland; and Private John H. Goale, a twenty-six-year-old recruit from Cincinnati.

"I hear you know where you're going, Blodgett," Bennett said as they rumbled across the slope.

"I been down this way more'n once," the civilian said. "We'll be there in no time."

Fact was, Blodgett had been in and through this part of Montana Territory before it even was Montana Territory. The first time was back in 1859, when the entire Bitterroot valley had no more than twenty-nine white settlers! Three years later he had guided supply wagons over from the bustling

---

*Such relationships between officers and slaves were not unheard of in the Indian-fighting army of the West. It was more often than not a relationship that was ignored by the higher echelons of the army, just as it was with Surgeon John FitzGerald's Negro cook and house servant, Jennie.

mining settlement of Bannack, by way of the Big Hole and this very same Trail Creek. His road was used two years later in '64 by a party of emigrants and again in '69 by another train of settlers bound for the Bitterroot. Using that path he knew so well, Blodgett got the gun crew down to the bluff overlooking the village just past daylight, after they had been hearing the gunfire for some time.

Bennett had glanced over his shoulder, just barely seeing Woodcock back up the trail, patiently leading that lone pack mule on foot.

Upon reaching the clearing Blodgett had picked out, the old private remained atop that howitzer's lead mule, coaxing that beast the best he could to get the team turned so the howitzer could be put into action. That's when the sergeants got the rest of the crew to unhitch the caisson and muscle it to the side, chocking the wheels, then throwing back the tops of both chests to expose the eight rounds held by each box.

"Give it to 'em down there where all them warriors are!" Sergeant Frederick ordered. "Bring its ass round this way!"

Their breath puffing in the cold morning air, the four others laid their shoulders into the wheels.

"Gimme some elevation," Frederick growled at them. "We gotta make it reach, boys."

"Which of these charges do you want?" Sergeant Daly asked as Corporal Sales went to work dropping the elevation screw.

"One of them spherical cases to start!" Frederick ordered. "This gun won't reach much more'n a thousand yards. But that spherical case'll give them warriors something to reckon with anyway, I'd wager."

Bennett kept a tight rein on the mule team when the howitzer belched that first time, jolting the piece as Frederick and the others scrambled to swab out the bore and reload, this time using one of the shells.

"Two pounds lighter!" Frederick was explaining when Blodgett suddenly gave the warning.

"We're gonna have company soon!" the civilian barked.

They all peered down the slope for but a moment, seeing how some of the Nez Perce horsemen were starting from the south end of the village toward their position.

"How sharp's that slope?" Frederick grumbled as he turned his back on the valley below. "Thirty degrees? Maybe more? Crank down that screw and gimme all the elevation you can by rolling the bloody gun up on these chocks! This'un's gotta reach farther for us to do any good for our men down below!"

"You damn well better hurry, boys!" Bennett roared about the time Blodgett leaped atop his horse and shot right on past him without a word of fare-thee-well, lunging up the back trail.

While Bennett had been concentrating his attention on those warriors streaming out of the village for a notch of timber north of their gun placement, he hadn't been at all aware of the Nez Perce dashing toward them *along* the slope just above their position—horsemen who had already fled the camp below and were well along in the process of flanking Gibbon's attack force. The first shot stung the lead mule low in the neck, not far from where the private gripped the harness straps. It whipped its head from side to side, then started kicking as a second shot struck it low in the belly—doing everything it could to pitch its rider off.

He cursed himself many times for blindly doing his best to stay on that wounded mule, even as it keeled to the side and crashed down on his right leg in a web of tangled harness, noisy, braying mules, and a maze of stomping, thrashing legs and hooves.

The first thing Bennett did when he caught his breath was try to pull himself free. No good. The second thing he thought to do was look around for what help he could call over.

"This is another Custer massacre!" one of the privates shrieked as he bounded away up the hill.

Bennett watched the backs of McGregor and Goale disappear up the hill through the shadows of the lodgepole pine. *Likely gonna run all the way to Fort Ellis—brave sons a bitches they are!*

He heard a loud slap of blood hitting flesh and bone—wondering if it were another one of these cantankerous mules as he brought up his arms to cover his face from their slashing hooves. Through the dancing legs he caught a glimpse of Corporal Sales sliding down against one of the caisson wheels, his Springfield still clutched in both hands, the front of his gray pullover dark with a shiny gravy stain. The corporal's chin slowly sank until it rested against his breastbone and he didn't move again.

"You hit, Bennett?"

"No, Sergeant Frederick!" he cried, recognizing the artilleryman's voice. "I can use your help gettin' my leg out—"

"I was hoping you could help me!" Frederick interrupted with a sputter. "I've took a bullet."

"Shit," Sergeant Daly grumbled aloud. "I s'pose neither of you's gonna be coming to help me get outta of me fix, are you now?"

"You wounded, too?" Frederick asked.

"Not so bad I can't make a run for it with you," Daly admitted.

Frederick said, "Get over here on this side of the gun and together we'll get up to them trees—"

"Sergeants!" Bennett cried.

"Shuddup and lay quiet!" Frederick ordered as he crabbed around the far side of the caisson in a crouch. "There ain't nothing we can do for you. Maybe they'll run right past you and come after us!"

Bennett listened as the two men shuffled away, half-dragging each other into the timber—the sound of their scuffing boots quickly drowned out by the chorus of victorious war cries headed his way.

"Shuddup and lay quiet, he says!" Bennett cursed. "Goddamn the sergeants of this world!"

He damn well wasn't going to take the chance those horsemen would rush on past him when they found a white man pinned down—prime pickings for some delicious torture. He thrashed to one side, pushing with his free leg again, then turned himself onto the other side, ready to thump the heaving animal on the back of the head—

When he felt the knot under his right thigh. His bloody folding knife!

Twisting slightly to drag it out of the front pocket of his britches, the private snapped it open as he stretched his body for all it was worth, struggling to get close enough to the mule's neck to do some good. Spitting out a mouthful of pine needles and dirt, Bennett jabbed the knife's tip into the mule's hide. The animal barely moved. Again he stabbed. And the beast moved a little more.

Finally he jabbed and jabbed, all the harder—heaving back on his leg at the same time.

It popped free!

Quickly looking around, he saw his Springfield was under the same damned mule, but he had that knife. The leg was coming alive with agonizing stabs of pain as blood surged back through the crushed, thirsty tissue. Bennett thought he should give it a try and shifted a little weight onto it—nearly falling—then whirled around suddenly at that war cry.

Across the clearing a warrior was charging him on foot.

Lunging on that half-asleep leg, Bennett scooped up Corporal Sales's rifle and immediately dropped to his knee. Firing off a shot that made the Nez Perce skid to a halt and duck for cover, Bennett clambered to his feet and started up the trail behind everyone else.

He wasn't sure how long that wooden leg of his leg would stay under him, what with the strain of his run, or how long his lungs would hold out, burning the way they were with such exertion at this high altitude—but Private Bennett wasn't about to turn belly-up now!

Not after the greasers down in Mexico and the Rebs down south had both tried to kill him more times than he cared to count . . . this was one soldier who wasn't about to turn his scalp over to these red bastards!

CHAPTER SIXTY-THREE

AUGUST 9, 1877

ILL THAT GODDAMN HORSE, WILL YOU, SIR!"

Lieutenant Charles Woodruff had listened to many of those pleas over the last few minutes . . . then reluctantly decided he had but one thing he could do.

His was the only horse that had reached the siege area alive. Colonel John Gibbon had abandoned his big gray down in the village with its broken leg, and by the time the retreat began none of the other handful of mounts a few of the civilians rode down from the wagon train ever managed to get out of the village alive.

Just as soon as they were completely surrounded, the Nez Perce began sighting in on Woodruff's animal—certainly the biggest target, easiest, too, since the men were religiously hugging the ground and digging in.

At first Woodruff had resisted the notion of killing the animal himself. If the Indians ended up doing it, he could accept that. But to kill such a magnificent horse himself?

For a long time as he brooded on it the lieutenant kept waiting to hear a third shot from that howitzer, knowing that the arrival of the fieldpiece was sure to drive off the warriors who had them surrounded, forcing them to flee on out of the village, raising their seige before his horse was wounded beyond any hope of recovery. But they heard no more than those two cannonshots—his hopes fading as quickly as had the hissing boom of that second, and final, blast from the mountain howitzer.

"Just shoot your horse and be done with it, Mr. Woodruff!" Gibbon finally growled himself, grown exasperated as the lieutenant's mount kicked and thrashed against the hold the lieutenant had on it, its wild gyrations endangering any of the men entrenching nearby as it danced this way and that.

"Yes, sir."

One of the civilians shouted, "We're gonna need them horse steaks for lunch, Lieutenant!"

Without paying the brittle laughter any heed, Woodruff grabbed hold of the stirrup, quickly dragged himself to his feet, then lunged alongside the nervous animal to its head. Before he had time to reconsider what he was doing he fired a pistol bullet into the horse's brain.

It dropped like a sack of buckshot, kicked a few times, then lay still with a final shudder as a bullet scuffed into the dirt beside his left foot. For an instant, that foot went numb; then his heel began to burn. Sinking to his knee as bullets whined through the trees, he twisted around to inspect his boot. A bullet had sliced through the back of the leather, making for an oozy flesh wound.

"Very good, Mr. Woodruff," Gibbon said. "Come with me and the others."

Woodruff rose to a crouch, slowly putting pressure on the wounded heel, finding that it didn't hurt nearly as bad as it looked. He stretched out on his belly, following the colonel and a handful of officers as they crawled to the end of their crude one-acre fortress, right to the very last of the skinny lodgepole pines, where they found themselves at the edge of a sharp embankment that fell away some twenty feet to the creek and willows below.

"Look there, General," Woodruff announced. "Warriors working their way at us."

"Should we fire at them?" Captain Rawn asked.

Gibbon wagged his head. "No. I came here only to have us a look at the village, reconnoiter the enemy's retaking of their camp."

Those warriors and the Nez Perce who had already closed in around them on the hillside, had Gibbon's command surrounded. It was clear from the discussion the officers held there at the edge of the embankment that there was no way to break out of the lines and rush the encampment in some desperate bid to locate more ammunition among the lodges. That became the overriding concern there and then: the fact that they were separated from their wagon train carrying a reserve of ammunition.

"But what if the Nez Perce ride back on our trail and find our wagon corral?" asked Captain Richard Comba.

Gibbon's face turned a solemn gray. "The train guard isn't big enough to hold off a stiff attack."

"I respectfully submit we've got to have our company commanders stop their men from throwing away their ammunition," Woodruff suggested.

Gibbon agreed as they heard an unearthly scream from one of the wounded men left in the creek bottom—those agonized cries from below filling the quiet pauses between gunshots on this hillside. "All of you, we must conserve our cartridges. Put a stop to rapid firing at the enemy. Shoot only when you are assured of a target."

As Woodruff was just starting to rock onto a knee to follow the others crabbing back to rejoin the men in that corral of rifle pits, a volley of shots persuaded the lieutenant to pitch himself onto the ground with the rest. He lay there a few moments, catching his breath, then realized his legs hurt like hell—probably from that excruciating climb up the slope.

But when he attempted to drag the legs under him preparing to get back onto his feet, Woodruff realized it was more than mere muscle fatigue. The pale sky blue of his wool britches was spotted with glistening blood. Both legs. Just above the knees.

Mortally scared, he immediately grabbed both burning wounds and squeezed, hopeful it would relieve the rising pain, then quickly felt along the big bones for any fractures.

"Thank you, God," he whispered.

Woodruff's head sagged back in his shoulders as he closed his eyes, grateful the bullet that had sliced through both legs had missed the bones. Otherwise, he would have lost both legs.

Oh, Louie, he thought of his wife as he opened his stinging eyes, smearing a tear across a powder-grimed cheek with the back of his bloody hand.

At least I can still dance with you on our next anniversary!

WHILE MOST OF the warriors who had taken part in the capture of the big wagon gun now went back to fight the soldiers who were hiding down in their hollows, Yellow Wolf and his mother's brother, Light in the Mountain, rode off up the slope, leading a small scouting party to search for more soldiers who must surely be coming their way.

Not far up the trail, the scouts divided, most continuing right on up the mountainside to put themselves above the soldiers who had escaped the village and taken refuge in the trees, while Yellow Wolf and Light in the Mountain stayed with the route the wagon gun soldiers had taken when they turned around and fled during the capture of their weapon. Farther and farther the two rode, without seeing any sign of the white men.

"These soldiers have run very fast," sighed Light in the Mountain as they finally brought their ponies to a halt.

"Do you think they have run all the way back to the settlers' valley?"* Yellow Wolf wondered.

"I hoped we could see Cut-Off Arm and his soldiers coming over the mountains," said his uncle. "At least to run across some of their big wagons filled with supplies and more ammunition."

"Listen, you can even hear the guns of *Ollokot*'s warriors firing from so far away," he told his uncle. "Since we did not find the soldiers, or their wagons, let's go back and see if we can help the families."

"Maybe there is something for us to do in the village, to help the wounded," Light in the Mountain suggested.

As they backtracked down that trail both the village and the soldiers had used to reach the Place of the Ground Squirrels, Yellow Wolf began to hear the first faint wails of grief rising from those in the encampment. As the pair reached the bottom and were beginning to angle left to see how the fight was going at the siege area, both riders heard a loud scream—one clearly made by a man.

Thinking one of their own might be in danger, they immediately kicked their ponies into a lope for the tall willows in the boggy bottom. It was there they came upon a scene of three older women hunched over a figure wearing the muddy pale blue britches of a soldier.** His legs kicked and flailed as two of the old women pinned him down and a third squatted over him, straddling her victim. She had a bloodied knife clutched in both of her hands, poised with it over her head, preparing to plunge it into the soldier a second time.

---

*The Bitterroot valley.

**Historical testimony reveals that this soldier was in all likelihood Private Michael Gallagher, musician, attached to D Company of the Seventh U. S. Infantry.

The wounded man screamed even louder this time, kicking with his legs as the two warriors came upon the brutal scene.

Down slashed the knife as the soldier attempted to twist out of the way. Just when he turned his head to the side, the woman jammed the big blade into the side of his neck, blood squirting from a ruptured vessel, spraying her in the face and across her breasts.

His back arched in agony, his legs thrashing. On and on the white man begged and pleaded, fighting from side to side as his clothing and the ground beneath him grew soggy with blood. For a brief instant his eyes caught and held on Yellow Wolf's, then rolled back in his head a little as the old woman plunged her knife into his neck a third time. The soldier went limp and stopped fighting.

The other two women slowly dragged themselves to their feet, wiping their blood-splattered hands and arms on the white man's britches. That's when the three noticed the two warriors.

"He was already wounded," the knife holder explained as she wiped off the man's blood on her torn and soot-smudged dress. "I wanted to help him die faster. Even though my son did not die fast this morning when one of these soldiers shot him. So I think this *suapie* got better than he deserved."

"Does he have any bullets on him?" Light in the Mountain asked.

The woman shook her head. "There was no gun or bullets near him. He must have lost them running from the village."

"Or," Yellow Wolf commented as he looked up the hillside to where the gunfire was sporadic, "the other soldiers took his gun and bullets for themselves when they left him behind to die a hard way."

"Let's go see these soldiers who would leave one of their own behind in battle," his uncle suggested.

"Yes—I want to see what sort of creature would leave his friends behind to die at the hands of women."*

NOW THAT HE and the other men had rallied and taken back their camp here in the river bottom, Lean Elk's curiosity was drawn by that loud roar of a wagon gun. He knew a little something about such weapons. The half-breed Frenchman galloped uphill to lead in the dismantling of the soldier cannon.

Showing the others how to use the white man's tools found in the wagon boxes, Poker Joe directed the loosening of each hub and the removal of the wheels. The warriors had great fun starting these heavy wheels spinning and

*Big Hole battle historians have documented that as many as eight of Gibbon's soldiers and Catlin's volunteers were indeed left behind in the retreat, eight white men still alive to one degree or another at that point when the rest made their mad dash to the hillside point of timber. These men were discovered by the women, old men, and boys who eagerly scoured through the brush to find any such white enemies still breathing. After *Ollokot*'s warriors had pulled back the following day and Howard's men had reached the scene a day after that, upon a search of the creek-bottom battlefield these eight bodies were discovered—not one of those wounded still alive after the Nez Perce had finished them off in a most horrific manner.

bounding down the hillside toward the creek bottom. With the gun eventually removed from its wagon, several of the stronger men worked hard to pitch the shiny brass barrel down the slope, watching it tumble and bound through the saplings trees and over the soft ground until it came to a stop just two short arrow flights below them.

That's when Bird Alighting took over the destruction, pulling his skinning knife from his belt and showing the others how they were going to dig a hole in which to bury the cannon.

"It's a great pity you destroyed this gun."

Turning at the words, Bird Alighting, Poker Joe, and the others looked up at the older horseman who had stopped above them. Of this warrior Joe did not know he asked, "Why such a pity?"

"I know how to use this kind of gun."

Very dubious of such a claim, Poker Joe got to his feet and walked over to the horseman. He asked, "How would you know such a thing?"

"I learned when I was with the soldier chief named Wright."

That almost sounded convincing to Joe. "You fought alongside the soldiers in that war with Wright?"

"Yes," the horseman answered. "Against the Cayuse and Yakima. That's where I learned."

"Did you ever fire the gun yourself?" Bird Alighting challenged.

"No, but I watched them load and fire it over and over again, so I know how the white men do it."

Poker Joe looked down at the half-buried fieldpiece and shrugged. "Too late."

"Yes," the horseman said as he eased away. "And too bad. We could have used it to dislodge those soldiers from their rabbit hollows over in the trees."

CHAPTER SIXTY-FOUR

August 9, 1877

LIEUTENANT CHARLES WOODRUFF FLINCHED AT THAT NEXT DULL THUD—more lead slamming into human flesh.

The distinctive slap made his own wounds ache all the more, his soul whimpering as the men around him were hit, one after another.

Sometimes he could tell when a bullet struck bone. Other times it was no more than a moist slap as lead penetrated soft tissue. Woodruff couldn't help cringing when he heard a man cry out in pain, begging for help from his bunkies.

One at a time, the wounded were adding up, not just the ones they had managed to drag up here with them in the retreat but also those wounded the snipers were accounting for as Nez Perce marksmen sighted in on the soldiers' perimeter. By now there wasn't a white man who still had his hat on—they made such fine targets of a fellow.

Without a surgeon along, they had no clean bandages for each new wound. Instead, the men did what they could, pulling free their long shirttails and using their dirty digging knives to hack off wide strips of greasy, soiled cloth. At first it had galled Woodruff to see how the old files and the civilians spit a little tobacco juice into the wounds of their comrades before knotting a bandage over the puckered hole, but it didn't take long for him to accept that this was the way of things with these veteran frontiersmen.

Still, for a few of the worst cases, mere tobacco juice wrapped up with a piece of shirttail wasn't nearly enough to stop the bleeding of a blood vessel nicked by a Nez Perce bullet.

An old sergeant was the first to crab over to a rifle pit to help two young soldiers with their seriously wounded comrade. Quickly fingering a rifle cartridge from a loop on his prairie belt, he snapped open his pocketknife and deftly pried the lead bullet loose from its copper casing.

"Hol' 'im down, boys," he grumbled as he positioned the open cartridge right over the oozy leg wound.

As the two soldiers rocked their weight on top of their reluctant comrade, the old file reached in one of his belt pouches and pulled out a sulphur-headed lucifer he stuffed between his front teeth. Now with the fingers of his left hand, the old sergeant gently spread apart the ragged edges of the gaping wound and up-ended the cartridge before tamping the last of the black powder grains into the hole with a dirty fingertip. He quickly brushed away the excess powder, then leaned back.

As the sergeant pulled the match from between his teeth, the wounded soldier on the ground quit thrashing a moment, gazing up at the old file, and said, "H-hell, that wasn't so bad, Sarge."

But when the old soldier dragged his thumbnail across the head of the match, the young soldier went cross-eyed staring at the sudden flare as the whitish-blue flame inched closer and closer to his wounded leg. "Wh-what you gonna do with that—"

His question was instantly answered as the sergeant laid the burning lucifer down against the pocket of black powder with a sudden fiery *phfffft.* Spitting a momentary tongue of flame, a narrow tendril of greasy smoke rising from the wound, the fire had done its work, cauterizing the injured blood vessel.

"Looks like he'll be out for a while," the sergeant said, inspecting the soldier by gently raising the unconscious man's eyelids. He rolled back onto his knees and crabbed away, passing the young lieutenant on the way to his rifle pit.

The sergeant nodded at Woodruff and said, "How your bullet holes, sir?"

"T-they aren't bleeding like his was, Sergeant."

The old file grinned, his eyes crinkling. "Call me if you need me, Lieutenant."

Woodruff gulped, knowing exactly what the soldier was referring to. "A fine job over there, Sergeant. Man won't bleed to death now."

"Thankee, sir," he said, a little embarrassed as he started to move on. "Jus' a lil' something I picked up many a year ago during the Great War."

WHEN YELLOW WOLF and his uncle reached the point of timber on the hillside overlooking the camp, a sporadic rattle of gunfire was still continuing as *Ollokot*'s warriors settled into the siege around the *suapies*. Many of the men on all sides were continuing to sing or chant their war and victory songs—each warrior calling on his *wyakin*, his individual spiritual power.

Yellow Wolf rode up to a knot of men surrounding Five Wounds, the famous warrior called *Pahkatos Owyeen.*

The grieving warrior stood in the middle, talking in low tones to the rest as Yellow Wolf slid off his pony, tied it to a nearby sapling, and stepped over to listen to their quiet discussion. He recognized the grave expressions on all the faces . . . but most especially that ghostly look on Five Wounds's face. His skin had taken on a gray pallor that only served to accentuate the reddened eyes, swollen from much crying.

That's when Yellow Wolf remembered the courageous death of Five Wounds's best friend, Rainbow, earlier that morning in the village fight.

"This sun, this time," Five Wounds was saying as he stared down at his repeater, "I am going to die."

"You are going to make a bravery run against the *suapies?*" asked *Ollokot.*

"No, this is not a run against them," Five Wounds explained. "I am going to charge right into their burrows and have them kill me when I reach them. Kill me when I am so close I can see the fear in their eyes."

His words, perhaps more the tone of Five Wounds's voice, immediately tugged at Yellow Wolf's heart. He knew the story—every *Nee-Me-Poo* knew that tale by heart—how these two had begun their friendship as small boys, a kinship that would be nurtured over more than two decades as they traveled ancestral lands and journeyed many times to *Illahe* together—sometimes fighting enemies, side by side, in that buffalo country far to the east.

Theirs was a bond not of blood but of the heart, even of their very spirits. And now that Rainbow had been killed, every man gathered there knew it was Five Wounds's day to die as well. Everyone knew that years ago the two brothers-in-arms had taken a vow that they would die on the same day.

No one dared stand in his way as he sought to fulfill his vow to Rainbow.

Otskai rode up and dismounted, holding out a soldier canteen as he stepped toward the group. "Five Wounds—see what I have found in the village."

"I am not thirsty," Five Wounds said.

Removing the stopper, *Otskai* held the canteen under Five Wounds's nose. "This isn't water, my brother."

"Whiskey," Five Wounds said, taking the canteen. "Yes, I will have a drink now."

"The white men drank whiskey before they attacked us?" Yellow Wolf asked as Five Wounds passed him the canteen, but he passed it right on. He never touched liquor.

"My brother is killed today," Five Wounds reminded those who needed no reminding while each man took a sip from the fragrant canteen. "And I shall go with him . . . while the sun is in this sky. We will die together the way his father and my father died together in the buffalo country. They lay side by side where the battle was the strongest. And now I shall lie down beside my warmate. He is no more and I shall see that I follow him."

Yellow Wolf remembered how the two fathers had been killed in a fight with Lakota over on the eastern plains. "Do you want us to lay down some cover fire as you make your charge?"

The dark, red-rimmed eyes in that tortured face turned to the younger man as Five Wounds said, "Yes. That would help me to get as close as I can to the white man's burrows before their bullets kill me."

Ollokot seized Five Wounds's forearm in his, and they shook, wrist to wrist. Several other men offered their arms, too, and Five Wounds took the forearm of each, to grasp in that manner of men who have suffered hardship together, men who have stood against powerful enemies together, men who have repeatedly placed their bodies between their families and the *suapies* . . . together in the brotherhood of warriors.

It made Yellow Wolf's eyes mist as Five Wounds turned away from him and the others, stepping to the edge of the shallow, narrow gulch that separated them from the soldiers.

Instead of immediately dashing for the white men's hollows, Five Wounds paused to look up at the sky, declaring, "Rainbow—may your spirit look over me now. I am coming! I am coming to join you!"

As those last words escaped his tongue, Five Wounds bolted away at a sprint, racing around the head of the ravine and dodging between trees as the first of the soldier bullets began to whine around him, some smacking the narrow trunks of lodgepole pines, others snapping off small branches.

They saw the first bullet hit Five Wounds, striking him in the shoulder, momentarily slowing his gait as the impact shoved him around to the side, knocking him off-stride but for an instant until he shrugged off the injury and ran even faster, half bent over, nearing the soldier burrows.

The others joined *Ollokot* as their war chief started singing his own war song in a loud, strong voice. Yellow Wolf raised his voice with the rest. In chanting their own medicine song, Five Wounds's warrior brothers were sending him on his way to meet his dearest friend—their songs his medicine songs at this fragile moment between life and death. Their combined strength would become his strength alone for as long as he needed theirs to accomplish this last great act of friendship.

A bullet ripped into Five Wounds's thigh, sending a shudder through his body, causing him to slow noticeably. He was limping—but still he plunged on, closer, ever closer, to the soldier burrows.

Now the white men were yelling, some of the men beginning to stand behind their rifle pits, shouting at one another and pointing their weapons at that lone oncoming warrior. It was as if all those rifles were suddenly trained on Five Wounds, fixed on him alone.

One of the bullets that snarled his way smacked into his chest, blowing out a large hole in his back—but it did nothing to stop the man now that he was nearing his goal. Five Wounds was almost close enough that he could throw his *kopluts* at the soldiers. . . .

Another bullet rocked him, striking him low in the other shoulder. He was so near the soldier hollows that the impact shoved him backward a faltering step. At that moment another bullet hit him low in the belly, knocking him sideways—before he visibly shook it off and bent over again, limping toward the hollows. But this time Five Wounds moved much, much slower.

Another bullet tore through his chest, leaving a second gaping hole in his back.

Yellow Wolf and many of the others stood there, every man openly weeping now as they watched this last selfless act of bravery for a friend.

"I am come this day to be with you, Rainbow!"

Though his body faltered, weaving and tottering very slowly toward the soldier burrows, Five Wounds's voice rang stronger than ever . . . even as another bullet rocked him, made him stumble and then collapse to his knees just short of the soldier lines.

Try as he might, he could not rise again, struggling to get his feet under him when two more bullets smacked into his body with the telltale breaking of bone as he was whirled one way, then the other, his weakened arms windmilling with the force of each impact. Still his head was held high as his undaunted will struggled to control his failing body. Collapsing forward, he planted both hands in front of him. Five Wounds crawled on.

Three more bullets hit him: one in the leg, another in the chest, and the third in the hip, breaking the big bone that could no longer support his weight.

And as Five Wounds wobbled there on one knee, he looked up at the sky, opening his mouth to speak—

"Rainbow, I am come to join—"

A bullet slammed into his forehead, snapping it backward violently, driving him off that one knee and hand, pitching his body backward onto his side . . . just short of his goal.

But Yellow Wolf knew better than to think Five Wounds hadn't finished his quest. As he wiped a hand down his face and cleared his eyes, he knew Five Wounds had reached his goal. Even though he hadn't made it into the heart of the soldier hollows, he had nonetheless gotten close enough to gaze into the eyes of the men who would kill him.

By now, this brave man was already reunited with Rainbow.

"DAMN—WILL YOU lookit that down there!"

Turning painfully at that exclamation from a nearby soldier, Lieutenant Charles Woodruff slowly crawled over to have himself a look from the edge of the bluff.

A warrior was coming out from the village, mounted on a showy pony. He guided the animal into the willow as he headed for the base of the soldiers' hill.

"Five dollars to the man who knocks him down afore me," proposed Second Cavalry Sergeant Edward Page, lying off to Woodruff's left.

After only two shots from the warrior, who reappeared in the brush below to fire up the slope—Page's head flopped backward, a neat, black hole below his chin, the top of his head blown off.

"I'll get that son of a bitch for you, Sarge," vowed one of the cavalrymen near Page's body. "An' you won't owe me a goddamned sawbuck!"

When that horseman next appeared, he didn't even have the time to raise his rifle before the trooper's bullet knocked him off the back of his pony.

"Watch 'im," the marksman warned those around him. "If he moves while I'm reloading, hit him again to make sure he's a good Injun—"

Down below in the creek bottom, a horrendous cry interrupted him. The sort of sound that would make any man's blood curdle.

" 'Spect they found 'nother of our wounded, Lieutenant," a soldier said quietly.

"Goddamn 'em to Hell!" a corporal cursed as they all listened to the pitiful screams of that white man—soldier or volunteer—whose life was slowly snuffed out in a most horrible fashion.

One of the older men ground his hands together, his words slipping out between clenched teeth: "If I just could get my hands on one of them monsters right now!"

Woodruff reclined back against a small mound of dirt thrown up by a long-fallen tree's roots. Swallowing down the rising pain in his left heel and both thighs, he wondered if they all would have that chance to get their hands on the Nez Perce soon enough . . . when the red bastards made one final charge.

CHAPTER SIXTY-FIVE

Wa-Wa-Mai-Khal, 1877

WHILE THE SUN ROSE HIGHER AND HOTTER THROUGH THAT LONG morning, Yellow Wolf had watched how Red Moccasin Tops had done such effective work with his soldier carbine against the *suapies*. This warrior, who was called *Sarpsis Ilppilp*, crouched behind a small boulder close to the hollows, where he undeniably had accounted for several of the soldiers who had fallen, either killed or badly wounded.

When his bullets struck a victim, Red Moccasin Tops celebrated and roared loudly, chanting his own strong-heart song while he reloaded and adjusted the white wolfskin cape he had tied around the shoulders of the red flannel shirt he had on—one of the powerful talismans he wore to ward off the death spirit. No other fighting man had dared crawl as close to the white enemies as Red Moccasin Tops.

"Where is White Bird now?" he shouted to the other warriors every time he hit one of the white men.

"He is not here!" a voice answered.

Someone else said, "Maybe still in the village."

Each time, the exchange was the same. Red Moccasin Tops told those who had the soldiers surrounded, "Don't you see that I am here and he is not! But this morning White Bird accused me of being a coward. *Wahlitits* and I were the only men brave enough to start this war. Who is this White Bird to call *us* cowards when Shore Crossing lies dead in the village—killed defending his home and family? He was a patriot killed defending his people and their freedom!"

Over time Yellow Wolf thought Red Moccasin Tops grew a little bolder as he popped out from the protection of his rock, quickly aimed, and fired a shot at the soldiers huddled like scared voles in their rifle pits.

"Who is White Bird to accuse me of being a coward because I started this war with my friend?" he shouted as he reloaded another cartridge into his soldier carbine. "See the soldiers cower from me in their hollows! Let no man question my courage now—"

At the instant he crept around the side of the boulder in a crouch, his rifle already at his shoulder, a bullet struck Red Moccasin Tops in the side of his throat, not only slashing open a massive blood vessel but also cutting the leather strand of his sacred dentalium-shell necklace, which he tied choker-style around his neck. For some weeks now *Sarpsis Ilppilp* had believed this necklace held *hattia tinukin*, the death spirit, at bay.

His body was hurtled to the side, landing in a heap, where he gurgled for a few moments, trying to speak, his legs pumping in anguish while blood spurted onto his sacred wolfskin cape.

For some time the others were stunned into complete silence.

"Who will bring Red Moccasin Tops out to safety?" someone finally cried from the late-morning shadows.

"Who among you is bravest?" immediately echoed a familiar voice. It belonged to the young warrior's father, Sun Necklace.

"Perhaps I am brave enough!" another voice called out.

His voice cracking with deep emotion, Sun Necklace hollered, "We do not want to leave Red Moccasin Tops there! We cannot leave him for the crazy white people to cut him up in pieces to make a fool of this brave warrior! Who will bring his body away, and carry him to me?"

"I am his good friend—I will bring *Sarpsis Ilppilp* away!" sang Strong Eagle. "Come along all those who want to save the body of a hero."

Yellow Wolf and six others hollered their agreement and hurried to follow Strong Eagle, the cousin of Red Moccasin Tops. Running and dodging in a crouch, they used the narrow trees the best they could to cover their intent. Inside their ring of rifle pits, the soldiers yelled their warnings at one another, becoming very animated. Yellow Wolf decided that, with Five Wounds having made his suicide charge not long ago, the white men believed that the rest of the warriors were now coming in for a massive assault.

The *suapies* laid down a murderous fire, knocking over the man beside Yellow Wolf. A bullet struck *Weweetsa*, called Log, in the collarbone and came out the opposite shoulder. The warriors left the wounded man where he lay and continued to sneak toward the boulder.

The remaining seven didn't get much closer when *Quiloishkish* had his right elbow shattered by a soldier bullet. He twisted to the ground, writhing in pain, groaning through clenched teeth.

"We should go back," Strong Eagle said regretfully.

Yellow Wolf reminded, "It is yours to decide: he is your cousin."

"His body is too close to the soldiers!" Strong Eagle snapped. "We will go back."

The six retreated, gathering up their two wounded on the way out.

It wasn't very long before Strong Eagle resentfully worked himself into a frenzy once more, desiring to retrieve the body of his cousin. "I will go again," he announced. "Come with me if you want to save his body."

For this attempt there were only five, since one of the warriors dropped out. And this time Strong Eagle led them in a different direction, staying at the bottom of a shallow draw that led down beneath the rifle pits to a spot not far from where Red Moccasin Tops lay.

"Wait here for me," Strong Eagle instructed the others. "I will bring his body back to this ravine."

Vaulting over the top of the shallow gully and surprising the *suapies*, the warrior scrambled on all fours to reach the boulder as bullets slammed against trees and plowed into the ground all around him. A moment after he reached the body, Strong Eagle shouted back to the others.

"My cousin is not dead! He still breathes!"

That was momentous news to Yellow Wolf as he watched Strong Eagle start away from the boulder, slowly standing with Red Moccasin Tops draped across his shoulder. He managed to lunge toward the ravine only a matter of steps before a soldier bullet found its mark, hitting Strong Eagle in the side. He pitched forward into the dirt and pine needles, dropping his cousin with a grunt.

Gasping in pain, Strong Eagle caught his breath, glancing down at the two wounds along his lower ribs. Then he crawled over to his cousin's body, grabbed hold of the belt, and started to pull Red Moccasin Tops onto his shoulder once more. Wobbly, Strong Eagle struggled to rise and eventually managed another half-dozen steps toward the ravine, when he collapsed under the weight, too weak from his loss of blood.

"My cousin, now he breathes no more," Strong Eagle announced some time later after he had rested on the ground.

"Come out by yourself!" Yellow Wolf shouted.

With a weak voice, Strong Eagle whimpered, "My heart feels small and cold that I cannot bring out the hero!"

His very soul aching for all the loss he had witnessed this day, Yellow Wolf said, "If your cousin is dead, he is beyond your help now."

"LIEUTENANT? I WAN'CHA lookit this bullet hole in me."

Charles Woodruff turned slightly as the enlisted man twisted about in his shallow rifle pit when the lieutenant was dragging himself past, sent by Gibbon to have someone check on the men and count the number of cartridges each of them still had available in the event of a rush by more than one warrior—the likes of which they had experienced a little while before.

"It can't be too bad now, can it?" he asked as the private inched toward him, pushing himself along with one hand, sliding on his hip. "If you can move that well—"

Charles Alberts* pulled his other bloody hand away from the damp, dark patch on his chest as the lieutenant bent forward to look. That's when Woodruff's words caught in his throat.

Moist blood not only continued to seep from the bullet hole the soldier had been pressing his hand over, but there were frothy bubbles escaping from the wound as well. From what little the lieutenant remembered of his basic human anatomy, the Nez Perce bullet had gone through the man's lungs. Woodruff took a deep breath, unsure what he would say to the soldier, since those bubbles did not bode well for the man surviving a lengthy siege.

"I near got myself killed by some women in a tepee this morning," Alberts confessed quietly. "Was ordered to search the tepees—them squaws tried to kill me, but I didn't hit till just a little while ago."

Woodruff could only stare at that dark, bubbling hole.

---

*See chapter 55.

"I'm asking you, Lieutenant," the private said, a slight quiver in the voice he consciously attempted to keep from wavering, " 'cause we don't have no surgeon along."

"You sure picked a poor substitute," Woodruff eventually replied, remembering to keep the gravity from showing in his eyes and his voice. "Here, let me take a look at your back. See the exit wound."

But when he looked at the soldier's shirt, then pulled up the blouse and peered at the back of the man's gray fatigue pullover, there was no hole. That meant no exit wound.

"Seems the bullet didn't come out, Private."

Alberts asked, "Wha-what's that mean, Lieutenant?"

"Means it's a serious wound, soldier."

Alberts swallowed hard, then coughed a little as he pressed his sticky fingers against the hole all the more firmly. "What you think of my chances, sir?"

Woodruff sighed, ruminating on what to say. It didn't make sense to tell the private just how bad things were, but . . . his conscience wouldn't let him lie to a man in that condition, either.

"Alberts, you have a serious wound—but there is no need of your dying . . . if you've got the nerve."

"The n-nerve, Lieutenant?"

"The nerve to hang on until relief comes and a surgeon gets here. You've already shown you had the nerve to see it through our difficult march and this hellish battle. If you've got the nerve to make it through this siege, you'll come out just fine on the other side."

It took a moment, but Private Charles Alberts finally grinned wanly. He said, "Thank you, Lieutenant. I promise I'll keep my nerve up."

Woodruff watched the soldier slide sideways around in his shallow rifle pit, lean back against the dirt breastwork, then close his eyes as another round came whining through their position—

"The red sonsabitches gonna burn us out!" came the pained yelp just as Woodruff's nose registered that peculiar stench of burning grass.

"Where's that coming from?" an officer called.

"Up the hill!"

"There—to the west!"

The first smudge of pale, whitish smoke wafted through the stand of lodgepole, assaulting their noses. The wounded began crying out all the more piteously with a new danger that only intensified their suffering from the heat and want of water. Now the very air around them was becoming a suffocating blanket too heavy to breathe.

"This can only mean the warriors are going to charge us!" Gibbon shouted from his place near the southern edge of the scene. "They're gonna rush in under cover of the smoke!"

Alberts reached out to snag Woodruff's arm. He pleaded, "Promise you'll kill me with your revolver afore they get their hands on me, Lieutenant."

"I don't want one more of our wounded to fall into their bloody hands," Woodruff vowed, instantly recalling the cries of those they had left in the creek bottom when they retreated to this little plateau. "This pistol is our last resort, soldier."

"Lieutenant Woodruff!"

"Yes, sir, General Gibbon?"

"Do you remember last year about this time, up at Fort Shaw, when Looking Glass himself and some of his warriors were on their way back home from the buffalo plains?"

Woodruff swallowed, the war cries and chants behind the smoke becoming louder still. The recollection was clear as rain-rinsed crystal.

"Yes, sir. Looking Glass held a sham battle for you on the broad plain near the stables—divided his warriors in two for the show."

"One band lit a grass fire," Gibbon recalled. "Made a charge in beneath all the smoke, driving the other side from the field."

"You heard the general, men!" Woodruff roared now with the certainty they had only moments to live. "This is a tactic the Nez Perce love to use in battle. Be prepared for a final charge. Make every one of your last cartridges count!"

As their throats became raw with coughing and their eyes stung with tears, attempting to peer through the billowing waves of grass smoke, Woodruff listened to the increasing amplitude of the war cries. They swelled in a seeming crescendo over several minutes as the breathless soldiers waited for the charge to come—a charge that meant the very real possibility of defeat and death . . . perhaps even worse.

"The smoke! My God—it's dyin' off!"

Sure as sun, the wind had suddenly shifted and blew the fire right back on the scorched hillside. Starved for fuel, the flames were swiftly snuffed out. No longer did the afternoon breeze carry the thick, stifling clouds of gray right into the soldier lines.

With his eyes tearing now that he could actually begin to see some distance beyond their ragged rectangle of rifle pits, Woodruff whispered a silent prayer, the first he had said in many a year.

He vowed to the Almighty that he would pray a little more often from here on out.

CHAPTER SIXTY-SIX

Wa-Wa-Mai-Khal, 1877

IN THEIR THIRD ATTEMPT TO RETRIEVE THE BODY OF RED MOCCASIN TOPS, a group of warriors led by Old Yellow Wolf managed to lay down enough harassing fire that Bighorn Bow, called *Tahwis Takaitat*, crawled under a barrage of soldier bullets and pulled *Sarpsis Ilppilp* away from the soldier hollows.

"You have done what I wanted!" roared Sun Necklace in relief.

By the time they carried the body out of the timber to the mouth of the ravine, a small crowd of old women had gathered in the creek bottom, patiently waiting to assist the family with the burial. It was not the first such ceremony those women had helped with that day. Yellow Wolf and his mother's brother stood by while the women cleaned the warrior's body, then wrapped it in a new blanket. After laying the body on a travois, they began walking their pony into the timbered hills, planning to leave Red Moccasin Tops in a secret place.

When the oldest among the women determined the spot, she signaled the others to halt. There they quickly went to work scraping at the soft forest floor, gouging out a final resting place for this hero's body.

"I remember a time early this summer, when he showed me his shell necklace," the dead man's father said quietly, standing to the side with Yellow Wolf and his uncle, joined by the oldest woman in charge of the burial party. "He said his medicine would be strong when he wore it into battle."

"He was right," the matriarch added, a slight lisp to her words due to the loss of so many of her front teeth. "Red Moccasin Tops *was* bullet-proof from the neck down when he wore it around his throat."

"Did you see how strong his medicine worked at that first battle against the soldiers?" Sun Necklace asked the woman proudly. "When the *suapies* attacked us in *Lahmotta?*"

"I did see with my own eyes," she replied, her old eyes filled with wonder. "After the fight was over and the soldiers all ran away . . . Red Moccasin Tops came back to the village and leaped off his horse in front of a big crowd of us who were singing the fighters' praises. I noticed how many bullet holes punctured his red flannel shirt and the blanket around his neck, but not a single bullet wound in his flesh!"

"After I gave him a hug of congratulation," Sun Necklace explained, "he took off the gun belt he had strapped around his waist—"

"Everyone standing there saw how many flattened, misshapen bullets fell from his shirt then," the old woman concluded. "Because they were trapped beneath his shirt and spilled out when he finally took off his belt."

"The *suapie* bullet hit him many times that day, yet not a one of them penetrated his flesh," his proud father remarked.

Then Sun Necklace fell silent for some time as the women laid the shroud into the long, shallow hole and started to scoop dirt back into it with their hands. "Some soldier made a lucky shot this day, to kill my son with a bullet that struck him above his medicine necklace."

"And what of your promise, Sun Necklace?" Old Yellow Wolf asked the father.

"Promise?"

"To give the wolf hide away to the man who rescued your son's body."

He nodded once. "Yes. I forgot about that. I will have to think about that—and talk to his mother, too."

"But that was a vow you made to those young warriors!"

Sun Necklace's face hardened like flint, his eyes glaring at Old Yellow Wolf and his nephew. "Why should I be held to a promise made in the heat of emotion—at the death of my son? His mother is a medicine woman. She made him that wolf-hide cape. It is she who should decide what becomes of her son's talisman."

"But *you* offered it—"

"That makes little difference," Sun Necklace interrupted. "It was never mine to offer."

Yellow Wolf watched the father turn his back on them as he stared down at the last of the burial process. The old women laid some rocks and several logs on the site before they stood and dusted their hands on their clothing.

This is not good, Yellow Wolf thought to himself. *First we had Looking Glass denying the strong medicine of several warriors who had bad visions about this Place of the Ground Squirrels . . . and now this revered war chief, Sun Necklace—who led so many of the first attacks on the Shadows in the early days of this war—he is breaking a blood oath made in battle, when death hovers near every man.*

Even though the *suapies* were huddled in their burrows and Cut-Off Arm was still far away, Yellow Wolf shuddered with a chill of defeat.

The white man had already defeated them.

While the *Nee-Me-Poo* might run to the buffalo country, they would never be the same people they had been before these troubles. No longer were the chiefs listening to quiet voices of the spirits around them. No longer would those spirits guide the actions of chiefs who broke their vows to the people.

How could such men of little honor ever hope to protect, much less lead, the *Nee-Me-Poo* . . . now that the People were running for their lives?

HENRY BUCK WONDERED if there would be anyone to bury him with such care and affection when he died.

Watching a few knots of women and old men as they went about their grim business of burying their dead in the creek bottom brush or dragging the bodies away toward the eastern plateau on travois, the civilian wondered if he would be missed nearly as much when his name was called from the great beyond.

As he sat alone with his thoughts, he brooded on how many of those victims were women and children—realizing now in the fading light of dusk that Gibbon had unleashed pent-up men on a sleeping village where shadowy figures darted from lodges in all directions, where every Nez Perce was a potential enemy. In the heat of that sort of warfare and battle, chances were more than good that many of those half-naked, blanket-wrapped forms hadn't been warriors at all.

But then . . . was anyone in that village entirely innocent of what outrages of murder and rape, theft and arson had been committed back in Idaho?

They were all guilty to one degree or another, he decided. Man, woman, child.

Henry tried to convince himself that the reason he suffered such gloomy thoughts was only because he had gone without sleep for so long. Because he was sitting here, pinned down without any food or water, surrounded by an enemy that might well kill him before sunrise, now that dark had come to bring an end to that bloody day.

Every time he tried to convince himself that Gibbon and the others were right in punishing these Nez Perce, some tiny hairline fractures began to splinter his certainty. All he had to do was watch the women, little ones, and old men go about their grim burials on the outskirts of that village for Henry Buck to finally realize this never had been a war of warriors. Right from the beginning of the troubles over on the Salmon River and the Camas Prairie, too, this hadn't been a story of men making war on men.

No, right from the first spasm of violence this had been a drama that swept up the women and children, a tragedy that made all the innocents not only unwitting victims but unwilling participants, too. The Nez Perce had started this tragedy by making war on *all* whites—not only men. So to Henry, it stood to reason that the army and its civilian volunteers made war on *all* Nez Perce . . . wherever they could find them.

The Indians gave the first hurt, attacking homes and families. The white man struck back, attacking homes and families.

Why had he ever thought that war was a honorable profession practiced between warriors? To consider it a noble art—practiced by fighting men, by those who truly understood its deadly risks? With this bloody day everything he had once believed had been turned on its head, his whole world yanked out from under him.

As the hours of siege had dragged by that afternoon, he kept reminding himself that once their families had cleared out of the village, the warriors would in all likelihood end their sniping and pull back. And once that red noose was loosened, the soldiers and Catlin's civilians could slip down to the creek to fill what few canteens they had among them, splash some cold water on the backs of their necks, and . . . and hell—he didn't know what the blazes any of them would do next.

But he watched those last three women attack a lodge cover together in the half-light of dusk, tearing it down, then tying all the belongings onto a travois suspended behind one of the ponies, many other pony drags already bearing what Henry took to be the wounded, slowly angling up the side of that plateau east of camp. At the top they struck out across the prairie.

South, he thought. Back for Idaho. Perhaps they were making for their homeland after this battle had proved so disastrous for both sides.

Home. It sounded damn good right then.

Then his heart clutched as he realized those Nez Perce never would have their old homes again—no matter how long they fought or where they ran. That was all a matter of long ago now. There could never be any heading *home* for them.

As the sun sank behind the mountains and threw an immediate darkness on the Big Hole, the night sounds began softly, slipping out of the forest around them, the slough somewhere below. Not just the chatter of the animals out there in the night, not only the frightening war cries and death oaths of the warriors who still made their presence known from time to time . . . but the whimpering sobs of a few of the soldiers and civilians as the cold black blanket of night settled over the hillside and a man felt much more anonymous, far more alone.

Many of the wounded begged for water. Some pleaded for a doctor. A few anguished for a bite of food when all any of them had to chew on was some raw, stringy horse that had been lying out in the sun all day, bloating and flyblown. To Henry's way of thinking, there was a thousand good reasons for any of them to cry.

No food but raw, rancid horse. No water, neither.

And precious little hope for what the new dawn would bring.

IT SEEMED AS if daylight never would come to Lieutenant Charles Woodruff. Nights in the mountains were always cold, even at the height of summer.

Before dawn that morning the men had abandoned their heavy coats, leaving them behind with the bedding and supplies back in Kirkendall's wagons. Woodruff wondered once or twice about those seventeen soldiers and three civilians left up the trail at the wagon camp. Had the same warriors who overran the howitzer grown curious and back-trailed to overwhelm the wagon guard?

Most, if not all, of the men in the compound began shivering as the night deepened and temperatures slid lower and lower. More than twelve hours ago they had all waded through that creek below, some of the men forced to make a crossing in water that lapped up to their armpits. In a wild retreat, they had splashed and slogged their way back through that deep creek and boggy slough to reach this hillside. So once the sun's relentless heat dissipated with the coming of night, the men began to tremble and quake in their damp clothing.

He did not want his thoughts to drift to his three wounds. So Woodruff willed his mind to busy itself with other things as the darkness deepened and some of the more than forty wounded men whimpered, sobbed, or outright cried for water, food, and a merciful relief. He knew that several of the men even suffered from more than one wound.

The rest of Gibbon's command put their anger, frustration, and fears into work: doing what they could in the dark to make their breastworks a bit higher, digging their rifle pits a little deeper. As the stars came out and a sliver of moon arose from the far horizon, he could hear soft scraping sounds of rocks being piled one on the other and the scratch of bayonet and knife where earth was slowly separated from itself at this corner or that of their little corral.

Charles wondered if these men who were still whole in body were soldiers and citizens who had never claimed to be totally without fear—merely men who struggled to keep their fear from paralyzing them as he did.

Of those one-hundred-eighty-three men who had pitched into the Nez Perce at dawn that morning, seven of Gibbon's seventeen officers were either dead or wounded . . . twenty-nine of the rank and file were dead, and forty more had suffered wounds—two of them mortal.

From time to time when the quiet of that night grew heavy, Woodruff even heard a man digging his fingernails across the bottom of his haversack, doing his best to peel free every last pasty residue of the hardtack he had packed into battle, his ration of tasteless crackers having suffered two unavoidable soakings. It was that or the flesh of the lieutenant's horse. Without the benefit of fire to roast a stringy strip he hacked from a rear flank, the lieutenant found he couldn't choke down the raw meat. One of the old files suggested their pry the bullets off their cartridges, the way some had done to cauterize a few of the most terrible wounds, using the powder now to season the uncooked raw meat . . . but Gibbon promptly issued an order against the wasting of even one of those precious cartridges.

Shortly before midnight three of the men, all recruits from G Company, came to the colonel and declared their willingness to make an attempt at bringing back some water from the creek below their plateau. As soon as they began to crawl out from the lines, each of them dragging four canteens strapped over his shoulders, the Nez Perce hollered their warnings to one another. Gibbon ordered a half-dozen volleys fired in the direction of the stream, in hopes of clearing a way for the water carriers. As the echo of those army guns faded, a few random Nez Perce carbines began to make some scattered noise. For those left behind in the compound to wait and wonder, intent upon every distinct sound the darkness brought to them, it was an eternity until they heard a lone white man cry out to the others that he was hit, but could still crawl.

By the time all three had slithered back in with one minor wound and their canteens refilled, one of the astonished trio announced that he had been so scared he forgot to get himself a drink at the stream while he was filling the canteens hung around his neck!

"I know it was only a hunnert yards, Lieutenant," exclaimed Private Homer Coon, "but it sure as hell seemed like a hunnert miles to me! An' lemme tell you—I never had no idea how much a canteen can hold while you're waiting on ever' one. Why, I thought them four'd never fill up!"

Woodruff figured it would have been a merciful death if any of the Nez Perce had caught those water carriers down by the stream in the dark: a bullet ending things quickly—before the warriors, or their squaws, scrounged through the brush to find him where he lay wounded and helpless. Better to go fast without any pain . . .

Not the way First Lieutenant William L. English was suffering with increasing agony from his numerous wounds to the wrist, the ear, the scalp, and a major penetration of his bowel. He was the worst of any, and Woodruff feared his fellow officer would not last out the night.

Not long after the water carriers returned, Gibbon called his officers together to assess their situation. Accounting for the expenditure or loss of more than nine thousand rounds, their desperate need for ammunition rested alone at the top of the list.

"One of the civilians, a half-breed named Matte," the colonel explained, "came up to report he knows the enemy's language. Said he overheard some of the Nez Perce talking out there in the dark. One of the chiefs was urging their men to be ready for a morning attack—because the white man's ammunition had to be nearly done for."

"We don't get more cartridges soon," Captain Rawn said, "they'll overrun us in one swift rush, sir. What can we do to assure the survival of the command?"

Reminding his officers that this very day, the ninth of August, commemorated his thirtieth year in the army, the colonel prepared to dispatch a runner, who would slip off through the dark, ordered to find the supply train and bring through the much-needed cartridges before their tiny compound ran out, making them helpless before a concerted charge by the Nez Perce come morning. Once he had started the train on its way, that courier was to continue on his way to next find General Oliver O. Howard—likely somewhere between them and the end of the Lolo Trail.

By pale starlight Gibbon wrote a brief message to Howard, penciling his words on a square piece of paper no bigger than a calling card:

> *GENERAL: We surprised the Nez Perce camp at daylight this morning, whipped them out of it, killing a considerable number. But they turned on us, forced us out of it, and compelled us to take the defensive. We are here near the mouth of Big Hole pass, with a number of wounded, and need medical assistance and assistance of all kinds, and hope you will hurry to our relief.*
>
> *GIBBON, COMM'DG*
> *Aug. 9, '77*

In addition, the colonel readied another two men—civilians both—to sneak off for the settlements, striking out to the east for Deer Lodge via Frenchman's Gulch, both to carry messages requesting food, ammunition, and medical supplies.

"My boots ain't worth a damn no more, Lieutenant," grumped William H. Edwards as he prepared to slip away in the darkness.

Woodruff looked down at the man's footwear. "You think we're about the same size?"

Edwards nodded. "Worth a try, Officer. If you don't mind, I got more'n sixty miles to walk to French Gulch, and these ol' boots of mine won't make it all that way."

"A noble donation to the cause," Woodruff announced, painfully dragging off one boot at a time to make the exchange with the civilian. "Besides, with these holes in my legs, I'm not fit to do much walking for the next few days anyway. Part of that leather heel got shot off."

Peering closely at the back of the fractured heel, Edwards said, "There's still enough here to hold me up till I get to Deer Lodge."

The civilian had stood, working his toes around in the unfamiliar boots, when Gibbon came up to stop in front of Edwards.

"I want you to remember, we need an escort sufficient to protect the wagons they'll send to relieve us," the colonel impressed upon his messenger. "Load the wagons as light as possible—for speed, you understand. Tell them how the Indians have cut us off from our own supply train. And take this message with you." He handed Edwards a folded paper.

The civilian said, "General?"

"At the first telegraph key you reach, it's to be wired to my commander, General Alfred Terry, headquarters in Minneapolis."

Big Hole Pass, August ninth

Surprised the Nez Perces camp here this morning, got possession of it after a hard fight in which both myself, Captain Williams and Lieuts Coolidge, Woodruff and English wounded, the last severely.

Gibbon, Comm'dg
Aug 9, '77

For a long time after the two couriers melted away into the dark, each taking his separate direction, those left behind listened to the night for some idea as to the success of their escape. Only an occasional shot whined into their dark compound. Just enough gunfire to keep Woodruff rattled, even more jealous of a civilian who continued to sleep nearby. The young volunteer lay on his back, hip-to-hip beside another citizen in their shallow rifle pit. His mouth had gone slack, and he began snoring loud enough that it eventually attracted the attention of an Indian sniper.

Just about the time Woodruff was finding himself in awe that anyone could sleep in such conditions, a bullet smacked the dirt piled up beside the rifle pit, filling the snoring man's mouth with soil and pine needles. Sputtering and choking, he flopped awake, spit, and wiped his tongue clean, then promptly rolled onto his side and fell right to sleep again.

Sometime in the middle of the night he heard two of the civilians whispering in a nearby rifle pit.*

"You wanna get out of this, Tom?"

"Why, what the hell do you mean?"

*This documented conversation took place at marker No. 7, hillside siege site.

"Well, there's several of us going tonight."

Tom asked, "All of you?"

"No, just a few, it appears."

Then Tom prodded in a softer whisper, "What about the wounded? What's to become of them?"

After a long pause, grave with silence, the other man answered, "We'll just have to let them go, Tom."

"That don't set right with me. Them wounded have to be took care of. I ain't going unless ever'body's pulling out together."

"Suit yourself, Tom. I just wanted you to know we was goin'."

Later that dark night, Woodruff overheard the scuffing of boots as the unnamed civilian crawled out of his rifle pit to join the half-dozen who were intending to make their escape through the Nez Perce lines. For a time after they had gone, he was jealous of them and their freedom to make the attempt—while his would be a soldier's fate.

Woodruff would wait for dawn and see what the morrow held in store for the stalwart and steadfast who had remained behind.

CHAPTER SIXTY-SEVEN

August 9, 1877

"Rider! Lookee—it's a goddamned rider comin' in!"

Henry Buck shook himself out of a fitful sleep with that yelp, instantly awake with the horseman's whooping and hoofbeats, accompanied by a few scattered shots from the Nez Perce who still had them surrounded this gray morning.

Buck got his knuckles out of his gritty eyes in time to watch the civilian's horse skidding to a halt in the middle of their rectangle of rifle pits. Dawn was coming.

"By God—is that you, McGilliam?" John Catlin roared as he leaped up to the side of the barely restrained horse.

Around them, the survivors in the compound were cheering lustily, many of them barking their own questions at the newcomer.

In the hubbub that lone rider held his hand down to Catlin and said, "Good to see you still standing on your pins, Cap'n Catlin. Where's your general?"

"Right over here," Gibbon announced from the spot where he was dragging his good leg under him and struggling onto his feet. "Where the hell did you come from and just how in blazes did you get through?"

"This is Nelse McGilliam, General," Catlin introduced the civilian who had just dropped to the ground.

"You come from Howard?"

"Yes, General—"

"So what do you know of our wagon train?"

McGilliam shrugged. "Nothing. Never saw it comin' through on my own."

"You're alone?"

"Yep."

"How do you come to be here?" Gibbon prodded.

"I slept back up the trail last night, in my saddle blanket—no more'n a mile from here, out in the black of night," the civilian explained as he swung out of the saddle. "I heard shooting now and again, so I didn't dare come any closer till I had enough light to see my way on in here."

"Can't believe the Injuns let you waltz on through 'em the way you did!" Catlin cheered, slapping McGilliam on the shoulder.

"I didn't see a damned Injun. Not one!"

"But they're out there," Catlin argued. "You heard 'em shooting as you rode in?"

"But I didn't see a one—"

"What's Howard got to say?" Gibbon demanded the courier's attention again. "When's he going to be here?"

"He's on his way behind me, bringing more'n two dozen riders on their best horses."

"T-two dozen?" Gibbon echoed. "That's all?"

"There's more coming up behind him, General," McGilliam explained. "With them first soldiers Howard's got some Bannock scouts, too. All of 'em riding hard. Should be here afore tomorrow morning."

It was easy for Henry Buck to see the disappointment from that register on Gibbon's face.

"Very well. We don't have much to offer you in the way of anything to eat—except for some half-rancid horse." Gibbon pointed out Woodruff's partially skinned horse, the flies not yet buzzing in the chill dawn air. The decomposing carcass had stewed and bloated with gases to a point where all four of its legs stuck straight out grotesquely.

"N-no thanks, General," McGilliam responded with a shake of his head. "I'll be fine—"

A sudden volley exploded outside their lines, bullets smacking the trees and whining through the men. Luckily, no one was hit as they dived in all directions, flopping to their bellies. McGilliam struggled to hold onto the reins from where he lay, his horse fighting to break free.

"May be some fresh horse meat soon, General!" the courier hollered.

"Do what you can to protect that animal, mister!" Gibbon ordered. "We're damn well gonna need it to ride out on before the day is out."

AS THAT SHORT summer night had worn on, more and more of *Ollokot*'s warriors had slipped away. But . . . their leaving was not a reflection upon their bravery.

By the time the light turned gray and foretold of dawn-coming, perhaps no more than the fingers on both hands still remained with the war chief and Yellow Wolf. Nowhere near enough to try rushing the *suapies*. No, the white men were safely corralled in their dirt hollows.

Besides, the families were a good distance away by now.

There had simply been too many dead to try carrying them all away from the battlefield for burial. Instead, the women and old men had done the best they could with the bodies of those who would be left behind at this tragic place. Many of the dead were carried to the edge of the creek, where they were laid beneath an overhanging cutbank before the earth was caved in over the bodies in a simple, but effective, grave.

A few families nonetheless chose to drag a loved one from the scene on a travois as the village started south toward Horse Prairie and on to the far pass over the mountains.

Whatever the sheer numbers of the dead—men, women, and children—Yellow Wolf realized that the loss of so many of their greatest warriors in this one fight was something that could never be measured in any terms.

At this Place of the Ground Squirrels, the *Nee-Me-Poo* had lost the flower of its young manhood. Their finest had fallen.

Rainbow.

Shore Crossing.

Five Wounds.

Red Moccasin Tops.

Five Fogs.

Red-Headed Woodpecker.

Black Owl.

No Heart—

And the list went on.

No matter trying to put a count to them. The loss was great by any measure. From here on out, the People would never be as strong, never be as capable of defending their families, as they had been when they had marched over the pass to this peaceful valley where the women had time to cut lodgepoles and the children to laugh. The *Nee-Me-Poo* hadn't had much of either lodgepoles or laughter since the war began.

Perhaps the most tragic death was that of No Heart.

In the very first moments of the fighting, Yellow Wolf had spotted Joseph and No Heart fording the stream and racing up the hillside opposite camp, making for the horse herd. How brave they were to assure that the white men could not steal the ponies. But because of a terrible rumor that the Flathead had come to steal the horses, one of *Toohoolhoolzote*'s men rushed across the creek and shot No Heart by mistake!

Late in the afternoon when Yellow Wolf heard about the death of this good warrior, he crept around to the hillside where the herd had been grazing, to see for himself this spot where No Heart was killed. To grieve where his friend had fallen. But he did not find the body where others said they had seen it during the fighting. For a long time while the last light remained in the evening sky Yellow Wolf had searched and searched, unable to find No Heart's body or the warrior's horse.

"Perhaps he came back to life after the others left," Yellow Wolf confided to *Ollokot* this gray morning.

"Maybe he got on his horse and went somewhere else to die,"* the chief replied.

Yellow Wolf shook his head sadly. "I think No Heart might still be alive—"

He jerked up at the sound of a horse's running hooves. Through the trees he saw a blur of movement, then heard cheering from the white man's corral of rifle pits.

Yellow Wolf thought that must mean it was a messenger coming in, breaking through their skimpy surround of the soldiers. With the sounds of those soldiers celebrating the man's arrival, Yellow Wolf remembered how

---

*Two years after the Battle of the Big Hole, when frontiersman Andrew Garcia and his Nez Perce wife, who had herself survived the battle, visited the Place of the Ground Squirrels, he stated in *A Tough Trip Through Paradise,* they located the grave of an Indian on the hillside where his wife reported No Heart was killed.

he had heard a Shadow voice in the dark of last night. A man apparently lost, calling for someone to answer. But no one responded and the voice eventually was heard no more. Had likely been this messenger, a rider who halted where he was until it was light enough to charge on in.

"It is better that he go on in, anyway," declared *Ollokot* as he turned to his horse. "Now we will have some good idea what news he brought the other Shadows."

Such loud cheering that accompanied the messenger's arrival could only mean one of two things. Either the man carried some more ammunition for the soldiers—which Yellow Wolf doubted; after all, how many cartridges could one man carry on one horse?

Or the Shadow was bringing word of another army coming to their rescue.

"I think more soldiers are coming," *Ollokot* commiserated as he got on the back of his pony.

"Perhaps we should look on their back trail to find those soldiers who are coming, maybe find their supplies to steal," Yellow Wolf suggested.

His chief agreed and that morning a handful of them moved up the trail, attempting to locate some sign of an advancing army. Hard as they scoured the hills on both sides of the creek, they discovered no sign, no wagons or horses, and no sighting of an army coming.

But later that second afternoon of the fight, there wasn't a man gathered around *Ollokot* near the south gulch who didn't feel in his marrow that more soldiers were already on their way. Cut-Off Arm would be there eventually. Even if he and his men were the "day after tomorrow army," they would get there soon.

"I want to see to my wife," *Ollokot* confessed to those faithful warriors who had remained with him even as their families had packed up and marched away a day ago. "Our people are buried, and our wounded are gone with the rest of the village. There is nothing more that we can do to these soldiers now."

"Do you want some of us to stay in the hills to watch for Cut-Off Arm and his soldiers?" Yellow Wolf asked. "To stay till we know the army is coming?"

Ollokot's eyes were as sad as any of them had ever seen the man. "Stay and spy if you want. As for me, I want to see my wife one more time before she dies."

BY NOW GENERAL Oliver Otis Howard was brutally aware that he should have pressed ahead more than a day earlier than he had when setting off from the Lolo hot springs.

Instead of starting out at dawn on 7 August when he dispatched Sergeant Oliver Sutherland with his message for Colonel Gibbon as originally planned, the general chose to leisurely lead his entire command down the Lolo Trail another nineteen miles to Woodman's Prairie, where they went into camp. It wasn't until the following day that he finally set off at a rapid gait with his advance unit of 200 horsemen, yet he and his staff took time out from their pursuit for a lengthy inspection of Rawn's barricades and riflepits at "Fort Fizzle" before continuing down to the mouth of the canyon, where Howard again halted, this time for more than two hours, while he dictated several more dispatches he wanted carried north to Missoula City. It had proven to be a good road that eighth day of August—his advance group of 200 horsemen made at least thirty-four miles before sundown.

But on the morning of the ninth, the strenuous pace of the previous day had told on the weakening horses. Howard's advance made less than twenty miles that Thursday—the first day of Gibbon's fight in the Big Hole. The following dawn, 10 August, Howard finally made the decision he should have back on the night of the sixth when Joe Pardee rode up the Lolo to the hot springs with the message that Colonel Gibbon was in pursuit of the fleeing Non-Treaty bands.

That morning the general selected twenty of the best troopers, mounting them on the best of his horses, and prepared to push ahead with all possible dispatch, accompanied by seventeen of "Captain" Orlando "Rube" Robbins's twenty Bannock scouts. Howard left the rest under the command of Major Edwin C. Mason of the First Cavalry to come along at all possible dispatch. With his twenty hand-picked men under First Lieutenant George R. Bacon, and aide de camp Wood, Howard set off, accompanied by correspondent Thomas Sutherland and a rival journalist, Mr. Bonny, who was also serving the column as Quartermaster Ebstein's clerk.

They moved out in a trot, column of twos. After they kept that pace for fifty minutes, a ten-minute halt was called every hour. Ride hard, then rest the horses, and ride hard for another fifty minutes. They took a brief midday rest at Ross's Hole; then both men and horses toiled up the steep, winding six-mile ascent to the top of the divide.

Despite their efforts at speed, these forty-some men managed to cover no more than twenty-five miles that day, beginning their climb over the divide to the Big Hole.

As grueling as the climb had been and as weary as the horses had become, they went into camp that Friday evening—10 August—far up on the eastern slope at the head of Trail Creek, where Howard sent frontiersman Robbins ahead, along with his Bannocks, to do some scouting while a little light remained in the sky. Just past dark a dozen of the Bannocks came back at a trot, escorting seven dismounted civilians.

"My God—you men are on foot!" Howard exclaimed as the Indians brought the exhausted volunteers huffing up to the general. "Where are your horses?"

"S-shot, most of 'em."

Another citizen confessed, "Rest of 'em got run off by the Injuns."

Howard tingled with the old excitement, mixed with a little envy. "Then Gibbon's had a fight."

"Oh, we had a fight, we did!" another one grumbled.

"What have you got to tell us?" the general prodded.

"General Gibbon pitched into them Injuns yesterday morning," began one. Said another, "Lost half his men by the time the sun come up."

"They was having a hard go of it when we left."

Concern crossed the general's face. He asked, "You—you ran off and left the rest behind?"

The man looked at Howard as if the general were daft. " 'Course we did.

We was gettin' whipped something terrible—gone with no sleep and nothing to eat in two days now. . . . You got something to eat here, don'cha, General?"

Howard looked aside at his aide, saying, "Lieutenant Wood, see that these men are given some bacon and hardbread. Bring them some cups for coffee, too." Then he turned back to the civilians warming their hands over the headquarters fire as the temperature dropped and the light drained from the sky.

"Your supper is coming," the general explained while Robbins and the last of the Bannock rode into camp. "Now, tell me everything."

They did, slowly, a bit here and a fragment there—at least what the seven had seen from their vantage point of things. After giving a graphic account of the early-morning assault and the capture of the village, they told of how the chiefs and their warriors had rallied to regain the camp and driven the white men to the hillside siege area. One of the seven, a civilian from the Bitterroot valley settlement of Corvallis, even had a brother* who had been wounded and forced to go into hiding near the boggy marsh when the rest failed to take him along with them in their retreat to the hillside.

Howard found himself repulsed that this volunteer had abandoned his brother in that escape to the timber, and again when he fled Gibbon's siege, apparently without suffering any shame or disgrace whatsoever. And now at the fire, the general discovered that no amount of money, not even the attraction of a brother wounded and sorely in need of rescue, could induce one of these seven brave citizens to guide Robbins and the Bannock to the battlefield!

Brave citizen militia indeed!

After they had wolfed down their dinner, even to licking the grease from the tin plates, the seven continued with their tales of Gibbon's fight up to the night they had slipped away through the warrior lines, enumerating the casualties and repeatedly expressing how gallantly the colonel and his soldiers had given back a struggle in their desperate fight, even though heavily outnumbered by the Nez Perce.

"How far do you figure you've come from where you left General Gibbon?" Howard asked as the stars came out.

One of the civilians dragged the back of his hand across his greasy lips and said, "Fifteen, no more'n twenty miles, General. But them are hard, hard miles gettin' down there from here."

Oliver Otis stood at last, his back kinked with knots from the hard riding along with sleeping on the cold ground. He knew the exhausted horses would not last another league that night.

"Lieutenant Bacon, have your men start and feed several fires here; scatter them across this clearing. Then barricade the best you can with what we have for saddles and baggage," Howard explained. "In case Joseph has his spies out in these hills, I want it to appear we are a much larger force than we are."

Bacon asked, "We'll push on at first light, General?"

"We'll move out as soon as we have enough light to see the trail ahead,"

---

*Campbell Mitchell, chapter 59.

he told his soldiers gathered close. “By the Almighty—we’ll lift that siege and drive the warriors off.”

As he turned aside to drag a trail-worn Bible from his haversack, Howard’s mind began to turn upon an offer he now made to God: praying they would find some of Gibbon’s soldiers alive.

EPILOGUE

AUGUST 10–11, 1877

AT SUNDOWN THAT NIGHT OF 10 AUGUST, HUGH KIRKENDALL'S WAGON train rattled into the siege compound without any interference from the Nez Perce everyone believed were still in the area.

It was accompanied by Captain George L. Browning and Second Lieutenant Francis Woodbridge, who, earlier that afternoon, had been directed by John Gibbon to lead twenty-five men up the mountainside and escort the wagons on down Trail Creek. Hours before at daybreak, the colonel had dispatched Sergeant Mildon H. Wilson of I Company and six men from K Company to reach the wagon corral and bring in the train. But as midday came and went Gibbon grew more apprehensive that Mildon's small squad had been ambushed; he had dispatched Browning's detail.

Those wagons arrived about 6:00 P.M., carrying all the coffee and hardtack the ravenous men could eat, along with their wool blankets. At least this night would be a shade more comfortable for the survivors.

"Wish we had some more of that bacon those two civilians brought in this morning," said the colonel.

"It didn't last long, did it, sir?" asked Lieutenant Charles Woodruff.

"A few bites for each man sure didn't go far." Gibbon sounded regretful. "There will be more coming when General Howard arrives."

The lieutenant prayed his words would come true.

Earlier that morning Sergeant Oliver Sutherland had himself come on down the trail after spending most of the previous day at Kirkendall's corral. He was carrying that message from Howard telling Gibbon how he was coming ahead with 200 horsemen and hoped to catch up to the infantry before Gibbon pitched into the Nez Perce.

"Why did you end up staying with the wagon train instead of riding on down here to deliver your message as ordered, Sergeant?" Woodruff asked the question he was sure Gibbon wanted to have answered.

"Made a try, sir," Sutherland admitted. "I started out with eight or nine of the wagon guard you left—but we was met on the trail by a big war party and drove back. A damn lucky thing they didn't follow us up the trail and find our wagons, Lieutenant."

That's when Gibbon had proposed, "I'm going to send an escort back right now—and bring those supplies in."

Minutes later two of Kirkendall's teamsters—Jerry Wallace and John Miller—rode in, having started down the trail right on the heels of Sergeant

Sutherland. Hung from Wallace's saddle horn was a grease-stained canvas bag that contained a side of bacon. It was promptly divided up among the famished men, disappearing down their gullets with an amazing speed. After suffering some thirty-six hours without anything more to eat than the pasty remains of hardtack scraped off the bottom of their haversacks and a few strips of raw meat butchered from Woodruff's bloated horse, Gibbon's compound was next to famished.

While this one side of bacon had done little to fill their shrunken bellies that morning, it had nonetheless gone far to lifting their sagging spirits for the rest of that day.

Not long after Kirkendall's wagons rattled in, it began to grow dark on that lonely rectangle of rifle pits for a second night. Twilight was deepening when one of the civilians called out, asking the rest to look at the three dim, flickering lights he had spotted to the southeast. Woodruff saw them, all three slowly bobbing, wavering, either on or against the plateau rising beyond the flat where much of the Nez Perce village still stood.

"What you make of that?" Charles asked the colonel.

Gibbon shook his head. "Can't be torches. Maybe they're small fires where their sharpshooters huddle to warm themselves."

"I didn't see any fires while they had us surrounded last night, General," Woodruff had replied. "Why would they light those three fires way off over there tonight, and nowhere close at all—"

Woodruff was interrupted with what he figured was the answer. A cluster of twelve distinct shots tore through their compound, some from each of the three sides. Then the echo of all that gunfire quickly faded, absorbed by the coal-cotton black of night.

Several discordant voices shouted at them from the river bottom—not in the manner of a war cry . . . but more so as a salutation.

"I think we've just been told they're leaving," Gibbon commented quietly.

Those mysterious lights, along with that final volley and farewell salutation, were just enough to keep Woodruff restless through that night. Despite his knotted belly finally being filled by hardbread and coffee and despite the warmth of a wool blanket to curl up inside, the lieutenant remained wary that the departure was all a ruse, right up till dawn on the eleventh of August.

"That lieutenant's in a bad way," confided Tom Sherrill, a civilian who had a rifle pit right beside Woodruff, the moment the lieutenant stirred.

First light was beginning to seep into the Big Hole.

"You mean English?"

Sherrill nodded, then whispered again. "Ain't a man here can't tell how bad he's suffering. That back wound of his is the worst I've ever seen."

"We'll have a surgeon here soon, Tom."

"The lieutenant, he asked me to take his boot off and rub his feet—saying they was getting stone-cold on him," Sherrill said in a hush. "But I couldn't get 'em off, everything was so wet. I ended up cutting the stitches on one of his boots with my folding knife, right down the back. Got it off that way. Started rubbing his foot. Wasn't long before he told me, 'It's no use; I'm done for this time.' "

Woodruff nodded knowingly. "I'd consider it a personal favor to me, if not to General Gibbon, if you'd do all in your power to make Lieutenant English as comfortable as you can until a surgeon arrives."

"How long you figure on that?" Sherrill asked. "Till Howard gets here with them reinforcements?"

"I'm praying they will show up tomorrow."

"IT'S MYRON! MY stars—it's Myron Lockwood!"

Lieutenant Woodruff looked up from an inspection of Private Edward D. Hunter's wound to his right forearm. Both bones had been shattered by a Nez Perce bullet, and without proper bandages the gaping hole—like the rotting horse carcass—had become flyblown. Try as Woodruff might to protect the wound with strips of the soldier's uniform these last two days, this morning it was a wriggling mass of maggots.

Getting to his feet, Charles thought he recognized that civilian slung between the two Sherrill brothers, Tom and his older brother, "Bunch."

"How bad is he?" John Gibbon asked as he rolled onto his hip and struggled to rise, dragging that wounded leg of his.

"He'll live!" Bunch Sherrill bellowed enthusiastically. "If those Nez Perce couldn't kill Lockwood in our attack and they never found 'im hiding in the bushes—by damn, this tough ol' nail ain't gonna die on us now, General!"

Just before daylight the brothers had slipped down to the mouth of the gulch* to look for their Bitterroot friend, the same Myron Lockwood who had horses stolen from him and his house looted as the Nez Perce meandered up the valley.

"I really 'spected to find 'im dead," Tom Sherrill confessed as they dragged Lockwood up to the fire and eased him down between them, the trio hunkered close to the flames.

To Woodruff's way of thinking, for the moment Lockwood hovered a little closer to death than he clung tenaciously to life.

"Found 'im sitting with his back against a wall of rock,"**
Bunch Sherrill declared. "From the looks of 'im, he's lost considerable blood."

"How is it he's still alive and the Nez Perce killed every other one of our wounded they got their hands on?" Gibbon asked. "He tell you that?"

Tom Sherrill shrugged. "Myron's so damned cold and stiff after these last two days and nights—he ain't been able to say a thing to us yet."

"Fortunate he kept that coat with him," Woodruff commented as the damp wool of the man's heavy hip-length coat steamed so near the warmth radiating from their fire.

"This wasn't his," Bunch Sherrill admitted quietly. "We took the coat off Elliott."†

"He won't mind now, Elliott won't," Tom assured the others as he

*Today's "Battle Gulch."

**Stake No. 50, Big Hole National Battlefield.

†Lynde C. Elliott, Stevensville volunteer.

kneaded one of Lockwood's hands between his. "Man's been dead for two days now."

"That's a dead man's coat?" asked Captain James Sanno.

"Don't appear it's making a damn bit of difference to Myron that's he's wearing a dead man's coat," Tom grumbled. "After them red bastards run off with his horses a few days back, sacked his house, and stole everything of value from him. Then this poor son of a bitch almost died down there in our attack on that village. That should show you Myron's a hard piece of iron. He ain't the sort what's easy to kill."

After sunrise, Colonel Gibbon asked Woodruff to select one of their best riders and put him on the strongest horse. "I have a sinking feeling that Mr. Edwards didn't get through the Nez Perce gauntlet when they had their noose tightened around us the other night."

"You're afraid he could be dead, sir?"

"Or worse," Gibbon admitted in a whisper. "A captive, tortured like the rest we heard being butchered down in the river bottom the day of our fight."

Sergeant Mildon H. Wilson was again the man for the assignment: a ride of more than eighty miles. While Gibbon completed another set of dispatches, Woodruff had the courier select his mount and saddle from what had been brought down with Kirkendall's wagons the afternoon before. When Wilson began to knot two small leather satchels behind his saddle, each one carrying an extra pistol and some ammunition for his Springfield, the lieutenant was struck with a sudden impulse.

"Sergeant, I want you to wait a few minutes before you ride out of here."

"Sir?"

"I've got something to write," he explained in a hush. "A letter I want you to see gets started back to Fort Shaw from Deer Lodge for me."

The older man nodded, his eyes crinkling with warmth. "Of course, Lieutenant. Something for your missus."

At the edge of his rifle pit, Lieutenant Charles A. Woodruff propped his dispatch ledger on his knees and began to scratch out a heartfelt communication to his wife, hopeful it would reach her at Fort Shaw before word of their terrible fight reached the telegraph keys of the outside world. Hoping to reassure her that he was alive, and whole. . . .

Camp on Ruby Creek
Aug. 11th 1877

My darling Louie:

I wrote you a note day before yesterday and will write to-day as we send out a courier.

I am getting along well, our train came up last evening and we expect Genl. Howard today. The Indians have all left

We had a hard fight lost 2 Officers Killed 10 Soldiers and 6 citizens, Wounded 5 officers 34 soldiers and 2 citizens. "K" Co., Sergt Stortz Private Kleis (the Carpenter) and Mus. Steinbacker were Killed.

I was shot in the heel of the left foot and in both legs above the knee, fortunately no bones broken. The Genl. and I were the only ones mounted, both our horses were shot, I got mine into camp and he was shot again, we ate some of him yesterday.

*I left the gun** *back the night we struck the village it started up at daylight and was attacked, one of the horses was shot and fell on Bennett, lamed him some, and of the three men with the gun one was killed and two wounded.*

Our men charged the village in fine shape and the reason we didn't hold it was there was so much brush and high bluffs that we couldn't occupy all the places at once The Indians suffered severely, I think their loss cannot be less than seventy-five or a hundred. We killed them right and left. Hurlburt of "K" killed the Indian that shot Bradley. Jacobs Killed three. Rawn two Hardin & Woodbridge one each, I didn't get a chance to Kill any of them I was carrying orders &c. The General and I were all over the field and were lucky to come off as well as we did.

The officers and men behaved well and gave the Indians the worst handling they ever seed before.

Bradley and Logan were both Killed dead.

It looked blue for us here on Thursday afternoon, the Indians set fire to the forest and kept up a fire from the brush and the hills, their idea was to follow up the fire and charge us when it reached us, I began to fear I should never see you again, some of the wounded covered up their heads and expected to be killed, I got my two revolvers said my prayers thought of you and Bertie and determined to kill a few Indians before I died, Our Heavenly Father was on our side and the wind changed and blew away from us.

I didn't know how much I loved you until I thought we would never see each other again.

We shall start this afternoon or tomorrow for Deer Lodge, I expect to get home in about ten-days . . .

Your loving husband,
Charles

*Howitzer.

AUTHOR'S AFTERWORD

As I began collecting my thoughts to write this wrap-up to *Lay the Mountains Low*, I discovered I had more than two dozen subjects I originally wanted to discuss here at the end of this second novel on the Nez Perce War. Trouble is, I feel compelled to pare away at that list of topics, because this has been the longest, most complex, book I've ever written.

While there are lots of interesting subjects I would like to tell my readers after researching and writing this dramatic, and ultimately tragic, story, *Lay the Mountains Low* is a big book to begin with. After muddling over every one of those two dozen topics I wanted to write about, I came to believe that while most are interesting at the very least, what I should do here in these next few pages is deal with only one of those subjects—a topic most compelling, downright intriguing. An unfinished story I promised you more about in the last book, *Cries from the Earth.*

Even though I am omitting the rest of those two dozen historical topics for now, I plan to eventually discuss the most important of them in a *final* author's afterword, the one I'll write at the conclusion of this trilogy on the Nez Perce War. For any of you who want to read about my ongoing research travels along this second segment of the Nez Perce Trail, I'll refer you to my annual news magazine, *WinterSong*, in every edition of which I recount my journey to go where this Indian Wars history actually happened. For more information on this publication, please see the "About the Author" section that follows this afterword.

Rather than reprinting the long list of titles I relied upon while researching and writing *Cries from the Earth* as well as the story you have just read, I will refer you back to the listing I gave in the Author's Afterword at the end of that previous book. Additional sources I have used for telling this second tragic tale in *Lay the Mountains Low* are:

An Elusive Victory—the Battle of the Big Hole, by Aubrey L. Haines

A Sharp Little Affair: The Archeology of the Big Hole Battlefield, by Douglas D. Scott

"Battle of the Big Hole," by General C. A. Woodruff, *Contributions to the Historical Society of Montana* 7 (1910)

"Chief Joseph's Flight Through Montana: 1877," by Verne Dusenberry, *The Montana Magazine of History* 2 (October, 1952)

Frontier Regulars: The United States Army and the Indian, 1866–1891, by Robert M. Utley

"Review of the Battle of the Big Hole," by Amos Buck, *Contributions to the Historical Society of Montana* 7 (1910)

Before jumping any further, I want to acknowledge the immeasurable help of two people, without whom this book could not have been written. The story you have just read is a chronicle, a rendering of the latest, most up-to-date research into the Nez Perce War.

I could not have researched this story over the past twenty-seven months without the assistance of my longtime friend Jerome A. Greene of the National Park Service's Rocky Mountain Regional Office. A few years ago Jerry began compiling his research for a soon-to-be-published volume on the *Nee-Me-Poo* Crisis, for the most part relying on primary accounts rather than secondary sources, along with his own intimate travels through Nez Perce country. His efforts serve as the framework for my three-book chronicle of the Nez Perce struggle: a trilogy of gut-wrenching novels that recount a five-month, fifteen-hundred-mile odyssey from tribal greatness to the "Hot Place" in Indian Territory. My hope is that Jerry's newest book, to be published by agreement between the National Park Service and the Montana Historical Society, will be available to the general reader sometime in the year 2000.

Since his work is not yet available to the public, I relied upon the kindness and generosity of both Jerry Greene himself and the research librarian at the Nez Perce National Historic Park in Spalding, Idaho, Rob Applegate. With Rob's timely assistance, I got my hands on a copy of Jerry Greene's monumental manuscript, which is undergoing a final copyedit at this time. After I met Rob on his first day at Spalding back in 1998, it wasn't long before I found him to be a real asset to the National Park Service—always cheerful and helpful with my obscure and ofttimes troublesome requests.

Again I want to emphasize that *Lay the Mountains Low* could not have been written without both Jerry and Rob being in the background to answer my questions and give me their support. If you find you've had some of your questions answered on this part of the Nez Perce War story or you simply enjoyed this captivating tale, then you must surely appreciate the efforts these two fine employees of the National Park Service gave to see this novel written.

Were you as tantalized as I was with the mystery of what became of Jennet Manuel and her infant son at the end of *Cries from the Earth?*

If you weren't as baffled or eager to find out as I was, you have no need of reading any further. The rest of this abbreviated afterword will deal with that little-known and heartrending tale of the Nez Perce War.

The shedding of blood is always answered. Almost two decades of assault, robbery, rape, and murder committed against the Non-Treaty *Nee-Me-Poo* brewed the foul-smelling recipe that boiled over along the Salmon River, then spilled across the Camas Prairie in mid-June 1877.

Blood cries out for blood. Following those outrages against innocent white women and children committed by drunken, revenge-seeking warriors from White Bird's and *Toohoolhoolzote*'s bands (and I use the term *warriors* very loosely, because I prefer to call them criminals, if not thugs), young men who felt very brave sweeping down upon unarmed or outnumbered civilians in overwhelming force, this mystery revolving around Jennet Manuel came to captivate an entire region of our country during that bloody summer. The speculation continues to this day.

Some of the contemporary testimony tells us that Mrs. Manuel, and perhaps her son, too, were taken along with the retreating warrior bands as they fled over the Lolo Trail to Montana Territory. Other reports have her being killed by a drunken and spiteful warrior just days after she was captured at her home (the former Ad Chapman homestead on White Bird Creek adjacent to the battlefield of 17 June). Some Nez Perce sources, who claim to have been at the scene, would have you believe mother and son were murdered and their bodies consumed in the fire that consumed the Manuel house—a few of the Indian stories admitting that Jennet Manuel was still alive and conscious when the drunken murderers set fire to the house—while other Nez Perce sources claim she was killed somewhere along the Lolo Trail.

Let's go back to chapter 18 in *Cries from the Earth*, when Maggie Manuel has crawled out of her house and into the timber, attempting to finding either her maternal grandfather, George Popham, or a local miner, Patrick Brice. She finds the Irish prospector and relates her story of how she watched from hiding as Joseph (who was widely reputed to abstain from whiskey—a fact testified to by even his most ardent spiritual enemy, Kate McBeth, the Christian schoolteacher at Kamiah, when she wrote: "Joseph had one good thing about him. He was a temperance man") and his drunken warriors clubbed both Maggie's mother and little brother before dragging them off to finish the murders. The story Maggie later told with consistency has her watching Joseph stab her mother in the breast, as she is nursing the infant, before Maggie herself is taken to another room, where she falls asleep.

This outrageous accusation that Joseph himself killed Mrs. Manuel simply refuses to die, especially among the Christian Nez Perce of today! Back in the summer of 1939, when Congress was considering a monument to Joseph, a Nez Perce from Lapwai, J. M. Parsons, wrote to U. S. Representative Usher L. Burdick to protest. Burdick had the Indian's letter read in the chamber and subsequently entered into the *Congressional Record:*

> Chief Joseph was not the man which history would place before the educational institutions as has been suggested along with the erection of the memorial. He is guilty of wantonly killing a white woman, Mrs. J. Manuel, while he was under the influence of liquor. On June 15, 1877, the chief and two companions, also under the influence of liquor, visited the home of the Manuels on White Bird

> Creek, where friendly Indians were keeping guard over the wounded Mrs. Manuel and baby with the understanding that the woman would be given aid in escaping to the white settlement. Joseph proceeded to wrangle over the succoring of the enemy white woman, and when the friendly Indians remonstrated,the chief reached out with a dagger and plunged it into her breast, killed her almost instantly . . . There is an old warrior living today who was present when the killing took place, and it has been generally known among the Nez Perce that Joseph committed the deed.

Upon learning of this claim, Nez Perce supporter and writer L.V. McWhorter wrote to Parsons, demanding he produce the "old warrior" and all evidence leading to Joseph's guilt. Parsons never answered any of McWhorter's entreaties.

In his book *Chief Joseph—the Biography of a Great Indian*, author Chester Anders Fee appears to have bought the whole of Maggie's story of how her mother was killed when he writes:

> . . . Mrs. Manuel, and her ten months old child fell injured when their horse stumbled. She with her baby and daughter, who had also broken her arm in the fall, were taken back to the ranch house by the Nez Perce, who then told her they would take no more lives if she gave them Mr. Manuel's rifle and ammunition. This she did, and the Indians left. But soon several others of the party returned and one plunged a knife into her breast, killing her, and later they also killed her baby.

A pretty convoluted explanation of how suddenly well mannered were that gang of murderers, while they were seizing everything and anything that suited them—including guns, ammunition, and white women. Mr. Fee simply can't have it both ways.

To continue with young Maggie's rendition of her story: When she awakens, the house is filled with an ominous silence. Opening the door to the main room, Maggie finds her mother's naked body lying in a pool of blood on the floor. That "blood oozed between my toes." Near her mother's head lay her baby brother, John. In her version of the story, when she located Brice outside in the woods, she took him back into the house to view the bodies before they both returned to the timber.

Although Brice would never confirm that part of the girl's story—he stated that when he went back to the house he found it empty—Maggie

Manuel remained consistent with every other detail of that night, right on into her adulthood.

First of all, let's lay to rest her allegation that Joseph killed her mother. Aside from whether or not Maggie herself had ever seen Joseph, chief of the *Wallowa* band, and would be able to identify him, the simple fact is that he could not have been in the White Bird Canyon the night of 15 June 1877. He and his brother, *Ollokot*, along with their families and the rest of the Wallamwatkin, were far, far to the north, sleeping in their camp near Cottonwood Creek after fleeing *Tepahlewam* at news of the murders and outrages against the whites on the Salmon.

When Brice left the White Bird Creek area with Maggie, he said the house was still standing. Later when the Irish miner was reunited with George Popham in Grangeville, Popham told him the house was burned to the ground. There should have been charred bodies, if not human skeletons, among the ashes as forensic evidence. When two local frontiersmen, Ad Chapman and James Conely, raked through the cinders of the Manuel place, they found some bones—but both men remained convinced the charred bones they discovered belonged to an animal.

But there were those who disagreed with this assessment. Writing a letter to the editor of the Lewiston *Teller* on 19 July, local resident J. W. Poe stated: "It was currently believed that Mrs. Manuel and the child were still alive until I had examined the ruins and found positive evidence to the contrary." On his journey back to his own looted store along the Salmon River after Howard's army marched into the area, H. C. "Hurdy Gurdy" Brown visited the Manuel homestead and declared his certainty that Jennet and little John had perished in the fire. However, historian Jack McDermott could not locate what "evidence" led Poe and Brown to unwaveringly declare both mother and son had died in the flames.

Perhaps it was nothing more conclusive than the jewelry someone unearthed in raking through the ashes of the Manuel home . . . earrings Maggie stated unequivocally that her mother was wearing the day of the attack.

The certainty that mother and son had been killed at their home was further solidified when local trader Harry Cone recorded his reminiscences as one of the settlers who took shelter behind the stockade at Slate Creek (see chapter 46 in *Cries from the Earth*). Cone remembered how one of the Nez Perce horsemen who came to the stockade wall to settle accounts with trader John Wood disclosed to an old Nez Perce woman, Tolo, who was in the stockade with the whites, how Mrs. Manuel was killed by a fellow warrior under the influence of whiskey: "She [Tolo] began to talk, upbraiding them for killing their friends and hers, and Mrs. Manuel, who, we learned from them, one of them had killed, who was full of bad whiskey."

Yet on 28 July, more than a month later, the Lewiston *Teller* stirred things up anew by announcing: "Squaws still report that Mrs. Manuel is living and a prisoner."

Additionally, here in *Lay the Mountains Low* we told you Henry Buck's story of seeing a blond-haired white woman among a small group of squaws he saw fleeing from the Nez Perce village at the time of Gibbon's attack at the Big Hole. But it wasn't until years later that a settler in the Bitterroot valley finally reported that he had spotted a blond-haired white woman with the Non-Treaty bands as they made their way to the Big Hole.

Two independent, and highly intriguing, sightings far, far from the charred remains of the Manuel house on White Bird Creek.

This story refused to take an entirely straight and uncompromising path, just as much of history itself refuses to do. A hint of something stuck its head up here, a rumor was reported there—and that's the way the mystery rested for almost a quarter of a century.

It wasn't until 1900 that the first Nez Perce account of the raid and abduction was given to a white man. Yellow Bull (who was called Sun Necklace at the time of the war) told his story to C. T. Stranahan—Nez Perce agent at the time—swearing the white man to keep his story secret until after Yellow Bull's death (which did not occur until July of 1919). According to the war chief, Mrs. Manuel was captured and kept a prisoner by an Indian Yellow Bull refused to name. Some time after the Non-Treaty bands had crossed the Lolo Pass into Montana Territory, Yellow Bull continued, her captor and another warrior began to quarrel over the white woman. The bickering escalated until friends had to keep the two apart.

As the village was preparing to march the morning after the heated argument, Yellow Bull and others discovered Mrs. Manuel missing. The war chief told Stranahan he believed she had been killed and her body hidden in the brush, somewhere off the Lolo Trail.

Around this same era on the reservation, one of L.V. McWhorter's informants said that Red Wolf (this is not the same "Josiah" Red Wolf who was but a young child at the time of the Big Hole fight, so the Red Wolf referred to might well have been the child's father or an uncle) attempted to abduct Mrs. Manuel from her ranch, riding with her on horseback, "when she snatched the knife from his belt and attempted to kill him. He struck her, felling her to the ground, and she died from the fall."

To that testimony McWhorter adds: "Presumably she was carried back to her home and the house then set afire."

Which, at least to me, is a convenient and blameless way to deflect a certain guilt for the murder—after all, the woman was "threatening" her kidnapper with his own knife—as well as a means to conceal the fact that Mrs. Manuel had started over the Lolo Trail with the Non-Treaty bands. Why are there so many different stories if every one of McWhorter's informants is telling the truth? There are so many attempts to have Jennet Manuel killed in her own home and her body conveniently consumed to ashes so the hunt for her would end.

Including the journalist who rendered a questionable version of Patrick Brice's story in 1911. Charles S. Moody chronicled the miner's experiences in an article for *Century Magazine*, "The Bravest Deed I Ever Knew." Brice carried the wounded Maggie Manuel back to her home, Moody writes, which was "only a heap of smoldering ashes. Among the embers lay the charred body of a woman and her infant. The Indians had taken Mrs. Manuel and her baby back to the house, killed them, and then fired the house."

Trouble is, Brice had testified that when he left the White Bird Canyon the Manuel house had not been destroyed.

It took nearly fourteen years after that before there arose any corroboration for Yellow Bull's account to Nez Perce agent Stranahan. Enter a young Treaty or Christian Indian named Many Wounds, who had taken the white name of Sam Lott. He approached an old warrior, who was embittered by the decades of struggle as he had watched the *Nee-Me-Poo* lose their land to white gold seekers and settlers. *Peopeo Tholekt*, known as Bird Alighting, had survived the many battles the Looking Glass band suffered during the war—a struggle that many of their people considered both their finest hour and their worst calamity.

Arriving at Bird Alighting's poor shack at the appointed hour on the appointed day, Many Wounds decided to begin their discussions by having the old warrior talk about many of the relics and artifacts Bird Alighting had in sight there at his tiny cabin. One of the very first Many Wounds took in hand to ask about was a blond scalp lock.

"Hair of white woman," Bird Alighting explained. "Mrs. Manuel."

He went on to relate how the woman was taken prisoner in the first raids and was subsequently taken with them as they started toward Montana Territory. On the way she took sick and died. The men buried her under some rocks beside the Lolo Trail. Bird Alighting related how Joseph took the woman's scalp after she was dead.

"The hair was beautiful," Bird Alighting explained the chief's motivation.

Years later, Bird Alighting somehow had fallen heir to the blond scalp lock. To Many Wounds he explained how sorry he was, how sorry Joseph himself was, for the woman's capture, her plight, and her death far from loved ones.

Personally, I don't know how much credence to put into the second part of this story, concerning Joseph scalping a dead woman on the Lolo Trail because he wanted to keep her blond locks. With what I know of the band structure at that time, it doesn't seem feasible that Joseph, a leader of the *Wallowa* people, would pass down such an important memento to an unrelated person like Bird Alighting, who was a member of Looking Glass's Alpowai band—especially when they were living apart on different reservations (remember, Joseph never was allowed to return to his homeland, living out his final days at the Colville agency). Perhaps that second part represents a little embellishment, while the kernel of the story remains intact and truthful.

A year after the Nez Perce War, Duncan McDonald undertook a journey to visit White Bird and those Nez Perce who made it across the Canadian border at the time of the Bear's Paw fight. A half-breed (McDonald's mother was Nez Perce and his father a factor with the Hudson's Bay Company), he served as the agency trader for the Flathead tribe at Jocko. He wrote a series of articles that appeared in the Deer Lodge, Montana, newspaper, the *New*

North-West, adding a colorful dimension to the entire story on the outbreak and war, including this confusing and controversial subject of Mrs. Manuel's disappearance.

McDonald muddied the waters about Joseph in specific, and this incident in general, even more than they already were when he wrote:

> It seems that at the earliest commencement of the Nez Perces war there were two white women murdered. One of them was murdered by an Indian who was drunk. The other white woman was burned in a house with her child. When her husband and others were murdered by the Nez Perces, she went upstairs. The Indians say they did not see her at the time of killing the men. When the Indians got possession of the house, Joseph, Jr. was present. He was sitting at one side of the place smoking his pipe. He was asked by the warriors what should be done—whether they should set fire to the house or leave without destroying it. All this time the woman and child were upstairs, but the Indians say they did not know it. Young Joseph answered, "You have done worse deeds than burning a house. You never asked our chiefs what was best to be done. You have murdered many men and not asked advice of your chiefs. You can do as you please about the house."
>
> Some of the young men lit a match and set fire to the building. They then went back a little and sat down to watch it burn. They were suddenly startled by the piercing screams of a woman in the second story of the house. Young Joseph ordered them to put out the fire. The young Indians ran down to the water, filled their hats, threw it on the flames, and tried every way they knew to extinguish the fire and to save the woman. But it was too late. She and her child perished.
>
> The same young warriors who were with Joseph, Jr., at the time told me that when he left the place, Joseph held down his head for a long time and, at last looking up, he said they had done very wrong in burning the woman, that he was very sorry, that he had believed the house empty.
>
> The burning of this poor, harmless woman looks very bad for the Indian side. Still there is some blame should attach to the white man. The white man does wrong in allowing the Indian to have whiskey. It is easy to reply that the Indians take the

> whiskey away from them by force, but there are
> many whites who are ready to sell whiskey to them
> in time of Indian Wars.

Both Duncan McDonald and L. V. McWhorter lived in and wrote about the final days of an intensely racist era in the American West. Since we know of their passionate support of the Nez Perce, it is reasonable to assume that they would do everything in their power to deflect blame from the raiders and murderers, but to place it instead on the white victims? Blaming them for bringing on themselves their own brutal deaths?

Neither George Popham (Jennet's father) nor Patrick Brice was a witness to what happened to Mrs. Manuel, so they can't be considered as anything resembling reliable witnesses. Nor was her husband, John, who had been left for dead out by the White Bird Road as told in *Cries from the Earth*; then we learned he had miraculously survived here in *Lay the Mountains Low*. John Manuel rarely, if ever, made any statements about the disappearance of his wife and son—but on one of the few occasions he ever talked about the tragedy, Manuel only said his family had been captured by the Nez Perce and "doubtless killed as they were never found afterwards."

As Jack McDermott sees it, John Manuel clearly harbored his own doubts about Maggie's and George Popham's cremation theory.

Friends and associates of the family throughout central Idaho refused to question Maggie's version of the story or her integrity. Everyone who ever talked to the child came away asserting, at the very least, that Maggie believed her own tale. Years later, some historians even purported that the girl must have suffered some traumatic hallucination—a reasonable assumption given the fact that she was a very young and impressionable child at the time of the brutal attack and had witnessed the killing of "Ol' man" James Baker, the murder of her father, and the long hours of terror that followed, culminating in what she claimed was Joseph's murder of her mother and brother before the warriors set fire to the house in an attempt to destroy evidence of their dastardly crime.

But . . . maybe there's a way to reconcile Maggie's account that does not rely on having to ignore her testimony or call her account a "post-traumatic stress" hallucination.

Clearly, Maggie saw some Nez Perce leader take a hand in the abduction of her mother. The fact that Joseph was the best known of the leaders in that locality and at that time must have played a major role in her testifying that Joseph was the murderer. Makes sense to me that a six- or seven-year-old girl could make such a claim and continue to believe it down to her dying day in Butte, Montana.

And perhaps she did actually see that Indian leader "stab" her mother and brother. Or perhaps the truth is as I chose to write it: that they were clubbed and dragged off, because Patrick Brice never saw the bodies, nor did he see the "pool of blood" Maggie claimed her mother and brother were lying in. The flow of Maggie's events is murky, but the truth may well be that the warrior who wanted Jennet Manuel for his own may have slashed her in a struggle over the infant she clutched in her arms. Then to subdue her, he or another of the attackers clubbed her over the head, as well as he or another warrior clubbing the child.

Here's where Maggie's story gets really muddied. It's entirely possible the drunken warriors left Jennet and baby John lying in a puddle of blood on the floor and departed, thinking them dead, when Maggie chanced to discover the bodies in the silent house—taking them for dead. As for me, I have a pretty good idea that Maggie found her baby brother in a pool of blood, but not her mother. Maggie concocted that part of the story.

Why kill one and not the other? Because the war chief wanted only Jennet Manuel and had killed the infant child so that she would not be dragging him along and tending to his needs. There are cases known to Western historians of such infanticides occurring during the Indian wars on the central and southern plains. White woman captured, her infant child has its brains dashed against the trunk of a nearby tree . . .

Perhaps some hours later when a little of the mind-numbing whiskey began to wear off, the raiding party returned for either or both of two purposes. First, to see about acquiring more whiskey. L.V. McWhorter, like many of the apologists, was well ahead of his time with what I will call "blame deflection." It's always good for someone who can't take personal responsibility for himself to blame his divorced parents, an alcoholic father, sexual abuse, or absentee parents. In the case of these first raids on the Salmon and Camas Prairie, McWhorter points his finger of blame not at the thugs and criminals who committed the murder and mayhem, rape and arson . . . but at the white man and his terrible whiskey!

> It is only fair to the Indians to call attention to the fact that the outrages against women and children did not occur until after the raiders became beastly drunk on whiskey found by the barrel at Benedict's store-saloon located on the lower reaches of White Bird Creek. That atrocities were committed by a few of the young Nez Perces, no one pretends to deny. But whiskey was at the bottom of all of them.

Or perhaps the raiding party returned for a second reason: As the murderer brooded long and hard on what he had done, perhaps he decided his best course would be to destroy the evidence of his crimes of kidnapping and murder. To his way of thinking, if he burned down the Manuel house, with the child's body therein, then the white man would think that both mother and child were burned—eliminating any need for the whites to pursue the war party to get the captive woman back.

I'm of the opinion that the whites at the Slate Creek stockade were told Jennet was dead because the Nez Perce warriors did not want the white men to know she was still alive and in the possession of one of their petty war chiefs. What Harry Cone and others heard doesn't serve as a discrepancy. I think it serves to prove that Jennet Manuel was still alive at the time.

And the presence of those earrings found among the ashes of the house is the flimsiest of circumstantial evidence. After all the time that had elapsed, and after what might have been the first stripping and rape of Mrs. Manuel there and then in her own house, the discovery of those earrings in the house proved one thing only—that some searcher found earrings belonging to Jennet Manuel in the ashes of the house where Jennet Manuel used to live. Nothing more.

When all is said and done, I believe that baby John was dead the night of 15 June. It was his bones discovered in the ashes by Ad Chapman and James Conely. Bones they said were those of an animal. Why would they say that? Because they were too small to be Jennet's? Could the bones have been those of baby John? But why weren't there enough bones found together for a savvy frontiersman to realize he was looking at a human skeleton?

And what of the stories left by Bird Alighting and Yellow Bull telling how Mrs. Manuel started the trip over the Lolo Trail with the Non-Treaty bands but either was killed in some sort of rage (according to Yellow Bull) or died of sickness, perhaps of exposure (according to *Peopeo Tholekt*)? It's hard to believe that either of them would have reason to lie at such a late date, what with the many years that had elapsed, not to mention that each man knew he was nearing the end of his life. I can't believe either man had anything to gain by concocting a bald-faced lie that many years after the crime. Especially after so many sources, down through the intervening years, had done their level best to convince journalists and writers that Jennet Manuel had died in her own house, where her body was consumed by the flames of revenge.

As I sit here on the hillside above the Big Hole Battlefield this cold, cold dawn in May of 1999, I ask myself again: Why am I so consumed by this mystery? Is it only because I sit here in the remnants of last night's crusty snow, staring down on the cones of skeletal lodgepoles erected where the Non-Treaty village once stood, thinking of that young blond-haired white woman Henry Buck glimpsed for two fleeting instants as she fled the pandemonium and terror in the camp, protectively surrounded by other squaws? If it was Jennet Manuel, and she did turn to look directly at the white civilian—why in hell didn't she cry out to him, yell something, anything, to beg for help?

Could it be that she had long ago decided she was already dead? Jennet had seen her husband fall from his horse, her young daughter, too. Although she would have known Maggie was going to survive her wounds, Jennet had to believe her husband dead. Then the young mother had watched the murder of her son, perhaps even witnessing the first flames starting their destruction of her home. After unimaginable abuse at the hands of some unnamed petty chief, could it be that Jennet believed nothing would ever be the same again, that she could never return home, that she was . . . as good as dead already?

Where did she go after the Big Hole? I brood on that simple mystery this subfreezing morning as the wind picks up and the sun finally emerges, briefly bubbling into that narrow ribbon of sky between the far mountains and the low gray hulking clouds that betray the reputation of this Big Sky Country.

There never was another report of the mysterious blond-haired woman spotted with the Non-Treaty bands. Did she live to make it to the Camas Meadow fight? And did she last out their perilous passage through Yellowstone National Park? The Canyon Creek fight? Cow Island? . . . And was Jennet Manuel still with the *Nee-Me-Poo* when they reached the cold, windswept hills at the foot of the Bears Paw Mountains when both a winter storm and Miles's Fifth Infantry caught them just short of the Medicine Line and the sanctuary of the Old Woman's Country?

Was Jennet Manuel still alive then?

Blood always answers blood.

This battlefield is like a lonely, hollow hole in the heart of the earth, especially now as I remember that all-too-quiet cemetery on a shady hillside back at Mount Idaho where stands a tall marble headstone erected for Jennet Manuel. I remember how I paused there, gazing down at that patch of ground, knowing hers was an empty grave . . . this silent haven adorned with a simple, beautiful piece of marble. If her body could not be laid to eternal rest, then I figure some of this war's survivors sought to put Jennet's soul at peace.

In a very real sense this morning, I feel a palpable connection between these two places—both sites are cemeteries. In both I sense the death of some innocence. You only have to walk among the tombstones and marble markers at the Mount Idaho cemetery to realize this was not a war between fighting men. In both places—the quiet cemetery and here at the hallowed Big Hole—lie the innocents: the women and children who gave a lie to the belief that this was a war between soldiers and warriors.

Right from the outbreak on the Salmon River, and on into Montana Territory, this was a dirty war that recognized no gender, nor youth.

The wind comes up as the sun disappears behind the low clouds, and I feel even colder than before. In chasing down the Nez Perce, Sherman and Sheridan once more had their "total war."

But blood will always demand more blood.

The great and deep wound Gibbon's men inflicted at this place of tears will now be answered in a frenzy of murder, an orgy of senseless killing that will mark with shame the return of the *Nee-Me-Poo* to Idaho and their migration through Yellowstone Park—pausing only when they discover that their old friends the Crow won't join them in a war against the soldiers.

I wipe the moisture from my eyes and stand, hoping I have what it will take to finish this sad story many months and many, many miles from here among the cold hills at the Bear's Paw. Blood always answers blood.

It has always been that way. I doubt anything man can ever do will change that.

Blood cries out for blood.

TERRY C. JOHNSTON
BIG HOLE NATIONAL BATTLEFIELD
13 MAY 1999

ABOUT THE AUTHOR

TERRY C. JOHNSTON was born on the first day of 1947 on the plains of Kansas and has lived all his life in the American West. His first novel, *Carry the Wind*, won the Medicine Pipe Bearer's Award from the Western Writers of America, and his subsequent books have appeared on best-seller lists throughout the country. He lives and writes in Big Sky Country near Billings, Montana.

Each year Terry and his wife, Vanette, publish their annual *WinterSong* newsmagazine. Twice every summer they take readers on one-week historical tours of the battlesites and hallowed ground Terry chronicles in volume after volume of this bestselling *Plainsmen* series.

All those wanting to write the author, those requesting a complimentary copy of the annual *WinterSong* newsmagazine, and those desiring information on taking part in the author's summer historical tours can write to him at:

Terry C. Johnston
P.O. Box 50594
Billings, MT 59105

Or you can E-mail him at:

tjohnston@imt.net

and visit his Web site at:

http://www.imt.net/~tjohnston